The Holy QURAN

ARABIC

ENGLISH

Translation by Talal Itani

“When you read the Quran, seek refuge with Allah from Satan the outcast. He has no authority over those who believe and trust in their Lord. His authority is only over those who follow him, and those who associate others with Him.” [The Bee 98-100]

فَإِذَا قَرَأْتَ ٱلْقُرْءَانَ فَٱسْتَعِذْ بِٱللَّهِ مِنَ ٱلشَّيْطَٰنِ ٱلرَّجِيمِ ﴿٩٨﴾
إِنَّهُۥ لَيْسَ لَهُۥ سُلْطَٰنٌ عَلَى ٱلَّذِينَ ءَامَنُوا۟ وَعَلَىٰ رَبِّهِمْ يَتَوَكَّلُونَ
﴿٩٩﴾ إِنَّمَا سُلْطَٰنُهُۥ عَلَى ٱلَّذِينَ يَتَوَلَّوْنَهُۥ وَٱلَّذِينَ هُم بِهِۦ مُشْرِكُونَ
﴿١٠٠﴾ سورة النحل

CHAPTERS - SURAS

1 The Opening الفاتحة

١ بِسْمِ ٱللَّهِ ٱلرَّحْمَٰنِ ٱلرَّحِيمِ	1 In the name of Allah, the Gracious, the Merciful.
٢ ٱلْحَمْدُ لِلَّهِ رَبِّ ٱلْعَٰلَمِينَ	2 Praise be to Allah, Lord of the Worlds.
٣ ٱلرَّحْمَٰنِ ٱلرَّحِيمِ	3 The Most Gracious, the Most Merciful.
٤ مَٰلِكِ يَوْمِ ٱلدِّينِ	4 Master of the Day of Judgment.
٥ إِيَّاكَ نَعْبُدُ وَإِيَّاكَ نَسْتَعِينُ	5 It is You we worship, and upon You we call for help.
٦ ٱهْدِنَا ٱلصِّرَٰطَ ٱلْمُسْتَقِيمَ	6 Guide us to the straight path.
٧ صِرَٰطَ ٱلَّذِينَ أَنْعَمْتَ عَلَيْهِمْ غَيْرِ ٱلْمَغْضُوبِ عَلَيْهِمْ وَلَا ٱلضَّآلِّينَ	7 The path of those You have blessed, not of those against whom there is anger, nor of those who are misguided.

2 The Heifer البقرة

بِسْمِ ٱللَّهِ ٱلرَّحْمَٰنِ ٱلرَّحِيمِ	In the name of Allah, the Gracious, the Merciful.
١ الٓمٓ	1 Alif, Lam, Meem.
٢ ذَٰلِكَ ٱلْكِتَٰبُ لَا رَيْبَ ۛ فِيهِ ۛ هُدًى لِّلْمُتَّقِينَ	2 This is the Book in which there is no doubt, a guide for the righteous.
٣ ٱلَّذِينَ يُؤْمِنُونَ بِٱلْغَيْبِ وَيُقِيمُونَ ٱلصَّلَوٰةَ وَمِمَّا رَزَقْنَٰهُمْ يُنفِقُونَ	3 Those who believe in the unseen, and perform the prayers, and give from what We have provided for them.
٤ وَٱلَّذِينَ يُؤْمِنُونَ بِمَآ أُنزِلَ إِلَيْكَ وَمَآ أُنزِلَ مِن قَبْلِكَ وَبِٱلْـَٔاخِرَةِ هُمْ يُوقِنُونَ	4 And those who believe in what was revealed to you, and in what was revealed before you, and are certain of the Hereafter.
٥ أُو۟لَٰٓئِكَ عَلَىٰ هُدًى مِّن رَّبِّهِمْ ۖ وَأُو۟لَٰٓئِكَ هُمُ ٱلْمُفْلِحُونَ	5 These are upon guidance from their Lord. These are the successful.

٦ إِنَّ ٱلَّذِينَ كَفَرُوا۟ سَوَآءٌ عَلَيْهِمْ ءَأَنذَرْتَهُمْ أَمْ
لَمْ تُنذِرْهُمْ لَا يُؤْمِنُونَ

6 As for those who disbelieve—it is the same for them, whether you have warned them, or have not warned them—they do not believe.

٧ خَتَمَ ٱللَّهُ عَلَىٰ قُلُوبِهِمْ وَعَلَىٰ سَمْعِهِمْ ۖ وَعَلَىٰٓ
أَبْصَٰرِهِمْ غِشَٰوَةٌ ۖ وَلَهُمْ عَذَابٌ عَظِيمٌ

7 Allah has set a seal on their hearts and on their hearing, and over their vision is a veil. They will have a severe torment.

٨ وَمِنَ ٱلنَّاسِ مَن يَقُولُ ءَامَنَّا بِٱللَّهِ وَبِٱلْيَوْمِ
ٱلْءَاخِرِ وَمَا هُم بِمُؤْمِنِينَ

8 Among the people are those who say, “We believe in Allah and in the Last Day,” but they are not believers.

٩ يُخَٰدِعُونَ ٱللَّهَ وَٱلَّذِينَ ءَامَنُوا۟ وَمَا يَخْدَعُونَ
إِلَّآ أَنفُسَهُمْ وَمَا يَشْعُرُونَ

9 They seek to deceive Allah and those who believe, but they deceive none but themselves, though they are not aware.

١٠ فِى قُلُوبِهِم مَّرَضٌ فَزَادَهُمُ ٱللَّهُ مَرَضًا ۖ وَلَهُمْ
عَذَابٌ أَلِيمٌۢ بِمَا كَانُوا۟ يَكْذِبُونَ

10 In their hearts is sickness, and Allah has increased their sickness. They will have a painful punishment because of their denial.

١١ وَإِذَا قِيلَ لَهُمْ لَا تُفْسِدُوا۟ فِى ٱلْأَرْضِ قَالُوٓا۟
إِنَّمَا نَحْنُ مُصْلِحُونَ

11 And when it is said to them, “Do not make trouble on earth,” they say, “We are only reformers.”

١٢ أَلَآ إِنَّهُمْ هُمُ ٱلْمُفْسِدُونَ وَلَٰكِن لَّا يَشْعُرُونَ

12 In fact, they are the troublemakers, but they are not aware.

١٣ وَإِذَا قِيلَ لَهُمْ ءَامِنُوا۟ كَمَآ ءَامَنَ ٱلنَّاسُ
قَالُوٓا۟ أَنُؤْمِنُ كَمَآ ءَامَنَ ٱلسُّفَهَآءُ ۗ أَلَآ إِنَّهُمْ هُمُ
ٱلسُّفَهَآءُ وَلَٰكِن لَّا يَعْلَمُونَ

13 And when it is said to them, “Believe as the people have believed,” they say, “Shall we believe as the fools have believed?” In fact, it is they who are the fools, but they do not know.

١٤ وَإِذَا لَقُوا۟ ٱلَّذِينَ ءَامَنُوا۟ قَالُوٓا۟ ءَامَنَّا وَإِذَا
خَلَوْا۟ إِلَىٰ شَيَٰطِينِهِمْ قَالُوٓا۟ إِنَّا مَعَكُمْ إِنَّمَا نَحْنُ
مُسْتَهْزِءُونَ

14 And when they come across those who believe, they say, “We believe”; but when they are alone with their devils, they say, “We are with you; we were only ridiculing.”

١٥ ٱللَّهُ يَسْتَهْزِئُ بِهِمْ وَيَمُدُّهُمْ فِى طُغْيَٰنِهِمْ
يَعْمَهُونَ

15 It is Allah who ridicules them, and leaves them bewildered in their transgression.

١٦ أُوْلَٰٓئِكَ ٱلَّذِينَ ٱشْتَرَوُاْ ٱلضَّلَٰلَةَ بِٱلْهُدَىٰ فَمَا
رَبِحَت تِّجَٰرَتُهُمْ وَمَا كَانُواْ مُهْتَدِينَ

16 Those are they who have bartered error for guidance; but their trade does not profit them, and they are not guided.

١٧ مَثَلُهُمْ كَمَثَلِ ٱلَّذِى ٱسْتَوْقَدَ نَارًا فَلَمَّآ
أَضَآءَتْ مَا حَوْلَهُۥ ذَهَبَ ٱللَّهُ بِنُورِهِمْ وَتَرَكَهُمْ
فِى ظُلُمَٰتٍ لَّا يُبْصِرُونَ

17 Their likeness is that of a person who kindled a fire; when it illuminated all around him, Allah took away their light, and left them in darkness, unable to see.

١٨ صُمٌّۢ بُكْمٌ عُمْىٌ فَهُمْ لَا يَرْجِعُونَ

18 Deaf, dumb, blind. They will not return.

١٩ أَوْ كَصَيِّبٍ مِّنَ ٱلسَّمَآءِ فِيهِ ظُلُمَٰتٌ وَرَعْدٌ
وَبَرْقٌ يَجْعَلُونَ أَصَٰبِعَهُمْ فِىٓ ءَاذَانِهِم مِّنَ
ٱلصَّوَٰعِقِ حَذَرَ ٱلْمَوْتِ ۚ وَٱللَّهُ مُحِيطٌۢ بِٱلْكَٰفِرِينَ

19 Or like a cloudburst from the sky, in which is darkness, and thunder, and lightning. They press their fingers into their ears from the thunderbolts, in fear of death. But Allah surrounds the disbelievers.

٢٠ يَكَادُ ٱلْبَرْقُ يَخْطَفُ أَبْصَٰرَهُمْ ۖ كُلَّمَآ أَضَآءَ
لَهُم مَّشَوْاْ فِيهِ وَإِذَآ أَظْلَمَ عَلَيْهِمْ قَامُواْ ۚ وَلَوْ
شَآءَ ٱللَّهُ لَذَهَبَ بِسَمْعِهِمْ وَأَبْصَٰرِهِمْ ۚ إِنَّ ٱللَّهَ
عَلَىٰ كُلِّ شَىْءٍ قَدِيرٌ

20 The lightning almost snatches their sight away. Whenever it illuminates for them, they walk in it; but when it grows dark over them, they stand still. Had Allah willed, He could have taken away their hearing and their sight. Allah is capable of everything.

٢١ يَٰٓأَيُّهَا ٱلنَّاسُ ٱعْبُدُواْ رَبَّكُمُ ٱلَّذِى خَلَقَكُمْ
وَٱلَّذِينَ مِن قَبْلِكُمْ لَعَلَّكُمْ تَتَّقُونَ

21 O people! Worship your Lord who created you and those before you, that you may attain piety.

٢٢ ٱلَّذِى جَعَلَ لَكُمُ ٱلْأَرْضَ فِرَٰشًا وَٱلسَّمَآءَ بِنَآءً
وَأَنزَلَ مِنَ ٱلسَّمَآءِ مَآءً فَأَخْرَجَ بِهِۦ مِنَ ٱلثَّمَرَٰتِ
رِزْقًا لَّكُمْ ۖ فَلَا تَجْعَلُواْ لِلَّهِ أَندَادًا وَأَنتُمْ تَعْلَمُونَ

22 He who made the earth a habitat for you, and the sky a structure, and sends water down from the sky, and brings out fruits thereby, as a sustenance for you. Therefore, do not assign rivals to Allah while you know.

٢٣ وَإِن كُنتُمْ فِى رَيْبٍ مِّمَّا نَزَّلْنَا عَلَىٰ عَبْدِنَا
فَأْتُواْ بِسُورَةٍ مِّن مِّثْلِهِۦ وَٱدْعُواْ شُهَدَآءَكُم مِّن
دُونِ ٱللَّهِ إِن كُنتُمْ صَٰدِقِينَ

23 And if you are in doubt about what We have revealed to Our servant, then produce a chapter like these, and call your witnesses apart from Allah, if you are truthful.

٢٤ فَإِن لَّمْ تَفْعَلُوا۟ وَلَن تَفْعَلُوا۟ فَٱتَّقُوا۟ ٱلنَّارَ ٱلَّتِى
وَقُودُهَا ٱلنَّاسُ وَٱلْحِجَارَةُ ۖ أُعِدَّتْ لِلْكَٰفِرِينَ

24 But if you do not—and you will not—then beware the Fire whose fuel is people and stones, prepared for the disbelievers.

٢٥ وَبَشِّرِ ٱلَّذِينَ ءَامَنُوا۟ وَعَمِلُوا۟ ٱلصَّٰلِحَٰتِ أَنَّ
لَهُمْ جَنَّٰتٍ تَجْرِى مِن تَحْتِهَا ٱلْأَنْهَٰرُ ۖ كُلَّمَا رُزِقُوا۟
مِنْهَا مِن ثَمَرَةٍ رِّزْقًا ۙ قَالُوا۟ هَٰذَا ٱلَّذِى رُزِقْنَا مِن
قَبْلُ ۖ وَأُتُوا۟ بِهِۦ مُتَشَٰبِهًا ۖ وَلَهُمْ فِيهَآ أَزْوَٰجٌ
مُّطَهَّرَةٌ ۖ وَهُمْ فِيهَا خَٰلِدُونَ

25 And give good news to those who believe and do righteous deeds; that they will have gardens beneath which rivers flow. Whenever they are provided with fruit therefrom as sustenance, they will say, “This is what we were provided with before,” and they will be given the like of it. And they will have pure spouses therein, and they will abide therein forever.

٢٦ إِنَّ ٱللَّهَ لَا يَسْتَحْىِۦٓ أَن يَضْرِبَ مَثَلًا مَّا
بَعُوضَةً فَمَا فَوْقَهَا ۚ فَأَمَّا ٱلَّذِينَ ءَامَنُوا۟
فَيَعْلَمُونَ أَنَّهُ ٱلْحَقُّ مِن رَّبِّهِمْ ۖ وَأَمَّا ٱلَّذِينَ
كَفَرُوا۟ فَيَقُولُونَ مَاذَآ أَرَادَ ٱللَّهُ بِهَٰذَا مَثَلًا ۘ يُضِلُّ
بِهِۦ كَثِيرًا وَيَهْدِى بِهِۦ كَثِيرًا ۚ وَمَا يُضِلُّ بِهِۦٓ إِلَّا
ٱلْفَٰسِقِينَ

26 Allah does not shy away from making an example of a gnat, or something above it. As for those who believe, they know that it is the Truth from their Lord. But as for those who disbelieve, they say, “What did Allah intend by this example?” He leads astray many thereby, and He guides many thereby; but He misleads thereby only the evildoers.

٢٧ ٱلَّذِينَ يَنقُضُونَ عَهْدَ ٱللَّهِ مِنۢ بَعْدِ مِيثَٰقِهِۦ
وَيَقْطَعُونَ مَآ أَمَرَ ٱللَّهُ بِهِۦٓ أَن يُوصَلَ
وَيُفْسِدُونَ فِى ٱلْأَرْضِ ۚ أُو۟لَٰٓئِكَ هُمُ ٱلْخَٰسِرُونَ

27 Those who violate Allah’s covenant after its confirmation, and sever what Allah has commanded to be joined, and commit evil on earth. These are the losers.

٢٨ كَيْفَ تَكْفُرُونَ بِٱللَّهِ وَكُنتُمْ أَمْوَٰتًا فَأَحْيَٰكُمْ ۖ
ثُمَّ يُمِيتُكُمْ ثُمَّ يُحْيِيكُمْ ثُمَّ إِلَيْهِ تُرْجَعُونَ

28 How can you deny Allah, when you were dead and He gave you life, then He will put you to death, then He will bring you to life, then to Him you will be returned?

٢٩ هُوَ ٱلَّذِى خَلَقَ لَكُم مَّا فِى ٱلْأَرْضِ جَمِيعًا ثُمَّ
ٱسْتَوَىٰٓ إِلَى ٱلسَّمَآءِ فَسَوَّىٰهُنَّ سَبْعَ سَمَٰوَٰتٍ ۚ
وَهُوَ بِكُلِّ شَىْءٍ عَلِيمٌ

29 It is He who created for you everything on earth, then turned to the heaven, and made them seven heavens. And He is aware of all things.

٣٠ وَإِذْ قَالَ رَبُّكَ لِلْمَلَٰٓئِكَةِ إِنِّى جَاعِلٌ فِى
ٱلْأَرْضِ خَلِيفَةً ۖ قَالُوٓا۟ أَتَجْعَلُ فِيهَا مَن يُفْسِدُ
فِيهَا وَيَسْفِكُ ٱلدِّمَآءَ وَنَحْنُ نُسَبِّحُ بِحَمْدِكَ
وَنُقَدِّسُ لَكَ ۖ قَالَ إِنِّىٓ أَعْلَمُ مَا لَا تَعْلَمُونَ

30 When your Lord said to the angels, “I am placing a successor on earth.” They said, “Will You place in it someone who will cause corruption in it and shed blood, while we declare Your praises and sanctify You?” He said, “I know what you do not know.”

٣١ وَعَلَّمَ ءَادَمَ ٱلْأَسْمَآءَ كُلَّهَا ثُمَّ عَرَضَهُمْ عَلَى
ٱلْمَلَٰٓئِكَةِ فَقَالَ أَنۢبِـُٔونِى بِأَسْمَآءِ هَٰٓؤُلَآءِ إِن كُنتُمْ
صَٰدِقِينَ

31 And He taught Adam the names, all of them; then he presented them to the angels, and said, “Tell Me the names of these, if you are sincere.”

٣٢ قَالُوا۟ سُبْحَٰنَكَ لَا عِلْمَ لَنَآ إِلَّا مَا عَلَّمْتَنَآ ۖ إِنَّكَ
أَنتَ ٱلْعَلِيمُ ٱلْحَكِيمُ

32 They said, “Glory be to You! We have no knowledge except what You have taught us. It is you who are the Knowledgeable, the Wise.”

٣٣ قَالَ يَٰٓـَٔادَمُ أَنۢبِئْهُم بِأَسْمَآئِهِمْ ۖ فَلَمَّآ أَنۢبَأَهُم
بِأَسْمَآئِهِمْ قَالَ أَلَمْ أَقُل لَّكُمْ إِنِّىٓ أَعْلَمُ غَيْبَ
ٱلسَّمَٰوَٰتِ وَٱلْأَرْضِ وَأَعْلَمُ مَا تُبْدُونَ وَمَا كُنتُمْ
تَكْتُمُونَ

33 He said, “O Adam, tell them their names.” And when he told them their names, He said, “Did I not tell you that I know the secrets of the heavens and the earth, and that I know what you reveal and what you conceal?”

٣٤ وَإِذْ قُلْنَا لِلْمَلَٰٓئِكَةِ ٱسْجُدُوا۟ لِءَادَمَ فَسَجَدُوٓا۟
إِلَّآ إِبْلِيسَ أَبَىٰ وَٱسْتَكْبَرَ وَكَانَ مِنَ ٱلْكَٰفِرِينَ

34 And We said to the angels, “Bow down to Adam.” They bowed down, except for Satan. He refused, was arrogant, and was one of the disbelievers.

٣٥ وَقُلْنَا يَٰٓـَٔادَمُ ٱسْكُنْ أَنتَ وَزَوْجُكَ ٱلْجَنَّةَ وَكُلَا
مِنْهَا رَغَدًا حَيْثُ شِئْتُمَا وَلَا تَقْرَبَا هَٰذِهِ ٱلشَّجَرَةَ
فَتَكُونَا مِنَ ٱلظَّٰلِمِينَ

35 We said, “O Adam, inhabit the Garden, you and your spouse, and eat from it freely as you please, but do not approach this tree, lest you become wrongdoers.”

٣٦ فَأَزَلَّهُمَا ٱلشَّيْطَٰنُ عَنْهَا فَأَخْرَجَهُمَا مِمَّا كَانَا
فِيهِ ۖ وَقُلْنَا ٱهْبِطُوا۟ بَعْضُكُمْ لِبَعْضٍ عَدُوٌّ ۖ وَلَكُمْ
فِى ٱلْأَرْضِ مُسْتَقَرٌّ وَمَتَٰعٌ إِلَىٰ حِينٍ

36 But Satan caused them to slip from it, and caused them to depart the state they were in. We said, “Go down, some of you enemies of one another. And you will have residence on earth, and enjoyment for a while.”

٣٧ فَتَلَقَّىٰٓ ءَادَمُ مِن رَّبِّهِۦ كَلِمَٰتٍ فَتَابَ عَلَيْهِ ۚ إِنَّهُۥ هُوَ ٱلتَّوَّابُ ٱلرَّحِيمُ

37 Then Adam received words from his Lord, so He relented towards him. He is the Relenting, the Merciful.

٣٨ قُلْنَا ٱهْبِطُوا۟ مِنْهَا جَمِيعًا ۖ فَإِمَّا يَأْتِيَنَّكُم مِّنِّى هُدًى فَمَن تَبِعَ هُدَاىَ فَلَا خَوْفٌ عَلَيْهِمْ وَلَا هُمْ يَحْزَنُونَ

38 We said, “Go down from it, all of you. Yet whenever guidance comes to you from Me, then whoever follows My guidance—they have nothing to fear, nor shall they grieve.

٣٩ وَٱلَّذِينَ كَفَرُوا۟ وَكَذَّبُوا۟ بِـَٔايَٰتِنَآ أُو۟لَٰٓئِكَ أَصْحَٰبُ ٱلنَّارِ ۖ هُمْ فِيهَا خَٰلِدُونَ

39 But as for those who disbelieve and reject Our signs—these are the inmates of the Fire—wherein they will remain forever.”

٤٠ يَٰبَنِىٓ إِسْرَٰٓءِيلَ ٱذْكُرُوا۟ نِعْمَتِىَ ٱلَّتِىٓ أَنْعَمْتُ عَلَيْكُمْ وَأَوْفُوا۟ بِعَهْدِىٓ أُوفِ بِعَهْدِكُمْ وَإِيَّٰىَ فَٱرْهَبُونِ

40 O Children of Israel! Remember My blessings which I bestowed upon you, and fulfill your pledge to Me, and I will fulfill My pledge to you, and fear Me.

٤١ وَءَامِنُوا۟ بِمَآ أَنزَلْتُ مُصَدِّقًا لِّمَا مَعَكُمْ وَلَا تَكُونُوٓا۟ أَوَّلَ كَافِرٍۭ بِهِۦ ۖ وَلَا تَشْتَرُوا۟ بِـَٔايَٰتِى ثَمَنًا قَلِيلًا وَإِيَّٰىَ فَٱتَّقُونِ

41 And believe in what I revealed, confirming what is with you; and do not be the first to deny it; and do not exchange My revelations for a small price; and be conscious of Me.

٤٢ وَلَا تَلْبِسُوا۟ ٱلْحَقَّ بِٱلْبَٰطِلِ وَتَكْتُمُوا۟ ٱلْحَقَّ وَأَنتُمْ تَعْلَمُونَ

42 And do not mix truth with falsehood, and do not conceal the truth while you know.

٤٣ وَأَقِيمُوا۟ ٱلصَّلَوٰةَ وَءَاتُوا۟ ٱلزَّكَوٰةَ وَٱرْكَعُوا۟ مَعَ ٱلرَّٰكِعِينَ

43 And attend to your prayers, and practice regular charity, and kneel with those who kneel.

٤٤ أَتَأْمُرُونَ ٱلنَّاسَ بِٱلْبِرِّ وَتَنسَوْنَ أَنفُسَكُمْ وَأَنتُمْ تَتْلُونَ ٱلْكِتَٰبَ ۚ أَفَلَا تَعْقِلُونَ

44 Do you command people to virtuous conduct, and forget yourselves, even though you read the Scripture? Do you not understand?

٤٥ وَٱسْتَعِينُوا۟ بِٱلصَّبْرِ وَٱلصَّلَوٰةِ ۚ وَإِنَّهَا لَكَبِيرَةٌ إِلَّا عَلَى ٱلْخَٰشِعِينَ

45 And seek help through patience and prayer. But it is difficult, except for the devout.

٤٦ ٱلَّذِينَ يَظُنُّونَ أَنَّهُم مُّلَٰقُوا۟ رَبِّهِمْ وَأَنَّهُمْ إِلَيْهِ رَٰجِعُونَ

46 Those who know that they will meet their Lord, and that to Him they will return.

٤٧ يَٰبَنِىٓ إِسْرَٰٓءِيلَ ٱذْكُرُوا۟ نِعْمَتِىَ ٱلَّتِىٓ أَنْعَمْتُ
عَلَيْكُمْ وَأَنِّى فَضَّلْتُكُمْ عَلَى ٱلْعَٰلَمِينَ

47 O Children of Israel! Remember My favor which I bestowed upon you, and I that favored you over all nations.

٤٨ وَٱتَّقُوا۟ يَوْمًا لَّا تَجْزِى نَفْسٌ عَن نَّفْسٍ شَيْـًٔا
وَلَا يُقْبَلُ مِنْهَا شَفَٰعَةٌ وَلَا يُؤْخَذُ مِنْهَا عَدْلٌ وَلَا
هُمْ يُنصَرُونَ

48 And beware of a Day when no soul will avail another in the least, nor will any intercession be accepted on its behalf, nor will any ransom be taken from it, nor will they be helped.

٤٩ وَإِذْ نَجَّيْنَٰكُم مِّنْ ءَالِ فِرْعَوْنَ يَسُومُونَكُمْ
سُوٓءَ ٱلْعَذَابِ يُذَبِّحُونَ أَبْنَآءَكُمْ وَيَسْتَحْيُونَ
نِسَآءَكُمْ ۚ وَفِى ذَٰلِكُم بَلَآءٌ مِّن رَّبِّكُمْ عَظِيمٌ

49 And recall that We delivered you from the people of Pharaoh. They inflicted on you terrible persecution, killing your sons and sparing your women. Therein was a tremendous trial from your Lord.

٥٠ وَإِذْ فَرَقْنَا بِكُمُ ٱلْبَحْرَ فَأَنجَيْنَٰكُمْ وَأَغْرَقْنَآ
ءَالَ فِرْعَوْنَ وَأَنتُمْ تَنظُرُونَ

50 And recall that We parted the sea for you, so We saved you, and We drowned the people of Pharaoh as you looked on.

٥١ وَإِذْ وَٰعَدْنَا مُوسَىٰٓ أَرْبَعِينَ لَيْلَةً ثُمَّ ٱتَّخَذْتُمُ
ٱلْعِجْلَ مِنۢ بَعْدِهِۦ وَأَنتُمْ ظَٰلِمُونَ

51 And recall that We appointed for Moses forty nights. Then you took to worshiping the calf after him, and you turned wicked.

٥٢ ثُمَّ عَفَوْنَا عَنكُم مِّنۢ بَعْدِ ذَٰلِكَ لَعَلَّكُمْ
تَشْكُرُونَ

52 Then We pardoned you after that, so that you might be grateful.

٥٣ وَإِذْ ءَاتَيْنَا مُوسَى ٱلْكِتَٰبَ وَٱلْفُرْقَانَ لَعَلَّكُمْ
تَهْتَدُونَ

53 And recall that We gave Moses the Scripture and the Criterion, so that you may be guided.

٥٤ وَإِذْ قَالَ مُوسَىٰ لِقَوْمِهِۦ يَٰقَوْمِ إِنَّكُمْ ظَلَمْتُمْ
أَنفُسَكُم بِٱتِّخَاذِكُمُ ٱلْعِجْلَ فَتُوبُوٓا۟ إِلَىٰ بَارِئِكُمْ
فَٱقْتُلُوٓا۟ أَنفُسَكُمْ ذَٰلِكُمْ خَيْرٌ لَّكُمْ عِندَ بَارِئِكُمْ
فَتَابَ عَلَيْكُمْ ۚ إِنَّهُۥ هُوَ ٱلتَّوَّابُ ٱلرَّحِيمُ

54 And recall that Moses said to his people, “O my people, you have done wrong to yourselves by worshiping the calf. So repent to your Maker, and kill your egos. That would be better for you with your Maker.” So He turned to you in repentance. He is the Accepter of Repentance, the Merciful.

٥٥ وَإِذْ قُلْتُمْ يَٰمُوسَىٰ لَن نُّؤْمِنَ لَكَ حَتَّىٰ نَرَى
ٱللَّهَ جَهْرَةً فَأَخَذَتْكُمُ ٱلصَّٰعِقَةُ وَأَنتُمْ تَنظُرُونَ

55 And recall that you said, “O Moses, we will not believe in you unless we see Allah plainly.”

Thereupon the thunderbolt struck you, as you looked on.

٥٦ ثُمَّ بَعَثْنَٰكُم مِّنۢ بَعْدِ مَوْتِكُمْ لَعَلَّكُمْ تَشْكُرُونَ

56 Then We revived you after your death, so that you may be appreciative.

٥٧ وَظَلَّلْنَا عَلَيْكُمُ ٱلْغَمَامَ وَأَنزَلْنَا عَلَيْكُمُ ٱلْمَنَّ
وَٱلسَّلْوَىٰ ۖ كُلُوا۟ مِن طَيِّبَٰتِ مَا رَزَقْنَٰكُمْ ۖ وَمَا
ظَلَمُونَا وَلَٰكِن كَانُوٓا۟ أَنفُسَهُمْ يَظْلِمُونَ

57 And We shaded you with clouds, and We sent down to you manna and quails: “Eat of the good things We have provided for you.” They did not wrong Us, but they used to wrong their own souls.

٥٨ وَإِذْ قُلْنَا ٱدْخُلُوا۟ هَٰذِهِ ٱلْقَرْيَةَ فَكُلُوا۟ مِنْهَا
حَيْثُ شِئْتُمْ رَغَدًا وَٱدْخُلُوا۟ ٱلْبَابَ سُجَّدًا
وَقُولُوا۟ حِطَّةٌ نَّغْفِرْ لَكُمْ خَطَٰيَٰكُمْ ۚ وَسَنَزِيدُ
ٱلْمُحْسِنِينَ

58 And recall that We said, “Enter this town, and eat plentifully from it whatever you wish; but enter the gate humbly, and say, 'Pardon.' We will forgive your sins, and give increase to the virtuous.”

٥٩ فَبَدَّلَ ٱلَّذِينَ ظَلَمُوا۟ قَوْلًا غَيْرَ ٱلَّذِى قِيلَ لَهُمْ
فَأَنزَلْنَا عَلَى ٱلَّذِينَ ظَلَمُوا۟ رِجْزًا مِّنَ ٱلسَّمَآءِ بِمَا
كَانُوا۟ يَفْسُقُونَ

59 But the wrongdoers among them substituted words other than those given to them, so We sent down on the wrongdoers a plague from heaven, because of their wicked behavior.

٦٠ وَإِذِ ٱسْتَسْقَىٰ مُوسَىٰ لِقَوْمِهِۦ فَقُلْنَا ٱضْرِب
بِّعَصَاكَ ٱلْحَجَرَ ۖ فَٱنفَجَرَتْ مِنْهُ ٱثْنَتَا عَشْرَةَ
عَيْنًا ۖ قَدْ عَلِمَ كُلُّ أُنَاسٍ مَّشْرَبَهُمْ ۖ كُلُوا۟
وَٱشْرَبُوا۟ مِن رِّزْقِ ٱللَّهِ وَلَا تَعْثَوْا۟ فِى ٱلْأَرْضِ
مُفْسِدِينَ

60 And recall when Moses prayed for water for his people. We said, “Strike the rock with your staff.” Thereupon twelve springs gushed out from it, and each tribe recognized its drinking-place. “Eat and drink from Allah’s provision, and do not corrupt the earth with disobedience.”

٦١ وَإِذْ قُلْتُمْ يَٰمُوسَىٰ لَن نَّصْبِرَ عَلَىٰ طَعَامٍ
وَٰحِدٍ فَٱدْعُ لَنَا رَبَّكَ يُخْرِجْ لَنَا مِمَّا تُنۢبِتُ
ٱلْأَرْضُ مِنۢ بَقْلِهَا وَقِثَّآئِهَا وَفُومِهَا وَعَدَسِهَا
وَبَصَلِهَا ۖ قَالَ أَتَسْتَبْدِلُونَ ٱلَّذِى هُوَ أَدْنَىٰ بِٱلَّذِى
هُوَ خَيْرٌ ۚ ٱهْبِطُوا۟ مِصْرًا فَإِنَّ لَكُم مَّا سَأَلْتُمْ ۗ
وَضُرِبَتْ عَلَيْهِمُ ٱلذِّلَّةُ وَٱلْمَسْكَنَةُ وَبَآءُو بِغَضَبٍ
مِّنَ ٱللَّهِ ۗ ذَٰلِكَ بِأَنَّهُمْ كَانُوا۟ يَكْفُرُونَ بِـَٔايَٰتِ ٱللَّهِ

61 And recall when you said, “O Moses, we cannot endure one kind of food, so call to your Lord to produce for us of what the earth grows: of its herbs, and its cucumbers, and its garlic, and its lentils, and its onions.” He said, “Would you substitute worse for better? Go down to Egypt, where you will have what you asked for.” They were struck with humiliation

وَيَقْتُلُونَ ٱلنَّبِيِّـۧنَ بِغَيْرِ ٱلْحَقِّ ۗ ذَٰلِكَ بِمَا عَصَوا۟
وَّكَانُوا۟ يَعْتَدُونَ

and poverty, and incurred wrath from Allah. That was because they rejected Allah's revelations and wrongfully killed the prophets. That was because they disobeyed and transgressed.

٦٢ إِنَّ ٱلَّذِينَ ءَامَنُوا۟ وَٱلَّذِينَ هَادُوا۟ وَٱلنَّصَـٰرَىٰ
وَٱلصَّـٰبِـِٔينَ مَنْ ءَامَنَ بِٱللَّهِ وَٱلْيَوْمِ ٱلْـَٔاخِرِ
وَعَمِلَ صَـٰلِحًا فَلَهُمْ أَجْرُهُمْ عِندَ رَبِّهِمْ وَلَا
خَوْفٌ عَلَيْهِمْ وَلَا هُمْ يَحْزَنُونَ

62 Those who believe, and those who are Jewish, and the Christians, and the Sabeans—any who believe in Allah and the Last Day, and act righteously—will have their reward with their Lord; they have nothing to fear, nor will they grieve.

٦٣ وَإِذْ أَخَذْنَا مِيثَـٰقَكُمْ وَرَفَعْنَا فَوْقَكُمُ ٱلطُّورَ
خُذُوا۟ مَآ ءَاتَيْنَـٰكُم بِقُوَّةٍ وَٱذْكُرُوا۟ مَا فِيهِ لَعَلَّكُمْ
تَتَّقُونَ

63 And recall when We received a pledge from you, and raised the Mount above you: "Take what We have given you earnestly, and remember what is in it, that you may attain righteousness."

٦٤ ثُمَّ تَوَلَّيْتُم مِّنۢ بَعْدِ ذَٰلِكَ ۖ فَلَوْلَا فَضْلُ ٱللَّهِ
عَلَيْكُمْ وَرَحْمَتُهُۥ لَكُنتُم مِّنَ ٱلْخَـٰسِرِينَ

64 But after that you turned away. Were it not for Allah's grace and mercy towards you, you would have been among the losers.

٦٥ وَلَقَدْ عَلِمْتُمُ ٱلَّذِينَ ٱعْتَدَوْا۟ مِنكُمْ فِى
ٱلسَّبْتِ فَقُلْنَا لَهُمْ كُونُوا۟ قِرَدَةً خَـٰسِـِٔينَ

65 And you surely knew those of you who violated the Sabbath. We said to them, "Be despicable apes!"

٦٦ فَجَعَلْنَـٰهَا نَكَـٰلًا لِّمَا بَيْنَ يَدَيْهَا وَمَا خَلْفَهَا
وَمَوْعِظَةً لِّلْمُتَّقِينَ

66 Thus We made it a deterrent for their generation, and for subsequent generations, and a lesson for the righteous.

٦٧ وَإِذْ قَالَ مُوسَىٰ لِقَوْمِهِۦٓ إِنَّ ٱللَّهَ يَأْمُرُكُمْ أَن
تَذْبَحُوا۟ بَقَرَةً ۖ قَالُوٓا۟ أَتَتَّخِذُنَا هُزُوًا ۖ قَالَ أَعُوذُ
بِٱللَّهِ أَنْ أَكُونَ مِنَ ٱلْجَـٰهِلِينَ

67 And recall when Moses said to his people, "Allah commands you to sacrifice a heifer." They said, "Do you make a mockery of us?" He said, "Allah forbid that I should be so ignorant."

٦٨ قَالُوا۟ ٱدْعُ لَنَا رَبَّكَ يُبَيِّن لَّنَا مَا هِىَ ۚ قَالَ إِنَّهُۥ
يَقُولُ إِنَّهَا بَقَرَةٌ لَّا فَارِضٌ وَلَا بِكْرٌ عَوَانٌۢ بَيْنَ
ذَٰلِكَ ۖ فَٱفْعَلُوا۟ مَا تُؤْمَرُونَ

68 They said, "Call upon your Lord to show us which one." He said, "He says she is a heifer, neither too old, nor too young, but in between. So do what you are commanded."

٦٩ قَالُوا۟ ٱدْعُ لَنَا رَبَّكَ يُبَيِّن لَّنَا مَا لَوْنُهَا ۚ قَالَ
إِنَّهُۥ يَقُولُ إِنَّهَا بَقَرَةٌ صَفْرَآءُ فَاقِعٌ لَّوْنُهَا تَسُرُّ
ٱلنَّـٰظِرِينَ

69 They said, “Call upon your Lord to show us what her color is.” He said, “He says she is a yellow heifer, bright in color, pleasing to the beholders.”

٧٠ قَالُوا۟ ٱدْعُ لَنَا رَبَّكَ يُبَيِّن لَّنَا مَا هِىَ إِنَّ ٱلْبَقَرَ
تَشَـٰبَهَ عَلَيْنَا وَإِنَّآ إِن شَآءَ ٱللَّهُ لَمُهْتَدُونَ

70 They said, “Call upon your Lord to show us which one; the heifers look alike to us; and Allah willing, we will be guided.”

٧١ قَالَ إِنَّهُۥ يَقُولُ إِنَّهَا بَقَرَةٌ لَّا ذَلُولٌ تُثِيرُ
ٱلْأَرْضَ وَلَا تَسْقِى ٱلْحَرْثَ مُسَلَّمَةٌ لَّا شِيَةَ
فِيهَا ۚ قَالُوا۟ ٱلْـَٔـٰنَ جِئْتَ بِٱلْحَقِّ ۚ فَذَبَحُوهَا وَمَا
كَادُوا۟ يَفْعَلُونَ

71 He said, “He says she is a heifer, neither yoked to plow the earth, nor to irrigate the field; sound without blemish.” They said, “Now you have brought the truth.” So they slew her; though they almost did not.

٧٢ وَإِذْ قَتَلْتُمْ نَفْسًا فَٱدَّٰرَْٔتُمْ فِيهَا ۖ وَٱللَّهُ
مُخْرِجٌ مَّا كُنتُمْ تَكْتُمُونَ

72 And recall when you killed a person, and disputed in the matter; but Allah was to expose what you were hiding.

٧٣ فَقُلْنَا ٱضْرِبُوهُ بِبَعْضِهَا ۚ كَذَٰلِكَ يُحْىِ ٱللَّهُ
ٱلْمَوْتَىٰ وَيُرِيكُمْ ءَايَـٰتِهِۦ لَعَلَّكُمْ تَعْقِلُونَ

73 We said, “Strike him with part of it.” Thus Allah brings the dead to life; and He shows you His signs, that you may understand.

٧٤ ثُمَّ قَسَتْ قُلُوبُكُم مِّنۢ بَعْدِ ذَٰلِكَ فَهِىَ
كَٱلْحِجَارَةِ أَوْ أَشَدُّ قَسْوَةً ۚ وَإِنَّ مِنَ ٱلْحِجَارَةِ
لَمَا يَتَفَجَّرُ مِنْهُ ٱلْأَنْهَـٰرُ ۚ وَإِنَّ مِنْهَا لَمَا يَشَّقَّقُ
فَيَخْرُجُ مِنْهُ ٱلْمَآءُ ۚ وَإِنَّ مِنْهَا لَمَا يَهْبِطُ مِنْ
خَشْيَةِ ٱللَّهِ ۗ وَمَا ٱللَّهُ بِغَـٰفِلٍ عَمَّا تَعْمَلُونَ

74 Then after that your hearts hardened. They were as rocks, or even harder. For there are some rocks from which rivers gush out, and others that splinter and water comes out from them, and others that sink in awe of Allah. Allah is not unaware of what you do.

٧٥ أَفَتَطْمَعُونَ أَن يُؤْمِنُوا۟ لَكُمْ وَقَدْ كَانَ فَرِيقٌ
مِّنْهُمْ يَسْمَعُونَ كَلَـٰمَ ٱللَّهِ ثُمَّ يُحَرِّفُونَهُۥ مِنۢ بَعْدِ
مَا عَقَلُوهُ وَهُمْ يَعْلَمُونَ

75 Do you hope that they will believe in you, when some of them used to hear the Word of Allah, and then deliberately distort it, even after understanding it?

٧٦ وَإِذَا لَقُوا۟ ٱلَّذِينَ ءَامَنُوا۟ قَالُوٓا۟ ءَامَنَّا وَإِذَا
خَلَا بَعْضُهُمْ إِلَىٰ بَعْضٍ قَالُوٓا۟ أَتُحَدِّثُونَهُم بِمَا

76 And when they come across those who believe, they say, “We believe,” but when they come together privately, they say, “Will you inform them of what Allah has disclosed to

فَتَحَ ٱللَّهُ عَلَيْكُمْ لِيُحَآجُّوكُم بِهِۦ عِندَ رَبِّكُمْۚ
أَفَلَا تَعْقِلُونَ

you, so that they might dispute with you concerning it before your Lord?" Do you not understand?

٧٧ أَوَلَا يَعْلَمُونَ أَنَّ ٱللَّهَ يَعْلَمُ مَا يُسِرُّونَ وَمَا
يُعْلِنُونَ

77 Do they not know that Allah knows what they conceal and what they reveal?

٧٨ وَمِنْهُمْ أُمِّيُّونَ لَا يَعْلَمُونَ ٱلْكِتَٰبَ إِلَّآ أَمَانِىَّ
وَإِنْ هُمْ إِلَّا يَظُنُّونَ

78 And among them are uneducated who know the Scripture only through hearsay, and they only speculate.

٧٩ فَوَيْلٌ لِّلَّذِينَ يَكْتُبُونَ ٱلْكِتَٰبَ بِأَيْدِيهِمْ ثُمَّ
يَقُولُونَ هَٰذَا مِنْ عِندِ ٱللَّهِ لِيَشْتَرُوا۟ بِهِۦ ثَمَنًا
قَلِيلًاۖ فَوَيْلٌ لَّهُم مِّمَّا كَتَبَتْ أَيْدِيهِمْ وَوَيْلٌ لَّهُم
مِّمَّا يَكْسِبُونَ

79 So woe to those who write the Scripture with their own hands, and then say, "This is from Allah," that they may exchange it for a little price. Woe to them for what their hands have written, and woe to them for what they earn.

٨٠ وَقَالُوا۟ لَن تَمَسَّنَا ٱلنَّارُ إِلَّآ أَيَّامًا مَّعْدُودَةًۚ قُلْ
أَتَّخَذْتُمْ عِندَ ٱللَّهِ عَهْدًا فَلَن يُخْلِفَ ٱللَّهُ عَهْدَهُۥٓۖ
أَمْ تَقُولُونَ عَلَى ٱللَّهِ مَا لَا تَعْلَمُونَ

80 And they say, "The Fire will not touch us except for a number of days." Say, "Have you received a promise from Allah—Allah never breaks His promise—or are you saying about Allah what you do not know?"

٨١ بَلَىٰ مَن كَسَبَ سَيِّئَةً وَأَحَٰطَتْ بِهِۦ خَطِيٓـَٔتُهُۥ
فَأُو۟لَٰٓئِكَ أَصْحَٰبُ ٱلنَّارِۖ هُمْ فِيهَا خَٰلِدُونَ

81 Indeed, whoever commits misdeeds, and becomes besieged by his iniquities—these are the inmates of the Fire, wherein they will dwell forever.

٨٢ وَٱلَّذِينَ ءَامَنُوا۟ وَعَمِلُوا۟ ٱلصَّٰلِحَٰتِ أُو۟لَٰٓئِكَ
أَصْحَٰبُ ٱلْجَنَّةِۖ هُمْ فِيهَا خَٰلِدُونَ

82 As for those who believe and do righteous deeds—these are the inhabitants of Paradise, wherein they will dwell forever.

٨٣ وَإِذْ أَخَذْنَا مِيثَٰقَ بَنِىٓ إِسْرَٰٓءِيلَ لَا تَعْبُدُونَ
إِلَّا ٱللَّهَ وَبِٱلْوَٰلِدَيْنِ إِحْسَانًا وَذِى ٱلْقُرْبَىٰ
وَٱلْيَتَٰمَىٰ وَٱلْمَسَٰكِينِ وَقُولُوا۟ لِلنَّاسِ حُسْنًا
وَأَقِيمُوا۟ ٱلصَّلَوٰةَ وَءَاتُوا۟ ٱلزَّكَوٰةَ ثُمَّ تَوَلَّيْتُمْ إِلَّا
قَلِيلًا مِّنكُمْ وَأَنتُم مُّعْرِضُونَ

83 We made a covenant with the Children of Israel: "Worship none but Allah; and be good to parents, and relatives, and orphans, and the needy; and speak nicely to people; and pray regularly, and give alms." Then you turned away, except for a few of you, recanting.

٨٤ وَإِذْ أَخَذْنَا مِيثَٰقَكُمْ لَا تَسْفِكُونَ دِمَآءَكُمْ وَلَا
تُخْرِجُونَ أَنفُسَكُم مِّن دِيَٰرِكُمْ ثُمَّ أَقْرَرْتُمْ
وَأَنتُمْ تَشْهَدُونَ

84 And We made a covenant with you: "You shall not shed the blood of your own, nor shall you evict your own from your homes." You agreed, and were all witnesses.

٨٥ ثُمَّ أَنتُمْ هَٰٓؤُلَآءِ تَقْتُلُونَ أَنفُسَكُمْ وَتُخْرِجُونَ
فَرِيقًا مِّنكُم مِّن دِيَٰرِهِمْ تَظَٰهَرُونَ عَلَيْهِم بِٱلْإِثْمِ
وَٱلْعُدْوَٰنِ وَإِن يَأْتُوكُمْ أُسَٰرَىٰ تُفَٰدُوهُمْ وَهُوَ
مُحَرَّمٌ عَلَيْكُمْ إِخْرَاجُهُمْ ۚ أَفَتُؤْمِنُونَ بِبَعْضِ
ٱلْكِتَٰبِ وَتَكْفُرُونَ بِبَعْضٍ ۚ فَمَا جَزَآءُ مَن يَفْعَلُ
ذَٰلِكَ مِنكُمْ إِلَّا خِزْيٌ فِى ٱلْحَيَوٰةِ ٱلدُّنْيَا ۖ وَيَوْمَ
ٱلْقِيَٰمَةِ يُرَدُّونَ إِلَىٰٓ أَشَدِّ ٱلْعَذَابِ ۗ وَمَا ٱللَّهُ بِغَٰفِلٍ
عَمَّا تَعْمَلُونَ

85 But here you are, killing your own, and expelling a group of your own from their homes—conspiring against them in wrongdoing and hostility. And if they come to you as captives, you ransom them, although it was forbidden to you. Is it that you believe in part of the Scripture, and disbelieve in part? What is the reward for those among you who do that but humiliation in this life? And on the Day of Resurrection, they will be assigned to the most severe torment. Allah is not unaware of what you do.

٨٦ أُو۟لَٰٓئِكَ ٱلَّذِينَ ٱشْتَرَوُا۟ ٱلْحَيَوٰةَ ٱلدُّنْيَا
بِٱلْءَاخِرَةِ ۖ فَلَا يُخَفَّفُ عَنْهُمُ ٱلْعَذَابُ وَلَا هُمْ
يُنصَرُونَ

86 Those are they who bought the present life for the Hereafter, so the punishment will not be lightened for them, nor will they be helped.

٨٧ وَلَقَدْ ءَاتَيْنَا مُوسَى ٱلْكِتَٰبَ وَقَفَّيْنَا مِنۢ
بَعْدِهِۦ بِٱلرُّسُلِ ۖ وَءَاتَيْنَا عِيسَى ٱبْنَ مَرْيَمَ
ٱلْبَيِّنَٰتِ وَأَيَّدْنَٰهُ بِرُوحِ ٱلْقُدُسِ ۗ أَفَكُلَّمَا جَآءَكُمْ
رَسُولٌۢ بِمَا لَا تَهْوَىٰٓ أَنفُسُكُمُ ٱسْتَكْبَرْتُمْ فَفَرِيقًا
كَذَّبْتُمْ وَفَرِيقًا تَقْتُلُونَ

87 We gave Moses the Scripture, and sent a succession of messengers after him. And We gave Jesus son of Mary the clear proofs, and We supported him with the Holy Spirit. Is it that whenever a messenger comes to you with anything your souls do not desire, you grew arrogant, calling some impostors, and killing others?

٨٨ وَقَالُوا۟ قُلُوبُنَا غُلْفٌۢ ۚ بَل لَّعَنَهُمُ ٱللَّهُ بِكُفْرِهِمْ
فَقَلِيلًا مَّا يُؤْمِنُونَ

88 And they said, "Our hearts are sealed." Rather, Allah has cursed them for their ingratitude. They have little faith.

٨٩ وَلَمَّا جَآءَهُمْ كِتَٰبٌ مِّنْ عِندِ ٱللَّهِ مُصَدِّقٌ لِّمَا
مَعَهُمْ وَكَانُوا۟ مِن قَبْلُ يَسْتَفْتِحُونَ عَلَى ٱلَّذِينَ

89 And when a scripture came to them from Allah, confirming what they have—although previously they

كَفَرُوا۟ فَلَمَّا جَآءَهُم مَّا عَرَفُوا۟ كَفَرُوا۟ بِهِۦ ۚ فَلَعْنَةُ
ٱللَّهِ عَلَى ٱلْكَٰفِرِينَ

were seeking victory against those who disbelieved—but when there came to them what they recognized, they disbelieved in it. So Allah's curse is upon the disbelievers.

٩٠ بِئْسَمَا ٱشْتَرَوْا۟ بِهِۦٓ أَنفُسَهُمْ أَن يَكْفُرُوا۟ بِمَآ
أَنزَلَ ٱللَّهُ بَغْيًا أَن يُنَزِّلَ ٱللَّهُ مِن فَضْلِهِۦ عَلَىٰ
مَن يَشَآءُ مِنْ عِبَادِهِۦ ۖ فَبَآءُو بِغَضَبٍ عَلَىٰ
غَضَبٍ ۚ وَلِلْكَٰفِرِينَ عَذَابٌ مُّهِينٌ

90 Miserable is what they sold their souls for—rejecting what Allah has revealed, out of resentment that Allah would send down His grace upon whomever He chooses from among His servants. Thus they incurred wrath upon wrath. And there is a demeaning punishment for the disbelievers.

٩١ وَإِذَا قِيلَ لَهُمْ ءَامِنُوا۟ بِمَآ أَنزَلَ ٱللَّهُ قَالُوا۟
نُؤْمِنُ بِمَآ أُنزِلَ عَلَيْنَا وَيَكْفُرُونَ بِمَا وَرَآءَهُۥ وَهُوَ
ٱلْحَقُّ مُصَدِّقًا لِّمَا مَعَهُمْ ۗ قُلْ فَلِمَ تَقْتُلُونَ
أَنۢبِيَآءَ ٱللَّهِ مِن قَبْلُ إِن كُنتُم مُّؤْمِنِينَ

91 And when it is said to them, "Believe in what Allah has revealed," they say, "We believe in what was revealed to us," and they reject anything beyond that, although it is the truth which confirms what they have. Say, "Why did you kill Allah's prophets before, if you were believers?"

٩٢ وَلَقَدْ جَآءَكُم مُّوسَىٰ بِٱلْبَيِّنَٰتِ ثُمَّ ٱتَّخَذْتُمُ
ٱلْعِجْلَ مِنۢ بَعْدِهِۦ وَأَنتُمْ ظَٰلِمُونَ

92 Moses came to you with clear proofs, yet you adopted the calf in his absence, and you were in the wrong.

٩٣ وَإِذْ أَخَذْنَا مِيثَٰقَكُمْ وَرَفَعْنَا فَوْقَكُمُ ٱلطُّورَ
خُذُوا۟ مَآ ءَاتَيْنَٰكُم بِقُوَّةٍ وَٱسْمَعُوا۟ ۖ قَالُوا۟ سَمِعْنَا
وَعَصَيْنَا وَأُشْرِبُوا۟ فِى قُلُوبِهِمُ ٱلْعِجْلَ بِكُفْرِهِمْ ۚ
قُلْ بِئْسَمَا يَأْمُرُكُم بِهِۦٓ إِيمَٰنُكُمْ إِن كُنتُم
مُّؤْمِنِينَ

93 And We made a covenant with you, and raised the Mount above you: "Take what We have given you firmly, and listen." They said, "We hear and disobey." And their hearts became filled with the love of the calf because of their disbelief. Say, "Wretched is what your faith commands you to do, if you are believers."

٩٤ قُلْ إِن كَانَتْ لَكُمُ ٱلدَّارُ ٱلْءَاخِرَةُ عِندَ ٱللَّهِ
خَالِصَةً مِّن دُونِ ٱلنَّاسِ فَتَمَنَّوُا۟ ٱلْمَوْتَ إِن
كُنتُمْ صَٰدِقِينَ

94 Say, "If the Final Home with Allah is yours alone, to the exclusion of all other people, then wish for death if you are sincere."

٩٥ وَلَن يَتَمَنَّوْهُ أَبَدًۢا بِمَا قَدَّمَتْ أَيْدِيهِمْ ۗ وَٱللَّهُ
عَلِيمٌۢ بِٱلظَّٰلِمِينَ

95 But they will never wish for it, because of what their hands have forwarded. Allah is aware of the evildoers.

٩٦ وَلَتَجِدَنَّهُمْ أَحْرَصَ ٱلنَّاسِ عَلَىٰ حَيَوٰةٍ وَمِنَ
ٱلَّذِينَ أَشْرَكُوا۟ ۚ يَوَدُّ أَحَدُهُمْ لَوْ يُعَمَّرُ أَلْفَ سَنَةٍ
وَمَا هُوَ بِمُزَحْزِحِهِۦ مِنَ ٱلْعَذَابِ أَن يُعَمَّرَ ۗ وَٱللَّهُ
بَصِيرٌۢ بِمَا يَعْمَلُونَ

96 You will find them, of all mankind, the most eager for life, even more than the polytheists. Every one of them wishes he could live a thousand years; but to be granted a long life will not nudge him from the punishment. Allah is Seeing of what they do.

٩٧ قُلْ مَن كَانَ عَدُوًّا لِّجِبْرِيلَ فَإِنَّهُۥ نَزَّلَهُۥ عَلَىٰ
قَلْبِكَ بِإِذْنِ ٱللَّهِ مُصَدِّقًا لِّمَا بَيْنَ يَدَيْهِ وَهُدًى
وَبُشْرَىٰ لِلْمُؤْمِنِينَ

97 Say, "Whoever is hostile to Gabriel—it is he who revealed it to your heart by Allah's leave, confirming what preceded it, and guidance and good news for the believers."

٩٨ مَن كَانَ عَدُوًّا لِّلَّهِ وَمَلَٰٓئِكَتِهِۦ وَرُسُلِهِۦ
وَجِبْرِيلَ وَمِيكَىٰلَ فَإِنَّ ٱللَّهَ عَدُوٌّ لِّلْكَٰفِرِينَ

98 Whoever is hostile to Allah, and His angels, and His messengers, and Gabriel, and Michael—Allah is hostile to the faithless.

٩٩ وَلَقَدْ أَنزَلْنَآ إِلَيْكَ ءَايَٰتٍۭ بَيِّنَٰتٍ ۖ وَمَا يَكْفُرُ بِهَآ
إِلَّا ٱلْفَٰسِقُونَ

99 We have revealed to you clear signs, and none rejects them except the sinners.

١٠٠ أَوَكُلَّمَا عَٰهَدُوا۟ عَهْدًا نَّبَذَهُۥ فَرِيقٌ مِّنْهُم ۚ بَلْ
أَكْثَرُهُمْ لَا يُؤْمِنُونَ

100 Is it not that whenever they make a covenant, some of them toss it aside? In fact, most of them do not believe.

١٠١ وَلَمَّا جَآءَهُمْ رَسُولٌ مِّنْ عِندِ ٱللَّهِ مُصَدِّقٌ
لِّمَا مَعَهُمْ نَبَذَ فَرِيقٌ مِّنَ ٱلَّذِينَ أُوتُوا۟ ٱلْكِتَٰبَ
كِتَٰبَ ٱللَّهِ وَرَآءَ ظُهُورِهِمْ كَأَنَّهُمْ لَا يَعْلَمُونَ

101 And when there came to them a messenger from Allah, confirming what they had, a faction of those who were given the Book threw the Book of Allah behind their backs, as if they do not know.

١٠٢ وَٱتَّبَعُوا۟ مَا تَتْلُوا۟ ٱلشَّيَٰطِينُ عَلَىٰ مُلْكِ
سُلَيْمَٰنَ ۖ وَمَا كَفَرَ سُلَيْمَٰنُ وَلَٰكِنَّ ٱلشَّيَٰطِينَ
كَفَرُوا۟ يُعَلِّمُونَ ٱلنَّاسَ ٱلسِّحْرَ وَمَآ أُنزِلَ عَلَى
ٱلْمَلَكَيْنِ بِبَابِلَ هَٰرُوتَ وَمَٰرُوتَ ۚ وَمَا يُعَلِّمَانِ مِنْ

102 And they followed what the devils taught during the reign of Solomon. It was not Solomon who disbelieved, but it was the devils who disbelieved. They taught the people witchcraft and what was revealed in

أَحَدٍ حَتَّىٰ يَقُولَآ إِنَّمَا نَحْنُ فِتْنَةٌ فَلَا تَكْفُرْ ۖ
فَيَتَعَلَّمُونَ مِنْهُمَا مَا يُفَرِّقُونَ بِهِۦ بَيْنَ ٱلْمَرْءِ
وَزَوْجِهِۦ ۚ وَمَا هُم بِضَآرِّينَ بِهِۦ مِنْ أَحَدٍ إِلَّا
بِإِذْنِ ٱللَّهِ ۚ وَيَتَعَلَّمُونَ مَا يَضُرُّهُمْ وَلَا يَنفَعُهُمْ ۚ
وَلَقَدْ عَلِمُوا۟ لَمَنِ ٱشْتَرَىٰهُ مَا لَهُۥ فِى ٱلْءَاخِرَةِ
مِنْ خَلَٰقٍ ۚ وَلَبِئْسَ مَا شَرَوْا۟ بِهِۦٓ أَنفُسَهُمْ ۚ لَوْ
كَانُوا۟ يَعْلَمُونَ

Babylon to the two angels Harut and Marut. They did not teach anybody until they had said, “We are a test, so do not lose faith.” But they learned from them the means to cause separation between man and his wife. But they cannot harm anyone except with Allah's permission. And they learned what would harm them and not benefit them. Yet they knew that whoever deals in it will have no share in the Hereafter. Miserable is what they sold their souls for, if they only knew.

١٠٣ وَلَوْ أَنَّهُمْ ءَامَنُوا۟ وَٱتَّقَوْا۟ لَمَثُوبَةٌ مِّنْ عِندِ
ٱللَّهِ خَيْرٌ ۖ لَّوْ كَانُوا۟ يَعْلَمُونَ

103 Had they believed and been righteous, the reward from Allah would have been better, if they only knew.

١٠٤ يَٰٓأَيُّهَا ٱلَّذِينَ ءَامَنُوا۟ لَا تَقُولُوا۟ رَٰعِنَا وَقُولُوا۟
ٱنظُرْنَا وَٱسْمَعُوا۟ ۗ وَلِلْكَٰفِرِينَ عَذَابٌ أَلِيمٌ

104 O you who believe! Do not say ambiguous words, but say words of respect, and listen. The disbelievers will have a painful torment.

١٠٥ مَّا يَوَدُّ ٱلَّذِينَ كَفَرُوا۟ مِنْ أَهْلِ ٱلْكِتَٰبِ وَلَا
ٱلْمُشْرِكِينَ أَن يُنَزَّلَ عَلَيْكُم مِّنْ خَيْرٍ مِّن رَّبِّكُمْ ۗ
وَٱللَّهُ يَخْتَصُّ بِرَحْمَتِهِۦ مَن يَشَآءُ ۚ وَٱللَّهُ ذُو
ٱلْفَضْلِ ٱلْعَظِيمِ

105 It is never the wish of the disbelievers from among the People of the Book, nor of the polytheists, that any good should be sent down to you from your Lord. But Allah chooses for His mercy whomever He wills. Allah is Possessor of Sublime Grace.

١٠٦ مَا نَنسَخْ مِنْ ءَايَةٍ أَوْ نُنسِهَا نَأْتِ بِخَيْرٍ
مِّنْهَآ أَوْ مِثْلِهَآ ۗ أَلَمْ تَعْلَمْ أَنَّ ٱللَّهَ عَلَىٰ كُلِّ شَىْءٍ
قَدِيرٌ

106 We never nullify a verse, nor cause it to be forgotten, unless We bring one better than it, or similar to it. Do you not know that Allah is capable of all things?

١٠٧ أَلَمْ تَعْلَمْ أَنَّ ٱللَّهَ لَهُۥ مُلْكُ ٱلسَّمَٰوَٰتِ
وَٱلْأَرْضِ ۗ وَمَا لَكُم مِّن دُونِ ٱللَّهِ مِن وَلِىٍّ وَلَا
نَصِيرٍ

107 Do you not know that to Allah belongs the sovereignty of the heavens and the earth, and that apart from Allah you have no guardian or helper?

١٠٨ أَمْ تُرِيدُونَ أَن تَسْـَٔلُوا۟ رَسُولَكُمْ كَمَا سُئِلَ
مُوسَىٰ مِن قَبْلُ ۗ وَمَن يَتَبَدَّلِ ٱلْكُفْرَ بِٱلْإِيمَٰنِ
فَقَدْ ضَلَّ سَوَآءَ ٱلسَّبِيلِ

108 Or do you want to question your Messenger as Moses was questioned before? Whoever exchanges faith for disbelief has strayed from the right path.

١٠٩ وَدَّ كَثِيرٌ مِّنْ أَهْلِ ٱلْكِتَٰبِ لَوْ يَرُدُّونَكُم مِّنۢ
بَعْدِ إِيمَٰنِكُمْ كُفَّارًا حَسَدًا مِّنْ عِندِ أَنفُسِهِم مِّنۢ
بَعْدِ مَا تَبَيَّنَ لَهُمُ ٱلْحَقُّ ۖ فَٱعْفُوا۟ وَٱصْفَحُوا۟
حَتَّىٰ يَأْتِىَ ٱللَّهُ بِأَمْرِهِۦٓ ۗ إِنَّ ٱللَّهَ عَلَىٰ كُلِّ شَىْءٍ
قَدِيرٌ

109 Many of the People of the Book wish to turn you back into unbelievers after you have believed, out of envy on their part, after the Truth has become clear to them. But pardon and overlook, until Allah brings His command. Allah has power over all things.

١١٠ وَأَقِيمُوا۟ ٱلصَّلَوٰةَ وَءَاتُوا۟ ٱلزَّكَوٰةَ ۚ وَمَا
تُقَدِّمُوا۟ لِأَنفُسِكُم مِّنْ خَيْرٍ تَجِدُوهُ عِندَ ٱللَّهِ ۗ
إِنَّ ٱللَّهَ بِمَا تَعْمَلُونَ بَصِيرٌ

110 And perform the prayer, and give alms. Whatever good you forward for yourselves, you will find it with Allah. Allah is Seeing of everything you do.

١١١ وَقَالُوا۟ لَن يَدْخُلَ ٱلْجَنَّةَ إِلَّا مَن كَانَ هُودًا
أَوْ نَصَٰرَىٰ ۗ تِلْكَ أَمَانِيُّهُمْ ۗ قُلْ هَاتُوا۟ بُرْهَٰنَكُمْ إِن
كُنتُمْ صَٰدِقِينَ

111 And they say, “None will enter Heaven unless he is a Jew or a Christian.” These are their wishes. Say, “Produce your proof, if you are truthful.”

١١٢ بَلَىٰ مَنْ أَسْلَمَ وَجْهَهُۥ لِلَّهِ وَهُوَ مُحْسِنٌ فَلَهُۥٓ
أَجْرُهُۥ عِندَ رَبِّهِۦ وَلَا خَوْفٌ عَلَيْهِمْ وَلَا هُمْ
يَحْزَنُونَ

112 In fact, whoever submits himself to Allah, and is a doer of good, will have his reward with his Lord—they have nothing to fear, nor shall they grieve.

١١٣ وَقَالَتِ ٱلْيَهُودُ لَيْسَتِ ٱلنَّصَٰرَىٰ عَلَىٰ شَىْءٍ
وَقَالَتِ ٱلنَّصَٰرَىٰ لَيْسَتِ ٱلْيَهُودُ عَلَىٰ شَىْءٍ
وَهُمْ يَتْلُونَ ٱلْكِتَٰبَ ۗ كَذَٰلِكَ قَالَ ٱلَّذِينَ لَا
يَعْلَمُونَ مِثْلَ قَوْلِهِمْ ۚ فَٱللَّهُ يَحْكُمُ بَيْنَهُمْ يَوْمَ
ٱلْقِيَٰمَةِ فِيمَا كَانُوا۟ فِيهِ يَخْتَلِفُونَ

113 The Jews say, “The Christians are not based on anything;” and the Christians say, “The Jews are not based on anything.” Yet they both read the Scripture. Similarly, the ignorant said the same thing. Allah will judge between them on the Day of Resurrection regarding their differences.

١١٤ وَمَنْ أَظْلَمُ مِمَّن مَّنَعَ مَسَٰجِدَ ٱللَّهِ أَن يُذْكَرَ
فِيهَا ٱسْمُهُۥ وَسَعَىٰ فِى خَرَابِهَآ ۚ أُو۟لَٰٓئِكَ مَا كَانَ

114 Who is more unjust than him who forbids the remembrance of Allah’s name in places of worship, and contributes to their ruin? These ought not to enter them except in

لَهُمْ أَن يَدْخُلُوهَآ إِلَّا خَآئِفِينَ ۚ لَهُمْ فِى ٱلدُّنْيَا
خِزْىٌ وَلَهُمْ فِى ٱلْءَاخِرَةِ عَذَابٌ عَظِيمٌ

fear. For them is disgrace in this world, and for them is a terrible punishment in the Hereafter.

١١٥ وَلِلَّهِ ٱلْمَشْرِقُ وَٱلْمَغْرِبُ ۚ فَأَيْنَمَا تُوَلُّوا۟ فَثَمَّ
وَجْهُ ٱللَّهِ ۚ إِنَّ ٱللَّهَ وَٰسِعٌ عَلِيمٌ

115 To Allah belong the East and the West. Whichever way you turn, there is Allah's presence. Allah is Omnipresent and Omniscient.

١١٦ وَقَالُوا۟ ٱتَّخَذَ ٱللَّهُ وَلَدًا ۗ سُبْحَٰنَهُۥ ۖ بَل لَّهُۥ مَا
فِى ٱلسَّمَٰوَٰتِ وَٱلْأَرْضِ ۖ كُلٌّ لَّهُۥ قَٰنِتُونَ

116 And they say, "Allah has begotten a son." Be He glorified. Rather, His is everything in the heavens and the earth; all are obedient to Him.

١١٧ بَدِيعُ ٱلسَّمَٰوَٰتِ وَٱلْأَرْضِ ۖ وَإِذَا قَضَىٰٓ أَمْرًا
فَإِنَّمَا يَقُولُ لَهُۥ كُن فَيَكُونُ

117 Originator of the heavens and the earth. Whenever He decrees a thing, He says to it, "Be," and it becomes.

١١٨ وَقَالَ ٱلَّذِينَ لَا يَعْلَمُونَ لَوْلَا يُكَلِّمُنَا ٱللَّهُ أَوْ
تَأْتِينَآ ءَايَةٌ ۗ كَذَٰلِكَ قَالَ ٱلَّذِينَ مِن قَبْلِهِم مِّثْلَ
قَوْلِهِمْ ۘ تَشَٰبَهَتْ قُلُوبُهُمْ ۗ قَدْ بَيَّنَّا ٱلْءَايَٰتِ
لِقَوْمٍ يُوقِنُونَ

118 Those who do not know say, "If only Allah would speak to us, or a sign would come to us." Thus said those who were before them. Their hearts are alike. We have made the signs clear for people who are certain.

١١٩ إِنَّآ أَرْسَلْنَٰكَ بِٱلْحَقِّ بَشِيرًا وَنَذِيرًا ۖ وَلَا تُسْـَٔلُ
عَنْ أَصْحَٰبِ ٱلْجَحِيمِ

119 We have sent you with the truth—bringing good news, and giving warnings. You will not be questioned about the inmates of Hell.

١٢٠ وَلَن تَرْضَىٰ عَنكَ ٱلْيَهُودُ وَلَا ٱلنَّصَٰرَىٰ حَتَّىٰ
تَتَّبِعَ مِلَّتَهُمْ ۗ قُلْ إِنَّ هُدَى ٱللَّهِ هُوَ ٱلْهُدَىٰ ۗ وَلَئِنِ
ٱتَّبَعْتَ أَهْوَآءَهُم بَعْدَ ٱلَّذِى جَآءَكَ مِنَ ٱلْعِلْمِ ۙ مَا
لَكَ مِنَ ٱللَّهِ مِن وَلِىٍّ وَلَا نَصِيرٍ

120 The Jews and the Christians will not approve of you, unless you follow their creed. Say, "Allah's guidance is the guidance." Should you follow their desires, after the knowledge that has come to you, you will have in Allah neither guardian nor helper.

١٢١ ٱلَّذِينَ ءَاتَيْنَٰهُمُ ٱلْكِتَٰبَ يَتْلُونَهُۥ حَقَّ تِلَاوَتِهِۦٓ
أُو۟لَٰٓئِكَ يُؤْمِنُونَ بِهِۦ ۗ وَمَن يَكْفُرْ بِهِۦ فَأُو۟لَٰٓئِكَ هُمُ
ٱلْخَٰسِرُونَ

121 Those to whom We have given the Scripture follow it, as it ought to be followed—these believe in it. But as for those who reject it—these are the losers.

١٢٢ يَٰبَنِىٓ إِسْرَٰٓءِيلَ ٱذْكُرُوا۟ نِعْمَتِىَ ٱلَّتِىٓ أَنْعَمْتُ
عَلَيْكُمْ وَأَنِّى فَضَّلْتُكُمْ عَلَى ٱلْعَٰلَمِينَ

122 O Children of Israel! Remember My blessing which I bestowed upon

you, and that I have favored you over all people.

١٢٣ وَٱتَّقُوا۟ يَوْمًا لَّا تَجْزِى نَفْسٌ عَن نَّفْسٍ شَيْـًٔا
وَلَا يُقْبَلُ مِنْهَا عَدْلٌ وَلَا تَنفَعُهَا شَفَٰعَةٌ وَلَا هُمْ
يُنصَرُونَ

123 And beware of a Day when no soul will avail another soul in any way, and no ransom will be accepted from it, and no intercession will benefit it, and they will not be helped.

١٢٤ وَإِذِ ٱبْتَلَىٰٓ إِبْرَٰهِۦمَ رَبُّهُۥ بِكَلِمَٰتٍ فَأَتَمَّهُنَّ ۖ قَالَ
إِنِّى جَاعِلُكَ لِلنَّاسِ إِمَامًا ۖ قَالَ وَمِن ذُرِّيَّتِى ۖ
قَالَ لَا يَنَالُ عَهْدِى ٱلظَّٰلِمِينَ

124 And when his Lord tested Abraham with certain words, and he fulfilled them. He said, “I am making you a leader of humanity.” He said, “And my descendants?” He said, “My pledge does not include the wrongdoers.”

١٢٥ وَإِذْ جَعَلْنَا ٱلْبَيْتَ مَثَابَةً لِّلنَّاسِ وَأَمْنًا
وَٱتَّخِذُوا۟ مِن مَّقَامِ إِبْرَٰهِۦمَ مُصَلًّى ۖ وَعَهِدْنَآ إِلَىٰٓ
إِبْرَٰهِۦمَ وَإِسْمَٰعِيلَ أَن طَهِّرَا بَيْتِىَ لِلطَّآئِفِينَ
وَٱلْعَٰكِفِينَ وَٱلرُّكَّعِ ٱلسُّجُودِ

125 And We made the House a focal point for the people, and a sanctuary. Use the shrine of Abraham as a place of prayer. And We commissioned Abraham and Ishmael, “Sanctify My House for those who circle around it, and those who seclude themselves in it, and those who kneel and prostrate.”

١٢٦ وَإِذْ قَالَ إِبْرَٰهِۦمُ رَبِّ ٱجْعَلْ هَٰذَا بَلَدًا ءَامِنًا
وَٱرْزُقْ أَهْلَهُۥ مِنَ ٱلثَّمَرَٰتِ مَنْ ءَامَنَ مِنْهُم بِٱللَّهِ
وَٱلْيَوْمِ ٱلْءَاخِرِ ۖ قَالَ وَمَن كَفَرَ فَأُمَتِّعُهُۥ قَلِيلًا
ثُمَّ أَضْطَرُّهُۥٓ إِلَىٰ عَذَابِ ٱلنَّارِ ۖ وَبِئْسَ ٱلْمَصِيرُ

126 When Abraham said, “O My Lord, make this a peaceful land, and provide its people with fruits—whoever of them believes in Allah and the Last Day.” He said, “And whoever disbelieves, I will give him a little enjoyment, then I will consign him to the punishment of the Fire; how miserable the destiny!”

١٢٧ وَإِذْ يَرْفَعُ إِبْرَٰهِۦمُ ٱلْقَوَاعِدَ مِنَ ٱلْبَيْتِ
وَإِسْمَٰعِيلُ رَبَّنَا تَقَبَّلْ مِنَّآ ۖ إِنَّكَ أَنتَ ٱلسَّمِيعُ
ٱلْعَلِيمُ

127 As Abraham raises the foundations of the House, together with Ishmael, “Our Lord, accept it from us, You are the Hearer, the Knower.

١٢٨ رَبَّنَا وَٱجْعَلْنَا مُسْلِمَيْنِ لَكَ وَمِن ذُرِّيَّتِنَآ أُمَّةً
مُّسْلِمَةً لَّكَ وَأَرِنَا مَنَاسِكَنَا وَتُبْ عَلَيْنَآ ۖ إِنَّكَ
أَنتَ ٱلتَّوَّابُ ٱلرَّحِيمُ

128 Our Lord, and make us submissive to You, and from our descendants a community submissive to You. And show us our rites, and accept our repentance. You are the Acceptor of Repentance, the Merciful.

١٢٩ رَبَّنَا وَٱبْعَثْ فِيهِمْ رَسُولًا مِّنْهُمْ يَتْلُوا۟
عَلَيْهِمْ ءَايَٰتِكَ وَيُعَلِّمُهُمُ ٱلْكِتَٰبَ وَٱلْحِكْمَةَ
وَيُزَكِّيهِمْ ۚ إِنَّكَ أَنتَ ٱلْعَزِيزُ ٱلْحَكِيمُ

129 Our Lord, and raise up among them a messenger, of themselves, who will recite to them Your revelations, and teach them the Book and wisdom, and purify them. You are the Almighty, the Wise."

١٣٠ وَمَن يَرْغَبُ عَن مِّلَّةِ إِبْرَٰهِـۧمَ إِلَّا مَن سَفِهَ
نَفْسَهُۥ ۚ وَلَقَدِ ٱصْطَفَيْنَٰهُ فِى ٱلدُّنْيَا ۖ وَإِنَّهُۥ فِى
ٱلْءَاخِرَةِ لَمِنَ ٱلصَّٰلِحِينَ

130 Who would forsake the religion of Abraham, except he who fools himself? We chose him in this world, and in the Hereafter he will be among the righteous.

١٣١ إِذْ قَالَ لَهُۥ رَبُّهُۥٓ أَسْلِمْ ۖ قَالَ أَسْلَمْتُ لِرَبِّ
ٱلْعَٰلَمِينَ

131 When his Lord said to him, "Submit!" He said, "I have submitted to the Lord of the Worlds."

١٣٢ وَوَصَّىٰ بِهَآ إِبْرَٰهِـۧمُ بَنِيهِ وَيَعْقُوبُ يَٰبَنِىَّ إِنَّ
ٱللَّهَ ٱصْطَفَىٰ لَكُمُ ٱلدِّينَ فَلَا تَمُوتُنَّ إِلَّا وَأَنتُم
مُّسْلِمُونَ

132 And Abraham exhorted his sons, and Jacob, "O my sons, Allah has chosen this religion for you, so do not die unless you have submitted."

١٣٣ أَمْ كُنتُمْ شُهَدَآءَ إِذْ حَضَرَ يَعْقُوبَ ٱلْمَوْتُ
إِذْ قَالَ لِبَنِيهِ مَا تَعْبُدُونَ مِنۢ بَعْدِى قَالُوا۟ نَعْبُدُ
إِلَٰهَكَ وَإِلَٰهَ ءَابَآئِكَ إِبْرَٰهِـۧمَ وَإِسْمَٰعِيلَ وَإِسْحَٰقَ
إِلَٰهًا وَٰحِدًا وَنَحْنُ لَهُۥ مُسْلِمُونَ

133 Or were you witnesses when death approached Jacob, and he said to his sons, "What will you worship after Me?" They said, "We will worship your God, and the God of your fathers, Abraham, Ishmael, and Isaac; One God; and to Him we submit."

١٣٤ تِلْكَ أُمَّةٌ قَدْ خَلَتْ ۖ لَهَا مَا كَسَبَتْ وَلَكُم مَّا
كَسَبْتُمْ ۖ وَلَا تُسْـَٔلُونَ عَمَّا كَانُوا۟ يَعْمَلُونَ

134 That was a community that has passed; for them is what they have earned, and for you is what you have earned; and you will not be questioned about what they used to do.

١٣٥ وَقَالُوا۟ كُونُوا۟ هُودًا أَوْ نَصَٰرَىٰ تَهْتَدُوا۟ ۗ قُلْ
بَلْ مِلَّةَ إِبْرَٰهِـۧمَ حَنِيفًا ۖ وَمَا كَانَ مِنَ ٱلْمُشْرِكِينَ

135 And they say, "Be Jews or Christians, and you will be guided." Say, "Rather, the religion of Abraham, the Monotheist; he was not an idolater."

١٣٦ قُولُوٓا۟ ءَامَنَّا بِٱللَّهِ وَمَآ أُنزِلَ إِلَيْنَا وَمَآ أُنزِلَ
إِلَىٰٓ إِبْرَٰهِـۧمَ وَإِسْمَٰعِيلَ وَإِسْحَٰقَ وَيَعْقُوبَ
وَٱلْأَسْبَاطِ وَمَآ أُوتِىَ مُوسَىٰ وَعِيسَىٰ وَمَآ
أُوتِىَ ٱلنَّبِيُّونَ مِن رَّبِّهِمْ لَا نُفَرِّقُ بَيْنَ أَحَدٍ
مِّنْهُمْ وَنَحْنُ لَهُۥ مُسْلِمُونَ

136 Say, "We believe in Allah; and in what was revealed to us; and in what was revealed to Abraham, and Ishmael, and Isaac, and Jacob, and the Patriarchs; and in what was given to Moses and Jesus; and in what was given to the prophets—from their Lord. We make no distinction between any of them, and to Him we surrender."

١٣٧ فَإِنْ ءَامَنُوا۟ بِمِثْلِ مَآ ءَامَنتُم بِهِۦ فَقَدِ
ٱهْتَدَوا۟ ۖ وَّإِن تَوَلَّوْا۟ فَإِنَّمَا هُمْ فِى شِقَاقٍ ۖ
فَسَيَكْفِيكَهُمُ ٱللَّهُ ۚ وَهُوَ ٱلسَّمِيعُ ٱلْعَلِيمُ

137 If they believe in the same as you have believed in, then they have been guided. But if they turn away, then they are in schism. Allah will protect you against them; for He is the Hearer, the Knower.

١٣٨ صِبْغَةَ ٱللَّهِ ۖ وَمَنْ أَحْسَنُ مِنَ ٱللَّهِ صِبْغَةً ۖ
وَنَحْنُ لَهُۥ عَٰبِدُونَ

138 Allah's coloring. And who gives better coloring than Allah? "And we are devoted to Him."

١٣٩ قُلْ أَتُحَآجُّونَنَا فِى ٱللَّهِ وَهُوَ رَبُّنَا وَرَبُّكُمْ
وَلَنَآ أَعْمَٰلُنَا وَلَكُمْ أَعْمَٰلُكُمْ وَنَحْنُ لَهُۥ مُخْلِصُونَ

139 Say, "Do you argue with us about Allah, when He is our Lord and your Lord, and We have our works, and you have your works, and we are sincere to Him?"

١٤٠ أَمْ تَقُولُونَ إِنَّ إِبْرَٰهِـۧمَ وَإِسْمَٰعِيلَ وَإِسْحَٰقَ
وَيَعْقُوبَ وَٱلْأَسْبَاطَ كَانُوا۟ هُودًا أَوْ نَصَٰرَىٰ ۗ قُلْ
ءَأَنتُمْ أَعْلَمُ أَمِ ٱللَّهُ ۗ وَمَنْ أَظْلَمُ مِمَّن كَتَمَ
شَهَٰدَةً عِندَهُۥ مِنَ ٱللَّهِ ۗ وَمَا ٱللَّهُ بِغَٰفِلٍ عَمَّا
تَعْمَلُونَ

140 Or do you say that Abraham, Ishmael, Isaac, Jacob, and the Patriarchs were Jews or Christians? Say, "Do you know better, or Allah?" And who does greater wrong than he who conceals a testimony he has from Allah? Allah is not unaware of what you do.

١٤١ تِلْكَ أُمَّةٌ قَدْ خَلَتْ ۖ لَهَا مَا كَسَبَتْ وَلَكُم مَّا
كَسَبْتُمْ ۖ وَلَا تُسْـَٔلُونَ عَمَّا كَانُوا۟ يَعْمَلُونَ

141 That was a community that has passed. To them is what they have earned, and to you is what you have earned. And you will not be

questioned about what they used to do.

١٤٢ سَيَقُولُ ٱلسُّفَهَآءُ مِنَ ٱلنَّاسِ مَا وَلَّىٰهُمْ عَن
قِبْلَتِهِمُ ٱلَّتِى كَانُوا۟ عَلَيْهَا ۚ قُل لِّلَّهِ ٱلْمَشْرِقُ
وَٱلْمَغْرِبُ ۚ يَهْدِى مَن يَشَآءُ إِلَىٰ صِرَٰطٍ مُّسْتَقِيمٍ

142 The ignorant among the people will say, "What has turned them away from the direction of prayer they once followed?" Say, "To Allah belong the East and the West. He guides whom He wills to a straight path."

١٤٣ وَكَذَٰلِكَ جَعَلْنَٰكُمْ أُمَّةً وَسَطًا لِّتَكُونُوا۟
شُهَدَآءَ عَلَى ٱلنَّاسِ وَيَكُونَ ٱلرَّسُولُ عَلَيْكُمْ
شَهِيدًا ۗ وَمَا جَعَلْنَا ٱلْقِبْلَةَ ٱلَّتِى كُنتَ عَلَيْهَآ إِلَّا
لِنَعْلَمَ مَن يَتَّبِعُ ٱلرَّسُولَ مِمَّن يَنقَلِبُ عَلَىٰ
عَقِبَيْهِ ۚ وَإِن كَانَتْ لَكَبِيرَةً إِلَّا عَلَى ٱلَّذِينَ هَدَى
ٱللَّهُ ۗ وَمَا كَانَ ٱللَّهُ لِيُضِيعَ إِيمَٰنَكُمْ ۚ إِنَّ ٱللَّهَ
بِٱلنَّاسِ لَرَءُوفٌ رَّحِيمٌ

143 Thus We made you a moderate community, that you may be witnesses to humanity, and that the Messenger may be a witness to you. We only established the direction of prayer, which you once followed, that We may distinguish those who follow the Messenger from those who turn on their heels. It is indeed difficult, except for those whom Allah has guided. But Allah would never let your faith go to waste. Allah is Kind towards the people, Merciful.

١٤٤ قَدْ نَرَىٰ تَقَلُّبَ وَجْهِكَ فِى ٱلسَّمَآءِ ۖ
فَلَنُوَلِّيَنَّكَ قِبْلَةً تَرْضَىٰهَا ۚ فَوَلِّ وَجْهَكَ شَطْرَ
ٱلْمَسْجِدِ ٱلْحَرَامِ ۚ وَحَيْثُ مَا كُنتُمْ فَوَلُّوا۟
وُجُوهَكُمْ شَطْرَهُۥ ۗ وَإِنَّ ٱلَّذِينَ أُوتُوا۟ ٱلْكِتَٰبَ
لَيَعْلَمُونَ أَنَّهُ ٱلْحَقُّ مِن رَّبِّهِمْ ۗ وَمَا ٱللَّهُ بِغَٰفِلٍ
عَمَّا يَعْمَلُونَ

144 We have seen your face turned towards the heaven. So We will turn you towards a direction that will satisfy you. So turn your face towards the Sacred Mosque. And wherever you may be, turn your faces towards it. Those who were given the Book know that it is the Truth from their Lord; and Allah is not unaware of what they do.

١٤٥ وَلَئِنْ أَتَيْتَ ٱلَّذِينَ أُوتُوا۟ ٱلْكِتَٰبَ بِكُلِّ ءَايَةٍ
مَّا تَبِعُوا۟ قِبْلَتَكَ ۚ وَمَآ أَنتَ بِتَابِعٍ قِبْلَتَهُمْ ۚ وَمَا
بَعْضُهُم بِتَابِعٍ قِبْلَةَ بَعْضٍ ۚ وَلَئِنِ ٱتَّبَعْتَ
أَهْوَآءَهُم مِّنۢ بَعْدِ مَا جَآءَكَ مِنَ ٱلْعِلْمِ ۙ إِنَّكَ إِذًا
لَّمِنَ ٱلظَّٰلِمِينَ

145 Even if you were to bring to those who were given the Book every proof, they would not follow your direction, nor are you to follow their direction, nor do they follow the direction of one another. And if you were to follow their desires, after the knowledge that has come to you, you would be in that case one of the wrongdoers.

١٤٦ ٱلَّذِينَ ءَاتَيْنَٰهُمُ ٱلْكِتَٰبَ يَعْرِفُونَهُۥ كَمَا
يَعْرِفُونَ أَبْنَآءَهُمْ ۖ وَإِنَّ فَرِيقًا مِّنْهُمْ لَيَكْتُمُونَ
ٱلْحَقَّ وَهُمْ يَعْلَمُونَ

146 Those to whom We have given the Book recognize it as they recognize their own children. But some of them conceal the truth while they know.

١٤٧ ٱلْحَقُّ مِن رَّبِّكَ ۖ فَلَا تَكُونَنَّ مِنَ ٱلْمُمْتَرِينَ

147 The truth is from your Lord, so do not be a skeptic.

١٤٨ وَلِكُلٍّ وِجْهَةٌ هُوَ مُوَلِّيهَا ۖ فَٱسْتَبِقُوا۟
ٱلْخَيْرَٰتِ ۚ أَيْنَ مَا تَكُونُوا۟ يَأْتِ بِكُمُ ٱللَّهُ جَمِيعًا ۚ
إِنَّ ٱللَّهَ عَلَىٰ كُلِّ شَىْءٍ قَدِيرٌ

148 To every community is a direction towards which it turns. Therefore, race towards goodness. Wherever you may be, Allah will bring you all together. Allah is capable of everything.

١٤٩ وَمِنْ حَيْثُ خَرَجْتَ فَوَلِّ وَجْهَكَ شَطْرَ
ٱلْمَسْجِدِ ٱلْحَرَامِ ۖ وَإِنَّهُۥ لَلْحَقُّ مِن رَّبِّكَ ۗ وَمَا ٱللَّهُ
بِغَٰفِلٍ عَمَّا تَعْمَلُونَ

149 And wherever you come from, turn your face towards the Sacred Mosque. This is the truth from your Lord, and Allah is not heedless of what you do.

١٥٠ وَمِنْ حَيْثُ خَرَجْتَ فَوَلِّ وَجْهَكَ شَطْرَ
ٱلْمَسْجِدِ ٱلْحَرَامِ ۚ وَحَيْثُ مَا كُنتُمْ فَوَلُّوا۟
وُجُوهَكُمْ شَطْرَهُۥ لِئَلَّا يَكُونَ لِلنَّاسِ عَلَيْكُمْ
حُجَّةٌ إِلَّا ٱلَّذِينَ ظَلَمُوا۟ مِنْهُمْ فَلَا تَخْشَوْهُمْ
وَٱخْشَوْنِى وَلِأُتِمَّ نِعْمَتِى عَلَيْكُمْ وَلَعَلَّكُمْ
تَهْتَدُونَ

150 And wherever you come from, turn your face towards the Sacred Mosque. And wherever you may be, turn your faces towards it. So that the people may not have any argument against you—except those who do wrong among them. So do not fear them, but fear Me, that I may complete My blessings upon you, and that you may be guided.

١٥١ كَمَآ أَرْسَلْنَا فِيكُمْ رَسُولًا مِّنكُمْ يَتْلُوا۟ عَلَيْكُمْ
ءَايَٰتِنَا وَيُزَكِّيكُمْ وَيُعَلِّمُكُمُ ٱلْكِتَٰبَ وَٱلْحِكْمَةَ
وَيُعَلِّمُكُم مَّا لَمْ تَكُونُوا۟ تَعْلَمُونَ

151 Just as We sent to you a messenger from among you, who recites Our revelations to you, and purifies you, and teaches you the Book and wisdom, and teaches you what you did not know.

١٥٢ فَٱذْكُرُونِىٓ أَذْكُرْكُمْ وَٱشْكُرُوا۟ لِى وَلَا
تَكْفُرُونِ

152 So remember Me, and I will remember you. And thank Me, and do not be ungrateful.

١٥٣ يَٰٓأَيُّهَا ٱلَّذِينَ ءَامَنُوا۟ ٱسْتَعِينُوا۟ بِٱلصَّبْرِ
وَٱلصَّلَوٰةِ ۚ إِنَّ ٱللَّهَ مَعَ ٱلصَّٰبِرِينَ

153 O you who believe! Seek help through patience and prayers. Allah is with the steadfast.

١٥٤ وَلَا تَقُولُوا۟ لِمَن يُقْتَلُ فِى سَبِيلِ ٱللَّهِ
أَمْوَٰتٌۢ ۚ بَلْ أَحْيَآءٌ وَلَٰكِن لَّا تَشْعُرُونَ

154 And do not say of those who are killed in the cause of Allah, "Dead." Rather, they are alive, but you do not perceive.

١٥٥ وَلَنَبْلُوَنَّكُم بِشَىْءٍ مِّنَ ٱلْخَوْفِ وَٱلْجُوعِ
وَنَقْصٍ مِّنَ ٱلْأَمْوَٰلِ وَٱلْأَنفُسِ وَٱلثَّمَرَٰتِ ۗ وَبَشِّرِ
ٱلصَّٰبِرِينَ

155 We will certainly test you with some fear and hunger, and some loss of possessions and lives and crops. But give good news to the steadfast.

١٥٦ ٱلَّذِينَ إِذَآ أَصَٰبَتْهُم مُّصِيبَةٌ قَالُوٓا۟ إِنَّا لِلَّهِ
وَإِنَّآ إِلَيْهِ رَٰجِعُونَ

156 Those who, when a calamity afflicts them, say, "To Allah we belong, and to Him we will return."

١٥٧ أُو۟لَٰٓئِكَ عَلَيْهِمْ صَلَوَٰتٌ مِّن رَّبِّهِمْ وَرَحْمَةٌ ۖ
وَأُو۟لَٰٓئِكَ هُمُ ٱلْمُهْتَدُونَ

157 Upon these are blessings and mercy from their Lord. These are the guided ones.

١٥٨ إِنَّ ٱلصَّفَا وَٱلْمَرْوَةَ مِن شَعَآئِرِ ٱللَّهِ ۖ فَمَنْ
حَجَّ ٱلْبَيْتَ أَوِ ٱعْتَمَرَ فَلَا جُنَاحَ عَلَيْهِ أَن
يَطَّوَّفَ بِهِمَا ۚ وَمَن تَطَوَّعَ خَيْرًا فَإِنَّ ٱللَّهَ شَاكِرٌ
عَلِيمٌ

158 Safa and Marwa are among the rites of Allah. Whoever makes the Pilgrimage to the House, or performs the Umrah, commits no error by circulating between them. Whoever volunteers good—Allah is Appreciative and Cognizant.

١٥٩ إِنَّ ٱلَّذِينَ يَكْتُمُونَ مَآ أَنزَلْنَا مِنَ ٱلْبَيِّنَٰتِ
وَٱلْهُدَىٰ مِنۢ بَعْدِ مَا بَيَّنَّٰهُ لِلنَّاسِ فِى ٱلْكِتَٰبِ ۙ
أُو۟لَٰٓئِكَ يَلْعَنُهُمُ ٱللَّهُ وَيَلْعَنُهُمُ ٱللَّٰعِنُونَ

159 Those who suppress the proofs and the guidance We have revealed, after We have clarified them to humanity in the Scripture—those—Allah curses them, and the cursers curse them.

١٦٠ إِلَّا ٱلَّذِينَ تَابُوا۟ وَأَصْلَحُوا۟ وَبَيَّنُوا۟ فَأُو۟لَٰٓئِكَ
أَتُوبُ عَلَيْهِمْ ۚ وَأَنَا ٱلتَّوَّابُ ٱلرَّحِيمُ

160 Except those who repent, and reform, and proclaim. Those—I will accept their repentance. I am the Acceptor of Repentance, the Merciful.

١٦١ إِنَّ ٱلَّذِينَ كَفَرُوا۟ وَمَاتُوا۟ وَهُمْ كُفَّارٌ أُو۟لَٰٓئِكَ
عَلَيْهِمْ لَعْنَةُ ٱللَّهِ وَٱلْمَلَٰٓئِكَةِ وَٱلنَّاسِ أَجْمَعِينَ

161 But as for those who reject faith, and die rejecting—those—upon them is the curse of Allah, and of the angels, and of all humanity.

١٦٢ خَٰلِدِينَ فِيهَا ۖ لَا يُخَفَّفُ عَنْهُمُ ٱلْعَذَابُ وَلَا
هُمْ يُنظَرُونَ

162 They will remain under it forever, and the torment will not be lightened for them, and they will not be reprieved.

١٦٣ وَإِلَٰهُكُمْ إِلَٰهٌ وَٰحِدٌۖ لَّآ إِلَٰهَ إِلَّا هُوَ ٱلرَّحْمَٰنُ
ٱلرَّحِيمُ

163 Your God is one God. There is no god but He, the Benevolent, the Compassionate.

١٦٤ إِنَّ فِى خَلْقِ ٱلسَّمَٰوَٰتِ وَٱلْأَرْضِ وَٱخْتِلَٰفِ
ٱلَّيْلِ وَٱلنَّهَارِ وَٱلْفُلْكِ ٱلَّتِى تَجْرِى فِى ٱلْبَحْرِ بِمَا
يَنفَعُ ٱلنَّاسَ وَمَآ أَنزَلَ ٱللَّهُ مِنَ ٱلسَّمَآءِ مِن مَّآءٍ
فَأَحْيَا بِهِ ٱلْأَرْضَ بَعْدَ مَوْتِهَا وَبَثَّ فِيهَا مِن كُلِّ
دَآبَّةٍ وَتَصْرِيفِ ٱلرِّيَٰحِ وَٱلسَّحَابِ ٱلْمُسَخَّرِ بَيْنَ
ٱلسَّمَآءِ وَٱلْأَرْضِ لَءَايَٰتٍ لِّقَوْمٍ يَعْقِلُونَ

164 In the creation of the heavens and the earth; in the alternation of night and day; in the ships that sail the oceans for the benefit of mankind; in the water that Allah sends down from the sky, and revives the earth with it after it had died, and scatters in it all kinds of creatures; in the changing of the winds, and the clouds disposed between the sky and the earth; are signs for people who understand.

١٦٥ وَمِنَ ٱلنَّاسِ مَن يَتَّخِذُ مِن دُونِ ٱللَّهِ أَندَادًا
يُحِبُّونَهُمْ كَحُبِّ ٱللَّهِۖ وَٱلَّذِينَ ءَامَنُوٓا۟ أَشَدُّ حُبًّا
لِّلَّهِۗ وَلَوْ يَرَى ٱلَّذِينَ ظَلَمُوٓا۟ إِذْ يَرَوْنَ ٱلْعَذَابَ أَنَّ
ٱلْقُوَّةَ لِلَّهِ جَمِيعًا وَأَنَّ ٱللَّهَ شَدِيدُ ٱلْعَذَابِ

165 Yet among the people are those who take other than Allah as equals to Him. They love them as the love of Allah. But those who believe have greater love for Allah. If only the wrongdoers would realize, when they see the torment; that all power is Allah's, and that Allah is severe in punishment.

١٦٦ إِذْ تَبَرَّأَ ٱلَّذِينَ ٱتُّبِعُوا۟ مِنَ ٱلَّذِينَ ٱتَّبَعُوا۟
وَرَأَوُا۟ ٱلْعَذَابَ وَتَقَطَّعَتْ بِهِمُ ٱلْأَسْبَابُ

166 Those who were followed will then disown those who followed them, and they will see the retribution, and ties between them will be severed.

١٦٧ وَقَالَ ٱلَّذِينَ ٱتَّبَعُوا۟ لَوْ أَنَّ لَنَا كَرَّةً فَنَتَبَرَّأَ
مِنْهُمْ كَمَا تَبَرَّءُوا۟ مِنَّاۗ كَذَٰلِكَ يُرِيهِمُ ٱللَّهُ
أَعْمَٰلَهُمْ حَسَرَٰتٍ عَلَيْهِمْۖ وَمَا هُم بِخَٰرِجِينَ مِنَ
ٱلنَّارِ

167 Those who followed will say, "If only we can have another chance, we will disown them, as they disowned us." Thus Allah will show them their deeds, as regrets to them, and they will not come out of the Fire.

١٦٨ يَٰٓأَيُّهَا ٱلنَّاسُ كُلُوا۟ مِمَّا فِى ٱلْأَرْضِ حَلَٰلًا
طَيِّبًا وَلَا تَتَّبِعُوا۟ خُطُوَٰتِ ٱلشَّيْطَٰنِ ۚ إِنَّهُۥ لَكُمْ
عَدُوٌّ مُّبِينٌ

168 O people! Eat of what is lawful and good on earth, and do not follow the footsteps of Satan. He is to you an open enemy.

١٦٩ إِنَّمَا يَأْمُرُكُم بِٱلسُّوٓءِ وَٱلْفَحْشَآءِ وَأَن
تَقُولُوا۟ عَلَى ٱللَّهِ مَا لَا تَعْلَمُونَ

169 He commands you to do evil and vice, and to say about Allah what you do not know.

١٧٠ وَإِذَا قِيلَ لَهُمُ ٱتَّبِعُوا۟ مَآ أَنزَلَ ٱللَّهُ قَالُوا۟ بَلْ
نَتَّبِعُ مَآ أَلْفَيْنَا عَلَيْهِ ءَابَآءَنَآ ۗ أَوَلَوْ كَانَ ءَابَآؤُهُمْ
لَا يَعْقِلُونَ شَيْـًٔا وَلَا يَهْتَدُونَ

170 And when it is said to them, "Follow what Allah has revealed," they say, "We will follow what we found our ancestors following." Even if their ancestors understood nothing, and were not guided?

١٧١ وَمَثَلُ ٱلَّذِينَ كَفَرُوا۟ كَمَثَلِ ٱلَّذِى يَنْعِقُ بِمَا لَا
يَسْمَعُ إِلَّا دُعَآءً وَنِدَآءً ۚ صُمٌّۢ بُكْمٌ عُمْىٌ فَهُمْ لَا
يَعْقِلُونَ

171 The parable of those who disbelieve is that of someone who calls upon someone who hears nothing except screaming and yelling. Deaf, dumb, and blind—they do not understand.

١٧٢ يَـٰٓأَيُّهَا ٱلَّذِينَ ءَامَنُوا۟ كُلُوا۟ مِن طَيِّبَـٰتِ مَا
رَزَقْنَـٰكُمْ وَٱشْكُرُوا۟ لِلَّهِ إِن كُنتُمْ إِيَّاهُ تَعْبُدُونَ

172 O you who believe! Eat of the good things We have provided for you, and give thanks to Allah, if it is Him that you serve.

١٧٣ إِنَّمَا حَرَّمَ عَلَيْكُمُ ٱلْمَيْتَةَ وَٱلدَّمَ وَلَحْمَ
ٱلْخِنزِيرِ وَمَآ أُهِلَّ بِهِۦ لِغَيْرِ ٱللَّهِ ۖ فَمَنِ ٱضْطُرَّ
غَيْرَ بَاغٍ وَلَا عَادٍ فَلَآ إِثْمَ عَلَيْهِ ۚ إِنَّ ٱللَّهَ غَفُورٌ
رَّحِيمٌ

173 He has forbidden you carrion, and blood, and the flesh of swine, and what was dedicated to other than Allah. But if anyone is compelled, without desiring or exceeding, he commits no sin. Allah is Forgiving and Merciful.

١٧٤ إِنَّ ٱلَّذِينَ يَكْتُمُونَ مَآ أَنزَلَ ٱللَّهُ مِنَ ٱلْكِتَـٰبِ
وَيَشْتَرُونَ بِهِۦ ثَمَنًا قَلِيلًا ۙ أُو۟لَـٰٓئِكَ مَا يَأْكُلُونَ
فِى بُطُونِهِمْ إِلَّا ٱلنَّارَ وَلَا يُكَلِّمُهُمُ ٱللَّهُ يَوْمَ
ٱلْقِيَـٰمَةِ وَلَا يُزَكِّيهِمْ وَلَهُمْ عَذَابٌ أَلِيمٌ

174 Those who conceal what Allah revealed in the Book, and exchange it for a small price—those swallow nothing but fire into their bellies. And Allah will not speak to them on the Day of Resurrection, nor will He purify them, and they will have a painful punishment.

١٧٥ أُو۟لَـٰٓئِكَ ٱلَّذِينَ ٱشْتَرَوُا۟ ٱلضَّلَـٰلَةَ بِٱلْهُدَىٰ
وَٱلْعَذَابَ بِٱلْمَغْفِرَةِ ۚ فَمَآ أَصْبَرَهُمْ عَلَى ٱلنَّارِ

175 It is they who exchange guidance for error, and forgiveness for punishment. But why do they insist on the Fire?

١٧٦ ذَٰلِكَ بِأَنَّ ٱللَّهَ نَزَّلَ ٱلْكِتَـٰبَ بِٱلْحَقِّ ۗ وَإِنَّ
ٱلَّذِينَ ٱخْتَلَفُوا۟ فِى ٱلْكِتَـٰبِ لَفِى شِقَاقٍۭ بَعِيدٍ

176 That is because Allah has revealed the Book in truth; and those

who differ about the Book are in deep discord.

١٧٧ لَّيۡسَ ٱلۡبِرَّ أَن تُوَلُّواْ وُجُوهَكُمۡ قِبَلَ ٱلۡمَشۡرِقِ
وَٱلۡمَغۡرِبِ وَلَٰكِنَّ ٱلۡبِرَّ مَنۡ ءَامَنَ بِٱللَّهِ وَٱلۡيَوۡمِ
ٱلۡأٓخِرِ وَٱلۡمَلَٰٓئِكَةِ وَٱلۡكِتَٰبِ وَٱلنَّبِيِّـۧنَ وَءَاتَى
ٱلۡمَالَ عَلَىٰ حُبِّهِۦ ذَوِي ٱلۡقُرۡبَىٰ وَٱلۡيَتَٰمَىٰ
وَٱلۡمَسَٰكِينَ وَٱبۡنَ ٱلسَّبِيلِ وَٱلسَّآئِلِينَ وَفِي
ٱلرِّقَابِ وَأَقَامَ ٱلصَّلَوٰةَ وَءَاتَى ٱلزَّكَوٰةَ
وَٱلۡمُوفُونَ بِعَهۡدِهِمۡ إِذَا عَٰهَدُواْۖ وَٱلصَّٰبِرِينَ فِي
ٱلۡبَأۡسَآءِ وَٱلضَّرَّآءِ وَحِينَ ٱلۡبَأۡسِۗ أُوْلَٰٓئِكَ ٱلَّذِينَ
صَدَقُواْۖ وَأُوْلَٰٓئِكَ هُمُ ٱلۡمُتَّقُونَ

177 Righteousness does not consist of turning your faces towards the East and the West. But righteous is he who believes in Allah, and the Last Day, and the angels, and the Scripture, and the prophets. Who gives money, though dear, to near relatives, and orphans, and the needy, and the homeless, and the beggars, and for the freeing of slaves; those who perform the prayers, and pay the obligatory charity, and fulfill their promise when they promise, and patiently persevere in the face of persecution, hardship, and in the time of conflict. These are the sincere; these are the pious.

١٧٨ يَٰٓأَيُّهَا ٱلَّذِينَ ءَامَنُواْ كُتِبَ عَلَيۡكُمُ ٱلۡقِصَاصُ
فِي ٱلۡقَتۡلَىۖ ٱلۡحُرُّ بِٱلۡحُرِّ وَٱلۡعَبۡدُ بِٱلۡعَبۡدِ وَٱلۡأُنثَىٰ
بِٱلۡأُنثَىٰۚ فَمَنۡ عُفِيَ لَهُۥ مِنۡ أَخِيهِ شَيۡءٞ فَٱتِّبَاعُۢ
بِٱلۡمَعۡرُوفِ وَأَدَآءٌ إِلَيۡهِ بِإِحۡسَٰنٖۗ ذَٰلِكَ تَخۡفِيفٞ
مِّن رَّبِّكُمۡ وَرَحۡمَةٞۗ فَمَنِ ٱعۡتَدَىٰ بَعۡدَ ذَٰلِكَ فَلَهُۥ
عَذَابٌ أَلِيمٞ

178 O you who believe! Retaliation for the murdered is ordained upon you: the free for the free, the slave for the slave, the female for the female. But if he is forgiven by his kin, then grant any reasonable demand, and pay with good will. This is a concession from your Lord, and a mercy. But whoever commits aggression after that, a painful torment awaits him.

١٧٩ وَلَكُمۡ فِي ٱلۡقِصَاصِ حَيَوٰةٞ يَٰٓأُوْلِي ٱلۡأَلۡبَٰبِ
لَعَلَّكُمۡ تَتَّقُونَ

179 There is life for you in retaliation, O people of understanding, so that you may refrain.

١٨٠ كُتِبَ عَلَيۡكُمۡ إِذَا حَضَرَ أَحَدَكُمُ ٱلۡمَوۡتُ إِن
تَرَكَ خَيۡرًا ٱلۡوَصِيَّةُ لِلۡوَٰلِدَيۡنِ وَٱلۡأَقۡرَبِينَ
بِٱلۡمَعۡرُوفِۖ حَقًّا عَلَى ٱلۡمُتَّقِينَ

180 It is decreed for you: when death approaches one of you, and he leaves wealth, to make a testament in favor of the parents and the relatives, fairly and correctly—a duty upon the righteous.

١٨١ فَمَنۢ بَدَّلَهُۥ بَعۡدَمَا سَمِعَهُۥ فَإِنَّمَآ إِثۡمُهُۥ عَلَى
ٱلَّذِينَ يُبَدِّلُونَهُۥٓۚ إِنَّ ٱللَّهَ سَمِيعٌ عَلِيمٞ

181 But whoever changes it after he has heard it, the guilt is upon those

who change it. Allah is All-Hearing, All-Knowing.

١٨٢ فَمَنْ خَافَ مِن مُّوصٍ جَنَفًا أَوْ إِثْمًا فَأَصْلَحَ
بَيْنَهُمْ فَلَآ إِثْمَ عَلَيْهِ ۚ إِنَّ ٱللَّهَ غَفُورٌ رَّحِيمٌ

182 Should someone suspect bias or injustice on the part of a testator, and then reconciles between them, he commits no sin. Allah is Forgiving and Merciful.

١٨٣ يَٰٓأَيُّهَا ٱلَّذِينَ ءَامَنُوا۟ كُتِبَ عَلَيْكُمُ ٱلصِّيَامُ
كَمَا كُتِبَ عَلَى ٱلَّذِينَ مِن قَبْلِكُمْ لَعَلَّكُمْ تَتَّقُونَ

183 O you who believe! Fasting is prescribed for you, as it was prescribed for those before you, that you may become righteous.

١٨٤ أَيَّامًا مَّعْدُودَٰتٍ ۚ فَمَن كَانَ مِنكُم مَّرِيضًا أَوْ
عَلَىٰ سَفَرٍ فَعِدَّةٌ مِّنْ أَيَّامٍ أُخَرَ ۚ وَعَلَى ٱلَّذِينَ
يُطِيقُونَهُۥ فِدْيَةٌ طَعَامُ مِسْكِينٍ ۖ فَمَن تَطَوَّعَ
خَيْرًا فَهُوَ خَيْرٌ لَّهُۥ ۚ وَأَن تَصُومُوا۟ خَيْرٌ لَّكُمْ ۖ إِن
كُنتُمْ تَعْلَمُونَ

184 For a specified number of days. But whoever among you is sick, or on a journey, then a number of other days. For those who are able: a ransom of feeding a needy person. But whoever volunteers goodness, it is better for him. But to fast is best for you, if you only knew.

١٨٥ شَهْرُ رَمَضَانَ ٱلَّذِىٓ أُنزِلَ فِيهِ ٱلْقُرْءَانُ هُدًى
لِّلنَّاسِ وَبَيِّنَٰتٍ مِّنَ ٱلْهُدَىٰ وَٱلْفُرْقَانِ ۚ فَمَن شَهِدَ
مِنكُمُ ٱلشَّهْرَ فَلْيَصُمْهُ ۖ وَمَن كَانَ مَرِيضًا أَوْ
عَلَىٰ سَفَرٍ فَعِدَّةٌ مِّنْ أَيَّامٍ أُخَرَ ۗ يُرِيدُ ٱللَّهُ بِكُمُ
ٱلْيُسْرَ وَلَا يُرِيدُ بِكُمُ ٱلْعُسْرَ وَلِتُكْمِلُوا۟ ٱلْعِدَّةَ
وَلِتُكَبِّرُوا۟ ٱللَّهَ عَلَىٰ مَا هَدَىٰكُمْ وَلَعَلَّكُمْ
تَشْكُرُونَ

185 Ramadan is the month in which the Quran was revealed. Guidance for humanity, and clear portents of guidance, and the Criterion. Whoever of you witnesses the month, shall fast it. But whoever is sick, or on a journey, then a number of other days. Allah desires ease for you, and does not desire hardship for you, that you may complete the number, and celebrate Allah for having guided you, so that you may be thankful.

١٨٦ وَإِذَا سَأَلَكَ عِبَادِى عَنِّى فَإِنِّى قَرِيبٌ ۖ
أُجِيبُ دَعْوَةَ ٱلدَّاعِ إِذَا دَعَانِ ۖ فَلْيَسْتَجِيبُوا۟ لِى
وَلْيُؤْمِنُوا۟ بِى لَعَلَّهُمْ يَرْشُدُونَ

186 And when My servants ask you about Me, I Am near; I answer the call of the caller when he calls on Me. So let them answer Me, and have faith in Me, that they may be rightly guided.

١٨٧ أُحِلَّ لَكُمْ لَيْلَةَ ٱلصِّيَامِ ٱلرَّفَثُ إِلَىٰ نِسَآئِكُمْ ۚ
هُنَّ لِبَاسٌ لَّكُمْ وَأَنتُمْ لِبَاسٌ لَّهُنَّ ۗ عَلِمَ ٱللَّهُ أَنَّكُمْ

187 Permitted for you is intercourse with your wives on the night of the fast. They are a garment for you, and you are a garment for them.

كُنتُمْ تَخْتَانُونَ أَنفُسَكُمْ فَتَابَ عَلَيْكُمْ وَعَفَا
عَنكُمْ ۖ فَٱلْـَٔـٰنَ بَـٰشِرُوهُنَّ وَٱبْتَغُوا۟ مَا كَتَبَ ٱللَّهُ
لَكُمْ ۚ وَكُلُوا۟ وَٱشْرَبُوا۟ حَتَّىٰ يَتَبَيَّنَ لَكُمُ ٱلْخَيْطُ
ٱلْأَبْيَضُ مِنَ ٱلْخَيْطِ ٱلْأَسْوَدِ مِنَ ٱلْفَجْرِ ۖ ثُمَّ
أَتِمُّوا۟ ٱلصِّيَامَ إِلَى ٱلَّيْلِ ۚ وَلَا تُبَـٰشِرُوهُنَّ وَأَنتُمْ
عَـٰكِفُونَ فِى ٱلْمَسَـٰجِدِ ۗ تِلْكَ حُدُودُ ٱللَّهِ فَلَا
تَقْرَبُوهَا ۗ كَذَٰلِكَ يُبَيِّنُ ٱللَّهُ ءَايَـٰتِهِۦ لِلنَّاسِ لَعَلَّهُمْ
يَتَّقُونَ

Allah knows that you used to betray yourselves, but He turned to you and pardoned you. So approach them now, and seek what Allah has ordained for you, and eat and drink until the white streak of dawn can be distinguished from the black streak. Then complete the fast until nightfall. But do not approach them while you are in retreat at the mosques. These are the limits of Allah, so do not come near them. Allah thus clarifies His revelations to the people, that they may attain piety.

١٨٨ وَلَا تَأْكُلُوٓا۟ أَمْوَٰلَكُم بَيْنَكُم بِٱلْبَـٰطِلِ وَتُدْلُوا۟
بِهَآ إِلَى ٱلْحُكَّامِ لِتَأْكُلُوا۟ فَرِيقًا مِّنْ أَمْوَٰلِ ٱلنَّاسِ
بِٱلْإِثْمِ وَأَنتُمْ تَعْلَمُونَ

188 And do not consume one another's wealth by unjust means, nor offer it as bribes to the officials in order to consume part of other people's wealth illicitly, while you know.

١٨٩ يَسْـَٔلُونَكَ عَنِ ٱلْأَهِلَّةِ ۖ قُلْ هِىَ مَوَٰقِيتُ
لِلنَّاسِ وَٱلْحَجِّ ۗ وَلَيْسَ ٱلْبِرُّ بِأَن تَأْتُوا۟ ٱلْبُيُوتَ
مِن ظُهُورِهَا وَلَـٰكِنَّ ٱلْبِرَّ مَنِ ٱتَّقَىٰ ۗ وَأْتُوا۟
ٱلْبُيُوتَ مِنْ أَبْوَٰبِهَا ۚ وَٱتَّقُوا۟ ٱللَّهَ لَعَلَّكُمْ تُفْلِحُونَ

189 They ask you about the crescents. Say, "They are timetables for people, and for the Hajj." It is not virtuous that you approach homes from their backs, but virtue is to be pious. So approach homes from their doors, and observe Allah, that you may succeed.

١٩٠ وَقَـٰتِلُوا۟ فِى سَبِيلِ ٱللَّهِ ٱلَّذِينَ يُقَـٰتِلُونَكُمْ وَلَا
تَعْتَدُوٓا۟ ۚ إِنَّ ٱللَّهَ لَا يُحِبُّ ٱلْمُعْتَدِينَ

190 And fight in the cause of Allah those who fight you, but do not commit aggression; Allah does not love the aggressors.

١٩١ وَٱقْتُلُوهُمْ حَيْثُ ثَقِفْتُمُوهُمْ وَأَخْرِجُوهُم
مِّنْ حَيْثُ أَخْرَجُوكُمْ ۚ وَٱلْفِتْنَةُ أَشَدُّ مِنَ ٱلْقَتْلِ ۚ
وَلَا تُقَـٰتِلُوهُمْ عِندَ ٱلْمَسْجِدِ ٱلْحَرَامِ حَتَّىٰ
يُقَـٰتِلُوكُمْ فِيهِ ۖ فَإِن قَـٰتَلُوكُمْ فَٱقْتُلُوهُمْ ۗ كَذَٰلِكَ
جَزَآءُ ٱلْكَـٰفِرِينَ

191 And kill them wherever you overtake them, and expel them from where they had expelled you. Oppression is more serious than murder. But do not fight them at the Sacred Mosque, unless they fight you there. If they fight you, then kill them. Such is the retribution of the disbelievers.

١٩٢ فَإِنِ ٱنتَهَوْا۟ فَإِنَّ ٱللَّهَ غَفُورٌ رَّحِيمٌ

192 But if they cease, then Allah is Forgiving and Merciful.

١٩٣ وَقَـٰتِلُوهُمْ حَتَّىٰ لَا تَكُونَ فِتْنَةٌ وَيَكُونَ
ٱلدِّينُ لِلَّهِ ۖ فَإِنِ ٱنتَهَوْا۟ فَلَا عُدْوَٰنَ إِلَّا عَلَى
ٱلظَّـٰلِمِينَ

193 And fight them until there is no oppression, and worship becomes devoted to Allah alone. But if they cease, then let there be no hostility except against the oppressors.

١٩٤ ٱلشَّهْرُ ٱلْحَرَامُ بِٱلشَّهْرِ ٱلْحَرَامِ وَٱلْحُرُمَـٰتُ
قِصَاصٌ ۚ فَمَنِ ٱعْتَدَىٰ عَلَيْكُمْ فَٱعْتَدُوا۟ عَلَيْهِ
بِمِثْلِ مَا ٱعْتَدَىٰ عَلَيْكُمْ ۚ وَٱتَّقُوا۟ ٱللَّهَ وَٱعْلَمُوٓا۟
أَنَّ ٱللَّهَ مَعَ ٱلْمُتَّقِينَ

194 The sacred month for the sacred month; and sacrilege calls for retaliation. Whoever commits aggression against you, retaliate against him in the same measure as he has committed against you. And be conscious of Allah, and know that Allah is with the righteous.

١٩٥ وَأَنفِقُوا۟ فِى سَبِيلِ ٱللَّهِ وَلَا تُلْقُوا۟ بِأَيْدِيكُمْ
إِلَى ٱلتَّهْلُكَةِ ۛ وَأَحْسِنُوٓا۟ ۛ إِنَّ ٱللَّهَ يُحِبُّ
ٱلْمُحْسِنِينَ

195 And spend in the cause of Allah, and do not throw yourselves with your own hands into ruin, and be charitable. Allah loves the charitable.

١٩٦ وَأَتِمُّوا۟ ٱلْحَجَّ وَٱلْعُمْرَةَ لِلَّهِ ۚ فَإِنْ أُحْصِرْتُمْ
فَمَا ٱسْتَيْسَرَ مِنَ ٱلْهَدْىِ ۖ وَلَا تَحْلِقُوا۟ رُءُوسَكُمْ
حَتَّىٰ يَبْلُغَ ٱلْهَدْىُ مَحِلَّهُۥ ۚ فَمَن كَانَ مِنكُم
مَّرِيضًا أَوْ بِهِۦٓ أَذًى مِّن رَّأْسِهِۦ فَفِدْيَةٌ مِّن
صِيَامٍ أَوْ صَدَقَةٍ أَوْ نُسُكٍ ۚ فَإِذَآ أَمِنتُمْ فَمَن
تَمَتَّعَ بِٱلْعُمْرَةِ إِلَى ٱلْحَجِّ فَمَا ٱسْتَيْسَرَ مِنَ
ٱلْهَدْىِ ۚ فَمَن لَّمْ يَجِدْ فَصِيَامُ ثَلَـٰثَةِ أَيَّامٍ فِى
ٱلْحَجِّ وَسَبْعَةٍ إِذَا رَجَعْتُمْ ۗ تِلْكَ عَشَرَةٌ كَامِلَةٌ ۗ
ذَٰلِكَ لِمَن لَّمْ يَكُنْ أَهْلُهُۥ حَاضِرِى ٱلْمَسْجِدِ
ٱلْحَرَامِ ۚ وَٱتَّقُوا۟ ٱللَّهَ وَٱعْلَمُوٓا۟ أَنَّ ٱللَّهَ شَدِيدُ
ٱلْعِقَابِ

196 And carry out the Hajj and the Umrah for Allah. But if you are prevented, then whatever is feasible of offerings. And do not shave your heads until the offering has reached its destination. Whoever of you is sick, or has an injury of the head, then redemption of fasting, or charity, or worship. When you are secure: whoever continues the Umrah until the Hajj, then whatever is feasible of offering. But if he lacks the means, then fasting for three days during the Hajj and seven when you have returned, making ten in all. This is for he whose household is not present at the Sacred Mosque. And remain conscious of Allah, and know that Allah is stern in retribution.

١٩٧ ٱلْحَجُّ أَشْهُرٌ مَّعْلُومَٰتٌ ۚ فَمَن فَرَضَ فِيهِنَّ
ٱلْحَجَّ فَلَا رَفَثَ وَلَا فُسُوقَ وَلَا جِدَالَ فِى
ٱلْحَجِّ ۗ وَمَا تَفْعَلُوا۟ مِنْ خَيْرٍ يَعْلَمْهُ ٱللَّهُ ۗ
وَتَزَوَّدُوا۟ فَإِنَّ خَيْرَ ٱلزَّادِ ٱلتَّقْوَىٰ ۚ وَٱتَّقُونِ
يَٰٓأُو۟لِى ٱلْأَلْبَٰبِ

197 The Hajj is during specific months. Whoever decides to perform the Hajj—there shall be no sexual relations, nor misconduct, nor quarrelling during the Hajj. And whatever good you do, Allah knows it. And take provisions, but the best provision is righteousness. And be mindful of Me, O people of understanding.

١٩٨ لَيْسَ عَلَيْكُمْ جُنَاحٌ أَن تَبْتَغُوا۟ فَضْلًا مِّن
رَّبِّكُمْ ۚ فَإِذَآ أَفَضْتُم مِّنْ عَرَفَٰتٍ فَٱذْكُرُوا۟ ٱللَّهَ
عِندَ ٱلْمَشْعَرِ ٱلْحَرَامِ ۖ وَٱذْكُرُوهُ كَمَا هَدَىٰكُمْ وَإِن
كُنتُم مِّن قَبْلِهِۦ لَمِنَ ٱلضَّآلِّينَ

198 You commit no error by seeking bounty from your Lord. When you disperse from Arafat, remember Allah at the Sacred Landmark. And remember Him as He has guided you. Although, before that, you were of those astray.

١٩٩ ثُمَّ أَفِيضُوا۟ مِنْ حَيْثُ أَفَاضَ ٱلنَّاسُ
وَٱسْتَغْفِرُوا۟ ٱللَّهَ ۚ إِنَّ ٱللَّهَ غَفُورٌ رَّحِيمٌ

199 Then disperse from where the people disperse, and ask Allah for forgiveness. Allah is Most Forgiving, Most Merciful.

٢٠٠ فَإِذَا قَضَيْتُم مَّنَٰسِكَكُمْ فَٱذْكُرُوا۟ ٱللَّهَ
كَذِكْرِكُمْ ءَابَآءَكُمْ أَوْ أَشَدَّ ذِكْرًا ۗ فَمِنَ ٱلنَّاسِ
مَن يَقُولُ رَبَّنَآ ءَاتِنَا فِى ٱلدُّنْيَا وَمَا لَهُۥ فِى
ٱلْءَاخِرَةِ مِنْ خَلَٰقٍ

200 When you have completed your rites, remember Allah as you remember your parents, or even more. Among the people is he who says, “Our Lord, give us in this world,” yet he has no share in the Hereafter.

٢٠١ وَمِنْهُم مَّن يَقُولُ رَبَّنَآ ءَاتِنَا فِى ٱلدُّنْيَا
حَسَنَةً وَفِى ٱلْءَاخِرَةِ حَسَنَةً وَقِنَا عَذَابَ ٱلنَّارِ

201 And among them is he who says, “Our Lord, give us goodness in this world, and goodness in the Hereafter, and protect us from the torment of the Fire.”

٢٠٢ أُو۟لَٰٓئِكَ لَهُمْ نَصِيبٌ مِّمَّا كَسَبُوا۟ ۚ وَٱللَّهُ سَرِيعُ
ٱلْحِسَابِ

202 These will have a share of what they have earned. Allah is swift in reckoning.

٢٠٣ وَٱذْكُرُوا۟ ٱللَّهَ فِىٓ أَيَّامٍ مَّعْدُودَٰتٍ ۚ فَمَن
تَعَجَّلَ فِى يَوْمَيْنِ فَلَآ إِثْمَ عَلَيْهِ وَمَن تَأَخَّرَ فَلَآ

203 And remember Allah during the designated days. But whoever hurries on in two days commits no wrong, and whoever stays on commits no wrong—provided he maintains righteousness. And obey

إِثۡمَ عَلَيۡهِۚ لِمَنِ ٱتَّقَىٰۗ وَٱتَّقُواْ ٱللَّهَ وَٱعۡلَمُوٓاْ أَنَّكُمۡ
إِلَيۡهِ تُحۡشَرُونَ

Allah, and know that to Him you will be gathered.

٢٠٤ وَمِنَ ٱلنَّاسِ مَن يُعۡجِبُكَ قَوۡلُهُۥ فِي ٱلۡحَيَوٰةِ
ٱلدُّنۡيَا وَيُشۡهِدُ ٱللَّهَ عَلَىٰ مَا فِي قَلۡبِهِۦ وَهُوَ أَلَدُّ
ٱلۡخِصَامِ

204 Among the people is he whose speech about the worldly life impresses you, and he calls Allah to witness what is in his heart, while he is the most hostile of adversaries.

٢٠٥ وَإِذَا تَوَلَّىٰ سَعَىٰ فِي ٱلۡأَرۡضِ لِيُفۡسِدَ فِيهَا
وَيُهۡلِكَ ٱلۡحَرۡثَ وَٱلنَّسۡلَۚ وَٱللَّهُ لَا يُحِبُّ ٱلۡفَسَادَ

205 When he gains power, he strives to spread corruption on earth, destroying properties and lives. Allah does not like corruption.

٢٠٦ وَإِذَا قِيلَ لَهُ ٱتَّقِ ٱللَّهَ أَخَذَتۡهُ ٱلۡعِزَّةُ بِٱلۡإِثۡمِۚ
فَحَسۡبُهُۥ جَهَنَّمُۖ وَلَبِئۡسَ ٱلۡمِهَادُ

206 And when he is told, “Beware of Allah,” his pride leads him to more sin. Hell is enough for him—a dreadful abode.

٢٠٧ وَمِنَ ٱلنَّاسِ مَن يَشۡرِي نَفۡسَهُ ٱبۡتِغَآءَ
مَرۡضَاتِ ٱللَّهِۚ وَٱللَّهُ رَءُوفُۢ بِٱلۡعِبَادِ

207 And among the people is he who sells himself seeking Allah’s approval. Allah is kind towards the servants.

٢٠٨ يَٰٓأَيُّهَا ٱلَّذِينَ ءَامَنُواْ ٱدۡخُلُواْ فِي ٱلسِّلۡمِ
كَآفَّةٗ وَلَا تَتَّبِعُواْ خُطُوَٰتِ ٱلشَّيۡطَٰنِۚ إِنَّهُۥ لَكُمۡ
عَدُوّٞ مُّبِينٞ

208 O you who believe! Enter into submission, wholeheartedly, and do not follow the footsteps of Satan; he is to you an outright enemy.

٢٠٩ فَإِن زَلَلۡتُم مِّنۢ بَعۡدِ مَا جَآءَتۡكُمُ ٱلۡبَيِّنَٰتُ
فَٱعۡلَمُوٓاْ أَنَّ ٱللَّهَ عَزِيزٌ حَكِيمٌ

209 But if you slip after the proofs have come to you, know that Allah is Powerful and Wise.

٢١٠ هَلۡ يَنظُرُونَ إِلَّآ أَن يَأۡتِيَهُمُ ٱللَّهُ فِي ظُلَلٖ
مِّنَ ٱلۡغَمَامِ وَٱلۡمَلَٰٓئِكَةُ وَقُضِيَ ٱلۡأَمۡرُۚ وَإِلَى ٱللَّهِ
تُرۡجَعُ ٱلۡأُمُورُ

210 Are they waiting for Allah Himself to come to them in the shadows of the clouds, together with the angels, and thus the matter is settled? All things are returned to Allah.

٢١١ سَلۡ بَنِيٓ إِسۡرَٰٓءِيلَ كَمۡ ءَاتَيۡنَٰهُم مِّنۡ ءَايَةِۭ
بَيِّنَةٖۗ وَمَن يُبَدِّلۡ نِعۡمَةَ ٱللَّهِ مِنۢ بَعۡدِ مَا جَآءَتۡهُ
فَإِنَّ ٱللَّهَ شَدِيدُ ٱلۡعِقَابِ

211 Ask the Children of Israel how many clear signs We have given them. Whoever alters the blessing of Allah after it has come to him—Allah is severe in retribution.

٢١٢ زُيِّنَ لِلَّذِينَ كَفَرُواْ ٱلۡحَيَوٰةُ ٱلدُّنۡيَا
وَيَسۡخَرُونَ مِنَ ٱلَّذِينَ ءَامَنُواْۘ وَٱلَّذِينَ ٱتَّقَوۡاْ

212 Beautified is the life of this world for those who disbelieve, and they ridicule those who believe. But the

فَوْقَهُمْ يَوْمَ ٱلْقِيَٰمَةِ ۗ وَٱللَّهُ يَرْزُقُ مَن يَشَآءُ
بِغَيْرِ حِسَابٍ

righteous will be above them on the Day of Resurrection. Allah provides to whomever He wills without measure.

٢١٣ كَانَ ٱلنَّاسُ أُمَّةً وَٰحِدَةً فَبَعَثَ ٱللَّهُ ٱلنَّبِيِّـۧنَ
مُبَشِّرِينَ وَمُنذِرِينَ وَأَنزَلَ مَعَهُمُ ٱلْكِتَٰبَ بِٱلْحَقِّ
لِيَحْكُمَ بَيْنَ ٱلنَّاسِ فِيمَا ٱخْتَلَفُوا۟ فِيهِ ۚ وَمَا
ٱخْتَلَفَ فِيهِ إِلَّا ٱلَّذِينَ أُوتُوهُ مِنۢ بَعْدِ مَا
جَآءَتْهُمُ ٱلْبَيِّنَٰتُ بَغْيًۢا بَيْنَهُمْ ۖ فَهَدَى ٱللَّهُ ٱلَّذِينَ
ءَامَنُوا۟ لِمَا ٱخْتَلَفُوا۟ فِيهِ مِنَ ٱلْحَقِّ بِإِذْنِهِۦ ۗ
وَٱللَّهُ يَهْدِى مَن يَشَآءُ إِلَىٰ صِرَٰطٍ مُّسْتَقِيمٍ

213 Humanity used to be one community; then Allah sent the prophets, bringing good news and giving warnings. And He sent down with them the Scripture, with the truth, to judge between people regarding their differences. But none differed over it except those who were given it—after the proofs had come to them—out of mutual envy between them. Then Allah guided those who believed to the truth they had disputed, in accordance with His will. Allah guides whom He wills to a straight path.

٢١٤ أَمْ حَسِبْتُمْ أَن تَدْخُلُوا۟ ٱلْجَنَّةَ وَلَمَّا يَأْتِكُم
مَّثَلُ ٱلَّذِينَ خَلَوْا۟ مِن قَبْلِكُم ۖ مَّسَّتْهُمُ ٱلْبَأْسَآءُ
وَٱلضَّرَّآءُ وَزُلْزِلُوا۟ حَتَّىٰ يَقُولَ ٱلرَّسُولُ وَٱلَّذِينَ
ءَامَنُوا۟ مَعَهُۥ مَتَىٰ نَصْرُ ٱللَّهِ ۗ أَلَآ إِنَّ نَصْرَ ٱللَّهِ
قَرِيبٌ

214 Or do you expect to enter Paradise before the example of those who came before you had reached you? Adversity and hardship had afflicted them, and they were so shaken up, that the Messenger and those who believed with him said, “When is Allah’s victory?” Indeed, Allah’s victory is near.

٢١٥ يَسْـَٔلُونَكَ مَاذَا يُنفِقُونَ ۖ قُلْ مَآ أَنفَقْتُم مِّنْ
خَيْرٍ فَلِلْوَٰلِدَيْنِ وَٱلْأَقْرَبِينَ وَٱلْيَتَٰمَىٰ وَٱلْمَسَٰكِينِ
وَٱبْنِ ٱلسَّبِيلِ ۗ وَمَا تَفْعَلُوا۟ مِنْ خَيْرٍ فَإِنَّ ٱللَّهَ
بِهِۦ عَلِيمٌ

215 They ask you what they should give. Say, “Whatever charity you give is for the parents, and the relatives, and the orphans, and the poor, and the wayfarer. Whatever good you do, Allah is aware of it.

٢١٦ كُتِبَ عَلَيْكُمُ ٱلْقِتَالُ وَهُوَ كُرْهٌ لَّكُمْ ۖ وَعَسَىٰٓ
أَن تَكْرَهُوا۟ شَيْـًٔا وَهُوَ خَيْرٌ لَّكُمْ ۖ وَعَسَىٰٓ أَن
تُحِبُّوا۟ شَيْـًٔا وَهُوَ شَرٌّ لَّكُمْ ۗ وَٱللَّهُ يَعْلَمُ وَأَنتُمْ لَا
تَعْلَمُونَ

216 Fighting is ordained for you, even though you dislike it. But it may be that you dislike something while it is good for you, and it may be that you like something while it is bad for you. Allah knows, and you do not know.

٢١٧ يَسْـَٔلُونَكَ عَنِ ٱلشَّهْرِ ٱلْحَرَامِ قِتَالٍ فِيهِ ۖ قُلْ
قِتَالٌ فِيهِ كَبِيرٌ ۖ وَصَدٌّ عَن سَبِيلِ ٱللَّهِ وَكُفْرٌۢ بِهِۦ
وَٱلْمَسْجِدِ ٱلْحَرَامِ وَإِخْرَاجُ أَهْلِهِۦ مِنْهُ أَكْبَرُ عِندَ
ٱللَّهِ ۚ وَٱلْفِتْنَةُ أَكْبَرُ مِنَ ٱلْقَتْلِ ۗ وَلَا يَزَالُونَ
يُقَٰتِلُونَكُمْ حَتَّىٰ يَرُدُّوكُمْ عَن دِينِكُمْ إِنِ
ٱسْتَطَٰعُوا۟ ۚ وَمَن يَرْتَدِدْ مِنكُمْ عَن دِينِهِۦ فَيَمُتْ
وَهُوَ كَافِرٌ فَأُو۟لَٰٓئِكَ حَبِطَتْ أَعْمَٰلُهُمْ فِى ٱلدُّنْيَا
وَٱلْءَاخِرَةِ ۖ وَأُو۟لَٰٓئِكَ أَصْحَٰبُ ٱلنَّارِ ۖ هُمْ فِيهَا
خَٰلِدُونَ

217 They ask you about fighting during the Holy Month. Say, "Fighting during it is deplorable; but to bar others from Allah's path, and to disbelieve in Him, and to prevent access to the Holy Mosque, and to expel its people from it, are more deplorable with Allah. And persecution is more serious than killing. They will not cease to fight you until they turn you back from your religion, if they can. Whoever among you turns back from his religion, and dies a disbeliever—those are they whose works will come to nothing, in this life, and in the Hereafter. Those are the inmates of the Fire, abiding in it forever.

٢١٨ إِنَّ ٱلَّذِينَ ءَامَنُوا۟ وَٱلَّذِينَ هَاجَرُوا۟ وَجَٰهَدُوا۟
فِى سَبِيلِ ٱللَّهِ أُو۟لَٰٓئِكَ يَرْجُونَ رَحْمَتَ ٱللَّهِ ۚ
وَٱللَّهُ غَفُورٌ رَّحِيمٌ

218 Those who believed, and those who migrated and fought for the sake of Allah—those look forward to Allah's mercy. Allah is Forgiving and Merciful.

٢١٩ يَسْـَٔلُونَكَ عَنِ ٱلْخَمْرِ وَٱلْمَيْسِرِ ۖ قُلْ فِيهِمَآ
إِثْمٌ كَبِيرٌ وَمَنَٰفِعُ لِلنَّاسِ وَإِثْمُهُمَآ أَكْبَرُ مِن
نَّفْعِهِمَا ۗ وَيَسْـَٔلُونَكَ مَاذَا يُنفِقُونَ قُلِ ٱلْعَفْوَ ۗ
كَذَٰلِكَ يُبَيِّنُ ٱللَّهُ لَكُمُ ٱلْءَايَٰتِ لَعَلَّكُمْ تَتَفَكَّرُونَ

219 They ask you about intoxicants and gambling. Say, "There is gross sin in them, and some benefits for people, but their sinfulness outweighs their benefit." And they ask you about what they should give: say, "The surplus." Thus Allah explains the revelations to you, so that you may think.

٢٢٠ فِى ٱلدُّنْيَا وَٱلْءَاخِرَةِ ۗ وَيَسْـَٔلُونَكَ عَنِ
ٱلْيَتَٰمَىٰ ۖ قُلْ إِصْلَاحٌ لَّهُمْ خَيْرٌ ۖ وَإِن تُخَالِطُوهُمْ
فَإِخْوَٰنُكُمْ ۚ وَٱللَّهُ يَعْلَمُ ٱلْمُفْسِدَ مِنَ ٱلْمُصْلِحِ ۚ
وَلَوْ شَآءَ ٱللَّهُ لَأَعْنَتَكُمْ ۚ إِنَّ ٱللَّهَ عَزِيزٌ حَكِيمٌ

220 About this world and the next. And they ask you about orphans. Say, "Improvement for them is best. And if you intermix with them, then they are your brethren." Allah knows the dishonest from the honest. Had Allah willed, He could have overburdened you. Allah is Mighty and Wise.

٢٢١ وَلَا تَنكِحُوا۟ ٱلْمُشْرِكَٰتِ حَتَّىٰ يُؤْمِنَّ ۚ وَلَأَمَةٌ
مُّؤْمِنَةٌ خَيْرٌ مِّن مُّشْرِكَةٍ وَلَوْ أَعْجَبَتْكُمْ ۗ وَلَا
تُنكِحُوا۟ ٱلْمُشْرِكِينَ حَتَّىٰ يُؤْمِنُوا۟ ۚ وَلَعَبْدٌ مُّؤْمِنٌ
خَيْرٌ مِّن مُّشْرِكٍ وَلَوْ أَعْجَبَكُمْ ۗ أُو۟لَٰٓئِكَ يَدْعُونَ
إِلَى ٱلنَّارِ ۖ وَٱللَّهُ يَدْعُوٓا۟ إِلَى ٱلْجَنَّةِ وَٱلْمَغْفِرَةِ
بِإِذْنِهِۦ ۖ وَيُبَيِّنُ ءَايَٰتِهِۦ لِلنَّاسِ لَعَلَّهُمْ يَتَذَكَّرُونَ

221 Do not marry idolatresses, unless they have believed. A believing maid is better than an idolatress, even if you like her. And do not marry idolaters, unless they have believed. A believing servant is better than an idolater, even if you like him. These call to the Fire, but Allah calls to the Garden and to forgiveness, by His leave. He makes clear His communications to the people, that they may be mindful.

٢٢٢ وَيَسْـَٔلُونَكَ عَنِ ٱلْمَحِيضِ ۖ قُلْ هُوَ أَذًى
فَٱعْتَزِلُوا۟ ٱلنِّسَآءَ فِى ٱلْمَحِيضِ ۖ وَلَا تَقْرَبُوهُنَّ
حَتَّىٰ يَطْهُرْنَ ۖ فَإِذَا تَطَهَّرْنَ فَأْتُوهُنَّ مِنْ حَيْثُ
أَمَرَكُمُ ٱللَّهُ ۚ إِنَّ ٱللَّهَ يُحِبُّ ٱلتَّوَّٰبِينَ وَيُحِبُّ
ٱلْمُتَطَهِّرِينَ

222 And they ask you about menstruation: say, “It is harmful, so keep away from women during menstruation. And do not approach them until they have become pure. Once they have become pure, approach them in the way Allah has directed you.” Allah loves the repentant, and He loves those who keep clean.”

٢٢٣ نِسَآؤُكُمْ حَرْثٌ لَّكُمْ فَأْتُوا۟ حَرْثَكُمْ أَنَّىٰ
شِئْتُمْ ۖ وَقَدِّمُوا۟ لِأَنفُسِكُمْ ۚ وَٱتَّقُوا۟ ٱللَّهَ وَٱعْلَمُوٓا۟
أَنَّكُم مُّلَٰقُوهُ ۗ وَبَشِّرِ ٱلْمُؤْمِنِينَ

223 Your women are cultivation for you; so approach your cultivation whenever you like, and send ahead for yourselves. And fear Allah, and know that you will meet Him. And give good news to the believers.

٢٢٤ وَلَا تَجْعَلُوا۟ ٱللَّهَ عُرْضَةً لِّأَيْمَٰنِكُمْ أَن تَبَرُّوا۟
وَتَتَّقُوا۟ وَتُصْلِحُوا۟ بَيْنَ ٱلنَّاسِ ۗ وَٱللَّهُ سَمِيعٌ
عَلِيمٌ

224 And do not allow your oaths in Allah's name to hinder you from virtue, and righteousness, and making peace between people. Allah is Listener and Knower.

٢٢٥ لَّا يُؤَاخِذُكُمُ ٱللَّهُ بِٱللَّغْوِ فِىٓ أَيْمَٰنِكُمْ وَلَٰكِن
يُؤَاخِذُكُم بِمَا كَسَبَتْ قُلُوبُكُمْ ۗ وَٱللَّهُ غَفُورٌ
حَلِيمٌ

225 Allah does not hold you responsible for your unintentional oaths, but He holds you responsible for your intentions. Allah is Forgiving and Forbearing.

٢٢٦ لِّلَّذِينَ يُؤْلُونَ مِن نِّسَآئِهِمْ تَرَبُّصُ أَرْبَعَةِ
أَشْهُرٍ ۖ فَإِن فَآءُو فَإِنَّ ٱللَّهَ غَفُورٌ رَّحِيمٌ

226 Those who vow abstinence from their wives must wait for four months. But if they reconcile—Allah is Forgiving and Merciful.

٢٢٧ وَإِنْ عَزَمُوا۟ ٱلطَّلَٰقَ فَإِنَّ ٱللَّهَ سَمِيعٌ عَلِيمٌ

227 And if they resolve to divorce—Allah is Hearing and Knowing.

٢٢٨ وَٱلْمُطَلَّقَٰتُ يَتَرَبَّصْنَ بِأَنفُسِهِنَّ ثَلَٰثَةَ قُرُوٓءٍ ۚ
وَلَا يَحِلُّ لَهُنَّ أَن يَكْتُمْنَ مَا خَلَقَ ٱللَّهُ فِىٓ
أَرْحَامِهِنَّ إِن كُنَّ يُؤْمِنَّ بِٱللَّهِ وَٱلْيَوْمِ ٱلْءَاخِرِ ۚ
وَبُعُولَتُهُنَّ أَحَقُّ بِرَدِّهِنَّ فِى ذَٰلِكَ إِنْ أَرَادُوٓا۟
إِصْلَٰحًا ۚ وَلَهُنَّ مِثْلُ ٱلَّذِى عَلَيْهِنَّ بِٱلْمَعْرُوفِ ۚ
وَلِلرِّجَالِ عَلَيْهِنَّ دَرَجَةٌ ۗ وَٱللَّهُ عَزِيزٌ حَكِيمٌ

228 Divorced women shall wait by themselves for three periods. And it is not lawful for them to conceal what Allah has created in their wombs, if they believe in Allah and the Last Day. Meanwhile, their husbands have the better right to take them back, if they desire reconciliation. And women have rights similar to their obligations, according to what is fair. But men have a degree over them. Allah is Mighty and Wise.

٢٢٩ ٱلطَّلَٰقُ مَرَّتَانِ ۖ فَإِمْسَاكٌۢ بِمَعْرُوفٍ أَوْ
تَسْرِيحٌۢ بِإِحْسَٰنٍ ۗ وَلَا يَحِلُّ لَكُمْ أَن تَأْخُذُوا۟ مِمَّآ
ءَاتَيْتُمُوهُنَّ شَيْـًٔا إِلَّآ أَن يَخَافَآ أَلَّا يُقِيمَا حُدُودَ
ٱللَّهِ ۖ فَإِنْ خِفْتُمْ أَلَّا يُقِيمَا حُدُودَ ٱللَّهِ فَلَا جُنَاحَ
عَلَيْهِمَا فِيمَا ٱفْتَدَتْ بِهِۦ ۗ تِلْكَ حُدُودُ ٱللَّهِ فَلَا
تَعْتَدُوهَا ۚ وَمَن يَتَعَدَّ حُدُودَ ٱللَّهِ فَأُو۟لَٰٓئِكَ هُمُ
ٱلظَّٰلِمُونَ

229 Divorce is allowed twice. Then, either honorable retention, or setting free kindly. It is not lawful for you to take back anything you have given them, unless they fear that they cannot maintain Allah's limits. If you fear that they cannot maintain Allah's limits, then there is no blame on them if she sacrifices something for her release. These are Allah's limits, so do not transgress them. Those who transgress Allah's limits are the unjust.

٢٣٠ فَإِن طَلَّقَهَا فَلَا تَحِلُّ لَهُۥ مِنۢ بَعْدُ حَتَّىٰ
تَنكِحَ زَوْجًا غَيْرَهُۥ ۗ فَإِن طَلَّقَهَا فَلَا جُنَاحَ
عَلَيْهِمَآ أَن يَتَرَاجَعَآ إِن ظَنَّآ أَن يُقِيمَا حُدُودَ
ٱللَّهِ ۗ وَتِلْكَ حُدُودُ ٱللَّهِ يُبَيِّنُهَا لِقَوْمٍ يَعْلَمُونَ

230 If he divorces her, she shall not be lawful for him again until she has married another husband. If the latter divorces her, then there is no blame on them for reuniting, provided they think they can maintain Allah's limits. These are Allah's limits; He makes them clear to people who know.

٢٣١ وَإِذَا طَلَّقْتُمُ ٱلنِّسَآءَ فَبَلَغْنَ أَجَلَهُنَّ
فَأَمْسِكُوهُنَّ بِمَعْرُوفٍ أَوْ سَرِّحُوهُنَّ بِمَعْرُوفٍ ۚ
وَلَا تُمْسِكُوهُنَّ ضِرَارًا لِّتَعْتَدُوا۟ ۚ وَمَن يَفْعَلْ

231 When you divorce women, and they have reached their term, either retain them amicably, or release them amicably. But do not retain them to hurt them and commit

ذَٰلِكَ فَقَدْ ظَلَمَ نَفْسَهُۥ ۚ وَلَا تَتَّخِذُوٓا۟ ءَايَٰتِ ٱللَّهِ
هُزُوًا ۚ وَٱذْكُرُوا۟ نِعْمَتَ ٱللَّهِ عَلَيْكُمْ وَمَآ أَنزَلَ
عَلَيْكُم مِّنَ ٱلْكِتَٰبِ وَٱلْحِكْمَةِ يَعِظُكُم بِهِۦ ۚ
وَٱتَّقُوا۟ ٱللَّهَ وَٱعْلَمُوٓا۟ أَنَّ ٱللَّهَ بِكُلِّ شَىْءٍ عَلِيمٌ

aggression. Whoever does that has wronged himself. And do not take Allah’s revelations for a joke. And remember Allah's favor to you, and that He revealed to you the Scripture and Wisdom to teach you. And fear Allah, and know that Allah is aware of everything.

٢٣٢ وَإِذَا طَلَّقْتُمُ ٱلنِّسَآءَ فَبَلَغْنَ أَجَلَهُنَّ فَلَا
تَعْضُلُوهُنَّ أَن يَنكِحْنَ أَزْوَٰجَهُنَّ إِذَا تَرَٰضَوْا۟
بَيْنَهُم بِٱلْمَعْرُوفِ ۗ ذَٰلِكَ يُوعَظُ بِهِۦ مَن كَانَ
مِنكُمْ يُؤْمِنُ بِٱللَّهِ وَٱلْيَوْمِ ٱلْءَاخِرِ ۗ ذَٰلِكُمْ أَزْكَىٰ
لَكُمْ وَأَطْهَرُ ۗ وَٱللَّهُ يَعْلَمُ وَأَنتُمْ لَا تَعْلَمُونَ

232 When you divorce women, and they have reached their term, do not prevent them from marrying their husbands, provided they agree on fair terms. Thereby is advised whoever among you believes in Allah and the Last Day. That is better and more decent for you. Allah knows, and you do not know.

٢٣٣ وَٱلْوَٰلِدَٰتُ يُرْضِعْنَ أَوْلَٰدَهُنَّ حَوْلَيْنِ كَامِلَيْنِ ۖ
لِمَنْ أَرَادَ أَن يُتِمَّ ٱلرَّضَاعَةَ ۚ وَعَلَى ٱلْمَوْلُودِ لَهُۥ
رِزْقُهُنَّ وَكِسْوَتُهُنَّ بِٱلْمَعْرُوفِ ۚ لَا تُكَلَّفُ نَفْسٌ
إِلَّا وُسْعَهَا ۚ لَا تُضَآرَّ وَٰلِدَةٌۢ بِوَلَدِهَا وَلَا مَوْلُودٌ لَّهُۥ
بِوَلَدِهِۦ ۚ وَعَلَى ٱلْوَارِثِ مِثْلُ ذَٰلِكَ ۗ فَإِنْ أَرَادَا
فِصَالًا عَن تَرَاضٍ مِّنْهُمَا وَتَشَاوُرٍ فَلَا جُنَاحَ
عَلَيْهِمَا ۗ وَإِنْ أَرَدتُّمْ أَن تَسْتَرْضِعُوٓا۟ أَوْلَٰدَكُمْ فَلَا
جُنَاحَ عَلَيْكُمْ إِذَا سَلَّمْتُم مَّآ ءَاتَيْتُم بِٱلْمَعْرُوفِ ۗ
وَٱتَّقُوا۟ ٱللَّهَ وَٱعْلَمُوٓا۟ أَنَّ ٱللَّهَ بِمَا تَعْمَلُونَ بَصِيرٌ

233 Mothers may nurse their infants for two whole years, for those who desire to complete the nursing-period. It is the duty of the father to provide for them and clothe them in a proper manner. No soul shall be burdened beyond its capacity. No mother shall be harmed on account of her child, and no father shall be harmed on account of his child. The same duty rests upon the heir. If the couple desire weaning, by mutual consent and consultation, they commit no error by doing so. You commit no error by hiring nursing-mothers, as long as you pay them fairly. And be wary of Allah, and know that Allah is Seeing of what you do.

٢٣٤ وَٱلَّذِينَ يُتَوَفَّوْنَ مِنكُمْ وَيَذَرُونَ أَزْوَٰجًا
يَتَرَبَّصْنَ بِأَنفُسِهِنَّ أَرْبَعَةَ أَشْهُرٍ وَعَشْرًا ۖ فَإِذَا
بَلَغْنَ أَجَلَهُنَّ فَلَا جُنَاحَ عَلَيْكُمْ فِيمَا فَعَلْنَ فِىٓ
أَنفُسِهِنَّ بِٱلْمَعْرُوفِ ۗ وَٱللَّهُ بِمَا تَعْمَلُونَ خَبِيرٌ

234 As for those among you who die and leave widows behind, their widows shall wait by themselves for four months and ten days. When they have reached their term, there is no blame on you regarding what they might honorably do with

themselves. Allah is fully acquainted with what you do.

٢٣٥ وَلَا جُنَاحَ عَلَيۡكُمۡ فِيمَا عَرَّضۡتُم بِهِۦ مِنۡ
خِطۡبَةِ ٱلنِّسَآءِ أَوۡ أَكۡنَنتُمۡ فِيٓ أَنفُسِكُمۡۚ عَلِمَ ٱللَّهُ
أَنَّكُمۡ سَتَذۡكُرُونَهُنَّ وَلَٰكِن لَّا تُوَاعِدُوهُنَّ سِرًّا إِلَّآ
أَن تَقُولُواْ قَوۡلٗا مَّعۡرُوفٗاۚ وَلَا تَعۡزِمُواْ عُقۡدَةَ
ٱلنِّكَاحِ حَتَّىٰ يَبۡلُغَ ٱلۡكِتَٰبُ أَجَلَهُۥۚ وَٱعۡلَمُوٓاْ أَنَّ
ٱللَّهَ يَعۡلَمُ مَا فِيٓ أَنفُسِكُمۡ فَٱحۡذَرُوهُۚ وَٱعۡلَمُوٓاْ
أَنَّ ٱللَّهَ غَفُورٌ حَلِيمٞ

235 You commit no error by announcing your engagement to women, or by keeping it to yourselves. Allah knows that you will be thinking about them. But do not meet them secretly, unless you have something proper to say. And do not confirm the marriage tie until the writing is fulfilled. And know that Allah knows what is in your souls, so beware of Him. And know that Allah is Forgiving and Forbearing.

٢٣٦ لَّا جُنَاحَ عَلَيۡكُمۡ إِن طَلَّقۡتُمُ ٱلنِّسَآءَ مَا لَمۡ
تَمَسُّوهُنَّ أَوۡ تَفۡرِضُواْ لَهُنَّ فَرِيضَةٗۚ وَمَتِّعُوهُنَّ
عَلَى ٱلۡمُوسِعِ قَدَرُهُۥ وَعَلَى ٱلۡمُقۡتِرِ قَدَرُهُۥ مَتَٰعَۢا
بِٱلۡمَعۡرُوفِۖ حَقًّا عَلَى ٱلۡمُحۡسِنِينَ

236 You commit no error by divorcing women before having touched them, or before having set the dowry for them. And compensate them—the wealthy according to his means, and the poor according to his means—with a fair compensation, a duty upon the doers of good.

٢٣٧ وَإِن طَلَّقۡتُمُوهُنَّ مِن قَبۡلِ أَن تَمَسُّوهُنَّ
وَقَدۡ فَرَضۡتُمۡ لَهُنَّ فَرِيضَةٗ فَنِصۡفُ مَا فَرَضۡتُمۡ
إِلَّآ أَن يَعۡفُونَ أَوۡ يَعۡفُوَاْ ٱلَّذِي بِيَدِهِۦ عُقۡدَةُ
ٱلنِّكَاحِۚ وَأَن تَعۡفُوٓاْ أَقۡرَبُ لِلتَّقۡوَىٰۚ وَلَا تَنسَوُاْ
ٱلۡفَضۡلَ بَيۡنَكُمۡۚ إِنَّ ٱللَّهَ بِمَا تَعۡمَلُونَ بَصِيرٌ

237 If you divorce them before you have touched them, but after you had set the dowry for them, give them half of what you specified—unless they forego the right, or the one in whose hand is the marriage contract foregoes it. But to forego is nearer to piety. And do not forget generosity between one another. Allah is seeing of everything you do.

٢٣٨ حَٰفِظُواْ عَلَى ٱلصَّلَوَٰتِ وَٱلصَّلَوٰةِ ٱلۡوُسۡطَىٰ
وَقُومُواْ لِلَّهِ قَٰنِتِينَ

238 Guard your prayers, and the middle prayer, and stand before Allah in devotion.

٢٣٩ فَإِنۡ خِفۡتُمۡ فَرِجَالًا أَوۡ رُكۡبَانٗاۖ فَإِذَآ أَمِنتُمۡ
فَٱذۡكُرُواْ ٱللَّهَ كَمَا عَلَّمَكُم مَّا لَمۡ تَكُونُواْ تَعۡلَمُونَ

239 But if you are in fear, then on foot, or riding. And when you are safe, remember Allah, as He taught you what you did not know.

٢٤٠ وَٱلَّذِينَ يُتَوَفَّوۡنَ مِنكُمۡ وَيَذَرُونَ أَزۡوَٰجٗا
وَصِيَّةٗ لِّأَزۡوَٰجِهِم مَّتَٰعًا إِلَى ٱلۡحَوۡلِ غَيۡرَ إِخۡرَاجٖۚ

240 Those of you who die and leave wives behind—a will shall provide their wives with support for a year,

فَإِنْ خَرَجْنَ فَلَا جُنَاحَ عَلَيْكُمْ فِى مَا فَعَلْنَ فِىٓ
أَنفُسِهِنَّ مِن مَّعْرُوفٍۗ وَٱللَّهُ عَزِيزٌ حَكِيمٌ

provided they do not leave. If they leave, you are not to blame for what they do with themselves, provided it is reasonable. Allah is Mighty and Wise.

٢٤١ وَلِلْمُطَلَّقَٰتِ مَتَٰعٌۢ بِٱلْمَعْرُوفِۖ حَقًّا عَلَى
ٱلْمُتَّقِينَ

241 And divorced women shall be provided for, equitably—a duty upon the righteous.

٢٤٢ كَذَٰلِكَ يُبَيِّنُ ٱللَّهُ لَكُمْ ءَايَٰتِهِۦ لَعَلَّكُمْ تَعْقِلُونَ

242 Allah thus explains His revelations to you, so that you may understand.

٢٤٣ أَلَمْ تَرَ إِلَى ٱلَّذِينَ خَرَجُوا۟ مِن دِيَٰرِهِمْ وَهُمْ
أُلُوفٌ حَذَرَ ٱلْمَوْتِ فَقَالَ لَهُمُ ٱللَّهُ مُوتُوا۟ ثُمَّ
أَحْيَٰهُمْۚ إِنَّ ٱللَّهَ لَذُو فَضْلٍ عَلَى ٱلنَّاسِ وَلَٰكِنَّ
أَكْثَرَ ٱلنَّاسِ لَا يَشْكُرُونَ

243 Have you not considered those who fled their homes, by the thousands, fearful of death? Allah said to them, “Die.” Then He revived them. Allah is Gracious towards the people, but most people are not appreciative.

٢٤٤ وَقَٰتِلُوا۟ فِى سَبِيلِ ٱللَّهِ وَٱعْلَمُوٓا۟ أَنَّ ٱللَّهَ
سَمِيعٌ عَلِيمٌ

244 Fight in the cause of Allah, and know that Allah is Hearing and Knowing.

٢٤٥ مَّن ذَا ٱلَّذِى يُقْرِضُ ٱللَّهَ قَرْضًا حَسَنًا
فَيُضَٰعِفَهُۥ لَهُۥٓ أَضْعَافًا كَثِيرَةًۚ وَٱللَّهُ يَقْبِضُ
وَيَبْصُۜطُ وَإِلَيْهِ تُرْجَعُونَ

245 Who is he who will offer Allah a generous loan, so He will multiply it for him manifold? Allah receives and amplifies, and to Him you will be returned.

٢٤٦ أَلَمْ تَرَ إِلَى ٱلْمَلَإِ مِنۢ بَنِىٓ إِسْرَٰٓءِيلَ مِنۢ بَعْدِ
مُوسَىٰٓ إِذْ قَالُوا۟ لِنَبِىٍّ لَّهُمُ ٱبْعَثْ لَنَا مَلِكًا نُّقَٰتِلْ
فِى سَبِيلِ ٱللَّهِۖ قَالَ هَلْ عَسَيْتُمْ إِن كُتِبَ
عَلَيْكُمُ ٱلْقِتَالُ أَلَّا تُقَٰتِلُوا۟ۖ قَالُوا۟ وَمَا لَنَآ أَلَّا نُقَٰتِلَ
فِى سَبِيلِ ٱللَّهِ وَقَدْ أُخْرِجْنَا مِن دِيَٰرِنَا وَأَبْنَآئِنَاۖ
فَلَمَّا كُتِبَ عَلَيْهِمُ ٱلْقِتَالُ تَوَلَّوْا۟ إِلَّا قَلِيلًا مِّنْهُمْۗ
وَٱللَّهُ عَلِيمٌۢ بِٱلظَّٰلِمِينَ

246 Have you not considered the notables of the Children of Israel after Moses? When they said to a prophet of theirs, “Appoint a king for us, and we will fight in the cause of Allah.” He said, “Is it possible that, if fighting was ordained for you, you would not fight?” They said, “Why would we not fight in the cause of Allah, when we were driven out of our homes, along with our children?” But when fighting was ordained for them, they turned away, except for a few of them. But Allah is aware of the wrongdoers.

٢٤٧ وَقَالَ لَهُمْ نَبِيُّهُمْ إِنَّ ٱللَّهَ قَدْ بَعَثَ لَكُمْ
طَالُوتَ مَلِكًا ۚ قَالُوٓا۟ أَنَّىٰ يَكُونُ لَهُ ٱلْمُلْكُ عَلَيْنَا
وَنَحْنُ أَحَقُّ بِٱلْمُلْكِ مِنْهُ وَلَمْ يُؤْتَ سَعَةً مِّنَ
ٱلْمَالِ ۚ قَالَ إِنَّ ٱللَّهَ ٱصْطَفَىٰهُ عَلَيْكُمْ وَزَادَهُۥ
بَسْطَةً فِى ٱلْعِلْمِ وَٱلْجِسْمِ ۖ وَٱللَّهُ يُؤْتِى مُلْكَهُۥ
مَن يَشَآءُ ۚ وَٱللَّهُ وَٰسِعٌ عَلِيمٌ

247 Their prophet said to them, “Allah has appointed Saul to be your king.” They said, “How can he have authority over us, when we are more worthy of authority than he, and he was not given plenty of wealth?” He said, “Allah has chosen him over you, and has increased him in knowledge and stature.” Allah bestows His sovereignty upon whomever He wills. Allah is Embracing and Knowing.

٢٤٨ وَقَالَ لَهُمْ نَبِيُّهُمْ إِنَّ ءَايَةَ مُلْكِهِۦٓ أَن
يَأْتِيَكُمُ ٱلتَّابُوتُ فِيهِ سَكِينَةٌ مِّن رَّبِّكُمْ وَبَقِيَّةٌ
مِّمَّا تَرَكَ ءَالُ مُوسَىٰ وَءَالُ هَٰرُونَ تَحْمِلُهُ
ٱلْمَلَٰٓئِكَةُ ۚ إِنَّ فِى ذَٰلِكَ لَءَايَةً لَّكُمْ إِن كُنتُم
مُّؤْمِنِينَ

248 And their prophet said to them, “The proof of his kingship is that the Ark will be restored to you, bringing tranquility from your Lord, and relics left by the family of Moses and the family of Aaron. It will be carried by the angels. In that is a sign for you, if you are believers.”

٢٤٩ فَلَمَّا فَصَلَ طَالُوتُ بِٱلْجُنُودِ قَالَ إِنَّ ٱللَّهَ
مُبْتَلِيكُم بِنَهَرٍ فَمَن شَرِبَ مِنْهُ فَلَيْسَ مِنِّى
وَمَن لَّمْ يَطْعَمْهُ فَإِنَّهُۥ مِنِّىٓ إِلَّا مَنِ ٱغْتَرَفَ
غُرْفَةًۢ بِيَدِهِۦ ۚ فَشَرِبُوا۟ مِنْهُ إِلَّا قَلِيلًا مِّنْهُمْ ۚ فَلَمَّا
جَاوَزَهُۥ هُوَ وَٱلَّذِينَ ءَامَنُوا۟ مَعَهُۥ قَالُوا۟ لَا طَاقَةَ
لَنَا ٱلْيَوْمَ بِجَالُوتَ وَجُنُودِهِۦ ۚ قَالَ ٱلَّذِينَ
يَظُنُّونَ أَنَّهُم مُّلَٰقُوا۟ ٱللَّهِ كَم مِّن فِئَةٍ قَلِيلَةٍ
غَلَبَتْ فِئَةً كَثِيرَةًۢ بِإِذْنِ ٱللَّهِ ۗ وَٱللَّهُ مَعَ ٱلصَّٰبِرِينَ

249 When Saul set out with the troops, he said, “Allah will be testing you with a river. Whoever drinks from it does not belong with me. But whoever does not drink from it, does belong with me, except for whoever scoops up a little with his hand.” But they drank from it, except for a few of them. Then, when he crossed it, he and those who believed with him, they said, “We have no strength to face Goliath and his troops today.” But those who knew that they would meet Allah said, “How many a small group has defeated a large group by Allah’s will. Allah is with the steadfast.”

٢٥٠ وَلَمَّا بَرَزُوا۟ لِجَالُوتَ وَجُنُودِهِۦ قَالُوا۟ رَبَّنَآ
أَفْرِغْ عَلَيْنَا صَبْرًا وَثَبِّتْ أَقْدَامَنَا وَٱنصُرْنَا عَلَى
ٱلْقَوْمِ ٱلْكَٰفِرِينَ

250 And when they confronted Goliath and his troops, they said, “Our Lord, pour down patience on us, and strengthen our foothold, and support us against the faithless people.”

٢٥١ فَهَزَمُوهُم بِإِذْنِ ٱللَّهِ وَقَتَلَ دَاوُۥدُ جَالُوتَ
وَءَاتَىٰهُ ٱللَّهُ ٱلْمُلْكَ وَٱلْحِكْمَةَ وَعَلَّمَهُۥ مِمَّا يَشَآءُ ۗ
وَلَوْلَا دَفْعُ ٱللَّهِ ٱلنَّاسَ بَعْضَهُم بِبَعْضٍ لَّفَسَدَتِ
ٱلْأَرْضُ وَلَٰكِنَّ ٱللَّهَ ذُو فَضْلٍ عَلَى ٱلْعَٰلَمِينَ

251 And they defeated them by Allah's leave, and David killed Goliath, and Allah gave him sovereignty and wisdom, and taught him as He willed. Were it not for Allah restraining the people, some by means of others, the earth would have gone to ruin. But Allah is gracious towards mankind.

٢٥٢ تِلْكَ ءَايَٰتُ ٱللَّهِ نَتْلُوهَا عَلَيْكَ بِٱلْحَقِّ ۚ وَإِنَّكَ
لَمِنَ ٱلْمُرْسَلِينَ

252 These are Allah's revelations, which We recite to you in truth. You are one of the messengers.

٢٥٣ تِلْكَ ٱلرُّسُلُ فَضَّلْنَا بَعْضَهُمْ عَلَىٰ بَعْضٍ ۘ
مِّنْهُم مَّن كَلَّمَ ٱللَّهُ ۖ وَرَفَعَ بَعْضَهُمْ دَرَجَٰتٍ ۚ
وَءَاتَيْنَا عِيسَى ٱبْنَ مَرْيَمَ ٱلْبَيِّنَٰتِ وَأَيَّدْنَٰهُ
بِرُوحِ ٱلْقُدُسِ ۗ وَلَوْ شَآءَ ٱللَّهُ مَا ٱقْتَتَلَ ٱلَّذِينَ
مِنۢ بَعْدِهِم مِّنۢ بَعْدِ مَا جَآءَتْهُمُ ٱلْبَيِّنَٰتُ وَلَٰكِنِ
ٱخْتَلَفُوا۟ فَمِنْهُم مَّنْ ءَامَنَ وَمِنْهُم مَّن كَفَرَ ۚ وَلَوْ
شَآءَ ٱللَّهُ مَا ٱقْتَتَلُوا۟ وَلَٰكِنَّ ٱللَّهَ يَفْعَلُ مَا يُرِيدُ

253 These messengers: We gave some advantage over others. To some of them Allah spoke directly, and some He raised in rank. We gave Jesus son of Mary the clear miracles, and We strengthened him with the Holy Spirit. Had Allah willed, those who succeeded them would not have fought one another, after the clear signs had come to them; but they disputed; some of them believed, and some of them disbelieved. Had Allah willed, they would not have fought one another; but Allah does whatever He desires.

٢٥٤ يَٰٓأَيُّهَا ٱلَّذِينَ ءَامَنُوٓا۟ أَنفِقُوا۟ مِمَّا رَزَقْنَٰكُم مِّن
قَبْلِ أَن يَأْتِىَ يَوْمٌ لَّا بَيْعٌ فِيهِ وَلَا خُلَّةٌ وَلَا
شَفَٰعَةٌ ۗ وَٱلْكَٰفِرُونَ هُمُ ٱلظَّٰلِمُونَ

254 O you who believe! Spend from what We have given you, before a Day comes in which there is neither trading, nor friendship, nor intercession. The disbelievers are the wrongdoers.

٢٥٥ ٱللَّهُ لَآ إِلَٰهَ إِلَّا هُوَ ٱلْحَىُّ ٱلْقَيُّومُ ۚ لَا تَأْخُذُهُۥ
سِنَةٌ وَلَا نَوْمٌ ۚ لَّهُۥ مَا فِى ٱلسَّمَٰوَٰتِ وَمَا فِى
ٱلْأَرْضِ ۗ مَن ذَا ٱلَّذِى يَشْفَعُ عِندَهُۥٓ إِلَّا بِإِذْنِهِۦ ۚ
يَعْلَمُ مَا بَيْنَ أَيْدِيهِمْ وَمَا خَلْفَهُمْ ۖ وَلَا يُحِيطُونَ
بِشَىْءٍ مِّنْ عِلْمِهِۦٓ إِلَّا بِمَا شَآءَ ۚ وَسِعَ كُرْسِيُّهُ

255 Allah! There is no god except He, the Living, the Everlasting. Neither slumber overtakes Him, nor sleep. To Him belongs everything in the heavens and everything on earth. Who is he that can intercede with Him except with His permission? He knows what is before them, and what is behind them; and they

ٱلسَّمَٰوَٰتِ وَٱلْأَرْضَۖ وَلَا يَـُٔودُهُۥ حِفْظُهُمَاۚ وَهُوَ
ٱلْعَلِيُّ ٱلْعَظِيمُ

cannot grasp any of His knowledge, except as He wills. His Throne extends over the heavens and the earth, and their preservation does not burden Him. He is the Most High, the Great.

٢٥٦ لَآ إِكْرَاهَ فِى ٱلدِّينِۖ قَد تَّبَيَّنَ ٱلرُّشْدُ مِنَ
ٱلْغَىِّۚ فَمَن يَكْفُرْ بِٱلطَّٰغُوتِ وَيُؤْمِنۢ بِٱللَّهِ فَقَدِ
ٱسْتَمْسَكَ بِٱلْعُرْوَةِ ٱلْوُثْقَىٰ لَا ٱنفِصَامَ لَهَاۗ وَٱللَّهُ
سَمِيعٌ عَلِيمٌ

256 There shall be no compulsion in religion; the right way has become distinct from the wrong way. Whoever renounces evil and believes in Allah has grasped the most trustworthy handle; which does not break. Allah is Hearing and Knowing.

٢٥٧ ٱللَّهُ وَلِىُّ ٱلَّذِينَ ءَامَنُوا۟ يُخْرِجُهُم مِّنَ
ٱلظُّلُمَٰتِ إِلَى ٱلنُّورِۖ وَٱلَّذِينَ كَفَرُوٓا۟ أَوْلِيَآؤُهُمُ
ٱلطَّٰغُوتُ يُخْرِجُونَهُم مِّنَ ٱلنُّورِ إِلَى ٱلظُّلُمَٰتِۗ
أُو۟لَٰٓئِكَ أَصْحَٰبُ ٱلنَّارِۖ هُمْ فِيهَا خَٰلِدُونَ

257 Allah is the Lord of those who believe; He brings them out of darkness and into light. As for those who disbelieve, their lords are the evil ones; they bring them out of light and into darkness—these are the inmates of the Fire, in which they will abide forever.

٢٥٨ أَلَمْ تَرَ إِلَى ٱلَّذِى حَآجَّ إِبْرَٰهِـۧمَ فِى رَبِّهِۦٓ أَنْ
ءَاتَىٰهُ ٱللَّهُ ٱلْمُلْكَ إِذْ قَالَ إِبْرَٰهِـۧمُ رَبِّىَ ٱلَّذِى
يُحْىِۦ وَيُمِيتُ قَالَ أَنَا۠ أُحْىِۦ وَأُمِيتُۖ قَالَ
إِبْرَٰهِـۧمُ فَإِنَّ ٱللَّهَ يَأْتِى بِٱلشَّمْسِ مِنَ ٱلْمَشْرِقِ
فَأْتِ بِهَا مِنَ ٱلْمَغْرِبِ فَبُهِتَ ٱلَّذِى كَفَرَۗ وَٱللَّهُ لَا
يَهْدِى ٱلْقَوْمَ ٱلظَّٰلِمِينَ

258 Have you not considered him who argued with Abraham about his Lord, because Allah had given him sovereignty? Abraham said, "My Lord is He who gives life and causes death." He said, "I give life and cause death." Abraham said, "Allah brings the sun from the East, so bring it from the West," so the blasphemer was confounded. Allah does not guide the wrongdoing people.

٢٥٩ أَوْ كَٱلَّذِى مَرَّ عَلَىٰ قَرْيَةٍ وَهِىَ خَاوِيَةٌ عَلَىٰ
عُرُوشِهَا قَالَ أَنَّىٰ يُحْىِۦ هَٰذِهِ ٱللَّهُ بَعْدَ مَوْتِهَاۖ
فَأَمَاتَهُ ٱللَّهُ مِا۟ئَةَ عَامٍ ثُمَّ بَعَثَهُۥۖ قَالَ كَمْ لَبِثْتَۖ
قَالَ لَبِثْتُ يَوْمًا أَوْ بَعْضَ يَوْمٍۖ قَالَ بَل لَّبِثْتَ
مِا۟ئَةَ عَامٍ فَٱنظُرْ إِلَىٰ طَعَامِكَ وَشَرَابِكَ لَمْ

259 Or like him who passed by a town collapsed on its foundations. He said, "How can Allah revive this after its demise?" Thereupon Allah caused him to die for a hundred years, and then resurrected him. He said, "For how long have you tarried?" He said, "I have tarried for

يَتَسَنَّهْۖ وَٱنظُرْ إِلَىٰ حِمَارِكَ وَلِنَجْعَلَكَ ءَايَةً
لِّلنَّاسِۖ وَٱنظُرْ إِلَى ٱلْعِظَامِ كَيْفَ نُنشِزُهَا ثُمَّ
نَكْسُوهَا لَحْمًاۚ فَلَمَّا تَبَيَّنَ لَهُۥ قَالَ أَعْلَمُ أَنَّ ٱللَّهَ
عَلَىٰ كُلِّ شَىْءٍ قَدِيرٌ

a day, or part of a day." He said, "No. You have tarried for a hundred years. Now look at your food and your drink—it has not spoiled—and look at your donkey. We will make you a wonder for mankind. And look at the bones, how We arrange them, and then clothe them with flesh." So when it became clear to him, he said, "I know that Allah has power over all things."

٢٦٠ وَإِذْ قَالَ إِبْرَٰهِـۧمُ رَبِّ أَرِنِى كَيْفَ تُحْىِ
ٱلْمَوْتَىٰۖ قَالَ أَوَلَمْ تُؤْمِنۖ قَالَ بَلَىٰ وَلَٰكِن
لِّيَطْمَئِنَّ قَلْبِىۖ قَالَ فَخُذْ أَرْبَعَةً مِّنَ ٱلطَّيْرِ
فَصُرْهُنَّ إِلَيْكَ ثُمَّ ٱجْعَلْ عَلَىٰ كُلِّ جَبَلٍ مِّنْهُنَّ
جُزْءًا ثُمَّ ٱدْعُهُنَّ يَأْتِينَكَ سَعْيًاۚ وَٱعْلَمْ أَنَّ ٱللَّهَ
عَزِيزٌ حَكِيمٌ

260 And when Abraham said, "My Lord, show me how You give life to the dead." He said, "Have you not believed?" He said, "Yes, but to put my heart at ease." He said, "Take four birds, and incline them to yourself, then place a part on each hill, then call to them; and they will come rushing to you. And know that Allah is Powerful and Wise."

٢٦١ مَّثَلُ ٱلَّذِينَ يُنفِقُونَ أَمْوَٰلَهُمْ فِى سَبِيلِ ٱللَّهِ
كَمَثَلِ حَبَّةٍ أَنۢبَتَتْ سَبْعَ سَنَابِلَ فِى كُلِّ سُنۢبُلَةٍ
مِّا۟ئَةُ حَبَّةٍۗ وَٱللَّهُ يُضَٰعِفُ لِمَن يَشَآءُۗ وَٱللَّهُ
وَٰسِعٌ عَلِيمٌ

261 The parable of those who spend their wealth in Allah's way is that of a grain that produces seven spikes; in each spike is a hundred grains. Allah multiplies for whom He wills. Allah is Bounteous and Knowing.

٢٦٢ ٱلَّذِينَ يُنفِقُونَ أَمْوَٰلَهُمْ فِى سَبِيلِ ٱللَّهِ ثُمَّ
لَا يُتْبِعُونَ مَآ أَنفَقُوا۟ مَنًّا وَلَآ أَذًىۙ لَّهُمْ أَجْرُهُمْ
عِندَ رَبِّهِمْ وَلَا خَوْفٌ عَلَيْهِمْ وَلَا هُمْ يَحْزَنُونَ

262 Those who spend their wealth in the way of Allah, and then do not follow up what they spent with reminders of their generosity or with insults, will have their reward with their Lord—they have nothing to fear, nor shall they grieve.

٢٦٣ قَوْلٌ مَّعْرُوفٌ وَمَغْفِرَةٌ خَيْرٌ مِّن صَدَقَةٍ
يَتْبَعُهَآ أَذًىۗ وَٱللَّهُ غَنِىٌّ حَلِيمٌ

263 Kind words and forgiveness are better than charity followed by insults. Allah is Rich and Clement.

٢٦٤ يَٰٓأَيُّهَا ٱلَّذِينَ ءَامَنُوا۟ لَا تُبْطِلُوا۟ صَدَقَٰتِكُم
بِٱلْمَنِّ وَٱلْأَذَىٰ كَٱلَّذِى يُنفِقُ مَالَهُۥ رِئَآءَ ٱلنَّاسِ
وَلَا يُؤْمِنُ بِٱللَّهِ وَٱلْيَوْمِ ٱلْءَاخِرِۖ فَمَثَلُهُۥ كَمَثَلِ

264 O you who believe! Do not nullify your charitable deeds with reminders and hurtful words, like him who spends his wealth to be seen by the people, and does not believe in Allah

صَفْوَانٍ عَلَيْهِ تُرَابٌ فَأَصَابَهُۥ وَابِلٌ فَتَرَكَهُۥ
صَلْدًا ۖ لَّا يَقْدِرُونَ عَلَىٰ شَىْءٍ مِّمَّا كَسَبُوا۟ ۗ
وَٱللَّهُ لَا يَهْدِى ٱلْقَوْمَ ٱلْكَٰفِرِينَ

and the Last Day. His likeness is that of a smooth rock covered with soil: a downpour strikes it, and leaves it bare—they gain nothing from their efforts. Allah does not guide the disbelieving people.

٢٦٥ وَمَثَلُ ٱلَّذِينَ يُنفِقُونَ أَمْوَٰلَهُمُ ٱبْتِغَآءَ
مَرْضَاتِ ٱللَّهِ وَتَثْبِيتًا مِّنْ أَنفُسِهِمْ كَمَثَلِ جَنَّةٍۭ
بِرَبْوَةٍ أَصَابَهَا وَابِلٌ فَـَٔاتَتْ أُكُلَهَا ضِعْفَيْنِ فَإِن
لَّمْ يُصِبْهَا وَابِلٌ فَطَلٌّ ۗ وَٱللَّهُ بِمَا تَعْمَلُونَ بَصِيرٌ

265 And the parable of those who spend their wealth seeking Allah's approval, and to strengthen their souls, is that of a garden on a hillside. If heavy rain falls on it, its produce is doubled; and if no heavy rain falls, then dew is enough. Allah is seeing of everything you do.

٢٦٦ أَيَوَدُّ أَحَدُكُمْ أَن تَكُونَ لَهُۥ جَنَّةٌ مِّن نَّخِيلٍ
وَأَعْنَابٍ تَجْرِى مِن تَحْتِهَا ٱلْأَنْهَٰرُ لَهُۥ فِيهَا مِن
كُلِّ ٱلثَّمَرَٰتِ وَأَصَابَهُ ٱلْكِبَرُ وَلَهُۥ ذُرِّيَّةٌ ضُعَفَآءُ
فَأَصَابَهَآ إِعْصَارٌ فِيهِ نَارٌ فَٱحْتَرَقَتْ ۗ كَذَٰلِكَ
يُبَيِّنُ ٱللَّهُ لَكُمُ ٱلْـَٔايَٰتِ لَعَلَّكُمْ تَتَفَكَّرُونَ

266 Would anyone of you like to have a garden of palms and vines, under which rivers flow—with all kinds of fruit in it for him, and old age has stricken him, and he has weak children—then a tornado with fire batters it, and it burns down? Thus Allah makes clear the signs for you, so that you may reflect.

٢٦٧ يَٰٓأَيُّهَا ٱلَّذِينَ ءَامَنُوٓا۟ أَنفِقُوا۟ مِن طَيِّبَٰتِ مَا
كَسَبْتُمْ وَمِمَّآ أَخْرَجْنَا لَكُم مِّنَ ٱلْأَرْضِ ۖ وَلَا
تَيَمَّمُوا۟ ٱلْخَبِيثَ مِنْهُ تُنفِقُونَ وَلَسْتُم بِـَٔاخِذِيهِ
إِلَّآ أَن تُغْمِضُوا۟ فِيهِ ۚ وَٱعْلَمُوٓا۟ أَنَّ ٱللَّهَ غَنِىٌّ
حَمِيدٌ

267 O you who believe! Give of the good things you have earned, and from what We have produced for you from the earth. And do not pick the inferior things to give away, when you yourselves would not accept it except with eyes closed. And know that Allah is Sufficient and Praiseworthy.

٢٦٨ ٱلشَّيْطَٰنُ يَعِدُكُمُ ٱلْفَقْرَ وَيَأْمُرُكُم
بِٱلْفَحْشَآءِ ۖ وَٱللَّهُ يَعِدُكُم مَّغْفِرَةً مِّنْهُ وَفَضْلًا ۗ
وَٱللَّهُ وَٰسِعٌ عَلِيمٌ

268 Satan promises you poverty, and urges you to immorality; but Allah promises you forgiveness from Himself, and grace. Allah is Embracing and Knowing.

٢٦٩ يُؤْتِى ٱلْحِكْمَةَ مَن يَشَآءُ ۚ وَمَن يُؤْتَ
ٱلْحِكْمَةَ فَقَدْ أُوتِىَ خَيْرًا كَثِيرًا ۗ وَمَا يَذَّكَّرُ إِلَّآ
أُو۟لُوا۟ ٱلْأَلْبَٰبِ

269 He gives wisdom to whomever He wills. Whoever is given wisdom has been given much good. But none pays heed except those with insight.

٢٧٠ وَمَآ أَنفَقْتُم مِّن نَّفَقَةٍ أَوْ نَذَرْتُم مِّن نَّذْرٍ
فَإِنَّ ٱللَّهَ يَعْلَمُهُۥ ۗ وَمَا لِلظَّٰلِمِينَ مِنْ أَنصَارٍ

270 Whatever charity you give, or a pledge you fulfill, Allah knows it. The wrongdoers have no helpers.

٢٧١ إِن تُبْدُوا۟ ٱلصَّدَقَٰتِ فَنِعِمَّا هِىَ ۖ وَإِن
تُخْفُوهَا وَتُؤْتُوهَا ٱلْفُقَرَآءَ فَهُوَ خَيْرٌ لَّكُمْ ۚ
وَيُكَفِّرُ عَنكُم مِّن سَيِّـَٔاتِكُمْ ۗ وَٱللَّهُ بِمَا تَعْمَلُونَ
خَبِيرٌ

271 If you give charity openly, that is good. But if you keep it secret, and give it to the needy in private, that is better for you. It will atone for some of your misdeeds. Allah is cognizant of what you do.

٢٧٢ لَّيْسَ عَلَيْكَ هُدَىٰهُمْ وَلَٰكِنَّ ٱللَّهَ يَهْدِى مَن
يَشَآءُ ۗ وَمَا تُنفِقُوا۟ مِنْ خَيْرٍ فَلِأَنفُسِكُمْ ۚ وَمَا
تُنفِقُونَ إِلَّا ٱبْتِغَآءَ وَجْهِ ٱللَّهِ ۚ وَمَا تُنفِقُوا۟ مِنْ
خَيْرٍ يُوَفَّ إِلَيْكُمْ وَأَنتُمْ لَا تُظْلَمُونَ

272 Their guidance is not your responsibility, but Allah guides whom He wills. Any charity you give is for your own good. Any charity you give shall be for the sake of Allah. Any charity you give will be repaid to you in full, and you will not be wronged.

٢٧٣ لِلْفُقَرَآءِ ٱلَّذِينَ أُحْصِرُوا۟ فِى سَبِيلِ ٱللَّهِ لَا
يَسْتَطِيعُونَ ضَرْبًا فِى ٱلْأَرْضِ يَحْسَبُهُمُ
ٱلْجَاهِلُ أَغْنِيَآءَ مِنَ ٱلتَّعَفُّفِ تَعْرِفُهُم بِسِيمَٰهُمْ
لَا يَسْـَٔلُونَ ٱلنَّاسَ إِلْحَافًا ۗ وَمَا تُنفِقُوا۟ مِنْ خَيْرٍ
فَإِنَّ ٱللَّهَ بِهِۦ عَلِيمٌ

273 It is for the poor; those who are restrained in the way of Allah, and unable to travel in the land. The unaware would think them rich, due to their dignity. You will recognize them by their features. They do not ask from people insistently. Whatever charity you give, Allah is aware of it.

٢٧٤ ٱلَّذِينَ يُنفِقُونَ أَمْوَٰلَهُم بِٱلَّيْلِ وَٱلنَّهَارِ سِرًّا
وَعَلَانِيَةً فَلَهُمْ أَجْرُهُمْ عِندَ رَبِّهِمْ وَلَا خَوْفٌ
عَلَيْهِمْ وَلَا هُمْ يَحْزَنُونَ

274 Those who spend their wealth by night and day, privately and publicly, will receive their reward from their Lord. They have nothing to fear, nor shall they grieve.

٢٧٥ ٱلَّذِينَ يَأْكُلُونَ ٱلرِّبَوٰا۟ لَا يَقُومُونَ إِلَّا كَمَا
يَقُومُ ٱلَّذِى يَتَخَبَّطُهُ ٱلشَّيْطَٰنُ مِنَ ٱلْمَسِّ ۚ ذَٰلِكَ
بِأَنَّهُمْ قَالُوٓا۟ إِنَّمَا ٱلْبَيْعُ مِثْلُ ٱلرِّبَوٰا۟ ۗ وَأَحَلَّ ٱللَّهُ
ٱلْبَيْعَ وَحَرَّمَ ٱلرِّبَوٰا۟ ۚ فَمَن جَآءَهُۥ مَوْعِظَةٌ مِّن
رَّبِّهِۦ فَٱنتَهَىٰ فَلَهُۥ مَا سَلَفَ وَأَمْرُهُۥٓ إِلَى ٱللَّهِ ۖ
وَمَنْ عَادَ فَأُو۟لَٰٓئِكَ أَصْحَٰبُ ٱلنَّارِ ۖ هُمْ فِيهَا
خَٰلِدُونَ

275 Those who swallow usury will not rise, except as someone driven mad by Satan's touch. That is because they say, “Commerce is like usury.” But Allah has permitted commerce, and has forbidden usury. Whoever, on receiving advice from his Lord, refrains, may keep his past earnings, and his case rests with Allah. But whoever resumes—these are the

dwellers of the Fire, wherein they will abide forever.

٢٧٦ يَمۡحَقُ ٱللَّهُ ٱلرِّبَوٰاْ وَيُرۡبِي ٱلصَّدَقَٰتِۗ وَٱللَّهُ
لَا يُحِبُّ كُلَّ كَفَّارٍ أَثِيمٍ

276 Allah condemns usury, and He blesses charities. Allah does not love any sinful ingrate.

٢٧٧ إِنَّ ٱلَّذِينَ ءَامَنُواْ وَعَمِلُواْ ٱلصَّٰلِحَٰتِ
وَأَقَامُواْ ٱلصَّلَوٰةَ وَءَاتَوُاْ ٱلزَّكَوٰةَ لَهُمۡ أَجۡرُهُمۡ
عِندَ رَبِّهِمۡ وَلَا خَوۡفٌ عَلَيۡهِمۡ وَلَا هُمۡ يَحۡزَنُونَ

277 Those who believe, and do good deeds, and pray regularly, and give charity—they will have their reward with their Lord; they will have no fear, nor shall they grieve.

٢٧٨ يَٰٓأَيُّهَا ٱلَّذِينَ ءَامَنُواْ ٱتَّقُواْ ٱللَّهَ وَذَرُواْ مَا
بَقِيَ مِنَ ٱلرِّبَوٰٓاْ إِن كُنتُم مُّؤۡمِنِينَ

278 O you who believe! Fear Allah, and forgo what remains of usury, if you are believers.

٢٧٩ فَإِن لَّمۡ تَفۡعَلُواْ فَأۡذَنُواْ بِحَرۡبٖ مِّنَ ٱللَّهِ
وَرَسُولِهِۦۖ وَإِن تُبۡتُمۡ فَلَكُمۡ رُءُوسُ أَمۡوَٰلِكُمۡ لَا
تَظۡلِمُونَ وَلَا تُظۡلَمُونَ

279 If you do not, then take notice of a war by Allah and His Messenger. But if you repent, you may keep your capital, neither wronging, nor being wronged.

٢٨٠ وَإِن كَانَ ذُو عُسۡرَةٖ فَنَظِرَةٌ إِلَىٰ مَيۡسَرَةٖۚ
وَأَن تَصَدَّقُواْ خَيۡرٞ لَّكُمۡۖ إِن كُنتُمۡ تَعۡلَمُونَ

280 But if he is in hardship, then deferment until a time of ease. But to remit it as charity is better for you, if you only knew.

٢٨١ وَٱتَّقُواْ يَوۡمٗا تُرۡجَعُونَ فِيهِ إِلَى ٱللَّهِۖ ثُمَّ
تُوَفَّىٰ كُلُّ نَفۡسٖ مَّا كَسَبَتۡ وَهُمۡ لَا يُظۡلَمُونَ

281 And guard yourselves against a Day when you will be returned to Allah; then each soul will be rewarded fully for what it has earned, and they will not be wronged.

٢٨٢ يَٰٓأَيُّهَا ٱلَّذِينَ ءَامَنُوٓاْ إِذَا تَدَايَنتُم بِدَيۡنٍ إِلَىٰٓ
أَجَلٖ مُّسَمّٗى فَٱكۡتُبُوهُۚ وَلۡيَكۡتُب بَّيۡنَكُمۡ كَاتِبُۢ
بِٱلۡعَدۡلِۚ وَلَا يَأۡبَ كَاتِبٌ أَن يَكۡتُبَ كَمَا عَلَّمَهُ
ٱللَّهُۚ فَلۡيَكۡتُبۡ وَلۡيُمۡلِلِ ٱلَّذِي عَلَيۡهِ ٱلۡحَقُّ وَلۡيَتَّقِ
ٱللَّهَ رَبَّهُۥ وَلَا يَبۡخَسۡ مِنۡهُ شَيۡـٔٗاۚ فَإِن كَانَ ٱلَّذِي
عَلَيۡهِ ٱلۡحَقُّ سَفِيهًا أَوۡ ضَعِيفًا أَوۡ لَا يَسۡتَطِيعُ أَن
يُمِلَّ هُوَ فَلۡيُمۡلِلۡ وَلِيُّهُۥ بِٱلۡعَدۡلِۚ وَٱسۡتَشۡهِدُواْ
شَهِيدَيۡنِ مِن رِّجَالِكُمۡۖ فَإِن لَّمۡ يَكُونَا رَجُلَيۡنِ

282 O you who believe! When you incur debt among yourselves for a certain period of time, write it down. And have a scribe write in your presence, in all fairness. And let no scribe refuse to write, as Allah has taught him. So let him write, and let the debtor dictate. And let him fear Allah, his Lord, and diminish nothing from it. But if the debtor is mentally deficient, or weak, or unable to dictate, then let his guardian dictate with honesty. And call to witness two

فَرَجُلٌ وَٱمْرَأَتَانِ مِمَّن تَرْضَوْنَ مِنَ ٱلشُّهَدَآءِ أَن
تَضِلَّ إِحْدَىٰهُمَا فَتُذَكِّرَ إِحْدَىٰهُمَا ٱلْأُخْرَىٰ ۚ وَلَا
يَأْبَ ٱلشُّهَدَآءُ إِذَا مَا دُعُوا۟ ۚ وَلَا تَسْـَٔمُوٓا۟ أَن
تَكْتُبُوهُ صَغِيرًا أَوْ كَبِيرًا إِلَىٰٓ أَجَلِهِۦ ۚ ذَٰلِكُمْ
أَقْسَطُ عِندَ ٱللَّهِ وَأَقْوَمُ لِلشَّهَٰدَةِ وَأَدْنَىٰٓ أَلَّا
تَرْتَابُوٓا۟ ۖ إِلَّآ أَن تَكُونَ تِجَٰرَةً حَاضِرَةً تُدِيرُونَهَا
بَيْنَكُمْ فَلَيْسَ عَلَيْكُمْ جُنَاحٌ أَلَّا تَكْتُبُوهَا ۗ
وَأَشْهِدُوٓا۟ إِذَا تَبَايَعْتُمْ ۚ وَلَا يُضَآرَّ كَاتِبٌ وَلَا
شَهِيدٌ ۚ وَإِن تَفْعَلُوا۟ فَإِنَّهُۥ فُسُوقٌۢ بِكُمْ ۗ وَٱتَّقُوا۟
ٱللَّهَ ۖ وَيُعَلِّمُكُمُ ٱللَّهُ ۗ وَٱللَّهُ بِكُلِّ شَىْءٍ عَلِيمٌ

men from among you. If two men are not available, then one man and two women whose testimony is acceptable to all—if one of them fails to remember, the other would remind her. Witnesses must not refuse when called upon. And do not think it too trivial to write down, whether small or large, including the time of repayment. That is more equitable with Allah, and stronger as evidence, and more likely to prevent doubt—except in the case of a spot transaction between you—then there is no blame on you if you do not write it down. And let there be witnesses whenever you conclude a contract, and let no harm be done to either scribe or witness. If you do that, it is corruption on your part. And fear Allah. Allah teaches you. Allah is aware of everything.

٢٨٣ وَإِن كُنتُمْ عَلَىٰ سَفَرٍ وَلَمْ تَجِدُوا۟ كَاتِبًا
فَرِهَٰنٌ مَّقْبُوضَةٌ ۖ فَإِنْ أَمِنَ بَعْضُكُم بَعْضًا فَلْيُؤَدِّ
ٱلَّذِى ٱؤْتُمِنَ أَمَٰنَتَهُۥ وَلْيَتَّقِ ٱللَّهَ رَبَّهُۥ ۗ وَلَا تَكْتُمُوا۟
ٱلشَّهَٰدَةَ ۚ وَمَن يَكْتُمْهَا فَإِنَّهُۥٓ ءَاثِمٌ قَلْبُهُۥ ۗ وَٱللَّهُ
بِمَا تَعْمَلُونَ عَلِيمٌ

283 If you are on a journey, and cannot find a scribe, then a security deposit should be handed over. But if you trust one another, let the trustee fulfill his trust, and let him fear Allah, his Lord. And do not conceal testimony. Whoever conceals it is sinner at heart. Allah is aware of what you do.

٢٨٤ لِّلَّهِ مَا فِى ٱلسَّمَٰوَٰتِ وَمَا فِى ٱلْأَرْضِ ۗ وَإِن
تُبْدُوا۟ مَا فِىٓ أَنفُسِكُمْ أَوْ تُخْفُوهُ يُحَاسِبْكُم بِهِ
ٱللَّهُ ۖ فَيَغْفِرُ لِمَن يَشَآءُ وَيُعَذِّبُ مَن يَشَآءُ ۗ
وَٱللَّهُ عَلَىٰ كُلِّ شَىْءٍ قَدِيرٌ

284 To Allah belongs everything in the heavens and the earth. Whether you reveal what is within your selves, or conceal it, Allah will call you to account for it. He forgives whom He wills, and He punishes whom He wills. Allah is Able to do all things.

٢٨٥ ءَامَنَ ٱلرَّسُولُ بِمَآ أُنزِلَ إِلَيْهِ مِن رَّبِّهِۦ
وَٱلْمُؤْمِنُونَ ۚ كُلٌّ ءَامَنَ بِٱللَّهِ وَمَلَٰٓئِكَتِهِۦ وَكُتُبِهِۦ

285 The Messenger has believed in what was revealed to him from his Lord, as did the believers. They all have believed in Allah, and His angels, and His scriptures, and His

وَرُسُلِهِۦ لَا نُفَرِّقُ بَيۡنَ أَحَدٖ مِّن رُّسُلِهِۦۚ وَقَالُواْ
سَمِعۡنَا وَأَطَعۡنَاۖ غُفۡرَانَكَ رَبَّنَا وَإِلَيۡكَ ٱلۡمَصِيرُ

messengers: "We make no distinction between any of His messengers." And they say, "We hear and we obey. Your forgiveness, our Lord. To you is the destiny."

٢٨٦ لَا يُكَلِّفُ ٱللَّهُ نَفۡسًا إِلَّا وُسۡعَهَاۚ لَهَا مَا
كَسَبَتۡ وَعَلَيۡهَا مَا ٱكۡتَسَبَتۡۗ رَبَّنَا لَا تُؤَاخِذۡنَآ إِن
نَّسِينَآ أَوۡ أَخۡطَأۡنَاۚ رَبَّنَا وَلَا تَحۡمِلۡ عَلَيۡنَآ إِصۡرٗا
كَمَا حَمَلۡتَهُۥ عَلَى ٱلَّذِينَ مِن قَبۡلِنَاۚ رَبَّنَا وَلَا
تُحَمِّلۡنَا مَا لَا طَاقَةَ لَنَا بِهِۦۖ وَٱعۡفُ عَنَّا وَٱغۡفِرۡ
لَنَا وَٱرۡحَمۡنَآۚ أَنتَ مَوۡلَىٰنَا فَٱنصُرۡنَا عَلَى ٱلۡقَوۡمِ
ٱلۡكَٰفِرِينَ

286 Allah does not burden any soul beyond its capacity. To its credit is what it earns, and against it is what it commits. "Our Lord, do not condemn us if we forget or make a mistake. Our Lord, do not burden us as You have burdened those before us. Our Lord, do not burden us with more than we have strength to bear; and pardon us, and forgive us, and have mercy on us. You are our Lord and Master, so help us against the disbelieving people."

3 Family of Imran آل عمران

بِسۡمِ ٱللَّهِ ٱلرَّحۡمَٰنِ ٱلرَّحِيمِ

In the name of Allah, the Gracious, the Merciful.

١ الٓمٓ

1 Alif, Lam, Meem.

٢ ٱللَّهُ لَآ إِلَٰهَ إِلَّا هُوَ ٱلۡحَيُّ ٱلۡقَيُّومُ

2 Allah, there is no god but He, the Living, the Eternal.

٣ نَزَّلَ عَلَيۡكَ ٱلۡكِتَٰبَ بِٱلۡحَقِّ مُصَدِّقٗا لِّمَا بَيۡنَ
يَدَيۡهِ وَأَنزَلَ ٱلتَّوۡرَىٰةَ وَٱلۡإِنجِيلَ

3 He sent down to you the Book with the Truth, confirming what came before it; and He sent down the Torah and the Gospel.

٤ مِن قَبۡلُ هُدٗى لِّلنَّاسِ وَأَنزَلَ ٱلۡفُرۡقَانَۗ إِنَّ
ٱلَّذِينَ كَفَرُواْ بِـَٔايَٰتِ ٱللَّهِ لَهُمۡ عَذَابٞ شَدِيدٞۗ
وَٱللَّهُ عَزِيزٞ ذُو ٱنتِقَامٍ

4 Aforetime, as guidance for mankind; and He sent down the Criterion. Those who have rejected Allah's signs will have a severe punishment. Allah is Mighty, Able to take revenge.

٥ إِنَّ ٱللَّهَ لَا يَخۡفَىٰ عَلَيۡهِ شَيۡءٞ فِي ٱلۡأَرۡضِ وَلَا
فِي ٱلسَّمَآءِ

5 Nothing is hidden from Allah, on earth or in the heaven.

٦ هُوَ ٱلَّذِى يُصَوِّرُكُمْ فِى ٱلْأَرْحَامِ كَيْفَ يَشَآءُ ۚ
لَآ إِلَٰهَ إِلَّا هُوَ ٱلْعَزِيزُ ٱلْحَكِيمُ

6 It is He who forms you in the wombs as He wills. There is no god except He, the Almighty, the Wise.

٧ هُوَ ٱلَّذِىٓ أَنزَلَ عَلَيْكَ ٱلْكِتَٰبَ مِنْهُ ءَايَٰتٌ
مُّحْكَمَٰتٌ هُنَّ أُمُّ ٱلْكِتَٰبِ وَأُخَرُ مُتَشَٰبِهَٰتٌ ۖ فَأَمَّا
ٱلَّذِينَ فِى قُلُوبِهِمْ زَيْغٌ فَيَتَّبِعُونَ مَا تَشَٰبَهَ مِنْهُ
ٱبْتِغَآءَ ٱلْفِتْنَةِ وَٱبْتِغَآءَ تَأْوِيلِهِۦ ۗ وَمَا يَعْلَمُ
تَأْوِيلَهُۥٓ إِلَّا ٱللَّهُ ۗ وَٱلرَّٰسِخُونَ فِى ٱلْعِلْمِ يَقُولُونَ
ءَامَنَّا بِهِۦ كُلٌّ مِّنْ عِندِ رَبِّنَا ۗ وَمَا يَذَّكَّرُ إِلَّآ أُو۟لُوا۟
ٱلْأَلْبَٰبِ

7 It is He who revealed to you the Book. Some of its verses are definitive; they are the foundation of the Book, and others are unspecific. As for those in whose hearts is deviation, they follow the unspecific part, seeking descent, and seeking to derive an interpretation. But none knows its interpretation except Allah and those firmly rooted in knowledge say, "We believe in it; all is from our Lord." But none recollects except those with understanding.

٨ رَبَّنَا لَا تُزِغْ قُلُوبَنَا بَعْدَ إِذْ هَدَيْتَنَا وَهَبْ لَنَا
مِن لَّدُنكَ رَحْمَةً ۚ إِنَّكَ أَنتَ ٱلْوَهَّابُ

8 "Our Lord, do not cause our hearts to swerve after You have guided us, and bestow on us mercy from Your presence; You are the Giver."

٩ رَبَّنَآ إِنَّكَ جَامِعُ ٱلنَّاسِ لِيَوْمٍ لَّا رَيْبَ فِيهِ ۚ إِنَّ
ٱللَّهَ لَا يُخْلِفُ ٱلْمِيعَادَ

9 "Our Lord, You will gather the people for a Day in which there is no doubt." Allah will never break His promise.

١٠ إِنَّ ٱلَّذِينَ كَفَرُوا۟ لَن تُغْنِىَ عَنْهُمْ أَمْوَٰلُهُمْ وَلَآ
أَوْلَٰدُهُم مِّنَ ٱللَّهِ شَيْـًٔا ۖ وَأُو۟لَٰٓئِكَ هُمْ وَقُودُ ٱلنَّارِ

10 As for those who disbelieve, neither their wealth nor their children will avail them anything against Allah. These will be fuel for the Fire.

١١ كَدَأْبِ ءَالِ فِرْعَوْنَ وَٱلَّذِينَ مِن قَبْلِهِمْ ۚ
كَذَّبُوا۟ بِـَٔايَٰتِنَا فَأَخَذَهُمُ ٱللَّهُ بِذُنُوبِهِمْ ۗ وَٱللَّهُ
شَدِيدُ ٱلْعِقَابِ

11 Like the behavior of Pharaoh's people and those before them. They rejected Our signs, so Allah seized them for their sins. Allah is Strict in retribution.

١٢ قُل لِّلَّذِينَ كَفَرُوا۟ سَتُغْلَبُونَ وَتُحْشَرُونَ إِلَىٰ
جَهَنَّمَ ۚ وَبِئْسَ ٱلْمِهَادُ

12 Say to those who disbelieve, "You will be defeated, and rounded up into Hell—an awful resting-place."

١٣ قَدْ كَانَ لَكُمْ ءَايَةٌ فِى فِئَتَيْنِ ٱلْتَقَتَا ۖ فِئَةٌ
تُقَٰتِلُ فِى سَبِيلِ ٱللَّهِ وَأُخْرَىٰ كَافِرَةٌ يَرَوْنَهُم

13 There was a sign for you in the two parties that met. One party fighting in the way of Allah, and the other was disbelieving. They saw them with their own eyes twice their

مِّثْلَيْهِمْ رَأْىَ ٱلْعَيْنِ ۚ وَٱللَّهُ يُؤَيِّدُ بِنَصْرِهِۦ مَن
يَشَآءُ ۗ إِنَّ فِى ذَٰلِكَ لَعِبْرَةً لِّأُو۟لِى ٱلْأَبْصَٰرِ

number. But Allah supports with His help whomever He wills. In that is a lesson for those with insight.

١٤ زُيِّنَ لِلنَّاسِ حُبُّ ٱلشَّهَوَٰتِ مِنَ ٱلنِّسَآءِ
وَٱلْبَنِينَ وَٱلْقَنَٰطِيرِ ٱلْمُقَنطَرَةِ مِنَ ٱلذَّهَبِ
وَٱلْفِضَّةِ وَٱلْخَيْلِ ٱلْمُسَوَّمَةِ وَٱلْأَنْعَٰمِ وَٱلْحَرْثِ ۗ
ذَٰلِكَ مَتَٰعُ ٱلْحَيَوٰةِ ٱلدُّنْيَا ۖ وَٱللَّهُ عِندَهُۥ حُسْنُ
ٱلْمَـَٔابِ

14 Adorned for the people is the love of desires, such as women, and children, and piles upon piles of gold and silver, and branded horses, and livestock, and fields. These are the conveniences of the worldly life, but with Allah lies the finest resort.

١٥ قُلْ أَؤُنَبِّئُكُم بِخَيْرٍ مِّن ذَٰلِكُمْ ۚ لِلَّذِينَ ٱتَّقَوْا۟
عِندَ رَبِّهِمْ جَنَّٰتٌ تَجْرِى مِن تَحْتِهَا ٱلْأَنْهَٰرُ
خَٰلِدِينَ فِيهَا وَأَزْوَٰجٌ مُّطَهَّرَةٌ وَرِضْوَٰنٌ مِّنَ ٱللَّهِ ۗ
وَٱللَّهُ بَصِيرٌۢ بِٱلْعِبَادِ

15 Say, “Shall I inform you of something better than that? For those who are righteous, with their Lord are Gardens beneath which rivers flow, where they will remain forever, and purified spouses, and acceptance from Allah.” Allah is Observant of the servants.

١٦ ٱلَّذِينَ يَقُولُونَ رَبَّنَآ إِنَّنَآ ءَامَنَّا فَٱغْفِرْ لَنَا
ذُنُوبَنَا وَقِنَا عَذَابَ ٱلنَّارِ

16 Those who say, “Our Lord, we have believed, so forgive us our sins, and save us from the suffering of the Fire.”

١٧ ٱلصَّٰبِرِينَ وَٱلصَّٰدِقِينَ وَٱلْقَٰنِتِينَ وَٱلْمُنفِقِينَ
وَٱلْمُسْتَغْفِرِينَ بِٱلْأَسْحَارِ

17 The patient, and the truthful, and the reverent, and the charitable, and the seekers of forgiveness at dawn.

١٨ شَهِدَ ٱللَّهُ أَنَّهُۥ لَآ إِلَٰهَ إِلَّا هُوَ وَٱلْمَلَٰٓئِكَةُ وَأُو۟لُوا۟
ٱلْعِلْمِ قَآئِمًۢا بِٱلْقِسْطِ ۚ لَآ إِلَٰهَ إِلَّا هُوَ ٱلْعَزِيزُ
ٱلْحَكِيمُ

18 Allah bears witness that there is no god but He, as do the angels, and those endowed with knowledge—upholding justice. There is no god but He, the Mighty, the Wise.

١٩ إِنَّ ٱلدِّينَ عِندَ ٱللَّهِ ٱلْإِسْلَٰمُ ۗ وَمَا ٱخْتَلَفَ
ٱلَّذِينَ أُوتُوا۟ ٱلْكِتَٰبَ إِلَّا مِنۢ بَعْدِ مَا جَآءَهُمُ
ٱلْعِلْمُ بَغْيًۢا بَيْنَهُمْ ۗ وَمَن يَكْفُرْ بِـَٔايَٰتِ ٱللَّهِ فَإِنَّ
ٱللَّهَ سَرِيعُ ٱلْحِسَابِ

19 Religion with Allah is Islam. Those to whom the Scripture was given differed only after knowledge came to them, out of envy among themselves. Whoever rejects the signs of Allah—Allah is quick to take account.

٢٠ فَإِنْ حَآجُّوكَ فَقُلْ أَسْلَمْتُ وَجْهِىَ لِلَّهِ وَمَنِ
ٱتَّبَعَنِ ۗ وَقُل لِّلَّذِينَ أُوتُوا۟ ٱلْكِتَـٰبَ وَٱلْأُمِّيِّـۧنَ
ءَأَسْلَمْتُمْ ۚ فَإِنْ أَسْلَمُوا۟ فَقَدِ ٱهْتَدَوا۟ ۖ وَّإِن تَوَلَّوْا۟
فَإِنَّمَا عَلَيْكَ ٱلْبَلَـٰغُ ۗ وَٱللَّهُ بَصِيرٌۢ بِٱلْعِبَادِ

20 If they argue with you, say, “I have surrendered myself to Allah, and those who follow me.” And say to those who were given the Scripture, and to the unlearned, “Have you surrendered?” If they have surrendered, then they are guided; but if they turn away, then your duty is to convey. Allah is Seeing of the servants.

٢١ إِنَّ ٱلَّذِينَ يَكْفُرُونَ بِـَٔايَـٰتِ ٱللَّهِ وَيَقْتُلُونَ
ٱلنَّبِيِّـۧنَ بِغَيْرِ حَقٍّ وَيَقْتُلُونَ ٱلَّذِينَ يَأْمُرُونَ
بِٱلْقِسْطِ مِنَ ٱلنَّاسِ فَبَشِّرْهُم بِعَذَابٍ أَلِيمٍ

21 As for those who defy Allah’s revelations, and kill the prophets unjustly, and kill those who advocate justice among the people—promise them a painful retribution.

٢٢ أُو۟لَـٰٓئِكَ ٱلَّذِينَ حَبِطَتْ أَعْمَـٰلُهُمْ فِى ٱلدُّنْيَا
وَٱلْـَٔاخِرَةِ وَمَا لَهُم مِّن نَّـٰصِرِينَ

22 They are those whose deeds will come to nothing, in this world and in the Hereafter; and they will have no saviors.

٢٣ أَلَمْ تَرَ إِلَى ٱلَّذِينَ أُوتُوا۟ نَصِيبًا مِّنَ ٱلْكِتَـٰبِ
يُدْعَوْنَ إِلَىٰ كِتَـٰبِ ٱللَّهِ لِيَحْكُمَ بَيْنَهُمْ ثُمَّ يَتَوَلَّىٰ
فَرِيقٌ مِّنْهُمْ وَهُم مُّعْرِضُونَ

23 Have you not considered those who were given a share of the Scripture, as they were called to the Scripture of Allah to arbitrate between them; then some of them turned back, and declined?

٢٤ ذَٰلِكَ بِأَنَّهُمْ قَالُوا۟ لَن تَمَسَّنَا ٱلنَّارُ إِلَّآ أَيَّامًا
مَّعْدُودَٰتٍ ۖ وَغَرَّهُمْ فِى دِينِهِم مَّا كَانُوا۟ يَفْتَرُونَ

24 That is because they said, “The Fire will not touch us except for a limited number of days.” They have been misled in their religion by the lies they fabricated.

٢٥ فَكَيْفَ إِذَا جَمَعْنَـٰهُمْ لِيَوْمٍ لَّا رَيْبَ فِيهِ
وَوُفِّيَتْ كُلُّ نَفْسٍ مَّا كَسَبَتْ وَهُمْ لَا يُظْلَمُونَ

25 How about when We gather them for a Day in which there is no doubt, and each soul will be paid in full for what it has earned, and they will not be wronged?

٢٦ قُلِ ٱللَّهُمَّ مَـٰلِكَ ٱلْمُلْكِ تُؤْتِى ٱلْمُلْكَ مَن تَشَآءُ
وَتَنزِعُ ٱلْمُلْكَ مِمَّن تَشَآءُ وَتُعِزُّ مَن تَشَآءُ وَتُذِلُّ
مَن تَشَآءُ ۖ بِيَدِكَ ٱلْخَيْرُ ۖ إِنَّكَ عَلَىٰ كُلِّ شَىْءٍ
قَدِيرٌ

26 Say, “O Allah, Owner of Sovereignty. You grant sovereignty to whom You will, and You strip sovereignty from whom you will. You honor whom you will, and You humiliate whom you will. In Your

hand is all goodness. You are Capable of all things."

٢٧ تُولِجُ ٱلَّيۡلَ فِى ٱلنَّهَارِ وَتُولِجُ ٱلنَّهَارَ فِى
ٱلَّيۡلِۖ وَتُخۡرِجُ ٱلۡحَىَّ مِنَ ٱلۡمَيِّتِ وَتُخۡرِجُ ٱلۡمَيِّتَ
مِنَ ٱلۡحَىِّۖ وَتَرۡزُقُ مَن تَشَآءُ بِغَيۡرِ حِسَابٍ

27 "You merge the night into the day, and You merge the day into the night; and you bring the living out of the dead, and You bring the dead out of the living; and You provide for whom you will without measure."

٢٨ لَّا يَتَّخِذِ ٱلۡمُؤۡمِنُونَ ٱلۡكَٰفِرِينَ أَوۡلِيَآءَ مِن
دُونِ ٱلۡمُؤۡمِنِينَۖ وَمَن يَفۡعَلۡ ذَٰلِكَ فَلَيۡسَ مِنَ
ٱللَّهِ فِى شَىۡءٍ إِلَّآ أَن تَتَّقُواْ مِنۡهُمۡ تُقَىٰةًۗ
وَيُحَذِّرُكُمُ ٱللَّهُ نَفۡسَهُۥۗ وَإِلَى ٱللَّهِ ٱلۡمَصِيرُ

28 Believers are not to take disbelievers for friends instead of believers. Whoever does that has nothing to do with Allah, unless it is to protect your own selves against them. Allah warns you to beware of Him. To Allah is the destiny.

٢٩ قُلۡ إِن تُخۡفُواْ مَا فِى صُدُورِكُمۡ أَوۡ تُبۡدُوهُ
يَعۡلَمۡهُ ٱللَّهُۗ وَيَعۡلَمُ مَا فِى ٱلسَّمَٰوَٰتِ وَمَا فِى
ٱلۡأَرۡضِۗ وَٱللَّهُ عَلَىٰ كُلِّ شَىۡءٍ قَدِيرٌ

29 Say, "Whether you conceal what is in your hearts, or disclose it, Allah knows it." He knows everything in the heavens and the earth. Allah is Powerful over everything.

٣٠ يَوۡمَ تَجِدُ كُلُّ نَفۡسٍ مَّا عَمِلَتۡ مِنۡ خَيۡرٍ
مُّحۡضَرًا وَمَا عَمِلَتۡ مِن سُوٓءٍ تَوَدُّ لَوۡ أَنَّ بَيۡنَهَا
وَبَيۡنَهُۥٓ أَمَدَۢا بَعِيدًاۗ وَيُحَذِّرُكُمُ ٱللَّهُ نَفۡسَهُۥۗ وَٱللَّهُ
رَءُوفُۢ بِٱلۡعِبَادِ

30 On the Day when every soul finds all the good it has done presented. And as for the evil it has done, it will wish there were a great distance between them. Allah cautions you of Himself. Allah is Kind towards the servants.

٣١ قُلۡ إِن كُنتُمۡ تُحِبُّونَ ٱللَّهَ فَٱتَّبِعُونِى يُحۡبِبۡكُمُ
ٱللَّهُ وَيَغۡفِرۡ لَكُمۡ ذُنُوبَكُمۡۗ وَٱللَّهُ غَفُورٌ رَّحِيمٌ

31 Say, "If you love Allah, then follow me, and Allah will love you, and will forgive you your sins." Allah is Forgiving and Merciful.

٣٢ قُلۡ أَطِيعُواْ ٱللَّهَ وَٱلرَّسُولَۖ فَإِن تَوَلَّوۡاْ فَإِنَّ
ٱللَّهَ لَا يُحِبُّ ٱلۡكَٰفِرِينَ

32 Say, "Obey Allah and the Messenger." But if they turn away—Allah does not love the faithless.

٣٣ إِنَّ ٱللَّهَ ٱصۡطَفَىٰٓ ءَادَمَ وَنُوحًا وَءَالَ
إِبۡرَٰهِيمَ وَءَالَ عِمۡرَٰنَ عَلَى ٱلۡعَٰلَمِينَ

33 Allah chose Adam, and Noah, and the family of Abraham, and the family of Imran, over all mankind.

٣٤ ذُرِّيَّةَۢ بَعۡضُهَا مِنۢ بَعۡضٍۗ وَٱللَّهُ سَمِيعٌ عَلِيمٌ

34 Offspring one of the other. Allah is Hearer and Knower.

٣٥ إِذْ قَالَتِ ٱمْرَأَتُ عِمْرَٰنَ رَبِّ إِنِّى نَذَرْتُ لَكَ
مَا فِى بَطْنِى مُحَرَّرًا فَتَقَبَّلْ مِنِّىٓ ۖ إِنَّكَ أَنتَ
ٱلسَّمِيعُ ٱلْعَلِيمُ

35 The wife of Imran said, “My Lord, I have vowed to You what is in my womb, dedicated, so accept from me; You are the Hearer and Knower.”

٣٦ فَلَمَّا وَضَعَتْهَا قَالَتْ رَبِّ إِنِّى وَضَعْتُهَآ أُنثَىٰ
وَٱللَّهُ أَعْلَمُ بِمَا وَضَعَتْ وَلَيْسَ ٱلذَّكَرُ كَٱلْأُنثَىٰ ۖ
وَإِنِّى سَمَّيْتُهَا مَرْيَمَ وَإِنِّىٓ أُعِيذُهَا بِكَ وَذُرِّيَّتَهَا
مِنَ ٱلشَّيْطَٰنِ ٱلرَّجِيمِ

36 And when she delivered her, she said, “My Lord, I have delivered a female,” and Allah was well aware of what she has delivered, “and the male is not like the female, and I have named her Mary, and have commended her and her descendants to Your protection, from Satan the outcast.”

٣٧ فَتَقَبَّلَهَا رَبُّهَا بِقَبُولٍ حَسَنٍ وَأَنۢبَتَهَا نَبَاتًا
حَسَنًا وَكَفَّلَهَا زَكَرِيَّا ۖ كُلَّمَا دَخَلَ عَلَيْهَا زَكَرِيَّا
ٱلْمِحْرَابَ وَجَدَ عِندَهَا رِزْقًا ۖ قَالَ يَٰمَرْيَمُ أَنَّىٰ
لَكِ هَٰذَا ۖ قَالَتْ هُوَ مِنْ عِندِ ٱللَّهِ ۖ إِنَّ ٱللَّهَ يَرْزُقُ
مَن يَشَآءُ بِغَيْرِ حِسَابٍ

37 Her Lord accepted her with a gracious reception, and brought her a beautiful upbringing, and entrusted her to the care of Zechariah. Whenever Zechariah entered upon her in the sanctuary, he found her with provision. He said, “O Mary, where did you get this from?” She said, “It is from Allah; Allah provides to whom He wills without reckoning.”

٣٨ هُنَالِكَ دَعَا زَكَرِيَّا رَبَّهُۥ ۖ قَالَ رَبِّ هَبْ لِى مِن
لَّدُنكَ ذُرِّيَّةً طَيِّبَةً ۖ إِنَّكَ سَمِيعُ ٱلدُّعَآءِ

38 Thereupon Zechariah prayed to his Lord; he said, “My Lord, bestow on me good offspring from Your presence; You are the Hearer of Prayers.”

٣٩ فَنَادَتْهُ ٱلْمَلَٰٓئِكَةُ وَهُوَ قَآئِمٌ يُصَلِّى فِى
ٱلْمِحْرَابِ أَنَّ ٱللَّهَ يُبَشِّرُكَ بِيَحْيَىٰ مُصَدِّقًۢا
بِكَلِمَةٍ مِّنَ ٱللَّهِ وَسَيِّدًا وَحَصُورًا وَنَبِيًّا مِّنَ
ٱلصَّٰلِحِينَ

39 Then the angels called out to him, as he stood praying in the sanctuary: “Allah gives you good news of John; confirming a Word from Allah, and honorable, and moral, and a prophet; one of the upright.”

٤٠ قَالَ رَبِّ أَنَّىٰ يَكُونُ لِى غُلَٰمٌ وَقَدْ بَلَغَنِىَ
ٱلْكِبَرُ وَٱمْرَأَتِى عَاقِرٌ ۖ قَالَ كَذَٰلِكَ ٱللَّهُ يَفْعَلُ مَا
يَشَآءُ

40 He said, “My Lord, how will I have a son, when old age has overtaken me, and my wife is barren?” He said, “Even so, Allah does whatever He wills.”

٤١ قَالَ رَبِّ ٱجْعَل لِّىٓ ءَايَةً ۖ قَالَ ءَايَتُكَ أَلَّا
تُكَلِّمَ ٱلنَّاسَ ثَلَٰثَةَ أَيَّامٍ إِلَّا رَمْزًا ۗ وَٱذْكُر رَّبَّكَ
كَثِيرًا وَسَبِّحْ بِٱلْعَشِىِّ وَٱلْإِبْكَٰرِ

41 He said, “My Lord, give me a sign.” He said, “Your sign is that you shall not speak to the people for three days, except by gestures. And remember your Lord much, and praise in the evening and the morning.”

٤٢ وَإِذْ قَالَتِ ٱلْمَلَٰٓئِكَةُ يَٰمَرْيَمُ إِنَّ ٱللَّهَ ٱصْطَفَىٰكِ
وَطَهَّرَكِ وَٱصْطَفَىٰكِ عَلَىٰ نِسَآءِ ٱلْعَٰلَمِينَ

42 The angels said, “O Mary, Allah has chosen you, and has purified you. He has chosen you over all the women of the world.

٤٣ يَٰمَرْيَمُ ٱقْنُتِى لِرَبِّكِ وَٱسْجُدِى وَٱرْكَعِى مَعَ
ٱلرَّٰكِعِينَ

43 “O Mary, be devoted to your Lord, and bow down, and kneel with those who kneel.”

٤٤ ذَٰلِكَ مِنْ أَنۢبَآءِ ٱلْغَيْبِ نُوحِيهِ إِلَيْكَ ۚ وَمَا
كُنتَ لَدَيْهِمْ إِذْ يُلْقُونَ أَقْلَٰمَهُمْ أَيُّهُمْ يَكْفُلُ مَرْيَمَ
وَمَا كُنتَ لَدَيْهِمْ إِذْ يَخْتَصِمُونَ

44 These are accounts from the Unseen, which We reveal to you. You were not with them when they cast their lots as to which of them would take charge of Mary; nor were you with them as they quarreled.

٤٥ إِذْ قَالَتِ ٱلْمَلَٰٓئِكَةُ يَٰمَرْيَمُ إِنَّ ٱللَّهَ يُبَشِّرُكِ
بِكَلِمَةٍ مِّنْهُ ٱسْمُهُ ٱلْمَسِيحُ عِيسَى ٱبْنُ مَرْيَمَ
وَجِيهًا فِى ٱلدُّنْيَا وَٱلْءَاخِرَةِ وَمِنَ ٱلْمُقَرَّبِينَ

45 The Angels said, “O Mary, Allah gives you good news of a Word from Him. His name is the Messiah, Jesus, son of Mary, well-esteemed in this world and the next, and one of the nearest.

٤٦ وَيُكَلِّمُ ٱلنَّاسَ فِى ٱلْمَهْدِ وَكَهْلًا وَمِنَ
ٱلصَّٰلِحِينَ

46 He will speak to the people from the crib, and in adulthood, and will be one of the righteous.”

٤٧ قَالَتْ رَبِّ أَنَّىٰ يَكُونُ لِى وَلَدٌ وَلَمْ يَمْسَسْنِى
بَشَرٌ ۖ قَالَ كَذَٰلِكِ ٱللَّهُ يَخْلُقُ مَا يَشَآءُ ۚ إِذَا
قَضَىٰٓ أَمْرًا فَإِنَّمَا يَقُولُ لَهُۥ كُن فَيَكُونُ

47 She said, “My Lord, how can I have a child, when no man has touched me?” He said, “It will be so. Allah creates whatever He wills. To have anything done, He only says to it, ‘Be,’ and it is.”

٤٨ وَيُعَلِّمُهُ ٱلْكِتَٰبَ وَٱلْحِكْمَةَ وَٱلتَّوْرَىٰةَ
وَٱلْإِنجِيلَ

48 And He will teach him the Scripture and wisdom, and the Torah and the Gospel.

٤٩ وَرَسُولًا إِلَىٰ بَنِىٓ إِسْرَٰٓءِيلَ أَنِّى قَدْ جِئْتُكُم
بِـَٔايَةٍ مِّن رَّبِّكُمْ ۖ أَنِّىٓ أَخْلُقُ لَكُم مِّنَ ٱلطِّينِ

49 A messenger to the Children of Israel: “I have come to you with a sign from your Lord. I make for you

كَهَيْـَٔةِ ٱلطَّيْرِ فَأَنفُخُ فِيهِ فَيَكُونُ طَيْرًۢا بِإِذْنِ
ٱللَّهِ ۖ وَأُبْرِئُ ٱلْأَكْمَهَ وَٱلْأَبْرَصَ وَأُحْىِ ٱلْمَوْتَىٰ
بِإِذْنِ ٱللَّهِ ۖ وَأُنَبِّئُكُم بِمَا تَأْكُلُونَ وَمَا تَدَّخِرُونَ
فِى بُيُوتِكُمْ ۚ إِنَّ فِى ذَٰلِكَ لَءَايَةً لَّكُمْ إِن كُنتُم
مُّؤْمِنِينَ

out of clay the figure of a bird; then I breathe into it, and it becomes a bird by Allah's leave. And I heal the blind and the leprous, and I revive the dead, by Allah's leave. And I inform you concerning what you eat, and what you store in your homes. In that is a sign for you, if you are believers."

٥٠ وَمُصَدِّقًا لِّمَا بَيْنَ يَدَىَّ مِنَ ٱلتَّوْرَىٰةِ وَلِأُحِلَّ
لَكُم بَعْضَ ٱلَّذِى حُرِّمَ عَلَيْكُمْ ۚ وَجِئْتُكُم بِـَٔايَةٍ
مِّن رَّبِّكُمْ فَٱتَّقُوا۟ ٱللَّهَ وَأَطِيعُونِ

50 "And verifying what lies before me of the Torah, and to make lawful for you some of what was forbidden to you. I have come to you with a sign from your Lord; so fear Allah, and obey me."

٥١ إِنَّ ٱللَّهَ رَبِّى وَرَبُّكُمْ فَٱعْبُدُوهُ ۗ هَٰذَا صِرَٰطٌ
مُّسْتَقِيمٌ

51 "Allah is my Lord and your Lord, so worship Him. That is a straight path."

٥٢ فَلَمَّآ أَحَسَّ عِيسَىٰ مِنْهُمُ ٱلْكُفْرَ قَالَ مَنْ
أَنصَارِىٓ إِلَى ٱللَّهِ ۖ قَالَ ٱلْحَوَارِيُّونَ نَحْنُ أَنصَارُ
ٱللَّهِ ءَامَنَّا بِٱللَّهِ وَٱشْهَدْ بِأَنَّا مُسْلِمُونَ

52 When Jesus sensed disbelief on their part, he said, "Who are my allies towards Allah?" The disciples said, "We are Allah's allies; we have believed in Allah, and bear witness that we submit."

٥٣ رَبَّنَآ ءَامَنَّا بِمَآ أَنزَلْتَ وَٱتَّبَعْنَا ٱلرَّسُولَ
فَٱكْتُبْنَا مَعَ ٱلشَّٰهِدِينَ

53 "Our Lord, we have believed in what You have revealed, and we have followed the Messenger, so count us among the witnesses."

٥٤ وَمَكَرُوا۟ وَمَكَرَ ٱللَّهُ ۖ وَٱللَّهُ خَيْرُ ٱلْمَٰكِرِينَ

54 They planned, and Allah planned; but Allah is the Best of planners.

٥٥ إِذْ قَالَ ٱللَّهُ يَٰعِيسَىٰٓ إِنِّى مُتَوَفِّيكَ وَرَافِعُكَ
إِلَىَّ وَمُطَهِّرُكَ مِنَ ٱلَّذِينَ كَفَرُوا۟ وَجَاعِلُ ٱلَّذِينَ
ٱتَّبَعُوكَ فَوْقَ ٱلَّذِينَ كَفَرُوٓا۟ إِلَىٰ يَوْمِ ٱلْقِيَٰمَةِ ۖ ثُمَّ
إِلَىَّ مَرْجِعُكُمْ فَأَحْكُمُ بَيْنَكُمْ فِيمَا كُنتُمْ فِيهِ
تَخْتَلِفُونَ

55 Allah said, "O Jesus, I am terminating your life, and raising you to Me, and clearing you of those who disbelieve. And I will make those who follow you superior to those who disbelieve, until the Day of Resurrection. Then to Me is your return; then I will judge between you regarding what you were disputing.

٥٦ فَأَمَّا ٱلَّذِينَ كَفَرُوا۟ فَأُعَذِّبُهُمْ عَذَابًا شَدِيدًا فِى ٱلدُّنْيَا وَٱلْـَٔاخِرَةِ وَمَا لَهُم مِّن نَّـٰصِرِينَ

56 As for those who disbelieve, I will punish them with a severe punishment, in this world and the next, and they will have no helpers.

٥٧ وَأَمَّا ٱلَّذِينَ ءَامَنُوا۟ وَعَمِلُوا۟ ٱلصَّـٰلِحَـٰتِ فَيُوَفِّيهِمْ أُجُورَهُمْ ۗ وَٱللَّهُ لَا يُحِبُّ ٱلظَّـٰلِمِينَ

57 And as for those who believe and do good works, He will give them their rewards in full. Allah does not love the unjust."

٥٨ ذَٰلِكَ نَتْلُوهُ عَلَيْكَ مِنَ ٱلْـَٔايَـٰتِ وَٱلذِّكْرِ ٱلْحَكِيمِ

58 This is what We recite to you of the Verses and the Wise Reminder.

٥٩ إِنَّ مَثَلَ عِيسَىٰ عِندَ ٱللَّهِ كَمَثَلِ ءَادَمَ ۖ خَلَقَهُۥ مِن تُرَابٍ ثُمَّ قَالَ لَهُۥ كُن فَيَكُونُ

59 The likeness of Jesus in Allah's sight is that of Adam: He created him from dust, then said to him, "Be," and he was.

٦٠ ٱلْحَقُّ مِن رَّبِّكَ فَلَا تَكُن مِّنَ ٱلْمُمْتَرِينَ

60 The truth is from your Lord, so do not be of those who doubt.

٦١ فَمَنْ حَآجَّكَ فِيهِ مِنۢ بَعْدِ مَا جَآءَكَ مِنَ ٱلْعِلْمِ فَقُلْ تَعَالَوْا۟ نَدْعُ أَبْنَآءَنَا وَأَبْنَآءَكُمْ وَنِسَآءَنَا وَنِسَآءَكُمْ وَأَنفُسَنَا وَأَنفُسَكُمْ ثُمَّ نَبْتَهِلْ فَنَجْعَل لَّعْنَتَ ٱللَّهِ عَلَى ٱلْكَـٰذِبِينَ

61 And if anyone disputes with you about him, after the knowledge that has come to you, say, "Come, let us call our children and your children, and our women and your women, and ourselves and yourselves, and let us invoke Allah's curse on the liars."

٦٢ إِنَّ هَـٰذَا لَهُوَ ٱلْقَصَصُ ٱلْحَقُّ ۚ وَمَا مِنْ إِلَـٰهٍ إِلَّا ٱللَّهُ ۚ وَإِنَّ ٱللَّهَ لَهُوَ ٱلْعَزِيزُ ٱلْحَكِيمُ

62 This is the narrative of truth: there is no god but Allah. Allah is the Mighty, the Wise.

٦٣ فَإِن تَوَلَّوْا۟ فَإِنَّ ٱللَّهَ عَلِيمٌۢ بِٱلْمُفْسِدِينَ

63 But if they turn away—Allah knows the corrupt.

٦٤ قُلْ يَـٰٓأَهْلَ ٱلْكِتَـٰبِ تَعَالَوْا۟ إِلَىٰ كَلِمَةٍ سَوَآءٍۭ بَيْنَنَا وَبَيْنَكُمْ أَلَّا نَعْبُدَ إِلَّا ٱللَّهَ وَلَا نُشْرِكَ بِهِۦ شَيْـًٔا وَلَا يَتَّخِذَ بَعْضُنَا بَعْضًا أَرْبَابًا مِّن دُونِ ٱللَّهِ ۚ فَإِن تَوَلَّوْا۟ فَقُولُوا۟ ٱشْهَدُوا۟ بِأَنَّا مُسْلِمُونَ

64 Say, "O People of the Book, come to terms common between us and you: that we worship none but Allah, and that we associate nothing with Him, and that none of us takes others as lords besides Allah." And if they turn away, say, "Bear witness that we have submitted."

٦٥ يَٰٓأَهْلَ ٱلْكِتَٰبِ لِمَ تُحَآجُّونَ فِىٓ إِبْرَٰهِيمَ وَمَآ
أُنزِلَتِ ٱلتَّوْرَىٰةُ وَٱلْإِنجِيلُ إِلَّا مِنۢ بَعْدِهِۦٓ ۚ أَفَلَا
تَعْقِلُونَ

65 O People of the Book! Why do you argue about Abraham, when the Torah and the Gospel were not revealed until after him? Will you not reason?

٦٦ هَٰٓأَنتُمْ هَٰٓؤُلَآءِ حَٰجَجْتُمْ فِيمَا لَكُم بِهِۦ عِلْمٌ
فَلِمَ تُحَآجُّونَ فِيمَا لَيْسَ لَكُم بِهِۦ عِلْمٌ ۚ وَٱللَّهُ
يَعْلَمُ وَأَنتُمْ لَا تَعْلَمُونَ

66 Here you are—you argue about things you know, but why do you argue about things you do not know? Allah knows, and you do not know.

٦٧ مَا كَانَ إِبْرَٰهِيمُ يَهُودِيًّا وَلَا نَصْرَانِيًّا وَلَٰكِن
كَانَ حَنِيفًا مُّسْلِمًا وَمَا كَانَ مِنَ ٱلْمُشْرِكِينَ

67 Abraham was neither a Jew nor a Christian, but he was a Monotheist, a Muslim. And he was not of the Polytheists.

٦٨ إِنَّ أَوْلَى ٱلنَّاسِ بِإِبْرَٰهِيمَ لَلَّذِينَ ٱتَّبَعُوهُ
وَهَٰذَا ٱلنَّبِىُّ وَٱلَّذِينَ ءَامَنُوا۟ ۗ وَٱللَّهُ وَلِىُّ
ٱلْمُؤْمِنِينَ

68 The people most deserving of Abraham are those who followed him, and this prophet, and those who believe. Allah is the Guardian of the believers.

٦٩ وَدَّت طَّآئِفَةٌ مِّنْ أَهْلِ ٱلْكِتَٰبِ لَوْ يُضِلُّونَكُمْ
وَمَا يُضِلُّونَ إِلَّآ أَنفُسَهُمْ وَمَا يَشْعُرُونَ

69 A party of the People of the Book would love to lead you astray, but they only lead themselves astray, and they do not realize it.

٧٠ يَٰٓأَهْلَ ٱلْكِتَٰبِ لِمَ تَكْفُرُونَ بِـَٔايَٰتِ ٱللَّهِ وَأَنتُمْ
تَشْهَدُونَ

70 O People of the Book! Why do you reject the revelations of Allah, even as you witness?

٧١ يَٰٓأَهْلَ ٱلْكِتَٰبِ لِمَ تَلْبِسُونَ ٱلْحَقَّ بِٱلْبَٰطِلِ
وَتَكْتُمُونَ ٱلْحَقَّ وَأَنتُمْ تَعْلَمُونَ

71 O People of the Book! Why do you confound the truth with falsehood, and knowingly conceal the truth?

٧٢ وَقَالَت طَّآئِفَةٌ مِّنْ أَهْلِ ٱلْكِتَٰبِ ءَامِنُوا۟
بِٱلَّذِىٓ أُنزِلَ عَلَى ٱلَّذِينَ ءَامَنُوا۟ وَجْهَ ٱلنَّهَارِ
وَٱكْفُرُوٓا۟ ءَاخِرَهُۥ لَعَلَّهُمْ يَرْجِعُونَ

72 Some of the People of the Book say, “Believe in what was revealed to the believers at the beginning of the day, and reject it at its end, so that they may return.”

٧٣ وَلَا تُؤْمِنُوٓا۟ إِلَّا لِمَن تَبِعَ دِينَكُمْ قُلْ إِنَّ ٱلْهُدَىٰ
هُدَى ٱللَّهِ أَن يُؤْتَىٰٓ أَحَدٌ مِّثْلَ مَآ أُوتِيتُمْ أَوْ
يُحَآجُّوكُمْ عِندَ رَبِّكُمْ ۗ قُلْ إِنَّ ٱلْفَضْلَ بِيَدِ ٱللَّهِ
يُؤْتِيهِ مَن يَشَآءُ ۗ وَٱللَّهُ وَٰسِعٌ عَلِيمٌ

73 And trust none except those who follow your religion.” Say, “Guidance is Allah’s guidance. If someone is given the like of what you were given, or they argue with you before your Lord, say, “All grace is in Allah’s hand; He gives it to

whomever He wills." Allah is Bounteous and Knowing.

٧٤ يَخْتَصُّ بِرَحْمَتِهِۦ مَن يَشَآءُ ۗ وَٱللَّهُ ذُو
ٱلْفَضْلِ ٱلْعَظِيمِ

74 He specifies His mercy for whomever He wills. Allah is Possessor of Sublime Grace.

٧٥ وَمِنْ أَهْلِ ٱلْكِتَٰبِ مَنْ إِن تَأْمَنْهُ بِقِنطَارٍ
يُؤَدِّهِۦٓ إِلَيْكَ وَمِنْهُم مَّنْ إِن تَأْمَنْهُ بِدِينَارٍ لَّا
يُؤَدِّهِۦٓ إِلَيْكَ إِلَّا مَا دُمْتَ عَلَيْهِ قَآئِمًا ۗ ذَٰلِكَ بِأَنَّهُمْ
قَالُوا۟ لَيْسَ عَلَيْنَا فِى ٱلْأُمِّيِّـۧنَ سَبِيلٌ وَيَقُولُونَ
عَلَى ٱللَّهِ ٱلْكَذِبَ وَهُمْ يَعْلَمُونَ

75 Among the People of the Book is he, who, if you entrust him with a heap of gold, he will give it back to you. And among them is he, who, if you entrust him with a single coin, he will not give it back to you, unless you keep after him. That is because they say, "We are under no obligation towards the gentiles." They tell lies about Allah, and they know it.

٧٦ بَلَىٰ مَنْ أَوْفَىٰ بِعَهْدِهِۦ وَٱتَّقَىٰ فَإِنَّ ٱللَّهَ
يُحِبُّ ٱلْمُتَّقِينَ

76 Indeed, whoever fulfills his commitments and maintains piety—Allah loves the pious.

٧٧ إِنَّ ٱلَّذِينَ يَشْتَرُونَ بِعَهْدِ ٱللَّهِ وَأَيْمَٰنِهِمْ ثَمَنًا
قَلِيلًا أُو۟لَٰٓئِكَ لَا خَلَٰقَ لَهُمْ فِى ٱلْءَاخِرَةِ وَلَا
يُكَلِّمُهُمُ ٱللَّهُ وَلَا يَنظُرُ إِلَيْهِمْ يَوْمَ ٱلْقِيَٰمَةِ وَلَا
يُزَكِّيهِمْ وَلَهُمْ عَذَابٌ أَلِيمٌ

77 Those who exchange the covenant of Allah, and their vows, for a small price, will have no share in the Hereafter, and Allah will not speak to them, nor will He look at them on the Day of Resurrection, nor will He purify them. They will have a painful punishment.

٧٨ وَإِنَّ مِنْهُمْ لَفَرِيقًا يَلْوُۥنَ أَلْسِنَتَهُم بِٱلْكِتَٰبِ
لِتَحْسَبُوهُ مِنَ ٱلْكِتَٰبِ وَمَا هُوَ مِنَ ٱلْكِتَٰبِ
وَيَقُولُونَ هُوَ مِنْ عِندِ ٱللَّهِ وَمَا هُوَ مِنْ عِندِ
ٱللَّهِ وَيَقُولُونَ عَلَى ٱللَّهِ ٱلْكَذِبَ وَهُمْ يَعْلَمُونَ

78 And among them are those who twist the Scripture with their tongues, that you may think it from the Scripture, when it is not from the Scripture. And they say, "It is from Allah," when it is not from Allah. They tell lies and attribute them to Allah, knowingly.

٧٩ مَا كَانَ لِبَشَرٍ أَن يُؤْتِيَهُ ٱللَّهُ ٱلْكِتَٰبَ وَٱلْحُكْمَ
وَٱلنُّبُوَّةَ ثُمَّ يَقُولَ لِلنَّاسِ كُونُوا۟ عِبَادًا لِّى مِن
دُونِ ٱللَّهِ وَلَٰكِن كُونُوا۟ رَبَّٰنِيِّـۧنَ بِمَا كُنتُمْ
تُعَلِّمُونَ ٱلْكِتَٰبَ وَبِمَا كُنتُمْ تَدْرُسُونَ

79 No person to whom Allah has given the Scripture, and wisdom, and prophethood would ever say to the people, "Be my worshipers rather than Allah's." Rather, "Be people of the Lord, according to the

Scripture you teach, and the teachings you learn."

٨٠ وَلَا يَأۡمُرَكُمۡ أَن تَتَّخِذُواْ ٱلۡمَلَٰٓئِكَةَ وَٱلنَّبِيِّـۧنَ
أَرۡبَابًاۗ أَيَأۡمُرُكُم بِٱلۡكُفۡرِ بَعۡدَ إِذۡ أَنتُم مُّسۡلِمُونَ

80 Nor would he command you to take the angels and the prophets as lords. Would he command you to infidelity after you have submitted?

٨١ وَإِذۡ أَخَذَ ٱللَّهُ مِيثَٰقَ ٱلنَّبِيِّـۧنَ لَمَآ ءَاتَيۡتُكُم
مِّن كِتَٰبٖ وَحِكۡمَةٖ ثُمَّ جَآءَكُمۡ رَسُولٞ مُّصَدِّقٞ
لِّمَا مَعَكُمۡ لَتُؤۡمِنُنَّ بِهِۦ وَلَتَنصُرُنَّهُۥۚ قَالَ
ءَأَقۡرَرۡتُمۡ وَأَخَذۡتُمۡ عَلَىٰ ذَٰلِكُمۡ إِصۡرِيۖ قَالُوٓاْ
أَقۡرَرۡنَاۚ قَالَ فَٱشۡهَدُواْ وَأَنَا۠ مَعَكُم مِّنَ ٱلشَّٰهِدِينَ

81 Allah received the covenant of the prophets, "Inasmuch as I have given you of scripture and wisdom; should a messenger come to you verifying what you have, you shall believe in him, and support him." He said, "Do you affirm My covenant and take it upon yourselves?" They said, "We affirm it." He said, "Then bear witness, and I am with you among the witnesses."

٨٢ فَمَن تَوَلَّىٰ بَعۡدَ ذَٰلِكَ فَأُوْلَٰٓئِكَ هُمُ ٱلۡفَٰسِقُونَ

82 Whoever turns away after that—these are the deceitful.

٨٣ أَفَغَيۡرَ دِينِ ٱللَّهِ يَبۡغُونَ وَلَهُۥٓ أَسۡلَمَ مَن فِي
ٱلسَّمَٰوَٰتِ وَٱلۡأَرۡضِ طَوۡعٗا وَكَرۡهٗا وَإِلَيۡهِ
يُرۡجَعُونَ

83 Do they desire other than the religion of Allah, when to Him has submitted everything in the heavens and the earth, willingly or unwillingly, and to Him they will be returned?

٨٤ قُلۡ ءَامَنَّا بِٱللَّهِ وَمَآ أُنزِلَ عَلَيۡنَا وَمَآ أُنزِلَ
عَلَىٰٓ إِبۡرَٰهِيمَ وَإِسۡمَٰعِيلَ وَإِسۡحَٰقَ وَيَعۡقُوبَ
وَٱلۡأَسۡبَاطِ وَمَآ أُوتِيَ مُوسَىٰ وَعِيسَىٰ
وَٱلنَّبِيُّونَ مِن رَّبِّهِمۡ لَا نُفَرِّقُ بَيۡنَ أَحَدٖ مِّنۡهُمۡ
وَنَحۡنُ لَهُۥ مُسۡلِمُونَ

84 Say, "We believe in Allah, and in what was revealed to us; and in what was revealed to Abraham, and Ishmael, and Isaac, and Jacob, and the Patriarchs; and in what was given to Moses, and Jesus, and the prophets from their Lord. We make no distinction between any of them, and to Him we submit."

٨٥ وَمَن يَبۡتَغِ غَيۡرَ ٱلۡإِسۡلَٰمِ دِينٗا فَلَن يُقۡبَلَ مِنۡهُ
وَهُوَ فِي ٱلۡأٓخِرَةِ مِنَ ٱلۡخَٰسِرِينَ

85 Whoever seeks other than Islam as a religion, it will not be accepted from him, and in the Hereafter he will be among the losers.

٨٦ كَيۡفَ يَهۡدِي ٱللَّهُ قَوۡمٗا كَفَرُواْ بَعۡدَ إِيمَٰنِهِمۡ
وَشَهِدُوٓاْ أَنَّ ٱلرَّسُولَ حَقّٞ وَجَآءَهُمُ ٱلۡبَيِّنَٰتُۚ
وَٱللَّهُ لَا يَهۡدِي ٱلۡقَوۡمَ ٱلظَّٰلِمِينَ

86 How will Allah guide a people who disbelieved after having believed, and had witnessed that the Messenger is true, and the clear

proofs had come to them? Allah does not guide the unjust people.

٨٧ أُوْلَٰٓئِكَ جَزَآؤُهُمْ أَنَّ عَلَيْهِمْ لَعْنَةَ ٱللَّهِ وَٱلْمَلَٰٓئِكَةِ وَٱلنَّاسِ أَجْمَعِينَ

87 Those—their penalty is that upon them falls the curse of Allah, and of the angels, and of all mankind.

٨٨ خَٰلِدِينَ فِيهَا لَا يُخَفَّفُ عَنْهُمُ ٱلْعَذَابُ وَلَا هُمْ يُنظَرُونَ

88 Remaining in it eternally, without their punishment being eased from them, and without being reprieved.

٨٩ إِلَّا ٱلَّذِينَ تَابُواْ مِنۢ بَعْدِ ذَٰلِكَ وَأَصْلَحُواْ فَإِنَّ ٱللَّهَ غَفُورٌ رَّحِيمٌ

89 Except those who repent afterwards, and reform; for Allah is Forgiving and Merciful.

٩٠ إِنَّ ٱلَّذِينَ كَفَرُواْ بَعْدَ إِيمَٰنِهِمْ ثُمَّ ٱزْدَادُواْ كُفْرًا لَّن تُقْبَلَ تَوْبَتُهُمْ وَأُوْلَٰٓئِكَ هُمُ ٱلضَّآلُّونَ

90 As for those who disbelieve after having believed, then plunge deeper into disbelief, their repentance will not be accepted; these are the lost.

٩١ إِنَّ ٱلَّذِينَ كَفَرُواْ وَمَاتُواْ وَهُمْ كُفَّارٌ فَلَن يُقْبَلَ مِنْ أَحَدِهِم مِّلْءُ ٱلْأَرْضِ ذَهَبًا وَلَوِ ٱفْتَدَىٰ بِهِۦٓ أُوْلَٰٓئِكَ لَهُمْ عَذَابٌ أَلِيمٌ وَمَا لَهُم مِّن نَّٰصِرِينَ

91 As for those who disbelieve and die disbelievers, even the earth full of gold would not be accepted from any of them, were he to offer it for ransom. These will have a painful torment, and will have no saviors.

٩٢ لَن تَنَالُواْ ٱلْبِرَّ حَتَّىٰ تُنفِقُواْ مِمَّا تُحِبُّونَ ۚ وَمَا تُنفِقُواْ مِن شَىْءٍ فَإِنَّ ٱللَّهَ بِهِۦ عَلِيمٌ

92 You will not attain virtuous conduct until you give of what you cherish. Whatever you give away, Allah is aware of it.

٩٣ كُلُّ ٱلطَّعَامِ كَانَ حِلًّا لِّبَنِىٓ إِسْرَٰٓءِيلَ إِلَّا مَا حَرَّمَ إِسْرَٰٓءِيلُ عَلَىٰ نَفْسِهِۦ مِن قَبْلِ أَن تُنَزَّلَ ٱلتَّوْرَىٰةُ ۗ قُلْ فَأْتُواْ بِٱلتَّوْرَىٰةِ فَٱتْلُوهَآ إِن كُنتُمْ صَٰدِقِينَ

93 All food was permissible to the Children of Israel, except what Israel forbade for itself before the Torah was revealed. Say, “Bring the Torah, and read it, if you are truthful.”

٩٤ فَمَنِ ٱفْتَرَىٰ عَلَى ٱللَّهِ ٱلْكَذِبَ مِنۢ بَعْدِ ذَٰلِكَ فَأُوْلَٰٓئِكَ هُمُ ٱلظَّٰلِمُونَ

94 Whoever forges lies about Allah after that—these are the unjust.

٩٥ قُلْ صَدَقَ ٱللَّهُ ۗ فَٱتَّبِعُواْ مِلَّةَ إِبْرَٰهِيمَ حَنِيفًا وَمَا كَانَ مِنَ ٱلْمُشْرِكِينَ

95 Say, “Allah has spoken the truth, so follow the religion of Abraham the Monotheist; he was not a Pagan.”

٩٦ إِنَّ أَوَّلَ بَيْتٍ وُضِعَ لِلنَّاسِ لَلَّذِى بِبَكَّةَ مُبَارَكًا وَهُدًى لِّلْعَٰلَمِينَ

96 The first house established for mankind is the one at Bekka; blessed, and guidance for all people.

٩٧ فِيهِ ءَايَٰتُۢ بَيِّنَٰتٌ مَّقَامُ إِبْرَٰهِيمَ ۖ وَمَن دَخَلَهُۥ
كَانَ ءَامِنًا ۗ وَلِلَّهِ عَلَى ٱلنَّاسِ حِجُّ ٱلْبَيْتِ مَنِ
ٱسْتَطَاعَ إِلَيْهِ سَبِيلًا ۚ وَمَن كَفَرَ فَإِنَّ ٱللَّهَ غَنِىٌّ
عَنِ ٱلْعَٰلَمِينَ

97 In it are evident signs; the Station of Abraham. Whoever enters it attains security. Pilgrimage to the House is a duty to Allah for all who can make the journey. But as for those who refuse—Allah is Independent of the worlds.

٩٨ قُلْ يَٰٓأَهْلَ ٱلْكِتَٰبِ لِمَ تَكْفُرُونَ بِـَٔايَٰتِ ٱللَّهِ
وَٱللَّهُ شَهِيدٌ عَلَىٰ مَا تَعْمَلُونَ

98 Say, “O People of the Scripture, why do you reject the Revelations of Allah, when Allah witnesses what you do?”

٩٩ قُلْ يَٰٓأَهْلَ ٱلْكِتَٰبِ لِمَ تَصُدُّونَ عَن سَبِيلِ ٱللَّهِ
مَنْ ءَامَنَ تَبْغُونَهَا عِوَجًا وَأَنتُمْ شُهَدَآءُ ۗ وَمَا
ٱللَّهُ بِغَٰفِلٍ عَمَّا تَعْمَلُونَ

99 Say, “O People of the Scripture, why do you hinder from Allah’s path those who believe, seeking to distort it, even though you are witnesses? Allah is not unaware of what you do.”

١٠٠ يَٰٓأَيُّهَا ٱلَّذِينَ ءَامَنُوٓا۟ إِن تُطِيعُوا۟ فَرِيقًا مِّنَ
ٱلَّذِينَ أُوتُوا۟ ٱلْكِتَٰبَ يَرُدُّوكُم بَعْدَ إِيمَٰنِكُمْ
كَٰفِرِينَ

100 O you who believe! If you obey a party of those who were given the Scripture, they will turn you, after your belief, into disbelievers.

١٠١ وَكَيْفَ تَكْفُرُونَ وَأَنتُمْ تُتْلَىٰ عَلَيْكُمْ ءَايَٰتُ
ٱللَّهِ وَفِيكُمْ رَسُولُهُۥ ۗ وَمَن يَعْتَصِم بِٱللَّهِ فَقَدْ
هُدِىَ إِلَىٰ صِرَٰطٍ مُّسْتَقِيمٍ

101 And how could you disbelieve, when Allah’s revelations are being recited to you, and among you is His Messenger? Whoever cleaves to Allah has been guided to a straight path.

١٠٢ يَٰٓأَيُّهَا ٱلَّذِينَ ءَامَنُوا۟ ٱتَّقُوا۟ ٱللَّهَ حَقَّ تُقَاتِهِۦ
وَلَا تَمُوتُنَّ إِلَّا وَأَنتُم مُّسْلِمُونَ

102 O you who believe! Revere Allah with due reverence, and do not die except as Muslims.

١٠٣ وَٱعْتَصِمُوا۟ بِحَبْلِ ٱللَّهِ جَمِيعًا وَلَا تَفَرَّقُوا۟ ۚ
وَٱذْكُرُوا۟ نِعْمَتَ ٱللَّهِ عَلَيْكُمْ إِذْ كُنتُمْ أَعْدَآءً
فَأَلَّفَ بَيْنَ قُلُوبِكُمْ فَأَصْبَحْتُم بِنِعْمَتِهِۦٓ إِخْوَٰنًا
وَكُنتُمْ عَلَىٰ شَفَا حُفْرَةٍ مِّنَ ٱلنَّارِ فَأَنقَذَكُم مِّنْهَا ۗ
كَذَٰلِكَ يُبَيِّنُ ٱللَّهُ لَكُمْ ءَايَٰتِهِۦ لَعَلَّكُمْ تَهْتَدُونَ

103 And hold fast to the rope of Allah, altogether, and do not become divided. And remember Allah’s blessings upon you; how you were enemies, and He reconciled your hearts, and by His grace you became brethren. And you were on the brink of a pit of fire, and He saved you from it. Allah thus clarifies His revelations for you, so that you may be guided.

١٠٤ وَلْتَكُن مِّنكُمْ أُمَّةٌ يَدْعُونَ إِلَى ٱلْخَيْرِ
وَيَأْمُرُونَ بِٱلْمَعْرُوفِ وَيَنْهَوْنَ عَنِ ٱلْمُنكَرِ ۚ
وَأُو۟لَٰٓئِكَ هُمُ ٱلْمُفْلِحُونَ

104 And let there be among you a community calling to virtue, and advocating righteousness, and deterring from evil. These are the successful.

١٠٥ وَلَا تَكُونُوا۟ كَٱلَّذِينَ تَفَرَّقُوا۟ وَٱخْتَلَفُوا۟ مِنۢ
بَعْدِ مَا جَآءَهُمُ ٱلْبَيِّنَٰتُ ۚ وَأُو۟لَٰٓئِكَ لَهُمْ عَذَابٌ
عَظِيمٌ

105 And do not be like those who separated and disputed after the clear proofs came to them; for them is a great punishment.

١٠٦ يَوْمَ تَبْيَضُّ وُجُوهٌ وَتَسْوَدُّ وُجُوهٌ ۚ فَأَمَّا
ٱلَّذِينَ ٱسْوَدَّتْ وُجُوهُهُمْ أَكَفَرْتُم بَعْدَ إِيمَٰنِكُمْ
فَذُوقُوا۟ ٱلْعَذَابَ بِمَا كُنتُمْ تَكْفُرُونَ

106 On the Day when some faces will be whitened, and some faces will be blackened. As for those whose faces are blackened: “Did you disbelieve after your belief?” Then taste the punishment for having disbelieved.

١٠٧ وَأَمَّا ٱلَّذِينَ ٱبْيَضَّتْ وُجُوهُهُمْ فَفِى رَحْمَةِ
ٱللَّهِ هُمْ فِيهَا خَٰلِدُونَ

107 But as for those whose faces are whitened: they are in Allah’s mercy, remaining in it forever.

١٠٨ تِلْكَ ءَايَٰتُ ٱللَّهِ نَتْلُوهَا عَلَيْكَ بِٱلْحَقِّ ۗ وَمَا
ٱللَّهُ يُرِيدُ ظُلْمًا لِّلْعَٰلَمِينَ

108 These are the revelations of Allah. We recite them to you in truth. Allah desires no injustice for mankind.

١٠٩ وَلِلَّهِ مَا فِى ٱلسَّمَٰوَٰتِ وَمَا فِى ٱلْأَرْضِ ۚ
وَإِلَى ٱللَّهِ تُرْجَعُ ٱلْأُمُورُ

109 To Allah belongs everything in the heavens and everything on earth, and to Allah all events are referred.

١١٠ كُنتُمْ خَيْرَ أُمَّةٍ أُخْرِجَتْ لِلنَّاسِ تَأْمُرُونَ
بِٱلْمَعْرُوفِ وَتَنْهَوْنَ عَنِ ٱلْمُنكَرِ وَتُؤْمِنُونَ بِٱللَّهِ ۗ
وَلَوْ ءَامَنَ أَهْلُ ٱلْكِتَٰبِ لَكَانَ خَيْرًا لَّهُم ۚ مِّنْهُمُ
ٱلْمُؤْمِنُونَ وَأَكْثَرُهُمُ ٱلْفَٰسِقُونَ

110 You are the best community that ever emerged for humanity: you advocate what is moral, and forbid what is immoral, and believe in Allah. Had the People of the Scripture believed, it would have been better for them. Among them are the believers, but most of them are sinners.

١١١ لَن يَضُرُّوكُمْ إِلَّآ أَذًى ۖ وَإِن يُقَٰتِلُوكُمْ يُوَلُّوكُمُ
ٱلْأَدْبَارَ ثُمَّ لَا يُنصَرُونَ

111 They will do you no harm, beyond insulting you. And if they fight you, they will turn around and flee, then they will not be helped.

١١٢ ضُرِبَتْ عَلَيْهِمُ ٱلذِّلَّةُ أَيْنَ مَا ثُقِفُوٓا۟ إِلَّا بِحَبْلٍ
مِّنَ ٱللَّهِ وَحَبْلٍ مِّنَ ٱلنَّاسِ وَبَآءُو بِغَضَبٍ مِّنَ
ٱللَّهِ وَضُرِبَتْ عَلَيْهِمُ ٱلْمَسْكَنَةُ ۚ ذَٰلِكَ بِأَنَّهُمْ كَانُوا۟
يَكْفُرُونَ بِـَٔايَٰتِ ٱللَّهِ وَيَقْتُلُونَ ٱلْأَنۢبِيَآءَ بِغَيْرِ
حَقٍّ ۚ ذَٰلِكَ بِمَا عَصَوا۟ وَّكَانُوا۟ يَعْتَدُونَ

112 They shall be humiliated wherever they are encountered, except through a rope from Allah, and a rope from the people; and they incurred wrath from Allah, and were stricken with misery. That is because they rejected Allah's revelations, and killed the prophets unjustly. That is because they rebelled and committed aggression.

١١٣ لَيْسُوا۟ سَوَآءً ۗ مِّنْ أَهْلِ ٱلْكِتَٰبِ أُمَّةٌ قَآئِمَةٌ
يَتْلُونَ ءَايَٰتِ ٱللَّهِ ءَانَآءَ ٱلَّيْلِ وَهُمْ يَسْجُدُونَ

113 They are not alike. Among the People of the Scripture is a community that is upright; they recite Allah's revelations throughout the night, and they prostrate themselves.

١١٤ يُؤْمِنُونَ بِٱللَّهِ وَٱلْيَوْمِ ٱلْءَاخِرِ وَيَأْمُرُونَ
بِٱلْمَعْرُوفِ وَيَنْهَوْنَ عَنِ ٱلْمُنكَرِ وَيُسَٰرِعُونَ فِى
ٱلْخَيْرَٰتِ وَأُو۟لَٰٓئِكَ مِنَ ٱلصَّٰلِحِينَ

114 They believe in Allah and the Last Day, and advocate righteousness and forbid evil, and are quick to do good deeds. These are among the righteous.

١١٥ وَمَا يَفْعَلُوا۟ مِنْ خَيْرٍ فَلَن يُكْفَرُوهُ ۗ وَٱللَّهُ
عَلِيمٌۢ بِٱلْمُتَّقِينَ

115 Whatever good they do, they will not be denied it. Allah knows the righteous.

١١٦ إِنَّ ٱلَّذِينَ كَفَرُوا۟ لَن تُغْنِىَ عَنْهُمْ أَمْوَٰلُهُمْ وَلَآ
أَوْلَٰدُهُم مِّنَ ٱللَّهِ شَيْـًٔا ۖ وَأُو۟لَٰٓئِكَ أَصْحَٰبُ ٱلنَّارِ ۚ
هُمْ فِيهَا خَٰلِدُونَ

116 As for those who disbelieve, neither their possessions nor their children will avail them anything against Allah. These are the inhabitants of the Fire, abiding therein forever.

١١٧ مَثَلُ مَا يُنفِقُونَ فِى هَٰذِهِ ٱلْحَيَوٰةِ ٱلدُّنْيَا
كَمَثَلِ رِيحٍ فِيهَا صِرٌّ أَصَابَتْ حَرْثَ قَوْمٍ ظَلَمُوٓا۟
أَنفُسَهُمْ فَأَهْلَكَتْهُ ۚ وَمَا ظَلَمَهُمُ ٱللَّهُ وَلَٰكِنْ
أَنفُسَهُمْ يَظْلِمُونَ

117 The parable of what they spend in this worldly life is that of a frosty wind that strikes the harvest of a people who have wronged their souls, and destroys it. Allah did not wrong them, but they wronged their own selves.

١١٨ يَٰٓأَيُّهَا ٱلَّذِينَ ءَامَنُوا۟ لَا تَتَّخِذُوا۟ بِطَانَةً مِّن
دُونِكُمْ لَا يَأْلُونَكُمْ خَبَالًا وَدُّوا۟ مَا عَنِتُّمْ قَدْ
بَدَتِ ٱلْبَغْضَآءُ مِنْ أَفْوَٰهِهِمْ وَمَا تُخْفِى

118 O you who believe! Do not befriend outsiders who never cease to wish you harm. They love to see you suffer. Hatred has already appeared from their mouths, but

صُدُورُهُمْ أَكْبَرُ ۚ قَدْ بَيَّنَّا لَكُمُ ٱلْءَايَٰتِ ۖ إِن كُنتُمْ
تَعْقِلُونَ

what their hearts conceal is worse. We have made the messages clear for you, if you understand.

١١٩ هَٰٓأَنتُمْ أُو۟لَآءِ تُحِبُّونَهُمْ وَلَا يُحِبُّونَكُمْ
وَتُؤْمِنُونَ بِٱلْكِتَٰبِ كُلِّهِۦ وَإِذَا لَقُوكُمْ قَالُوٓا۟ ءَامَنَّا
وَإِذَا خَلَوْا۟ عَضُّوا۟ عَلَيْكُمُ ٱلْأَنَامِلَ مِنَ ٱلْغَيْظِ ۚ
قُلْ مُوتُوا۟ بِغَيْظِكُمْ ۗ إِنَّ ٱللَّهَ عَلِيمٌۢ بِذَاتِ
ٱلصُّدُورِ

119 There you are, you love them, but they do not love you, and you believe in the entire scripture. And when they meet you, they say, “We believe;” but when they are alone, they bite their fingers in rage at you. Say, “Die in your rage; Allah knows what is within the hearts.”

١٢٠ إِن تَمْسَسْكُمْ حَسَنَةٌ تَسُؤْهُمْ وَإِن تُصِبْكُمْ
سَيِّئَةٌ يَفْرَحُوا۟ بِهَا ۖ وَإِن تَصْبِرُوا۟ وَتَتَّقُوا۟ لَا
يَضُرُّكُمْ كَيْدُهُمْ شَيْـًٔا ۗ إِنَّ ٱللَّهَ بِمَا يَعْمَلُونَ
مُحِيطٌ

120 If something good happens to you, it upsets them; but if something bad befalls you, they rejoice at it. But if you persevere and maintain righteousness, their schemes will not harm you at all. Allah comprehends what they do.

١٢١ وَإِذْ غَدَوْتَ مِنْ أَهْلِكَ تُبَوِّئُ ٱلْمُؤْمِنِينَ
مَقَٰعِدَ لِلْقِتَالِ ۗ وَٱللَّهُ سَمِيعٌ عَلِيمٌ

121 Remember when you left your home in the morning, to assign battle-positions for the believers. Allah is Hearing and Knowing.

١٢٢ إِذْ هَمَّت طَّآئِفَتَانِ مِنكُمْ أَن تَفْشَلَا وَٱللَّهُ
وَلِيُّهُمَا ۗ وَعَلَى ٱللَّهِ فَلْيَتَوَكَّلِ ٱلْمُؤْمِنُونَ

122 When two groups among you almost faltered, but Allah was their Protector. So in Allah let the believers put their trust.

١٢٣ وَلَقَدْ نَصَرَكُمُ ٱللَّهُ بِبَدْرٍ وَأَنتُمْ أَذِلَّةٌ ۖ فَٱتَّقُوا۟
ٱللَّهَ لَعَلَّكُمْ تَشْكُرُونَ

123 Allah had given you victory at Badr, when you were weak. So fear Allah, that you may be thankful.

١٢٤ إِذْ تَقُولُ لِلْمُؤْمِنِينَ أَلَن يَكْفِيَكُمْ أَن يُمِدَّكُمْ
رَبُّكُم بِثَلَٰثَةِ ءَالَٰفٍ مِّنَ ٱلْمَلَٰٓئِكَةِ مُنزَلِينَ

124 When you said to the believers, “Is it not enough for you that your Lord has reinforced you with three thousand angels, sent down?”

١٢٥ بَلَىٰٓ ۚ إِن تَصْبِرُوا۟ وَتَتَّقُوا۟ وَيَأْتُوكُم مِّن
فَوْرِهِمْ هَٰذَا يُمْدِدْكُمْ رَبُّكُم بِخَمْسَةِ ءَالَٰفٍ مِّنَ
ٱلْمَلَٰٓئِكَةِ مُسَوِّمِينَ

125 It is; but if you persevere and remain cautious, and they attack you suddenly, your Lord will reinforce you with five thousand angels, well trained.

١٢٦ وَمَا جَعَلَهُ ٱللَّهُ إِلَّا بُشْرَىٰ لَكُمْ وَلِتَطْمَئِنَّ
قُلُوبُكُم بِهِۦ ۗ وَمَا ٱلنَّصْرُ إِلَّا مِنْ عِندِ ٱللَّهِ ٱلْعَزِيزِ
ٱلْحَكِيمِ

126 Allah made it but a message of hope for you, and to reassure your hearts thereby. Victory comes only from Allah the Almighty, the Wise.

١٢٧ لِيَقْطَعَ طَرَفًا مِّنَ ٱلَّذِينَ كَفَرُوٓا۟ أَوْ يَكْبِتَهُمْ
فَيَنقَلِبُوا۟ خَآئِبِينَ

127 He thus cuts off a section of those who disbelieved, or subdues them, so they retreat disappointed.

١٢٨ لَيْسَ لَكَ مِنَ ٱلْأَمْرِ شَىْءٌ أَوْ يَتُوبَ عَلَيْهِمْ
أَوْ يُعَذِّبَهُمْ فَإِنَّهُمْ ظَٰلِمُونَ

128 It is no concern of yours whether He redeems them or punishes them. They are wrongdoers.

١٢٩ وَلِلَّهِ مَا فِى ٱلسَّمَٰوَٰتِ وَمَا فِى ٱلْأَرْضِ ۚ
يَغْفِرُ لِمَن يَشَآءُ وَيُعَذِّبُ مَن يَشَآءُ ۚ وَٱللَّهُ غَفُورٌ
رَّحِيمٌ

129 To Allah belongs everything in the heavens and the earth. He forgives whom He wills, and He punishes whom He wills. Allah is Most Forgiving, Most Merciful.

١٣٠ يَٰٓأَيُّهَا ٱلَّذِينَ ءَامَنُوا۟ لَا تَأْكُلُوا۟ ٱلرِّبَوٰٓا۟ أَضْعَٰفًا
مُّضَٰعَفَةً ۖ وَٱتَّقُوا۟ ٱللَّهَ لَعَلَّكُمْ تُفْلِحُونَ

130 O you who believe! Do not feed on usury, compounded over and over, and fear Allah, so that you may prosper.

١٣١ وَٱتَّقُوا۟ ٱلنَّارَ ٱلَّتِىٓ أُعِدَّتْ لِلْكَٰفِرِينَ

131 And guard yourselves against the Fire that is prepared for the disbelievers.

١٣٢ وَأَطِيعُوا۟ ٱللَّهَ وَٱلرَّسُولَ لَعَلَّكُمْ تُرْحَمُونَ

132 And obey Allah and the Messenger, that you may obtain mercy.

١٣٣ وَسَارِعُوٓا۟ إِلَىٰ مَغْفِرَةٍ مِّن رَّبِّكُمْ وَجَنَّةٍ
عَرْضُهَا ٱلسَّمَٰوَٰتُ وَٱلْأَرْضُ أُعِدَّتْ لِلْمُتَّقِينَ

133 And race towards forgiveness from your Lord, and a Garden as wide as the heavens and the earth, prepared for the righteous.

١٣٤ ٱلَّذِينَ يُنفِقُونَ فِى ٱلسَّرَّآءِ وَٱلضَّرَّآءِ
وَٱلْكَٰظِمِينَ ٱلْغَيْظَ وَٱلْعَافِينَ عَنِ ٱلنَّاسِ ۗ وَٱللَّهُ
يُحِبُّ ٱلْمُحْسِنِينَ

134 Those who give in prosperity and adversity, and those who restrain anger, and those who forgive people. Allah loves the doers of good.

١٣٥ وَٱلَّذِينَ إِذَا فَعَلُوا۟ فَٰحِشَةً أَوْ ظَلَمُوٓا۟
أَنفُسَهُمْ ذَكَرُوا۟ ٱللَّهَ فَٱسْتَغْفَرُوا۟ لِذُنُوبِهِمْ وَمَن
يَغْفِرُ ٱلذُّنُوبَ إِلَّا ٱللَّهُ وَلَمْ يُصِرُّوا۟ عَلَىٰ مَا
فَعَلُوا۟ وَهُمْ يَعْلَمُونَ

135 And those who, when they commit an indecency or wrong themselves, remember Allah and ask forgiveness for their sins—and who forgives sins except Allah? And

they do not persist in their wrongdoing while they know.

١٣٦ أُولَٰٓئِكَ جَزَآؤُهُم مَّغْفِرَةٌ مِّن رَّبِّهِمْ وَجَنَّٰتٌ
تَجْرِى مِن تَحْتِهَا ٱلْأَنْهَٰرُ خَٰلِدِينَ فِيهَا ۚ وَنِعْمَ
أَجْرُ ٱلْعَٰمِلِينَ

136 Those—their reward is forgiveness from their Lord, and gardens beneath which rivers flow, abiding therein forever. How excellent is the reward of the workers.

١٣٧ قَدْ خَلَتْ مِن قَبْلِكُمْ سُنَنٌ فَسِيرُوا۟ فِى
ٱلْأَرْضِ فَٱنظُرُوا۟ كَيْفَ كَانَ عَٰقِبَةُ ٱلْمُكَذِّبِينَ

137 Many societies have passed away before you. So travel the earth and note the fate of the deniers.

١٣٨ هَٰذَا بَيَانٌ لِّلنَّاسِ وَهُدًى وَمَوْعِظَةٌ لِّلْمُتَّقِينَ

138 This is a proclamation to humanity, and guidance, and advice for the righteous.

١٣٩ وَلَا تَهِنُوا۟ وَلَا تَحْزَنُوا۟ وَأَنتُمُ ٱلْأَعْلَوْنَ إِن
كُنتُم مُّؤْمِنِينَ

139 And do not waver, nor feel remorse. You are the superior ones, if you are believers.

١٤٠ إِن يَمْسَسْكُمْ قَرْحٌ فَقَدْ مَسَّ ٱلْقَوْمَ قَرْحٌ
مِّثْلُهُۥ ۚ وَتِلْكَ ٱلْأَيَّامُ نُدَاوِلُهَا بَيْنَ ٱلنَّاسِ وَلِيَعْلَمَ
ٱللَّهُ ٱلَّذِينَ ءَامَنُوا۟ وَيَتَّخِذَ مِنكُمْ شُهَدَآءَ ۗ وَٱللَّهُ
لَا يُحِبُّ ٱلظَّٰلِمِينَ

140 If a wound afflicts you, a similar wound has afflicted the others. Such days We alternate between the people, that Allah may know those who believe, and take martyrs from among you. Allah does not love the evildoers.

١٤١ وَلِيُمَحِّصَ ٱللَّهُ ٱلَّذِينَ ءَامَنُوا۟ وَيَمْحَقَ
ٱلْكَٰفِرِينَ

141 So that Allah may prove those who believe, and eliminate the disbelievers.

١٤٢ أَمْ حَسِبْتُمْ أَن تَدْخُلُوا۟ ٱلْجَنَّةَ وَلَمَّا يَعْلَمِ
ٱللَّهُ ٱلَّذِينَ جَٰهَدُوا۟ مِنكُمْ وَيَعْلَمَ ٱلصَّٰبِرِينَ

142 Or do you expect to enter Paradise, before Allah has distinguished those among you who strive, and before He has distinguished the steadfast?

١٤٣ وَلَقَدْ كُنتُمْ تَمَنَّوْنَ ٱلْمَوْتَ مِن قَبْلِ أَن
تَلْقَوْهُ فَقَدْ رَأَيْتُمُوهُ وَأَنتُمْ تَنظُرُونَ

143 You used to wish for death before you have faced it. Now you have seen it before your own eyes.

١٤٤ وَمَا مُحَمَّدٌ إِلَّا رَسُولٌ قَدْ خَلَتْ مِن قَبْلِهِ
ٱلرُّسُلُ ۚ أَفَإِي۟ن مَّاتَ أَوْ قُتِلَ ٱنقَلَبْتُمْ عَلَىٰٓ

144 Muhammad is no more than a messenger. Messengers have passed on before him. If he dies or gets killed, will you turn on your heels? He who turns on his heels

أَعْقَٰبِكُمْ ۚ وَمَن يَنقَلِبْ عَلَىٰ عَقِبَيْهِ فَلَن يَضُرَّ ٱللَّهَ شَيْـًٔا ۗ وَسَيَجْزِى ٱللَّهُ ٱلشَّٰكِرِينَ

will not harm Allah in any way. And Allah will reward the appreciative.

١٤٥ وَمَا كَانَ لِنَفْسٍ أَن تَمُوتَ إِلَّا بِإِذْنِ ٱللَّهِ كِتَٰبًا مُّؤَجَّلًا ۗ وَمَن يُرِدْ ثَوَابَ ٱلدُّنْيَا نُؤْتِهِۦ مِنْهَا وَمَن يُرِدْ ثَوَابَ ٱلْءَاخِرَةِ نُؤْتِهِۦ مِنْهَا ۚ وَسَنَجْزِى ٱلشَّٰكِرِينَ

145 No soul can die except by Allah's leave, at a predetermined time. Whoever desires the reward of the world, We will give him some of it; and whoever desires the reward of the Hereafter, We will give him some of it; and We will reward the appreciative.

١٤٦ وَكَأَيِّن مِّن نَّبِىٍّ قَٰتَلَ مَعَهُۥ رِبِّيُّونَ كَثِيرٌ فَمَا وَهَنُوا۟ لِمَآ أَصَابَهُمْ فِى سَبِيلِ ٱللَّهِ وَمَا ضَعُفُوا۟ وَمَا ٱسْتَكَانُوا۟ ۗ وَٱللَّهُ يُحِبُّ ٱلصَّٰبِرِينَ

146 How many a prophet fought alongside him numerous godly people? They did not waver for what afflicted them in the cause of Allah, nor did they weaken, nor did they give in. Allah loves those who endure.

١٤٧ وَمَا كَانَ قَوْلَهُمْ إِلَّآ أَن قَالُوا۟ رَبَّنَا ٱغْفِرْ لَنَا ذُنُوبَنَا وَإِسْرَافَنَا فِىٓ أَمْرِنَا وَثَبِّتْ أَقْدَامَنَا وَٱنصُرْنَا عَلَى ٱلْقَوْمِ ٱلْكَٰفِرِينَ

147 Their only words were, "Our Lord, forgive us our offences, and our excesses in our conduct, and strengthen our foothold, and help us against the disbelieving people."

١٤٨ فَـَٔاتَىٰهُمُ ٱللَّهُ ثَوَابَ ٱلدُّنْيَا وَحُسْنَ ثَوَابِ ٱلْءَاخِرَةِ ۗ وَٱللَّهُ يُحِبُّ ٱلْمُحْسِنِينَ

148 So Allah gave them the reward of this world, and the excellent reward of the Hereafter. Allah loves the doers of good.

١٤٩ يَٰٓأَيُّهَا ٱلَّذِينَ ءَامَنُوٓا۟ إِن تُطِيعُوا۟ ٱلَّذِينَ كَفَرُوا۟ يَرُدُّوكُمْ عَلَىٰٓ أَعْقَٰبِكُمْ فَتَنقَلِبُوا۟ خَٰسِرِينَ

149 O you who believe! If you obey those who disbelieve, they will turn you back on your heels, and you end up losers.

١٥٠ بَلِ ٱللَّهُ مَوْلَىٰكُمْ ۖ وَهُوَ خَيْرُ ٱلنَّٰصِرِينَ

150 Allah is your Master, and He is the Best of Helpers.

١٥١ سَنُلْقِى فِى قُلُوبِ ٱلَّذِينَ كَفَرُوا۟ ٱلرُّعْبَ بِمَآ أَشْرَكُوا۟ بِٱللَّهِ مَا لَمْ يُنَزِّلْ بِهِۦ سُلْطَٰنًا ۖ وَمَأْوَىٰهُمُ ٱلنَّارُ ۚ وَبِئْسَ مَثْوَى ٱلظَّٰلِمِينَ

151 We will throw terror into the hearts of those who disbelieve, because they attribute to Allah partners for which He revealed no sanction. Their lodging is the Fire. Miserable is the lodging of the evildoers.

١٥٢ وَلَقَدْ صَدَقَكُمُ ٱللَّهُ وَعْدَهُۥٓ إِذْ تَحُسُّونَهُم
بِإِذْنِهِۦ ۖ حَتَّىٰٓ إِذَا فَشِلْتُمْ وَتَنَٰزَعْتُمْ فِى ٱلْأَمْرِ
وَعَصَيْتُم مِّنۢ بَعْدِ مَآ أَرَىٰكُم مَّا تُحِبُّونَ ۚ مِنكُم
مَّن يُرِيدُ ٱلدُّنْيَا وَمِنكُم مَّن يُرِيدُ ٱلْءَاخِرَةَ ۚ ثُمَّ
صَرَفَكُمْ عَنْهُمْ لِيَبْتَلِيَكُمْ ۖ وَلَقَدْ عَفَا عَنكُمْ ۗ
وَٱللَّهُ ذُو فَضْلٍ عَلَى ٱلْمُؤْمِنِينَ

152 Allah has fulfilled His promise to you, and you defeated them by His leave; until when you faltered, and disputed the command, and disobeyed after He had shown you what you like. Some of you want this world, and some of you want the next. Then He turned you away from them, to test you; but He pardoned you. Allah is Gracious towards the believers.

١٥٣ إِذْ تُصْعِدُونَ وَلَا تَلْوُۥنَ عَلَىٰٓ أَحَدٍ وَٱلرَّسُولُ
يَدْعُوكُمْ فِىٓ أُخْرَىٰكُمْ فَأَثَٰبَكُمْ غَمًّۢا بِغَمٍّ لِّكَيْلَا
تَحْزَنُوا۟ عَلَىٰ مَا فَاتَكُمْ وَلَا مَآ أَصَٰبَكُمْ ۗ وَٱللَّهُ
خَبِيرٌۢ بِمَا تَعْمَلُونَ

153 Remember when you fled, not caring for anyone, even though the Messenger was calling you from your rear. Then He repaid you with sorrow upon sorrow, so that you would not grieve over what you missed, or for what afflicted you. Allah is Informed of what you do.

١٥٤ ثُمَّ أَنزَلَ عَلَيْكُم مِّنۢ بَعْدِ ٱلْغَمِّ أَمَنَةً نُّعَاسًا
يَغْشَىٰ طَآئِفَةً مِّنكُمْ ۖ وَطَآئِفَةٌ قَدْ أَهَمَّتْهُمْ
أَنفُسُهُمْ يَظُنُّونَ بِٱللَّهِ غَيْرَ ٱلْحَقِّ ظَنَّ ٱلْجَٰهِلِيَّةِ ۖ
يَقُولُونَ هَل لَّنَا مِنَ ٱلْأَمْرِ مِن شَىْءٍ ۗ قُلْ إِنَّ
ٱلْأَمْرَ كُلَّهُۥ لِلَّهِ ۗ يُخْفُونَ فِىٓ أَنفُسِهِم مَّا لَا
يُبْدُونَ لَكَ ۖ يَقُولُونَ لَوْ كَانَ لَنَا مِنَ ٱلْأَمْرِ شَىْءٌ
مَّا قُتِلْنَا هَٰهُنَا ۗ قُل لَّوْ كُنتُمْ فِى بُيُوتِكُمْ لَبَرَزَ
ٱلَّذِينَ كُتِبَ عَلَيْهِمُ ٱلْقَتْلُ إِلَىٰ مَضَاجِعِهِمْ ۖ
وَلِيَبْتَلِىَ ٱللَّهُ مَا فِى صُدُورِكُمْ وَلِيُمَحِّصَ مَا
فِى قُلُوبِكُمْ ۗ وَٱللَّهُ عَلِيمٌۢ بِذَاتِ ٱلصُّدُورِ

154 Then after the setback, He sent down security upon you. Slumber overcame some of you, while others cared only for themselves, thinking of Allah thoughts that were untrue—thoughts of ignorance—saying, "Is anything up to us?" Say, "Everything is up to Allah." They conceal within themselves what they do not reveal to you. And they say, "If it was up to us, none of us would have been killed here." Say, "Even if you Had stayed in your homes, those destined to be killed would have marched into their death beds." Allah thus tests what is in your minds, and purifies what is in your hearts. Allah knows what the hearts contain.

١٥٥ إِنَّ ٱلَّذِينَ تَوَلَّوْا۟ مِنكُمْ يَوْمَ ٱلْتَقَى ٱلْجَمْعَانِ
إِنَّمَا ٱسْتَزَلَّهُمُ ٱلشَّيْطَٰنُ بِبَعْضِ مَا كَسَبُوا۟ ۖ وَلَقَدْ
عَفَا ٱللَّهُ عَنْهُمْ ۗ إِنَّ ٱللَّهَ غَفُورٌ حَلِيمٌ

155 Those of you who turned back on the day when the two armies clashed—it was Satan who caused them to backslide, on account of some of what they have earned. But

Allah has forgiven them. Allah is Forgiving and Prudent.

١٥٦ يَٰٓأَيُّهَا ٱلَّذِينَ ءَامَنُواْ لَا تَكُونُواْ كَٱلَّذِينَ
كَفَرُواْ وَقَالُواْ لِإِخۡوَٰنِهِمۡ إِذَا ضَرَبُواْ فِي ٱلۡأَرۡضِ
أَوۡ كَانُواْ غُزّٗى لَّوۡ كَانُواْ عِندَنَا مَا مَاتُواْ وَمَا
قُتِلُواْ لِيَجۡعَلَ ٱللَّهُ ذَٰلِكَ حَسۡرَةٗ فِي قُلُوبِهِمۡۗ
وَٱللَّهُ يُحۡيِۦ وَيُمِيتُۗ وَٱللَّهُ بِمَا تَعۡمَلُونَ بَصِيرٞ

156 O you who believe! Do not be like those who disbelieved, and said of their brethren who marched in the land, or went on the offensive, “Had they stayed with us, they would not have died or been killed.” So that Allah may make it a cause of regret in their hearts. Allah gives life and causes death. Allah is Seeing of what you do.

١٥٧ وَلَئِن قُتِلۡتُمۡ فِي سَبِيلِ ٱللَّهِ أَوۡ مُتُّمۡ لَمَغۡفِرَةٞ
مِّنَ ٱللَّهِ وَرَحۡمَةٌ خَيۡرٞ مِّمَّا يَجۡمَعُونَ

157 If you are killed in the cause of Allah, or die—forgiveness and mercy from Allah are better than what they hoard.

١٥٨ وَلَئِن مُّتُّمۡ أَوۡ قُتِلۡتُمۡ لَإِلَى ٱللَّهِ تُحۡشَرُونَ

158 If you die, or are killed—to Allah you will be gathered up.

١٥٩ فَبِمَا رَحۡمَةٖ مِّنَ ٱللَّهِ لِنتَ لَهُمۡۖ وَلَوۡ كُنتَ
فَظًّا غَلِيظَ ٱلۡقَلۡبِ لَٱنفَضُّواْ مِنۡ حَوۡلِكَۖ فَٱعۡفُ
عَنۡهُمۡ وَٱسۡتَغۡفِرۡ لَهُمۡ وَشَاوِرۡهُمۡ فِي ٱلۡأَمۡرِۖ فَإِذَا
عَزَمۡتَ فَتَوَكَّلۡ عَلَى ٱللَّهِۚ إِنَّ ٱللَّهَ يُحِبُّ
ٱلۡمُتَوَكِّلِينَ

159 It is by of grace from Allah that you were gentle with them. Had you been harsh, hardhearted, they would have dispersed from around you. So pardon them, and ask forgiveness for them, and consult them in the conduct of affairs. And when you make a decision, put your trust in Allah; Allah loves the trusting.

١٦٠ إِن يَنصُرۡكُمُ ٱللَّهُ فَلَا غَالِبَ لَكُمۡۖ وَإِن
يَخۡذُلۡكُمۡ فَمَن ذَا ٱلَّذِي يَنصُرُكُم مِّنۢ بَعۡدِهِۦۗ
وَعَلَى ٱللَّهِ فَلۡيَتَوَكَّلِ ٱلۡمُؤۡمِنُونَ

160 If Allah supports you, there is none who can overcome you. But if He fails you, who is there to help you after Him? So in Allah let the believers put their trust.

١٦١ وَمَا كَانَ لِنَبِيٍّ أَن يَغُلَّۚ وَمَن يَغۡلُلۡ يَأۡتِ بِمَا
غَلَّ يَوۡمَ ٱلۡقِيَٰمَةِۚ ثُمَّ تُوَفَّىٰ كُلُّ نَفۡسٖ مَّا كَسَبَتۡ
وَهُمۡ لَا يُظۡلَمُونَ

161 It is not for a prophet to act dishonestly. Whoever acts dishonestly will bring his dishonesty on the Day of Resurrection. Then every soul will be paid in full for what it has earned, and they will not be wronged.

١٦٢ أَفَمَنِ ٱتَّبَعَ رِضْوَٰنَ ٱللَّهِ كَمَنۢ بَآءَ بِسَخَطٍ
مِّنَ ٱللَّهِ وَمَأْوَىٰهُ جَهَنَّمُ ۚ وَبِئْسَ ٱلْمَصِيرُ

162 Is someone who pursues Allah's approval the same as someone who incurs Allah's wrath and his refuge is Hell—the miserable destination?

١٦٣ هُمْ دَرَجَٰتٌ عِندَ ٱللَّهِ ۗ وَٱللَّهُ بَصِيرٌۢ بِمَا
يَعْمَلُونَ

163 They have different ranks with Allah, and Allah is Seeing of what they do.

١٦٤ لَقَدْ مَنَّ ٱللَّهُ عَلَى ٱلْمُؤْمِنِينَ إِذْ بَعَثَ فِيهِمْ
رَسُولًا مِّنْ أَنفُسِهِمْ يَتْلُوا۟ عَلَيْهِمْ ءَايَٰتِهِۦ
وَيُزَكِّيهِمْ وَيُعَلِّمُهُمُ ٱلْكِتَٰبَ وَٱلْحِكْمَةَ وَإِن كَانُوا۟
مِن قَبْلُ لَفِى ضَلَٰلٍ مُّبِينٍ

164 Allah has blessed the believers, as He raised up among them a messenger from among themselves, who recites to them His revelations, and purifies them, and teaches them the Scripture and wisdom; although before that they were in evident error.

١٦٥ أَوَلَمَّآ أَصَٰبَتْكُم مُّصِيبَةٌ قَدْ أَصَبْتُم مِّثْلَيْهَا
قُلْتُمْ أَنَّىٰ هَٰذَا ۖ قُلْ هُوَ مِنْ عِندِ أَنفُسِكُمْ ۗ إِنَّ
ٱللَّهَ عَلَىٰ كُلِّ شَىْءٍ قَدِيرٌ

165 And when a calamity befell you, even after you had inflicted twice as much, you said, “How is this?” Say, “It is from your own selves.” Allah is Able to do all things.

١٦٦ وَمَآ أَصَٰبَكُمْ يَوْمَ ٱلْتَقَى ٱلْجَمْعَانِ فَبِإِذْنِ
ٱللَّهِ وَلِيَعْلَمَ ٱلْمُؤْمِنِينَ

166 What befell you on the day the two armies clashed was with Allah’s permission; that He may know the believers.

١٦٧ وَلِيَعْلَمَ ٱلَّذِينَ نَافَقُوا۟ ۚ وَقِيلَ لَهُمْ تَعَالَوْا۟
قَٰتِلُوا۟ فِى سَبِيلِ ٱللَّهِ أَوِ ٱدْفَعُوا۟ ۖ قَالُوا۟ لَوْ نَعْلَمُ
قِتَالًا لَّٱتَّبَعْنَٰكُمْ ۗ هُمْ لِلْكُفْرِ يَوْمَئِذٍ أَقْرَبُ مِنْهُمْ
لِلْإِيمَٰنِ ۚ يَقُولُونَ بِأَفْوَٰهِهِم مَّا لَيْسَ فِى
قُلُوبِهِمْ ۗ وَٱللَّهُ أَعْلَمُ بِمَا يَكْتُمُونَ

167 And that He may know the hypocrites. And it was said to them, “Come, fight in the cause of Allah, or contribute.” They said, “If we knew how to fight, we would have followed you.” On that day they were closer to infidelity than they were to faith. They say with their mouths what is not in their hearts; but Allah knows what they hide.

١٦٨ ٱلَّذِينَ قَالُوا۟ لِإِخْوَٰنِهِمْ وَقَعَدُوا۟ لَوْ أَطَاعُونَا
مَا قُتِلُوا۟ ۗ قُلْ فَٱدْرَءُوا۟ عَنْ أَنفُسِكُمُ ٱلْمَوْتَ إِن
كُنتُمْ صَٰدِقِينَ

168 Those who said of their brethren, as they stayed behind, “Had they obeyed us, they would not have been killed.” Say, “Then avert death from yourselves, if you are truthful.”

١٦٩ وَلَا تَحۡسَبَنَّ ٱلَّذِينَ قُتِلُواْ فِي سَبِيلِ ٱللَّهِ
أَمۡوَٰتَۢاۚ بَلۡ أَحۡيَآءٌ عِندَ رَبِّهِمۡ يُرۡزَقُونَ

169 Do not consider those killed in the cause of Allah as dead. In fact, they are alive, at their Lord, well provided for.

١٧٠ فَرِحِينَ بِمَآ ءَاتَىٰهُمُ ٱللَّهُ مِن فَضۡلِهِۦ
وَيَسۡتَبۡشِرُونَ بِٱلَّذِينَ لَمۡ يَلۡحَقُواْ بِهِم مِّنۡ
خَلۡفِهِمۡ أَلَّا خَوۡفٌ عَلَيۡهِمۡ وَلَا هُمۡ يَحۡزَنُونَ

170 Delighting in what Allah has given them out of His grace, and happy for those who have not yet joined them; that they have nothing to fear, nor will they grieve.

١٧١ يَسۡتَبۡشِرُونَ بِنِعۡمَةٖ مِّنَ ٱللَّهِ وَفَضۡلٖ وَأَنَّ
ٱللَّهَ لَا يُضِيعُ أَجۡرَ ٱلۡمُؤۡمِنِينَ

171 They rejoice in grace from Allah, and bounty, and that Allah will not waste the reward of the faithful.

١٧٢ ٱلَّذِينَ ٱسۡتَجَابُواْ لِلَّهِ وَٱلرَّسُولِ مِنۢ بَعۡدِ مَآ
أَصَابَهُمُ ٱلۡقَرۡحُۚ لِلَّذِينَ أَحۡسَنُواْ مِنۡهُمۡ وَٱتَّقَوۡاْ
أَجۡرٌ عَظِيمٌ

172 Those who responded to Allah and the Messenger, despite the persecution they had suffered. For the virtuous and the pious among them is a great reward.

١٧٣ ٱلَّذِينَ قَالَ لَهُمُ ٱلنَّاسُ إِنَّ ٱلنَّاسَ قَدۡ
جَمَعُواْ لَكُمۡ فَٱخۡشَوۡهُمۡ فَزَادَهُمۡ إِيمَٰنٗا وَقَالُواْ
حَسۡبُنَا ٱللَّهُ وَنِعۡمَ ٱلۡوَكِيلُ

173 Those to whom the people have said, “The people have mobilized against you, so fear them.” But this only increased them in faith, and they said, “Allah is enough for us; He is the Excellent Protector.”

١٧٤ فَٱنقَلَبُواْ بِنِعۡمَةٖ مِّنَ ٱللَّهِ وَفَضۡلٖ لَّمۡ
يَمۡسَسۡهُمۡ سُوٓءٞ وَٱتَّبَعُواْ رِضۡوَٰنَ ٱللَّهِۗ وَٱللَّهُ ذُو
فَضۡلٍ عَظِيمٍ

174 So they came back with grace from Allah, and bounty, and no harm having touched them. They pursued what pleases Allah. Allah possesses immense grace.

١٧٥ إِنَّمَا ذَٰلِكُمُ ٱلشَّيۡطَٰنُ يُخَوِّفُ أَوۡلِيَآءَهُۥ فَلَا
تَخَافُوهُمۡ وَخَافُونِ إِن كُنتُم مُّؤۡمِنِينَ

175 That is only Satan frightening his partisans; so do not fear them, but fear Me, if you are believers.

١٧٦ وَلَا يَحۡزُنكَ ٱلَّذِينَ يُسَٰرِعُونَ فِي ٱلۡكُفۡرِۚ
إِنَّهُمۡ لَن يَضُرُّواْ ٱللَّهَ شَيۡـٔٗاۗ يُرِيدُ ٱللَّهُ أَلَّا يَجۡعَلَ
لَهُمۡ حَظّٗا فِي ٱلۡأٓخِرَةِۖ وَلَهُمۡ عَذَابٌ عَظِيمٌ

176 And do not be saddened by those who rush into disbelief. They will not harm Allah in the least. Allah desires to give them no share in the Hereafter. A terrible torment awaits them.

١٧٧ إِنَّ ٱلَّذِينَ ٱشۡتَرَوُاْ ٱلۡكُفۡرَ بِٱلۡإِيمَٰنِ لَن يَضُرُّواْ
ٱللَّهَ شَيۡـٔٗا وَلَهُمۡ عَذَابٌ أَلِيمٞ

177 Those who exchange blasphemy for faith will not harm Allah in the least. A painful torment awaits them.

١٧٨ وَلَا يَحْسَبَنَّ ٱلَّذِينَ كَفَرُوٓا۟ أَنَّمَا نُمْلِى لَهُمْ
خَيْرٌ لِّأَنفُسِهِمْ ۚ إِنَّمَا نُمْلِى لَهُمْ لِيَزْدَادُوٓا۟ إِثْمًا ۚ
وَلَهُمْ عَذَابٌ مُّهِينٌ

178 Those who disbelieve should not assume that We respite them for their own good. In fact, We only respite them so that they may increase in sinfulness. A humiliating torment awaits them.

١٧٩ مَّا كَانَ ٱللَّهُ لِيَذَرَ ٱلْمُؤْمِنِينَ عَلَىٰ مَآ أَنتُمْ
عَلَيْهِ حَتَّىٰ يَمِيزَ ٱلْخَبِيثَ مِنَ ٱلطَّيِّبِ ۗ وَمَا كَانَ
ٱللَّهُ لِيُطْلِعَكُمْ عَلَى ٱلْغَيْبِ وَلَٰكِنَّ ٱللَّهَ يَجْتَبِى
مِن رُّسُلِهِۦ مَن يَشَآءُ ۖ فَـَٔامِنُوا۟ بِٱللَّهِ وَرُسُلِهِۦ ۚ
وَإِن تُؤْمِنُوا۟ وَتَتَّقُوا۟ فَلَكُمْ أَجْرٌ عَظِيمٌ

179 Allah will not leave the believers as you are, without distinguishing the wicked from the sincere. Nor will Allah inform you of the future, but Allah elects from among His messengers whom He wills. So believe in Allah and His messengers. If you believe and practice piety, you will have a splendid reward.

١٨٠ وَلَا يَحْسَبَنَّ ٱلَّذِينَ يَبْخَلُونَ بِمَآ ءَاتَىٰهُمُ ٱللَّهُ
مِن فَضْلِهِۦ هُوَ خَيْرًا لَّهُم ۖ بَلْ هُوَ شَرٌّ لَّهُمْ ۖ
سَيُطَوَّقُونَ مَا بَخِلُوا۟ بِهِۦ يَوْمَ ٱلْقِيَٰمَةِ ۗ وَلِلَّهِ
مِيرَٰثُ ٱلسَّمَٰوَٰتِ وَٱلْأَرْضِ ۗ وَٱللَّهُ بِمَا تَعْمَلُونَ
خَبِيرٌ

180 Those who withhold what Allah has given them of his bounty should not assume that is good for them. In fact, it is bad for them. They will be encircled by their hoardings on the Day of Resurrection. To Allah belongs the inheritance of the heavens and the earth, and Allah is well acquainted with what you do.

١٨١ لَّقَدْ سَمِعَ ٱللَّهُ قَوْلَ ٱلَّذِينَ قَالُوٓا۟ إِنَّ ٱللَّهَ
فَقِيرٌ وَنَحْنُ أَغْنِيَآءُ ۘ سَنَكْتُبُ مَا قَالُوا۟ وَقَتْلَهُمُ
ٱلْأَنۢبِيَآءَ بِغَيْرِ حَقٍّ وَنَقُولُ ذُوقُوا۟ عَذَابَ
ٱلْحَرِيقِ

181 Allah has heard the statement of those who said, “Allah is poor, and we are rich.” We will write down what they said, and their wrongful killing of the prophets; and We will say, “Taste the torment of the burning.”

١٨٢ ذَٰلِكَ بِمَا قَدَّمَتْ أَيْدِيكُمْ وَأَنَّ ٱللَّهَ لَيْسَ
بِظَلَّامٍ لِّلْعَبِيدِ

182 “This is on account of what your hands have forwarded, and because Allah is not unjust towards the creatures.”

١٨٣ ٱلَّذِينَ قَالُوٓا۟ إِنَّ ٱللَّهَ عَهِدَ إِلَيْنَآ أَلَّا نُؤْمِنَ
لِرَسُولٍ حَتَّىٰ يَأْتِيَنَا بِقُرْبَانٍ تَأْكُلُهُ ٱلنَّارُ ۗ قُلْ قَدْ
جَآءَكُمْ رُسُلٌ مِّن قَبْلِى بِٱلْبَيِّنَٰتِ وَبِٱلَّذِى قُلْتُمْ
فَلِمَ قَتَلْتُمُوهُمْ إِن كُنتُمْ صَٰدِقِينَ

183 Those who said, “Allah has made a covenant with us, that we shall not believe in any messenger unless he brings us an offering to be consumed by fire.” Say, “Messengers have come to you

before me with proofs, and with what you asked for; so why did you assassinate them, if you are truthful?"

١٨٤ فَإِن كَذَّبُوكَ فَقَدْ كُذِّبَ رُسُلٌ مِّن قَبْلِكَ
جَآءُو بِٱلْبَيِّنَٰتِ وَٱلزُّبُرِ وَٱلْكِتَٰبِ ٱلْمُنِيرِ

184 If they accuse you of lying, messengers before you were accused of lying. They came with the proofs, and the Psalms, and the Illuminating Scripture.

١٨٥ كُلُّ نَفْسٍ ذَآئِقَةُ ٱلْمَوْتِ ۗ وَإِنَّمَا تُوَفَّوْنَ
أُجُورَكُمْ يَوْمَ ٱلْقِيَٰمَةِ ۖ فَمَن زُحْزِحَ عَنِ ٱلنَّارِ
وَأُدْخِلَ ٱلْجَنَّةَ فَقَدْ فَازَ ۗ وَمَا ٱلْحَيَوٰةُ ٱلدُّنْيَآ إِلَّا
مَتَٰعُ ٱلْغُرُورِ

185 Every soul will have a taste of death, and you will receive your recompense on the Day of Resurrection. Whoever is swayed from the Fire, and admitted to Paradise, has won. The life of this world is merely enjoyment of delusion.

١٨٦ لَتُبْلَوُنَّ فِىٓ أَمْوَٰلِكُمْ وَأَنفُسِكُمْ وَلَتَسْمَعُنَّ
مِنَ ٱلَّذِينَ أُوتُوا۟ ٱلْكِتَٰبَ مِن قَبْلِكُمْ وَمِنَ ٱلَّذِينَ
أَشْرَكُوٓا۟ أَذًى كَثِيرًا ۚ وَإِن تَصْبِرُوا۟ وَتَتَّقُوا۟ فَإِنَّ
ذَٰلِكَ مِنْ عَزْمِ ٱلْأُمُورِ

186 You will be tested through your possessions and your persons; and you will hear from those who received the Scripture before you, and from the idol worshipers, much abuse. But if you persevere and lead a righteous life—that indeed is a mark of great determination.

١٨٧ وَإِذْ أَخَذَ ٱللَّهُ مِيثَٰقَ ٱلَّذِينَ أُوتُوا۟ ٱلْكِتَٰبَ
لَتُبَيِّنُنَّهُۥ لِلنَّاسِ وَلَا تَكْتُمُونَهُۥ فَنَبَذُوهُ وَرَآءَ
ظُهُورِهِمْ وَٱشْتَرَوْا۟ بِهِۦ ثَمَنًا قَلِيلًا ۖ فَبِئْسَ مَا
يَشْتَرُونَ

187 Allah received a pledge from those who were given the Scripture: "You shall proclaim it to the people, and not conceal it." But they disregarded it behind their backs, and exchanged it for a small price. What a miserable exchange they made.

١٨٨ لَا تَحْسَبَنَّ ٱلَّذِينَ يَفْرَحُونَ بِمَآ أَتَوا۟
وَّيُحِبُّونَ أَن يُحْمَدُوا۟ بِمَا لَمْ يَفْعَلُوا۟ فَلَا
تَحْسَبَنَّهُم بِمَفَازَةٍ مِّنَ ٱلْعَذَابِ ۖ وَلَهُمْ عَذَابٌ
أَلِيمٌ

188 Do not think that those who rejoice in what they have done, and love to be praised for what they have not done—do not think they can evade the punishment. They will have a painful punishment.

١٨٩ وَلِلَّهِ مُلْكُ ٱلسَّمَٰوَٰتِ وَٱلْأَرْضِ ۗ وَٱللَّهُ عَلَىٰ
كُلِّ شَىْءٍ قَدِيرٌ

189 To Allah belongs the sovereignty of the heavens and the earth. Allah has power over all things.

١٩٠ إِنَّ فِى خَلْقِ ٱلسَّمَٰوَٰتِ وَٱلْأَرْضِ وَٱخْتِلَٰفِ
ٱلَّيْلِ وَٱلنَّهَارِ لَءَايَٰتٍ لِّأُو۟لِى ٱلْأَلْبَٰبِ

190 In the creation of the heavens and the earth, and in the alternation of night and day, are signs for people of understanding.

١٩١ ٱلَّذِينَ يَذْكُرُونَ ٱللَّهَ قِيَٰمًا وَقُعُودًا وَعَلَىٰ
جُنُوبِهِمْ وَيَتَفَكَّرُونَ فِى خَلْقِ ٱلسَّمَٰوَٰتِ
وَٱلْأَرْضِ رَبَّنَا مَا خَلَقْتَ هَٰذَا بَٰطِلًا سُبْحَٰنَكَ فَقِنَا
عَذَابَ ٱلنَّارِ

191 Those who remember Allah while standing, and sitting, and on their sides; and they reflect upon the creation of the heavens and the earth: “Our Lord, You did not create this in vain, glory to You, so protect us from the punishment of the Fire.”

١٩٢ رَبَّنَآ إِنَّكَ مَن تُدْخِلِ ٱلنَّارَ فَقَدْ أَخْزَيْتَهُۥ ۖ وَمَا
لِلظَّٰلِمِينَ مِنْ أَنصَارٍ

192 “Our Lord, whomever You commit to the Fire, You have disgraced. The wrongdoers will have no helpers.”

١٩٣ رَّبَّنَآ إِنَّنَا سَمِعْنَا مُنَادِيًا يُنَادِى لِلْإِيمَٰنِ أَنْ
ءَامِنُوا۟ بِرَبِّكُمْ فَـَٔامَنَّا ۚ رَبَّنَا فَٱغْفِرْ لَنَا ذُنُوبَنَا
وَكَفِّرْ عَنَّا سَيِّـَٔاتِنَا وَتَوَفَّنَا مَعَ ٱلْأَبْرَارِ

193 “Our Lord, we have heard a caller calling to the faith: `Believe in your Lord,' and we have believed. Our Lord! Forgive us our sins, and remit our misdeeds, and make us die in the company of the virtuous.”

١٩٤ رَبَّنَا وَءَاتِنَا مَا وَعَدتَّنَا عَلَىٰ رُسُلِكَ وَلَا
تُخْزِنَا يَوْمَ ٱلْقِيَٰمَةِ ۗ إِنَّكَ لَا تُخْلِفُ ٱلْمِيعَادَ

194 “Our Lord, and give us what You have promised us through Your messengers, and do not disgrace us on the Day of Resurrection. Surely You never break a promise.”

١٩٥ فَٱسْتَجَابَ لَهُمْ رَبُّهُمْ أَنِّى لَآ أُضِيعُ عَمَلَ
عَٰمِلٍ مِّنكُم مِّن ذَكَرٍ أَوْ أُنثَىٰ ۖ بَعْضُكُم مِّنۢ
بَعْضٍ ۖ فَٱلَّذِينَ هَاجَرُوا۟ وَأُخْرِجُوا۟ مِن دِيَٰرِهِمْ
وَأُوذُوا۟ فِى سَبِيلِى وَقَٰتَلُوا۟ وَقُتِلُوا۟ لَأُكَفِّرَنَّ
عَنْهُمْ سَيِّـَٔاتِهِمْ وَلَأُدْخِلَنَّهُمْ جَنَّٰتٍ تَجْرِى مِن
تَحْتِهَا ٱلْأَنْهَٰرُ ثَوَابًا مِّنْ عِندِ ٱللَّهِ ۗ وَٱللَّهُ عِندَهُۥ
حُسْنُ ٱلثَّوَابِ

195 And so their Lord answered them: “I will not waste the work of any worker among you, whether male or female. You are one of another. For those who emigrated, and were expelled from their homes, and were persecuted because of Me, and fought and were killed—I will remit for them their sins, and will admit them into gardens beneath which rivers flow—a reward from Allah. With Allah is the ultimate reward.”

١٩٦ لَا يَغُرَّنَّكَ تَقَلُّبُ ٱلَّذِينَ كَفَرُوا۟ فِى ٱلْبِلَٰدِ

196 Do not be impressed by the disbelievers' movements in the land.

١٩٧ مَتَٰعٌ قَلِيلٌ ثُمَّ مَأْوَىٰهُمْ جَهَنَّمُ ۚ وَبِئْسَ ٱلْمِهَادُ

197 A brief enjoyment, then their abode is Hell. What a miserable resort.

١٩٨ لَٰكِنِ ٱلَّذِينَ ٱتَّقَوْا۟ رَبَّهُمْ لَهُمْ جَنَّٰتٌ تَجْرِى
مِن تَحْتِهَا ٱلْأَنْهَٰرُ خَٰلِدِينَ فِيهَا نُزُلًا مِّنْ عِندِ
ٱللَّهِ ۗ وَمَا عِندَ ٱللَّهِ خَيْرٌ لِّلْأَبْرَارِ

198 As for those who feared their Lord: for them will be gardens beneath which rivers flow, wherein they will abide forever—hospitality from Allah. What Allah possesses is best for the just.

١٩٩ وَإِنَّ مِنْ أَهْلِ ٱلْكِتَٰبِ لَمَن يُؤْمِنُ بِٱللَّهِ وَمَآ
أُنزِلَ إِلَيْكُمْ وَمَآ أُنزِلَ إِلَيْهِمْ خَٰشِعِينَ لِلَّهِ لَا
يَشْتَرُونَ بِـَٔايَٰتِ ٱللَّهِ ثَمَنًا قَلِيلًا ۗ أُو۟لَٰٓئِكَ لَهُمْ
أَجْرُهُمْ عِندَ رَبِّهِمْ ۗ إِنَّ ٱللَّهَ سَرِيعُ ٱلْحِسَابِ

199 Among the People of the Scripture are those who believe in Allah, and in what was revealed to you, and in what was revealed to them. They are humble before Allah, and they do not sell Allah's revelations for a cheap price. These will have their reward with their Lord. Allah is swift in reckoning.

٢٠٠ يَٰٓأَيُّهَا ٱلَّذِينَ ءَامَنُوا۟ ٱصْبِرُوا۟ وَصَابِرُوا۟
وَرَابِطُوا۟ وَٱتَّقُوا۟ ٱللَّهَ لَعَلَّكُمْ تُفْلِحُونَ

200 O you who believe! Be patient, and advocate patience, and be united, and revere Allah, so that you may thrive.

4 Women النساء

بِسْمِ ٱللَّهِ ٱلرَّحْمَٰنِ ٱلرَّحِيمِ

In the name of Allah, the Gracious, the Merciful.

١ يَٰٓأَيُّهَا ٱلنَّاسُ ٱتَّقُوا۟ رَبَّكُمُ ٱلَّذِى خَلَقَكُم مِّن
نَّفْسٍ وَٰحِدَةٍ وَخَلَقَ مِنْهَا زَوْجَهَا وَبَثَّ مِنْهُمَا
رِجَالًا كَثِيرًا وَنِسَآءً ۚ وَٱتَّقُوا۟ ٱللَّهَ ٱلَّذِى
تَسَآءَلُونَ بِهِۦ وَٱلْأَرْحَامَ ۚ إِنَّ ٱللَّهَ كَانَ عَلَيْكُمْ
رَقِيبًا

1 O people! Fear your Lord, who created you from a single soul, and created from it its mate, and propagated from them many men and women. And revere Allah whom you ask about, and the parents. Surely, Allah is Watchful over you.

٢ وَءَاتُوا۟ ٱلْيَتَٰمَىٰٓ أَمْوَٰلَهُمْ ۖ وَلَا تَتَبَدَّلُوا۟ ٱلْخَبِيثَ
بِٱلطَّيِّبِ ۖ وَلَا تَأْكُلُوٓا۟ أَمْوَٰلَهُمْ إِلَىٰٓ أَمْوَٰلِكُمْ ۚ إِنَّهُۥ
كَانَ حُوبًا كَبِيرًا

2 And give orphans their properties, and do not substitute the bad for the good. And do not consume their properties by combining them with yours, for that would be a serious sin.

٣ وَإِنْ خِفْتُمْ أَلَّا تُقْسِطُوا۟ فِى ٱلْيَتَٰمَىٰ فَٱنكِحُوا۟
مَا طَابَ لَكُم مِّنَ ٱلنِّسَآءِ مَثْنَىٰ وَثُلَٰثَ وَرُبَٰعَ ۖ
فَإِنْ خِفْتُمْ أَلَّا تَعْدِلُوا۟ فَوَٰحِدَةً أَوْ مَا مَلَكَتْ
أَيْمَٰنُكُمْ ۚ ذَٰلِكَ أَدْنَىٰٓ أَلَّا تَعُولُوا۟

3 If you fear you cannot act fairly towards the orphans—then marry the women you like—two, or three, or four. But if you fear you will not be fair, then one, or what you already have. That makes it more likely that you avoid bias.

٤ وَءَاتُوا۟ ٱلنِّسَآءَ صَدُقَٰتِهِنَّ نِحْلَةً ۚ فَإِن طِبْنَ
لَكُمْ عَن شَىْءٍ مِّنْهُ نَفْسًا فَكُلُوهُ هَنِيٓـًٔا مَّرِيٓـًٔا

4 Give women their dowries graciously. But if they willingly forego some of it, then consume it with enjoyment and pleasure.

٥ وَلَا تُؤْتُوا۟ ٱلسُّفَهَآءَ أَمْوَٰلَكُمُ ٱلَّتِى جَعَلَ ٱللَّهُ
لَكُمْ قِيَٰمًا وَٱرْزُقُوهُمْ فِيهَا وَٱكْسُوهُمْ وَقُولُوا۟
لَهُمْ قَوْلًا مَّعْرُوفًا

5 Do not give the immature your money which Allah has assigned to you for support. But provide for them from it, and clothe them, and speak to them with kind words.

٦ وَٱبْتَلُوا۟ ٱلْيَتَٰمَىٰ حَتَّىٰٓ إِذَا بَلَغُوا۟ ٱلنِّكَاحَ فَإِنْ
ءَانَسْتُم مِّنْهُمْ رُشْدًا فَٱدْفَعُوٓا۟ إِلَيْهِمْ أَمْوَٰلَهُمْ ۖ
وَلَا تَأْكُلُوهَآ إِسْرَافًا وَبِدَارًا أَن يَكْبَرُوا۟ ۚ وَمَن
كَانَ غَنِيًّا فَلْيَسْتَعْفِفْ ۖ وَمَن كَانَ فَقِيرًا فَلْيَأْكُلْ
بِٱلْمَعْرُوفِ ۚ فَإِذَا دَفَعْتُمْ إِلَيْهِمْ أَمْوَٰلَهُمْ
فَأَشْهِدُوا۟ عَلَيْهِمْ ۚ وَكَفَىٰ بِٱللَّهِ حَسِيبًا

6 Test the orphans until they reach the age of marriage. If you find them to be mature enough, hand over their properties to them. And do not consume it extravagantly or hastily before they grow up. The rich shall not charge any wage, but the poor may charge fairly. When you hand over their properties to them, have it witnessed for them. Allah suffices as a Reckoner.

٧ لِّلرِّجَالِ نَصِيبٌ مِّمَّا تَرَكَ ٱلْوَٰلِدَانِ وَٱلْأَقْرَبُونَ
وَلِلنِّسَآءِ نَصِيبٌ مِّمَّا تَرَكَ ٱلْوَٰلِدَانِ وَٱلْأَقْرَبُونَ
مِمَّا قَلَّ مِنْهُ أَوْ كَثُرَ ۚ نَصِيبًا مَّفْرُوضًا

7 Men receive a share of what their parents and relatives leave, and women receive a share of what their parents and relatives leave; be it little or much—a legal share.

٨ وَإِذَا حَضَرَ ٱلْقِسْمَةَ أُو۟لُوا۟ ٱلْقُرْبَىٰ وَٱلْيَتَـٰمَىٰ
وَٱلْمَسَـٰكِينُ فَٱرْزُقُوهُم مِّنْهُ وَقُولُوا۟ لَهُمْ قَوْلًا
مَّعْرُوفًا

8 If the distribution is attended by the relatives, and the orphans, and the needy, give them something out of it, and speak to them kindly.

٩ وَلْيَخْشَ ٱلَّذِينَ لَوْ تَرَكُوا۟ مِنْ خَلْفِهِمْ ذُرِّيَّةً
ضِعَـٰفًا خَافُوا۟ عَلَيْهِمْ فَلْيَتَّقُوا۟ ٱللَّهَ وَلْيَقُولُوا۟
قَوْلًا سَدِيدًا

9 Those who are concerned about the fate of their weak children, in case they leave them behind, should fear Allah, and speak appropriate words.

١٠ إِنَّ ٱلَّذِينَ يَأْكُلُونَ أَمْوَٰلَ ٱلْيَتَـٰمَىٰ ظُلْمًا إِنَّمَا
يَأْكُلُونَ فِى بُطُونِهِمْ نَارًا ۖ وَسَيَصْلَوْنَ سَعِيرًا

10 Those who consume the wealth of orphans illicitly consume only fire into their bellies; and they will roast in a Blaze.

١١ يُوصِيكُمُ ٱللَّهُ فِىٓ أَوْلَـٰدِكُمْ ۖ لِلذَّكَرِ مِثْلُ حَظِّ
ٱلْأُنثَيَيْنِ ۚ فَإِن كُنَّ نِسَآءً فَوْقَ ٱثْنَتَيْنِ فَلَهُنَّ
ثُلُثَا مَا تَرَكَ ۖ وَإِن كَانَتْ وَٰحِدَةً فَلَهَا ٱلنِّصْفُ ۚ
وَلِأَبَوَيْهِ لِكُلِّ وَٰحِدٍ مِّنْهُمَا ٱلسُّدُسُ مِمَّا تَرَكَ إِن
كَانَ لَهُۥ وَلَدٌ ۚ فَإِن لَّمْ يَكُن لَّهُۥ وَلَدٌ وَوَرِثَهُۥٓ أَبَوَاهُ
فَلِأُمِّهِ ٱلثُّلُثُ ۚ فَإِن كَانَ لَهُۥٓ إِخْوَةٌ فَلِأُمِّهِ
ٱلسُّدُسُ ۚ مِنۢ بَعْدِ وَصِيَّةٍ يُوصِى بِهَآ أَوْ دَيْنٍ ۗ
ءَابَآؤُكُمْ وَأَبْنَآؤُكُمْ لَا تَدْرُونَ أَيُّهُمْ أَقْرَبُ لَكُمْ
نَفْعًا ۚ فَرِيضَةً مِّنَ ٱللَّهِ ۗ إِنَّ ٱللَّهَ كَانَ عَلِيمًا
حَكِيمًا

11 Allah instructs you regarding your children: The male receives the equivalent of the share of two females. If they are daughters, more than two, they get two-thirds of what he leaves. If there is only one, she gets one-half. As for the parents, each gets one-sixth of what he leaves, if he had children. If he had no children, and his parents inherit from him, his mother gets one-third. If he has siblings, his mother gets one-sixth. After fulfilling any bequest and paying off debts. Your parents and your children—you do not know which are closer to you in welfare. This is Allah's Law. Allah is Knowing and Judicious.

١٢ وَلَكُمْ نِصْفُ مَا تَرَكَ أَزْوَٰجُكُمْ إِن لَّمْ يَكُن
لَّهُنَّ وَلَدٌ ۚ فَإِن كَانَ لَهُنَّ وَلَدٌ فَلَكُمُ ٱلرُّبُعُ مِمَّا
تَرَكْنَ ۚ مِنۢ بَعْدِ وَصِيَّةٍ يُوصِينَ بِهَآ أَوْ دَيْنٍ ۚ
وَلَهُنَّ ٱلرُّبُعُ مِمَّا تَرَكْتُمْ إِن لَّمْ يَكُن لَّكُمْ وَلَدٌ ۚ
فَإِن كَانَ لَكُمْ وَلَدٌ فَلَهُنَّ ٱلثُّمُنُ مِمَّا تَرَكْتُم ۚ مِّنۢ
بَعْدِ وَصِيَّةٍ تُوصُونَ بِهَآ أَوْ دَيْنٍ ۗ وَإِن كَانَ
رَجُلٌ يُورَثُ كَلَـٰلَةً أَوِ ٱمْرَأَةٌ وَلَهُۥٓ أَخٌ أَوْ أُخْتٌ

12 You get one-half of what your wives leave behind, if they had no children. If they had children, you get one-fourth of what they leave. After fulfilling any bequest and paying off debts. They get one-fourth of what you leave behind, if you have no children. If you have children, they get one-eighth of what you leave. After fulfilling any bequest and paying off debts. If a man or woman

فَلِكُلِّ وَٰحِدٍ مِّنْهُمَا ٱلسُّدُسُ ۚ فَإِن كَانُوٓا۟ أَكْثَرَ مِن
ذَٰلِكَ فَهُمْ شُرَكَآءُ فِى ٱلثُّلُثِ ۚ مِنۢ بَعْدِ وَصِيَّةٍ
يُوصَىٰ بِهَآ أَوْ دَيْنٍ غَيْرَ مُضَآرٍّ ۚ وَصِيَّةً مِّنَ ٱللَّهِ ۗ
وَٱللَّهُ عَلِيمٌ حَلِيمٌ

leaves neither parents nor children, but has a brother or sister, each of them gets one-sixth. If there are more siblings, they share one-third. After fulfilling any bequest and paying off debts, without any prejudice. This is a will from Allah. Allah is Knowing and Clement.

١٣ تِلْكَ حُدُودُ ٱللَّهِ ۚ وَمَن يُطِعِ ٱللَّهَ وَرَسُولَهُۥ
يُدْخِلْهُ جَنَّٰتٍ تَجْرِى مِن تَحْتِهَا ٱلْأَنْهَٰرُ خَٰلِدِينَ
فِيهَا ۚ وَذَٰلِكَ ٱلْفَوْزُ ٱلْعَظِيمُ

13 These are the bounds set by Allah. Whoever obeys Allah and His Messenger, He will admit him into Gardens beneath which rivers flow, to abide therein forever. That is the great attainment.

١٤ وَمَن يَعْصِ ٱللَّهَ وَرَسُولَهُۥ وَيَتَعَدَّ حُدُودَهُۥ
يُدْخِلْهُ نَارًا خَٰلِدًا فِيهَا وَلَهُۥ عَذَابٌ مُّهِينٌ

14 But whoever disobeys Allah and His Messenger, and oversteps His bounds, He will admit him into a Fire, wherein he abides forever, and he will have a shameful punishment.

١٥ وَٱلَّٰتِى يَأْتِينَ ٱلْفَٰحِشَةَ مِن نِّسَآئِكُمْ
فَٱسْتَشْهِدُوا۟ عَلَيْهِنَّ أَرْبَعَةً مِّنكُمْ ۖ فَإِن شَهِدُوا۟
فَأَمْسِكُوهُنَّ فِى ٱلْبُيُوتِ حَتَّىٰ يَتَوَفَّىٰهُنَّ
ٱلْمَوْتُ أَوْ يَجْعَلَ ٱللَّهُ لَهُنَّ سَبِيلًا

15 Those of your women who commit lewdness, you must have four witnesses against them, from among you. If they testify, confine them to the homes until death claims them, or Allah makes a way for them.

١٦ وَٱلَّذَانِ يَأْتِيَٰنِهَا مِنكُمْ فَـَٔاذُوهُمَا ۖ فَإِن تَابَا
وَأَصْلَحَا فَأَعْرِضُوا۟ عَنْهُمَآ ۗ إِنَّ ٱللَّهَ كَانَ تَوَّابًا
رَّحِيمًا

16 If two men among you commit it, punish them both. But if they repent and reform, leave them alone. Allah is Redeemer, Full of Mercy.

١٧ إِنَّمَا ٱلتَّوْبَةُ عَلَى ٱللَّهِ لِلَّذِينَ يَعْمَلُونَ ٱلسُّوٓءَ
بِجَهَٰلَةٍ ثُمَّ يَتُوبُونَ مِن قَرِيبٍ فَأُو۟لَٰٓئِكَ يَتُوبُ
ٱللَّهُ عَلَيْهِمْ ۗ وَكَانَ ٱللَّهُ عَلِيمًا حَكِيمًا

17 Repentance is available from Allah for those who commit evil out of ignorance, and then repent soon after. These—Allah will relent towards them. Allah is Knowing and Wise.

١٨ وَلَيْسَتِ ٱلتَّوْبَةُ لِلَّذِينَ يَعْمَلُونَ ٱلسَّيِّـَٔاتِ
حَتَّىٰٓ إِذَا حَضَرَ أَحَدَهُمُ ٱلْمَوْتُ قَالَ إِنِّى تُبْتُ
ٱلْـَٰٔنَ وَلَا ٱلَّذِينَ يَمُوتُونَ وَهُمْ كُفَّارٌ ۚ أُو۟لَٰٓئِكَ
أَعْتَدْنَا لَهُمْ عَذَابًا أَلِيمًا

18 But repentance is not available for those who commit evils, until when death approaches one of them, he says, “Now I repent,” nor for those who die as disbelievers. These—We

have prepared for them a painful torment.

١٩ يَٰٓأَيُّهَا ٱلَّذِينَ ءَامَنُوا۟ لَا يَحِلُّ لَكُمْ أَن تَرِثُوا۟
ٱلنِّسَآءَ كَرْهًا ۖ وَلَا تَعْضُلُوهُنَّ لِتَذْهَبُوا۟ بِبَعْضِ مَآ
ءَاتَيْتُمُوهُنَّ إِلَّآ أَن يَأْتِينَ بِفَٰحِشَةٍ مُّبَيِّنَةٍ ۚ
وَعَاشِرُوهُنَّ بِٱلْمَعْرُوفِ ۚ فَإِن كَرِهْتُمُوهُنَّ
فَعَسَىٰٓ أَن تَكْرَهُوا۟ شَيْـًٔا وَيَجْعَلَ ٱللَّهُ فِيهِ خَيْرًا
كَثِيرًا

19 O you who believe! It is not permitted for you to inherit women against their will. And do not coerce them in order to take away some of what you had given them, unless they commit a proven adultery. And live with them in kindness. If you dislike them, it may be that you dislike something in which Allah has placed much good.

٢٠ وَإِنْ أَرَدتُّمُ ٱسْتِبْدَالَ زَوْجٍ مَّكَانَ زَوْجٍ
وَءَاتَيْتُمْ إِحْدَىٰهُنَّ قِنطَارًا فَلَا تَأْخُذُوا۟ مِنْهُ
شَيْـًٔا ۚ أَتَأْخُذُونَهُۥ بُهْتَٰنًا وَإِثْمًا مُّبِينًا

20 If you wish to replace one wife with another, and you have given one of them a fortune, take nothing back from it. Would you take it back fraudulently and sinfully?

٢١ وَكَيْفَ تَأْخُذُونَهُۥ وَقَدْ أَفْضَىٰ بَعْضُكُمْ إِلَىٰ
بَعْضٍ وَأَخَذْنَ مِنكُم مِّيثَٰقًا غَلِيظًا

21 And how can you take it back, when you have been intimate with one another, and they have received from you a solid commitment?

٢٢ وَلَا تَنكِحُوا۟ مَا نَكَحَ ءَابَآؤُكُم مِّنَ ٱلنِّسَآءِ إِلَّا
مَا قَدْ سَلَفَ ۚ إِنَّهُۥ كَانَ فَٰحِشَةً وَمَقْتًا وَسَآءَ
سَبِيلًا

22 Do not marry women whom your fathers married, except what is already past. That is improper, indecent, and a bad custom.

٢٣ حُرِّمَتْ عَلَيْكُمْ أُمَّهَٰتُكُمْ وَبَنَاتُكُمْ وَأَخَوَٰتُكُمْ
وَعَمَّٰتُكُمْ وَخَٰلَٰتُكُمْ وَبَنَاتُ ٱلْأَخِ وَبَنَاتُ ٱلْأُخْتِ
وَأُمَّهَٰتُكُمُ ٱلَّٰتِىٓ أَرْضَعْنَكُمْ وَأَخَوَٰتُكُم مِّنَ
ٱلرَّضَٰعَةِ وَأُمَّهَٰتُ نِسَآئِكُمْ وَرَبَٰٓئِبُكُمُ ٱلَّٰتِى فِى
حُجُورِكُم مِّن نِّسَآئِكُمُ ٱلَّٰتِى دَخَلْتُم بِهِنَّ فَإِن
لَّمْ تَكُونُوا۟ دَخَلْتُم بِهِنَّ فَلَا جُنَاحَ عَلَيْكُمْ
وَحَلَٰٓئِلُ أَبْنَآئِكُمُ ٱلَّذِينَ مِنْ أَصْلَٰبِكُمْ وَأَن
تَجْمَعُوا۟ بَيْنَ ٱلْأُخْتَيْنِ إِلَّا مَا قَدْ سَلَفَ ۗ إِنَّ ٱللَّهَ
كَانَ غَفُورًا رَّحِيمًا

23 Forbidden for you are your mothers, your daughters, your sisters, your paternal aunts, your maternal aunts, your brother's daughters, your sister's daughters, your foster-mothers who nursed you, your sisters through nursing, your wives' mothers, and your stepdaughters in your guardianship—born of wives you have gone into—but if you have not gone into them, there is no blame on you. And the wives of your genetic sons, and marrying two sisters simultaneously. Except what is past. Allah is Oft-Forgiving, Most Merciful.

٢٤ وَٱلْمُحْصَنَٰتُ مِنَ ٱلنِّسَآءِ إِلَّا مَا مَلَكَتْ
أَيْمَٰنُكُمْ ۖ كِتَٰبَ ٱللَّهِ عَلَيْكُمْ ۚ وَأُحِلَّ لَكُم مَّا وَرَآءَ
ذَٰلِكُمْ أَن تَبْتَغُوا۟ بِأَمْوَٰلِكُم مُّحْصِنِينَ غَيْرَ
مُسَٰفِحِينَ ۚ فَمَا ٱسْتَمْتَعْتُم بِهِۦ مِنْهُنَّ فَـَٔاتُوهُنَّ
أُجُورَهُنَّ فَرِيضَةً ۚ وَلَا جُنَاحَ عَلَيْكُمْ فِيمَا
تَرَٰضَيْتُم بِهِۦ مِنۢ بَعْدِ ٱلْفَرِيضَةِ ۚ إِنَّ ٱللَّهَ كَانَ
عَلِيمًا حَكِيمًا

24 And all married women, except those you rightfully possess. This is Allah's decree, binding upon you. Permitted for you are those that lie outside these limits, provided you seek them in legal marriage, with gifts from your property, seeking wedlock, not prostitution. If you wish to enjoy them, then give them their dowry—a legal obligation. You commit no error by agreeing to any change to the dowry. Allah is All-Knowing, Most Wise.

٢٥ وَمَن لَّمْ يَسْتَطِعْ مِنكُمْ طَوْلًا أَن يَنكِحَ
ٱلْمُحْصَنَٰتِ ٱلْمُؤْمِنَٰتِ فَمِن مَّا مَلَكَتْ أَيْمَٰنُكُم
مِّن فَتَيَٰتِكُمُ ٱلْمُؤْمِنَٰتِ ۚ وَٱللَّهُ أَعْلَمُ بِإِيمَٰنِكُم ۚ
بَعْضُكُم مِّنۢ بَعْضٍ ۚ فَٱنكِحُوهُنَّ بِإِذْنِ أَهْلِهِنَّ
وَءَاتُوهُنَّ أُجُورَهُنَّ بِٱلْمَعْرُوفِ مُحْصَنَٰتٍ غَيْرَ
مُسَٰفِحَٰتٍ وَلَا مُتَّخِذَٰتِ أَخْدَانٍ ۚ فَإِذَآ أُحْصِنَّ
فَإِنْ أَتَيْنَ بِفَٰحِشَةٍ فَعَلَيْهِنَّ نِصْفُ مَا عَلَى
ٱلْمُحْصَنَٰتِ مِنَ ٱلْعَذَابِ ۚ ذَٰلِكَ لِمَنْ خَشِىَ ٱلْعَنَتَ
مِنكُمْ ۚ وَأَن تَصْبِرُوا۟ خَيْرٌ لَّكُمْ ۗ وَٱللَّهُ غَفُورٌ
رَّحِيمٌ

25 If any of you lack the means to marry free believing women, he may marry one of the believing maids under your control. Allah is well aware of your faith. You are from one another. Marry them with the permission of their guardians, and give them their recompense fairly—to be protected—neither committing adultery, nor taking secret lovers. When they are married, if they commit adultery, their punishment shall be half that of free women. That is for those among you who fear falling into decadence. But to practice self-restraint is better for you. Allah is Most Forgiving, Most Merciful.

٢٦ يُرِيدُ ٱللَّهُ لِيُبَيِّنَ لَكُمْ وَيَهْدِيَكُمْ سُنَنَ ٱلَّذِينَ
مِن قَبْلِكُمْ وَيَتُوبَ عَلَيْكُمْ ۗ وَٱللَّهُ عَلِيمٌ حَكِيمٌ

26 Allah intends to make things clear to you, and to guide you in the ways of those before you, and to redeem you. Allah is Most Knowing, Most Wise.

٢٧ وَٱللَّهُ يُرِيدُ أَن يَتُوبَ عَلَيْكُمْ وَيُرِيدُ ٱلَّذِينَ
يَتَّبِعُونَ ٱلشَّهَوَٰتِ أَن تَمِيلُوا۟ مَيْلًا عَظِيمًا

27 Allah intends to redeem you, but those who follow their desires want you to turn away utterly.

٢٨ يُرِيدُ ٱللَّهُ أَن يُخَفِّفَ عَنكُمْ ۚ وَخُلِقَ ٱلْإِنسَٰنُ
ضَعِيفًا

28 Allah intends to lighten your burden, for the human being was created weak.

٢٩ يَٰٓأَيُّهَا ٱلَّذِينَ ءَامَنُواْ لَا تَأۡكُلُوٓاْ أَمۡوَٰلَكُم بَيۡنَكُم
بِٱلۡبَٰطِلِ إِلَّآ أَن تَكُونَ تِجَٰرَةً عَن تَرَاضٖ مِّنكُمۡۚ
وَلَا تَقۡتُلُوٓاْ أَنفُسَكُمۡۚ إِنَّ ٱللَّهَ كَانَ بِكُمۡ رَحِيمٗا

29 O you who believe! Do not consume each other's wealth illicitly, but trade by mutual consent. And do not kill yourselves, for Allah is Merciful towards you.

٣٠ وَمَن يَفۡعَلۡ ذَٰلِكَ عُدۡوَٰنٗا وَظُلۡمٗا فَسَوۡفَ
نُصۡلِيهِ نَارٗاۚ وَكَانَ ذَٰلِكَ عَلَى ٱللَّهِ يَسِيرًا

30 Whoever does that, out of hostility and wrongdoing, We will cast him into a Fire. And that would be easy for Allah.

٣١ إِن تَجۡتَنِبُواْ كَبَآئِرَ مَا تُنۡهَوۡنَ عَنۡهُ نُكَفِّرۡ عَنكُمۡ
سَيِّـَٔاتِكُمۡ وَنُدۡخِلۡكُم مُّدۡخَلٗا كَرِيمٗا

31 If you avoid the worst of what you are forbidden, We will remit your sins, and admit you by a Gate of Honor.

٣٢ وَلَا تَتَمَنَّوۡاْ مَا فَضَّلَ ٱللَّهُ بِهِۦ بَعۡضَكُمۡ عَلَىٰ
بَعۡضٖۚ لِّلرِّجَالِ نَصِيبٞ مِّمَّا ٱكۡتَسَبُواْۖ وَلِلنِّسَآءِ
نَصِيبٞ مِّمَّا ٱكۡتَسَبۡنَۚ وَسۡـَٔلُواْ ٱللَّهَ مِن فَضۡلِهِۦٓۗ
إِنَّ ٱللَّهَ كَانَ بِكُلِّ شَيۡءٍ عَلِيمٗا

32 Do not covet what Allah has given to some of you in preference to others. For men is a share of what they have earned, and for women is a share of what they have earned. And ask Allah of his bounty. Allah has knowledge of everything.

٣٣ وَلِكُلّٖ جَعَلۡنَا مَوَٰلِيَ مِمَّا تَرَكَ ٱلۡوَٰلِدَانِ
وَٱلۡأَقۡرَبُونَۚ وَٱلَّذِينَ عَقَدَتۡ أَيۡمَٰنُكُمۡ فَـَٔاتُوهُمۡ
نَصِيبَهُمۡۚ إِنَّ ٱللَّهَ كَانَ عَلَىٰ كُلِّ شَيۡءٖ شَهِيدًا

33 To everyone We have assigned beneficiaries in what is left by parents and relatives. Those with whom you have made an agreement, give them their share. Allah is Witness over all things.

٣٤ ٱلرِّجَالُ قَوَّٰمُونَ عَلَى ٱلنِّسَآءِ بِمَا فَضَّلَ ٱللَّهُ
بَعۡضَهُمۡ عَلَىٰ بَعۡضٖ وَبِمَآ أَنفَقُواْ مِنۡ أَمۡوَٰلِهِمۡۚ
فَٱلصَّٰلِحَٰتُ قَٰنِتَٰتٌ حَٰفِظَٰتٞ لِّلۡغَيۡبِ بِمَا حَفِظَ
ٱللَّهُۚ وَٱلَّٰتِي تَخَافُونَ نُشُوزَهُنَّ فَعِظُوهُنَّ
وَٱهۡجُرُوهُنَّ فِي ٱلۡمَضَاجِعِ وَٱضۡرِبُوهُنَّۖ فَإِنۡ
أَطَعۡنَكُمۡ فَلَا تَبۡغُواْ عَلَيۡهِنَّ سَبِيلًاۗ إِنَّ ٱللَّهَ كَانَ
عَلِيّٗا كَبِيرٗا

34 Men are the protectors and maintainers of women, as Allah has given some of them an advantage over others, and because they spend out of their wealth. The good women are obedient, guarding what Allah would have them guard. As for those from whom you fear disloyalty, admonish them, and abandon them in their beds, then strike them. But if they obey you, seek no way against them. Allah is Sublime, Great.

٣٥ وَإِنْ خِفْتُمْ شِقَاقَ بَيْنِهِمَا فَٱبْعَثُوا۟ حَكَمًا مِّنْ أَهْلِهِۦ وَحَكَمًا مِّنْ أَهْلِهَآ إِن يُرِيدَآ إِصْلَٰحًا يُوَفِّقِ ٱللَّهُ بَيْنَهُمَآ ۗ إِنَّ ٱللَّهَ كَانَ عَلِيمًا خَبِيرًا	35 If you fear a breach between the two, appoint an arbiter from his family and an arbiter from her family. If they wish to reconcile, Allah will bring them together. Allah is Knowledgeable, Expert.
٣٦ وَٱعْبُدُوا۟ ٱللَّهَ وَلَا تُشْرِكُوا۟ بِهِۦ شَيْـًٔا ۖ وَبِٱلْوَٰلِدَيْنِ إِحْسَٰنًا وَبِذِى ٱلْقُرْبَىٰ وَٱلْيَتَٰمَىٰ وَٱلْمَسَٰكِينِ وَٱلْجَارِ ذِى ٱلْقُرْبَىٰ وَٱلْجَارِ ٱلْجُنُبِ وَٱلصَّاحِبِ بِٱلْجَنۢبِ وَٱبْنِ ٱلسَّبِيلِ وَمَا مَلَكَتْ أَيْمَٰنُكُمْ ۗ إِنَّ ٱللَّهَ لَا يُحِبُّ مَن كَانَ مُخْتَالًا فَخُورًا	36 Worship Allah, and ascribe no partners to Him, and be good to the parents, and the relatives, and the orphans, and the poor, and the neighbor next door, and the distant neighbor, and the close associate, and the traveler, and your servants. Allah does not love the arrogant showoff.
٣٧ ٱلَّذِينَ يَبْخَلُونَ وَيَأْمُرُونَ ٱلنَّاسَ بِٱلْبُخْلِ وَيَكْتُمُونَ مَآ ءَاتَىٰهُمُ ٱللَّهُ مِن فَضْلِهِۦ ۗ وَأَعْتَدْنَا لِلْكَٰفِرِينَ عَذَابًا مُّهِينًا	37 Those who are stingy, and exhort people to stinginess, and conceal what Allah has given them from His bounty. We have prepared for the disbelievers a disgraceful punishment.
٣٨ وَٱلَّذِينَ يُنفِقُونَ أَمْوَٰلَهُمْ رِئَآءَ ٱلنَّاسِ وَلَا يُؤْمِنُونَ بِٱللَّهِ وَلَا بِٱلْيَوْمِ ٱلْءَاخِرِ ۗ وَمَن يَكُنِ ٱلشَّيْطَٰنُ لَهُۥ قَرِينًا فَسَآءَ قَرِينًا	38 And those who spend their money to be seen by people, and believe neither in Allah nor in the Last Day. Whoever has Satan as a companion—what an evil companion.
٣٩ وَمَاذَا عَلَيْهِمْ لَوْ ءَامَنُوا۟ بِٱللَّهِ وَٱلْيَوْمِ ٱلْءَاخِرِ وَأَنفَقُوا۟ مِمَّا رَزَقَهُمُ ٱللَّهُ ۚ وَكَانَ ٱللَّهُ بِهِمْ عَلِيمًا	39 What would they have lost, had they believed in Allah and the Last Day, and gave out of what Allah has provided for them? Allah knows them very well.
٤٠ إِنَّ ٱللَّهَ لَا يَظْلِمُ مِثْقَالَ ذَرَّةٍ ۖ وَإِن تَكُ حَسَنَةً يُضَٰعِفْهَا وَيُؤْتِ مِن لَّدُنْهُ أَجْرًا عَظِيمًا	40 Allah does not commit an atom's weight of injustice; and if there is a good deed, He doubles it, and gives from His Presence a sublime compensation.
٤١ فَكَيْفَ إِذَا جِئْنَا مِن كُلِّ أُمَّةٍۭ بِشَهِيدٍ وَجِئْنَا بِكَ عَلَىٰ هَٰٓؤُلَآءِ شَهِيدًا	41 Then how will it be, when We bring a witness from every community, and We bring you as a witness against these?

٤٢ يَوْمَئِذٍ يَوَدُّ ٱلَّذِينَ كَفَرُوا۟ وَعَصَوُا۟ ٱلرَّسُولَ
لَوْ تُسَوَّىٰ بِهِمُ ٱلْأَرْضُ وَلَا يَكْتُمُونَ ٱللَّهَ حَدِيثًا

42 On that Day, those who disbelieved and disobeyed the Messenger will wish that the earth were leveled over them. They will conceal nothing from Allah.

٤٣ يَٰٓأَيُّهَا ٱلَّذِينَ ءَامَنُوا۟ لَا تَقْرَبُوا۟ ٱلصَّلَوٰةَ وَأَنتُمْ
سُكَٰرَىٰ حَتَّىٰ تَعْلَمُوا۟ مَا تَقُولُونَ وَلَا جُنُبًا إِلَّا
عَابِرِى سَبِيلٍ حَتَّىٰ تَغْتَسِلُوا۟ ۚ وَإِن كُنتُم
مَّرْضَىٰٓ أَوْ عَلَىٰ سَفَرٍ أَوْ جَآءَ أَحَدٌ مِّنكُم مِّنَ
ٱلْغَآئِطِ أَوْ لَٰمَسْتُمُ ٱلنِّسَآءَ فَلَمْ تَجِدُوا۟ مَآءً
فَتَيَمَّمُوا۟ صَعِيدًا طَيِّبًا فَٱمْسَحُوا۟ بِوُجُوهِكُمْ
وَأَيْدِيكُمْ ۗ إِنَّ ٱللَّهَ كَانَ عَفُوًّا غَفُورًا

43 O you who believe! Do not approach the prayer while you are drunk, so that you know what you say; nor after sexual orgasm—unless you are travelling—until you have bathed. If you are sick, or traveling, or one of you comes from the toilet, or you have had intercourse with women, and cannot find water, find clean sand and wipe your faces and your hands with it. Allah is Pardoning and Forgiving.

٤٤ أَلَمْ تَرَ إِلَى ٱلَّذِينَ أُوتُوا۟ نَصِيبًا مِّنَ ٱلْكِتَٰبِ
يَشْتَرُونَ ٱلضَّلَٰلَةَ وَيُرِيدُونَ أَن تَضِلُّوا۟ ٱلسَّبِيلَ

44 Have you not considered those who were given a share of the Book? They buy error, and wish you would lose the way.

٤٥ وَٱللَّهُ أَعْلَمُ بِأَعْدَآئِكُمْ ۚ وَكَفَىٰ بِٱللَّهِ وَلِيًّا
وَكَفَىٰ بِٱللَّهِ نَصِيرًا

45 But Allah knows your enemies best. Allah is sufficient as a Protector, and Allah is sufficient as a Supporter.

٤٦ مِّنَ ٱلَّذِينَ هَادُوا۟ يُحَرِّفُونَ ٱلْكَلِمَ عَن
مَّوَاضِعِهِۦ وَيَقُولُونَ سَمِعْنَا وَعَصَيْنَا وَٱسْمَعْ
غَيْرَ مُسْمَعٍ وَرَٰعِنَا لَيًّۢا بِأَلْسِنَتِهِمْ وَطَعْنًا فِى
ٱلدِّينِ ۚ وَلَوْ أَنَّهُمْ قَالُوا۟ سَمِعْنَا وَأَطَعْنَا وَٱسْمَعْ
وَٱنظُرْنَا لَكَانَ خَيْرًا لَّهُمْ وَأَقْوَمَ وَلَٰكِن لَّعَنَهُمُ
ٱللَّهُ بِكُفْرِهِمْ فَلَا يُؤْمِنُونَ إِلَّا قَلِيلًا

46 Among the Jews are some who take words out of context, and say, “We hear and we disobey”, and “Hear without listening”, and “Observe us,” twisting with their tongues and slandering the religion. Had they said, “We hear and we obey”, and “Listen”, and “Give us your attention,” it would have been better for them, and more upright. But Allah has cursed them for their disbelief; they do not believe except a little.

٤٧ يَٰٓأَيُّهَا ٱلَّذِينَ أُوتُوا۟ ٱلْكِتَٰبَ ءَامِنُوا۟ بِمَا نَزَّلْنَا
مُصَدِّقًا لِّمَا مَعَكُم مِّن قَبْلِ أَن نَّطْمِسَ وُجُوهًا

47 O you who were given the Book! Believe in what We sent down, confirming what you have, before We obliterate faces and turn them

فَنَرُدَّهَا عَلَىٰٓ أَدْبَارِهَآ أَوْ نَلْعَنَهُمْ كَمَا لَعَنَّآ
أَصْحَٰبَ ٱلسَّبْتِ ۚ وَكَانَ أَمْرُ ٱللَّهِ مَفْعُولًا

inside out, or curse them as We cursed the Sabbath-breakers. The command of Allah is always done.

٤٨ إِنَّ ٱللَّهَ لَا يَغْفِرُ أَن يُشْرَكَ بِهِۦ وَيَغْفِرُ مَا
دُونَ ذَٰلِكَ لِمَن يَشَآءُ ۚ وَمَن يُشْرِكْ بِٱللَّهِ فَقَدِ
ٱفْتَرَىٰٓ إِثْمًا عَظِيمًا

48 Allah does not forgive association with Him, but He forgives anything less than that to whomever He wills. Whoever associates anything with Allah has devised a monstrous sin.

٤٩ أَلَمْ تَرَ إِلَى ٱلَّذِينَ يُزَكُّونَ أَنفُسَهُم ۚ بَلِ ٱللَّهُ
يُزَكِّى مَن يَشَآءُ وَلَا يُظْلَمُونَ فَتِيلًا

49 Have you not considered those who claim purity for themselves? Rather, Allah purifies whom He wills, and they will not be wronged a whit.

٥٠ ٱنظُرْ كَيْفَ يَفْتَرُونَ عَلَى ٱللَّهِ ٱلْكَذِبَ ۖ وَكَفَىٰ
بِهِۦٓ إِثْمًا مُّبِينًا

50 See how they devise lies against Allah. That alone is an outright sin.

٥١ أَلَمْ تَرَ إِلَى ٱلَّذِينَ أُوتُوا۟ نَصِيبًا مِّنَ ٱلْكِتَٰبِ
يُؤْمِنُونَ بِٱلْجِبْتِ وَٱلطَّٰغُوتِ وَيَقُولُونَ لِلَّذِينَ
كَفَرُوا۟ هَٰٓؤُلَآءِ أَهْدَىٰ مِنَ ٱلَّذِينَ ءَامَنُوا۟ سَبِيلًا

51 Have you not considered those who were given a share of the Book? They believe in superstition and evil powers, and say of those who disbelieve, “These are better guided on the way than the believers.”

٥٢ أُو۟لَٰٓئِكَ ٱلَّذِينَ لَعَنَهُمُ ٱللَّهُ ۖ وَمَن يَلْعَنِ ٱللَّهُ
فَلَن تَجِدَ لَهُۥ نَصِيرًا

52 Those are they whom Allah has cursed. Whomever Allah curses, you will find no savior for him.

٥٣ أَمْ لَهُمْ نَصِيبٌ مِّنَ ٱلْمُلْكِ فَإِذًا لَّا يُؤْتُونَ
ٱلنَّاسَ نَقِيرًا

53 Or do they own a share of the kingdom? Then they would not give people a speck.

٥٤ أَمْ يَحْسُدُونَ ٱلنَّاسَ عَلَىٰ مَآ ءَاتَىٰهُمُ ٱللَّهُ
مِن فَضْلِهِۦ ۖ فَقَدْ ءَاتَيْنَآ ءَالَ إِبْرَٰهِيمَ ٱلْكِتَٰبَ
وَٱلْحِكْمَةَ وَءَاتَيْنَٰهُم مُّلْكًا عَظِيمًا

54 Or do they envy the people for what Allah has given them of His grace? We have given the family of Abraham the Book and wisdom, and We have given them a great kingdom.

٥٥ فَمِنْهُم مَّنْ ءَامَنَ بِهِۦ وَمِنْهُم مَّن صَدَّ عَنْهُ ۚ
وَكَفَىٰ بِجَهَنَّمَ سَعِيرًا

55 Among them are those who believed in it, and among them are those who held back from it. Hell is a sufficient Inferno.

٥٦ إِنَّ ٱلَّذِينَ كَفَرُوا۟ بِـَٔايَٰتِنَا سَوْفَ نُصْلِيهِمْ نَارًا
كُلَّمَا نَضِجَتْ جُلُودُهُم بَدَّلْنَٰهُمْ جُلُودًا غَيْرَهَا
لِيَذُوقُوا۟ ٱلْعَذَابَ ۗ إِنَّ ٱللَّهَ كَانَ عَزِيزًا حَكِيمًا

56 Those who reject Our revelations—We will scorch them in a Fire. Every time their skins are cooked, We will replace them with other skins, so they will experience the suffering. Allah is Most Powerful, Most Wise.

٥٧ وَٱلَّذِينَ ءَامَنُوا۟ وَعَمِلُوا۟ ٱلصَّٰلِحَٰتِ سَنُدْخِلُهُمْ
جَنَّٰتٍ تَجْرِى مِن تَحْتِهَا ٱلْأَنْهَٰرُ خَٰلِدِينَ فِيهَآ
أَبَدًا ۖ لَّهُمْ فِيهَآ أَزْوَٰجٌ مُّطَهَّرَةٌ ۖ وَنُدْخِلُهُمْ ظِلًّا
ظَلِيلًا

57 As for those who believe and do good deeds, We will admit them into Gardens beneath which rivers flow, abiding therein forever. They will have purified spouses therein, and We will admit them into a shady shade.

٥٨ إِنَّ ٱللَّهَ يَأْمُرُكُمْ أَن تُؤَدُّوا۟ ٱلْأَمَٰنَٰتِ إِلَىٰٓ أَهْلِهَا
وَإِذَا حَكَمْتُم بَيْنَ ٱلنَّاسِ أَن تَحْكُمُوا۟ بِٱلْعَدْلِ ۚ
إِنَّ ٱللَّهَ نِعِمَّا يَعِظُكُم بِهِۦٓ ۗ إِنَّ ٱللَّهَ كَانَ سَمِيعًۢا
بَصِيرًا

58 Allah instructs you to give back things entrusted to you to their owners. And when you judge between people, judge with justice. Allah's instructions to you are excellent. Allah is All-Hearing, All-Seeing.

٥٩ يَٰٓأَيُّهَا ٱلَّذِينَ ءَامَنُوٓا۟ أَطِيعُوا۟ ٱللَّهَ وَأَطِيعُوا۟
ٱلرَّسُولَ وَأُو۟لِى ٱلْأَمْرِ مِنكُمْ ۖ فَإِن تَنَٰزَعْتُمْ فِى
شَىْءٍ فَرُدُّوهُ إِلَى ٱللَّهِ وَٱلرَّسُولِ إِن كُنتُمْ
تُؤْمِنُونَ بِٱللَّهِ وَٱلْيَوْمِ ٱلْءَاخِرِ ۚ ذَٰلِكَ خَيْرٌ
وَأَحْسَنُ تَأْوِيلًا

59 O you who believe! Obey Allah and obey the Messenger and those in authority among you. And if you dispute over anything, refer it to Allah and the Messenger, if you believe in Allah and the Last Day. That is best, and a most excellent determination.

٦٠ أَلَمْ تَرَ إِلَى ٱلَّذِينَ يَزْعُمُونَ أَنَّهُمْ ءَامَنُوا۟ بِمَآ
أُنزِلَ إِلَيْكَ وَمَآ أُنزِلَ مِن قَبْلِكَ يُرِيدُونَ أَن
يَتَحَاكَمُوٓا۟ إِلَى ٱلطَّٰغُوتِ وَقَدْ أُمِرُوٓا۟ أَن يَكْفُرُوا۟
بِهِۦ وَيُرِيدُ ٱلشَّيْطَٰنُ أَن يُضِلَّهُمْ ضَلَٰلًۢا بَعِيدًا

60 Have you not observed those who claim that they believe in what was revealed to you, and in what was revealed before you, yet they seek Satanic sources for legislation, in spite of being commanded to reject them? Satan means to mislead them far away.

٦١ وَإِذَا قِيلَ لَهُمْ تَعَالَوْا۟ إِلَىٰ مَآ أَنزَلَ ٱللَّهُ وَإِلَى
ٱلرَّسُولِ رَأَيْتَ ٱلْمُنَٰفِقِينَ يَصُدُّونَ عَنكَ صُدُودًا

61 And when it is said to them, "Come to what Allah has revealed, and to the Messenger," you see the hypocrites shunning you completely.

٦٢ فَكَيْفَ إِذَآ أَصَٰبَتْهُم مُّصِيبَةٌۢ بِمَا قَدَّمَتْ
أَيْدِيهِمْ ثُمَّ جَآءُوكَ يَحْلِفُونَ بِٱللَّهِ إِنْ أَرَدْنَآ إِلَّآ
إِحْسَٰنًا وَتَوْفِيقًا

62 How about when a disaster strikes them because what their hands have put forward, and then they come to you swearing by Allah: "We only intended goodwill and reconciliation"?

٦٣ أُو۟لَٰٓئِكَ ٱلَّذِينَ يَعْلَمُ ٱللَّهُ مَا فِى قُلُوبِهِمْ
فَأَعْرِضْ عَنْهُمْ وَعِظْهُمْ وَقُل لَّهُمْ فِىٓ أَنفُسِهِمْ
قَوْلًۢا بَلِيغًا

63 They are those whom Allah knows what is in their hearts. So ignore them, and admonish them, and say to them concerning themselves penetrating words.

٦٤ وَمَآ أَرْسَلْنَا مِن رَّسُولٍ إِلَّا لِيُطَاعَ بِإِذْنِ ٱللَّهِ ۚ
وَلَوْ أَنَّهُمْ إِذ ظَّلَمُوٓا۟ أَنفُسَهُمْ جَآءُوكَ
فَٱسْتَغْفَرُوا۟ ٱللَّهَ وَٱسْتَغْفَرَ لَهُمُ ٱلرَّسُولُ لَوَجَدُوا۟
ٱللَّهَ تَوَّابًا رَّحِيمًا

64 We did not send any messenger except to be obeyed by Allah's leave. Had they, when they wronged themselves, come to you, and prayed for Allah's forgiveness, and the Messenger had prayed for their forgiveness, they would have found Allah Relenting and Merciful.

٦٥ فَلَا وَرَبِّكَ لَا يُؤْمِنُونَ حَتَّىٰ يُحَكِّمُوكَ فِيمَا
شَجَرَ بَيْنَهُمْ ثُمَّ لَا يَجِدُوا۟ فِىٓ أَنفُسِهِمْ حَرَجًا
مِّمَّا قَضَيْتَ وَيُسَلِّمُوا۟ تَسْلِيمًا

65 But no, by your Lord, they will not believe until they call you to arbitrate in their disputes, and then find within themselves no resentment regarding your decisions, and submit themselves completely.

٦٦ وَلَوْ أَنَّا كَتَبْنَا عَلَيْهِمْ أَنِ ٱقْتُلُوٓا۟ أَنفُسَكُمْ أَوِ
ٱخْرُجُوا۟ مِن دِيَٰرِكُم مَّا فَعَلُوهُ إِلَّا قَلِيلٌ مِّنْهُمْ ۖ
وَلَوْ أَنَّهُمْ فَعَلُوا۟ مَا يُوعَظُونَ بِهِۦ لَكَانَ خَيْرًا
لَّهُمْ وَأَشَدَّ تَثْبِيتًا

66 Had We decreed for them: "Kill yourselves," or "Leave your homes," they would not have done it, except for a few of them. But had they done what they were instructed to do, it would have been better for them, and a firmer confirmation.

٦٧ وَإِذًا لَّءَاتَيْنَٰهُم مِّن لَّدُنَّآ أَجْرًا عَظِيمًا

67 And We would have given them from Our presence a rich compensation.

٦٨ وَلَهَدَيْنَٰهُمْ صِرَٰطًا مُّسْتَقِيمًا

68 And We would have guided them on a straight path.

٦٩ وَمَن يُطِعِ ٱللَّهَ وَٱلرَّسُولَ فَأُو۟لَٰٓئِكَ مَعَ ٱلَّذِينَ
أَنْعَمَ ٱللَّهُ عَلَيْهِم مِّنَ ٱلنَّبِيِّۦنَ وَٱلصِّدِّيقِينَ
وَٱلشُّهَدَآءِ وَٱلصَّٰلِحِينَ ۚ وَحَسُنَ أُو۟لَٰٓئِكَ رَفِيقًا

69 Whoever obeys Allah and the Messenger—these are with those whom Allah has blessed—among the prophets, and the sincere, and

the martyrs, and the upright. Excellent are those as companions.

٧٠ ذَٰلِكَ ٱلْفَضْلُ مِنَ ٱللَّهِ ۚ وَكَفَىٰ بِٱللَّهِ عَلِيمًا

70 That is the grace from Allah. Allah suffices as Knower.

٧١ يَٰٓأَيُّهَا ٱلَّذِينَ ءَامَنُوا۟ خُذُوا۟ حِذْرَكُمْ فَٱنفِرُوا۟
ثُبَاتٍ أَوِ ٱنفِرُوا۟ جَمِيعًا

71 O you who believe! Take your precautions, and mobilize in groups, or mobilize altogether.

٧٢ وَإِنَّ مِنكُمْ لَمَن لَّيُبَطِّئَنَّ فَإِنْ أَصَٰبَتْكُم
مُّصِيبَةٌ قَالَ قَدْ أَنْعَمَ ٱللَّهُ عَلَىَّ إِذْ لَمْ أَكُن
مَّعَهُمْ شَهِيدًا

72 Among you is he who lags behind. Then, when a calamity befalls you, he says, “Allah has favored me, that I was not martyred with them.”

٧٣ وَلَئِنْ أَصَٰبَكُمْ فَضْلٌ مِّنَ ٱللَّهِ لَيَقُولَنَّ كَأَن لَّمْ
تَكُنۢ بَيْنَكُمْ وَبَيْنَهُۥ مَوَدَّةٌ يَٰلَيْتَنِى كُنتُ مَعَهُمْ
فَأَفُوزَ فَوْزًا عَظِيمًا

73 But when some bounty from Allah comes to you, he says—as if no affection existed between you and him—“If only I had been with them, I would have achieved a great victory.”

٧٤ فَلْيُقَٰتِلْ فِى سَبِيلِ ٱللَّهِ ٱلَّذِينَ يَشْرُونَ
ٱلْحَيَوٰةَ ٱلدُّنْيَا بِٱلْءَاخِرَةِ ۚ وَمَن يُقَٰتِلْ فِى
سَبِيلِ ٱللَّهِ فَيُقْتَلْ أَوْ يَغْلِبْ فَسَوْفَ نُؤْتِيهِ
أَجْرًا عَظِيمًا

74 Let those who sell the life of this world for the Hereafter fight in the cause of Allah. Whoever fights in the cause of Allah, and then is killed, or achieves victory, We will grant him a great compensation.

٧٥ وَمَا لَكُمْ لَا تُقَٰتِلُونَ فِى سَبِيلِ ٱللَّهِ
وَٱلْمُسْتَضْعَفِينَ مِنَ ٱلرِّجَالِ وَٱلنِّسَآءِ وَٱلْوِلْدَٰنِ
ٱلَّذِينَ يَقُولُونَ رَبَّنَآ أَخْرِجْنَا مِنْ هَٰذِهِ ٱلْقَرْيَةِ
ٱلظَّالِمِ أَهْلُهَا وَٱجْعَل لَّنَا مِن لَّدُنكَ وَلِيًّا وَٱجْعَل
لَّنَا مِن لَّدُنكَ نَصِيرًا

75 And why would you not fight in the cause of Allah, and the helpless men, and women, and children, cry out, “Our Lord, deliver us from this town whose people are oppressive, and appoint for us from Your Presence a Protector, and appoint for us from Your Presence a Victor.”

٧٦ ٱلَّذِينَ ءَامَنُوا۟ يُقَٰتِلُونَ فِى سَبِيلِ ٱللَّهِ ۖ
وَٱلَّذِينَ كَفَرُوا۟ يُقَٰتِلُونَ فِى سَبِيلِ ٱلطَّٰغُوتِ
فَقَٰتِلُوٓا۟ أَوْلِيَآءَ ٱلشَّيْطَٰنِ ۖ إِنَّ كَيْدَ ٱلشَّيْطَٰنِ كَانَ
ضَعِيفًا

76 Those who believe fight in the cause of Allah, while those who disbelieve fight in the cause of Evil. So fight the allies of the Devil. Surely the strategy of the Devil is weak.

٧٧ أَلَمْ تَرَ إِلَى ٱلَّذِينَ قِيلَ لَهُمْ كُفُّوٓا۟ أَيْدِيَكُمْ
وَأَقِيمُوا۟ ٱلصَّلَوٰةَ وَءَاتُوا۟ ٱلزَّكَوٰةَ فَلَمَّا كُتِبَ

77 Have you not considered those who were told, “Restrain your hands, and perform your prayers, and

عَلَيْهِمُ ٱلْقِتَالُ إِذَا فَرِيقٌ مِّنْهُمْ يَخْشَوْنَ ٱلنَّاسَ
كَخَشْيَةِ ٱللَّهِ أَوْ أَشَدَّ خَشْيَةً ۚ وَقَالُوا۟ رَبَّنَا لِمَ
كَتَبْتَ عَلَيْنَا ٱلْقِتَالَ لَوْلَآ أَخَّرْتَنَآ إِلَىٰٓ أَجَلٍ
قَرِيبٍ ۗ قُلْ مَتَٰعُ ٱلدُّنْيَا قَلِيلٌ وَٱلْءَاخِرَةُ خَيْرٌ
لِّمَنِ ٱتَّقَىٰ وَلَا تُظْلَمُونَ فَتِيلًا

spend in regular charity"? But when fighting was ordained for them, a faction of them feared the people as Allah is ought to be feared, or even more. And they said, "Our Lord, why did You ordain fighting for us? If only You would postpone it for us for a short while." Say, "The enjoyments of this life are brief, but the Hereafter is better for the righteous, and you will not be wronged one bit."

٧٨ أَيْنَمَا تَكُونُوا۟ يُدْرِككُّمُ ٱلْمَوْتُ وَلَوْ كُنتُمْ فِى
بُرُوجٍ مُّشَيَّدَةٍ ۗ وَإِن تُصِبْهُمْ حَسَنَةٌ يَقُولُوا۟
هَٰذِهِۦ مِنْ عِندِ ٱللَّهِ ۖ وَإِن تُصِبْهُمْ سَيِّئَةٌ يَقُولُوا۟
هَٰذِهِۦ مِنْ عِندِكَ ۚ قُلْ كُلٌّ مِّنْ عِندِ ٱللَّهِ ۖ فَمَالِ
هَٰٓؤُلَآءِ ٱلْقَوْمِ لَا يَكَادُونَ يَفْقَهُونَ حَدِيثًا

78 Wherever you may be, death will catch up with you, even if you were in fortified towers. When a good fortune comes their way, they say, "This is from Allah." But when a misfortune befalls them, they say, "This is from you." Say, "All is from Allah." So what is the matter with these people, that they hardly understand a thing?

٧٩ مَّآ أَصَابَكَ مِنْ حَسَنَةٍ فَمِنَ ٱللَّهِ ۖ وَمَآ أَصَابَكَ
مِن سَيِّئَةٍ فَمِن نَّفْسِكَ ۚ وَأَرْسَلْنَٰكَ لِلنَّاسِ
رَسُولًا ۚ وَكَفَىٰ بِٱللَّهِ شَهِيدًا

79 Whatever good happens to you is from Allah, and whatever bad happens to you is from your own self. We sent you to humanity as a messenger, and Allah is Witness enough.

٨٠ مَّن يُطِعِ ٱلرَّسُولَ فَقَدْ أَطَاعَ ٱللَّهَ ۖ وَمَن
تَوَلَّىٰ فَمَآ أَرْسَلْنَٰكَ عَلَيْهِمْ حَفِيظًا

80 Whoever obeys the Messenger is obeying Allah. And whoever turns away—We did not send you as a watcher over them.

٨١ وَيَقُولُونَ طَاعَةٌ فَإِذَا بَرَزُوا۟ مِنْ عِندِكَ بَيَّتَ
طَآئِفَةٌ مِّنْهُمْ غَيْرَ ٱلَّذِى تَقُولُ ۖ وَٱللَّهُ يَكْتُبُ مَا
يُبَيِّتُونَ ۖ فَأَعْرِضْ عَنْهُمْ وَتَوَكَّلْ عَلَى ٱللَّهِ ۚ
وَكَفَىٰ بِٱللَّهِ وَكِيلًا

81 They profess obedience, but when they leave your presence, some of them conspire something contrary to what you said. But Allah writes down what they conspire. So avoid them, and put your trust in Allah. Allah is Guardian enough.

٨٢ أَفَلَا يَتَدَبَّرُونَ ٱلْقُرْءَانَ ۚ وَلَوْ كَانَ مِنْ عِندِ
غَيْرِ ٱللَّهِ لَوَجَدُوا۟ فِيهِ ٱخْتِلَٰفًا كَثِيرًا

82 Do they not ponder the Quran? Had it been from any other than Allah, they would have found in it much discrepancy.

٨٣ وَإِذَا جَآءَهُمْ أَمْرٌ مِّنَ ٱلْأَمْنِ أَوِ ٱلْخَوْفِ
أَذَاعُوا۟ بِهِۦ ۖ وَلَوْ رَدُّوهُ إِلَى ٱلرَّسُولِ وَإِلَىٰٓ أُو۟لِى
ٱلْأَمْرِ مِنْهُمْ لَعَلِمَهُ ٱلَّذِينَ يَسْتَنۢبِطُونَهُۥ مِنْهُمْ ۗ
وَلَوْلَا فَضْلُ ٱللَّهِ عَلَيْكُمْ وَرَحْمَتُهُۥ لَٱتَّبَعْتُمُ
ٱلشَّيْطَٰنَ إِلَّا قَلِيلًا

83 When some news of security or alarm comes their way, they broadcast it. But had they referred it to the Messenger, and to those in authority among them, those who can draw conclusions from it would have comprehended it. Were it not for Allah's blessing and mercy upon you, you would have followed the Devil, except for a few.

٨٤ فَقَٰتِلْ فِى سَبِيلِ ٱللَّهِ لَا تُكَلَّفُ إِلَّا نَفْسَكَ ۚ
وَحَرِّضِ ٱلْمُؤْمِنِينَ ۖ عَسَى ٱللَّهُ أَن يَكُفَّ بَأْسَ
ٱلَّذِينَ كَفَرُوا۟ ۚ وَٱللَّهُ أَشَدُّ بَأْسًا وَأَشَدُّ تَنكِيلًا

84 So fight in the cause of Allah; you are responsible only for yourself. And rouse the believers. Perhaps Allah will restrain the might of those who disbelieve. Allah is Stronger in Might, and More Punishing.

٨٥ مَّن يَشْفَعْ شَفَٰعَةً حَسَنَةً يَكُن لَّهُۥ نَصِيبٌ
مِّنْهَا ۖ وَمَن يَشْفَعْ شَفَٰعَةً سَيِّئَةً يَكُن لَّهُۥ كِفْلٌ
مِّنْهَا ۗ وَكَانَ ٱللَّهُ عَلَىٰ كُلِّ شَىْءٍ مُّقِيتًا

85 Whoever intercedes for a good cause has a share in it, and whoever intercedes for an evil cause shares in its burdens. Allah keeps watch over everything.

٨٦ وَإِذَا حُيِّيتُم بِتَحِيَّةٍ فَحَيُّوا۟ بِأَحْسَنَ مِنْهَآ أَوْ
رُدُّوهَآ ۗ إِنَّ ٱللَّهَ كَانَ عَلَىٰ كُلِّ شَىْءٍ حَسِيبًا

86 When you are greeted with a greeting, respond with a better greeting, or return it. Allah keeps count of everything.

٨٧ ٱللَّهُ لَآ إِلَٰهَ إِلَّا هُوَ ۚ لَيَجْمَعَنَّكُمْ إِلَىٰ يَوْمِ
ٱلْقِيَٰمَةِ لَا رَيْبَ فِيهِ ۗ وَمَنْ أَصْدَقُ مِنَ ٱللَّهِ
حَدِيثًا

87 Allah—there is no god except He. He will gather you to the Day of Resurrection, in which there is no doubt. And who speaks more truly than Allah?

٨٨ فَمَا لَكُمْ فِى ٱلْمُنَٰفِقِينَ فِئَتَيْنِ وَٱللَّهُ أَرْكَسَهُم
بِمَا كَسَبُوٓا۟ ۚ أَتُرِيدُونَ أَن تَهْدُوا۟ مَنْ أَضَلَّ ٱللَّهُ ۖ
وَمَن يُضْلِلِ ٱللَّهُ فَلَن تَجِدَ لَهُۥ سَبِيلًا

88 What is the matter with you, divided into two factions regarding the hypocrites, when Allah Himself has overwhelmed them on account of what they did? Do you want to guide those whom Allah has led astray? Whomever Allah leads astray—you will never find for him a way.

٨٩ وَدُّوا۟ لَوْ تَكْفُرُونَ كَمَا كَفَرُوا۟ فَتَكُونُونَ
سَوَآءً ۖ فَلَا تَتَّخِذُوا۟ مِنْهُمْ أَوْلِيَآءَ حَتَّىٰ

89 They would love to see you disbelieve, just as they disbelieve, so you would become equal. So do

يُهَاجِرُوا۟ فِى سَبِيلِ ٱللَّهِ ۚ فَإِن تَوَلَّوْا۟ فَخُذُوهُمْ
وَٱقْتُلُوهُمْ حَيْثُ وَجَدتُّمُوهُمْ ۖ وَلَا تَتَّخِذُوا۟
مِنْهُمْ وَلِيًّا وَلَا نَصِيرًا

not befriend any of them, unless they emigrate in the way of Allah. If they turn away, seize them and execute them wherever you may find them; and do not take from among them allies or supporters.

٩٠ إِلَّا ٱلَّذِينَ يَصِلُونَ إِلَىٰ قَوْمٍۭ بَيْنَكُمْ وَبَيْنَهُم
مِّيثَٰقٌ أَوْ جَآءُوكُمْ حَصِرَتْ صُدُورُهُمْ أَن
يُقَٰتِلُوكُمْ أَوْ يُقَٰتِلُوا۟ قَوْمَهُمْ ۚ وَلَوْ شَآءَ ٱللَّهُ
لَسَلَّطَهُمْ عَلَيْكُمْ فَلَقَٰتَلُوكُمْ ۚ فَإِنِ ٱعْتَزَلُوكُمْ فَلَمْ
يُقَٰتِلُوكُمْ وَأَلْقَوْا۟ إِلَيْكُمُ ٱلسَّلَمَ فَمَا جَعَلَ ٱللَّهُ
لَكُمْ عَلَيْهِمْ سَبِيلًا

90 Except those who join people with whom you have a treaty, or those who come to you reluctant to fight you or fight their own people. Had Allah willed, He would have given them power over you, and they would have fought you. If they withdraw from you, and do not fight you, and offer you peace, then Allah assigns no excuse for you against them.

٩١ سَتَجِدُونَ ءَاخَرِينَ يُرِيدُونَ أَن يَأْمَنُوكُمْ
وَيَأْمَنُوا۟ قَوْمَهُمْ كُلَّ مَا رُدُّوٓا۟ إِلَى ٱلْفِتْنَةِ
أُرْكِسُوا۟ فِيهَا ۚ فَإِن لَّمْ يَعْتَزِلُوكُمْ وَيُلْقُوٓا۟ إِلَيْكُمُ
ٱلسَّلَمَ وَيَكُفُّوٓا۟ أَيْدِيَهُمْ فَخُذُوهُمْ وَٱقْتُلُوهُمْ
حَيْثُ ثَقِفْتُمُوهُمْ ۚ وَأُو۟لَٰٓئِكُمْ جَعَلْنَا لَكُمْ عَلَيْهِمْ
سُلْطَٰنًا مُّبِينًا

91 You will find others who want security from you, and security from their own people. But whenever they are tempted into civil discord, they plunge into it. So if they do not withdraw from you, nor offer you peace, nor restrain their hands, seize them and execute them wherever you find them. Against these, We have given you clear authorization.

٩٢ وَمَا كَانَ لِمُؤْمِنٍ أَن يَقْتُلَ مُؤْمِنًا إِلَّا خَطَـًٔا ۚ
وَمَن قَتَلَ مُؤْمِنًا خَطَـًٔا فَتَحْرِيرُ رَقَبَةٍ مُّؤْمِنَةٍ
وَدِيَةٌ مُّسَلَّمَةٌ إِلَىٰٓ أَهْلِهِۦٓ إِلَّآ أَن يَصَّدَّقُوا۟ ۚ فَإِن
كَانَ مِن قَوْمٍ عَدُوٍّ لَّكُمْ وَهُوَ مُؤْمِنٌ فَتَحْرِيرُ
رَقَبَةٍ مُّؤْمِنَةٍ ۖ وَإِن كَانَ مِن قَوْمٍۭ بَيْنَكُمْ وَبَيْنَهُم
مِّيثَٰقٌ فَدِيَةٌ مُّسَلَّمَةٌ إِلَىٰٓ أَهْلِهِۦ وَتَحْرِيرُ رَقَبَةٍ
مُّؤْمِنَةٍ ۖ فَمَن لَّمْ يَجِدْ فَصِيَامُ شَهْرَيْنِ
مُتَتَابِعَيْنِ تَوْبَةً مِّنَ ٱللَّهِ ۗ وَكَانَ ٱللَّهُ عَلِيمًا
حَكِيمًا

92 Never should a believer kill another believer, unless by error. Anyone who kills a believer by error must set free a believing slave, and pay compensation to the victim's family, unless they remit it as charity. If the victim belonged to a people who are hostile to you, but is a believer, then the compensation is to free a believing slave. If he belonged to a people with whom you have a treaty, then compensation should be handed over to his family, and a believing slave set free. Anyone who lacks the means must fast for two

consecutive months, by way of repentance to Allah. Allah is All-Knowing, Most Wise.

٩٣ وَمَن يَقْتُلْ مُؤْمِنًا مُّتَعَمِّدًا فَجَزَآؤُهُۥ جَهَنَّمُ
خَٰلِدًا فِيهَا وَغَضِبَ ٱللَّهُ عَلَيْهِ وَلَعَنَهُۥ وَأَعَدَّ لَهُۥ
عَذَابًا عَظِيمًا

93 Whoever kills a believer deliberately, the penalty for him is Hell, where he will remain forever. And Allah will be angry with him, and will curse him, and will prepare for him a terrible punishment.

٩٤ يَٰٓأَيُّهَا ٱلَّذِينَ ءَامَنُوٓا۟ إِذَا ضَرَبْتُمْ فِى سَبِيلِ
ٱللَّهِ فَتَبَيَّنُوا۟ وَلَا تَقُولُوا۟ لِمَنْ أَلْقَىٰٓ إِلَيْكُمُ ٱلسَّلَٰمَ
لَسْتَ مُؤْمِنًا تَبْتَغُونَ عَرَضَ ٱلْحَيَوٰةِ ٱلدُّنْيَا
فَعِندَ ٱللَّهِ مَغَانِمُ كَثِيرَةٌ ۚ كَذَٰلِكَ كُنتُم مِّن قَبْلُ
فَمَنَّ ٱللَّهُ عَلَيْكُمْ فَتَبَيَّنُوٓا۟ ۚ إِنَّ ٱللَّهَ كَانَ بِمَا
تَعْمَلُونَ خَبِيرًا

94 O you who believe! When you journey in the way of Allah, investigate, and do not say to him who offers you peace, “You are not a believer,” aspiring for the goods of this world. With Allah are abundant riches. You yourselves were like this before, and Allah bestowed favor on you; so investigate. Allah is well aware of what you do.

٩٥ لَّا يَسْتَوِى ٱلْقَٰعِدُونَ مِنَ ٱلْمُؤْمِنِينَ غَيْرُ أُو۟لِى
ٱلضَّرَرِ وَٱلْمُجَٰهِدُونَ فِى سَبِيلِ ٱللَّهِ بِأَمْوَٰلِهِمْ
وَأَنفُسِهِمْ ۚ فَضَّلَ ٱللَّهُ ٱلْمُجَٰهِدِينَ بِأَمْوَٰلِهِمْ
وَأَنفُسِهِمْ عَلَى ٱلْقَٰعِدِينَ دَرَجَةً ۚ وَكُلًّا وَعَدَ ٱللَّهُ
ٱلْحُسْنَىٰ ۚ وَفَضَّلَ ٱللَّهُ ٱلْمُجَٰهِدِينَ عَلَى ٱلْقَٰعِدِينَ
أَجْرًا عَظِيمًا

95 Not equal are the inactive among the believers—except the disabled—and the strivers in the cause of Allah with their possessions and their persons. Allah prefers the strivers with their possessions and their persons above the inactive, by a degree. But Allah has promised goodness to both. Yet Allah favors the strivers, over the inactive, with a great reward.

٩٦ دَرَجَٰتٍ مِّنْهُ وَمَغْفِرَةً وَرَحْمَةً ۚ وَكَانَ ٱللَّهُ
غَفُورًا رَّحِيمًا

96 Degrees from Him, and forgiveness, and mercy. Allah is Forgiving and Merciful.

٩٧ إِنَّ ٱلَّذِينَ تَوَفَّىٰهُمُ ٱلْمَلَٰٓئِكَةُ ظَالِمِىٓ أَنفُسِهِمْ
قَالُوا۟ فِيمَ كُنتُمْ ۖ قَالُوا۟ كُنَّا مُسْتَضْعَفِينَ فِى
ٱلْأَرْضِ ۚ قَالُوٓا۟ أَلَمْ تَكُنْ أَرْضُ ٱللَّهِ وَٰسِعَةً
فَتُهَاجِرُوا۟ فِيهَا ۚ فَأُو۟لَٰٓئِكَ مَأْوَىٰهُمْ جَهَنَّمُ ۖ
وَسَآءَتْ مَصِيرًا

97 While the angels are removing the souls of those who have wronged themselves, they will say, “What was the matter with you?” They will say, “We were oppressed in the land.” They will say, “Was Allah’s earth not vast enough for you to emigrate in it?” These—their refuge is Hell. What a wretched retreat!

٩٨ إِلَّا ٱلۡمُسۡتَضۡعَفِينَ مِنَ ٱلرِّجَالِ وَٱلنِّسَآءِ
وَٱلۡوِلۡدَٰنِ لَا يَسۡتَطِيعُونَ حِيلَةٗ وَلَا يَهۡتَدُونَ
سَبِيلٗا

98 Except for the weak among men, and women, and children who have no means to act, and no means to find a way out.

٩٩ فَأُوْلَٰٓئِكَ عَسَى ٱللَّهُ أَن يَعۡفُوَ عَنۡهُمۡۚ وَكَانَ
ٱللَّهُ عَفُوًّا غَفُورٗا

99 These—Allah may well pardon them. Allah is Pardoning and Forgiving.

١٠٠ وَمَن يُهَاجِرۡ فِي سَبِيلِ ٱللَّهِ يَجِدۡ فِي
ٱلۡأَرۡضِ مُرَٰغَمٗا كَثِيرٗا وَسَعَةٗۚ وَمَن يَخۡرُجۡ مِنۢ
بَيۡتِهِۦ مُهَاجِرًا إِلَى ٱللَّهِ وَرَسُولِهِۦ ثُمَّ يُدۡرِكۡهُ
ٱلۡمَوۡتُ فَقَدۡ وَقَعَ أَجۡرُهُۥ عَلَى ٱللَّهِۗ وَكَانَ ٱللَّهُ
غَفُورٗا رَّحِيمٗا

100 Anyone who emigrates for the sake of Allah will find on earth many places of refuge, and plentitude. Anyone who leaves his home, emigrating to Allah and His Messenger, and then is overtaken by death, his compensation falls on Allah. Allah is Forgiver, Most Merciful.

١٠١ وَإِذَا ضَرَبۡتُمۡ فِي ٱلۡأَرۡضِ فَلَيۡسَ عَلَيۡكُمۡ
جُنَاحٌ أَن تَقۡصُرُواْ مِنَ ٱلصَّلَوٰةِ إِنۡ خِفۡتُمۡ أَن
يَفۡتِنَكُمُ ٱلَّذِينَ كَفَرُوٓاْۚ إِنَّ ٱلۡكَٰفِرِينَ كَانُواْ لَكُمۡ
عَدُوّٗا مُّبِينٗا

101 When you travel in the land, there is no blame on you for shortening the prayers, if you fear that the disbelievers may harm you. The disbelievers are your manifest enemies.

١٠٢ وَإِذَا كُنتَ فِيهِمۡ فَأَقَمۡتَ لَهُمُ ٱلصَّلَوٰةَ فَلۡتَقُمۡ
طَآئِفَةٞ مِّنۡهُم مَّعَكَ وَلۡيَأۡخُذُوٓاْ أَسۡلِحَتَهُمۡ فَإِذَا
سَجَدُواْ فَلۡيَكُونُواْ مِن وَرَآئِكُمۡ وَلۡتَأۡتِ طَآئِفَةٌ
أُخۡرَىٰ لَمۡ يُصَلُّواْ فَلۡيُصَلُّواْ مَعَكَ وَلۡيَأۡخُذُواْ
حِذۡرَهُمۡ وَأَسۡلِحَتَهُمۡۗ وَدَّ ٱلَّذِينَ كَفَرُواْ لَوۡ
تَغۡفُلُونَ عَنۡ أَسۡلِحَتِكُمۡ وَأَمۡتِعَتِكُمۡ فَيَمِيلُونَ
عَلَيۡكُم مَّيۡلَةٗ وَٰحِدَةٗۚ وَلَا جُنَاحَ عَلَيۡكُمۡ إِن كَانَ
بِكُمۡ أَذٗى مِّن مَّطَرٍ أَوۡ كُنتُم مَّرۡضَىٰٓ أَن تَضَعُوٓاْ
أَسۡلِحَتَكُمۡۖ وَخُذُواْ حِذۡرَكُمۡۗ إِنَّ ٱللَّهَ أَعَدَّ
لِلۡكَٰفِرِينَ عَذَابٗا مُّهِينٗا

102 When you are among them, and you stand to lead them in prayer, let a group of them stand with you, and let them hold their weapons. Then, when they have done their prostrations, let them withdraw to the rear, and let another group, that have not prayed yet, come forward and pray with you; and let them take their precautions and their weapons. Those who disbelieve would like you to neglect your weapons and your equipment, so they can attack you in a single assault. You commit no error, if you are hampered by rain or are sick, by putting down your weapons; but take precautions. Indeed, Allah has prepared for the

disbelievers a demeaning punishment.

١٠٣ فَإِذَا قَضَيْتُمُ ٱلصَّلَوٰةَ فَٱذْكُرُوا۟ ٱللَّهَ قِيَٰمًا
وَقُعُودًا وَعَلَىٰ جُنُوبِكُمْ ۚ فَإِذَا ٱطْمَأْنَنتُمْ
فَأَقِيمُوا۟ ٱلصَّلَوٰةَ ۚ إِنَّ ٱلصَّلَوٰةَ كَانَتْ عَلَى
ٱلْمُؤْمِنِينَ كِتَٰبًا مَّوْقُوتًا

103 When you have completed the prayer, remember Allah, standing, or sitting, or on your sides. And when you feel secure, perform the prayer. The prayer is obligatory for believers at specific times.

١٠٤ وَلَا تَهِنُوا۟ فِى ٱبْتِغَآءِ ٱلْقَوْمِ ۖ إِن تَكُونُوا۟
تَأْلَمُونَ فَإِنَّهُمْ يَأْلَمُونَ كَمَا تَأْلَمُونَ ۖ وَتَرْجُونَ
مِنَ ٱللَّهِ مَا لَا يَرْجُونَ ۗ وَكَانَ ٱللَّهُ عَلِيمًا حَكِيمًا

104 And do not falter in the pursuit of the enemy. If you are aching, they are aching as you are aching, but you expect from Allah what they cannot expect. Allah is Knowledgeable and Wise.

١٠٥ إِنَّآ أَنزَلْنَآ إِلَيْكَ ٱلْكِتَٰبَ بِٱلْحَقِّ لِتَحْكُمَ بَيْنَ
ٱلنَّاسِ بِمَآ أَرَىٰكَ ٱللَّهُ ۚ وَلَا تَكُن لِّلْخَآئِنِينَ
خَصِيمًا

105 We have revealed to you the Scripture, with the truth, so that you judge between people in accordance with what Allah has shown you. And do not be an advocate for the traitors.

١٠٦ وَٱسْتَغْفِرِ ٱللَّهَ ۖ إِنَّ ٱللَّهَ كَانَ غَفُورًا رَّحِيمًا

106 And ask Allah for forgiveness. Allah is Forgiver and Merciful.

١٠٧ وَلَا تُجَٰدِلْ عَنِ ٱلَّذِينَ يَخْتَانُونَ أَنفُسَهُمْ ۚ
إِنَّ ٱللَّهَ لَا يُحِبُّ مَن كَانَ خَوَّانًا أَثِيمًا

107 And do not argue on behalf of those who deceive themselves. Allah does not love the deceitful sinner.

١٠٨ يَسْتَخْفُونَ مِنَ ٱلنَّاسِ وَلَا يَسْتَخْفُونَ مِنَ
ٱللَّهِ وَهُوَ مَعَهُمْ إِذْ يُبَيِّتُونَ مَا لَا يَرْضَىٰ مِنَ
ٱلْقَوْلِ ۚ وَكَانَ ٱللَّهُ بِمَا يَعْمَلُونَ مُحِيطًا

108 They hide from the people, but they cannot hide from Allah. He is with them, as they plot by night with words He does not approve. Allah comprehends what they do.

١٠٩ هَٰٓأَنتُمْ هَٰٓؤُلَآءِ جَٰدَلْتُمْ عَنْهُمْ فِى ٱلْحَيَوٰةِ
ٱلدُّنْيَا فَمَن يُجَٰدِلُ ٱللَّهَ عَنْهُمْ يَوْمَ ٱلْقِيَٰمَةِ أَم
مَّن يَكُونُ عَلَيْهِمْ وَكِيلًا

109 There you are, arguing on their behalf in the present life, but who will argue with Allah on their behalf on the Day of Resurrection? Or who will be their representative?

١١٠ وَمَن يَعْمَلْ سُوٓءًا أَوْ يَظْلِمْ نَفْسَهُۥ ثُمَّ
يَسْتَغْفِرِ ٱللَّهَ يَجِدِ ٱللَّهَ غَفُورًا رَّحِيمًا

110 Whoever commits evil, or wrongs his soul, then implores Allah for forgiveness, will find Allah Forgiving and Merciful.

١١١ وَمَن يَكْسِبْ إِثْمًا فَإِنَّمَا يَكْسِبُهُۥ عَلَىٰ
نَفْسِهِۦ ۚ وَكَانَ ٱللَّهُ عَلِيمًا حَكِيمًا

111 And Whoever earns a sin, earns it against himself. Allah is Aware and Wise.

١١٢ وَمَن يَكْسِبْ خَطِيٓـَٔةً أَوْ إِثْمًا ثُمَّ يَرْمِ بِهِۦ
بَرِيٓـًٔا فَقَدِ ٱحْتَمَلَ بُهْتَٰنًا وَإِثْمًا مُّبِينًا

112 And whoever commits a mistake, or a sin, and then blames it on an innocent person, has taken a slander and a clear sin.

١١٣ وَلَوْلَا فَضْلُ ٱللَّهِ عَلَيْكَ وَرَحْمَتُهُۥ لَهَمَّت
طَّآئِفَةٌ مِّنْهُمْ أَن يُضِلُّوكَ وَمَا يُضِلُّونَ إِلَّآ
أَنفُسَهُمْ ۖ وَمَا يَضُرُّونَكَ مِن شَىْءٍ ۚ وَأَنزَلَ ٱللَّهُ
عَلَيْكَ ٱلْكِتَٰبَ وَٱلْحِكْمَةَ وَعَلَّمَكَ مَا لَمْ تَكُن
تَعْلَمُ ۚ وَكَانَ فَضْلُ ٱللَّهِ عَلَيْكَ عَظِيمًا

113 Were it not for Allah's grace towards you, and His mercy, a faction of them would have managed to mislead you. But they only mislead themselves, and they cannot harm you in any way. Allah has revealed to you the Scripture and wisdom, and has taught you what you did not know. Allah's goodness towards you is great.

١١٤ لَّا خَيْرَ فِى كَثِيرٍ مِّن نَّجْوَىٰهُمْ إِلَّا مَنْ أَمَرَ
بِصَدَقَةٍ أَوْ مَعْرُوفٍ أَوْ إِصْلَٰحٍۭ بَيْنَ ٱلنَّاسِ ۚ وَمَن
يَفْعَلْ ذَٰلِكَ ٱبْتِغَآءَ مَرْضَاتِ ٱللَّهِ فَسَوْفَ نُؤْتِيهِ
أَجْرًا عَظِيمًا

114 There is no good in much of their private counsels, except for him who advocates charity, or kindness, or reconciliation between people. Whoever does that, seeking Allah's approval, We will give him a great compensation.

١١٥ وَمَن يُشَاقِقِ ٱلرَّسُولَ مِنۢ بَعْدِ مَا تَبَيَّنَ لَهُ
ٱلْهُدَىٰ وَيَتَّبِعْ غَيْرَ سَبِيلِ ٱلْمُؤْمِنِينَ نُوَلِّهِۦ مَا
تَوَلَّىٰ وَنُصْلِهِۦ جَهَنَّمَ ۖ وَسَآءَتْ مَصِيرًا

115 Whoever makes a breach with the Messenger, after the guidance has become clear to him, and follows other than the path of the believers, We will direct him in the direction he has chosen, and commit him to Hell—what a terrible destination!

١١٦ إِنَّ ٱللَّهَ لَا يَغْفِرُ أَن يُشْرَكَ بِهِۦ وَيَغْفِرُ مَا
دُونَ ذَٰلِكَ لِمَن يَشَآءُ ۚ وَمَن يُشْرِكْ بِٱللَّهِ فَقَدْ
ضَلَّ ضَلَٰلًۢا بَعِيدًا

116 Allah will not forgive that partners be associated with Him; but will forgive anything less than that, to whomever He wills. Anyone who ascribes partners to Allah has strayed into far error.

١١٧ إِن يَدْعُونَ مِن دُونِهِۦٓ إِلَّآ إِنَٰثًا وَإِن يَدْعُونَ
إِلَّا شَيْطَٰنًا مَّرِيدًا

117 They invoke in His stead only females. In fact, they invoke none but a rebellious devil.

١١٨ لَّعَنَهُ ٱللَّهُ ۘ وَقَالَ لَأَتَّخِذَنَّ مِنْ عِبَادِكَ نَصِيبًا
مَّفْرُوضًا

118 Allah has cursed him. And he said, “I will take to myself my due share of Your servants.”

١١٩ وَلَأُضِلَّنَّهُمْ وَلَأُمَنِّيَنَّهُمْ وَلَءَامُرَنَّهُمْ فَلَيُبَتِّكُنَّ
ءَاذَانَ ٱلْأَنْعَٰمِ وَلَءَامُرَنَّهُمْ فَلَيُغَيِّرُنَّ خَلْقَ ٱللَّهِ ۚ
وَمَن يَتَّخِذِ ٱلشَّيْطَٰنَ وَلِيًّا مِّن دُونِ ٱللَّهِ فَقَدْ
خَسِرَ خُسْرَانًا مُّبِينًا

119 “And I will mislead them, and I will entice them, and I will prompt them to slit the ears of cattle, and I will prompt them to alter the creation of Allah.” Whoever takes Satan as a lord, instead of Allah, has surely suffered a profound loss.

١٢٠ يَعِدُهُمْ وَيُمَنِّيهِمْ ۖ وَمَا يَعِدُهُمُ ٱلشَّيْطَٰنُ إِلَّا
غُرُورًا

120 He promises them, and he raises their expectations, but Satan promises them nothing but delusions.

١٢١ أُو۟لَٰٓئِكَ مَأْوَىٰهُمْ جَهَنَّمُ وَلَا يَجِدُونَ عَنْهَا
مَحِيصًا

121 These—their place is Hell, and they will find no escape from it.

١٢٢ وَٱلَّذِينَ ءَامَنُوا۟ وَعَمِلُوا۟ ٱلصَّٰلِحَٰتِ
سَنُدْخِلُهُمْ جَنَّٰتٍ تَجْرِى مِن تَحْتِهَا ٱلْأَنْهَٰرُ
خَٰلِدِينَ فِيهَآ أَبَدًا ۖ وَعْدَ ٱللَّهِ حَقًّا ۚ وَمَنْ أَصْدَقُ
مِنَ ٱللَّهِ قِيلًا

122 But as for those who believe and do righteous deeds, We will admit them into gardens beneath which rivers flow, where they will abide forever. The promise of Allah is true—and who is more truthful in speech than Allah?

١٢٣ لَّيْسَ بِأَمَانِيِّكُمْ وَلَآ أَمَانِىِّ أَهْلِ ٱلْكِتَٰبِ ۗ مَن
يَعْمَلْ سُوٓءًا يُجْزَ بِهِۦ وَلَا يَجِدْ لَهُۥ مِن دُونِ ٱللَّهِ
وَلِيًّا وَلَا نَصِيرًا

123 It is not in accordance with your wishes, nor in accordance with the wishes of the People of the Scripture. Whoever works evil will pay for it, and will not find for himself, besides Allah, any protector or savior.

١٢٤ وَمَن يَعْمَلْ مِنَ ٱلصَّٰلِحَٰتِ مِن ذَكَرٍ أَوْ أُنثَىٰ
وَهُوَ مُؤْمِنٌ فَأُو۟لَٰٓئِكَ يَدْخُلُونَ ٱلْجَنَّةَ وَلَا
يُظْلَمُونَ نَقِيرًا

124 But whoever works righteousness, whether male or female, and is a believer—those will enter Paradise, and will not be wronged a whit.

١٢٥ وَمَنْ أَحْسَنُ دِينًا مِّمَّنْ أَسْلَمَ وَجْهَهُۥ لِلَّهِ
وَهُوَ مُحْسِنٌ وَٱتَّبَعَ مِلَّةَ إِبْرَٰهِيمَ حَنِيفًا ۗ وَٱتَّخَذَ
ٱللَّهُ إِبْرَٰهِيمَ خَلِيلًا

125 And who is better in religion than he who submits himself wholly to Allah, and is a doer of good, and follows the faith of Abraham the

Monotheist? Allah has chosen
Abraham for a friend.

١٢٦ وَلِلَّهِ مَا فِى ٱلسَّمَٰوَٰتِ وَمَا فِى ٱلْأَرْضِ ۚ
وَكَانَ ٱللَّهُ بِكُلِّ شَىْءٍ مُّحِيطًا

126 To Allah belongs what is in the
heavens and what is on earth, and
Allah encompasses everything.

١٢٧ وَيَسْتَفْتُونَكَ فِى ٱلنِّسَآءِ ۖ قُلِ ٱللَّهُ يُفْتِيكُمْ
فِيهِنَّ وَمَا يُتْلَىٰ عَلَيْكُمْ فِى ٱلْكِتَٰبِ فِى يَتَٰمَى
ٱلنِّسَآءِ ٱلَّٰتِى لَا تُؤْتُونَهُنَّ مَا كُتِبَ لَهُنَّ
وَتَرْغَبُونَ أَن تَنكِحُوهُنَّ وَٱلْمُسْتَضْعَفِينَ مِنَ
ٱلْوِلْدَٰنِ وَأَن تَقُومُوا۟ لِلْيَتَٰمَىٰ بِٱلْقِسْطِ ۚ وَمَا
تَفْعَلُوا۟ مِنْ خَيْرٍ فَإِنَّ ٱللَّهَ كَانَ بِهِۦ عَلِيمًا

127 They ask you for a ruling about
women. Say, "Allah gives you a
ruling about them, and so does what
is stated to you in the Book about
widowed women from whom you
withhold what is decreed for them,
yet you desire to marry them, and
about helpless children: that you
should treat the orphans fairly."
Whatever good you do, Allah knows
it.

١٢٨ وَإِنِ ٱمْرَأَةٌ خَافَتْ مِنۢ بَعْلِهَا نُشُوزًا أَوْ
إِعْرَاضًا فَلَا جُنَاحَ عَلَيْهِمَآ أَن يُصْلِحَا بَيْنَهُمَا
صُلْحًا ۚ وَٱلصُّلْحُ خَيْرٌ ۗ وَأُحْضِرَتِ ٱلْأَنفُسُ
ٱلشُّحَّ ۚ وَإِن تُحْسِنُوا۟ وَتَتَّقُوا۟ فَإِنَّ ٱللَّهَ كَانَ بِمَا
تَعْمَلُونَ خَبِيرًا

128 If a woman fears maltreatment or
desertion from her husband, there is
no fault in them if they reconcile their
differences, for reconciliation is best.
Souls are prone to avarice; yet if you
do what is good, and practice
piety—Allah is Cognizant of what
you do.

١٢٩ وَلَن تَسْتَطِيعُوٓا۟ أَن تَعْدِلُوا۟ بَيْنَ ٱلنِّسَآءِ وَلَوْ
حَرَصْتُمْ ۖ فَلَا تَمِيلُوا۟ كُلَّ ٱلْمَيْلِ فَتَذَرُوهَا
كَٱلْمُعَلَّقَةِ ۚ وَإِن تُصْلِحُوا۟ وَتَتَّقُوا۟ فَإِنَّ ٱللَّهَ كَانَ
غَفُورًا رَّحِيمًا

129 You will not be able to treat
women with equal fairness, no
matter how much you desire it. But
do not be so biased as to leave
another suspended. If you make
amends, and act righteously—Allah
is Forgiving and Merciful.

١٣٠ وَإِن يَتَفَرَّقَا يُغْنِ ٱللَّهُ كُلًّا مِّن سَعَتِهِۦ ۚ وَكَانَ
ٱللَّهُ وَٰسِعًا حَكِيمًا

130 And if they separate, Allah will
enrich each from His abundance.
Allah is Bounteous and Wise.

١٣١ وَلِلَّهِ مَا فِى ٱلسَّمَٰوَٰتِ وَمَا فِى ٱلْأَرْضِ ۗ وَلَقَدْ
وَصَّيْنَا ٱلَّذِينَ أُوتُوا۟ ٱلْكِتَٰبَ مِن قَبْلِكُمْ وَإِيَّاكُمْ
أَنِ ٱتَّقُوا۟ ٱللَّهَ ۚ وَإِن تَكْفُرُوا۟ فَإِنَّ لِلَّهِ مَا فِى
ٱلسَّمَٰوَٰتِ وَمَا فِى ٱلْأَرْضِ ۚ وَكَانَ ٱللَّهُ غَنِيًّا
حَمِيدًا

131 To Allah belongs everything in the
heavens and everything on earth.
We have instructed those who were
given the Book before you, and you,
to be conscious of Allah. But if you
refuse—to Allah belongs everything
in the heavens and everything on

earth. Allah is in no need,
Praiseworthy.

١٣٢ وَلِلَّهِ مَا فِى ٱلسَّمَٰوَٰتِ وَمَا فِى ٱلْأَرْضِ ۚ
وَكَفَىٰ بِٱللَّهِ وَكِيلًا

132 To Allah belongs everything in the heavens and everything on earth. Allah suffices as Manager.

١٣٣ إِن يَشَأْ يُذْهِبْكُمْ أَيُّهَا ٱلنَّاسُ وَيَأْتِ
بِـَٔاخَرِينَ ۚ وَكَانَ ٱللَّهُ عَلَىٰ ذَٰلِكَ قَدِيرًا

133 If He wills, He can do away with you, O people, and bring others. Allah is Able to do that.

١٣٤ مَّن كَانَ يُرِيدُ ثَوَابَ ٱلدُّنْيَا فَعِندَ ٱللَّهِ ثَوَابُ
ٱلدُّنْيَا وَٱلْـَٔاخِرَةِ ۚ وَكَانَ ٱللَّهُ سَمِيعًۢا بَصِيرًا

134 Whoever desires the reward of this world—with Allah is the reward of this world and the next. Allah is All-Hearing, All-Seeing.

١٣٥ يَـٰٓأَيُّهَا ٱلَّذِينَ ءَامَنُوا۟ كُونُوا۟ قَوَّٰمِينَ بِٱلْقِسْطِ
شُهَدَآءَ لِلَّهِ وَلَوْ عَلَىٰٓ أَنفُسِكُمْ أَوِ ٱلْوَٰلِدَيْنِ
وَٱلْأَقْرَبِينَ ۚ إِن يَكُنْ غَنِيًّا أَوْ فَقِيرًا فَٱللَّهُ أَوْلَىٰ
بِهِمَا ۖ فَلَا تَتَّبِعُوا۟ ٱلْهَوَىٰٓ أَن تَعْدِلُوا۟ ۚ وَإِن تَلْوُۥٓا۟ أَوْ
تُعْرِضُوا۟ فَإِنَّ ٱللَّهَ كَانَ بِمَا تَعْمَلُونَ خَبِيرًا

135 O you who believe! Stand firmly for justice, as witnesses to Allah, even if against yourselves, or your parents, or your relatives. Whether one is rich or poor, Allah takes care of both. So do not follow your desires, lest you swerve. If you deviate, or turn away—then Allah is Aware of what you do.

١٣٦ يَـٰٓأَيُّهَا ٱلَّذِينَ ءَامَنُوٓا۟ ءَامِنُوا۟ بِٱللَّهِ وَرَسُولِهِۦ
وَٱلْكِتَـٰبِ ٱلَّذِى نَزَّلَ عَلَىٰ رَسُولِهِۦ وَٱلْكِتَـٰبِ ٱلَّذِىٓ
أَنزَلَ مِن قَبْلُ ۚ وَمَن يَكْفُرْ بِٱللَّهِ وَمَلَـٰٓئِكَتِهِۦ
وَكُتُبِهِۦ وَرُسُلِهِۦ وَٱلْيَوْمِ ٱلْـَٔاخِرِ فَقَدْ ضَلَّ
ضَلَـٰلًۢا بَعِيدًا

136 O you who believe! Believe in Allah and His messenger, and the Book He sent down to His messenger, and the Book He sent down before. Whoever rejects Allah, His angels, His Books, His messengers, and the Last Day, has strayed far in error.

١٣٧ إِنَّ ٱلَّذِينَ ءَامَنُوا۟ ثُمَّ كَفَرُوا۟ ثُمَّ ءَامَنُوا۟ ثُمَّ
كَفَرُوا۟ ثُمَّ ٱزْدَادُوا۟ كُفْرًا لَّمْ يَكُنِ ٱللَّهُ لِيَغْفِرَ لَهُمْ
وَلَا لِيَهْدِيَهُمْ سَبِيلًۢا

137 Those who believe, then disbelieve, then believe, then disbelieve, then increase in disbelief, Allah will not forgive them, nor will He guide them to a way.

١٣٨ بَشِّرِ ٱلْمُنَـٰفِقِينَ بِأَنَّ لَهُمْ عَذَابًا أَلِيمًا

138 Inform the hypocrites that they will have a painful punishment.

١٣٩ ٱلَّذِينَ يَتَّخِذُونَ ٱلْكَـٰفِرِينَ أَوْلِيَآءَ مِن دُونِ
ٱلْمُؤْمِنِينَ ۚ أَيَبْتَغُونَ عِندَهُمُ ٱلْعِزَّةَ فَإِنَّ ٱلْعِزَّةَ
لِلَّهِ جَمِيعًا

139 Those who ally themselves with the disbelievers instead of the believers. Do they seek glory in them? All glory belongs to Allah.

١٤٠ وَقَدْ نَزَّلَ عَلَيْكُمْ فِى ٱلْكِتَٰبِ أَنْ إِذَا سَمِعْتُمْ
ءَايَٰتِ ٱللَّهِ يُكْفَرُ بِهَا وَيُسْتَهْزَأُ بِهَا فَلَا تَقْعُدُوا۟
مَعَهُمْ حَتَّىٰ يَخُوضُوا۟ فِى حَدِيثٍ غَيْرِهِۦٓ ۚ إِنَّكُمْ
إِذًا مِّثْلُهُمْ ۗ إِنَّ ٱللَّهَ جَامِعُ ٱلْمُنَٰفِقِينَ وَٱلْكَٰفِرِينَ
فِى جَهَنَّمَ جَمِيعًا

140 He has revealed to you in the Book that when you hear Allah's revelations being rejected, or ridiculed, do not sit with them until they engage in some other subject. Otherwise, you would be like them. Allah will gather the hypocrites and the disbelievers, into Hell, altogether.

١٤١ ٱلَّذِينَ يَتَرَبَّصُونَ بِكُمْ فَإِن كَانَ لَكُمْ فَتْحٌ
مِّنَ ٱللَّهِ قَالُوٓا۟ أَلَمْ نَكُن مَّعَكُمْ وَإِن كَانَ لِلْكَٰفِرِينَ
نَصِيبٌ قَالُوٓا۟ أَلَمْ نَسْتَحْوِذْ عَلَيْكُمْ وَنَمْنَعْكُم مِّنَ
ٱلْمُؤْمِنِينَ ۚ فَٱللَّهُ يَحْكُمُ بَيْنَكُمْ يَوْمَ ٱلْقِيَٰمَةِ ۗ وَلَن
يَجْعَلَ ٱللَّهُ لِلْكَٰفِرِينَ عَلَى ٱلْمُؤْمِنِينَ سَبِيلًا

141 Those who lie in wait for you: if you attain victory from Allah, they say, "Were we not with you?" But if the disbelievers get a turn, they say, "Did we not side with you, and defend you from the believers?" Allah will judge between you on the Day of Resurrection; and Allah will give the disbelievers no means of overcoming the believers.

١٤٢ إِنَّ ٱلْمُنَٰفِقِينَ يُخَٰدِعُونَ ٱللَّهَ وَهُوَ خَٰدِعُهُمْ
وَإِذَا قَامُوٓا۟ إِلَى ٱلصَّلَوٰةِ قَامُوا۟ كُسَالَىٰ يُرَآءُونَ
ٱلنَّاسَ وَلَا يَذْكُرُونَ ٱللَّهَ إِلَّا قَلِيلًا

142 The hypocrites try to deceive Allah, but He is deceiving them. And when they stand for prayer, they stand lazily, showing off in front of people, and remembering Allah only a little.

١٤٣ مُّذَبْذَبِينَ بَيْنَ ذَٰلِكَ لَآ إِلَىٰ هَٰٓؤُلَآءِ وَلَآ إِلَىٰ
هَٰٓؤُلَآءِ ۚ وَمَن يُضْلِلِ ٱللَّهُ فَلَن تَجِدَ لَهُۥ سَبِيلًا

143 Wavering in between, neither with these, nor with those. Whomever Allah sends astray, you will never find for him a way.

١٤٤ يَٰٓأَيُّهَا ٱلَّذِينَ ءَامَنُوا۟ لَا تَتَّخِذُوا۟ ٱلْكَٰفِرِينَ
أَوْلِيَآءَ مِن دُونِ ٱلْمُؤْمِنِينَ ۚ أَتُرِيدُونَ أَن
تَجْعَلُوا۟ لِلَّهِ عَلَيْكُمْ سُلْطَٰنًا مُّبِينًا

144 O you who believe! Do not befriend disbelievers rather than believers. Do you want to give Allah a clear case against you?

١٤٥ إِنَّ ٱلْمُنَٰفِقِينَ فِى ٱلدَّرْكِ ٱلْأَسْفَلِ مِنَ ٱلنَّارِ
وَلَن تَجِدَ لَهُمْ نَصِيرًا

145 The hypocrites will be in the lowest level of the Fire, and you will find no helper for them.

١٤٦ إِلَّا ٱلَّذِينَ تَابُوا۟ وَأَصْلَحُوا۟ وَٱعْتَصَمُوا۟ بِٱللَّهِ
وَأَخْلَصُوا۟ دِينَهُمْ لِلَّهِ فَأُو۟لَٰٓئِكَ مَعَ ٱلْمُؤْمِنِينَ ۖ
وَسَوْفَ يُؤْتِ ٱللَّهُ ٱلْمُؤْمِنِينَ أَجْرًا عَظِيمًا

146 Except those who repent, and reform, and hold fast to Allah, and dedicate their religion to Allah alone. These are with the believers; and

Allah will give the believers a great reward.

١٤٧ مَّا يَفْعَلُ ٱللَّهُ بِعَذَابِكُمْ إِن شَكَرْتُمْ
وَءَامَنتُمْ ۚ وَكَانَ ٱللَّهُ شَاكِرًا عَلِيمًا

147 What would Allah accomplish by your punishment, if you have given thanks, and have believed? Allah is Appreciative and Cognizant.

١٤٨ لَّا يُحِبُّ ٱللَّهُ ٱلْجَهْرَ بِٱلسُّوٓءِ مِنَ ٱلْقَوْلِ إِلَّا
مَن ظُلِمَ ۚ وَكَانَ ٱللَّهُ سَمِيعًا عَلِيمًا

148 Allah does not like the public uttering of bad language, unless someone was wronged. Allah is Hearing and Knowing.

١٤٩ إِن تُبْدُوا۟ خَيْرًا أَوْ تُخْفُوهُ أَوْ تَعْفُوا۟ عَن
سُوٓءٍ فَإِنَّ ٱللَّهَ كَانَ عَفُوًّا قَدِيرًا

149 If you let a good deed be shown, or conceal it, or pardon an offense—Allah is Pardoning and Capable.

١٥٠ إِنَّ ٱلَّذِينَ يَكْفُرُونَ بِٱللَّهِ وَرُسُلِهِۦ وَيُرِيدُونَ
أَن يُفَرِّقُوا۟ بَيْنَ ٱللَّهِ وَرُسُلِهِۦ وَيَقُولُونَ نُؤْمِنُ
بِبَعْضٍ وَنَكْفُرُ بِبَعْضٍ وَيُرِيدُونَ أَن يَتَّخِذُوا۟
بَيْنَ ذَٰلِكَ سَبِيلًا

150 Those who disbelieve in Allah and His messengers, and want to separate between Allah and His messengers, and say, "We believe in some, and reject some," and wish to take a path in between.

١٥١ أُو۟لَٰٓئِكَ هُمُ ٱلْكَٰفِرُونَ حَقًّا ۚ وَأَعْتَدْنَا لِلْكَٰفِرِينَ
عَذَابًا مُّهِينًا

151 These are the unbelievers, truly. We have prepared for the unbelievers a shameful punishment.

١٥٢ وَٱلَّذِينَ ءَامَنُوا۟ بِٱللَّهِ وَرُسُلِهِۦ وَلَمْ يُفَرِّقُوا۟
بَيْنَ أَحَدٍ مِّنْهُمْ أُو۟لَٰٓئِكَ سَوْفَ يُؤْتِيهِمْ أُجُورَهُمْ ۗ
وَكَانَ ٱللَّهُ غَفُورًا رَّحِيمًا

152 As for those who believe in Allah and His messengers, and make no distinction between any of them—He will give them their rewards. Allah is Forgiver and Merciful.

١٥٣ يَسْـَٔلُكَ أَهْلُ ٱلْكِتَٰبِ أَن تُنَزِّلَ عَلَيْهِمْ كِتَٰبًا
مِّنَ ٱلسَّمَآءِ ۚ فَقَدْ سَأَلُوا۟ مُوسَىٰٓ أَكْبَرَ مِن ذَٰلِكَ
فَقَالُوٓا۟ أَرِنَا ٱللَّهَ جَهْرَةً فَأَخَذَتْهُمُ ٱلصَّٰعِقَةُ
بِظُلْمِهِمْ ۚ ثُمَّ ٱتَّخَذُوا۟ ٱلْعِجْلَ مِنۢ بَعْدِ مَا
جَآءَتْهُمُ ٱلْبَيِّنَٰتُ فَعَفَوْنَا عَن ذَٰلِكَ ۚ وَءَاتَيْنَا
مُوسَىٰ سُلْطَٰنًا مُّبِينًا

153 The People of the Scripture challenge you to bring down to them a book from the sky. They had asked Moses for something even greater. They said, "Show us Allah plainly." The thunderbolt struck them for their wickedness. Then they took the calf for worship, even after the clear proofs had come to them. Yet We pardoned that, and We gave Moses a clear authority.

١٥٤ وَرَفَعْنَا فَوْقَهُمُ ٱلطُّورَ بِمِيثَٰقِهِمْ وَقُلْنَا لَهُمُ
ٱدْخُلُوا۟ ٱلْبَابَ سُجَّدًا وَقُلْنَا لَهُمْ لَا تَعْدُوا۟ فِى
ٱلسَّبْتِ وَأَخَذْنَا مِنْهُم مِّيثَٰقًا غَلِيظًا

154 And We raised the Mount above them in accordance with their covenant, and We said to them, "Enter the gate humbly", and We said to them, "Do not violate the Sabbath", and We received from them a solemn pledge.

١٥٥ فَبِمَا نَقْضِهِم مِّيثَٰقَهُمْ وَكُفْرِهِم بِـَٔايَٰتِ ٱللَّهِ
وَقَتْلِهِمُ ٱلْأَنۢبِيَآءَ بِغَيْرِ حَقٍّ وَقَوْلِهِمْ قُلُوبُنَا
غُلْفٌۢ ۚ بَلْ طَبَعَ ٱللَّهُ عَلَيْهَا بِكُفْرِهِمْ فَلَا يُؤْمِنُونَ
إِلَّا قَلِيلًا

155 But for their violation of their covenant, and their denial of Allah's revelations, and their killing of the prophets unjustly, and their saying, "Our minds are closed." In fact, Allah has sealed them for their disbelief, so they do not believe, except for a few.

١٥٦ وَبِكُفْرِهِمْ وَقَوْلِهِمْ عَلَىٰ مَرْيَمَ بُهْتَٰنًا عَظِيمًا

156 And for their faithlessness, and their saying against Mary a monstrous slander.

١٥٧ وَقَوْلِهِمْ إِنَّا قَتَلْنَا ٱلْمَسِيحَ عِيسَى ٱبْنَ
مَرْيَمَ رَسُولَ ٱللَّهِ وَمَا قَتَلُوهُ وَمَا صَلَبُوهُ وَلَٰكِن
شُبِّهَ لَهُمْ ۚ وَإِنَّ ٱلَّذِينَ ٱخْتَلَفُوا۟ فِيهِ لَفِى شَكٍّ
مِّنْهُ ۚ مَا لَهُم بِهِۦ مِنْ عِلْمٍ إِلَّا ٱتِّبَاعَ ٱلظَّنِّ ۚ وَمَا
قَتَلُوهُ يَقِينًۢا

157 And for their saying, "We have killed the Messiah, Jesus, the son of Mary, the Messenger of Allah." In fact, they did not kill him, nor did they crucify him, but it appeared to them as if they did. Indeed, those who differ about him are in doubt about it. They have no knowledge of it, except the following of assumptions. Certainly, they did not kill him.

١٥٨ بَل رَّفَعَهُ ٱللَّهُ إِلَيْهِ ۚ وَكَانَ ٱللَّهُ عَزِيزًا حَكِيمًا

158 Rather, Allah raised him up to Himself. Allah is Mighty and Wise.

١٥٩ وَإِن مِّنْ أَهْلِ ٱلْكِتَٰبِ إِلَّا لَيُؤْمِنَنَّ بِهِۦ قَبْلَ
مَوْتِهِۦ ۖ وَيَوْمَ ٱلْقِيَٰمَةِ يَكُونُ عَلَيْهِمْ شَهِيدًا

159 There is none from the People of the Scripture but will believe in him before his death, and on the Day of Resurrection he will be a witness against them.

١٦٠ فَبِظُلْمٍ مِّنَ ٱلَّذِينَ هَادُوا۟ حَرَّمْنَا عَلَيْهِمْ
طَيِّبَٰتٍ أُحِلَّتْ لَهُمْ وَبِصَدِّهِمْ عَن سَبِيلِ ٱللَّهِ
كَثِيرًا

160 Due to wrongdoing on the part of the Jews, We forbade them good things that used to be lawful for them; and for deterring many from Allah's path.

١٦١ وَأَخْذِهِمُ ٱلرِّبَوٰا۟ وَقَدْ نُهُوا۟ عَنْهُ وَأَكْلِهِمْ
أَمْوَٰلَ ٱلنَّاسِ بِٱلْبَٰطِلِ ۚ وَأَعْتَدْنَا لِلْكَٰفِرِينَ مِنْهُمْ
عَذَابًا أَلِيمًا

161 And for their taking usury, although they were forbidden it; and for their consuming people's wealth dishonestly. We have prepared for the faithless among them a painful torment.

١٦٢ لَّٰكِنِ ٱلرَّٰسِخُونَ فِى ٱلْعِلْمِ مِنْهُمْ وَٱلْمُؤْمِنُونَ
يُؤْمِنُونَ بِمَآ أُنزِلَ إِلَيْكَ وَمَآ أُنزِلَ مِن قَبْلِكَ ۚ
وَٱلْمُقِيمِينَ ٱلصَّلَوٰةَ ۚ وَٱلْمُؤْتُونَ ٱلزَّكَوٰةَ
وَٱلْمُؤْمِنُونَ بِٱللَّهِ وَٱلْيَوْمِ ٱلْءَاخِرِ أُو۟لَٰٓئِكَ
سَنُؤْتِيهِمْ أَجْرًا عَظِيمًا

162 But those among them firmly rooted in knowledge, and the believers, believe in what was revealed to you, and in what was revealed before you; and the observers of prayers, and the givers of charity, and the believers in Allah and the Last Day—upon these We will bestow an immense reward.

١٦٣ إِنَّآ أَوْحَيْنَآ إِلَيْكَ كَمَآ أَوْحَيْنَآ إِلَىٰ نُوحٍ
وَٱلنَّبِيِّۦنَ مِنۢ بَعْدِهِۦ ۚ وَأَوْحَيْنَآ إِلَىٰٓ إِبْرَٰهِيمَ
وَإِسْمَٰعِيلَ وَإِسْحَٰقَ وَيَعْقُوبَ وَٱلْأَسْبَاطِ
وَعِيسَىٰ وَأَيُّوبَ وَيُونُسَ وَهَٰرُونَ وَسُلَيْمَٰنَ ۚ
وَءَاتَيْنَا دَاوُۥدَ زَبُورًا

163 We have inspired you, as We had inspired Noah and the prophets after him. And We inspired Abraham, and Ishmael, and Isaac, and Jacob, and the Patriarchs, and Jesus, and Job, and Jonah, and Aaron, and Solomon. And We gave David the Psalms.

١٦٤ وَرُسُلًا قَدْ قَصَصْنَٰهُمْ عَلَيْكَ مِن قَبْلُ
وَرُسُلًا لَّمْ نَقْصُصْهُمْ عَلَيْكَ ۚ وَكَلَّمَ ٱللَّهُ مُوسَىٰ
تَكْلِيمًا

164 Some messengers We have already told you about, while some messengers We have not told you about. And Allah spoke to Moses directly.

١٦٥ رُّسُلًا مُّبَشِّرِينَ وَمُنذِرِينَ لِئَلَّا يَكُونَ لِلنَّاسِ
عَلَى ٱللَّهِ حُجَّةٌۢ بَعْدَ ٱلرُّسُلِ ۚ وَكَانَ ٱللَّهُ عَزِيزًا
حَكِيمًا

165 Messengers delivering good news, and bringing warnings; so that people may have no excuse before Allah after the coming of the messengers. Allah is Powerful and Wise.

١٦٦ لَّٰكِنِ ٱللَّهُ يَشْهَدُ بِمَآ أَنزَلَ إِلَيْكَ ۖ أَنزَلَهُۥ
بِعِلْمِهِۦ ۖ وَٱلْمَلَٰٓئِكَةُ يَشْهَدُونَ ۚ وَكَفَىٰ بِٱللَّهِ شَهِيدًا

166 But Allah bears witness to what He revealed to you. He revealed it with His knowledge. And the angels bear witness. Though Allah is a sufficient witness.

١٦٧ إِنَّ ٱلَّذِينَ كَفَرُوا۟ وَصَدُّوا۟ عَن سَبِيلِ ٱللَّهِ قَدْ
ضَلُّوا۟ ضَلَٰلًۢا بَعِيدًا

167 Those who disbelieve and repel from Allah's path have gone far astray.

١٦٨ إِنَّ ٱلَّذِينَ كَفَرُوا۟ وَظَلَمُوا۟ لَمْ يَكُنِ ٱللَّهُ لِيَغْفِرَ
لَهُمْ وَلَا لِيَهْدِيَهُمْ طَرِيقًا

168 Those who disbelieve and transgress; Allah is not about to forgive them, nor will He guide them to any path.

١٦٩ إِلَّا طَرِيقَ جَهَنَّمَ خَٰلِدِينَ فِيهَآ أَبَدًا ۚ وَكَانَ
ذَٰلِكَ عَلَى ٱللَّهِ يَسِيرًا

169 Except to the path of Hell, where they will dwell forever. And that is easy for Allah.

١٧٠ يَٰٓأَيُّهَا ٱلنَّاسُ قَدْ جَآءَكُمُ ٱلرَّسُولُ بِٱلْحَقِّ
مِن رَّبِّكُمْ فَـَٔامِنُوا۟ خَيْرًا لَّكُمْ ۚ وَإِن تَكْفُرُوا۟ فَإِنَّ
لِلَّهِ مَا فِى ٱلسَّمَٰوَٰتِ وَٱلْأَرْضِ ۚ وَكَانَ ٱللَّهُ عَلِيمًا
حَكِيمًا

170 O people! The Messenger has come to you with the truth from your Lord, so believe—that is best for you. But if you disbelieve, to Allah belongs everything in the heavens and the earth. Allah is Omniscient and Wise.

١٧١ يَٰٓأَهْلَ ٱلْكِتَٰبِ لَا تَغْلُوا۟ فِى دِينِكُمْ وَلَا تَقُولُوا۟
عَلَى ٱللَّهِ إِلَّا ٱلْحَقَّ ۚ إِنَّمَا ٱلْمَسِيحُ عِيسَى ٱبْنُ
مَرْيَمَ رَسُولُ ٱللَّهِ وَكَلِمَتُهُۥٓ أَلْقَىٰهَآ إِلَىٰ مَرْيَمَ
وَرُوحٌ مِّنْهُ ۖ فَـَٔامِنُوا۟ بِٱللَّهِ وَرُسُلِهِۦ ۖ وَلَا تَقُولُوا۟
ثَلَٰثَةٌ ۚ ٱنتَهُوا۟ خَيْرًا لَّكُمْ ۚ إِنَّمَا ٱللَّهُ إِلَٰهٌ وَٰحِدٌ ۖ
سُبْحَٰنَهُۥٓ أَن يَكُونَ لَهُۥ وَلَدٌ ۘ لَّهُۥ مَا فِى ٱلسَّمَٰوَٰتِ
وَمَا فِى ٱلْأَرْضِ ۗ وَكَفَىٰ بِٱللَّهِ وَكِيلًا

171 O People of the Scripture! Do not exaggerate in your religion, and do not say about Allah except the truth. The Messiah, Jesus, the son of Mary, is the Messenger of Allah, and His Word that He conveyed to Mary, and a Spirit from Him. So believe in Allah and His messengers, and do not say, "Three." Refrain—it is better for you. Allah is only one God. Glory be to Him—that He should have a son. To Him belongs everything in the heavens and the earth, and Allah is a sufficient Protector.

١٧٢ لَّن يَسْتَنكِفَ ٱلْمَسِيحُ أَن يَكُونَ عَبْدًا لِّلَّهِ
وَلَا ٱلْمَلَٰٓئِكَةُ ٱلْمُقَرَّبُونَ ۚ وَمَن يَسْتَنكِفْ عَنْ
عِبَادَتِهِۦ وَيَسْتَكْبِرْ فَسَيَحْشُرُهُمْ إِلَيْهِ جَمِيعًا

172 The Messiah does not disdain to be a servant of Allah, nor do the favored angels. Whoever disdains His worship, and is too arrogant—He will round them up to Himself altogether.

١٧٣ فَأَمَّا ٱلَّذِينَ ءَامَنُوا۟ وَعَمِلُوا۟ ٱلصَّٰلِحَٰتِ
فَيُوَفِّيهِمْ أُجُورَهُمْ وَيَزِيدُهُم مِّن فَضْلِهِۦ ۖ وَأَمَّا
ٱلَّذِينَ ٱسْتَنكَفُوا۟ وَٱسْتَكْبَرُوا۟ فَيُعَذِّبُهُمْ عَذَابًا

173 But as for those who believe and do good works, He will pay them their wages in full, and will increase His grace for them. But as for those who disdain and are too proud, He

أَلِيمًا وَلَا يَجِدُونَ لَهُم مِّن دُونِ ٱللَّهِ وَلِيًّا وَلَا
نَصِيرًا

will punish them with an agonizing punishment. And they will find for themselves, apart from Allah, no lord and no savior.

١٧٤ يَٰٓأَيُّهَا ٱلنَّاسُ قَدْ جَآءَكُم بُرْهَٰنٌ مِّن رَّبِّكُمْ
وَأَنزَلْنَآ إِلَيْكُمْ نُورًا مُّبِينًا

174 O people! A proof has come to you from your Lord, and We sent down to you a clear light.

١٧٥ فَأَمَّا ٱلَّذِينَ ءَامَنُوا۟ بِٱللَّهِ وَٱعْتَصَمُوا۟ بِهِۦ
فَسَيُدْخِلُهُمْ فِى رَحْمَةٍ مِّنْهُ وَفَضْلٍ وَيَهْدِيهِمْ
إِلَيْهِ صِرَٰطًا مُّسْتَقِيمًا

175 As for those who believe in Allah, and hold fast to Him, He will admit them into mercy and grace from Him, and will guide them to Himself in a straight path.

١٧٦ يَسْتَفْتُونَكَ قُلِ ٱللَّهُ يُفْتِيكُمْ فِى ٱلْكَلَٰلَةِ ۚ إِنِ
ٱمْرُؤٌا۟ هَلَكَ لَيْسَ لَهُۥ وَلَدٌ وَلَهُۥٓ أُخْتٌ فَلَهَا نِصْفُ
مَا تَرَكَ ۚ وَهُوَ يَرِثُهَآ إِن لَّمْ يَكُن لَّهَا وَلَدٌ ۚ فَإِن
كَانَتَا ٱثْنَتَيْنِ فَلَهُمَا ٱلثُّلُثَانِ مِمَّا تَرَكَ ۚ وَإِن كَانُوٓا۟
إِخْوَةً رِّجَالًا وَنِسَآءً فَلِلذَّكَرِ مِثْلُ حَظِّ
ٱلْأُنثَيَيْنِ ۗ يُبَيِّنُ ٱللَّهُ لَكُمْ أَن تَضِلُّوا۟ ۗ وَٱللَّهُ بِكُلِّ
شَىْءٍ عَلِيمٌۢ

176 They ask you for a ruling. Say, "Allah gives you a ruling concerning the person who has neither parents nor children." If a man dies, and leaves no children, and he had a sister, she receives one-half of what he leaves. And he inherits from her if she leaves no children. But if there are two sisters, they receive two-thirds of what he leaves. If the siblings are men and women, the male receives the share of two females." Allah makes things clear for you, lest you err. Allah is Aware of everything.

5 The Table المائدة

بِسْمِ ٱللَّهِ ٱلرَّحْمَٰنِ ٱلرَّحِيمِ

In the name of Allah, the Gracious, the Merciful.

١ يَٰٓأَيُّهَا ٱلَّذِينَ ءَامَنُوٓا۟ أَوْفُوا۟ بِٱلْعُقُودِ ۚ أُحِلَّتْ
لَكُم بَهِيمَةُ ٱلْأَنْعَٰمِ إِلَّا مَا يُتْلَىٰ عَلَيْكُمْ غَيْرَ
مُحِلِّى ٱلصَّيْدِ وَأَنتُمْ حُرُمٌ ۗ إِنَّ ٱللَّهَ يَحْكُمُ مَا
يُرِيدُ

1 O you who believe! Fulfill your commitments. Livestock animals are permitted for you, except those specified to you; but not wild game while you are in pilgrim sanctity. Allah decrees whatever He wills.

٢ يَٰٓأَيُّهَا ٱلَّذِينَ ءَامَنُوا۟ لَا تُحِلُّوا۟ شَعَٰٓئِرَ ٱللَّهِ وَلَا
ٱلشَّهْرَ ٱلْحَرَامَ وَلَا ٱلْهَدْىَ وَلَا ٱلْقَلَٰٓئِدَ وَلَآ ءَآمِّينَ

2 O you who believe! Do not violate Allah's sacraments, nor the Sacred Month, nor the offerings, nor the

ٱلْبَيْتَ ٱلْحَرَامَ يَبْتَغُونَ فَضْلًا مِّن رَّبِّهِمْ
وَرِضْوَٰنًا ۚ وَإِذَا حَلَلْتُمْ فَٱصْطَادُوا۟ ۚ وَلَا
يَجْرِمَنَّكُمْ شَنَـَٔانُ قَوْمٍ أَن صَدُّوكُمْ عَنِ
ٱلْمَسْجِدِ ٱلْحَرَامِ أَن تَعْتَدُوا۟ ۘ وَتَعَاوَنُوا۟ عَلَى
ٱلْبِرِّ وَٱلتَّقْوَىٰ ۖ وَلَا تَعَاوَنُوا۟ عَلَى ٱلْإِثْمِ
وَٱلْعُدْوَٰنِ ۚ وَٱتَّقُوا۟ ٱللَّهَ ۖ إِنَّ ٱللَّهَ شَدِيدُ ٱلْعِقَابِ

garlanded, nor those heading for the Sacred House seeking blessings from their Lord and approval. When you have left the pilgrim sanctity, you may hunt. And let not the hatred of people who barred you from the Sacred Mosque incite you to aggression. And cooperate with one another in virtuous conduct and conscience, and do not cooperate with one another in sin and hostility. And fear Allah. Allah is severe in punishment.

٣ حُرِّمَتْ عَلَيْكُمُ ٱلْمَيْتَةُ وَٱلدَّمُ وَلَحْمُ ٱلْخِنزِيرِ
وَمَآ أُهِلَّ لِغَيْرِ ٱللَّهِ بِهِۦ وَٱلْمُنْخَنِقَةُ وَٱلْمَوْقُوذَةُ
وَٱلْمُتَرَدِّيَةُ وَٱلنَّطِيحَةُ وَمَآ أَكَلَ ٱلسَّبُعُ إِلَّا مَا
ذَكَّيْتُمْ وَمَا ذُبِحَ عَلَى ٱلنُّصُبِ وَأَن تَسْتَقْسِمُوا۟
بِٱلْأَزْلَـٰمِ ۚ ذَٰلِكُمْ فِسْقٌ ۗ ٱلْيَوْمَ يَئِسَ ٱلَّذِينَ كَفَرُوا۟
مِن دِينِكُمْ فَلَا تَخْشَوْهُمْ وَٱخْشَوْنِ ۚ ٱلْيَوْمَ
أَكْمَلْتُ لَكُمْ دِينَكُمْ وَأَتْمَمْتُ عَلَيْكُمْ نِعْمَتِى
وَرَضِيتُ لَكُمُ ٱلْإِسْلَـٰمَ دِينًا ۚ فَمَنِ ٱضْطُرَّ فِى
مَخْمَصَةٍ غَيْرَ مُتَجَانِفٍ لِّإِثْمٍ ۙ فَإِنَّ ٱللَّهَ غَفُورٌ
رَّحِيمٌ

3 Prohibited for you are carrion, blood, the flesh of swine, and animals dedicated to other than Allah; also the flesh of animals strangled, killed violently, killed by a fall, gored to death, mangled by wild animals—except what you rescue, and animals sacrificed on altars; and the practice of drawing lots. For it is immoral. Today, those who disbelieve have despaired of your religion, so do not fear them, but fear Me. Today I have perfected your religion for you, and have completed My favor upon you, and have approved Islam as a religion for you. But whoever is compelled by hunger, with no intent of wrongdoing—Allah is Forgiving and Merciful.

٤ يَسْـَٔلُونَكَ مَاذَآ أُحِلَّ لَهُمْ ۖ قُلْ أُحِلَّ لَكُمُ
ٱلطَّيِّبَـٰتُ ۙ وَمَا عَلَّمْتُم مِّنَ ٱلْجَوَارِحِ مُكَلِّبِينَ
تُعَلِّمُونَهُنَّ مِمَّا عَلَّمَكُمُ ٱللَّهُ ۖ فَكُلُوا۟ مِمَّآ أَمْسَكْنَ
عَلَيْكُمْ وَٱذْكُرُوا۟ ٱسْمَ ٱللَّهِ عَلَيْهِ ۖ وَٱتَّقُوا۟ ٱللَّهَ ۚ إِنَّ
ٱللَّهَ سَرِيعُ ٱلْحِسَابِ

4 They ask you what is permitted for them. Say, “Permitted for you are all good things, including what trained dogs and falcons catch for you.” You train them according to what Allah has taught you. So eat from what they catch for you, and pronounce Allah’s name over it. And fear Allah. Allah is Swift in reckoning.

٥ ٱلْيَوْمَ أُحِلَّ لَكُمُ ٱلطَّيِّبَٰتُ ۖ وَطَعَامُ ٱلَّذِينَ
أُوتُوا۟ ٱلْكِتَٰبَ حِلٌّ لَّكُمْ وَطَعَامُكُمْ حِلٌّ لَّهُمْ ۖ
وَٱلْمُحْصَنَٰتُ مِنَ ٱلْمُؤْمِنَٰتِ وَٱلْمُحْصَنَٰتُ مِنَ
ٱلَّذِينَ أُوتُوا۟ ٱلْكِتَٰبَ مِن قَبْلِكُمْ إِذَآ ءَاتَيْتُمُوهُنَّ
أُجُورَهُنَّ مُحْصِنِينَ غَيْرَ مُسَٰفِحِينَ وَلَا
مُتَّخِذِىٓ أَخْدَانٍ ۗ وَمَن يَكْفُرْ بِٱلْإِيمَٰنِ فَقَدْ حَبِطَ
عَمَلُهُۥ وَهُوَ فِى ٱلْءَاخِرَةِ مِنَ ٱلْخَٰسِرِينَ

5 Today all good things are made lawful for you. And the food of those given the Scripture is lawful for you, and your food is lawful for them. So are chaste believing women, and chaste women from the people who were given the Scripture before you, provided you give them their dowries, and take them in marriage, not in adultery, nor as mistresses. But whoever rejects faith, his work will be in vain, and in the Hereafter he will be among the losers.

٦ يَٰٓأَيُّهَا ٱلَّذِينَ ءَامَنُوٓا۟ إِذَا قُمْتُمْ إِلَى ٱلصَّلَوٰةِ
فَٱغْسِلُوا۟ وُجُوهَكُمْ وَأَيْدِيَكُمْ إِلَى ٱلْمَرَافِقِ
وَٱمْسَحُوا۟ بِرُءُوسِكُمْ وَأَرْجُلَكُمْ إِلَى ٱلْكَعْبَيْنِ ۚ
وَإِن كُنتُمْ جُنُبًا فَٱطَّهَّرُوا۟ ۚ وَإِن كُنتُم مَّرْضَىٰٓ أَوْ
عَلَىٰ سَفَرٍ أَوْ جَآءَ أَحَدٌ مِّنكُم مِّنَ ٱلْغَآئِطِ أَوْ
لَٰمَسْتُمُ ٱلنِّسَآءَ فَلَمْ تَجِدُوا۟ مَآءً فَتَيَمَّمُوا۟
صَعِيدًا طَيِّبًا فَٱمْسَحُوا۟ بِوُجُوهِكُمْ وَأَيْدِيكُم
مِّنْهُ ۚ مَا يُرِيدُ ٱللَّهُ لِيَجْعَلَ عَلَيْكُم مِّنْ حَرَجٍ
وَلَٰكِن يُرِيدُ لِيُطَهِّرَكُمْ وَلِيُتِمَّ نِعْمَتَهُۥ عَلَيْكُمْ
لَعَلَّكُمْ تَشْكُرُونَ

6 O you who believe! When you rise to pray, wash your faces and your hands and arms to the elbows, and wipe your heads, and your feet to the ankles. If you had intercourse, then purify yourselves. If you are ill, or travelling, or one of you returns from the toilet, or you had contact with women, and could not find water, then use some clean sand and wipe your faces and hands with it. Allah does not intend to burden you, but He intends to purify you, and to complete His blessing upon you, that you may be thankful.

٧ وَٱذْكُرُوا۟ نِعْمَةَ ٱللَّهِ عَلَيْكُمْ وَمِيثَٰقَهُ ٱلَّذِى
وَاثَقَكُم بِهِۦٓ إِذْ قُلْتُمْ سَمِعْنَا وَأَطَعْنَا ۖ وَٱتَّقُوا۟
ٱللَّهَ ۚ إِنَّ ٱللَّهَ عَلِيمٌۢ بِذَاتِ ٱلصُّدُورِ

7 And Remember Allah's blessings upon you, and His covenant which He covenanted with you; when you said, "We hear and we obey." And remain conscious of Allah, for Allah knows what the hearts contain.

٨ يَٰٓأَيُّهَا ٱلَّذِينَ ءَامَنُوا۟ كُونُوا۟ قَوَّٰمِينَ لِلَّهِ
شُهَدَآءَ بِٱلْقِسْطِ ۖ وَلَا يَجْرِمَنَّكُمْ شَنَـَٔانُ قَوْمٍ
عَلَىٰٓ أَلَّا تَعْدِلُوا۟ ۚ ٱعْدِلُوا۟ هُوَ أَقْرَبُ لِلتَّقْوَىٰ ۖ
وَٱتَّقُوا۟ ٱللَّهَ ۚ إِنَّ ٱللَّهَ خَبِيرٌۢ بِمَا تَعْمَلُونَ

8 O you who believe! Be upright to Allah, witnessing with justice; and let not the hatred of a certain people prevent you from acting justly. Adhere to justice, for that is nearer to piety; and fear Allah. Allah is informed of what you do.

٩ وَعَدَ ٱللَّهُ ٱلَّذِينَ ءَامَنُوا۟ وَعَمِلُوا۟ ٱلصَّٰلِحَٰتِ ۙ
لَهُم مَّغْفِرَةٌ وَأَجْرٌ عَظِيمٌ

9 Allah has promised those who believe and work righteousness: they will have forgiveness and a great reward.

١٠ وَٱلَّذِينَ كَفَرُوا۟ وَكَذَّبُوا۟ بِـَٔايَٰتِنَآ أُو۟لَٰٓئِكَ أَصْحَٰبُ
ٱلْجَحِيمِ

10 As for those who disbelieve and reject Our revelations—these are the inmates of Hell.

١١ يَٰٓأَيُّهَا ٱلَّذِينَ ءَامَنُوا۟ ٱذْكُرُوا۟ نِعْمَتَ ٱللَّهِ
عَلَيْكُمْ إِذْ هَمَّ قَوْمٌ أَن يَبْسُطُوٓا۟ إِلَيْكُمْ أَيْدِيَهُمْ
فَكَفَّ أَيْدِيَهُمْ عَنكُمْ ۖ وَٱتَّقُوا۟ ٱللَّهَ ۚ وَعَلَى ٱللَّهِ
فَلْيَتَوَكَّلِ ٱلْمُؤْمِنُونَ

11 O you who believe! Remember Allah's blessings upon you; when certain people intended to extend their hands against you, and He restrained their hands from you. So reverence Allah, and in Allah let the believers put their trust.

١٢ وَلَقَدْ أَخَذَ ٱللَّهُ مِيثَٰقَ بَنِىٓ إِسْرَٰٓءِيلَ وَبَعَثْنَا
مِنْهُمُ ٱثْنَىْ عَشَرَ نَقِيبًا ۖ وَقَالَ ٱللَّهُ إِنِّى مَعَكُمْ ۖ
لَئِنْ أَقَمْتُمُ ٱلصَّلَوٰةَ وَءَاتَيْتُمُ ٱلزَّكَوٰةَ وَءَامَنتُم
بِرُسُلِى وَعَزَّرْتُمُوهُمْ وَأَقْرَضْتُمُ ٱللَّهَ قَرْضًا
حَسَنًا لَّأُكَفِّرَنَّ عَنكُمْ سَيِّـَٔاتِكُمْ وَلَأُدْخِلَنَّكُمْ
جَنَّٰتٍ تَجْرِى مِن تَحْتِهَا ٱلْأَنْهَٰرُ ۚ فَمَن كَفَرَ بَعْدَ
ذَٰلِكَ مِنكُمْ فَقَدْ ضَلَّ سَوَآءَ ٱلسَّبِيلِ

12 Allah received a pledge from the Children of Israel, and We raised among them twelve chiefs. Allah said, "I am with you; if you perform the prayer, and pay the alms, and believe in My messengers and support them, and lend Allah a loan of righteousness; I will remit your sins, and admit you into Gardens beneath which rivers flow. But whoever among you disbelieves afterwards has strayed from the right way."

١٣ فَبِمَا نَقْضِهِم مِّيثَٰقَهُمْ لَعَنَّٰهُمْ وَجَعَلْنَا قُلُوبَهُمْ
قَٰسِيَةً ۖ يُحَرِّفُونَ ٱلْكَلِمَ عَن مَّوَاضِعِهِۦ ۙ وَنَسُوا۟
حَظًّا مِّمَّا ذُكِّرُوا۟ بِهِۦ ۚ وَلَا تَزَالُ تَطَّلِعُ عَلَىٰ
خَآئِنَةٍ مِّنْهُمْ إِلَّا قَلِيلًا مِّنْهُمْ ۖ فَٱعْفُ عَنْهُمْ
وَٱصْفَحْ ۚ إِنَّ ٱللَّهَ يُحِبُّ ٱلْمُحْسِنِينَ

13 Because of their breaking their pledge, We cursed them, and made their hearts hard. They twist the words out of their context, and they disregarded some of what they were reminded of. You will always witness deceit from them, except for a few of them. But pardon them, and overlook. Allah loves the doers of good.

١٤ وَمِنَ ٱلَّذِينَ قَالُوٓا۟ إِنَّا نَصَٰرَىٰٓ أَخَذْنَا مِيثَٰقَهُمْ
فَنَسُوا۟ حَظًّا مِّمَّا ذُكِّرُوا۟ بِهِۦ فَأَغْرَيْنَا بَيْنَهُمُ

14 And from those who say, "We are Christians," We received their pledge, but they neglected some of what they were reminded of. So We provoked enmity and hatred among

ٱلْعَدَاوَةَ وَٱلْبَغْضَآءَ إِلَىٰ يَوْمِ ٱلْقِيَٰمَةِ ۚ وَسَوْفَ
يُنَبِّئُهُمُ ٱللَّهُ بِمَا كَانُوا۟ يَصْنَعُونَ

them until the Day of Resurrection; Allah will then inform them of what they used to craft.

١٥ يَٰٓأَهْلَ ٱلْكِتَٰبِ قَدْ جَآءَكُمْ رَسُولُنَا يُبَيِّنُ لَكُمْ
كَثِيرًا مِّمَّا كُنتُمْ تُخْفُونَ مِنَ ٱلْكِتَٰبِ وَيَعْفُوا۟
عَن كَثِيرٍ ۚ قَدْ جَآءَكُم مِّنَ ٱللَّهِ نُورٌ وَكِتَٰبٌ مُّبِينٌ

15 O People of the Book! Our Messenger has come to you, clarifying for you much of what you kept hidden of the Book, and overlooking much. A light from Allah has come to you, and a clear Book.

١٦ يَهْدِى بِهِ ٱللَّهُ مَنِ ٱتَّبَعَ رِضْوَٰنَهُۥ سُبُلَ ٱلسَّلَٰمِ
وَيُخْرِجُهُم مِّنَ ٱلظُّلُمَٰتِ إِلَى ٱلنُّورِ بِإِذْنِهِۦ
وَيَهْدِيهِمْ إِلَىٰ صِرَٰطٍ مُّسْتَقِيمٍ

16 Allah guides with it whoever follows His approval to the ways of peace, and He brings them out of darkness into light, by His permission, and He guides them in a straight path.

١٧ لَّقَدْ كَفَرَ ٱلَّذِينَ قَالُوٓا۟ إِنَّ ٱللَّهَ هُوَ ٱلْمَسِيحُ
ٱبْنُ مَرْيَمَ ۚ قُلْ فَمَن يَمْلِكُ مِنَ ٱللَّهِ شَيْـًٔا إِنْ أَرَادَ
أَن يُهْلِكَ ٱلْمَسِيحَ ٱبْنَ مَرْيَمَ وَأُمَّهُۥ وَمَن فِى
ٱلْأَرْضِ جَمِيعًا ۗ وَلِلَّهِ مُلْكُ ٱلسَّمَٰوَٰتِ وَٱلْأَرْضِ
وَمَا بَيْنَهُمَا ۚ يَخْلُقُ مَا يَشَآءُ ۚ وَٱللَّهُ عَلَىٰ كُلِّ
شَىْءٍ قَدِيرٌ

17 They disbelieve those who say, “Allah is the Christ, the son of Mary.” Say, “Who can prevent Allah, if He willed, from annihilating the Christ son of Mary, and his mother, and everyone on earth?” To Allah belongs the sovereignty of the heavens and the earth and what is between them. He creates whatever He wills, and Allah has power over everything.

١٨ وَقَالَتِ ٱلْيَهُودُ وَٱلنَّصَٰرَىٰ نَحْنُ أَبْنَٰٓؤُا۟ ٱللَّهِ
وَأَحِبَّٰٓؤُهُۥ ۚ قُلْ فَلِمَ يُعَذِّبُكُم بِذُنُوبِكُم ۖ بَلْ أَنتُم
بَشَرٌ مِّمَّنْ خَلَقَ ۚ يَغْفِرُ لِمَن يَشَآءُ وَيُعَذِّبُ مَن
يَشَآءُ ۚ وَلِلَّهِ مُلْكُ ٱلسَّمَٰوَٰتِ وَٱلْأَرْضِ وَمَا
بَيْنَهُمَا ۖ وَإِلَيْهِ ٱلْمَصِيرُ

18 The Jews and the Christians say, “We are the children of Allah, and His beloved.” Say, “Why then does He punish you for your sins?” In fact, you are humans from among those He created. He forgives whom He wills, and He punishes whom He wills. To Allah belongs the dominion of the heavens and the earth and what lies between them, and to Him is the return.

١٩ يَٰٓأَهْلَ ٱلْكِتَٰبِ قَدْ جَآءَكُمْ رَسُولُنَا يُبَيِّنُ لَكُمْ
عَلَىٰ فَتْرَةٍ مِّنَ ٱلرُّسُلِ أَن تَقُولُوا۟ مَا جَآءَنَا مِن

19 O People of the Book! Our Messenger has come to you, making things clear to you—after a cessation of messengers—so that you cannot say, “No preacher has

بَشِيرٍ وَلَا نَذِيرٍ فَقَدْ جَآءَكُم بَشِيرٌ وَنَذِيرٌ وَٱللَّهُ عَلَىٰ كُلِّ شَيْءٍ قَدِيرٌ

come to us, and no warner." In fact, a preacher has come to you, and a warner; and Allah is Capable of everything.

٢٠ وَإِذْ قَالَ مُوسَىٰ لِقَوْمِهِۦ يَٰقَوْمِ ٱذْكُرُوا۟ نِعْمَةَ ٱللَّهِ عَلَيْكُمْ إِذْ جَعَلَ فِيكُمْ أَنۢبِيَآءَ وَجَعَلَكُم مُّلُوكًا وَءَاتَىٰكُم مَّا لَمْ يُؤْتِ أَحَدًا مِّنَ ٱلْعَٰلَمِينَ

20 When Moses said to his people, "O my people, remember Allah's blessings upon you, when He placed prophets among you, and made you kings, and gave you what He never gave any other people."

٢١ يَٰقَوْمِ ٱدْخُلُوا۟ ٱلْأَرْضَ ٱلْمُقَدَّسَةَ ٱلَّتِى كَتَبَ ٱللَّهُ لَكُمْ وَلَا تَرْتَدُّوا۟ عَلَىٰٓ أَدْبَارِكُمْ فَتَنقَلِبُوا۟ خَٰسِرِينَ

21 "O my people, enter the Holy Land which Allah has assigned for you, and do not turn back, lest you return as losers."

٢٢ قَالُوا۟ يَٰمُوسَىٰٓ إِنَّ فِيهَا قَوْمًا جَبَّارِينَ وَإِنَّا لَن نَّدْخُلَهَا حَتَّىٰ يَخْرُجُوا۟ مِنْهَا فَإِن يَخْرُجُوا۟ مِنْهَا فَإِنَّا دَٰخِلُونَ

22 They said, "O Moses, there are tyrannical people in it; we will not enter it until they leave it. If they leave it, we will be entering."

٢٣ قَالَ رَجُلَانِ مِنَ ٱلَّذِينَ يَخَافُونَ أَنْعَمَ ٱللَّهُ عَلَيْهِمَا ٱدْخُلُوا۟ عَلَيْهِمُ ٱلْبَابَ فَإِذَا دَخَلْتُمُوهُ فَإِنَّكُمْ غَٰلِبُونَ وَعَلَى ٱللَّهِ فَتَوَكَّلُوٓا۟ إِن كُنتُم مُّؤْمِنِينَ

23 Two men of those who feared, but whom Allah had blessed, said, "Go at them by the gate; and when you have entered it, you will prevail. And put your trust in Allah, if you are believers."

٢٤ قَالُوا۟ يَٰمُوسَىٰٓ إِنَّا لَن نَّدْخُلَهَآ أَبَدًا مَّا دَامُوا۟ فِيهَا فَٱذْهَبْ أَنتَ وَرَبُّكَ فَقَٰتِلَآ إِنَّا هَٰهُنَا قَٰعِدُونَ

24 They said, "O Moses, we will not enter it, ever, as long as they are in it. So go ahead, you and your Lord, and fight. We are staying right here."

٢٥ قَالَ رَبِّ إِنِّى لَآ أَمْلِكُ إِلَّا نَفْسِى وَأَخِى فَٱفْرُقْ بَيْنَنَا وَبَيْنَ ٱلْقَوْمِ ٱلْفَٰسِقِينَ

25 He said, "My Lord! I have control only over myself and my brother, so separate between us and between the wicked people."

٢٦ قَالَ فَإِنَّهَا مُحَرَّمَةٌ عَلَيْهِمْ أَرْبَعِينَ سَنَةً يَتِيهُونَ فِى ٱلْأَرْضِ فَلَا تَأْسَ عَلَى ٱلْقَوْمِ ٱلْفَٰسِقِينَ

26 He said, "It is forbidden for them for forty years. They will wander aimlessly in the land. So do not grieve over the defiant people."

٢٧ وَٱتْلُ عَلَيْهِمْ نَبَأَ ٱبْنَىْ ءَادَمَ بِٱلْحَقِّ إِذْ قَرَّبَا قُرْبَانًا فَتُقُبِّلَ مِنْ أَحَدِهِمَا وَلَمْ يُتَقَبَّلْ مِنَ ٱلْءَاخَرِ قَالَ لَأَقْتُلَنَّكَ ۖ قَالَ إِنَّمَا يَتَقَبَّلُ ٱللَّهُ مِنَ ٱلْمُتَّقِينَ

27 And relate to them the true story of Adam's two sons: when they offered an offering, and it was accepted from one of them, but it was not accepted from the other. He Said, "I will kill you." He Said, "Allah accepts only from the righteous."

٢٨ لَئِنۢ بَسَطتَ إِلَىَّ يَدَكَ لِتَقْتُلَنِى مَآ أَنَا۠ بِبَاسِطٍ يَدِىَ إِلَيْكَ لِأَقْتُلَكَ ۖ إِنِّىٓ أَخَافُ ٱللَّهَ رَبَّ ٱلْعَٰلَمِينَ

28 "If you extend your hand to kill me, I will not extend my hand to kill you; for I fear Allah, Lord of the Worlds."

٢٩ إِنِّىٓ أُرِيدُ أَن تَبُوٓأَ بِإِثْمِى وَإِثْمِكَ فَتَكُونَ مِنْ أَصْحَٰبِ ٱلنَّارِ ۚ وَذَٰلِكَ جَزَٰٓؤُا۟ ٱلظَّٰلِمِينَ

29 "I would rather you bear my sin and your sin, and you become among the inmates of the Fire. Such is the reward for the evildoers."

٣٠ فَطَوَّعَتْ لَهُۥ نَفْسُهُۥ قَتْلَ أَخِيهِ فَقَتَلَهُۥ فَأَصْبَحَ مِنَ ٱلْخَٰسِرِينَ

30 Then His soul prompted him to kill his brother, so he killed him, and became one of the losers.

٣١ فَبَعَثَ ٱللَّهُ غُرَابًا يَبْحَثُ فِى ٱلْأَرْضِ لِيُرِيَهُۥ كَيْفَ يُوَٰرِى سَوْءَةَ أَخِيهِ ۚ قَالَ يَٰوَيْلَتَىٰٓ أَعَجَزْتُ أَنْ أَكُونَ مِثْلَ هَٰذَا ٱلْغُرَابِ فَأُوَٰرِىَ سَوْءَةَ أَخِى ۖ فَأَصْبَحَ مِنَ ٱلنَّٰدِمِينَ

31 Then Allah sent a raven digging the ground, to show him how to cover his brother's corpse. He said, "Woe to me! I was unable to be like this raven, and bury my brother's corpse." So he became full of regrets.

٣٢ مِنْ أَجْلِ ذَٰلِكَ كَتَبْنَا عَلَىٰ بَنِىٓ إِسْرَٰٓءِيلَ أَنَّهُۥ مَن قَتَلَ نَفْسًۢا بِغَيْرِ نَفْسٍ أَوْ فَسَادٍ فِى ٱلْأَرْضِ فَكَأَنَّمَا قَتَلَ ٱلنَّاسَ جَمِيعًا وَمَنْ أَحْيَاهَا فَكَأَنَّمَآ أَحْيَا ٱلنَّاسَ جَمِيعًا ۚ وَلَقَدْ جَآءَتْهُمْ رُسُلُنَا بِٱلْبَيِّنَٰتِ ثُمَّ إِنَّ كَثِيرًا مِّنْهُم بَعْدَ ذَٰلِكَ فِى ٱلْأَرْضِ لَمُسْرِفُونَ

32 Because of that We ordained for the Children of Israel: that whoever kills a person—unless it is for murder or corruption on earth—it is as if he killed the whole of mankind; and whoever saves it, it is as if he saved the whole of mankind. Our messengers came to them with clarifications, but even after that, many of them continue to commit excesses in the land.

٣٣ إِنَّمَا جَزَٰٓؤُا۟ ٱلَّذِينَ يُحَارِبُونَ ٱللَّهَ وَرَسُولَهُۥ وَيَسْعَوْنَ فِى ٱلْأَرْضِ فَسَادًا أَن يُقَتَّلُوٓا۟ أَوْ يُصَلَّبُوٓا۟ أَوْ تُقَطَّعَ أَيْدِيهِمْ وَأَرْجُلُهُم مِّنْ خِلَٰفٍ

33 The punishment for those who fight Allah and His Messenger, and strive to spread corruption on earth, is that they be killed, or crucified, or have their hands and feet cut off on

أَوْ يُنفَوْا۟ مِنَ ٱلْأَرْضِ ۚ ذَٰلِكَ لَهُمْ خِزْىٌ فِى ٱلدُّنْيَا ۖ
وَلَهُمْ فِى ٱلْءَاخِرَةِ عَذَابٌ عَظِيمٌ

opposite sides, or be banished from the land. That is to disgrace them in this life; and in the Hereafter they will have a terrible punishment.

٣٤ إِلَّا ٱلَّذِينَ تَابُوا۟ مِن قَبْلِ أَن تَقْدِرُوا۟ عَلَيْهِمْ ۖ
فَٱعْلَمُوٓا۟ أَنَّ ٱللَّهَ غَفُورٌ رَّحِيمٌ

34 Except for those who repent before you apprehend them. So know that Allah is Forgiving and Merciful.

٣٥ يَٰٓأَيُّهَا ٱلَّذِينَ ءَامَنُوا۟ ٱتَّقُوا۟ ٱللَّهَ وَٱبْتَغُوٓا۟ إِلَيْهِ
ٱلْوَسِيلَةَ وَجَٰهِدُوا۟ فِى سَبِيلِهِۦ لَعَلَّكُمْ تُفْلِحُونَ

35 O you who believe! Be conscious of Allah, and seek the means of approach to Him, and strive in His cause, so that you may succeed.

٣٦ إِنَّ ٱلَّذِينَ كَفَرُوا۟ لَوْ أَنَّ لَهُم مَّا فِى ٱلْأَرْضِ
جَمِيعًا وَمِثْلَهُۥ مَعَهُۥ لِيَفْتَدُوا۟ بِهِۦ مِنْ عَذَابِ يَوْمِ
ٱلْقِيَٰمَةِ مَا تُقُبِّلَ مِنْهُمْ ۖ وَلَهُمْ عَذَابٌ أَلِيمٌ

36 As for those who disbelieve, even if they owned everything on earth, and the like of it with it, and they offered it to ransom themselves from the torment of the Day of Resurrection, it will not be accepted from them. For them is a painful punishment.

٣٧ يُرِيدُونَ أَن يَخْرُجُوا۟ مِنَ ٱلنَّارِ وَمَا هُم
بِخَٰرِجِينَ مِنْهَا ۖ وَلَهُمْ عَذَابٌ مُّقِيمٌ

37 They will want to leave the Fire, but they will not leave it. For them is a lasting punishment.

٣٨ وَٱلسَّارِقُ وَٱلسَّارِقَةُ فَٱقْطَعُوٓا۟ أَيْدِيَهُمَا جَزَآءًۢ
بِمَا كَسَبَا نَكَٰلًا مِّنَ ٱللَّهِ ۗ وَٱللَّهُ عَزِيزٌ حَكِيمٌ

38 As for the thief, whether male or female, cut their hands as a penalty for what they have reaped—a deterrent from Allah. Allah is Mighty and Wise.

٣٩ فَمَن تَابَ مِنۢ بَعْدِ ظُلْمِهِۦ وَأَصْلَحَ فَإِنَّ ٱللَّهَ
يَتُوبُ عَلَيْهِ ۗ إِنَّ ٱللَّهَ غَفُورٌ رَّحِيمٌ

39 But whoever repents after his crime, and reforms, Allah will accept his repentance. Allah is Forgiving and Merciful.

٤٠ أَلَمْ تَعْلَمْ أَنَّ ٱللَّهَ لَهُۥ مُلْكُ ٱلسَّمَٰوَٰتِ وَٱلْأَرْضِ
يُعَذِّبُ مَن يَشَآءُ وَيَغْفِرُ لِمَن يَشَآءُ ۗ وَٱللَّهُ عَلَىٰ
كُلِّ شَىْءٍ قَدِيرٌ

40 Do you not know that to Allah belongs the kingdom of the heavens and the earth? He punishes whom He wills, and He forgives whom He wills. And Allah is Capable of everything.

٤١ يَٰٓأَيُّهَا ٱلرَّسُولُ لَا يَحْزُنكَ ٱلَّذِينَ يُسَٰرِعُونَ
فِى ٱلْكُفْرِ مِنَ ٱلَّذِينَ قَالُوٓا۟ ءَامَنَّا بِأَفْوَٰهِهِمْ وَلَمْ

41 O Messenger! Do not let those who are quick to disbelief grieve you—from among those who say

تُؤْمِن قُلُوبُهُمْ ۛ وَمِنَ ٱلَّذِينَ هَادُوا۟ ۛ سَمَّٰعُونَ
لِلْكَذِبِ سَمَّٰعُونَ لِقَوْمٍ ءَاخَرِينَ لَمْ يَأْتُوكَ ۖ
يُحَرِّفُونَ ٱلْكَلِمَ مِنۢ بَعْدِ مَوَاضِعِهِۦ ۖ يَقُولُونَ إِنْ
أُوتِيتُمْ هَٰذَا فَخُذُوهُ وَإِن لَّمْ تُؤْتَوْهُ فَٱحْذَرُوا۟ ۚ
وَمَن يُرِدِ ٱللَّهُ فِتْنَتَهُۥ فَلَن تَمْلِكَ لَهُۥ مِنَ ٱللَّهِ
شَيْـًٔا ۚ أُو۟لَٰٓئِكَ ٱلَّذِينَ لَمْ يُرِدِ ٱللَّهُ أَن يُطَهِّرَ
قُلُوبَهُمْ ۚ لَهُمْ فِى ٱلدُّنْيَا خِزْىٌ ۖ وَلَهُمْ فِى
ٱلْءَاخِرَةِ عَذَابٌ عَظِيمٌ

with their mouths, "We believe," but their hearts do not believe; and from among the Jews—listeners to lies, listeners to other people who did not come to you. They distort words from their places, and they say, "If you are given this, accept it; but if you are not given it, beware." Whomever Allah has willed to divert, you have nothing for him from Allah. Those are they whose hearts Allah does not intend to purify. For them is disgrace in this world, and for them is a great punishment in the Hereafter.

٤٢ سَمَّٰعُونَ لِلْكَذِبِ أَكَّٰلُونَ لِلسُّحْتِ ۚ فَإِن
جَآءُوكَ فَٱحْكُم بَيْنَهُمْ أَوْ أَعْرِضْ عَنْهُمْ ۖ وَإِن
تُعْرِضْ عَنْهُمْ فَلَن يَضُرُّوكَ شَيْـًٔا ۖ وَإِنْ حَكَمْتَ
فَٱحْكُم بَيْنَهُم بِٱلْقِسْطِ ۚ إِنَّ ٱللَّهَ يُحِبُّ
ٱلْمُقْسِطِينَ

42 Listeners to falsehoods, eaters of illicit earnings. If they come to you, judge between them, or turn away from them. If you turn away from them, they will not harm you in the least. But if you judge, judge between them equitably. Allah loves the equitable.

٤٣ وَكَيْفَ يُحَكِّمُونَكَ وَعِندَهُمُ ٱلتَّوْرَىٰةُ فِيهَا
حُكْمُ ٱللَّهِ ثُمَّ يَتَوَلَّوْنَ مِنۢ بَعْدِ ذَٰلِكَ ۚ وَمَآ أُو۟لَٰٓئِكَ
بِٱلْمُؤْمِنِينَ

43 But why do they come to you for judgment, when they have the Torah, in which is Allah's Law? Yet they turn away after that. These are not believers.

٤٤ إِنَّآ أَنزَلْنَا ٱلتَّوْرَىٰةَ فِيهَا هُدًى وَنُورٌ ۚ يَحْكُمُ
بِهَا ٱلنَّبِيُّونَ ٱلَّذِينَ أَسْلَمُوا۟ لِلَّذِينَ هَادُوا۟
وَٱلرَّبَّٰنِيُّونَ وَٱلْأَحْبَارُ بِمَا ٱسْتُحْفِظُوا۟ مِن كِتَٰبِ
ٱللَّهِ وَكَانُوا۟ عَلَيْهِ شُهَدَآءَ ۚ فَلَا تَخْشَوُا۟ ٱلنَّاسَ
وَٱخْشَوْنِ وَلَا تَشْتَرُوا۟ بِـَٔايَٰتِى ثَمَنًا قَلِيلًا ۚ وَمَن
لَّمْ يَحْكُم بِمَآ أَنزَلَ ٱللَّهُ فَأُو۟لَٰٓئِكَ هُمُ ٱلْكَٰفِرُونَ

44 We have revealed the Torah, wherein is guidance and light. The submissive prophets ruled the Jews according to it, so did the rabbis and the scholars, as they were required to protect Allah's Book, and were witnesses to it. So do not fear people, but fear Me. And do not sell My revelations for a cheap price. Those who do not rule according to what Allah revealed are the unbelievers.

٤٥ وَكَتَبْنَا عَلَيْهِمْ فِيهَآ أَنَّ ٱلنَّفْسَ بِٱلنَّفْسِ
وَٱلْعَيْنَ بِٱلْعَيْنِ وَٱلْأَنفَ بِٱلْأَنفِ وَٱلْأُذُنَ بِٱلْأُذُنِ
وَٱلسِّنَّ بِٱلسِّنِّ وَٱلْجُرُوحَ قِصَاصٌ ۚ فَمَن تَصَدَّقَ
بِهِۦ فَهُوَ كَفَّارَةٌ لَّهُۥ ۚ وَمَن لَّمْ يَحْكُم بِمَآ أَنزَلَ ٱللَّهُ
فَأُو۟لَٰٓئِكَ هُمُ ٱلظَّٰلِمُونَ

45 And We wrote for them in it: a life for a life, an eye for an eye, a nose for a nose, an ear for an ear, a tooth for a tooth, and an equal wound for a wound; but whoever forgoes it in charity, it will serve as atonement for him. Those who do not rule according to what Allah revealed are the evildoers.

٤٦ وَقَفَّيْنَا عَلَىٰٓ ءَاثَٰرِهِم بِعِيسَى ٱبْنِ مَرْيَمَ
مُصَدِّقًا لِّمَا بَيْنَ يَدَيْهِ مِنَ ٱلتَّوْرَىٰةِ ۖ وَءَاتَيْنَٰهُ
ٱلْإِنجِيلَ فِيهِ هُدًى وَنُورٌ وَمُصَدِّقًا لِّمَا بَيْنَ
يَدَيْهِ مِنَ ٱلتَّوْرَىٰةِ وَهُدًى وَمَوْعِظَةً لِّلْمُتَّقِينَ

46 In their footsteps, We sent Jesus son of Mary, fulfilling the Torah that preceded him; and We gave him the Gospel, wherein is guidance and light, and confirming the Torah that preceded him, and guidance and counsel for the righteous.

٤٧ وَلْيَحْكُمْ أَهْلُ ٱلْإِنجِيلِ بِمَآ أَنزَلَ ٱللَّهُ فِيهِ ۚ
وَمَن لَّمْ يَحْكُم بِمَآ أَنزَلَ ٱللَّهُ فَأُو۟لَٰٓئِكَ هُمُ
ٱلْفَٰسِقُونَ

47 So let the people of the Gospel rule according to what Allah revealed in it. Those who do not rule according to what Allah revealed are the sinners.

٤٨ وَأَنزَلْنَآ إِلَيْكَ ٱلْكِتَٰبَ بِٱلْحَقِّ مُصَدِّقًا لِّمَا بَيْنَ
يَدَيْهِ مِنَ ٱلْكِتَٰبِ وَمُهَيْمِنًا عَلَيْهِ ۖ فَٱحْكُم بَيْنَهُم
بِمَآ أَنزَلَ ٱللَّهُ ۖ وَلَا تَتَّبِعْ أَهْوَآءَهُمْ عَمَّا جَآءَكَ
مِنَ ٱلْحَقِّ ۚ لِكُلٍّ جَعَلْنَا مِنكُمْ شِرْعَةً وَمِنْهَاجًا ۚ
وَلَوْ شَآءَ ٱللَّهُ لَجَعَلَكُمْ أُمَّةً وَٰحِدَةً وَلَٰكِن
لِّيَبْلُوَكُمْ فِى مَآ ءَاتَىٰكُمْ ۖ فَٱسْتَبِقُوا۟ ٱلْخَيْرَٰتِ ۚ
إِلَى ٱللَّهِ مَرْجِعُكُمْ جَمِيعًا فَيُنَبِّئُكُم بِمَا كُنتُمْ
فِيهِ تَخْتَلِفُونَ

48 And We revealed to you the Book, with truth, confirming the Scripture that preceded it, and superseding it. So judge between them according to what Allah revealed, and do not follow their desires if they differ from the truth that has come to you. For each of you We have assigned a law and a method. Had Allah willed, He could have made you a single nation, but He tests you through what He has given you. So compete in righteousness. To Allah is your return, all of you; then He will inform you of what you had disputed.

٤٩ وَأَنِ ٱحْكُم بَيْنَهُم بِمَآ أَنزَلَ ٱللَّهُ وَلَا تَتَّبِعْ
أَهْوَآءَهُمْ وَٱحْذَرْهُمْ أَن يَفْتِنُوكَ عَنۢ بَعْضِ مَآ
أَنزَلَ ٱللَّهُ إِلَيْكَ ۖ فَإِن تَوَلَّوْا۟ فَٱعْلَمْ أَنَّمَا يُرِيدُ

49 And judge between them according to what Allah revealed, and do not follow their desires. And beware of them, lest they lure you away from some of what Allah has revealed to you. But if they turn

ٱللَّهُ أَن يُصِيبَهُم بِبَعْضِ ذُنُوبِهِمْ ۗ وَإِنَّ كَثِيرًا
مِّنَ ٱلنَّاسِ لَفَٰسِقُونَ

away, know that Allah intends to strike them with some of their sins. In fact, a great many people are corrupt.

٥٠ أَفَحُكْمَ ٱلْجَٰهِلِيَّةِ يَبْغُونَ ۚ وَمَنْ أَحْسَنُ مِنَ
ٱللَّهِ حُكْمًا لِّقَوْمٍ يُوقِنُونَ

50 Is it the laws of the time of ignorance that they desire? Who is better than Allah in judgment for people who are certain?

٥١ يَٰٓأَيُّهَا ٱلَّذِينَ ءَامَنُوا۟ لَا تَتَّخِذُوا۟ ٱلْيَهُودَ
وَٱلنَّصَٰرَىٰٓ أَوْلِيَآءَ ۘ بَعْضُهُمْ أَوْلِيَآءُ بَعْضٍ ۚ وَمَن
يَتَوَلَّهُم مِّنكُمْ فَإِنَّهُۥ مِنْهُمْ ۗ إِنَّ ٱللَّهَ لَا يَهْدِى
ٱلْقَوْمَ ٱلظَّٰلِمِينَ

51 O you who believe! Do not take the Jews and the Christians as allies; some of them are allies of one another. Whoever of you allies himself with them is one of them. Allah does not guide the wrongdoing people.

٥٢ فَتَرَى ٱلَّذِينَ فِى قُلُوبِهِم مَّرَضٌ يُسَٰرِعُونَ
فِيهِمْ يَقُولُونَ نَخْشَىٰٓ أَن تُصِيبَنَا دَآئِرَةٌ ۚ
فَعَسَى ٱللَّهُ أَن يَأْتِىَ بِٱلْفَتْحِ أَوْ أَمْرٍ مِّنْ عِندِهِۦ
فَيُصْبِحُوا۟ عَلَىٰ مَآ أَسَرُّوا۟ فِىٓ أَنفُسِهِمْ نَٰدِمِينَ

52 You will see those in whose hearts is sickness racing towards them. They say, “We fear the wheel of fate may turn against us.” But perhaps Allah will bring about victory, or some event of His making; thereupon they will regret what they concealed within themselves.

٥٣ وَيَقُولُ ٱلَّذِينَ ءَامَنُوٓا۟ أَهَٰٓؤُلَآءِ ٱلَّذِينَ
أَقْسَمُوا۟ بِٱللَّهِ جَهْدَ أَيْمَٰنِهِمْ ۙ إِنَّهُمْ لَمَعَكُمْ ۚ
حَبِطَتْ أَعْمَٰلُهُمْ فَأَصْبَحُوا۟ خَٰسِرِينَ

53 Those who believe will say, “Are these the ones who swore by Allah with their strongest oaths that they are with you?” Their works have failed, so they became losers.

٥٤ يَٰٓأَيُّهَا ٱلَّذِينَ ءَامَنُوا۟ مَن يَرْتَدَّ مِنكُمْ عَن
دِينِهِۦ فَسَوْفَ يَأْتِى ٱللَّهُ بِقَوْمٍ يُحِبُّهُمْ
وَيُحِبُّونَهُۥٓ أَذِلَّةٍ عَلَى ٱلْمُؤْمِنِينَ أَعِزَّةٍ عَلَى
ٱلْكَٰفِرِينَ يُجَٰهِدُونَ فِى سَبِيلِ ٱللَّهِ وَلَا يَخَافُونَ
لَوْمَةَ لَآئِمٍ ۚ ذَٰلِكَ فَضْلُ ٱللَّهِ يُؤْتِيهِ مَن يَشَآءُ ۚ
وَٱللَّهُ وَٰسِعٌ عَلِيمٌ

54 O you who believe! Whoever of you goes back on his religion—Allah will bring a people whom He loves and who love Him, kind towards the believers, stern with the disbelievers. They strive in the way of Allah, and do not fear the blame of the critic. That is the grace of Allah; He bestows it upon whomever He wills. Allah is Embracing and Knowing.

٥٥ إِنَّمَا وَلِيُّكُمُ ٱللَّهُ وَرَسُولُهُۥ وَٱلَّذِينَ ءَامَنُوا۟
ٱلَّذِينَ يُقِيمُونَ ٱلصَّلَوٰةَ وَيُؤْتُونَ ٱلزَّكَوٰةَ وَهُمْ
رَٰكِعُونَ

55 Your allies are Allah, and His Messenger, and those who believe—those who pray regularly, and give charity, and bow down.

٥٦ وَمَن يَتَوَلَّ ٱللَّهَ وَرَسُولَهُۥ وَٱلَّذِينَ ءَامَنُوا۟
فَإِنَّ حِزْبَ ٱللَّهِ هُمُ ٱلْغَٰلِبُونَ

56 Whoever allies himself with Allah, and His Messenger, and those who believe—surely the Party of Allah is the victorious.

٥٧ يَٰٓأَيُّهَا ٱلَّذِينَ ءَامَنُوا۟ لَا تَتَّخِذُوا۟ ٱلَّذِينَ
ٱتَّخَذُوا۟ دِينَكُمْ هُزُوًا وَلَعِبًا مِّنَ ٱلَّذِينَ أُوتُوا۟
ٱلْكِتَٰبَ مِن قَبْلِكُمْ وَٱلْكُفَّارَ أَوْلِيَآءَ ۚ وَٱتَّقُوا۟ ٱللَّهَ
إِن كُنتُم مُّؤْمِنِينَ

57 O you who believe! Do not befriend those who take your religion in mockery and as a sport, be they from among those who were given the Scripture before you, or the disbelievers. And obey Allah, if you are believers.

٥٨ وَإِذَا نَادَيْتُمْ إِلَى ٱلصَّلَوٰةِ ٱتَّخَذُوهَا هُزُوًا
وَلَعِبًا ۚ ذَٰلِكَ بِأَنَّهُمْ قَوْمٌ لَّا يَعْقِلُونَ

58 When you call to the prayer, they take it as a joke and a trifle. That is because they are people who do not reason.

٥٩ قُلْ يَٰٓأَهْلَ ٱلْكِتَٰبِ هَلْ تَنقِمُونَ مِنَّآ إِلَّآ أَنْ
ءَامَنَّا بِٱللَّهِ وَمَآ أُنزِلَ إِلَيْنَا وَمَآ أُنزِلَ مِن قَبْلُ
وَأَنَّ أَكْثَرَكُمْ فَٰسِقُونَ

59 Say, "O People of the Scripture! Do you resent us only because we believe in Allah, and in what was revealed to us, and in what was revealed previously; and most of you are sinners?"

٦٠ قُلْ هَلْ أُنَبِّئُكُم بِشَرٍّ مِّن ذَٰلِكَ مَثُوبَةً عِندَ
ٱللَّهِ ۚ مَن لَّعَنَهُ ٱللَّهُ وَغَضِبَ عَلَيْهِ وَجَعَلَ مِنْهُمُ
ٱلْقِرَدَةَ وَٱلْخَنَازِيرَ وَعَبَدَ ٱلطَّٰغُوتَ ۚ أُو۟لَٰٓئِكَ شَرٌّ
مَّكَانًا وَأَضَلُّ عَن سَوَآءِ ٱلسَّبِيلِ

60 Say, "Shall I inform you of worse than that for retribution from Allah? He whom Allah has cursed, and with whom He became angry; and He turned some of them into apes, and swine, and idol worshipers. These are in a worse position, and further away from the right way."

٦١ وَإِذَا جَآءُوكُمْ قَالُوٓا۟ ءَامَنَّا وَقَد دَّخَلُوا۟
بِٱلْكُفْرِ وَهُمْ قَدْ خَرَجُوا۟ بِهِۦ ۚ وَٱللَّهُ أَعْلَمُ بِمَا
كَانُوا۟ يَكْتُمُونَ

61 When they come to you, they say, "We believe," though they have entered with disbelief, and they have departed with it. But Allah is well aware of what they hide.

٦٢ وَتَرَىٰ كَثِيرًا مِّنْهُمْ يُسَٰرِعُونَ فِى ٱلْإِثْمِ
وَٱلْعُدْوَٰنِ وَأَكْلِهِمُ ٱلسُّحْتَ ۚ لَبِئْسَ مَا كَانُوا۟
يَعْمَلُونَ

62 You see many of them competing with one another in sin and hostility, and their consuming of what is illicit. What they have been doing is truly evil.

٦٣ لَوْلَا يَنْهَىٰهُمُ ٱلرَّبَّٰنِيُّونَ وَٱلْأَحْبَارُ عَن قَوْلِهِمُ
ٱلْإِثْمَ وَأَكْلِهِمُ ٱلسُّحْتَ ۚ لَبِئْسَ مَا كَانُوا۟
يَصْنَعُونَ

63 Why do the rabbis and the priests not prevent them from speaking sinfully and from consuming forbidden wealth? Evil is what they have been doing.

٦٤ وَقَالَتِ ٱلْيَهُودُ يَدُ ٱللَّهِ مَغْلُولَةٌ ۚ غُلَّتْ أَيْدِيهِمْ
وَلُعِنُوا۟ بِمَا قَالُوا۟ ۘ بَلْ يَدَاهُ مَبْسُوطَتَانِ يُنفِقُ
كَيْفَ يَشَآءُ ۚ وَلَيَزِيدَنَّ كَثِيرًا مِّنْهُم مَّآ أُنزِلَ
إِلَيْكَ مِن رَّبِّكَ طُغْيَٰنًا وَكُفْرًا ۚ وَأَلْقَيْنَا بَيْنَهُمُ
ٱلْعَدَٰوَةَ وَٱلْبَغْضَآءَ إِلَىٰ يَوْمِ ٱلْقِيَٰمَةِ ۚ كُلَّمَآ
أَوْقَدُوا۟ نَارًا لِّلْحَرْبِ أَطْفَأَهَا ٱللَّهُ ۚ وَيَسْعَوْنَ فِى
ٱلْأَرْضِ فَسَادًا ۚ وَٱللَّهُ لَا يُحِبُّ ٱلْمُفْسِدِينَ

64 The Jews say, "Allah's hand is tied." It is their hands that are tied, and they are cursed for what they say. In fact, His hands are outstretched; He gives as He wills. Certainly, what was revealed to your from your Lord will increase many of them in defiance and blasphemy. And We placed between them enmity and hatred, until the Day of Resurrection. Whenever they kindle the fire of war, Allah extinguishes it. And they strive to spread corruption on earth. Allah does not love the corrupters.

٦٥ وَلَوْ أَنَّ أَهْلَ ٱلْكِتَٰبِ ءَامَنُوا۟ وَٱتَّقَوْا۟ لَكَفَّرْنَا
عَنْهُمْ سَيِّـَٔاتِهِمْ وَلَأَدْخَلْنَٰهُمْ جَنَّٰتِ ٱلنَّعِيمِ

65 Had the People of the Scripture believed and been righteous, We would have remitted their sins, and admitted them into the Gardens of Bliss.

٦٦ وَلَوْ أَنَّهُمْ أَقَامُوا۟ ٱلتَّوْرَىٰةَ وَٱلْإِنجِيلَ وَمَآ
أُنزِلَ إِلَيْهِم مِّن رَّبِّهِمْ لَأَكَلُوا۟ مِن فَوْقِهِمْ وَمِن
تَحْتِ أَرْجُلِهِم ۚ مِّنْهُمْ أُمَّةٌ مُّقْتَصِدَةٌ ۖ وَكَثِيرٌ
مِّنْهُمْ سَآءَ مَا يَعْمَلُونَ

66 Had they observed the Torah, and the Gospel, and what was revealed to them from their Lord, they would have consumed amply from above them, and from beneath their feet. Among them is a moderate community, but evil is what many of them are doing.

٦٧ يَٰٓأَيُّهَا ٱلرَّسُولُ بَلِّغْ مَآ أُنزِلَ إِلَيْكَ مِن رَّبِّكَ ۖ
وَإِن لَّمْ تَفْعَلْ فَمَا بَلَّغْتَ رِسَالَتَهُۥ ۚ وَٱللَّهُ

67 O Messenger, convey what was revealed to you from your Lord. But if you do not, then you would not have delivered His message. And

يَعْصِمُكَ مِنَ ٱلنَّاسِ ۗ إِنَّ ٱللَّهَ لَا يَهْدِى ٱلْقَوْمَ
ٱلْكَٰفِرِينَ

Allah will protect you from the
people. Allah does not guide the
disbelieving people.

٦٨ قُلْ يَٰٓأَهْلَ ٱلْكِتَٰبِ لَسْتُمْ عَلَىٰ شَىْءٍ حَتَّىٰ
تُقِيمُوا۟ ٱلتَّوْرَىٰةَ وَٱلْإِنجِيلَ وَمَآ أُنزِلَ إِلَيْكُم مِّن
رَّبِّكُمْ ۗ وَلَيَزِيدَنَّ كَثِيرًا مِّنْهُم مَّآ أُنزِلَ إِلَيْكَ مِن
رَّبِّكَ طُغْيَٰنًا وَكُفْرًا ۖ فَلَا تَأْسَ عَلَى ٱلْقَوْمِ
ٱلْكَٰفِرِينَ

68 Say, “O People of the Scripture!
You have no basis until you uphold
the Torah, and the Gospel, and what
is revealed to you from your Lord.”
But what is revealed to you from
your Lord will increase many of them
in rebellion and disbelief, so do not
be sorry for the disbelieving people.

٦٩ إِنَّ ٱلَّذِينَ ءَامَنُوا۟ وَٱلَّذِينَ هَادُوا۟ وَٱلصَّٰبِـُٔونَ
وَٱلنَّصَٰرَىٰ مَنْ ءَامَنَ بِٱللَّهِ وَٱلْيَوْمِ ٱلْءَاخِرِ
وَعَمِلَ صَٰلِحًا فَلَا خَوْفٌ عَلَيْهِمْ وَلَا هُمْ
يَحْزَنُونَ

69 Those who believe, and the Jews,
and the Sabians, and the
Christians—whoever believes in
Allah and the Last Day, and does
what is right—they have nothing to
fear, nor shall they grieve.

٧٠ لَقَدْ أَخَذْنَا مِيثَٰقَ بَنِىٓ إِسْرَٰٓءِيلَ وَأَرْسَلْنَآ
إِلَيْهِمْ رُسُلًا ۖ كُلَّمَا جَآءَهُمْ رَسُولٌۢ بِمَا لَا تَهْوَىٰٓ
أَنفُسُهُمْ فَرِيقًا كَذَّبُوا۟ وَفَرِيقًا يَقْتُلُونَ

70 We made a covenant with the
Children of Israel, and We sent to
them messengers. Whenever a
messenger came to them with what
their souls did not desire, some of
them they accused of lying, and
others they put to death.

٧١ وَحَسِبُوٓا۟ أَلَّا تَكُونَ فِتْنَةٌ فَعَمُوا۟ وَصَمُّوا۟ ثُمَّ
تَابَ ٱللَّهُ عَلَيْهِمْ ثُمَّ عَمُوا۟ وَصَمُّوا۟ كَثِيرٌ مِّنْهُمْ ۚ
وَٱللَّهُ بَصِيرٌۢ بِمَا يَعْمَلُونَ

71 They assumed there would be no
punishment, so they turned blind
and deaf. Then Allah redeemed
them, but then again many of them
turned blind and deaf. But Allah is
Seeing of what they do.

٧٢ لَقَدْ كَفَرَ ٱلَّذِينَ قَالُوٓا۟ إِنَّ ٱللَّهَ هُوَ ٱلْمَسِيحُ
ٱبْنُ مَرْيَمَ ۖ وَقَالَ ٱلْمَسِيحُ يَٰبَنِىٓ إِسْرَٰٓءِيلَ
ٱعْبُدُوا۟ ٱللَّهَ رَبِّى وَرَبَّكُمْ ۖ إِنَّهُۥ مَن يُشْرِكْ بِٱللَّهِ
فَقَدْ حَرَّمَ ٱللَّهُ عَلَيْهِ ٱلْجَنَّةَ وَمَأْوَىٰهُ ٱلنَّارُ ۖ وَمَا
لِلظَّٰلِمِينَ مِنْ أَنصَارٍ

72 They disbelieve those who say,
“Allah is the Messiah the son of
Mary.” But the Messiah himself said,
“O Children of Israel, worship Allah,
my Lord and your Lord. Whoever
associates others with Allah, Allah
has forbidden him Paradise, and his
dwelling is the Fire. The wrongdoers
have no saviors.”

٧٣ لَّقَدْ كَفَرَ ٱلَّذِينَ قَالُوٓا۟ إِنَّ ٱللَّهَ ثَالِثُ ثَلَٰثَةٍ ۘ وَمَا
مِنْ إِلَٰهٍ إِلَّآ إِلَٰهٌ وَٰحِدٌ ۚ وَإِن لَّمْ يَنتَهُوا۟ عَمَّا
يَقُولُونَ لَيَمَسَّنَّ ٱلَّذِينَ كَفَرُوا۟ مِنْهُمْ عَذَابٌ أَلِيمٌ

73 They disbelieve those who say, “Allah is the third of three.” But there is no deity except the One God. If they do not refrain from what they say, a painful torment will befall those among them who disbelieve.

٧٤ أَفَلَا يَتُوبُونَ إِلَى ٱللَّهِ وَيَسْتَغْفِرُونَهُۥ ۚ وَٱللَّهُ
غَفُورٌ رَّحِيمٌ

74 Will they not repent to Allah and ask His forgiveness? Allah is Forgiving and Merciful.

٧٥ مَّا ٱلْمَسِيحُ ٱبْنُ مَرْيَمَ إِلَّا رَسُولٌ قَدْ خَلَتْ
مِن قَبْلِهِ ٱلرُّسُلُ وَأُمُّهُۥ صِدِّيقَةٌ ۖ كَانَا يَأْكُلَانِ
ٱلطَّعَامَ ۗ ٱنظُرْ كَيْفَ نُبَيِّنُ لَهُمُ ٱلْءَايَٰتِ ثُمَّ ٱنظُرْ
أَنَّىٰ يُؤْفَكُونَ

75 The Messiah son of Mary was only a messenger, before whom other Messengers had passed away, and his mother was a woman of truth. They both used to eat food. Note how We make clear the revelations to them; then note how deluded they are.

٧٦ قُلْ أَتَعْبُدُونَ مِن دُونِ ٱللَّهِ مَا لَا يَمْلِكُ لَكُمْ
ضَرًّا وَلَا نَفْعًا ۚ وَٱللَّهُ هُوَ ٱلسَّمِيعُ ٱلْعَلِيمُ

76 Say, “Do you worship, besides Allah, what has no power to harm or benefit you?” But Allah: He is the Hearer, the Knower.

٧٧ قُلْ يَٰٓأَهْلَ ٱلْكِتَٰبِ لَا تَغْلُوا۟ فِى دِينِكُمْ غَيْرَ
ٱلْحَقِّ وَلَا تَتَّبِعُوٓا۟ أَهْوَآءَ قَوْمٍ قَدْ ضَلُّوا۟ مِن قَبْلُ
وَأَضَلُّوا۟ كَثِيرًا وَضَلُّوا۟ عَن سَوَآءِ ٱلسَّبِيلِ

77 Say, “O People of the Scripture! Do not exaggerate in your religion beyond the truth; and do not follow the opinions of people who went astray before, and misled many, and themselves strayed off the balanced way.”

٧٨ لُعِنَ ٱلَّذِينَ كَفَرُوا۟ مِنۢ بَنِىٓ إِسْرَٰٓءِيلَ عَلَىٰ
لِسَانِ دَاوُۥدَ وَعِيسَى ٱبْنِ مَرْيَمَ ۚ ذَٰلِكَ بِمَا عَصَوا۟
وَّكَانُوا۟ يَعْتَدُونَ

78 Cursed were those who disbelieved from among the Children of Israel by the tongue of David and Jesus son of Mary. That is because they rebelled and used to transgress.

٧٩ كَانُوا۟ لَا يَتَنَاهَوْنَ عَن مُّنكَرٍ فَعَلُوهُ ۚ لَبِئْسَ مَا
كَانُوا۟ يَفْعَلُونَ

79 They used not to prevent one another from the wrongs they used to commit. Evil is what they used to do.

٨٠ تَرَىٰ كَثِيرًا مِّنْهُمْ يَتَوَلَّوْنَ ٱلَّذِينَ كَفَرُوا۟ ۚ
لَبِئْسَ مَا قَدَّمَتْ لَهُمْ أَنفُسُهُمْ أَن سَخِطَ ٱللَّهُ
عَلَيْهِمْ وَفِى ٱلْعَذَابِ هُمْ خَٰلِدُونَ

80 You will see many of them befriending those who disbelieve. Terrible is what their souls prompts them to do. The wrath of Allah fell upon them, and in the torment they will remain.

٨١ وَلَوْ كَانُوا۟ يُؤْمِنُونَ بِٱللَّهِ وَٱلنَّبِىِّ وَمَآ أُنزِلَ
إِلَيْهِ مَا ٱتَّخَذُوهُمْ أَوْلِيَآءَ وَلَٰكِنَّ كَثِيرًا مِّنْهُمْ
فَٰسِقُونَ

81 Had they believed in Allah and the Prophet, and in what was revealed to him, they would not have befriended them. But many of them are immoral.

٨٢ لَتَجِدَنَّ أَشَدَّ ٱلنَّاسِ عَدَٰوَةً لِّلَّذِينَ ءَامَنُوا۟
ٱلْيَهُودَ وَٱلَّذِينَ أَشْرَكُوا۟ ۖ وَلَتَجِدَنَّ أَقْرَبَهُم مَّوَدَّةً
لِّلَّذِينَ ءَامَنُوا۟ ٱلَّذِينَ قَالُوٓا۟ إِنَّا نَصَٰرَىٰ ۚ ذَٰلِكَ بِأَنَّ
مِنْهُمْ قِسِّيسِينَ وَرُهْبَانًا وَأَنَّهُمْ لَا يَسْتَكْبِرُونَ

82 You will find that the people most hostile towards the believers are the Jews and the polytheists. And you will find that the nearest in affection towards the believers are those who say, "We are Christians." That is because among them are priests and monks, and they are not arrogant.

٨٣ وَإِذَا سَمِعُوا۟ مَآ أُنزِلَ إِلَى ٱلرَّسُولِ تَرَىٰٓ
أَعْيُنَهُمْ تَفِيضُ مِنَ ٱلدَّمْعِ مِمَّا عَرَفُوا۟ مِنَ
ٱلْحَقِّ ۖ يَقُولُونَ رَبَّنَآ ءَامَنَّا فَٱكْتُبْنَا مَعَ ٱلشَّٰهِدِينَ

83 And when they hear what was revealed to the Messenger, you see their eyes overflowing with tears, as they recognize the truth in it. They say, "Our Lord, we have believed, so count us among the witnesses."

٨٤ وَمَا لَنَا لَا نُؤْمِنُ بِٱللَّهِ وَمَا جَآءَنَا مِنَ ٱلْحَقِّ
وَنَطْمَعُ أَن يُدْخِلَنَا رَبُّنَا مَعَ ٱلْقَوْمِ ٱلصَّٰلِحِينَ

84 "And why should we not believe in Allah, and in the truth that has come to us, and hope that our Lord will include us among the righteous people?"

٨٥ فَأَثَٰبَهُمُ ٱللَّهُ بِمَا قَالُوا۟ جَنَّٰتٍ تَجْرِى مِن
تَحْتِهَا ٱلْأَنْهَٰرُ خَٰلِدِينَ فِيهَا ۚ وَذَٰلِكَ جَزَآءُ
ٱلْمُحْسِنِينَ

85 Allah will reward them for what they say—Gardens beneath which rivers flow, where they will stay forever. Such is the reward of the righteous.

٨٦ وَٱلَّذِينَ كَفَرُوا۟ وَكَذَّبُوا۟ بِـَٔايَٰتِنَآ أُو۟لَٰٓئِكَ
أَصْحَٰبُ ٱلْجَحِيمِ

86 But as for those who disbelieve and deny Our signs—these are the inmates of the Fire.

٨٧ يَٰٓأَيُّهَا ٱلَّذِينَ ءَامَنُوا۟ لَا تُحَرِّمُوا۟ طَيِّبَٰتِ مَآ
أَحَلَّ ٱللَّهُ لَكُمْ وَلَا تَعْتَدُوٓا۟ ۚ إِنَّ ٱللَّهَ لَا يُحِبُّ
ٱلْمُعْتَدِينَ

87 O you who believe! Do not prohibit the good things Allah has permitted for you, and do not commit aggression. Allah does not love the aggressors.

٨٨ وَكُلُوا۟ مِمَّا رَزَقَكُمُ ٱللَّهُ حَلَٰلًا طَيِّبًا ۚ وَٱتَّقُوا۟
ٱللَّهَ ٱلَّذِىٓ أَنتُم بِهِۦ مُؤْمِنُونَ

88 And eat of the lawful and good things Allah has provided for you; and be conscious of Allah, in whom you are believers.

٨٩ لَا يُؤَاخِذُكُمُ ٱللَّهُ بِٱللَّغْوِ فِىٓ أَيْمَٰنِكُمْ وَلَٰكِن
يُؤَاخِذُكُم بِمَا عَقَّدتُّمُ ٱلْأَيْمَٰنَ ۖ فَكَفَّٰرَتُهُۥٓ إِطْعَامُ
عَشَرَةِ مَسَٰكِينَ مِنْ أَوْسَطِ مَا تُطْعِمُونَ أَهْلِيكُمْ
أَوْ كِسْوَتُهُمْ أَوْ تَحْرِيرُ رَقَبَةٍ ۖ فَمَن لَّمْ يَجِدْ
فَصِيَامُ ثَلَٰثَةِ أَيَّامٍ ۚ ذَٰلِكَ كَفَّٰرَةُ أَيْمَٰنِكُمْ إِذَا
حَلَفْتُمْ ۚ وَٱحْفَظُوٓا۟ أَيْمَٰنَكُمْ ۚ كَذَٰلِكَ يُبَيِّنُ ٱللَّهُ
لَكُمْ ءَايَٰتِهِۦ لَعَلَّكُمْ تَشْكُرُونَ

89 Allah does not hold you accountable for your unintended oaths, but He holds you accountable for your binding oaths. The atonement for it is by feeding ten needy people from the average of what you feed your families, or by clothing them, or by freeing a slave. Anyone who lacks the means shall fast for three days. That is the atonement for breaking your oaths when you have sworn them. So keep your oaths. Thus Allah makes clear His Revelations to you, that you may be grateful.

٩٠ يَٰٓأَيُّهَا ٱلَّذِينَ ءَامَنُوٓا۟ إِنَّمَا ٱلْخَمْرُ وَٱلْمَيْسِرُ
وَٱلْأَنصَابُ وَٱلْأَزْلَٰمُ رِجْسٌ مِّنْ عَمَلِ ٱلشَّيْطَٰنِ
فَٱجْتَنِبُوهُ لَعَلَّكُمْ تُفْلِحُونَ

90 O you who believe! Intoxicants, gambling, idolatry, and divination are abominations of Satan's doing. Avoid them, so that you may prosper.

٩١ إِنَّمَا يُرِيدُ ٱلشَّيْطَٰنُ أَن يُوقِعَ بَيْنَكُمُ ٱلْعَدَٰوَةَ
وَٱلْبَغْضَآءَ فِى ٱلْخَمْرِ وَٱلْمَيْسِرِ وَيَصُدَّكُمْ عَن
ذِكْرِ ٱللَّهِ وَعَنِ ٱلصَّلَوٰةِ ۖ فَهَلْ أَنتُم مُّنتَهُونَ

91 Satan wants to provoke strife and hatred among you through intoxicants and gambling, and to prevent you from the remembrance of Allah, and from prayer. Will you not desist?

٩٢ وَأَطِيعُوا۟ ٱللَّهَ وَأَطِيعُوا۟ ٱلرَّسُولَ وَٱحْذَرُوا۟ ۚ
فَإِن تَوَلَّيْتُمْ فَٱعْلَمُوٓا۟ أَنَّمَا عَلَىٰ رَسُولِنَا ٱلْبَلَٰغُ
ٱلْمُبِينُ

92 Obey Allah and obey the Messenger, and be cautious. If you turn away—know that the duty of Our Messenger is clear communication.

٩٣ لَيْسَ عَلَى ٱلَّذِينَ ءَامَنُوا۟ وَعَمِلُوا۟ ٱلصَّٰلِحَٰتِ
جُنَاحٌ فِيمَا طَعِمُوٓا۟ إِذَا مَا ٱتَّقَوا۟ وَّءَامَنُوا۟
وَعَمِلُوا۟ ٱلصَّٰلِحَٰتِ ثُمَّ ٱتَّقَوا۟ وَّءَامَنُوا۟ ثُمَّ ٱتَّقَوا۟
وَّأَحْسَنُوا۟ ۗ وَٱللَّهُ يُحِبُّ ٱلْمُحْسِنِينَ

93 Those who believe and do righteous deeds will not be blamed for what they may have eaten, provided they obey, and believe, and do good deeds, then maintain piety and faith, then remain righteous and charitable. Allah loves the charitable.

٩٤ يَٰٓأَيُّهَا ٱلَّذِينَ ءَامَنُوا۟ لَيَبْلُوَنَّكُمُ ٱللَّهُ بِشَىْءٍ
مِّنَ ٱلصَّيْدِ تَنَالُهُۥٓ أَيْدِيكُمْ وَرِمَاحُكُمْ لِيَعْلَمَ ٱللَّهُ
مَن يَخَافُهُۥ بِٱلْغَيْبِ ۚ فَمَنِ ٱعْتَدَىٰ بَعْدَ ذَٰلِكَ فَلَهُۥ
عَذَابٌ أَلِيمٌ

94 O you who believe! Allah will test you with something of the game your hands and spears obtain, that Allah may know who fears Him at heart. Whoever commits aggression after that will have a painful punishment.

٩٥ يَٰٓأَيُّهَا ٱلَّذِينَ ءَامَنُوا۟ لَا تَقْتُلُوا۟ ٱلصَّيْدَ وَأَنتُمْ
حُرُمٌ ۚ وَمَن قَتَلَهُۥ مِنكُم مُّتَعَمِّدًا فَجَزَآءٌ مِّثْلُ مَا
قَتَلَ مِنَ ٱلنَّعَمِ يَحْكُمُ بِهِۦ ذَوَا عَدْلٍ مِّنكُمْ هَدْيًۢا
بَٰلِغَ ٱلْكَعْبَةِ أَوْ كَفَّٰرَةٌ طَعَامُ مَسَٰكِينَ أَوْ عَدْلُ
ذَٰلِكَ صِيَامًا لِّيَذُوقَ وَبَالَ أَمْرِهِۦ ۗ عَفَا ٱللَّهُ عَمَّا
سَلَفَ ۚ وَمَنْ عَادَ فَيَنتَقِمُ ٱللَّهُ مِنْهُ ۗ وَٱللَّهُ عَزِيزٌ
ذُو ٱنتِقَامٍ

95 O you who believe! do not kill game while you are in pilgrim sanctity. Whoever of you kills any intentionally, its penalty shall be a domestic animal comparable to what he killed, as determined by two honest persons among you—an offering delivered to the Kaabah. Or he may atone by feeding the needy, or its equivalent in fasting, so that he may taste the consequences of his conduct. Allah forgives what is past. But whoever repeats, Allah will take revenge on him. Allah is Almighty, Avenger.

٩٦ أُحِلَّ لَكُمْ صَيْدُ ٱلْبَحْرِ وَطَعَامُهُۥ مَتَٰعًا لَّكُمْ
وَلِلسَّيَّارَةِ ۖ وَحُرِّمَ عَلَيْكُمْ صَيْدُ ٱلْبَرِّ مَا دُمْتُمْ
حُرُمًا ۗ وَٱتَّقُوا۟ ٱللَّهَ ٱلَّذِىٓ إِلَيْهِ تُحْشَرُونَ

96 Permitted for you is the catch of sea, and its food—as sustenance for you and for travelers. But forbidden for you is the game of land while you are in pilgrim sanctity. And fear Allah, to whom you will be gathered.

٩٧ جَعَلَ ٱللَّهُ ٱلْكَعْبَةَ ٱلْبَيْتَ ٱلْحَرَامَ قِيَٰمًا لِّلنَّاسِ
وَٱلشَّهْرَ ٱلْحَرَامَ وَٱلْهَدْىَ وَٱلْقَلَٰٓئِدَ ۚ ذَٰلِكَ لِتَعْلَمُوٓا۟
أَنَّ ٱللَّهَ يَعْلَمُ مَا فِى ٱلسَّمَٰوَٰتِ وَمَا فِى ٱلْأَرْضِ
وَأَنَّ ٱللَّهَ بِكُلِّ شَىْءٍ عَلِيمٌ

97 Allah has appointed the Kaabah, the Sacred House, a sanctuary for the people, and the Sacred Month, and the offerings, and the garlanded. That you may know that Allah knows everything in the heavens and the earth, and that Allah is Cognizant of all things.

٩٨ ٱعْلَمُوٓا۟ أَنَّ ٱللَّهَ شَدِيدُ ٱلْعِقَابِ وَأَنَّ ٱللَّهَ
غَفُورٌ رَّحِيمٌ

98 Know that Allah is severe in retribution, and that Allah is Forgiving and Merciful.

٩٩ مَّا عَلَى ٱلرَّسُولِ إِلَّا ٱلْبَلَٰغُ ۗ وَٱللَّهُ يَعْلَمُ مَا
تُبْدُونَ وَمَا تَكْتُمُونَ

99 The Messenger's sole duty is to convey. Allah knows what you reveal and what you conceal.

١٠٠ قُل لَّا يَسْتَوِى ٱلْخَبِيثُ وَٱلطَّيِّبُ وَلَوْ
أَعْجَبَكَ كَثْرَةُ ٱلْخَبِيثِ ۚ فَٱتَّقُوا۟ ٱللَّهَ يَٰٓأُو۟لِى
ٱلْأَلْبَٰبِ لَعَلَّكُمْ تُفْلِحُونَ

100 Say: "The bad and the good are not equal, even though the abundance of the bad may impress you. So be conscious of Allah, O you who possess intelligence, that you may succeed."

١٠١ يَٰٓأَيُّهَا ٱلَّذِينَ ءَامَنُوا۟ لَا تَسْـَٔلُوا۟ عَنْ أَشْيَآءَ إِن
تُبْدَ لَكُمْ تَسُؤْكُمْ وَإِن تَسْـَٔلُوا۟ عَنْهَا حِينَ يُنَزَّلُ
ٱلْقُرْءَانُ تُبْدَ لَكُمْ عَفَا ٱللَّهُ عَنْهَا ۗ وَٱللَّهُ غَفُورٌ
حَلِيمٌ

101 O you who believe! Do not ask about things that would trouble you if disclosed to you. But if you were to ask about them while the Quran is being revealed, they will become obvious to you. Allah forgives that. Allah is Forgiving and Clement.

١٠٢ قَدْ سَأَلَهَا قَوْمٌ مِّن قَبْلِكُمْ ثُمَّ أَصْبَحُوا۟ بِهَا
كَٰفِرِينَ

102 A people before you asked about them, but then came to reject them.

١٠٣ مَا جَعَلَ ٱللَّهُ مِنۢ بَحِيرَةٍ وَلَا سَآئِبَةٍ وَلَا
وَصِيلَةٍ وَلَا حَامٍ ۙ وَلَٰكِنَّ ٱلَّذِينَ كَفَرُوا۟ يَفْتَرُونَ
عَلَى ٱللَّهِ ٱلْكَذِبَ ۖ وَأَكْثَرُهُمْ لَا يَعْقِلُونَ

103 Allah did not institute the superstitions of Bahirah, Saibah, Wasilah, or of Hami; but those who disbelieve fabricate lies about Allah—most of them do not understand.

١٠٤ وَإِذَا قِيلَ لَهُمْ تَعَالَوْا۟ إِلَىٰ مَآ أَنزَلَ ٱللَّهُ وَإِلَى
ٱلرَّسُولِ قَالُوا۟ حَسْبُنَا مَا وَجَدْنَا عَلَيْهِ ءَابَآءَنَآ ۚ
أَوَلَوْ كَانَ ءَابَآؤُهُمْ لَا يَعْلَمُونَ شَيْـًٔا وَلَا يَهْتَدُونَ

104 And when it is said to them, "Come to what Allah has revealed, and to the Messenger," they say, "Sufficient for us is what we found our forefathers upon." Even if their forefathers knew nothing, and were not guided?

١٠٥ يَٰٓأَيُّهَا ٱلَّذِينَ ءَامَنُوا۟ عَلَيْكُمْ أَنفُسَكُمْ ۖ لَا
يَضُرُّكُم مَّن ضَلَّ إِذَا ٱهْتَدَيْتُمْ ۚ إِلَى ٱللَّهِ
مَرْجِعُكُمْ جَمِيعًا فَيُنَبِّئُكُم بِمَا كُنتُمْ تَعْمَلُونَ

105 O you who believe! You are responsible for your own souls. He who has strayed cannot harm you if you are guided. To Allah is you return, all of you, and He will inform you of what you used to do.

١٠٦ يَٰٓأَيُّهَا ٱلَّذِينَ ءَامَنُوا۟ شَهَٰدَةُ بَيْنِكُمْ إِذَا حَضَرَ
أَحَدَكُمُ ٱلْمَوْتُ حِينَ ٱلْوَصِيَّةِ ٱثْنَانِ ذَوَا عَدْلٍ
مِّنكُمْ أَوْ ءَاخَرَانِ مِنْ غَيْرِكُمْ إِنْ أَنتُمْ ضَرَبْتُمْ
فِى ٱلْأَرْضِ فَأَصَٰبَتْكُم مُّصِيبَةُ ٱلْمَوْتِ ۚ
تَحْبِسُونَهُمَا مِنۢ بَعْدِ ٱلصَّلَوٰةِ فَيُقْسِمَانِ بِٱللَّهِ
إِنِ ٱرْتَبْتُمْ لَا نَشْتَرِى بِهِۦ ثَمَنًا وَلَوْ كَانَ ذَا
قُرْبَىٰ ۙ وَلَا نَكْتُمُ شَهَٰدَةَ ٱللَّهِ إِنَّآ إِذًا لَّمِنَ
ٱلْءَاثِمِينَ

106 O you who believe! When death approaches one of you, let two reliable persons from among you act as witnesses to the making of a bequest, or two persons from another people if you are travelling in the land and the event of death approaches you. Engage them after the prayer. If you have doubts, let them swear by Allah: "We will not sell our testimony for any price, even if he was a near relative, and we will not conceal Allah's testimony, for then we would be sinners."

١٠٧ فَإِنْ عُثِرَ عَلَىٰٓ أَنَّهُمَا ٱسْتَحَقَّآ إِثْمًا فَـَٔاخَرَانِ
يَقُومَانِ مَقَامَهُمَا مِنَ ٱلَّذِينَ ٱسْتَحَقَّ عَلَيْهِمُ
ٱلْأَوْلَيَٰنِ فَيُقْسِمَانِ بِٱللَّهِ لَشَهَٰدَتُنَآ أَحَقُّ مِن
شَهَٰدَتِهِمَا وَمَا ٱعْتَدَيْنَآ إِنَّآ إِذًا لَّمِنَ ٱلظَّٰلِمِينَ

107 If it is discovered that they are guilty of perjury: let two others take their place, two from among those responsible for the claim, and have them swear by Allah, "Our testimony is more truthful than their testimony, and we will not be biased, for then we would be wrongdoers."

١٠٨ ذَٰلِكَ أَدْنَىٰٓ أَن يَأْتُوا۟ بِٱلشَّهَٰدَةِ عَلَىٰ وَجْهِهَآ
أَوْ يَخَافُوٓا۟ أَن تُرَدَّ أَيْمَٰنٌۢ بَعْدَ أَيْمَٰنِهِمْ ۗ وَٱتَّقُوا۟
ٱللَّهَ وَٱسْمَعُوا۟ ۗ وَٱللَّهُ لَا يَهْدِى ٱلْقَوْمَ ٱلْفَٰسِقِينَ

108 That makes it more likely that they will give true testimony, fearing that their oaths might be contradicted by subsequent oaths. So fear Allah, and listen. Allah does not guide the disobedient people.

١٠٩ يَوْمَ يَجْمَعُ ٱللَّهُ ٱلرُّسُلَ فَيَقُولُ مَاذَآ أُجِبْتُمْ ۖ
قَالُوا۟ لَا عِلْمَ لَنَآ ۖ إِنَّكَ أَنتَ عَلَّٰمُ ٱلْغُيُوبِ

109 On the Day when Allah will gather the messengers, then say, "What response were you given?" They will say, "We have no knowledge; it is you who are the Knower of the unseen."

١١٠ إِذْ قَالَ ٱللَّهُ يَٰعِيسَى ٱبْنَ مَرْيَمَ ٱذْكُرْ نِعْمَتِى
عَلَيْكَ وَعَلَىٰ وَٰلِدَتِكَ إِذْ أَيَّدتُّكَ بِرُوحِ ٱلْقُدُسِ
تُكَلِّمُ ٱلنَّاسَ فِى ٱلْمَهْدِ وَكَهْلًا ۖ وَإِذْ عَلَّمْتُكَ
ٱلْكِتَٰبَ وَٱلْحِكْمَةَ وَٱلتَّوْرَىٰةَ وَٱلْإِنجِيلَ ۖ وَإِذْ
تَخْلُقُ مِنَ ٱلطِّينِ كَهَيْـَٔةِ ٱلطَّيْرِ بِإِذْنِى فَتَنفُخُ

110 When Allah will say, "O Jesus son of Mary, recall My favor upon you and upon your mother, how I supported you with the Holy Spirit. You spoke to the people from the crib, and in maturity. How I taught you the Scripture and wisdom, and the Torah and the Gospel. And recall

فِيهَا فَتَكُونُ طَيْرًۢا بِإِذْنِى ۖ وَتُبْرِئُ ٱلْأَكْمَهَ
وَٱلْأَبْرَصَ بِإِذْنِى ۖ وَإِذْ تُخْرِجُ ٱلْمَوْتَىٰ بِإِذْنِى ۖ
وَإِذْ كَفَفْتُ بَنِىٓ إِسْرَٰٓءِيلَ عَنكَ إِذْ جِئْتَهُم
بِٱلْبَيِّنَٰتِ فَقَالَ ٱلَّذِينَ كَفَرُوا۟ مِنْهُمْ إِنْ هَٰذَآ إِلَّا
سِحْرٌ مُّبِينٌ

that you molded from clay the shape of a bird, by My leave, and then you breathed into it, and it became a bird, by My leave. And you healed the blind and the leprous, by My leave; and you revived the dead, by My leave. And recall that I restrained the Children of Israel from you when you brought them the clear miracles. But those who disbelieved among them said, `This is nothing but obvious sorcery.'"

١١١ وَإِذْ أَوْحَيْتُ إِلَى ٱلْحَوَارِيِّـۧنَ أَنْ ءَامِنُوا۟ بِى
وَبِرَسُولِى قَالُوٓا۟ ءَامَنَّا وَٱشْهَدْ بِأَنَّنَا مُسْلِمُونَ

111 "And when I inspired the disciples: `Believe in Me and in My Messenger.' They said, `We have believed, so bear witness that We have submitted.'"

١١٢ إِذْ قَالَ ٱلْحَوَارِيُّونَ يَٰعِيسَى ٱبْنَ مَرْيَمَ هَلْ
يَسْتَطِيعُ رَبُّكَ أَن يُنَزِّلَ عَلَيْنَا مَآئِدَةً مِّنَ
ٱلسَّمَآءِ ۖ قَالَ ٱتَّقُوا۟ ٱللَّهَ إِن كُنتُم مُّؤْمِنِينَ

112 "And when the disciples said, 'O Jesus son of Mary, is your Lord able to bring down for us a feast from heaven?' He said, 'Fear Allah, if you are believers.'"

١١٣ قَالُوا۟ نُرِيدُ أَن نَّأْكُلَ مِنْهَا وَتَطْمَئِنَّ قُلُوبُنَا
وَنَعْلَمَ أَن قَدْ صَدَقْتَنَا وَنَكُونَ عَلَيْهَا مِنَ
ٱلشَّٰهِدِينَ

113 They said, "We wish to eat from it, so that our hearts may be reassured, and know that you have told us the truth, and be among those who witness it."

١١٤ قَالَ عِيسَى ٱبْنُ مَرْيَمَ ٱللَّهُمَّ رَبَّنَآ أَنزِلْ عَلَيْنَا
مَآئِدَةً مِّنَ ٱلسَّمَآءِ تَكُونُ لَنَا عِيدًا لِّأَوَّلِنَا
وَءَاخِرِنَا وَءَايَةً مِّنكَ ۖ وَٱرْزُقْنَا وَأَنتَ خَيْرُ
ٱلرَّٰزِقِينَ

114 Jesus son of Mary said, "O Allah, our Lord, send down for us a table from heaven, to be a festival for us, for the first of us, and the last of us, and a sign from You; and provide for us; You are the Best of providers."

١١٥ قَالَ ٱللَّهُ إِنِّى مُنَزِّلُهَا عَلَيْكُمْ ۖ فَمَن يَكْفُرْ بَعْدُ
مِنكُمْ فَإِنِّىٓ أُعَذِّبُهُۥ عَذَابًا لَّآ أُعَذِّبُهُۥٓ أَحَدًا مِّنَ
ٱلْعَٰلَمِينَ

115 Allah said, "I will send it down to you. But whoever among you disbelieves thereafter, I will punish him with a punishment the like of which I never punish any other being."

١١٦ وَإِذْ قَالَ ٱللَّهُ يَٰعِيسَى ٱبْنَ مَرْيَمَ ءَأَنتَ قُلْتَ
لِلنَّاسِ ٱتَّخِذُونِى وَأُمِّىَ إِلَٰهَيْنِ مِن دُونِ ٱللَّهِ ۖ
قَالَ سُبْحَٰنَكَ مَا يَكُونُ لِىٓ أَنْ أَقُولَ مَا لَيْسَ
لِى بِحَقٍّ ۚ إِن كُنتُ قُلْتُهُۥ فَقَدْ عَلِمْتَهُۥ ۚ تَعْلَمُ مَا
فِى نَفْسِى وَلَآ أَعْلَمُ مَا فِى نَفْسِكَ ۚ إِنَّكَ أَنتَ
عَلَّٰمُ ٱلْغُيُوبِ

116 And Allah will say, “O Jesus son of Mary, did you say to the people, `Take me and my mother as gods rather than Allah?'“ He will say, “Glory be to You! It is not for me to say what I have no right to. Had I said it, You would have known it. You know what is in my soul, and I do not know what is in your soul. You are the Knower of the hidden.

١١٧ مَا قُلْتُ لَهُمْ إِلَّا مَآ أَمَرْتَنِى بِهِۦٓ أَنِ ٱعْبُدُوا۟
ٱللَّهَ رَبِّى وَرَبَّكُمْ ۚ وَكُنتُ عَلَيْهِمْ شَهِيدًا مَّا دُمْتُ
فِيهِمْ ۖ فَلَمَّا تَوَفَّيْتَنِى كُنتَ أَنتَ ٱلرَّقِيبَ
عَلَيْهِمْ ۚ وَأَنتَ عَلَىٰ كُلِّ شَىْءٍ شَهِيدٌ

117 I only told them what You commanded me: that you shall worship Allah, my Lord and your Lord. And I was a witness over them while I was among them; but when You took me to Yourself, you became the Watcher over them—You are Witness over everything.

١١٨ إِن تُعَذِّبْهُمْ فَإِنَّهُمْ عِبَادُكَ ۖ وَإِن تَغْفِرْ لَهُمْ
فَإِنَّكَ أَنتَ ٱلْعَزِيزُ ٱلْحَكِيمُ

118 If You punish them, they are Your servants; but if You forgive them, You are the Mighty and Wise.”

١١٩ قَالَ ٱللَّهُ هَٰذَا يَوْمُ يَنفَعُ ٱلصَّٰدِقِينَ صِدْقُهُمْ ۚ
لَهُمْ جَنَّٰتٌ تَجْرِى مِن تَحْتِهَا ٱلْأَنْهَٰرُ خَٰلِدِينَ
فِيهَآ أَبَدًا ۚ رَّضِىَ ٱللَّهُ عَنْهُمْ وَرَضُوا۟ عَنْهُ ۚ ذَٰلِكَ
ٱلْفَوْزُ ٱلْعَظِيمُ

119 Allah will say, “This is a Day when the truthful will benefit from their truthfulness.” They will have Gardens beneath which rivers flow, wherein they will remain forever. Allah is pleased with them, and they are pleased with Him. That is the great attainment.

١٢٠ لِلَّهِ مُلْكُ ٱلسَّمَٰوَٰتِ وَٱلْأَرْضِ وَمَا فِيهِنَّ ۚ وَهُوَ
عَلَىٰ كُلِّ شَىْءٍ قَدِيرٌۢ

120 To Allah belongs the sovereignty of the heavens and the earth and what lies in them, and He has power over everything.

6 Livestock الأنعام

بِسْمِ ٱللَّهِ ٱلرَّحْمَٰنِ ٱلرَّحِيمِ

In the name of Allah, the Gracious, the Merciful.

١ ٱلْحَمْدُ لِلَّهِ ٱلَّذِى خَلَقَ ٱلسَّمَٰوَٰتِ وَٱلْأَرْضَ
وَجَعَلَ ٱلظُّلُمَٰتِ وَٱلنُّورَ ۖ ثُمَّ ٱلَّذِينَ كَفَرُوا۟ بِرَبِّهِمْ
يَعْدِلُونَ

1 Praise be to Allah, Who created the heavens and the earth, and made the darkness and the light. Yet those who disbelieve ascribe equals to their Lord.

٢ هُوَ ٱلَّذِى خَلَقَكُم مِّن طِينٍ ثُمَّ قَضَىٰٓ أَجَلًا ۖ
وَأَجَلٌ مُّسَمًّى عِندَهُۥ ۖ ثُمَّ أَنتُمْ تَمْتَرُونَ

2 It is He who created you from clay, then decided a term—a term determined by him. Yet you doubt.

٣ وَهُوَ ٱللَّهُ فِى ٱلسَّمَٰوَٰتِ وَفِى ٱلْأَرْضِ ۖ يَعْلَمُ
سِرَّكُمْ وَجَهْرَكُمْ وَيَعْلَمُ مَا تَكْسِبُونَ

3 He is Allah in the heavens and the earth. He knows what you keep secret and what you make public; and He knows what you earn.

٤ وَمَا تَأْتِيهِم مِّنْ ءَايَةٍ مِّنْ ءَايَٰتِ رَبِّهِمْ إِلَّا
كَانُوا۟ عَنْهَا مُعْرِضِينَ

4 Not one of their Lord's signs comes to them, but they turn away from it.

٥ فَقَدْ كَذَّبُوا۟ بِٱلْحَقِّ لَمَّا جَآءَهُمْ ۖ فَسَوْفَ
يَأْتِيهِمْ أَنۢبَٰٓؤُا۟ مَا كَانُوا۟ بِهِۦ يَسْتَهْزِءُونَ

5 They denied the truth when it has come to them; but soon will reach them the news of what they used to ridicule.

٦ أَلَمْ يَرَوْا۟ كَمْ أَهْلَكْنَا مِن قَبْلِهِم مِّن قَرْنٍ
مَّكَّنَّٰهُمْ فِى ٱلْأَرْضِ مَا لَمْ نُمَكِّن لَّكُمْ وَأَرْسَلْنَا
ٱلسَّمَآءَ عَلَيْهِم مِّدْرَارًا وَجَعَلْنَا ٱلْأَنْهَٰرَ تَجْرِى
مِن تَحْتِهِمْ فَأَهْلَكْنَٰهُم بِذُنُوبِهِمْ وَأَنشَأْنَا مِنۢ
بَعْدِهِمْ قَرْنًا ءَاخَرِينَ

6 Have they not considered how many generations We destroyed before them? We had established them on earth more firmly than We established you, and We sent the clouds pouring down abundant rain on them, and We made rivers flow beneath them. But We destroyed them for their sins, and established other civilizations after them.

٧ وَلَوْ نَزَّلْنَا عَلَيْكَ كِتَٰبًا فِى قِرْطَاسٍ فَلَمَسُوهُ
بِأَيْدِيهِمْ لَقَالَ ٱلَّذِينَ كَفَرُوٓا۟ إِنْ هَٰذَآ إِلَّا سِحْرٌ
مُّبِينٌ

7 Had We sent down upon you a book on paper, and they had touched it with their hands, those who disbelieve would have said, "This is nothing but plain magic."

٨ وَقَالُوا۟ لَوْلَآ أُنزِلَ عَلَيْهِ مَلَكٌ ۖ وَلَوْ أَنزَلْنَا مَلَكًا
لَّقُضِىَ ٱلْأَمْرُ ثُمَّ لَا يُنظَرُونَ

8 And they say, "Why was an angel not sent down to him." Had We sent down an angel, the matter would have been settled, and they would not have been reprieved.

٩ وَلَوْ جَعَلْنَٰهُ مَلَكًا لَّجَعَلْنَٰهُ رَجُلًا وَلَلَبَسْنَا عَلَيْهِم
مَّا يَلْبِسُونَ

9 Had We made him an angel, We would have made him a man, and confused them when they are already confused.

١٠ وَلَقَدِ ٱسْتُهْزِئَ بِرُسُلٍ مِّن قَبْلِكَ فَحَاقَ
بِٱلَّذِينَ سَخِرُوا۟ مِنْهُم مَّا كَانُوا۟ بِهِۦ يَسْتَهْزِءُونَ

10 Messengers before you were ridiculed, but those who mocked them became besieged by what they ridiculed.

١١ قُلْ سِيرُوا۟ فِى ٱلْأَرْضِ ثُمَّ ٱنظُرُوا۟ كَيْفَ كَانَ
عَٰقِبَةُ ٱلْمُكَذِّبِينَ

11 Say, “Travel the earth and observe the final fate of the deniers.”

١٢ قُل لِّمَن مَّا فِى ٱلسَّمَٰوَٰتِ وَٱلْأَرْضِ ۖ قُل لِّلَّهِ ۚ
كَتَبَ عَلَىٰ نَفْسِهِ ٱلرَّحْمَةَ ۚ لَيَجْمَعَنَّكُمْ إِلَىٰ يَوْمِ
ٱلْقِيَٰمَةِ لَا رَيْبَ فِيهِ ۚ ٱلَّذِينَ خَسِرُوٓا۟ أَنفُسَهُمْ
فَهُمْ لَا يُؤْمِنُونَ

12 Say, “To whom belongs what is in the heavens and the earth?” Say, “To Allah.” He has inscribed for Himself mercy. He will gather you to the Day of Resurrection, in which there is no doubt. Those who lost their souls do not believe.

١٣ وَلَهُۥ مَا سَكَنَ فِى ٱلَّيْلِ وَٱلنَّهَارِ ۚ وَهُوَ ٱلسَّمِيعُ
ٱلْعَلِيمُ

13 To Him belongs whatever rests in the night and the day. He is the Hearing, the Knowing.

١٤ قُلْ أَغَيْرَ ٱللَّهِ أَتَّخِذُ وَلِيًّا فَاطِرِ ٱلسَّمَٰوَٰتِ
وَٱلْأَرْضِ وَهُوَ يُطْعِمُ وَلَا يُطْعَمُ ۗ قُلْ إِنِّىٓ أُمِرْتُ
أَنْ أَكُونَ أَوَّلَ مَنْ أَسْلَمَ ۖ وَلَا تَكُونَنَّ مِنَ
ٱلْمُشْرِكِينَ

14 Say, “Shall I take for myself a protector other than Allah, Originator of the heavens and the earth, and He feeds and is not fed?” Say, “I am instructed to be the first of those who submit.” And do not be among the idolaters.

١٥ قُلْ إِنِّىٓ أَخَافُ إِنْ عَصَيْتُ رَبِّى عَذَابَ يَوْمٍ
عَظِيمٍ

15 Say, “I fear, should I defy my Lord, the punishment of a tremendous Day.”

١٦ مَّن يُصْرَفْ عَنْهُ يَوْمَئِذٍ فَقَدْ رَحِمَهُۥ ۚ وَذَٰلِكَ
ٱلْفَوْزُ ٱلْمُبِينُ

16 Whoever is spared on that Day—He had mercy on him. That is the clear victory.

١٧ وَإِن يَمْسَسْكَ ٱللَّهُ بِضُرٍّ فَلَا كَاشِفَ لَهُۥٓ إِلَّا
هُوَ ۖ وَإِن يَمْسَسْكَ بِخَيْرٍ فَهُوَ عَلَىٰ كُلِّ شَىْءٍ
قَدِيرٌ

17 If Allah touches you with adversity, none can remove it except He. And if He touches you with good—He is Capable of everything.

١٨ وَهُوَ ٱلْقَاهِرُ فَوْقَ عِبَادِهِۦ ۚ وَهُوَ ٱلْحَكِيمُ ٱلْخَبِيرُ

18 He is the Supreme over His servants. He is the Wise, the Expert.

١٩ قُلْ أَىُّ شَىْءٍ أَكْبَرُ شَهَٰدَةً ۖ قُلِ ٱللَّهُ ۖ شَهِيدٌۢ بَيْنِى وَبَيْنَكُمْ ۚ وَأُوحِىَ إِلَىَّ هَٰذَا ٱلْقُرْءَانُ لِأُنذِرَكُم بِهِۦ وَمَنۢ بَلَغَ ۚ أَئِنَّكُمْ لَتَشْهَدُونَ أَنَّ مَعَ ٱللَّهِ ءَالِهَةً أُخْرَىٰ ۚ قُل لَّآ أَشْهَدُ ۚ قُلْ إِنَّمَا هُوَ إِلَٰهٌ وَٰحِدٌ وَإِنَّنِى بَرِىٓءٌ مِّمَّا تُشْرِكُونَ

19 Say, "What thing is more solemn in testimony?" Say, "Allah is Witness between you and me. This Quran was revealed to me, that I may warn you with it, and whomever it may reach. Do you indeed testify that there are other gods with Allah?" Say, "I myself do not testify." Say, "He is but One God, and I am innocent of your idolatry."

٢٠ ٱلَّذِينَ ءَاتَيْنَٰهُمُ ٱلْكِتَٰبَ يَعْرِفُونَهُۥ كَمَا يَعْرِفُونَ أَبْنَآءَهُمُ ۘ ٱلَّذِينَ خَسِرُوٓا۟ أَنفُسَهُمْ فَهُمْ لَا يُؤْمِنُونَ

20 Those to whom We have given the Book recognize it as they recognize their own children; but those who have lost their souls do not believe.

٢١ وَمَنْ أَظْلَمُ مِمَّنِ ٱفْتَرَىٰ عَلَى ٱللَّهِ كَذِبًا أَوْ كَذَّبَ بِـَٔايَٰتِهِۦٓ ۗ إِنَّهُۥ لَا يُفْلِحُ ٱلظَّٰلِمُونَ

21 Who does greater wrong than someone who fabricates lies against Allah, or denies His revelations? The wrongdoers will not succeed.

٢٢ وَيَوْمَ نَحْشُرُهُمْ جَمِيعًا ثُمَّ نَقُولُ لِلَّذِينَ أَشْرَكُوٓا۟ أَيْنَ شُرَكَآؤُكُمُ ٱلَّذِينَ كُنتُمْ تَزْعُمُونَ

22 On the Day when We gather them all together, then say to the idolaters, "Where are your idols, those you used to claim?"

٢٣ ثُمَّ لَمْ تَكُن فِتْنَتُهُمْ إِلَّآ أَن قَالُوا۟ وَٱللَّهِ رَبِّنَا مَا كُنَّا مُشْرِكِينَ

23 Then their only argument will be to say, "By Allah, our Lord, we were not idolaters."

٢٤ ٱنظُرْ كَيْفَ كَذَبُوا۟ عَلَىٰٓ أَنفُسِهِمْ ۚ وَضَلَّ عَنْهُم مَّا كَانُوا۟ يَفْتَرُونَ

24 Look how they lied to themselves. And what they invented deserted them.

٢٥ وَمِنْهُم مَّن يَسْتَمِعُ إِلَيْكَ ۖ وَجَعَلْنَا عَلَىٰ قُلُوبِهِمْ أَكِنَّةً أَن يَفْقَهُوهُ وَفِىٓ ءَاذَانِهِمْ وَقْرًا ۚ وَإِن يَرَوْا۟ كُلَّ ءَايَةٍ لَّا يُؤْمِنُوا۟ بِهَا ۚ حَتَّىٰٓ إِذَا جَآءُوكَ يُجَٰدِلُونَكَ يَقُولُ ٱلَّذِينَ كَفَرُوٓا۟ إِنْ هَٰذَآ إِلَّآ أَسَٰطِيرُ ٱلْأَوَّلِينَ

25 Among them are those who listen to you; but We place covers over their hearts, to prevent them from understanding it, and heaviness in their ears. Even if they see every sign, they will not believe in it. Until, when they come to you, to argue with you, those who disbelieve will

say, “These are nothing but myths of the ancients.”

٢٦ وَهُمْ يَنْهَوْنَ عَنْهُ وَيَنْـَٔوْنَ عَنْهُ ۖ وَإِن يُهْلِكُونَ
إِلَّآ أَنفُسَهُمْ وَمَا يَشْعُرُونَ

26 They keep others from it, and avoid it themselves; but they ruin only their own souls, and they do not realize.

٢٧ وَلَوْ تَرَىٰٓ إِذْ وُقِفُوا۟ عَلَى ٱلنَّارِ فَقَالُوا۟ يَـٰلَيْتَنَا
نُرَدُّ وَلَا نُكَذِّبَ بِـَٔايَـٰتِ رَبِّنَا وَنَكُونَ مِنَ ٱلْمُؤْمِنِينَ

27 If only you could see, when they are made to stand before the Fire; they will say, “If only we could be sent back, and not reject the revelations of our Lord, and be among the faithful.”

٢٨ بَلْ بَدَا لَهُم مَّا كَانُوا۟ يُخْفُونَ مِن قَبْلُ ۖ وَلَوْ
رُدُّوا۟ لَعَادُوا۟ لِمَا نُهُوا۟ عَنْهُ وَإِنَّهُمْ لَكَـٰذِبُونَ

28 What they used to conceal before will become clear to them. And even if they were sent back, they would revert to what they were forbidden. They are liars.

٢٩ وَقَالُوٓا۟ إِنْ هِىَ إِلَّا حَيَاتُنَا ٱلدُّنْيَا وَمَا نَحْنُ
بِمَبْعُوثِينَ

29 And they say, “There is nothing but our life in this world, and we will not be resurrected.”

٣٠ وَلَوْ تَرَىٰٓ إِذْ وُقِفُوا۟ عَلَىٰ رَبِّهِمْ ۚ قَالَ أَلَيْسَ
هَـٰذَا بِٱلْحَقِّ ۚ قَالُوا۟ بَلَىٰ وَرَبِّنَا ۚ قَالَ فَذُوقُوا۟
ٱلْعَذَابَ بِمَا كُنتُمْ تَكْفُرُونَ

30 If only you could see, when they are stationed before their Lord. He will say, “Is this not real?” They will say, “Yes indeed, by our Lord.” He will say, “Then taste the torment for having disbelieved.”

٣١ قَدْ خَسِرَ ٱلَّذِينَ كَذَّبُوا۟ بِلِقَآءِ ٱللَّهِ ۖ حَتَّىٰٓ إِذَا
جَآءَتْهُمُ ٱلسَّاعَةُ بَغْتَةً قَالُوا۟ يَـٰحَسْرَتَنَا عَلَىٰ مَا
فَرَّطْنَا فِيهَا وَهُمْ يَحْمِلُونَ أَوْزَارَهُمْ عَلَىٰ
ظُهُورِهِمْ ۚ أَلَا سَآءَ مَا يَزِرُونَ

31 Losers are those who deny the encounter with Allah. Then, when the Hour comes upon them suddenly, they will say, “Alas for us, how we have neglected it.” And they will carry their burdens on their backs—evil is what they carry.

٣٢ وَمَا ٱلْحَيَوٰةُ ٱلدُّنْيَآ إِلَّا لَعِبٌ وَلَهْوٌ ۖ وَلَلدَّارُ
ٱلْـَٔاخِرَةُ خَيْرٌ لِّلَّذِينَ يَتَّقُونَ ۗ أَفَلَا تَعْقِلُونَ

32 The life of this world is nothing but game and distraction, but the Home of the Hereafter is better for those who are righteous. Do you not understand?

٣٣ قَدْ نَعْلَمُ إِنَّهُۥ لَيَحْزُنُكَ ٱلَّذِى يَقُولُونَ ۖ فَإِنَّهُمْ
لَا يُكَذِّبُونَكَ وَلَٰكِنَّ ٱلظَّٰلِمِينَ بِـَٔايَٰتِ ٱللَّهِ
يَجْحَدُونَ

33 We know that what they say grieves you. It is not you they reject, but it is Allah's revelations that the wicked deny.

٣٤ وَلَقَدْ كُذِّبَتْ رُسُلٌ مِّن قَبْلِكَ فَصَبَرُوا۟ عَلَىٰ
مَا كُذِّبُوا۟ وَأُوذُوا۟ حَتَّىٰٓ أَتَىٰهُمْ نَصْرُنَا ۚ وَلَا مُبَدِّلَ
لِكَلِمَٰتِ ٱللَّهِ ۚ وَلَقَدْ جَآءَكَ مِن نَّبَإِى۟ ٱلْمُرْسَلِينَ

34 Other messengers before you were rejected, but they endured rejection and persecution until Our help came to them. There can be no change to Allah's words. News of the Messengers has already reached you.

٣٥ وَإِن كَانَ كَبُرَ عَلَيْكَ إِعْرَاضُهُمْ فَإِنِ
ٱسْتَطَعْتَ أَن تَبْتَغِىَ نَفَقًا فِى ٱلْأَرْضِ أَوْ سُلَّمًا
فِى ٱلسَّمَآءِ فَتَأْتِيَهُم بِـَٔايَةٍ ۚ وَلَوْ شَآءَ ٱللَّهُ
لَجَمَعَهُمْ عَلَى ٱلْهُدَىٰ ۚ فَلَا تَكُونَنَّ مِنَ ٱلْجَٰهِلِينَ

35 If you find their rejection hard to bear, then if you can, seek a tunnel into the earth, or a stairway into the heaven, and bring them a sign. Had Allah willed, He could have gathered them to guidance. So do not be of the ignorant.

٣٦ إِنَّمَا يَسْتَجِيبُ ٱلَّذِينَ يَسْمَعُونَ ۘ وَٱلْمَوْتَىٰ
يَبْعَثُهُمُ ٱللَّهُ ثُمَّ إِلَيْهِ يُرْجَعُونَ

36 Only those who listen will respond. As for the dead, Allah will resurrect them; then to Him they will be returned.

٣٧ وَقَالُوا۟ لَوْلَا نُزِّلَ عَلَيْهِ ءَايَةٌ مِّن رَّبِّهِۦ ۚ قُلْ
إِنَّ ٱللَّهَ قَادِرٌ عَلَىٰٓ أَن يُنَزِّلَ ءَايَةً وَلَٰكِنَّ أَكْثَرَهُمْ
لَا يَعْلَمُونَ

37 And they say, "If only a sign could come down to him from his Lord." Say, "Allah is Able to send down a sign, but most of them do not know."

٣٨ وَمَا مِن دَآبَّةٍ فِى ٱلْأَرْضِ وَلَا طَٰٓئِرٍ يَطِيرُ
بِجَنَاحَيْهِ إِلَّآ أُمَمٌ أَمْثَالُكُم ۚ مَّا فَرَّطْنَا فِى
ٱلْكِتَٰبِ مِن شَىْءٍ ۚ ثُمَّ إِلَىٰ رَبِّهِمْ يُحْشَرُونَ

38 There is no animal on land, nor a bird flying with its wings, but are communities like you. We neglected nothing in the Scripture. Then to their Lord they will be gathered.

٣٩ وَٱلَّذِينَ كَذَّبُوا۟ بِـَٔايَٰتِنَا صُمٌّ وَبُكْمٌ فِى
ٱلظُّلُمَٰتِ ۗ مَن يَشَإِ ٱللَّهُ يُضْلِلْهُ وَمَن يَشَأْ يَجْعَلْهُ
عَلَىٰ صِرَٰطٍ مُّسْتَقِيمٍ

39 Those who reject Our revelations are deaf and dumb, in total darkness. Whomever Allah wills, He leaves astray; and whomever He wills, He sets on a straight path.

٤٠ قُلْ أَرَءَيْتَكُمْ إِنْ أَتَىٰكُمْ عَذَابُ ٱللَّهِ أَوْ أَتَتْكُمُ
ٱلسَّاعَةُ أَغَيْرَ ٱللَّهِ تَدْعُونَ إِن كُنتُمْ صَٰدِقِينَ

40 Say, "Have you considered? if Allah's punishment came upon you, or the Hour overtook you, would you

call upon any other than Allah, if you are sincere?"

٤١ بَلْ إِيَّاهُ تَدْعُونَ فَيَكْشِفُ مَا تَدْعُونَ إِلَيْهِ إِن
شَآءَ وَتَنسَوْنَ مَا تُشْرِكُونَ

41 In fact, it is Him you will call upon; and if He wills, he will remove what you called Him for, and you will forget what you idolized.

٤٢ وَلَقَدْ أَرْسَلْنَآ إِلَىٰٓ أُمَمٍ مِّن قَبْلِكَ فَأَخَذْنَٰهُم
بِٱلْبَأْسَآءِ وَٱلضَّرَّآءِ لَعَلَّهُمْ يَتَضَرَّعُونَ

42 We sent messengers to communities before you, and We afflicted them with suffering and hardship, that they may humble themselves.

٤٣ فَلَوْلَآ إِذْ جَآءَهُم بَأْسُنَا تَضَرَّعُوا۟ وَلَٰكِن
قَسَتْ قُلُوبُهُمْ وَزَيَّنَ لَهُمُ ٱلشَّيْطَٰنُ مَا كَانُوا۟
يَعْمَلُونَ

43 If only, when Our calamity came upon them, they humbled themselves. But their hearts hardened, and Satan made their deeds appear good to them.

٤٤ فَلَمَّا نَسُوا۟ مَا ذُكِّرُوا۟ بِهِۦ فَتَحْنَا عَلَيْهِمْ أَبْوَٰبَ
كُلِّ شَىْءٍ حَتَّىٰٓ إِذَا فَرِحُوا۟ بِمَآ أُوتُوٓا۟ أَخَذْنَٰهُم
بَغْتَةً فَإِذَا هُم مُّبْلِسُونَ

44 Then, when they disregarded what they were reminded of, We opened for them the gates of all things. Until, when they delighted in what they were given, We seized them suddenly; and at once, they were in despair.

٤٥ فَقُطِعَ دَابِرُ ٱلْقَوْمِ ٱلَّذِينَ ظَلَمُوا۟ ۚ وَٱلْحَمْدُ لِلَّهِ
رَبِّ ٱلْعَٰلَمِينَ

45 Thus the last remnant of the people who did wrong was cut off. And praise be to Allah, Lord of the Worlds.

٤٦ قُلْ أَرَءَيْتُمْ إِنْ أَخَذَ ٱللَّهُ سَمْعَكُمْ وَأَبْصَٰرَكُمْ
وَخَتَمَ عَلَىٰ قُلُوبِكُم مَّنْ إِلَٰهٌ غَيْرُ ٱللَّهِ يَأْتِيكُم
بِهِ ۗ ٱنظُرْ كَيْفَ نُصَرِّفُ ٱلْءَايَٰتِ ثُمَّ هُمْ
يَصْدِفُونَ

46 Say, "Have you considered? If Allah took away your hearing and your sight, and set a seal on your hearts, what god other than Allah would restore them to you?" Note how We explain the revelations in various ways, yet they still turn away.

٤٧ قُلْ أَرَءَيْتَكُمْ إِنْ أَتَىٰكُمْ عَذَابُ ٱللَّهِ بَغْتَةً أَوْ
جَهْرَةً هَلْ يُهْلَكُ إِلَّا ٱلْقَوْمُ ٱلظَّٰلِمُونَ

47 Say, "Have you considered? if Allah's punishment descended on you suddenly or gradually, would any be destroyed except the wrongdoing people?"

٤٨ وَمَا نُرْسِلُ ٱلْمُرْسَلِينَ إِلَّا مُبَشِّرِينَ
وَمُنذِرِينَ ۖ فَمَنْ ءَامَنَ وَأَصْلَحَ فَلَا خَوْفٌ
عَلَيْهِمْ وَلَا هُمْ يَحْزَنُونَ

48 We sent the messengers only as bearers of good news and as warners. Those who believe and reform have nothing to fear, nor shall they grieve.

٤٩ وَٱلَّذِينَ كَذَّبُوا۟ بِـَٔايَـٰتِنَا يَمَسُّهُمُ ٱلْعَذَابُ بِمَا
كَانُوا۟ يَفْسُقُونَ

49 But as for those who reject Our revelations, torment will afflict them because of their defiance.

٥٠ قُل لَّآ أَقُولُ لَكُمْ عِندِى خَزَآئِنُ ٱللَّهِ وَلَآ أَعْلَمُ
ٱلْغَيْبَ وَلَآ أَقُولُ لَكُمْ إِنِّى مَلَكٌ ۖ إِنْ أَتَّبِعُ إِلَّا مَا
يُوحَىٰٓ إِلَىَّ ۚ قُلْ هَلْ يَسْتَوِى ٱلْأَعْمَىٰ وَٱلْبَصِيرُ ۚ
أَفَلَا تَتَفَكَّرُونَ

50 Say, “I do not say to you that I possess the treasuries of Allah, nor do I know the future, nor do I say to you that I am an angel. I only follow what is inspired to me.” Say, “Are the blind and the seeing alike? Do you not think?”

٥١ وَأَنذِرْ بِهِ ٱلَّذِينَ يَخَافُونَ أَن يُحْشَرُوٓا۟ إِلَىٰ
رَبِّهِمْ ۙ لَيْسَ لَهُم مِّن دُونِهِۦ وَلِىٌّ وَلَا شَفِيعٌ
لَّعَلَّهُمْ يَتَّقُونَ

51 And warn with it those who fear to be gathered before their Lord—they have no protector or intercessor apart from him—perhaps they will grow in piety.

٥٢ وَلَا تَطْرُدِ ٱلَّذِينَ يَدْعُونَ رَبَّهُم بِٱلْغَدَوٰةِ
وَٱلْعَشِىِّ يُرِيدُونَ وَجْهَهُۥ ۖ مَا عَلَيْكَ مِنْ
حِسَابِهِم مِّن شَىْءٍ وَمَا مِنْ حِسَابِكَ عَلَيْهِم
مِّن شَىْءٍ فَتَطْرُدَهُمْ فَتَكُونَ مِنَ ٱلظَّـٰلِمِينَ

52 And do not drive away those who call upon their Lord, morning and evening, seeking His attention. You are not accountable for them in any way, nor are they accountable for you in any way. If you drive them away, you would be one of the unjust.

٥٣ وَكَذَٰلِكَ فَتَنَّا بَعْضَهُم بِبَعْضٍ لِّيَقُولُوٓا۟ أَهَـٰٓؤُلَآءِ
مَنَّ ٱللَّهُ عَلَيْهِم مِّنۢ بَيْنِنَآ ۗ أَلَيْسَ ٱللَّهُ بِأَعْلَمَ
بِٱلشَّـٰكِرِينَ

53 Thus We try some of them by means of others, that they may say, “Are these the ones whom Allah has favored from among us?” Is Allah not aware of the appreciative?

٥٤ وَإِذَا جَآءَكَ ٱلَّذِينَ يُؤْمِنُونَ بِـَٔايَـٰتِنَا فَقُلْ سَلَـٰمٌ
عَلَيْكُمْ ۖ كَتَبَ رَبُّكُمْ عَلَىٰ نَفْسِهِ ٱلرَّحْمَةَ ۖ أَنَّهُۥ مَنْ
عَمِلَ مِنكُمْ سُوٓءًۢا بِجَهَـٰلَةٍ ثُمَّ تَابَ مِنۢ بَعْدِهِۦ
وَأَصْلَحَ فَأَنَّهُۥ غَفُورٌ رَّحِيمٌ

54 When those who believe in Our revelations come to you, say, “Peace be upon you, your Lord has prescribed mercy for Himself. Whoever among you does wrong out of ignorance, and then repents afterwards and reforms—He is Forgiving and Merciful.”

٥٥ وَكَذَٰلِكَ نُفَصِّلُ ٱلْءَايَٰتِ وَلِتَسْتَبِينَ سَبِيلُ
ٱلْمُجْرِمِينَ

55 Thus We explain the revelations, and expose the path of the unrighteous.

٥٦ قُلْ إِنِّى نُهِيتُ أَنْ أَعْبُدَ ٱلَّذِينَ تَدْعُونَ مِن
دُونِ ٱللَّهِ ۚ قُل لَّآ أَتَّبِعُ أَهْوَآءَكُمْ ۙ قَدْ ضَلَلْتُ إِذًا
وَمَآ أَنَا۠ مِنَ ٱلْمُهْتَدِينَ

56 Say, "I am forbidden from worshiping those you pray to besides Allah." Say, "I will not follow your desires; else I would be lost and not be of those guided."

٥٧ قُلْ إِنِّى عَلَىٰ بَيِّنَةٍ مِّن رَّبِّى وَكَذَّبْتُم بِهِۦ ۚ مَا
عِندِى مَا تَسْتَعْجِلُونَ بِهِۦٓ ۚ إِنِ ٱلْحُكْمُ إِلَّا لِلَّهِ ۖ
يَقُصُّ ٱلْحَقَّ ۖ وَهُوَ خَيْرُ ٱلْفَٰصِلِينَ

57 Say, "I stand on clear evidence from my Lord, and you have rejected Him. I do not possess what you seek me to hasten; the decision belongs solely to Allah. He states the truth, and He is the Best of Judges."

٥٨ قُل لَّوْ أَنَّ عِندِى مَا تَسْتَعْجِلُونَ بِهِۦ لَقُضِىَ
ٱلْأَمْرُ بَيْنِى وَبَيْنَكُمْ ۗ وَٱللَّهُ أَعْلَمُ بِٱلظَّٰلِمِينَ

58 Say, "If I possessed what you seek me to hasten, the matter between you and me would have been settled. Allah is well aware of the unjust."

٥٩ وَعِندَهُۥ مَفَاتِحُ ٱلْغَيْبِ لَا يَعْلَمُهَآ إِلَّا هُوَ ۚ
وَيَعْلَمُ مَا فِى ٱلْبَرِّ وَٱلْبَحْرِ ۚ وَمَا تَسْقُطُ مِن
وَرَقَةٍ إِلَّا يَعْلَمُهَا وَلَا حَبَّةٍ فِى ظُلُمَٰتِ ٱلْأَرْضِ
وَلَا رَطْبٍ وَلَا يَابِسٍ إِلَّا فِى كِتَٰبٍ مُّبِينٍ

59 With Him are the keys of the unseen; none knows them except He. And He knows everything on land and in the sea. Not a leaf falls but He knows it; and there is not a single grain in the darkness of earth, nor is there anything wet or dry, but is in a clear record.

٦٠ وَهُوَ ٱلَّذِى يَتَوَفَّىٰكُم بِٱلَّيْلِ وَيَعْلَمُ مَا
جَرَحْتُم بِٱلنَّهَارِ ثُمَّ يَبْعَثُكُمْ فِيهِ لِيُقْضَىٰٓ أَجَلٌ
مُّسَمًّى ۖ ثُمَّ إِلَيْهِ مَرْجِعُكُمْ ثُمَّ يُنَبِّئُكُم بِمَا كُنتُمْ
تَعْمَلُونَ

60 It is He Who takes you by night, and He knows what you earn by day. Then He raises you up in it, until a fixed term is fulfilled. Then to Him is your return, then He will inform you of what you used to do.

٦١ وَهُوَ ٱلْقَاهِرُ فَوْقَ عِبَادِهِۦ ۖ وَيُرْسِلُ عَلَيْكُمْ
حَفَظَةً حَتَّىٰٓ إِذَا جَآءَ أَحَدَكُمُ ٱلْمَوْتُ تَوَفَّتْهُ
رُسُلُنَا وَهُمْ لَا يُفَرِّطُونَ

61 He is the Conqueror over His servants, and He sends guardians over you, until, when death overtakes one of you, Our envoys take him away, and they never fail.

٦٢ ثُمَّ رُدُّوٓا۟ إِلَى ٱللَّهِ مَوْلَىٰهُمُ ٱلْحَقِّ ۚ أَلَا لَهُ
ٱلْحُكْمُ وَهُوَ أَسْرَعُ ٱلْحَٰسِبِينَ

62 Then they are brought back to Allah, their True Master.

Unquestionably, His is the judgment, and He is the Swiftest of reckoners.

٦٣ قُلْ مَن يُنَجِّيكُم مِّن ظُلُمَٰتِ ٱلْبَرِّ وَٱلْبَحْرِ
تَدْعُونَهُۥ تَضَرُّعًا وَخُفْيَةً لَّئِنْ أَنجَىٰنَا مِنْ هَٰذِهِۦ
لَنَكُونَنَّ مِنَ ٱلشَّٰكِرِينَ

63 Say, "Who delivers you from the darkness of land and sea?" You call upon Him humbly and inwardly: "If He delivers us from this, We will surely be among the thankful."

٦٤ قُلِ ٱللَّهُ يُنَجِّيكُم مِّنْهَا وَمِن كُلِّ كَرْبٍ ثُمَّ
أَنتُمْ تُشْرِكُونَ

64 Say, "It is Allah who delivers you from it, and from every disaster. Yet then you associate others with Him."

٦٥ قُلْ هُوَ ٱلْقَادِرُ عَلَىٰٓ أَن يَبْعَثَ عَلَيْكُمْ عَذَابًا
مِّن فَوْقِكُمْ أَوْ مِن تَحْتِ أَرْجُلِكُمْ أَوْ يَلْبِسَكُمْ
شِيَعًا وَيُذِيقَ بَعْضَكُم بَأْسَ بَعْضٍ ۗ ٱنظُرْ كَيْفَ
نُصَرِّفُ ٱلْءَايَٰتِ لَعَلَّهُمْ يَفْقَهُونَ

65 Say, "He is Able to send upon you an affliction, from above you, or from under your feet. Or He can divide you into factions, and make you taste the violence of one another. Note how We explain the revelations, so that they may understand."

٦٦ وَكَذَّبَ بِهِۦ قَوْمُكَ وَهُوَ ٱلْحَقُّ ۚ قُل لَّسْتُ
عَلَيْكُم بِوَكِيلٍ

66 But your people rejected it, though it is the truth. Say, "I am not responsible for you."

٦٧ لِّكُلِّ نَبَإٍ مُّسْتَقَرٌّ ۚ وَسَوْفَ تَعْلَمُونَ

67 For every happening is a finality, and you will surely know.

٦٨ وَإِذَا رَأَيْتَ ٱلَّذِينَ يَخُوضُونَ فِىٓ ءَايَٰتِنَا
فَأَعْرِضْ عَنْهُمْ حَتَّىٰ يَخُوضُوا۟ فِى حَدِيثٍ
غَيْرِهِۦ ۚ وَإِمَّا يُنسِيَنَّكَ ٱلشَّيْطَٰنُ فَلَا تَقْعُدْ بَعْدَ
ٱلذِّكْرَىٰ مَعَ ٱلْقَوْمِ ٱلظَّٰلِمِينَ

68 When you encounter those who gossip about Our revelations, turn away from them, until they engage in another topic. But should Satan make you forget, do not sit after the recollection with the wicked people.

٦٩ وَمَا عَلَى ٱلَّذِينَ يَتَّقُونَ مِنْ حِسَابِهِم مِّن
شَىْءٍ وَلَٰكِن ذِكْرَىٰ لَعَلَّهُمْ يَتَّقُونَ

69 The righteous are in no way accountable for them; it is only a reminder, that they may be careful.

٧٠ وَذَرِ ٱلَّذِينَ ٱتَّخَذُوا۟ دِينَهُمْ لَعِبًا وَلَهْوًا
وَغَرَّتْهُمُ ٱلْحَيَوٰةُ ٱلدُّنْيَا ۚ وَذَكِّرْ بِهِۦٓ أَن تُبْسَلَ
نَفْسٌۢ بِمَا كَسَبَتْ لَيْسَ لَهَا مِن دُونِ ٱللَّهِ وَلِىٌّ
وَلَا شَفِيعٌ وَإِن تَعْدِلْ كُلَّ عَدْلٍ لَّا يُؤْخَذْ مِنْهَآ ۗ

70 So leave alone those who take their religion for play and pastime, and whom the worldly life has deceived. But remind with it, lest a soul becomes damned on account of what it has earned. It has no helper or intercessor besides Allah. Even if it offers every equivalent, none will be accepted from it. These are the

أُولَٰٓئِكَ ٱلَّذِينَ أُبْسِلُوا۟ بِمَا كَسَبُوا۟ ۖ لَهُمْ شَرَابٌ مِّنْ حَمِيمٍ وَعَذَابٌ أَلِيمٌۢ بِمَا كَانُوا۟ يَكْفُرُونَ	ones who are delivered to perdition by their actions. They will have a drink of scalding water, and a painful punishment, because they used to disbelieve.
٧١ قُلْ أَنَدْعُوا۟ مِن دُونِ ٱللَّهِ مَا لَا يَنفَعُنَا وَلَا يَضُرُّنَا وَنُرَدُّ عَلَىٰٓ أَعْقَابِنَا بَعْدَ إِذْ هَدَىٰنَا ٱللَّهُ كَٱلَّذِى ٱسْتَهْوَتْهُ ٱلشَّيَٰطِينُ فِى ٱلْأَرْضِ حَيْرَانَ لَهُۥٓ أَصْحَٰبٌ يَدْعُونَهُۥٓ إِلَى ٱلْهُدَى ٱئْتِنَا ۗ قُلْ إِنَّ هُدَى ٱللَّهِ هُوَ ٱلْهُدَىٰ ۖ وَأُمِرْنَا لِنُسْلِمَ لِرَبِّ ٱلْعَٰلَمِينَ	71 Say, “Shall we invoke besides Allah something that can neither benefit us nor harm us, and turn back on our heels after Allah has guided us; like someone seduced by the devils and confused on earth, who has friends calling him to guidance: 'Come to us'?” Say, “The guidance of Allah is the guidance, and we are commanded to surrender to the Lord of the Universe.”
٧٢ وَأَنْ أَقِيمُوا۟ ٱلصَّلَوٰةَ وَٱتَّقُوهُ ۚ وَهُوَ ٱلَّذِىٓ إِلَيْهِ تُحْشَرُونَ	72 “And to perform the prayers, and to revere Him; it is to Him that you will be gathered.”
٧٣ وَهُوَ ٱلَّذِى خَلَقَ ٱلسَّمَٰوَٰتِ وَٱلْأَرْضَ بِٱلْحَقِّ ۖ وَيَوْمَ يَقُولُ كُن فَيَكُونُ ۚ قَوْلُهُ ٱلْحَقُّ ۚ وَلَهُ ٱلْمُلْكُ يَوْمَ يُنفَخُ فِى ٱلصُّورِ ۚ عَٰلِمُ ٱلْغَيْبِ وَٱلشَّهَٰدَةِ ۚ وَهُوَ ٱلْحَكِيمُ ٱلْخَبِيرُ	73 It is He who created the heavens and the earth in truth. On the Day when He says: “Be,” it will be. His saying is the truth, and His is the sovereignty on the Day when the trumpet is blown. The Knower of secrets and declarations. He is the Wise, the Expert.
٧٤ وَإِذْ قَالَ إِبْرَٰهِيمُ لِأَبِيهِ ءَازَرَ أَتَتَّخِذُ أَصْنَامًا ءَالِهَةً ۖ إِنِّىٓ أَرَىٰكَ وَقَوْمَكَ فِى ضَلَٰلٍ مُّبِينٍ	74 Abraham said to his father Azar, “Do you take idols for gods? I see that you and your people are in evident error.”
٧٥ وَكَذَٰلِكَ نُرِىٓ إِبْرَٰهِيمَ مَلَكُوتَ ٱلسَّمَٰوَٰتِ وَٱلْأَرْضِ وَلِيَكُونَ مِنَ ٱلْمُوقِنِينَ	75 Thus We showed Abraham the empire of the heavens and the earth, that he might be one of those with certainty.
٧٦ فَلَمَّا جَنَّ عَلَيْهِ ٱلَّيْلُ رَءَا كَوْكَبًا ۖ قَالَ هَٰذَا رَبِّى ۖ فَلَمَّآ أَفَلَ قَالَ لَآ أُحِبُّ ٱلْءَافِلِينَ	76 When the night fell over him, he saw a planet. He said, “This is my lord.” But when it set, he said, “I do not love those that set.”

٧٧ فَلَمَّا رَءَا ٱلْقَمَرَ بَازِغًا قَالَ هَٰذَا رَبِّى ۖ فَلَمَّآ
أَفَلَ قَالَ لَئِن لَّمْ يَهْدِنِى رَبِّى لَأَكُونَنَّ مِنَ ٱلْقَوْمِ
ٱلضَّآلِّينَ

77 Then, when he saw the moon rising, he said, "This is my lord." But when it set, he said, "If my Lord does not guide me, I will be one of the erring people."

٧٨ فَلَمَّا رَءَا ٱلشَّمْسَ بَازِغَةً قَالَ هَٰذَا رَبِّى هَٰذَآ
أَكْبَرُ ۖ فَلَمَّآ أَفَلَتْ قَالَ يَٰقَوْمِ إِنِّى بَرِىٓءٌ مِّمَّا
تُشْرِكُونَ

78 Then, when he saw the sun rising, he said, "This is my lord, this is bigger." But when it set, he said, "O my people, I am innocent of your idolatry.

٧٩ إِنِّى وَجَّهْتُ وَجْهِىَ لِلَّذِى فَطَرَ ٱلسَّمَٰوَٰتِ
وَٱلْأَرْضَ حَنِيفًا ۖ وَمَآ أَنَا۠ مِنَ ٱلْمُشْرِكِينَ

79 I have directed my attention towards Him Who created the heavens and the earth—a monotheist—and I am not of the idolaters."

٨٠ وَحَآجَّهُۥ قَوْمُهُۥ ۚ قَالَ أَتُحَٰٓجُّوٓنِّى فِى ٱللَّهِ وَقَدْ
هَدَىٰنِ ۚ وَلَآ أَخَافُ مَا تُشْرِكُونَ بِهِۦٓ إِلَّآ أَن يَشَآءَ
رَبِّى شَيْـًٔا ۗ وَسِعَ رَبِّى كُلَّ شَىْءٍ عِلْمًا ۗ أَفَلَا
تَتَذَكَّرُونَ

80 And his people argued with him. He said, "Do you argue with me about Allah, when He has guided me? I do not fear what you associate with Him, unless my Lord wills it. My Lord comprehends all things in knowledge. Will you not reconsider?

٨١ وَكَيْفَ أَخَافُ مَآ أَشْرَكْتُمْ وَلَا تَخَافُونَ أَنَّكُمْ
أَشْرَكْتُم بِٱللَّهِ مَا لَمْ يُنَزِّلْ بِهِۦ عَلَيْكُمْ سُلْطَٰنًا ۚ
فَأَىُّ ٱلْفَرِيقَيْنِ أَحَقُّ بِٱلْأَمْنِ ۖ إِن كُنتُمْ تَعْلَمُونَ

81 And why should I fear those you associate with Him, and you do not fear associating others with Allah for which He sent down to you no authority? Which side is more entitled to security, if you are aware?"

٨٢ ٱلَّذِينَ ءَامَنُوا۟ وَلَمْ يَلْبِسُوٓا۟ إِيمَٰنَهُم بِظُلْمٍ
أُو۟لَٰٓئِكَ لَهُمُ ٱلْأَمْنُ وَهُم مُّهْتَدُونَ

82 Those who believe, and do not obscure their faith with wrongdoing—those will have security, and they are guided.

٨٣ وَتِلْكَ حُجَّتُنَآ ءَاتَيْنَٰهَآ إِبْرَٰهِيمَ عَلَىٰ قَوْمِهِۦ ۚ
نَرْفَعُ دَرَجَٰتٍ مَّن نَّشَآءُ ۗ إِنَّ رَبَّكَ حَكِيمٌ عَلِيمٌ

83 That was Our argument which We gave to Abraham against his people. We elevate by degrees whomever We will. Your Lord is Wise and Informed.

٨٤ وَوَهَبْنَا لَهُۥٓ إِسْحَٰقَ وَيَعْقُوبَ ۚ كُلًّا هَدَيْنَا ۚ
وَنُوحًا هَدَيْنَا مِن قَبْلُ ۖ وَمِن ذُرِّيَّتِهِۦ دَاوُۥدَ

84 And We gave him Isaac and Jacob—each of them We guided. And We guided Noah previously;

وَسُلَيْمَٰنَ وَأَيُّوبَ وَيُوسُفَ وَمُوسَىٰ وَهَٰرُونَ ۚ
وَكَذَٰلِكَ نَجْزِى ٱلْمُحْسِنِينَ

and from his descendants David, and Solomon, and Job, and Joseph, and Moses, and Aaron. Thus We reward the righteous.

٨٥ وَزَكَرِيَّا وَيَحْيَىٰ وَعِيسَىٰ وَإِلْيَاسَ ۖ كُلٌّ مِّنَ
ٱلصَّٰلِحِينَ

85 And Zechariah, and John, and Jesus, and Elias—every one of them was of the upright.

٨٦ وَإِسْمَٰعِيلَ وَٱلْيَسَعَ وَيُونُسَ وَلُوطًا ۚ وَكُلًّا
فَضَّلْنَا عَلَى ٱلْعَٰلَمِينَ

86 And Ishmael, and Elijah, and Jonah, and Lot—We favored each one of them over all other people.

٨٧ وَمِنْ ءَابَآئِهِمْ وَذُرِّيَّٰتِهِمْ وَإِخْوَٰنِهِمْ ۖ
وَٱجْتَبَيْنَٰهُمْ وَهَدَيْنَٰهُمْ إِلَىٰ صِرَٰطٍ مُّسْتَقِيمٍ

87 And of their ancestors, and their descendants, and their siblings—We chose them, and guided them to a straight path.

٨٨ ذَٰلِكَ هُدَى ٱللَّهِ يَهْدِى بِهِۦ مَن يَشَآءُ مِنْ
عِبَادِهِۦ ۚ وَلَوْ أَشْرَكُوا۟ لَحَبِطَ عَنْهُم مَّا كَانُوا۟
يَعْمَلُونَ

88 Such is Allah's guidance. He guides with it whomever He wills of His servants. Had they associated, their deeds would have gone in vain.

٨٩ أُو۟لَٰٓئِكَ ٱلَّذِينَ ءَاتَيْنَٰهُمُ ٱلْكِتَٰبَ وَٱلْحُكْمَ
وَٱلنُّبُوَّةَ ۚ فَإِن يَكْفُرْ بِهَا هَٰٓؤُلَآءِ فَقَدْ وَكَّلْنَا بِهَا
قَوْمًا لَّيْسُوا۟ بِهَا بِكَٰفِرِينَ

89 Those are they to whom We gave the Book, and wisdom, and prophethood. If these reject them, We have entrusted them to others who do not reject them.

٩٠ أُو۟لَٰٓئِكَ ٱلَّذِينَ هَدَى ٱللَّهُ ۖ فَبِهُدَىٰهُمُ ٱقْتَدِهْ ۗ قُل
لَّآ أَسْـَٔلُكُمْ عَلَيْهِ أَجْرًا ۖ إِنْ هُوَ إِلَّا ذِكْرَىٰ لِلْعَٰلَمِينَ

90 Those are they whom Allah has guided, so follow their guidance. Say, "I ask of you no compensation for it; it is just a reminder for all mankind."

٩١ وَمَا قَدَرُوا۟ ٱللَّهَ حَقَّ قَدْرِهِۦٓ إِذْ قَالُوا۟ مَآ أَنزَلَ
ٱللَّهُ عَلَىٰ بَشَرٍ مِّن شَىْءٍ ۗ قُلْ مَنْ أَنزَلَ ٱلْكِتَٰبَ
ٱلَّذِى جَآءَ بِهِۦ مُوسَىٰ نُورًا وَهُدًى لِّلنَّاسِ ۖ
تَجْعَلُونَهُۥ قَرَاطِيسَ تُبْدُونَهَا وَتُخْفُونَ كَثِيرًا ۖ
وَعُلِّمْتُم مَّا لَمْ تَعْلَمُوٓا۟ أَنتُمْ وَلَآ ءَابَآؤُكُمْ ۖ قُلِ
ٱللَّهُ ۖ ثُمَّ ذَرْهُمْ فِى خَوْضِهِمْ يَلْعَبُونَ

91 They do not value Allah as He should be valued, when they say, "Allah did not reveal anything to any human being." Say, "Who revealed the Scripture which Moses brought—a light and guidance for humanity?" You put it on scrolls, displaying them, yet concealing much. And you were taught what you did not know—neither you, nor your ancestors. Say, "Allah;" then leave them toying away in their speculation.

٩٢ وَهَٰذَا كِتَٰبٌ أَنزَلْنَٰهُ مُبَارَكٌ مُّصَدِّقُ ٱلَّذِى بَيْنَ
يَدَيْهِ وَلِتُنذِرَ أُمَّ ٱلْقُرَىٰ وَمَنْ حَوْلَهَا ۚ وَٱلَّذِينَ
يُؤْمِنُونَ بِٱلْءَاخِرَةِ يُؤْمِنُونَ بِهِۦ ۖ وَهُمْ عَلَىٰ
صَلَاتِهِمْ يُحَافِظُونَ

92 This too is a Scripture that We revealed—blessed—verifying what preceded it, that you may warn the Mother of Cities and all around it. Those who believe in the Hereafter believe in it, and are dedicated to their prayers.

٩٣ وَمَنْ أَظْلَمُ مِمَّنِ ٱفْتَرَىٰ عَلَى ٱللَّهِ كَذِبًا أَوْ
قَالَ أُوحِىَ إِلَىَّ وَلَمْ يُوحَ إِلَيْهِ شَىْءٌ وَمَن قَالَ
سَأُنزِلُ مِثْلَ مَآ أَنزَلَ ٱللَّهُ ۗ وَلَوْ تَرَىٰٓ إِذِ ٱلظَّٰلِمُونَ
فِى غَمَرَٰتِ ٱلْمَوْتِ وَٱلْمَلَٰٓئِكَةُ بَاسِطُوٓا۟ أَيْدِيهِمْ
أَخْرِجُوٓا۟ أَنفُسَكُمُ ۖ ٱلْيَوْمَ تُجْزَوْنَ عَذَابَ ٱلْهُونِ
بِمَا كُنتُمْ تَقُولُونَ عَلَى ٱللَّهِ غَيْرَ ٱلْحَقِّ وَكُنتُمْ
عَنْ ءَايَٰتِهِۦ تَسْتَكْبِرُونَ

93 Who does greater wrong than someone who invents falsehood against Allah, or says, “It was revealed to me,” when nothing was revealed to him, or says, “I will reveal the like of what Allah revealed”? If only you could see the wrongdoers in the floods of death, as the angels with arms outstretched: “Give up your souls. Today you are being repaid with the torment of shame for having said about Allah other than the truth, and for being too proud to accept His revelations.”

٩٤ وَلَقَدْ جِئْتُمُونَا فُرَٰدَىٰ كَمَا خَلَقْنَٰكُمْ أَوَّلَ مَرَّةٍ
وَتَرَكْتُم مَّا خَوَّلْنَٰكُمْ وَرَآءَ ظُهُورِكُمْ ۖ وَمَا نَرَىٰ
مَعَكُمْ شُفَعَآءَكُمُ ٱلَّذِينَ زَعَمْتُمْ أَنَّهُمْ فِيكُمْ
شُرَكَٰٓؤُا۟ ۚ لَقَد تَّقَطَّعَ بَيْنَكُمْ وَضَلَّ عَنكُم مَّا كُنتُمْ
تَزْعُمُونَ

94 “You have come to Us individually, just as We created you the first time, leaving behind you everything We gave you. We do not see with you your intercessors—those you claimed were your partners. The link between you is cut, and what you had asserted has failed you.”

٩٥ إِنَّ ٱللَّهَ فَالِقُ ٱلْحَبِّ وَٱلنَّوَىٰ ۖ يُخْرِجُ ٱلْحَىَّ
مِنَ ٱلْمَيِّتِ وَمُخْرِجُ ٱلْمَيِّتِ مِنَ ٱلْحَىِّ ۚ ذَٰلِكُمُ
ٱللَّهُ ۖ فَأَنَّىٰ تُؤْفَكُونَ

95 It is Allah Who splits the grain and the seed. He brings the living from the dead, and He brings the dead from the living. Such is Allah. So how could you deviate?

٩٦ فَالِقُ ٱلْإِصْبَاحِ وَجَعَلَ ٱلَّيْلَ سَكَنًا وَٱلشَّمْسَ
وَٱلْقَمَرَ حُسْبَانًا ۚ ذَٰلِكَ تَقْدِيرُ ٱلْعَزِيزِ ٱلْعَلِيمِ

96 It is He Who breaks the dawn. And He made the night for rest, and the sun and the moon for calculation. Such is the disposition of the Almighty, the All-Knowing.

٩٧ وَهُوَ ٱلَّذِى جَعَلَ لَكُمُ ٱلنُّجُومَ لِتَهۡتَدُواْ بِهَا
فِى ظُلُمَٰتِ ٱلۡبَرِّ وَٱلۡبَحۡرِۗ قَدۡ فَصَّلۡنَا ٱلۡءَايَٰتِ
لِقَوۡمٖ يَعۡلَمُونَ

97 And it is He Who created the stars for you, that you may be guided by them in the darkness of land and sea. We thus explain the revelations for people who know.

٩٨ وَهُوَ ٱلَّذِىٓ أَنشَأَكُم مِّن نَّفۡسٖ وَٰحِدَةٖ
فَمُسۡتَقَرّٞ وَمُسۡتَوۡدَعٞۗ قَدۡ فَصَّلۡنَا ٱلۡءَايَٰتِ لِقَوۡمٖ
يَفۡقَهُونَ

98 And it is He who produced you from a single person, then a repository, then a depository. We have detailed the revelations for people who understand.

٩٩ وَهُوَ ٱلَّذِىٓ أَنزَلَ مِنَ ٱلسَّمَآءِ مَآءٗ فَأَخۡرَجۡنَا
بِهِۦ نَبَاتَ كُلِّ شَىۡءٖ فَأَخۡرَجۡنَا مِنۡهُ خَضِرٗا
نُّخۡرِجُ مِنۡهُ حَبّٗا مُّتَرَاكِبٗا وَمِنَ ٱلنَّخۡلِ مِن طَلۡعِهَا
قِنۡوَانٞ دَانِيَةٞ وَجَنَّٰتٖ مِّنۡ أَعۡنَابٖ وَٱلزَّيۡتُونَ
وَٱلرُّمَّانَ مُشۡتَبِهٗا وَغَيۡرَ مُتَشَٰبِهٍۗ ٱنظُرُوٓاْ إِلَىٰ
ثَمَرِهِۦٓ إِذَآ أَثۡمَرَ وَيَنۡعِهِۦٓۚ إِنَّ فِى ذَٰلِكُمۡ لَأٓيَٰتٖ
لِّقَوۡمٖ يُؤۡمِنُونَ

99 And it is He who sends down water from the sky. With it We produce vegetation of all kinds, from which We bring greenery, from which We produce grains in clusters. And palm-trees with hanging clusters, and vineyards, and olives, and pomegranates—similar and dissimilar. Watch their fruits as they grow and ripen. Surely in this are signs for people who believe.

١٠٠ وَجَعَلُواْ لِلَّهِ شُرَكَآءَ ٱلۡجِنَّ وَخَلَقَهُمۡۖ
وَخَرَقُواْ لَهُۥ بَنِينَ وَبَنَٰتِۭ بِغَيۡرِ عِلۡمٖۚ سُبۡحَٰنَهُۥ
وَتَعَٰلَىٰ عَمَّا يَصِفُونَ

100 Yet they attributed to Allah partners—the sprites—although He created them. And they invented for Him sons and daughters, without any knowledge. Glory be to Him. He is exalted, beyond what they describe.

١٠١ بَدِيعُ ٱلسَّمَٰوَٰتِ وَٱلۡأَرۡضِۖ أَنَّىٰ يَكُونُ لَهُۥ وَلَدٞ
وَلَمۡ تَكُن لَّهُۥ صَٰحِبَةٞۖ وَخَلَقَ كُلَّ شَىۡءٖۖ وَهُوَ
بِكُلِّ شَىۡءٍ عَلِيمٞ

101 Originator of the heavens and the earth—how can He have a son when He never had a companion? He created all things, and He has knowledge of all things.

١٠٢ ذَٰلِكُمُ ٱللَّهُ رَبُّكُمۡۖ لَآ إِلَٰهَ إِلَّا هُوَۖ خَٰلِقُ كُلِّ
شَىۡءٖ فَٱعۡبُدُوهُۚ وَهُوَ عَلَىٰ كُلِّ شَىۡءٖ وَكِيلٞ

102 Such is Allah, your Lord. There is no god except He, the Creator of all things; so worship Him. He is responsible for everything.

١٠٣ لَّا تُدۡرِكُهُ ٱلۡأَبۡصَٰرُ وَهُوَ يُدۡرِكُ ٱلۡأَبۡصَٰرَۖ وَهُوَ
ٱللَّطِيفُ ٱلۡخَبِيرُ

103 No vision can grasp Him, but His grasp is over all vision. He is the Subtle, the Expert.

١٠٤ قَدْ جَآءَكُم بَصَآئِرُ مِن رَّبِّكُمْ ۖ فَمَنْ أَبْصَرَ
فَلِنَفْسِهِۦ ۖ وَمَنْ عَمِىَ فَعَلَيْهَا ۚ وَمَآ أَنَا۠ عَلَيْكُم
بِحَفِيظٍ

104 "Insights have come to you from your Lord. Whoever sees, it is to the benefit of his soul; and whoever remains blind, it is to its detriment. I am not a guardian over you."

١٠٥ وَكَذَٰلِكَ نُصَرِّفُ ٱلْـَٔايَـٰتِ وَلِيَقُولُوا۟ دَرَسْتَ
وَلِنُبَيِّنَهُۥ لِقَوْمٍ يَعْلَمُونَ

105 We thus diversify the revelations, lest they say, "You have studied," and to clarify them for people who know.

١٠٦ ٱتَّبِعْ مَآ أُوحِىَ إِلَيْكَ مِن رَّبِّكَ ۖ لَآ إِلَـٰهَ إِلَّا هُوَ ۖ
وَأَعْرِضْ عَنِ ٱلْمُشْرِكِينَ

106 Follow what was revealed to you from your Lord. There is no god but He. And turn away from the polytheists.

١٠٧ وَلَوْ شَآءَ ٱللَّهُ مَآ أَشْرَكُوا۟ ۗ وَمَا جَعَلْنَـٰكَ
عَلَيْهِمْ حَفِيظًا ۖ وَمَآ أَنتَ عَلَيْهِم بِوَكِيلٍ

107 Had Allah willed, they would not have practiced idolatry. We did not appoint you as a guardian over them, and you are not a manager over them.

١٠٨ وَلَا تَسُبُّوا۟ ٱلَّذِينَ يَدْعُونَ مِن دُونِ ٱللَّهِ
فَيَسُبُّوا۟ ٱللَّهَ عَدْوًۢا بِغَيْرِ عِلْمٍ ۗ كَذَٰلِكَ زَيَّنَّا لِكُلِّ
أُمَّةٍ عَمَلَهُمْ ثُمَّ إِلَىٰ رَبِّهِم مَّرْجِعُهُمْ فَيُنَبِّئُهُم بِمَا
كَانُوا۟ يَعْمَلُونَ

108 Do not insult those they call upon besides Allah, lest they insult Allah out of hostility and ignorance. We made attractive to every community their deeds. Then to their Lord is their return, and He will inform them of what they used to do.

١٠٩ وَأَقْسَمُوا۟ بِٱللَّهِ جَهْدَ أَيْمَـٰنِهِمْ لَئِن جَآءَتْهُمْ
ءَايَةٌ لَّيُؤْمِنُنَّ بِهَا ۚ قُلْ إِنَّمَا ٱلْـَٔايَـٰتُ عِندَ ٱللَّهِ ۖ
وَمَا يُشْعِرُكُمْ أَنَّهَآ إِذَا جَآءَتْ لَا يُؤْمِنُونَ

109 They swear by Allah, with their most solemn oaths, that if a miracle were to come to them, they would believe in it. Say, "The miracles are only with Allah." But how do you know? Even if it did come, they still would not believe.

١١٠ وَنُقَلِّبُ أَفْـِٔدَتَهُمْ وَأَبْصَـٰرَهُمْ كَمَا لَمْ يُؤْمِنُوا۟
بِهِۦٓ أَوَّلَ مَرَّةٍ وَنَذَرُهُمْ فِى طُغْيَـٰنِهِمْ يَعْمَهُونَ

110 And We turn away their hearts and their visions, as they refused to believe in it the first time, and We leave them blundering in their rebellion.

١١١ وَلَوْ أَنَّنَا نَزَّلْنَآ إِلَيْهِمُ ٱلْمَلَـٰٓئِكَةَ وَكَلَّمَهُمُ ٱلْمَوْتَىٰ
وَحَشَرْنَا عَلَيْهِمْ كُلَّ شَىْءٍ قُبُلًا مَّا كَانُوا۟

111 Even if We sent down the angels to them, and the dead spoke to them, and We gathered all things before them, they still would not

لِيُؤْمِنُوٓاْ إِلَّآ أَن يَشَآءَ ٱللَّهُ وَلَٰكِنَّ أَكْثَرَهُمْ
يَجْهَلُونَ

believe, unless Allah wills; but most of them are ignorant.

١١٢ وَكَذَٰلِكَ جَعَلْنَا لِكُلِّ نَبِيٍّ عَدُوًّا شَيَٰطِينَ
ٱلْإِنسِ وَٱلْجِنِّ يُوحِى بَعْضُهُمْ إِلَىٰ بَعْضٍ
زُخْرُفَ ٱلْقَوْلِ غُرُورًا ۚ وَلَوْ شَآءَ رَبُّكَ مَا فَعَلُوهُ ۖ
فَذَرْهُمْ وَمَا يَفْتَرُونَ

112 Likewise, We have assigned for every prophet an enemy—human and jinn devils—inspiring one another with fancy words in order to deceive. But had your Lord willed, they would not have done it. So leave them to their fabrications.

١١٣ وَلِتَصْغَىٰٓ إِلَيْهِ أَفْـِٔدَةُ ٱلَّذِينَ لَا يُؤْمِنُونَ
بِٱلْءَاخِرَةِ وَلِيَرْضَوْهُ وَلِيَقْتَرِفُوا۟ مَا هُم
مُّقْتَرِفُونَ

113 So that the hearts of those who do not believe in the Hereafter may incline to it, and be content with it, and that they may perpetrate whatever they perpetrate.

١١٤ أَفَغَيْرَ ٱللَّهِ أَبْتَغِى حَكَمًا وَهُوَ ٱلَّذِىٓ أَنزَلَ
إِلَيْكُمُ ٱلْكِتَٰبَ مُفَصَّلًا ۚ وَٱلَّذِينَ ءَاتَيْنَٰهُمُ ٱلْكِتَٰبَ
يَعْلَمُونَ أَنَّهُۥ مُنَزَّلٌ مِّن رَّبِّكَ بِٱلْحَقِّ ۖ فَلَا تَكُونَنَّ
مِنَ ٱلْمُمْتَرِينَ

114 “Shall I seek a judge other than Allah, when He is the One who revealed to you the Book, explained in detail?” Those to whom We gave the Book know that it is the truth revealed from your Lord. So do not be of those who doubt.

١١٥ وَتَمَّتْ كَلِمَتُ رَبِّكَ صِدْقًا وَعَدْلًا ۚ لَّا مُبَدِّلَ
لِكَلِمَٰتِهِۦ ۚ وَهُوَ ٱلسَّمِيعُ ٱلْعَلِيمُ

115 The Word of your Lord has been completed, in truth and justice. There is no changing to His words. He is the Hearer, the Knower.

١١٦ وَإِن تُطِعْ أَكْثَرَ مَن فِى ٱلْأَرْضِ يُضِلُّوكَ عَن
سَبِيلِ ٱللَّهِ ۚ إِن يَتَّبِعُونَ إِلَّا ٱلظَّنَّ وَإِنْ هُمْ إِلَّا
يَخْرُصُونَ

116 If you were to obey most of those on earth, they would divert you from Allah’s path. They follow nothing but assumptions, and they only conjecture.

١١٧ إِنَّ رَبَّكَ هُوَ أَعْلَمُ مَن يَضِلُّ عَن سَبِيلِهِۦ ۖ
وَهُوَ أَعْلَمُ بِٱلْمُهْتَدِينَ

117 Your Lord knows best who strays from His path, and He knows best the guided ones.

١١٨ فَكُلُوا۟ مِمَّا ذُكِرَ ٱسْمُ ٱللَّهِ عَلَيْهِ إِن كُنتُم
بِـَٔايَٰتِهِۦ مُؤْمِنِينَ

118 So eat of that over which the Name of Allah was pronounced, if you indeed believe in His revelations.

١١٩ وَمَا لَكُمْ أَلَّا تَأْكُلُوا۟ مِمَّا ذُكِرَ ٱسْمُ ٱللَّهِ عَلَيْهِ
وَقَدْ فَصَّلَ لَكُم مَّا حَرَّمَ عَلَيْكُمْ إِلَّا مَا

119 And why should you not eat of that over which the Name of Allah is pronounced, when He has detailed

ٱضْطُرِرْتُمْ إِلَيْهِ ۗ وَإِنَّ كَثِيرًا لَّيُضِلُّونَ بِأَهْوَآئِهِم بِغَيْرِ عِلْمٍ ۗ إِنَّ رَبَّكَ هُوَ أَعْلَمُ بِٱلْمُعْتَدِينَ	for you what is prohibited for you, unless you are compelled by necessity? Many lead astray with their opinions, through lack of knowledge. Your Lord knows best the transgressors.
١٢٠ وَذَرُوا۟ ظَٰهِرَ ٱلْإِثْمِ وَبَاطِنَهُۥٓ ۚ إِنَّ ٱلَّذِينَ يَكْسِبُونَ ٱلْإِثْمَ سَيُجْزَوْنَ بِمَا كَانُوا۟ يَقْتَرِفُونَ	120 So abandon sin, outward and inward. Those who commit sins will be repaid for what they used to perpetrate.
١٢١ وَلَا تَأْكُلُوا۟ مِمَّا لَمْ يُذْكَرِ ٱسْمُ ٱللَّهِ عَلَيْهِ وَإِنَّهُۥ لَفِسْقٌ ۗ وَإِنَّ ٱلشَّيَٰطِينَ لَيُوحُونَ إِلَىٰٓ أَوْلِيَآئِهِمْ لِيُجَٰدِلُوكُمْ ۖ وَإِنْ أَطَعْتُمُوهُمْ إِنَّكُمْ لَمُشْرِكُونَ	121 And do not eat from that over which the Name of Allah was not pronounced, for it is abomination. The devils inspire their followers to argue with you; but if you obey them, you would be polytheists.
١٢٢ أَوَمَن كَانَ مَيْتًا فَأَحْيَيْنَٰهُ وَجَعَلْنَا لَهُۥ نُورًا يَمْشِى بِهِۦ فِى ٱلنَّاسِ كَمَن مَّثَلُهُۥ فِى ٱلظُّلُمَٰتِ لَيْسَ بِخَارِجٍ مِّنْهَا ۚ كَذَٰلِكَ زُيِّنَ لِلْكَٰفِرِينَ مَا كَانُوا۟ يَعْمَلُونَ	122 Is he who was dead, then We gave him life, and made for him a light by which he walks among the people, like he who is in total darkness, and cannot get out of it? Thus the doings of disbelievers are made to appear good to them.
١٢٣ وَكَذَٰلِكَ جَعَلْنَا فِى كُلِّ قَرْيَةٍ أَكَٰبِرَ مُجْرِمِيهَا لِيَمْكُرُوا۟ فِيهَا ۖ وَمَا يَمْكُرُونَ إِلَّا بِأَنفُسِهِمْ وَمَا يَشْعُرُونَ	123 And thus We set up in every city its leading wicked sinners, to conspire in it, but they conspire only against themselves, and they do not realize it.
١٢٤ وَإِذَا جَآءَتْهُمْ ءَايَةٌ قَالُوا۟ لَن نُّؤْمِنَ حَتَّىٰ نُؤْتَىٰ مِثْلَ مَآ أُوتِىَ رُسُلُ ٱللَّهِ ۘ ٱللَّهُ أَعْلَمُ حَيْثُ يَجْعَلُ رِسَالَتَهُۥ ۗ سَيُصِيبُ ٱلَّذِينَ أَجْرَمُوا۟ صَغَارٌ عِندَ ٱللَّهِ وَعَذَابٌ شَدِيدٌۢ بِمَا كَانُوا۟ يَمْكُرُونَ	124 When a sign comes to them, they say, “We will not believe unless we are given the like of what was given to Allah’s messengers.” Allah knows best where to place His message. Humiliation from Allah and severe torment will afflict the criminals for their scheming.
١٢٥ فَمَن يُرِدِ ٱللَّهُ أَن يَهْدِيَهُۥ يَشْرَحْ صَدْرَهُۥ لِلْإِسْلَٰمِ ۖ وَمَن يُرِدْ أَن يُضِلَّهُۥ يَجْعَلْ صَدْرَهُۥ	125 Whomever Allah desires to guide, He spreads open his heart to Islam; and whomever He desires to misguide, He makes his heart narrow, constricted, as though he were climbing up the sky. Allah thus

ضَيِّقًا حَرَجًا كَأَنَّمَا يَصَّعَّدُ فِى ٱلسَّمَآءِ ۚ كَذَٰلِكَ
يَجْعَلُ ٱللَّهُ ٱلرِّجْسَ عَلَى ٱلَّذِينَ لَا يُؤْمِنُونَ

lays defilement upon those who do not believe.

١٢٦ وَهَٰذَا صِرَٰطُ رَبِّكَ مُسْتَقِيمًا ۗ قَدْ فَصَّلْنَا
ٱلْءَايَٰتِ لِقَوْمٍ يَذَّكَّرُونَ

126 This is the straight path of your Lord. We have explained the revelations in detail for people who recollect.

١٢٧ لَهُمْ دَارُ ٱلسَّلَٰمِ عِندَ رَبِّهِمْ ۖ وَهُوَ وَلِيُّهُم بِمَا
كَانُوا۟ يَعْمَلُونَ

127 For them is the Home of Peace with their Lord, and He is their Master—because of what they used to do.

١٢٨ وَيَوْمَ يَحْشُرُهُمْ جَمِيعًا يَٰمَعْشَرَ ٱلْجِنِّ قَدِ
ٱسْتَكْثَرْتُم مِّنَ ٱلْإِنسِ ۖ وَقَالَ أَوْلِيَآؤُهُم مِّنَ
ٱلْإِنسِ رَبَّنَا ٱسْتَمْتَعَ بَعْضُنَا بِبَعْضٍ وَبَلَغْنَآ أَجَلَنَا
ٱلَّذِىٓ أَجَّلْتَ لَنَا ۚ قَالَ ٱلنَّارُ مَثْوَىٰكُمْ خَٰلِدِينَ فِيهَآ
إِلَّا مَا شَآءَ ٱللَّهُ ۗ إِنَّ رَبَّكَ حَكِيمٌ عَلِيمٌ

128 On the Day when He gathers them all together: “O assembly of jinn, you have exploited multitudes of humans.” Their adherents among mankind will say, “Our Lord, we have profited from one another, but we have reached the term that you have assigned for us.” He will say, “The Fire is your dwelling, wherein you will remain, except as Allah wills. Your Lord is Wise and Informed.

١٢٩ وَكَذَٰلِكَ نُوَلِّى بَعْضَ ٱلظَّٰلِمِينَ بَعْضًۢا بِمَا
كَانُوا۟ يَكْسِبُونَ

129 Thus We make some of the wrongdoers befriend one another, because of what they used to do.

١٣٠ يَٰمَعْشَرَ ٱلْجِنِّ وَٱلْإِنسِ أَلَمْ يَأْتِكُمْ رُسُلٌ
مِّنكُمْ يَقُصُّونَ عَلَيْكُمْ ءَايَٰتِى وَيُنذِرُونَكُمْ لِقَآءَ
يَوْمِكُمْ هَٰذَا ۚ قَالُوا۟ شَهِدْنَا عَلَىٰٓ أَنفُسِنَا ۖ
وَغَرَّتْهُمُ ٱلْحَيَوٰةُ ٱلدُّنْيَا وَشَهِدُوا۟ عَلَىٰٓ أَنفُسِهِمْ
أَنَّهُمْ كَانُوا۟ كَٰفِرِينَ

130 “O assembly of jinn and humans, did there not come to you messengers from among you, relating to you My revelations, and warning you of the meeting of this Day of yours?” They will say, “We testify against ourselves.” The life of the world seduced them. They will testify against themselves that they were disbelievers.

١٣١ ذَٰلِكَ أَن لَّمْ يَكُن رَّبُّكَ مُهْلِكَ ٱلْقُرَىٰ بِظُلْمٍ
وَأَهْلُهَا غَٰفِلُونَ

131 That is because your Lord would not destroy towns for injustice while their inhabitants are unaware.

١٣٢ وَلِكُلّٖ دَرَجَٰتٞ مِّمَّا عَمِلُواْۚ وَمَا رَبُّكَ بِغَٰفِلٍ
عَمَّا يَعۡمَلُونَ

132 They all have ranks according to what they did; and your Lord is not unaware of what they do.

١٣٣ وَرَبُّكَ ٱلۡغَنِيُّ ذُو ٱلرَّحۡمَةِۚ إِن يَشَأۡ يُذۡهِبۡكُمۡ
وَيَسۡتَخۡلِفۡ مِنۢ بَعۡدِكُم مَّا يَشَآءُ كَمَآ أَنشَأَكُم
مِّن ذُرِّيَّةِ قَوۡمٍ ءَاخَرِينَ

133 Your Lord is the Rich Beyond Need, the Possessor of Mercy. If He wills, He can do away with you, and substitute whomever He wills in your place, just as He produced you from the descendants of another people.

١٣٤ إِنَّ مَا تُوعَدُونَ لَأٓتٖۖ وَمَآ أَنتُم
بِمُعۡجِزِينَ

134 What you are promised is coming, and you cannot thwart it.

١٣٥ قُلۡ يَٰقَوۡمِ ٱعۡمَلُواْ عَلَىٰ مَكَانَتِكُمۡ إِنِّي عَامِلٞۖ
فَسَوۡفَ تَعۡلَمُونَ مَن تَكُونُ لَهُۥ عَٰقِبَةُ ٱلدَّارِۚ إِنَّهُۥ
لَا يُفۡلِحُ ٱلظَّٰلِمُونَ

135 Say, "O my people! Work according to your ability, and so will I." You will come to know to whom will belong the sequel of the abode." The wrongdoers will not prevail.

١٣٦ وَجَعَلُواْ لِلَّهِ مِمَّا ذَرَأَ مِنَ ٱلۡحَرۡثِ وَٱلۡأَنۡعَٰمِ
نَصِيبٗا فَقَالُواْ هَٰذَا لِلَّهِ بِزَعۡمِهِمۡ وَهَٰذَا لِشُرَكَآئِنَاۖ
فَمَا كَانَ لِشُرَكَآئِهِمۡ فَلَا يَصِلُ إِلَى ٱللَّهِۖ وَمَا كَانَ
لِلَّهِ فَهُوَ يَصِلُ إِلَىٰ شُرَكَآئِهِمۡۗ سَآءَ مَا يَحۡكُمُونَ

136 And they set aside for Allah a share of the crops and the livestock He created, and they say, "This is for Allah," according to their claim, "and this is for our idols." But the share of their idols does not reach Allah, yet the share of Allah reaches their idols. Evil is their judgment.

١٣٧ وَكَذَٰلِكَ زَيَّنَ لِكَثِيرٖ مِّنَ ٱلۡمُشۡرِكِينَ قَتۡلَ
أَوۡلَٰدِهِمۡ شُرَكَآؤُهُمۡ لِيُرۡدُوهُمۡ وَلِيَلۡبِسُواْ عَلَيۡهِمۡ
دِينَهُمۡۖ وَلَوۡ شَآءَ ٱللَّهُ مَا فَعَلُوهُۖ فَذَرۡهُمۡ وَمَا
يَفۡتَرُونَ

137 Likewise, their idols entice many idolaters to kill their children, in order to lead them to their ruin, and confuse them in their religion. Had Allah willed, they would not have done it; so leave them to their fraud.

١٣٨ وَقَالُواْ هَٰذِهِۦٓ أَنۡعَٰمٞ وَحَرۡثٌ حِجۡرٞ لَّا يَطۡعَمُهَآ
إِلَّا مَن نَّشَآءُ بِزَعۡمِهِمۡ وَأَنۡعَٰمٌ حُرِّمَتۡ ظُهُورُهَا
وَأَنۡعَٰمٞ لَّا يَذۡكُرُونَ ٱسۡمَ ٱللَّهِ عَلَيۡهَا ٱفۡتِرَآءً عَلَيۡهِۚ
سَيَجۡزِيهِم بِمَا كَانُواْ يَفۡتَرُونَ

138 And they say, "These animals and crops are restricted; none may eat them except those we permit," by their claims, and animals whose backs are forbidden, and animals over which they do not pronounce the name of Allah—fabricating lies against Him. He will repay them for what they used to invent.

١٣٩ وَقَالُوا۟ مَا فِى بُطُونِ هَٰذِهِ ٱلْأَنْعَٰمِ خَالِصَةٌ
لِّذُكُورِنَا وَمُحَرَّمٌ عَلَىٰٓ أَزْوَٰجِنَا ۖ وَإِن يَكُن مَّيْتَةً
فَهُمْ فِيهِ شُرَكَآءُ ۚ سَيَجْزِيهِمْ وَصْفَهُمْ ۚ إِنَّهُۥ
حَكِيمٌ عَلِيمٌ

139 And they say, “What lies in the wombs of these animals is exclusively for our males, and prohibited to our wives.” But if it is stillborn, they can share in it. He will surely punish them for their allegations. He is Wise and Knowing.

١٤٠ قَدْ خَسِرَ ٱلَّذِينَ قَتَلُوٓا۟ أَوْلَٰدَهُمْ سَفَهًۢا بِغَيْرِ
عِلْمٍ وَحَرَّمُوا۟ مَا رَزَقَهُمُ ٱللَّهُ ٱفْتِرَآءً عَلَى ٱللَّهِ ۚ
قَدْ ضَلُّوا۟ وَمَا كَانُوا۟ مُهْتَدِينَ

140 Lost are those who kill their children foolishly, with no basis in knowledge, and forbid what Allah has provided for them—innovations about Allah. They have gone astray. They are not guided.

١٤١ وَهُوَ ٱلَّذِىٓ أَنشَأَ جَنَّٰتٍ مَّعْرُوشَٰتٍ وَغَيْرَ
مَعْرُوشَٰتٍ وَٱلنَّخْلَ وَٱلزَّرْعَ مُخْتَلِفًا أُكُلُهُۥ
وَٱلزَّيْتُونَ وَٱلرُّمَّانَ مُتَشَٰبِهًا وَغَيْرَ مُتَشَٰبِهٍ ۚ كُلُوا۟
مِن ثَمَرِهِۦٓ إِذَآ أَثْمَرَ وَءَاتُوا۟ حَقَّهُۥ يَوْمَ حَصَادِهِۦ ۖ
وَلَا تُسْرِفُوٓا۟ ۚ إِنَّهُۥ لَا يُحِبُّ ٱلْمُسْرِفِينَ

141 It is He who produces gardens, both cultivated and wild, and date-palms, and crops of diverse tastes, and olives and pomegranates, similar and dissimilar. Eat of its fruit when it yields, and give its due on the day of its harvest, and do not waste. He does not love the wasteful.

١٤٢ وَمِنَ ٱلْأَنْعَٰمِ حَمُولَةً وَفَرْشًا ۚ كُلُوا۟ مِمَّا
رَزَقَكُمُ ٱللَّهُ وَلَا تَتَّبِعُوا۟ خُطُوَٰتِ ٱلشَّيْطَٰنِ ۚ إِنَّهُۥ
لَكُمْ عَدُوٌّ مُّبِينٌ

142 Among the livestock are some for transportation, and some for clothing. Eat of what Allah has provided for you, and do not follow the footsteps of Satan. He is to you an outright enemy.

١٤٣ ثَمَٰنِيَةَ أَزْوَٰجٍ ۖ مِّنَ ٱلضَّأْنِ ٱثْنَيْنِ وَمِنَ ٱلْمَعْزِ
ٱثْنَيْنِ ۗ قُلْ ءَآلذَّكَرَيْنِ حَرَّمَ أَمِ ٱلْأُنثَيَيْنِ أَمَّا
ٱشْتَمَلَتْ عَلَيْهِ أَرْحَامُ ٱلْأُنثَيَيْنِ ۖ نَبِّـُٔونِى بِعِلْمٍ إِن
كُنتُمْ صَٰدِقِينَ

143 Eight pairs: two of the sheep, and two of the goats. Say, “Did He forbid the two males, or the two females, or what the wombs of the two females contain? Inform me with knowledge, if you are truthful.”

١٤٤ وَمِنَ ٱلْإِبِلِ ٱثْنَيْنِ وَمِنَ ٱلْبَقَرِ ٱثْنَيْنِ ۗ قُلْ
ءَآلذَّكَرَيْنِ حَرَّمَ أَمِ ٱلْأُنثَيَيْنِ أَمَّا ٱشْتَمَلَتْ عَلَيْهِ
أَرْحَامُ ٱلْأُنثَيَيْنِ ۖ أَمْ كُنتُمْ شُهَدَآءَ إِذْ وَصَّىٰكُمُ
ٱللَّهُ بِهَٰذَا ۚ فَمَنْ أَظْلَمُ مِمَّنِ ٱفْتَرَىٰ عَلَى ٱللَّهِ

144 And two of the camels, and two of the cattle. Say, “Did He forbid the two males, or the two females, or what the wombs of the two females contain? Were you present when Allah enjoined this upon you?” Who does greater wrong than he who

كَذِبًا لِّيُضِلَّ ٱلنَّاسَ بِغَيْرِ عِلْمٍ ۗ إِنَّ ٱللَّهَ لَا يَهْدِى
ٱلْقَوْمَ ٱلظَّٰلِمِينَ

invents lies and attributes them to Allah, in order to mislead people without knowledge? Allah does not guide the wicked people.

١٤٥ قُل لَّآ أَجِدُ فِى مَآ أُوحِىَ إِلَىَّ مُحَرَّمًا عَلَىٰ
طَاعِمٍ يَطْعَمُهُۥٓ إِلَّآ أَن يَكُونَ مَيْتَةً أَوْ دَمًا
مَّسْفُوحًا أَوْ لَحْمَ خِنزِيرٍ فَإِنَّهُۥ رِجْسٌ أَوْ فِسْقًا
أُهِلَّ لِغَيْرِ ٱللَّهِ بِهِۦ ۚ فَمَنِ ٱضْطُرَّ غَيْرَ بَاغٍ وَلَا
عَادٍ فَإِنَّ رَبَّكَ غَفُورٌ رَّحِيمٌ

145 Say, “In what was revealed to me, I find nothing forbidden to a consumer who eats it, except carrion, or spilled blood, or the flesh of swine—because it is impure—or a sinful offering dedicated to other than Allah. But if someone is compelled by necessity, without being deliberate or malicious—your Lord is Forgiving and Merciful.

١٤٦ وَعَلَى ٱلَّذِينَ هَادُوا۟ حَرَّمْنَا كُلَّ ذِى ظُفُرٍ ۖ
وَمِنَ ٱلْبَقَرِ وَٱلْغَنَمِ حَرَّمْنَا عَلَيْهِمْ شُحُومَهُمَآ إِلَّا
مَا حَمَلَتْ ظُهُورُهُمَآ أَوِ ٱلْحَوَايَآ أَوْ مَا ٱخْتَلَطَ
بِعَظْمٍ ۚ ذَٰلِكَ جَزَيْنَٰهُم بِبَغْيِهِمْ ۖ وَإِنَّا لَصَٰدِقُونَ

146 For the Jews We forbade everything with claws. As of cattle and sheep: We forbade them their fat, except what adheres to their backs, or the entrails, or what is mixed with bone. This is how We penalized them for their inequity. We are indeed truthful.

١٤٧ فَإِن كَذَّبُوكَ فَقُل رَّبُّكُمْ ذُو رَحْمَةٍ وَٰسِعَةٍ
وَلَا يُرَدُّ بَأْسُهُۥ عَنِ ٱلْقَوْمِ ٱلْمُجْرِمِينَ

147 If they accuse you of lying, say, “Your Lord is Possessor of infinite mercy, but His wrath cannot be averted from the guilty people.”

١٤٨ سَيَقُولُ ٱلَّذِينَ أَشْرَكُوا۟ لَوْ شَآءَ ٱللَّهُ مَآ
أَشْرَكْنَا وَلَآ ءَابَآؤُنَا وَلَا حَرَّمْنَا مِن شَىْءٍ ۚ
كَذَٰلِكَ كَذَّبَ ٱلَّذِينَ مِن قَبْلِهِمْ حَتَّىٰ ذَاقُوا۟
بَأْسَنَا ۗ قُلْ هَلْ عِندَكُم مِّنْ عِلْمٍ فَتُخْرِجُوهُ لَنَآ ۖ
إِن تَتَّبِعُونَ إِلَّا ٱلظَّنَّ وَإِنْ أَنتُمْ إِلَّا تَخْرُصُونَ

148 The polytheists will say, “Had Allah willed, we would not have practiced idolatry, nor would have our forefathers, nor would we have prohibited anything.” Likewise those before them lied, until they tasted Our might. Say, “Do you have any knowledge that you can produce for us? You follow nothing but conjecture, and you only guess.”

١٤٩ قُلْ فَلِلَّهِ ٱلْحُجَّةُ ٱلْبَٰلِغَةُ ۖ فَلَوْ شَآءَ لَهَدَىٰكُمْ
أَجْمَعِينَ

149 Say, “To Allah belongs the conclusive argument. Had He willed, He would have guided you all.”

١٥٠ قُلْ هَلُمَّ شُهَدَآءَكُمُ ٱلَّذِينَ يَشْهَدُونَ أَنَّ ٱللَّهَ
حَرَّمَ هَٰذَا ۖ فَإِن شَهِدُوا۟ فَلَا تَشْهَدْ مَعَهُمْ ۚ وَلَا

150 Say, “Produce your witnesses who would testify that Allah has prohibited this.” If they testify, do not

تَتَّبِعْ أَهْوَآءَ ٱلَّذِينَ كَذَّبُوا۟ بِـَٔايَـٰتِنَا وَٱلَّذِينَ لَا
يُؤْمِنُونَ بِٱلْـَٔاخِرَةِ وَهُم بِرَبِّهِمْ يَعْدِلُونَ

testify with them. And do not follow the whims of those who deny Our revelation, and those who do not believe in the Hereafter, and those who equate others with their Lord.

١٥١ قُلْ تَعَالَوْا۟ أَتْلُ مَا حَرَّمَ رَبُّكُمْ عَلَيْكُمْ ۖ أَلَّا
تُشْرِكُوا۟ بِهِۦ شَيْـًٔا ۖ وَبِٱلْوَٰلِدَيْنِ إِحْسَـٰنًا ۖ وَلَا
تَقْتُلُوٓا۟ أَوْلَـٰدَكُم مِّنْ إِمْلَـٰقٍ ۖ نَّحْنُ نَرْزُقُكُمْ
وَإِيَّاهُمْ ۖ وَلَا تَقْرَبُوا۟ ٱلْفَوَٰحِشَ مَا ظَهَرَ مِنْهَا وَمَا
بَطَنَ ۖ وَلَا تَقْتُلُوا۟ ٱلنَّفْسَ ٱلَّتِى حَرَّمَ ٱللَّهُ إِلَّا
بِٱلْحَقِّ ۚ ذَٰلِكُمْ وَصَّىٰكُم بِهِۦ لَعَلَّكُمْ تَعْقِلُونَ

151 Say, "Come, let me tell you what your Lord has forbidden you: that you associate nothing with Him; that you honor your parents; that you do not kill your children because of poverty—We provide for you and for them; that you do not come near indecencies, whether outward or inward; and that you do not kill the soul which Allah has sanctified—except in the course of justice. All this He has enjoined upon you, so that you may understand."

١٥٢ وَلَا تَقْرَبُوا۟ مَالَ ٱلْيَتِيمِ إِلَّا بِٱلَّتِى هِىَ
أَحْسَنُ حَتَّىٰ يَبْلُغَ أَشُدَّهُۥ ۖ وَأَوْفُوا۟ ٱلْكَيْلَ
وَٱلْمِيزَانَ بِٱلْقِسْطِ ۖ لَا نُكَلِّفُ نَفْسًا إِلَّا وُسْعَهَا ۖ
وَإِذَا قُلْتُمْ فَٱعْدِلُوا۟ وَلَوْ كَانَ ذَا قُرْبَىٰ ۖ وَبِعَهْدِ
ٱللَّهِ أَوْفُوا۟ ۚ ذَٰلِكُمْ وَصَّىٰكُم بِهِۦ لَعَلَّكُمْ تَذَكَّرُونَ

152 And do not come near the property of the orphan, except with the best intentions, until he reaches maturity. And give full weight and full measure, equitably. We do not burden any soul beyond its capacity. And when you speak, be fair, even if it concerns a close relative. And fulfill your covenant with Allah. All this He has enjoined upon you, so that you may take heed.

١٥٣ وَأَنَّ هَـٰذَا صِرَٰطِى مُسْتَقِيمًا فَٱتَّبِعُوهُ ۖ وَلَا
تَتَّبِعُوا۟ ٱلسُّبُلَ فَتَفَرَّقَ بِكُمْ عَن سَبِيلِهِۦ ۚ ذَٰلِكُمْ
وَصَّىٰكُم بِهِۦ لَعَلَّكُمْ تَتَّقُونَ

153 This is My path, straight, so follow it. And do not follow the other paths, lest they divert you from His path. All this He has enjoined upon you, that you may refrain from wrongdoing.

١٥٤ ثُمَّ ءَاتَيْنَا مُوسَى ٱلْكِتَـٰبَ تَمَامًا عَلَى ٱلَّذِىٓ
أَحْسَنَ وَتَفْصِيلًا لِّكُلِّ شَىْءٍ وَهُدًى وَرَحْمَةً
لَّعَلَّهُم بِلِقَآءِ رَبِّهِمْ يُؤْمِنُونَ

154 Then We gave Moses the Scripture, perfect for the righteous, and explaining everything clearly, and a beacon, and mercy, that they may believe in the encounter with their Lord.

155 This too is a blessed Scripture that We revealed; so follow it, and be righteous, that you may receive mercy.

١٥٥ وَهَٰذَا كِتَٰبٌ أَنزَلۡنَٰهُ مُبَارَكٌ فَٱتَّبِعُوهُ وَٱتَّقُواْ
لَعَلَّكُمۡ تُرۡحَمُونَ

156 Lest you say, "The Scripture was revealed to two parties before us, and we were unaware of their teachings."

١٥٦ أَن تَقُولُوٓاْ إِنَّمَآ أُنزِلَ ٱلۡكِتَٰبُ عَلَىٰ طَآئِفَتَيۡنِ
مِن قَبۡلِنَا وَإِن كُنَّا عَن دِرَاسَتِهِمۡ لَغَٰفِلِينَ

157 Or lest you say, "Had the Scripture been revealed to us, we would have been better guided than they." Clarification has come to you from your Lord, and guidance, and mercy. Who then does greater wrong than he who gives the lie to Allah's messages, and turns away from them? We will repay those who turn away from Our messages with the worst kind of punishment, because of their turning away.

١٥٧ أَوۡ تَقُولُواْ لَوۡ أَنَّآ أُنزِلَ عَلَيۡنَا ٱلۡكِتَٰبُ لَكُنَّآ
أَهۡدَىٰ مِنۡهُمۡۚ فَقَدۡ جَآءَكُم بَيِّنَةٞ مِّن رَّبِّكُمۡ
وَهُدٗى وَرَحۡمَةٞۚ فَمَنۡ أَظۡلَمُ مِمَّن كَذَّبَ بِـَٔايَٰتِ
ٱللَّهِ وَصَدَفَ عَنۡهَاۗ سَنَجۡزِي ٱلَّذِينَ يَصۡدِفُونَ
عَنۡ ءَايَٰتِنَا سُوٓءَ ٱلۡعَذَابِ بِمَا كَانُواْ يَصۡدِفُونَ

158 Are they waiting for anything but for the angels to come to them, or for your Lord to arrive, or for some of your Lord's signs to come? On the Day when some of your Lord's signs come, no soul will benefit from its faith unless it had believed previously, or had earned goodness through its faith. Say, "Wait, we too are waiting."

١٥٨ هَلۡ يَنظُرُونَ إِلَّآ أَن تَأۡتِيَهُمُ ٱلۡمَلَٰٓئِكَةُ أَوۡ
يَأۡتِيَ رَبُّكَ أَوۡ يَأۡتِيَ بَعۡضُ ءَايَٰتِ رَبِّكَۗ يَوۡمَ
يَأۡتِي بَعۡضُ ءَايَٰتِ رَبِّكَ لَا يَنفَعُ نَفۡسًا إِيمَٰنُهَا لَمۡ
تَكُنۡ ءَامَنَتۡ مِن قَبۡلُ أَوۡ كَسَبَتۡ فِيٓ إِيمَٰنِهَا
خَيۡرٗاۗ قُلِ ٱنتَظِرُوٓاْ إِنَّا مُنتَظِرُونَ

159 As for those who divided their religion and became sects—you have nothing to do with them. Their case rests with Allah; then He will inform them of what they used to do.

١٥٩ إِنَّ ٱلَّذِينَ فَرَّقُواْ دِينَهُمۡ وَكَانُواْ شِيَعٗا لَّسۡتَ
مِنۡهُمۡ فِي شَيۡءٍۚ إِنَّمَآ أَمۡرُهُمۡ إِلَى ٱللَّهِ ثُمَّ
يُنَبِّئُهُم بِمَا كَانُواْ يَفۡعَلُونَ

160 Whoever comes up with a good deed will have ten times its like; and whoever comes up with an evil deed will be repaid only with its equivalent—they will not be wronged.

١٦٠ مَن جَآءَ بِٱلۡحَسَنَةِ فَلَهُۥ عَشۡرُ أَمۡثَالِهَاۖ وَمَن
جَآءَ بِٱلسَّيِّئَةِ فَلَا يُجۡزَىٰٓ إِلَّا مِثۡلَهَا وَهُمۡ لَا
يُظۡلَمُونَ

١٦١ قُلْ إِنَّنِى هَدَىٰنِى رَبِّىٓ إِلَىٰ صِرَٰطٍ مُّسْتَقِيمٍ دِينًا قِيَمًا مِّلَّةَ إِبْرَٰهِيمَ حَنِيفًا ۚ وَمَا كَانَ مِنَ ٱلْمُشْرِكِينَ	161 Say, “My Lord has guided me to a straight path, an upright religion, the creed of Abraham the Monotheist, who was not a polytheist.”
١٦٢ قُلْ إِنَّ صَلَاتِى وَنُسُكِى وَمَحْيَاىَ وَمَمَاتِى لِلَّهِ رَبِّ ٱلْعَٰلَمِينَ	162 Say, “My prayer and my worship, and my life and my death, are devoted to Allah, the Lord of the Worlds.
١٦٣ لَا شَرِيكَ لَهُۥ ۖ وَبِذَٰلِكَ أُمِرْتُ وَأَنَا۠ أَوَّلُ ٱلْمُسْلِمِينَ	163 No associate has He. Thus I am commanded, and I am the first of those who submit.
١٦٤ قُلْ أَغَيْرَ ٱللَّهِ أَبْغِى رَبًّا وَهُوَ رَبُّ كُلِّ شَىْءٍ ۚ وَلَا تَكْسِبُ كُلُّ نَفْسٍ إِلَّا عَلَيْهَا ۚ وَلَا تَزِرُ وَازِرَةٌ وِزْرَ أُخْرَىٰ ۚ ثُمَّ إِلَىٰ رَبِّكُم مَّرْجِعُكُمْ فَيُنَبِّئُكُم بِمَا كُنتُمْ فِيهِ تَخْتَلِفُونَ	164 Say, “Am I to seek a Lord other than Allah, when He is the Lord of all things?” No soul gets except what it is due, and no soul bears the burdens of another. Then to your Lord is your return, then He will inform you regarding your disputes.
١٦٥ وَهُوَ ٱلَّذِى جَعَلَكُمْ خَلَٰٓئِفَ ٱلْأَرْضِ وَرَفَعَ بَعْضَكُمْ فَوْقَ بَعْضٍ دَرَجَٰتٍ لِّيَبْلُوَكُمْ فِى مَآ ءَاتَىٰكُمْ ۗ إِنَّ رَبَّكَ سَرِيعُ ٱلْعِقَابِ وَإِنَّهُۥ لَغَفُورٌ رَّحِيمٌۢ	165 It is He who made you successors on the earth, and raised some of you in ranks over others, in order to test you through what He has given you. Your Lord is Quick in retribution, and He is Forgiving and Merciful.

7 The Elevations الأعراف

بِسْمِ ٱللَّهِ ٱلرَّحْمَٰنِ ٱلرَّحِيمِ	In the name of Allah, the Gracious, the Merciful.
١ الٓمٓصٓ	1 Alif, Lam, Meem, Saad.
٢ كِتَٰبٌ أُنزِلَ إِلَيْكَ فَلَا يَكُن فِى صَدْرِكَ حَرَجٌ مِّنْهُ لِتُنذِرَ بِهِۦ وَذِكْرَىٰ لِلْمُؤْمِنِينَ	2 A Scripture was revealed to you, so let there be no anxiety in your heart because of it. You are to warn with it—and a reminder for the believers.
٣ ٱتَّبِعُوا۟ مَآ أُنزِلَ إِلَيْكُم مِّن رَّبِّكُمْ وَلَا تَتَّبِعُوا۟ مِن دُونِهِۦٓ أَوْلِيَآءَ ۗ قَلِيلًا مَّا تَذَكَّرُونَ	3 Follow what is revealed to you from your Lord, and do not follow other masters beside Him. Little you recollect.

٤ وَكَم مِّن قَرْيَةٍ أَهْلَكْنَٰهَا فَجَآءَهَا بَأْسُنَا بَيَٰتًا أَوْ
هُمْ قَآئِلُونَ

4 How many a town have We destroyed? Our might came upon them by night, or while they were napping.

٥ فَمَا كَانَ دَعْوَىٰهُمْ إِذْ جَآءَهُم بَأْسُنَآ إِلَّآ أَن
قَالُوٓا۟ إِنَّا كُنَّا ظَٰلِمِينَ

5 When Our might came upon them, their only cry was, "We were indeed wrongdoers."

٦ فَلَنَسْـَٔلَنَّ ٱلَّذِينَ أُرْسِلَ إِلَيْهِمْ وَلَنَسْـَٔلَنَّ
ٱلْمُرْسَلِينَ

6 We will question those to whom messengers were sent, and We will question the messengers.

٧ فَلَنَقُصَّنَّ عَلَيْهِم بِعِلْمٍ ۖ وَمَا كُنَّا غَآئِبِينَ

7 We will narrate to them with knowledge, for We were never absent.

٨ وَٱلْوَزْنُ يَوْمَئِذٍ ٱلْحَقُّ ۚ فَمَن ثَقُلَتْ مَوَٰزِينُهُۥ
فَأُو۟لَٰٓئِكَ هُمُ ٱلْمُفْلِحُونَ

8 The scales on that Day will be just. Those whose weights are heavy—it is they who are the successful.

٩ وَمَنْ خَفَّتْ مَوَٰزِينُهُۥ فَأُو۟لَٰٓئِكَ ٱلَّذِينَ خَسِرُوٓا۟
أَنفُسَهُم بِمَا كَانُوا۟ بِـَٔايَٰتِنَا يَظْلِمُونَ

9 But as for those whose weights are light—it is they who have lost their souls, because they used to mistreat Our revelations.

١٠ وَلَقَدْ مَكَّنَّٰكُمْ فِى ٱلْأَرْضِ وَجَعَلْنَا لَكُمْ فِيهَا
مَعَٰيِشَ ۗ قَلِيلًا مَّا تَشْكُرُونَ

10 We have established you firmly on earth, and made for you in it livelihood—but rarely do you give thanks.

١١ وَلَقَدْ خَلَقْنَٰكُمْ ثُمَّ صَوَّرْنَٰكُمْ ثُمَّ قُلْنَا لِلْمَلَٰٓئِكَةِ
ٱسْجُدُوا۟ لِءَادَمَ فَسَجَدُوٓا۟ إِلَّآ إِبْلِيسَ لَمْ يَكُن
مِّنَ ٱلسَّٰجِدِينَ

11 We created you, then We shaped you, then We said to the angels, "Bow down before Adam;" so they bowed down, except for Satan; he was not of those who bowed down.

١٢ قَالَ مَا مَنَعَكَ أَلَّا تَسْجُدَ إِذْ أَمَرْتُكَ ۖ قَالَ أَنَا۠
خَيْرٌ مِّنْهُ خَلَقْتَنِى مِن نَّارٍ وَخَلَقْتَهُۥ مِن طِينٍ

12 He said, "What prevented you from bowing down when I have commanded you?" He said, "I am better than he; You created me from fire, and You created him from mud."

١٣ قَالَ فَٱهْبِطْ مِنْهَا فَمَا يَكُونُ لَكَ أَن تَتَكَبَّرَ
فِيهَا فَٱخْرُجْ إِنَّكَ مِنَ ٱلصَّٰغِرِينَ

13 He said, "Get down from it! It is not for you to act arrogantly in it. Get out! You are one of the lowly!"

١٤ قَالَ أَنظِرْنِىٓ إِلَىٰ يَوْمِ يُبْعَثُونَ

14 He said, "Give me respite, until the Day they are resurrected."

١٥ قَالَ إِنَّكَ مِنَ ٱلْمُنظَرِينَ

15 He said, "You are of those given respite."

١٦ قَالَ فَبِمَآ أَغْوَيْتَنِى لَأَقْعُدَنَّ لَهُمْ صِرَٰطَكَ
ٱلْمُسْتَقِيمَ

16 He said, "Because you have lured me, I will waylay them on Your straight path.

١٧ ثُمَّ لَـَٔاتِيَنَّهُم مِّنۢ بَيْنِ أَيْدِيهِمْ وَمِنْ خَلْفِهِمْ
وَعَنْ أَيْمَٰنِهِمْ وَعَن شَمَآئِلِهِمْ ۖ وَلَا تَجِدُ أَكْثَرَهُمْ
شَٰكِرِينَ

17 Then I will come at them from before them, and from behind them, and from their right, and from their left; and you will not find most of them appreciative."

١٨ قَالَ ٱخْرُجْ مِنْهَا مَذْءُومًا مَّدْحُورًا ۖ لَّمَن
تَبِعَكَ مِنْهُمْ لَأَمْلَأَنَّ جَهَنَّمَ مِنكُمْ أَجْمَعِينَ

18 He said, "Get out of it, despised and vanquished. Whoever among them follows you—I will fill up Hell with you all.

١٩ وَيَٰٓـَٔادَمُ ٱسْكُنْ أَنتَ وَزَوْجُكَ ٱلْجَنَّةَ فَكُلَا مِنْ
حَيْثُ شِئْتُمَا وَلَا تَقْرَبَا هَٰذِهِ ٱلشَّجَرَةَ فَتَكُونَا
مِنَ ٱلظَّٰلِمِينَ

19 And you, Adam, inhabit the Garden, you and your wife, and eat whatever you wish; but do not approach this tree, lest you become sinners."

٢٠ فَوَسْوَسَ لَهُمَا ٱلشَّيْطَٰنُ لِيُبْدِىَ لَهُمَا مَا وُۥرِىَ
عَنْهُمَا مِن سَوْءَٰتِهِمَا وَقَالَ مَا نَهَىٰكُمَا رَبُّكُمَا عَنْ
هَٰذِهِ ٱلشَّجَرَةِ إِلَّآ أَن تَكُونَا مَلَكَيْنِ أَوْ تَكُونَا مِنَ
ٱلْخَٰلِدِينَ

20 But Satan whispered to them, to reveal to them their nakedness, which was invisible to them. He said, "Your Lord has only forbidden you this tree, lest you become angels, or become immortals."

٢١ وَقَاسَمَهُمَآ إِنِّى لَكُمَا لَمِنَ ٱلنَّٰصِحِينَ

21 And he swore to them, "I am a sincere advisor to you."

٢٢ فَدَلَّىٰهُمَا بِغُرُورٍ ۚ فَلَمَّا ذَاقَا ٱلشَّجَرَةَ بَدَتْ لَهُمَا
سَوْءَٰتُهُمَا وَطَفِقَا يَخْصِفَانِ عَلَيْهِمَا مِن وَرَقِ
ٱلْجَنَّةِ ۖ وَنَادَىٰهُمَا رَبُّهُمَآ أَلَمْ أَنْهَكُمَا عَن تِلْكُمَا
ٱلشَّجَرَةِ وَأَقُل لَّكُمَآ إِنَّ ٱلشَّيْطَٰنَ لَكُمَا عَدُوٌّ
مُّبِينٌ

22 So he lured them with deceit. And when they tasted the tree, their nakedness became evident to them, and they began covering themselves with the leaves of the Garden. And their Lord called out to them, "Did I not forbid you from this tree, and say to you that Satan is a sworn enemy to you?"

٢٣ قَالَا رَبَّنَا ظَلَمْنَآ أَنفُسَنَا وَإِن لَّمْ تَغْفِرْ لَنَا
وَتَرْحَمْنَا لَنَكُونَنَّ مِنَ ٱلْخَٰسِرِينَ

23 They said, "Our Lord, we have done wrong to ourselves. Unless You forgive us, and have mercy on us, we will be among the losers."

٢٤ قَالَ ٱهْبِطُوا۟ بَعْضُكُمْ لِبَعْضٍ عَدُوٌّ ۖ وَلَكُمْ فِى
ٱلْأَرْضِ مُسْتَقَرٌّ وَمَتَـٰعٌ إِلَىٰ حِينٍ

24 He said, "Fall, some of you enemies to one another. On earth you will have residence and livelihood for a while."

٢٥ قَالَ فِيهَا تَحْيَوْنَ وَفِيهَا تَمُوتُونَ وَمِنْهَا
تُخْرَجُونَ

25 He said, "In it you will live, and in it you will die, and from it you will be brought out."

٢٦ يَـٰبَنِىٓ ءَادَمَ قَدْ أَنزَلْنَا عَلَيْكُمْ لِبَاسًا يُوَٰرِى
سَوْءَٰتِكُمْ وَرِيشًا ۖ وَلِبَاسُ ٱلتَّقْوَىٰ ذَٰلِكَ خَيْرٌ ۚ
ذَٰلِكَ مِنْ ءَايَـٰتِ ٱللَّهِ لَعَلَّهُمْ يَذَّكَّرُونَ

26 O children of Adam! We have provided you with clothing to cover your bodies, and for luxury. But the clothing of piety—that is best. These are some of Allah's revelations, so that they may take heed.

٢٧ يَـٰبَنِىٓ ءَادَمَ لَا يَفْتِنَنَّكُمُ ٱلشَّيْطَـٰنُ كَمَآ أَخْرَجَ
أَبَوَيْكُم مِّنَ ٱلْجَنَّةِ يَنزِعُ عَنْهُمَا لِبَاسَهُمَا لِيُرِيَهُمَا
سَوْءَٰتِهِمَآ ۗ إِنَّهُۥ يَرَىٰكُمْ هُوَ وَقَبِيلُهُۥ مِنْ حَيْثُ لَا
تَرَوْنَهُمْ ۗ إِنَّا جَعَلْنَا ٱلشَّيَـٰطِينَ أَوْلِيَآءَ لِلَّذِينَ لَا
يُؤْمِنُونَ

27 O Children of Adam! Do not let Satan seduce you, as he drove your parents out of the Garden, stripping them of their garments, to show them their nakedness. He sees you, him and his clan, from where you cannot see them. We have made the devils friends of those who do not believe.

٢٨ وَإِذَا فَعَلُوا۟ فَـٰحِشَةً قَالُوا۟ وَجَدْنَا عَلَيْهَآ
ءَابَآءَنَا وَٱللَّهُ أَمَرَنَا بِهَا ۗ قُلْ إِنَّ ٱللَّهَ لَا يَأْمُرُ
بِٱلْفَحْشَآءِ ۖ أَتَقُولُونَ عَلَى ٱللَّهِ مَا لَا تَعْلَمُونَ

28 And when they commit an indecency, they say, "We found our parents doing this, and Allah has commanded us to do it." Say, "Allah does not command indecencies. Are you attributing to Allah what you do not know?"

٢٩ قُلْ أَمَرَ رَبِّى بِٱلْقِسْطِ ۖ وَأَقِيمُوا۟ وُجُوهَكُمْ
عِندَ كُلِّ مَسْجِدٍ وَٱدْعُوهُ مُخْلِصِينَ لَهُ ٱلدِّينَ ۚ
كَمَا بَدَأَكُمْ تَعُودُونَ

29 Say, "My Lord commands justice, and to stand devoted at every place of worship. So call upon Him, and dedicate your faith to Him alone. Just as He originated you, so you will return."

٣٠ فَرِيقًا هَدَىٰ وَفَرِيقًا حَقَّ عَلَيْهِمُ ٱلضَّلَـٰلَةُ ۗ
إِنَّهُمُ ٱتَّخَذُوا۟ ٱلشَّيَـٰطِينَ أَوْلِيَآءَ مِن دُونِ ٱللَّهِ
وَيَحْسَبُونَ أَنَّهُم مُّهْتَدُونَ

30 Some He has guided, and some have deserved misguidance. They have adopted the devils for patrons rather than Allah, and they assume that they are guided.

٣١ يَٰبَنِيٓ ءَادَمَ خُذُواْ زِينَتَكُمۡ عِندَ كُلِّ مَسۡجِدٖ
وَكُلُواْ وَٱشۡرَبُواْ وَلَا تُسۡرِفُوٓاْۚ إِنَّهُۥ لَا يُحِبُّ
ٱلۡمُسۡرِفِينَ

31 O Children of Adam! Dress properly at every place of worship, and eat and drink, but do not be excessive. He does not love the excessive.

٣٢ قُلۡ مَنۡ حَرَّمَ زِينَةَ ٱللَّهِ ٱلَّتِيٓ أَخۡرَجَ لِعِبَادِهِۦ
وَٱلطَّيِّبَٰتِ مِنَ ٱلرِّزۡقِۚ قُلۡ هِيَ لِلَّذِينَ ءَامَنُواْ
فِي ٱلۡحَيَوٰةِ ٱلدُّنۡيَا خَالِصَةٗ يَوۡمَ ٱلۡقِيَٰمَةِۗ كَذَٰلِكَ
نُفَصِّلُ ٱلۡأٓيَٰتِ لِقَوۡمٖ يَعۡلَمُونَ

32 Say, “Who forbade Allah’s finery which He has produced for His servants, and the delights of livelihood?” Say, “They are for those who believe, in this present world, but exclusively theirs on the Day of Resurrection.” We thus detail the revelations for people who know.

٣٣ قُلۡ إِنَّمَا حَرَّمَ رَبِّيَ ٱلۡفَوَٰحِشَ مَا ظَهَرَ مِنۡهَا
وَمَا بَطَنَ وَٱلۡإِثۡمَ وَٱلۡبَغۡيَ بِغَيۡرِ ٱلۡحَقِّ وَأَن
تُشۡرِكُواْ بِٱللَّهِ مَا لَمۡ يُنَزِّلۡ بِهِۦ سُلۡطَٰنٗا وَأَن
تَقُولُواْ عَلَى ٱللَّهِ مَا لَا تَعۡلَمُونَ

33 Say, “My Lord has forbidden immoralities—both open and secret—and sin, and unjustified aggression, and that you associate with Allah anything for which He revealed no sanction, and that you say about Allah what you do not know.”

٣٤ وَلِكُلِّ أُمَّةٍ أَجَلٞۖ فَإِذَا جَآءَ أَجَلُهُمۡ لَا
يَسۡتَأۡخِرُونَ سَاعَةٗ وَلَا يَسۡتَقۡدِمُونَ

34 For every nation is an appointed time. When their time has come, they cannot delay it by one hour, nor can they advance it.

٣٥ يَٰبَنِيٓ ءَادَمَ إِمَّا يَأۡتِيَنَّكُمۡ رُسُلٞ مِّنكُمۡ
يَقُصُّونَ عَلَيۡكُمۡ ءَايَٰتِي فَمَنِ ٱتَّقَىٰ وَأَصۡلَحَ فَلَا
خَوۡفٌ عَلَيۡهِمۡ وَلَا هُمۡ يَحۡزَنُونَ

35 O Children of Adam! When messengers from among you come to you, relating to you My revelations—whoever practices piety and reforms—upon them shall be no fear, nor shall they grieve.

٣٦ وَٱلَّذِينَ كَذَّبُواْ بِـَٔايَٰتِنَا وَٱسۡتَكۡبَرُواْ عَنۡهَآ
أُوْلَٰٓئِكَ أَصۡحَٰبُ ٱلنَّارِۖ هُمۡ فِيهَا خَٰلِدُونَ

36 But as for those who reject Our revelations, and are too proud to accept them—these are the inmates of the Fire, where they will remain forever.

٣٧ فَمَنۡ أَظۡلَمُ مِمَّنِ ٱفۡتَرَىٰ عَلَى ٱللَّهِ كَذِبًا أَوۡ
كَذَّبَ بِـَٔايَٰتِهِۦٓۚ أُوْلَٰٓئِكَ يَنَالُهُمۡ نَصِيبُهُم مِّنَ
ٱلۡكِتَٰبِۖ حَتَّىٰٓ إِذَا جَآءَتۡهُمۡ رُسُلُنَا يَتَوَفَّوۡنَهُمۡ

37 Who does greater wrong than he who invents lies about Allah, or denies His revelations? These—their share of the decree will reach them. Until, when Our envoys come to them, to take their souls away, they

قَالُوٓا۟ أَيْنَ مَا كُنتُمْ تَدْعُونَ مِن دُونِ ٱللَّهِ ۖ قَالُوا۟
ضَلُّوا۟ عَنَّا وَشَهِدُوا۟ عَلَىٰٓ أَنفُسِهِمْ أَنَّهُمْ كَانُوا۟
كَٰفِرِينَ

will say, "Where are they whom you used to pray to besides Allah?" They will say, "They have abandoned us," and they will testify against themselves that they were faithless.

٣٨ قَالَ ٱدْخُلُوا۟ فِىٓ أُمَمٍ قَدْ خَلَتْ مِن قَبْلِكُم
مِّنَ ٱلْجِنِّ وَٱلْإِنسِ فِى ٱلنَّارِ ۖ كُلَّمَا دَخَلَتْ أُمَّةٌ
لَّعَنَتْ أُخْتَهَا ۖ حَتَّىٰٓ إِذَا ٱدَّارَكُوا۟ فِيهَا جَمِيعًا
قَالَتْ أُخْرَىٰهُمْ لِأُولَىٰهُمْ رَبَّنَا هَٰٓؤُلَآءِ أَضَلُّونَا
فَـَٔاتِهِمْ عَذَابًا ضِعْفًا مِّنَ ٱلنَّارِ ۖ قَالَ لِكُلٍّ ضِعْفٌ
وَلَٰكِن لَّا تَعْلَمُونَ

38 He will say, "Join the crowds of jinn and humans who have gone into the Fire before you." Every time a crowd enters, it will curse its sister-crowd. Until, when they are all in it, the last of them will say to the first of them, "Our Lord, these are the ones who misled us, so inflict on them a double punishment in the Fire." He will say, "Each will have a double, but you do not know."

٣٩ وَقَالَتْ أُولَىٰهُمْ لِأُخْرَىٰهُمْ فَمَا كَانَ لَكُمْ عَلَيْنَا
مِن فَضْلٍ فَذُوقُوا۟ ٱلْعَذَابَ بِمَا كُنتُمْ تَكْسِبُونَ

39 The first of them will say to the last of them, "You have no advantage over us, so taste the torment for what you used to earn."

٤٠ إِنَّ ٱلَّذِينَ كَذَّبُوا۟ بِـَٔايَٰتِنَا وَٱسْتَكْبَرُوا۟ عَنْهَا لَا
تُفَتَّحُ لَهُمْ أَبْوَٰبُ ٱلسَّمَآءِ وَلَا يَدْخُلُونَ ٱلْجَنَّةَ
حَتَّىٰ يَلِجَ ٱلْجَمَلُ فِى سَمِّ ٱلْخِيَاطِ ۚ وَكَذَٰلِكَ
نَجْزِى ٱلْمُجْرِمِينَ

40 Those who reject Our revelations and are too arrogant to uphold them—the doors of Heaven will not be opened for them, nor will they enter Paradise, until the camel passes through the eye of the needle. Thus We repay the guilty.

٤١ لَهُم مِّن جَهَنَّمَ مِهَادٌ وَمِن فَوْقِهِمْ غَوَاشٍ ۚ
وَكَذَٰلِكَ نَجْزِى ٱلظَّٰلِمِينَ

41 For them is a couch of hell, and above them are sheets of fire. Thus We repay the wrongdoers.

٤٢ وَٱلَّذِينَ ءَامَنُوا۟ وَعَمِلُوا۟ ٱلصَّٰلِحَٰتِ لَا نُكَلِّفُ
نَفْسًا إِلَّا وُسْعَهَآ أُو۟لَٰٓئِكَ أَصْحَٰبُ ٱلْجَنَّةِ ۖ هُمْ
فِيهَا خَٰلِدُونَ

42 As for those who believe and do righteous works—We never burden any soul beyond its capacity—these are the inhabitants of the Garden; abiding therein eternally.

٤٣ وَنَزَعْنَا مَا فِى صُدُورِهِم مِّنْ غِلٍّ تَجْرِى مِن
تَحْتِهِمُ ٱلْأَنْهَٰرُ ۖ وَقَالُوا۟ ٱلْحَمْدُ لِلَّهِ ٱلَّذِى هَدَىٰنَا
لِهَٰذَا وَمَا كُنَّا لِنَهْتَدِىَ لَوْلَآ أَنْ هَدَىٰنَا ٱللَّهُ ۖ لَقَدْ

43 We will remove whatever rancor is in their hearts. Rivers will flow beneath them. And they will say, "Praise be to Allah, who has guided us to this. Had Allah not guided us, we would never be guided. The messengers of our Lord did come

جَآءَتْ رُسُلُ رَبِّنَا بِٱلْحَقِّ ۖ وَنُودُوٓا۟ أَن تِلْكُمُ
ٱلْجَنَّةُ أُورِثْتُمُوهَا بِمَا كُنتُمْ تَعْمَلُونَ

with the truth." And it will be proclaimed to them, "This is the Garden you are made to inherit, on account of what you used to do."

٤٤ وَنَادَىٰٓ أَصْحَٰبُ ٱلْجَنَّةِ أَصْحَٰبَ ٱلنَّارِ أَن قَدْ
وَجَدْنَا مَا وَعَدَنَا رَبُّنَا حَقًّا فَهَلْ وَجَدتُّم مَّا
وَعَدَ رَبُّكُمْ حَقًّا ۖ قَالُوا۟ نَعَمْ ۚ فَأَذَّنَ مُؤَذِّنٌۢ بَيْنَهُمْ
أَن لَّعْنَةُ ٱللَّهِ عَلَى ٱلظَّٰلِمِينَ

44 And the inhabitants of the Garden will call out to the inmates of the Fire, "We found what our Lord promised us to be true; did you find what your Lord promised you to be true?" They will say, "Yes." Thereupon a caller will announce in their midst, "The curse of Allah is upon the wrongdoers."

٤٥ ٱلَّذِينَ يَصُدُّونَ عَن سَبِيلِ ٱللَّهِ وَيَبْغُونَهَا
عِوَجًا وَهُم بِٱلْءَاخِرَةِ كَٰفِرُونَ

45 "Those who hinder from the path of Allah, and seek to distort it, and who deny the Hereafter."

٤٦ وَبَيْنَهُمَا حِجَابٌ ۚ وَعَلَى ٱلْأَعْرَافِ رِجَالٌ
يَعْرِفُونَ كُلًّۢا بِسِيمَىٰهُمْ ۚ وَنَادَوْا۟ أَصْحَٰبَ ٱلْجَنَّةِ
أَن سَلَٰمٌ عَلَيْكُمْ ۚ لَمْ يَدْخُلُوهَا وَهُمْ يَطْمَعُونَ

46 And between them is a partition, and on the Elevations are men who recognize everyone by their features. They will call to the inhabitants of the Garden, "Peace be upon you." They have not entered it, but they are hoping.

٤٧ وَإِذَا صُرِفَتْ أَبْصَٰرُهُمْ تِلْقَآءَ أَصْحَٰبِ ٱلنَّارِ
قَالُوا۟ رَبَّنَا لَا تَجْعَلْنَا مَعَ ٱلْقَوْمِ ٱلظَّٰلِمِينَ

47 And when their eyes are directed towards the inmates of the Fire, they will say, "Our Lord, do not place us among the wrongdoing people."

٤٨ وَنَادَىٰٓ أَصْحَٰبُ ٱلْأَعْرَافِ رِجَالًا يَعْرِفُونَهُم
بِسِيمَىٰهُمْ قَالُوا۟ مَآ أَغْنَىٰ عَنكُمْ جَمْعُكُمْ وَمَا
كُنتُمْ تَسْتَكْبِرُونَ

48 And the dwellers of the Elevations will call to men they recognize by their features, saying, "Your hoardings did not avail you, nor did your arrogance."

٤٩ أَهَٰٓؤُلَآءِ ٱلَّذِينَ أَقْسَمْتُمْ لَا يَنَالُهُمُ ٱللَّهُ
بِرَحْمَةٍ ۚ ٱدْخُلُوا۟ ٱلْجَنَّةَ لَا خَوْفٌ عَلَيْكُمْ وَلَآ
أَنتُمْ تَحْزَنُونَ

49 "Are these the ones you swore Allah will not touch with mercy?" "Enter the Garden; you have nothing to fear, and you will not grieve."

٥٠ وَنَادَىٰٓ أَصْحَٰبُ ٱلنَّارِ أَصْحَٰبَ ٱلْجَنَّةِ أَنْ
أَفِيضُوا۟ عَلَيْنَا مِنَ ٱلْمَآءِ أَوْ مِمَّا رَزَقَكُمُ ٱللَّهُ ۚ
قَالُوٓا۟ إِنَّ ٱللَّهَ حَرَّمَهُمَا عَلَى ٱلْكَٰفِرِينَ

50 The inmates of the Fire will call on the inhabitants of the Garden, "Pour some water over us, or some of what Allah has provided for you."

They will say, “Allah has forbidden them for the disbelievers.”

٥١ ٱلَّذِينَ ٱتَّخَذُواْ دِينَهُمْ لَهْوًا وَلَعِبًا وَغَرَّتْهُمُ
ٱلْحَيَوٰةُ ٱلدُّنْيَا ۚ فَٱلْيَوْمَ نَنسَىٰهُمْ كَمَا نَسُواْ لِقَآءَ
يَوْمِهِمْ هَٰذَا وَمَا كَانُواْ بِـَٔايَٰتِنَا يَجْحَدُونَ

51 Those who took their religion lightly, and in jest, and whom the worldly life deceived. Today We will ignore them, as they ignored the meeting on this Day of theirs, and they used to deny Our revelations.

٥٢ وَلَقَدْ جِئْنَٰهُم بِكِتَٰبٍ فَصَّلْنَٰهُ عَلَىٰ عِلْمٍ هُدًى
وَرَحْمَةً لِّقَوْمٍ يُؤْمِنُونَ

52 We have given them a Scripture, which We detailed with knowledge—guidance and mercy for people who believe.

٥٣ هَلْ يَنظُرُونَ إِلَّا تَأْوِيلَهُۥ ۚ يَوْمَ يَأْتِى تَأْوِيلُهُۥ
يَقُولُ ٱلَّذِينَ نَسُوهُ مِن قَبْلُ قَدْ جَآءَتْ رُسُلُ
رَبِّنَا بِٱلْحَقِّ فَهَل لَّنَا مِن شُفَعَآءَ فَيَشْفَعُواْ لَنَآ أَوْ
نُرَدُّ فَنَعْمَلَ غَيْرَ ٱلَّذِى كُنَّا نَعْمَلُ ۚ قَدْ خَسِرُوٓاْ
أَنفُسَهُمْ وَضَلَّ عَنْهُم مَّا كَانُواْ يَفْتَرُونَ

53 Are they waiting for anything but its fulfillment? The Day its fulfillment comes true, those who disregarded it before will say, “The messengers of our Lord did come with the truth. Have we any intercessors to intercede for us? Or, could we be sent back, to behave differently from the way we behaved before?” They ruined their souls, and what they used to invent has failed them.

٥٤ إِنَّ رَبَّكُمُ ٱللَّهُ ٱلَّذِى خَلَقَ ٱلسَّمَٰوَٰتِ وَٱلْأَرْضَ
فِى سِتَّةِ أَيَّامٍ ثُمَّ ٱسْتَوَىٰ عَلَى ٱلْعَرْشِ يُغْشِى
ٱلَّيْلَ ٱلنَّهَارَ يَطْلُبُهُۥ حَثِيثًا وَٱلشَّمْسَ وَٱلْقَمَرَ
وَٱلنُّجُومَ مُسَخَّرَٰتٍۭ بِأَمْرِهِۦٓ ۗ أَلَا لَهُ ٱلْخَلْقُ
وَٱلْأَمْرُ ۗ تَبَارَكَ ٱللَّهُ رَبُّ ٱلْعَٰلَمِينَ

54 Your Lord is Allah; He who created the heavens and the earth in six days, then established Himself on the Throne. The night overtakes the day, as it pursues it persistently; and the sun, and the moon, and the stars are subservient by His command. His is the creation, and His is the command. Blessed is Allah, Lord of all beings.

٥٥ ٱدْعُواْ رَبَّكُمْ تَضَرُّعًا وَخُفْيَةً ۚ إِنَّهُۥ لَا يُحِبُّ
ٱلْمُعْتَدِينَ

55 Call upon your Lord humbly and privately. He does not love the aggressors.

٥٦ وَلَا تُفْسِدُواْ فِى ٱلْأَرْضِ بَعْدَ إِصْلَٰحِهَا
وَٱدْعُوهُ خَوْفًا وَطَمَعًا ۚ إِنَّ رَحْمَتَ ٱللَّهِ قَرِيبٌ
مِّنَ ٱلْمُحْسِنِينَ

56 And do not corrupt on earth after its reformation, and pray to Him with fear and hope. Allah’s mercy is close to the doers of good.

٥٧ وَهُوَ ٱلَّذِى يُرْسِلُ ٱلرِّيَٰحَ بُشْرًۢا بَيْنَ يَدَىْ
رَحْمَتِهِۦ ۖ حَتَّىٰٓ إِذَآ أَقَلَّتْ سَحَابًا ثِقَالًا سُقْنَٰهُ
لِبَلَدٍ مَّيِّتٍ فَأَنزَلْنَا بِهِ ٱلْمَآءَ فَأَخْرَجْنَا بِهِۦ مِن
كُلِّ ٱلثَّمَرَٰتِ ۚ كَذَٰلِكَ نُخْرِجُ ٱلْمَوْتَىٰ لَعَلَّكُمْ
تَذَكَّرُونَ

57 It is He who sends the wind ahead of His mercy. Then, when they have gathered up heavy clouds, We drive them to a dead land, where We make water come down, and with it We bring out all kinds of fruits. Thus We bring out the dead—perhaps you will reflect.

٥٨ وَٱلْبَلَدُ ٱلطَّيِّبُ يَخْرُجُ نَبَاتُهُۥ بِإِذْنِ رَبِّهِۦ ۖ
وَٱلَّذِى خَبُثَ لَا يَخْرُجُ إِلَّا نَكِدًا ۚ كَذَٰلِكَ نُصَرِّفُ
ٱلْءَايَٰتِ لِقَوْمٍ يَشْكُرُونَ

58 As for the good land, it yields its produce by the leave of its Lord. But as for the bad, it produces nothing but hardship and misery. Thus We explain the revelations in various ways for people who are thankful.

٥٩ لَقَدْ أَرْسَلْنَا نُوحًا إِلَىٰ قَوْمِهِۦ فَقَالَ يَٰقَوْمِ
ٱعْبُدُوا۟ ٱللَّهَ مَا لَكُم مِّنْ إِلَٰهٍ غَيْرُهُۥٓ إِنِّىٓ أَخَافُ
عَلَيْكُمْ عَذَابَ يَوْمٍ عَظِيمٍ

59 We sent Noah to his people. He said, "O my people! Worship Allah; you have no god other than Him. I fear for you the punishment of a tremendous Day."

٦٠ قَالَ ٱلْمَلَأُ مِن قَوْمِهِۦٓ إِنَّا لَنَرَىٰكَ فِى ضَلَٰلٍ
مُّبِينٍ

60 The dignitaries among his people said, "We see that you are in obvious error."

٦١ قَالَ يَٰقَوْمِ لَيْسَ بِى ضَلَٰلَةٌ وَلَٰكِنِّى رَسُولٌ
مِّن رَّبِّ ٱلْعَٰلَمِينَ

61 He said, "O my people, I am not in error, but I am a messenger from the Lord of the Worlds."

٦٢ أُبَلِّغُكُمْ رِسَٰلَٰتِ رَبِّى وَأَنصَحُ لَكُمْ وَأَعْلَمُ مِنَ
ٱللَّهِ مَا لَا تَعْلَمُونَ

62 "I deliver to you the messages of my Lord, and I advise you, and I know from Allah what you do not know."

٦٣ أَوَعَجِبْتُمْ أَن جَآءَكُمْ ذِكْرٌ مِّن رَّبِّكُمْ عَلَىٰ
رَجُلٍ مِّنكُمْ لِيُنذِرَكُمْ وَلِتَتَّقُوا۟ وَلَعَلَّكُمْ تُرْحَمُونَ

63 "Do you wonder that a reminder has come to you from your Lord, through a man from among you, to warn you, and to lead you to righteousness, so that you may attain mercy?"

٦٤ فَكَذَّبُوهُ فَأَنجَيْنَٰهُ وَٱلَّذِينَ مَعَهُۥ فِى ٱلْفُلْكِ
وَأَغْرَقْنَا ٱلَّذِينَ كَذَّبُوا۟ بِـَٔايَٰتِنَآ ۚ إِنَّهُمْ كَانُوا۟ قَوْمًا
عَمِينَ

64 But they called him a liar. So We saved him and those with him in the Ark, and We drowned those who rejected Our revelations. They were blind people.

٦٥ وَإِلَىٰ عَادٍ أَخَاهُمْ هُودًا ۗ قَالَ يَٰقَوْمِ ٱعْبُدُوا۟
ٱللَّهَ مَا لَكُم مِّنْ إِلَٰهٍ غَيْرُهُۥٓ ۚ أَفَلَا تَتَّقُونَ

65 And to Aad, their brother Hud. He said, “O my people! Worship Allah; you have no god other than Him. Will you not take heed?”

٦٦ قَالَ ٱلْمَلَأُ ٱلَّذِينَ كَفَرُوا۟ مِن قَوْمِهِۦٓ إِنَّا لَنَرَىٰكَ
فِى سَفَاهَةٍ وَإِنَّا لَنَظُنُّكَ مِنَ ٱلْكَٰذِبِينَ

66 The elite of his people who disbelieved said, “We see foolishness in you, and we think that you are a liar.”

٦٧ قَالَ يَٰقَوْمِ لَيْسَ بِى سَفَاهَةٌ وَلَٰكِنِّى رَسُولٌ
مِّن رَّبِّ ٱلْعَٰلَمِينَ

67 He said, “O my people! There is no foolishness in me, but I am a messenger from the Lord of the Worlds.

٦٨ أُبَلِّغُكُمْ رِسَٰلَٰتِ رَبِّى وَأَنَا۠ لَكُمْ نَاصِحٌ أَمِينٌ

68 “I convey to you the messages of my Lord, and I am a trustworthy adviser to you.”

٦٩ أَوَعَجِبْتُمْ أَن جَآءَكُمْ ذِكْرٌ مِّن رَّبِّكُمْ عَلَىٰ
رَجُلٍ مِّنكُمْ لِيُنذِرَكُمْ ۚ وَٱذْكُرُوٓا۟ إِذْ جَعَلَكُمْ
خُلَفَآءَ مِنۢ بَعْدِ قَوْمِ نُوحٍ وَزَادَكُمْ فِى ٱلْخَلْقِ
بَصْۜطَةً ۖ فَٱذْكُرُوٓا۟ ءَالَآءَ ٱللَّهِ لَعَلَّكُمْ تُفْلِحُونَ

69 “Are you surprised that a reminder has come to you from your Lord, through a man from among you, to warn you? Remember how He made you successors after the people of Noah, and increased you greatly in stature. And remember Allah’s blessings, so that you may prosper.”

٧٠ قَالُوٓا۟ أَجِئْتَنَا لِنَعْبُدَ ٱللَّهَ وَحْدَهُۥ وَنَذَرَ مَا كَانَ
يَعْبُدُ ءَابَآؤُنَا ۖ فَأْتِنَا بِمَا تَعِدُنَآ إِن كُنتَ مِنَ
ٱلصَّٰدِقِينَ

70 They said, “Did you come to us to make us worship Allah alone, and abandon what our ancestors used to worship? Then bring us what you threaten us with, if you are truthful.”

٧١ قَالَ قَدْ وَقَعَ عَلَيْكُم مِّن رَّبِّكُمْ رِجْسٌ
وَغَضَبٌ ۖ أَتُجَٰدِلُونَنِى فِىٓ أَسْمَآءٍ سَمَّيْتُمُوهَآ
أَنتُمْ وَءَابَآؤُكُم مَّا نَزَّلَ ٱللَّهُ بِهَا مِن سُلْطَٰنٍ ۚ
فَٱنتَظِرُوٓا۟ إِنِّى مَعَكُم مِّنَ ٱلْمُنتَظِرِينَ

71 He said, “Condemnation and wrath have befallen you from your Lord. Are you arguing with me over names, which you and your ancestors invented, for which Allah sent down no authority? Just wait; I am waiting with you.”

٧٢ فَأَنجَيْنَٰهُ وَٱلَّذِينَ مَعَهُۥ بِرَحْمَةٍ مِّنَّا وَقَطَعْنَا
دَابِرَ ٱلَّذِينَ كَذَّبُوا۟ بِـَٔايَٰتِنَا ۖ وَمَا كَانُوا۟ مُؤْمِنِينَ

72 So We saved him and those with him, by mercy from Us, and We cut off the roots of those who rejected Our revelations and were not believers.

٧٣ وَإِلَىٰ ثَمُودَ أَخَاهُمْ صَٰلِحًاۗ قَالَ يَٰقَوْمِ
ٱعْبُدُوا۟ ٱللَّهَ مَا لَكُم مِّنْ إِلَٰهٍ غَيْرُهُۥۖ قَدْ جَآءَتْكُم
بَيِّنَةٌ مِّن رَّبِّكُمْۖ هَٰذِهِۦ نَاقَةُ ٱللَّهِ لَكُمْ ءَايَةًۖ
فَذَرُوهَا تَأْكُلْ فِىٓ أَرْضِ ٱللَّهِۖ وَلَا تَمَسُّوهَا
بِسُوٓءٍ فَيَأْخُذَكُمْ عَذَابٌ أَلِيمٌ

73 And to Thamood, their brother Saleh. He said, "O my people! Worship Allah; you have no god other than Him. Clarification has come to you from your Lord. This she-camel of Allah is a sign for you. So leave her to graze on Allah's earth, and do her no harm, lest a painful penalty seizes you."

٧٤ وَٱذْكُرُوٓا۟ إِذْ جَعَلَكُمْ خُلَفَآءَ مِنۢ بَعْدِ عَادٍ
وَبَوَّأَكُمْ فِى ٱلْأَرْضِ تَتَّخِذُونَ مِن سُهُولِهَا
قُصُورًا وَتَنْحِتُونَ ٱلْجِبَالَ بُيُوتًاۖ فَٱذْكُرُوٓا۟
ءَالَآءَ ٱللَّهِ وَلَا تَعْثَوْا۟ فِى ٱلْأَرْضِ مُفْسِدِينَ

74 "And remember how He made you successors after Aad, and settled you in the land. You make for yourselves mansions on its plains, and carve out dwellings in the mountains. So remember Allah's benefits, and do not roam the earth corruptingly."

٧٥ قَالَ ٱلْمَلَأُ ٱلَّذِينَ ٱسْتَكْبَرُوا۟ مِن قَوْمِهِۦ
لِلَّذِينَ ٱسْتُضْعِفُوا۟ لِمَنْ ءَامَنَ مِنْهُمْ أَتَعْلَمُونَ أَنَّ
صَٰلِحًا مُّرْسَلٌ مِّن رَّبِّهِۦۚ قَالُوٓا۟ إِنَّا بِمَآ أُرْسِلَ بِهِۦ
مُؤْمِنُونَ

75 The elite of his people, who were arrogant, said to the common people who had believed, "Do you know that Saleh is sent from his Lord?" They said, "We are believers in what he was sent with."

٧٦ قَالَ ٱلَّذِينَ ٱسْتَكْبَرُوٓا۟ إِنَّا بِٱلَّذِىٓ ءَامَنتُم بِهِۦ
كَٰفِرُونَ

76 Those who were arrogant said, "We reject what you believe in."

٧٧ فَعَقَرُوا۟ ٱلنَّاقَةَ وَعَتَوْا۟ عَنْ أَمْرِ رَبِّهِمْ وَقَالُوا۟
يَٰصَٰلِحُ ٱئْتِنَا بِمَا تَعِدُنَآ إِن كُنتَ مِنَ ٱلْمُرْسَلِينَ

77 So they hamstrung the she-camel, and defied the command of their Lord, and said, "O Saleh, bring upon us what you threaten us with, if you are one of the messengers."

٧٨ فَأَخَذَتْهُمُ ٱلرَّجْفَةُ فَأَصْبَحُوا۟ فِى دَارِهِمْ
جَٰثِمِينَ

78 Whereupon the quake overtook them, and they became lifeless bodies in their homes.

٧٩ فَتَوَلَّىٰ عَنْهُمْ وَقَالَ يَٰقَوْمِ لَقَدْ أَبْلَغْتُكُمْ
رِسَالَةَ رَبِّى وَنَصَحْتُ لَكُمْ وَلَٰكِن لَّا تُحِبُّونَ
ٱلنَّٰصِحِينَ

79 Then he turned away from them, and said, "O my people, I have delivered to you the message of my Lord, and I have advised you, but you do not like those who give advice."

٨٠ وَلُوطًا إِذْ قَالَ لِقَوْمِهِۦٓ أَتَأْتُونَ ٱلْفَٰحِشَةَ مَا
سَبَقَكُم بِهَا مِنْ أَحَدٍ مِّنَ ٱلْعَٰلَمِينَ

80 And Lot, when he said to his people, "Do you commit lewdness no people anywhere have ever committed before you?"

٨١ إِنَّكُمْ لَتَأْتُونَ ٱلرِّجَالَ شَهْوَةً مِّن دُونِ
ٱلنِّسَآءِ ۚ بَلْ أَنتُمْ قَوْمٌ مُّسْرِفُونَ

81 "You lust after men rather than women. You are an excessive people."

٨٢ وَمَا كَانَ جَوَابَ قَوْمِهِۦٓ إِلَّآ أَن قَالُوٓا۟
أَخْرِجُوهُم مِّن قَرْيَتِكُمْ ۖ إِنَّهُمْ أُنَاسٌ يَتَطَهَّرُونَ

82 And his people's only answer was to say, "Expel them from your town; they are purist people."

٨٣ فَأَنجَيْنَٰهُ وَأَهْلَهُۥٓ إِلَّا ٱمْرَأَتَهُۥ كَانَتْ مِنَ
ٱلْغَٰبِرِينَ

83 But We saved him and his family, except for his wife; she was of those who lagged behind.

٨٤ وَأَمْطَرْنَا عَلَيْهِم مَّطَرًا ۖ فَٱنظُرْ كَيْفَ كَانَ
عَٰقِبَةُ ٱلْمُجْرِمِينَ

84 And We rained down on them a rain; note the consequences for the sinners.

٨٥ وَإِلَىٰ مَدْيَنَ أَخَاهُمْ شُعَيْبًا ۗ قَالَ يَٰقَوْمِ
ٱعْبُدُوا۟ ٱللَّهَ مَا لَكُم مِّنْ إِلَٰهٍ غَيْرُهُۥ ۖ قَدْ جَآءَتْكُم
بَيِّنَةٌ مِّن رَّبِّكُمْ ۖ فَأَوْفُوا۟ ٱلْكَيْلَ وَٱلْمِيزَانَ وَلَا
تَبْخَسُوا۟ ٱلنَّاسَ أَشْيَآءَهُمْ وَلَا تُفْسِدُوا۟ فِى
ٱلْأَرْضِ بَعْدَ إِصْلَٰحِهَا ۚ ذَٰلِكُمْ خَيْرٌ لَّكُمْ إِن كُنتُم
مُّؤْمِنِينَ

85 And to Median, their brother Shuaib. He said, "O my people, worship Allah; you have no god other than Him. A clear proof has come to you from your Lord. Give full measure and weight, and do not cheat people out of their rights, and do not corrupt the land once it has been set right. This is better for you, if you are believers."

٨٦ وَلَا تَقْعُدُوا۟ بِكُلِّ صِرَٰطٍ تُوعِدُونَ وَتَصُدُّونَ
عَن سَبِيلِ ٱللَّهِ مَنْ ءَامَنَ بِهِۦ وَتَبْغُونَهَا عِوَجًا ۚ
وَٱذْكُرُوٓا۟ إِذْ كُنتُمْ قَلِيلًا فَكَثَّرَكُمْ ۖ وَٱنظُرُوا۟ كَيْفَ
كَانَ عَٰقِبَةُ ٱلْمُفْسِدِينَ

86 "And do not lurk on every path, making threats and turning away from the path of Allah those who believe in Him, seeking to distort it. And remember how you were few, and how He made you numerous. So note the consequences for the corrupters."

٨٧ وَإِن كَانَ طَآئِفَةٌ مِّنكُمْ ءَامَنُوا۟ بِٱلَّذِىٓ
أُرْسِلْتُ بِهِۦ وَطَآئِفَةٌ لَّمْ يُؤْمِنُوا۟ فَٱصْبِرُوا۟ حَتَّىٰ
يَحْكُمَ ٱللَّهُ بَيْنَنَا ۚ وَهُوَ خَيْرُ ٱلْحَٰكِمِينَ

87 "Since some of you believed in what I was sent with, and some did not believe, be patient until Allah judges between us; for He is the Best of Judges."

٨٨ قَالَ ٱلْمَلَأُ ٱلَّذِينَ ٱسْتَكْبَرُوا۟ مِن قَوْمِهِۦ
لَنُخْرِجَنَّكَ يَٰشُعَيْبُ وَٱلَّذِينَ ءَامَنُوا۟ مَعَكَ مِن
قَرْيَتِنَآ أَوْ لَتَعُودُنَّ فِى مِلَّتِنَا ۚ قَالَ أَوَلَوْ كُنَّا
كَٰرِهِينَ

88 The arrogant elite among his
people said, "O Shuaib, We will evict
you from our town, along with those
who believe with you, unless you
return to our religion." He said,
"Even if we are unwilling?"

٨٩ قَدِ ٱفْتَرَيْنَا عَلَى ٱللَّهِ كَذِبًا إِنْ عُدْنَا فِى
مِلَّتِكُم بَعْدَ إِذْ نَجَّىٰنَا ٱللَّهُ مِنْهَا ۚ وَمَا يَكُونُ لَنَآ
أَن نَّعُودَ فِيهَآ إِلَّآ أَن يَشَآءَ ٱللَّهُ رَبُّنَا ۚ وَسِعَ رَبُّنَا
كُلَّ شَىْءٍ عِلْمًا ۚ عَلَى ٱللَّهِ تَوَكَّلْنَا ۚ رَبَّنَا ٱفْتَحْ
بَيْنَنَا وَبَيْنَ قَوْمِنَا بِٱلْحَقِّ وَأَنتَ خَيْرُ ٱلْفَٰتِحِينَ

89 "We would be fabricating
falsehood against Allah, if we were
to return to your religion, after Allah
has saved us from it. It is not for us
to return to it, unless Allah, our Lord,
wills. Our Lord embraces all things in
knowledge. In Allah we place our
trust. Our Lord, decide between us
and our people in truth, for You are
the Best of Deciders."

٩٠ وَقَالَ ٱلْمَلَأُ ٱلَّذِينَ كَفَرُوا۟ مِن قَوْمِهِۦ لَئِنِ
ٱتَّبَعْتُمْ شُعَيْبًا إِنَّكُمْ إِذًا لَّخَٰسِرُونَ

90 The elite of his people who
disbelieved said, "If you follow
Shuaib, you will be losers."

٩١ فَأَخَذَتْهُمُ ٱلرَّجْفَةُ فَأَصْبَحُوا۟ فِى دَارِهِمْ
جَٰثِمِينَ

91 Thereupon, the quake struck
them; and they became lifeless
bodies in their homes.

٩٢ ٱلَّذِينَ كَذَّبُوا۟ شُعَيْبًا كَأَن لَّمْ يَغْنَوْا۟ فِيهَا ۚ
ٱلَّذِينَ كَذَّبُوا۟ شُعَيْبًا كَانُوا۟ هُمُ ٱلْخَٰسِرِينَ

92 Those who rejected Shuaib—as if
they never prospered therein. Those
who rejected Shuaib—it was they
who were the losers.

٩٣ فَتَوَلَّىٰ عَنْهُمْ وَقَالَ يَٰقَوْمِ لَقَدْ أَبْلَغْتُكُمْ
رِسَٰلَٰتِ رَبِّى وَنَصَحْتُ لَكُمْ ۖ فَكَيْفَ ءَاسَىٰ عَلَىٰ
قَوْمٍ كَٰفِرِينَ

93 So he turned away from them, and
said, "O my people, I have delivered
to you the messages of my Lord,
and I have advised you, so why
should I grieve over a disbelieving
people?"

٩٤ وَمَآ أَرْسَلْنَا فِى قَرْيَةٍ مِّن نَّبِىٍّ إِلَّآ أَخَذْنَآ
أَهْلَهَا بِٱلْبَأْسَآءِ وَٱلضَّرَّآءِ لَعَلَّهُمْ يَضَّرَّعُونَ

94 We did not send any prophet to
any town but We afflicted its people
with misery and adversity, so that
they may humble themselves.

٩٥ ثُمَّ بَدَّلْنَا مَكَانَ ٱلسَّيِّئَةِ ٱلْحَسَنَةَ حَتَّىٰ عَفَوا۟
وَّقَالُوا۟ قَدْ مَسَّ ءَابَآءَنَا ٱلضَّرَّآءُ وَٱلسَّرَّآءُ
فَأَخَذْنَٰهُم بَغْتَةً وَهُمْ لَا يَشْعُرُونَ

95 Then We substituted prosperity in
place of hardship. Until they
increased in number, and said,
"Adversity and prosperity has
touched our ancestors." Then We

seized them suddenly, while they were unaware.

٩٦ وَلَوْ أَنَّ أَهْلَ ٱلْقُرَىٰٓ ءَامَنُوا۟ وَٱتَّقَوْا۟ لَفَتَحْنَا
عَلَيْهِم بَرَكَٰتٍ مِّنَ ٱلسَّمَآءِ وَٱلْأَرْضِ وَلَٰكِن كَذَّبُوا۟
فَأَخَذْنَٰهُم بِمَا كَانُوا۟ يَكْسِبُونَ

96 Had the people of the towns believed and turned righteous, We would have opened for them the blessings of the heaven and the earth; but they rejected the truth, so We seized them by what they were doing.

٩٧ أَفَأَمِنَ أَهْلُ ٱلْقُرَىٰٓ أَن يَأْتِيَهُم بَأْسُنَا بَيَٰتًا
وَهُمْ نَآئِمُونَ

97 Do the people of the towns feel secure that Our might will not come upon them by night, while they sleep?

٩٨ أَوَأَمِنَ أَهْلُ ٱلْقُرَىٰٓ أَن يَأْتِيَهُم بَأْسُنَا ضُحًى
وَهُمْ يَلْعَبُونَ

98 Do the people of the towns feel secure that Our might will not come upon them by day, while they play?

٩٩ أَفَأَمِنُوا۟ مَكْرَ ٱللَّهِ ۚ فَلَا يَأْمَنُ مَكْرَ ٱللَّهِ إِلَّا
ٱلْقَوْمُ ٱلْخَٰسِرُونَ

99 Do they feel safe from Allah's plan? None feel safe from Allah's plan except the losing people.

١٠٠ أَوَلَمْ يَهْدِ لِلَّذِينَ يَرِثُونَ ٱلْأَرْضَ مِنۢ بَعْدِ
أَهْلِهَآ أَن لَّوْ نَشَآءُ أَصَبْنَٰهُم بِذُنُوبِهِمْ ۚ وَنَطْبَعُ
عَلَىٰ قُلُوبِهِمْ فَهُمْ لَا يَسْمَعُونَ

100 Is it not guidance for those who inherit the land after its inhabitants, that if We willed, We could strike them for their sins? And seal up their hearts, so that they would not hear?

١٠١ تِلْكَ ٱلْقُرَىٰ نَقُصُّ عَلَيْكَ مِنْ أَنۢبَآئِهَا ۚ وَلَقَدْ
جَآءَتْهُمْ رُسُلُهُم بِٱلْبَيِّنَٰتِ فَمَا كَانُوا۟ لِيُؤْمِنُوا۟ بِمَا
كَذَّبُوا۟ مِن قَبْلُ ۚ كَذَٰلِكَ يَطْبَعُ ٱللَّهُ عَلَىٰ قُلُوبِ
ٱلْكَٰفِرِينَ

101 These towns—We narrate to you some of their tales. Their messengers came to them with the clear signs, but they would not believe in what they had rejected previously. Thus Allah seals the hearts of the disbelievers.

١٠٢ وَمَا وَجَدْنَا لِأَكْثَرِهِم مِّنْ عَهْدٍ ۖ وَإِن وَجَدْنَآ
أَكْثَرَهُمْ لَفَٰسِقِينَ

102 We found most of them untrue to their covenants; We found most of them corrupt.

١٠٣ ثُمَّ بَعَثْنَا مِنۢ بَعْدِهِم مُّوسَىٰ بِـَٔايَٰتِنَآ إِلَىٰ
فِرْعَوْنَ وَمَلَإِي۟هِۦ فَظَلَمُوا۟ بِهَا ۖ فَٱنظُرْ كَيْفَ كَانَ
عَٰقِبَةُ ٱلْمُفْسِدِينَ

103 Then, after them, We sent Moses with Our miracles to Pharaoh and his establishment, but they denounced them. So consider the end of the evildoers.

١٠٤ وَقَالَ مُوسَىٰ يَٰفِرْعَوْنُ إِنِّى رَسُولٌ مِّن رَّبِّ ٱلْعَٰلَمِينَ	104 Moses said, "O Pharaoh, I am a messenger from the Lord of the Worlds."
١٠٥ حَقِيقٌ عَلَىٰٓ أَن لَّآ أَقُولَ عَلَى ٱللَّهِ إِلَّا ٱلْحَقَّ ۚ قَدْ جِئْتُكُم بِبَيِّنَةٍ مِّن رَّبِّكُمْ فَأَرْسِلْ مَعِىَ بَنِىٓ إِسْرَٰٓءِيلَ	105 "It is only proper that I should not say about Allah anything other than the truth. I have come to you with clear evidence from your Lord, so let the Children of Israel go with me."
١٠٦ قَالَ إِن كُنتَ جِئْتَ بِـَٔايَةٍ فَأْتِ بِهَآ إِن كُنتَ مِنَ ٱلصَّٰدِقِينَ	106 He said, "If you brought a miracle, then present it, if you are truthful."
١٠٧ فَأَلْقَىٰ عَصَاهُ فَإِذَا هِىَ ثُعْبَانٌ مُّبِينٌ	107 So he threw his staff, and it was an apparent serpent.
١٠٨ وَنَزَعَ يَدَهُۥ فَإِذَا هِىَ بَيْضَآءُ لِلنَّٰظِرِينَ	108 And He pulled out his hand, and it was white to the onlookers.
١٠٩ قَالَ ٱلْمَلَأُ مِن قَوْمِ فِرْعَوْنَ إِنَّ هَٰذَا لَسَٰحِرٌ عَلِيمٌ	109 The notables among Pharaoh's people said, "This is really a skilled magician."
١١٠ يُرِيدُ أَن يُخْرِجَكُم مِّنْ أَرْضِكُمْ ۖ فَمَاذَا تَأْمُرُونَ	110 "He wants to evict you from your land, so what do you recommend?"
١١١ قَالُوٓا۟ أَرْجِهْ وَأَخَاهُ وَأَرْسِلْ فِى ٱلْمَدَآئِنِ حَٰشِرِينَ	111 They said, "Put him off, and his brother, and send heralds to the cities."
١١٢ يَأْتُوكَ بِكُلِّ سَٰحِرٍ عَلِيمٍ	112 "And let them bring you every skillful magician."
١١٣ وَجَآءَ ٱلسَّحَرَةُ فِرْعَوْنَ قَالُوٓا۟ إِنَّ لَنَا لَأَجْرًا إِن كُنَّا نَحْنُ ٱلْغَٰلِبِينَ	113 The magicians came to Pharaoh, and said, "Surely there is a reward for us, if we are the victors."
١١٤ قَالَ نَعَمْ وَإِنَّكُمْ لَمِنَ ٱلْمُقَرَّبِينَ	114 He said, "Yes, and you will be among my favorites."
١١٥ قَالُوا۟ يَٰمُوسَىٰٓ إِمَّآ أَن تُلْقِىَ وَإِمَّآ أَن نَّكُونَ نَحْنُ ٱلْمُلْقِينَ	115 They said, "O Moses! Either you throw, or we are the ones to throw."
١١٦ قَالَ أَلْقُوا۟ ۖ فَلَمَّآ أَلْقَوْا۟ سَحَرُوٓا۟ أَعْيُنَ ٱلنَّاسِ وَٱسْتَرْهَبُوهُمْ وَجَآءُو بِسِحْرٍ عَظِيمٍ	116 He said, "You throw!" And when they threw, they beguiled the eyes of the people, and intimidated them, and produced a mighty magic.

١١٧ وَأَوْحَيْنَآ إِلَىٰ مُوسَىٰٓ أَنْ أَلْقِ عَصَاكَ ۖ فَإِذَا هِىَ تَلْقَفُ مَا يَأْفِكُونَ	117 And We inspired Moses: "Throw your staff." And at once, it swallowed what they were faking.
١١٨ فَوَقَعَ ٱلْحَقُّ وَبَطَلَ مَا كَانُوا۟ يَعْمَلُونَ	118 So the truth came to pass, and what they were producing came to nothing.
١١٩ فَغُلِبُوا۟ هُنَالِكَ وَٱنقَلَبُوا۟ صَٰغِرِينَ	119 There they were defeated, and utterly reduced.
١٢٠ وَأُلْقِىَ ٱلسَّحَرَةُ سَٰجِدِينَ	120 And the magicians fell to their knees.
١٢١ قَالُوٓا۟ ءَامَنَّا بِرَبِّ ٱلْعَٰلَمِينَ	121 They said, "We have believed in the Lord of the Worlds."
١٢٢ رَبِّ مُوسَىٰ وَهَٰرُونَ	122 "The Lord of Moses and Aaron."
١٢٣ قَالَ فِرْعَوْنُ ءَامَنتُم بِهِۦ قَبْلَ أَنْ ءَاذَنَ لَكُمْ ۖ إِنَّ هَٰذَا لَمَكْرٌ مَّكَرْتُمُوهُ فِى ٱلْمَدِينَةِ لِتُخْرِجُوا۟ مِنْهَآ أَهْلَهَا ۖ فَسَوْفَ تَعْلَمُونَ	123 Pharaoh said, "Did you believe in Him before I have given you permission? This is surely a conspiracy you schemed in the city, in order to expel its people from it. You will surely know."
١٢٤ لَأُقَطِّعَنَّ أَيْدِيَكُمْ وَأَرْجُلَكُم مِّنْ خِلَٰفٍ ثُمَّ لَأُصَلِّبَنَّكُمْ أَجْمَعِينَ	124 "I will cut off your hands and your feet on opposite sides; then I will crucify you all."
١٢٥ قَالُوٓا۟ إِنَّآ إِلَىٰ رَبِّنَا مُنقَلِبُونَ	125 They said, "It is to our Lord that we will return."
١٢٦ وَمَا تَنقِمُ مِنَّآ إِلَّآ أَنْ ءَامَنَّا بِـَٔايَٰتِ رَبِّنَا لَمَّا جَآءَتْنَا ۚ رَبَّنَآ أَفْرِغْ عَلَيْنَا صَبْرًا وَتَوَفَّنَا مُسْلِمِينَ	126 "You are taking vengeance on us only because we have believed in the signs of our Lord when they have come to us." "Our Lord! Pour out patience upon us, and receive our souls in submission."
١٢٧ وَقَالَ ٱلْمَلَأُ مِن قَوْمِ فِرْعَوْنَ أَتَذَرُ مُوسَىٰ وَقَوْمَهُۥ لِيُفْسِدُوا۟ فِى ٱلْأَرْضِ وَيَذَرَكَ وَءَالِهَتَكَ ۚ قَالَ سَنُقَتِّلُ أَبْنَآءَهُمْ وَنَسْتَحْىِۦ نِسَآءَهُمْ وَإِنَّا فَوْقَهُمْ قَٰهِرُونَ	127 The chiefs of Pharaoh's people said, "Will you let Moses and his people cause trouble in the land, and forsake you and your gods?" He said, "We will kill their sons, and spare their women. We have absolute power over them."

١٢٨ قَالَ مُوسَىٰ لِقَوْمِهِ ٱسْتَعِينُوا۟ بِٱللَّهِ
وَٱصْبِرُوٓا۟ ۖ إِنَّ ٱلْأَرْضَ لِلَّهِ يُورِثُهَا مَن يَشَآءُ مِنْ
عِبَادِهِۦ ۖ وَٱلْعَٰقِبَةُ لِلْمُتَّقِينَ

128 Moses said to his people, “Seek help in Allah, and be patient. The earth belongs to Allah. He gives it in inheritance to whomever He wills of His servants, and the future belongs to the righteous.”

١٢٩ قَالُوٓا۟ أُوذِينَا مِن قَبْلِ أَن تَأْتِيَنَا وَمِنۢ بَعْدِ مَا
جِئْتَنَا ۚ قَالَ عَسَىٰ رَبُّكُمْ أَن يُهْلِكَ عَدُوَّكُمْ
وَيَسْتَخْلِفَكُمْ فِى ٱلْأَرْضِ فَيَنظُرَ كَيْفَ تَعْمَلُونَ

129 They said, “We were persecuted before you came to us, and after you came to us.” He said, “Perhaps your Lord will destroy your enemy, and make you successors in the land; then He will see how you behave.”

١٣٠ وَلَقَدْ أَخَذْنَآ ءَالَ فِرْعَوْنَ بِٱلسِّنِينَ وَنَقْصٍ
مِّنَ ٱلثَّمَرَٰتِ لَعَلَّهُمْ يَذَّكَّرُونَ

130 And We afflicted the people of Pharaoh with barren years, and with shortage of crops, that they may take heed.

١٣١ فَإِذَا جَآءَتْهُمُ ٱلْحَسَنَةُ قَالُوا۟ لَنَا هَٰذِهِۦ ۖ وَإِن
تُصِبْهُمْ سَيِّئَةٌ يَطَّيَّرُوا۟ بِمُوسَىٰ وَمَن مَّعَهُۥٓ ۗ أَلَآ
إِنَّمَا طَٰٓئِرُهُمْ عِندَ ٱللَّهِ وَلَٰكِنَّ أَكْثَرَهُمْ لَا يَعْلَمُونَ

131 When something good came their way, they said, “This is ours.” And when something bad happened to them, they ascribed the evil omen to Moses and those with him. In fact, their omen is with Allah, but most of them do not know.

١٣٢ وَقَالُوا۟ مَهْمَا تَأْتِنَا بِهِۦ مِنْ ءَايَةٍ لِّتَسْحَرَنَا
بِهَا فَمَا نَحْنُ لَكَ بِمُؤْمِنِينَ

132 And they said, “No matter what sign you bring us, to bewitch us with, we will not believe in you.”

١٣٣ فَأَرْسَلْنَا عَلَيْهِمُ ٱلطُّوفَانَ وَٱلْجَرَادَ وَٱلْقُمَّلَ
وَٱلضَّفَادِعَ وَٱلدَّمَ ءَايَٰتٍ مُّفَصَّلَٰتٍ فَٱسْتَكْبَرُوا۟
وَكَانُوا۟ قَوْمًا مُّجْرِمِينَ

133 So We let loose upon them the flood, and the locusts, and the lice, and the frogs, and blood—all explicit signs—but they were too arrogant. They were a sinful people.

١٣٤ وَلَمَّا وَقَعَ عَلَيْهِمُ ٱلرِّجْزُ قَالُوا۟ يَٰمُوسَى ٱدْعُ
لَنَا رَبَّكَ بِمَا عَهِدَ عِندَكَ ۖ لَئِن كَشَفْتَ عَنَّا ٱلرِّجْزَ
لَنُؤْمِنَنَّ لَكَ وَلَنُرْسِلَنَّ مَعَكَ بَنِىٓ إِسْرَٰٓءِيلَ

134 Whenever a plague befell them, they would say, “O Moses, pray to your Lord for us, according to the covenant He made with you. If you lift the plague from us, we will believe in you, and let the Children of Israel go with you.”

١٣٥ فَلَمَّا كَشَفْنَا عَنْهُمُ ٱلرِّجْزَ إِلَىٰٓ أَجَلٍ هُم
بَٰلِغُوهُ إِذَا هُمْ يَنكُثُونَ

135 But when We lifted the plague from them, for a term they were to fulfill, they broke their promise.

١٣٦ فَٱنتَقَمْنَا مِنْهُمْ فَأَغْرَقْنَٰهُمْ فِى ٱلْيَمِّ بِأَنَّهُمْ كَذَّبُوا۟ بِـَٔايَٰتِنَا وَكَانُوا۟ عَنْهَا غَٰفِلِينَ

136 So We took vengeance on them, and drowned them in the sea—because they rejected Our signs, and paid no heed to them.

١٣٧ وَأَوْرَثْنَا ٱلْقَوْمَ ٱلَّذِينَ كَانُوا۟ يُسْتَضْعَفُونَ مَشَٰرِقَ ٱلْأَرْضِ وَمَغَٰرِبَهَا ٱلَّتِى بَٰرَكْنَا فِيهَا ۖ وَتَمَّتْ كَلِمَتُ رَبِّكَ ٱلْحُسْنَىٰ عَلَىٰ بَنِىٓ إِسْرَٰٓءِيلَ بِمَا صَبَرُوا۟ ۖ وَدَمَّرْنَا مَا كَانَ يَصْنَعُ فِرْعَوْنُ وَقَوْمُهُۥ وَمَا كَانُوا۟ يَعْرِشُونَ

137 And We made the oppressed people inherit the eastern and western parts of the land, which We had blessed. Thus the fair promise of your Lord to the Children of Israel was fulfilled, because of their endurance. And We destroyed what Pharaoh and his people had built, and what they had harvested.

١٣٨ وَجَٰوَزْنَا بِبَنِىٓ إِسْرَٰٓءِيلَ ٱلْبَحْرَ فَأَتَوْا۟ عَلَىٰ قَوْمٍ يَعْكُفُونَ عَلَىٰٓ أَصْنَامٍ لَّهُمْ ۚ قَالُوا۟ يَٰمُوسَى ٱجْعَل لَّنَآ إِلَٰهًا كَمَا لَهُمْ ءَالِهَةٌ ۚ قَالَ إِنَّكُمْ قَوْمٌ تَجْهَلُونَ

138 And We delivered the Children of Israel across the sea. And when they came upon a people who were devoted to some statues of theirs, they said, "O Moses, make for us a god, as they have gods." He said, "You are truly an ignorant people."

١٣٩ إِنَّ هَٰٓؤُلَآءِ مُتَبَّرٌ مَّا هُمْ فِيهِ وَبَٰطِلٌ مَّا كَانُوا۟ يَعْمَلُونَ

139 "What these people are concerned with is perdition, and their deeds are based on falsehoods."

١٤٠ قَالَ أَغَيْرَ ٱللَّهِ أَبْغِيكُمْ إِلَٰهًا وَهُوَ فَضَّلَكُمْ عَلَى ٱلْعَٰلَمِينَ

140 He said, "Shall I seek for you a god other than Allah, when He has favored you over all other people?"

١٤١ وَإِذْ أَنجَيْنَٰكُم مِّنْ ءَالِ فِرْعَوْنَ يَسُومُونَكُمْ سُوٓءَ ٱلْعَذَابِ ۖ يُقَتِّلُونَ أَبْنَآءَكُمْ وَيَسْتَحْيُونَ نِسَآءَكُمْ ۚ وَفِى ذَٰلِكُم بَلَآءٌ مِّن رَّبِّكُمْ عَظِيمٌ

141 Remember how We saved you from Pharaoh's people, who subjected you to the worst of sufferings—killing your sons and sparing your women. In that was a tremendous trial from your Lord.

١٤٢ وَوَٰعَدْنَا مُوسَىٰ ثَلَٰثِينَ لَيْلَةً وَأَتْمَمْنَٰهَا بِعَشْرٍ فَتَمَّ مِيقَٰتُ رَبِّهِۦٓ أَرْبَعِينَ لَيْلَةً ۚ وَقَالَ مُوسَىٰ لِأَخِيهِ هَٰرُونَ ٱخْلُفْنِى فِى قَوْمِى وَأَصْلِحْ وَلَا تَتَّبِعْ سَبِيلَ ٱلْمُفْسِدِينَ

142 And We appointed to Moses thirty nights, and completed them with ten; and thus the time appointed by his Lord was forty nights. And Moses said to his brother Aaron: "Take my place among my people, and be upright, and do not follow the way of the mischief-makers."

١٤٣ وَلَمَّا جَآءَ مُوسَىٰ لِمِيقَٰتِنَا وَكَلَّمَهُۥ رَبُّهُۥ قَالَ
رَبِّ أَرِنِىٓ أَنظُرْ إِلَيْكَ ۚ قَالَ لَن تَرَىٰنِى وَلَٰكِنِ
ٱنظُرْ إِلَى ٱلْجَبَلِ فَإِنِ ٱسْتَقَرَّ مَكَانَهُۥ فَسَوْفَ
تَرَىٰنِى ۚ فَلَمَّا تَجَلَّىٰ رَبُّهُۥ لِلْجَبَلِ جَعَلَهُۥ دَكًّا وَخَرَّ
مُوسَىٰ صَعِقًا ۚ فَلَمَّآ أَفَاقَ قَالَ سُبْحَٰنَكَ تُبْتُ
إِلَيْكَ وَأَنَا۠ أَوَّلُ ٱلْمُؤْمِنِينَ

143 And when Moses came to Our appointment, and his Lord spoke to him, he said, “My Lord, allow me to look and see You.” He said, “You will not see Me, but look at the mountain; if it stays in its place, you will see Me.” But when his Lord manifested Himself to the mountain, He turned it into dust, and Moses fell down unconscious. Then, when he recovered, he said, “Glory be to you, I repent to you, and I am the first of the believers.”

١٤٤ قَالَ يَٰمُوسَىٰٓ إِنِّى ٱصْطَفَيْتُكَ عَلَى ٱلنَّاسِ
بِرِسَٰلَٰتِى وَبِكَلَٰمِى فَخُذْ مَآ ءَاتَيْتُكَ وَكُن مِّنَ
ٱلشَّٰكِرِينَ

144 He said, “O Moses, I have chosen you over all people for My messages and for My Words. So take what I have given you, and be one of the thankful.”

١٤٥ وَكَتَبْنَا لَهُۥ فِى ٱلْأَلْوَاحِ مِن كُلِّ شَىْءٍ
مَّوْعِظَةً وَتَفْصِيلًا لِّكُلِّ شَىْءٍ فَخُذْهَا بِقُوَّةٍ
وَأْمُرْ قَوْمَكَ يَأْخُذُوا۟ بِأَحْسَنِهَا ۚ سَأُو۟رِيكُمْ دَارَ
ٱلْفَٰسِقِينَ

145 And We inscribed for him in the Tablets all kinds of enlightenments, and decisive explanation of all things. “Hold fast to them, and exhort your people to adopt the best of them. I will show you the fate of the sinners.”

١٤٦ سَأَصْرِفُ عَنْ ءَايَٰتِىَ ٱلَّذِينَ يَتَكَبَّرُونَ فِى
ٱلْأَرْضِ بِغَيْرِ ٱلْحَقِّ وَإِن يَرَوْا۟ كُلَّ ءَايَةٍ لَّا
يُؤْمِنُوا۟ بِهَا وَإِن يَرَوْا۟ سَبِيلَ ٱلرُّشْدِ لَا يَتَّخِذُوهُ
سَبِيلًا وَإِن يَرَوْا۟ سَبِيلَ ٱلْغَىِّ يَتَّخِذُوهُ سَبِيلًا ۚ
ذَٰلِكَ بِأَنَّهُمْ كَذَّبُوا۟ بِـَٔايَٰتِنَا وَكَانُوا۟ عَنْهَا غَٰفِلِينَ

146 I will turn away from My revelations those who behave proudly on earth without justification. Even if they see every sign, they will not believe in it; and if they see the path of rectitude, they will not adopt it for a path; and if they see the path of error, they will adopt it for a path. That is because they denied Our revelations, and paid no attention to them.

١٤٧ وَٱلَّذِينَ كَذَّبُوا۟ بِـَٔايَٰتِنَا وَلِقَآءِ ٱلْءَاخِرَةِ
حَبِطَتْ أَعْمَٰلُهُمْ ۚ هَلْ يُجْزَوْنَ إِلَّا مَا كَانُوا۟
يَعْمَلُونَ

147 Those who deny Our revelations and the meeting of the Hereafter—their deeds will come to nothing. Will they be repaid except according to what they used to do?

١٤٨ وَٱتَّخَذَ قَوۡمُ مُوسَىٰ مِنۢ بَعۡدِهِۦ مِنۡ حُلِيِّهِمۡ
عِجۡلٗا جَسَدٗا لَّهُۥ خُوَارٌۚ أَلَمۡ يَرَوۡاْ أَنَّهُۥ لَا يُكَلِّمُهُمۡ
وَلَا يَهۡدِيهِمۡ سَبِيلًاۘ ٱتَّخَذُوهُ وَكَانُواْ ظَٰلِمِينَ

148 In his absence, the people of Moses adopted a calf made from their ornaments—a body which lowed. Did they not see that it could not speak to them, nor guide them in any way? They took it for worship. They were in the wrong.

١٤٩ وَلَمَّا سُقِطَ فِيٓ أَيۡدِيهِمۡ وَرَأَوۡاْ أَنَّهُمۡ قَدۡ
ضَلُّواْ قَالُواْ لَئِن لَّمۡ يَرۡحَمۡنَا رَبُّنَا وَيَغۡفِرۡ لَنَا
لَنَكُونَنَّ مِنَ ٱلۡخَٰسِرِينَ

149 Then, when they regretted, and realized that they had erred, they said, “Unless our Lord extends His mercy to us, and forgives us, we will be among the losers.”

١٥٠ وَلَمَّا رَجَعَ مُوسَىٰٓ إِلَىٰ قَوۡمِهِۦ غَضۡبَٰنَ أَسِفٗا
قَالَ بِئۡسَمَا خَلَفۡتُمُونِي مِنۢ بَعۡدِيٓۖ أَعَجِلۡتُمۡ أَمۡرَ
رَبِّكُمۡۖ وَأَلۡقَى ٱلۡأَلۡوَاحَ وَأَخَذَ بِرَأۡسِ أَخِيهِ يَجُرُّهُۥٓ
إِلَيۡهِۚ قَالَ ٱبۡنَ أُمَّ إِنَّ ٱلۡقَوۡمَ ٱسۡتَضۡعَفُونِي
وَكَادُواْ يَقۡتُلُونَنِي فَلَا تُشۡمِتۡ بِيَ ٱلۡأَعۡدَآءَ وَلَا
تَجۡعَلۡنِي مَعَ ٱلۡقَوۡمِ ٱلظَّٰلِمِينَ

150 And when Moses returned to his people, angry and disappointed, he said, “What an awful thing you did in my absence. Did you forsake the commandments of your Lord so hastily?” And he threw down the tablets; and he took hold of his brother’s head, dragging him towards himself. He said, “Son of my mother, the people have overpowered me, and were about to kill me; so do not allow the enemies to gloat over me, and do not count me among the unjust people.”

١٥١ قَالَ رَبِّ ٱغۡفِرۡ لِي وَلِأَخِي وَأَدۡخِلۡنَا فِي
رَحۡمَتِكَۖ وَأَنتَ أَرۡحَمُ ٱلرَّٰحِمِينَ

151 He said, “My Lord, forgive me and my brother, and admit us into Your mercy; for you are the Most Merciful of the merciful.”

١٥٢ إِنَّ ٱلَّذِينَ ٱتَّخَذُواْ ٱلۡعِجۡلَ سَيَنَالُهُمۡ غَضَبٞ
مِّن رَّبِّهِمۡ وَذِلَّةٞ فِي ٱلۡحَيَوٰةِ ٱلدُّنۡيَاۚ وَكَذَٰلِكَ
نَجۡزِي ٱلۡمُفۡتَرِينَ

152 Those who idolized the calf have incurred wrath from their Lord, and humiliation in this life. We thus requite the innovators.

١٥٣ وَٱلَّذِينَ عَمِلُواْ ٱلسَّيِّـَٔاتِ ثُمَّ تَابُواْ مِنۢ بَعۡدِهَا
وَءَامَنُوٓاْ إِنَّ رَبَّكَ مِنۢ بَعۡدِهَا لَغَفُورٞ رَّحِيمٞ

153 As for those who commit sins, and then repent afterwards and believe—your Lord, thereafter, is Forgiving and Merciful.

١٥٤ وَلَمَّا سَكَتَ عَن مُّوسَى ٱلْغَضَبُ أَخَذَ
ٱلْأَلْوَاحَ ۖ وَفِى نُسْخَتِهَا هُدًى وَرَحْمَةٌ لِّلَّذِينَ هُمْ
لِرَبِّهِمْ يَرْهَبُونَ

154 When the anger abated in Moses, he took up the tablets. In their transcript is guidance and mercy for those in awe of their Lord.

١٥٥ وَٱخْتَارَ مُوسَىٰ قَوْمَهُۥ سَبْعِينَ رَجُلًا
لِّمِيقَٰتِنَا ۖ فَلَمَّآ أَخَذَتْهُمُ ٱلرَّجْفَةُ قَالَ رَبِّ لَوْ
شِئْتَ أَهْلَكْتَهُم مِّن قَبْلُ وَإِيَّٰىَ ۖ أَتُهْلِكُنَا بِمَا فَعَلَ
ٱلسُّفَهَآءُ مِنَّآ ۖ إِنْ هِىَ إِلَّا فِتْنَتُكَ تُضِلُّ بِهَا مَن
تَشَآءُ وَتَهْدِى مَن تَشَآءُ ۖ أَنتَ وَلِيُّنَا فَٱغْفِرْ لَنَا
وَٱرْحَمْنَا ۖ وَأَنتَ خَيْرُ ٱلْغَٰفِرِينَ

155 And Moses chose from his people seventy men for Our appointment. When the tremor shook them, he said, "My Lord, had You willed, You could have destroyed them before, and me too. Will you destroy us for what the fools among us have done? This is but Your test—with it You misguide whomever You will, and guide whomever You will. You are our Protector, so forgive us, and have mercy on us. You are the Best of Forgivers."

١٥٦ وَٱكْتُبْ لَنَا فِى هَٰذِهِ ٱلدُّنْيَا حَسَنَةً وَفِى
ٱلْءَاخِرَةِ إِنَّا هُدْنَآ إِلَيْكَ ۚ قَالَ عَذَابِىٓ أُصِيبُ
بِهِۦ مَنْ أَشَآءُ ۖ وَرَحْمَتِى وَسِعَتْ كُلَّ شَىْءٍ ۚ
فَسَأَكْتُبُهَا لِلَّذِينَ يَتَّقُونَ وَيُؤْتُونَ ٱلزَّكَوٰةَ
وَٱلَّذِينَ هُم بِـَٔايَٰتِنَا يُؤْمِنُونَ

156 "And inscribe for us goodness in this world, and in the Hereafter. We have turned to You." He said, "My punishment—I inflict it upon whomever I will, but My mercy encompasses all things. I will specify it for those who act righteously and practice regular charity, and those who believe in Our signs."

١٥٧ ٱلَّذِينَ يَتَّبِعُونَ ٱلرَّسُولَ ٱلنَّبِىَّ ٱلْأُمِّىَّ ٱلَّذِى
يَجِدُونَهُۥ مَكْتُوبًا عِندَهُمْ فِى ٱلتَّوْرَىٰةِ
وَٱلْإِنجِيلِ يَأْمُرُهُم بِٱلْمَعْرُوفِ وَيَنْهَىٰهُمْ عَنِ
ٱلْمُنكَرِ وَيُحِلُّ لَهُمُ ٱلطَّيِّبَٰتِ وَيُحَرِّمُ عَلَيْهِمُ
ٱلْخَبَٰٓئِثَ وَيَضَعُ عَنْهُمْ إِصْرَهُمْ وَٱلْأَغْلَٰلَ ٱلَّتِى
كَانَتْ عَلَيْهِمْ ۚ فَٱلَّذِينَ ءَامَنُوا۟ بِهِۦ وَعَزَّرُوهُ
وَنَصَرُوهُ وَٱتَّبَعُوا۟ ٱلنُّورَ ٱلَّذِىٓ أُنزِلَ مَعَهُۥٓ ۙ أُو۟لَٰٓئِكَ
هُمُ ٱلْمُفْلِحُونَ

157 Those who follow the Messenger, the Unlettered Prophet, whom they find mentioned in the Torah and the Gospel in their possession. He directs them to righteousness, and deters them from evil, and allows for them all good things, and prohibits for them wickedness, and unloads the burdens and the shackles that are upon them. Those who believe in him, and respect him, and support him, and follow the light that came down with him—these are the successful.

١٥٨ قُلْ يَٰٓأَيُّهَا ٱلنَّاسُ إِنِّى رَسُولُ ٱللَّهِ إِلَيْكُمْ
جَمِيعًا ٱلَّذِى لَهُۥ مُلْكُ ٱلسَّمَٰوَٰتِ وَٱلْأَرْضِ ۖ لَآ إِلَٰهَ
إِلَّا هُوَ يُحْىِۦ وَيُمِيتُ ۖ فَـَٔامِنُوا۟ بِٱللَّهِ وَرَسُولِهِ
ٱلنَّبِىِّ ٱلْأُمِّىِّ ٱلَّذِى يُؤْمِنُ بِٱللَّهِ وَكَلِمَٰتِهِۦ
وَٱتَّبِعُوهُ لَعَلَّكُمْ تَهْتَدُونَ

158 Say, "O people, I am the Messenger of Allah to you all—He to whom belongs the kingdom of the heavens and the earth. There is no god but He. He gives life and causes death." So believe in Allah and His Messenger, the Unlettered Prophet, who believes in Allah and His words. And follow him, that you may be guided.

١٥٩ وَمِن قَوْمِ مُوسَىٰٓ أُمَّةٌ يَهْدُونَ بِٱلْحَقِّ وَبِهِۦ
يَعْدِلُونَ

159 Among the people of Moses is a community that guides by truth, and thereby does justice.

١٦٠ وَقَطَّعْنَٰهُمُ ٱثْنَتَىْ عَشْرَةَ أَسْبَاطًا أُمَمًا ۚ
وَأَوْحَيْنَآ إِلَىٰ مُوسَىٰٓ إِذِ ٱسْتَسْقَىٰهُ قَوْمُهُۥٓ أَنِ
ٱضْرِب بِّعَصَاكَ ٱلْحَجَرَ ۖ فَٱنۢبَجَسَتْ مِنْهُ ٱثْنَتَا
عَشْرَةَ عَيْنًا ۖ قَدْ عَلِمَ كُلُّ أُنَاسٍ مَّشْرَبَهُمْ ۚ
وَظَلَّلْنَا عَلَيْهِمُ ٱلْغَمَٰمَ وَأَنزَلْنَا عَلَيْهِمُ ٱلْمَنَّ
وَٱلسَّلْوَىٰ ۖ كُلُوا۟ مِن طَيِّبَٰتِ مَا رَزَقْنَٰكُمْ ۚ وَمَا
ظَلَمُونَا وَلَٰكِن كَانُوٓا۟ أَنفُسَهُمْ يَظْلِمُونَ

160 We divided them into twelve tribal communities. And We inspired Moses, when his people asked him for something to drink: "Strike the rock with your staff." Whereupon twelve springs gushed from it. Each group recognized its drinking-place. And We shaded them with clouds, and We sent down upon them manna and quails: "Eat of the good things We have provided for you." They did not wrong Us, but they used to wrong their own selves.

١٦١ وَإِذْ قِيلَ لَهُمُ ٱسْكُنُوا۟ هَٰذِهِ ٱلْقَرْيَةَ وَكُلُوا۟
مِنْهَا حَيْثُ شِئْتُمْ وَقُولُوا۟ حِطَّةٌ وَٱدْخُلُوا۟ ٱلْبَابَ
سُجَّدًا نَّغْفِرْ لَكُمْ خَطِيٓـَٰٔتِكُمْ ۚ سَنَزِيدُ ٱلْمُحْسِنِينَ

161 And it was said to them, "Settle this town, and eat therein whatever you wish, and speak modestly, and enter the gate in humility—We will forgive your sins, and will promote the righteous."

١٦٢ فَبَدَّلَ ٱلَّذِينَ ظَلَمُوا۟ مِنْهُمْ قَوْلًا غَيْرَ ٱلَّذِى
قِيلَ لَهُمْ فَأَرْسَلْنَا عَلَيْهِمْ رِجْزًا مِّنَ ٱلسَّمَآءِ بِمَا
كَانُوا۟ يَظْلِمُونَ

162 But the wicked among them substituted other words for the words given to them; so We sent down upon them a plague from the sky, because of their wrongdoing.

١٦٣ وَسْـَٔلْهُمْ عَنِ ٱلْقَرْيَةِ ٱلَّتِى كَانَتْ حَاضِرَةَ
ٱلْبَحْرِ إِذْ يَعْدُونَ فِى ٱلسَّبْتِ إِذْ تَأْتِيهِمْ

163 Ask them about the town by the sea, when they violated the Sabbath. When they observed the Sabbath, their fish would come to them abundantly. But when they

حِيتَانُهُمْ يَوْمَ سَبْتِهِمْ شُرَّعًا وَيَوْمَ لَا يَسْبِتُونَ ۙ
لَا تَأْتِيهِمْ ۚ كَذَٰلِكَ نَبْلُوهُم بِمَا كَانُوا۟ يَفْسُقُونَ

violated the Sabbath, their fish would not come to them. Thus We tried them because they disobeyed.

١٦٤ وَإِذْ قَالَتْ أُمَّةٌ مِّنْهُمْ لِمَ تَعِظُونَ قَوْمًا ۙ ٱللَّهُ
مُهْلِكُهُمْ أَوْ مُعَذِّبُهُمْ عَذَابًا شَدِيدًا ۖ قَالُوا۟ مَعْذِرَةً
إِلَىٰ رَبِّكُمْ وَلَعَلَّهُمْ يَتَّقُونَ

164 And when a group of them said, “Why do you counsel a people whom Allah will annihilate, or punish with a severe punishment?” They said, “As an excuse to your Lord, and so that they may become righteous.”

١٦٥ فَلَمَّا نَسُوا۟ مَا ذُكِّرُوا۟ بِهِۦٓ أَنجَيْنَا ٱلَّذِينَ
يَنْهَوْنَ عَنِ ٱلسُّوٓءِ وَأَخَذْنَا ٱلَّذِينَ ظَلَمُوا۟
بِعَذَابٍۭ بَـِٔيسٍۭ بِمَا كَانُوا۟ يَفْسُقُونَ

165 Then, when they neglected what they were reminded of, We saved those who prohibited evil, and We seized those who did wrong with a terrible punishment, because of their sinfulness.

١٦٦ فَلَمَّا عَتَوْا۟ عَن مَّا نُهُوا۟ عَنْهُ قُلْنَا لَهُمْ كُونُوا۟
قِرَدَةً خَـٰسِـِٔينَ

166 Then, when they rebelled against the commands to refrain, We said to them, “Be despicable apes.”

١٦٧ وَإِذْ تَأَذَّنَ رَبُّكَ لَيَبْعَثَنَّ عَلَيْهِمْ إِلَىٰ يَوْمِ
ٱلْقِيَـٰمَةِ مَن يَسُومُهُمْ سُوٓءَ ٱلْعَذَابِ ۗ إِنَّ رَبَّكَ
لَسَرِيعُ ٱلْعِقَابِ ۖ وَإِنَّهُۥ لَغَفُورٌ رَّحِيمٌ

167 Your Lord has announced that, He would send against them, until the Day of Resurrection, those who would inflict terrible suffering upon them. Your Lord is swift in retribution, yet He is Forgiving and Merciful.

١٦٨ وَقَطَّعْنَـٰهُمْ فِى ٱلْأَرْضِ أُمَمًا ۖ مِّنْهُمُ
ٱلصَّـٰلِحُونَ وَمِنْهُمْ دُونَ ذَٰلِكَ ۖ وَبَلَوْنَـٰهُم
بِٱلْحَسَنَـٰتِ وَٱلسَّيِّـَٔاتِ لَعَلَّهُمْ يَرْجِعُونَ

168 And We scattered them into communities on earth. Some of them righteous, and some of them short of that. And We tested them with fortunes and misfortunes, so that they may return.

١٦٩ فَخَلَفَ مِنۢ بَعْدِهِمْ خَلْفٌ وَرِثُوا۟ ٱلْكِتَـٰبَ
يَأْخُذُونَ عَرَضَ هَـٰذَا ٱلْأَدْنَىٰ وَيَقُولُونَ سَيُغْفَرُ
لَنَا وَإِن يَأْتِهِمْ عَرَضٌ مِّثْلُهُۥ يَأْخُذُوهُ ۚ أَلَمْ يُؤْخَذْ
عَلَيْهِم مِّيثَـٰقُ ٱلْكِتَـٰبِ أَن لَّا يَقُولُوا۟ عَلَى ٱللَّهِ إِلَّا
ٱلْحَقَّ وَدَرَسُوا۟ مَا فِيهِ ۗ وَٱلدَّارُ ٱلْـَٔاخِرَةُ خَيْرٌ
لِّلَّذِينَ يَتَّقُونَ ۗ أَفَلَا تَعْقِلُونَ

169 They were succeeded by generations who inherited the Scripture and chose the materials of this world, saying, “We will be forgiven.” And should similar materials come their way, they would again seize them. Did they not make a covenant to uphold the Scripture, and to not say about Allah except the truth? Did they not study

its contents? But the Home of the Hereafter is better for the cautious; will you not understand?

١٧٠ وَٱلَّذِينَ يُمَسِّكُونَ بِٱلْكِتَٰبِ وَأَقَامُوا۟ ٱلصَّلَوٰةَ
إِنَّا لَا نُضِيعُ أَجْرَ ٱلْمُصْلِحِينَ

170 Those who adhere to the Scripture, and practice prayer—We will not waste the reward of the reformers.

١٧١ وَإِذْ نَتَقْنَا ٱلْجَبَلَ فَوْقَهُمْ كَأَنَّهُۥ ظُلَّةٌ وَظَنُّوٓا۟
أَنَّهُۥ وَاقِعٌۢ بِهِمْ خُذُوا۟ مَآ ءَاتَيْنَٰكُم بِقُوَّةٍ وَٱذْكُرُوا۟
مَا فِيهِ لَعَلَّكُمْ تَتَّقُونَ

171 And when We suspended the mountain over them, as if it was an umbrella, and they thought it would fall on them: “Hold fast to what We have given you, and remember what it contains, so that you may be saved.”

١٧٢ وَإِذْ أَخَذَ رَبُّكَ مِنۢ بَنِىٓ ءَادَمَ مِن ظُهُورِهِمْ
ذُرِّيَّتَهُمْ وَأَشْهَدَهُمْ عَلَىٰٓ أَنفُسِهِمْ أَلَسْتُ بِرَبِّكُمْ ۖ
قَالُوا۟ بَلَىٰ ۛ شَهِدْنَآ ۛ أَن تَقُولُوا۟ يَوْمَ ٱلْقِيَٰمَةِ إِنَّا
كُنَّا عَنْ هَٰذَا غَٰفِلِينَ

172 And when Your Lord summoned the descendants of Adam, and made them testify about themselves. “Am I not your Lord?” They said, “Yes, we testify.” Thus you cannot say on the Day of Resurrection, “We were unaware of this.”

١٧٣ أَوْ تَقُولُوٓا۟ إِنَّمَآ أَشْرَكَ ءَابَآؤُنَا مِن قَبْلُ وَكُنَّا
ذُرِّيَّةً مِّنۢ بَعْدِهِمْ ۖ أَفَتُهْلِكُنَا بِمَا فَعَلَ ٱلْمُبْطِلُونَ

173 Nor can you Say, “Our ancestors practiced idolatry before; and we are their descendants who came after them; will you destroy us for what the falsifiers did?”

١٧٤ وَكَذَٰلِكَ نُفَصِّلُ ٱلْءَايَٰتِ وَلَعَلَّهُمْ يَرْجِعُونَ

174 We thus elaborate the revelations, so that they may return.

١٧٥ وَٱتْلُ عَلَيْهِمْ نَبَأَ ٱلَّذِىٓ ءَاتَيْنَٰهُ ءَايَٰتِنَا
فَٱنسَلَخَ مِنْهَا فَأَتْبَعَهُ ٱلشَّيْطَٰنُ فَكَانَ مِنَ
ٱلْغَاوِينَ

175 And relate to them the story of him to whom We delivered Our signs, but he detached himself from them, so Satan went after him, and he became one of the perverts.

١٧٦ وَلَوْ شِئْنَا لَرَفَعْنَٰهُ بِهَا وَلَٰكِنَّهُۥٓ أَخْلَدَ إِلَى
ٱلْأَرْضِ وَٱتَّبَعَ هَوَىٰهُ ۚ فَمَثَلُهُۥ كَمَثَلِ ٱلْكَلْبِ إِن
تَحْمِلْ عَلَيْهِ يَلْهَثْ أَوْ تَتْرُكْهُ يَلْهَث ۚ ذَّٰلِكَ مَثَلُ
ٱلْقَوْمِ ٱلَّذِينَ كَذَّبُوا۟ بِـَٔايَٰتِنَا ۚ فَٱقْصُصِ ٱلْقَصَصَ
لَعَلَّهُمْ يَتَفَكَّرُونَ

176 Had We willed, We could have elevated him through them; but he clung to the ground, and followed his desires. His metaphor is that of a dog: if you chase it, it pants; and if you leave it alone, it pants. Such is the metaphor of the people who

deny Our signs. So tell the tale, so that they may ponder.

١٧٧ سَآءَ مَثَلًا ٱلْقَوْمُ ٱلَّذِينَ كَذَّبُوا۟ بِـَٔايَٰتِنَا
وَأَنفُسَهُمْ كَانُوا۟ يَظْلِمُونَ

177 Evil is the metaphor of the people who reject Our signs and wrong themselves.

١٧٨ مَن يَهْدِ ٱللَّهُ فَهُوَ ٱلْمُهْتَدِى ۖ وَمَن يُضْلِلْ
فَأُو۟لَٰٓئِكَ هُمُ ٱلْخَٰسِرُونَ

178 Whomever Allah guides is the guided one. And whomever He sends astray—these are the losers.

١٧٩ وَلَقَدْ ذَرَأْنَا لِجَهَنَّمَ كَثِيرًا مِّنَ ٱلْجِنِّ
وَٱلْإِنسِ ۖ لَهُمْ قُلُوبٌ لَّا يَفْقَهُونَ بِهَا وَلَهُمْ أَعْيُنٌ
لَّا يُبْصِرُونَ بِهَا وَلَهُمْ ءَاذَانٌ لَّا يَسْمَعُونَ بِهَآ ۚ
أُو۟لَٰٓئِكَ كَٱلْأَنْعَٰمِ بَلْ هُمْ أَضَلُّ ۚ أُو۟لَٰٓئِكَ هُمُ
ٱلْغَٰفِلُونَ

179 We have destined for Hell multitudes of jinn and humans. They have hearts with which they do not understand. They have eyes with which they do not see. They have ears with which they do not hear. These are like cattle. In fact, they are further astray. These are the heedless.

١٨٠ وَلِلَّهِ ٱلْأَسْمَآءُ ٱلْحُسْنَىٰ فَٱدْعُوهُ بِهَا ۖ وَذَرُوا۟
ٱلَّذِينَ يُلْحِدُونَ فِىٓ أَسْمَٰٓئِهِۦ ۚ سَيُجْزَوْنَ مَا
كَانُوا۟ يَعْمَلُونَ

180 To Allah belong the Most Beautiful Names, so call Him by them, and disregard those who blaspheme His names. They will be repaid for what they used to do.

١٨١ وَمِمَّنْ خَلَقْنَآ أُمَّةٌ يَهْدُونَ بِٱلْحَقِّ وَبِهِۦ
يَعْدِلُونَ

181 Among those We created is a community—they guide by truth, and do justice thereby.

١٨٢ وَٱلَّذِينَ كَذَّبُوا۟ بِـَٔايَٰتِنَا سَنَسْتَدْرِجُهُم مِّنْ
حَيْثُ لَا يَعْلَمُونَ

182 As for those who reject Our messages, We will gradually lead them from where they do not know.

١٨٣ وَأُمْلِى لَهُمْ ۚ إِنَّ كَيْدِى مَتِينٌ

183 And I will encourage them. My plan is firm.

١٨٤ أَوَلَمْ يَتَفَكَّرُوا۟ ۗ مَا بِصَاحِبِهِم مِّن جِنَّةٍ ۚ إِنْ
هُوَ إِلَّا نَذِيرٌ مُّبِينٌ

184 Do they not think? There is no madness in their friend. He is but a plain warner.

١٨٥ أَوَلَمْ يَنظُرُوا۟ فِى مَلَكُوتِ ٱلسَّمَٰوَٰتِ
وَٱلْأَرْضِ وَمَا خَلَقَ ٱللَّهُ مِن شَىْءٍ وَأَنْ عَسَىٰٓ
أَن يَكُونَ قَدِ ٱقْتَرَبَ أَجَلُهُمْ ۖ فَبِأَىِّ حَدِيثٍۭ
بَعْدَهُۥ يُؤْمِنُونَ

185 Have they not observed the government of the heavens and the earth, and all the things that Allah created, and that their time may have drawn near? Which message, besides this, will they believe in?

١٨٦ مَن يُضْلِلِ ٱللَّهُ فَلَا هَادِىَ لَهُۥ ۚ وَيَذَرُهُمْ فِى
طُغْيَٰنِهِمْ يَعْمَهُونَ

186 Whomever Allah misguides has no guide. And He leaves them blundering in their transgression.

١٨٧ يَسْـَٔلُونَكَ عَنِ ٱلسَّاعَةِ أَيَّانَ مُرْسَىٰهَا ۖ قُلْ
إِنَّمَا عِلْمُهَا عِندَ رَبِّى ۖ لَا يُجَلِّيهَا لِوَقْتِهَآ إِلَّا هُوَ ۚ
ثَقُلَتْ فِى ٱلسَّمَٰوَٰتِ وَٱلْأَرْضِ ۚ لَا تَأْتِيكُمْ إِلَّا
بَغْتَةً ۗ يَسْـَٔلُونَكَ كَأَنَّكَ حَفِىٌّ عَنْهَا ۖ قُلْ إِنَّمَا
عِلْمُهَا عِندَ ٱللَّهِ وَلَٰكِنَّ أَكْثَرَ ٱلنَّاسِ لَا يَعْلَمُونَ

187 They ask you about the Hour, "When will it come?" Say, "Knowledge of it rests with my Lord. None can reveal its coming except He. It weighs heavily on the heavens and the earth. It will not come upon you except suddenly." They ask you as if you are responsible for it. Say, "Knowledge of it rests with Allah," but most people do not know.

١٨٨ قُل لَّآ أَمْلِكُ لِنَفْسِى نَفْعًا وَلَا ضَرًّا إِلَّا مَا
شَآءَ ٱللَّهُ ۚ وَلَوْ كُنتُ أَعْلَمُ ٱلْغَيْبَ لَٱسْتَكْثَرْتُ
مِنَ ٱلْخَيْرِ وَمَا مَسَّنِىَ ٱلسُّوٓءُ ۚ إِنْ أَنَا۠ إِلَّا نَذِيرٌ
وَبَشِيرٌ لِّقَوْمٍ يُؤْمِنُونَ

188 Say, "I have no control over any benefit or harm to myself, except as Allah wills. Had I known the future, I would have acquired much good, and no harm would have touched me. I am only a warner, and a herald of good news to a people who believe."

١٨٩ هُوَ ٱلَّذِى خَلَقَكُم مِّن نَّفْسٍ وَٰحِدَةٍ وَجَعَلَ
مِنْهَا زَوْجَهَا لِيَسْكُنَ إِلَيْهَا ۖ فَلَمَّا تَغَشَّىٰهَا حَمَلَتْ
حَمْلًا خَفِيفًا فَمَرَّتْ بِهِۦ ۖ فَلَمَّآ أَثْقَلَت دَّعَوَا ٱللَّهَ
رَبَّهُمَا لَئِنْ ءَاتَيْتَنَا صَٰلِحًا لَّنَكُونَنَّ مِنَ ٱلشَّٰكِرِينَ

189 It is He who created you from a single person, and made from it its mate, that he may find comfort with her. Then, when he has covered her, she conceives a light load, and she carries it around. But when she has grown heavy, they pray to Allah their Lord, "if You give us a good child, we will be among the thankful."

١٩٠ فَلَمَّآ ءَاتَىٰهُمَا صَٰلِحًا جَعَلَا لَهُۥ شُرَكَآءَ فِيمَآ
ءَاتَىٰهُمَا ۚ فَتَعَٰلَى ٱللَّهُ عَمَّا يُشْرِكُونَ

190 But when He has given them a good child, they attribute partners to Him in what He has given them. Allah is exalted above what they associate.

١٩١ أَيُشْرِكُونَ مَا لَا يَخْلُقُ شَيْـًٔا وَهُمْ يُخْلَقُونَ

191 Do they idolize those who create nothing, and are themselves created?

١٩٢ وَلَا يَسْتَطِيعُونَ لَهُمْ نَصْرًا وَلَآ أَنفُسَهُمْ
يَنصُرُونَ

192 And can neither help them, nor help their own selves?

١٩٣ وَإِن تَدْعُوهُمْ إِلَى ٱلْهُدَىٰ لَا يَتَّبِعُوكُمْ ۚ
سَوَآءٌ عَلَيْكُمْ أَدَعَوْتُمُوهُمْ أَمْ أَنتُمْ صَٰمِتُونَ

193 And if you invite them to guidance, they will not follow you. It is the same for you, whether you invite them, or remain silent.

١٩٤ إِنَّ ٱلَّذِينَ تَدْعُونَ مِن دُونِ ٱللَّهِ عِبَادٌ
أَمْثَالُكُمْ ۖ فَٱدْعُوهُمْ فَلْيَسْتَجِيبُوا۟ لَكُمْ إِن كُنتُمْ
صَٰدِقِينَ

194 Those you call upon besides Allah are servants like you. So call upon them, and let them answer you, if you are truthful.

١٩٥ أَلَهُمْ أَرْجُلٌ يَمْشُونَ بِهَآ ۖ أَمْ لَهُمْ أَيْدٍ
يَبْطِشُونَ بِهَآ ۖ أَمْ لَهُمْ أَعْيُنٌ يُبْصِرُونَ بِهَآ ۖ أَمْ
لَهُمْ ءَاذَانٌ يَسْمَعُونَ بِهَا ۗ قُلِ ٱدْعُوا۟ شُرَكَآءَكُمْ
ثُمَّ كِيدُونِ فَلَا تُنظِرُونِ

195 Do they have feet with which they walk? Or do they have hands with which they strike? Or do they have eyes with which they see? Or do they have ears with which they hear? Say, "Call upon your partners, then plot against me, and do not wait."

١٩٦ إِنَّ وَلِۦِّىَ ٱللَّهُ ٱلَّذِى نَزَّلَ ٱلْكِتَٰبَ ۖ وَهُوَ
يَتَوَلَّى ٱلصَّٰلِحِينَ

196 "My Master is Allah, He Who sent down the Book, and He takes care of the righteous."

١٩٧ وَٱلَّذِينَ تَدْعُونَ مِن دُونِهِۦ لَا يَسْتَطِيعُونَ
نَصْرَكُمْ وَلَآ أَنفُسَهُمْ يَنصُرُونَ

197 Those you call upon besides Him cannot help you, nor can they help themselves.

١٩٨ وَإِن تَدْعُوهُمْ إِلَى ٱلْهُدَىٰ لَا يَسْمَعُوا۟ ۖ
وَتَرَىٰهُمْ يَنظُرُونَ إِلَيْكَ وَهُمْ لَا يُبْصِرُونَ

198 And if you call them to guidance, they will not hear. And you see them looking at you, yet they do not see.

١٩٩ خُذِ ٱلْعَفْوَ وَأْمُرْ بِٱلْعُرْفِ وَأَعْرِضْ عَنِ
ٱلْجَٰهِلِينَ

199 Be tolerant, and command decency, and avoid the ignorant.

٢٠٠ وَإِمَّا يَنزَغَنَّكَ مِنَ ٱلشَّيْطَٰنِ نَزْغٌ فَٱسْتَعِذْ
بِٱللَّهِ ۚ إِنَّهُۥ سَمِيعٌ عَلِيمٌ

200 And when a suggestion from Satan assails you, take refuge with Allah. He is Hearing and Knowing.

٢٠١ إِنَّ ٱلَّذِينَ ٱتَّقَوْا۟ إِذَا مَسَّهُمْ طَٰٓئِفٌ مِّنَ
ٱلشَّيْطَٰنِ تَذَكَّرُوا۟ فَإِذَا هُم مُّبْصِرُونَ

201 Those who are righteous—when an impulse from Satan strikes them, they remind themselves, and immediately see clearly.

٢٠٢ وَإِخْوَٰنُهُمْ يَمُدُّونَهُمْ فِى ٱلْغَىِّ ثُمَّ لَا
يُقْصِرُونَ

202 But their brethren lead them relentlessly into error, and they never stop short.

203 If you do not produce a miracle for them, they say, “Why don’t you improvise one.” Say, “I only follow what is inspired to me from my Lord.” These are insights from your Lord, and guidance, and mercy, for a people who believe.

٢٠٣ وَإِذَا لَمْ تَأْتِهِم بِـَٔايَةٍ قَالُواْ لَوْلَا ٱجْتَبَيْتَهَا ۚ قُلْ إِنَّمَآ أَتَّبِعُ مَا يُوحَىٰٓ إِلَىَّ مِن رَّبِّى ۚ هَٰذَا بَصَآئِرُ مِن رَّبِّكُمْ وَهُدًى وَرَحْمَةٌ لِّقَوْمٍ يُؤْمِنُونَ

204 When the Quran is recited, listen to it, and pay attention, so that you may experience mercy.

٢٠٤ وَإِذَا قُرِئَ ٱلْقُرْءَانُ فَٱسْتَمِعُواْ لَهُۥ وَأَنصِتُواْ لَعَلَّكُمْ تُرْحَمُونَ

205 And remember your Lord within yourself, humbly and fearfully, and quietly, in the morning and the evening, and do not be of the neglectful.

٢٠٥ وَٱذْكُر رَّبَّكَ فِى نَفْسِكَ تَضَرُّعًا وَخِيفَةً وَدُونَ ٱلْجَهْرِ مِنَ ٱلْقَوْلِ بِٱلْغُدُوِّ وَٱلْءَاصَالِ وَلَا تَكُن مِّنَ ٱلْغَٰفِلِينَ

206 Those who are in the presence of your Lord are not too proud to worship Him. They recite His praises, and to Him they bow down.

٢٠٦ إِنَّ ٱلَّذِينَ عِندَ رَبِّكَ لَا يَسْتَكْبِرُونَ عَنْ عِبَادَتِهِۦ وَيُسَبِّحُونَهُۥ وَلَهُۥ يَسْجُدُونَ ۩

8 The Spoils الأنفال

In the name of Allah, the Gracious, the Merciful.

بِسْمِ ٱللَّهِ ٱلرَّحْمَٰنِ ٱلرَّحِيمِ

1 They ask you about the bounties. Say, “The bounties are for Allah and the Messenger.” So be mindful of Allah, and settle your differences, and obey Allah and His Messenger, if you are believers.

١ يَسْـَٔلُونَكَ عَنِ ٱلْأَنفَالِ ۖ قُلِ ٱلْأَنفَالُ لِلَّهِ وَٱلرَّسُولِ ۖ فَٱتَّقُواْ ٱللَّهَ وَأَصْلِحُواْ ذَاتَ بَيْنِكُمْ ۖ وَأَطِيعُواْ ٱللَّهَ وَرَسُولَهُۥٓ إِن كُنتُم مُّؤْمِنِينَ

2 The believers are those whose hearts tremble when Allah is mentioned, and when His revelations are recited to them, they strengthen them in faith, and upon their Lord they rely.

٢ إِنَّمَا ٱلْمُؤْمِنُونَ ٱلَّذِينَ إِذَا ذُكِرَ ٱللَّهُ وَجِلَتْ قُلُوبُهُمْ وَإِذَا تُلِيَتْ عَلَيْهِمْ ءَايَٰتُهُۥ زَادَتْهُمْ إِيمَٰنًا وَعَلَىٰ رَبِّهِمْ يَتَوَكَّلُونَ

3 Those who perform the prayer; and from Our provisions to them, they spend.

٣ ٱلَّذِينَ يُقِيمُونَ ٱلصَّلَوٰةَ وَمِمَّا رَزَقْنَٰهُمْ يُنفِقُونَ

٤ أُو۟لَٰٓئِكَ هُمُ ٱلْمُؤْمِنُونَ حَقًّا ۚ لَّهُمْ دَرَجَٰتٌ عِندَ
رَبِّهِمْ وَمَغْفِرَةٌ وَرِزْقٌ كَرِيمٌ

4 These are the true believers. They have high standing with their Lord, and forgiveness, and a generous provision.

٥ كَمَآ أَخْرَجَكَ رَبُّكَ مِنۢ بَيْتِكَ بِٱلْحَقِّ وَإِنَّ
فَرِيقًا مِّنَ ٱلْمُؤْمِنِينَ لَكَٰرِهُونَ

5 Even as your Lord brought you out of your home with the truth, some believers were reluctant.

٦ يُجَٰدِلُونَكَ فِى ٱلْحَقِّ بَعْدَمَا تَبَيَّنَ كَأَنَّمَا
يُسَاقُونَ إِلَى ٱلْمَوْتِ وَهُمْ يَنظُرُونَ

6 Arguing with you about the truth after it was made clear, as if they were being driven to death as they looked on.

٧ وَإِذْ يَعِدُكُمُ ٱللَّهُ إِحْدَى ٱلطَّآئِفَتَيْنِ أَنَّهَا لَكُمْ
وَتَوَدُّونَ أَنَّ غَيْرَ ذَاتِ ٱلشَّوْكَةِ تَكُونُ لَكُمْ
وَيُرِيدُ ٱللَّهُ أَن يُحِقَّ ٱلْحَقَّ بِكَلِمَٰتِهِۦ وَيَقْطَعَ
دَابِرَ ٱلْكَٰفِرِينَ

7 Allah has promised you one of the two groups—that it would be yours—but you wanted the unarmed group to be yours. Allah intends to prove the truth with His words, and to uproot the disbelievers.

٨ لِيُحِقَّ ٱلْحَقَّ وَيُبْطِلَ ٱلْبَٰطِلَ وَلَوْ كَرِهَ
ٱلْمُجْرِمُونَ

8 In order to confirm the truth and nullify falsehood, even though the guilty dislike it.

٩ إِذْ تَسْتَغِيثُونَ رَبَّكُمْ فَٱسْتَجَابَ لَكُمْ أَنِّى
مُمِدُّكُم بِأَلْفٍ مِّنَ ٱلْمَلَٰٓئِكَةِ مُرْدِفِينَ

9 When you appealed to your Lord for help, He answered you, "I am reinforcing you with one thousand angels in succession."

١٠ وَمَا جَعَلَهُ ٱللَّهُ إِلَّا بُشْرَىٰ وَلِتَطْمَئِنَّ بِهِۦ
قُلُوبُكُمْ ۚ وَمَا ٱلنَّصْرُ إِلَّا مِنْ عِندِ ٱللَّهِ ۚ إِنَّ ٱللَّهَ
عَزِيزٌ حَكِيمٌ

10 Allah only made it a message of hope, and to set your hearts at rest. Victory comes only from Allah. Allah is Mighty and Wise.

١١ إِذْ يُغَشِّيكُمُ ٱلنُّعَاسَ أَمَنَةً مِّنْهُ وَيُنَزِّلُ عَلَيْكُم
مِّنَ ٱلسَّمَآءِ مَآءً لِّيُطَهِّرَكُم بِهِۦ وَيُذْهِبَ عَنكُمْ
رِجْزَ ٱلشَّيْطَٰنِ وَلِيَرْبِطَ عَلَىٰ قُلُوبِكُمْ وَيُثَبِّتَ بِهِ
ٱلْأَقْدَامَ

11 He made drowsiness overcome you, as a security from Him. And He sent down upon you water from the sky, to cleanse you with it, and to rid you of Satan's pollution, and to fortify your hearts, and to strengthen your foothold.

١٢ إِذْ يُوحِى رَبُّكَ إِلَى ٱلْمَلَٰٓئِكَةِ أَنِّى مَعَكُمْ
فَثَبِّتُوا۟ ٱلَّذِينَ ءَامَنُوا۟ ۚ سَأُلْقِى فِى قُلُوبِ ٱلَّذِينَ

12 Your Lord inspired the angels: "I am with you, so support those who believe. I will cast terror into the hearts of those who disbelieve. So

كَفَرُوا۟ ٱلرُّعْبَ فَٱضْرِبُوا۟ فَوْقَ ٱلْأَعْنَاقِ وَٱضْرِبُوا۟
مِنْهُمْ كُلَّ بَنَانٍ

strike above the necks, and strike off every fingertip of theirs."

١٣ ذَٰلِكَ بِأَنَّهُمْ شَآقُّوا۟ ٱللَّهَ وَرَسُولَهُۥ ۚ وَمَن
يُشَاقِقِ ٱللَّهَ وَرَسُولَهُۥ فَإِنَّ ٱللَّهَ شَدِيدُ ٱلْعِقَابِ

13 That is because they opposed Allah and His Messenger. Whoever opposes Allah and His Messenger—Allah is severe in retribution.

١٤ ذَٰلِكُمْ فَذُوقُوهُ وَأَنَّ لِلْكَٰفِرِينَ عَذَابَ ٱلنَّارِ

14 "Here it is; so taste it." For the disbelievers there is the suffering of the Fire.

١٥ يَٰٓأَيُّهَا ٱلَّذِينَ ءَامَنُوٓا۟ إِذَا لَقِيتُمُ ٱلَّذِينَ كَفَرُوا۟
زَحْفًا فَلَا تُوَلُّوهُمُ ٱلْأَدْبَارَ

15 O you who believe! When you meet those who disbelieve on the march, never turn your backs on them.

١٦ وَمَن يُوَلِّهِمْ يَوْمَئِذٍ دُبُرَهُۥٓ إِلَّا مُتَحَرِّفًا لِّقِتَالٍ
أَوْ مُتَحَيِّزًا إِلَىٰ فِئَةٍ فَقَدْ بَآءَ بِغَضَبٍ مِّنَ ٱللَّهِ
وَمَأْوَىٰهُ جَهَنَّمُ ۖ وَبِئْسَ ٱلْمَصِيرُ

16 Anyone who turns his back on them on that Day, except while maneuvering for battle, or to join another group, has incurred wrath from Allah, and his abode is Hell—what a miserable destination!

١٧ فَلَمْ تَقْتُلُوهُمْ وَلَٰكِنَّ ٱللَّهَ قَتَلَهُمْ ۚ وَمَا رَمَيْتَ
إِذْ رَمَيْتَ وَلَٰكِنَّ ٱللَّهَ رَمَىٰ ۚ وَلِيُبْلِىَ ٱلْمُؤْمِنِينَ
مِنْهُ بَلَآءً حَسَنًا ۚ إِنَّ ٱللَّهَ سَمِيعٌ عَلِيمٌ

17 It was not you who killed them, but it was Allah who killed them. And it was not you who launched when you launched, but it was Allah who launched. That He may bestow upon the believers an excellent reward. Allah is Hearing and Knowing.

١٨ ذَٰلِكُمْ وَأَنَّ ٱللَّهَ مُوهِنُ كَيْدِ ٱلْكَٰفِرِينَ

18 Such is the case. Allah will undermine the strategy of the disbelievers.

١٩ إِن تَسْتَفْتِحُوا۟ فَقَدْ جَآءَكُمُ ٱلْفَتْحُ ۖ وَإِن
تَنتَهُوا۟ فَهُوَ خَيْرٌ لَّكُمْ ۖ وَإِن تَعُودُوا۟ نَعُدْ وَلَن
تُغْنِىَ عَنكُمْ فِئَتُكُمْ شَيْـًٔا وَلَوْ كَثُرَتْ وَأَنَّ ٱللَّهَ
مَعَ ٱلْمُؤْمِنِينَ

19 If you desire a verdict, the verdict has come to you. And if you desist, it would be best for you. And if you return, We will return; and your troops, however numerous, will not benefit you. Allah is with the believers.

٢٠ يَٰٓأَيُّهَا ٱلَّذِينَ ءَامَنُوٓا۟ أَطِيعُوا۟ ٱللَّهَ وَرَسُولَهُۥ
وَلَا تَوَلَّوْا۟ عَنْهُ وَأَنتُمْ تَسْمَعُونَ

20 O you who believe! Obey Allah and His Messenger, and do not turn away from him when you hear.

٢١ وَلَا تَكُونُوا۟ كَٱلَّذِينَ قَالُوا۟ سَمِعْنَا وَهُمْ لَا
يَسْمَعُونَ

21 And be not like those who say, "We hear," when they do not hear.

٢٢ إِنَّ شَرَّ ٱلدَّوَآبِّ عِندَ ٱللَّهِ ٱلصُّمُّ ٱلْبُكْمُ ٱلَّذِينَ
لَا يَعْقِلُونَ

22 The worst of animals to Allah are the deaf and dumb—those who do not reason.

٢٣ وَلَوْ عَلِمَ ٱللَّهُ فِيهِمْ خَيْرًا لَّأَسْمَعَهُمْ ۖ وَلَوْ
أَسْمَعَهُمْ لَتَوَلَّوا۟ وَّهُم مُّعْرِضُونَ

23 Had Allah recognized any good in them, He would have made them hear; and had He made them hear, they would have turned away defiantly.

٢٤ يَٰٓأَيُّهَا ٱلَّذِينَ ءَامَنُوا۟ ٱسْتَجِيبُوا۟ لِلَّهِ وَلِلرَّسُولِ
إِذَا دَعَاكُمْ لِمَا يُحْيِيكُمْ ۖ وَٱعْلَمُوٓا۟ أَنَّ ٱللَّهَ
يَحُولُ بَيْنَ ٱلْمَرْءِ وَقَلْبِهِۦ وَأَنَّهُۥٓ إِلَيْهِ تُحْشَرُونَ

24 O you who believe! Respond to Allah and to the Messenger when He calls you to what will revive you. And know that Allah stands between a man and his heart, and that to Him you will be gathered.

٢٥ وَٱتَّقُوا۟ فِتْنَةً لَّا تُصِيبَنَّ ٱلَّذِينَ ظَلَمُوا۟ مِنكُمْ
خَآصَّةً ۖ وَٱعْلَمُوٓا۟ أَنَّ ٱللَّهَ شَدِيدُ ٱلْعِقَابِ

25 And beware of discord which does not afflict the wrongdoers among you exclusively; and know that Allah is severe in retribution.

٢٦ وَٱذْكُرُوٓا۟ إِذْ أَنتُمْ قَلِيلٌ مُّسْتَضْعَفُونَ فِى
ٱلْأَرْضِ تَخَافُونَ أَن يَتَخَطَّفَكُمُ ٱلنَّاسُ فَـَٔاوَىٰكُمْ
وَأَيَّدَكُم بِنَصْرِهِۦ وَرَزَقَكُم مِّنَ ٱلطَّيِّبَٰتِ لَعَلَّكُمْ
تَشْكُرُونَ

26 And remember when you were few, oppressed in the land, fearing that people may capture you; but He sheltered you, and supported you with His victory, and provided you with good things—so that you may be thankful.

٢٧ يَٰٓأَيُّهَا ٱلَّذِينَ ءَامَنُوا۟ لَا تَخُونُوا۟ ٱللَّهَ
وَٱلرَّسُولَ وَتَخُونُوٓا۟ أَمَٰنَٰتِكُمْ وَأَنتُمْ تَعْلَمُونَ

27 O you who believe! Do not betray Allah and the Messenger, nor betray your trusts, while you know.

٢٨ وَٱعْلَمُوٓا۟ أَنَّمَآ أَمْوَٰلُكُمْ وَأَوْلَٰدُكُمْ فِتْنَةٌ وَأَنَّ
ٱللَّهَ عِندَهُۥٓ أَجْرٌ عَظِيمٌ

28 And know that your possessions and your children are a test, and that Allah possesses an immense reward.

٢٩ يَٰٓأَيُّهَا ٱلَّذِينَ ءَامَنُوٓا۟ إِن تَتَّقُوا۟ ٱللَّهَ يَجْعَل
لَّكُمْ فُرْقَانًا وَيُكَفِّرْ عَنكُمْ سَيِّـَٔاتِكُمْ وَيَغْفِرْ لَكُمْ ۗ
وَٱللَّهُ ذُو ٱلْفَضْلِ ٱلْعَظِيمِ

29 O you who believe! If you remain conscious of Allah, He will give you a criterion, and will remit from you your sins, and will forgive you. Allah is possessor of infinite grace.

٣٠ وَإِذْ يَمْكُرُ بِكَ ٱلَّذِينَ كَفَرُوا۟ لِيُثْبِتُوكَ أَوْ
يَقْتُلُوكَ أَوْ يُخْرِجُوكَ ۚ وَيَمْكُرُونَ وَيَمْكُرُ ٱللَّهُ ۖ
وَٱللَّهُ خَيْرُ ٱلْمَٰكِرِينَ

30 When the disbelievers plotted against you, to imprison you, or kill you, or expel you. They planned, and Allah planned, but Allah is the Best of planners.

٣١ وَإِذَا تُتْلَىٰ عَلَيْهِمْ ءَايَٰتُنَا قَالُوا۟ قَدْ سَمِعْنَا لَوْ
نَشَآءُ لَقُلْنَا مِثْلَ هَٰذَآ ۙ إِنْ هَٰذَآ إِلَّآ أَسَٰطِيرُ
ٱلْأَوَّلِينَ

31 And when Our revelations are recited to them, they say, “We have heard. Had we wanted, we could have said the like of this; these are nothing but myths of the ancients.”

٣٢ وَإِذْ قَالُوا۟ ٱللَّهُمَّ إِن كَانَ هَٰذَا هُوَ ٱلْحَقَّ مِنْ
عِندِكَ فَأَمْطِرْ عَلَيْنَا حِجَارَةً مِّنَ ٱلسَّمَآءِ أَوِ
ٱئْتِنَا بِعَذَابٍ أَلِيمٍ

32 And they said, “Our God, if this is the truth from You, then rain down on us stones from the sky, or visit us with a painful affliction.”

٣٣ وَمَا كَانَ ٱللَّهُ لِيُعَذِّبَهُمْ وَأَنتَ فِيهِمْ ۚ وَمَا
كَانَ ٱللَّهُ مُعَذِّبَهُمْ وَهُمْ يَسْتَغْفِرُونَ

33 But Allah would not punish them while you are amongst them. And Allah would not punish them as long as they seek forgiveness.

٣٤ وَمَا لَهُمْ أَلَّا يُعَذِّبَهُمُ ٱللَّهُ وَهُمْ يَصُدُّونَ عَنِ
ٱلْمَسْجِدِ ٱلْحَرَامِ وَمَا كَانُوٓا۟ أَوْلِيَآءَهُۥٓ ۚ إِنْ
أَوْلِيَآؤُهُۥٓ إِلَّا ٱلْمُتَّقُونَ وَلَٰكِنَّ أَكْثَرَهُمْ لَا يَعْلَمُونَ

34 Yet why should Allah not punish them, when they are turning others away from the Sacred Mosque, although they are not its custodians? Its rightful custodians are the pious; but most of them do not know.

٣٥ وَمَا كَانَ صَلَاتُهُمْ عِندَ ٱلْبَيْتِ إِلَّا مُكَآءً
وَتَصْدِيَةً ۚ فَذُوقُوا۟ ٱلْعَذَابَ بِمَا كُنتُمْ تَكْفُرُونَ

35 Their prayer at the House was nothing but whistling and clapping—so taste the punishment for your blasphemy.

٣٦ إِنَّ ٱلَّذِينَ كَفَرُوا۟ يُنفِقُونَ أَمْوَٰلَهُمْ لِيَصُدُّوا۟
عَن سَبِيلِ ٱللَّهِ ۚ فَسَيُنفِقُونَهَا ثُمَّ تَكُونُ عَلَيْهِمْ
حَسْرَةً ثُمَّ يُغْلَبُونَ ۗ وَٱلَّذِينَ كَفَرُوٓا۟ إِلَىٰ جَهَنَّمَ
يُحْشَرُونَ

36 Those who disbelieve spend their wealth to repel from Allah’s path. They will spend it, then it will become a source of sorrow for them, and then they will be defeated. Those who disbelieve will be herded into Hell.

٣٧ لِيَمِيزَ ٱللَّهُ ٱلْخَبِيثَ مِنَ ٱلطَّيِّبِ وَيَجْعَلَ
ٱلْخَبِيثَ بَعْضَهُۥ عَلَىٰ بَعْضٍ فَيَرْكُمَهُۥ جَمِيعًا
فَيَجْعَلَهُۥ فِى جَهَنَّمَ ۚ أُو۟لَٰٓئِكَ هُمُ ٱلْخَٰسِرُونَ

37 That Allah may distinguish the bad from the good, and heap the bad on top of one another, and pile them together, and throw them in Hell. These are the losers.

٣٨ قُل لِّلَّذِينَ كَفَرُوٓاْ إِن يَنتَهُواْ يُغْفَرْ لَهُم مَّا قَدْ
سَلَفَ وَإِن يَعُودُواْ فَقَدْ مَضَتْ سُنَّتُ ٱلْأَوَّلِينَ

38 Say to those who disbelieve: if they desist, their past will be forgiven. But if they persist—the practice of the ancients has passed away.

٣٩ وَقَٰتِلُوهُمْ حَتَّىٰ لَا تَكُونَ فِتْنَةٌ وَيَكُونَ
ٱلدِّينُ كُلُّهُۥ لِلَّهِ ۚ فَإِنِ ٱنتَهَوْاْ فَإِنَّ ٱللَّهَ بِمَا يَعْمَلُونَ
بَصِيرٌ

39 Fight them until there is no more persecution, and religion becomes exclusively for Allah. But if they desist—Allah is Seeing of what they do.

٤٠ وَإِن تَوَلَّوْاْ فَٱعْلَمُوٓاْ أَنَّ ٱللَّهَ مَوْلَىٰكُمْ ۚ نِعْمَ
ٱلْمَوْلَىٰ وَنِعْمَ ٱلنَّصِيرُ

40 And if they turn away, know that Allah is your Protector. The Best Protector, and the Best Supporter.

٤١ وَٱعْلَمُوٓاْ أَنَّمَا غَنِمْتُم مِّن شَىْءٍ فَأَنَّ لِلَّهِ
خُمُسَهُۥ وَلِلرَّسُولِ وَلِذِى ٱلْقُرْبَىٰ وَٱلْيَتَٰمَىٰ
وَٱلْمَسَٰكِينِ وَٱبْنِ ٱلسَّبِيلِ إِن كُنتُمْ ءَامَنتُم بِٱللَّهِ
وَمَآ أَنزَلْنَا عَلَىٰ عَبْدِنَا يَوْمَ ٱلْفُرْقَانِ يَوْمَ ٱلْتَقَى
ٱلْجَمْعَانِ ۗ وَٱللَّهُ عَلَىٰ كُلِّ شَىْءٍ قَدِيرٌ

41 And know that whatever spoils you gain, to Allah belongs its fifth, and to the Messenger, and the relatives, and the orphans, and the poor, and to the wayfarer, provided you believe in Allah and in what We revealed to Our servant on the Day of Distinction, the day when the two armies met. Allah is Capable of everything.

٤٢ إِذْ أَنتُم بِٱلْعُدْوَةِ ٱلدُّنْيَا وَهُم بِٱلْعُدْوَةِ
ٱلْقُصْوَىٰ وَٱلرَّكْبُ أَسْفَلَ مِنكُمْ ۚ وَلَوْ تَوَاعَدتُّمْ
لَٱخْتَلَفْتُمْ فِى ٱلْمِيعَٰدِ ۙ وَلَٰكِن لِّيَقْضِىَ ٱللَّهُ أَمْرًا
كَانَ مَفْعُولًا لِّيَهْلِكَ مَنْ هَلَكَ عَنۢ بَيِّنَةٍ وَيَحْيَىٰ
مَنْ حَىَّ عَنۢ بَيِّنَةٍ ۗ وَإِنَّ ٱللَّهَ لَسَمِيعٌ عَلِيمٌ

42 Recall when you were on the nearer bank, and they were on the further bank, and the caravan was below you. Had you planned for this meeting, you would have disagreed on the timing, but Allah was to carry out a predetermined matter, so that those who perish would perish by clear evidence, and those who survive would survive by clear evidence. Allah is Hearing and Knowing.

٤٣ إِذْ يُرِيكَهُمُ ٱللَّهُ فِى مَنَامِكَ قَلِيلًا ۖ وَلَوْ
أَرَىٰكَهُمْ كَثِيرًا لَّفَشِلْتُمْ وَلَتَنَٰزَعْتُمْ فِى ٱلْأَمْرِ
وَلَٰكِنَّ ٱللَّهَ سَلَّمَ ۗ إِنَّهُۥ عَلِيمٌۢ بِذَاتِ ٱلصُّدُورِ

43 Allah made them appear in your dream as few. Had He made them appear as many, you would have lost heart, and disputed in the matter. But Allah saved the situation. He knows what the hearts contain.

٤٤ وَإِذْ يُرِيكُمُوهُمْ إِذِ ٱلْتَقَيْتُمْ فِىٓ أَعْيُنِكُمْ
قَلِيلًا وَيُقَلِّلُكُمْ فِىٓ أَعْيُنِهِمْ لِيَقْضِىَ ٱللَّهُ أَمْرًا
كَانَ مَفْعُولًا ۗ وَإِلَى ٱللَّهِ تُرْجَعُ ٱلْأُمُورُ

44 When you met, He made them appear as few in your eyes, and made you appear fewer in their eyes, so that Allah may conclude a predetermined matter. To Allah all matters revert.

٤٥ يَٰٓأَيُّهَا ٱلَّذِينَ ءَامَنُوٓا۟ إِذَا لَقِيتُمْ فِئَةً فَٱثْبُتُوا۟
وَٱذْكُرُوا۟ ٱللَّهَ كَثِيرًا لَّعَلَّكُمْ تُفْلِحُونَ

45 O you who believe! When you meet a force, stand firm, and remember Allah much, so that you may prevail.

٤٦ وَأَطِيعُوا۟ ٱللَّهَ وَرَسُولَهُۥ وَلَا تَنَٰزَعُوا۟ فَتَفْشَلُوا۟
وَتَذْهَبَ رِيحُكُمْ ۖ وَٱصْبِرُوٓا۟ ۚ إِنَّ ٱللَّهَ مَعَ
ٱلصَّٰبِرِينَ

46 And obey Allah and His Messenger, and do not dispute, lest you falter and lose your courage. And be steadfast. Allah is with the steadfast.

٤٧ وَلَا تَكُونُوا۟ كَٱلَّذِينَ خَرَجُوا۟ مِن دِيَٰرِهِم بَطَرًا
وَرِئَآءَ ٱلنَّاسِ وَيَصُدُّونَ عَن سَبِيلِ ٱللَّهِ ۚ وَٱللَّهُ
بِمَا يَعْمَلُونَ مُحِيطٌ

47 And do not be like those who left their homes boastfully, showing off before the people, and barring others from the path of Allah. Allah comprehends what they do.

٤٨ وَإِذْ زَيَّنَ لَهُمُ ٱلشَّيْطَٰنُ أَعْمَٰلَهُمْ وَقَالَ لَا
غَالِبَ لَكُمُ ٱلْيَوْمَ مِنَ ٱلنَّاسِ وَإِنِّى جَارٌ لَّكُمْ ۖ
فَلَمَّا تَرَآءَتِ ٱلْفِئَتَانِ نَكَصَ عَلَىٰ عَقِبَيْهِ وَقَالَ
إِنِّى بَرِىٓءٌ مِّنكُمْ إِنِّىٓ أَرَىٰ مَا لَا تَرَوْنَ إِنِّىٓ
أَخَافُ ٱللَّهَ ۚ وَٱللَّهُ شَدِيدُ ٱلْعِقَابِ

48 Satan made their deeds appear good to them, and said, “You cannot be defeated by any people today, and I am at your side.” But when the two armies came in sight of one another, he turned on his heels, and said, “I am innocent of you; I see what you do not see; I fear Allah; Allah is severe in punishment.”

٤٩ إِذْ يَقُولُ ٱلْمُنَٰفِقُونَ وَٱلَّذِينَ فِى قُلُوبِهِم
مَّرَضٌ غَرَّ هَٰٓؤُلَآءِ دِينُهُمْ ۗ وَمَن يَتَوَكَّلْ عَلَى ٱللَّهِ
فَإِنَّ ٱللَّهَ عَزِيزٌ حَكِيمٌ

49 The hypocrites and those in whose hearts is sickness said, “Their religion has deluded these people.” But whoever puts his trust in Allah—Allah is Mighty and Wise.

٥٠ وَلَوْ تَرَىٰٓ إِذْ يَتَوَفَّى ٱلَّذِينَ كَفَرُوا۟ ۙ ٱلْمَلَٰٓئِكَةُ
يَضْرِبُونَ وُجُوهَهُمْ وَأَدْبَٰرَهُمْ وَذُوقُوا۟ عَذَابَ
ٱلْحَرِيقِ

50 If only you could see, as the angels take away those who disbelieve, striking their faces and their backs: “Taste the agony of the Burning.”

٥١ ذَٰلِكَ بِمَا قَدَّمَتْ أَيْدِيكُمْ وَأَنَّ ٱللَّهَ لَيْسَ
بِظَلَّٰمٍ لِّلْعَبِيدِ

51 “That is because of what your hands have committed, and because Allah is not unjust to the servants.”

٥٢ كَدَأْبِ ءَالِ فِرْعَوْنَ ۙ وَٱلَّذِينَ مِن قَبْلِهِمْ ۚ
كَفَرُوا۟ بِـَٔايَٰتِ ٱللَّهِ فَأَخَذَهُمُ ٱللَّهُ بِذُنُوبِهِمْ ۗ إِنَّ
ٱللَّهَ قَوِىٌّ شَدِيدُ ٱلْعِقَابِ

52 Like the behavior of the people of Pharaoh, and those before them. They rejected the signs of Allah, so Allah seized them for their sins. Allah is Powerful, Severe in punishment.

٥٣ ذَٰلِكَ بِأَنَّ ٱللَّهَ لَمْ يَكُ مُغَيِّرًا نِّعْمَةً أَنْعَمَهَا
عَلَىٰ قَوْمٍ حَتَّىٰ يُغَيِّرُوا۟ مَا بِأَنفُسِهِمْ ۙ وَأَنَّ ٱللَّهَ
سَمِيعٌ عَلِيمٌ

53 That is because Allah would never change a blessing He has bestowed on a people unless they change what is within themselves, and because Allah is Hearing and Knowing.

٥٤ كَدَأْبِ ءَالِ فِرْعَوْنَ ۙ وَٱلَّذِينَ مِن قَبْلِهِمْ ۚ
كَذَّبُوا۟ بِـَٔايَٰتِ رَبِّهِمْ فَأَهْلَكْنَٰهُم بِذُنُوبِهِمْ وَأَغْرَقْنَآ
ءَالَ فِرْعَوْنَ ۚ وَكُلٌّ كَانُوا۟ ظَٰلِمِينَ

54 Such was the case with the people of Pharaoh, and those before them. They denied the signs of their Lord, so We annihilated them for their wrongs, and We drowned the people of Pharaoh—they were all evildoers.

٥٥ إِنَّ شَرَّ ٱلدَّوَآبِّ عِندَ ٱللَّهِ ٱلَّذِينَ كَفَرُوا۟ فَهُمْ
لَا يُؤْمِنُونَ

55 The worst of creatures in Allah's view are those who disbelieve. They have no faith.

٥٦ ٱلَّذِينَ عَٰهَدتَّ مِنْهُمْ ثُمَّ يَنقُضُونَ عَهْدَهُمْ
فِى كُلِّ مَرَّةٍ وَهُمْ لَا يَتَّقُونَ

56 Those of them with whom you made a treaty, but they violate their agreement every time. They are not righteous.

٥٧ فَإِمَّا تَثْقَفَنَّهُمْ فِى ٱلْحَرْبِ فَشَرِّدْ بِهِم مَّنْ
خَلْفَهُمْ لَعَلَّهُمْ يَذَّكَّرُونَ

57 If you confront them in battle, make of them a fearsome example for those who follow them, that they may take heed.

٥٨ وَإِمَّا تَخَافَنَّ مِن قَوْمٍ خِيَانَةً فَٱنۢبِذْ إِلَيْهِمْ
عَلَىٰ سَوَآءٍ ۚ إِنَّ ٱللَّهَ لَا يُحِبُّ ٱلْخَآئِنِينَ

58 If you fear treachery on the part of a people, break off with them in a like manner. Allah does not like the treacherous.

٥٩ وَلَا يَحْسَبَنَّ ٱلَّذِينَ كَفَرُوا۟ سَبَقُوٓا۟ ۚ إِنَّهُمْ لَا
يُعْجِزُونَ

59 Let not the disbelievers assume that they are ahead. They will not escape.

٦٠ وَأَعِدُّوا۟ لَهُم مَّا ٱسْتَطَعْتُم مِّن قُوَّةٍ وَمِن
رِّبَاطِ ٱلْخَيْلِ تُرْهِبُونَ بِهِۦ عَدُوَّ ٱللَّهِ وَعَدُوَّكُمْ
وَءَاخَرِينَ مِن دُونِهِمْ لَا تَعْلَمُونَهُمُ ٱللَّهُ يَعْلَمُهُمْ ۚ
وَمَا تُنفِقُوا۟ مِن شَىْءٍ فِى سَبِيلِ ٱللَّهِ يُوَفَّ
إِلَيْكُمْ وَأَنتُمْ لَا تُظْلَمُونَ

60 And prepare against them all the power you can muster, and all the cavalry you can mobilize, to terrify thereby Allah's enemies and your enemies, and others besides them whom you do not know, but Allah knows them. Whatever you spend in Allah's way will be repaid to you in full, and you will not be wronged.

٦١ وَإِن جَنَحُوا۟ لِلسَّلْمِ فَٱجْنَحْ لَهَا وَتَوَكَّلْ عَلَى
ٱللَّهِ ۚ إِنَّهُۥ هُوَ ٱلسَّمِيعُ ٱلْعَلِيمُ

61 But if they incline towards peace, then incline towards it, and put your trust in Allah. He is the Hearer, the Knower.

٦٢ وَإِن يُرِيدُوٓا۟ أَن يَخْدَعُوكَ فَإِنَّ حَسْبَكَ ٱللَّهُ ۚ
هُوَ ٱلَّذِىٓ أَيَّدَكَ بِنَصْرِهِۦ وَبِٱلْمُؤْمِنِينَ

62 If they intend to deceive you—Allah is sufficient for you. It is He who supported you with His aid, and with the believers.

٦٣ وَأَلَّفَ بَيْنَ قُلُوبِهِمْ ۚ لَوْ أَنفَقْتَ مَا فِى ٱلْأَرْضِ
جَمِيعًا مَّآ أَلَّفْتَ بَيْنَ قُلُوبِهِمْ وَلَٰكِنَّ ٱللَّهَ أَلَّفَ
بَيْنَهُمْ ۚ إِنَّهُۥ عَزِيزٌ حَكِيمٌ

63 And He united their hearts. Had you spent everything on earth, you would not have united their hearts, but Allah united them together. He is Mighty and Wise.

٦٤ يَٰٓأَيُّهَا ٱلنَّبِىُّ حَسْبُكَ ٱللَّهُ وَمَنِ ٱتَّبَعَكَ مِنَ
ٱلْمُؤْمِنِينَ

64 O prophet! Count on Allah, and on the believers who have followed you.

٦٥ يَٰٓأَيُّهَا ٱلنَّبِىُّ حَرِّضِ ٱلْمُؤْمِنِينَ عَلَى ٱلْقِتَالِ ۚ
إِن يَكُن مِّنكُمْ عِشْرُونَ صَٰبِرُونَ يَغْلِبُوا۟ مِا۟ئَتَيْنِ ۚ
وَإِن يَكُن مِّنكُم مِّا۟ئَةٌ يَغْلِبُوٓا۟ أَلْفًا مِّنَ ٱلَّذِينَ
كَفَرُوا۟ بِأَنَّهُمْ قَوْمٌ لَّا يَفْقَهُونَ

65 O prophet! Rouse the believers to battle. If there are twenty steadfast among you, they will defeat two hundred; and if there are a hundred of you, they will defeat a thousand of those who disbelieve; because they are a people who do not understand.

٦٦ ٱلْـَٰٔنَ خَفَّفَ ٱللَّهُ عَنكُمْ وَعَلِمَ أَنَّ فِيكُمْ ضَعْفًا ۚ
فَإِن يَكُن مِّنكُم مِّا۟ئَةٌ صَابِرَةٌ يَغْلِبُوا۟ مِا۟ئَتَيْنِ ۚ
وَإِن يَكُن مِّنكُمْ أَلْفٌ يَغْلِبُوٓا۟ أَلْفَيْنِ بِإِذْنِ ٱللَّهِ ۗ
وَٱللَّهُ مَعَ ٱلصَّٰبِرِينَ

66 Allah has now lightened your burden, knowing that there is weakness in you. If there are a hundred steadfast among you, they will defeat two hundred; and if there are a thousand of you, they will defeat two thousand by Allah's leave. Allah is with the steadfast.

٦٧ مَا كَانَ لِنَبِيٍّ أَن يَكُونَ لَهُۥٓ أَسْرَىٰ حَتَّىٰ
يُثْخِنَ فِى ٱلْأَرْضِ ۚ تُرِيدُونَ عَرَضَ ٱلدُّنْيَا وَٱللَّهُ
يُرِيدُ ٱلْـَٔاخِرَةَ ۗ وَٱللَّهُ عَزِيزٌ حَكِيمٌ

67 It is not for a prophet to take prisoners before he has subdued the land. You desire the materials of this world, but Allah desires the Hereafter. Allah is Strong and Wise.

٦٨ لَّوْلَا كِتَٰبٌ مِّنَ ٱللَّهِ سَبَقَ لَمَسَّكُمْ فِيمَآ
أَخَذْتُمْ عَذَابٌ عَظِيمٌ

68 Were it not for a predetermined decree from Allah, an awful punishment would have afflicted you for what you have taken.

٦٩ فَكُلُوا۟ مِمَّا غَنِمْتُمْ حَلَٰلًا طَيِّبًا ۚ وَٱتَّقُوا۟ ٱللَّهَ ۚ
إِنَّ ٱللَّهَ غَفُورٌ رَّحِيمٌ

69 So consume what you have gained, legitimate and wholesome; and remain conscious of Allah. Allah is Forgiving and Merciful.

٧٠ يَٰٓأَيُّهَا ٱلنَّبِىُّ قُل لِّمَن فِىٓ أَيْدِيكُم مِّنَ ٱلْأَسْرَىٰٓ
إِن يَعْلَمِ ٱللَّهُ فِى قُلُوبِكُمْ خَيْرًا يُؤْتِكُمْ خَيْرًا
مِّمَّآ أُخِذَ مِنكُمْ وَيَغْفِرْ لَكُمْ ۗ وَٱللَّهُ غَفُورٌ رَّحِيمٌ

70 O prophet! Say to those you hold prisoners, “If Allah finds any good in your hearts, He will give you better than what was taken from you, and He will forgive you. Allah is Forgiving and Merciful.”

٧١ وَإِن يُرِيدُوا۟ خِيَانَتَكَ فَقَدْ خَانُوا۟ ٱللَّهَ مِن
قَبْلُ فَأَمْكَنَ مِنْهُمْ ۗ وَٱللَّهُ عَلِيمٌ حَكِيمٌ

71 But if they intend to betray you, they have already betrayed Allah, and He has overpowered them. Allah is Knowing and Wise.

٧٢ إِنَّ ٱلَّذِينَ ءَامَنُوا۟ وَهَاجَرُوا۟ وَجَٰهَدُوا۟
بِأَمْوَٰلِهِمْ وَأَنفُسِهِمْ فِى سَبِيلِ ٱللَّهِ وَٱلَّذِينَ
ءَاوَوا۟ وَّنَصَرُوٓا۟ أُو۟لَٰٓئِكَ بَعْضُهُمْ أَوْلِيَآءُ بَعْضٍ ۚ
وَٱلَّذِينَ ءَامَنُوا۟ وَلَمْ يُهَاجِرُوا۟ مَا لَكُم مِّن
وَلَٰيَتِهِم مِّن شَىْءٍ حَتَّىٰ يُهَاجِرُوا۟ ۚ وَإِنِ
ٱسْتَنصَرُوكُمْ فِى ٱلدِّينِ فَعَلَيْكُمُ ٱلنَّصْرُ إِلَّا عَلَىٰ
قَوْمٍۭ بَيْنَكُمْ وَبَيْنَهُم مِّيثَٰقٌ ۗ وَٱللَّهُ بِمَا تَعْمَلُونَ
بَصِيرٌ

72 Those who believed, and emigrated, and struggled in Allah’s cause with their possessions and their persons, and those who provided shelter and support—these are allies of one another. As for those who believed, but did not emigrate, you owe them no protection, until they have emigrated. But if they ask you for help in religion, you must come to their aid, except against a people with whom you have a treaty. Allah is Seeing of what you do.

٧٣ وَٱلَّذِينَ كَفَرُوا۟ بَعْضُهُمْ أَوْلِيَآءُ بَعْضٍ ۚ إِلَّا
تَفْعَلُوهُ تَكُن فِتْنَةٌ فِى ٱلْأَرْضِ وَفَسَادٌ كَبِيرٌ

73 As for those who disbelieve, they are allies of one another. Unless you do this, there will be turmoil in the land, and much corruption.

٧٤ وَٱلَّذِينَ ءَامَنُوا۟ وَهَاجَرُوا۟ وَجَٰهَدُوا۟ فِى سَبِيلِ ٱللَّهِ وَٱلَّذِينَ ءَاوَوا۟ وَّنَصَرُوٓا۟ أُو۟لَٰٓئِكَ هُمُ ٱلْمُؤْمِنُونَ حَقًّا ۚ لَّهُم مَّغْفِرَةٌ وَرِزْقٌ كَرِيمٌ

74 Those who believed, and emigrated, and struggled for Allah's cause, and those who gave shelter and support—these are the true believers. They will have forgiveness, and a bountiful provision.

٧٥ وَٱلَّذِينَ ءَامَنُوا۟ مِنۢ بَعْدُ وَهَاجَرُوا۟ وَجَٰهَدُوا۟ مَعَكُمْ فَأُو۟لَٰٓئِكَ مِنكُمْ ۚ وَأُو۟لُوا۟ ٱلْأَرْحَامِ بَعْضُهُمْ أَوْلَىٰ بِبَعْضٍ فِى كِتَٰبِ ٱللَّهِ ۗ إِنَّ ٱللَّهَ بِكُلِّ شَىْءٍ عَلِيمٌۢ

75 As for those who believed afterwards, and emigrated and struggled with you—these belong with you. But family members are nearer to one another in the Book of Allah. Allah is Cognizant of everything.

9 Repentance التوبة

١ بَرَآءَةٌ مِّنَ ٱللَّهِ وَرَسُولِهِۦٓ إِلَى ٱلَّذِينَ عَٰهَدتُّم مِّنَ ٱلْمُشْرِكِينَ

1 A declaration of immunity from Allah and His Messenger to the polytheists with whom you had made a treaty.

٢ فَسِيحُوا۟ فِى ٱلْأَرْضِ أَرْبَعَةَ أَشْهُرٍ وَٱعْلَمُوٓا۟ أَنَّكُمْ غَيْرُ مُعْجِزِى ٱللَّهِ ۙ وَأَنَّ ٱللَّهَ مُخْزِى ٱلْكَٰفِرِينَ

2 So travel the land for four months, and know that you cannot escape Allah, and that Allah will disgrace the disbelievers.

٣ وَأَذَٰنٌ مِّنَ ٱللَّهِ وَرَسُولِهِۦٓ إِلَى ٱلنَّاسِ يَوْمَ ٱلْحَجِّ ٱلْأَكْبَرِ أَنَّ ٱللَّهَ بَرِىٓءٌ مِّنَ ٱلْمُشْرِكِينَ ۙ وَرَسُولُهُۥ ۚ فَإِن تُبْتُمْ فَهُوَ خَيْرٌ لَّكُمْ ۖ وَإِن تَوَلَّيْتُمْ فَٱعْلَمُوٓا۟ أَنَّكُمْ غَيْرُ مُعْجِزِى ٱللَّهِ ۗ وَبَشِّرِ ٱلَّذِينَ كَفَرُوا۟ بِعَذَابٍ أَلِيمٍ

3 And a proclamation from Allah and His Messenger to the people on the day of the Greater Pilgrimage, that Allah has disowned the polytheists, and so did His Messenger. If you repent, it will be better for you. But if you turn away, know that you cannot escape Allah. And announce to those who disbelieve a painful punishment.

٤ إِلَّا ٱلَّذِينَ عَٰهَدتُّم مِّنَ ٱلْمُشْرِكِينَ ثُمَّ لَمْ يَنقُصُوكُمْ شَيْـًٔا وَلَمْ يُظَٰهِرُوا۟ عَلَيْكُمْ أَحَدًا

4 Except for those among the polytheists with whom you had made a treaty, and did not violate any of its terms, nor aided anyone against you. So fulfill the treaty with them to

فَأَتِمُّوٓاْ إِلَيۡهِمۡ عَهۡدَهُمۡ إِلَىٰ مُدَّتِهِمۡۚ إِنَّ ٱللَّهَ
يُحِبُّ ٱلۡمُتَّقِينَ

the end of its term. Allah loves the righteous.

٥ فَإِذَا ٱنسَلَخَ ٱلۡأَشۡهُرُ ٱلۡحُرُمُ فَٱقۡتُلُواْ
ٱلۡمُشۡرِكِينَ حَيۡثُ وَجَدتُّمُوهُمۡ وَخُذُوهُمۡ
وَٱحۡصُرُوهُمۡ وَٱقۡعُدُواْ لَهُمۡ كُلَّ مَرۡصَدٖۚ فَإِن
تَابُواْ وَأَقَامُواْ ٱلصَّلَوٰةَ وَءَاتَوُاْ ٱلزَّكَوٰةَ فَخَلُّواْ
سَبِيلَهُمۡۚ إِنَّ ٱللَّهَ غَفُورٞ رَّحِيمٞ

5 When the Sacred Months have passed, kill the polytheists wherever you find them. And capture them, and besiege them, and lie in wait for them at every ambush. But if they repent, and perform the prayers, and pay the alms, then let them go their way. Allah is Most Forgiving, Most Merciful.

٦ وَإِنۡ أَحَدٞ مِّنَ ٱلۡمُشۡرِكِينَ ٱسۡتَجَارَكَ فَأَجِرۡهُ
حَتَّىٰ يَسۡمَعَ كَلَٰمَ ٱللَّهِ ثُمَّ أَبۡلِغۡهُ مَأۡمَنَهُۥۚ ذَٰلِكَ
بِأَنَّهُمۡ قَوۡمٞ لَّا يَعۡلَمُونَ

6 And if anyone of the polytheists asks you for protection, give him protection so that he may hear the Word of Allah; then escort him to his place of safety. That is because they are a people who do not know.

٧ كَيۡفَ يَكُونُ لِلۡمُشۡرِكِينَ عَهۡدٌ عِندَ ٱللَّهِ وَعِندَ
رَسُولِهِۦٓ إِلَّا ٱلَّذِينَ عَٰهَدتُّمۡ عِندَ ٱلۡمَسۡجِدِ
ٱلۡحَرَامِۖ فَمَا ٱسۡتَقَٰمُواْ لَكُمۡ فَٱسۡتَقِيمُواْ لَهُمۡۚ إِنَّ
ٱللَّهَ يُحِبُّ ٱلۡمُتَّقِينَ

7 How can there be a treaty with the polytheists on the part of Allah and His Messenger, except for those with whom you made a treaty at the Sacred Mosque? As long as they are upright with you, be upright with them. Allah loves the pious.

٨ كَيۡفَ وَإِن يَظۡهَرُواْ عَلَيۡكُمۡ لَا يَرۡقُبُواْ فِيكُمۡ إِلّٗا
وَلَا ذِمَّةٗۚ يُرۡضُونَكُم بِأَفۡوَٰهِهِمۡ وَتَأۡبَىٰ قُلُوبُهُمۡ
وَأَكۡثَرُهُمۡ فَٰسِقُونَ

8 How? Whenever they overcome you, they respect neither kinship nor treaty with you. They satisfy you with lip service, but their hearts refuse, and most of them are immoral.

٩ ٱشۡتَرَوۡاْ بِـَٔايَٰتِ ٱللَّهِ ثَمَنٗا قَلِيلٗا فَصَدُّواْ عَن
سَبِيلِهِۦٓۚ إِنَّهُمۡ سَآءَ مَا كَانُواْ يَعۡمَلُونَ

9 They traded away Allah's revelations for a cheap price, so they barred others from His path. How evil is what they did.

١٠ لَا يَرۡقُبُونَ فِي مُؤۡمِنٍ إِلّٗا وَلَا ذِمَّةٗۚ وَأُوْلَٰٓئِكَ
هُمُ ٱلۡمُعۡتَدُونَ

10 Towards a believer they respect neither kinship nor treaty. These are the transgressors.

١١ فَإِن تَابُواْ وَأَقَامُواْ ٱلصَّلَوٰةَ وَءَاتَوُاْ ٱلزَّكَوٰةَ
فَإِخۡوَٰنُكُمۡ فِي ٱلدِّينِۗ وَنُفَصِّلُ ٱلۡأٓيَٰتِ لِقَوۡمٖ
يَعۡلَمُونَ

11 But if they repent, and perform the prayers, and give the obligatory charity, then they are your brethren

in faith. We detail the revelations for
a people who know.

١٢ وَإِن نَّكَثُوٓاْ أَيۡمَٰنَهُم مِّنۢ بَعۡدِ عَهۡدِهِمۡ وَطَعَنُواْ
فِي دِينِكُمۡ فَقَٰتِلُوٓاْ أَئِمَّةَ ٱلۡكُفۡرِ إِنَّهُمۡ لَآ أَيۡمَٰنَ
لَهُمۡ لَعَلَّهُمۡ يَنتَهُونَ

12 But if they violate their oaths after
their pledge, and attack your
religion, then fight the leaders of
disbelief—they have no faith—so
that they may desist.

١٣ أَلَا تُقَٰتِلُونَ قَوۡمٗا نَّكَثُوٓاْ أَيۡمَٰنَهُمۡ وَهَمُّواْ
بِإِخۡرَاجِ ٱلرَّسُولِ وَهُم بَدَءُوكُمۡ أَوَّلَ مَرَّةٍۚ
أَتَخۡشَوۡنَهُمۡۚ فَٱللَّهُ أَحَقُّ أَن تَخۡشَوۡهُ إِن كُنتُم
مُّؤۡمِنِينَ

13 Will you not fight a people who
violated their oaths, and planned to
exile the Messenger, and initiated
hostilities against you? Do you fear
them? It is Allah you should fear, if
you are believers.

١٤ قَٰتِلُوهُمۡ يُعَذِّبۡهُمُ ٱللَّهُ بِأَيۡدِيكُمۡ وَيُخۡزِهِمۡ
وَيَنصُرۡكُمۡ عَلَيۡهِمۡ وَيَشۡفِ صُدُورَ قَوۡمٖ مُّؤۡمِنِينَ

14 Fight them. Allah will punish them
at your hands, and humiliate them,
and help you against them, and heal
the hearts of a believing people.

١٥ وَيُذۡهِبۡ غَيۡظَ قُلُوبِهِمۡۗ وَيَتُوبُ ٱللَّهُ عَلَىٰ
مَن يَشَآءُۗ وَٱللَّهُ عَلِيمٌ حَكِيمٌ

15 And He will remove the anger of
their hearts. Allah redeems
whomever He wills. Allah is
Knowledgeable and Wise.

١٦ أَمۡ حَسِبۡتُمۡ أَن تُتۡرَكُواْ وَلَمَّا يَعۡلَمِ ٱللَّهُ ٱلَّذِينَ
جَٰهَدُواْ مِنكُمۡ وَلَمۡ يَتَّخِذُواْ مِن دُونِ ٱللَّهِ وَلَا
رَسُولِهِۦ وَلَا ٱلۡمُؤۡمِنِينَ وَلِيجَةٗۚ وَٱللَّهُ خَبِيرُۢ بِمَا
تَعۡمَلُونَ

16 Or do you think that you will be left
alone, without Allah identifying which
of you will strive, and take no
supporters apart from Allah, His
Messenger, and the believers? Allah
is well Aware of what you do.

١٧ مَا كَانَ لِلۡمُشۡرِكِينَ أَن يَعۡمُرُواْ مَسَٰجِدَ ٱللَّهِ
شَٰهِدِينَ عَلَىٰٓ أَنفُسِهِم بِٱلۡكُفۡرِۚ أُوْلَٰٓئِكَ حَبِطَتۡ
أَعۡمَٰلُهُمۡ وَفِي ٱلنَّارِ هُمۡ خَٰلِدُونَ

17 It is not for the polytheists to
attend Allah's places of worship
while professing their disbelief.
These—their works are in vain, and
in the Fire they will abide.

١٨ إِنَّمَا يَعۡمُرُ مَسَٰجِدَ ٱللَّهِ مَنۡ ءَامَنَ بِٱللَّهِ
وَٱلۡيَوۡمِ ٱلۡأٓخِرِ وَأَقَامَ ٱلصَّلَوٰةَ وَءَاتَى ٱلزَّكَوٰةَ
وَلَمۡ يَخۡشَ إِلَّا ٱللَّهَۖ فَعَسَىٰٓ أُوْلَٰٓئِكَ أَن يَكُونُواْ
مِنَ ٱلۡمُهۡتَدِينَ

18 The only people to attend Allah's
places of worship are those who
believe in Allah and the Last Day,
and pray regularly, and practice
regular charity, and fear none but
Allah. These are most likely to be
guided.

١٩ أَجَعَلْتُمْ سِقَايَةَ ٱلْحَآجِّ وَعِمَارَةَ ٱلْمَسْجِدِ
ٱلْحَرَامِ كَمَنْ ءَامَنَ بِٱللَّهِ وَٱلْيَوْمِ ٱلْءَاخِرِ
وَجَٰهَدَ فِى سَبِيلِ ٱللَّهِ ۚ لَا يَسْتَوُۥنَ عِندَ ٱللَّهِ ۗ
وَٱللَّهُ لَا يَهْدِى ٱلْقَوْمَ ٱلظَّٰلِمِينَ

19 Do you consider giving water to pilgrims and maintaining the Sacred Mosque the same as believing in Allah and the Last Day and striving in Allah's path? They are not equal in Allah's sight. Allah does not guide the unjust people.

٢٠ ٱلَّذِينَ ءَامَنُوا۟ وَهَاجَرُوا۟ وَجَٰهَدُوا۟ فِى سَبِيلِ
ٱللَّهِ بِأَمْوَٰلِهِمْ وَأَنفُسِهِمْ أَعْظَمُ دَرَجَةً عِندَ ٱللَّهِ ۚ
وَأُو۟لَٰٓئِكَ هُمُ ٱلْفَآئِزُونَ

20 Those who believe, and emigrate, and strive in Allah's path with their possessions and their persons, are of a higher rank with Allah. These are the winners.

٢١ يُبَشِّرُهُمْ رَبُّهُم بِرَحْمَةٍ مِّنْهُ وَرِضْوَٰنٍ وَجَنَّٰتٍ
لَّهُمْ فِيهَا نَعِيمٌ مُّقِيمٌ

21 Their Lord announces to them good news of mercy from Him, and acceptance, and gardens wherein they will have lasting bliss.

٢٢ خَٰلِدِينَ فِيهَآ أَبَدًا ۚ إِنَّ ٱللَّهَ عِندَهُۥٓ أَجْرٌ عَظِيمٌ

22 Abiding therein forever. With Allah is a great reward.

٢٣ يَٰٓأَيُّهَا ٱلَّذِينَ ءَامَنُوا۟ لَا تَتَّخِذُوٓا۟ ءَابَآءَكُمْ
وَإِخْوَٰنَكُمْ أَوْلِيَآءَ إِنِ ٱسْتَحَبُّوا۟ ٱلْكُفْرَ عَلَى
ٱلْإِيمَٰنِ ۚ وَمَن يَتَوَلَّهُم مِّنكُمْ فَأُو۟لَٰٓئِكَ هُمُ
ٱلظَّٰلِمُونَ

23 O you who believe! Do not ally yourselves with your parents and your siblings if they prefer disbelief to belief. Whoever of you allies himself with them—these are the wrongdoers.

٢٤ قُلْ إِن كَانَ ءَابَآؤُكُمْ وَأَبْنَآؤُكُمْ وَإِخْوَٰنُكُمْ
وَأَزْوَٰجُكُمْ وَعَشِيرَتُكُمْ وَأَمْوَٰلٌ ٱقْتَرَفْتُمُوهَا
وَتِجَٰرَةٌ تَخْشَوْنَ كَسَادَهَا وَمَسَٰكِنُ تَرْضَوْنَهَآ
أَحَبَّ إِلَيْكُم مِّنَ ٱللَّهِ وَرَسُولِهِۦ وَجِهَادٍ فِى
سَبِيلِهِۦ فَتَرَبَّصُوا۟ حَتَّىٰ يَأْتِىَ ٱللَّهُ بِأَمْرِهِۦ ۗ وَٱللَّهُ
لَا يَهْدِى ٱلْقَوْمَ ٱلْفَٰسِقِينَ

24 Say, "If your parents, and your children, and your siblings, and your spouses, and your relatives, and the wealth you have acquired, and a business you worry about, and homes you love, are more dear to you than Allah, and His Messenger, and the struggle in His cause, then wait until Allah executes His judgment." Allah does not guide the sinful people.

٢٥ لَقَدْ نَصَرَكُمُ ٱللَّهُ فِى مَوَاطِنَ كَثِيرَةٍ ۙ وَيَوْمَ
حُنَيْنٍ ۙ إِذْ أَعْجَبَتْكُمْ كَثْرَتُكُمْ فَلَمْ تُغْنِ عَنكُمْ
شَيْـًٔا وَضَاقَتْ عَلَيْكُمُ ٱلْأَرْضُ بِمَا رَحُبَتْ ثُمَّ
وَلَّيْتُم مُّدْبِرِينَ

25 Allah has given you victory in numerous regions; but on the day of Hunayn, your great number impressed you, but it availed you nothing; and the land, as spacious

as it was, narrowed for you; and you turned your backs in retreat.

٢٦ ثُمَّ أَنزَلَ ٱللَّهُ سَكِينَتَهُۥ عَلَىٰ رَسُولِهِۦ وَعَلَى
ٱلْمُؤْمِنِينَ وَأَنزَلَ جُنُودًا لَّمْ تَرَوْهَا وَعَذَّبَ
ٱلَّذِينَ كَفَرُوا۟ ۚ وَذَٰلِكَ جَزَآءُ ٱلْكَٰفِرِينَ

26 Then Allah sent down His serenity upon His Messenger, and upon the believers; and He sent down troops you did not see; and He punished those who disbelieved. Such is the recompense of the disbelievers.

٢٧ ثُمَّ يَتُوبُ ٱللَّهُ مِنۢ بَعْدِ ذَٰلِكَ عَلَىٰ مَن يَشَآءُ ۗ
وَٱللَّهُ غَفُورٌ رَّحِيمٌ

27 Then, after that, Allah will relent towards whomever He wills. Allah is Forgiving and Merciful.

٢٨ يَٰٓأَيُّهَا ٱلَّذِينَ ءَامَنُوٓا۟ إِنَّمَا ٱلْمُشْرِكُونَ نَجَسٌ
فَلَا يَقْرَبُوا۟ ٱلْمَسْجِدَ ٱلْحَرَامَ بَعْدَ عَامِهِمْ هَٰذَا ۚ
وَإِنْ خِفْتُمْ عَيْلَةً فَسَوْفَ يُغْنِيكُمُ ٱللَّهُ مِن
فَضْلِهِۦٓ إِن شَآءَ ۚ إِنَّ ٱللَّهَ عَلِيمٌ حَكِيمٌ

28 O you who believe! The polytheists are polluted, so let them not approach the Sacred Mosque after this year of theirs. And if you fear poverty, Allah will enrich you from His grace, if He wills. Allah is Aware and Wise.

٢٩ قَٰتِلُوا۟ ٱلَّذِينَ لَا يُؤْمِنُونَ بِٱللَّهِ وَلَا بِٱلْيَوْمِ
ٱلْءَاخِرِ وَلَا يُحَرِّمُونَ مَا حَرَّمَ ٱللَّهُ وَرَسُولُهُۥ
وَلَا يَدِينُونَ دِينَ ٱلْحَقِّ مِنَ ٱلَّذِينَ أُوتُوا۟ ٱلْكِتَٰبَ
حَتَّىٰ يُعْطُوا۟ ٱلْجِزْيَةَ عَن يَدٍ وَهُمْ صَٰغِرُونَ

29 Fight those who do not believe in Allah, nor in the Last Day, nor forbid what Allah and His Messenger have forbidden, nor abide by the religion of truth—from among those who received the Scripture—until they pay the due tax, willingly or unwillingly.

٣٠ وَقَالَتِ ٱلْيَهُودُ عُزَيْرٌ ٱبْنُ ٱللَّهِ وَقَالَتِ
ٱلنَّصَٰرَى ٱلْمَسِيحُ ٱبْنُ ٱللَّهِ ۖ ذَٰلِكَ قَوْلُهُم
بِأَفْوَٰهِهِمْ ۖ يُضَٰهِـُٔونَ قَوْلَ ٱلَّذِينَ كَفَرُوا۟ مِن قَبْلُ ۚ
قَٰتَلَهُمُ ٱللَّهُ ۚ أَنَّىٰ يُؤْفَكُونَ

30 The Jews said, “Ezra is the son of Allah,” and the Christians said, “The Messiah is the son of Allah.” These are their statements, out of their mouths. They emulate the statements of those who blasphemed before. May Allah assail them! How deceived they are!

٣١ ٱتَّخَذُوٓا۟ أَحْبَارَهُمْ وَرُهْبَٰنَهُمْ أَرْبَابًا مِّن دُونِ
ٱللَّهِ وَٱلْمَسِيحَ ٱبْنَ مَرْيَمَ وَمَآ أُمِرُوٓا۟ إِلَّا لِيَعْبُدُوٓا۟
إِلَٰهًا وَٰحِدًا ۖ لَّآ إِلَٰهَ إِلَّا هُوَ ۚ سُبْحَٰنَهُۥ عَمَّا يُشْرِكُونَ

31 They have taken their rabbis and their priests as lords instead of Allah, as well as the Messiah son of Mary. Although they were commanded to worship none but The One God. There is no god except He. Glory be to Him; High above what they associate with Him.

٣٢ يُرِيدُونَ أَن يُطْفِـُٔوا۟ نُورَ ٱللَّهِ بِأَفْوَٰهِهِمْ
وَيَأْبَى ٱللَّهُ إِلَّآ أَن يُتِمَّ نُورَهُۥ وَلَوْ كَرِهَ ٱلْكَـٰفِرُونَ

32 They want to extinguish Allah's light with their mouths, but Allah refuses except to complete His light, even though the disbelievers dislike it.

٣٣ هُوَ ٱلَّذِىٓ أَرْسَلَ رَسُولَهُۥ بِٱلْهُدَىٰ وَدِينِ ٱلْحَقِّ
لِيُظْهِرَهُۥ عَلَى ٱلدِّينِ كُلِّهِۦ وَلَوْ كَرِهَ ٱلْمُشْرِكُونَ

33 It is He who sent His Messenger with the guidance and the religion of truth, in order to make it prevail over all religions, even though the idolaters dislike it.

٣٤ يَـٰٓأَيُّهَا ٱلَّذِينَ ءَامَنُوٓا۟ إِنَّ كَثِيرًا مِّنَ ٱلْأَحْبَارِ
وَٱلرُّهْبَانِ لَيَأْكُلُونَ أَمْوَٰلَ ٱلنَّاسِ بِٱلْبَـٰطِلِ
وَيَصُدُّونَ عَن سَبِيلِ ٱللَّهِ ۗ وَٱلَّذِينَ يَكْنِزُونَ
ٱلذَّهَبَ وَٱلْفِضَّةَ وَلَا يُنفِقُونَهَا فِى سَبِيلِ ٱللَّهِ
فَبَشِّرْهُم بِعَذَابٍ أَلِيمٍ

34 O you who believe! Many of the rabbis and priests consume people's wealth illicitly, and hinder from Allah's path. Those who hoard gold and silver, and do not spend them in Allah's cause, inform them of a painful punishment.

٣٥ يَوْمَ يُحْمَىٰ عَلَيْهَا فِى نَارِ جَهَنَّمَ فَتُكْوَىٰ بِهَا
جِبَاهُهُمْ وَجُنُوبُهُمْ وَظُهُورُهُمْ ۖ هَـٰذَا مَا كَنَزْتُمْ
لِأَنفُسِكُمْ فَذُوقُوا۟ مَا كُنتُمْ تَكْنِزُونَ

35 On the Day when they will be heated in the Fire of Hell, then their foreheads, and their sides, and their backs will be branded with them: "This is what you hoarded for yourselves; so taste what you used to hoard."

٣٦ إِنَّ عِدَّةَ ٱلشُّهُورِ عِندَ ٱللَّهِ ٱثْنَا عَشَرَ شَهْرًا
فِى كِتَـٰبِ ٱللَّهِ يَوْمَ خَلَقَ ٱلسَّمَـٰوَٰتِ وَٱلْأَرْضَ
مِنْهَآ أَرْبَعَةٌ حُرُمٌ ۚ ذَٰلِكَ ٱلدِّينُ ٱلْقَيِّمُ ۚ فَلَا تَظْلِمُوا۟
فِيهِنَّ أَنفُسَكُمْ ۚ وَقَـٰتِلُوا۟ ٱلْمُشْرِكِينَ كَآفَّةً كَمَا
يُقَـٰتِلُونَكُمْ كَآفَّةً ۚ وَٱعْلَمُوٓا۟ أَنَّ ٱللَّهَ مَعَ ٱلْمُتَّقِينَ

36 The number of months, according to Allah, is twelve months—in the decree of Allah—since the Day He created the heavens and the earth, of which four are sacred. This is the correct religion. So do not wrong yourselves during them. And fight the polytheists collectively, as they fight you collectively, and know that Allah is with the righteous.

٣٧ إِنَّمَا ٱلنَّسِىٓءُ زِيَادَةٌ فِى ٱلْكُفْرِ ۖ يُضَلُّ بِهِ
ٱلَّذِينَ كَفَرُوا۟ يُحِلُّونَهُۥ عَامًا وَيُحَرِّمُونَهُۥ عَامًا
لِّيُوَاطِـُٔوا۟ عِدَّةَ مَا حَرَّمَ ٱللَّهُ فَيُحِلُّوا۟ مَا حَرَّمَ

37 Postponement is an increase in disbelief—by which those who disbelieve are led astray. They allow it one year, and forbid it another year, in order to conform to the number made sacred by Allah, thus permitting what Allah has forbidden.

ٱللَّهُۚ زُيِّنَ لَهُمْ سُوٓءُ أَعْمَـٰلِهِمْۗ وَٱللَّهُ لَا يَهْدِى
ٱلْقَوْمَ ٱلْكَـٰفِرِينَ

The evil of their deeds seems good to them. Allah does not guide the disbelieving people.

٣٨ يَـٰٓأَيُّهَا ٱلَّذِينَ ءَامَنُوا۟ مَا لَكُمْ إِذَا قِيلَ لَكُمُ
ٱنفِرُوا۟ فِى سَبِيلِ ٱللَّهِ ٱثَّاقَلْتُمْ إِلَى ٱلْأَرْضِۚ
أَرَضِيتُم بِٱلْحَيَوٰةِ ٱلدُّنْيَا مِنَ ٱلْـَٔاخِرَةِۚ فَمَا
مَتَـٰعُ ٱلْحَيَوٰةِ ٱلدُّنْيَا فِى ٱلْـَٔاخِرَةِ إِلَّا قَلِيلٌ

38 O you who believe! What is the matter with you, when it is said to you, “Mobilize in the cause of Allah,” you cling heavily to the earth? Do you prefer the present life to the Hereafter? The enjoyment of the present life, compared to the Hereafter, is only a little.

٣٩ إِلَّا تَنفِرُوا۟ يُعَذِّبْكُمْ عَذَابًا أَلِيمًا وَيَسْتَبْدِلْ
قَوْمًا غَيْرَكُمْ وَلَا تَضُرُّوهُ شَيْـًٔاۗ وَٱللَّهُ عَلَىٰ كُلِّ
شَىْءٍ قَدِيرٌ

39 Unless you mobilize, He will punish you most painfully, and will replace you with another people, and you will not harm Him at all. Allah has power over all things.

٤٠ إِلَّا تَنصُرُوهُ فَقَدْ نَصَرَهُ ٱللَّهُ إِذْ أَخْرَجَهُ
ٱلَّذِينَ كَفَرُوا۟ ثَانِىَ ٱثْنَيْنِ إِذْ هُمَا فِى ٱلْغَارِ إِذْ
يَقُولُ لِصَـٰحِبِهِۦ لَا تَحْزَنْ إِنَّ ٱللَّهَ مَعَنَاۖ فَأَنزَلَ
ٱللَّهُ سَكِينَتَهُۥ عَلَيْهِ وَأَيَّدَهُۥ بِجُنُودٍ لَّمْ تَرَوْهَا
وَجَعَلَ كَلِمَةَ ٱلَّذِينَ كَفَرُوا۟ ٱلسُّفْلَىٰۗ وَكَلِمَةُ ٱللَّهِ
هِىَ ٱلْعُلْيَاۗ وَٱللَّهُ عَزِيزٌ حَكِيمٌ

40 If you do not help him, Allah has already helped him, when those who disbelieved expelled him, and he was the second of two in the cave. He said to his friend, “Do not worry, Allah is with us.” And Allah made His tranquility descend upon him, and supported him with forces you did not see, and made the word of those who disbelieved the lowest, while the Word of Allah is the Highest. Allah is Mighty and Wise.

٤١ ٱنفِرُوا۟ خِفَافًا وَثِقَالًا وَجَـٰهِدُوا۟ بِأَمْوَٰلِكُمْ
وَأَنفُسِكُمْ فِى سَبِيلِ ٱللَّهِۚ ذَٰلِكُمْ خَيْرٌ لَّكُمْ إِن
كُنتُمْ تَعْلَمُونَ

41 Mobilize, light or heavy, and strive with your possessions and your lives in the cause of Allah. That is better for you, if you only knew.

٤٢ لَوْ كَانَ عَرَضًا قَرِيبًا وَسَفَرًا قَاصِدًا لَّٱتَّبَعُوكَ
وَلَـٰكِنۢ بَعُدَتْ عَلَيْهِمُ ٱلشُّقَّةُۚ وَسَيَحْلِفُونَ بِٱللَّهِ
لَوِ ٱسْتَطَعْنَا لَخَرَجْنَا مَعَكُمْ يُهْلِكُونَ أَنفُسَهُمْ
وَٱللَّهُ يَعْلَمُ إِنَّهُمْ لَكَـٰذِبُونَ

42 Had the gain been immediate, and the journey shorter, they would have followed you; but the distance seemed too long for them. Still they swear by Allah: “Had we been able, we would have marched out with you.” They damn their own souls, and Allah knows that they are lying.

٤٣ عَفَا ٱللَّهُ عَنكَ لِمَ أَذِنتَ لَهُمْ حَتَّىٰ يَتَبَيَّنَ لَكَ
ٱلَّذِينَ صَدَقُوا۟ وَتَعْلَمَ ٱلْكَـٰذِبِينَ

43 May Allah pardon you! Why did you give them permission before it became clear to you who are the truthful ones, and who are the liars?

٤٤ لَا يَسْتَـْٔذِنُكَ ٱلَّذِينَ يُؤْمِنُونَ بِٱللَّهِ وَٱلْيَوْمِ
ٱلْـَٔاخِرِ أَن يُجَـٰهِدُوا۟ بِأَمْوَٰلِهِمْ وَأَنفُسِهِمْ ۗ وَٱللَّهُ
عَلِيمٌۢ بِٱلْمُتَّقِينَ

44 Those who believe in Allah and the Last Day do not ask you for exemption from striving with their possessions and their lives. Allah is fully aware of the righteous.

٤٥ إِنَّمَا يَسْتَـْٔذِنُكَ ٱلَّذِينَ لَا يُؤْمِنُونَ بِٱللَّهِ
وَٱلْيَوْمِ ٱلْـَٔاخِرِ وَٱرْتَابَتْ قُلُوبُهُمْ فَهُمْ فِى
رَيْبِهِمْ يَتَرَدَّدُونَ

45 Only those who do not believe in Allah and the Last Day ask you for exemption. Their hearts are full of doubts, so they waver in their doubts.

٤٦ وَلَوْ أَرَادُوا۟ ٱلْخُرُوجَ لَأَعَدُّوا۟ لَهُۥ عُدَّةً وَلَـٰكِن
كَرِهَ ٱللَّهُ ٱنۢبِعَاثَهُمْ فَثَبَّطَهُمْ وَقِيلَ ٱقْعُدُوا۟ مَعَ
ٱلْقَـٰعِدِينَ

46 Had they wanted to mobilize, they would have made preparations for it; but Allah disliked their participation, so he held them back, and it was said, “Stay behind with those who stay behind.”

٤٧ لَوْ خَرَجُوا۟ فِيكُم مَّا زَادُوكُمْ إِلَّا خَبَالًا
وَلَأَوْضَعُوا۟ خِلَـٰلَكُمْ يَبْغُونَكُمُ ٱلْفِتْنَةَ وَفِيكُمْ
سَمَّـٰعُونَ لَهُمْ ۗ وَٱللَّهُ عَلِيمٌۢ بِٱلظَّـٰلِمِينَ

47 Had they mobilized with you, they would have added only to your difficulties, and they would have spread rumors in your midst, trying to sow discord among you. Some of you are avid listeners to them. Allah is Aware of the wrongdoers.

٤٨ لَقَدِ ٱبْتَغَوُا۟ ٱلْفِتْنَةَ مِن قَبْلُ وَقَلَّبُوا۟ لَكَ
ٱلْأُمُورَ حَتَّىٰ جَآءَ ٱلْحَقُّ وَظَهَرَ أَمْرُ ٱللَّهِ وَهُمْ
كَـٰرِهُونَ

48 They tried to cause conflict before, and they hatched plots against you, until the truth prevailed, and the command of Allah became evident—in spite of their dislike.

٤٩ وَمِنْهُم مَّن يَقُولُ ٱئْذَن لِّى وَلَا تَفْتِنِّىٓ ۚ أَلَا
فِى ٱلْفِتْنَةِ سَقَطُوا۟ ۗ وَإِنَّ جَهَنَّمَ لَمُحِيطَةٌۢ
بِٱلْكَـٰفِرِينَ

49 Among them is he who says, “Excuse me, and do not trouble me.” In fact, they sunk into trouble. In fact, Hell will engulf the disbelievers.

٥٠ إِن تُصِبْكَ حَسَنَةٌ تَسُؤْهُمْ ۖ وَإِن تُصِبْكَ
مُصِيبَةٌ يَقُولُوا۟ قَدْ أَخَذْنَآ أَمْرَنَا مِن قَبْلُ
وَيَتَوَلَّوا۟ وَّهُمْ فَرِحُونَ

50 If something good happens to you, it upsets them; and if a calamity befalls you, they say, “We took our precautions in advance,” and they depart, happy.

٥١ قُل لَّن يُصِيبَنَآ إِلَّا مَا كَتَبَ ٱللَّهُ لَنَا هُوَ
مَوْلَىٰنَا ۚ وَعَلَى ٱللَّهِ فَلْيَتَوَكَّلِ ٱلْمُؤْمِنُونَ

51 Say, “Nothing will happen to us except what Allah has ordained for us; He is our Protector.” In Allah let the faithful put their trust.

٥٢ قُلْ هَلْ تَرَبَّصُونَ بِنَآ إِلَّآ إِحْدَى ٱلْحُسْنَيَيْنِ ۖ
وَنَحْنُ نَتَرَبَّصُ بِكُمْ أَن يُصِيبَكُمُ ٱللَّهُ بِعَذَابٍ
مِّنْ عِندِهِۦٓ أَوْ بِأَيْدِينَا ۖ فَتَرَبَّصُوٓا۟ إِنَّا مَعَكُم
مُّتَرَبِّصُونَ

52 Say, “Are you expecting for us anything other than one of the two excellences? As for us: we are expecting that Allah will afflict you with a punishment from Himself, or at our hands. So wait, we are waiting with you.”

٥٣ قُلْ أَنفِقُوا۟ طَوْعًا أَوْ كَرْهًا لَّن يُتَقَبَّلَ مِنكُمْ ۖ
إِنَّكُمْ كُنتُمْ قَوْمًا فَٰسِقِينَ

53 Say, “Whether you spend willingly or unwillingly, it will not be accepted from you. You are evil people.”

٥٤ وَمَا مَنَعَهُمْ أَن تُقْبَلَ مِنْهُمْ نَفَقَٰتُهُمْ إِلَّآ أَنَّهُمْ
كَفَرُوا۟ بِٱللَّهِ وَبِرَسُولِهِۦ وَلَا يَأْتُونَ ٱلصَّلَوٰةَ إِلَّا
وَهُمْ كُسَالَىٰ وَلَا يُنفِقُونَ إِلَّا وَهُمْ كَٰرِهُونَ

54 What prevents the acceptance of their contributions is nothing but the fact that they disbelieved in Allah and His Messenger, and that they do not approach the prayer except lazily, and that they do not spend except grudgingly.

٥٥ فَلَا تُعْجِبْكَ أَمْوَٰلُهُمْ وَلَآ أَوْلَٰدُهُمْ ۚ إِنَّمَا يُرِيدُ
ٱللَّهُ لِيُعَذِّبَهُم بِهَا فِى ٱلْحَيَوٰةِ ٱلدُّنْيَا وَتَزْهَقَ
أَنفُسُهُمْ وَهُمْ كَٰفِرُونَ

55 Let neither their possessions nor their children impress you. Allah intends to torment them through them in this worldly life, and that their souls depart while they are disbelievers.

٥٦ وَيَحْلِفُونَ بِٱللَّهِ إِنَّهُمْ لَمِنكُمْ وَمَا هُم مِّنكُمْ
وَلَٰكِنَّهُمْ قَوْمٌ يَفْرَقُونَ

56 They swear by Allah that they are of you. But they are not of you. They are divisive people.

٥٧ لَوْ يَجِدُونَ مَلْجَـًٔا أَوْ مَغَٰرَٰتٍ أَوْ مُدَّخَلًا لَّوَلَّوْا۟
إِلَيْهِ وَهُمْ يَجْمَحُونَ

57 Were they to find a shelter, or a cave, or a hideout, they would go to it, rushing.

٥٨ وَمِنْهُم مَّن يَلْمِزُكَ فِى ٱلصَّدَقَٰتِ فَإِنْ أُعْطُوا۟
مِنْهَا رَضُوا۟ وَإِن لَّمْ يُعْطَوْا۟ مِنْهَآ إِذَا هُمْ
يَسْخَطُونَ

58 And among them are those who criticize you in regard to charities. If they are given some of it, they become pleased; but if they are not given any, they grow resentful.

٥٩ وَلَوْ أَنَّهُمْ رَضُوا۟ مَآ ءَاتَىٰهُمُ ٱللَّهُ وَرَسُولُهُۥ
وَقَالُوا۟ حَسْبُنَا ٱللَّهُ سَيُؤْتِينَا ٱللَّهُ مِن فَضْلِهِۦ
وَرَسُولُهُۥٓ إِنَّآ إِلَى ٱللَّهِ رَٰغِبُونَ

59 If only they were content with what Allah and His Messenger have given them, and said, “Allah is sufficient for us; Allah will give us of His bounty, and so will His Messenger; to Allah we eagerly turn.”

٦٠ إِنَّمَا ٱلصَّدَقَٰتُ لِلْفُقَرَآءِ وَٱلْمَسَٰكِينِ وَٱلْعَٰمِلِينَ
عَلَيْهَا وَٱلْمُؤَلَّفَةِ قُلُوبُهُمْ وَفِى ٱلرِّقَابِ
وَٱلْغَٰرِمِينَ وَفِى سَبِيلِ ٱللَّهِ وَٱبْنِ ٱلسَّبِيلِ ۖ
فَرِيضَةً مِّنَ ٱللَّهِ ۗ وَٱللَّهُ عَلِيمٌ حَكِيمٌ

60 Charities are for the poor, and the destitute, and those who administer them, and for reconciling hearts, and for freeing slaves, and for those in debt, and in the path of Allah, and for the traveler in need—an obligation from Allah. Allah is All-Knowing, Most Wise.

٦١ وَمِنْهُمُ ٱلَّذِينَ يُؤْذُونَ ٱلنَّبِىَّ وَيَقُولُونَ هُوَ
أُذُنٌ ۚ قُلْ أُذُنُ خَيْرٍ لَّكُمْ يُؤْمِنُ بِٱللَّهِ وَيُؤْمِنُ
لِلْمُؤْمِنِينَ وَرَحْمَةٌ لِّلَّذِينَ ءَامَنُوا۟ مِنكُمْ ۚ وَٱلَّذِينَ
يُؤْذُونَ رَسُولَ ٱللَّهِ لَهُمْ عَذَابٌ أَلِيمٌ

61 And among them are those who insult the Prophet, and say, “He is all ears.” Say, “He listens for your own good. He believes in Allah, and trusts the believers, and is mercy for those of you who believe.” Those who insult the Messenger of Allah will have a painful penalty.

٦٢ يَحْلِفُونَ بِٱللَّهِ لَكُمْ لِيُرْضُوكُمْ وَٱللَّهُ وَرَسُولُهُۥٓ
أَحَقُّ أَن يُرْضُوهُ إِن كَانُوا۟ مُؤْمِنِينَ

62 They swear to you by Allah to please you. But it is more proper for them to please Allah and His Messenger, if they are believers.

٦٣ أَلَمْ يَعْلَمُوٓا۟ أَنَّهُۥ مَن يُحَادِدِ ٱللَّهَ وَرَسُولَهُۥ فَأَنَّ
لَهُۥ نَارَ جَهَنَّمَ خَٰلِدًا فِيهَا ۚ ذَٰلِكَ ٱلْخِزْىُ ٱلْعَظِيمُ

63 Do they not know that whoever opposes Allah and His Messenger, will have the Fire of Hell, abiding in it forever? That is the supreme disgrace.

٦٤ يَحْذَرُ ٱلْمُنَٰفِقُونَ أَن تُنَزَّلَ عَلَيْهِمْ سُورَةٌ
تُنَبِّئُهُم بِمَا فِى قُلُوبِهِمْ ۚ قُلِ ٱسْتَهْزِءُوٓا۟ إِنَّ ٱللَّهَ
مُخْرِجٌ مَّا تَحْذَرُونَ

64 The hypocrites worry lest a chapter may be revealed about them, informing them of what is in their hearts. Say, “Go on mocking; Allah will bring out what you fear.”

٦٥ وَلَئِن سَأَلْتَهُمْ لَيَقُولُنَّ إِنَّمَا كُنَّا نَخُوضُ
وَنَلْعَبُ ۚ قُلْ أَبِٱللَّهِ وَءَايَٰتِهِۦ وَرَسُولِهِۦ كُنتُمْ
تَسْتَهْزِءُونَ

65 If you ask them, they will say, “We were just joking and playing.” Say, “Were you making jokes about Allah, His revelations, and His Messenger?”

٦٦ لَا تَعْتَذِرُوا۟ قَدْ كَفَرْتُم بَعْدَ إِيمَٰنِكُمْ ۚ إِن نَّعْفُ
عَن طَآئِفَةٍ مِّنكُمْ نُعَذِّبْ طَآئِفَةًۢ بِأَنَّهُمْ كَانُوا۟
مُجْرِمِينَ

66 Do not apologize. You have disbelieved after your belief. If We pardon some of you, We will punish others, because they are guilty.

٦٧ ٱلْمُنَٰفِقُونَ وَٱلْمُنَٰفِقَٰتُ بَعْضُهُم مِّنۢ بَعْضٍ ۚ
يَأْمُرُونَ بِٱلْمُنكَرِ وَيَنْهَوْنَ عَنِ ٱلْمَعْرُوفِ
وَيَقْبِضُونَ أَيْدِيَهُمْ ۚ نَسُوا۟ ٱللَّهَ فَنَسِيَهُمْ ۗ إِنَّ
ٱلْمُنَٰفِقِينَ هُمُ ٱلْفَٰسِقُونَ

67 The hypocrite men and hypocrite women are of one another. They advocate evil, and prohibit righteousness, and withhold their hands. They forgot Allah, so He forgot them. The hypocrites are the sinners.

٦٨ وَعَدَ ٱللَّهُ ٱلْمُنَٰفِقِينَ وَٱلْمُنَٰفِقَٰتِ وَٱلْكُفَّارَ نَارَ
جَهَنَّمَ خَٰلِدِينَ فِيهَا ۚ هِىَ حَسْبُهُمْ ۚ وَلَعَنَهُمُ ٱللَّهُ ۖ
وَلَهُمْ عَذَابٌ مُّقِيمٌ

68 Allah has promised the hypocrite men and hypocrite women, and the disbelievers, the Fire of Hell, abiding therein forever. It is their due. And Allah has cursed them. They will have a lasting punishment.

٦٩ كَٱلَّذِينَ مِن قَبْلِكُمْ كَانُوٓا۟ أَشَدَّ مِنكُمْ قُوَّةً
وَأَكْثَرَ أَمْوَٰلًا وَأَوْلَٰدًا فَٱسْتَمْتَعُوا۟ بِخَلَٰقِهِمْ
فَٱسْتَمْتَعْتُم بِخَلَٰقِكُمْ كَمَا ٱسْتَمْتَعَ ٱلَّذِينَ مِن
قَبْلِكُم بِخَلَٰقِهِمْ وَخُضْتُمْ كَٱلَّذِى خَاضُوٓا۟ ۚ أُو۟لَٰٓئِكَ
حَبِطَتْ أَعْمَٰلُهُمْ فِى ٱلدُّنْيَا وَٱلْءَاخِرَةِ ۖ وَأُو۟لَٰٓئِكَ
هُمُ ٱلْخَٰسِرُونَ

69 Like those before you. They were more powerful than you, and had more wealth and children. They enjoyed their share, and you enjoyed your share, as those before you enjoyed their share. And you indulged, as they indulged. It is they whose works will fail in this world and in the Hereafter. It is they who are the losers.

٧٠ أَلَمْ يَأْتِهِمْ نَبَأُ ٱلَّذِينَ مِن قَبْلِهِمْ قَوْمِ نُوحٍ
وَعَادٍ وَثَمُودَ وَقَوْمِ إِبْرَٰهِيمَ وَأَصْحَٰبِ مَدْيَنَ
وَٱلْمُؤْتَفِكَٰتِ ۚ أَتَتْهُمْ رُسُلُهُم بِٱلْبَيِّنَٰتِ ۖ فَمَا كَانَ
ٱللَّهُ لِيَظْلِمَهُمْ وَلَٰكِن كَانُوٓا۟ أَنفُسَهُمْ يَظْلِمُونَ

70 Have they not heard the stories of those before them? The people of Noah, and Aad, and Thamood; and the people of Abraham, and the inhabitants of Median, and the Overturned Cities? Their messengers came to them with the clear proofs. Allah never wronged them, but they used to wrong their own selves.

٧١ وَٱلْمُؤْمِنُونَ وَٱلْمُؤْمِنَٰتُ بَعْضُهُمْ أَوْلِيَآءُ
بَعْضٍ ۚ يَأْمُرُونَ بِٱلْمَعْرُوفِ وَيَنْهَوْنَ عَنِ ٱلْمُنكَرِ
وَيُقِيمُونَ ٱلصَّلَوٰةَ وَيُؤْتُونَ ٱلزَّكَوٰةَ وَيُطِيعُونَ

71 The believing men and believing women are friends of one another. They advocate virtue, forbid evil, perform the prayers, practice charity,

ٱللَّهَ وَرَسُولَهُۥٓۚ أُوْلَٰٓئِكَ سَيَرۡحَمُهُمُ ٱللَّهُۗ إِنَّ ٱللَّهَ
عَزِيزٌ حَكِيمٞ

and obey Allah and His Messenger. These—Allah will have mercy on them. Allah is Noble and Wise.

٧٢ وَعَدَ ٱللَّهُ ٱلۡمُؤۡمِنِينَ وَٱلۡمُؤۡمِنَٰتِ جَنَّٰتٖ تَجۡرِي
مِن تَحۡتِهَا ٱلۡأَنۡهَٰرُ خَٰلِدِينَ فِيهَا وَمَسَٰكِنَ طَيِّبَةٗ
فِي جَنَّٰتِ عَدۡنٖۚ وَرِضۡوَٰنٞ مِّنَ ٱللَّهِ أَكۡبَرُۚ ذَٰلِكَ
هُوَ ٱلۡفَوۡزُ ٱلۡعَظِيمُ

72 Allah promises the believers, men and women, gardens beneath which rivers flow, abiding therein forever, and fine homes in the Gardens of Eden. But approval from Allah is even greater. That is the supreme achievement.

٧٣ يَٰٓأَيُّهَا ٱلنَّبِيُّ جَٰهِدِ ٱلۡكُفَّارَ وَٱلۡمُنَٰفِقِينَ وَٱغۡلُظۡ
عَلَيۡهِمۡۚ وَمَأۡوَىٰهُمۡ جَهَنَّمُۖ وَبِئۡسَ ٱلۡمَصِيرُ

73 O Prophet! Strive against the disbelievers and the hypocrites, and be stern with them. Their abode is Hell—what a miserable destination!

٧٤ يَحۡلِفُونَ بِٱللَّهِ مَا قَالُواْ وَلَقَدۡ قَالُواْ كَلِمَةَ
ٱلۡكُفۡرِ وَكَفَرُواْ بَعۡدَ إِسۡلَٰمِهِمۡ وَهَمُّواْ بِمَا لَمۡ
يَنَالُواْۚ وَمَا نَقَمُوٓاْ إِلَّآ أَنۡ أَغۡنَىٰهُمُ ٱللَّهُ وَرَسُولُهُۥ
مِن فَضۡلِهِۦۚ فَإِن يَتُوبُواْ يَكُ خَيۡرٗا لَّهُمۡۖ وَإِن
يَتَوَلَّوۡاْ يُعَذِّبۡهُمُ ٱللَّهُ عَذَابًا أَلِيمٗا فِي ٱلدُّنۡيَا
وَٱلۡأٓخِرَةِۚ وَمَا لَهُمۡ فِي ٱلۡأَرۡضِ مِن وَلِيّٖ وَلَا
نَصِيرٖ

74 They swear by Allah that they said nothing; but they did utter the word of blasphemy, and they renounced faith after their submission. And they plotted what they could not attain. They were resentful only because Allah and His Messenger have enriched them out of His grace. If they repent, it would be best for them; but if they turn away, Allah will afflict them with a painful punishment—in this life and in the Hereafter—and they will have on earth no protector and no savior.

٧٥ وَمِنۡهُم مَّنۡ عَٰهَدَ ٱللَّهَ لَئِنۡ ءَاتَىٰنَا مِن فَضۡلِهِۦ
لَنَصَّدَّقَنَّ وَلَنَكُونَنَّ مِنَ ٱلصَّٰلِحِينَ

75 Among them are those who promised Allah: “If He gives us of His bounty, we will donate and be among the upright.”

٧٦ فَلَمَّآ ءَاتَىٰهُم مِّن فَضۡلِهِۦ بَخِلُواْ بِهِۦ وَتَوَلَّواْ
وَّهُم مُّعۡرِضُونَ

76 But when He has given them of His bounty, they became stingy with it, and turned away in aversion.

٧٧ فَأَعۡقَبَهُمۡ نِفَاقٗا فِي قُلُوبِهِمۡ إِلَىٰ يَوۡمِ يَلۡقَوۡنَهُۥ
بِمَآ أَخۡلَفُواْ ٱللَّهَ مَا وَعَدُوهُ وَبِمَا كَانُواْ يَكۡذِبُونَ

77 So He penalized them with hypocrisy in their hearts, until the Day they face Him—because they broke their promise to Allah, and because they used to lie.

٧٨ أَلَمْ يَعْلَمُوٓا۟ أَنَّ ٱللَّهَ يَعْلَمُ سِرَّهُمْ وَنَجْوَىٰهُمْ وَأَنَّ ٱللَّهَ عَلَّـٰمُ ٱلْغُيُوبِ

78 Do they not know that Allah knows their secrets and their conspiracies? And that Allah is the Knower of the unseen?

٧٩ ٱلَّذِينَ يَلْمِزُونَ ٱلْمُطَّوِّعِينَ مِنَ ٱلْمُؤْمِنِينَ فِى ٱلصَّدَقَـٰتِ وَٱلَّذِينَ لَا يَجِدُونَ إِلَّا جُهْدَهُمْ فَيَسْخَرُونَ مِنْهُمْ ۙ سَخِرَ ٱللَّهُ مِنْهُمْ وَلَهُمْ عَذَابٌ أَلِيمٌ

79 Those who criticize the believers who give charity voluntarily, and ridicule those who find nothing to give except their own efforts—Allah ridicules them. They will have a painful punishment.

٨٠ ٱسْتَغْفِرْ لَهُمْ أَوْ لَا تَسْتَغْفِرْ لَهُمْ إِن تَسْتَغْفِرْ لَهُمْ سَبْعِينَ مَرَّةً فَلَن يَغْفِرَ ٱللَّهُ لَهُمْ ۚ ذَٰلِكَ بِأَنَّهُمْ كَفَرُوا۟ بِٱللَّهِ وَرَسُولِهِۦ ۗ وَٱللَّهُ لَا يَهْدِى ٱلْقَوْمَ ٱلْفَـٰسِقِينَ

80 Whether you ask forgiveness for them, or do not ask forgiveness for them—even if you ask forgiveness for them seventy times, Allah will not forgive them. That is because they disbelieved in Allah and His Messenger. Allah does not guide the immoral people.

٨١ فَرِحَ ٱلْمُخَلَّفُونَ بِمَقْعَدِهِمْ خِلَـٰفَ رَسُولِ ٱللَّهِ وَكَرِهُوٓا۟ أَن يُجَـٰهِدُوا۟ بِأَمْوَٰلِهِمْ وَأَنفُسِهِمْ فِى سَبِيلِ ٱللَّهِ وَقَالُوا۟ لَا تَنفِرُوا۟ فِى ٱلْحَرِّ ۗ قُلْ نَارُ جَهَنَّمَ أَشَدُّ حَرًّا ۚ لَّوْ كَانُوا۟ يَفْقَهُونَ

81 Those who stayed behind rejoiced at their staying behind the Messenger of Allah. And they hated to strive with their wealth and their lives in Allah's way. And they said, "Do not venture out in the heat." Say, "The Fire of Hell is much hotter, if they only understood."

٨٢ فَلْيَضْحَكُوا۟ قَلِيلًا وَلْيَبْكُوا۟ كَثِيرًا جَزَآءًۢ بِمَا كَانُوا۟ يَكْسِبُونَ

82 Let them laugh a little, and weep much; in recompense for what they used to earn.

٨٣ فَإِن رَّجَعَكَ ٱللَّهُ إِلَىٰ طَآئِفَةٍ مِّنْهُمْ فَٱسْتَـْٔذَنُوكَ لِلْخُرُوجِ فَقُل لَّن تَخْرُجُوا۟ مَعِىَ أَبَدًا وَلَن تُقَـٰتِلُوا۟ مَعِىَ عَدُوًّا ۖ إِنَّكُمْ رَضِيتُم بِٱلْقُعُودِ أَوَّلَ مَرَّةٍ فَٱقْعُدُوا۟ مَعَ ٱلْخَـٰلِفِينَ

83 If Allah brings you back to a party of them, and they ask your permission to go out, say, "You will not go out with me, ever, nor will you ever fight an enemy with me. You were content to sit back the first time, so sit back with those who stay behind."

٨٤ وَلَا تُصَلِّ عَلَىٰٓ أَحَدٍ مِّنْهُم مَّاتَ أَبَدًا وَلَا تَقُمْ عَلَىٰ قَبْرِهِۦٓ ۖ إِنَّهُمْ كَفَرُوا۟ بِٱللَّهِ وَرَسُولِهِۦ وَمَاتُوا۟ وَهُمْ فَـٰسِقُونَ

84 You are never to pray over anyone of them who dies, nor are you to stand at his graveside. They rejected

Allah and His Messenger, and died while they were sinners.

٨٥ وَلَا تُعۡجِبۡكَ أَمۡوَٰلُهُمۡ وَأَوۡلَٰدُهُمۡۚ إِنَّمَا يُرِيدُ
ٱللَّهُ أَن يُعَذِّبَهُم بِهَا فِى ٱلدُّنۡيَا وَتَزۡهَقَ أَنفُسُهُمۡ
وَهُمۡ كَٰفِرُونَ

85 Do not let their possessions and their children impress you. Allah desires to torment them through them in this world, and their souls expire while they are disbelievers.

٨٦ وَإِذَآ أُنزِلَتۡ سُورَةٌ أَنۡ ءَامِنُواْ بِٱللَّهِ وَجَٰهِدُواْ
مَعَ رَسُولِهِ ٱسۡتَـٔۡذَنَكَ أُوْلُواْ ٱلطَّوۡلِ مِنۡهُمۡ وَقَالُواْ
ذَرۡنَا نَكُن مَّعَ ٱلۡقَٰعِدِينَ

86 When a chapter is revealed, stating: "Believe in Allah and strive with His Messenger," the prominent among them ask you for exemption. They say, "Allow us to stay with those who stay behind."

٨٧ رَضُواْ بِأَن يَكُونُواْ مَعَ ٱلۡخَوَالِفِ وَطُبِعَ عَلَىٰ
قُلُوبِهِمۡ فَهُمۡ لَا يَفۡقَهُونَ

87 They prefer to be with those who stay behind. Their hearts were sealed, so they do not understand.

٨٨ لَٰكِنِ ٱلرَّسُولُ وَٱلَّذِينَ ءَامَنُواْ مَعَهُۥ جَٰهَدُواْ
بِأَمۡوَٰلِهِمۡ وَأَنفُسِهِمۡۚ وَأُوْلَٰٓئِكَ لَهُمُ ٱلۡخَيۡرَٰتُۖ
وَأُوْلَٰٓئِكَ هُمُ ٱلۡمُفۡلِحُونَ

88 But the Messenger and those who believe with him struggle with their possessions and their lives. These have deserved the good things. These are the successful.

٨٩ أَعَدَّ ٱللَّهُ لَهُمۡ جَنَّٰتٍ تَجۡرِى مِن تَحۡتِهَا ٱلۡأَنۡهَٰرُ
خَٰلِدِينَ فِيهَاۚ ذَٰلِكَ ٱلۡفَوۡزُ ٱلۡعَظِيمُ

89 Allah has prepared for them gardens beneath which rivers flow, wherein they will abide forever. That is the great victory.

٩٠ وَجَآءَ ٱلۡمُعَذِّرُونَ مِنَ ٱلۡأَعۡرَابِ لِيُؤۡذَنَ لَهُمۡ
وَقَعَدَ ٱلَّذِينَ كَذَبُواْ ٱللَّهَ وَرَسُولَهُۥۚ سَيُصِيبُ
ٱلَّذِينَ كَفَرُواْ مِنۡهُمۡ عَذَابٌ أَلِيمٌ

90 Some of the Desert-Arabs came to make excuses, asking to be granted exemption, while those who were untrue to Allah and His Messenger stayed behind. A painful punishment will afflict those among them who disbelieved.

٩١ لَّيۡسَ عَلَى ٱلضُّعَفَآءِ وَلَا عَلَى ٱلۡمَرۡضَىٰ وَلَا
عَلَى ٱلَّذِينَ لَا يَجِدُونَ مَا يُنفِقُونَ حَرَجٌ إِذَا
نَصَحُواْ لِلَّهِ وَرَسُولِهِۦۚ مَا عَلَى ٱلۡمُحۡسِنِينَ مِن
سَبِيلٍۚ وَٱللَّهُ غَفُورٌ رَّحِيمٌ

91 There is no blame on the weak, nor on the sick, nor on those who have nothing to give, provided they are true to Allah and His Messenger. In no way can the righteous be blamed. Allah is Forgiving and Merciful.

٩٢ وَلَا عَلَى ٱلَّذِينَ إِذَا مَآ أَتَوۡكَ لِتَحۡمِلَهُمۡ قُلۡتَ
لَآ أَجِدُ مَآ أَحۡمِلُكُمۡ عَلَيۡهِ تَوَلَّواْ وَّأَعۡيُنُهُمۡ تَفِيضُ
مِنَ ٱلدَّمۡعِ حَزَنًا أَلَّا يَجِدُواْ مَا يُنفِقُونَ

92 Nor on those who approach you, wishing to ride with you, and you said, "I have nothing to carry you on." So they went away, with their eyes overflowing with tears, sorrowing for not finding the means to spend.

٩٣ إِنَّمَا ٱلسَّبِيلُ عَلَى ٱلَّذِينَ يَسۡتَـٔۡذِنُونَكَ وَهُمۡ
أَغۡنِيَآءُۚ رَضُواْ بِأَن يَكُونُواْ مَعَ ٱلۡخَوَالِفِ وَطَبَعَ
ٱللَّهُ عَلَىٰ قُلُوبِهِمۡ فَهُمۡ لَا يَعۡلَمُونَ

93 But blame is on those who ask you for exemption, although they are rich. They are content to be with those who stay behind. Allah has sealed their hearts, so they do not know.

٩٤ يَعۡتَذِرُونَ إِلَيۡكُمۡ إِذَا رَجَعۡتُمۡ إِلَيۡهِمۡۚ قُل لَّا
تَعۡتَذِرُواْ لَن نُّؤۡمِنَ لَكُمۡ قَدۡ نَبَّأَنَا ٱللَّهُ مِنۡ
أَخۡبَارِكُمۡۚ وَسَيَرَى ٱللَّهُ عَمَلَكُمۡ وَرَسُولُهُۥ ثُمَّ
تُرَدُّونَ إِلَىٰ عَٰلِمِ ٱلۡغَيۡبِ وَٱلشَّهَٰدَةِ فَيُنَبِّئُكُم بِمَا
كُنتُمۡ تَعۡمَلُونَ

94 They present excuses to you when you return to them. Say, "Do not offer excuses; we do not trust you; Allah has informed us of you. And Allah will watch your actions, and so will the Messenger; then you will be returned to the Knower of the Invisible and the Visible, and He will inform you of what you used to do."

٩٥ سَيَحۡلِفُونَ بِٱللَّهِ لَكُمۡ إِذَا ٱنقَلَبۡتُمۡ إِلَيۡهِمۡ
لِتُعۡرِضُواْ عَنۡهُمۡۖ فَأَعۡرِضُواْ عَنۡهُمۡۖ إِنَّهُمۡ رِجۡسٌۖ
وَمَأۡوَىٰهُمۡ جَهَنَّمُ جَزَآءَۢ بِمَا كَانُواْ يَكۡسِبُونَ

95 They will swear to you by Allah, when you return to them, that you may leave them alone. So leave them alone. They are a disgrace, and their destiny is Hell; a reward for what they used to earn.

٩٦ يَحۡلِفُونَ لَكُمۡ لِتَرۡضَوۡاْ عَنۡهُمۡۖ فَإِن تَرۡضَوۡاْ
عَنۡهُمۡ فَإِنَّ ٱللَّهَ لَا يَرۡضَىٰ عَنِ ٱلۡقَوۡمِ ٱلۡفَٰسِقِينَ

96 They will swear to you that you may accept them. But even if you accept them, Allah does not accept the wicked people.

٩٧ ٱلۡأَعۡرَابُ أَشَدُّ كُفۡرٗا وَنِفَاقٗا وَأَجۡدَرُ أَلَّا يَعۡلَمُواْ
حُدُودَ مَآ أَنزَلَ ٱللَّهُ عَلَىٰ رَسُولِهِۦۗ وَٱللَّهُ عَلِيمٌ
حَكِيمٞ

97 The Desert-Arabs are the most steeped in disbelief and hypocrisy, and the most likely to ignore the limits that Allah revealed to His Messenger. Allah is Knowing and Wise.

٩٨ وَمِنَ ٱلْأَعْرَابِ مَن يَتَّخِذُ مَا يُنفِقُ مَغْرَمًا
وَيَتَرَبَّصُ بِكُمُ ٱلدَّوَآئِرَ ۚ عَلَيْهِمْ دَآئِرَةُ ٱلسَّوْءِ ۗ
وَٱللَّهُ سَمِيعٌ عَلِيمٌ

98 And among the Desert-Arabs are those who consider their contribution to be a fine. And they wait for a reversal of your fortunes. Upon them will fall the cycle of misfortune. Allah is Hearing and Knowing.

٩٩ وَمِنَ ٱلْأَعْرَابِ مَن يُؤْمِنُ بِٱللَّهِ وَٱلْيَوْمِ
ٱلْءَاخِرِ وَيَتَّخِذُ مَا يُنفِقُ قُرُبَٰتٍ عِندَ ٱللَّهِ
وَصَلَوَٰتِ ٱلرَّسُولِ ۚ أَلَآ إِنَّهَا قُرْبَةٌ لَّهُمْ ۚ
سَيُدْخِلُهُمُ ٱللَّهُ فِى رَحْمَتِهِۦٓ ۗ إِنَّ ٱللَّهَ غَفُورٌ
رَّحِيمٌ

99 Yet among the Desert-Arabs are those who believe in Allah and the Last Day, and consider their contribution to be a means towards Allah, and the prayers of the Messenger. Surely it will draw them closer, and Allah will admit them into His mercy. Allah is Forgiving and Compassionate.

١٠٠ وَٱلسَّٰبِقُونَ ٱلْأَوَّلُونَ مِنَ ٱلْمُهَٰجِرِينَ وَٱلْأَنصَارِ
وَٱلَّذِينَ ٱتَّبَعُوهُم بِإِحْسَٰنٍ رَّضِىَ ٱللَّهُ عَنْهُمْ
وَرَضُوا۟ عَنْهُ وَأَعَدَّ لَهُمْ جَنَّٰتٍ تَجْرِى تَحْتَهَا
ٱلْأَنْهَٰرُ خَٰلِدِينَ فِيهَآ أَبَدًا ۚ ذَٰلِكَ ٱلْفَوْزُ ٱلْعَظِيمُ

100 The Pioneers—The first of the Migrants and the Supporters, and those who followed them in righteousness. Allah is pleased with them, and they are pleased with Him. He has prepared for them Gardens beneath which rivers flow, where they will abide forever. That is the sublime triumph.

١٠١ وَمِمَّنْ حَوْلَكُم مِّنَ ٱلْأَعْرَابِ مُنَٰفِقُونَ ۖ وَمِنْ
أَهْلِ ٱلْمَدِينَةِ ۖ مَرَدُوا۟ عَلَى ٱلنِّفَاقِ لَا تَعْلَمُهُمْ ۖ
نَحْنُ نَعْلَمُهُمْ ۚ سَنُعَذِّبُهُم مَّرَّتَيْنِ ثُمَّ يُرَدُّونَ إِلَىٰ
عَذَابٍ عَظِيمٍ

101 Among the Desert-Arabs around you there are some hypocrites, and among the inhabitants of Medina too. They have become adamant in hypocrisy. You do not know them, but We know them. We will punish them twice; then they will be returned to a severe torment.

١٠٢ وَءَاخَرُونَ ٱعْتَرَفُوا۟ بِذُنُوبِهِمْ خَلَطُوا۟ عَمَلًا
صَٰلِحًا وَءَاخَرَ سَيِّئًا عَسَى ٱللَّهُ أَن يَتُوبَ
عَلَيْهِمْ ۚ إِنَّ ٱللَّهَ غَفُورٌ رَّحِيمٌ

102 Others have confessed their sins, having mixed good deeds with bad deeds. Perhaps Allah will redeem them. Allah is Forgiving and Merciful.

١٠٣ خُذْ مِنْ أَمْوَٰلِهِمْ صَدَقَةً تُطَهِّرُهُمْ وَتُزَكِّيهِم
بِهَا وَصَلِّ عَلَيْهِمْ ۖ إِنَّ صَلَوٰتَكَ سَكَنٌ لَّهُمْ ۗ وَٱللَّهُ
سَمِيعٌ عَلِيمٌ

103 Receive contributions from their wealth, to purify them and sanctify them with it; and pray for them. Your prayer is comfort for them. Allah is Hearing and Knowing.

١٠٤ أَلَمْ يَعْلَمُوٓا۟ أَنَّ ٱللَّهَ هُوَ يَقْبَلُ ٱلتَّوْبَةَ عَنْ
عِبَادِهِۦ وَيَأْخُذُ ٱلصَّدَقَـٰتِ وَأَنَّ ٱللَّهَ هُوَ ٱلتَّوَّابُ
ٱلرَّحِيمُ

104 Do they not know that Allah accepts the repentance of His servants, and that He receives the contributions, and that Allah is the Acceptor of Repentance, the Merciful?

١٠٥ وَقُلِ ٱعْمَلُوا۟ فَسَيَرَى ٱللَّهُ عَمَلَكُمْ وَرَسُولُهُۥ
وَٱلْمُؤْمِنُونَ ۖ وَسَتُرَدُّونَ إِلَىٰ عَـٰلِمِ ٱلْغَيْبِ
وَٱلشَّهَـٰدَةِ فَيُنَبِّئُكُم بِمَا كُنتُمْ تَعْمَلُونَ

105 Say, “Work. Allah will see your work, and so will His Messenger, and the believers. Then you will be returned to the Knower of secrets and declarations, and He will inform you of what you used to do.”

١٠٦ وَءَاخَرُونَ مُرْجَوْنَ لِأَمْرِ ٱللَّهِ إِمَّا يُعَذِّبُهُمْ
وَإِمَّا يَتُوبُ عَلَيْهِمْ ۗ وَٱللَّهُ عَلِيمٌ حَكِيمٌ

106 Others are held in suspense, awaiting Allah’s decree, as to whether He will punish them, or accept their repentance. Allah is Aware and Wise.

١٠٧ وَٱلَّذِينَ ٱتَّخَذُوا۟ مَسْجِدًا ضِرَارًا وَكُفْرًا
وَتَفْرِيقًۢا بَيْنَ ٱلْمُؤْمِنِينَ وَإِرْصَادًا لِّمَنْ حَارَبَ
ٱللَّهَ وَرَسُولَهُۥ مِن قَبْلُ ۚ وَلَيَحْلِفُنَّ إِنْ أَرَدْنَآ إِلَّا
ٱلْحُسْنَىٰ ۖ وَٱللَّهُ يَشْهَدُ إِنَّهُمْ لَكَـٰذِبُونَ

107 Then there are those who establish a mosque to cause harm, and disbelief, and disunity among the believers, and as an outpost for those who fight Allah and His Messenger. They will swear: “Our intentions are nothing but good.” But Allah bears witness that they are liars.

١٠٨ لَا تَقُمْ فِيهِ أَبَدًا ۚ لَّمَسْجِدٌ أُسِّسَ عَلَى
ٱلتَّقْوَىٰ مِنْ أَوَّلِ يَوْمٍ أَحَقُّ أَن تَقُومَ فِيهِ ۚ فِيهِ
رِجَالٌ يُحِبُّونَ أَن يَتَطَهَّرُوا۟ ۚ وَٱللَّهُ يُحِبُّ
ٱلْمُطَّهِّرِينَ

108 Do not stand in it, ever. A mosque founded upon piety from the first day is worthier of your standing in it. In it are men who love to be purified. Allah loves those who purify themselves.

١٠٩ أَفَمَنْ أَسَّسَ بُنْيَـٰنَهُۥ عَلَىٰ تَقْوَىٰ مِنَ ٱللَّهِ
وَرِضْوَٰنٍ خَيْرٌ أَم مَّنْ أَسَّسَ بُنْيَـٰنَهُۥ عَلَىٰ شَفَا
جُرُفٍ هَارٍ فَٱنْهَارَ بِهِۦ فِى نَارِ جَهَنَّمَ ۗ وَٱللَّهُ لَا
يَهْدِى ٱلْقَوْمَ ٱلظَّـٰلِمِينَ

109 Is he who founds his structure upon piety and acceptance from Allah better, or he who founds his structure on the brink of a cliff that is about to tumble, so it tumbles with him into the Fire of Hell? Allah does not guide the unjust people.

١١٠ لَا يَزَالُ بُنْيَٰنُهُمُ ٱلَّذِى بَنَوْا۟ رِيبَةً فِى قُلُوبِهِمْ
إِلَّآ أَن تَقَطَّعَ قُلُوبُهُمْ ۗ وَٱللَّهُ عَلِيمٌ حَكِيمٌ

110 The structure which they built will remain questionable in their hearts, until their hearts are stopped. Allah is Knowing and Wise.

١١١ إِنَّ ٱللَّهَ ٱشْتَرَىٰ مِنَ ٱلْمُؤْمِنِينَ أَنفُسَهُمْ
وَأَمْوَٰلَهُم بِأَنَّ لَهُمُ ٱلْجَنَّةَ ۚ يُقَٰتِلُونَ فِى سَبِيلِ
ٱللَّهِ فَيَقْتُلُونَ وَيُقْتَلُونَ ۖ وَعْدًا عَلَيْهِ حَقًّا فِى
ٱلتَّوْرَىٰةِ وَٱلْإِنجِيلِ وَٱلْقُرْءَانِ ۚ وَمَنْ أَوْفَىٰ
بِعَهْدِهِۦ مِنَ ٱللَّهِ ۚ فَٱسْتَبْشِرُوا۟ بِبَيْعِكُمُ ٱلَّذِى
بَايَعْتُم بِهِۦ ۚ وَذَٰلِكَ هُوَ ٱلْفَوْزُ ٱلْعَظِيمُ

111 Allah has purchased from the believers their lives and their properties in exchange for Paradise. They fight in Allah's way, and they kill and get killed. It is a promise binding on Him in the Torah, and the Gospel, and the Quran. And who is more true to his promise than Allah? So rejoice in making such an exchange—that is the supreme triumph.

١١٢ ٱلتَّٰٓئِبُونَ ٱلْعَٰبِدُونَ ٱلْحَٰمِدُونَ ٱلسَّٰٓئِحُونَ
ٱلرَّٰكِعُونَ ٱلسَّٰجِدُونَ ٱلْءَامِرُونَ بِٱلْمَعْرُوفِ
وَٱلنَّاهُونَ عَنِ ٱلْمُنكَرِ وَٱلْحَٰفِظُونَ لِحُدُودِ ٱللَّهِ ۗ
وَبَشِّرِ ٱلْمُؤْمِنِينَ

112 Those who repent, those who worship, those who praise, those who journey, those who kneel, those who bow down, those who advocate righteousness and forbid evil, and those who keep Allah's limits—give good news to the believers.

١١٣ مَا كَانَ لِلنَّبِىِّ وَٱلَّذِينَ ءَامَنُوٓا۟ أَن يَسْتَغْفِرُوا۟
لِلْمُشْرِكِينَ وَلَوْ كَانُوٓا۟ أُو۟لِى قُرْبَىٰ مِنۢ بَعْدِ مَا
تَبَيَّنَ لَهُمْ أَنَّهُمْ أَصْحَٰبُ ٱلْجَحِيمِ

113 It is not for the Prophet and those who believe to ask forgiveness for the polytheists, even if they are near relatives, after it has become clear to them that they are people of Hellfire.

١١٤ وَمَا كَانَ ٱسْتِغْفَارُ إِبْرَٰهِيمَ لِأَبِيهِ إِلَّا عَن
مَّوْعِدَةٍ وَعَدَهَآ إِيَّاهُ فَلَمَّا تَبَيَّنَ لَهُۥٓ أَنَّهُۥ عَدُوٌّ لِّلَّهِ
تَبَرَّأَ مِنْهُ ۚ إِنَّ إِبْرَٰهِيمَ لَأَوَّٰهٌ حَلِيمٌ

114 Abraham asked forgiveness for his father only because of a promise he had made to him. But when it became clear to him that he was an enemy of Allah, he disowned him. Abraham was kind and clement.

١١٥ وَمَا كَانَ ٱللَّهُ لِيُضِلَّ قَوْمًۢا بَعْدَ إِذْ هَدَىٰهُمْ
حَتَّىٰ يُبَيِّنَ لَهُم مَّا يَتَّقُونَ ۚ إِنَّ ٱللَّهَ بِكُلِّ شَىْءٍ
عَلِيمٌ

115 Allah would never lead a people astray, after He had guided them, until He makes clear to them what they should guard against. Allah has knowledge of all things.

١١٦ إِنَّ ٱللَّهَ لَهُۥ مُلْكُ ٱلسَّمَٰوَٰتِ وَٱلْأَرْضِ ۖ يُحْىِۦ
وَيُمِيتُ ۚ وَمَا لَكُم مِّن دُونِ ٱللَّهِ مِن وَلِىٍّ وَلَا
نَصِيرٍ

116 To Allah belongs the dominion of the heavens and the earth. He gives life, and He causes death. And besides Allah, you have neither protector, nor supporter.

١١٧ لَّقَد تَّابَ ٱللَّهُ عَلَى ٱلنَّبِىِّ وَٱلْمُهَٰجِرِينَ
وَٱلْأَنصَارِ ٱلَّذِينَ ٱتَّبَعُوهُ فِى سَاعَةِ ٱلْعُسْرَةِ مِنۢ
بَعْدِ مَا كَادَ يَزِيغُ قُلُوبُ فَرِيقٍ مِّنْهُمْ ثُمَّ تَابَ
عَلَيْهِمْ ۚ إِنَّهُۥ بِهِمْ رَءُوفٌ رَّحِيمٌ

117 Allah has redeemed the Prophet, and the Emigrants, and the Supporters—those who followed him in the hour of difficulty—after the hearts of some of them almost swerved. Then He pardoned them. He is Kind towards them, Compassionate.

١١٨ وَعَلَى ٱلثَّلَٰثَةِ ٱلَّذِينَ خُلِّفُوا۟ حَتَّىٰٓ إِذَا
ضَاقَتْ عَلَيْهِمُ ٱلْأَرْضُ بِمَا رَحُبَتْ وَضَاقَتْ
عَلَيْهِمْ أَنفُسُهُمْ وَظَنُّوٓا۟ أَن لَّا مَلْجَأَ مِنَ ٱللَّهِ إِلَّآ
إِلَيْهِ ثُمَّ تَابَ عَلَيْهِمْ لِيَتُوبُوٓا۟ ۚ إِنَّ ٱللَّهَ هُوَ
ٱلتَّوَّابُ ٱلرَّحِيمُ

118 Also towards the three who were left behind. Then, when the earth, as vast as it is, closed in on them, and their very souls closed in on them, and they realized that there was no refuge from Allah, except in Him, He redeemed them, so that they may repent. Allah is the Redeemer, the Merciful.

١١٩ يَٰٓأَيُّهَا ٱلَّذِينَ ءَامَنُوا۟ ٱتَّقُوا۟ ٱللَّهَ وَكُونُوا۟ مَعَ
ٱلصَّٰدِقِينَ

119 O you who believe! Be conscious of Allah, and be with the sincere.

١٢٠ مَا كَانَ لِأَهْلِ ٱلْمَدِينَةِ وَمَنْ حَوْلَهُم مِّنَ
ٱلْأَعْرَابِ أَن يَتَخَلَّفُوا۟ عَن رَّسُولِ ٱللَّهِ وَلَا
يَرْغَبُوا۟ بِأَنفُسِهِمْ عَن نَّفْسِهِۦ ۚ ذَٰلِكَ بِأَنَّهُمْ لَا
يُصِيبُهُمْ ظَمَأٌ وَلَا نَصَبٌ وَلَا مَخْمَصَةٌ فِى
سَبِيلِ ٱللَّهِ وَلَا يَطَـُٔونَ مَوْطِئًا يَغِيظُ ٱلْكُفَّارَ وَلَا
يَنَالُونَ مِنْ عَدُوٍّ نَّيْلًا إِلَّا كُتِبَ لَهُم بِهِۦ عَمَلٌ
صَٰلِحٌ ۚ إِنَّ ٱللَّهَ لَا يُضِيعُ أَجْرَ ٱلْمُحْسِنِينَ

120 It is not for the inhabitants of Medina and the Desert-Arabs around them to stay behind the Messenger of Allah, nor to prefer themselves to him. That is because they never suffer any thirst, nor fatigue, nor hunger in the cause of Allah, nor do they take one step that enrages the disbelievers, nor do they gain anything from an enemy, but it is recorded to their credit as a righteous deed. Allah does not waste the reward of the righteous.

١٢١ وَلَا يُنفِقُونَ نَفَقَةً صَغِيرَةً وَلَا كَبِيرَةً وَلَا يَقْطَعُونَ وَادِيًا إِلَّا كُتِبَ لَهُمْ لِيَجْزِيَهُمُ ٱللَّهُ أَحْسَنَ مَا كَانُوا۟ يَعْمَلُونَ	121 Nor do they spend any expenditure, small or large, nor do they cross any valley, but it is recorded to their credit. That Allah may reward them in accordance with the best of their deeds.
١٢٢ وَمَا كَانَ ٱلْمُؤْمِنُونَ لِيَنفِرُوا۟ كَآفَّةً ۚ فَلَوْلَا نَفَرَ مِن كُلِّ فِرْقَةٍ مِّنْهُمْ طَآئِفَةٌ لِّيَتَفَقَّهُوا۟ فِى ٱلدِّينِ وَلِيُنذِرُوا۟ قَوْمَهُمْ إِذَا رَجَعُوٓا۟ إِلَيْهِمْ لَعَلَّهُمْ يَحْذَرُونَ	122 It is not advisable for the believers to march out altogether. Of every division that marches out, let a group remain behind, to gain understanding of the religion, and to notify their people when they have returned to them, that they may beware.
١٢٣ يَٰٓأَيُّهَا ٱلَّذِينَ ءَامَنُوا۟ قَٰتِلُوا۟ ٱلَّذِينَ يَلُونَكُم مِّنَ ٱلْكُفَّارِ وَلْيَجِدُوا۟ فِيكُمْ غِلْظَةً ۚ وَٱعْلَمُوٓا۟ أَنَّ ٱللَّهَ مَعَ ٱلْمُتَّقِينَ	123 O you who believe! Fight those of the disbelievers who attack you, and let them find severity in you, and know that Allah is with the righteous.
١٢٤ وَإِذَا مَآ أُنزِلَتْ سُورَةٌ فَمِنْهُم مَّن يَقُولُ أَيُّكُمْ زَادَتْهُ هَٰذِهِۦٓ إِيمَٰنًا ۚ فَأَمَّا ٱلَّذِينَ ءَامَنُوا۟ فَزَادَتْهُمْ إِيمَٰنًا وَهُمْ يَسْتَبْشِرُونَ	124 Whenever a chapter is revealed, some of them say, "Which of you has this increased in faith?" As for those who believe: it increases them in faith, and they rejoice.
١٢٥ وَأَمَّا ٱلَّذِينَ فِى قُلُوبِهِم مَّرَضٌ فَزَادَتْهُمْ رِجْسًا إِلَىٰ رِجْسِهِمْ وَمَاتُوا۟ وَهُمْ كَٰفِرُونَ	125 But as for those in whose hearts is sickness: it adds disgrace to their disgrace, and they die as unbelievers.
١٢٦ أَوَلَا يَرَوْنَ أَنَّهُمْ يُفْتَنُونَ فِى كُلِّ عَامٍ مَّرَّةً أَوْ مَرَّتَيْنِ ثُمَّ لَا يَتُوبُونَ وَلَا هُمْ يَذَّكَّرُونَ	126 Do they not see that they are tested once or twice every year? Yet they do not repent, and they do not learn.
١٢٧ وَإِذَا مَآ أُنزِلَتْ سُورَةٌ نَّظَرَ بَعْضُهُمْ إِلَىٰ بَعْضٍ هَلْ يَرَىٰكُم مِّنْ أَحَدٍ ثُمَّ ٱنصَرَفُوا۟ ۚ صَرَفَ ٱللَّهُ قُلُوبَهُم بِأَنَّهُمْ قَوْمٌ لَّا يَفْقَهُونَ	127 And whenever a chapter is revealed, they look at one another, "Does anyone see you?" Then they slip away. Allah has diverted their hearts, because they are a people who do not understand.

١٢٨ لَقَدْ جَآءَكُمْ رَسُولٌ مِّنْ أَنفُسِكُمْ عَزِيزٌ عَلَيْهِ
مَا عَنِتُّمْ حَرِيصٌ عَلَيْكُم بِٱلْمُؤْمِنِينَ رَءُوفٌ
رَّحِيمٌ

128 There has come to you a messenger from among yourselves, concerned over your suffering, anxious over you. Towards the believers, he is compassionate and merciful.

١٢٩ فَإِن تَوَلَّوْا۟ فَقُلْ حَسْبِىَ ٱللَّهُ لَآ إِلَٰهَ إِلَّا هُوَ ۖ
عَلَيْهِ تَوَكَّلْتُ ۖ وَهُوَ رَبُّ ٱلْعَرْشِ ٱلْعَظِيمِ

129 If they turn away, say, “Allah is enough for me; there is no god except He; in Him I have put my trust; He is the Lord of the Sublime Throne.”

10 Jonah يونس

بِسْمِ ٱللَّهِ ٱلرَّحْمَٰنِ ٱلرَّحِيمِ

In the name of Allah, the Gracious, the Merciful.

١ الٓر ۚ تِلْكَ ءَايَٰتُ ٱلْكِتَٰبِ ٱلْحَكِيمِ

1 Alif, Lam, Ra. These are the Verses of the Wise Book.

٢ أَكَانَ لِلنَّاسِ عَجَبًا أَنْ أَوْحَيْنَآ إِلَىٰ رَجُلٍ مِّنْهُمْ
أَنْ أَنذِرِ ٱلنَّاسَ وَبَشِّرِ ٱلَّذِينَ ءَامَنُوٓا۟ أَنَّ لَهُمْ
قَدَمَ صِدْقٍ عِندَ رَبِّهِمْ ۗ قَالَ ٱلْكَٰفِرُونَ إِنَّ هَٰذَا
لَسَٰحِرٌ مُّبِينٌ

2 Is it a wonder to the people that We inspired a man from among them: “Warn mankind, and give good news to those who believe that they are on a sound footing with their Lord”? The disbelievers said, “This is a manifest sorcerer.”

٣ إِنَّ رَبَّكُمُ ٱللَّهُ ٱلَّذِى خَلَقَ ٱلسَّمَٰوَٰتِ وَٱلْأَرْضَ
فِى سِتَّةِ أَيَّامٍ ثُمَّ ٱسْتَوَىٰ عَلَى ٱلْعَرْشِ ۖ يُدَبِّرُ
ٱلْأَمْرَ ۖ مَا مِن شَفِيعٍ إِلَّا مِنۢ بَعْدِ إِذْنِهِۦ ۚ ذَٰلِكُمُ
ٱللَّهُ رَبُّكُمْ فَٱعْبُدُوهُ ۚ أَفَلَا تَذَكَّرُونَ

3 Your Lord is Allah, who created the heavens and the earth in six days, then settled over the Throne, governing all things. There is no intercessor except after His permission. Such is Allah, your Lord—so serve Him. Will you not reflect?

٤ إِلَيْهِ مَرْجِعُكُمْ جَمِيعًا ۖ وَعْدَ ٱللَّهِ حَقًّا ۚ إِنَّهُۥ
يَبْدَؤُا۟ ٱلْخَلْقَ ثُمَّ يُعِيدُهُۥ لِيَجْزِىَ ٱلَّذِينَ ءَامَنُوا۟
وَعَمِلُوا۟ ٱلصَّٰلِحَٰتِ بِٱلْقِسْطِ ۚ وَٱلَّذِينَ كَفَرُوا۟ لَهُمْ
شَرَابٌ مِّنْ حَمِيمٍ وَعَذَابٌ أَلِيمٌۢ بِمَا كَانُوا۟
يَكْفُرُونَ

4 To Him is your return, altogether. The promise of Allah is true. He originates creation, and then He repeats it, to reward those who believe and do good deeds with equity. As for those who disbelieve, for them is a drink of boiling water,

and agonizing torment, on account of their disbelief.

٥ هُوَ ٱلَّذِى جَعَلَ ٱلشَّمْسَ ضِيَآءً وَٱلْقَمَرَ نُورًا
وَقَدَّرَهُۥ مَنَازِلَ لِتَعْلَمُوا۟ عَدَدَ ٱلسِّنِينَ وَٱلْحِسَابَ ۚ
مَا خَلَقَ ٱللَّهُ ذَٰلِكَ إِلَّا بِٱلْحَقِّ ۚ يُفَصِّلُ ٱلْـَٔايَٰتِ
لِقَوْمٍ يَعْلَمُونَ

5 It is He who made the sun radiant, and the moon a light, and determined phases for it—that you may know the number of years and the calculation. Allah did not create all this except with truth. He details the revelations for a people who know.

٦ إِنَّ فِى ٱخْتِلَٰفِ ٱلَّيْلِ وَٱلنَّهَارِ وَمَا خَلَقَ ٱللَّهُ
فِى ٱلسَّمَٰوَٰتِ وَٱلْأَرْضِ لَـَٔايَٰتٍ لِّقَوْمٍ يَتَّقُونَ

6 In the alternation of night and day, and in what Allah created in the heavens and the earth, are signs for people who are aware.

٧ إِنَّ ٱلَّذِينَ لَا يَرْجُونَ لِقَآءَنَا وَرَضُوا۟ بِٱلْحَيَوٰةِ
ٱلدُّنْيَا وَٱطْمَأَنُّوا۟ بِهَا وَٱلَّذِينَ هُمْ عَنْ ءَايَٰتِنَا
غَٰفِلُونَ

7 Those who do not hope to meet Us, and are content with the worldly life, and are at ease in it, and those who pay no heed to Our signs.

٨ أُو۟لَٰٓئِكَ مَأْوَىٰهُمُ ٱلنَّارُ بِمَا كَانُوا۟ يَكْسِبُونَ

8 These—their dwelling is the Fire—on account of what they used to do.

٩ إِنَّ ٱلَّذِينَ ءَامَنُوا۟ وَعَمِلُوا۟ ٱلصَّٰلِحَٰتِ يَهْدِيهِمْ
رَبُّهُم بِإِيمَٰنِهِمْ ۖ تَجْرِى مِن تَحْتِهِمُ ٱلْأَنْهَٰرُ فِى
جَنَّٰتِ ٱلنَّعِيمِ

9 As for those who believe and do good deeds, their Lord guides them in their faith. Rivers will flow beneath them in the Gardens of Bliss.

١٠ دَعْوَىٰهُمْ فِيهَا سُبْحَٰنَكَ ٱللَّهُمَّ وَتَحِيَّتُهُمْ فِيهَا
سَلَٰمٌ ۚ وَءَاخِرُ دَعْوَىٰهُمْ أَنِ ٱلْحَمْدُ لِلَّهِ رَبِّ
ٱلْعَٰلَمِينَ

10 Their call therein is, “Glory be to You, our God.” And their greeting therein is, “Peace.” And the last of their call is, “Praise be to Allah, Lord of the Worlds.”

١١ وَلَوْ يُعَجِّلُ ٱللَّهُ لِلنَّاسِ ٱلشَّرَّ ٱسْتِعْجَالَهُم
بِٱلْخَيْرِ لَقُضِىَ إِلَيْهِمْ أَجَلُهُمْ ۖ فَنَذَرُ ٱلَّذِينَ لَا
يَرْجُونَ لِقَآءَنَا فِى طُغْيَٰنِهِمْ يَعْمَهُونَ

11 If Allah were to accelerate the ill for the people, as they wish to accelerate the good, their term would have been fulfilled. But We leave those who do not expect Our encounter to blunder in their excesses.

١٢ وَإِذَا مَسَّ ٱلْإِنسَٰنَ ٱلضُّرُّ دَعَانَا لِجَنۢبِهِۦٓ أَوْ
قَاعِدًا أَوْ قَآئِمًا فَلَمَّا كَشَفْنَا عَنْهُ ضُرَّهُۥ مَرَّ كَأَن

12 Whenever adversity touches the human being, he prays to Us—reclining on his side, or sitting, or standing. But when We have

لَمْ يَدْعُنَآ إِلَىٰ ضُرٍّ مَّسَّهُۥ ۚ كَذَٰلِكَ زُيِّنَ لِلْمُسْرِفِينَ
مَا كَانُوا۟ يَعْمَلُونَ

relieved his adversity from him, he goes away, as though he had never called on Us for trouble that had afflicted him. Thus the deeds of the transgressors appear good to them.

١٣ وَلَقَدْ أَهْلَكْنَا ٱلْقُرُونَ مِن قَبْلِكُمْ لَمَّا ظَلَمُوا۟ ۙ
وَجَآءَتْهُمْ رُسُلُهُم بِٱلْبَيِّنَٰتِ وَمَا كَانُوا۟ لِيُؤْمِنُوا۟ ۚ
كَذَٰلِكَ نَجْزِى ٱلْقَوْمَ ٱلْمُجْرِمِينَ

13 We destroyed generations before you when they did wrong. Their messengers came to them with clear signs, but they would not believe. Thus We requite the sinful people.

١٤ ثُمَّ جَعَلْنَٰكُمْ خَلَٰٓئِفَ فِى ٱلْأَرْضِ مِنۢ بَعْدِهِمْ
لِنَنظُرَ كَيْفَ تَعْمَلُونَ

14 Then We made you successors on earth after them, to see how you would behave.

١٥ وَإِذَا تُتْلَىٰ عَلَيْهِمْ ءَايَاتُنَا بَيِّنَٰتٍ ۙ قَالَ ٱلَّذِينَ
لَا يَرْجُونَ لِقَآءَنَا ٱئْتِ بِقُرْءَانٍ غَيْرِ هَٰذَآ أَوْ
بَدِّلْهُ ۚ قُلْ مَا يَكُونُ لِىٓ أَنْ أُبَدِّلَهُۥ مِن تِلْقَآئِ
نَفْسِىٓ ۖ إِنْ أَتَّبِعُ إِلَّا مَا يُوحَىٰٓ إِلَىَّ ۖ إِنِّىٓ أَخَافُ
إِنْ عَصَيْتُ رَبِّى عَذَابَ يَوْمٍ عَظِيمٍ

15 And when Our clear revelations are recited to them, those who do not hope to meet Us say, “Bring a Quran other than this, or change it.” Say, “It is not for me to change it of my own accord. I only follow what is revealed to me. I fear, if I disobeyed my Lord, the torment of a terrible Day.”

١٦ قُل لَّوْ شَآءَ ٱللَّهُ مَا تَلَوْتُهُۥ عَلَيْكُمْ وَلَآ أَدْرَىٰكُم
بِهِۦ ۖ فَقَدْ لَبِثْتُ فِيكُمْ عُمُرًا مِّن قَبْلِهِۦٓ ۚ أَفَلَا
تَعْقِلُونَ

16 Say, “Had Allah willed, I would not have recited it to you, and He would not have made it known to you. I have lived among you for a lifetime before it. Do you not understand?”

١٧ فَمَنْ أَظْلَمُ مِمَّنِ ٱفْتَرَىٰ عَلَى ٱللَّهِ كَذِبًا أَوْ
كَذَّبَ بِـَٔايَٰتِهِۦٓ ۚ إِنَّهُۥ لَا يُفْلِحُ ٱلْمُجْرِمُونَ

17 Who does greater wrong than someone who fabricates lies about Allah, or denies His revelations? The guilty will never prosper.

١٨ وَيَعْبُدُونَ مِن دُونِ ٱللَّهِ مَا لَا يَضُرُّهُمْ وَلَا
يَنفَعُهُمْ وَيَقُولُونَ هَٰٓؤُلَآءِ شُفَعَٰٓؤُنَا عِندَ ٱللَّهِ ۚ قُلْ
أَتُنَبِّـُٔونَ ٱللَّهَ بِمَا لَا يَعْلَمُ فِى ٱلسَّمَٰوَٰتِ وَلَا فِى
ٱلْأَرْضِ ۚ سُبْحَٰنَهُۥ وَتَعَٰلَىٰ عَمَّا يُشْرِكُونَ

18 And they worship, besides Allah, what neither harms them nor benefits them. And they say, “These are our intercessors with Allah.” Say, “Are you informing Allah about what He does not know in the heavens or on earth?” Glorified be He, High above the associations they make.

١٩ وَمَا كَانَ ٱلنَّاسُ إِلَّآ أُمَّةً وَٰحِدَةً فَٱخْتَلَفُوا۟ ۚ
وَلَوْلَا كَلِمَةٌ سَبَقَتْ مِن رَّبِّكَ لَقُضِىَ بَيْنَهُمْ فِيمَا
فِيهِ يَخْتَلِفُونَ

19 Mankind was a single community; then they differed. Were it not for a prior decree from your Lord, the matters over which they had disputed would have been settled.

٢٠ وَيَقُولُونَ لَوْلَآ أُنزِلَ عَلَيْهِ ءَايَةٌ مِّن رَّبِّهِۦ ۖ
فَقُلْ إِنَّمَا ٱلْغَيْبُ لِلَّهِ فَٱنتَظِرُوٓا۟ إِنِّى مَعَكُم مِّنَ
ٱلْمُنتَظِرِينَ

20 And they say, “If only a miracle was sent down to him from his Lord.” Say, “The realm of the unseen belongs to Allah; so wait, I am waiting with you.”

٢١ وَإِذَآ أَذَقْنَا ٱلنَّاسَ رَحْمَةً مِّنۢ بَعْدِ ضَرَّآءَ
مَسَّتْهُمْ إِذَا لَهُم مَّكْرٌ فِىٓ ءَايَاتِنَا ۚ قُلِ ٱللَّهُ
أَسْرَعُ مَكْرًا ۚ إِنَّ رُسُلَنَا يَكْتُبُونَ مَا تَمْكُرُونَ

21 When We make the people taste mercy after some adversity has touched them, they begin to scheme against Our revelations. Say, “Allah is swifter in scheming.” Our envoys are writing down what you scheme.

٢٢ هُوَ ٱلَّذِى يُسَيِّرُكُمْ فِى ٱلْبَرِّ وَٱلْبَحْرِ ۖ حَتَّىٰٓ
إِذَا كُنتُمْ فِى ٱلْفُلْكِ وَجَرَيْنَ بِهِم بِرِيحٍ طَيِّبَةٍ
وَفَرِحُوا۟ بِهَا جَآءَتْهَا رِيحٌ عَاصِفٌ وَجَآءَهُمُ
ٱلْمَوْجُ مِن كُلِّ مَكَانٍ وَظَنُّوٓا۟ أَنَّهُمْ أُحِيطَ بِهِمْ ۙ
دَعَوُا۟ ٱللَّهَ مُخْلِصِينَ لَهُ ٱلدِّينَ لَئِنْ أَنجَيْتَنَا مِنْ
هَٰذِهِۦ لَنَكُونَنَّ مِنَ ٱلشَّٰكِرِينَ

22 It is He who transports you across land and sea. Until, when you are on ships, sailing in a favorable wind, and rejoicing in it, a raging wind arrives. The waves surge over them from every side, and they realize that they are besieged. Thereupon they pray to Allah, professing sincere devotion to Him: “If You save us from this, we will be among the appreciative.”

٢٣ فَلَمَّآ أَنجَىٰهُمْ إِذَا هُمْ يَبْغُونَ فِى ٱلْأَرْضِ
بِغَيْرِ ٱلْحَقِّ ۗ يَٰٓأَيُّهَا ٱلنَّاسُ إِنَّمَا بَغْيُكُمْ عَلَىٰٓ
أَنفُسِكُم ۖ مَّتَٰعَ ٱلْحَيَوٰةِ ٱلدُّنْيَا ۖ ثُمَّ إِلَيْنَا مَرْجِعُكُمْ
فَنُنَبِّئُكُم بِمَا كُنتُمْ تَعْمَلُونَ

23 But then, when He has saved them, they commit violations on earth, and oppose justice. O people! Your violations are against your own souls. It is the enjoyment of the present life. Then to Us is your return, and We will inform you of what you used to do.

٢٤ إِنَّمَا مَثَلُ ٱلْحَيَوٰةِ ٱلدُّنْيَا كَمَآءٍ أَنزَلْنَٰهُ مِنَ
ٱلسَّمَآءِ فَٱخْتَلَطَ بِهِۦ نَبَاتُ ٱلْأَرْضِ مِمَّا يَأْكُلُ
ٱلنَّاسُ وَٱلْأَنْعَٰمُ حَتَّىٰٓ إِذَآ أَخَذَتِ ٱلْأَرْضُ
زُخْرُفَهَا وَٱزَّيَّنَتْ وَظَنَّ أَهْلُهَآ أَنَّهُمْ قَٰدِرُونَ

24 The likeness of the present life is this: water that We send down from the sky is absorbed by the plants of the earth, from which the people and the animals eat. Until, when the earth puts on its fine appearance, and is beautified, and its inhabitants

عَلَيْهَآ أَتَىٰهَآ أَمْرُنَا لَيْلًا أَوْ نَهَارًا فَجَعَلْنَٰهَا
حَصِيدًا كَأَن لَّمْ تَغْنَ بِٱلْأَمْسِ ۚ كَذَٰلِكَ نُفَصِّلُ
ٱلْءَايَٰتِ لِقَوْمٍ يَتَفَكَّرُونَ

think that they have mastered it, Our command descends upon it by night or by day, and We turn it into stubble, as if it had not flourished the day before. We thus clarify the revelations for people who reflect.

٢٥ وَٱللَّهُ يَدْعُوٓا۟ إِلَىٰ دَارِ ٱلسَّلَٰمِ وَيَهْدِى مَن
يَشَآءُ إِلَىٰ صِرَٰطٍ مُّسْتَقِيمٍ

25 Allah invites to the Home of Peace, and guides whomever He wills to a straight path.

٢٦ لِّلَّذِينَ أَحْسَنُوا۟ ٱلْحُسْنَىٰ وَزِيَادَةٌ ۖ وَلَا يَرْهَقُ
وُجُوهَهُمْ قَتَرٌ وَلَا ذِلَّةٌ ۚ أُو۟لَٰٓئِكَ أَصْحَٰبُ ٱلْجَنَّةِ ۖ
هُمْ فِيهَا خَٰلِدُونَ

26 For those who have done good is goodness, and more. Neither gloom nor shame will come over their faces. These are the inhabitants of Paradise, abiding therein forever.

٢٧ وَٱلَّذِينَ كَسَبُوا۟ ٱلسَّيِّـَٔاتِ جَزَآءُ سَيِّئَةٍۭ بِمِثْلِهَا
وَتَرْهَقُهُمْ ذِلَّةٌ ۖ مَّا لَهُم مِّنَ ٱللَّهِ مِنْ عَاصِمٍ ۖ
كَأَنَّمَآ أُغْشِيَتْ وُجُوهُهُمْ قِطَعًا مِّنَ ٱلَّيْلِ مُظْلِمًا ۚ
أُو۟لَٰٓئِكَ أَصْحَٰبُ ٱلنَّارِ ۖ هُمْ فِيهَا خَٰلِدُونَ

27 As for those who have earned evil deeds: a reward of similar evil, and shame will cover them. They will have no defense against Allah—as if their faces are covered with dark patches of night. These are the inmates of the Fire, abiding therein forever.

٢٨ وَيَوْمَ نَحْشُرُهُمْ جَمِيعًا ثُمَّ نَقُولُ لِلَّذِينَ
أَشْرَكُوا۟ مَكَانَكُمْ أَنتُمْ وَشُرَكَآؤُكُمْ ۚ فَزَيَّلْنَا
بَيْنَهُمْ ۖ وَقَالَ شُرَكَآؤُهُم مَّا كُنتُمْ إِيَّانَا تَعْبُدُونَ

28 On the Day when We will gather them altogether, then say to those who ascribed partners, "To your place, you and your partners." Then We will separate between them, and their partners will say, "It was not us you were worshiping."

٢٩ فَكَفَىٰ بِٱللَّهِ شَهِيدًۢا بَيْنَنَا وَبَيْنَكُمْ إِن كُنَّا عَنْ
عِبَادَتِكُمْ لَغَٰفِلِينَ

29 "Allah is sufficient witness between us and you. We were unaware of your worshiping us."

٣٠ هُنَالِكَ تَبْلُوا۟ كُلُّ نَفْسٍ مَّآ أَسْلَفَتْ ۚ وَرُدُّوٓا۟
إِلَى ٱللَّهِ مَوْلَىٰهُمُ ٱلْحَقِّ ۖ وَضَلَّ عَنْهُم مَّا كَانُوا۟
يَفْتَرُونَ

30 There, every soul will experience what it had done previously; and they will be returned to Allah, their True Master; and what they used to invent will fail them.

٣١ قُلْ مَن يَرْزُقُكُم مِّنَ ٱلسَّمَآءِ وَٱلْأَرْضِ أَمَّن
يَمْلِكُ ٱلسَّمْعَ وَٱلْأَبْصَٰرَ وَمَن يُخْرِجُ ٱلْحَىَّ مِنَ

31 Say, "Who provides for you from the heaven and the earth? And who controls the hearing and the sight? And who produces the living from

ٱلْمَيِّتِ وَيُخْرِجُ ٱلْمَيِّتَ مِنَ ٱلْحَىِّ وَمَن يُدَبِّرُ
ٱلْأَمْرَ ۚ فَسَيَقُولُونَ ٱللَّهُ ۚ فَقُلْ أَفَلَا تَتَّقُونَ

the dead, and produces the dead from the living? And who governs the Order?" They will say, "Allah." Say, "Will you not be careful?"

٣٢ فَذَٰلِكُمُ ٱللَّهُ رَبُّكُمُ ٱلْحَقُّ ۖ فَمَاذَا بَعْدَ ٱلْحَقِّ إِلَّا
ٱلضَّلَٰلُ ۖ فَأَنَّىٰ تُصْرَفُونَ

32 Such is Allah, your Lord—the True. What is there, beyond the truth, except falsehood? How are you turned away?

٣٣ كَذَٰلِكَ حَقَّتْ كَلِمَتُ رَبِّكَ عَلَى ٱلَّذِينَ فَسَقُوٓا۟
أَنَّهُمْ لَا يُؤْمِنُونَ

33 Thus your Lord's Word proved true against those who disobeyed, for they do not believe.

٣٤ قُلْ هَلْ مِن شُرَكَآئِكُم مَّن يَبْدَؤُا۟ ٱلْخَلْقَ ثُمَّ
يُعِيدُهُۥ ۚ قُلِ ٱللَّهُ يَبْدَؤُا۟ ٱلْخَلْقَ ثُمَّ يُعِيدُهُۥ ۖ فَأَنَّىٰ
تُؤْفَكُونَ

34 Say, "Can any of your partners initiate creation, and then repeat it?" Say, "Allah initiates creation, and then repeats it. How are you so deluded?"

٣٥ قُلْ هَلْ مِن شُرَكَآئِكُم مَّن يَهْدِىٓ إِلَى ٱلْحَقِّ ۚ
قُلِ ٱللَّهُ يَهْدِى لِلْحَقِّ ۗ أَفَمَن يَهْدِىٓ إِلَى ٱلْحَقِّ
أَحَقُّ أَن يُتَّبَعَ أَمَّن لَّا يَهِدِّىٓ إِلَّآ أَن يُهْدَىٰ ۖ فَمَا
لَكُمْ كَيْفَ تَحْكُمُونَ

35 Say, "Can any of your partners guide to the truth?" Say, "Allah guides to the truth. Is He who guides to the truth more worthy of being followed, or he who does not guide, unless he himself is guided? What is the matter with you? How do you judge?"

٣٦ وَمَا يَتَّبِعُ أَكْثَرُهُمْ إِلَّا ظَنًّا ۚ إِنَّ ٱلظَّنَّ لَا يُغْنِى
مِنَ ٱلْحَقِّ شَيْـًٔا ۚ إِنَّ ٱللَّهَ عَلِيمٌۢ بِمَا يَفْعَلُونَ

36 Most of them follow nothing but assumptions; and assumptions avail nothing against the truth. Allah is fully aware of what they do.

٣٧ وَمَا كَانَ هَٰذَا ٱلْقُرْءَانُ أَن يُفْتَرَىٰ مِن دُونِ
ٱللَّهِ وَلَٰكِن تَصْدِيقَ ٱلَّذِى بَيْنَ يَدَيْهِ وَتَفْصِيلَ
ٱلْكِتَٰبِ لَا رَيْبَ فِيهِ مِن رَّبِّ ٱلْعَٰلَمِينَ

37 This Quran could not have been produced by anyone other than Allah. In fact, it is a confirmation of what preceded it, and an elaboration of the Book. There is no doubt about it—it is from the Lord of the Universe.

٣٨ أَمْ يَقُولُونَ ٱفْتَرَىٰهُ ۖ قُلْ فَأْتُوا۟ بِسُورَةٍ مِّثْلِهِۦ
وَٱدْعُوا۟ مَنِ ٱسْتَطَعْتُم مِّن دُونِ ٱللَّهِ إِن كُنتُمْ
صَٰدِقِينَ

38 Or do they say, "He has forged it"? Say, "Then produce a single chapter like it, and call upon whomever you can, apart from Allah, if you are truthful."

٣٩ بَلْ كَذَّبُوا۟ بِمَا لَمْ يُحِيطُوا۟ بِعِلْمِهِۦ وَلَمَّا
يَأْتِهِمْ تَأْوِيلُهُۥ ۚ كَذَٰلِكَ كَذَّبَ ٱلَّذِينَ مِن قَبْلِهِمْ ۖ
فَٱنظُرْ كَيْفَ كَانَ عَٰقِبَةُ ٱلظَّٰلِمِينَ

39 In fact, they deny what is beyond the limits of their knowledge, and whose explanation has not yet reached them. Thus those before them refused to believe. So note the consequences for the wrongdoers.

٤٠ وَمِنْهُم مَّن يُؤْمِنُ بِهِۦ وَمِنْهُم مَّن لَّا يُؤْمِنُ
بِهِۦ ۚ وَرَبُّكَ أَعْلَمُ بِٱلْمُفْسِدِينَ

40 Among them are those who believe in it, and among them are those who do not believe in it. Your Lord is fully aware of the mischief-makers.

٤١ وَإِن كَذَّبُوكَ فَقُل لِّى عَمَلِى وَلَكُمْ عَمَلُكُمْ ۖ
أَنتُم بَرِيٓـُٔونَ مِمَّآ أَعْمَلُ وَأَنَا۠ بَرِىٓءٌ مِّمَّا تَعْمَلُونَ

41 If they accuse you of lying, say, “I have my deeds, and you have your deeds. You are quit of what I do, and I am quit of what you do.”

٤٢ وَمِنْهُم مَّن يَسْتَمِعُونَ إِلَيْكَ ۚ أَفَأَنتَ تُسْمِعُ
ٱلصُّمَّ وَلَوْ كَانُوا۟ لَا يَعْقِلُونَ

42 And among them are those who listen to you. But can you make the deaf hear, even though they do not understand?

٤٣ وَمِنْهُم مَّن يَنظُرُ إِلَيْكَ ۚ أَفَأَنتَ تَهْدِى ٱلْعُمْىَ
وَلَوْ كَانُوا۟ لَا يُبْصِرُونَ

43 And among them are those who look at you. But can you guide the blind, even though they do not see?

٤٤ إِنَّ ٱللَّهَ لَا يَظْلِمُ ٱلنَّاسَ شَيْـًٔا وَلَٰكِنَّ ٱلنَّاسَ
أَنفُسَهُمْ يَظْلِمُونَ

44 Allah does not wrong the people in the least, but the people wrong their own selves.

٤٥ وَيَوْمَ يَحْشُرُهُمْ كَأَن لَّمْ يَلْبَثُوٓا۟ إِلَّا سَاعَةً
مِّنَ ٱلنَّهَارِ يَتَعَارَفُونَ بَيْنَهُمْ ۚ قَدْ خَسِرَ ٱلَّذِينَ
كَذَّبُوا۟ بِلِقَآءِ ٱللَّهِ وَمَا كَانُوا۟ مُهْتَدِينَ

45 On the Day when He rounds them up—as if they had tarried only one hour of a day—they will recognize one another. Those who denied the meeting with Allah will be the losers. They were not guided.

٤٦ وَإِمَّا نُرِيَنَّكَ بَعْضَ ٱلَّذِى نَعِدُهُمْ أَوْ نَتَوَفَّيَنَّكَ
فَإِلَيْنَا مَرْجِعُهُمْ ثُمَّ ٱللَّهُ شَهِيدٌ عَلَىٰ مَا يَفْعَلُونَ

46 Whether We show you some of what We promise them, or take you, to Us is their return. Allah is witness to everything they do.

٤٧ وَلِكُلِّ أُمَّةٍ رَّسُولٌ ۖ فَإِذَا جَآءَ رَسُولُهُمْ قُضِىَ
بَيْنَهُم بِٱلْقِسْطِ وَهُمْ لَا يُظْلَمُونَ

47 Every community has a messenger. When their messenger has come, judgment will be passed between them with fairness, and they will not be wronged.

٤٨ وَيَقُولُونَ مَتَىٰ هَٰذَا ٱلْوَعْدُ إِن كُنتُمْ صَٰدِقِينَ

48 And they say, “When will this promise be fulfilled, if you are truthful?”

٤٩ قُل لَّآ أَمْلِكُ لِنَفْسِى ضَرًّا وَلَا نَفْعًا إِلَّا مَا
شَآءَ ٱللَّهُ ۗ لِكُلِّ أُمَّةٍ أَجَلٌ ۚ إِذَا جَآءَ أَجَلُهُمْ فَلَا
يَسْتَـْٔخِرُونَ سَاعَةً ۖ وَلَا يَسْتَقْدِمُونَ

49 Say, “I have no power to harm or benefit myself, except as Allah wills. To every nation is an appointed time. Then, when their time arrives, they can neither postpone it by one hour, nor advance it.

٥٠ قُلْ أَرَءَيْتُمْ إِنْ أَتَىٰكُمْ عَذَابُهُۥ بَيَٰتًا أَوْ نَهَارًا
مَّاذَا يَسْتَعْجِلُ مِنْهُ ٱلْمُجْرِمُونَ

50 Say, “Have you considered? If His punishment overtakes you by night or by day, what part of it will the guilty seek to hasten?”

٥١ أَثُمَّ إِذَا مَا وَقَعَ ءَامَنتُم بِهِۦٓ ۚ ءَآلْـَٰٔنَ وَقَدْ كُنتُم
بِهِۦ تَسْتَعْجِلُونَ

51 “Then, when it falls, will you believe in it? Now? When before you tried to hasten it?”

٥٢ ثُمَّ قِيلَ لِلَّذِينَ ظَلَمُوا۟ ذُوقُوا۟ عَذَابَ ٱلْخُلْدِ
هَلْ تُجْزَوْنَ إِلَّا بِمَا كُنتُمْ تَكْسِبُونَ

52 Then it will be said to those who did wrong, “Taste the torment of eternity. Will you be rewarded except for what you used to do?”

٥٣ وَيَسْتَنۢبِـُٔونَكَ أَحَقٌّ هُوَ ۖ قُلْ إِى وَرَبِّىٓ إِنَّهُۥ
لَحَقٌّ ۖ وَمَآ أَنتُم بِمُعْجِزِينَ

53 And they inquire of you, “Is it true?” Say, “Yes, by my Lord, it is true, and you cannot evade it.”

٥٤ وَلَوْ أَنَّ لِكُلِّ نَفْسٍ ظَلَمَتْ مَا فِى ٱلْأَرْضِ
لَٱفْتَدَتْ بِهِۦ ۗ وَأَسَرُّوا۟ ٱلنَّدَامَةَ لَمَّا رَأَوُا۟ ٱلْعَذَابَ ۖ
وَقُضِىَ بَيْنَهُم بِٱلْقِسْطِ ۚ وَهُمْ لَا يُظْلَمُونَ

54 Had every soul which had done wrong possessed everything on earth, it would offer it as a ransom. They will hide the remorse when they witness the suffering, and it will be judged between them equitably, and they will not be wronged.

٥٥ أَلَآ إِنَّ لِلَّهِ مَا فِى ٱلسَّمَٰوَٰتِ وَٱلْأَرْضِ ۗ أَلَآ إِنَّ
وَعْدَ ٱللَّهِ حَقٌّ وَلَٰكِنَّ أَكْثَرَهُمْ لَا يَعْلَمُونَ

55 Assuredly, to Allah belongs everything in the heavens and the earth. Assuredly, the promise of Allah is true. But most of them do not know.

٥٦ هُوَ يُحْىِۦ وَيُمِيتُ وَإِلَيْهِ تُرْجَعُونَ

56 He gives life and causes death, and to Him you will be returned.

57 O people! There has come to you advice from your Lord, and healing for what is in the hearts, and guidance and mercy for the believers.

٥٧ يَٰٓأَيُّهَا ٱلنَّاسُ قَدْ جَآءَتْكُم مَّوْعِظَةٌ مِّن رَّبِّكُمْ
وَشِفَآءٌ لِّمَا فِى ٱلصُّدُورِ وَهُدًى وَرَحْمَةٌ
لِّلْمُؤْمِنِينَ

58 Say, "In Allah's grace and mercy let them rejoice. That is better than what they hoard."

٥٨ قُلْ بِفَضْلِ ٱللَّهِ وَبِرَحْمَتِهِۦ فَبِذَٰلِكَ فَلْيَفْرَحُوا۟
هُوَ خَيْرٌ مِّمَّا يَجْمَعُونَ

59 Say, "Have you considered the sustenance Allah has sent down for you, some of which you made unlawful, and some lawful?" Say, "Did Allah give you permission, or do you fabricate lies and attribute them to Allah?"

٥٩ قُلْ أَرَءَيْتُم مَّآ أَنزَلَ ٱللَّهُ لَكُم مِّن رِّزْقٍ
فَجَعَلْتُم مِّنْهُ حَرَامًا وَحَلَٰلًا قُلْ ءَآللَّهُ أَذِنَ لَكُمْ ۖ
أَمْ عَلَى ٱللَّهِ تَفْتَرُونَ

60 What will they think—those who fabricate lies and attribute them to Allah—on the Day of Resurrection? Allah is bountiful towards the people, but most of them do not give thanks.

٦٠ وَمَا ظَنُّ ٱلَّذِينَ يَفْتَرُونَ عَلَى ٱللَّهِ ٱلْكَذِبَ
يَوْمَ ٱلْقِيَٰمَةِ ۗ إِنَّ ٱللَّهَ لَذُو فَضْلٍ عَلَى ٱلنَّاسِ
وَلَٰكِنَّ أَكْثَرَهُمْ لَا يَشْكُرُونَ

61 You do not get into any situation, nor do you recite any Quran, nor do you do anything, but We are watching over you as you undertake it. Not even the weight of an atom, on earth or in the sky, escapes your Lord, nor is there anything smaller or larger, but is in a clear record.

٦١ وَمَا تَكُونُ فِى شَأْنٍ وَمَا تَتْلُوا۟ مِنْهُ مِن
قُرْءَانٍ وَلَا تَعْمَلُونَ مِنْ عَمَلٍ إِلَّا كُنَّا عَلَيْكُمْ
شُهُودًا إِذْ تُفِيضُونَ فِيهِ ۚ وَمَا يَعْزُبُ عَن رَّبِّكَ
مِن مِّثْقَالِ ذَرَّةٍ فِى ٱلْأَرْضِ وَلَا فِى ٱلسَّمَآءِ وَلَآ
أَصْغَرَ مِن ذَٰلِكَ وَلَآ أَكْبَرَ إِلَّا فِى كِتَٰبٍ مُّبِينٍ

62 Unquestionably, Allah's friends have nothing to fear, nor shall they grieve.

٦٢ أَلَآ إِنَّ أَوْلِيَآءَ ٱللَّهِ لَا خَوْفٌ عَلَيْهِمْ وَلَا هُمْ
يَحْزَنُونَ

63 Those who believe and are aware.

٦٣ ٱلَّذِينَ ءَامَنُوا۟ وَكَانُوا۟ يَتَّقُونَ

64 For them is good news in this life, and in the Hereafter. There is no alteration to the words of Allah. That is the supreme triumph.

٦٤ لَهُمُ ٱلْبُشْرَىٰ فِى ٱلْحَيَوٰةِ ٱلدُّنْيَا وَفِى
ٱلْءَاخِرَةِ ۚ لَا تَبْدِيلَ لِكَلِمَٰتِ ٱللَّهِ ۚ ذَٰلِكَ هُوَ ٱلْفَوْزُ
ٱلْعَظِيمُ

65 And let not their sayings dishearten you. All power is Allah's. He is the Hearer, the Knower.

٦٥ وَلَا يَحْزُنكَ قَوْلُهُمْ ۘ إِنَّ ٱلْعِزَّةَ لِلَّهِ جَمِيعًا ۚ هُوَ
ٱلسَّمِيعُ ٱلْعَلِيمُ

٦٦ أَلَآ إِنَّ لِلَّهِ مَن فِى ٱلسَّمَٰوَٰتِ وَمَن فِى
ٱلْأَرْضِ ۗ وَمَا يَتَّبِعُ ٱلَّذِينَ يَدْعُونَ مِن دُونِ ٱللَّهِ
شُرَكَآءَ ۚ إِن يَتَّبِعُونَ إِلَّا ٱلظَّنَّ وَإِنْ هُمْ إِلَّا
يَخْرُصُونَ

66 Certainly, to Allah belongs everyone in the heavens and everyone on earth. Those who invoke other than Allah do not follow partners; they follow only assumptions, and they only guess.

٦٧ هُوَ ٱلَّذِى جَعَلَ لَكُمُ ٱلَّيْلَ لِتَسْكُنُوا۟ فِيهِ
وَٱلنَّهَارَ مُبْصِرًا ۚ إِنَّ فِى ذَٰلِكَ لَءَايَٰتٍ لِّقَوْمٍ
يَسْمَعُونَ

67 It is He who made the night for your rest, and the daylight for visibility. Surely in that are signs for people who listen.

٦٨ قَالُوا۟ ٱتَّخَذَ ٱللَّهُ وَلَدًا ۗ سُبْحَٰنَهُۥ ۖ هُوَ ٱلْغَنِىُّ ۖ لَهُۥ
مَا فِى ٱلسَّمَٰوَٰتِ وَمَا فِى ٱلْأَرْضِ ۚ إِنْ عِندَكُم
مِّن سُلْطَٰنٍۭ بِهَٰذَآ ۚ أَتَقُولُونَ عَلَى ٱللَّهِ مَا لَا
تَعْلَمُونَ

68 And they said, “Allah has taken a son.” Be He glorified. He is the Self-Sufficient. His is everything in the heavens and everything on earth. Do you have any proof for this? Or are you saying about Allah what you do not know?

٦٩ قُلْ إِنَّ ٱلَّذِينَ يَفْتَرُونَ عَلَى ٱللَّهِ ٱلْكَذِبَ لَا
يُفْلِحُونَ

69 Say, “Those who fabricate lies about Allah will not succeed.”

٧٠ مَتَٰعٌ فِى ٱلدُّنْيَا ثُمَّ إِلَيْنَا مَرْجِعُهُمْ ثُمَّ
نُذِيقُهُمُ ٱلْعَذَابَ ٱلشَّدِيدَ بِمَا كَانُوا۟ يَكْفُرُونَ

70 Some enjoyment in this world; then to Us is their return; then We will make them taste the severe punishment on account of their disbelief.

٧١ وَٱتْلُ عَلَيْهِمْ نَبَأَ نُوحٍ إِذْ قَالَ لِقَوْمِهِۦ يَٰقَوْمِ
إِن كَانَ كَبُرَ عَلَيْكُم مَّقَامِى وَتَذْكِيرِى بِـَٔايَٰتِ
ٱللَّهِ فَعَلَى ٱللَّهِ تَوَكَّلْتُ فَأَجْمِعُوٓا۟ أَمْرَكُمْ
وَشُرَكَآءَكُمْ ثُمَّ لَا يَكُنْ أَمْرُكُمْ عَلَيْكُمْ غُمَّةً ثُمَّ
ٱقْضُوٓا۟ إِلَىَّ وَلَا تُنظِرُونِ

71 And relate to them the story of Noah, when he said to his people, “O my people, if my presence among you and my reminding you of Allah’s signs is too much for you, then in Allah I have put my trust. So come to a decision, you and your partners, and do not let the matter perplex you; then carry out your decision on me, and do not hold back.”

٧٢ فَإِن تَوَلَّيْتُمْ فَمَا سَأَلْتُكُم مِّنْ أَجْرٍ ۖ إِنْ أَجْرِىَ
إِلَّا عَلَى ٱللَّهِ ۖ وَأُمِرْتُ أَنْ أَكُونَ مِنَ ٱلْمُسْلِمِينَ

72 “But if you turn away, I have not asked you for any wage. My wage falls only on Allah, and I was commanded to be of those who submit.”

٧٣ فَكَذَّبُوهُ فَنَجَّيْنَٰهُ وَمَن مَّعَهُۥ فِى ٱلْفُلْكِ
وَجَعَلْنَٰهُمْ خَلَٰٓئِفَ وَأَغْرَقْنَا ٱلَّذِينَ كَذَّبُوا۟ بِـَٔايَٰتِنَا ۖ
فَٱنظُرْ كَيْفَ كَانَ عَٰقِبَةُ ٱلْمُنذَرِينَ

73 But they denounced him, so We saved him and those with him in the Ark, and We made them successors, and We drowned those who rejected Our signs. So consider the fate of those who were warned.

٧٤ ثُمَّ بَعَثْنَا مِنۢ بَعْدِهِۦ رُسُلًا إِلَىٰ قَوْمِهِمْ
فَجَآءُوهُم بِٱلْبَيِّنَٰتِ فَمَا كَانُوا۟ لِيُؤْمِنُوا۟ بِمَا
كَذَّبُوا۟ بِهِۦ مِن قَبْلُ ۚ كَذَٰلِكَ نَطْبَعُ عَلَىٰ قُلُوبِ
ٱلْمُعْتَدِينَ

74 Then, after him, We sent messengers to their people. They came to them with the clear proofs, but they would not believe in anything they had already rejected. Thus We set a seal on the hearts of the hostile.

٧٥ ثُمَّ بَعَثْنَا مِنۢ بَعْدِهِم مُّوسَىٰ وَهَٰرُونَ إِلَىٰ
فِرْعَوْنَ وَمَلَإِي۟هِۦ بِـَٔايَٰتِنَا فَٱسْتَكْبَرُوا۟ وَكَانُوا۟
قَوْمًا مُّجْرِمِينَ

75 Then, after them, We sent Moses and Aaron with Our proofs to Pharaoh and his dignitaries. But they acted arrogantly. They were sinful people.

٧٦ فَلَمَّا جَآءَهُمُ ٱلْحَقُّ مِنْ عِندِنَا قَالُوٓا۟ إِنَّ هَٰذَا
لَسِحْرٌ مُّبِينٌ

76 And when the truth came to them from Us, they said, “This is clearly sorcery.”

٧٧ قَالَ مُوسَىٰٓ أَتَقُولُونَ لِلْحَقِّ لَمَّا جَآءَكُمْ ۖ
أَسِحْرٌ هَٰذَا وَلَا يُفْلِحُ ٱلسَّٰحِرُونَ

77 Moses said, “Is this what you say of the truth when it has come to you? Is this sorcery? Sorcerers do not succeed.”

٧٨ قَالُوٓا۟ أَجِئْتَنَا لِتَلْفِتَنَا عَمَّا وَجَدْنَا عَلَيْهِ
ءَابَآءَنَا وَتَكُونَ لَكُمَا ٱلْكِبْرِيَآءُ فِى ٱلْأَرْضِ وَمَا
نَحْنُ لَكُمَا بِمُؤْمِنِينَ

78 They said, “Did you come to us to divert us from what we found our ancestors following, and so that you become prominent in the land? We will never believe in you.”

٧٩ وَقَالَ فِرْعَوْنُ ٱئْتُونِى بِكُلِّ سَٰحِرٍ عَلِيمٍ

79 Pharaoh said, “Bring me every experienced sorcerer.”

٨٠ فَلَمَّا جَآءَ ٱلسَّحَرَةُ قَالَ لَهُم مُّوسَىٰٓ أَلْقُوا۟ مَآ
أَنتُم مُّلْقُونَ

80 And when the sorcerers came, Moses said to them, “Throw whatever you have to throw.”

٨١ فَلَمَّآ أَلْقَوْا۟ قَالَ مُوسَىٰ مَا جِئْتُم بِهِ ٱلسِّحْرُ ۖ
إِنَّ ٱللَّهَ سَيُبْطِلُهُۥٓ ۖ إِنَّ ٱللَّهَ لَا يُصْلِحُ عَمَلَ
ٱلْمُفْسِدِينَ

81 And when they threw, Moses said, “What you produced is sorcery, and Allah will make it fail. Allah does not foster the efforts of the corrupt.”

٨٢ وَيُحِقُّ ٱللَّهُ ٱلْحَقَّ بِكَلِمَٰتِهِۦ وَلَوْ كَرِهَ ٱلْمُجْرِمُونَ

82 "And Allah upholds the truth with His words, even though the sinners detest it."

٨٣ فَمَآ ءَامَنَ لِمُوسَىٰٓ إِلَّا ذُرِّيَّةٌ مِّن قَوْمِهِۦ عَلَىٰ خَوْفٍ مِّن فِرْعَوْنَ وَمَلَإِيْهِمْ أَن يَفْتِنَهُمْ ۚ وَإِنَّ فِرْعَوْنَ لَعَالٍ فِى ٱلْأَرْضِ وَإِنَّهُۥ لَمِنَ ٱلْمُسْرِفِينَ

83 But none believed in Moses except some children of his people, for fear that Pharaoh and his chiefs would persecute them. Pharaoh was high and mighty in the land. He was a tyrant.

٨٤ وَقَالَ مُوسَىٰ يَٰقَوْمِ إِن كُنتُمْ ءَامَنتُم بِٱللَّهِ فَعَلَيْهِ تَوَكَّلُوٓا۟ إِن كُنتُم مُّسْلِمِينَ

84 Moses said, "O my people, if you have believed in Allah, then put your trust in Him, if you have submitted."

٨٥ فَقَالُوا۟ عَلَى ٱللَّهِ تَوَكَّلْنَا رَبَّنَا لَا تَجْعَلْنَا فِتْنَةً لِّلْقَوْمِ ٱلظَّٰلِمِينَ

85 They said, "In Allah we have put our trust. Our Lord, do not make us victims of the oppressive people."

٨٦ وَنَجِّنَا بِرَحْمَتِكَ مِنَ ٱلْقَوْمِ ٱلْكَٰفِرِينَ

86 "And deliver us, by Your mercy, from the disbelieving people."

٨٧ وَأَوْحَيْنَآ إِلَىٰ مُوسَىٰ وَأَخِيهِ أَن تَبَوَّءَا لِقَوْمِكُمَا بِمِصْرَ بُيُوتًا وَٱجْعَلُوا۟ بُيُوتَكُمْ قِبْلَةً وَأَقِيمُوا۟ ٱلصَّلَوٰةَ ۗ وَبَشِّرِ ٱلْمُؤْمِنِينَ

87 And We inspired Moses and his brother, "Settle your people in Egypt, and make your homes places of worship, and perform the prayer, and give good news to the believers."

٨٨ وَقَالَ مُوسَىٰ رَبَّنَآ إِنَّكَ ءَاتَيْتَ فِرْعَوْنَ وَمَلَأَهُۥ زِينَةً وَأَمْوَٰلًا فِى ٱلْحَيَوٰةِ ٱلدُّنْيَا رَبَّنَا لِيُضِلُّوا۟ عَن سَبِيلِكَ ۖ رَبَّنَا ٱطْمِسْ عَلَىٰٓ أَمْوَٰلِهِمْ وَٱشْدُدْ عَلَىٰ قُلُوبِهِمْ فَلَا يُؤْمِنُوا۟ حَتَّىٰ يَرَوُا۟ ٱلْعَذَابَ ٱلْأَلِيمَ

88 Moses said, "Our Lord, you have given Pharaoh and his chiefs splendor and wealth in the worldly life. Our Lord, for them to lead away from Your path. Our Lord, obliterate their wealth, and harden their hearts, they will not believe until they see the painful torment."

٨٩ قَالَ قَدْ أُجِيبَت دَّعْوَتُكُمَا فَٱسْتَقِيمَا وَلَا تَتَّبِعَآنِّ سَبِيلَ ٱلَّذِينَ لَا يَعْلَمُونَ

89 He said, "Your prayer has been answered, so go straight, and do not follow the path of those who do not know."

٩٠ وَجَٰوَزْنَا بِبَنِىٓ إِسْرَٰٓءِيلَ ٱلْبَحْرَ فَأَتْبَعَهُمْ فِرْعَوْنُ وَجُنُودُهُۥ بَغْيًا وَعَدْوًا ۖ حَتَّىٰٓ إِذَآ أَدْرَكَهُ ٱلْغَرَقُ قَالَ ءَامَنتُ أَنَّهُۥ لَآ إِلَٰهَ إِلَّا ٱلَّذِىٓ ءَامَنَتْ بِهِۦ بَنُوٓا۟ إِسْرَٰٓءِيلَ وَأَنَا۠ مِنَ ٱلْمُسْلِمِينَ

90 And We delivered the Children of Israel across the sea. Pharaoh and his troops pursued them, defiantly and aggressively. Until, when he was about to drown, he said, "I believe that there is no god except

the One the Children of Israel believe in, and I am of those who submit."

٩١ ءَآلْـَٰٔنَ وَقَدْ عَصَيْتَ قَبْلُ وَكُنتَ مِنَ
ٱلْمُفْسِدِينَ

91 Now? When you have rebelled before, and been of the mischief-makers?

٩٢ فَٱلْيَوْمَ نُنَجِّيكَ بِبَدَنِكَ لِتَكُونَ لِمَنْ خَلْفَكَ
ءَايَةً ۚ وَإِنَّ كَثِيرًا مِّنَ ٱلنَّاسِ عَنْ ءَايَٰتِنَا لَغَٰفِلُونَ

92 Today We will preserve your body, so that you become a sign for those after you. But most people are heedless of Our signs.

٩٣ وَلَقَدْ بَوَّأْنَا بَنِىٓ إِسْرَٰٓءِيلَ مُبَوَّأَ صِدْقٍ
وَرَزَقْنَٰهُم مِّنَ ٱلطَّيِّبَٰتِ فَمَا ٱخْتَلَفُوا۟ حَتَّىٰ
جَآءَهُمُ ٱلْعِلْمُ ۚ إِنَّ رَبَّكَ يَقْضِى بَيْنَهُمْ يَوْمَ
ٱلْقِيَٰمَةِ فِيمَا كَانُوا۟ فِيهِ يَخْتَلِفُونَ

93 And We settled the Children of Israel in a position of honor, and provided them with good things. They did not differ until knowledge came to them. Your Lord will judge between them on the Day of Resurrection regarding their differences.

٩٤ فَإِن كُنتَ فِى شَكٍّ مِّمَّآ أَنزَلْنَآ إِلَيْكَ فَسْـَٔلِ
ٱلَّذِينَ يَقْرَءُونَ ٱلْكِتَٰبَ مِن قَبْلِكَ ۚ لَقَدْ جَآءَكَ
ٱلْحَقُّ مِن رَّبِّكَ فَلَا تَكُونَنَّ مِنَ ٱلْمُمْتَرِينَ

94 If you are in doubt about what We revealed to you, ask those who read the Scripture before you. The truth has come to you from your Lord, so do not be of those who doubt.

٩٥ وَلَا تَكُونَنَّ مِنَ ٱلَّذِينَ كَذَّبُوا۟ بِـَٔايَٰتِ ٱللَّهِ
فَتَكُونَ مِنَ ٱلْخَٰسِرِينَ

95 And do not be of those who deny Allah's revelations, lest you become one of the losers.

٩٦ إِنَّ ٱلَّذِينَ حَقَّتْ عَلَيْهِمْ كَلِمَتُ رَبِّكَ لَا
يُؤْمِنُونَ

96 Those against whom your Lord's Word is justified will not believe.

٩٧ وَلَوْ جَآءَتْهُمْ كُلُّ ءَايَةٍ حَتَّىٰ يَرَوُا۟ ٱلْعَذَابَ
ٱلْأَلِيمَ

97 Even if every sign comes to them—until they see the painful punishment.

٩٨ فَلَوْلَا كَانَتْ قَرْيَةٌ ءَامَنَتْ فَنَفَعَهَآ إِيمَٰنُهَآ إِلَّا
قَوْمَ يُونُسَ لَمَّآ ءَامَنُوا۟ كَشَفْنَا عَنْهُمْ عَذَابَ
ٱلْخِزْىِ فِى ٱلْحَيَوٰةِ ٱلدُّنْيَا وَمَتَّعْنَٰهُمْ إِلَىٰ حِينٍ

98 If only there was one town that believed and benefited by its belief. Except for the people of Jonah. When they believed, We removed from them the suffering of disgrace in the worldly life, and We gave them comfort for a while.

٩٩ وَلَوْ شَآءَ رَبُّكَ لَءَامَنَ مَن فِى ٱلْأَرْضِ كُلُّهُمْ
جَمِيعًا ۚ أَفَأَنتَ تُكْرِهُ ٱلنَّاسَ حَتَّىٰ يَكُونُوا۟
مُؤْمِنِينَ

99 Had your Lord willed, everyone on earth would have believed. Will you compel people to become believers?

١٠٠ وَمَا كَانَ لِنَفْسٍ أَن تُؤْمِنَ إِلَّا بِإِذْنِ ٱللَّهِ ۚ
وَيَجْعَلُ ٱلرِّجْسَ عَلَى ٱلَّذِينَ لَا يَعْقِلُونَ

100 No soul can believe except by Allah's leave; and He lays disgrace upon those who refuse to understand.

١٠١ قُلِ ٱنظُرُوا۟ مَاذَا فِى ٱلسَّمَٰوَٰتِ وَٱلْأَرْضِ ۚ
وَمَا تُغْنِى ٱلْءَايَٰتُ وَٱلنُّذُرُ عَن قَوْمٍ لَّا يُؤْمِنُونَ

101 Say, "Look at what is in the heavens and the earth." But signs and warnings are of no avail for people who do not believe.

١٠٢ فَهَلْ يَنتَظِرُونَ إِلَّا مِثْلَ أَيَّامِ ٱلَّذِينَ خَلَوْا۟
مِن قَبْلِهِمْ ۚ قُلْ فَٱنتَظِرُوٓا۟ إِنِّى مَعَكُم مِّنَ
ٱلْمُنتَظِرِينَ

102 Do they expect anything but the likes of the days of those who passed away before them? Say, "Then wait, I will be waiting with you."

١٠٣ ثُمَّ نُنَجِّى رُسُلَنَا وَٱلَّذِينَ ءَامَنُوا۟ ۚ كَذَٰلِكَ
حَقًّا عَلَيْنَا نُنجِ ٱلْمُؤْمِنِينَ

103 Then We save Our messengers and those who believe. It is binding on Us to save the believers.

١٠٤ قُلْ يَٰٓأَيُّهَا ٱلنَّاسُ إِن كُنتُمْ فِى شَكٍّ مِّن
دِينِى فَلَآ أَعْبُدُ ٱلَّذِينَ تَعْبُدُونَ مِن دُونِ ٱللَّهِ
وَلَٰكِنْ أَعْبُدُ ٱللَّهَ ٱلَّذِى يَتَوَفَّىٰكُمْ ۖ وَأُمِرْتُ أَنْ
أَكُونَ مِنَ ٱلْمُؤْمِنِينَ

104 Say, "O people, if you are in doubt about my religion—I do not serve those you serve apart from Allah. But I serve Allah, the one who will terminate your lives. And I was commanded to be of the believers."

١٠٥ وَأَنْ أَقِمْ وَجْهَكَ لِلدِّينِ حَنِيفًا وَلَا تَكُونَنَّ
مِنَ ٱلْمُشْرِكِينَ

105 And dedicate yourself to the true religion—a monotheist—and never be of the polytheists.

١٠٦ وَلَا تَدْعُ مِن دُونِ ٱللَّهِ مَا لَا يَنفَعُكَ وَلَا
يَضُرُّكَ ۖ فَإِن فَعَلْتَ فَإِنَّكَ إِذًا مِّنَ ٱلظَّٰلِمِينَ

106 And do not call, apart from Allah, on what neither benefits you nor harms you. If you do, you are then one of the wrongdoers.

١٠٧ وَإِن يَمْسَسْكَ ٱللَّهُ بِضُرٍّ فَلَا كَاشِفَ لَهُۥٓ إِلَّا
هُوَ ۖ وَإِن يُرِدْكَ بِخَيْرٍ فَلَا رَآدَّ لِفَضْلِهِۦ ۚ يُصِيبُ
بِهِۦ مَن يَشَآءُ مِنْ عِبَادِهِۦ ۚ وَهُوَ ٱلْغَفُورُ ٱلرَّحِيمُ

107 If Allah afflicts you with harm, none can remove it except He. And if He wants good for you, none can repel His grace. He makes it reach whomever He wills of His servants. He is the Forgiver, the Merciful.

١٠٨ قُلْ يَٰٓأَيُّهَا ٱلنَّاسُ قَدْ جَآءَكُمُ ٱلْحَقُّ مِن رَّبِّكُمْ ۖ فَمَنِ ٱهْتَدَىٰ فَإِنَّمَا يَهْتَدِى لِنَفْسِهِۦ ۖ وَمَن ضَلَّ فَإِنَّمَا يَضِلُّ عَلَيْهَا ۖ وَمَآ أَنَا۠ عَلَيْكُم بِوَكِيلٍ	108 Say, "O people, the truth has come to you from your Lord. Whoever accepts guidance is guided for his own soul; and whoever strays only strays to its detriment. I am not a guardian over you."
١٠٩ وَٱتَّبِعْ مَا يُوحَىٰٓ إِلَيْكَ وَٱصْبِرْ حَتَّىٰ يَحْكُمَ ٱللَّهُ ۚ وَهُوَ خَيْرُ ٱلْحَٰكِمِينَ	109 And follow what is revealed to you, and be patient until Allah issues His judgment, for He is the Best of judges.

11 Hud هود

بِسْمِ ٱللَّهِ ٱلرَّحْمَٰنِ ٱلرَّحِيمِ	In the name of Allah, the Gracious, the Merciful.
١ الٓر ۚ كِتَٰبٌ أُحْكِمَتْ ءَايَٰتُهُۥ ثُمَّ فُصِّلَتْ مِن لَّدُنْ حَكِيمٍ خَبِيرٍ	1 Alif, Lam, Ra. A Scripture whose Verses were perfected, then elaborated, from One who is Wise and Informed.
٢ أَلَّا تَعْبُدُوٓا۟ إِلَّا ٱللَّهَ ۚ إِنَّنِى لَكُم مِّنْهُ نَذِيرٌ وَبَشِيرٌ	2 That you shall worship none but Allah. "I am a warner to you from Him, and a bearer of good news."
٣ وَأَنِ ٱسْتَغْفِرُوا۟ رَبَّكُمْ ثُمَّ تُوبُوٓا۟ إِلَيْهِ يُمَتِّعْكُم مَّتَٰعًا حَسَنًا إِلَىٰٓ أَجَلٍ مُّسَمًّى وَيُؤْتِ كُلَّ ذِى فَضْلٍ فَضْلَهُۥ ۖ وَإِن تَوَلَّوْا۟ فَإِنِّىٓ أَخَافُ عَلَيْكُمْ عَذَابَ يَوْمٍ كَبِيرٍ	3 "And ask your Lord for forgiveness, and repent to Him. He will provide you with good sustenance until a stated term, and will bestow His grace on every possessor of virtue. But if you turn away, then I fear for you the punishment of a grievous Day."
٤ إِلَى ٱللَّهِ مَرْجِعُكُمْ ۖ وَهُوَ عَلَىٰ كُلِّ شَىْءٍ قَدِيرٌ	4 "To Allah is your return, and He is Capable of all things."
٥ أَلَآ إِنَّهُمْ يَثْنُونَ صُدُورَهُمْ لِيَسْتَخْفُوا۟ مِنْهُ ۚ أَلَا حِينَ يَسْتَغْشُونَ ثِيَابَهُمْ يَعْلَمُ مَا يُسِرُّونَ وَمَا يُعْلِنُونَ ۚ إِنَّهُۥ عَلِيمٌۢ بِذَاتِ ٱلصُّدُورِ	5 They wrap their chests to hide from Him. But even as they cover themselves with their clothes, He knows what they conceal and what they reveal. He knows what lies within the hearts.

٦ وَمَا مِن دَآبَّةٍ فِى ٱلْأَرْضِ إِلَّا عَلَى ٱللَّهِ رِزْقُهَا
وَيَعْلَمُ مُسْتَقَرَّهَا وَمُسْتَوْدَعَهَا ۚ كُلٌّ فِى كِتَٰبٍ
مُّبِينٍ

6 There is no moving creature on earth but its sustenance depends on Allah. And He knows where it lives and where it rests. Everything is in a Clear Book.

٧ وَهُوَ ٱلَّذِى خَلَقَ ٱلسَّمَٰوَٰتِ وَٱلْأَرْضَ فِى سِتَّةِ
أَيَّامٍ وَكَانَ عَرْشُهُۥ عَلَى ٱلْمَآءِ لِيَبْلُوَكُمْ أَيُّكُمْ
أَحْسَنُ عَمَلًا ۗ وَلَئِن قُلْتَ إِنَّكُم مَّبْعُوثُونَ مِنۢ
بَعْدِ ٱلْمَوْتِ لَيَقُولَنَّ ٱلَّذِينَ كَفَرُوٓا۟ إِنْ هَٰذَآ إِلَّا
سِحْرٌ مُّبِينٌ

7 It is He who created the heavens and the earth in six days—and His Throne was upon the waters—in order to test you—which of you is best in conduct. And if you were to say, “You will be resurrected after death,” those who disbelieve would say, “This is nothing but plain witchcraft.”

٨ وَلَئِنْ أَخَّرْنَا عَنْهُمُ ٱلْعَذَابَ إِلَىٰٓ أُمَّةٍ مَّعْدُودَةٍ
لَّيَقُولُنَّ مَا يَحْبِسُهُۥٓ ۗ أَلَا يَوْمَ يَأْتِيهِمْ لَيْسَ
مَصْرُوفًا عَنْهُمْ وَحَاقَ بِهِم مَّا كَانُوا۟ بِهِۦ
يَسْتَهْزِءُونَ

8 And if We postponed their punishment until a stated time, they would say, “What holds it back?” On the Day when it reaches them, it will not be averted from them, and what they used to ridicule will besiege them.

٩ وَلَئِنْ أَذَقْنَا ٱلْإِنسَٰنَ مِنَّا رَحْمَةً ثُمَّ نَزَعْنَٰهَا مِنْهُ
إِنَّهُۥ لَيَـُٔوسٌ كَفُورٌ

9 If We give the human being a taste of mercy from Us, and then withdraw it from him, he becomes despairing and ungrateful.

١٠ وَلَئِنْ أَذَقْنَٰهُ نَعْمَآءَ بَعْدَ ضَرَّآءَ مَسَّتْهُ لَيَقُولَنَّ
ذَهَبَ ٱلسَّيِّـَٔاتُ عَنِّىٓ ۚ إِنَّهُۥ لَفَرِحٌ فَخُورٌ

10 And if We give him a taste of prosperity, after some adversity has afflicted him, he will say, “Troubles have gone away from me.” He becomes excited and proud.

١١ إِلَّا ٱلَّذِينَ صَبَرُوا۟ وَعَمِلُوا۟ ٱلصَّٰلِحَٰتِ أُو۟لَٰٓئِكَ
لَهُم مَّغْفِرَةٌ وَأَجْرٌ كَبِيرٌ

11 Except those who are patient and do good deeds—these will have forgiveness and a great reward.

١٢ فَلَعَلَّكَ تَارِكٌۢ بَعْضَ مَا يُوحَىٰٓ إِلَيْكَ وَضَآئِقٌۢ
بِهِۦ صَدْرُكَ أَن يَقُولُوا۟ لَوْلَآ أُنزِلَ عَلَيْهِ كَنزٌ أَوْ
جَآءَ مَعَهُۥ مَلَكٌ ۚ إِنَّمَآ أَنتَ نَذِيرٌ ۚ وَٱللَّهُ عَلَىٰ كُلِّ
شَىْءٍ وَكِيلٌ

12 Perhaps you wish to disregard some of what is revealed to you, and you may be stressed because of it, since they say, “If only a treasure was sent down to him, or an angel came with him.” You are only a warner, and Allah is Responsible for all things.

١٣ أَمْ يَقُولُونَ ٱفْتَرَىٰهُ ۖ قُلْ فَأْتُوا۟ بِعَشْرِ سُوَرٍ
مِّثْلِهِۦ مُفْتَرَيَـٰتٍ وَٱدْعُوا۟ مَنِ ٱسْتَطَعْتُم مِّن دُونِ
ٱللَّهِ إِن كُنتُمْ صَـٰدِقِينَ

13 Or do they say, “He invented it?” Say, “Then produce ten chapters like it, invented, and call upon whomever you can, besides Allah, if you are truthful.”

١٤ فَإِلَّمْ يَسْتَجِيبُوا۟ لَكُمْ فَٱعْلَمُوٓا۟ أَنَّمَآ أُنزِلَ بِعِلْمِ
ٱللَّهِ وَأَن لَّآ إِلَـٰهَ إِلَّا هُوَ ۖ فَهَلْ أَنتُم مُّسْلِمُونَ

14 But if they fail to answer you, know that it was revealed with Allah’s knowledge, and that there is no god but He. Will you then submit?

١٥ مَن كَانَ يُرِيدُ ٱلْحَيَوٰةَ ٱلدُّنْيَا وَزِينَتَهَا نُوَفِّ
إِلَيْهِمْ أَعْمَـٰلَهُمْ فِيهَا وَهُمْ فِيهَا لَا يُبْخَسُونَ

15 Whoever desires the worldly life and its glitter—We will fully recompense them for their deeds therein, and therein they will not be defrauded.

١٦ أُو۟لَـٰٓئِكَ ٱلَّذِينَ لَيْسَ لَهُمْ فِى ٱلْـَٔاخِرَةِ إِلَّا
ٱلنَّارُ ۖ وَحَبِطَ مَا صَنَعُوا۟ فِيهَا وَبَـٰطِلٌ مَّا كَانُوا۟
يَعْمَلُونَ

16 These—they will have nothing but the Fire in the Hereafter. Their deeds are in vain therein, and their works are null.

١٧ أَفَمَن كَانَ عَلَىٰ بَيِّنَةٍ مِّن رَّبِّهِۦ وَيَتْلُوهُ شَاهِدٌ
مِّنْهُ وَمِن قَبْلِهِۦ كِتَـٰبُ مُوسَىٰٓ إِمَامًا وَرَحْمَةً ۚ
أُو۟لَـٰٓئِكَ يُؤْمِنُونَ بِهِۦ ۚ وَمَن يَكْفُرْ بِهِۦ مِنَ
ٱلْأَحْزَابِ فَٱلنَّارُ مَوْعِدُهُۥ ۚ فَلَا تَكُ فِى مِرْيَةٍ مِّنْهُ ۚ
إِنَّهُ ٱلْحَقُّ مِن رَّبِّكَ وَلَـٰكِنَّ أَكْثَرَ ٱلنَّاسِ لَا
يُؤْمِنُونَ

17 Is he who possesses a clear proof from his Lord, recited by a witness from Him, and before it the Book of Moses, a guide and a mercy? These believe in it. But whoever defies it from among the various factions, the Fire is his promise. So have no doubt about it. It is the truth from your Lord, but most people do not believe.

١٨ وَمَنْ أَظْلَمُ مِمَّنِ ٱفْتَرَىٰ عَلَى ٱللَّهِ كَذِبًا ۚ
أُو۟لَـٰٓئِكَ يُعْرَضُونَ عَلَىٰ رَبِّهِمْ وَيَقُولُ ٱلْأَشْهَـٰدُ
هَـٰٓؤُلَآءِ ٱلَّذِينَ كَذَبُوا۟ عَلَىٰ رَبِّهِمْ ۚ أَلَا لَعْنَةُ ٱللَّهِ
عَلَى ٱلظَّـٰلِمِينَ

18 Who does greater wrong than he who fabricates lies about Allah? These will be presented before their Lord, and the witnesses will say, “These are they who lied about their Lord.” Indeed, the curse of Allah is upon the wrongdoers.

١٩ ٱلَّذِينَ يَصُدُّونَ عَن سَبِيلِ ٱللَّهِ وَيَبْغُونَهَا
عِوَجًا وَهُم بِٱلْـَٔاخِرَةِ هُمْ كَـٰفِرُونَ

19 Those who hinder others from the path of Allah, and seek to make it crooked; and regarding the Hereafter, they are in denial.

٢٠ أُو۟لَـٰٓئِكَ لَمْ يَكُونُوا۟ مُعْجِزِينَ فِى ٱلْأَرْضِ وَمَا
كَانَ لَهُم مِّن دُونِ ٱللَّهِ مِنْ أَوْلِيَآءَ ۘ يُضَـٰعَفُ لَهُمُ
ٱلْعَذَابُ ۚ مَا كَانُوا۟ يَسْتَطِيعُونَ ٱلسَّمْعَ وَمَا كَانُوا۟
يُبْصِرُونَ

20 These will not escape on earth, and they have no protectors besides Allah. The punishment will be doubled for them. They have failed to hear, and they have failed to see.

٢١ أُو۟لَـٰٓئِكَ ٱلَّذِينَ خَسِرُوٓا۟ أَنفُسَهُمْ وَضَلَّ عَنْهُم
مَّا كَانُوا۟ يَفْتَرُونَ

21 Those are the ones who lost their souls, and what they had invented has strayed away from them.

٢٢ لَا جَرَمَ أَنَّهُمْ فِى ٱلْـَٔاخِرَةِ هُمُ ٱلْأَخْسَرُونَ

22 Without a doubt, in the Hereafter, they will be the biggest losers.

٢٣ إِنَّ ٱلَّذِينَ ءَامَنُوا۟ وَعَمِلُوا۟ ٱلصَّـٰلِحَـٰتِ
وَأَخْبَتُوٓا۟ إِلَىٰ رَبِّهِمْ أُو۟لَـٰٓئِكَ أَصْحَـٰبُ ٱلْجَنَّةِ ۖ هُمْ
فِيهَا خَـٰلِدُونَ

23 As for those who believe and do good deeds, and humble themselves before their Lord—these are the inhabitants of Paradise, where they will abide forever.

٢٤ مَثَلُ ٱلْفَرِيقَيْنِ كَٱلْأَعْمَىٰ وَٱلْأَصَمِّ وَٱلْبَصِيرِ
وَٱلسَّمِيعِ ۚ هَلْ يَسْتَوِيَانِ مَثَلًا ۚ أَفَلَا تَذَكَّرُونَ

24 The parable of the two groups is that of the blind and the deaf, and the seeing and the hearing. Are they equal in comparison? Will you not reflect?

٢٥ وَلَقَدْ أَرْسَلْنَا نُوحًا إِلَىٰ قَوْمِهِۦٓ إِنِّى لَكُمْ نَذِيرٌ
مُّبِينٌ

25 We sent Noah to his people, "I am to you a clear warner."

٢٦ أَن لَّا تَعْبُدُوٓا۟ إِلَّا ٱللَّهَ ۖ إِنِّىٓ أَخَافُ عَلَيْكُمْ
عَذَابَ يَوْمٍ أَلِيمٍ

26 "That you shall worship none but Allah. I fear for you the agony of a painful Day."

٢٧ فَقَالَ ٱلْمَلَأُ ٱلَّذِينَ كَفَرُوا۟ مِن قَوْمِهِۦ مَا نَرَىٰكَ
إِلَّا بَشَرًا مِّثْلَنَا وَمَا نَرَىٰكَ ٱتَّبَعَكَ إِلَّا ٱلَّذِينَ هُمْ
أَرَاذِلُنَا بَادِىَ ٱلرَّأْىِ وَمَا نَرَىٰ لَكُمْ عَلَيْنَا مِن
فَضْلٍۭ بَلْ نَظُنُّكُمْ كَـٰذِبِينَ

27 The notables who disbelieved among his people said, "We see in you nothing but a man like us, and we see that only the worst among us have followed you, those of immature judgment. And we see that you have no advantage over us. In fact, we think you are liars."

٢٨ قَالَ يَـٰقَوْمِ أَرَءَيْتُمْ إِن كُنتُ عَلَىٰ بَيِّنَةٍ مِّن
رَّبِّى وَءَاتَىٰنِى رَحْمَةً مِّنْ عِندِهِۦ فَعُمِّيَتْ عَلَيْكُمْ
أَنُلْزِمُكُمُوهَا وَأَنتُمْ لَهَا كَـٰرِهُونَ

28 He said, "O my people, Have you considered? If I stand on clear evidence from my Lord, and He has given me a mercy from Himself, but you were blind to it, can we compel

you to accept it, even though you dislike it?"

٢٩ وَيَٰقَوْمِ لَآ أَسْـَٔلُكُمْ عَلَيْهِ مَالًاۖ إِنْ أَجْرِىَ إِلَّا
عَلَى ٱللَّهِۚ وَمَآ أَنَا۠ بِطَارِدِ ٱلَّذِينَ ءَامَنُوٓاْۚ إِنَّهُم
مُّلَٰقُواْ رَبِّهِمْ وَلَٰكِنِّىٓ أَرَىٰكُمْ قَوْمًا تَجْهَلُونَ

29 "O my people! I ask of you no money for it. My reward lies only with Allah. And I am not about to dismiss those who believed; they will surely meet their Lord. And I see that you are ignorant people."

٣٠ وَيَٰقَوْمِ مَن يَنصُرُنِى مِنَ ٱللَّهِ إِن طَرَدتُّهُمْۚ
أَفَلَا تَذَكَّرُونَ

30 "O my people! Who will support me against Allah, if I dismiss them? Will you not give a thought?"

٣١ وَلَآ أَقُولُ لَكُمْ عِندِى خَزَآئِنُ ٱللَّهِ وَلَآ أَعْلَمُ
ٱلْغَيْبَ وَلَآ أَقُولُ إِنِّى مَلَكٌ وَلَآ أَقُولُ لِلَّذِينَ
تَزْدَرِىٓ أَعْيُنُكُمْ لَن يُؤْتِيَهُمُ ٱللَّهُ خَيْرًاۖ ٱللَّهُ أَعْلَمُ
بِمَا فِىٓ أَنفُسِهِمْۖ إِنِّىٓ إِذًا لَّمِنَ ٱلظَّٰلِمِينَ

31 "I do not say to you that I possess the treasures of Allah, nor do I know the future, nor do I say that I am an angel. Nor do I say of those who are despicable in your eyes that Allah will never give them any good. Allah is Aware of what lies in their souls. If I did, I would be one of the wrongdoers."

٣٢ قَالُواْ يَٰنُوحُ قَدْ جَٰدَلْتَنَا فَأَكْثَرْتَ جِدَٰلَنَا فَأْتِنَا
بِمَا تَعِدُنَآ إِن كُنتَ مِنَ ٱلصَّٰدِقِينَ

32 They said, "O Noah, you have argued with us, and argued a great deal. Now bring upon us what you threaten us with, if you are truthful."

٣٣ قَالَ إِنَّمَا يَأْتِيكُم بِهِ ٱللَّهُ إِن شَآءَ وَمَآ أَنتُم
بِمُعْجِزِينَ

33 He said, "It is Allah who will bring it upon you, if He wills, and you will not be able to escape."

٣٤ وَلَا يَنفَعُكُمْ نُصْحِىٓ إِنْ أَرَدتُّ أَنْ أَنصَحَ
لَكُمْ إِن كَانَ ٱللَّهُ يُرِيدُ أَن يُغْوِيَكُمْۚ هُوَ رَبُّكُمْ
وَإِلَيْهِ تُرْجَعُونَ

34 "My advice will not benefit you, much as I may want to advise you, if Allah desires to confound you. He is your Lord, and to Him you will be returned."

٣٥ أَمْ يَقُولُونَ ٱفْتَرَىٰهُۖ قُلْ إِنِ ٱفْتَرَيْتُهُۥ فَعَلَىَّ
إِجْرَامِى وَأَنَا۠ بَرِىٓءٌ مِّمَّا تُجْرِمُونَ

35 Or do they say, "He made it up?" Say, "If I made it up, upon me falls my crime, and I am innocent of the crimes you commit."

٣٦ وَأُوحِىَ إِلَىٰ نُوحٍ أَنَّهُۥ لَن يُؤْمِنَ مِن قَوْمِكَ
إِلَّا مَن قَدْ ءَامَنَ فَلَا تَبْتَئِسْ بِمَا كَانُواْ يَفْعَلُونَ

36 And it was revealed to Noah: "None of your people will believe, except those who have already believed, so do not grieve over what they do."

٣٧ وَٱصْنَعِ ٱلْفُلْكَ بِأَعْيُنِنَا وَوَحْيِنَا وَلَا تُخَٰطِبْنِى
فِى ٱلَّذِينَ ظَلَمُوٓا۟ ۚ إِنَّهُم مُّغْرَقُونَ

37 “And build the Ark, under Our eyes, and with Our inspiration, and do not address Me regarding those who did wrong; they are to be drowned.”

٣٨ وَيَصْنَعُ ٱلْفُلْكَ وَكُلَّمَا مَرَّ عَلَيْهِ مَلَأٌ مِّن
قَوْمِهِۦ سَخِرُوا۟ مِنْهُ ۚ قَالَ إِن تَسْخَرُوا۟ مِنَّا فَإِنَّا
نَسْخَرُ مِنكُمْ كَمَا تَسْخَرُونَ

38 As he was building the ark, whenever some of his people passed by him, they ridiculed him. He said, “If you ridicule us, we will ridicule you, just as you ridicule.”

٣٩ فَسَوْفَ تَعْلَمُونَ مَن يَأْتِيهِ عَذَابٌ يُخْزِيهِ
وَيَحِلُّ عَلَيْهِ عَذَابٌ مُّقِيمٌ

39 “You will surely know upon whom will come a torment that will abase him, and upon whom will fall a lasting torment.”

٤٠ حَتَّىٰٓ إِذَا جَآءَ أَمْرُنَا وَفَارَ ٱلتَّنُّورُ قُلْنَا ٱحْمِلْ
فِيهَا مِن كُلٍّ زَوْجَيْنِ ٱثْنَيْنِ وَأَهْلَكَ إِلَّا مَن
سَبَقَ عَلَيْهِ ٱلْقَوْلُ وَمَنْ ءَامَنَ ۚ وَمَآ ءَامَنَ مَعَهُۥٓ
إِلَّا قَلِيلٌ

40 Until, when Our command came, and the volcano erupted, We said, “Board into it a pair of every kind, and your family—except those against whom the sentence has already been passed—and those who have believed.” But those who believed with him were only a few.

٤١ وَقَالَ ٱرْكَبُوا۟ فِيهَا بِسْمِ ٱللَّهِ مَجْر۪ىٰهَا
وَمُرْسَىٰهَآ ۚ إِنَّ رَبِّى لَغَفُورٌ رَّحِيمٌ

41 He said, “Embark in it. In the name of Allah shall be its sailing and its anchorage. My Lord is indeed Forgiving and Merciful.”

٤٢ وَهِىَ تَجْرِى بِهِمْ فِى مَوْجٍ كَٱلْجِبَالِ وَنَادَىٰ
نُوحٌ ٱبْنَهُۥ وَكَانَ فِى مَعْزِلٍ يَٰبُنَىَّ ٱرْكَب مَّعَنَا وَلَا
تَكُن مَّعَ ٱلْكَٰفِرِينَ

42 And so it sailed with them amidst waves like hills. And Noah called to his son, who had kept away, “O my son! Embark with us, and do not be with the disbelievers.”

٤٣ قَالَ سَـَٔاوِىٓ إِلَىٰ جَبَلٍ يَعْصِمُنِى مِنَ ٱلْمَآءِ ۚ
قَالَ لَا عَاصِمَ ٱلْيَوْمَ مِنْ أَمْرِ ٱللَّهِ إِلَّا مَن رَّحِمَ ۚ
وَحَالَ بَيْنَهُمَا ٱلْمَوْجُ فَكَانَ مِنَ ٱلْمُغْرَقِينَ

43 He said, “I will take refuge on a mountain—it will protect me from the water.” He said, “There is no protection from Allah’s decree today, except for him on whom He has mercy.” And the waves surged between them, and he was among the drowned.

٤٤ وَقِيلَ يَٰٓأَرْضُ ٱبْلَعِى مَآءَكِ وَيَٰسَمَآءُ أَقْلِعِى
وَغِيضَ ٱلْمَآءُ وَقُضِىَ ٱلْأَمْرُ وَٱسْتَوَتْ عَلَى
ٱلْجُودِىِّ ۖ وَقِيلَ بُعْدًا لِّلْقَوْمِ ٱلظَّٰلِمِينَ

44 And it was said, “O earth, swallow your waters,” and “O heaven, clear up.” And the waters receded, and the event was concluded, and it settled on Judi, and it was proclaimed: “Away with the wicked people.”

٤٥ وَنَادَىٰ نُوحٌ رَّبَّهُۥ فَقَالَ رَبِّ إِنَّ ٱبْنِى مِنْ
أَهْلِى وَإِنَّ وَعْدَكَ ٱلْحَقُّ وَأَنتَ أَحْكَمُ ٱلْحَٰكِمِينَ

45 And Noah called to his Lord. He said, “O My Lord, my son is of my family, and Your promise is true, and You are the Wisest of the wise.”

٤٦ قَالَ يَٰنُوحُ إِنَّهُۥ لَيْسَ مِنْ أَهْلِكَ ۖ إِنَّهُۥ عَمَلٌ
غَيْرُ صَٰلِحٍ ۖ فَلَا تَسْـَٔلْنِ مَا لَيْسَ لَكَ بِهِۦ عِلْمٌ ۖ
إِنِّىٓ أَعِظُكَ أَن تَكُونَ مِنَ ٱلْجَٰهِلِينَ

46 He said, “O Noah, he is not of your family. It is an unrighteous deed. So do not ask Me about something you know nothing about. I admonish you, lest you be one of the ignorant.”

٤٧ قَالَ رَبِّ إِنِّىٓ أَعُوذُ بِكَ أَنْ أَسْـَٔلَكَ مَا لَيْسَ
لِى بِهِۦ عِلْمٌ ۖ وَإِلَّا تَغْفِرْ لِى وَتَرْحَمْنِىٓ أَكُن مِّنَ
ٱلْخَٰسِرِينَ

47 He said, “O My Lord, I seek refuge with You, from asking You about what I have no knowledge of. Unless You forgive me, and have mercy on me, I will be one of the losers.”

٤٨ قِيلَ يَٰنُوحُ ٱهْبِطْ بِسَلَٰمٍ مِّنَّا وَبَرَكَٰتٍ عَلَيْكَ
وَعَلَىٰٓ أُمَمٍ مِّمَّن مَّعَكَ ۚ وَأُمَمٌ سَنُمَتِّعُهُمْ ثُمَّ
يَمَسُّهُم مِّنَّا عَذَابٌ أَلِيمٌ

48 It was said, “O Noah, disembark with peace from Us; and with blessings upon you, and upon communities from those with you. And other communities We will grant prosperity, and then a painful torment from Us will befall them.”

٤٩ تِلْكَ مِنْ أَنۢبَآءِ ٱلْغَيْبِ نُوحِيهَآ إِلَيْكَ ۖ مَا كُنتَ
تَعْلَمُهَآ أَنتَ وَلَا قَوْمُكَ مِن قَبْلِ هَٰذَا ۖ فَٱصْبِرْ ۖ
إِنَّ ٱلْعَٰقِبَةَ لِلْمُتَّقِينَ

49 These are some stories from the past that we reveal to you. Neither you, nor your people knew them before this. So be patient. The future belongs to the pious.

٥٠ وَإِلَىٰ عَادٍ أَخَاهُمْ هُودًا ۚ قَالَ يَٰقَوْمِ ٱعْبُدُوا۟
ٱللَّهَ مَا لَكُم مِّنْ إِلَٰهٍ غَيْرُهُۥٓ ۖ إِنْ أَنتُمْ إِلَّا مُفْتَرُونَ

50 And to Aad, their brother Hud. He said, “O my people, worship Allah, you have no other god besides Him. You do nothing but invent lies.”

٥١ يَٰقَوْمِ لَآ أَسْـَٔلُكُمْ عَلَيْهِ أَجْرًا ۖ إِنْ أَجْرِىَ إِلَّا
عَلَى ٱلَّذِى فَطَرَنِىٓ ۚ أَفَلَا تَعْقِلُونَ

51 “O my people, I ask you no wage for it; my wage lies with Him who originated me. Do you not understand?”

٥٢ وَيَٰقَوۡمِ ٱسۡتَغۡفِرُواْ رَبَّكُمۡ ثُمَّ تُوبُوٓاْ إِلَيۡهِ
يُرۡسِلِ ٱلسَّمَآءَ عَلَيۡكُم مِّدۡرَارٗا وَيَزِدۡكُمۡ قُوَّةً إِلَىٰ
قُوَّتِكُمۡ وَلَا تَتَوَلَّوۡاْ مُجۡرِمِينَ

52 "O my people, ask forgiveness from your Lord, and repent to Him. He will release the sky pouring down upon you, and will add strength to your strength. And do not turn away and be wicked."

٥٣ قَالُواْ يَٰهُودُ مَا جِئۡتَنَا بِبَيِّنَةٖ وَمَا نَحۡنُ
بِتَارِكِيٓ ءَالِهَتِنَا عَن قَوۡلِكَ وَمَا نَحۡنُ لَكَ
بِمُؤۡمِنِينَ

53 They said, "O Hud, you did not bring us any evidence, and we are not about to abandon our gods at your word, and we are not believers in you."

٥٤ إِن نَّقُولُ إِلَّا ٱعۡتَرَىٰكَ بَعۡضُ ءَالِهَتِنَا بِسُوٓءٖۗ
قَالَ إِنِّيٓ أُشۡهِدُ ٱللَّهَ وَٱشۡهَدُوٓاْ أَنِّي بَرِيٓءٞ مِّمَّا
تُشۡرِكُونَ

54 "We only say that some of our gods have possessed you with evil." He said, "I call Allah to witness, and you to witness, that I am innocent of what you associate.

٥٥ مِن دُونِهِۦۖ فَكِيدُونِي جَمِيعٗا ثُمَّ لَا تُنظِرُونِ

55 Besides Him. So scheme against me, all of you, and do not hesitate.

٥٦ إِنِّي تَوَكَّلۡتُ عَلَى ٱللَّهِ رَبِّي وَرَبِّكُمۚ مَّا مِن
دَآبَّةٍ إِلَّا هُوَ ءَاخِذُۢ بِنَاصِيَتِهَآۚ إِنَّ رَبِّي عَلَىٰ
صِرَٰطٖ مُّسۡتَقِيمٖ

56 I have placed my trust in Allah, my Lord and your Lord. There is not a creature but He holds it by the forelock. My Lord is on a straight path.

٥٧ فَإِن تَوَلَّوۡاْ فَقَدۡ أَبۡلَغۡتُكُم مَّآ أُرۡسِلۡتُ بِهِۦٓ
إِلَيۡكُمۡۚ وَيَسۡتَخۡلِفُ رَبِّي قَوۡمًا غَيۡرَكُمۡ وَلَا
تَضُرُّونَهُۥ شَيۡـًٔاۚ إِنَّ رَبِّي عَلَىٰ كُلِّ شَيۡءٍ حَفِيظٞ

57 If you turn away, I have conveyed to you what I was sent to you with; and my Lord will replace you with another people, and you will not cause Him any harm. My Lord is Guardian over all things."

٥٨ وَلَمَّا جَآءَ أَمۡرُنَا نَجَّيۡنَا هُودٗا وَٱلَّذِينَ ءَامَنُواْ
مَعَهُۥ بِرَحۡمَةٖ مِّنَّا وَنَجَّيۡنَٰهُم مِّنۡ عَذَابٍ غَلِيظٖ

58 And when Our decree came, We saved Hud and those who believed with him, by a mercy from Us, and We delivered them from a harsh punishment.

٥٩ وَتِلۡكَ عَادٞۖ جَحَدُواْ بِـَٔايَٰتِ رَبِّهِمۡ وَعَصَوۡاْ
رُسُلَهُۥ وَٱتَّبَعُوٓاْ أَمۡرَ كُلِّ جَبَّارٍ عَنِيدٖ

59 That was Aad; they denied the signs of their Lord, and defied His messengers, and followed the lead of every stubborn tyrant.

٦٠ وَأُتۡبِعُواْ فِي هَٰذِهِ ٱلدُّنۡيَا لَعۡنَةٗ وَيَوۡمَ ٱلۡقِيَٰمَةِۗ
أَلَآ إِنَّ عَادٗا كَفَرُواْ رَبَّهُمۡۗ أَلَا بُعۡدٗا لِّعَادٖ قَوۡمِ هُودٖ

60 And they were pursued by a curse in this world, and on the Day of Resurrection. Indeed, Aad

blasphemed against their Lord—so away with Aad, the people of Hud.

٦١ وَإِلَىٰ ثَمُودَ أَخَاهُمْ صَٰلِحًا ۚ قَالَ يَٰقَوْمِ
ٱعْبُدُوا۟ ٱللَّهَ مَا لَكُم مِّنْ إِلَٰهٍ غَيْرُهُۥ ۖ هُوَ أَنشَأَكُم
مِّنَ ٱلْأَرْضِ وَٱسْتَعْمَرَكُمْ فِيهَا فَٱسْتَغْفِرُوهُ ثُمَّ
تُوبُوٓا۟ إِلَيْهِ ۚ إِنَّ رَبِّى قَرِيبٌ مُّجِيبٌ

61 And to Thamood, their brother Saleh. He said, “O my people, worship Allah, you have no god other than Him. He initiated you from the earth, and settled you in it. So seek His forgiveness, and repent to Him. My Lord is Near and Responsive.”

٦٢ قَالُوا۟ يَٰصَٰلِحُ قَدْ كُنتَ فِينَا مَرْجُوًّا قَبْلَ هَٰذَآ ۖ
أَتَنْهَىٰنَآ أَن نَّعْبُدَ مَا يَعْبُدُ ءَابَآؤُنَا وَإِنَّنَا لَفِى شَكٍّ
مِّمَّا تَدْعُونَآ إِلَيْهِ مُرِيبٍ

62 They said, “O Saleh, we had hopes in you before this. Are you trying to prevent us from worshiping what our parents worship? We are in serious doubt regarding what you are calling us to.”

٦٣ قَالَ يَٰقَوْمِ أَرَءَيْتُمْ إِن كُنتُ عَلَىٰ بَيِّنَةٍ مِّن
رَّبِّى وَءَاتَىٰنِى مِنْهُ رَحْمَةً فَمَن يَنصُرُنِى مِنَ
ٱللَّهِ إِنْ عَصَيْتُهُۥ ۖ فَمَا تَزِيدُونَنِى غَيْرَ تَخْسِيرٍ

63 He said, “O my people, have you considered? If I stand upon clear evidence from my Lord, and He has given me mercy from Him, who would protect me from Allah, if I disobeyed Him? You add nothing for me except loss.”

٦٤ وَيَٰقَوْمِ هَٰذِهِۦ نَاقَةُ ٱللَّهِ لَكُمْ ءَايَةً فَذَرُوهَا
تَأْكُلْ فِىٓ أَرْضِ ٱللَّهِ وَلَا تَمَسُّوهَا بِسُوٓءٍ
فَيَأْخُذَكُمْ عَذَابٌ قَرِيبٌ

64 “O my people, this is the she-camel of Allah, a sign for you. Let her graze on Allah’s land, and do not harm her, lest an imminent punishment overtakes you.”

٦٥ فَعَقَرُوهَا فَقَالَ تَمَتَّعُوا۟ فِى دَارِكُمْ ثَلَٰثَةَ
أَيَّامٍ ۖ ذَٰلِكَ وَعْدٌ غَيْرُ مَكْذُوبٍ

65 But they hamstrung her, and so He said, “Enjoy yourselves in your homes for three days. This is a prophecy that is infallible.”

٦٦ فَلَمَّا جَآءَ أَمْرُنَا نَجَّيْنَا صَٰلِحًا وَٱلَّذِينَ
ءَامَنُوا۟ مَعَهُۥ بِرَحْمَةٍ مِّنَّا وَمِنْ خِزْىِ يَوْمِئِذٍ ۗ إِنَّ
رَبَّكَ هُوَ ٱلْقَوِىُّ ٱلْعَزِيزُ

66 Then, when Our command came, We saved Saleh and those who believed with him, by a mercy from Us, from the disgrace of that day. Your Lord is the Strong, the Mighty.

٦٧ وَأَخَذَ ٱلَّذِينَ ظَلَمُوا۟ ٱلصَّيْحَةُ فَأَصْبَحُوا۟ فِى
دِيَٰرِهِمْ جَٰثِمِينَ

67 And the Scream struck those who transgressed, and they became motionless bodies in their homes.

٦٨ كَأَن لَّمْ يَغْنَوْا۟ فِيهَآ ۗ أَلَآ إِنَّ ثَمُودَا۟ كَفَرُوا۟
رَبَّهُمْ ۗ أَلَا بُعْدًا لِّثَمُودَ

68 As if they had never prospered therein. Indeed, Thamood rejected their Lord, so away with Thamood.

٦٩ وَلَقَدْ جَآءَتْ رُسُلُنَآ إِبْرَٰهِيمَ بِٱلْبُشْرَىٰ قَالُوا۟
سَلَٰمًا ۖ قَالَ سَلَٰمٌ ۖ فَمَا لَبِثَ أَن جَآءَ بِعِجْلٍ حَنِيذٍ

69 Our messengers came to Abraham with good news. They said, “Peace.” He said, “Peace.” Soon after, he came with a roasted calf.

٧٠ فَلَمَّا رَءَآ أَيْدِيَهُمْ لَا تَصِلُ إِلَيْهِ نَكِرَهُمْ
وَأَوْجَسَ مِنْهُمْ خِيفَةً ۚ قَالُوا۟ لَا تَخَفْ إِنَّآ أُرْسِلْنَآ
إِلَىٰ قَوْمِ لُوطٍ

70 But when he saw their hands not reaching towards it, he became suspicious of them, and conceived a fear of them. They said, “Do not fear, we were sent to the people of Lot.”

٧١ وَٱمْرَأَتُهُۥ قَآئِمَةٌ فَضَحِكَتْ فَبَشَّرْنَٰهَا بِإِسْحَٰقَ
وَمِن وَرَآءِ إِسْحَٰقَ يَعْقُوبَ

71 His wife was standing by, so she laughed. And We gave her good news of Isaac; and after Isaac, Jacob.

٧٢ قَالَتْ يَٰوَيْلَتَىٰٓ ءَأَلِدُ وَأَنَا۠ عَجُوزٌ وَهَٰذَا بَعْلِى
شَيْخًا ۖ إِنَّ هَٰذَا لَشَىْءٌ عَجِيبٌ

72 She said, “Alas for me. Shall I give birth, when I am an old woman, and this, my husband, is an old man? This is truly a strange thing.”

٧٣ قَالُوٓا۟ أَتَعْجَبِينَ مِنْ أَمْرِ ٱللَّهِ ۖ رَحْمَتُ ٱللَّهِ
وَبَرَكَٰتُهُۥ عَلَيْكُمْ أَهْلَ ٱلْبَيْتِ ۚ إِنَّهُۥ حَمِيدٌ مَّجِيدٌ

73 They said, “Do you marvel at the decree of Allah? The mercy and blessings of Allah are upon you, O people of the house. He is Praiseworthy and Glorious.”

٧٤ فَلَمَّا ذَهَبَ عَنْ إِبْرَٰهِيمَ ٱلرَّوْعُ وَجَآءَتْهُ
ٱلْبُشْرَىٰ يُجَٰدِلُنَا فِى قَوْمِ لُوطٍ

74 When Abraham's fear subsided, and the good news had reached him, he started pleading with Us concerning the people of Lot.

٧٥ إِنَّ إِبْرَٰهِيمَ لَحَلِيمٌ أَوَّٰهٌ مُّنِيبٌ

75 Abraham was gentle, kind, penitent.

٧٦ يَٰٓإِبْرَٰهِيمُ أَعْرِضْ عَنْ هَٰذَآ ۖ إِنَّهُۥ قَدْ جَآءَ أَمْرُ
رَبِّكَ ۖ وَإِنَّهُمْ ءَاتِيهِمْ عَذَابٌ غَيْرُ مَرْدُودٍ

76 “O Abraham, refrain from this. The command of your Lord has come; they have incurred an irreversible punishment.”

٧٧ وَلَمَّا جَآءَتْ رُسُلُنَا لُوطًا سِىٓءَ بِهِمْ وَضَاقَ
بِهِمْ ذَرْعًا وَقَالَ هَٰذَا يَوْمٌ عَصِيبٌ

77 And when Our envoys came to Lot, he was anxious for them, and concerned for them. He said, “This is a dreadful day.”

٧٨ وَجَآءَهُۥ قَوْمُهُۥ يُهْرَعُونَ إِلَيْهِ وَمِن قَبْلُ كَانُوا۟
يَعْمَلُونَ ٱلسَّيِّـَٔاتِ ۚ قَالَ يَٰقَوْمِ هَٰٓؤُلَآءِ بَنَاتِى هُنَّ
أَطْهَرُ لَكُمْ ۖ فَٱتَّقُوا۟ ٱللَّهَ وَلَا تُخْزُونِ فِى ضَيْفِىٓ ۖ
أَلَيْسَ مِنكُمْ رَجُلٌ رَّشِيدٌ

78 And his people came rushing towards him—they were in the habit of committing sins. He said, “O my people, these are my daughters; they are purer for you. So fear Allah, and do not embarrass me before my guests. Is there not one reasonable man among you?”

٧٩ قَالُوا۟ لَقَدْ عَلِمْتَ مَا لَنَا فِى بَنَاتِكَ مِنْ حَقٍّ
وَإِنَّكَ لَتَعْلَمُ مَا نُرِيدُ

79 They said, “You know well that we have no right to your daughters, and you know well what we want.”

٨٠ قَالَ لَوْ أَنَّ لِى بِكُمْ قُوَّةً أَوْ ءَاوِىٓ إِلَىٰ رُكْنٍ
شَدِيدٍ

80 He said, “If only I had the strength to stop you, or could rely on some strong support.”

٨١ قَالُوا۟ يَٰلُوطُ إِنَّا رُسُلُ رَبِّكَ لَن يَصِلُوٓا۟ إِلَيْكَ ۖ
فَأَسْرِ بِأَهْلِكَ بِقِطْعٍ مِّنَ ٱلَّيْلِ وَلَا يَلْتَفِتْ مِنكُمْ
أَحَدٌ إِلَّا ٱمْرَأَتَكَ ۖ إِنَّهُۥ مُصِيبُهَا مَآ أَصَابَهُمْ ۚ إِنَّ
مَوْعِدَهُمُ ٱلصُّبْحُ ۚ أَلَيْسَ ٱلصُّبْحُ بِقَرِيبٍ

81 They said, “O Lot, we are the envoys of your Lord; they will not reach you. So set out with your family during the cover of the night, and let none of you look back, except for your wife. She will be struck by what will strike them. Their appointed time is the morning. Is not the morning near?”

٨٢ فَلَمَّا جَآءَ أَمْرُنَا جَعَلْنَا عَٰلِيَهَا سَافِلَهَا
وَأَمْطَرْنَا عَلَيْهَا حِجَارَةً مِّن سِجِّيلٍ مَّنضُودٍ

82 And when Our command came about, We turned it upside down, and We rained down on it stones of baked clay.

٨٣ مُّسَوَّمَةً عِندَ رَبِّكَ ۖ وَمَا هِىَ مِنَ ٱلظَّٰلِمِينَ
بِبَعِيدٍ

83 Marked from your Lord, and never far from the wrongdoers.

٨٤ وَإِلَىٰ مَدْيَنَ أَخَاهُمْ شُعَيْبًا ۚ قَالَ يَٰقَوْمِ
ٱعْبُدُوا۟ ٱللَّهَ مَا لَكُم مِّنْ إِلَٰهٍ غَيْرُهُۥ ۖ وَلَا تَنقُصُوا۟
ٱلْمِكْيَالَ وَٱلْمِيزَانَ ۚ إِنِّىٓ أَرَىٰكُم بِخَيْرٍ وَإِنِّىٓ
أَخَافُ عَلَيْكُمْ عَذَابَ يَوْمٍ مُّحِيطٍ

84 And to Median, their brother Shuaib. He said, “O my people, worship Allah; you have no god other than Him. And do not short measure or short weight. I see you in good circumstances, but I fear for you the agony of an encompassing Day.”

٨٥ وَيَٰقَوۡمِ أَوۡفُواْ ٱلۡمِكۡيَالَ وَٱلۡمِيزَانَ بِٱلۡقِسۡطِۖ
وَلَا تَبۡخَسُواْ ٱلنَّاسَ أَشۡيَآءَهُمۡ وَلَا تَعۡثَوۡاْ فِي
ٱلۡأَرۡضِ مُفۡسِدِينَ

85 "O my people! Give full measure and full weight, in all fairness, and do not cheat the people out of their rights, and do not spread corruption in the land.

٨٦ بَقِيَّتُ ٱللَّهِ خَيۡرٞ لَّكُمۡ إِن كُنتُم مُّؤۡمِنِينَۚ وَمَآ
أَنَا۠ عَلَيۡكُم بِحَفِيظٖ

86 What is left by Allah is best for you, if you are believers. And I am not a guardian over you."

٨٧ قَالُواْ يَٰشُعَيۡبُ أَصَلَوٰتُكَ تَأۡمُرُكَ أَن نَّتۡرُكَ مَا
يَعۡبُدُ ءَابَآؤُنَآ أَوۡ أَن نَّفۡعَلَ فِيٓ أَمۡوَٰلِنَا مَا نَشَٰٓؤُاْۖ
إِنَّكَ لَأَنتَ ٱلۡحَلِيمُ ٱلرَّشِيدُ

87 They said, "O Shuaib, does your prayer command you that we abandon what our ancestors worshiped, or doing with our wealth what we want? You are the one who is intelligent and wise."

٨٨ قَالَ يَٰقَوۡمِ أَرَءَيۡتُمۡ إِن كُنتُ عَلَىٰ بَيِّنَةٖ مِّن
رَّبِّي وَرَزَقَنِي مِنۡهُ رِزۡقًا حَسَنٗاۚ وَمَآ أُرِيدُ أَنۡ
أُخَالِفَكُمۡ إِلَىٰ مَآ أَنۡهَىٰكُمۡ عَنۡهُۚ إِنۡ أُرِيدُ إِلَّا
ٱلۡإِصۡلَٰحَ مَا ٱسۡتَطَعۡتُۚ وَمَا تَوۡفِيقِيٓ إِلَّا بِٱللَّهِۚ
عَلَيۡهِ تَوَكَّلۡتُ وَإِلَيۡهِ أُنِيبُ

88 He said, "O my people, have you considered? What if I have clear evidence from my Lord, and He has given me good livelihood from Himself? I have no desire to do what I forbid you from doing. I desire nothing but reform, as far as I can. My success lies only with Allah. In Him I trust, and to Him I turn."

٨٩ وَيَٰقَوۡمِ لَا يَجۡرِمَنَّكُمۡ شِقَاقِيٓ أَن يُصِيبَكُم
مِّثۡلُ مَآ أَصَابَ قَوۡمَ نُوحٍ أَوۡ قَوۡمَ هُودٍ أَوۡ قَوۡمَ
صَٰلِحٖۚ وَمَا قَوۡمُ لُوطٖ مِّنكُم بِبَعِيدٖ

89 "O my people, let not your hostility towards me cause you to suffer what was suffered by the people of Noah, or the people of Hud, or the people of Saleh. The people of Lot are not far away from you."

٩٠ وَٱسۡتَغۡفِرُواْ رَبَّكُمۡ ثُمَّ تُوبُوٓاْ إِلَيۡهِۚ إِنَّ رَبِّي
رَحِيمٞ وَدُودٞ

90 "And ask your Lord for forgiveness, and repent to Him. My Lord is Merciful and Loving."

٩١ قَالُواْ يَٰشُعَيۡبُ مَا نَفۡقَهُ كَثِيرٗا مِّمَّا تَقُولُ وَإِنَّا
لَنَرَىٰكَ فِينَا ضَعِيفٗاۖ وَلَوۡلَا رَهۡطُكَ لَرَجَمۡنَٰكَۖ
وَمَآ أَنتَ عَلَيۡنَا بِعَزِيزٖ

91 They said, "O Shuaib, we do not understand much of what you say, and we see that you are weak among us. Were it not for your tribe, we would have stoned you. You are of no value to us."

٩٢ قَالَ يَٰقَوْمِ أَرَهْطِىٓ أَعَزُّ عَلَيْكُم مِّنَ ٱللَّهِ
وَٱتَّخَذْتُمُوهُ وَرَآءَكُمْ ظِهْرِيًّا ۖ إِنَّ رَبِّى بِمَا
تَعْمَلُونَ مُحِيطٌ

92 He said, "O my people, is my tribe more important to you than Allah? And you have turned your backs on Him? My Lord comprehends everything you do."

٩٣ وَيَٰقَوْمِ ٱعْمَلُوا۟ عَلَىٰ مَكَانَتِكُمْ إِنِّى عَٰمِلٌ ۖ
سَوْفَ تَعْلَمُونَ مَن يَأْتِيهِ عَذَابٌ يُخْزِيهِ وَمَنْ
هُوَ كَٰذِبٌ ۖ وَٱرْتَقِبُوٓا۟ إِنِّى مَعَكُمْ رَقِيبٌ

93 "O my people, do as you may, and so will I. You will know to whom will come a punishment that will shame him, and who is a liar. So look out; I am on the lookout with you."

٩٤ وَلَمَّا جَآءَ أَمْرُنَا نَجَّيْنَا شُعَيْبًا وَٱلَّذِينَ
ءَامَنُوا۟ مَعَهُۥ بِرَحْمَةٍ مِّنَّا وَأَخَذَتِ ٱلَّذِينَ ظَلَمُوا۟
ٱلصَّيْحَةُ فَأَصْبَحُوا۟ فِى دِيَٰرِهِمْ جَٰثِمِينَ

94 And when Our command came, We saved Shuaib and those who believed with him, by mercy from Us, and the Blast struck the wrongdoers, and they became motionless bodies in their homes.

٩٥ كَأَن لَّمْ يَغْنَوْا۟ فِيهَآ ۗ أَلَا بُعْدًا لِّمَدْيَنَ كَمَا
بَعِدَتْ ثَمُودُ

95 As though they never flourished therein. Away with Median, as was done away with Thamood.

٩٦ وَلَقَدْ أَرْسَلْنَا مُوسَىٰ بِـَٔايَٰتِنَا وَسُلْطَٰنٍ مُّبِينٍ

96 And We sent Moses with Our signs and a clear mandate.

٩٧ إِلَىٰ فِرْعَوْنَ وَمَلَإِي۟هِۦ فَٱتَّبَعُوٓا۟ أَمْرَ فِرْعَوْنَ ۖ
وَمَآ أَمْرُ فِرْعَوْنَ بِرَشِيدٍ

97 To Pharaoh and his nobles, but they followed the command of Pharaoh, and the command of Pharaoh was not wise.

٩٨ يَقْدُمُ قَوْمَهُۥ يَوْمَ ٱلْقِيَٰمَةِ فَأَوْرَدَهُمُ ٱلنَّارَ ۖ
وَبِئْسَ ٱلْوِرْدُ ٱلْمَوْرُودُ

98 He will precede his people on the Day of Resurrection, and will lead them into the Fire. Miserable is the place he placed them in.

٩٩ وَأُتْبِعُوا۟ فِى هَٰذِهِۦ لَعْنَةً وَيَوْمَ ٱلْقِيَٰمَةِ ۚ بِئْسَ
ٱلرِّفْدُ ٱلْمَرْفُودُ

99 They were followed by a curse in this, and on the Day of Resurrection. Miserable is the path they followed.

١٠٠ ذَٰلِكَ مِنْ أَنۢبَآءِ ٱلْقُرَىٰ نَقُصُّهُۥ عَلَيْكَ ۖ مِنْهَا
قَآئِمٌ وَحَصِيدٌ

100 These are of the reports of the towns—We relate them to you. Some are still standing, and some have withered away.

١٠١ وَمَا ظَلَمْنَٰهُمْ وَلَٰكِن ظَلَمُوٓا۟ أَنفُسَهُمْ ۖ فَمَآ
أَغْنَتْ عَنْهُمْ ءَالِهَتُهُمُ ٱلَّتِى يَدْعُونَ مِن دُونِ

101 We did not wrong them, but they wronged themselves. Their gods, whom they invoked besides Allah, availed them nothing when the

ٱللَّهِ مِن شَىْءٍ لَّمَّا جَآءَ أَمْرُ رَبِّكَ ۖ وَمَا زَادُوهُمْ
غَيْرَ تَتْبِيبٍ

command of your Lord arrived. In fact, they added only to their ruin.

١٠٢ وَكَذَٰلِكَ أَخْذُ رَبِّكَ إِذَآ أَخَذَ ٱلْقُرَىٰ وَهِىَ
ظَٰلِمَةٌ ۚ إِنَّ أَخْذَهُۥٓ أَلِيمٌ شَدِيدٌ

102 Such is the grip of your Lord when He seizes the towns in the midst of their sins. His grip is most painful, most severe.

١٠٣ إِنَّ فِى ذَٰلِكَ لَءَايَةً لِّمَنْ خَافَ عَذَابَ
ٱلْءَاخِرَةِ ۚ ذَٰلِكَ يَوْمٌ مَّجْمُوعٌ لَّهُ ٱلنَّاسُ وَذَٰلِكَ
يَوْمٌ مَّشْهُودٌ

103 In that is a sign for whoever fears the punishment of the Hereafter. That is a Day for which humanity will be gathered together—that is a Day to be witnessed.

١٠٤ وَمَا نُؤَخِّرُهُۥٓ إِلَّا لِأَجَلٍ مَّعْدُودٍ

104 We only postpone it until a predetermined time.

١٠٥ يَوْمَ يَأْتِ لَا تَكَلَّمُ نَفْسٌ إِلَّا بِإِذْنِهِۦ ۚ فَمِنْهُمْ
شَقِىٌّ وَسَعِيدٌ

105 On the Day when it arrives, no soul will speak without His permission. Some will be miserable, and some will be happy.

١٠٦ فَأَمَّا ٱلَّذِينَ شَقُوا۟ فَفِى ٱلنَّارِ لَهُمْ فِيهَا زَفِيرٌ
وَشَهِيقٌ

106 As for those who are miserable, they will be in the Fire. They will have therein sighing and wailing.

١٠٧ خَٰلِدِينَ فِيهَا مَا دَامَتِ ٱلسَّمَٰوَٰتُ وَٱلْأَرْضُ
إِلَّا مَا شَآءَ رَبُّكَ ۚ إِنَّ رَبَّكَ فَعَّالٌ لِّمَا يُرِيدُ

107 Remaining therein for as long as the heavens and the earth endure, except as your Lord wills. Your Lord is Doer of whatever He wills.

١٠٨ وَأَمَّا ٱلَّذِينَ سُعِدُوا۟ فَفِى ٱلْجَنَّةِ خَٰلِدِينَ
فِيهَا مَا دَامَتِ ٱلسَّمَٰوَٰتُ وَٱلْأَرْضُ إِلَّا مَا شَآءَ
رَبُّكَ ۖ عَطَآءً غَيْرَ مَجْذُوذٍ

108 And as for those who are happy, they will be in Paradise, remaining therein for as long as the heavens and the earth endure, except as your Lord wills—a reward without end.

١٠٩ فَلَا تَكُ فِى مِرْيَةٍ مِّمَّا يَعْبُدُ هَٰٓؤُلَآءِ ۚ مَا
يَعْبُدُونَ إِلَّا كَمَا يَعْبُدُ ءَابَآؤُهُم مِّن قَبْلُ ۚ وَإِنَّا
لَمُوَفُّوهُمْ نَصِيبَهُمْ غَيْرَ مَنقُوصٍ

109 So be not in doubt regarding what these people worship. They worship only as their ancestors worshiped before. We will pay them their due in full, without any reduction.

١١٠ وَلَقَدْ ءَاتَيْنَا مُوسَى ٱلْكِتَٰبَ فَٱخْتُلِفَ فِيهِ ۚ
وَلَوْلَا كَلِمَةٌ سَبَقَتْ مِن رَّبِّكَ لَقُضِىَ بَيْنَهُمْ ۚ
وَإِنَّهُمْ لَفِى شَكٍّ مِّنْهُ مُرِيبٍ

110 We gave Moses the Scripture, but it was disputed. Were it not for a prior word from your Lord, it would have been settled between them. They are in serious doubt concerning it.

١١١ وَإِنَّ كُلًّا لَّمَّا لَيُوَفِّيَنَّهُمْ رَبُّكَ أَعْمَٰلَهُمْ ۚ إِنَّهُۥ بِمَا
يَعْمَلُونَ خَبِيرٌ

111 Your Lord will repay each one of them in full for their deeds. He is Aware of everything they do.

١١٢ فَٱسْتَقِمْ كَمَآ أُمِرْتَ وَمَن تَابَ مَعَكَ وَلَا
تَطْغَوْا۟ ۚ إِنَّهُۥ بِمَا تَعْمَلُونَ بَصِيرٌ

112 So be upright, as you are commanded, along with those who repented with you, and do not transgress. He is Seeing of everything you do.

١١٣ وَلَا تَرْكَنُوٓا۟ إِلَى ٱلَّذِينَ ظَلَمُوا۟ فَتَمَسَّكُمُ ٱلنَّارُ
وَمَا لَكُم مِّن دُونِ ٱللَّهِ مِنْ أَوْلِيَآءَ ثُمَّ لَا
تُنصَرُونَ

113 And do not incline towards those who do wrong, or the Fire may touch you; and you will have no protectors besides Allah, and you will not be saved.

١١٤ وَأَقِمِ ٱلصَّلَوٰةَ طَرَفَىِ ٱلنَّهَارِ وَزُلَفًا مِّنَ ٱلَّيْلِ ۚ
إِنَّ ٱلْحَسَنَٰتِ يُذْهِبْنَ ٱلسَّيِّـَٔاتِ ۚ ذَٰلِكَ ذِكْرَىٰ
لِلذَّٰكِرِينَ

114 Perform the prayer at the borders of the day, and during the approaches of the night. The good deeds take away the bad deeds. This is a reminder for those who remember.

١١٥ وَٱصْبِرْ فَإِنَّ ٱللَّهَ لَا يُضِيعُ أَجْرَ ٱلْمُحْسِنِينَ

115 And be patient. Allah will not waste the reward of the virtuous.

١١٦ فَلَوْلَا كَانَ مِنَ ٱلْقُرُونِ مِن قَبْلِكُمْ أُو۟لُوا۟
بَقِيَّةٍ يَنْهَوْنَ عَنِ ٱلْفَسَادِ فِى ٱلْأَرْضِ إِلَّا قَلِيلًا
مِّمَّنْ أَنجَيْنَا مِنْهُمْ ۗ وَٱتَّبَعَ ٱلَّذِينَ ظَلَمُوا۟ مَآ
أُتْرِفُوا۟ فِيهِ وَكَانُوا۟ مُجْرِمِينَ

116 If only there were, among the generations before you, people with wisdom, who spoke against corruption on earth—except for the few whom We saved. But the wrongdoers pursued the luxuries they were indulged in, and thus became guilty.

١١٧ وَمَا كَانَ رَبُّكَ لِيُهْلِكَ ٱلْقُرَىٰ بِظُلْمٍ وَأَهْلُهَا
مُصْلِحُونَ

117 Your Lord would never destroy the towns wrongfully, while their inhabitants are righteous.

١١٨ وَلَوْ شَآءَ رَبُّكَ لَجَعَلَ ٱلنَّاسَ أُمَّةً وَٰحِدَةً ۖ وَلَا
يَزَالُونَ مُخْتَلِفِينَ

118 Had your Lord willed, He could have made humanity one community, but they continue to differ.

١١٩ إِلَّا مَن رَّحِمَ رَبُّكَ ۚ وَلِذَٰلِكَ خَلَقَهُمْ ۗ وَتَمَّتْ
كَلِمَةُ رَبِّكَ لَأَمْلَأَنَّ جَهَنَّمَ مِنَ ٱلْجِنَّةِ وَٱلنَّاسِ
أَجْمَعِينَ

119 Except those on whom your Lord has mercy—for that reason He created them. The Word of your Lord is final: “I will fill Hell with jinn and humans, altogether.”

١٢٠ وَكُلًّا نَّقُصُّ عَلَيْكَ مِنْ أَنۢبَآءِ ٱلرُّسُلِ مَا نُثَبِّتُ بِهِۦ فُؤَادَكَ ۚ وَجَآءَكَ فِى هَٰذِهِ ٱلْحَقُّ وَمَوْعِظَةٌ وَذِكْرَىٰ لِلْمُؤْمِنِينَ	120 Everything We narrate to you of the history of the messengers is to strengthen your heart therewith. The truth has come to you in this, and a lesson, and a reminder for the believers.
١٢١ وَقُل لِّلَّذِينَ لَا يُؤْمِنُونَ ٱعْمَلُوا۟ عَلَىٰ مَكَانَتِكُمْ إِنَّا عَٰمِلُونَ	121 And say to those who do not believe, "Act according to your ability; and so will we."
١٢٢ وَٱنتَظِرُوٓا۟ إِنَّا مُنتَظِرُونَ	122 "And wait; we too are waiting."
١٢٣ وَلِلَّهِ غَيْبُ ٱلسَّمَٰوَٰتِ وَٱلْأَرْضِ وَإِلَيْهِ يُرْجَعُ ٱلْأَمْرُ كُلُّهُۥ فَٱعْبُدْهُ وَتَوَكَّلْ عَلَيْهِ ۚ وَمَا رَبُّكَ بِغَٰفِلٍ عَمَّا تَعْمَلُونَ	123 To Allah belongs the future of the heavens and the earth, and to Him all authority goes back. So worship Him, and rely on Him. Your Lord is never unaware of what you do.

12 Joseph يوسف

بِسْمِ ٱللَّهِ ٱلرَّحْمَٰنِ ٱلرَّحِيمِ	In the name of Allah, the Gracious, the Merciful.
١ الٓر ۚ تِلْكَ ءَايَٰتُ ٱلْكِتَٰبِ ٱلْمُبِينِ	1 Alif, Lam, Ra. These are the Verses of the Clear Book.
٢ إِنَّآ أَنزَلْنَٰهُ قُرْءَٰنًا عَرَبِيًّا لَّعَلَّكُمْ تَعْقِلُونَ	2 We have revealed it an Arabic Quran, so that you may understand.
٣ نَحْنُ نَقُصُّ عَلَيْكَ أَحْسَنَ ٱلْقَصَصِ بِمَآ أَوْحَيْنَآ إِلَيْكَ هَٰذَا ٱلْقُرْءَانَ وَإِن كُنتَ مِن قَبْلِهِۦ لَمِنَ ٱلْغَٰفِلِينَ	3 We narrate to you the most accurate history, by revealing to you this Quran. Although, prior to it, you were of the unaware.
٤ إِذْ قَالَ يُوسُفُ لِأَبِيهِ يَٰٓأَبَتِ إِنِّى رَأَيْتُ أَحَدَ عَشَرَ كَوْكَبًا وَٱلشَّمْسَ وَٱلْقَمَرَ رَأَيْتُهُمْ لِى سَٰجِدِينَ	4 When Joseph said to his father, "O my father, I saw eleven planets, and the sun, and the moon; I saw them bowing down to me."
٥ قَالَ يَٰبُنَىَّ لَا تَقْصُصْ رُءْيَاكَ عَلَىٰٓ إِخْوَتِكَ فَيَكِيدُوا۟ لَكَ كَيْدًا ۖ إِنَّ ٱلشَّيْطَٰنَ لِلْإِنسَٰنِ عَدُوٌّ مُّبِينٌ	5 He said, "O my son, do not relate your vision to your brothers, lest they plot and scheme against you. Satan is man's sworn enemy.

٦ وَكَذَٰلِكَ يَجْتَبِيكَ رَبُّكَ وَيُعَلِّمُكَ مِن تَأْوِيلِ
ٱلْأَحَادِيثِ وَيُتِمُّ نِعْمَتَهُۥ عَلَيْكَ وَعَلَىٰٓ ءَالِ
يَعْقُوبَ كَمَآ أَتَمَّهَا عَلَىٰٓ أَبَوَيْكَ مِن قَبْلُ إِبْرَٰهِيمَ
وَإِسْحَٰقَ ۚ إِنَّ رَبَّكَ عَلِيمٌ حَكِيمٌ

6 And thus your Lord will choose you, and will teach you the interpretation of events, and will complete His blessing upon you and upon the family of Jacob, as He has completed it before upon your forefathers Abraham and Isaac. Your Lord is Knowing and Wise.

٧ لَّقَدْ كَانَ فِى يُوسُفَ وَإِخْوَتِهِۦٓ ءَايَٰتٌ
لِّلسَّآئِلِينَ

7 In Joseph and his brothers are lessons for the seekers.

٨ إِذْ قَالُوا۟ لَيُوسُفُ وَأَخُوهُ أَحَبُّ إِلَىٰٓ أَبِينَا مِنَّا
وَنَحْنُ عُصْبَةٌ إِنَّ أَبَانَا لَفِى ضَلَٰلٍ مُّبِينٍ

8 When they said, "Joseph and his brother are dearer to our father than we are, although we are a whole group. Our father is obviously in the wrong.

٩ ٱقْتُلُوا۟ يُوسُفَ أَوِ ٱطْرَحُوهُ أَرْضًا يَخْلُ لَكُمْ
وَجْهُ أَبِيكُمْ وَتَكُونُوا۟ مِنۢ بَعْدِهِۦ قَوْمًا صَٰلِحِينَ

9 "Kill Joseph, or throw him somewhere in the land, and your father's attention will be yours. Afterwards, you will be decent people."

١٠ قَالَ قَآئِلٌ مِّنْهُمْ لَا تَقْتُلُوا۟ يُوسُفَ وَأَلْقُوهُ
فِى غَيَٰبَتِ ٱلْجُبِّ يَلْتَقِطْهُ بَعْضُ ٱلسَّيَّارَةِ إِن
كُنتُمْ فَٰعِلِينَ

10 One of them said, "Do not kill Joseph, but throw him into the bottom of the well; some caravan may pick him up—if you must do something."

١١ قَالُوا۟ يَٰٓأَبَانَا مَا لَكَ لَا تَأْمَ۫نَّا عَلَىٰ يُوسُفَ وَإِنَّا
لَهُۥ لَنَٰصِحُونَ

11 They said, "Father, why do you not trust us with Joseph, although we care for him?"

١٢ أَرْسِلْهُ مَعَنَا غَدًا يَرْتَعْ وَيَلْعَبْ وَإِنَّا لَهُۥ
لَحَٰفِظُونَ

12 "Send him with us tomorrow, that he may roam and play; we will take care of him."

١٣ قَالَ إِنِّى لَيَحْزُنُنِىٓ أَن تَذْهَبُوا۟ بِهِۦ وَأَخَافُ
أَن يَأْكُلَهُ ٱلذِّئْبُ وَأَنتُمْ عَنْهُ غَٰفِلُونَ

13 He said, "It worries me that you would take him away. And I fear the wolf may eat him while you are careless of him."

١٤ قَالُوا۟ لَئِنْ أَكَلَهُ ٱلذِّئْبُ وَنَحْنُ عُصْبَةٌ إِنَّآ إِذًا
لَّخَٰسِرُونَ

14 They said, "If the wolf ate him, and we are many, we would be good for nothing."

١٥ فَلَمَّا ذَهَبُوا۟ بِهِۦ وَأَجْمَعُوٓا۟ أَن يَجْعَلُوهُ فِى
غَيَٰبَتِ ٱلْجُبِّ ۚ وَأَوْحَيْنَآ إِلَيْهِ لَتُنَبِّئَنَّهُم بِأَمْرِهِمْ
هَٰذَا وَهُمْ لَا يَشْعُرُونَ

15 So they went away with him, and agreed to put him at the bottom of the well. And We inspired him, "You will inform them of this deed of theirs when they are unaware."

١٦ وَجَآءُوٓ أَبَاهُمْ عِشَآءً يَبْكُونَ

16 And they came to their father in the evening weeping.

١٧ قَالُوا۟ يَٰٓأَبَانَآ إِنَّا ذَهَبْنَا نَسْتَبِقُ وَتَرَكْنَا يُوسُفَ
عِندَ مَتَٰعِنَا فَأَكَلَهُ ٱلذِّئْبُ ۖ وَمَآ أَنتَ بِمُؤْمِنٍ لَّنَا
وَلَوْ كُنَّا صَٰدِقِينَ

17 They said, "O father, we went off racing one another, and left Joseph by our belongings; and the wolf ate him. But you will not believe us, even though we are being truthful."

١٨ وَجَآءُو عَلَىٰ قَمِيصِهِۦ بِدَمٍ كَذِبٍ ۚ قَالَ بَلْ
سَوَّلَتْ لَكُمْ أَنفُسُكُمْ أَمْرًا ۖ فَصَبْرٌ جَمِيلٌ ۖ وَٱللَّهُ
ٱلْمُسْتَعَانُ عَلَىٰ مَا تَصِفُونَ

18 And they brought his shirt, with fake blood on it. He said, "Your souls enticed you to do something. But patience is beautiful, and Allah is my Help against what you describe."

١٩ وَجَآءَتْ سَيَّارَةٌ فَأَرْسَلُوا۟ وَارِدَهُمْ فَأَدْلَىٰ
دَلْوَهُۥ ۖ قَالَ يَٰبُشْرَىٰ هَٰذَا غُلَٰمٌ ۚ وَأَسَرُّوهُ بِضَٰعَةً ۚ
وَٱللَّهُ عَلِيمٌۢ بِمَا يَعْمَلُونَ

19 A caravan passed by, and they sent their water-carrier. He lowered his bucket, and said, "Good news. Here is a boy." And they hid him as merchandise. But Allah was aware of what they did.

٢٠ وَشَرَوْهُ بِثَمَنٍۭ بَخْسٍ دَرَٰهِمَ مَعْدُودَةٍ وَكَانُوا۟
فِيهِ مِنَ ٱلزَّٰهِدِينَ

20 And they sold him for a cheap price—a few coins—they considered him to be of little value.

٢١ وَقَالَ ٱلَّذِى ٱشْتَرَىٰهُ مِن مِّصْرَ لِٱمْرَأَتِهِۦٓ
أَكْرِمِى مَثْوَىٰهُ عَسَىٰٓ أَن يَنفَعَنَآ أَوْ نَتَّخِذَهُۥ وَلَدًا ۚ
وَكَذَٰلِكَ مَكَّنَّا لِيُوسُفَ فِى ٱلْأَرْضِ وَلِنُعَلِّمَهُۥ مِن
تَأْوِيلِ ٱلْأَحَادِيثِ ۚ وَٱللَّهُ غَالِبٌ عَلَىٰٓ أَمْرِهِۦ
وَلَٰكِنَّ أَكْثَرَ ٱلنَّاسِ لَا يَعْلَمُونَ

21 The Egyptian who bought him said to his wife, "Take good care of him; he may be useful to us, or we may adopt him as a son." We thus established Joseph in the land, to teach him the interpretation of events. Allah has control over His affairs, but most people do not know.

٢٢ وَلَمَّا بَلَغَ أَشُدَّهُۥٓ ءَاتَيْنَٰهُ حُكْمًا وَعِلْمًا ۚ وَكَذَٰلِكَ
نَجْزِى ٱلْمُحْسِنِينَ

22 When he reached his maturity, We gave him wisdom and knowledge. We thus reward the righteous.

٢٣ وَرَٰوَدَتْهُ ٱلَّتِى هُوَ فِى بَيْتِهَا عَن نَّفْسِهِۦ
وَغَلَّقَتِ ٱلْأَبْوَٰبَ وَقَالَتْ هَيْتَ لَكَ ۚ قَالَ مَعَاذَ

23 She in whose house he was living tried to seduce him. She shut the doors, and said, "I am yours." He said, "Allah forbid! He is my Lord. He

ٱللَّهِ ۖ إِنَّهُۥ رَبِّىٓ أَحْسَنَ مَثْوَاىَ ۖ إِنَّهُۥ لَا يُفْلِحُ
ٱلظَّٰلِمُونَ

has given me a good home. Sinners never succeed."

٢٤ وَلَقَدْ هَمَّتْ بِهِۦ ۖ وَهَمَّ بِهَا لَوْلَآ أَن رَّءَا بُرْهَٰنَ
رَبِّهِۦ ۚ كَذَٰلِكَ لِنَصْرِفَ عَنْهُ ٱلسُّوٓءَ وَٱلْفَحْشَآءَ ۚ
إِنَّهُۥ مِنْ عِبَادِنَا ٱلْمُخْلَصِينَ

24 She desired him, and he desired her, had he not seen the proof of his Lord. It was thus that We diverted evil and indecency away from him. He was one of Our loyal servants.

٢٥ وَٱسْتَبَقَا ٱلْبَابَ وَقَدَّتْ قَمِيصَهُۥ مِن دُبُرٍ
وَأَلْفَيَا سَيِّدَهَا لَدَا ٱلْبَابِ ۚ قَالَتْ مَا جَزَآءُ مَنْ
أَرَادَ بِأَهْلِكَ سُوٓءًا إِلَّآ أَن يُسْجَنَ أَوْ عَذَابٌ أَلِيمٌ

25 As they raced towards the door, she tore his shirt from behind. At the door, they ran into her husband. She said, "What is the penalty for him who desired to dishonor your wife, except imprisonment or a painful punishment?"

٢٦ قَالَ هِىَ رَٰوَدَتْنِى عَن نَّفْسِى ۚ وَشَهِدَ شَاهِدٌ
مِّنْ أَهْلِهَآ إِن كَانَ قَمِيصُهُۥ قُدَّ مِن قُبُلٍ
فَصَدَقَتْ وَهُوَ مِنَ ٱلْكَٰذِبِينَ

26 He said, "It was she who tried to seduce me." A witness from her household suggested: "If his shirt is torn from the front: then she has told the truth, and he is the liar.

٢٧ وَإِن كَانَ قَمِيصُهُۥ قُدَّ مِن دُبُرٍ فَكَذَبَتْ وَهُوَ
مِنَ ٱلصَّٰدِقِينَ

27 But if his shirt is torn from the back: then she has lied, and he is the truthful."

٢٨ فَلَمَّا رَءَا قَمِيصَهُۥ قُدَّ مِن دُبُرٍ قَالَ إِنَّهُۥ مِن
كَيْدِكُنَّ ۖ إِنَّ كَيْدَكُنَّ عَظِيمٌ

28 And when he saw that his shirt was torn from the back, he said, "This is a woman's scheme. Your scheming is serious indeed."

٢٩ يُوسُفُ أَعْرِضْ عَنْ هَٰذَا ۚ وَٱسْتَغْفِرِى لِذَنۢبِكِ ۖ
إِنَّكِ كُنتِ مِنَ ٱلْخَاطِـِٔينَ

29 "Joseph, turn away from this. And you, woman, ask forgiveness for your sin; you are indeed in the wrong."

٣٠ وَقَالَ نِسْوَةٌ فِى ٱلْمَدِينَةِ ٱمْرَأَتُ ٱلْعَزِيزِ
تُرَٰوِدُ فَتَىٰهَا عَن نَّفْسِهِۦ ۖ قَدْ شَغَفَهَا حُبًّا ۖ إِنَّا
لَنَرَىٰهَا فِى ضَلَٰلٍ مُّبِينٍ

30 Some ladies in the city said, "The governor's wife is trying to seduce her servant. She is deeply in love with him. We see she has gone astray."

٣١ فَلَمَّا سَمِعَتْ بِمَكْرِهِنَّ أَرْسَلَتْ إِلَيْهِنَّ
وَأَعْتَدَتْ لَهُنَّ مُتَّكَـًٔا وَءَاتَتْ كُلَّ وَٰحِدَةٍ مِّنْهُنَّ
سِكِّينًا وَقَالَتِ ٱخْرُجْ عَلَيْهِنَّ ۖ فَلَمَّا رَأَيْنَهُۥٓ أَكْبَرْنَهُۥ

31 And when she heard of their gossip, she invited them, and prepared for them a banquet, and she gave each one of them a knife. She said, "Come out before them."

وَقَطَّعْنَ أَيْدِيَهُنَّ وَقُلْنَ حَٰشَ لِلَّهِ مَا هَٰذَا بَشَرًا
إِنْ هَٰذَآ إِلَّا مَلَكٌ كَرِيمٌ

And when they saw him, they marveled at him, and cut their hands. They said, “Good Allah, this is not a human, this must be a precious angel.”

٣٢ قَالَتْ فَذَٰلِكُنَّ ٱلَّذِى لُمْتُنَّنِى فِيهِ ۖ وَلَقَدْ
رَٰوَدتُّهُۥ عَن نَّفْسِهِۦ فَٱسْتَعْصَمَ ۖ وَلَئِن لَّمْ يَفْعَلْ
مَآ ءَامُرُهُۥ لَيُسْجَنَنَّ وَلَيَكُونًا مِّنَ ٱلصَّٰغِرِينَ

32 She said, “Here he is, the one you blamed me for. I did try to seduce him, but he resisted. But if he does not do what I tell him to do, he will be imprisoned, and will be one of the despised.”

٣٣ قَالَ رَبِّ ٱلسِّجْنُ أَحَبُّ إِلَىَّ مِمَّا يَدْعُونَنِىٓ
إِلَيْهِ ۖ وَإِلَّا تَصْرِفْ عَنِّى كَيْدَهُنَّ أَصْبُ إِلَيْهِنَّ
وَأَكُن مِّنَ ٱلْجَٰهِلِينَ

33 He said, “My Lord, prison is more desirable to me than what they call me to. Unless You turn their scheming away from me, I may yield to them, and become one of the ignorant.”

٣٤ فَٱسْتَجَابَ لَهُۥ رَبُّهُۥ فَصَرَفَ عَنْهُ كَيْدَهُنَّ ۚ إِنَّهُۥ
هُوَ ٱلسَّمِيعُ ٱلْعَلِيمُ

34 Thereupon his Lord answered him, and diverted their scheming away from him. He is the Hearer, the Knower.

٣٥ ثُمَّ بَدَا لَهُم مِّنۢ بَعْدِ مَا رَأَوُا۟ ٱلْءَايَٰتِ
لَيَسْجُنُنَّهُۥ حَتَّىٰ حِينٍ

35 Then it occurred to them, after they had seen the signs, to imprison him for a while.

٣٦ وَدَخَلَ مَعَهُ ٱلسِّجْنَ فَتَيَانِ ۖ قَالَ أَحَدُهُمَآ
إِنِّىٓ أَرَىٰنِىٓ أَعْصِرُ خَمْرًا ۖ وَقَالَ ٱلْءَاخَرُ إِنِّىٓ
أَرَىٰنِىٓ أَحْمِلُ فَوْقَ رَأْسِى خُبْزًا تَأْكُلُ ٱلطَّيْرُ
مِنْهُ ۖ نَبِّئْنَا بِتَأْوِيلِهِۦٓ ۖ إِنَّا نَرَىٰكَ مِنَ ٱلْمُحْسِنِينَ

36 Two youth entered the prison with him. One of them said, “I see myself pressing wine.” The other said, “I see myself carrying bread on my head, from which the birds are eating. Tell us their interpretation—we see that you are one of the righteous.”

٣٧ قَالَ لَا يَأْتِيكُمَا طَعَامٌ تُرْزَقَانِهِۦٓ إِلَّا نَبَّأْتُكُمَا
بِتَأْوِيلِهِۦ قَبْلَ أَن يَأْتِيَكُمَا ۚ ذَٰلِكُمَا مِمَّا عَلَّمَنِى
رَبِّىٓ ۚ إِنِّى تَرَكْتُ مِلَّةَ قَوْمٍ لَّا يُؤْمِنُونَ بِٱللَّهِ
وَهُم بِٱلْءَاخِرَةِ هُمْ كَٰفِرُونَ

37 He said, “No food is served to you, but I have informed you about it before you have received it. That is some of what my Lord has taught me. I have forsaken the tradition of people who do not believe in Allah; and regarding the Hereafter, they are deniers.”

٣٨ وَٱتَّبَعْتُ مِلَّةَ ءَابَآءِىٓ إِبْرَٰهِيمَ وَإِسْحَٰقَ وَيَعْقُوبَ ۚ مَا كَانَ لَنَآ أَن نُّشْرِكَ بِٱللَّهِ مِن شَىْءٍ ۚ ذَٰلِكَ مِن فَضْلِ ٱللَّهِ عَلَيْنَا وَعَلَى ٱلنَّاسِ وَلَٰكِنَّ أَكْثَرَ ٱلنَّاسِ لَا يَشْكُرُونَ

38 "And I have followed the faith of my forefathers, Abraham, and Isaac, and Jacob. It is not for us to associate anything with Allah. This is by virtue of Allah's grace upon us and upon the people, but most people do not give thanks.

٣٩ يَٰصَىٰحِبَىِ ٱلسِّجْنِ ءَأَرْبَابٌ مُّتَفَرِّقُونَ خَيْرٌ أَمِ ٱللَّهُ ٱلْوَٰحِدُ ٱلْقَهَّارُ

39 "O My fellow inmates, are diverse lords better, or Allah, the One, the Supreme?"

٤٠ مَا تَعْبُدُونَ مِن دُونِهِۦٓ إِلَّآ أَسْمَآءً سَمَّيْتُمُوهَآ أَنتُمْ وَءَابَآؤُكُم مَّآ أَنزَلَ ٱللَّهُ بِهَا مِن سُلْطَٰنٍ ۚ إِنِ ٱلْحُكْمُ إِلَّا لِلَّهِ ۚ أَمَرَ أَلَّا تَعْبُدُوٓا۟ إِلَّآ إِيَّاهُ ۚ ذَٰلِكَ ٱلدِّينُ ٱلْقَيِّمُ وَلَٰكِنَّ أَكْثَرَ ٱلنَّاسِ لَا يَعْلَمُونَ

40 "You do not worship, besides Him, except names you have named, you and your ancestors, for which Allah has sent down no authority. Judgment belongs to none but Allah. He has commanded that you worship none but Him. This is the right religion, but most people do not know.

٤١ يَٰصَىٰحِبَىِ ٱلسِّجْنِ أَمَّآ أَحَدُكُمَا فَيَسْقِى رَبَّهُۥ خَمْرًا ۖ وَأَمَّا ٱلْءَاخَرُ فَيُصْلَبُ فَتَأْكُلُ ٱلطَّيْرُ مِن رَّأْسِهِۦ ۚ قُضِىَ ٱلْأَمْرُ ٱلَّذِى فِيهِ تَسْتَفْتِيَانِ

41 "O my fellow inmates! One of you will serve his master wine; while the other will be crucified, and the birds will eat from his head. Thus the matter you are inquiring about is settled."

٤٢ وَقَالَ لِلَّذِى ظَنَّ أَنَّهُۥ نَاجٍ مِّنْهُمَا ٱذْكُرْنِى عِندَ رَبِّكَ فَأَنسَىٰهُ ٱلشَّيْطَٰنُ ذِكْرَ رَبِّهِۦ فَلَبِثَ فِى ٱلسِّجْنِ بِضْعَ سِنِينَ

42 And he said to the one he thought would be released, "Mention me to your master." But Satan caused him to forget mentioning him to his master, so he remained in prison for several years.

٤٣ وَقَالَ ٱلْمَلِكُ إِنِّىٓ أَرَىٰ سَبْعَ بَقَرَٰتٍ سِمَانٍ يَأْكُلُهُنَّ سَبْعٌ عِجَافٌ وَسَبْعَ سُنۢبُلَٰتٍ خُضْرٍ وَأُخَرَ يَابِسَٰتٍ ۖ يَٰٓأَيُّهَا ٱلْمَلَأُ أَفْتُونِى فِى رُءْيَٰىَ إِن كُنتُمْ لِلرُّءْيَا تَعْبُرُونَ

43 The king said, "I see seven fat cows being eaten by seven lean ones, and seven green spikes, and others dried up. O elders, explain to me my vision, if you are able to interpret visions."

٤٤ قَالُوٓا۟ أَضْغَٰثُ أَحْلَٰمٍ ۖ وَمَا نَحْنُ بِتَأْوِيلِ ٱلْأَحْلَٰمِ بِعَٰلِمِينَ

44 They said, "Jumbles of dreams, and we know nothing of the interpretation of dreams."

٤٥ وَقَالَ ٱلَّذِى نَجَا مِنْهُمَا وَٱدَّكَرَ بَعْدَ أُمَّةٍ أَنَا۠
أُنَبِّئُكُم بِتَأْوِيلِهِۦ فَأَرْسِلُونِ

45 The one who was released said, having remembered after a time, “I will inform you of its interpretation, so send me out.”

٤٦ يُوسُفُ أَيُّهَا ٱلصِّدِّيقُ أَفْتِنَا فِى سَبْعِ بَقَرَٰتٍ
سِمَانٍ يَأْكُلُهُنَّ سَبْعٌ عِجَافٌ وَسَبْعِ سُنۢبُلَٰتٍ
خُضْرٍ وَأُخَرَ يَابِسَٰتٍ لَّعَلِّىٓ أَرْجِعُ إِلَى ٱلنَّاسِ
لَعَلَّهُمْ يَعْلَمُونَ

46 “Joseph, O man of truth, inform us concerning seven fat cows being eaten by seven lean ones, and seven green spikes, and others dried up, so that I may return to the people, so that they may know.”

٤٧ قَالَ تَزْرَعُونَ سَبْعَ سِنِينَ دَأَبًا فَمَا حَصَدتُّمْ
فَذَرُوهُ فِى سُنۢبُلِهِۦٓ إِلَّا قَلِيلًا مِّمَّا تَأْكُلُونَ

47 He said, “You will farm for seven consecutive years. But whatever you harvest, leave it in its spikes, except for the little that you eat.”

٤٨ ثُمَّ يَأْتِى مِنۢ بَعْدِ ذَٰلِكَ سَبْعٌ شِدَادٌ يَأْكُلْنَ مَا
قَدَّمْتُمْ لَهُنَّ إِلَّا قَلِيلًا مِّمَّا تُحْصِنُونَ

48 Then after that will come seven difficult ones, which will consume what you have stored for them, except for the little that you have preserved.

٤٩ ثُمَّ يَأْتِى مِنۢ بَعْدِ ذَٰلِكَ عَامٌ فِيهِ يُغَاثُ
ٱلنَّاسُ وَفِيهِ يَعْصِرُونَ

49 Then after that will come a year that brings relief to the people, and during which they will press.

٥٠ وَقَالَ ٱلْمَلِكُ ٱئْتُونِى بِهِۦ ۖ فَلَمَّا جَآءَهُ
ٱلرَّسُولُ قَالَ ٱرْجِعْ إِلَىٰ رَبِّكَ فَسْـَٔلْهُ مَا بَالُ
ٱلنِّسْوَةِ ٱلَّٰتِى قَطَّعْنَ أَيْدِيَهُنَّ ۚ إِنَّ رَبِّى بِكَيْدِهِنَّ
عَلِيمٌ

50 The king said, “Bring him to me.” And when the envoy came to him, he said, “Go back to your master, and ask him about the intentions of the women who cut their hands; my Lord is well aware of their schemes.”

٥١ قَالَ مَا خَطْبُكُنَّ إِذْ رَٰوَدتُّنَّ يُوسُفَ عَن
نَّفْسِهِۦ ۚ قُلْنَ حَٰشَ لِلَّهِ مَا عَلِمْنَا عَلَيْهِ مِن سُوٓءٍ ۚ
قَالَتِ ٱمْرَأَتُ ٱلْعَزِيزِ ٱلْـَٰٔنَ حَصْحَصَ ٱلْحَقُّ أَنَا۠
رَٰوَدتُّهُۥ عَن نَّفْسِهِۦ وَإِنَّهُۥ لَمِنَ ٱلصَّٰدِقِينَ

51 He said, “What was the matter with you, women, when you tried to seduce Joseph?” They said, “Allah forbid! We knew of no evil committed by him.” The governor’s wife then said, “Now the truth is out. It was I who tried to seduce him, and he is telling the truth.”

٥٢ ذَٰلِكَ لِيَعْلَمَ أَنِّى لَمْ أَخُنْهُ بِٱلْغَيْبِ وَأَنَّ ٱللَّهَ لَا
يَهْدِى كَيْدَ ٱلْخَآئِنِينَ

52 “This is that he may know that I did not betray him in secret, and that Allah does not guide the scheming of the betrayers.”

٥٣ وَمَآ أُبَرِّئُ نَفْسِىٓ ۚ إِنَّ ٱلنَّفْسَ لَأَمَّارَةٌۢ بِٱلسُّوٓءِ
إِلَّا مَا رَحِمَ رَبِّىٓ ۚ إِنَّ رَبِّى غَفُورٌ رَّحِيمٌ

53 “Yet I do not claim to be innocent. The soul commands evil, except those on whom my Lord has mercy. Truly my Lord is Forgiving and Merciful.”

٥٤ وَقَالَ ٱلْمَلِكُ ٱئْتُونِى بِهِۦٓ أَسْتَخْلِصْهُ لِنَفْسِى ۖ
فَلَمَّا كَلَّمَهُۥ قَالَ إِنَّكَ ٱلْيَوْمَ لَدَيْنَا مَكِينٌ أَمِينٌ

54 The king said, “Bring him to me, and I will reserve him for myself.” And when he spoke to him, he said, “This day you are with us established and secure.”

٥٥ قَالَ ٱجْعَلْنِى عَلَىٰ خَزَآئِنِ ٱلْأَرْضِ ۖ إِنِّى
حَفِيظٌ عَلِيمٌ

55 He said, “Put me in charge of the storehouses of the land; I am honest and knowledgeable.”

٥٦ وَكَذَٰلِكَ مَكَّنَّا لِيُوسُفَ فِى ٱلْأَرْضِ يَتَبَوَّأُ
مِنْهَا حَيْثُ يَشَآءُ ۚ نُصِيبُ بِرَحْمَتِنَا مَن نَّشَآءُ ۖ
وَلَا نُضِيعُ أَجْرَ ٱلْمُحْسِنِينَ

56 And thus We established Joseph in the land, to live therein wherever he wished. We touch with Our mercy whomever We will, and We never waste the reward of the righteous.

٥٧ وَلَأَجْرُ ٱلْءَاخِرَةِ خَيْرٌ لِّلَّذِينَ ءَامَنُوا۟ وَكَانُوا۟
يَتَّقُونَ

57 But the reward of the Hereafter is better for those who believe and observed piety.

٥٨ وَجَآءَ إِخْوَةُ يُوسُفَ فَدَخَلُوا۟ عَلَيْهِ فَعَرَفَهُمْ
وَهُمْ لَهُۥ مُنكِرُونَ

58 And Joseph's brothers came, and entered into his presence. He recognized them, but they did not recognize him.

٥٩ وَلَمَّا جَهَّزَهُم بِجَهَازِهِمْ قَالَ ٱئْتُونِى بِأَخٍ
لَّكُم مِّنْ أَبِيكُمْ ۚ أَلَا تَرَوْنَ أَنِّىٓ أُوفِى ٱلْكَيْلَ وَأَنَا۠
خَيْرُ ٱلْمُنزِلِينَ

59 When he provided them with their provisions, he said, “Bring me a brother of yours from your father. Do you not see that I fill up the measure, and I am the best of hosts?”

٦٠ فَإِن لَّمْ تَأْتُونِى بِهِۦ فَلَا كَيْلَ لَكُمْ عِندِى وَلَا
تَقْرَبُونِ

60 “But if you do not bring him to me, you will have no measure from me, and you will not come near me.”

٦١ قَالُوا۟ سَنُرَٰوِدُ عَنْهُ أَبَاهُ وَإِنَّا لَفَٰعِلُونَ

61 They said, “We will solicit him from his father. We will surely do.”

٦٢ وَقَالَ لِفِتْيَٰنِهِ ٱجْعَلُوا۟ بِضَٰعَتَهُمْ فِى رِحَالِهِمْ
لَعَلَّهُمْ يَعْرِفُونَهَآ إِذَا ٱنقَلَبُوٓا۟ إِلَىٰٓ أَهْلِهِمْ لَعَلَّهُمْ
يَرْجِعُونَ

62 He said to his servants, “Put their goods in their saddlebags; perhaps they will recognize them when they

return to their families, and maybe they will come back."

٦٣ فَلَمَّا رَجَعُوٓاْ إِلَىٰٓ أَبِيهِمۡ قَالُواْ يَٰٓأَبَانَا مُنِعَ مِنَّا ٱلۡكَيۡلُ فَأَرۡسِلۡ مَعَنَآ أَخَانَا نَكۡتَلۡ وَإِنَّا لَهُۥ لَحَٰفِظُونَ

63 When they returned to their father, they said, "O father, we were denied measure, but send our brother with us, and we will obtain measure. We will take care of him."

٦٤ قَالَ هَلۡ ءَامَنُكُمۡ عَلَيۡهِ إِلَّا كَمَآ أَمِنتُكُمۡ عَلَىٰٓ أَخِيهِ مِن قَبۡلُۖ فَٱللَّهُ خَيۡرٌ حَٰفِظٗاۖ وَهُوَ أَرۡحَمُ ٱلرَّٰحِمِينَ

64 He said, "Shall I trust you with him, as I trusted you with his brother before? Allah is the Best Guardian, and He is the Most Merciful of the merciful."

٦٥ وَلَمَّا فَتَحُواْ مَتَٰعَهُمۡ وَجَدُواْ بِضَٰعَتَهُمۡ رُدَّتۡ إِلَيۡهِمۡۖ قَالُواْ يَٰٓأَبَانَا مَا نَبۡغِيۖ هَٰذِهِۦ بِضَٰعَتُنَا رُدَّتۡ إِلَيۡنَاۖ وَنَمِيرُ أَهۡلَنَا وَنَحۡفَظُ أَخَانَا وَنَزۡدَادُ كَيۡلَ بَعِيرٖۖ ذَٰلِكَ كَيۡلٞ يَسِيرٞ

65 And when they opened their baggage, they found that their goods were returned to them. They said, "Father, what more do we want? Here are our goods, returned to us. We will provide for our family, and protect our brother, and have an additional camel-load. This is easy commerce."

٦٦ قَالَ لَنۡ أُرۡسِلَهُۥ مَعَكُمۡ حَتَّىٰ تُؤۡتُونِ مَوۡثِقٗا مِّنَ ٱللَّهِ لَتَأۡتُنَّنِي بِهِۦٓ إِلَّآ أَن يُحَاطَ بِكُمۡۖ فَلَمَّآ ءَاتَوۡهُ مَوۡثِقَهُمۡ قَالَ ٱللَّهُ عَلَىٰ مَا نَقُولُ وَكِيلٞ

66 He said, "I will not send him with you, unless you give me a pledge before Allah that you will bring him back to me, unless you get trapped." And when they gave him their pledge, he said, "Allah is witness to what we say."

٦٧ وَقَالَ يَٰبَنِيَّ لَا تَدۡخُلُواْ مِنۢ بَابٖ وَٰحِدٖ وَٱدۡخُلُواْ مِنۡ أَبۡوَٰبٖ مُّتَفَرِّقَةٖۖ وَمَآ أُغۡنِي عَنكُم مِّنَ ٱللَّهِ مِن شَيۡءٍۖ إِنِ ٱلۡحُكۡمُ إِلَّا لِلَّهِۖ عَلَيۡهِ تَوَكَّلۡتُۖ وَعَلَيۡهِ فَلۡيَتَوَكَّلِ ٱلۡمُتَوَكِّلُونَ

67 And he said, "O my sons, do not enter by one gate, but enter by different gates. I cannot avail you anything against Allah. The decision rests only with Allah. On Him I rely, and on Him let the reliant rely."

٦٨ وَلَمَّا دَخَلُواْ مِنۡ حَيۡثُ أَمَرَهُمۡ أَبُوهُم مَّا كَانَ يُغۡنِي عَنۡهُم مِّنَ ٱللَّهِ مِن شَيۡءٍ إِلَّا حَاجَةٗ فِي نَفۡسِ يَعۡقُوبَ قَضَىٰهَاۚ وَإِنَّهُۥ لَذُو عِلۡمٖ لِّمَا عَلَّمۡنَٰهُ وَلَٰكِنَّ أَكۡثَرَ ٱلنَّاسِ لَا يَعۡلَمُونَ

68 And when they entered as their father had instructed them, it did not avail them anything against Allah; it was just a need in the soul of Jacob, which he carried out. He was a person of knowledge inasmuch as

We had taught him, but most people do not know.

٦٩ وَلَمَّا دَخَلُوا۟ عَلَىٰ يُوسُفَ ءَاوَىٰٓ إِلَيْهِ أَخَاهُ ۖ
قَالَ إِنِّىٓ أَنَا۠ أَخُوكَ فَلَا تَبْتَئِسْ بِمَا كَانُوا۟
يَعْمَلُونَ

69 And when they entered into the presence of Joseph, he embraced his brother, and said, "I am your brother; do not be saddened by what they used to do."

٧٠ فَلَمَّا جَهَّزَهُم بِجَهَازِهِمْ جَعَلَ ٱلسِّقَايَةَ فِى
رَحْلِ أَخِيهِ ثُمَّ أَذَّنَ مُؤَذِّنٌ أَيَّتُهَا ٱلْعِيرُ إِنَّكُمْ
لَسَٰرِقُونَ

70 Then, when he provided them with their provisions, he placed the drinking-cup in his brother's saddlebag. Then an announcer called out, "O people of the caravan, you are thieves."

٧١ قَالُوا۟ وَأَقْبَلُوا۟ عَلَيْهِم مَّاذَا تَفْقِدُونَ

71 They said, as they came towards them, "What are you missing?"

٧٢ قَالُوا۟ نَفْقِدُ صُوَاعَ ٱلْمَلِكِ وَلِمَن جَآءَ بِهِۦ
حِمْلُ بَعِيرٍ وَأَنَا۠ بِهِۦ زَعِيمٌ

72 They said, "We are missing the king's goblet. Whoever brings it will have a camel-load; and I personally guarantee it."

٧٣ قَالُوا۟ تَٱللَّهِ لَقَدْ عَلِمْتُم مَّا جِئْنَا لِنُفْسِدَ فِى
ٱلْأَرْضِ وَمَا كُنَّا سَٰرِقِينَ

73 They said, "By Allah, you know we did not come to cause trouble in the land, and we are not thieves."

٧٤ قَالُوا۟ فَمَا جَزَٰٓؤُهُۥٓ إِن كُنتُمْ كَٰذِبِينَ

74 They said, "What shall be his punishment, if you are lying?"

٧٥ قَالُوا۟ جَزَٰٓؤُهُۥ مَن وُجِدَ فِى رَحْلِهِۦ فَهُوَ
جَزَٰٓؤُهُۥ ۚ كَذَٰلِكَ نَجْزِى ٱلظَّٰلِمِينَ

75 They said, "His punishment, if it is found in his bag: he will belong to you. Thus we penalize the guilty."

٧٦ فَبَدَأَ بِأَوْعِيَتِهِمْ قَبْلَ وِعَآءِ أَخِيهِ ثُمَّ
ٱسْتَخْرَجَهَا مِن وِعَآءِ أَخِيهِ ۚ كَذَٰلِكَ كِدْنَا
لِيُوسُفَ ۖ مَا كَانَ لِيَأْخُذَ أَخَاهُ فِى دِينِ ٱلْمَلِكِ
إِلَّآ أَن يَشَآءَ ٱللَّهُ ۚ نَرْفَعُ دَرَجَٰتٍ مَّن نَّشَآءُ ۗ
وَفَوْقَ كُلِّ ذِى عِلْمٍ عَلِيمٌ

76 So he began with their bags, before his brother's bag. Then he pulled it out of his brother's bag. Thus We devised a plan for Joseph; he could not have detained his brother under the king's law, unless Allah so willed. We elevate by degrees whomever We will; and above every person of knowledge, there is one more learned.

٧٧ قَالُوٓاْ إِن يَسْرِقْ فَقَدْ سَرَقَ أَخٌ لَّهُۥ مِن قَبْلُ ۚ
فَأَسَرَّهَا يُوسُفُ فِى نَفْسِهِۦ وَلَمْ يُبْدِهَا لَهُمْ ۚ
قَالَ أَنتُمْ شَرٌّ مَّكَانًا ۖ وَٱللَّهُ أَعْلَمُ بِمَا تَصِفُونَ

77 They said, "If he has stolen, a brother of his has stolen before." But Joseph kept it to himself, and did not reveal it to them. He said, "You are in a worse situation, and Allah is Aware of what you allege."

٧٨ قَالُواْ يَٰٓأَيُّهَا ٱلْعَزِيزُ إِنَّ لَهُۥٓ أَبًا شَيْخًا كَبِيرًا
فَخُذْ أَحَدَنَا مَكَانَهُۥٓ ۖ إِنَّا نَرَىٰكَ مِنَ ٱلْمُحْسِنِينَ

78 They said, "O noble prince, he has a father, a very old man, so take one of us in his place. We see that you are a good person."

٧٩ قَالَ مَعَاذَ ٱللَّهِ أَن نَّأْخُذَ إِلَّا مَن وَجَدْنَا مَتَٰعَنَا
عِندَهُۥٓ إِنَّآ إِذًا لَّظَٰلِمُونَ

79 He said, "Allah forbid that we should arrest anyone except him in whose possession we found our property; for then we would be unjust."

٨٠ فَلَمَّا ٱسْتَيْـَٔسُواْ مِنْهُ خَلَصُواْ نَجِيًّا ۖ قَالَ
كَبِيرُهُمْ أَلَمْ تَعْلَمُوٓاْ أَنَّ أَبَاكُمْ قَدْ أَخَذَ عَلَيْكُم
مَّوْثِقًا مِّنَ ٱللَّهِ وَمِن قَبْلُ مَا فَرَّطتُمْ فِى
يُوسُفَ ۖ فَلَنْ أَبْرَحَ ٱلْأَرْضَ حَتَّىٰ يَأْذَنَ لِىٓ أَبِىٓ
أَوْ يَحْكُمَ ٱللَّهُ لِى ۖ وَهُوَ خَيْرُ ٱلْحَٰكِمِينَ

80 And when they despaired of him, they conferred privately. Their eldest said, "Don't you know that your father received a pledge from you before Allah, and in the past you failed with regard to Joseph? I will not leave this land until my father permits me, or Allah decides for me; for He is the Best of Deciders."

٨١ ٱرْجِعُوٓاْ إِلَىٰٓ أَبِيكُمْ فَقُولُواْ يَٰٓأَبَانَآ إِنَّ ٱبْنَكَ
سَرَقَ وَمَا شَهِدْنَآ إِلَّا بِمَا عَلِمْنَا وَمَا كُنَّا لِلْغَيْبِ
حَٰفِظِينَ

81 "Go back to your father, and say, 'Our father, your son has stolen. We testify only to what we know, and we could not have prevented the unforeseen.'"

٨٢ وَسْـَٔلِ ٱلْقَرْيَةَ ٱلَّتِى كُنَّا فِيهَا وَٱلْعِيرَ ٱلَّتِىٓ
أَقْبَلْنَا فِيهَا ۖ وَإِنَّا لَصَٰدِقُونَ

82 "Ask the town where we were, and the caravan in which we came. We are being truthful."

٨٣ قَالَ بَلْ سَوَّلَتْ لَكُمْ أَنفُسُكُمْ أَمْرًا ۖ فَصَبْرٌ
جَمِيلٌ ۖ عَسَى ٱللَّهُ أَن يَأْتِيَنِى بِهِمْ جَمِيعًا ۚ إِنَّهُۥ
هُوَ ٱلْعَلِيمُ ٱلْحَكِيمُ

83 He said, "Rather, your souls have contrived something for you. Patience is a virtue. Perhaps Allah will bring them all back to me. He is the Knowing, the Wise."

٨٤ وَتَوَلَّىٰ عَنْهُمْ وَقَالَ يَٰٓأَسَفَىٰ عَلَىٰ يُوسُفَ
وَٱبْيَضَّتْ عَيْنَاهُ مِنَ ٱلْحُزْنِ فَهُوَ كَظِيمٌ

84 Then he turned away from them, and said, "O my bitterness for Joseph." And his eyes turned white

from sorrow, and he became depressed.

٨٥ قَالُواْ تَٱللَّهِ تَفْتَؤُاْ تَذْكُرُ يُوسُفَ حَتَّىٰ تَكُونَ
حَرَضًا أَوْ تَكُونَ مِنَ ٱلْهَٰلِكِينَ

85 They said, “By Allah, you will not stop remembering Joseph, until you have ruined your health, or you have passed away.”

٨٦ قَالَ إِنَّمَآ أَشْكُواْ بَثِّى وَحُزْنِىٓ إِلَى ٱللَّهِ
وَأَعْلَمُ مِنَ ٱللَّهِ مَا لَا تَعْلَمُونَ

86 He said, “I only complain of my grief and sorrow to Allah, and I know from Allah what you do not know.”

٨٧ يَٰبَنِىَّ ٱذْهَبُواْ فَتَحَسَّسُواْ مِن يُوسُفَ وَأَخِيهِ
وَلَا تَاْيْـَٔسُواْ مِن رَّوْحِ ٱللَّهِ ۖ إِنَّهُۥ لَا يَاْيْـَٔسُ مِن
رَّوْحِ ٱللَّهِ إِلَّا ٱلْقَوْمُ ٱلْكَٰفِرُونَ

87 “O my sons, go and inquire about Joseph and his brother, and do not despair of Allah's comfort. None despairs of Allah's comfort except the disbelieving people.”

٨٨ فَلَمَّا دَخَلُواْ عَلَيْهِ قَالُواْ يَٰٓأَيُّهَا ٱلْعَزِيزُ مَسَّنَا
وَأَهْلَنَا ٱلضُّرُّ وَجِئْنَا بِبِضَٰعَةٍ مُّزْجَىٰةٍ فَأَوْفِ لَنَا
ٱلْكَيْلَ وَتَصَدَّقْ عَلَيْنَآ ۖ إِنَّ ٱللَّهَ يَجْزِى
ٱلْمُتَصَدِّقِينَ

88 Then, when they entered into his presence, they said, “Mighty governor, adversity has befallen us, and our family. We have brought scant merchandise. But give us full measure, and be charitable towards us—Allah rewards the charitable.”

٨٩ قَالَ هَلْ عَلِمْتُم مَّا فَعَلْتُم بِيُوسُفَ وَأَخِيهِ
إِذْ أَنتُمْ جَٰهِلُونَ

89 He said, “Do you realize what you did with Joseph and his brother, in your ignorance?”

٩٠ قَالُوٓاْ أَءِنَّكَ لَأَنتَ يُوسُفُ ۖ قَالَ أَنَا۠ يُوسُفُ
وَهَٰذَآ أَخِى ۖ قَدْ مَنَّ ٱللَّهُ عَلَيْنَآ ۖ إِنَّهُۥ مَن يَتَّقِ
وَيَصْبِرْ فَإِنَّ ٱللَّهَ لَا يُضِيعُ أَجْرَ ٱلْمُحْسِنِينَ

90 They said, “Is that you, Joseph?” He said, “I am Joseph, and this is my brother. Allah has been gracious to us. He who practices piety and patience—Allah never fails to reward the righteous.”

٩١ قَالُواْ تَٱللَّهِ لَقَدْ ءَاثَرَكَ ٱللَّهُ عَلَيْنَا وَإِن كُنَّا
لَخَٰطِـِٔينَ

91 They said, “By Allah, Allah has preferred you over us. We were definitely in the wrong.”

٩٢ قَالَ لَا تَثْرِيبَ عَلَيْكُمُ ٱلْيَوْمَ ۖ يَغْفِرُ ٱللَّهُ لَكُمْ ۖ
وَهُوَ أَرْحَمُ ٱلرَّٰحِمِينَ

92 He said, “There is no blame upon you today. Allah will forgive you. He is the Most Merciful of the merciful.”

٩٣ ٱذْهَبُواْ بِقَمِيصِى هَٰذَا فَأَلْقُوهُ عَلَىٰ وَجْهِ أَبِى
يَأْتِ بَصِيرًا وَأْتُونِى بِأَهْلِكُمْ أَجْمَعِينَ

93 “Take this shirt of mine, and lay it over my father’s face, and he will recover his sight. And bring your whole family to me.”

٩٤ وَلَمَّا فَصَلَتِ ٱلْعِيرُ قَالَ أَبُوهُمْ إِنِّى لَأَجِدُ
رِيحَ يُوسُفَ ۖ لَوْلَآ أَن تُفَنِّدُونِ

94 As the caravan set out, their father said, “I sense the presence of Joseph, though you may think I am senile.”

٩٥ قَالُوا۟ تَٱللَّهِ إِنَّكَ لَفِى ضَلَـٰلِكَ ٱلْقَدِيمِ

95 They said, “By Allah, you are still in your old confusion.”

٩٦ فَلَمَّآ أَن جَآءَ ٱلْبَشِيرُ أَلْقَىٰهُ عَلَىٰ وَجْهِهِۦ
فَٱرْتَدَّ بَصِيرًا ۖ قَالَ أَلَمْ أَقُل لَّكُمْ إِنِّىٓ أَعْلَمُ مِنَ
ٱللَّهِ مَا لَا تَعْلَمُونَ

96 Then, when the bearer of good news arrived, he laid it over his face, and he regained his sight. He said, “Did I not say to you that I know from Allah what you do not know?”

٩٧ قَالُوا۟ يَـٰٓأَبَانَا ٱسْتَغْفِرْ لَنَا ذُنُوبَنَآ إِنَّا كُنَّا
خَـٰطِـِٔينَ

97 They said, “Father, pray for the forgiveness of our sins; we were indeed at fault.”

٩٨ قَالَ سَوْفَ أَسْتَغْفِرُ لَكُمْ رَبِّىٓ ۖ إِنَّهُۥ هُوَ
ٱلْغَفُورُ ٱلرَّحِيمُ

98 He said, “I will ask my Lord to forgive you. He is the Forgiver, the Most Merciful.”

٩٩ فَلَمَّا دَخَلُوا۟ عَلَىٰ يُوسُفَ ءَاوَىٰٓ إِلَيْهِ أَبَوَيْهِ
وَقَالَ ٱدْخُلُوا۟ مِصْرَ إِن شَآءَ ٱللَّهُ ءَامِنِينَ

99 Then, when they entered into the presence of Joseph, he embraced his parents, and said, “Enter Egypt, Allah willing, safe and secure.”

١٠٠ وَرَفَعَ أَبَوَيْهِ عَلَى ٱلْعَرْشِ وَخَرُّوا۟ لَهُۥ سُجَّدًا ۖ
وَقَالَ يَـٰٓأَبَتِ هَـٰذَا تَأْوِيلُ رُءْيَـٰىَ مِن قَبْلُ قَدْ
جَعَلَهَا رَبِّى حَقًّا ۖ وَقَدْ أَحْسَنَ بِىٓ إِذْ أَخْرَجَنِى
مِنَ ٱلسِّجْنِ وَجَآءَ بِكُم مِّنَ ٱلْبَدْوِ مِنۢ بَعْدِ أَن
نَّزَغَ ٱلشَّيْطَـٰنُ بَيْنِى وَبَيْنَ إِخْوَتِىٓ ۚ إِنَّ رَبِّى
لَطِيفٌ لِّمَا يَشَآءُ ۚ إِنَّهُۥ هُوَ ٱلْعَلِيمُ ٱلْحَكِيمُ

100 And he elevated his parents on the throne, and they fell prostrate before him. He said, “Father, this is the fulfillment of my vision of long ago. My Lord has made it come true. He has blessed me, when he released me from prison, and brought you out of the wilderness, after the devil had sown conflict between me and my brothers. My Lord is Most Kind towards whomever He wills. He is the All-knowing, the Most Wise.”

١٠١ رَبِّ قَدْ ءَاتَيْتَنِى مِنَ ٱلْمُلْكِ وَعَلَّمْتَنِى مِن
تَأْوِيلِ ٱلْأَحَادِيثِ ۚ فَاطِرَ ٱلسَّمَـٰوَٰتِ وَٱلْأَرْضِ
أَنتَ وَلِىِّۦ فِى ٱلدُّنْيَا وَٱلْـَٔاخِرَةِ ۖ تَوَفَّنِى
مُسْلِمًا وَأَلْحِقْنِى بِٱلصَّـٰلِحِينَ

101 “My Lord, You have given me some authority, and taught me some interpretation of events. Initiator of the heavens and the earth; You are my Protector in this life and in the Hereafter. Receive my soul in

submission, and unite me with the righteous.”

١٠٢ ذَٰلِكَ مِنْ أَنۢبَآءِ ٱلْغَيْبِ نُوحِيهِ إِلَيْكَ ۖ وَمَا
كُنتَ لَدَيْهِمْ إِذْ أَجْمَعُوٓا۟ أَمْرَهُمْ وَهُمْ يَمْكُرُونَ

102 This is news from the past that We reveal to you. You were not present with them when they plotted and agreed on a plan.

١٠٣ وَمَآ أَكْثَرُ ٱلنَّاسِ وَلَوْ حَرَصْتَ بِمُؤْمِنِينَ

103 But most people, for all your eagerness, are not believers.

١٠٤ وَمَا تَسْـَٔلُهُمْ عَلَيْهِ مِنْ أَجْرٍ ۚ إِنْ هُوَ إِلَّا ذِكْرٌ
لِّلْعَٰلَمِينَ

104 You ask them no wage for it. It is only a reminder for all mankind.

١٠٥ وَكَأَيِّن مِّنْ ءَايَةٍ فِى ٱلسَّمَٰوَٰتِ وَٱلْأَرْضِ
يَمُرُّونَ عَلَيْهَا وَهُمْ عَنْهَا مُعْرِضُونَ

105 How many a sign in the heavens and the earth do they pass by, paying no attention to them?

١٠٦ وَمَا يُؤْمِنُ أَكْثَرُهُم بِٱللَّهِ إِلَّا وَهُم مُّشْرِكُونَ

106 And most of them do not believe in Allah unless they associate others.

١٠٧ أَفَأَمِنُوٓا۟ أَن تَأْتِيَهُمْ غَٰشِيَةٌ مِّنْ عَذَابِ ٱللَّهِ
أَوْ تَأْتِيَهُمُ ٱلسَّاعَةُ بَغْتَةً وَهُمْ لَا يَشْعُرُونَ

107 Do they feel secure that a covering of Allah’s punishment will not come upon them, or that the Hour will not come upon them suddenly, while they are unaware?

١٠٨ قُلْ هَٰذِهِۦ سَبِيلِىٓ أَدْعُوٓا۟ إِلَى ٱللَّهِ ۚ عَلَىٰ
بَصِيرَةٍ أَنَا۠ وَمَنِ ٱتَّبَعَنِى ۖ وَسُبْحَٰنَ ٱللَّهِ وَمَآ أَنَا۠
مِنَ ٱلْمُشْرِكِينَ

108 Say, “This is my way; I invite to Allah, based on clear knowledge—I and whoever follows me. Glory be to Allah; and I am not of the polytheists.”

١٠٩ وَمَآ أَرْسَلْنَا مِن قَبْلِكَ إِلَّا رِجَالًا نُّوحِىٓ
إِلَيْهِم مِّنْ أَهْلِ ٱلْقُرَىٰٓ ۗ أَفَلَمْ يَسِيرُوا۟ فِى ٱلْأَرْضِ
فَيَنظُرُوا۟ كَيْفَ كَانَ عَٰقِبَةُ ٱلَّذِينَ مِن قَبْلِهِمْ ۗ
وَلَدَارُ ٱلْءَاخِرَةِ خَيْرٌ لِّلَّذِينَ ٱتَّقَوْا۟ ۗ أَفَلَا تَعْقِلُونَ

109 We did not send before you except men, whom We inspired, from the people of the towns. Have they not roamed the earth and seen the consequences for those before them? The Home of the Hereafter is better for those who are righteous. Do you not understand?

١١٠ حَتَّىٰٓ إِذَا ٱسْتَيْـَٔسَ ٱلرُّسُلُ وَظَنُّوٓا۟ أَنَّهُمْ قَدْ
كُذِبُوا۟ جَآءَهُمْ نَصْرُنَا فَنُجِّىَ مَن نَّشَآءُ ۖ وَلَا
يُرَدُّ بَأْسُنَا عَنِ ٱلْقَوْمِ ٱلْمُجْرِمِينَ

110 Until, when the messengers have despaired, and thought that they were rejected, Our help came to them. We save whomever We will, and Our severity is not averted from the guilty people.

١١١ لَقَدْ كَانَ فِى قَصَصِهِمْ عِبْرَةٌ لِّأُو۟لِى ٱلْأَلْبَٰبِ ۗ
مَا كَانَ حَدِيثًا يُفْتَرَىٰ وَلَٰكِن تَصْدِيقَ ٱلَّذِى بَيْنَ
يَدَيْهِ وَتَفْصِيلَ كُلِّ شَىْءٍ وَهُدًى وَرَحْمَةً لِّقَوْمٍ
يُؤْمِنُونَ

111 In their stories is a lesson for those who possess intelligence. This is not a fabricated tale, but a confirmation of what came before it, and a detailed explanation of all things, and guidance, and mercy for people who believe.

13 Thunder الرعد

بِسْمِ ٱللَّهِ ٱلرَّحْمَٰنِ ٱلرَّحِيمِ

In the name of Allah, the Gracious, the Merciful.

١ الٓمٓر ۚ تِلْكَ ءَايَٰتُ ٱلْكِتَٰبِ ۗ وَٱلَّذِىٓ أُنزِلَ إِلَيْكَ
مِن رَّبِّكَ ٱلْحَقُّ وَلَٰكِنَّ أَكْثَرَ ٱلنَّاسِ لَا يُؤْمِنُونَ

1 Alif, Lam, Meem, Ra. These are the signs of the Scripture. What is revealed to you from your Lord is the truth, but most people do not believe.

٢ ٱللَّهُ ٱلَّذِى رَفَعَ ٱلسَّمَٰوَٰتِ بِغَيْرِ عَمَدٍ تَرَوْنَهَا ۖ ثُمَّ
ٱسْتَوَىٰ عَلَى ٱلْعَرْشِ ۖ وَسَخَّرَ ٱلشَّمْسَ وَٱلْقَمَرَ ۖ
كُلٌّ يَجْرِى لِأَجَلٍ مُّسَمًّى ۚ يُدَبِّرُ ٱلْأَمْرَ يُفَصِّلُ
ٱلْءَايَٰتِ لَعَلَّكُم بِلِقَآءِ رَبِّكُمْ تُوقِنُونَ

2 Allah is He who raised the heavens without pillars that you can see, and then settled on the Throne. And He regulated the sun and the moon, each running for a specified period. He manages all affairs, and He explains the signs, that you may be certain of the meeting with your Lord.

٣ وَهُوَ ٱلَّذِى مَدَّ ٱلْأَرْضَ وَجَعَلَ فِيهَا رَوَٰسِىَ
وَأَنْهَٰرًا ۖ وَمِن كُلِّ ٱلثَّمَرَٰتِ جَعَلَ فِيهَا زَوْجَيْنِ
ٱثْنَيْنِ ۖ يُغْشِى ٱلَّيْلَ ٱلنَّهَارَ ۚ إِنَّ فِى ذَٰلِكَ لَءَايَٰتٍ
لِّقَوْمٍ يَتَفَكَّرُونَ

3 And it is He who spread the earth, and placed in it mountains and rivers. And He placed in it two kinds of every fruit. He causes the night to overlap the day. In that are signs for people who reflect.

٤ وَفِى ٱلْأَرْضِ قِطَعٌ مُّتَجَٰوِرَٰتٌ وَجَنَّٰتٌ مِّنْ
أَعْنَٰبٍ وَزَرْعٌ وَنَخِيلٌ صِنْوَانٌ وَغَيْرُ صِنْوَانٍ
يُسْقَىٰ بِمَآءٍ وَٰحِدٍ وَنُفَضِّلُ بَعْضَهَا عَلَىٰ بَعْضٍ
فِى ٱلْأُكُلِ ۚ إِنَّ فِى ذَٰلِكَ لَءَايَٰتٍ لِّقَوْمٍ يَعْقِلُونَ

4 On earth are adjacent terrains, and gardens of vines, and crops, and date-palms, from the same root or from distinct roots, irrigated with the same water. We make some taste better than others. In that are proofs for people who reason.

٥ وَإِن تَعۡجَبۡ فَعَجَبٞ قَوۡلُهُمۡ أَءِذَا كُنَّا تُرَٰبًا أَءِنَّا
لَفِي خَلۡقٖ جَدِيدٍۗ أُوْلَٰٓئِكَ ٱلَّذِينَ كَفَرُواْ بِرَبِّهِمۡۖ
وَأُوْلَٰٓئِكَ ٱلۡأَغۡلَٰلُ فِيٓ أَعۡنَاقِهِمۡۖ وَأُوْلَٰٓئِكَ أَصۡحَٰبُ
ٱلنَّارِۖ هُمۡ فِيهَا خَٰلِدُونَ

5 Should you wonder—the real wonder is their saying: “When we have become dust, will we be in a new creation?” Those are they who defied their Lord. Those are they who will have yokes around their necks. Those are the inhabitants of the Fire, where they will remain forever.

٦ وَيَسۡتَعۡجِلُونَكَ بِٱلسَّيِّئَةِ قَبۡلَ ٱلۡحَسَنَةِ وَقَدۡ
خَلَتۡ مِن قَبۡلِهِمُ ٱلۡمَثُلَٰتُۗ وَإِنَّ رَبَّكَ لَذُو مَغۡفِرَةٖ
لِّلنَّاسِ عَلَىٰ ظُلۡمِهِمۡۖ وَإِنَّ رَبَّكَ لَشَدِيدُ ٱلۡعِقَابِ

6 And they urge you to hasten evil before good, though examples have passed away before them. Your Lord is full of forgiveness towards the people for their wrongdoings, yet your Lord is severe in retribution.

٧ وَيَقُولُ ٱلَّذِينَ كَفَرُواْ لَوۡلَآ أُنزِلَ عَلَيۡهِ ءَايَةٞ
مِّن رَّبِّهِۦٓۗ إِنَّمَآ أَنتَ مُنذِرٞۖ وَلِكُلِّ قَوۡمٍ هَادٍ

7 Those who disbelieve say, “Why was a miracle not sent down to him from his Lord?” You are only a warner, and to every community is a guide.

٨ ٱللَّهُ يَعۡلَمُ مَا تَحۡمِلُ كُلُّ أُنثَىٰ وَمَا تَغِيضُ
ٱلۡأَرۡحَامُ وَمَا تَزۡدَادُۖ وَكُلُّ شَيۡءٍ عِندَهُۥ بِمِقۡدَارٍ

8 Allah knows what every female bears, and every increase and decrease of the wombs. With Him, everything is by measure.

٩ عَٰلِمُ ٱلۡغَيۡبِ وَٱلشَّهَٰدَةِ ٱلۡكَبِيرُ ٱلۡمُتَعَالِ

9 The Knower of the Invisible and the Visible; the Grand, the Supreme.

١٠ سَوَآءٞ مِّنكُم مَّنۡ أَسَرَّ ٱلۡقَوۡلَ وَمَن جَهَرَ بِهِۦ
وَمَنۡ هُوَ مُسۡتَخۡفِۭ بِٱلَّيۡلِ وَسَارِبُۢ بِٱلنَّهَارِ

10 It is the same; whether one of you conceals his speech, or declares it; whether he goes into hiding by night, or goes out by day.

١١ لَهُۥ مُعَقِّبَٰتٞ مِّنۢ بَيۡنِ يَدَيۡهِ وَمِنۡ خَلۡفِهِۦ
يَحۡفَظُونَهُۥ مِنۡ أَمۡرِ ٱللَّهِۗ إِنَّ ٱللَّهَ لَا يُغَيِّرُ مَا
بِقَوۡمٍ حَتَّىٰ يُغَيِّرُواْ مَا بِأَنفُسِهِمۡۗ وَإِذَآ أَرَادَ ٱللَّهُ
بِقَوۡمٖ سُوٓءٗا فَلَا مَرَدَّ لَهُۥۚ وَمَا لَهُم مِّن دُونِهِۦ مِن
وَالٍ

11 He has a succession; before him and behind him, protecting him by Allah’s command. Allah does not change the condition of a people until they change what is within themselves. And if Allah wills any hardship for a people, there is no turning it back; and apart from Him they have no protector.

١٢ هُوَ ٱلَّذِى يُرِيكُمُ ٱلْبَرْقَ خَوْفًا وَطَمَعًا
وَيُنشِئُ ٱلسَّحَابَ ٱلثِّقَالَ

12 It is He who shows you the lightening, causing fear and hope. And He produces the heavy clouds.

١٣ وَيُسَبِّحُ ٱلرَّعْدُ بِحَمْدِهِۦ وَٱلْمَلَٰٓئِكَةُ مِنْ
خِيفَتِهِۦ وَيُرْسِلُ ٱلصَّوَٰعِقَ فَيُصِيبُ بِهَا مَن
يَشَآءُ وَهُمْ يُجَٰدِلُونَ فِى ٱللَّهِ وَهُوَ شَدِيدُ
ٱلْمِحَالِ

13 The thunder praises His glory, and so do the angels, in awe of Him. And He sends the thunderbolts, striking with them whomever He wills. Yet they argue about Allah, while He is Tremendous in might.

١٤ لَهُۥ دَعْوَةُ ٱلْحَقِّ ۖ وَٱلَّذِينَ يَدْعُونَ مِن دُونِهِۦ
لَا يَسْتَجِيبُونَ لَهُم بِشَىْءٍ إِلَّا كَبَٰسِطِ كَفَّيْهِ إِلَى
ٱلْمَآءِ لِيَبْلُغَ فَاهُ وَمَا هُوَ بِبَٰلِغِهِۦ ۚ وَمَا دُعَآءُ
ٱلْكَٰفِرِينَ إِلَّا فِى ضَلَٰلٍ

14 To Him belongs the call to truth. Those they call upon besides Him do not respond to them with anything—except as someone who stretches his hands towards water, so that it may reach his mouth, but it does not reach it. The prayers of the unbelievers are only in vain.

١٥ وَلِلَّهِ يَسْجُدُ مَن فِى ٱلسَّمَٰوَٰتِ وَٱلْأَرْضِ
طَوْعًا وَكَرْهًا وَظِلَٰلُهُم بِٱلْغُدُوِّ وَٱلْءَاصَالِ ۩

15 To Allah prostrates everyone in the heavens and the earth, willingly or unwillingly, as do their shadows, in the morning and in the evening.

١٦ قُلْ مَن رَّبُّ ٱلسَّمَٰوَٰتِ وَٱلْأَرْضِ قُلِ ٱللَّهُ ۚ قُلْ
أَفَٱتَّخَذْتُم مِّن دُونِهِۦٓ أَوْلِيَآءَ لَا يَمْلِكُونَ
لِأَنفُسِهِمْ نَفْعًا وَلَا ضَرًّا ۚ قُلْ هَلْ يَسْتَوِى
ٱلْأَعْمَىٰ وَٱلْبَصِيرُ أَمْ هَلْ تَسْتَوِى ٱلظُّلُمَٰتُ
وَٱلنُّورُ ۗ أَمْ جَعَلُوا۟ لِلَّهِ شُرَكَآءَ خَلَقُوا۟ كَخَلْقِهِۦ
فَتَشَٰبَهَ ٱلْخَلْقُ عَلَيْهِمْ ۚ قُلِ ٱللَّهُ خَٰلِقُ كُلِّ شَىْءٍ
وَهُوَ ٱلْوَٰحِدُ ٱلْقَهَّٰرُ

16 Say, "Who is the Lord of the heavens and the earth?" Say, "Allah." Say, "Have you taken besides Him protectors, who have no power to profit or harm even themselves?" Say, "Are the blind and the seeing equal? Or are darkness and light equal? Or have they assigned to Allah associates, who created the likes of His creation, so that the creations seemed to them alike? Say, "Allah is the Creator of all things, and He is The One, the Irresistible."

١٧ أَنزَلَ مِنَ ٱلسَّمَآءِ مَآءً فَسَالَتْ أَوْدِيَةٌۢ بِقَدَرِهَا
فَٱحْتَمَلَ ٱلسَّيْلُ زَبَدًا رَّابِيًا ۚ وَمِمَّا يُوقِدُونَ
عَلَيْهِ فِى ٱلنَّارِ ٱبْتِغَآءَ حِلْيَةٍ أَوْ مَتَٰعٍ زَبَدٌ مِّثْلُهُۥ ۚ
كَذَٰلِكَ يَضْرِبُ ٱللَّهُ ٱلْحَقَّ وَٱلْبَٰطِلَ ۚ فَأَمَّا ٱلزَّبَدُ

17 He sends down water from the sky, and riverbeds flow according to their capacity. The current carries swelling froth. And from what they heat in fire of ornaments or utensils comes a similar froth. Thus Allah exemplifies truth and falsehood. As

فَيَذْهَبُ جُفَآءً ۖ وَأَمَّا مَا يَنفَعُ ٱلنَّاسَ فَيَمْكُثُ
فِى ٱلْأَرْضِ ۚ كَذَٰلِكَ يَضْرِبُ ٱللَّهُ ٱلْأَمْثَالَ

for the froth, it is swept away, but what benefits the people remains in the ground. Thus Allah presents the analogies.

١٨ لِلَّذِينَ ٱسْتَجَابُوا۟ لِرَبِّهِمُ ٱلْحُسْنَىٰ ۚ وَٱلَّذِينَ لَمْ
يَسْتَجِيبُوا۟ لَهُۥ لَوْ أَنَّ لَهُم مَّا فِى ٱلْأَرْضِ جَمِيعًا
وَمِثْلَهُۥ مَعَهُۥ لَٱفْتَدَوْا۟ بِهِۦٓ ۚ أُو۟لَٰٓئِكَ لَهُمْ سُوٓءُ
ٱلْحِسَابِ وَمَأْوَىٰهُمْ جَهَنَّمُ ۖ وَبِئْسَ ٱلْمِهَادُ

18 For those who respond to their Lord is the best. But as for those who do not respond to Him, even if they possessed everything on earth, and twice as much, they could not redeem themselves with it. Those will have the worst reckoning; and their home is Hell—a miserable destination.

١٩ أَفَمَن يَعْلَمُ أَنَّمَآ أُنزِلَ إِلَيْكَ مِن رَّبِّكَ ٱلْحَقُّ
كَمَنْ هُوَ أَعْمَىٰٓ ۚ إِنَّمَا يَتَذَكَّرُ أُو۟لُوا۟ ٱلْأَلْبَٰبِ

19 Is he who knows that what was revealed to your from your Lord is the truth, like him who is blind? Only those who reason will remember.

٢٠ ٱلَّذِينَ يُوفُونَ بِعَهْدِ ٱللَّهِ وَلَا يَنقُضُونَ
ٱلْمِيثَٰقَ

20 Those who fulfill the promise to Allah, and do not violate the agreement.

٢١ وَٱلَّذِينَ يَصِلُونَ مَآ أَمَرَ ٱللَّهُ بِهِۦٓ أَن يُوصَلَ
وَيَخْشَوْنَ رَبَّهُمْ وَيَخَافُونَ سُوٓءَ ٱلْحِسَابِ

21 And those who join what Allah has commanded to be joined, and fear their Lord, and dread the dire reckoning.

٢٢ وَٱلَّذِينَ صَبَرُوا۟ ٱبْتِغَآءَ وَجْهِ رَبِّهِمْ وَأَقَامُوا۟
ٱلصَّلَوٰةَ وَأَنفَقُوا۟ مِمَّا رَزَقْنَٰهُمْ سِرًّا وَعَلَانِيَةً
وَيَدْرَءُونَ بِٱلْحَسَنَةِ ٱلسَّيِّئَةَ أُو۟لَٰٓئِكَ لَهُمْ عُقْبَى
ٱلدَّارِ

22 And those who patiently seek the presence of their Lord, and pray regularly, and spend from Our provisions to them, secretly and openly, and repel evil with good. These will have the Ultimate Home.

٢٣ جَنَّٰتُ عَدْنٍ يَدْخُلُونَهَا وَمَن صَلَحَ مِنْ
ءَابَآئِهِمْ وَأَزْوَٰجِهِمْ وَذُرِّيَّٰتِهِمْ ۖ وَٱلْمَلَٰٓئِكَةُ
يَدْخُلُونَ عَلَيْهِم مِّن كُلِّ بَابٍ

23 Everlasting Gardens, which they will enter, along with the righteous among their parents, and their spouses, and their descendants. And the angels will enter upon them from every gate.

٢٤ سَلَٰمٌ عَلَيْكُم بِمَا صَبَرْتُمْ ۚ فَنِعْمَ عُقْبَى ٱلدَّارِ

24 “Peace be upon you, because you endured patiently. How excellent is the Final Home.”

٢٥ وَٱلَّذِينَ يَنقُضُونَ عَهْدَ ٱللَّهِ مِنۢ بَعْدِ مِيثَٰقِهِۦ
وَيَقْطَعُونَ مَآ أَمَرَ ٱللَّهُ بِهِۦٓ أَن يُوصَلَ
وَيُفْسِدُونَ فِى ٱلْأَرْضِ ۙ أُو۟لَٰٓئِكَ لَهُمُ ٱللَّعْنَةُ وَلَهُمْ
سُوٓءُ ٱلدَّارِ

25 As for those who violate the promise to Allah, after pledging to keep it, and sever what Allah has commanded to be joined, and spread corruption on earth—these, the curse will be upon them, and they will have the Worst Home.

٢٦ ٱللَّهُ يَبْسُطُ ٱلرِّزْقَ لِمَن يَشَآءُ وَيَقْدِرُ ۚ
وَفَرِحُوا۟ بِٱلْحَيَوٰةِ ٱلدُّنْيَا وَمَا ٱلْحَيَوٰةُ ٱلدُّنْيَا فِى
ٱلْءَاخِرَةِ إِلَّا مَتَٰعٌ

26 Allah dispenses the provisions to whomever He wills, and restricts. And they delight in the worldly life; yet the worldly life, compared to the Hereafter, is only enjoyment.

٢٧ وَيَقُولُ ٱلَّذِينَ كَفَرُوا۟ لَوْلَآ أُنزِلَ عَلَيْهِ ءَايَةٌ
مِّن رَّبِّهِۦ ۗ قُلْ إِنَّ ٱللَّهَ يُضِلُّ مَن يَشَآءُ وَيَهْدِىٓ
إِلَيْهِ مَنْ أَنَابَ

27 Those who disbelieve say, “If only a miracle was sent down to him from his Lord.” Say, “Allah leads astray whomever He wills, and He guides to Himself whoever repents.”

٢٨ ٱلَّذِينَ ءَامَنُوا۟ وَتَطْمَئِنُّ قُلُوبُهُم بِذِكْرِ ٱللَّهِ ۗ
أَلَا بِذِكْرِ ٱللَّهِ تَطْمَئِنُّ ٱلْقُلُوبُ

28 Those who believe, and whose hearts find comfort in the remembrance of Allah. Surely, it is in the remembrance of Allah that hearts find comfort.”

٢٩ ٱلَّذِينَ ءَامَنُوا۟ وَعَمِلُوا۟ ٱلصَّٰلِحَٰتِ طُوبَىٰ لَهُمْ
وَحُسْنُ مَـَٔابٍ

29 For those who believe and do righteous deeds—for them is happiness and a beautiful return.

٣٠ كَذَٰلِكَ أَرْسَلْنَٰكَ فِىٓ أُمَّةٍ قَدْ خَلَتْ مِن قَبْلِهَآ
أُمَمٌ لِّتَتْلُوَا۟ عَلَيْهِمُ ٱلَّذِىٓ أَوْحَيْنَآ إِلَيْكَ وَهُمْ
يَكْفُرُونَ بِٱلرَّحْمَٰنِ ۚ قُلْ هُوَ رَبِّى لَآ إِلَٰهَ إِلَّا هُوَ
عَلَيْهِ تَوَكَّلْتُ وَإِلَيْهِ مَتَابِ

30 Thus We sent you among a community before which other communities have passed away, that you may recite to them what We revealed to you. Yet they deny the Benevolent One. Say, “He is my Lord; there is no god but He; in Him I trust, and to Him is my repentance.”

٣١ وَلَوْ أَنَّ قُرْءَانًا سُيِّرَتْ بِهِ ٱلْجِبَالُ أَوْ قُطِّعَتْ
بِهِ ٱلْأَرْضُ أَوْ كُلِّمَ بِهِ ٱلْمَوْتَىٰ ۗ بَل لِّلَّهِ ٱلْأَمْرُ
جَمِيعًا ۗ أَفَلَمْ يَا۟يْـَٔسِ ٱلَّذِينَ ءَامَنُوٓا۟ أَن لَّوْ يَشَآءُ
ٱللَّهُ لَهَدَى ٱلنَّاسَ جَمِيعًا ۗ وَلَا يَزَالُ ٱلَّذِينَ
كَفَرُوا۟ تُصِيبُهُم بِمَا صَنَعُوا۟ قَارِعَةٌ أَوْ تَحُلُّ

31 Even if there were a Quran, by which mountains could be set in motion, or by which the earth could be shattered, or by which the dead could be made to speak. In fact, every decision rests with Allah. Did the believers not give up and realize that had Allah willed, He would have guided all humanity? Disasters will

قَرِيبًا مِّن دَارِهِمْ حَتَّىٰ يَأْتِىَ وَعْدُ ٱللَّهِ ۚ إِنَّ ٱللَّهَ
لَا يُخْلِفُ ٱلْمِيعَادَ

continue to strike those who disbelieve, because of their deeds, or they fall near their homes, until Allah's promise comes true. Allah never breaks a promise.

٣٢ وَلَقَدِ ٱسْتُهْزِئَ بِرُسُلٍ مِّن قَبْلِكَ فَأَمْلَيْتُ
لِلَّذِينَ كَفَرُوا۟ ثُمَّ أَخَذْتُهُمْ ۖ فَكَيْفَ كَانَ عِقَابِ

32 Messengers before you were ridiculed, but I granted the disbelievers respite, and then I seized them. What a punishment it was!

٣٣ أَفَمَنْ هُوَ قَآئِمٌ عَلَىٰ كُلِّ نَفْسٍۭ بِمَا كَسَبَتْ ۗ
وَجَعَلُوا۟ لِلَّهِ شُرَكَآءَ قُلْ سَمُّوهُمْ ۚ أَمْ تُنَبِّـُٔونَهُۥ بِمَا
لَا يَعْلَمُ فِى ٱلْأَرْضِ أَم بِظَٰهِرٍ مِّنَ ٱلْقَوْلِ ۗ بَلْ
زُيِّنَ لِلَّذِينَ كَفَرُوا۟ مَكْرُهُمْ وَصُدُّوا۟ عَنِ ٱلسَّبِيلِ ۗ
وَمَن يُضْلِلِ ٱللَّهُ فَمَا لَهُۥ مِنْ هَادٍ

33 Is He who is watchful over the deeds of every soul? Yet they ascribe associates to Allah. Say, "Name them! Or are you informing Him of something on earth He does not know, or is it a show of words?" In fact, the scheming of those who disbelieve is made to appear good to them, and they are averted from the path. Whomever Allah misguides has no guide.

٣٤ لَّهُمْ عَذَابٌ فِى ٱلْحَيَوٰةِ ٱلدُّنْيَا ۖ وَلَعَذَابُ
ٱلْـَٔاخِرَةِ أَشَقُّ ۖ وَمَا لَهُم مِّنَ ٱللَّهِ مِن وَاقٍ

34 There is for them torment in the worldly life, but the torment of the Hereafter is harsher. And they have no defender against Allah.

٣٥ مَّثَلُ ٱلْجَنَّةِ ٱلَّتِى وُعِدَ ٱلْمُتَّقُونَ ۖ تَجْرِى مِن
تَحْتِهَا ٱلْأَنْهَٰرُ ۖ أُكُلُهَا دَآئِمٌ وَظِلُّهَا ۚ تِلْكَ عُقْبَى
ٱلَّذِينَ ٱتَّقَوا۟ ۖ وَّعُقْبَى ٱلْكَٰفِرِينَ ٱلنَّارُ

35 The likeness of the Garden promised to the righteous: rivers flowing beneath it; its food is perpetual, and so is its shade. Such is the sequel for those who guard against evil, but the sequel of the disbelievers is the Fire.

٣٦ وَٱلَّذِينَ ءَاتَيْنَٰهُمُ ٱلْكِتَٰبَ يَفْرَحُونَ بِمَآ أُنزِلَ
إِلَيْكَ ۖ وَمِنَ ٱلْأَحْزَابِ مَن يُنكِرُ بَعْضَهُۥ ۚ قُلْ إِنَّمَآ
أُمِرْتُ أَنْ أَعْبُدَ ٱللَّهَ وَلَآ أُشْرِكَ بِهِۦٓ ۚ إِلَيْهِ أَدْعُوا۟
وَإِلَيْهِ مَـَٔابِ

36 Those to whom We gave the Scripture rejoice in what was revealed to you, while some factions reject parts of it. Say, "I am commanded to worship Allah, and to never associate anything with Him. To Him I invite, and to Him is my return."

٣٧ وَكَذَٰلِكَ أَنزَلْنَٰهُ حُكْمًا عَرَبِيًّا ۚ وَلَئِنِ ٱتَّبَعْتَ
أَهْوَآءَهُم بَعْدَمَا جَآءَكَ مِنَ ٱلْعِلْمِ مَا لَكَ مِنَ
ٱللَّهِ مِن وَلِىٍّ وَلَا وَاقٍ

37 Thus We revealed it an Arabic code of law. Were you to follow their desires, after the knowledge that has come to you, you would have neither ally nor defender against Allah.

٣٨ وَلَقَدْ أَرْسَلْنَا رُسُلًا مِّن قَبْلِكَ وَجَعَلْنَا لَهُمْ
أَزْوَٰجًا وَذُرِّيَّةً ۚ وَمَا كَانَ لِرَسُولٍ أَن يَأْتِىَ بِـَٔايَةٍ
إِلَّا بِإِذْنِ ٱللَّهِ ۗ لِكُلِّ أَجَلٍ كِتَابٌ

38 We sent messengers before you, and We assigned for them wives and offspring. No messenger could bring a sign except with the permission of Allah. For every era is a scripture.

٣٩ يَمْحُوا۟ ٱللَّهُ مَا يَشَآءُ وَيُثْبِتُ ۖ وَعِندَهُۥٓ أُمُّ
ٱلْكِتَٰبِ

39 Allah abolishes whatever He wills, and He affirms. With Him is the source of the Scripture.

٤٠ وَإِن مَّا نُرِيَنَّكَ بَعْضَ ٱلَّذِى نَعِدُهُمْ أَوْ
نَتَوَفَّيَنَّكَ فَإِنَّمَا عَلَيْكَ ٱلْبَلَٰغُ وَعَلَيْنَا ٱلْحِسَابُ

40 Whether We show you some of what We have promised them, or We cause you to die—your duty is to inform, and Ours is the reckoning.

٤١ أَوَلَمْ يَرَوْا۟ أَنَّا نَأْتِى ٱلْأَرْضَ نَنقُصُهَا مِنْ
أَطْرَافِهَا ۚ وَٱللَّهُ يَحْكُمُ لَا مُعَقِّبَ لِحُكْمِهِۦ ۚ وَهُوَ
سَرِيعُ ٱلْحِسَابِ

41 Do they not see how We deal with the earth, diminishing it at its edges? Allah judges; and nothing can hold back His judgment. And He is quick to settle accounts.

٤٢ وَقَدْ مَكَرَ ٱلَّذِينَ مِن قَبْلِهِمْ فَلِلَّهِ ٱلْمَكْرُ
جَمِيعًا ۖ يَعْلَمُ مَا تَكْسِبُ كُلُّ نَفْسٍ ۗ وَسَيَعْلَمُ
ٱلْكُفَّٰرُ لِمَنْ عُقْبَى ٱلدَّارِ

42 Those before them planned, but the entire plan is up to Allah. He knows what every soul earns. Those who disbelieve will know to whom the Ultimate Home is.

٤٣ وَيَقُولُ ٱلَّذِينَ كَفَرُوا۟ لَسْتَ مُرْسَلًا ۚ قُلْ كَفَىٰ
بِٱللَّهِ شَهِيدًۢا بَيْنِى وَبَيْنَكُمْ وَمَنْ عِندَهُۥ عِلْمُ
ٱلْكِتَٰبِ

43 Those who disbelieve say, "You are not a messenger." Say, "Allah is a sufficient witness between me and you, and whoever has knowledge of the Scripture."

14 Abraham إبراهيم

بِسْمِ ٱللَّهِ ٱلرَّحْمَٰنِ ٱلرَّحِيمِ

In the name of Allah, the Gracious, the Merciful.

١ الٓرۚ كِتَٰبٌ أَنزَلۡنَٰهُ إِلَيۡكَ لِتُخۡرِجَ ٱلنَّاسَ مِنَ
ٱلظُّلُمَٰتِ إِلَى ٱلنُّورِ بِإِذۡنِ رَبِّهِمۡ إِلَىٰ صِرَٰطِ
ٱلۡعَزِيزِ ٱلۡحَمِيدِ

1 Alif, Lam, Ra. A Scripture that We revealed to you, that you may bring humanity from darkness to light—with the permission of their Lord—to the path of the Almighty, the Praiseworthy.

٢ ٱللَّهِ ٱلَّذِي لَهُۥ مَا فِي ٱلسَّمَٰوَٰتِ وَمَا فِي
ٱلۡأَرۡضِۗ وَوَيۡلٞ لِّلۡكَٰفِرِينَ مِنۡ عَذَابٖ شَدِيدٍ

2 Allah—to whom belongs what is in the heavens and the earth. And woe to the disbelievers from a severe torment.

٣ ٱلَّذِينَ يَسۡتَحِبُّونَ ٱلۡحَيَوٰةَ ٱلدُّنۡيَا عَلَى
ٱلۡأٓخِرَةِ وَيَصُدُّونَ عَن سَبِيلِ ٱللَّهِ وَيَبۡغُونَهَا
عِوَجًاۚ أُوْلَٰٓئِكَ فِي ضَلَٰلِۭ بَعِيدٖ

3 Those who prefer the present life to the Hereafter, and repel from the path of Allah, and seek to make it crooked—these are far astray.

٤ وَمَآ أَرۡسَلۡنَا مِن رَّسُولٍ إِلَّا بِلِسَانِ قَوۡمِهِۦ
لِيُبَيِّنَ لَهُمۡۖ فَيُضِلُّ ٱللَّهُ مَن يَشَآءُ وَيَهۡدِي مَن
يَشَآءُۚ وَهُوَ ٱلۡعَزِيزُ ٱلۡحَكِيمُ

4 We never sent any messenger except in the language of his people, to make things clear for them. Allah leads astray whom He wills, and guides whom He wills. He is the Mighty, the Wise.

٥ وَلَقَدۡ أَرۡسَلۡنَا مُوسَىٰ بِـَٔايَٰتِنَآ أَنۡ أَخۡرِجۡ قَوۡمَكَ
مِنَ ٱلظُّلُمَٰتِ إِلَى ٱلنُّورِ وَذَكِّرۡهُم بِأَيَّىٰمِ ٱللَّهِۚ إِنَّ
فِي ذَٰلِكَ لَأٓيَٰتٖ لِّكُلِّ صَبَّارٖ شَكُورٖ

5 We sent Moses with Our signs: “Bring your people out of darkness into light, and remind them of the Days of Allah.” In that are signs for every patient and thankful person.”

٦ وَإِذۡ قَالَ مُوسَىٰ لِقَوۡمِهِ ٱذۡكُرُواْ نِعۡمَةَ ٱللَّهِ
عَلَيۡكُمۡ إِذۡ أَنجَىٰكُم مِّنۡ ءَالِ فِرۡعَوۡنَ
يَسُومُونَكُمۡ سُوٓءَ ٱلۡعَذَابِ وَيُذَبِّحُونَ أَبۡنَآءَكُمۡ
وَيَسۡتَحۡيُونَ نِسَآءَكُمۡۚ وَفِي ذَٰلِكُم بَلَآءٞ مِّن
رَّبِّكُمۡ عَظِيمٞ

6 Moses said to his people, “Remember Allah’s blessings upon you, as He delivered you from the people of Pharaoh, who inflicted on you terrible suffering, slaughtering your sons while sparing your daughters. In that was a serious trial from your Lord.”

٧ وَإِذۡ تَأَذَّنَ رَبُّكُمۡ لَئِن شَكَرۡتُمۡ لَأَزِيدَنَّكُمۡۖ وَلَئِن
كَفَرۡتُمۡ إِنَّ عَذَابِي لَشَدِيدٞ

7 And when your Lord proclaimed: “If you give thanks, I will grant you increase; but if you are ungrateful, My punishment is severe.”

٨ وَقَالَ مُوسَىٰٓ إِن تَكۡفُرُوٓاْ أَنتُمۡ وَمَن فِي
ٱلۡأَرۡضِ جَمِيعٗا فَإِنَّ ٱللَّهَ لَغَنِيٌّ حَمِيدٌ

8 And Moses said, “Even if you are ungrateful, together with everyone on earth—Allah is in no need, Worthy of Praise.”

٩ أَلَمْ يَأْتِكُمْ نَبَؤُا۟ ٱلَّذِينَ مِن قَبْلِكُمْ قَوْمِ نُوحٍ
وَعَادٍ وَثَمُودَ ۛ وَٱلَّذِينَ مِنۢ بَعْدِهِمْ ۛ لَا يَعْلَمُهُمْ إِلَّا
ٱللَّهُ ۚ جَآءَتْهُمْ رُسُلُهُم بِٱلْبَيِّنَٰتِ فَرَدُّوٓا۟ أَيْدِيَهُمْ
فِىٓ أَفْوَٰهِهِمْ وَقَالُوٓا۟ إِنَّا كَفَرْنَا بِمَآ أُرْسِلْتُم بِهِۦ
وَإِنَّا لَفِى شَكٍّ مِّمَّا تَدْعُونَنَآ إِلَيْهِ مُرِيبٍ

9 Has not the story reached you, of those before you, the people of Noah, and Aad, and Thamood—and those after them? None knows them except Allah. Their messengers came to them with the clear proofs, but they tried to silence them, and said, "We reject what you are sent with, and we are in serious doubt regarding what you are calling us to."

١٠ قَالَتْ رُسُلُهُمْ أَفِى ٱللَّهِ شَكٌّ فَاطِرِ ٱلسَّمَٰوَٰتِ
وَٱلْأَرْضِ ۖ يَدْعُوكُمْ لِيَغْفِرَ لَكُم مِّن ذُنُوبِكُمْ
وَيُؤَخِّرَكُمْ إِلَىٰٓ أَجَلٍ مُّسَمًّى ۚ قَالُوٓا۟ إِنْ أَنتُمْ إِلَّا
بَشَرٌ مِّثْلُنَا تُرِيدُونَ أَن تَصُدُّونَا عَمَّا كَانَ يَعْبُدُ
ءَابَآؤُنَا فَأْتُونَا بِسُلْطَٰنٍ مُّبِينٍ

10 Their messengers said, "Is there any doubt about Allah, Maker of the heavens and the earth? He calls you to forgive you your sins, and to defer you until a stated term." They said, "You are only humans like us; you want to turn us away from what our ancestors worshiped; so bring us a clear proof."

١١ قَالَتْ لَهُمْ رُسُلُهُمْ إِن نَّحْنُ إِلَّا بَشَرٌ مِّثْلُكُمْ
وَلَٰكِنَّ ٱللَّهَ يَمُنُّ عَلَىٰ مَن يَشَآءُ مِنْ عِبَادِهِۦ ۖ وَمَا
كَانَ لَنَآ أَن نَّأْتِيَكُم بِسُلْطَٰنٍ إِلَّا بِإِذْنِ ٱللَّهِ ۚ وَعَلَى
ٱللَّهِ فَلْيَتَوَكَّلِ ٱلْمُؤْمِنُونَ

11 Their messengers said to them, "We are only humans like you, but Allah favors whomever He wills from among His servants. We cannot possibly show you any proof, except by leave of Allah. In Allah let the faithful put their trust."

١٢ وَمَا لَنَآ أَلَّا نَتَوَكَّلَ عَلَى ٱللَّهِ وَقَدْ هَدَىٰنَا
سُبُلَنَا ۚ وَلَنَصْبِرَنَّ عَلَىٰ مَآ ءَاذَيْتُمُونَا ۚ وَعَلَى
ٱللَّهِ فَلْيَتَوَكَّلِ ٱلْمُتَوَكِّلُونَ

12 "And why should we not trust in Allah, when He has guided us in our ways? We will persevere in the face of your persecution. And upon Allah the reliant should rely."

١٣ وَقَالَ ٱلَّذِينَ كَفَرُوا۟ لِرُسُلِهِمْ لَنُخْرِجَنَّكُم مِّنْ
أَرْضِنَآ أَوْ لَتَعُودُنَّ فِى مِلَّتِنَا ۖ فَأَوْحَىٰٓ إِلَيْهِمْ
رَبُّهُمْ لَنُهْلِكَنَّ ٱلظَّٰلِمِينَ

13 Those who disbelieved said to their messengers, "We will expel you from our land, unless you return to our religion." And their Lord inspired them: "We will destroy the wrongdoers."

١٤ وَلَنُسْكِنَنَّكُمُ ٱلْأَرْضَ مِنۢ بَعْدِهِمْ ۚ ذَٰلِكَ لِمَنْ
خَافَ مَقَامِى وَخَافَ وَعِيدِ

14 "And We will settle you in the land after them. That is for him who fears My Majesty, and fears My threats."

١٥ وَٱسْتَفْتَحُوا۟ وَخَابَ كُلُّ جَبَّارٍ عَنِيدٍ

15 And they prayed for victory, and every stubborn tyrant came to disappointment.

١٦ مِّن وَرَآئِهِۦ جَهَنَّمُ وَيُسْقَىٰ مِن مَّآءٍ صَدِيدٍ

16 Beyond him lies Hell, and he will be given to drink putrid water.

١٧ يَتَجَرَّعُهُۥ وَلَا يَكَادُ يُسِيغُهُۥ وَيَأْتِيهِ ٱلْمَوْتُ مِن كُلِّ مَكَانٍ وَمَا هُوَ بِمَيِّتٍ ۖ وَمِن وَرَآئِهِۦ عَذَابٌ غَلِيظٌ

17 He will guzzle it, but he will not swallow it. Death will come at him from every direction, but he will not die. And beyond this is relentless suffering.

١٨ مَّثَلُ ٱلَّذِينَ كَفَرُوا۟ بِرَبِّهِمْ ۖ أَعْمَٰلُهُمْ كَرَمَادٍ ٱشْتَدَّتْ بِهِ ٱلرِّيحُ فِى يَوْمٍ عَاصِفٍ ۖ لَّا يَقْدِرُونَ مِمَّا كَسَبُوا۟ عَلَىٰ شَىْءٍ ۚ ذَٰلِكَ هُوَ ٱلضَّلَٰلُ ٱلْبَعِيدُ

18 The likeness of those who disbelieve in their Lord: their works are like ashes, in a fierce wind, on a stormy day. They have no control over anything they have earned. That is the utmost misguidance.

١٩ أَلَمْ تَرَ أَنَّ ٱللَّهَ خَلَقَ ٱلسَّمَٰوَٰتِ وَٱلْأَرْضَ بِٱلْحَقِّ ۚ إِن يَشَأْ يُذْهِبْكُمْ وَيَأْتِ بِخَلْقٍ جَدِيدٍ

19 Do you not see that Allah created the heavens and the earth with truth? If He wills, He can do away with you, and bring a new creation.

٢٠ وَمَا ذَٰلِكَ عَلَى ٱللَّهِ بِعَزِيزٍ

20 And that is not difficult for Allah.

٢١ وَبَرَزُوا۟ لِلَّهِ جَمِيعًا فَقَالَ ٱلضُّعَفَٰٓؤُا۟ لِلَّذِينَ ٱسْتَكْبَرُوٓا۟ إِنَّا كُنَّا لَكُمْ تَبَعًا فَهَلْ أَنتُم مُّغْنُونَ عَنَّا مِنْ عَذَابِ ٱللَّهِ مِن شَىْءٍ ۚ قَالُوا۟ لَوْ هَدَىٰنَا ٱللَّهُ لَهَدَيْنَٰكُمْ ۖ سَوَآءٌ عَلَيْنَآ أَجَزِعْنَآ أَمْ صَبَرْنَا مَا لَنَا مِن مَّحِيصٍ

21 They will emerge before Allah, altogether. The weak will say to those who were proud, “We were your followers, can you protect us at all against Allah’s punishment?” They will say, “Had Allah guided us, we would have guided you. It is the same for us; whether we mourn, or are patient; there is no asylum for us.”

٢٢ وَقَالَ ٱلشَّيْطَٰنُ لَمَّا قُضِىَ ٱلْأَمْرُ إِنَّ ٱللَّهَ وَعَدَكُمْ وَعْدَ ٱلْحَقِّ وَوَعَدتُّكُمْ فَأَخْلَفْتُكُمْ ۖ وَمَا كَانَ لِىَ عَلَيْكُم مِّن سُلْطَٰنٍ إِلَّآ أَن دَعَوْتُكُمْ فَٱسْتَجَبْتُمْ لِى ۖ فَلَا تَلُومُونِى وَلُومُوٓا۟ أَنفُسَكُم ۖ مَّآ أَنَا۠ بِمُصْرِخِكُمْ وَمَآ أَنتُم بِمُصْرِخِىَّ ۖ إِنِّى

22 And Satan will say, when the issue is settled, “Allah has promised you the promise of truth, and I promised you, but I failed you. I had no authority over you, except that I called you, and you answered me. So do not blame me, but blame yourselves. I cannot come to your aid, nor can you come to my aid. I reject your associating with me in

كَفَرْتُ بِمَآ أَشْرَكْتُمُونِ مِن قَبْلُ ۗ إِنَّ ٱلظَّٰلِمِينَ
لَهُمْ عَذَابٌ أَلِيمٌ

the past. The wrongdoers will have a torment most painful."

٢٣ وَأُدْخِلَ ٱلَّذِينَ ءَامَنُوا۟ وَعَمِلُوا۟ ٱلصَّٰلِحَٰتِ
جَنَّٰتٍ تَجْرِى مِن تَحْتِهَا ٱلْأَنْهَٰرُ خَٰلِدِينَ فِيهَا
بِإِذْنِ رَبِّهِمْ ۖ تَحِيَّتُهُمْ فِيهَا سَلَٰمٌ

23 But those who believed and did good deeds will be admitted into gardens beneath which rivers flow, to remain therein forever, by leave of their Lord. Their greeting therein will be: "Peace."

٢٤ أَلَمْ تَرَ كَيْفَ ضَرَبَ ٱللَّهُ مَثَلًا كَلِمَةً طَيِّبَةً
كَشَجَرَةٍ طَيِّبَةٍ أَصْلُهَا ثَابِتٌ وَفَرْعُهَا فِى
ٱلسَّمَآءِ

24 Do you not see how Allah presents a parable? A good word is like a good tree—its root is firm, and its branches are in the sky.

٢٥ تُؤْتِىٓ أُكُلَهَا كُلَّ حِينٍۭ بِإِذْنِ رَبِّهَا ۗ وَيَضْرِبُ
ٱللَّهُ ٱلْأَمْثَالَ لِلنَّاسِ لَعَلَّهُمْ يَتَذَكَّرُونَ

25 It yields its fruits every season by the will of its Lord. Allah presents the parables to the people, so that they may reflect.

٢٦ وَمَثَلُ كَلِمَةٍ خَبِيثَةٍ كَشَجَرَةٍ خَبِيثَةٍ ٱجْتُثَّتْ
مِن فَوْقِ ٱلْأَرْضِ مَا لَهَا مِن قَرَارٍ

26 And the parable of a bad word is that of a bad tree—it is uprooted from the ground; it has no stability.

٢٧ يُثَبِّتُ ٱللَّهُ ٱلَّذِينَ ءَامَنُوا۟ بِٱلْقَوْلِ ٱلثَّابِتِ فِى
ٱلْحَيَوٰةِ ٱلدُّنْيَا وَفِى ٱلْءَاخِرَةِ ۖ وَيُضِلُّ ٱللَّهُ
ٱلظَّٰلِمِينَ ۚ وَيَفْعَلُ ٱللَّهُ مَا يَشَآءُ

27 Allah gives firmness to those who believe, with the firm word, in this life, and in the Hereafter. And Allah leads the wicked astray. Allah does whatever He wills.

٢٨ أَلَمْ تَرَ إِلَى ٱلَّذِينَ بَدَّلُوا۟ نِعْمَتَ ٱللَّهِ كُفْرًا
وَأَحَلُّوا۟ قَوْمَهُمْ دَارَ ٱلْبَوَارِ

28 Have you not seen those who exchanged the blessing of Allah with blasphemy, and landed their people into the house of perdition?

٢٩ جَهَنَّمَ يَصْلَوْنَهَا ۖ وَبِئْسَ ٱلْقَرَارُ

29 Hell—they will roast in it. What a miserable settlement.

٣٠ وَجَعَلُوا۟ لِلَّهِ أَندَادًا لِّيُضِلُّوا۟ عَن سَبِيلِهِۦ ۗ قُلْ
تَمَتَّعُوا۟ فَإِنَّ مَصِيرَكُمْ إِلَى ٱلنَّارِ

30 And they set up rivals to Allah, in order to lead away from His path. Say, "Enjoy yourselves; your destination is the Fire."

٣١ قُل لِّعِبَادِىَ ٱلَّذِينَ ءَامَنُوا۟ يُقِيمُوا۟ ٱلصَّلَوٰةَ
وَيُنفِقُوا۟ مِمَّا رَزَقْنَٰهُمْ سِرًّا وَعَلَانِيَةً مِّن قَبْلِ أَن
يَأْتِىَ يَوْمٌ لَّا بَيْعٌ فِيهِ وَلَا خِلَٰلٌ

31 Tell My servants who have believed to perform the prayers, and to give from what We have given them, secretly and publicly, before a

Day comes in which there is neither trading nor friendship.

٣٢ ٱللَّهُ ٱلَّذِى خَلَقَ ٱلسَّمَٰوَٰتِ وَٱلْأَرْضَ وَأَنزَلَ
مِنَ ٱلسَّمَآءِ مَآءً فَأَخْرَجَ بِهِۦ مِنَ ٱلثَّمَرَٰتِ رِزْقًا
لَّكُمْ ۖ وَسَخَّرَ لَكُمُ ٱلْفُلْكَ لِتَجْرِىَ فِى ٱلْبَحْرِ
بِأَمْرِهِۦ ۖ وَسَخَّرَ لَكُمُ ٱلْأَنْهَٰرَ

32 Allah is He Who created the heavens and the earth, and sends down water from the sky, and with it produces fruits for your sustenance. And He committed the ships to your service, sailing through the sea by His command, and He committed the rivers to your service.

٣٣ وَسَخَّرَ لَكُمُ ٱلشَّمْسَ وَٱلْقَمَرَ دَآئِبَيْنِ ۖ وَسَخَّرَ
لَكُمُ ٱلَّيْلَ وَٱلنَّهَارَ

33 And He committed the sun and the moon to your service, both continuously pursuing their courses, and He committed the night and the day to your service.

٣٤ وَءَاتَىٰكُم مِّن كُلِّ مَا سَأَلْتُمُوهُ ۚ وَإِن تَعُدُّوا۟
نِعْمَتَ ٱللَّهِ لَا تُحْصُوهَآ ۗ إِنَّ ٱلْإِنسَٰنَ لَظَلُومٌ كَفَّارٌ

34 And He has given you something of all what you asked. And if you were to count Allah's blessings, you would not be able to enumerate them. The human being is unfair and ungrateful.

٣٥ وَإِذْ قَالَ إِبْرَٰهِيمُ رَبِّ ٱجْعَلْ هَٰذَا ٱلْبَلَدَ ءَامِنًا
وَٱجْنُبْنِى وَبَنِىَّ أَن نَّعْبُدَ ٱلْأَصْنَامَ

35 Recall that Abraham said, "O my Lord, make this land peaceful, and keep me and my sons from worshiping idols."

٣٦ رَبِّ إِنَّهُنَّ أَضْلَلْنَ كَثِيرًا مِّنَ ٱلنَّاسِ ۖ فَمَن
تَبِعَنِى فَإِنَّهُۥ مِنِّى ۖ وَمَنْ عَصَانِى فَإِنَّكَ غَفُورٌ
رَّحِيمٌ

36 "My Lord, they have led many people astray. Whoever follows me belongs with me; and whoever disobeys me—You are Forgiving and Merciful.

٣٧ رَّبَّنَآ إِنِّىٓ أَسْكَنتُ مِن ذُرِّيَّتِى بِوَادٍ غَيْرِ ذِى
زَرْعٍ عِندَ بَيْتِكَ ٱلْمُحَرَّمِ رَبَّنَا لِيُقِيمُوا۟ ٱلصَّلَوٰةَ
فَٱجْعَلْ أَفْـِٔدَةً مِّنَ ٱلنَّاسِ تَهْوِىٓ إِلَيْهِمْ وَٱرْزُقْهُم
مِّنَ ٱلثَّمَرَٰتِ لَعَلَّهُمْ يَشْكُرُونَ

37 "Our Lord, I have settled some of my offspring in a valley of no vegetation, by Your Sacred House, our Lord, so that they may perform the prayers. So make the hearts of some people incline towards them, and provide them with fruits, that they may be thankful."

٣٨ رَبَّنَآ إِنَّكَ تَعْلَمُ مَا نُخْفِى وَمَا نُعْلِنُ ۗ وَمَا
يَخْفَىٰ عَلَى ٱللَّهِ مِن شَىْءٍ فِى ٱلْأَرْضِ وَلَا فِى
ٱلسَّمَآءِ

38 “Our Lord, You know what we conceal and what we reveal. And nothing is hidden from Allah, on earth or in the heaven.”

٣٩ ٱلْحَمْدُ لِلَّهِ ٱلَّذِى وَهَبَ لِى عَلَى ٱلْكِبَرِ
إِسْمَٰعِيلَ وَإِسْحَٰقَ ۚ إِنَّ رَبِّى لَسَمِيعُ ٱلدُّعَآءِ

39 “Praise be to Allah, Who has given me, in my old age, Ishmael and Isaac. My Lord is the Hearer of Prayers.”

٤٠ رَبِّ ٱجْعَلْنِى مُقِيمَ ٱلصَّلَوٰةِ وَمِن ذُرِّيَّتِى ۚ
رَبَّنَا وَتَقَبَّلْ دُعَآءِ

40 “My Lord, make me one who performs the prayer, and from my offspring. Our Lord, accept my supplication.”

٤١ رَبَّنَا ٱغْفِرْ لِى وَلِوَٰلِدَىَّ وَلِلْمُؤْمِنِينَ يَوْمَ يَقُومُ
ٱلْحِسَابُ

41 “Our Lord, forgive me, and my parents, and the believers, on the Day the Reckoning takes place.”

٤٢ وَلَا تَحْسَبَنَّ ٱللَّهَ غَٰفِلًا عَمَّا يَعْمَلُ ٱلظَّٰلِمُونَ ۚ
إِنَّمَا يُؤَخِّرُهُمْ لِيَوْمٍ تَشْخَصُ فِيهِ ٱلْأَبْصَٰرُ

42 Do not ever think that Allah is unaware of what the wrongdoers do. He only defers them until a Day when the sights stare.

٤٣ مُهْطِعِينَ مُقْنِعِى رُءُوسِهِمْ لَا يَرْتَدُّ إِلَيْهِمْ
طَرْفُهُمْ ۖ وَأَفْـِٔدَتُهُمْ هَوَآءٌ

43 Their necks outstretched, their heads upraised, their gaze unblinking, their hearts void.

٤٤ وَأَنذِرِ ٱلنَّاسَ يَوْمَ يَأْتِيهِمُ ٱلْعَذَابُ فَيَقُولُ
ٱلَّذِينَ ظَلَمُوا۟ رَبَّنَآ أَخِّرْنَآ إِلَىٰٓ أَجَلٍ قَرِيبٍ نُّجِبْ
دَعْوَتَكَ وَنَتَّبِعِ ٱلرُّسُلَ ۗ أَوَلَمْ تَكُونُوٓا۟ أَقْسَمْتُم
مِّن قَبْلُ مَا لَكُم مِّن زَوَالٍ

44 And warn mankind of the Day when the punishment will come upon them, and the wicked will say, “Our Lord, defer us for a little while, and we will answer Your call and follow the messengers.” Did you not swear before that there will be no passing away for you?

٤٥ وَسَكَنتُمْ فِى مَسَٰكِنِ ٱلَّذِينَ ظَلَمُوٓا۟ أَنفُسَهُمْ
وَتَبَيَّنَ لَكُمْ كَيْفَ فَعَلْنَا بِهِمْ وَضَرَبْنَا لَكُمُ
ٱلْأَمْثَالَ

45 And you inhabited the homes of those who wronged themselves, and it became clear to you how We dealt with them, and We cited for you the examples.

٤٦ وَقَدْ مَكَرُوا۟ مَكْرَهُمْ وَعِندَ ٱللَّهِ مَكْرُهُمْ وَإِن
كَانَ مَكْرُهُمْ لِتَزُولَ مِنْهُ ٱلْجِبَالُ

46 They planned their plans, but their plans are known to Allah, even if their plans can eliminate mountains.

٤٧ فَلَا تَحْسَبَنَّ ٱللَّهَ مُخْلِفَ وَعْدِهِۦ رُسُلَهُۥٓ ۚ إِنَّ ٱللَّهَ عَزِيزٌ ذُو ٱنتِقَامٍ	47 Do not ever think that Allah will break His promise to His messengers. Allah is Strong, Able to Avenge.
٤٨ يَوْمَ تُبَدَّلُ ٱلْأَرْضُ غَيْرَ ٱلْأَرْضِ وَٱلسَّمَٰوَٰتُ ۖ وَبَرَزُوا۟ لِلَّهِ ٱلْوَٰحِدِ ٱلْقَهَّارِ	48 On the Day when the earth is changed into another earth, and the heavens, and they will emerge before Allah, the One, the Irresistible.
٤٩ وَتَرَى ٱلْمُجْرِمِينَ يَوْمَئِذٍ مُّقَرَّنِينَ فِى ٱلْأَصْفَادِ	49 On that Day, you will see the sinners bound together in chains.
٥٠ سَرَابِيلُهُم مِّن قَطِرَانٍ وَتَغْشَىٰ وُجُوهَهُمُ ٱلنَّارُ	50 Their garments made of tar, and the Fire covering their faces.
٥١ لِيَجْزِىَ ٱللَّهُ كُلَّ نَفْسٍ مَّا كَسَبَتْ ۚ إِنَّ ٱللَّهَ سَرِيعُ ٱلْحِسَابِ	51 That Allah may repay each soul according to what it has earned. Allah is Quick in reckoning.
٥٢ هَٰذَا بَلَٰغٌ لِّلنَّاسِ وَلِيُنذَرُوا۟ بِهِۦ وَلِيَعْلَمُوٓا۟ أَنَّمَا هُوَ إِلَٰهٌ وَٰحِدٌ وَلِيَذَّكَّرَ أُو۟لُوا۟ ٱلْأَلْبَٰبِ	52 This is a proclamation for mankind, that they may be warned thereby, and know that He is One God, and that people of understanding may remember.

15 The Rock الحجر

بِسْمِ ٱللَّهِ ٱلرَّحْمَٰنِ ٱلرَّحِيمِ	In the name of Allah, the Gracious, the Merciful.
١ الٓر ۚ تِلْكَ ءَايَٰتُ ٱلْكِتَٰبِ وَقُرْءَانٍ مُّبِينٍ	1 Alif, Lam, Ra. These are the Verses of the Book; a Quran that makes things clear.
٢ رُّبَمَا يَوَدُّ ٱلَّذِينَ كَفَرُوا۟ لَوْ كَانُوا۟ مُسْلِمِينَ	2 Perhaps those who disbelieve would like to become Muslims.
٣ ذَرْهُمْ يَأْكُلُوا۟ وَيَتَمَتَّعُوا۟ وَيُلْهِهِمُ ٱلْأَمَلُ ۖ فَسَوْفَ يَعْلَمُونَ	3 Leave them to eat, and enjoy, and be lulled by hope. They will find out.
٤ وَمَآ أَهْلَكْنَا مِن قَرْيَةٍ إِلَّا وَلَهَا كِتَابٌ مَّعْلُومٌ	4 We have never destroyed a town unless it had a set time.

٥ مَّا تَسۡبِقُ مِنۡ أُمَّةٍ أَجَلَهَا وَمَا يَسۡتَـٔۡخِرُونَ

5 No nation can bring its time forward, nor can they delay it.

٦ وَقَالُواْ يَٰٓأَيُّهَا ٱلَّذِي نُزِّلَ عَلَيۡهِ ٱلذِّكۡرُ إِنَّكَ
لَمَجۡنُونٞ

6 And they said, “O you who received the message, you are insane.”

٧ لَّوۡ مَا تَأۡتِينَا بِٱلۡمَلَٰٓئِكَةِ إِن كُنتَ مِنَ ٱلصَّٰدِقِينَ

7 Why do you not bring us the angels, if you are truthful?”

٨ مَا نُنَزِّلُ ٱلۡمَلَٰٓئِكَةَ إِلَّا بِٱلۡحَقِّ وَمَا كَانُوٓاْ إِذٗا
مُّنظَرِينَ

8 We do not send the angels down except with reason, and they will not be held back.

٩ إِنَّا نَحۡنُ نَزَّلۡنَا ٱلذِّكۡرَ وَإِنَّا لَهُۥ لَحَٰفِظُونَ

9 Surely We revealed the Message, and We will surely preserve it.

١٠ وَلَقَدۡ أَرۡسَلۡنَا مِن قَبۡلِكَ فِي شِيَعِ ٱلۡأَوَّلِينَ

10 We sent others before you, to the former communities.

١١ وَمَا يَأۡتِيهِم مِّن رَّسُولٍ إِلَّا كَانُواْ بِهِۦ
يَسۡتَهۡزِءُونَ

11 But no messenger came to them, but they ridiculed him.

١٢ كَذَٰلِكَ نَسۡلُكُهُۥ فِي قُلُوبِ ٱلۡمُجۡرِمِينَ

12 Thus We slip it into the hearts of the guilty.

١٣ لَا يُؤۡمِنُونَ بِهِۦۖ وَقَدۡ خَلَتۡ سُنَّةُ ٱلۡأَوَّلِينَ

13 They do not believe in it, though the ways of the ancients have passed away.

١٤ وَلَوۡ فَتَحۡنَا عَلَيۡهِم بَابٗا مِّنَ ٱلسَّمَآءِ فَظَلُّواْ
فِيهِ يَعۡرُجُونَ

14 Even if We opened for them a gateway into the sky, and they began to ascend through it.

١٥ لَقَالُوٓاْ إِنَّمَا سُكِّرَتۡ أَبۡصَٰرُنَا بَلۡ نَحۡنُ قَوۡمٞ
مَّسۡحُورُونَ

15 They would still say, “Our eyes are hallucinating; in fact, we are people bewitched.”

١٦ وَلَقَدۡ جَعَلۡنَا فِي ٱلسَّمَآءِ بُرُوجٗا وَزَيَّنَّٰهَا
لِلنَّٰظِرِينَ

16 We placed constellations in the sky, and made them beautiful to the beholders.

١٧ وَحَفِظۡنَٰهَا مِن كُلِّ شَيۡطَٰنٖ رَّجِيمٍ

17 And We guarded them from every outcast devil.

١٨ إِلَّا مَنِ ٱسۡتَرَقَ ٱلسَّمۡعَ فَأَتۡبَعَهُۥ شِهَابٞ مُّبِينٞ

18 Except one who steals a hearing, and is followed by a visible projectile.

١٩ وَٱلۡأَرۡضَ مَدَدۡنَٰهَا وَأَلۡقَيۡنَا فِيهَا رَوَٰسِيَ وَأَنۢبَتۡنَا
فِيهَا مِن كُلِّ شَيۡءٖ مَّوۡزُونٖ

19 We spread the earth, and placed stabilizers in it, and in it We grew all things in proper measure.

٢٠ وَجَعَلْنَا لَكُمْ فِيهَا مَعَـٰيِشَ وَمَن لَّسْتُمْ لَهُۥ
بِرَٰزِقِينَ

20 And in it We created livelihoods for you, and for those for whom you are not the providers.

٢١ وَإِن مِّن شَىْءٍ إِلَّا عِندَنَا خَزَآئِنُهُۥ وَمَا نُنَزِّلُهُۥٓ
إِلَّا بِقَدَرٍ مَّعْلُومٍ

21 There is not a thing but with Us are its stores, and We send it down only in precise measure.

٢٢ وَأَرْسَلْنَا ٱلرِّيَـٰحَ لَوَٰقِحَ فَأَنزَلْنَا مِنَ ٱلسَّمَآءِ
مَآءً فَأَسْقَيْنَـٰكُمُوهُ وَمَآ أَنتُمْ لَهُۥ بِخَـٰزِنِينَ

22 We send the fertilizing winds; and send down water from the sky, and give it to you to drink, and you are not the ones who store it.

٢٣ وَإِنَّا لَنَحْنُ نُحْىِۦ وَنُمِيتُ وَنَحْنُ ٱلْوَٰرِثُونَ

23 It is We who give life and cause death, and We are the Inheritors.

٢٤ وَلَقَدْ عَلِمْنَا ٱلْمُسْتَقْدِمِينَ مِنكُمْ وَلَقَدْ عَلِمْنَا
ٱلْمُسْتَـْٔخِرِينَ

24 And We know those of you who go forward, and We know those who lag behind.

٢٥ وَإِنَّ رَبَّكَ هُوَ يَحْشُرُهُمْ ۚ إِنَّهُۥ حَكِيمٌ عَلِيمٌ

25 It is your Lord who will gather them together. He is the Wise, the Knowing.

٢٦ وَلَقَدْ خَلَقْنَا ٱلْإِنسَـٰنَ مِن صَلْصَـٰلٍ مِّنْ حَمَإٍ
مَّسْنُونٍ

26 We created the human being from clay, from molded mud.

٢٧ وَٱلْجَآنَّ خَلَقْنَـٰهُ مِن قَبْلُ مِن نَّارِ ٱلسَّمُومِ

27 And the jinn We created before, from piercing fire.

٢٨ وَإِذْ قَالَ رَبُّكَ لِلْمَلَـٰٓئِكَةِ إِنِّى خَـٰلِقٌۢ بَشَرًا مِّن
صَلْصَـٰلٍ مِّنْ حَمَإٍ مَّسْنُونٍ

28 Your Lord said to the angels, "I am creating a human being from clay, from molded mud."

٢٩ فَإِذَا سَوَّيْتُهُۥ وَنَفَخْتُ فِيهِ مِن رُّوحِى فَقَعُوا۟
لَهُۥ سَـٰجِدِينَ

29 "When I have formed him, and breathed into him of My spirit, fall down prostrating before him."

٣٠ فَسَجَدَ ٱلْمَلَـٰٓئِكَةُ كُلُّهُمْ أَجْمَعُونَ

30 So the angels prostrated themselves, all together.

٣١ إِلَّآ إِبْلِيسَ أَبَىٰٓ أَن يَكُونَ مَعَ ٱلسَّـٰجِدِينَ

31 Except for Satan. He refused to be among those who prostrated themselves.

٣٢ قَالَ يَـٰٓإِبْلِيسُ مَا لَكَ أَلَّا تَكُونَ مَعَ ٱلسَّـٰجِدِينَ

32 He said, "O Satan, what kept you from being among those who prostrated themselves?"

٣٣ قَالَ لَمْ أَكُن لِّأَسْجُدَ لِبَشَرٍ خَلَقْتَهُۥ مِن صَلْصَٰلٍ مِّنْ حَمَإٍ مَّسْنُونٍ	33 He said, "I am not about to prostrate myself before a human being, whom You created from clay, from molded mud."
٣٤ قَالَ فَٱخْرُجْ مِنْهَا فَإِنَّكَ رَجِيمٌ	34 He said, "Then get out of here, for you are an outcast".
٣٥ وَإِنَّ عَلَيْكَ ٱللَّعْنَةَ إِلَىٰ يَوْمِ ٱلدِّينِ	35 "And the curse will be upon you until the Day of Judgment."
٣٦ قَالَ رَبِّ فَأَنظِرْنِىٓ إِلَىٰ يَوْمِ يُبْعَثُونَ	36 He said, "My Lord, reprieve me until the Day they are resurrected."
٣٧ قَالَ فَإِنَّكَ مِنَ ٱلْمُنظَرِينَ	37 He said, "You are of those reprieved."
٣٨ إِلَىٰ يَوْمِ ٱلْوَقْتِ ٱلْمَعْلُومِ	38 "Until the Day of the time appointed."
٣٩ قَالَ رَبِّ بِمَآ أَغْوَيْتَنِى لَأُزَيِّنَنَّ لَهُمْ فِى ٱلْأَرْضِ وَلَأُغْوِيَنَّهُمْ أَجْمَعِينَ	39 He said, "My Lord, since You have lured me away, I will glamorize for them on earth, and I will lure them all away."
٤٠ إِلَّا عِبَادَكَ مِنْهُمُ ٱلْمُخْلَصِينَ	40 "Except for Your sincere servants among them."
٤١ قَالَ هَٰذَا صِرَٰطٌ عَلَىَّ مُسْتَقِيمٌ	41 He said, "This is a right way with Me."
٤٢ إِنَّ عِبَادِى لَيْسَ لَكَ عَلَيْهِمْ سُلْطَٰنٌ إِلَّا مَنِ ٱتَّبَعَكَ مِنَ ٱلْغَاوِينَ	42 "Over My servants you have no authority, except for the sinners who follow you."
٤٣ وَإِنَّ جَهَنَّمَ لَمَوْعِدُهُمْ أَجْمَعِينَ	43 And Hell is the meeting-place for them all.
٤٤ لَهَا سَبْعَةُ أَبْوَٰبٍ لِّكُلِّ بَابٍ مِّنْهُمْ جُزْءٌ مَّقْسُومٌ	44 "It has seven doors; for each door is an assigned class."
٤٥ إِنَّ ٱلْمُتَّقِينَ فِى جَنَّٰتٍ وَعُيُونٍ	45 But the righteous will be in gardens with springs.
٤٦ ٱدْخُلُوهَا بِسَلَٰمٍ ءَامِنِينَ	46 "Enter it in peace and security."
٤٧ وَنَزَعْنَا مَا فِى صُدُورِهِم مِّنْ غِلٍّ إِخْوَٰنًا عَلَىٰ سُرُرٍ مُّتَقَٰبِلِينَ	47 And We will remove all ill-feelings from their hearts—brothers and sisters, on couches facing one another.

٤٨ لَا يَمَسُّهُمْ فِيهَا نَصَبٌ وَمَا هُم مِّنْهَا بِمُخْرَجِينَ	48 No fatigue will ever touch them therein, nor will they be asked to leave it.
٤٩ نَبِّئْ عِبَادِىٓ أَنِّىٓ أَنَا ٱلْغَفُورُ ٱلرَّحِيمُ	49 Inform My servants that I am the Forgiver, the Merciful.
٥٠ وَأَنَّ عَذَابِى هُوَ ٱلْعَذَابُ ٱلْأَلِيمُ	50 And that My punishment is the painful punishment.
٥١ وَنَبِّئْهُمْ عَن ضَيْفِ إِبْرَٰهِيمَ	51 And inform them of the guests of Abraham.
٥٢ إِذْ دَخَلُوا۟ عَلَيْهِ فَقَالُوا۟ سَلَٰمًا قَالَ إِنَّا مِنكُمْ وَجِلُونَ	52 When they entered upon him, and said, “Peace.” He said, “We are wary of you.”
٥٣ قَالُوا۟ لَا تَوْجَلْ إِنَّا نُبَشِّرُكَ بِغُلَٰمٍ عَلِيمٍ	53 They said, “Do not fear; we bring you good news of a boy endowed with knowledge.”
٥٤ قَالَ أَبَشَّرْتُمُونِى عَلَىٰٓ أَن مَّسَّنِىَ ٱلْكِبَرُ فَبِمَ تُبَشِّرُونَ	54 He said, “Do you bring me good news, when old age has overtaken me? What good news do you bring?”
٥٥ قَالُوا۟ بَشَّرْنَٰكَ بِٱلْحَقِّ فَلَا تَكُن مِّنَ ٱلْقَٰنِطِينَ	55 They said, “We bring you good news in truth, so do not despair.”
٥٦ قَالَ وَمَن يَقْنَطُ مِن رَّحْمَةِ رَبِّهِۦٓ إِلَّا ٱلضَّآلُّونَ	56 He said, “And who despairs of his Lord’s mercy but the lost?”
٥٧ قَالَ فَمَا خَطْبُكُمْ أَيُّهَا ٱلْمُرْسَلُونَ	57 He said, “So what is your business, O envoys?”
٥٨ قَالُوٓا۟ إِنَّآ أُرْسِلْنَآ إِلَىٰ قَوْمٍ مُّجْرِمِينَ	58 They said, “We were sent to a sinful people.”
٥٩ إِلَّآ ءَالَ لُوطٍ إِنَّا لَمُنَجُّوهُمْ أَجْمَعِينَ	59 “Except for the family of Lot; we will save them all.”
٦٠ إِلَّا ٱمْرَأَتَهُۥ قَدَّرْنَآ ۙ إِنَّهَا لَمِنَ ٱلْغَٰبِرِينَ	60 “Except for his wife.” We have determined that she will be of those who lag behind.
٦١ فَلَمَّا جَآءَ ءَالَ لُوطٍ ٱلْمُرْسَلُونَ	61 And when the envoys came to the family of Lot.
٦٢ قَالَ إِنَّكُمْ قَوْمٌ مُّنكَرُونَ	62 He said, “You are a people unknown to me.”
٦٣ قَالُوا۟ بَلْ جِئْنَٰكَ بِمَا كَانُوا۟ فِيهِ يَمْتَرُونَ	63 They said, “We bring you what they have doubts about.”

٦٤ وَأَتَيْنَٰكَ بِٱلْحَقِّ وَإِنَّا لَصَٰدِقُونَ

64 "We bring you the truth, and we are truthful."

٦٥ فَأَسْرِ بِأَهْلِكَ بِقِطْعٍ مِّنَ ٱلَّيْلِ وَٱتَّبِعْ أَدْبَٰرَهُمْ
وَلَا يَلْتَفِتْ مِنكُمْ أَحَدٌ وَٱمْضُوا۟ حَيْثُ تُؤْمَرُونَ

65 "Travel with your family at the dead of the night, and follow up behind them, and let none of you look back, and proceed as commanded."

٦٦ وَقَضَيْنَآ إِلَيْهِ ذَٰلِكَ ٱلْأَمْرَ أَنَّ دَابِرَ هَٰٓؤُلَآءِ
مَقْطُوعٌ مُّصْبِحِينَ

66 And We informed him of Our decree: the last remnant of these will be uprooted by early morning.

٦٧ وَجَآءَ أَهْلُ ٱلْمَدِينَةِ يَسْتَبْشِرُونَ

67 And the people of the town came joyfully.

٦٨ قَالَ إِنَّ هَٰٓؤُلَآءِ ضَيْفِى فَلَا تَفْضَحُونِ

68 He said, "These are my guests, so do not embarrass me."

٦٩ وَٱتَّقُوا۟ ٱللَّهَ وَلَا تُخْزُونِ

69 "And fear Allah, and do not disgrace me."

٧٠ قَالُوٓا۟ أَوَلَمْ نَنْهَكَ عَنِ ٱلْعَٰلَمِينَ

70 They said, "Did we not forbid you from strangers?"

٧١ قَالَ هَٰٓؤُلَآءِ بَنَاتِىٓ إِن كُنتُمْ فَٰعِلِينَ

71 He said, "These are my daughters, if you must."

٧٢ لَعَمْرُكَ إِنَّهُمْ لَفِى سَكْرَتِهِمْ يَعْمَهُونَ

72 By your life, they were blundering in their drunkenness.

٧٣ فَأَخَذَتْهُمُ ٱلصَّيْحَةُ مُشْرِقِينَ

73 So the Blast struck them at sunrise.

٧٤ فَجَعَلْنَا عَٰلِيَهَا سَافِلَهَا وَأَمْطَرْنَا عَلَيْهِمْ
حِجَارَةً مِّن سِجِّيلٍ

74 And We turned it upside down, and rained down upon them stones of baked clay.

٧٥ إِنَّ فِى ذَٰلِكَ لَءَايَٰتٍ لِّلْمُتَوَسِّمِينَ

75 Surely in that are lessons for those who read signs.

٧٦ وَإِنَّهَا لَبِسَبِيلٍ مُّقِيمٍ

76 And it is on an existing road.

٧٧ إِنَّ فِى ذَٰلِكَ لَءَايَةً لِّلْمُؤْمِنِينَ

77 Surely in that is a sign for the believers.

٧٨ وَإِن كَانَ أَصْحَٰبُ ٱلْأَيْكَةِ لَظَٰلِمِينَ

78 The people of the Woods were also wrongdoers.

٧٩ فَٱنتَقَمْنَا مِنْهُمْ وَإِنَّهُمَا لَبِإِمَامٍ مُّبِينٍ

79 So We took revenge upon them. Both are clearly documented.

٨٠ وَلَقَدْ كَذَّبَ أَصْحَٰبُ ٱلْحِجْرِ ٱلْمُرْسَلِينَ

80 The people of the Rock also rejected the messengers.

٨١ وَءَاتَيْنَٰهُمْ ءَايَٰتِنَا فَكَانُوا۟ عَنْهَا مُعْرِضِينَ

81 We gave them Our revelations, but they turned away from them.

٨٢ وَكَانُوا۟ يَنْحِتُونَ مِنَ ٱلْجِبَالِ بُيُوتًا ءَامِنِينَ

82 They used to carve homes in the mountains, feeling secure.

٨٣ فَأَخَذَتْهُمُ ٱلصَّيْحَةُ مُصْبِحِينَ

83 But the Blast struck them in the morning.

٨٤ فَمَآ أَغْنَىٰ عَنْهُم مَّا كَانُوا۟ يَكْسِبُونَ

84 All they had acquired was of no avail to them.

٨٥ وَمَا خَلَقْنَا ٱلسَّمَٰوَٰتِ وَٱلْأَرْضَ وَمَا بَيْنَهُمَآ إِلَّا
بِٱلْحَقِّ ۗ وَإِنَّ ٱلسَّاعَةَ لَءَاتِيَةٌ ۖ فَٱصْفَحِ ٱلصَّفْحَ
ٱلْجَمِيلَ

85 We did not create the heavens and the earth, and what lies between them, except with truth. The Hour is coming, so forgive with gracious forgiveness.

٨٦ إِنَّ رَبَّكَ هُوَ ٱلْخَلَّٰقُ ٱلْعَلِيمُ

86 Your Lord is the All-Knowing Creator.

٨٧ وَلَقَدْ ءَاتَيْنَٰكَ سَبْعًا مِّنَ ٱلْمَثَانِى وَٱلْقُرْءَانَ
ٱلْعَظِيمَ

87 We have given you seven of the pairs, and the Grand Quran.

٨٨ لَا تَمُدَّنَّ عَيْنَيْكَ إِلَىٰ مَا مَتَّعْنَا بِهِۦٓ أَزْوَٰجًا
مِّنْهُمْ وَلَا تَحْزَنْ عَلَيْهِمْ وَٱخْفِضْ جَنَاحَكَ
لِلْمُؤْمِنِينَ

88 Do not extend your eyes towards what We have bestowed on some couples of them to enjoy, and do not grieve over them, and lower your wing to the believers.

٨٩ وَقُلْ إِنِّىٓ أَنَا ٱلنَّذِيرُ ٱلْمُبِينُ

89 And say, “I am the clear warner.”

٩٠ كَمَآ أَنزَلْنَا عَلَى ٱلْمُقْتَسِمِينَ

90 Just as We sent down to the separatists.

٩١ ٱلَّذِينَ جَعَلُوا۟ ٱلْقُرْءَانَ عِضِينَ

91 Those who made the Quran obsolete.

٩٢ فَوَرَبِّكَ لَنَسْـَٔلَنَّهُمْ أَجْمَعِينَ

92 By your Lord, we will question them all.

٩٣ عَمَّا كَانُوا۟ يَعْمَلُونَ

93 About what they used to do.

٩٤ فَٱصْدَعْ بِمَا تُؤْمَرُ وَأَعْرِضْ عَنِ ٱلْمُشْرِكِينَ

94 So proclaim openly what you are commanded, and turn away from the polytheists.

٩٥ إِنَّا كَفَيْنَٰكَ ٱلْمُسْتَهْزِءِينَ

95 We are enough for you against the mockers.

٩٦ ٱلَّذِينَ يَجۡعَلُونَ مَعَ ٱللَّهِ إِلَٰهًا ءَاخَرَۚ فَسَوۡفَ يَعۡلَمُونَ	96 Those who set up another god with Allah. They will come to know.
٩٧ وَلَقَدۡ نَعۡلَمُ أَنَّكَ يَضِيقُ صَدۡرُكَ بِمَا يَقُولُونَ	97 We are aware that your heart is strained by what they say.
٩٨ فَسَبِّحۡ بِحَمۡدِ رَبِّكَ وَكُن مِّنَ ٱلسَّٰجِدِينَ	98 So glorify the praise of your Lord, and be among those who bow down.
٩٩ وَٱعۡبُدۡ رَبَّكَ حَتَّىٰ يَأۡتِيَكَ ٱلۡيَقِينُ	99 And worship your Lord in order to attain certainty.

16 The Bee النحل

بِسۡمِ ٱللَّهِ ٱلرَّحۡمَٰنِ ٱلرَّحِيمِ	In the name of Allah, the Gracious, the Merciful.
١ أَتَىٰٓ أَمۡرُ ٱللَّهِ فَلَا تَسۡتَعۡجِلُوهُۚ سُبۡحَٰنَهُۥ وَتَعَٰلَىٰ عَمَّا يُشۡرِكُونَ	1 The command of Allah has come, so do not rush it. Glory be to Him; exalted above what they associate.
٢ يُنَزِّلُ ٱلۡمَلَٰٓئِكَةَ بِٱلرُّوحِ مِنۡ أَمۡرِهِۦ عَلَىٰ مَن يَشَآءُ مِنۡ عِبَادِهِۦٓ أَنۡ أَنذِرُوٓاْ أَنَّهُۥ لَآ إِلَٰهَ إِلَّآ أَنَا۠ فَٱتَّقُونِ	2 He sends down the angels with the Spirit by His command, upon whom He wills of His servants: "Give warning that there is no god but Me, and fear Me."
٣ خَلَقَ ٱلسَّمَٰوَٰتِ وَٱلۡأَرۡضَ بِٱلۡحَقِّۚ تَعَٰلَىٰ عَمَّا يُشۡرِكُونَ	3 He created the heavens and the earth with justice. He is exalted above the associations they attribute.
٤ خَلَقَ ٱلۡإِنسَٰنَ مِن نُّطۡفَةٖ فَإِذَا هُوَ خَصِيمٞ مُّبِينٞ	4 He created the human being from a drop of fluid, yet he becomes an open adversary.
٥ وَٱلۡأَنۡعَٰمَ خَلَقَهَاۖ لَكُمۡ فِيهَا دِفۡءٞ وَمَنَٰفِعُ وَمِنۡهَا تَأۡكُلُونَ	5 And the livestock—He created them for you. In them are warmth and benefits for you, and of them you eat.
٦ وَلَكُمۡ فِيهَا جَمَالٌ حِينَ تُرِيحُونَ وَحِينَ تَسۡرَحُونَ	6 And there is beauty in them for you, when you bring them home, and when you drive them to pasture.
٧ وَتَحۡمِلُ أَثۡقَالَكُمۡ إِلَىٰ بَلَدٖ لَّمۡ تَكُونُواْ بَٰلِغِيهِ إِلَّا بِشِقِّ ٱلۡأَنفُسِۚ إِنَّ رَبَّكُمۡ لَرَءُوفٞ رَّحِيمٞ	7 And they carry your loads to territory you could not have reached

without great hardship. Your Lord is Clement and Merciful.

٨ وَٱلْخَيْلَ وَٱلْبِغَالَ وَٱلْحَمِيرَ لِتَرْكَبُوهَا وَزِينَةً ۚ
وَيَخْلُقُ مَا لَا تَعْلَمُونَ

8 And the horses, and the mules, and the donkeys—for you to ride, and for luxury. And He creates what you do not know.

٩ وَعَلَى ٱللَّهِ قَصْدُ ٱلسَّبِيلِ وَمِنْهَا جَآئِرٌ ۚ وَلَوْ
شَآءَ لَهَدَىٰكُمْ أَجْمَعِينَ

9 It is for Allah to point out the paths, but some of them are flawed. Had He willed, He could have guided you all.

١٠ هُوَ ٱلَّذِىٓ أَنزَلَ مِنَ ٱلسَّمَآءِ مَآءً ۖ لَّكُم مِّنْهُ
شَرَابٌ وَمِنْهُ شَجَرٌ فِيهِ تُسِيمُونَ

10 It is He Who sends down for you from the sky water. From it is drink, and with it grows vegetation for grazing.

١١ يُنۢبِتُ لَكُم بِهِ ٱلزَّرْعَ وَٱلزَّيْتُونَ وَٱلنَّخِيلَ
وَٱلْأَعْنَـٰبَ وَمِن كُلِّ ٱلثَّمَرَٰتِ ۗ إِنَّ فِى ذَٰلِكَ
لَءَايَةً لِّقَوْمٍ يَتَفَكَّرُونَ

11 And He produces for you grains with it, and olives, and date-palms, and grapes, and all kinds of fruits. Surely in that is a sign for people who think.

١٢ وَسَخَّرَ لَكُمُ ٱلَّيْلَ وَٱلنَّهَارَ وَٱلشَّمْسَ وَٱلْقَمَرَ ۖ
وَٱلنُّجُومُ مُسَخَّرَٰتٌۢ بِأَمْرِهِۦٓ ۗ إِنَّ فِى ذَٰلِكَ
لَءَايَـٰتٍ لِّقَوْمٍ يَعْقِلُونَ

12 And He regulated for you the night and the day; and the sun, and the moon, and the stars are disposed by His command. Surely in that are signs for people who ponder.

١٣ وَمَا ذَرَأَ لَكُمْ فِى ٱلْأَرْضِ مُخْتَلِفًا أَلْوَٰنُهُۥٓ ۗ إِنَّ
فِى ذَٰلِكَ لَءَايَةً لِّقَوْمٍ يَذَّكَّرُونَ

13 And whatsoever He created for you on earth is of diverse colors. Surely in that is a sign for people who are mindful.

١٤ وَهُوَ ٱلَّذِى سَخَّرَ ٱلْبَحْرَ لِتَأْكُلُوا۟ مِنْهُ لَحْمًا
طَرِيًّا وَتَسْتَخْرِجُوا۟ مِنْهُ حِلْيَةً تَلْبَسُونَهَا وَتَرَى
ٱلْفُلْكَ مَوَاخِرَ فِيهِ وَلِتَبْتَغُوا۟ مِن فَضْلِهِۦ وَلَعَلَّكُمْ
تَشْكُرُونَ

14 And it is He who made the sea to serve you, that you may eat from it tender meat, and extract from it ornaments that you wear. And you see the ships plowing through it, as you seek His bounties, so that you may give thanks.

١٥ وَأَلْقَىٰ فِى ٱلْأَرْضِ رَوَٰسِىَ أَن تَمِيدَ بِكُمْ
وَأَنْهَـٰرًا وَسُبُلًا لَّعَلَّكُمْ تَهْتَدُونَ

15 And he cast mountains on the earth, lest it shifts with you; and rivers, and roads, so that you may be guided.

١٦ وَعَلَـٰمَـٰتٍ ۚ وَبِٱلنَّجْمِ هُمْ يَهْتَدُونَ

16 And landmarks. And by the stars they guide themselves.

١٧ أَفَمَن يَخْلُقُ كَمَن لَّا يَخْلُقُ ۗ أَفَلَا تَذَكَّرُونَ

17 Is He who creates like him who does not create? Will you not take a lesson?

١٨ وَإِن تَعُدُّوا۟ نِعْمَةَ ٱللَّهِ لَا تُحْصُوهَآ ۗ إِنَّ ٱللَّهَ
لَغَفُورٌ رَّحِيمٌ

18 And if you tried to enumerate the favors of Allah, you will not be able to count them. Allah is Forgiving and Merciful.

١٩ وَٱللَّهُ يَعْلَمُ مَا تُسِرُّونَ وَمَا تُعْلِنُونَ

19 And Allah knows what you hide and what you disclose.

٢٠ وَٱلَّذِينَ يَدْعُونَ مِن دُونِ ٱللَّهِ لَا يَخْلُقُونَ
شَيْـًٔا وَهُمْ يُخْلَقُونَ

20 Those they invoke besides Allah create nothing, but are themselves created.

٢١ أَمْوَٰتٌ غَيْرُ أَحْيَآءٍ ۖ وَمَا يَشْعُرُونَ أَيَّانَ
يُبْعَثُونَ

21 They are dead, not alive; and they do not know when they will be resurrected.

٢٢ إِلَٰهُكُمْ إِلَٰهٌ وَٰحِدٌ ۚ فَٱلَّذِينَ لَا يُؤْمِنُونَ
بِٱلْـَٔاخِرَةِ قُلُوبُهُم مُّنكِرَةٌ وَهُم مُّسْتَكْبِرُونَ

22 Your God is one God. As for those who do not believe in the Hereafter, their hearts are in denial, and they are arrogant.

٢٣ لَا جَرَمَ أَنَّ ٱللَّهَ يَعْلَمُ مَا يُسِرُّونَ وَمَا
يُعْلِنُونَ ۚ إِنَّهُۥ لَا يُحِبُّ ٱلْمُسْتَكْبِرِينَ

23 Without a doubt, Allah knows what they conceal and what they reveal. He does not like the arrogant.

٢٤ وَإِذَا قِيلَ لَهُم مَّاذَآ أَنزَلَ رَبُّكُمْ ۙ قَالُوٓا۟
أَسَٰطِيرُ ٱلْأَوَّلِينَ

24 And when it is said to them, “What has your Lord sent down?” They say, “Legends of the ancients.”

٢٥ لِيَحْمِلُوٓا۟ أَوْزَارَهُمْ كَامِلَةً يَوْمَ ٱلْقِيَٰمَةِ ۙ وَمِنْ
أَوْزَارِ ٱلَّذِينَ يُضِلُّونَهُم بِغَيْرِ عِلْمٍ ۗ أَلَا سَآءَ مَا
يَزِرُونَ

25 So let them carry their loads complete on the Day of Resurrection, and some of the loads of those they misguided without knowledge. Evil is what they carry.

٢٦ قَدْ مَكَرَ ٱلَّذِينَ مِن قَبْلِهِمْ فَأَتَى ٱللَّهُ بُنْيَٰنَهُم
مِّنَ ٱلْقَوَاعِدِ فَخَرَّ عَلَيْهِمُ ٱلسَّقْفُ مِن فَوْقِهِمْ
وَأَتَىٰهُمُ ٱلْعَذَابُ مِنْ حَيْثُ لَا يَشْعُرُونَ

26 Those before them also schemed, but Allah took their structures from the foundations, and the roof caved in on them. The punishment came at them from where they did not perceive.

٢٧ ثُمَّ يَوْمَ ٱلْقِيَٰمَةِ يُخْزِيهِمْ وَيَقُولُ أَيْنَ
شُرَكَآءِىَ ٱلَّذِينَ كُنتُمْ تُشَٰٓقُّونَ فِيهِمْ ۚ قَالَ

27 Then, on the Day of Resurrection, He will disgrace them, and say, “Where are My associates for whose sake you used to dispute?” Those

ٱلَّذِينَ أُوتُوا۟ ٱلْعِلْمَ إِنَّ ٱلْخِزْىَ ٱلْيَوْمَ وَٱلسُّوٓءَ
عَلَى ٱلْكَـٰفِرِينَ

who were given knowledge will say, “Today shame and misery are upon the disbelievers.”

٢٨ ٱلَّذِينَ تَتَوَفَّىٰهُمُ ٱلْمَلَـٰٓئِكَةُ ظَالِمِىٓ أَنفُسِهِمْ ۖ
فَأَلْقَوُا۟ ٱلسَّلَمَ مَا كُنَّا نَعْمَلُ مِن سُوٓءٍۭ ۚ بَلَىٰٓ إِنَّ
ٱللَّهَ عَلِيمٌۢ بِمَا كُنتُمْ تَعْمَلُونَ

28 Those wronging their souls while the angels are taking them away—they will propose peace: “We did no wrong.” Yes you did. Allah is aware of what you used to do.”

٢٩ فَٱدْخُلُوٓا۟ أَبْوَٰبَ جَهَنَّمَ خَـٰلِدِينَ فِيهَا ۖ فَلَبِئْسَ
مَثْوَى ٱلْمُتَكَبِّرِينَ

29 Enter the gates of Hell, to dwell therein forever. Miserable is the residence of the arrogant.

٣٠ وَقِيلَ لِلَّذِينَ ٱتَّقَوْا۟ مَاذَآ أَنزَلَ رَبُّكُمْ ۚ قَالُوا۟
خَيْرًا ۗ لِّلَّذِينَ أَحْسَنُوا۟ فِى هَـٰذِهِ ٱلدُّنْيَا حَسَنَةٌ ۚ
وَلَدَارُ ٱلْـَٔاخِرَةِ خَيْرٌ ۚ وَلَنِعْمَ دَارُ ٱلْمُتَّقِينَ

30 And it will be said to those who maintained piety, “What has your Lord revealed?” They will say, “Goodness.” To those who do good in this world is goodness, and the Home of the Hereafter is even better. How wonderful is the residence of the pious.

٣١ جَنَّـٰتُ عَدْنٍ يَدْخُلُونَهَا تَجْرِى مِن تَحْتِهَا
ٱلْأَنْهَـٰرُ ۖ لَهُمْ فِيهَا مَا يَشَآءُونَ ۚ كَذَٰلِكَ يَجْزِى ٱللَّهُ
ٱلْمُتَّقِينَ

31 The Gardens of Perpetuity, which they will enter, beneath which rivers flow, where they will have whatever they desire. Thus Allah rewards the pious.

٣٢ ٱلَّذِينَ تَتَوَفَّىٰهُمُ ٱلْمَلَـٰٓئِكَةُ طَيِّبِينَ ۙ يَقُولُونَ
سَلَـٰمٌ عَلَيْكُمُ ٱدْخُلُوا۟ ٱلْجَنَّةَ بِمَا كُنتُمْ تَعْمَلُونَ

32 Those who are in a wholesome state when the angels take them—will say, “Peace be upon you; enter Paradise, for what you used to do.”

٣٣ هَلْ يَنظُرُونَ إِلَّآ أَن تَأْتِيَهُمُ ٱلْمَلَـٰٓئِكَةُ أَوْ يَأْتِىَ
أَمْرُ رَبِّكَ ۚ كَذَٰلِكَ فَعَلَ ٱلَّذِينَ مِن قَبْلِهِمْ ۚ وَمَا
ظَلَمَهُمُ ٱللَّهُ وَلَـٰكِن كَانُوٓا۟ أَنفُسَهُمْ يَظْلِمُونَ

33 Are they but waiting for the angels to come to them, or for the command of your Lord to arrive? Those before them did likewise. Allah did not wrong them, but they used to wrong their own souls.

٣٤ فَأَصَابَهُمْ سَيِّـَٔاتُ مَا عَمِلُوا۟ وَحَاقَ بِهِم مَّا
كَانُوا۟ بِهِۦ يَسْتَهْزِءُونَ

34 So the evils of their deeds assailed them, and what they used to ridicule engulfed them.

٣٥ وَقَالَ ٱلَّذِينَ أَشْرَكُوا۟ لَوْ شَآءَ ٱللَّهُ مَا عَبَدْنَا
مِن دُونِهِۦ مِن شَىْءٍ نَّحْنُ وَلَآ ءَابَآؤُنَا وَلَا

35 The idolaters say, “Had Allah willed, we would not have worshiped anything besides Him, neither us, nor our ancestors, nor would we

حَرَّمْنَا مِن دُونِهِۦ مِن شَىْءٍۢ ۚ كَذَٰلِكَ فَعَلَ ٱلَّذِينَ
مِن قَبْلِهِمْ ۚ فَهَلْ عَلَى ٱلرُّسُلِ إِلَّا ٱلْبَلَٰغُ ٱلْمُبِينُ

have prohibited anything besides His prohibitions." Those before them did likewise. Are the messengers responsible for anything but clear communication?

٣٦ وَلَقَدْ بَعَثْنَا فِى كُلِّ أُمَّةٍۢ رَّسُولًا أَنِ ٱعْبُدُوا۟
ٱللَّهَ وَٱجْتَنِبُوا۟ ٱلطَّٰغُوتَ ۖ فَمِنْهُم مَّنْ هَدَى ٱللَّهُ
وَمِنْهُم مَّنْ حَقَّتْ عَلَيْهِ ٱلضَّلَٰلَةُ ۚ فَسِيرُوا۟ فِى
ٱلْأَرْضِ فَٱنظُرُوا۟ كَيْفَ كَانَ عَٰقِبَةُ ٱلْمُكَذِّبِينَ

36 To every community We sent a messenger: "Worship Allah, and avoid idolatry." Some of them Allah guided, while others deserved misguidance. So travel through the earth, and see what the fate of the deniers was.

٣٧ إِن تَحْرِصْ عَلَىٰ هُدَىٰهُمْ فَإِنَّ ٱللَّهَ لَا يَهْدِى
مَن يُضِلُّ ۖ وَمَا لَهُم مِّن نَّٰصِرِينَ

37 Even though you may be concerned about their guidance, Allah does not guide those who misguide. And they will have no saviors.

٣٨ وَأَقْسَمُوا۟ بِٱللَّهِ جَهْدَ أَيْمَٰنِهِمْ ۙ لَا يَبْعَثُ ٱللَّهُ
مَن يَمُوتُ ۚ بَلَىٰ وَعْدًا عَلَيْهِ حَقًّا وَلَٰكِنَّ أَكْثَرَ
ٱلنَّاسِ لَا يَعْلَمُونَ

38 And they swear by Allah with their most solemn oaths, "Allah will not resurrect anyone who dies." Yes indeed, it is a promise binding on Him, but most people do not know.

٣٩ لِيُبَيِّنَ لَهُمُ ٱلَّذِى يَخْتَلِفُونَ فِيهِ وَلِيَعْلَمَ
ٱلَّذِينَ كَفَرُوٓا۟ أَنَّهُمْ كَانُوا۟ كَٰذِبِينَ

39 To clarify for them what they differed about, and for the faithless to know that they were liars.

٤٠ إِنَّمَا قَوْلُنَا لِشَىْءٍ إِذَآ أَرَدْنَٰهُ أَن نَّقُولَ لَهُۥ كُن
فَيَكُونُ

40 When We intend for something to happen, We say to it, "Be," and it becomes.

٤١ وَٱلَّذِينَ هَاجَرُوا۟ فِى ٱللَّهِ مِنۢ بَعْدِ مَا ظُلِمُوا۟
لَنُبَوِّئَنَّهُمْ فِى ٱلدُّنْيَا حَسَنَةً ۖ وَلَأَجْرُ ٱلْءَاخِرَةِ
أَكْبَرُ ۚ لَوْ كَانُوا۟ يَعْلَمُونَ

41 Those who emigrate for Allah's sake after being persecuted, We will settle them in a good place in this world; but the reward of the Hereafter is greater, if they only knew.

٤٢ ٱلَّذِينَ صَبَرُوا۟ وَعَلَىٰ رَبِّهِمْ يَتَوَكَّلُونَ

42 Those who endure patiently, and in their Lord they put their trust.

٤٣ وَمَآ أَرْسَلْنَا مِن قَبْلِكَ إِلَّا رِجَالًا نُّوحِىٓ
إِلَيْهِمْ ۚ فَسْـَٔلُوٓا۟ أَهْلَ ٱلذِّكْرِ إِن كُنتُمْ لَا تَعْلَمُونَ

43 We did not send before you except men whom We inspired. So ask the people of knowledge, if you do not know.

٤٤ بِٱلْبَيِّنَٰتِ وَٱلزُّبُرِ ۗ وَأَنزَلْنَآ إِلَيْكَ ٱلذِّكْرَ لِتُبَيِّنَ
لِلنَّاسِ مَا نُزِّلَ إِلَيْهِمْ وَلَعَلَّهُمْ يَتَفَكَّرُونَ

44 With the clarifications and the scriptures. And We revealed to you the Reminder, that you may clarify to the people what was revealed to them, and that they may reflect.

٤٥ أَفَأَمِنَ ٱلَّذِينَ مَكَرُوا۟ ٱلسَّيِّـَٔاتِ أَن يَخْسِفَ
ٱللَّهُ بِهِمُ ٱلْأَرْضَ أَوْ يَأْتِيَهُمُ ٱلْعَذَابُ مِنْ حَيْثُ لَا
يَشْعُرُونَ

45 Do those who scheme evils feel secure that Allah will not cause the earth to cave in with them, or that the punishment will not come upon them from where they do not perceive?

٤٦ أَوْ يَأْخُذَهُمْ فِى تَقَلُّبِهِمْ فَمَا هُم بِمُعْجِزِينَ

46 Or that He will not seize them during their activities? And they will not be able to prevent it.

٤٧ أَوْ يَأْخُذَهُمْ عَلَىٰ تَخَوُّفٍ فَإِنَّ رَبَّكُمْ لَرَءُوفٌ
رَّحِيمٌ

47 Or that He will not seize them while in dread? Your Lord is Gentle and Merciful.

٤٨ أَوَلَمْ يَرَوْا۟ إِلَىٰ مَا خَلَقَ ٱللَّهُ مِن شَىْءٍ
يَتَفَيَّؤُا۟ ظِلَٰلُهُۥ عَنِ ٱلْيَمِينِ وَٱلشَّمَآئِلِ سُجَّدًا لِّلَّهِ
وَهُمْ دَٰخِرُونَ

48 Have they not observed what Allah has created? Their shadows revolve from the right and the left, bowing to Allah as they shrink away.

٤٩ وَلِلَّهِ يَسْجُدُ مَا فِى ٱلسَّمَٰوَٰتِ وَمَا فِى
ٱلْأَرْضِ مِن دَآبَّةٍ وَٱلْمَلَٰٓئِكَةُ وَهُمْ لَا يَسْتَكْبِرُونَ

49 To Allah bows down everything in the heavens and everything on earth—every living creature, and the angels, and without being proud.

٥٠ يَخَافُونَ رَبَّهُم مِّن فَوْقِهِمْ وَيَفْعَلُونَ مَا
يُؤْمَرُونَ ۩

50 They fear their Lord above them, and they do what they are commanded.

٥١ وَقَالَ ٱللَّهُ لَا تَتَّخِذُوٓا۟ إِلَٰهَيْنِ ٱثْنَيْنِ ۖ إِنَّمَا هُوَ
إِلَٰهٌ وَٰحِدٌ ۖ فَإِيَّٰىَ فَٱرْهَبُونِ

51 Allah has said: “Do not take two gods; He is only One God; so fear only Me.”

٥٢ وَلَهُۥ مَا فِى ٱلسَّمَٰوَٰتِ وَٱلْأَرْضِ وَلَهُ ٱلدِّينُ
وَاصِبًا ۚ أَفَغَيْرَ ٱللَّهِ تَتَّقُونَ

52 To Him belongs everything in the heavens and the earth; and to Him obedience is due always. Do you, then, fear anyone other than Allah?

٥٣ وَمَا بِكُم مِّن نِّعْمَةٍ فَمِنَ ٱللَّهِ ۖ ثُمَّ إِذَا مَسَّكُمُ
ٱلضُّرُّ فَإِلَيْهِ تَجْـَٔرُونَ

53 Whatever blessing you have is from Allah. And when harm touches you, it is to Him that you groan.

٥٤ ثُمَّ إِذَا كَشَفَ ٱلضُّرَّ عَنكُمْ إِذَا فَرِيقٌ مِّنكُم
بِرَبِّهِمْ يُشْرِكُونَ

54 But when He lifts the harm from you, some of you associate others with their Lord.

٥٥ لِيَكْفُرُواْ بِمَآ ءَاتَيْنَٰهُمْ ۚ فَتَمَتَّعُواْ ۖ فَسَوْفَ
تَعْلَمُونَ

55 To show ingratitude for what We have given them. Enjoy yourselves. You will soon know.

٥٦ وَيَجْعَلُونَ لِمَا لَا يَعْلَمُونَ نَصِيبًا مِّمَّا
رَزَقْنَٰهُمْ ۗ تَٱللَّهِ لَتُسْـَٔلُنَّ عَمَّا كُنتُمْ تَفْتَرُونَ

56 And they allocate, to something they do not know, a share of what We have provided for them. By Allah, you will be questioned about what you have been inventing.

٥٧ وَيَجْعَلُونَ لِلَّهِ ٱلْبَنَٰتِ سُبْحَٰنَهُۥ ۙ وَلَهُم مَّا
يَشْتَهُونَ

57 And they attribute to Allah daughters—exalted is He—and for themselves what they desire.

٥٨ وَإِذَا بُشِّرَ أَحَدُهُم بِٱلْأُنثَىٰ ظَلَّ وَجْهُهُۥ
مُسْوَدًّا وَهُوَ كَظِيمٌ

58 And when one of them is given news of a female infant, his face darkens, and he chokes with grief.

٥٩ يَتَوَٰرَىٰ مِنَ ٱلْقَوْمِ مِن سُوٓءِ مَا بُشِّرَ بِهِۦٓ ۚ
أَيُمْسِكُهُۥ عَلَىٰ هُونٍ أَمْ يَدُسُّهُۥ فِى ٱلتُّرَابِ ۗ أَلَا
سَآءَ مَا يَحْكُمُونَ

59 He hides from the people because of the bad news given to him. Shall he keep it in humiliation, or bury it in the dust? Evil is the decision they make.

٦٠ لِلَّذِينَ لَا يُؤْمِنُونَ بِٱلْءَاخِرَةِ مَثَلُ ٱلسَّوْءِ ۖ
وَلِلَّهِ ٱلْمَثَلُ ٱلْأَعْلَىٰ ۚ وَهُوَ ٱلْعَزِيزُ ٱلْحَكِيمُ

60 Those who do not believe in the Hereafter set a bad example, while Allah sets the Highest Example. He is the Mighty, the Wise.

٦١ وَلَوْ يُؤَاخِذُ ٱللَّهُ ٱلنَّاسَ بِظُلْمِهِم مَّا تَرَكَ
عَلَيْهَا مِن دَآبَّةٍ وَلَٰكِن يُؤَخِّرُهُمْ إِلَىٰٓ أَجَلٍ
مُّسَمًّى ۖ فَإِذَا جَآءَ أَجَلُهُمْ لَا يَسْتَـْٔخِرُونَ سَاعَةً ۖ
وَلَا يَسْتَقْدِمُونَ

61 If Allah were to hold mankind for their injustices, He would not leave upon it a single creature, but He postpones them until an appointed time. Then, when their time arrives, they will not delay it by one hour, nor will they advance it.

٦٢ وَيَجْعَلُونَ لِلَّهِ مَا يَكْرَهُونَ وَتَصِفُ أَلْسِنَتُهُمُ
ٱلْكَذِبَ أَنَّ لَهُمُ ٱلْحُسْنَىٰ ۖ لَا جَرَمَ أَنَّ لَهُمُ ٱلنَّارَ
وَأَنَّهُم مُّفْرَطُونَ

62 And they attribute to Allah what they themselves dislike, while their tongues utter the lie that theirs is the goodness. Without a doubt, for them is the Fire, and they will be neglected.

٦٣ تَٱللَّهِ لَقَدْ أَرْسَلْنَآ إِلَىٰٓ أُمَمٍ مِّن قَبْلِكَ فَزَيَّنَ
لَهُمُ ٱلشَّيْطَٰنُ أَعْمَٰلَهُمْ فَهُوَ وَلِيُّهُمُ ٱلْيَوْمَ وَلَهُمْ
عَذَابٌ أَلِيمٌ

63 By Allah, We sent messengers to communities before you, but Satan made their deeds appear alluring to them. He is their master today, and they will have a painful punishment.

٦٤ وَمَآ أَنزَلْنَا عَلَيْكَ ٱلْكِتَٰبَ إِلَّا لِتُبَيِّنَ لَهُمُ ٱلَّذِى
ٱخْتَلَفُوا۟ فِيهِ ۙ وَهُدًى وَرَحْمَةً لِّقَوْمٍ يُؤْمِنُونَ

64 We revealed to you the Scripture only to clarify for them what they differ about, and guidance and mercy for people who believe.

٦٥ وَٱللَّهُ أَنزَلَ مِنَ ٱلسَّمَآءِ مَآءً فَأَحْيَا بِهِ
ٱلْأَرْضَ بَعْدَ مَوْتِهَآ ۚ إِنَّ فِى ذَٰلِكَ لَءَايَةً لِّقَوْمٍ
يَسْمَعُونَ

65 Allah sends down water from the sky, with which He revives the earth after its death. In this is a sign for people who listen.

٦٦ وَإِنَّ لَكُمْ فِى ٱلْأَنْعَٰمِ لَعِبْرَةً ۖ نُّسْقِيكُم مِّمَّا
فِى بُطُونِهِۦ مِنۢ بَيْنِ فَرْثٍ وَدَمٍ لَّبَنًا خَالِصًا
سَآئِغًا لِّلشَّٰرِبِينَ

66 And there is a lesson for you in cattle: We give you a drink from their bellies, from between waste and blood, pure milk, refreshing to the drinkers.

٦٧ وَمِن ثَمَرَٰتِ ٱلنَّخِيلِ وَٱلْأَعْنَٰبِ تَتَّخِذُونَ مِنْهُ
سَكَرًا وَرِزْقًا حَسَنًا ۗ إِنَّ فِى ذَٰلِكَ لَءَايَةً لِّقَوْمٍ
يَعْقِلُونَ

67 And from the fruits of date-palms and grapevines, you derive sugar and wholesome food. In this is a sign for people who understand.

٦٨ وَأَوْحَىٰ رَبُّكَ إِلَى ٱلنَّحْلِ أَنِ ٱتَّخِذِى مِنَ
ٱلْجِبَالِ بُيُوتًا وَمِنَ ٱلشَّجَرِ وَمِمَّا يَعْرِشُونَ

68 And your Lord inspired the bee: “Set up hives in the mountains, and in the trees, and in what they construct.”

٦٩ ثُمَّ كُلِى مِن كُلِّ ٱلثَّمَرَٰتِ فَٱسْلُكِى سُبُلَ رَبِّكِ
ذُلُلًا ۚ يَخْرُجُ مِنۢ بُطُونِهَا شَرَابٌ مُّخْتَلِفٌ أَلْوَٰنُهُۥ
فِيهِ شِفَآءٌ لِّلنَّاسِ ۗ إِنَّ فِى ذَٰلِكَ لَءَايَةً لِّقَوْمٍ
يَتَفَكَّرُونَ

69 Then eat of all the fruits, and go along the pathways of your Lord, with precision. From their bellies emerges a fluid of diverse colors, containing healing for the people. Surely in this is a sign for people who reflect.

٧٠ وَٱللَّهُ خَلَقَكُمْ ثُمَّ يَتَوَفَّىٰكُمْ ۚ وَمِنكُم مَّن يُرَدُّ
إِلَىٰٓ أَرْذَلِ ٱلْعُمُرِ لِكَىْ لَا يَعْلَمَ بَعْدَ عِلْمٍ شَيْـًٔا ۚ إِنَّ
ٱللَّهَ عَلِيمٌ قَدِيرٌ

70 Allah created you; then He takes you away. Some of you will be brought back to the worst age, so that he will no longer know anything, after having acquired knowledge. Allah is Omniscient and Omnipotent.

٧١ وَٱللَّهُ فَضَّلَ بَعْضَكُمْ عَلَىٰ بَعْضٍ فِى ٱلرِّزْقِ ۚ
فَمَا ٱلَّذِينَ فُضِّلُوا۟ بِرَآدِّى رِزْقِهِمْ عَلَىٰ مَا مَلَكَتْ
أَيْمَـٰنُهُمْ فَهُمْ فِيهِ سَوَآءٌ ۚ أَفَبِنِعْمَةِ ٱللَّهِ
يَجْحَدُونَ

71 Allah has favored some of you over others in livelihood. Those who are favored would not give their properties to their servants, to the extent of making them partners in it. Will they then renounce Allah's blessings?

٧٢ وَٱللَّهُ جَعَلَ لَكُم مِّنْ أَنفُسِكُمْ أَزْوَٰجًا وَجَعَلَ
لَكُم مِّنْ أَزْوَٰجِكُم بَنِينَ وَحَفَدَةً وَرَزَقَكُم مِّنَ
ٱلطَّيِّبَـٰتِ ۚ أَفَبِٱلْبَـٰطِلِ يُؤْمِنُونَ وَبِنِعْمَتِ ٱللَّهِ هُمْ
يَكْفُرُونَ

72 Allah has given you mates from among yourselves; and has produced for you, from your mates, children and grandchildren; and has provided you with good things. Will they then believe in falsehood, and refuse Allah's favors?

٧٣ وَيَعْبُدُونَ مِن دُونِ ٱللَّهِ مَا لَا يَمْلِكُ لَهُمْ
رِزْقًا مِّنَ ٱلسَّمَـٰوَٰتِ وَٱلْأَرْضِ شَيْـًٔا وَلَا
يَسْتَطِيعُونَ

73 And yet they serve besides Allah what possesses no provisions for them in the heavens, nor on earth, nor are they capable.

٧٤ فَلَا تَضْرِبُوا۟ لِلَّهِ ٱلْأَمْثَالَ ۚ إِنَّ ٱللَّهَ يَعْلَمُ
وَأَنتُمْ لَا تَعْلَمُونَ

74 So do not cite the examples for Allah. Allah knows, and you do not know.

٧٥ ضَرَبَ ٱللَّهُ مَثَلًا عَبْدًا مَّمْلُوكًا لَّا يَقْدِرُ عَلَىٰ
شَىْءٍ وَمَن رَّزَقْنَـٰهُ مِنَّا رِزْقًا حَسَنًا فَهُوَ يُنفِقُ
مِنْهُ سِرًّا وَجَهْرًا ۖ هَلْ يَسْتَوُۥنَ ۚ ٱلْحَمْدُ لِلَّهِ ۚ بَلْ
أَكْثَرُهُمْ لَا يَعْلَمُونَ

75 Allah cites the example of a bonded slave, who has no power over anything; and someone to whom We have given plentiful provision, from which he gives secretly and openly. Are they equal in comparison? All praise belongs to Allah, but most of them do not know.

٧٦ وَضَرَبَ ٱللَّهُ مَثَلًا رَّجُلَيْنِ أَحَدُهُمَآ أَبْكَمُ لَا
يَقْدِرُ عَلَىٰ شَىْءٍ وَهُوَ كَلٌّ عَلَىٰ مَوْلَىٰهُ أَيْنَمَا
يُوَجِّههُّ لَا يَأْتِ بِخَيْرٍ ۖ هَلْ يَسْتَوِى هُوَ وَمَن
يَأْمُرُ بِٱلْعَدْلِ ۙ وَهُوَ عَلَىٰ صِرَٰطٍ مُّسْتَقِيمٍ

76 And Allah cites the example of two men: one of them dumb, unable to do anything, and is a burden on his master; whichever way he directs him, he achieves nothing good. Is he equal to him who commands justice, and is on a straight path?

٧٧ وَلِلَّهِ غَيْبُ ٱلسَّمَـٰوَٰتِ وَٱلْأَرْضِ ۚ وَمَآ أَمْرُ
ٱلسَّاعَةِ إِلَّا كَلَمْحِ ٱلْبَصَرِ أَوْ هُوَ أَقْرَبُ ۚ إِنَّ ٱللَّهَ
عَلَىٰ كُلِّ شَىْءٍ قَدِيرٌ

77 To Allah belongs the unseen of the heavens and the earth. The coming of the Hour is only as the twinkling of the eye, or even nearer. Allah has power over everything.

٧٨ وَٱللَّهُ أَخْرَجَكُم مِّنۢ بُطُونِ أُمَّهَٰتِكُمْ لَا تَعْلَمُونَ شَيْـًٔا وَجَعَلَ لَكُمُ ٱلسَّمْعَ وَٱلْأَبْصَٰرَ وَٱلْأَفْـِٔدَةَ ۙ لَعَلَّكُمْ تَشْكُرُونَ

78 Allah brought you out of your mothers' wombs, not knowing anything; and He gave you the hearing, and the eyesight, and the brains; that you may give thanks.

٧٩ أَلَمْ يَرَوْا۟ إِلَى ٱلطَّيْرِ مُسَخَّرَٰتٍ فِى جَوِّ ٱلسَّمَآءِ مَا يُمْسِكُهُنَّ إِلَّا ٱللَّهُ ۗ إِنَّ فِى ذَٰلِكَ لَءَايَٰتٍ لِّقَوْمٍ يُؤْمِنُونَ

79 Have they not seen the birds, flying in the midst of the sky? None sustains them except Allah. In this are signs for people who believe.

٨٠ وَٱللَّهُ جَعَلَ لَكُم مِّنۢ بُيُوتِكُمْ سَكَنًا وَجَعَلَ لَكُم مِّن جُلُودِ ٱلْأَنْعَٰمِ بُيُوتًا تَسْتَخِفُّونَهَا يَوْمَ ظَعْنِكُمْ وَيَوْمَ إِقَامَتِكُمْ ۙ وَمِنْ أَصْوَافِهَا وَأَوْبَارِهَا وَأَشْعَارِهَآ أَثَٰثًا وَمَتَٰعًا إِلَىٰ حِينٍ

80 And Allah has given you in your homes habitats for you, and has provided for you out of the hides of livestock portable homes for you, so you can use them when you travel, and when you camp; and from their wool, and fur, and hair, furnishings and comfort for a while.

٨١ وَٱللَّهُ جَعَلَ لَكُم مِّمَّا خَلَقَ ظِلَٰلًا وَجَعَلَ لَكُم مِّنَ ٱلْجِبَالِ أَكْنَٰنًا وَجَعَلَ لَكُمْ سَرَٰبِيلَ تَقِيكُمُ ٱلْحَرَّ وَسَرَٰبِيلَ تَقِيكُم بَأْسَكُمْ ۚ كَذَٰلِكَ يُتِمُّ نِعْمَتَهُۥ عَلَيْكُمْ لَعَلَّكُمْ تُسْلِمُونَ

81 And Allah has made for you shade out of what He has created, and has given you resorts in the mountains, and has given you garments to protect you from the heat, and garments to protect you from your violence. Thus He completes His blessings upon you, so that you may submit.

٨٢ فَإِن تَوَلَّوْا۟ فَإِنَّمَا عَلَيْكَ ٱلْبَلَٰغُ ٱلْمُبِينُ

82 But if they turn away, your only duty is clear communication.

٨٣ يَعْرِفُونَ نِعْمَتَ ٱللَّهِ ثُمَّ يُنكِرُونَهَا وَأَكْثَرُهُمُ ٱلْكَٰفِرُونَ

83 They recognize Allah's blessing, but then deny it, as most of them are ungrateful.

٨٤ وَيَوْمَ نَبْعَثُ مِن كُلِّ أُمَّةٍ شَهِيدًا ثُمَّ لَا يُؤْذَنُ لِلَّذِينَ كَفَرُوا۟ وَلَا هُمْ يُسْتَعْتَبُونَ

84 On the Day when We raise up a witness from every community—those who disbelieved will not be permitted, nor will they be excused.

٨٥ وَإِذَا رَءَا ٱلَّذِينَ ظَلَمُوا۟ ٱلْعَذَابَ فَلَا يُخَفَّفُ عَنْهُمْ وَلَا هُمْ يُنظَرُونَ

85 When those who did wrong see the punishment, it will not be lightened for them, nor will they be reprieved.

٨٦ وَإِذَا رَءَا ٱلَّذِينَ أَشْرَكُوا۟ شُرَكَآءَهُمْ قَالُوا۟ رَبَّنَا هَٰٓؤُلَآءِ شُرَكَآؤُنَا ٱلَّذِينَ كُنَّا نَدْعُوا۟ مِن دُونِكَ ۖ فَأَلْقَوْا۟ إِلَيْهِمُ ٱلْقَوْلَ إِنَّكُمْ لَكَٰذِبُونَ

86 And when the idolaters see their associates, they will say, “Our Lord, these are our associates whom we used to invoke besides You.” They will strike back at them with the saying, “Surely you are liars.”

٨٧ وَأَلْقَوْا۟ إِلَى ٱللَّهِ يَوْمَئِذٍ ٱلسَّلَمَ ۖ وَضَلَّ عَنْهُم مَّا كَانُوا۟ يَفْتَرُونَ

87 On that Day they will offer their submission to Allah, and what they had invented will abandon them.

٨٨ ٱلَّذِينَ كَفَرُوا۟ وَصَدُّوا۟ عَن سَبِيلِ ٱللَّهِ زِدْنَٰهُمْ عَذَابًا فَوْقَ ٱلْعَذَابِ بِمَا كَانُوا۟ يُفْسِدُونَ

88 Those who disbelieve and obstruct from Allah’s path—We will add punishment to their punishment, on account of the mischief they used to make.

٨٩ وَيَوْمَ نَبْعَثُ فِى كُلِّ أُمَّةٍ شَهِيدًا عَلَيْهِم مِّنْ أَنفُسِهِمْ ۖ وَجِئْنَا بِكَ شَهِيدًا عَلَىٰ هَٰٓؤُلَآءِ ۚ وَنَزَّلْنَا عَلَيْكَ ٱلْكِتَٰبَ تِبْيَٰنًا لِّكُلِّ شَىْءٍ وَهُدًى وَرَحْمَةً وَبُشْرَىٰ لِلْمُسْلِمِينَ

89 On the Day when We raise in every community a witness against them, from among them, and bring you as a witness against these. We have revealed to you the Book, as an explanation of all things, and guidance, and mercy and good news for those who submit.

٩٠ إِنَّ ٱللَّهَ يَأْمُرُ بِٱلْعَدْلِ وَٱلْإِحْسَٰنِ وَإِيتَآئِ ذِى ٱلْقُرْبَىٰ وَيَنْهَىٰ عَنِ ٱلْفَحْشَآءِ وَٱلْمُنكَرِ وَٱلْبَغْىِ ۚ يَعِظُكُمْ لَعَلَّكُمْ تَذَكَّرُونَ

90 Allah commands justice, and goodness, and generosity towards relatives. And He forbids immorality, and injustice, and oppression. He advises you, so that you may take heed.

٩١ وَأَوْفُوا۟ بِعَهْدِ ٱللَّهِ إِذَا عَٰهَدتُّمْ وَلَا تَنقُضُوا۟ ٱلْأَيْمَٰنَ بَعْدَ تَوْكِيدِهَا وَقَدْ جَعَلْتُمُ ٱللَّهَ عَلَيْكُمْ كَفِيلًا ۚ إِنَّ ٱللَّهَ يَعْلَمُ مَا تَفْعَلُونَ

91 Fulfill Allah’s covenant when you make a covenant, and do not break your oaths after ratifying them. You have made Allah your guarantor, and Allah knows what you do.

٩٢ وَلَا تَكُونُوا۟ كَٱلَّتِى نَقَضَتْ غَزْلَهَا مِنۢ بَعْدِ قُوَّةٍ أَنكَٰثًا تَتَّخِذُونَ أَيْمَٰنَكُمْ دَخَلًۢا بَيْنَكُمْ أَن تَكُونَ أُمَّةٌ هِىَ أَرْبَىٰ مِنْ أُمَّةٍ ۚ إِنَّمَا يَبْلُوكُمُ ٱللَّهُ بِهِۦ ۚ وَلَيُبَيِّنَنَّ لَكُمْ يَوْمَ ٱلْقِيَٰمَةِ مَا كُنتُمْ فِيهِ تَخْتَلِفُونَ

92 And do not be like her who unravels her yarn, breaking it into pieces, after she has spun it strongly. Nor use your oaths as means of deception among you, because one community is more prosperous than another. Allah is testing you thereby. On the Day of Resurrection, He will make clear to

you everything you had disputed about.

٩٣ وَلَوْ شَآءَ ٱللَّهُ لَجَعَلَكُمْ أُمَّةً وَٰحِدَةً وَلَٰكِن
يُضِلُّ مَن يَشَآءُ وَيَهْدِى مَن يَشَآءُ ۚ وَلَتُسْـَٔلُنَّ
عَمَّا كُنتُمْ تَعْمَلُونَ

93 Had Allah willed, He would have made you one congregation, but He leaves astray whom He wills, and He guides whom He wills. And you will surely be questioned about what you used to do.

٩٤ وَلَا تَتَّخِذُوٓا۟ أَيْمَٰنَكُمْ دَخَلًۢا بَيْنَكُمْ فَتَزِلَّ قَدَمٌۢ
بَعْدَ ثُبُوتِهَا وَتَذُوقُوا۟ ٱلسُّوٓءَ بِمَا صَدَدتُّمْ عَن
سَبِيلِ ٱللَّهِ ۖ وَلَكُمْ عَذَابٌ عَظِيمٌ

94 And do not use your oaths to deceive one another, so that a foot may not slip after being firm, and you taste misery because you hindered from Allah's path, and incur a terrible torment.

٩٥ وَلَا تَشْتَرُوا۟ بِعَهْدِ ٱللَّهِ ثَمَنًا قَلِيلًا ۚ إِنَّمَا عِندَ
ٱللَّهِ هُوَ خَيْرٌ لَّكُمْ إِن كُنتُمْ تَعْلَمُونَ

95 And do not exchange Allah's covenant for a small price. What is with Allah is better for you, if you only knew.

٩٦ مَا عِندَكُمْ يَنفَدُ ۖ وَمَا عِندَ ٱللَّهِ بَاقٍ ۗ
وَلَنَجْزِيَنَّ ٱلَّذِينَ صَبَرُوٓا۟ أَجْرَهُم بِأَحْسَنِ مَا
كَانُوا۟ يَعْمَلُونَ

96 What you have runs out, but what is with Allah remains. We will reward those who are patient according to the best of their deeds.

٩٧ مَنْ عَمِلَ صَٰلِحًا مِّن ذَكَرٍ أَوْ أُنثَىٰ وَهُوَ
مُؤْمِنٌ فَلَنُحْيِيَنَّهُۥ حَيَوٰةً طَيِّبَةً ۖ وَلَنَجْزِيَنَّهُمْ
أَجْرَهُم بِأَحْسَنِ مَا كَانُوا۟ يَعْمَلُونَ

97 Whoever works righteousness, whether male or female, while being a believer, We will grant him a good life—and We will reward them according to the best of what they used to do.

٩٨ فَإِذَا قَرَأْتَ ٱلْقُرْءَانَ فَٱسْتَعِذْ بِٱللَّهِ مِنَ
ٱلشَّيْطَٰنِ ٱلرَّجِيمِ

98 When you read the Quran, seek refuge with Allah from Satan the outcast.

٩٩ إِنَّهُۥ لَيْسَ لَهُۥ سُلْطَٰنٌ عَلَى ٱلَّذِينَ ءَامَنُوا۟
وَعَلَىٰ رَبِّهِمْ يَتَوَكَّلُونَ

99 He has no authority over those who believe and trust in their Lord.

١٠٠ إِنَّمَا سُلْطَٰنُهُۥ عَلَى ٱلَّذِينَ يَتَوَلَّوْنَهُۥ وَٱلَّذِينَ
هُم بِهِۦ مُشْرِكُونَ

100 His authority is only over those who follow him, and those who associate others with Him.

١٠١ وَإِذَا بَدَّلْنَآ ءَايَةً مَّكَانَ ءَايَةٍ ۙ وَٱللَّهُ أَعْلَمُ بِمَا
يُنَزِّلُ قَالُوٓا۟ إِنَّمَآ أَنتَ مُفْتَرٍۭ ۚ بَلْ أَكْثَرُهُمْ لَا
يَعْلَمُونَ

101 When We substitute a verse in place of another verse—and Allah knows best what He reveals—they say, “You are an impostor.” But most of them do not know.

١٠٢ قُلْ نَزَّلَهُۥ رُوحُ ٱلْقُدُسِ مِن رَّبِّكَ بِٱلْحَقِّ
لِيُثَبِّتَ ٱلَّذِينَ ءَامَنُوا۟ وَهُدًى وَبُشْرَىٰ لِلْمُسْلِمِينَ

102 Say, “The Holy Spirit has brought it down from your Lord, truthfully, in order to stabilize those who believe, and as guidance and good news for those who submit.”

١٠٣ وَلَقَدْ نَعْلَمُ أَنَّهُمْ يَقُولُونَ إِنَّمَا يُعَلِّمُهُۥ بَشَرٌ ۗ
لِّسَانُ ٱلَّذِى يُلْحِدُونَ إِلَيْهِ أَعْجَمِىٌّ وَهَٰذَا لِسَانٌ
عَرَبِىٌّ مُّبِينٌ

103 We are well aware that they say, “It is a human being who is teaching him.” But the tongue of him they allude to is foreign, while this is a clear Arabic tongue.

١٠٤ إِنَّ ٱلَّذِينَ لَا يُؤْمِنُونَ بِـَٔايَٰتِ ٱللَّهِ لَا يَهْدِيهِمُ
ٱللَّهُ وَلَهُمْ عَذَابٌ أَلِيمٌ

104 Those who do not believe in Allah’s revelations—Allah will not guide them, and for them is a painful punishment.

١٠٥ إِنَّمَا يَفْتَرِى ٱلْكَذِبَ ٱلَّذِينَ لَا يُؤْمِنُونَ بِـَٔايَٰتِ
ٱللَّهِ ۖ وَأُو۟لَٰٓئِكَ هُمُ ٱلْكَٰذِبُونَ

105 It is those who do not believe in Allah’s revelations who fabricate falsehood. These are the liars.

١٠٦ مَن كَفَرَ بِٱللَّهِ مِنۢ بَعْدِ إِيمَٰنِهِۦٓ إِلَّا مَنْ أُكْرِهَ
وَقَلْبُهُۥ مُطْمَئِنٌّۢ بِٱلْإِيمَٰنِ وَلَٰكِن مَّن شَرَحَ بِٱلْكُفْرِ
صَدْرًا فَعَلَيْهِمْ غَضَبٌ مِّنَ ٱللَّهِ وَلَهُمْ عَذَابٌ
عَظِيمٌ

106 Whoever renounces faith in Allah after having believed—except for someone who is compelled, while his heart rests securely in faith—but whoever willingly opens up his heart to disbelief—upon them falls wrath from Allah, and for them is a tremendous torment.

١٠٧ ذَٰلِكَ بِأَنَّهُمُ ٱسْتَحَبُّوا۟ ٱلْحَيَوٰةَ ٱلدُّنْيَا عَلَى
ٱلْءَاخِرَةِ وَأَنَّ ٱللَّهَ لَا يَهْدِى ٱلْقَوْمَ ٱلْكَٰفِرِينَ

107 That is because they have preferred the worldly life to the Hereafter, and because Allah does not guide the people who refuse.

١٠٨ أُو۟لَٰٓئِكَ ٱلَّذِينَ طَبَعَ ٱللَّهُ عَلَىٰ قُلُوبِهِمْ
وَسَمْعِهِمْ وَأَبْصَٰرِهِمْ ۖ وَأُو۟لَٰٓئِكَ هُمُ ٱلْغَٰفِلُونَ

108 It is they whom Allah has sealed their hearts, and their hearing, and their sight. It is they who are the heedless.

١٠٩ لَا جَرَمَ أَنَّهُمْ فِى ٱلْءَاخِرَةِ هُمُ ٱلْخَٰسِرُونَ

109 There is no doubt that in the Hereafter they will be the losers.

١١٠ ثُمَّ إِنَّ رَبَّكَ لِلَّذِينَ هَاجَرُوا۟ مِنۢ بَعْدِ مَا
فُتِنُوا۟ ثُمَّ جَٰهَدُوا۟ وَصَبَرُوٓا۟ إِنَّ رَبَّكَ مِنۢ بَعْدِهَا
لَغَفُورٌ رَّحِيمٌ

110 But then your Lord—for those who emigrated after being persecuted, then struggled and persevered—your Lord thereafter is Forgiving and Merciful.

١١١ يَوْمَ تَأْتِى كُلُّ نَفْسٍ تُجَٰدِلُ عَن نَّفْسِهَا
وَتُوَفَّىٰ كُلُّ نَفْسٍ مَّا عَمِلَتْ وَهُمْ لَا يُظْلَمُونَ

111 On the Day when every soul will come pleading for itself, and every soul will be paid in full for what it has done, and they will not be wronged.

١١٢ وَضَرَبَ ٱللَّهُ مَثَلًا قَرْيَةً كَانَتْ ءَامِنَةً
مُّطْمَئِنَّةً يَأْتِيهَا رِزْقُهَا رَغَدًا مِّن كُلِّ مَكَانٍ
فَكَفَرَتْ بِأَنْعُمِ ٱللَّهِ فَأَذَٰقَهَا ٱللَّهُ لِبَاسَ ٱلْجُوعِ
وَٱلْخَوْفِ بِمَا كَانُوا۟ يَصْنَعُونَ

112 And Allah cites the example of a town that was secure and peaceful, with its livelihood coming to it abundantly from every direction. But then it turned unappreciative of Allah's blessings, so Allah made it taste the robe of hunger and fear, because of what they used to craft.

١١٣ وَلَقَدْ جَآءَهُمْ رَسُولٌ مِّنْهُمْ فَكَذَّبُوهُ
فَأَخَذَهُمُ ٱلْعَذَابُ وَهُمْ ظَٰلِمُونَ

113 A messenger from among them had come to them, but they denounced him, so the punishment seized them in the midst of their wrongdoing.

١١٤ فَكُلُوا۟ مِمَّا رَزَقَكُمُ ٱللَّهُ حَلَٰلًا طَيِّبًا وَٱشْكُرُوا۟
نِعْمَتَ ٱللَّهِ إِن كُنتُمْ إِيَّاهُ تَعْبُدُونَ

114 Eat of the lawful and good things Allah has provided for you, and be thankful for Allah's blessings, if it is Him that you serve.

١١٥ إِنَّمَا حَرَّمَ عَلَيْكُمُ ٱلْمَيْتَةَ وَٱلدَّمَ وَلَحْمَ
ٱلْخِنزِيرِ وَمَآ أُهِلَّ لِغَيْرِ ٱللَّهِ بِهِۦ فَمَنِ ٱضْطُرَّ
غَيْرَ بَاغٍ وَلَا عَادٍ فَإِنَّ ٱللَّهَ غَفُورٌ رَّحِيمٌ

115 He has forbidden you carrion, and blood, and the flesh of swine, and anything consecrated to other than Allah. But if anyone is compelled by necessity, without being deliberate or malicious, then Allah is Forgiving and Merciful.

١١٦ وَلَا تَقُولُوا۟ لِمَا تَصِفُ أَلْسِنَتُكُمُ ٱلْكَذِبَ هَٰذَا
حَلَٰلٌ وَهَٰذَا حَرَامٌ لِّتَفْتَرُوا۟ عَلَى ٱللَّهِ ٱلْكَذِبَ ۚ إِنَّ
ٱلَّذِينَ يَفْتَرُونَ عَلَى ٱللَّهِ ٱلْكَذِبَ لَا يُفْلِحُونَ

116 And do not say of falsehood asserted by your tongues, "This is lawful, and this is unlawful," in order to invent lies and attribute them to Allah. Those who invent lies and attribute them to Allah will not succeed.

١١٧ مَتَٰعٌ قَلِيلٌ وَلَهُمْ عَذَابٌ أَلِيمٌ

117 A brief enjoyment—then they will have a painful punishment.

١١٨ وَعَلَى ٱلَّذِينَ هَادُوا۟ حَرَّمْنَا مَا قَصَصْنَا
عَلَيْكَ مِن قَبْلُ ۖ وَمَا ظَلَمْنَٰهُمْ وَلَٰكِن كَانُوٓا۟
أَنفُسَهُمْ يَظْلِمُونَ

118 For those who are Jews, We have prohibited what We related to you before. We did not wrong them, but they used to wrong their own selves.

١١٩ ثُمَّ إِنَّ رَبَّكَ لِلَّذِينَ عَمِلُوا۟ ٱلسُّوٓءَ بِجَهَٰلَةٍ ثُمَّ
تَابُوا۟ مِنۢ بَعْدِ ذَٰلِكَ وَأَصْلَحُوٓا۟ إِنَّ رَبَّكَ مِنۢ
بَعْدِهَا لَغَفُورٌ رَّحِيمٌ

119 But towards those who do wrongs in ignorance, and then repent afterwards and reform, your Lord thereafter is Forgiving and Merciful.

١٢٠ إِنَّ إِبْرَٰهِيمَ كَانَ أُمَّةً قَانِتًا لِّلَّهِ حَنِيفًا وَلَمْ
يَكُ مِنَ ٱلْمُشْرِكِينَ

120 Abraham was an exemplary leader, devoted to Allah, a monotheist, and was not of the polytheists.

١٢١ شَاكِرًا لِّأَنْعُمِهِ ۚ ٱجْتَبَىٰهُ وَهَدَىٰهُ إِلَىٰ صِرَٰطٍ
مُّسْتَقِيمٍ

121 Thankful for His blessings. He chose him, and guided him to a straight path.

١٢٢ وَءَاتَيْنَٰهُ فِى ٱلدُّنْيَا حَسَنَةً ۖ وَإِنَّهُۥ فِى
ٱلْءَاخِرَةِ لَمِنَ ٱلصَّٰلِحِينَ

122 And We gave him goodness in this world, and in the Hereafter he will be among the righteous.

١٢٣ ثُمَّ أَوْحَيْنَآ إِلَيْكَ أَنِ ٱتَّبِعْ مِلَّةَ إِبْرَٰهِيمَ
حَنِيفًا ۖ وَمَا كَانَ مِنَ ٱلْمُشْرِكِينَ

123 Then We inspired you: “Follow the religion of Abraham, the Monotheist. He was not an idol-worshiper.”

١٢٤ إِنَّمَا جُعِلَ ٱلسَّبْتُ عَلَى ٱلَّذِينَ ٱخْتَلَفُوا۟ فِيهِ ۚ
وَإِنَّ رَبَّكَ لَيَحْكُمُ بَيْنَهُمْ يَوْمَ ٱلْقِيَٰمَةِ فِيمَا كَانُوا۟
فِيهِ يَخْتَلِفُونَ

124 The Sabbath was decreed only for those who differed about it. Your Lord will judge between them on the Day of Resurrection regarding their differences.

١٢٥ ٱدْعُ إِلَىٰ سَبِيلِ رَبِّكَ بِٱلْحِكْمَةِ وَٱلْمَوْعِظَةِ
ٱلْحَسَنَةِ ۖ وَجَٰدِلْهُم بِٱلَّتِى هِىَ أَحْسَنُ ۚ إِنَّ رَبَّكَ
هُوَ أَعْلَمُ بِمَن ضَلَّ عَن سَبِيلِهِۦ ۖ وَهُوَ أَعْلَمُ
بِٱلْمُهْتَدِينَ

125 Invite to the way of your Lord with wisdom and good advice, and debate with them in the most dignified manner. Your Lord is aware of those who stray from His path, and He is aware of those who are guided.

١٢٦ وَإِنْ عَاقَبْتُمْ فَعَاقِبُوا۟ بِمِثْلِ مَا عُوقِبْتُم بِهِۦ ۖ
وَلَئِن صَبَرْتُمْ لَهُوَ خَيْرٌ لِّلصَّٰبِرِينَ

126 If you were to retaliate, retaliate to the same degree as the injury done

to you. But if you resort to patience—it is better for the patient.

١٢٧ وَٱصْبِرْ وَمَا صَبْرُكَ إِلَّا بِٱللَّهِ ۚ وَلَا تَحْزَنْ
عَلَيْهِمْ وَلَا تَكُ فِى ضَيْقٍ مِّمَّا يَمْكُرُونَ

127 So be patient. Your patience is solely from Allah. And do not grieve over them, and do not be stressed by their schemes.

١٢٨ إِنَّ ٱللَّهَ مَعَ ٱلَّذِينَ ٱتَّقَوا۟ وَّٱلَّذِينَ هُم
مُّحْسِنُونَ

128 Allah is with those who are righteous and those who are virtuous.

17 The Night Journey الإسراء

بِسْمِ ٱللَّهِ ٱلرَّحْمَٰنِ ٱلرَّحِيمِ

In the name of Allah, the Gracious, the Merciful.

١ سُبْحَٰنَ ٱلَّذِىٓ أَسْرَىٰ بِعَبْدِهِۦ لَيْلًا مِّنَ ٱلْمَسْجِدِ
ٱلْحَرَامِ إِلَى ٱلْمَسْجِدِ ٱلْأَقْصَا ٱلَّذِى بَٰرَكْنَا حَوْلَهُۥ
لِنُرِيَهُۥ مِنْ ءَايَٰتِنَآ ۚ إِنَّهُۥ هُوَ ٱلسَّمِيعُ ٱلْبَصِيرُ

1 Glory to Him who journeyed His servant by night, from the Sacred Mosque, to the Farthest Mosque, whose precincts We have blessed, in order to show him of Our wonders. He is the Listener, the Beholder.

٢ وَءَاتَيْنَا مُوسَى ٱلْكِتَٰبَ وَجَعَلْنَٰهُ هُدًى لِّبَنِىٓ
إِسْرَٰٓءِيلَ أَلَّا تَتَّخِذُوا۟ مِن دُونِى وَكِيلًا

2 And We gave Moses the Scripture, and made it a guide for the Children of Israel: Take none for protector other than Me.

٣ ذُرِّيَّةَ مَنْ حَمَلْنَا مَعَ نُوحٍ ۚ إِنَّهُۥ كَانَ عَبْدًا
شَكُورًا

3 The descendants of those We carried with Noah. He was an appreciative servant.

٤ وَقَضَيْنَآ إِلَىٰ بَنِىٓ إِسْرَٰٓءِيلَ فِى ٱلْكِتَٰبِ
لَتُفْسِدُنَّ فِى ٱلْأَرْضِ مَرَّتَيْنِ وَلَتَعْلُنَّ عُلُوًّا كَبِيرًا

4 And We conveyed to the Children of Israel in the Scripture: You will commit evil on earth twice, and you will rise to a great height.

٥ فَإِذَا جَآءَ وَعْدُ أُولَىٰهُمَا بَعَثْنَا عَلَيْكُمْ عِبَادًا لَّنَآ
أُو۟لِى بَأْسٍ شَدِيدٍ فَجَاسُوا۟ خِلَٰلَ ٱلدِّيَارِ ۚ وَكَانَ
وَعْدًا مَّفْعُولًا

5 When the first of the two promises came true, We sent against you servants of Ours, possessing great might, and they ransacked your homes. It was a promise fulfilled.

٦ ثُمَّ رَدَدْنَا لَكُمُ ٱلْكَرَّةَ عَلَيْهِمْ وَأَمْدَدْنَٰكُم بِأَمْوَٰلٍ
وَبَنِينَ وَجَعَلْنَٰكُمْ أَكْثَرَ نَفِيرًا

6 Then We gave you back your turn against them, and supplied you with

wealth and children, and made you more numerous.

٧ إِنْ أَحْسَنتُمْ أَحْسَنتُمْ لِأَنفُسِكُمْ ۖ وَإِنْ أَسَأْتُمْ
فَلَهَا ۚ فَإِذَا جَآءَ وَعْدُ ٱلْـَٔاخِرَةِ لِيَسُـۥٓـُٔوا۟
وُجُوهَكُمْ وَلِيَدْخُلُوا۟ ٱلْمَسْجِدَ كَمَا دَخَلُوهُ أَوَّلَ
مَرَّةٍ وَلِيُتَبِّرُوا۟ مَا عَلَوْا۟ تَتْبِيرًا

7 If you work righteousness, you work righteousness for yourselves; and if you commit evil, you do so against yourselves. Then, when the second promise comes true, they will make your faces filled with sorrow, and enter the Temple as they entered it the first time, and utterly destroy all that falls into their power.

٨ عَسَىٰ رَبُّكُمْ أَن يَرْحَمَكُمْ ۚ وَإِنْ عُدتُّمْ عُدْنَا ۘ
وَجَعَلْنَا جَهَنَّمَ لِلْكَٰفِرِينَ حَصِيرًا

8 Perhaps your Lord will have mercy on you. But if you revert, We will revert. We have made Hell a prison for the disbelievers.

٩ إِنَّ هَٰذَا ٱلْقُرْءَانَ يَهْدِى لِلَّتِى هِىَ أَقْوَمُ
وَيُبَشِّرُ ٱلْمُؤْمِنِينَ ٱلَّذِينَ يَعْمَلُونَ ٱلصَّٰلِحَٰتِ أَنَّ
لَهُمْ أَجْرًا كَبِيرًا

9 This Quran guides to what is most upright; and it gives good news to the believers who do good deeds, that they will have a great reward.

١٠ وَأَنَّ ٱلَّذِينَ لَا يُؤْمِنُونَ بِٱلْـَٔاخِرَةِ أَعْتَدْنَا
لَهُمْ عَذَابًا أَلِيمًا

10 And those who do not believe in the Hereafter—We have prepared for them a painful punishment.

١١ وَيَدْعُ ٱلْإِنسَٰنُ بِٱلشَّرِّ دُعَآءَهُۥ بِٱلْخَيْرِ ۖ وَكَانَ
ٱلْإِنسَٰنُ عَجُولًا

11 The human being prays for evil as he prays for good. The human being is very hasty.

١٢ وَجَعَلْنَا ٱلَّيْلَ وَٱلنَّهَارَ ءَايَتَيْنِ ۖ فَمَحَوْنَآ ءَايَةَ
ٱلَّيْلِ وَجَعَلْنَآ ءَايَةَ ٱلنَّهَارِ مُبْصِرَةً لِّتَبْتَغُوا۟ فَضْلًا
مِّن رَّبِّكُمْ وَلِتَعْلَمُوا۟ عَدَدَ ٱلسِّنِينَ وَٱلْحِسَابَ ۚ
وَكُلَّ شَىْءٍ فَصَّلْنَٰهُ تَفْصِيلًا

12 We have made the night and the day two wonders. We erased the wonder of the night, and made the wonder of the day revealing, that you may seek bounty from your Lord, and know the number of years, and the calculation. We have explained all things in detail.

١٣ وَكُلَّ إِنسَٰنٍ أَلْزَمْنَٰهُ طَٰٓئِرَهُۥ فِى عُنُقِهِۦ ۖ
وَنُخْرِجُ لَهُۥ يَوْمَ ٱلْقِيَٰمَةِ كِتَٰبًا يَلْقَىٰهُ مَنشُورًا

13 For every person We have attached his fate to his neck. And on the Day of Resurrection, We will bring out for him a book which he will find spread open.

١٤ ٱقْرَأْ كِتَٰبَكَ كَفَىٰ بِنَفْسِكَ ٱلْيَوْمَ عَلَيْكَ
حَسِيبًا

14 "Read your book; today there will be none but yourself to call you to account."

١٥ مَّنِ ٱهْتَدَىٰ فَإِنَّمَا يَهْتَدِى لِنَفْسِهِۦ ۖ وَمَن ضَلَّ
فَإِنَّمَا يَضِلُّ عَلَيْهَا ۚ وَلَا تَزِرُ وَازِرَةٌ وِزْرَ أُخْرَىٰ ۗ
وَمَا كُنَّا مُعَذِّبِينَ حَتَّىٰ نَبْعَثَ رَسُولًا

15 Whoever is guided—is guided for his own good. And whoever goes astray—goes astray to his detriment. No burdened soul carries the burdens of another, nor do We ever punish until We have sent a messenger.

١٦ وَإِذَآ أَرَدْنَآ أَن نُّهْلِكَ قَرْيَةً أَمَرْنَا مُتْرَفِيهَا
فَفَسَقُوا۟ فِيهَا فَحَقَّ عَلَيْهَا ٱلْقَوْلُ فَدَمَّرْنَٰهَا
تَدْمِيرًا

16 When We decide to destroy a town, We command its affluent ones, they transgress in it, so the word becomes justified against it, and We destroy it completely.

١٧ وَكَمْ أَهْلَكْنَا مِنَ ٱلْقُرُونِ مِنۢ بَعْدِ نُوحٍ ۗ وَكَفَىٰ
بِرَبِّكَ بِذُنُوبِ عِبَادِهِۦ خَبِيرًۢا بَصِيرًا

17 How many generations have We destroyed after Noah? Your Lord is sufficient as Knower and Beholder of the sins of his servants.

١٨ مَّن كَانَ يُرِيدُ ٱلْعَاجِلَةَ عَجَّلْنَا لَهُۥ فِيهَا مَا
نَشَآءُ لِمَن نُّرِيدُ ثُمَّ جَعَلْنَا لَهُۥ جَهَنَّمَ يَصْلَىٰهَا
مَذْمُومًا مَّدْحُورًا

18 Whoever desires the fleeting life, We expedite for him what We decide to give him, to whomever We desire. Then We consign him to Hell, where he will roast, condemned and defeated.

١٩ وَمَنْ أَرَادَ ٱلْءَاخِرَةَ وَسَعَىٰ لَهَا سَعْيَهَا وَهُوَ
مُؤْمِنٌ فَأُو۟لَٰٓئِكَ كَانَ سَعْيُهُم مَّشْكُورًا

19 But whoever desires the Hereafter, and pursues it as it should be pursued, while he is a believer; these—their effort will be appreciated.

٢٠ كُلًّا نُّمِدُّ هَٰٓؤُلَآءِ وَهَٰٓؤُلَآءِ مِنْ عَطَآءِ رَبِّكَ ۚ وَمَا
كَانَ عَطَآءُ رَبِّكَ مَحْظُورًا

20 To all—these and those—We extend from the gifts of your Lord. The gifts of your Lord are not restricted.

٢١ ٱنظُرْ كَيْفَ فَضَّلْنَا بَعْضَهُمْ عَلَىٰ بَعْضٍ ۚ
وَلَلْءَاخِرَةُ أَكْبَرُ دَرَجَٰتٍ وَأَكْبَرُ تَفْضِيلًا

21 See how We have favored some of them over others; yet the Hereafter is greater in ranks, and greater in favors.

٢٢ لَّا تَجْعَلْ مَعَ ٱللَّهِ إِلَٰهًا ءَاخَرَ فَتَقْعُدَ مَذْمُومًا
مَّخْذُولًا

22 Do not set up another god with Allah, lest you become condemned and damned.

٢٣ وَقَضَىٰ رَبُّكَ أَلَّا تَعۡبُدُوٓاْ إِلَّآ إِيَّاهُ وَبِٱلۡوَٰلِدَيۡنِ
إِحۡسَٰنًاۚ إِمَّا يَبۡلُغَنَّ عِندَكَ ٱلۡكِبَرَ أَحَدُهُمَآ أَوۡ
كِلَاهُمَا فَلَا تَقُل لَّهُمَآ أُفّٖ وَلَا تَنۡهَرۡهُمَا وَقُل لَّهُمَا
قَوۡلٗا كَرِيمٗا

23 Your Lord has commanded that you worship none but Him, and that you be good to your parents. If either of them or both of them reach old age with you, do not say to them a word of disrespect, nor scold them, but say to them kind words.

٢٤ وَٱخۡفِضۡ لَهُمَا جَنَاحَ ٱلذُّلِّ مِنَ ٱلرَّحۡمَةِ وَقُل
رَّبِّ ٱرۡحَمۡهُمَا كَمَا رَبَّيَانِي صَغِيرٗا

24 And lower to them the wing of humility, out of mercy, and say, “My Lord, have mercy on them, as they raised me when I was a child.”

٢٥ رَّبُّكُمۡ أَعۡلَمُ بِمَا فِي نُفُوسِكُمۡۚ إِن تَكُونُواْ
صَٰلِحِينَ فَإِنَّهُۥ كَانَ لِلۡأَوَّٰبِينَ غَفُورٗا

25 Your Lord knows best what is in your minds. If you are righteous—He is Forgiving to the obedient.

٢٦ وَءَاتِ ذَا ٱلۡقُرۡبَىٰ حَقَّهُۥ وَٱلۡمِسۡكِينَ وَٱبۡنَ
ٱلسَّبِيلِ وَلَا تُبَذِّرۡ تَبۡذِيرًا

26 And give the relative his rights, and the poor, and the wayfarer, and do not squander wastefully.

٢٧ إِنَّ ٱلۡمُبَذِّرِينَ كَانُوٓاْ إِخۡوَٰنَ ٱلشَّيَٰطِينِۖ وَكَانَ
ٱلشَّيۡطَٰنُ لِرَبِّهِۦ كَفُورٗا

27 The extravagant are brethren of the devils, and the devil is ever ungrateful to his Lord.

٢٨ وَإِمَّا تُعۡرِضَنَّ عَنۡهُمُ ٱبۡتِغَآءَ رَحۡمَةٖ مِّن رَّبِّكَ
تَرۡجُوهَا فَقُل لَّهُمۡ قَوۡلٗا مَّيۡسُورٗا

28 But if you turn away from them, seeking mercy from your Lord which you hope for, then say to them words of comfort.

٢٩ وَلَا تَجۡعَلۡ يَدَكَ مَغۡلُولَةً إِلَىٰ عُنُقِكَ وَلَا
تَبۡسُطۡهَا كُلَّ ٱلۡبَسۡطِ فَتَقۡعُدَ مَلُومٗا مَّحۡسُورًا

29 And do not keep your hand tied to your neck, nor spread it out fully, lest you end up liable and regretful.

٣٠ إِنَّ رَبَّكَ يَبۡسُطُ ٱلرِّزۡقَ لِمَن يَشَآءُ وَيَقۡدِرُۚ إِنَّهُۥ
كَانَ بِعِبَادِهِۦ خَبِيرَۢا بَصِيرٗا

30 Your Lord expands the provision for whomever He wills, and restricts it. He is fully Informed, Observant of His servants.

٣١ وَلَا تَقۡتُلُوٓاْ أَوۡلَٰدَكُمۡ خَشۡيَةَ إِمۡلَٰقٖۖ نَّحۡنُ
نَرۡزُقُهُمۡ وَإِيَّاكُمۡۚ إِنَّ قَتۡلَهُمۡ كَانَ خِطۡـٔٗا كَبِيرٗا

31 And do not kill your children for fear of poverty. We provide for them, and for you. Killing them is a grave sin.

٣٢ وَلَا تَقۡرَبُواْ ٱلزِّنَىٰٓۖ إِنَّهُۥ كَانَ فَٰحِشَةٗ وَسَآءَ
سَبِيلٗا

32 And do not come near adultery. It is immoral, and an evil way.

٣٣ وَلَا تَقْتُلُوا۟ ٱلنَّفْسَ ٱلَّتِى حَرَّمَ ٱللَّهُ إِلَّا بِٱلْحَقِّ ۗ
وَمَن قُتِلَ مَظْلُومًا فَقَدْ جَعَلْنَا لِوَلِيِّهِۦ سُلْطَـٰنًا
فَلَا يُسْرِف فِّى ٱلْقَتْلِ ۖ إِنَّهُۥ كَانَ مَنصُورًا

33 And do not kill the soul which Allah has made sacred, except in the course of justice. If someone is killed unjustly, We have given his next of kin certain authority. But he should not be excessive in killing, for he will be supported.

٣٤ وَلَا تَقْرَبُوا۟ مَالَ ٱلْيَتِيمِ إِلَّا بِٱلَّتِى هِىَ أَحْسَنُ
حَتَّىٰ يَبْلُغَ أَشُدَّهُۥ ۚ وَأَوْفُوا۟ بِٱلْعَهْدِ ۖ إِنَّ ٱلْعَهْدَ كَانَ
مَسْـُٔولًا

34 And do not go near the orphan's property, except with the best of intentions, until he has reached his maturity. And honor your pledge, because the pledge involves responsibility.

٣٥ وَأَوْفُوا۟ ٱلْكَيْلَ إِذَا كِلْتُمْ وَزِنُوا۟ بِٱلْقِسْطَاسِ
ٱلْمُسْتَقِيمِ ۚ ذَٰلِكَ خَيْرٌ وَأَحْسَنُ تَأْوِيلًا

35 And give full measure when you measure, and weigh with accurate scales. That is fair, and the best determination.

٣٦ وَلَا تَقْفُ مَا لَيْسَ لَكَ بِهِۦ عِلْمٌ ۚ إِنَّ ٱلسَّمْعَ
وَٱلْبَصَرَ وَٱلْفُؤَادَ كُلُّ أُو۟لَـٰٓئِكَ كَانَ عَنْهُ مَسْـُٔولًا

36 And do not occupy yourself with what you have no knowledge of. The hearing, and the sight, and the brains—all these will be questioned.

٣٧ وَلَا تَمْشِ فِى ٱلْأَرْضِ مَرَحًا ۖ إِنَّكَ لَن تَخْرِقَ
ٱلْأَرْضَ وَلَن تَبْلُغَ ٱلْجِبَالَ طُولًا

37 And do not walk proudly on earth. You can neither pierce the earth, nor can you match the mountains in height.

٣٨ كُلُّ ذَٰلِكَ كَانَ سَيِّئُهُۥ عِندَ رَبِّكَ مَكْرُوهًا

38 The evil of all these is disliked by your Lord.

٣٩ ذَٰلِكَ مِمَّآ أَوْحَىٰٓ إِلَيْكَ رَبُّكَ مِنَ ٱلْحِكْمَةِ ۗ وَلَا
تَجْعَلْ مَعَ ٱللَّهِ إِلَـٰهًا ءَاخَرَ فَتُلْقَىٰ فِى جَهَنَّمَ
مَلُومًا مَّدْحُورًا

39 That is some of the wisdom your Lord has revealed to you. Do not set up with Allah another god, or else you will be thrown in Hell, rebuked and banished.

٤٠ أَفَأَصْفَىٰكُمْ رَبُّكُم بِٱلْبَنِينَ وَٱتَّخَذَ مِنَ ٱلْمَلَـٰٓئِكَةِ
إِنَـٰثًا ۚ إِنَّكُمْ لَتَقُولُونَ قَوْلًا عَظِيمًا

40 Has your Lord favored you with sons, while choosing for Himself daughters from among the angels? You are indeed saying a terrible thing.

٤١ وَلَقَدْ صَرَّفْنَا فِى هَـٰذَا ٱلْقُرْءَانِ لِيَذَّكَّرُوا۟ وَمَا
يَزِيدُهُمْ إِلَّا نُفُورًا

41 We have explained in this Quran in various ways, that they may remember, but it only adds to their rebellion.

٤٢ قُل لَّوْ كَانَ مَعَهُۥٓ ءَالِهَةٌ كَمَا يَقُولُونَ إِذًا
لَّٱبْتَغَوْا۟ إِلَىٰ ذِى ٱلْعَرْشِ سَبِيلًا

42 Say, “If there were other gods with Him, as they say, they would have sought a way to the Lord of the Throne.”

٤٣ سُبْحَٰنَهُۥ وَتَعَٰلَىٰ عَمَّا يَقُولُونَ عُلُوًّا كَبِيرًا

43 Be He glorified. He is exalted, far above what they say.

٤٤ تُسَبِّحُ لَهُ ٱلسَّمَٰوَٰتُ ٱلسَّبْعُ وَٱلْأَرْضُ وَمَن
فِيهِنَّ ۚ وَإِن مِّن شَىْءٍ إِلَّا يُسَبِّحُ بِحَمْدِهِۦ وَلَٰكِن
لَّا تَفْقَهُونَ تَسْبِيحَهُمْ ۗ إِنَّهُۥ كَانَ حَلِيمًا غَفُورًا

44 Praising Him are the seven heavens, and the earth, and everyone in them. There is not a thing that does not glorify Him with praise, but you do not understand their praises. He is indeed Forbearing and Forgiving.

٤٥ وَإِذَا قَرَأْتَ ٱلْقُرْءَانَ جَعَلْنَا بَيْنَكَ وَبَيْنَ
ٱلَّذِينَ لَا يُؤْمِنُونَ بِٱلْءَاخِرَةِ حِجَابًا مَّسْتُورًا

45 When you read the Quran, We place between you and those who do not believe in the Hereafter an invisible barrier.

٤٦ وَجَعَلْنَا عَلَىٰ قُلُوبِهِمْ أَكِنَّةً أَن يَفْقَهُوهُ وَفِىٓ
ءَاذَانِهِمْ وَقْرًا ۚ وَإِذَا ذَكَرْتَ رَبَّكَ فِى ٱلْقُرْءَانِ
وَحْدَهُۥ وَلَّوْا۟ عَلَىٰٓ أَدْبَٰرِهِمْ نُفُورًا

46 And We drape veils over their hearts, preventing them from understanding it, and heaviness in their ears. And when you mention your Lord alone in the Quran, they turn their backs in aversion.

٤٧ نَّحْنُ أَعْلَمُ بِمَا يَسْتَمِعُونَ بِهِۦٓ إِذْ يَسْتَمِعُونَ
إِلَيْكَ وَإِذْ هُمْ نَجْوَىٰٓ إِذْ يَقُولُ ٱلظَّٰلِمُونَ إِن
تَتَّبِعُونَ إِلَّا رَجُلًا مَّسْحُورًا

47 We know well what they listen to, when they listen to you, as they conspire, when the wrongdoers say, “You only follow a man bewitched.”

٤٨ ٱنظُرْ كَيْفَ ضَرَبُوا۟ لَكَ ٱلْأَمْثَالَ فَضَلُّوا۟ فَلَا
يَسْتَطِيعُونَ سَبِيلًا

48 Note what they compared you to. They are lost, and unable to find a way.

٤٩ وَقَالُوٓا۟ أَءِذَا كُنَّا عِظَٰمًا وَرُفَٰتًا أَءِنَّا لَمَبْعُوثُونَ
خَلْقًا جَدِيدًا

49 And they say, “When we have become bones and fragments, shall we really be resurrected as a new creation?”

٥٠ قُلْ كُونُوا۟ حِجَارَةً أَوْ حَدِيدًا

50 Say, “Even if you become rocks or iron.

٥١ أَوْ خَلْقًا مِّمَّا يَكْبُرُ فِى صُدُورِكُمْ ۚ فَسَيَقُولُونَ
مَن يُعِيدُنَا ۖ قُلِ ٱلَّذِى فَطَرَكُمْ أَوَّلَ مَرَّةٍ ۚ

51 Or some substance, which, in your minds, is even harder.” Then they will say, “Who will restore us?” Say, “The One who originated you the

فَسَيُنْغِضُونَ إِلَيْكَ رُءُوسَهُمْ وَيَقُولُونَ مَتَىٰ
هُوَ ۖ قُلْ عَسَىٰٓ أَن يَكُونَ قَرِيبًا

first time." Then they will nod their heads at you, and say, "When will it be?" Say, "Perhaps it will be soon."

٥٢ يَوْمَ يَدْعُوكُمْ فَتَسْتَجِيبُونَ بِحَمْدِهِۦ
وَتَظُنُّونَ إِن لَّبِثْتُمْ إِلَّا قَلِيلًا

52 On the Day when He calls you, you will respond with His praise, and you will realize that you stayed only a little.

٥٣ وَقُل لِّعِبَادِى يَقُولُوا۟ ٱلَّتِى هِىَ أَحْسَنُ ۚ إِنَّ
ٱلشَّيْطَـٰنَ يَنزَغُ بَيْنَهُمْ ۚ إِنَّ ٱلشَّيْطَـٰنَ كَانَ لِلْإِنسَـٰنِ
عَدُوًّا مُّبِينًا

53 Tell My servants to say what is best. Satan sows discord among them. Satan is to man an open enemy.

٥٤ رَّبُّكُمْ أَعْلَمُ بِكُمْ ۖ إِن يَشَأْ يَرْحَمْكُمْ أَوْ إِن
يَشَأْ يُعَذِّبْكُمْ ۚ وَمَآ أَرْسَلْنَـٰكَ عَلَيْهِمْ وَكِيلًا

54 Your Lord knows you best. If He wills, He will have mercy on you; and if He wills, He will punish you. We did not send you as their advocate.

٥٥ وَرَبُّكَ أَعْلَمُ بِمَن فِى ٱلسَّمَـٰوَٰتِ وَٱلْأَرْضِ ۗ
وَلَقَدْ فَضَّلْنَا بَعْضَ ٱلنَّبِيِّـۧنَ عَلَىٰ بَعْضٍ ۖ
وَءَاتَيْنَا دَاوُۥدَ زَبُورًا

55 Your Lord knows well everyone in the heavens and the earth. We have given some prophets advantage over others; and to David We gave the Psalms.

٥٦ قُلِ ٱدْعُوا۟ ٱلَّذِينَ زَعَمْتُم مِّن دُونِهِۦ فَلَا
يَمْلِكُونَ كَشْفَ ٱلضُّرِّ عَنكُمْ وَلَا تَحْوِيلًا

56 Say, "Call upon those you claim besides Him. They have no power to relieve your adversity, nor can they change it."

٥٧ أُو۟لَـٰٓئِكَ ٱلَّذِينَ يَدْعُونَ يَبْتَغُونَ إِلَىٰ رَبِّهِمُ
ٱلْوَسِيلَةَ أَيُّهُمْ أَقْرَبُ وَيَرْجُونَ رَحْمَتَهُۥ
وَيَخَافُونَ عَذَابَهُۥٓ ۚ إِنَّ عَذَابَ رَبِّكَ كَانَ مَحْذُورًا

57 Those they call upon are themselves seeking means of access to their Lord, vying to be nearer, and hoping for His mercy, and fearing His punishment. The punishment of your Lord is to be dreaded.

٥٨ وَإِن مِّن قَرْيَةٍ إِلَّا نَحْنُ مُهْلِكُوهَا قَبْلَ يَوْمِ
ٱلْقِيَـٰمَةِ أَوْ مُعَذِّبُوهَا عَذَابًا شَدِيدًا ۚ كَانَ ذَٰلِكَ
فِى ٱلْكِتَـٰبِ مَسْطُورًا

58 There is no city but We will destroy before the Day of Resurrection, or punish it with a severe punishment. This is inscribed in the Book.

٥٩ وَمَا مَنَعَنَآ أَن نُّرْسِلَ بِٱلْـَٔايَـٰتِ إِلَّآ أَن كَذَّبَ
بِهَا ٱلْأَوَّلُونَ ۚ وَءَاتَيْنَا ثَمُودَ ٱلنَّاقَةَ مُبْصِرَةً
فَظَلَمُوا۟ بِهَا ۚ وَمَا نُرْسِلُ بِٱلْـَٔايَـٰتِ إِلَّا تَخْوِيفًا

59 Nothing prevents Us from sending miraculous signs, except that the ancients called them lies. We gave Thamood the she-camel, a visible

sign, but they mistreated her. We do not send the signs except to instill reverence.

٦٠ وَإِذْ قُلْنَا لَكَ إِنَّ رَبَّكَ أَحَاطَ بِٱلنَّاسِ ۚ وَمَا
جَعَلْنَا ٱلرُّءْيَا ٱلَّتِىٓ أَرَيْنَٰكَ إِلَّا فِتْنَةً لِّلنَّاسِ
وَٱلشَّجَرَةَ ٱلْمَلْعُونَةَ فِى ٱلْقُرْءَانِ ۚ وَنُخَوِّفُهُمْ
فَمَا يَزِيدُهُمْ إِلَّا طُغْيَٰنًا كَبِيرًا

60 We said to you that your Lord encompasses humanity. We did not make the vision We showed you, except as a test for the people, and the tree cursed in the Quran. We frighten them, but that only increases their defiance.

٦١ وَإِذْ قُلْنَا لِلْمَلَٰٓئِكَةِ ٱسْجُدُوا۟ لِءَادَمَ فَسَجَدُوٓا۟
إِلَّآ إِبْلِيسَ قَالَ ءَأَسْجُدُ لِمَنْ خَلَقْتَ طِينًا

61 When We said to the angels, “Bow down before Adam,” they bowed down, except for Satan. He said, “Shall I bow down before someone You created from mud?”

٦٢ قَالَ أَرَءَيْتَكَ هَٰذَا ٱلَّذِى كَرَّمْتَ عَلَىَّ لَئِنْ
أَخَّرْتَنِ إِلَىٰ يَوْمِ ٱلْقِيَٰمَةِ لَأَحْتَنِكَنَّ ذُرِّيَّتَهُۥٓ إِلَّا
قَلِيلًا

62 He said, “Do You see this one whom You have honored more than me? If You reprieve me until the Day of Resurrection, I will bring his descendants under my sway, except for a few.”

٦٣ قَالَ ٱذْهَبْ فَمَن تَبِعَكَ مِنْهُمْ فَإِنَّ جَهَنَّمَ
جَزَآؤُكُمْ جَزَآءً مَّوْفُورًا

63 He said, “Begone! Whoever of them follows you—Hell is your reward, an ample reward.”

٦٤ وَٱسْتَفْزِزْ مَنِ ٱسْتَطَعْتَ مِنْهُم بِصَوْتِكَ
وَأَجْلِبْ عَلَيْهِم بِخَيْلِكَ وَرَجِلِكَ وَشَارِكْهُمْ فِى
ٱلْأَمْوَٰلِ وَٱلْأَوْلَٰدِ وَعِدْهُمْ ۚ وَمَا يَعِدُهُمُ ٱلشَّيْطَٰنُ
إِلَّا غُرُورًا

64 “And entice whomever of them you can with your voice, and rally against them your cavalry and your infantry, and share with them in wealth and children, and make promises to them.” But Satan promises them nothing but delusion.

٦٥ إِنَّ عِبَادِى لَيْسَ لَكَ عَلَيْهِمْ سُلْطَٰنٌ ۚ وَكَفَىٰ
بِرَبِّكَ وَكِيلًا

65 “As for My devotees, you have no authority over them.” Your Lord is an adequate Guardian.

٦٦ رَّبُّكُمُ ٱلَّذِى يُزْجِى لَكُمُ ٱلْفُلْكَ فِى ٱلْبَحْرِ
لِتَبْتَغُوا۟ مِن فَضْلِهِۦٓ ۚ إِنَّهُۥ كَانَ بِكُمْ رَحِيمًا

66 Your Lord is He who propels for you the ships at sea, that you may seek of His bounty. He is towards you Most Merciful.

٦٧ وَإِذَا مَسَّكُمُ ٱلضُّرُّ فِى ٱلْبَحْرِ ضَلَّ مَن
تَدْعُونَ إِلَّآ إِيَّاهُ ۖ فَلَمَّا نَجَّىٰكُمْ إِلَى ٱلْبَرِّ
أَعْرَضْتُمْ ۚ وَكَانَ ٱلْإِنسَٰنُ كَفُورًا

67 When harm afflicts you at sea, those you pray to vanish, except for Him. But when He saves you to land, you turn away. The human being is ever thankless.

٦٨ أَفَأَمِنتُمْ أَن يَخْسِفَ بِكُمْ جَانِبَ ٱلْبَرِّ أَوْ
يُرْسِلَ عَلَيْكُمْ حَاصِبًا ثُمَّ لَا تَجِدُوا۟ لَكُمْ وَكِيلًا

68 Are you confident that He will not cause a track of land to cave in beneath you, or unleash a tornado against you, and then you find no protector?

٦٩ أَمْ أَمِنتُمْ أَن يُعِيدَكُمْ فِيهِ تَارَةً أُخْرَىٰ
فَيُرْسِلَ عَلَيْكُمْ قَاصِفًا مِّنَ ٱلرِّيحِ فَيُغْرِقَكُم بِمَا
كَفَرْتُمْ ۙ ثُمَّ لَا تَجِدُوا۟ لَكُمْ عَلَيْنَا بِهِۦ تَبِيعًا

69 Or are you confident that He will not return you to it once again, and unleash a hurricane against you, and drown you for your ingratitude? Then you will find no helper against Us.

٧٠ وَلَقَدْ كَرَّمْنَا بَنِىٓ ءَادَمَ وَحَمَلْنَٰهُمْ فِى ٱلْبَرِّ
وَٱلْبَحْرِ وَرَزَقْنَٰهُم مِّنَ ٱلطَّيِّبَٰتِ وَفَضَّلْنَٰهُمْ عَلَىٰ
كَثِيرٍ مِّمَّنْ خَلَقْنَا تَفْضِيلًا

70 We have honored the Children of Adam, and carried them on land and sea, and provided them with good things, and greatly favored them over many of those We created.

٧١ يَوْمَ نَدْعُوا۟ كُلَّ أُنَاسٍۭ بِإِمَٰمِهِمْ ۖ فَمَنْ أُوتِىَ
كِتَٰبَهُۥ بِيَمِينِهِۦ فَأُو۟لَٰٓئِكَ يَقْرَءُونَ كِتَٰبَهُمْ وَلَا
يُظْلَمُونَ فَتِيلًا

71 On the Day when We call every people with their leader. Whoever is given his record in his right hand—these will read their record, and they will not be wronged one bit.

٧٢ وَمَن كَانَ فِى هَٰذِهِۦٓ أَعْمَىٰ فَهُوَ فِى
ٱلْءَاخِرَةِ أَعْمَىٰ وَأَضَلُّ سَبِيلًا

72 But whoever is blind in this, he will be blind in the Hereafter, and further astray from the way.

٧٣ وَإِن كَادُوا۟ لَيَفْتِنُونَكَ عَنِ ٱلَّذِىٓ أَوْحَيْنَآ
إِلَيْكَ لِتَفْتَرِىَ عَلَيْنَا غَيْرَهُۥ ۖ وَإِذًا لَّٱتَّخَذُوكَ
خَلِيلًا

73 They almost lured you away from what We have revealed to you, so that you would invent something else in Our name. In that case, they would have taken you for a friend.

٧٤ وَلَوْلَآ أَن ثَبَّتْنَٰكَ لَقَدْ كِدتَّ تَرْكَنُ إِلَيْهِمْ شَيْـًٔا
قَلِيلًا

74 Had We not given you stability, you might have inclined towards them a little.

٧٥ إِذًا لَّأَذَقْنَٰكَ ضِعْفَ ٱلْحَيَوٰةِ وَضِعْفَ ٱلْمَمَاتِ
ثُمَّ لَا تَجِدُ لَكَ عَلَيْنَا نَصِيرًا

75 Then We would have made you taste double in life, and double at death; then you would have found for yourself no helper against Us.

٧٦ وَإِن كَادُوا۟ لَيَسْتَفِزُّونَكَ مِنَ ٱلْأَرْضِ
لِيُخْرِجُوكَ مِنْهَا ۖ وَإِذًا لَّا يَلْبَثُونَ خِلَٰفَكَ إِلَّا
قَلِيلًا

76 They almost provoked you, to expel you from the land. In that case, they would not have lasted after you, except briefly.

٧٧ سُنَّةَ مَن قَدْ أَرْسَلْنَا قَبْلَكَ مِن رُّسُلِنَا ۖ وَلَا
تَجِدُ لِسُنَّتِنَا تَحْوِيلًا

77 The tradition of the messengers We sent before you—you will find no change in Our rules.

٧٨ أَقِمِ ٱلصَّلَوٰةَ لِدُلُوكِ ٱلشَّمْسِ إِلَىٰ غَسَقِ ٱلَّيْلِ
وَقُرْءَانَ ٱلْفَجْرِ ۖ إِنَّ قُرْءَانَ ٱلْفَجْرِ كَانَ مَشْهُودًا

78 Perform the prayer at the decline of the sun, until the darkness of the night; and the Quran at dawn. The Quran at dawn is witnessed.

٧٩ وَمِنَ ٱلَّيْلِ فَتَهَجَّدْ بِهِۦ نَافِلَةً لَّكَ عَسَىٰٓ أَن
يَبْعَثَكَ رَبُّكَ مَقَامًا مَّحْمُودًا

79 And keep vigil with it during parts of the night, as an extra prayer. Perhaps your Lord will raise you to a laudable position.

٨٠ وَقُل رَّبِّ أَدْخِلْنِى مُدْخَلَ صِدْقٍ وَأَخْرِجْنِى
مُخْرَجَ صِدْقٍ وَٱجْعَل لِّى مِن لَّدُنكَ سُلْطَٰنًا
نَّصِيرًا

80 And say, “My Lord, lead me in through an entry of truth, and lead me out through an exit of truth, and grant me from You a supporting power.”

٨١ وَقُلْ جَآءَ ٱلْحَقُّ وَزَهَقَ ٱلْبَٰطِلُ ۚ إِنَّ ٱلْبَٰطِلَ
كَانَ زَهُوقًا

81 And say, “The truth has come, and falsehood has withered away; for falsehood is bound to wither away.”

٨٢ وَنُنَزِّلُ مِنَ ٱلْقُرْءَانِ مَا هُوَ شِفَآءٌ وَرَحْمَةٌ
لِّلْمُؤْمِنِينَ ۙ وَلَا يَزِيدُ ٱلظَّٰلِمِينَ إِلَّا خَسَارًا

82 We send down in the Quran healing and mercy for the believers, but it increases the wrongdoers only in loss.

٨٣ وَإِذَآ أَنْعَمْنَا عَلَى ٱلْإِنسَٰنِ أَعْرَضَ وَنَـَٔا
بِجَانِبِهِۦ ۖ وَإِذَا مَسَّهُ ٱلشَّرُّ كَانَ يَـُٔوسًا

83 When We bless the human being, he turns away and distances himself. But when adversity touches him, he is in despair.

٨٤ قُلْ كُلٌّ يَعْمَلُ عَلَىٰ شَاكِلَتِهِۦ فَرَبُّكُمْ أَعْلَمُ
بِمَنْ هُوَ أَهْدَىٰ سَبِيلًا

84 Say, “Each does according to his disposition. Your Lord knows best who is better guided in the way.”

٨٥ وَيَسْـَٔلُونَكَ عَنِ ٱلرُّوحِ ۖ قُلِ ٱلرُّوحُ مِنْ أَمْرِ
رَبِّى وَمَآ أُوتِيتُم مِّنَ ٱلْعِلْمِ إِلَّا قَلِيلًا

85 And they ask you about the Spirit. Say, “The Spirit belongs to the domain of my Lord; and you were given only little knowledge.”

86 If We willed, We could take away what We revealed to you. Then you will find for yourself no protecting guardian against Us.

٨٦ وَلَئِن شِئْنَا لَنَذْهَبَنَّ بِٱلَّذِىٓ أَوْحَيْنَآ إِلَيْكَ ثُمَّ
لَا تَجِدُ لَكَ بِهِۦ عَلَيْنَا وَكِيلًا

87 Except through a mercy from your Lord. His favors upon you have been great.

٨٧ إِلَّا رَحْمَةً مِّن رَّبِّكَ ۚ إِنَّ فَضْلَهُۥ كَانَ عَلَيْكَ
كَبِيرًا

88 Say, "If mankind and jinn came together to produce the like of this Quran, they could never produce the like of it, even if they backed up one another."

٨٨ قُل لَّئِنِ ٱجْتَمَعَتِ ٱلْإِنسُ وَٱلْجِنُّ عَلَىٰٓ أَن
يَأْتُوا۟ بِمِثْلِ هَٰذَا ٱلْقُرْءَانِ لَا يَأْتُونَ بِمِثْلِهِۦ وَلَوْ
كَانَ بَعْضُهُمْ لِبَعْضٍ ظَهِيرًا

89 We have displayed for mankind in this Quran every kind of similitude, but most people insist on denying the truth.

٨٩ وَلَقَدْ صَرَّفْنَا لِلنَّاسِ فِى هَٰذَا ٱلْقُرْءَانِ مِن
كُلِّ مَثَلٍ فَأَبَىٰٓ أَكْثَرُ ٱلنَّاسِ إِلَّا كُفُورًا

90 And they said, "We will not believe in you unless you make a spring burst from the ground for us.

٩٠ وَقَالُوا۟ لَن نُّؤْمِنَ لَكَ حَتَّىٰ تَفْجُرَ لَنَا مِنَ
ٱلْأَرْضِ يَنۢبُوعًا

91 Or you have a garden of palms and vines; then cause rivers to gush pouring through them.

٩١ أَوْ تَكُونَ لَكَ جَنَّةٌ مِّن نَّخِيلٍ وَعِنَبٍ فَتُفَجِّرَ
ٱلْأَنْهَٰرَ خِلَٰلَهَا تَفْجِيرًا

92 Or make the sky fall on us in pieces, as you claim, or bring Allah and the angels before us.

٩٢ أَوْ تُسْقِطَ ٱلسَّمَآءَ كَمَا زَعَمْتَ عَلَيْنَا كِسَفًا أَوْ
تَأْتِىَ بِٱللَّهِ وَٱلْمَلَٰٓئِكَةِ قَبِيلًا

93 Or you possess a house of gold. Or you ascend into the sky. Even then, we will not believe in your ascension, unless you bring down for us a book that we can read." Say, "Glory be to my Lord. Am I anything but a human messenger?"

٩٣ أَوْ يَكُونَ لَكَ بَيْتٌ مِّن زُخْرُفٍ أَوْ تَرْقَىٰ فِى
ٱلسَّمَآءِ وَلَن نُّؤْمِنَ لِرُقِيِّكَ حَتَّىٰ تُنَزِّلَ عَلَيْنَا
كِتَٰبًا نَّقْرَؤُهُۥ ۗ قُلْ سُبْحَانَ رَبِّى هَلْ كُنتُ إِلَّا
بَشَرًا رَّسُولًا

94 Nothing prevented the people from believing, when guidance has come to them, except that they said, "Did Allah send a human messenger?"

٩٤ وَمَا مَنَعَ ٱلنَّاسَ أَن يُؤْمِنُوٓا۟ إِذْ جَآءَهُمُ
ٱلْهُدَىٰٓ إِلَّآ أَن قَالُوٓا۟ أَبَعَثَ ٱللَّهُ بَشَرًا رَّسُولًا

95 Say, "If there were angels on earth, walking around in peace, We would have sent down to them from heaven an angel messenger."

٩٥ قُل لَّوْ كَانَ فِى ٱلْأَرْضِ مَلَٰٓئِكَةٌ يَمْشُونَ
مُطْمَئِنِّينَ لَنَزَّلْنَا عَلَيْهِم مِّنَ ٱلسَّمَآءِ مَلَكًا رَّسُولًا

٩٦ قُلْ كَفَىٰ بِٱللَّهِ شَهِيدًۢا بَيْنِى وَبَيْنَكُمْ ۚ إِنَّهُۥ
كَانَ بِعِبَادِهِۦ خَبِيرًۢا بَصِيرًا

96 Say, "Allah is enough witness between you and me. He is fully aware of His servants, and He sees them well."

٩٧ وَمَن يَهْدِ ٱللَّهُ فَهُوَ ٱلْمُهْتَدِ ۖ وَمَن يُضْلِلْ فَلَن
تَجِدَ لَهُمْ أَوْلِيَآءَ مِن دُونِهِۦ ۖ وَنَحْشُرُهُمْ يَوْمَ
ٱلْقِيَٰمَةِ عَلَىٰ وُجُوهِهِمْ عُمْيًا وَبُكْمًا وَصُمًّا ۖ
مَّأْوَىٰهُمْ جَهَنَّمُ ۖ كُلَّمَا خَبَتْ زِدْنَٰهُمْ سَعِيرًا

97 Whomever Allah guides is the guided one. And whomever He leaves astray—for them you will find no protectors apart from Him. And We will gather them on the Day of Resurrection, on their faces, blind, dumb, and deaf. Their abode is Hell; whenever it abates, We intensify the blaze for them.

٩٨ ذَٰلِكَ جَزَآؤُهُم بِأَنَّهُمْ كَفَرُوا۟ بِـَٔايَٰتِنَا وَقَالُوٓا۟
أَءِذَا كُنَّا عِظَٰمًا وَرُفَٰتًا أَءِنَّا لَمَبْعُوثُونَ خَلْقًا
جَدِيدًا

98 This is their repayment for having blasphemed against Our revelations, and having said, "Shall we, when we have become bones and fragments, be resurrected as a new creation?"

٩٩ أَوَلَمْ يَرَوْا۟ أَنَّ ٱللَّهَ ٱلَّذِى خَلَقَ ٱلسَّمَٰوَٰتِ
وَٱلْأَرْضَ قَادِرٌ عَلَىٰٓ أَن يَخْلُقَ مِثْلَهُمْ وَجَعَلَ
لَهُمْ أَجَلًا لَّا رَيْبَ فِيهِ فَأَبَى ٱلظَّٰلِمُونَ إِلَّا كُفُورًا

99 Do they not consider that Allah, Who created the heavens and the earth, is Able to create the likes of them? He has assigned for them a term, in which there is no doubt. But the wrongdoers persist in denying the truth.

١٠٠ قُل لَّوْ أَنتُمْ تَمْلِكُونَ خَزَآئِنَ رَحْمَةِ رَبِّىٓ إِذًا
لَّأَمْسَكْتُمْ خَشْيَةَ ٱلْإِنفَاقِ ۚ وَكَانَ ٱلْإِنسَٰنُ قَتُورًا

100 Say, "If you possessed the treasuries of my Lord's mercy, you would have withheld them for fear of spending." The human being has always been stingy.

١٠١ وَلَقَدْ ءَاتَيْنَا مُوسَىٰ تِسْعَ ءَايَٰتٍۭ بَيِّنَٰتٍ ۖ
فَسْـَٔلْ بَنِىٓ إِسْرَٰٓءِيلَ إِذْ جَآءَهُمْ فَقَالَ لَهُۥ
فِرْعَوْنُ إِنِّى لَأَظُنُّكَ يَٰمُوسَىٰ مَسْحُورًا

101 We gave Moses nine clear signs—ask the Children of Israel. When he went to them, Pharaoh said to him, "I think that you, Moses, are bewitched."

١٠٢ قَالَ لَقَدْ عَلِمْتَ مَآ أَنزَلَ هَٰٓؤُلَآءِ إِلَّا رَبُّ
ٱلسَّمَٰوَٰتِ وَٱلْأَرْضِ بَصَآئِرَ وَإِنِّى لَأَظُنُّكَ
يَٰفِرْعَوْنُ مَثْبُورًا

102 He said, "You know that none sent these down except the Lord of the heavens and the earth—eye openers; and I think that you, Pharaoh, are doomed."

١٠٣ فَأَرَادَ أَن يَسْتَفِزَّهُم مِّنَ ٱلْأَرْضِ فَأَغْرَقْنَٰهُ
وَمَن مَّعَهُۥ جَمِيعًا

103 He resolved to scare them off the land, but We drowned him, and those with him, altogether.

١٠٤ وَقُلْنَا مِنۢ بَعْدِهِۦ لِبَنِىٓ إِسْرَٰٓءِيلَ ٱسْكُنُوا۟
ٱلْأَرْضَ فَإِذَا جَآءَ وَعْدُ ٱلْـَٔاخِرَةِ جِئْنَا بِكُمْ
لَفِيفًا

104 After him, We said to the Children of Israel, "Inhabit the land, and when the promise of the Hereafter arrives, We will bring you all together."

١٠٥ وَبِٱلْحَقِّ أَنزَلْنَٰهُ وَبِٱلْحَقِّ نَزَلَ ۗ وَمَآ أَرْسَلْنَٰكَ
إِلَّا مُبَشِّرًا وَنَذِيرًا

105 With the truth We sent it down, and with the truth it descended. We sent you only as a bearer of good news and a warner.

١٠٦ وَقُرْءَانًا فَرَقْنَٰهُ لِتَقْرَأَهُۥ عَلَى ٱلنَّاسِ عَلَىٰ
مُكْثٍ وَنَزَّلْنَٰهُ تَنزِيلًا

106 A Quran which We unfolded gradually, that you may recite to the people over time. And We revealed it in stages.

١٠٧ قُلْ ءَامِنُوا۟ بِهِۦٓ أَوْ لَا تُؤْمِنُوٓا۟ ۚ إِنَّ ٱلَّذِينَ
أُوتُوا۟ ٱلْعِلْمَ مِن قَبْلِهِۦٓ إِذَا يُتْلَىٰ عَلَيْهِمْ يَخِرُّونَ
لِلْأَذْقَانِ سُجَّدًا

107 Say, "Believe in it, or do not believe." Those who were given knowledge before it, when it is recited to them, they fall to their chins, prostrating.

١٠٨ وَيَقُولُونَ سُبْحَٰنَ رَبِّنَآ إِن كَانَ وَعْدُ رَبِّنَا
لَمَفْعُولًا

108 And they say, "Glory to our Lord. The promise of our Lord is fulfilled."

١٠٩ وَيَخِرُّونَ لِلْأَذْقَانِ يَبْكُونَ وَيَزِيدُهُمْ
خُشُوعًا ۩

109 And they fall to their chins, weeping, and it adds to their humility.

١١٠ قُلِ ٱدْعُوا۟ ٱللَّهَ أَوِ ٱدْعُوا۟ ٱلرَّحْمَٰنَ ۖ أَيًّا مَّا
تَدْعُوا۟ فَلَهُ ٱلْأَسْمَآءُ ٱلْحُسْنَىٰ ۚ وَلَا تَجْهَرْ
بِصَلَاتِكَ وَلَا تُخَافِتْ بِهَا وَٱبْتَغِ بَيْنَ ذَٰلِكَ سَبِيلًا

110 Say, "Call Him Allah, or call Him the Most Merciful. Whichever name you use, to Him belong the Best Names." And be neither loud in your prayer, nor silent in it, but follow a course in between.

١١١ وَقُلِ ٱلْحَمْدُ لِلَّهِ ٱلَّذِى لَمْ يَتَّخِذْ وَلَدًا وَلَمْ
يَكُن لَّهُۥ شَرِيكٌ فِى ٱلْمُلْكِ وَلَمْ يَكُن لَّهُۥ وَلِىٌّ مِّنَ
ٱلذُّلِّ ۖ وَكَبِّرْهُ تَكْبِيرًۢا

111 And say, "Praise be to Allah, who has not begotten a son, nor has He a partner in sovereignty, nor has He an ally out of weakness, and glorify Him constantly."

18 The Cave الكهف

بِسْمِ ٱللَّهِ ٱلرَّحْمَٰنِ ٱلرَّحِيمِ	In the name of Allah, the Gracious, the Merciful.
١ ٱلْحَمْدُ لِلَّهِ ٱلَّذِىٓ أَنزَلَ عَلَىٰ عَبْدِهِ ٱلْكِتَٰبَ وَلَمْ يَجْعَل لَّهُۥ عِوَجَا ۜ	1 Praise be to Allah, who revealed the Book to His servant, and allowed in it no distortion.
٢ قَيِّمًا لِّيُنذِرَ بَأْسًا شَدِيدًا مِّن لَّدُنْهُ وَيُبَشِّرَ ٱلْمُؤْمِنِينَ ٱلَّذِينَ يَعْمَلُونَ ٱلصَّٰلِحَٰتِ أَنَّ لَهُمْ أَجْرًا حَسَنًا	2 Valuable—to warn of severe punishment from Himself; and to deliver good news to the believers who do righteous deeds, that they will have an excellent reward.
٣ مَّٰكِثِينَ فِيهِ أَبَدًا	3 In which they will abide forever.
٤ وَيُنذِرَ ٱلَّذِينَ قَالُوا۟ ٱتَّخَذَ ٱللَّهُ وَلَدًا	4 And to warn those who say, “Allah has begotten a son.”
٥ مَّا لَهُم بِهِۦ مِنْ عِلْمٍ وَلَا لِءَابَآئِهِمْ ۚ كَبُرَتْ كَلِمَةً تَخْرُجُ مِنْ أَفْوَٰهِهِمْ ۚ إِن يَقُولُونَ إِلَّا كَذِبًا	5 They have no knowledge of this, nor did their forefathers. Grave is the word that comes out of their mouths. They say nothing but a lie.
٦ فَلَعَلَّكَ بَٰخِعٌ نَّفْسَكَ عَلَىٰٓ ءَاثَٰرِهِمْ إِن لَّمْ يُؤْمِنُوا۟ بِهَٰذَا ٱلْحَدِيثِ أَسَفًا	6 Perhaps you may destroy yourself with grief, chasing after them, if they do not believe in this information.
٧ إِنَّا جَعَلْنَا مَا عَلَى ٱلْأَرْضِ زِينَةً لَّهَا لِنَبْلُوَهُمْ أَيُّهُمْ أَحْسَنُ عَمَلًا	7 We made what is upon the earth an ornament for it, to test them as to which of them is best in conduct.
٨ وَإِنَّا لَجَٰعِلُونَ مَا عَلَيْهَا صَعِيدًا جُرُزًا	8 And We will turn what is on it into barren waste.
٩ أَمْ حَسِبْتَ أَنَّ أَصْحَٰبَ ٱلْكَهْفِ وَٱلرَّقِيمِ كَانُوا۟ مِنْ ءَايَٰتِنَا عَجَبًا	9 Did you know that the People of the Cave and the Inscription were of Our wondrous signs?
١٠ إِذْ أَوَى ٱلْفِتْيَةُ إِلَى ٱلْكَهْفِ فَقَالُوا۟ رَبَّنَآ ءَاتِنَا مِن لَّدُنكَ رَحْمَةً وَهَيِّئْ لَنَا مِنْ أَمْرِنَا رَشَدًا	10 When the youths took shelter in the cave, they said, “Our Lord, give us mercy from Yourself, and bless our affair with guidance.”
١١ فَضَرَبْنَا عَلَىٰٓ ءَاذَانِهِمْ فِى ٱلْكَهْفِ سِنِينَ عَدَدًا	11 Then We sealed their ears in the cave for a number of years.

١٢ ثُمَّ بَعَثْنَٰهُمْ لِنَعْلَمَ أَىُّ ٱلْحِزْبَيْنِ أَحْصَىٰ لِمَا
لَبِثُوٓا۟ أَمَدًا

12 Then We awakened them to know which of the two groups could better calculate the length of their stay.

١٣ نَّحْنُ نَقُصُّ عَلَيْكَ نَبَأَهُم بِٱلْحَقِّ ۚ إِنَّهُمْ فِتْيَةٌ
ءَامَنُوا۟ بِرَبِّهِمْ وَزِدْنَٰهُمْ هُدًى

13 We relate to you their story in truth. They were youths who believed in their Lord, and We increased them in guidance.

١٤ وَرَبَطْنَا عَلَىٰ قُلُوبِهِمْ إِذْ قَامُوا۟ فَقَالُوا۟ رَبُّنَا
رَبُّ ٱلسَّمَٰوَٰتِ وَٱلْأَرْضِ لَن نَّدْعُوَا۟ مِن دُونِهِۦٓ
إِلَٰهًا ۖ لَّقَدْ قُلْنَآ إِذًا شَطَطًا

14 And We strengthened their hearts, when they stood up and said, “Our Lord is the Lord of the heavens and the earth; we will not call on any god besides Him, for then we would have spoken an outrage.”

١٥ هَٰٓؤُلَآءِ قَوْمُنَا ٱتَّخَذُوا۟ مِن دُونِهِۦٓ ءَالِهَةً ۖ لَّوْلَا
يَأْتُونَ عَلَيْهِم بِسُلْطَٰنٍۭ بَيِّنٍ ۖ فَمَنْ أَظْلَمُ مِمَّنِ
ٱفْتَرَىٰ عَلَى ٱللَّهِ كَذِبًا

15 “These people, our people, have taken to themselves gods other than Him. Why do they not bring a clear proof concerning them? Who, then, does greater wrong than he who invents lies and attributes them to Allah?”

١٦ وَإِذِ ٱعْتَزَلْتُمُوهُمْ وَمَا يَعْبُدُونَ إِلَّا ٱللَّهَ فَأْوُۥٓا۟
إِلَى ٱلْكَهْفِ يَنشُرْ لَكُمْ رَبُّكُم مِّن رَّحْمَتِهِۦ
وَيُهَيِّئْ لَكُم مِّنْ أَمْرِكُم مِّرْفَقًا

16 “Now that you have withdrawn from them, and from what they worship besides Allah, take shelter in the cave. And your Lord will unfold His mercy for you, and will set your affair towards ease.”

١٧ وَتَرَى ٱلشَّمْسَ إِذَا طَلَعَت تَّزَٰوَرُ عَن كَهْفِهِمْ
ذَاتَ ٱلْيَمِينِ وَإِذَا غَرَبَت تَّقْرِضُهُمْ ذَاتَ ٱلشِّمَالِ
وَهُمْ فِى فَجْوَةٍ مِّنْهُ ۚ ذَٰلِكَ مِنْ ءَايَٰتِ ٱللَّهِ ۗ مَن
يَهْدِ ٱللَّهُ فَهُوَ ٱلْمُهْتَدِ ۖ وَمَن يُضْلِلْ فَلَن تَجِدَ لَهُۥ
وَلِيًّا مُّرْشِدًا

17 You would have seen the sun, when it rose, veering away from their cave towards the right, and when it sets, moving away from them to the left, as they lay in the midst of the cave. That was one of Allah’s wonders. He whom Allah guides is truly guided; but he whom He misguides, for him you will find no directing friend.

١٨ وَتَحْسَبُهُمْ أَيْقَاظًا وَهُمْ رُقُودٌ ۚ وَنُقَلِّبُهُمْ ذَاتَ
ٱلْيَمِينِ وَذَاتَ ٱلشِّمَالِ ۖ وَكَلْبُهُم بَٰسِطٌ ذِرَاعَيْهِ

18 You would think them awake, although they were asleep. And We turned them over to the right, and to the left, with their dog stretching its paws across the threshold. Had you looked at them, you would have

بِٱلْوَصِيدِ ۚ لَوِ ٱطَّلَعْتَ عَلَيْهِمْ لَوَلَّيْتَ مِنْهُمْ فِرَارًا
وَلَمُلِئْتَ مِنْهُمْ رُعْبًا

turned away from them in flight, and been filled with fear of them.

١٩ وَكَذَٰلِكَ بَعَثْنَٰهُمْ لِيَتَسَآءَلُوا۟ بَيْنَهُمْ ۚ قَالَ قَآئِلٌ
مِّنْهُمْ كَمْ لَبِثْتُمْ ۖ قَالُوا۟ لَبِثْنَا يَوْمًا أَوْ بَعْضَ يَوْمٍ ۚ
قَالُوا۟ رَبُّكُمْ أَعْلَمُ بِمَا لَبِثْتُمْ فَٱبْعَثُوٓا۟ أَحَدَكُم
بِوَرِقِكُمْ هَٰذِهِۦٓ إِلَى ٱلْمَدِينَةِ فَلْيَنظُرْ أَيُّهَآ أَزْكَىٰ
طَعَامًا فَلْيَأْتِكُم بِرِزْقٍ مِّنْهُ وَلْيَتَلَطَّفْ وَلَا
يُشْعِرَنَّ بِكُمْ أَحَدًا

19 Even so, We awakened them, so that they may ask one another. A speaker among them said, “How long have you stayed?” They said, “We have stayed a day, or part of a day.” They said, “Your Lord knows best how long you have stayed.” “Send one of you to the city, with this money of yours, and let him see which food is most suitable, and let him bring you some provision thereof. And let him be gentle, and let no one become aware of you.”

٢٠ إِنَّهُمْ إِن يَظْهَرُوا۟ عَلَيْكُمْ يَرْجُمُوكُمْ أَوْ
يُعِيدُوكُمْ فِى مِلَّتِهِمْ وَلَن تُفْلِحُوٓا۟ إِذًا أَبَدًا

20 “If they discover you, they will stone you, or force you back into their religion; then you will never be saved.”

٢١ وَكَذَٰلِكَ أَعْثَرْنَا عَلَيْهِمْ لِيَعْلَمُوٓا۟ أَنَّ وَعْدَ ٱللَّهِ
حَقٌّ وَأَنَّ ٱلسَّاعَةَ لَا رَيْبَ فِيهَآ إِذْ يَتَنَٰزَعُونَ
بَيْنَهُمْ أَمْرَهُمْ ۖ فَقَالُوا۟ ٱبْنُوا۟ عَلَيْهِم بُنْيَٰنًا ۖ رَّبُّهُمْ
أَعْلَمُ بِهِمْ ۚ قَالَ ٱلَّذِينَ غَلَبُوا۟ عَلَىٰٓ أَمْرِهِمْ
لَنَتَّخِذَنَّ عَلَيْهِم مَّسْجِدًا

21 So it was, that We caused them to be discovered, that they would know that the promise of Allah is true, and that of the Hour there is no doubt. As they were disputing their case among themselves, they said, “Build over them a building.” Their Lord knows best about them. Those who prevailed over their case said, “We will set up over them a place of worship.”

٢٢ سَيَقُولُونَ ثَلَٰثَةٌ رَّابِعُهُمْ كَلْبُهُمْ وَيَقُولُونَ
خَمْسَةٌ سَادِسُهُمْ كَلْبُهُمْ رَجْمًۢا بِٱلْغَيْبِ ۖ
وَيَقُولُونَ سَبْعَةٌ وَثَامِنُهُمْ كَلْبُهُمْ ۚ قُل رَّبِّىٓ أَعْلَمُ
بِعِدَّتِهِم مَّا يَعْلَمُهُمْ إِلَّا قَلِيلٌ ۗ فَلَا تُمَارِ فِيهِمْ إِلَّا
مِرَآءً ظَٰهِرًا وَلَا تَسْتَفْتِ فِيهِم مِّنْهُمْ أَحَدًا

22 They will say, “Three, and their fourth being their dog.” And they will say, “Five, and their sixth being their dog,” guessing at the unknown. And they will say, “Seven, and their eighth being their dog.” Say, “My Lord knows best their number.” None knows them except a few. So do not argue concerning them except with an obvious argument,

and do not consult any of them about them.

٢٣ وَلَا تَقُولَنَّ لِشَاْىْءٍ إِنِّى فَاعِلٌ ذَٰلِكَ غَدًا

23 And never say about anything, "I will do that tomorrow."

٢٤ إِلَّآ أَن يَشَآءَ ٱللَّهُ ۚ وَٱذْكُر رَّبَّكَ إِذَا نَسِيتَ
وَقُلْ عَسَىٰٓ أَن يَهْدِيَنِ رَبِّى لِأَقْرَبَ مِنْ هَٰذَا
رَشَدًا

24 Without saying, "If Allah wills." And remember your Lord if you forget, and say, "Perhaps my Lord will guide me to nearer than this in integrity."

٢٥ وَلَبِثُوا۟ فِى كَهْفِهِمْ ثَلَٰثَ مِا۟ئَةٍ سِنِينَ
وَٱزْدَادُوا۟ تِسْعًا

25 And they stayed in their cave for three hundred years, adding nine.

٢٦ قُلِ ٱللَّهُ أَعْلَمُ بِمَا لَبِثُوا۟ ۖ لَهُۥ غَيْبُ ٱلسَّمَٰوَٰتِ
وَٱلْأَرْضِ ۖ أَبْصِرْ بِهِۦ وَأَسْمِعْ ۚ مَا لَهُم مِّن دُونِهِۦ
مِن وَلِىٍّ وَلَا يُشْرِكُ فِى حُكْمِهِۦٓ أَحَدًا

26 Say, "Allah knows best how long they stayed." His is the mystery of the heavens and the earth. By Him you see and hear. They have no guardian apart from Him, and He shares His Sovereignty with no one.

٢٧ وَٱتْلُ مَآ أُوحِىَ إِلَيْكَ مِن كِتَابِ رَبِّكَ ۖ لَا
مُبَدِّلَ لِكَلِمَٰتِهِۦ وَلَن تَجِدَ مِن دُونِهِۦ مُلْتَحَدًا

27 And recite what was revealed to you from the Book of your Lord. There is no changing His words, and you will find no refuge except in Him.

٢٨ وَٱصْبِرْ نَفْسَكَ مَعَ ٱلَّذِينَ يَدْعُونَ رَبَّهُم
بِٱلْغَدَوٰةِ وَٱلْعَشِىِّ يُرِيدُونَ وَجْهَهُۥ ۖ وَلَا تَعْدُ
عَيْنَاكَ عَنْهُمْ تُرِيدُ زِينَةَ ٱلْحَيَوٰةِ ٱلدُّنْيَا ۖ وَلَا
تُطِعْ مَنْ أَغْفَلْنَا قَلْبَهُۥ عَن ذِكْرِنَا وَٱتَّبَعَ هَوَىٰهُ
وَكَانَ أَمْرُهُۥ فُرُطًا

28 And content yourself with those who pray to their Lord morning and evening, desiring His Presence. And do not turn your eyes away from them, desiring the glitter of this world. And do not obey him whose heart We have made heedless of Our remembrance—so he follows his own desires—and his priorities are confused.

٢٩ وَقُلِ ٱلْحَقُّ مِن رَّبِّكُمْ ۖ فَمَن شَآءَ فَلْيُؤْمِن
وَمَن شَآءَ فَلْيَكْفُرْ ۚ إِنَّآ أَعْتَدْنَا لِلظَّٰلِمِينَ نَارًا
أَحَاطَ بِهِمْ سُرَادِقُهَا ۚ وَإِن يَسْتَغِيثُوا۟ يُغَاثُوا۟
بِمَآءٍ كَٱلْمُهْلِ يَشْوِى ٱلْوُجُوهَ ۚ بِئْسَ ٱلشَّرَابُ
وَسَآءَتْ مُرْتَفَقًا

29 And say, "The truth is from your Lord. Whoever wills—let him believe. And whoever wills—let him disbelieve". We have prepared for the unjust a Fire, whose curtains will hem them in. And when they cry for relief, they will be relieved with water like molten brass, which scalds the

faces. What a miserable drink, and what a terrible place.

٣٠ إِنَّ ٱلَّذِينَ ءَامَنُواْ وَعَمِلُواْ ٱلصَّٰلِحَٰتِ إِنَّا لَا
نُضِيعُ أَجْرَ مَنْ أَحْسَنَ عَمَلًا

30 As for those who believe and lead a righteous life—We will not waste the reward of those who work righteousness.

٣١ أُوْلَٰٓئِكَ لَهُمْ جَنَّٰتُ عَدْنٍ تَجْرِى مِن تَحْتِهِمُ
ٱلْأَنْهَٰرُ يُحَلَّوْنَ فِيهَا مِنْ أَسَاوِرَ مِن ذَهَبٍ
وَيَلْبَسُونَ ثِيَابًا خُضْرًا مِّن سُندُسٍ وَإِسْتَبْرَقٍ
مُّتَّكِـِٔينَ فِيهَا عَلَى ٱلْأَرَآئِكِ ۚ نِعْمَ ٱلثَّوَابُ
وَحَسُنَتْ مُرْتَفَقًا

31 These will have the Gardens of Eden, beneath which rivers flow. Reclining on comfortable furnishings, they will be adorned with bracelets of gold, and will wear green garments of silk and brocade. What a wonderful reward, and what an excellent resting-place.

٣٢ وَٱضْرِبْ لَهُم مَّثَلًا رَّجُلَيْنِ جَعَلْنَا لِأَحَدِهِمَا
جَنَّتَيْنِ مِنْ أَعْنَٰبٍ وَحَفَفْنَٰهُمَا بِنَخْلٍ وَجَعَلْنَا
بَيْنَهُمَا زَرْعًا

32 And cite for them the parable of two men. To one of them We gave two gardens of vine, and We surrounded them with palm-trees, and We placed between them crops.

٣٣ كِلْتَا ٱلْجَنَّتَيْنِ ءَاتَتْ أُكُلَهَا وَلَمْ تَظْلِم مِّنْهُ
شَيْـًٔا ۚ وَفَجَّرْنَا خِلَٰلَهُمَا نَهَرًا

33 Both gardens produced their harvest in full, and suffered no loss. And We made a river flow through them.

٣٤ وَكَانَ لَهُۥ ثَمَرٌ فَقَالَ لِصَٰحِبِهِۦ وَهُوَ يُحَاوِرُهُۥٓ
أَنَا أَكْثَرُ مِنكَ مَالًا وَأَعَزُّ نَفَرًا

34 And thus he had abundant fruits. He said to his friend, as he conversed with him, “I am wealthier than you, and greater in manpower.”

٣٥ وَدَخَلَ جَنَّتَهُۥ وَهُوَ ظَالِمٌ لِّنَفْسِهِۦ قَالَ مَآ
أَظُنُّ أَن تَبِيدَ هَٰذِهِۦٓ أَبَدًا

35 And he entered his garden, wronging himself. He said, “I do not think this will ever perish.”

٣٦ وَمَآ أَظُنُّ ٱلسَّاعَةَ قَآئِمَةً وَلَئِن رُّدِدتُّ إِلَىٰ
رَبِّى لَأَجِدَنَّ خَيْرًا مِّنْهَا مُنقَلَبًا

36 “And I do not think the Hour is coming. And even if I am returned to my Lord, I will find something better than this in return.”

٣٧ قَالَ لَهُۥ صَاحِبُهُۥ وَهُوَ يُحَاوِرُهُۥٓ أَكَفَرْتَ بِٱلَّذِى
خَلَقَكَ مِن تُرَابٍ ثُمَّ مِن نُّطْفَةٍ ثُمَّ سَوَّىٰكَ رَجُلًا

37 His friend said to him, as he conversed with him, “Are you being ungrateful to Him who created you from dust, then from a sperm-drop, then evolved you into a man?

٣٨ لَّٰكِنَّا۠ هُوَ ٱللَّهُ رَبِّى وَلَآ أُشْرِكُ بِرَبِّىٓ أَحَدًا

38 But as for me, He is Allah, my Lord, and I never associate with my Lord anyone.

٣٩ وَلَوْلَآ إِذْ دَخَلْتَ جَنَّتَكَ قُلْتَ مَا شَآءَ ٱللَّهُ لَا
قُوَّةَ إِلَّا بِٱللَّهِ ۚ إِن تَرَنِ أَنَا۠ أَقَلَّ مِنكَ مَالًا وَوَلَدًا

39 When you entered your garden, why did you not say, "As Allah wills; there is no power except through Allah"? Although you see me inferior to you in wealth and children.

٤٠ فَعَسَىٰ رَبِّىٓ أَن يُؤْتِيَنِ خَيْرًا مِّن جَنَّتِكَ
وَيُرْسِلَ عَلَيْهَا حُسْبَانًا مِّنَ ٱلسَّمَآءِ فَتُصْبِحَ
صَعِيدًا زَلَقًا

40 Perhaps my Lord will give me something better than your garden, and release upon it thunderbolts from the sky, so it becomes barren waste.

٤١ أَوْ يُصْبِحَ مَآؤُهَا غَوْرًا فَلَن تَسْتَطِيعَ لَهُۥ طَلَبًا

41 Or its water will sink into the ground, and you will be unable to draw it."

٤٢ وَأُحِيطَ بِثَمَرِهِۦ فَأَصْبَحَ يُقَلِّبُ كَفَّيْهِ عَلَىٰ مَآ
أَنفَقَ فِيهَا وَهِىَ خَاوِيَةٌ عَلَىٰ عُرُوشِهَا وَيَقُولُ
يَٰلَيْتَنِى لَمْ أُشْرِكْ بِرَبِّىٓ أَحَدًا

42 And ruin closed in on his crops, and so he began wringing his hands over what he had invested in it, as it lays fallen upon its trellises. And he was saying, "I wish I never associated anyone with my Lord."

٤٣ وَلَمْ تَكُن لَّهُۥ فِئَةٌ يَنصُرُونَهُۥ مِن دُونِ ٱللَّهِ
وَمَا كَانَ مُنتَصِرًا

43 He had no faction to help him besides Allah, and he was helpless.

٤٤ هُنَالِكَ ٱلْوَلَٰيَةُ لِلَّهِ ٱلْحَقِّ ۚ هُوَ خَيْرٌ ثَوَابًا
وَخَيْرٌ عُقْبًا

44 That is because authority belongs to Allah, the True. He is Best in rewarding, and Best in requiting.

٤٥ وَٱضْرِبْ لَهُم مَّثَلَ ٱلْحَيَوٰةِ ٱلدُّنْيَا كَمَآءٍ
أَنزَلْنَٰهُ مِنَ ٱلسَّمَآءِ فَٱخْتَلَطَ بِهِۦ نَبَاتُ ٱلْأَرْضِ
فَأَصْبَحَ هَشِيمًا تَذْرُوهُ ٱلرِّيَٰحُ ۗ وَكَانَ ٱللَّهُ عَلَىٰ
كُلِّ شَىْءٍ مُّقْتَدِرًا

45 And cite for them the parable of the present life: it is like water that We send down from the sky; the plants of the earth absorb it; but then it becomes debris, scattered by the wind. Allah has absolute power over everything.

٤٦ ٱلْمَالُ وَٱلْبَنُونَ زِينَةُ ٱلْحَيَوٰةِ ٱلدُّنْيَا ۖ
وَٱلْبَٰقِيَٰتُ ٱلصَّٰلِحَٰتُ خَيْرٌ عِندَ رَبِّكَ ثَوَابًا وَخَيْرٌ
أَمَلًا

46 Wealth and children are the adornments of the present life. But the things that last, the virtuous deeds, are better with your Lord for reward, and better for hope.

٤٧ وَيَوْمَ نُسَيِّرُ ٱلْجِبَالَ وَتَرَى ٱلْأَرْضَ بَارِزَةً
وَحَشَرْنَٰهُمْ فَلَمْ نُغَادِرْ مِنْهُمْ أَحَدًا

47 On the Day when We set the mountains in motion; and you see the earth emerging; and We gather them together, and leave none of them behind.

٤٨ وَعُرِضُوا۟ عَلَىٰ رَبِّكَ صَفًّا لَّقَدْ جِئْتُمُونَا كَمَا
خَلَقْنَٰكُمْ أَوَّلَ مَرَّةٍۭ ۚ بَلْ زَعَمْتُمْ أَلَّن نَّجْعَلَ لَكُم
مَّوْعِدًا

48 They will be presented before your Lord in a row. "You have come to Us as We created you the first time. Although you claimed We would not set a meeting for you."

٤٩ وَوُضِعَ ٱلْكِتَٰبُ فَتَرَى ٱلْمُجْرِمِينَ مُشْفِقِينَ
مِمَّا فِيهِ وَيَقُولُونَ يَٰوَيْلَتَنَا مَالِ هَٰذَا ٱلْكِتَٰبِ لَا
يُغَادِرُ صَغِيرَةً وَلَا كَبِيرَةً إِلَّآ أَحْصَىٰهَا ۚ وَوَجَدُوا۟
مَا عَمِلُوا۟ حَاضِرًا ۗ وَلَا يَظْلِمُ رَبُّكَ أَحَدًا

49 And the book will be placed, and you will see the sinners fearful of its contents. And they will say, "Woe to us! What is with this book that leaves nothing, small or big, but it has enumerated it?" They will find everything they had done present. Your Lord does not wrong anyone.

٥٠ وَإِذْ قُلْنَا لِلْمَلَٰٓئِكَةِ ٱسْجُدُوا۟ لِءَادَمَ فَسَجَدُوٓا۟
إِلَّآ إِبْلِيسَ كَانَ مِنَ ٱلْجِنِّ فَفَسَقَ عَنْ أَمْرِ رَبِّهِۦٓ ۗ
أَفَتَتَّخِذُونَهُۥ وَذُرِّيَّتَهُۥٓ أَوْلِيَآءَ مِن دُونِى وَهُمْ
لَكُمْ عَدُوٌّۢ ۚ بِئْسَ لِلظَّٰلِمِينَ بَدَلًا

50 We said to the angels, "Bow down to Adam." So they bowed down, except for Satan. He was of the jinn, and he defied the command of his Lord. Will you take him and his offspring as lords instead of Me, when they are an enemy to you? Evil is the exchange for the wrongdoers.

٥١ مَّآ أَشْهَدتُّهُمْ خَلْقَ ٱلسَّمَٰوَٰتِ وَٱلْأَرْضِ وَلَا
خَلْقَ أَنفُسِهِمْ وَمَا كُنتُ مُتَّخِذَ ٱلْمُضِلِّينَ عَضُدًا

51 I did not call them to witness the creation of the heavens and the earth, nor their own creation; and I do not take the misleaders for assistants.

٥٢ وَيَوْمَ يَقُولُ نَادُوا۟ شُرَكَآءِىَ ٱلَّذِينَ زَعَمْتُمْ
فَدَعَوْهُمْ فَلَمْ يَسْتَجِيبُوا۟ لَهُمْ وَجَعَلْنَا بَيْنَهُم
مَّوْبِقًا

52 On the Day when He will say, "Call on My partners whom you have claimed." They will call on them, but they will not answer them. And We will place between them a barrier.

٥٣ وَرَءَا ٱلْمُجْرِمُونَ ٱلنَّارَ فَظَنُّوٓا۟ أَنَّهُم
مُّوَاقِعُوهَا وَلَمْ يَجِدُوا۟ عَنْهَا مَصْرِفًا

53 And the sinners will see the Fire, and will realize that they will tumble into it. They will find no deliverance from it.

٥٤ وَلَقَدْ صَرَّفْنَا فِى هَٰذَا ٱلْقُرْءَانِ لِلنَّاسِ مِن
كُلِّ مَثَلٍۚ وَكَانَ ٱلْإِنسَٰنُ أَكْثَرَ شَىْءٍ جَدَلًا

54 We have elaborated in this Quran for the people every kind of example, but the human being is a most argumentative being.

٥٥ وَمَا مَنَعَ ٱلنَّاسَ أَن يُؤْمِنُوٓا۟ إِذْ جَآءَهُمُ
ٱلْهُدَىٰ وَيَسْتَغْفِرُوا۟ رَبَّهُمْ إِلَّآ أَن تَأْتِيَهُمْ سُنَّةُ
ٱلْأَوَّلِينَ أَوْ يَأْتِيَهُمُ ٱلْعَذَابُ قُبُلًا

55 What prevented people from accepting faith, when guidance has come to them, and from seeking their Lord's forgiveness? Unless they are waiting for the precedent of the ancients to befall them, or to have the punishment come upon them face to face.

٥٦ وَمَا نُرْسِلُ ٱلْمُرْسَلِينَ إِلَّا مُبَشِّرِينَ
وَمُنذِرِينَۚ وَيُجَٰدِلُ ٱلَّذِينَ كَفَرُوا۟ بِٱلْبَٰطِلِ
لِيُدْحِضُوا۟ بِهِ ٱلْحَقَّۖ وَٱتَّخَذُوٓا۟ ءَايَٰتِى وَمَآ
أُنذِرُوا۟ هُزُوًا

56 We send the messengers only as deliverers of good news and warners. Those who disbelieve argue with false argument, in order to defeat the truth thereby. They take My Verses, and the warnings, for a joke.

٥٧ وَمَنْ أَظْلَمُ مِمَّن ذُكِّرَ بِـَٔايَٰتِ رَبِّهِۦ فَأَعْرَضَ
عَنْهَا وَنَسِىَ مَا قَدَّمَتْ يَدَاهُۚ إِنَّا جَعَلْنَا عَلَىٰ
قُلُوبِهِمْ أَكِنَّةً أَن يَفْقَهُوهُ وَفِىٓ ءَاذَانِهِمْ وَقْرًاۖ
وَإِن تَدْعُهُمْ إِلَى ٱلْهُدَىٰ فَلَن يَهْتَدُوٓا۟ إِذًا أَبَدًا

57 Who does greater wrong than he, who, when reminded of his Lord's revelations, turns away from them, and forgets what his hands have put forward? We have placed coverings over their hearts, lest they understand it, and heaviness in their ears. And if you call them to guidance, they will not be guided, ever.

٥٨ وَرَبُّكَ ٱلْغَفُورُ ذُو ٱلرَّحْمَةِۖ لَوْ يُؤَاخِذُهُم بِمَا
كَسَبُوا۟ لَعَجَّلَ لَهُمُ ٱلْعَذَابَۚ بَل لَّهُم مَّوْعِدٌ لَّن
يَجِدُوا۟ مِن دُونِهِۦ مَوْئِلًا

58 Your Lord is the Forgiver, Possessor of Mercy. Were He to call them to account for what they have earned, He would have hastened the punishment for them. But they have an appointment from which they will find no escape.

٥٩ وَتِلْكَ ٱلْقُرَىٰٓ أَهْلَكْنَٰهُمْ لَمَّا ظَلَمُوا۟ وَجَعَلْنَا
لِمَهْلِكِهِم مَّوْعِدًا

59 And these towns—We destroyed them when they committed injustices, and We set for their destruction an appointed time.

٦٠ وَإِذْ قَالَ مُوسَىٰ لِفَتَىٰهُ لَآ أَبْرَحُ حَتَّىٰٓ أَبْلُغَ
مَجْمَعَ ٱلْبَحْرَيْنِ أَوْ أَمْضِىَ حُقُبًا

60 Recall when Moses said to his servant, “I will not give up until I reach the junction of the two rivers, even if it takes me years.”

٦١ فَلَمَّا بَلَغَا مَجْمَعَ بَيْنِهِمَا نَسِيَا حُوتَهُمَا فَٱتَّخَذَ
سَبِيلَهُۥ فِى ٱلْبَحْرِ سَرَبًا

61 Then, when they reached the junction between them, they forgot about their fish. It found its way into the river, slipping away.

٦٢ فَلَمَّا جَاوَزَا قَالَ لِفَتَىٰهُ ءَاتِنَا غَدَآءَنَا لَقَدْ
لَقِينَا مِن سَفَرِنَا هَٰذَا نَصَبًا

62 When they went further, he said to his servant, “Bring us our lunch; we were exposed in our travel to much fatigue.”

٦٣ قَالَ أَرَءَيْتَ إِذْ أَوَيْنَآ إِلَى ٱلصَّخْرَةِ فَإِنِّى
نَسِيتُ ٱلْحُوتَ وَمَآ أَنسَىٰنِيهُ إِلَّا ٱلشَّيْطَٰنُ أَنْ
أَذْكُرَهُۥ ۚ وَٱتَّخَذَ سَبِيلَهُۥ فِى ٱلْبَحْرِ عَجَبًا

63 He said, “Do you remember when we rested by the rock? I forgot about the fish. It was only the devil who made me forget it. And so it found its way to the river, amazingly.”

٦٤ قَالَ ذَٰلِكَ مَا كُنَّا نَبْغِ ۚ فَٱرْتَدَّا عَلَىٰٓ ءَاثَارِهِمَا
قَصَصًا

64 He said, “This is what we were seeking.” And so they turned back retracing their steps.

٦٥ فَوَجَدَا عَبْدًا مِّنْ عِبَادِنَآ ءَاتَيْنَٰهُ رَحْمَةً مِّنْ
عِندِنَا وَعَلَّمْنَٰهُ مِن لَّدُنَّا عِلْمًا

65 Then they came upon a servant of Ours, whom We had blessed with mercy from Us, and had taught him knowledge from Our Own.

٦٦ قَالَ لَهُۥ مُوسَىٰ هَلْ أَتَّبِعُكَ عَلَىٰٓ أَن تُعَلِّمَنِ
مِمَّا عُلِّمْتَ رُشْدًا

66 Moses said to him, “May I follow you, so that you may teach me some of the guidance you were taught?”

٦٧ قَالَ إِنَّكَ لَن تَسْتَطِيعَ مَعِىَ صَبْرًا

67 He said, “You will not be able to endure with me.

٦٨ وَكَيْفَ تَصْبِرُ عَلَىٰ مَا لَمْ تُحِطْ بِهِۦ خُبْرًا

68 And how will you endure what you have no knowledge of?”

٦٩ قَالَ سَتَجِدُنِىٓ إِن شَآءَ ٱللَّهُ صَابِرًا وَلَآ
أَعْصِى لَكَ أَمْرًا

69 He said, “You will find me, Allah willing, patient; and I will not disobey you in any order of yours.”

٧٠ قَالَ فَإِنِ ٱتَّبَعْتَنِى فَلَا تَسْـَٔلْنِى عَن شَىْءٍ
حَتَّىٰٓ أُحْدِثَ لَكَ مِنْهُ ذِكْرًا

70 He said, “If you follow me, do not ask me about anything, until I myself make mention of it to you.”

٧١ فَٱنطَلَقَا حَتَّىٰٓ إِذَا رَكِبَا فِى ٱلسَّفِينَةِ خَرَقَهَا ۖ
قَالَ أَخَرَقْتَهَا لِتُغْرِقَ أَهْلَهَا لَقَدْ جِئْتَ شَيْـًٔا إِمْرًا

71 So they set out. Until, when they had boarded the boat, he holed it. He said, “Did you hole it, to drown its

passengers? You have done something awful.”

٧٢ قَالَ أَلَمْ أَقُلْ إِنَّكَ لَن تَسْتَطِيعَ مَعِىَ صَبْرًا

72 He said, “Did I not tell you that you will not be able to endure with me?”

٧٣ قَالَ لَا تُؤَاخِذْنِى بِمَا نَسِيتُ وَلَا تُرْهِقْنِى
مِنْ أَمْرِى عُسْرًا

73 He said, “Do not rebuke me for forgetting, and do not make my course difficult for me.”

٧٤ فَٱنطَلَقَا حَتَّىٰٓ إِذَا لَقِيَا غُلَٰمًا فَقَتَلَهُۥ قَالَ
أَقَتَلْتَ نَفْسًا زَكِيَّةًۢ بِغَيْرِ نَفْسٍ لَّقَدْ جِئْتَ شَيْـًٔا
نُّكْرًا

74 Then they set out. Until, when they encountered a boy, he killed him. He said, “Did you kill a pure soul, who killed no one? You have done something terrible.”

٧٥ قَالَ أَلَمْ أَقُل لَّكَ إِنَّكَ لَن تَسْتَطِيعَ مَعِىَ
صَبْرًا

75 He said, “Did I not tell you that you will not be able to endure with me?”

٧٦ قَالَ إِن سَأَلْتُكَ عَن شَىْءٍۭ بَعْدَهَا فَلَا
تُصَٰحِبْنِى ۖ قَدْ بَلَغْتَ مِن لَّدُنِّى عُذْرًا

76 He said, “If I ask you about anything after this, then do not keep company with me. You have received excuses from me.”

٧٧ فَٱنطَلَقَا حَتَّىٰٓ إِذَآ أَتَيَآ أَهْلَ قَرْيَةٍ ٱسْتَطْعَمَآ
أَهْلَهَا فَأَبَوْا۟ أَن يُضَيِّفُوهُمَا فَوَجَدَا فِيهَا جِدَارًا
يُرِيدُ أَن يَنقَضَّ فَأَقَامَهُۥ ۖ قَالَ لَوْ شِئْتَ لَتَّخَذْتَ
عَلَيْهِ أَجْرًا

77 So they set out. Until, when they reached the people of a town, they asked them for food, but they refused to offer them hospitality. There they found a wall about to collapse, and he repaired it. He said, “If you wanted, you could have obtained a payment for it.”

٧٨ قَالَ هَٰذَا فِرَاقُ بَيْنِى وَبَيْنِكَ ۚ سَأُنَبِّئُكَ
بِتَأْوِيلِ مَا لَمْ تَسْتَطِع عَّلَيْهِ صَبْرًا

78 He said, “This is the parting between you and me. I will tell you the interpretation of what you were unable to endure.

٧٩ أَمَّا ٱلسَّفِينَةُ فَكَانَتْ لِمَسَٰكِينَ يَعْمَلُونَ فِى
ٱلْبَحْرِ فَأَرَدتُّ أَنْ أَعِيبَهَا وَكَانَ وَرَآءَهُم مَّلِكٌ
يَأْخُذُ كُلَّ سَفِينَةٍ غَصْبًا

79 As for the boat, it belonged to paupers working at sea. I wanted to damage it because there was a king coming after them seizing every boat by force.

٨٠ وَأَمَّا ٱلْغُلَٰمُ فَكَانَ أَبَوَاهُ مُؤْمِنَيْنِ فَخَشِينَآ أَن
يُرْهِقَهُمَا طُغْيَٰنًا وَكُفْرًا

80 As for the boy, his parents were believers, and we feared he would overwhelm them with oppression and disbelief.

٨١ فَأَرَدْنَآ أَن يُبْدِلَهُمَا رَبُّهُمَا خَيْرًا مِّنْهُ زَكَوٰةً
وَأَقْرَبَ رُحْمًا

81 So we wanted their Lord to replace him with someone better in purity, and closer to mercy.

٨٢ وَأَمَّا ٱلْجِدَارُ فَكَانَ لِغُلَٰمَيْنِ يَتِيمَيْنِ فِى
ٱلْمَدِينَةِ وَكَانَ تَحْتَهُۥ كَنزٌ لَّهُمَا وَكَانَ أَبُوهُمَا
صَٰلِحًا فَأَرَادَ رَبُّكَ أَن يَبْلُغَآ أَشُدَّهُمَا
وَيَسْتَخْرِجَا كَنزَهُمَا رَحْمَةً مِّن رَّبِّكَ ۚ وَمَا
فَعَلْتُهُۥ عَنْ أَمْرِى ۚ ذَٰلِكَ تَأْوِيلُ مَا لَمْ تَسْطِع
عَّلَيْهِ صَبْرًا

82 And as for the wall, it belonged to two orphaned boys in the town. Beneath it was a treasure that belonged to them. Their father was a righteous man. Your Lord wanted them to reach their maturity, and then extract their treasure—as a mercy from your Lord. I did not do it of my own accord. This is the interpretation of what you were unable to endure."

٨٣ وَيَسْـَٔلُونَكَ عَن ذِى ٱلْقَرْنَيْنِ ۖ قُلْ سَأَتْلُوا۟
عَلَيْكُم مِّنْهُ ذِكْرًا

83 And they ask you about Zul-Qarnain. Say, "I will tell you something about him."

٨٤ إِنَّا مَكَّنَّا لَهُۥ فِى ٱلْأَرْضِ وَءَاتَيْنَٰهُ مِن كُلِّ
شَىْءٍ سَبَبًا

84 We established him on earth, and gave him all kinds of means.

٨٥ فَأَتْبَعَ سَبَبًا

85 He pursued a certain course.

٨٦ حَتَّىٰٓ إِذَا بَلَغَ مَغْرِبَ ٱلشَّمْسِ وَجَدَهَا تَغْرُبُ
فِى عَيْنٍ حَمِئَةٍ وَوَجَدَ عِندَهَا قَوْمًا ۗ قُلْنَا يَٰذَا
ٱلْقَرْنَيْنِ إِمَّآ أَن تُعَذِّبَ وَإِمَّآ أَن تَتَّخِذَ فِيهِمْ
حُسْنًا

86 Until, when he reached the setting of the sun, he found it setting in a murky spring, and found a people in its vicinity. We said, "O Zul-Qarnain, you may either inflict a penalty, or else treat them kindly."

٨٧ قَالَ أَمَّا مَن ظَلَمَ فَسَوْفَ نُعَذِّبُهُۥ ثُمَّ يُرَدُّ إِلَىٰ
رَبِّهِۦ فَيُعَذِّبُهُۥ عَذَابًا نُّكْرًا

87 He said, "As for him who does wrong, we will penalize him, then he will be returned to his Lord, and He will punish him with an unheard-of torment.

٨٨ وَأَمَّا مَنْ ءَامَنَ وَعَمِلَ صَٰلِحًا فَلَهُۥ جَزَآءً
ٱلْحُسْنَىٰ ۖ وَسَنَقُولُ لَهُۥ مِنْ أَمْرِنَا يُسْرًا

88 "But as for him who believes and acts righteously, he will have the finest reward, and We will speak to him of Our command with ease."

٨٩ ثُمَّ أَتْبَعَ سَبَبًا

89 Then he pursued a course.

٩٠ حَتَّىٰٓ إِذَا بَلَغَ مَطْلِعَ ٱلشَّمْسِ وَجَدَهَا تَطْلُعُ
عَلَىٰ قَوْمٍ لَّمْ نَجْعَل لَّهُم مِّن دُونِهَا سِتْرًا

90 Until, when he reached the rising of the sun, he found it rising on a people for whom We had provided no shelter from it.

٩١ كَذَٰلِكَ وَقَدْ أَحَطْنَا بِمَا لَدَيْهِ خُبْرًا

91 And so it was. We had full knowledge of what he had.

٩٢ ثُمَّ أَتْبَعَ سَبَبًا

92 Then he pursued a course.

٩٣ حَتَّىٰٓ إِذَا بَلَغَ بَيْنَ ٱلسَّدَّيْنِ وَجَدَ مِن دُونِهِمَا
قَوْمًا لَّا يَكَادُونَ يَفْقَهُونَ قَوْلًا

93 Until, when he reached the point separating the two barriers, he found beside them a people who could barely understand what is said.

٩٤ قَالُوا۟ يَٰذَا ٱلْقَرْنَيْنِ إِنَّ يَأْجُوجَ وَمَأْجُوجَ
مُفْسِدُونَ فِى ٱلْأَرْضِ فَهَلْ نَجْعَلُ لَكَ خَرْجًا
عَلَىٰٓ أَن تَجْعَلَ بَيْنَنَا وَبَيْنَهُمْ سَدًّا

94 They said, "O Zul-Qarnain, the Gog and Magog are spreading chaos in the land. Can we pay you, to build between us and them a wall?"

٩٥ قَالَ مَا مَكَّنِّى فِيهِ رَبِّى خَيْرٌ فَأَعِينُونِى
بِقُوَّةٍ أَجْعَلْ بَيْنَكُمْ وَبَيْنَهُمْ رَدْمًا

95 He said, "What my Lord has empowered me with is better. But assist me with strength, and I will build between you and them a dam."

٩٦ ءَاتُونِى زُبَرَ ٱلْحَدِيدِ ۖ حَتَّىٰٓ إِذَا سَاوَىٰ بَيْنَ
ٱلصَّدَفَيْنِ قَالَ ٱنفُخُوا۟ ۖ حَتَّىٰٓ إِذَا جَعَلَهُۥ نَارًا
قَالَ ءَاتُونِىٓ أُفْرِغْ عَلَيْهِ قِطْرًا

96 "Bring me blocks of iron." So that, when he had leveled up between the two cliffs, he said, "Blow." And having turned it into a fire, he said, "Bring me tar to pour over it."

٩٧ فَمَا ٱسْطَٰعُوٓا۟ أَن يَظْهَرُوهُ وَمَا ٱسْتَطَٰعُوا۟ لَهُۥ
نَقْبًا

97 So they were unable to climb it, and they could not penetrate it.

٩٨ قَالَ هَٰذَا رَحْمَةٌ مِّن رَّبِّى ۖ فَإِذَا جَآءَ وَعْدُ
رَبِّى جَعَلَهُۥ دَكَّآءَ ۖ وَكَانَ وَعْدُ رَبِّى حَقًّا

98 He said, "This is a mercy from my Lord. But when the promise of my Lord comes true, He will turn it into rubble, and the promise of my Lord is always true."

٩٩ وَتَرَكْنَا بَعْضَهُمْ يَوْمَئِذٍ يَمُوجُ فِى بَعْضٍ ۖ
وَنُفِخَ فِى ٱلصُّورِ فَجَمَعْنَٰهُمْ جَمْعًا

99 On that Day, We will leave them surging upon one another. And the Trumpet will be blown, and We will gather them together.

١٠٠ وَعَرَضْنَا جَهَنَّمَ يَوْمَئِذٍ لِّلْكَٰفِرِينَ عَرْضًا

100 On that Day, We will present the disbelievers to Hell, all displayed.

١٠١ ٱلَّذِينَ كَانَتْ أَعْيُنُهُمْ فِى غِطَآءٍ عَن ذِكْرِى
وَكَانُوا۟ لَا يَسْتَطِيعُونَ سَمْعًا

101 Those whose eyes were screened to My message, and were unable to hear.

١٠٢ أَفَحَسِبَ ٱلَّذِينَ كَفَرُوٓا۟ أَن يَتَّخِذُوا۟ عِبَادِى
مِن دُونِىٓ أَوْلِيَآءَ ۚ إِنَّآ أَعْتَدْنَا جَهَنَّمَ لِلْكَٰفِرِينَ
نُزُلًا

102 Do those who disbelieve think that they can take My servants for masters instead of Me? We have prepared Hell for the hospitality of the faithless.

١٠٣ قُلْ هَلْ نُنَبِّئُكُم بِٱلْأَخْسَرِينَ أَعْمَٰلًا

103 Say, "Shall We inform you of the greatest losers in their works?"

١٠٤ ٱلَّذِينَ ضَلَّ سَعْيُهُمْ فِى ٱلْحَيَوٰةِ ٱلدُّنْيَا وَهُمْ
يَحْسَبُونَ أَنَّهُمْ يُحْسِنُونَ صُنْعًا

104 "Those whose efforts in this world are misguided, while they assume that they are doing well."

١٠٥ أُو۟لَٰٓئِكَ ٱلَّذِينَ كَفَرُوا۟ بِـَٔايَٰتِ رَبِّهِمْ وَلِقَآئِهِۦ
فَحَبِطَتْ أَعْمَٰلُهُمْ فَلَا نُقِيمُ لَهُمْ يَوْمَ ٱلْقِيَٰمَةِ
وَزْنًا

105 It is they who rejected the communications of their Lord, and the encounter with Him. So their works are in vain. And on the Day of Resurrection, We will consider them of no weight.

١٠٦ ذَٰلِكَ جَزَآؤُهُمْ جَهَنَّمُ بِمَا كَفَرُوا۟ وَٱتَّخَذُوٓا۟
ءَايَٰتِى وَرُسُلِى هُزُوًا

106 That is their requital—Hell—on account of their disbelief, and their taking My revelations and My messengers in mockery.

١٠٧ إِنَّ ٱلَّذِينَ ءَامَنُوا۟ وَعَمِلُوا۟ ٱلصَّٰلِحَٰتِ كَانَتْ
لَهُمْ جَنَّٰتُ ٱلْفِرْدَوْسِ نُزُلًا

107 As for those who believe and do righteous deeds, they will have the Gardens of Paradise for hospitality.

١٠٨ خَٰلِدِينَ فِيهَا لَا يَبْغُونَ عَنْهَا حِوَلًا

108 Abiding therein forever, without desiring any change therefrom.

١٠٩ قُل لَّوْ كَانَ ٱلْبَحْرُ مِدَادًا لِّكَلِمَٰتِ رَبِّى لَنَفِدَ
ٱلْبَحْرُ قَبْلَ أَن تَنفَدَ كَلِمَٰتُ رَبِّى وَلَوْ جِئْنَا
بِمِثْلِهِۦ مَدَدًا

109 Say, "If the ocean were ink for the words of my Lord, the ocean would run out, before the words of my Lord run out," even if We were to bring the like of it in addition to it.

١١٠ قُلْ إِنَّمَآ أَنَا۠ بَشَرٌ مِّثْلُكُمْ يُوحَىٰٓ إِلَىَّ أَنَّمَآ
إِلَٰهُكُمْ إِلَٰهٌ وَٰحِدٌ ۖ فَمَن كَانَ يَرْجُوا۟ لِقَآءَ رَبِّهِۦ
فَلْيَعْمَلْ عَمَلًا صَٰلِحًا وَلَا يُشْرِكْ بِعِبَادَةِ رَبِّهِۦٓ
أَحَدًا

110 Say, "I am only a human being like you, being inspired that your god is One God. Whoever hopes to meet his Lord, let him work righteousness, and never associate anyone with the service of his Lord."

19 Mary مريم

بِسْمِ ٱللَّهِ ٱلرَّحْمَٰنِ ٱلرَّحِيمِ	In the name of Allah, the Gracious, the Merciful.
١ كٓهيعٓصٓ	1 Kaf, Ha, Ya, Ayn, Saad.
٢ ذِكْرُ رَحْمَتِ رَبِّكَ عَبْدَهُۥ زَكَرِيَّآ	2 A mention of the mercy of your Lord towards His servant Zechariah.
٣ إِذْ نَادَىٰ رَبَّهُۥ نِدَآءً خَفِيًّا	3 When he called on his Lord, a call in seclusion.
٤ قَالَ رَبِّ إِنِّى وَهَنَ ٱلْعَظْمُ مِنِّى وَٱشْتَعَلَ ٱلرَّأْسُ شَيْبًا وَلَمْ أَكُنۢ بِدُعَآئِكَ رَبِّ شَقِيًّا	4 He said, “My Lord, my bones have become feeble, and my hair is aflame with gray, and never, Lord, have I been disappointed in my prayer to you.
٥ وَإِنِّى خِفْتُ ٱلْمَوَٰلِىَ مِن وَرَآءِى وَكَانَتِ ٱمْرَأَتِى عَاقِرًا فَهَبْ لِى مِن لَّدُنكَ وَلِيًّا	5 “And I fear for my dependents after me, and my wife is barren. So grant me, from Yourself, an heir.
٦ يَرِثُنِى وَيَرِثُ مِنْ ءَالِ يَعْقُوبَ ۖ وَٱجْعَلْهُ رَبِّ رَضِيًّا	6 To inherit me, and inherit from the House of Jacob, and make him, my Lord, pleasing.”
٧ يَٰزَكَرِيَّآ إِنَّا نُبَشِّرُكَ بِغُلَٰمٍ ٱسْمُهُۥ يَحْيَىٰ لَمْ نَجْعَل لَّهُۥ مِن قَبْلُ سَمِيًّا	7 “O Zechariah, We give you good news of a son, whose name is John, a name We have never given before.”
٨ قَالَ رَبِّ أَنَّىٰ يَكُونُ لِى غُلَٰمٌ وَكَانَتِ ٱمْرَأَتِى عَاقِرًا وَقَدْ بَلَغْتُ مِنَ ٱلْكِبَرِ عِتِيًّا	8 He said, “My Lord, how can I have a son, when my wife is barren, and I have become decrepit with old age?”
٩ قَالَ كَذَٰلِكَ قَالَ رَبُّكَ هُوَ عَلَىَّ هَيِّنٌ وَقَدْ خَلَقْتُكَ مِن قَبْلُ وَلَمْ تَكُ شَيْـًٔا	9 He said, “It will be so, your Lord says, ‘it is easy for me, and I created you before, when you were nothing.’”
١٠ قَالَ رَبِّ ٱجْعَل لِّىٓ ءَايَةً ۚ قَالَ ءَايَتُكَ أَلَّا تُكَلِّمَ ٱلنَّاسَ ثَلَٰثَ لَيَالٍ سَوِيًّا	10 He said, “My Lord, give me a sign.” He said, “Your sign is that you will not speak to the people for three nights straight.”
١١ فَخَرَجَ عَلَىٰ قَوْمِهِۦ مِنَ ٱلْمِحْرَابِ فَأَوْحَىٰٓ إِلَيْهِمْ أَن سَبِّحُوا۟ بُكْرَةً وَعَشِيًّا	11 And he came out to his people, from the sanctuary, and signaled to them to praise morning and evening.

١٢ يَٰيَحْيَىٰ خُذِ ٱلْكِتَٰبَ بِقُوَّةٍ ۖ وَءَاتَيْنَٰهُ ٱلْحُكْمَ صَبِيًّا	12 "O John, hold on to the Scripture firmly," and We gave him wisdom in his youth.
١٣ وَحَنَانًا مِّن لَّدُنَّا وَزَكَوٰةً ۖ وَكَانَ تَقِيًّا	13 And tenderness from Us, and innocence. He was devout.
١٤ وَبَرًّۢا بِوَٰلِدَيْهِ وَلَمْ يَكُن جَبَّارًا عَصِيًّا	14 And kind to his parents; and he was not a disobedient tyrant.
١٥ وَسَلَٰمٌ عَلَيْهِ يَوْمَ وُلِدَ وَيَوْمَ يَمُوتُ وَيَوْمَ يُبْعَثُ حَيًّا	15 And peace be upon him the day he was born, and the day he dies, and the Day he is raised alive.
١٦ وَٱذْكُرْ فِى ٱلْكِتَٰبِ مَرْيَمَ إِذِ ٱنتَبَذَتْ مِنْ أَهْلِهَا مَكَانًا شَرْقِيًّا	16 And mention in the Scripture Mary, when she withdrew from her people to an eastern location.
١٧ فَٱتَّخَذَتْ مِن دُونِهِمْ حِجَابًا فَأَرْسَلْنَآ إِلَيْهَا رُوحَنَا فَتَمَثَّلَ لَهَا بَشَرًا سَوِيًّا	17 She screened herself away from them, and We sent to her Our spirit, and He appeared to her as an immaculate human.
١٨ قَالَتْ إِنِّىٓ أَعُوذُ بِٱلرَّحْمَٰنِ مِنكَ إِن كُنتَ تَقِيًّا	18 She said, "I take refuge from you in the Most Merciful, should you be righteous."
١٩ قَالَ إِنَّمَآ أَنَا۠ رَسُولُ رَبِّكِ لِأَهَبَ لَكِ غُلَٰمًا زَكِيًّا	19 He said, "I am only the messenger of your Lord, to give you the gift of a pure son."
٢٠ قَالَتْ أَنَّىٰ يَكُونُ لِى غُلَٰمٌ وَلَمْ يَمْسَسْنِى بَشَرٌ وَلَمْ أَكُ بَغِيًّا	20 She said, "How can I have a son, when no man has touched me, and I was never unchaste?"
٢١ قَالَ كَذَٰلِكِ قَالَ رَبُّكِ هُوَ عَلَىَّ هَيِّنٌ ۖ وَلِنَجْعَلَهُۥٓ ءَايَةً لِّلنَّاسِ وَرَحْمَةً مِّنَّا ۚ وَكَانَ أَمْرًا مَّقْضِيًّا	21 He said, "Thus said your Lord, `It is easy for Me, and We will make him a sign for humanity, and a mercy from Us. It is a matter already decided.'"
٢٢ فَحَمَلَتْهُ فَٱنتَبَذَتْ بِهِۦ مَكَانًا قَصِيًّا	22 So she carried him, and secluded herself with him in a remote place.
٢٣ فَأَجَآءَهَا ٱلْمَخَاضُ إِلَىٰ جِذْعِ ٱلنَّخْلَةِ قَالَتْ يَٰلَيْتَنِى مِتُّ قَبْلَ هَٰذَا وَكُنتُ نَسْيًا مَّنسِيًّا	23 The labor-pains came upon her, by the trunk of a palm-tree. She said, "I wish I had died before this, and been completely forgotten."
٢٤ فَنَادَىٰهَا مِن تَحْتِهَآ أَلَّا تَحْزَنِى قَدْ جَعَلَ رَبُّكِ تَحْتَكِ سَرِيًّا	24 Whereupon he called her from beneath her: "Do not worry; your

Lord has placed a stream beneath you.

٢٥ وَهُزِّىٓ إِلَيْكِ بِجِذْعِ ٱلنَّخْلَةِ تُسَٰقِطْ عَلَيْكِ رُطَبًا جَنِيًّا

25 And shake the trunk of the palm-tree towards you, and it will drop ripe dates by you."

٢٦ فَكُلِى وَٱشْرَبِى وَقَرِّى عَيْنًا ۖ فَإِمَّا تَرَيِنَّ مِنَ ٱلْبَشَرِ أَحَدًا فَقُولِىٓ إِنِّى نَذَرْتُ لِلرَّحْمَٰنِ صَوْمًا فَلَنْ أُكَلِّمَ ٱلْيَوْمَ إِنسِيًّا

26 "So eat, and drink, and be consoled. And if you see any human, say, 'I have vowed a fast to the Most Gracious, so I will not speak to any human today.'"

٢٧ فَأَتَتْ بِهِۦ قَوْمَهَا تَحْمِلُهُۥ ۖ قَالُوا۟ يَٰمَرْيَمُ لَقَدْ جِئْتِ شَيْـًٔا فَرِيًّا

27 Then she came to her people, carrying him. They said, "O Mary, you have done something terrible.

٢٨ يَٰٓأُخْتَ هَٰرُونَ مَا كَانَ أَبُوكِ ٱمْرَأَ سَوْءٍ وَمَا كَانَتْ أُمُّكِ بَغِيًّا

28 O sister of Aaron, your father was not an evil man, and your mother was not a whore."

٢٩ فَأَشَارَتْ إِلَيْهِ ۖ قَالُوا۟ كَيْفَ نُكَلِّمُ مَن كَانَ فِى ٱلْمَهْدِ صَبِيًّا

29 So she pointed to him. They said, "How can we speak to an infant in the crib?"

٣٠ قَالَ إِنِّى عَبْدُ ٱللَّهِ ءَاتَىٰنِىَ ٱلْكِتَٰبَ وَجَعَلَنِى نَبِيًّا

30 He said, "I am the servant of Allah. He has given me the Scripture, and made me a prophet.

٣١ وَجَعَلَنِى مُبَارَكًا أَيْنَ مَا كُنتُ وَأَوْصَٰنِى بِٱلصَّلَوٰةِ وَٱلزَّكَوٰةِ مَا دُمْتُ حَيًّا

31 And has made me blessed wherever I may be; and has enjoined on me prayer and charity, so long as I live.

٣٢ وَبَرًّۢا بِوَٰلِدَتِى وَلَمْ يَجْعَلْنِى جَبَّارًا شَقِيًّا

32 And kind to my mother, and He did not make me a disobedient rebel.

٣٣ وَٱلسَّلَٰمُ عَلَىَّ يَوْمَ وُلِدتُّ وَيَوْمَ أَمُوتُ وَيَوْمَ أُبْعَثُ حَيًّا

33 So Peace is upon me the day I was born, and the day I die, and the Day I get resurrected alive."

٣٤ ذَٰلِكَ عِيسَى ٱبْنُ مَرْيَمَ ۚ قَوْلَ ٱلْحَقِّ ٱلَّذِى فِيهِ يَمْتَرُونَ

34 That is Jesus son of Mary—the Word of truth about which they doubt.

٣٥ مَا كَانَ لِلَّهِ أَن يَتَّخِذَ مِن وَلَدٍ ۖ سُبْحَٰنَهُۥٓ ۚ إِذَا قَضَىٰٓ أَمْرًا فَإِنَّمَا يَقُولُ لَهُۥ كُن فَيَكُونُ

35 It is not for Allah to have a child—glory be to Him. To have anything done, He says to it, "Be," and it becomes.

٣٦ وَإِنَّ ٱللَّهَ رَبِّى وَرَبُّكُمْ فَٱعْبُدُوهُ ۚ هَٰذَا صِرَٰطٌ
مُّسْتَقِيمٌ

36 "Allah is my Lord and your Lord, so worship Him. That is a straight path."

٣٧ فَٱخْتَلَفَ ٱلْأَحْزَابُ مِنۢ بَيْنِهِمْ ۖ فَوَيْلٌ لِّلَّذِينَ
كَفَرُوا۟ مِن مَّشْهَدِ يَوْمٍ عَظِيمٍ

37 But the various factions differed among themselves. So woe to those who disbelieve from the scene of a tremendous Day.

٣٨ أَسْمِعْ بِهِمْ وَأَبْصِرْ يَوْمَ يَأْتُونَنَا ۖ لَٰكِنِ
ٱلظَّٰلِمُونَ ٱلْيَوْمَ فِى ضَلَٰلٍ مُّبِينٍ

38 Listen to them and watch for them the Day they come to Us. But the wrongdoers today are completely lost.

٣٩ وَأَنذِرْهُمْ يَوْمَ ٱلْحَسْرَةِ إِذْ قُضِىَ ٱلْأَمْرُ وَهُمْ
فِى غَفْلَةٍ وَهُمْ لَا يُؤْمِنُونَ

39 And warn them of the Day of Regret, when the matter will be concluded. Yet they are heedless, and they do not believe.

٤٠ إِنَّا نَحْنُ نَرِثُ ٱلْأَرْضَ وَمَنْ عَلَيْهَا وَإِلَيْنَا
يُرْجَعُونَ

40 It is We who will inherit the earth and everyone on it, and to Us they will be returned.

٤١ وَٱذْكُرْ فِى ٱلْكِتَٰبِ إِبْرَٰهِيمَ ۚ إِنَّهُۥ كَانَ صِدِّيقًا
نَّبِيًّا

41 And mention in the Scripture Abraham. He was a man of truth, a prophet.

٤٢ إِذْ قَالَ لِأَبِيهِ يَٰٓأَبَتِ لِمَ تَعْبُدُ مَا لَا يَسْمَعُ وَلَا
يُبْصِرُ وَلَا يُغْنِى عَنكَ شَيْـًٔا

42 He said to his father, "O my father, why do you worship what can neither hear, nor see, nor benefit you in any way?

٤٣ يَٰٓأَبَتِ إِنِّى قَدْ جَآءَنِى مِنَ ٱلْعِلْمِ مَا لَمْ يَأْتِكَ
فَٱتَّبِعْنِىٓ أَهْدِكَ صِرَٰطًا سَوِيًّا

43 O my father, there has come to me knowledge that never came to you. So follow me, and I will guide you along a straight way.

٤٤ يَٰٓأَبَتِ لَا تَعْبُدِ ٱلشَّيْطَٰنَ ۖ إِنَّ ٱلشَّيْطَٰنَ كَانَ
لِلرَّحْمَٰنِ عَصِيًّا

44 O my father, do not worship the devil. The devil is disobedient to the Most Gracious.

٤٥ يَٰٓأَبَتِ إِنِّىٓ أَخَافُ أَن يَمَسَّكَ عَذَابٌ مِّنَ
ٱلرَّحْمَٰنِ فَتَكُونَ لِلشَّيْطَٰنِ وَلِيًّا

45 O my father, I fear that a punishment from the Most Gracious will afflict you, and you become an ally of the devil."

٤٦ قَالَ أَرَاغِبٌ أَنتَ عَنْ ءَالِهَتِى يَٰٓإِبْرَٰهِيمُ ۖ لَئِن
لَّمْ تَنتَهِ لَأَرْجُمَنَّكَ ۖ وَٱهْجُرْنِى مَلِيًّا

46 He said, "Are you renouncing my gods, O Abraham? If you do not desist, I will stone you. So leave me alone for a while."

٤٧ قَالَ سَلَٰمٌ عَلَيْكَ ۖ سَأَسْتَغْفِرُ لَكَ رَبِّىٓ ۖ إِنَّهُۥ
كَانَ بِى حَفِيًّا

47 He said, “Peace be upon you. I will ask my Lord to forgive you; He has been Kind to me.

٤٨ وَأَعْتَزِلُكُمْ وَمَا تَدْعُونَ مِن دُونِ ٱللَّهِ
وَأَدْعُوا۟ رَبِّى عَسَىٰٓ أَلَّآ أَكُونَ بِدُعَآءِ رَبِّى شَقِيًّا

48 And I will withdraw from you, and from what you pray to instead of Allah. And I will pray to my Lord, and I hope I will not be disappointed in my prayer to my Lord.”

٤٩ فَلَمَّا ٱعْتَزَلَهُمْ وَمَا يَعْبُدُونَ مِن دُونِ ٱللَّهِ
وَهَبْنَا لَهُۥٓ إِسْحَٰقَ وَيَعْقُوبَ ۖ وَكُلًّا جَعَلْنَا نَبِيًّا

49 When he withdrew from them, and from what they worship besides Allah, We granted him Isaac and Jacob. And each We made a prophet.

٥٠ وَوَهَبْنَا لَهُم مِّن رَّحْمَتِنَا وَجَعَلْنَا لَهُمْ لِسَانَ
صِدْقٍ عَلِيًّا

50 And We gave them freely of Our mercy, and gave them a noble reputation of truth.

٥١ وَٱذْكُرْ فِى ٱلْكِتَٰبِ مُوسَىٰٓ ۚ إِنَّهُۥ كَانَ مُخْلَصًا
وَكَانَ رَسُولًا نَّبِيًّا

51 And mention in the Scripture Moses. He was dedicated. He was a messenger and a prophet.

٥٢ وَنَٰدَيْنَٰهُ مِن جَانِبِ ٱلطُّورِ ٱلْأَيْمَنِ وَقَرَّبْنَٰهُ
نَجِيًّا

52 And We called him from the right side of the Mount, and brought him near in communion.

٥٣ وَوَهَبْنَا لَهُۥ مِن رَّحْمَتِنَآ أَخَاهُ هَٰرُونَ نَبِيًّا

53 And We granted him, out of Our mercy, his brother Aaron, a prophet.

٥٤ وَٱذْكُرْ فِى ٱلْكِتَٰبِ إِسْمَٰعِيلَ ۚ إِنَّهُۥ كَانَ صَادِقَ
ٱلْوَعْدِ وَكَانَ رَسُولًا نَّبِيًّا

54 And mention in the Scripture Ishmael. He was true to his promise, and was a messenger, a prophet.

٥٥ وَكَانَ يَأْمُرُ أَهْلَهُۥ بِٱلصَّلَوٰةِ وَٱلزَّكَوٰةِ وَكَانَ
عِندَ رَبِّهِۦ مَرْضِيًّا

55 And he used to enjoin on his people prayer and charity, and he was pleasing to his Lord.

٥٦ وَٱذْكُرْ فِى ٱلْكِتَٰبِ إِدْرِيسَ ۚ إِنَّهُۥ كَانَ صِدِّيقًا
نَّبِيًّا

56 And mention in the Scripture Enoch. He was a man of truth, a prophet.

٥٧ وَرَفَعْنَٰهُ مَكَانًا عَلِيًّا

57 And We raised him to a high position.

٥٨ أُو۟لَٰٓئِكَ ٱلَّذِينَ أَنْعَمَ ٱللَّهُ عَلَيْهِم مِّنَ ٱلنَّبِيِّـۧنَ
مِن ذُرِّيَّةِ ءَادَمَ وَمِمَّنْ حَمَلْنَا مَعَ نُوحٍ وَمِن
ذُرِّيَّةِ إِبْرَٰهِيمَ وَإِسْرَٰٓءِيلَ وَمِمَّنْ هَدَيْنَا

58 These are some of the prophets Allah has blessed, from the descendants of Adam, and from those We carried with Noah, and from the descendants of Abraham

وَٱجْتَبَيْنَآ ۚ إِذَا تُتْلَىٰ عَلَيْهِمْ ءَايَٰتُ ٱلرَّحْمَٰنِ
خَرُّوا۟ سُجَّدًا وَبُكِيًّا ۩

and Israel, and from those We guided and selected. Whenever the revelations of the Most Gracious are recited to them, they would fall down, prostrating and weeping.

٥٩ فَخَلَفَ مِنۢ بَعْدِهِمْ خَلْفٌ أَضَاعُوا۟ ٱلصَّلَوٰةَ
وَٱتَّبَعُوا۟ ٱلشَّهَوَٰتِ ۖ فَسَوْفَ يَلْقَوْنَ غَيًّا

59 But they were succeeded by generations who lost the prayers and followed their appetites. They will meet perdition.

٦٠ إِلَّا مَن تَابَ وَءَامَنَ وَعَمِلَ صَٰلِحًا فَأُو۟لَٰٓئِكَ
يَدْخُلُونَ ٱلْجَنَّةَ وَلَا يُظْلَمُونَ شَيْـًٔا

60 Except for those who repent, and believe, and act righteously. These will enter Paradise, and will not be wronged in the least.

٦١ جَنَّٰتِ عَدْنٍ ٱلَّتِى وَعَدَ ٱلرَّحْمَٰنُ عِبَادَهُۥ
بِٱلْغَيْبِ ۚ إِنَّهُۥ كَانَ وَعْدُهُۥ مَأْتِيًّا

61 The Gardens of Eden, promised by the Most Merciful to His servants in the Unseen. His promise will certainly come true.

٦٢ لَّا يَسْمَعُونَ فِيهَا لَغْوًا إِلَّا سَلَٰمًا ۖ وَلَهُمْ رِزْقُهُمْ
فِيهَا بُكْرَةً وَعَشِيًّا

62 They will hear no nonsense therein, but only peace. And they will have their provision therein, morning and evening.

٦٣ تِلْكَ ٱلْجَنَّةُ ٱلَّتِى نُورِثُ مِنْ عِبَادِنَا مَن كَانَ
تَقِيًّا

63 Such is Paradise which We will give as inheritance to those of Our servants who are devout.

٦٤ وَمَا نَتَنَزَّلُ إِلَّا بِأَمْرِ رَبِّكَ ۖ لَهُۥ مَا بَيْنَ أَيْدِينَا
وَمَا خَلْفَنَا وَمَا بَيْنَ ذَٰلِكَ ۚ وَمَا كَانَ رَبُّكَ نَسِيًّا

64 "We do not descend except by the command of your Lord. His is what is before us, and what is behind us, and what is between them. Your Lord is never forgetful."

٦٥ رَّبُّ ٱلسَّمَٰوَٰتِ وَٱلْأَرْضِ وَمَا بَيْنَهُمَا فَٱعْبُدْهُ
وَٱصْطَبِرْ لِعِبَٰدَتِهِۦ ۚ هَلْ تَعْلَمُ لَهُۥ سَمِيًّا

65 Lord of the heavens and the earth and what is between them. So worship Him, and persevere in His service. Do you know of anyone equal to Him?

٦٦ وَيَقُولُ ٱلْإِنسَٰنُ أَءِذَا مَا مِتُّ لَسَوْفَ أُخْرَجُ
حَيًّا

66 And the human being says, "When I am dead, will I be brought back alive?"

٦٧ أَوَلَا يَذْكُرُ ٱلْإِنسَٰنُ أَنَّا خَلَقْنَٰهُ مِن قَبْلُ وَلَمْ
يَكُ شَيْـًٔا

67 Does the human being not remember that We created him before, when he was nothing?

٦٨ فَوَرَبِّكَ لَنَحْشُرَنَّهُمْ وَٱلشَّيَـٰطِينَ ثُمَّ لَنُحْضِرَنَّهُمْ حَوْلَ جَهَنَّمَ جِثِيًّا

68 By your Lord, We will round them up, and the devils, then We will bring them around Hell, on their knees.

٦٩ ثُمَّ لَنَنزِعَنَّ مِن كُلِّ شِيعَةٍ أَيُّهُمْ أَشَدُّ عَلَى ٱلرَّحْمَـٰنِ عِتِيًّا

69 Then, out of every sect, We will snatch those most defiant to the Most Merciful.

٧٠ ثُمَّ لَنَحْنُ أَعْلَمُ بِٱلَّذِينَ هُمْ أَوْلَىٰ بِهَا صِلِيًّا

70 We are fully aware of those most deserving to scorch in it.

٧١ وَإِن مِّنكُمْ إِلَّا وَارِدُهَا ۚ كَانَ عَلَىٰ رَبِّكَ حَتْمًا مَّقْضِيًّا

71 There is not one of you but will go down to it. This has been an unavoidable decree of your Lord.

٧٢ ثُمَّ نُنَجِّى ٱلَّذِينَ ٱتَّقَوا۟ وَّنَذَرُ ٱلظَّـٰلِمِينَ فِيهَا جِثِيًّا

72 Then We will rescue those who were devout, and leave the wrongdoers in it, on their knees.

٧٣ وَإِذَا تُتْلَىٰ عَلَيْهِمْ ءَايَـٰتُنَا بَيِّنَـٰتٍ قَالَ ٱلَّذِينَ كَفَرُوا۟ لِلَّذِينَ ءَامَنُوٓا۟ أَىُّ ٱلْفَرِيقَيْنِ خَيْرٌ مَّقَامًا وَأَحْسَنُ نَدِيًّا

73 When Our clear revelations are recited to them, those who disbelieve say to those who believe, “Which of the two parties is better in position, and superior in influence?”

٧٤ وَكَمْ أَهْلَكْنَا قَبْلَهُم مِّن قَرْنٍ هُمْ أَحْسَنُ أَثَـٰثًا وَرِءْيًا

74 How many a generation have We destroyed before them, who surpassed them in riches and splendor?

٧٥ قُلْ مَن كَانَ فِى ٱلضَّلَـٰلَةِ فَلْيَمْدُدْ لَهُ ٱلرَّحْمَـٰنُ مَدًّا ۚ حَتَّىٰٓ إِذَا رَأَوْا۟ مَا يُوعَدُونَ إِمَّا ٱلْعَذَابَ وَإِمَّا ٱلسَّاعَةَ فَسَيَعْلَمُونَ مَنْ هُوَ شَرٌّ مَّكَانًا وَأَضْعَفُ جُندًا

75 Say, “Whoever is in error, the Most Merciful will lead him on.” Until, when they see what they were promised—either the punishment, or the Hour. Then they will know who was in worse position and weaker in forces.

٧٦ وَيَزِيدُ ٱللَّهُ ٱلَّذِينَ ٱهْتَدَوْا۟ هُدًى ۗ وَٱلْبَـٰقِيَـٰتُ ٱلصَّـٰلِحَـٰتُ خَيْرٌ عِندَ رَبِّكَ ثَوَابًا وَخَيْرٌ مَّرَدًّا

76 Allah increases in guidance those who accept guidance. And the things that endure—the righteous deeds—have the best reward with your Lord, and the best outcome.

٧٧ أَفَرَءَيْتَ ٱلَّذِى كَفَرَ بِـَٔايَـٰتِنَا وَقَالَ لَأُوتَيَنَّ مَالًا وَوَلَدًا

77 Have you seen him who denied Our revelations, and said, “I will be given wealth and children”?

٧٨ أَطَّلَعَ ٱلْغَيْبَ أَمِ ٱتَّخَذَ عِندَ ٱلرَّحْمَٰنِ عَهْدًا

78 Did he look into the future, or did he receive a promise from the Most Merciful?

٧٩ كَلَّا ۚ سَنَكْتُبُ مَا يَقُولُ وَنَمُدُّ لَهُۥ مِنَ ٱلْعَذَابِ مَدًّا

79 No indeed! We will write what he says, and will keep extending the agony for him.

٨٠ وَنَرِثُهُۥ مَا يَقُولُ وَيَأْتِينَا فَرْدًا

80 Then We will inherit from him what he speaks of, and he will come to Us alone.

٨١ وَٱتَّخَذُوا۟ مِن دُونِ ٱللَّهِ ءَالِهَةً لِّيَكُونُوا۟ لَهُمْ عِزًّا

81 And they took, besides Allah, other gods, to be for them a source of strength.

٨٢ كَلَّا ۚ سَيَكْفُرُونَ بِعِبَادَتِهِمْ وَيَكُونُونَ عَلَيْهِمْ ضِدًّا

82 By no means! They will reject their worship of them, and become opponents to them.

٨٣ أَلَمْ تَرَ أَنَّآ أَرْسَلْنَا ٱلشَّيَٰطِينَ عَلَى ٱلْكَٰفِرِينَ تَؤُزُّهُمْ أَزًّا

83 Have you not considered how We dispatch the devils against the disbelievers, exciting them with incitement?

٨٤ فَلَا تَعْجَلْ عَلَيْهِمْ ۖ إِنَّمَا نَعُدُّ لَهُمْ عَدًّا

84 So do not hurry against them. We are counting for them a countdown.

٨٥ يَوْمَ نَحْشُرُ ٱلْمُتَّقِينَ إِلَى ٱلرَّحْمَٰنِ وَفْدًا

85 On the Day when We will gather the righteous to the Most Merciful, as guests.

٨٦ وَنَسُوقُ ٱلْمُجْرِمِينَ إِلَىٰ جَهَنَّمَ وِرْدًا

86 And herd the sinners into hell, like animals to water.

٨٧ لَّا يَمْلِكُونَ ٱلشَّفَٰعَةَ إِلَّا مَنِ ٱتَّخَذَ عِندَ ٱلرَّحْمَٰنِ عَهْدًا

87 They will have no power of intercession, except for someone who has an agreement with the Most Merciful.

٨٨ وَقَالُوا۟ ٱتَّخَذَ ٱلرَّحْمَٰنُ وَلَدًا

88 And they say, “The Most Merciful has begotten a son.”

٨٩ لَّقَدْ جِئْتُمْ شَيْـًٔا إِدًّا

89 You have come up with something monstrous.

٩٠ تَكَادُ ٱلسَّمَٰوَٰتُ يَتَفَطَّرْنَ مِنْهُ وَتَنشَقُّ ٱلْأَرْضُ وَتَخِرُّ ٱلْجِبَالُ هَدًّا

90 At which the heavens almost rupture, and the earth splits, and the mountains fall and crumble.

٩١ أَن دَعَوْا۟ لِلرَّحْمَٰنِ وَلَدًا

91 Because they attribute a son to the Most Merciful.

٩٢ وَمَا يَنۢبَغِى لِلرَّحۡمَٰنِ أَن يَتَّخِذَ وَلَدًا

92 It is not fitting for the Most Merciful to have a son.

٩٣ إِن كُلُّ مَن فِى ٱلسَّمَٰوَٰتِ وَٱلۡأَرۡضِ إِلَّآ ءَاتِى ٱلرَّحۡمَٰنِ عَبۡدًا

93 There is none in the heavens and the earth but will come to the Most Merciful as a servant.

٩٤ لَّقَدۡ أَحۡصَىٰهُمۡ وَعَدَّهُمۡ عَدًّا

94 He has enumerated them, and counted them one by one.

٩٥ وَكُلُّهُمۡ ءَاتِيهِ يَوۡمَ ٱلۡقِيَٰمَةِ فَرۡدًا

95 And each one of them will come to Him on the Day of Resurrection alone.

٩٦ إِنَّ ٱلَّذِينَ ءَامَنُواْ وَعَمِلُواْ ٱلصَّٰلِحَٰتِ سَيَجۡعَلُ لَهُمُ ٱلرَّحۡمَٰنُ وُدًّا

96 Those who believe and do righteous deeds, the Most Merciful will give them love.

٩٧ فَإِنَّمَا يَسَّرۡنَٰهُ بِلِسَانِكَ لِتُبَشِّرَ بِهِ ٱلۡمُتَّقِينَ وَتُنذِرَ بِهِۦ قَوۡمًا لُّدًّا

97 We made it easy in your tongue, in order to deliver good news to the righteous, and to warn with it a hostile people.

٩٨ وَكَمۡ أَهۡلَكۡنَا قَبۡلَهُم مِّن قَرۡنٍ هَلۡ تُحِسُّ مِنۡهُم مِّنۡ أَحَدٍ أَوۡ تَسۡمَعُ لَهُمۡ رِكۡزًۢا

98 How many a generation have We destroyed before them? Can you feel a single one of them, or hear from them the slightest whisper?

20 Ta-Ha طه

بِسۡمِ ٱللَّهِ ٱلرَّحۡمَٰنِ ٱلرَّحِيمِ

In the name of Allah, the Gracious, the Merciful.

١ طه

1 Ta, Ha.

٢ مَآ أَنزَلۡنَا عَلَيۡكَ ٱلۡقُرۡءَانَ لِتَشۡقَىٰٓ

2 We did not reveal the Quran to you to make you suffer.

٣ إِلَّا تَذۡكِرَةً لِّمَن يَخۡشَىٰ

3 But only as a reminder for him who fears.

٤ تَنزِيلًا مِّمَّنۡ خَلَقَ ٱلۡأَرۡضَ وَٱلسَّمَٰوَٰتِ ٱلۡعُلَى

4 A revelation from He who created the earth and the high heavens.

٥ ٱلرَّحۡمَٰنُ عَلَى ٱلۡعَرۡشِ ٱسۡتَوَىٰ

5 The Most Merciful; on the Throne He settled.

٦ لَهُۥ مَا فِى ٱلسَّمَٰوَٰتِ وَمَا فِى ٱلۡأَرۡضِ وَمَا بَيۡنَهُمَا وَمَا تَحۡتَ ٱلثَّرَىٰ

6 To Him belongs everything in the heavens and the earth, and

everything between them, and everything beneath the soil.

٧ وَإِن تَجْهَرْ بِٱلْقَوْلِ فَإِنَّهُۥ يَعْلَمُ ٱلسِّرَّ وَأَخْفَى

7 If you speak aloud—He knows the secret, and the most hidden.

٨ ٱللَّهُ لَآ إِلَـٰهَ إِلَّا هُوَ ۖ لَهُ ٱلْأَسْمَآءُ ٱلْحُسْنَىٰ

8 Allah, there is no god but He, His are the Most Beautiful Names.

٩ وَهَلْ أَتَىٰكَ حَدِيثُ مُوسَىٰٓ

9 Has the story of Moses reached you?

١٠ إِذْ رَءَا نَارًا فَقَالَ لِأَهْلِهِ ٱمْكُثُوٓا۟ إِنِّىٓ ءَانَسْتُ
نَارًا لَّعَلِّىٓ ءَاتِيكُم مِّنْهَا بِقَبَسٍ أَوْ أَجِدُ عَلَى
ٱلنَّارِ هُدًى

10 When he saw a fire, he said to his family, “Stay; I have noticed a fire; Perhaps I can bring you a torch therefrom, or find some guidance by the fire.”

١١ فَلَمَّآ أَتَىٰهَا نُودِىَ يَـٰمُوسَىٰٓ

11 Then, when he reached it, he was called, “O Moses.

١٢ إِنِّىٓ أَنَا۠ رَبُّكَ فَٱخْلَعْ نَعْلَيْكَ ۖ إِنَّكَ بِٱلْوَادِ
ٱلْمُقَدَّسِ طُوًى

12 I—I am your Lord. Take off your shoes. You are in the sacred valley of Tuwa.

١٣ وَأَنَا ٱخْتَرْتُكَ فَٱسْتَمِعْ لِمَا يُوحَىٰٓ

13 I have chosen you, so listen to what is revealed.

١٤ إِنَّنِىٓ أَنَا ٱللَّهُ لَآ إِلَـٰهَ إِلَّآ أَنَا۠ فَٱعْبُدْنِى وَأَقِمِ
ٱلصَّلَوٰةَ لِذِكْرِىٓ

14 I—I am Allah. There is no God but I. So serve Me, and practice the prayer for My remembrance.

١٥ إِنَّ ٱلسَّاعَةَ ءَاتِيَةٌ أَكَادُ أُخْفِيهَا لِتُجْزَىٰ كُلُّ
نَفْسٍۭ بِمَا تَسْعَىٰ

15 The Hour is coming—but I keep it almost hidden—so that each soul will be paid for what it endeavors.

١٦ فَلَا يَصُدَّنَّكَ عَنْهَا مَن لَّا يُؤْمِنُ بِهَا وَٱتَّبَعَ
هَوَىٰهُ فَتَرْدَىٰ

16 And do not let him who denies it and follows his desire turn you away from it, lest you fall.

١٧ وَمَا تِلْكَ بِيَمِينِكَ يَـٰمُوسَىٰ

17 And what is that in your right-hand, O Moses?”

١٨ قَالَ هِىَ عَصَاىَ أَتَوَكَّؤُا۟ عَلَيْهَا وَأَهُشُّ بِهَا
عَلَىٰ غَنَمِى وَلِىَ فِيهَا مَـَٔارِبُ أُخْرَىٰ

18 He said, “This is my staff. I lean on it, and herd my sheep with it, and I have other uses for it.”

١٩ قَالَ أَلْقِهَا يَـٰمُوسَىٰ

19 He said, “Throw it, O Moses.”

٢٠ فَأَلْقَىٰهَا فَإِذَا هِىَ حَيَّةٌ تَسْعَىٰ

20 So he threw it—thereupon it became a moving serpent.

٢١ قَالَ خُذْهَا وَلَا تَخَفْ ۖ سَنُعِيدُهَا سِيرَتَهَا ٱلْأُولَىٰ

21 He said, "Take hold of it, and do not fear. We will restore it to its original condition.

٢٢ وَٱضْمُمْ يَدَكَ إِلَىٰ جَنَاحِكَ تَخْرُجْ بَيْضَآءَ مِنْ غَيْرِ سُوٓءٍ ءَايَةً أُخْرَىٰ

22 And press your hand to your side; it will come out white, without a blemish—another sign.

٢٣ لِنُرِيَكَ مِنْ ءَايَٰتِنَا ٱلْكُبْرَى

23 That We may show you some of Our greatest signs.

٢٤ ٱذْهَبْ إِلَىٰ فِرْعَوْنَ إِنَّهُۥ طَغَىٰ

24 Go to Pharaoh; He has transgressed."

٢٥ قَالَ رَبِّ ٱشْرَحْ لِى صَدْرِى

25 He said, "My Lord, put my heart at peace for me.

٢٦ وَيَسِّرْ لِىٓ أَمْرِى

26 And ease my task for me.

٢٧ وَٱحْلُلْ عُقْدَةً مِّن لِّسَانِى

27 And untie the knot from my tongue.

٢٨ يَفْقَهُوا۟ قَوْلِى

28 So they can understand my speech.

٢٩ وَٱجْعَل لِّى وَزِيرًا مِّنْ أَهْلِى

29 And appoint an assistant for me, from my family.

٣٠ هَٰرُونَ أَخِى

30 Aaron, my brother.

٣١ ٱشْدُدْ بِهِۦٓ أَزْرِى

31 Strengthen me with him.

٣٢ وَأَشْرِكْهُ فِىٓ أَمْرِى

32 And have him share in my mission.

٣٣ كَىْ نُسَبِّحَكَ كَثِيرًا

33 That we may glorify You much.

٣٤ وَنَذْكُرَكَ كَثِيرًا

34 And remember You much.

٣٥ إِنَّكَ كُنتَ بِنَا بَصِيرًا

35 You are always watching over us."

٣٦ قَالَ قَدْ أُوتِيتَ سُؤْلَكَ يَٰمُوسَىٰ

36 He said, "You are granted your request, O Moses.

٣٧ وَلَقَدْ مَنَنَّا عَلَيْكَ مَرَّةً أُخْرَىٰٓ

37 We had favored you another time.

٣٨ إِذْ أَوْحَيْنَآ إِلَىٰٓ أُمِّكَ مَا يُوحَىٰٓ

38 When We inspired your mother with the inspiration.

٣٩ أَنِ ٱقْذِفِيهِ فِى ٱلتَّابُوتِ فَٱقْذِفِيهِ فِى ٱلْيَمِّ فَلْيُلْقِهِ ٱلْيَمُّ بِٱلسَّاحِلِ يَأْخُذْهُ عَدُوٌّ لِّى وَعَدُوٌّ

39 `Put him in the chest; then cast him into the river. The river will wash him to shore, where an enemy of Mine and an enemy of his will pick

لَهُۥۚ وَأَلْقَيْتُ عَلَيْكَ مَحَبَّةً مِّنِّى وَلِتُصْنَعَ عَلَىٰ
عَيْنِىٓ

him up. And I have bestowed upon you love from Me, so that you may be reared before My eye.

٤٠ إِذْ تَمْشِىٓ أُخْتُكَ فَتَقُولُ هَلْ أَدُلُّكُمْ عَلَىٰ مَن
يَكْفُلُهُۥ ۖ فَرَجَعْنَٰكَ إِلَىٰٓ أُمِّكَ كَىْ تَقَرَّ عَيْنُهَا وَلَا
تَحْزَنَ ۚ وَقَتَلْتَ نَفْسًا فَنَجَّيْنَٰكَ مِنَ ٱلْغَمِّ وَفَتَنَّٰكَ
فُتُونًا ۚ فَلَبِثْتَ سِنِينَ فِىٓ أَهْلِ مَدْيَنَ ثُمَّ جِئْتَ
عَلَىٰ قَدَرٍ يَٰمُوسَىٰ

40 When your sister walked along, and said, 'Shall I tell you about someone who will take care of him?' So We returned you to your mother, that she may be comforted, and not sorrow. And you killed a person, but We saved you from stress; and We tested you thoroughly. And you stayed years among the people of Median. Then you came back, as ordained, O Moses.

٤١ وَٱصْطَنَعْتُكَ لِنَفْسِى

41 And I made you for Myself.

٤٢ ٱذْهَبْ أَنتَ وَأَخُوكَ بِـَٔايَٰتِى وَلَا تَنِيَا فِى
ذِكْرِى

42 Go, you and your brother, with My signs, and do not neglect My remembrance.

٤٣ ٱذْهَبَآ إِلَىٰ فِرْعَوْنَ إِنَّهُۥ طَغَىٰ

43 Go to Pharaoh. He has tyrannized.

٤٤ فَقُولَا لَهُۥ قَوْلًا لَّيِّنًا لَّعَلَّهُۥ يَتَذَكَّرُ أَوْ يَخْشَىٰ

44 But speak to him nicely. Perhaps he will remember, or have some fear."

٤٥ قَالَا رَبَّنَآ إِنَّنَا نَخَافُ أَن يَفْرُطَ عَلَيْنَآ أَوْ أَن
يَطْغَىٰ

45 They said, "Lord, we fear he may persecute us, or become violent."

٤٦ قَالَ لَا تَخَافَآ ۖ إِنَّنِى مَعَكُمَآ أَسْمَعُ وَأَرَىٰ

46 He said, "Do not fear, I am with you, I hear and I see.

٤٧ فَأْتِيَاهُ فَقُولَآ إِنَّا رَسُولَا رَبِّكَ فَأَرْسِلْ مَعَنَا
بَنِىٓ إِسْرَٰٓءِيلَ وَلَا تُعَذِّبْهُمْ ۖ قَدْ جِئْنَٰكَ بِـَٔايَةٍ مِّن
رَّبِّكَ ۖ وَٱلسَّلَٰمُ عَلَىٰ مَنِ ٱتَّبَعَ ٱلْهُدَىٰٓ

47 Approach him and say, `We are the messengers of your Lord; so let the Children of Israel go with us, and do not torment them. We bring you a sign from your Lord, and peace be upon him who follows guidance.

٤٨ إِنَّا قَدْ أُوحِىَ إِلَيْنَآ أَنَّ ٱلْعَذَابَ عَلَىٰ مَن
كَذَّبَ وَتَوَلَّىٰ

48 It was revealed to us that the punishment falls upon him who disbelieves and turns away.'"

٤٩ قَالَ فَمَن رَّبُّكُمَا يَٰمُوسَىٰ

49 He said, "Who is your Lord, O Moses."

٥٠ قَالَ رَبُّنَا ٱلَّذِىٓ أَعْطَىٰ كُلَّ شَىْءٍ خَلْقَهُۥ ثُمَّ
هَدَىٰ

50 He said, "Our Lord is He who gave everything its existence, then guided it."

٥١ قَالَ فَمَا بَالُ ٱلْقُرُونِ ٱلْأُولَىٰ

51 He said, "What about the first generations?"

٥٢ قَالَ عِلْمُهَا عِندَ رَبِّى فِى كِتَٰبٍۖ لَّا يَضِلُّ رَبِّى
وَلَا يَنسَى

52 He said, "Knowledge thereof is with my Lord, in a Book. My Lord never errs, nor does He forget."

٥٣ ٱلَّذِى جَعَلَ لَكُمُ ٱلْأَرْضَ مَهْدًا وَسَلَكَ لَكُمْ
فِيهَا سُبُلًا وَأَنزَلَ مِنَ ٱلسَّمَآءِ مَآءً فَأَخْرَجْنَا
بِهِۦٓ أَزْوَٰجًا مِّن نَّبَاتٍ شَتَّىٰ

53 He who made the earth a habitat for you; and traced in it routes for you; and sent down water from the sky, with which We produce pairs of diverse plants.

٥٤ كُلُوا۟ وَٱرْعَوْا۟ أَنْعَٰمَكُمْۗ إِنَّ فِى ذَٰلِكَ لَءَايَٰتٍ
لِّأُو۟لِى ٱلنُّهَىٰ

54 Eat and pasture your livestock. In that are signs for those with understanding.

٥٥ مِنْهَا خَلَقْنَٰكُمْ وَفِيهَا نُعِيدُكُمْ وَمِنْهَا
نُخْرِجُكُمْ تَارَةً أُخْرَىٰ

55 From it We created you, and into it We will return you, and from it We will bring you out another time.

٥٦ وَلَقَدْ أَرَيْنَٰهُ ءَايَٰتِنَا كُلَّهَا فَكَذَّبَ وَأَبَىٰ

56 We showed him Our signs, all of them, but he denied and refused.

٥٧ قَالَ أَجِئْتَنَا لِتُخْرِجَنَا مِنْ أَرْضِنَا بِسِحْرِكَ
يَٰمُوسَىٰ

57 He said, "Did you come to us to drive us out of our land with your magic, O Moses?

٥٨ فَلَنَأْتِيَنَّكَ بِسِحْرٍ مِّثْلِهِۦ فَٱجْعَلْ بَيْنَنَا وَبَيْنَكَ
مَوْعِدًا لَّا نُخْلِفُهُۥ نَحْنُ وَلَآ أَنتَ مَكَانًا سُوًى

58 We will produce for you magic like it; so make an appointment between us and you, which we will not miss—neither us, nor you—in a central place."

٥٩ قَالَ مَوْعِدُكُمْ يَوْمُ ٱلزِّينَةِ وَأَن يُحْشَرَ
ٱلنَّاسُ ضُحًى

59 He said, "Your appointment is the day of the festival, so let the people be gathered together at mid-morning."

٦٠ فَتَوَلَّىٰ فِرْعَوْنُ فَجَمَعَ كَيْدَهُۥ ثُمَّ أَتَىٰ

60 Pharaoh turned away, put together his plan, and then came back.

٦١ قَالَ لَهُم مُّوسَىٰ وَيْلَكُمْ لَا تَفْتَرُوا۟ عَلَى ٱللَّهِ
كَذِبًا فَيُسْحِتَكُم بِعَذَابٍۖ وَقَدْ خَابَ مَنِ ٱفْتَرَىٰ

61 Moses said to them, "Woe to you. Do not fabricate lies against Allah, or He will destroy you with a punishment. He who invents lies will fail."

٦٢ فَتَنَٰزَعُوٓاْ أَمۡرَهُم بَيۡنَهُمۡ وَأَسَرُّواْ ٱلنَّجۡوَىٰ

62 They disagreed among themselves over their affair, and conferred secretly.

٦٣ قَالُوٓاْ إِنۡ هَٰذَٰنِ لَسَٰحِرَٰنِ يُرِيدَانِ أَن
يُخۡرِجَاكُم مِّنۡ أَرۡضِكُم بِسِحۡرِهِمَا وَيَذۡهَبَا
بِطَرِيقَتِكُمُ ٱلۡمُثۡلَىٰ

63 They said, "These two are magicians who want to drive you out of your land with their magic, and to abolish your exemplary way of life.

٦٤ فَأَجۡمِعُواْ كَيۡدَكُمۡ ثُمَّ ٱئۡتُواْ صَفّٗاۚ وَقَدۡ أَفۡلَحَ
ٱلۡيَوۡمَ مَنِ ٱسۡتَعۡلَىٰ

64 So settle your plan, and come as one front. Today, whoever gains the upper hand will succeed."

٦٥ قَالُواْ يَٰمُوسَىٰٓ إِمَّآ أَن تُلۡقِيَ وَإِمَّآ أَن نَّكُونَ
أَوَّلَ مَنۡ أَلۡقَىٰ

65 They said, "O Moses, either you throw, or we will be the first to throw."

٦٦ قَالَ بَلۡ أَلۡقُواْۖ فَإِذَا حِبَالُهُمۡ وَعِصِيُّهُمۡ يُخَيَّلُ
إِلَيۡهِ مِن سِحۡرِهِمۡ أَنَّهَا تَسۡعَىٰ

66 He said, "You throw." And suddenly, their ropes and sticks appeared to him, because of their magic, to be crawling swiftly.

٦٧ فَأَوۡجَسَ فِي نَفۡسِهِۦ خِيفَةٗ مُّوسَىٰ

67 So Moses felt apprehensive within himself.

٦٨ قُلۡنَا لَا تَخَفۡ إِنَّكَ أَنتَ ٱلۡأَعۡلَىٰ

68 We said, "Do not be afraid, you are the uppermost.

٦٩ وَأَلۡقِ مَا فِي يَمِينِكَ تَلۡقَفۡ مَا صَنَعُوٓاْۖ إِنَّمَا
صَنَعُواْ كَيۡدُ سَٰحِرٖۖ وَلَا يُفۡلِحُ ٱلسَّاحِرُ حَيۡثُ
أَتَىٰ

69 Now throw down what is in your right hand—it will swallow what they have crafted. What they have crafted is only a magician's trickery. But the magician will not succeed, no matter what he does."

٧٠ فَأُلۡقِيَ ٱلسَّحَرَةُ سُجَّدٗا قَالُوٓاْ ءَامَنَّا بِرَبِّ
هَٰرُونَ وَمُوسَىٰ

70 And the magicians fell down prostrate. They said, "We have believed in the Lord of Aaron and Moses."

٧١ قَالَ ءَامَنتُمۡ لَهُۥ قَبۡلَ أَنۡ ءَاذَنَ لَكُمۡۖ إِنَّهُۥ
لَكَبِيرُكُمُ ٱلَّذِي عَلَّمَكُمُ ٱلسِّحۡرَۖ فَلَأُقَطِّعَنَّ
أَيۡدِيَكُمۡ وَأَرۡجُلَكُم مِّنۡ خِلَٰفٖ وَلَأُصَلِّبَنَّكُمۡ فِي
جُذُوعِ ٱلنَّخۡلِ وَلَتَعۡلَمُنَّ أَيُّنَآ أَشَدُّ عَذَابٗا وَأَبۡقَىٰ

71 He said, "Did you believe in him before I have given you permission? He must be your chief, who has taught you magic. I will cut off your hands and your feet on alternate sides, and I will crucify you on the trunks of the palm-trees. Then you will know which of us is more severe in punishment, and more lasting."

٧٢ قَالُوا۟ لَن نُّؤْثِرَكَ عَلَىٰ مَا جَآءَنَا مِنَ ٱلْبَيِّنَٰتِ وَٱلَّذِى فَطَرَنَا ۖ فَٱقْضِ مَآ أَنتَ قَاضٍ ۖ إِنَّمَا تَقْضِى هَٰذِهِ ٱلْحَيَوٰةَ ٱلدُّنْيَآ	72 They said, "We will not prefer you to the proofs that have come to us, and Him who created us. So issue whatever judgment you wish to issue. You can only rule in this lowly life.
٧٣ إِنَّآ ءَامَنَّا بِرَبِّنَا لِيَغْفِرَ لَنَا خَطَٰيَٰنَا وَمَآ أَكْرَهْتَنَا عَلَيْهِ مِنَ ٱلسِّحْرِ ۗ وَٱللَّهُ خَيْرٌ وَأَبْقَىٰٓ	73 We have believed in our Lord, so that He may forgive us our sins, and the magic you have compelled us to practice. Allah is Better, and more Lasting."
٧٤ إِنَّهُۥ مَن يَأْتِ رَبَّهُۥ مُجْرِمًا فَإِنَّ لَهُۥ جَهَنَّمَ لَا يَمُوتُ فِيهَا وَلَا يَحْيَىٰ	74 Whoever comes to his Lord guilty, for him is Hell, where he neither dies nor lives.
٧٥ وَمَن يَأْتِهِۦ مُؤْمِنًا قَدْ عَمِلَ ٱلصَّٰلِحَٰتِ فَأُو۟لَٰٓئِكَ لَهُمُ ٱلدَّرَجَٰتُ ٱلْعُلَىٰ	75 But whoever comes to Him a believer, having worked righteousness—these will have the highest ranks.
٧٦ جَنَّٰتُ عَدْنٍ تَجْرِى مِن تَحْتِهَا ٱلْأَنْهَٰرُ خَٰلِدِينَ فِيهَا ۚ وَذَٰلِكَ جَزَآءُ مَن تَزَكَّىٰ	76 The Gardens of Perpetuity, beneath which rivers flow, dwelling therein forever. That is the reward for him who purifies himself.
٧٧ وَلَقَدْ أَوْحَيْنَآ إِلَىٰ مُوسَىٰٓ أَنْ أَسْرِ بِعِبَادِى فَٱضْرِبْ لَهُمْ طَرِيقًا فِى ٱلْبَحْرِ يَبَسًا لَّا تَخَٰفُ دَرَكًا وَلَا تَخْشَىٰ	77 And We inspired Moses: "Travel by night with My servants, and strike for them a dry path across the sea, not fearing being overtaken, nor worrying."
٧٨ فَأَتْبَعَهُمْ فِرْعَوْنُ بِجُنُودِهِۦ فَغَشِيَهُم مِّنَ ٱلْيَمِّ مَا غَشِيَهُمْ	78 Pharaoh pursued them with his troops, but the sea overwhelmed them, and completely engulfed them.
٧٩ وَأَضَلَّ فِرْعَوْنُ قَوْمَهُۥ وَمَا هَدَىٰ	79 Pharaoh misled his people, and did not guide them.
٨٠ يَٰبَنِىٓ إِسْرَٰٓءِيلَ قَدْ أَنجَيْنَٰكُم مِّنْ عَدُوِّكُمْ وَوَٰعَدْنَٰكُمْ جَانِبَ ٱلطُّورِ ٱلْأَيْمَنَ وَنَزَّلْنَا عَلَيْكُمُ ٱلْمَنَّ وَٱلسَّلْوَىٰ	80 O Children of Israel! We have delivered you from your enemy, and promised you by the right side of the Mount, and sent down to you manna and quails.

٨١ كُلُوا۟ مِن طَيِّبَٰتِ مَا رَزَقْنَٰكُمْ وَلَا تَطْغَوْا۟ فِيهِ
فَيَحِلَّ عَلَيْكُمْ غَضَبِى ۖ وَمَن يَحْلِلْ عَلَيْهِ
غَضَبِى فَقَدْ هَوَىٰ

81 Eat of the good things We have provided for you, but do not be excessive therein, lest My wrath descends upon you. He upon whom My wrath descends has fallen.

٨٢ وَإِنِّى لَغَفَّارٌ لِّمَن تَابَ وَءَامَنَ وَعَمِلَ صَٰلِحًا
ثُمَّ ٱهْتَدَىٰ

82 And I am Forgiving towards him who repents, believes, acts righteously, and then remains guided.

٨٣ وَمَآ أَعْجَلَكَ عَن قَوْمِكَ يَٰمُوسَىٰ

83 "And what made you rush ahead of your people, O Moses?"

٨٤ قَالَ هُمْ أُو۟لَآءِ عَلَىٰٓ أَثَرِى وَعَجِلْتُ إِلَيْكَ
رَبِّ لِتَرْضَىٰ

84 He said, "They are following in my footsteps; and I hurried on to You, my Lord, that you may be pleased."

٨٥ قَالَ فَإِنَّا قَدْ فَتَنَّا قَوْمَكَ مِنۢ بَعْدِكَ وَأَضَلَّهُمُ
ٱلسَّامِرِىُّ

85 He said, "We have tested your people in your absence, and the Samarian misled them."

٨٦ فَرَجَعَ مُوسَىٰٓ إِلَىٰ قَوْمِهِۦ غَضْبَٰنَ أَسِفًا ۚ قَالَ
يَٰقَوْمِ أَلَمْ يَعِدْكُمْ رَبُّكُمْ وَعْدًا حَسَنًا ۚ أَفَطَالَ
عَلَيْكُمُ ٱلْعَهْدُ أَمْ أَرَدتُّمْ أَن يَحِلَّ عَلَيْكُمْ غَضَبٌ
مِّن رَّبِّكُمْ فَأَخْلَفْتُم مَّوْعِدِى

86 So Moses returned to his people, angry and disappointed. He said, "O my people, did your Lord not promise you a good promise? Was the time too long for you? Or did you want wrath from your Lord to descend upon you, so you broke your promise to me?"

٨٧ قَالُوا۟ مَآ أَخْلَفْنَا مَوْعِدَكَ بِمَلْكِنَا وَلَٰكِنَّا حُمِّلْنَآ
أَوْزَارًا مِّن زِينَةِ ٱلْقَوْمِ فَقَذَفْنَٰهَا فَكَذَٰلِكَ أَلْقَى
ٱلسَّامِرِىُّ

87 They said, "We did not break our promise to you by our choice, but we were made to carry loads of the people's ornaments, and we cast them in. That was what the Samarian suggested."

٨٨ فَأَخْرَجَ لَهُمْ عِجْلًا جَسَدًا لَّهُۥ خُوَارٌ فَقَالُوا۟
هَٰذَآ إِلَٰهُكُمْ وَإِلَٰهُ مُوسَىٰ فَنَسِىَ

88 So he produced for them a calf—a mere body which lowed. And they said, "This is your god, and the god of Moses, but he has forgotten."

٨٩ أَفَلَا يَرَوْنَ أَلَّا يَرْجِعُ إِلَيْهِمْ قَوْلًا وَلَا يَمْلِكُ
لَهُمْ ضَرًّا وَلَا نَفْعًا

89 Did they not see that it cannot return a word to them, and has no power to harm them or benefit them?

٩٠ وَلَقَدْ قَالَ لَهُمْ هَٰرُونُ مِن قَبْلُ يَٰقَوْمِ إِنَّمَا
فُتِنتُم بِهِۦ ۖ وَإِنَّ رَبَّكُمُ ٱلرَّحْمَٰنُ فَٱتَّبِعُونِى
وَأَطِيعُوٓا۟ أَمْرِى

90 Aaron had said to them before, "O my people, you are being tested by this. And your Lord is the Merciful, so follow me, and obey my command."

٩١ قَالُوا۟ لَن نَّبْرَحَ عَلَيْهِ عَٰكِفِينَ حَتَّىٰ يَرْجِعَ
إِلَيْنَا مُوسَىٰ

91 They said, "We will not give up our devotion to it, until Moses returns to us."

٩٢ قَالَ يَٰهَٰرُونُ مَا مَنَعَكَ إِذْ رَأَيْتَهُمْ ضَلُّوٓا۟

92 He said, "O Aaron, what prevented you, when you saw them going astray.

٩٣ أَلَّا تَتَّبِعَنِ ۖ أَفَعَصَيْتَ أَمْرِى

93 From following me? Did you disobey my command?"

٩٤ قَالَ يَبْنَؤُمَّ لَا تَأْخُذْ بِلِحْيَتِى وَلَا بِرَأْسِىٓ ۖ
إِنِّى خَشِيتُ أَن تَقُولَ فَرَّقْتَ بَيْنَ بَنِىٓ
إِسْرَٰٓءِيلَ وَلَمْ تَرْقُبْ قَوْلِى

94 He said, "Son of my mother, do not seize me by my beard or my head. I feared you would say, `You have caused division among the Children of Israel, and did not regard my word.'"

٩٥ قَالَ فَمَا خَطْبُكَ يَٰسَٰمِرِىُّ

95 He said, "What do you have to say, O Samarian?"

٩٦ قَالَ بَصُرْتُ بِمَا لَمْ يَبْصُرُوا۟ بِهِۦ فَقَبَضْتُ
قَبْضَةً مِّنْ أَثَرِ ٱلرَّسُولِ فَنَبَذْتُهَا وَكَذَٰلِكَ سَوَّلَتْ
لِى نَفْسِى

96 He said, "I saw what they did not see, so I grasped a handful from the Messenger's traces, and I flung it away. Thus my soul prompted me."

٩٧ قَالَ فَٱذْهَبْ فَإِنَّ لَكَ فِى ٱلْحَيَوٰةِ أَن تَقُولَ
لَا مِسَاسَ ۖ وَإِنَّ لَكَ مَوْعِدًا لَّن تُخْلَفَهُۥ ۖ وَٱنظُرْ
إِلَىٰٓ إِلَٰهِكَ ٱلَّذِى ظَلْتَ عَلَيْهِ عَاكِفًا ۖ لَّنُحَرِّقَنَّهُۥ ثُمَّ
لَنَنسِفَنَّهُۥ فِى ٱلْيَمِّ نَسْفًا

97 He said, "Begone! Your lot in this life is to say, 'No contact.' And you have an appointment that you will not miss. Now look at your god that you remained devoted to—we will burn it up, and then blow it away into the sea, as powder."

٩٨ إِنَّمَآ إِلَٰهُكُمُ ٱللَّهُ ٱلَّذِى لَآ إِلَٰهَ إِلَّا هُوَ ۚ وَسِعَ كُلَّ
شَىْءٍ عِلْمًا

98 Surely your god is Allah, the One besides whom there is no other god. He comprehends everything in knowledge.

٩٩ كَذَٰلِكَ نَقُصُّ عَلَيْكَ مِنْ أَنۢبَآءِ مَا قَدْ سَبَقَ ۚ
وَقَدْ ءَاتَيْنَٰكَ مِن لَّدُنَّا ذِكْرًا

99 Thus We narrate to you reports of times gone by; and We have given you a message from Our Presence.

١٠٠ مَّنْ أَعْرَضَ عَنْهُ فَإِنَّهُۥ يَحْمِلُ يَوْمَ ٱلْقِيَٰمَةِ وِزْرًا	100 Whoever turns away from it will carry on the Day of Resurrection a burden.
١٠١ خَٰلِدِينَ فِيهِ ۖ وَسَآءَ لَهُمْ يَوْمَ ٱلْقِيَٰمَةِ حِمْلًا	101 Abiding therein forever. And wretched is their burden on the Day of Resurrection.
١٠٢ يَوْمَ يُنفَخُ فِى ٱلصُّورِ ۚ وَنَحْشُرُ ٱلْمُجْرِمِينَ يَوْمَئِذٍ زُرْقًا	102 On the Day when the Trumpet is blown—We will gather the sinners on that Day, blue.
١٠٣ يَتَخَٰفَتُونَ بَيْنَهُمْ إِن لَّبِثْتُمْ إِلَّا عَشْرًا	103 Murmuring among themselves: “You have lingered only for ten.”
١٠٤ نَّحْنُ أَعْلَمُ بِمَا يَقُولُونَ إِذْ يَقُولُ أَمْثَلُهُمْ طَرِيقَةً إِن لَّبِثْتُمْ إِلَّا يَوْمًا	104 We are fully aware of what they say, when the most exemplary of them in conduct will say, “You have lingered only a day.”
١٠٥ وَيَسْـَٔلُونَكَ عَنِ ٱلْجِبَالِ فَقُلْ يَنسِفُهَا رَبِّى نَسْفًا	105 And they ask you about the mountains. Say, “My Lord will crumble them utterly.”
١٠٦ فَيَذَرُهَا قَاعًا صَفْصَفًا	106 And leave them desolate waste.
١٠٧ لَّا تَرَىٰ فِيهَا عِوَجًا وَلَآ أَمْتًا	107 You will see in them neither crookedness, nor deviation.”
١٠٨ يَوْمَئِذٍ يَتَّبِعُونَ ٱلدَّاعِىَ لَا عِوَجَ لَهُۥ ۖ وَخَشَعَتِ ٱلْأَصْوَاتُ لِلرَّحْمَٰنِ فَلَا تَسْمَعُ إِلَّا هَمْسًا	108 On that Day, they will follow the caller, without any deviation. Voices will be hushed before the Merciful, and you will hear nothing but murmur.
١٠٩ يَوْمَئِذٍ لَّا تَنفَعُ ٱلشَّفَٰعَةُ إِلَّا مَنْ أَذِنَ لَهُ ٱلرَّحْمَٰنُ وَرَضِىَ لَهُۥ قَوْلًا	109 On that Day, intercession will not avail, except for him permitted by the Merciful, and whose words He has approved.
١١٠ يَعْلَمُ مَا بَيْنَ أَيْدِيهِمْ وَمَا خَلْفَهُمْ وَلَا يُحِيطُونَ بِهِۦ عِلْمًا	110 He knows what is before them and what is behind them, and they cannot comprehend Him in their knowledge.
١١١ وَعَنَتِ ٱلْوُجُوهُ لِلْحَىِّ ٱلْقَيُّومِ ۖ وَقَدْ خَابَ مَنْ حَمَلَ ظُلْمًا	111 Faces will be humbled before the Living, the Eternal. Whoever carries injustice will despair.

١١٢ وَمَن يَعْمَلْ مِنَ ٱلصَّٰلِحَٰتِ وَهُوَ مُؤْمِنٌ فَلَا
يَخَافُ ظُلْمًا وَلَا هَضْمًا

112 But whoever has done righteous deeds, while being a believer—will fear neither injustice, nor grievance.

١١٣ وَكَذَٰلِكَ أَنزَلْنَٰهُ قُرْءَانًا عَرَبِيًّا وَصَرَّفْنَا فِيهِ
مِنَ ٱلْوَعِيدِ لَعَلَّهُمْ يَتَّقُونَ أَوْ يُحْدِثُ لَهُمْ ذِكْرًا

113 Thus We have revealed it an Arabic Quran, and We have diversified the warnings in it, that perhaps they would become righteous, or it may produce a lesson for them.

١١٤ فَتَعَٰلَى ٱللَّهُ ٱلْمَلِكُ ٱلْحَقُّ ۗ وَلَا تَعْجَلْ
بِٱلْقُرْءَانِ مِن قَبْلِ أَن يُقْضَىٰٓ إِلَيْكَ وَحْيُهُۥ ۖ وَقُل
رَّبِّ زِدْنِى عِلْمًا

114 Exalted is Allah, the True King. Do not be hasty with the Quran before its inspiration to you is concluded, and say, “My Lord, increase me in knowledge.”

١١٥ وَلَقَدْ عَهِدْنَآ إِلَىٰٓ ءَادَمَ مِن قَبْلُ فَنَسِىَ وَلَمْ
نَجِدْ لَهُۥ عَزْمًا

115 And We covenanted with Adam before, but he forgot, and We found in him no resolve.

١١٦ وَإِذْ قُلْنَا لِلْمَلَٰٓئِكَةِ ٱسْجُدُوا۟ لِءَادَمَ فَسَجَدُوٓا۟
إِلَّآ إِبْلِيسَ أَبَىٰ

116 And when We said to the angels, “Bow down to Adam.” They bowed down, except for Satan; he refused.

١١٧ فَقُلْنَا يَٰٓـَٔادَمُ إِنَّ هَٰذَا عَدُوٌّ لَّكَ وَلِزَوْجِكَ فَلَا
يُخْرِجَنَّكُمَا مِنَ ٱلْجَنَّةِ فَتَشْقَىٰٓ

117 We said, “O Adam, this is an enemy to you and to your wife. So do not let him make you leave the Garden, for then you will suffer.

١١٨ إِنَّ لَكَ أَلَّا تَجُوعَ فِيهَا وَلَا تَعْرَىٰ

118 In it you will never go hungry, nor be naked.

١١٩ وَأَنَّكَ لَا تَظْمَؤُا۟ فِيهَا وَلَا تَضْحَىٰ

119 Nor will you be thirsty in it, nor will you swelter.”

١٢٠ فَوَسْوَسَ إِلَيْهِ ٱلشَّيْطَٰنُ قَالَ يَٰٓـَٔادَمُ هَلْ
أَدُلُّكَ عَلَىٰ شَجَرَةِ ٱلْخُلْدِ وَمُلْكٍ لَّا يَبْلَىٰ

120 But Satan whispered to him. He said, “O Adam, shall I show you the Tree of Immortality, and a kingdom that never decays?”

١٢١ فَأَكَلَا مِنْهَا فَبَدَتْ لَهُمَا سَوْءَٰتُهُمَا وَطَفِقَا
يَخْصِفَانِ عَلَيْهِمَا مِن وَرَقِ ٱلْجَنَّةِ ۚ وَعَصَىٰٓ
ءَادَمُ رَبَّهُۥ فَغَوَىٰ

121 And so they ate from it; whereupon their bodies became visible to them, and they started covering themselves with the leaves of the Garden. Thus Adam disobeyed his Lord, and fell.

١٢٢ ثُمَّ ٱجْتَبَٰهُ رَبُّهُۥ فَتَابَ عَلَيْهِ وَهَدَىٰ

122 But then his Lord recalled him, and pardoned him, and guided him.

١٢٣ قَالَ ٱهْبِطَا مِنْهَا جَمِيعًۢا ۖ بَعْضُكُمْ لِبَعْضٍ
عَدُوٌّ ۖ فَإِمَّا يَأْتِيَنَّكُم مِّنِّى هُدًى فَمَنِ ٱتَّبَعَ هُدَاىَ
فَلَا يَضِلُّ وَلَا يَشْقَىٰ

123 He said, "Go down from it, altogether; some of you enemies of some others. But whenever guidance comes to you from Me, whoever follows My guidance, will not go astray, nor suffer.

١٢٤ وَمَنْ أَعْرَضَ عَن ذِكْرِى فَإِنَّ لَهُۥ مَعِيشَةً
ضَنكًا وَنَحْشُرُهُۥ يَوْمَ ٱلْقِيَٰمَةِ أَعْمَىٰ

124 But whoever turns away from My Reminder, for him is a confined life. And We will raise him on the Day of Resurrection blind."

١٢٥ قَالَ رَبِّ لِمَ حَشَرْتَنِىٓ أَعْمَىٰ وَقَدْ كُنتُ
بَصِيرًا

125 He will say, "My Lord, why did You raise me blind, though I was seeing?"

١٢٦ قَالَ كَذَٰلِكَ أَتَتْكَ ءَايَٰتُنَا فَنَسِيتَهَا ۖ وَكَذَٰلِكَ
ٱلْيَوْمَ تُنسَىٰ

126 He will say, "Just as Our revelations came to you, and you forgot them, today you will be forgotten."

١٢٧ وَكَذَٰلِكَ نَجْزِى مَنْ أَسْرَفَ وَلَمْ يُؤْمِنۢ بِـَٔايَٰتِ
رَبِّهِۦ ۚ وَلَعَذَابُ ٱلْءَاخِرَةِ أَشَدُّ وَأَبْقَىٰٓ

127 Thus We recompense him who transgresses and does not believe in the revelations of his Lord. The punishment of the Hereafter is more severe, and more lasting.

١٢٨ أَفَلَمْ يَهْدِ لَهُمْ كَمْ أَهْلَكْنَا قَبْلَهُم مِّنَ ٱلْقُرُونِ
يَمْشُونَ فِى مَسَٰكِنِهِمْ ۗ إِنَّ فِى ذَٰلِكَ لَءَايَٰتٍ
لِّأُو۟لِى ٱلنُّهَىٰ

128 Is it not instructive to them, how many generations before them We destroyed, in whose settlements they walk? Surely in that are signs for people of understanding.

١٢٩ وَلَوْلَا كَلِمَةٌ سَبَقَتْ مِن رَّبِّكَ لَكَانَ لِزَامًا
وَأَجَلٌ مُّسَمًّى

129 Were it not for a word that issued from your Lord, the inevitable would have happened, but there is an appointed term.

١٣٠ فَٱصْبِرْ عَلَىٰ مَا يَقُولُونَ وَسَبِّحْ بِحَمْدِ رَبِّكَ
قَبْلَ طُلُوعِ ٱلشَّمْسِ وَقَبْلَ غُرُوبِهَا ۖ وَمِنْ ءَانَآئِ
ٱلَّيْلِ فَسَبِّحْ وَأَطْرَافَ ٱلنَّهَارِ لَعَلَّكَ تَرْضَىٰ

130 So bear patiently what they say, and celebrate the praises of your Lord before the rising of the sun, and before its setting. And during the hours of the night glorify Him, and at the borders of the day, that you may be satisfied.

١٣١ وَلَا تَمُدَّنَّ عَيْنَيْكَ إِلَىٰ مَا مَتَّعْنَا بِهِۦٓ أَزْوَٰجًا
مِّنْهُمْ زَهْرَةَ ٱلْحَيَوٰةِ ٱلدُّنْيَا لِنَفْتِنَهُمْ فِيهِ ۚ وَرِزْقُ
رَبِّكَ خَيْرٌ وَأَبْقَىٰ

131 And do not extend your glance towards what We have given some classes of them to enjoy—the splendor of the life of this world—that We may test them thereby. Your Lord's provision is better, and more lasting.

١٣٢ وَأْمُرْ أَهْلَكَ بِٱلصَّلَوٰةِ وَٱصْطَبِرْ عَلَيْهَا ۖ لَا
نَسْـَٔلُكَ رِزْقًا ۖ نَّحْنُ نَرْزُقُكَ ۗ وَٱلْعَٰقِبَةُ لِلتَّقْوَىٰ

132 And exhort your people to pray, and patiently adhere to it. We ask of you no sustenance, but it is We who sustain you. The good ending is that for righteousness.

١٣٣ وَقَالُوا۟ لَوْلَا يَأْتِينَا بِـَٔايَةٍ مِّن رَّبِّهِۦٓ ۚ أَوَلَمْ
تَأْتِهِم بَيِّنَةُ مَا فِى ٱلصُّحُفِ ٱلْأُولَىٰ

133 And they say, "Why does he not bring us a miracle from his Lord?" Were they not given enough miracles in the former scriptures?

١٣٤ وَلَوْ أَنَّآ أَهْلَكْنَٰهُم بِعَذَابٍ مِّن قَبْلِهِۦ لَقَالُوا۟
رَبَّنَا لَوْلَآ أَرْسَلْتَ إِلَيْنَا رَسُولًا فَنَتَّبِعَ ءَايَٰتِكَ مِن
قَبْلِ أَن نَّذِلَّ وَنَخْزَىٰ

134 Had We destroyed them with a punishment before him, they would have said, "Our Lord, if only You had sent us a messenger, we would have followed Your revelations before we were humiliated and disgraced."

١٣٥ قُلْ كُلٌّ مُّتَرَبِّصٌ فَتَرَبَّصُوا۟ ۖ فَسَتَعْلَمُونَ مَنْ
أَصْحَٰبُ ٱلصِّرَٰطِ ٱلسَّوِىِّ وَمَنِ ٱهْتَدَىٰ

135 Say, "Everybody is waiting, so wait. You will know who the people of the straight path are, and who is rightly-guided.

21 The Prophets الأنبياء

بِسْمِ ٱللَّهِ ٱلرَّحْمَٰنِ ٱلرَّحِيمِ

In the name of Allah, the Gracious, the Merciful.

١ ٱقْتَرَبَ لِلنَّاسِ حِسَابُهُمْ وَهُمْ فِى غَفْلَةٍ
مُّعْرِضُونَ

1 Mankind's reckoning has drawn near, but they turn away heedlessly.

٢ مَا يَأْتِيهِم مِّن ذِكْرٍ مِّن رَّبِّهِم مُّحْدَثٍ إِلَّا
ٱسْتَمَعُوهُ وَهُمْ يَلْعَبُونَ

2 No fresh reminder comes to them from their Lord, but they listen to it playfully.

٣ لَاهِيَةً قُلُوبُهُمْ ۗ وَأَسَرُّوا۟ ٱلنَّجْوَى ٱلَّذِينَ ظَلَمُوا۟ هَلْ هَٰذَآ إِلَّا بَشَرٌ مِّثْلُكُمْ ۖ أَفَتَأْتُونَ ٱلسِّحْرَ وَأَنتُمْ تُبْصِرُونَ	3 Their hearts distracted, the wrongdoers confer secretly, "Is this anything but a mortal like you? Will you take to sorcery, with open-eyes?"
٤ قَالَ رَبِّى يَعْلَمُ ٱلْقَوْلَ فِى ٱلسَّمَآءِ وَٱلْأَرْضِ ۖ وَهُوَ ٱلسَّمِيعُ ٱلْعَلِيمُ	4 He said, "My Lord knows what is said in the heaven and the earth; and He is the Hearer, the Knower."
٥ بَلْ قَالُوٓا۟ أَضْغَٰثُ أَحْلَٰمٍۭ بَلِ ٱفْتَرَىٰهُ بَلْ هُوَ شَاعِرٌ فَلْيَأْتِنَا بِـَٔايَةٍ كَمَآ أُرْسِلَ ٱلْأَوَّلُونَ	5 And they said, "A jumble of dreams," and, "He made it up," and, "He is a poet," "let him bring us a sign, like those sent to the ancients."
٦ مَآ ءَامَنَتْ قَبْلَهُم مِّن قَرْيَةٍ أَهْلَكْنَٰهَآ ۖ أَفَهُمْ يُؤْمِنُونَ	6 None of the towns We destroyed before them had believed. Will they, then, believe?
٧ وَمَآ أَرْسَلْنَا قَبْلَكَ إِلَّا رِجَالًا نُّوحِىٓ إِلَيْهِمْ ۖ فَسْـَٔلُوٓا۟ أَهْلَ ٱلذِّكْرِ إِن كُنتُمْ لَا تَعْلَمُونَ	7 We did not send before you except men, whom We inspired. Ask the people of knowledge, if you do not know.
٨ وَمَا جَعَلْنَٰهُمْ جَسَدًا لَّا يَأْكُلُونَ ٱلطَّعَامَ وَمَا كَانُوا۟ خَٰلِدِينَ	8 We did not make them mere bodies that ate no food, nor were they immortal.
٩ ثُمَّ صَدَقْنَٰهُمُ ٱلْوَعْدَ فَأَنجَيْنَٰهُمْ وَمَن نَّشَآءُ وَأَهْلَكْنَا ٱلْمُسْرِفِينَ	9 Then We fulfilled Our promise to them, and We saved them together with whomever We willed, and We destroyed the extravagant.
١٠ لَقَدْ أَنزَلْنَآ إِلَيْكُمْ كِتَٰبًا فِيهِ ذِكْرُكُمْ ۖ أَفَلَا تَعْقِلُونَ	10 We have sent down to you a Book, containing your message. Do you not understand?
١١ وَكَمْ قَصَمْنَا مِن قَرْيَةٍ كَانَتْ ظَالِمَةً وَأَنشَأْنَا بَعْدَهَا قَوْمًا ءَاخَرِينَ	11 How many a guilty town have We crushed, and established thereafter another people?
١٢ فَلَمَّآ أَحَسُّوا۟ بَأْسَنَآ إِذَا هُم مِّنْهَا يَرْكُضُونَ	12 Then, when they sensed Our might, they started running away from it.
١٣ لَا تَرْكُضُوا۟ وَٱرْجِعُوٓا۟ إِلَىٰ مَآ أُتْرِفْتُمْ فِيهِ وَمَسَٰكِنِكُمْ لَعَلَّكُمْ تُسْـَٔلُونَ	13 Do not run, but come back to your luxuries, and to your homes, that you may be questioned.
١٤ قَالُوا۟ يَٰوَيْلَنَآ إِنَّا كُنَّا ظَٰلِمِينَ	14 They said, "Woe to us; we were unfair."

١٥ فَمَا زَالَت تِّلْكَ دَعْوَىٰهُمْ حَتَّىٰ جَعَلْنَٰهُمْ
حَصِيدًا خَٰمِدِينَ

15 This continued to be their cry, until We made them silent ashes.

١٦ وَمَا خَلَقْنَا ٱلسَّمَآءَ وَٱلْأَرْضَ وَمَا بَيْنَهُمَا
لَٰعِبِينَ

16 We did not create the sky and the earth and what is between them for amusement.

١٧ لَوْ أَرَدْنَآ أَن نَّتَّخِذَ لَهْوًا لَّٱتَّخَذْنَٰهُ مِن لَّدُنَّآ إِن
كُنَّا فَٰعِلِينَ

17 If We wanted amusement, We could have found it within Us, were We to do so.

١٨ بَلْ نَقْذِفُ بِٱلْحَقِّ عَلَى ٱلْبَٰطِلِ فَيَدْمَغُهُۥ فَإِذَا
هُوَ زَاهِقٌ ۚ وَلَكُمُ ٱلْوَيْلُ مِمَّا تَصِفُونَ

18 In fact, We hurl the truth against falsehood, and it crushes it, so it vanishes. Woe unto you, for what you describe.

١٩ وَلَهُۥ مَن فِى ٱلسَّمَٰوَٰتِ وَٱلْأَرْضِ ۚ وَمَنْ عِندَهُۥ
لَا يَسْتَكْبِرُونَ عَنْ عِبَادَتِهِۦ وَلَا يَسْتَحْسِرُونَ

19 To Him belongs everyone in the heavens and the earth. Those near Him are not too proud to worship Him, nor do they waver.

٢٠ يُسَبِّحُونَ ٱلَّيْلَ وَٱلنَّهَارَ لَا يَفْتُرُونَ

20 They praise night and day, without ever tiring.

٢١ أَمِ ٱتَّخَذُوٓا۟ ءَالِهَةً مِّنَ ٱلْأَرْضِ هُمْ يُنشِرُونَ

21 Or have they taken to themselves gods from the earth who resurrect?

٢٢ لَوْ كَانَ فِيهِمَآ ءَالِهَةٌ إِلَّا ٱللَّهُ لَفَسَدَتَا ۚ
فَسُبْحَٰنَ ٱللَّهِ رَبِّ ٱلْعَرْشِ عَمَّا يَصِفُونَ

22 If there were in them gods other than Allah, they would have gone to ruin. So glory be to Allah, Lord of the Throne, beyond what they allege.

٢٣ لَا يُسْـَٔلُ عَمَّا يَفْعَلُ وَهُمْ يُسْـَٔلُونَ

23 He will not be questioned about what He does, but they will be questioned.

٢٤ أَمِ ٱتَّخَذُوا۟ مِن دُونِهِۦٓ ءَالِهَةً ۖ قُلْ هَاتُوا۟
بُرْهَٰنَكُمْ ۖ هَٰذَا ذِكْرُ مَن مَّعِىَ وَذِكْرُ مَن قَبْلِى ۗ بَلْ
أَكْثَرُهُمْ لَا يَعْلَمُونَ ٱلْحَقَّ ۖ فَهُم مُّعْرِضُونَ

24 Or have they taken, besides Him, other gods? Say, “Bring your proof. This is a message for those with me, and a message of those before me.” But most of them do not know the truth, so they turn away.

٢٥ وَمَآ أَرْسَلْنَا مِن قَبْلِكَ مِن رَّسُولٍ إِلَّا نُوحِىٓ
إِلَيْهِ أَنَّهُۥ لَآ إِلَٰهَ إِلَّآ أَنَا۠ فَٱعْبُدُونِ

25 We never sent a messenger before you without inspiring him that: “There is no god but I, so worship Me.”

٢٦ وَقَالُوا۟ ٱتَّخَذَ ٱلرَّحْمَٰنُ وَلَدًا ۗ سُبْحَٰنَهُۥ ۚ بَلْ
عِبَادٌ مُّكْرَمُونَ

26 And they say, "The Most Merciful has taken to himself a son." Be He glorified; they are but honored servants.

٢٧ لَا يَسْبِقُونَهُۥ بِٱلْقَوْلِ وَهُم بِأَمْرِهِۦ يَعْمَلُونَ

27 They never speak before He has spoken, and they only act on His command.

٢٨ يَعْلَمُ مَا بَيْنَ أَيْدِيهِمْ وَمَا خَلْفَهُمْ وَلَا
يَشْفَعُونَ إِلَّا لِمَنِ ٱرْتَضَىٰ وَهُم مِّنْ خَشْيَتِهِۦ
مُشْفِقُونَ

28 He knows what is before them, and what is behind them; and they do not intercede except for him whom He approves; and they tremble in awe of Him.

٢٩ وَمَن يَقُلْ مِنْهُمْ إِنِّىٓ إِلَٰهٌ مِّن دُونِهِۦ فَذَٰلِكَ
نَجْزِيهِ جَهَنَّمَ ۚ كَذَٰلِكَ نَجْزِى ٱلظَّٰلِمِينَ

29 And whoever of them says, "I am a god besides Him," We will reward him with Hell. Thus We reward the wrongdoers.

٣٠ أَوَلَمْ يَرَ ٱلَّذِينَ كَفَرُوٓا۟ أَنَّ ٱلسَّمَٰوَٰتِ وَٱلْأَرْضَ
كَانَتَا رَتْقًا فَفَتَقْنَٰهُمَا ۖ وَجَعَلْنَا مِنَ ٱلْمَآءِ كُلَّ
شَىْءٍ حَىٍّ ۖ أَفَلَا يُؤْمِنُونَ

30 Do the disbelievers not see that the heavens and the earth were one mass, and We tore them apart? And We made from water every living thing. Will they not believe?

٣١ وَجَعَلْنَا فِى ٱلْأَرْضِ رَوَٰسِىَ أَن تَمِيدَ بِهِمْ
وَجَعَلْنَا فِيهَا فِجَاجًا سُبُلًا لَّعَلَّهُمْ يَهْتَدُونَ

31 And We placed on earth stabilizers, lest it sways with them, and We placed therein signposts and passages, that they may be guided.

٣٢ وَجَعَلْنَا ٱلسَّمَآءَ سَقْفًا مَّحْفُوظًا ۖ وَهُمْ عَنْ
ءَايَٰتِهَا مُعْرِضُونَ

32 And We made the sky a protected ceiling; yet they turn away from its wonders.

٣٣ وَهُوَ ٱلَّذِى خَلَقَ ٱلَّيْلَ وَٱلنَّهَارَ وَٱلشَّمْسَ
وَٱلْقَمَرَ ۖ كُلٌّ فِى فَلَكٍ يَسْبَحُونَ

33 It is He who created the night and the day, and the sun and the moon; each floating in an orbit.

٣٤ وَمَا جَعَلْنَا لِبَشَرٍ مِّن قَبْلِكَ ٱلْخُلْدَ ۖ أَفَإِي۟ن
مِّتَّ فَهُمُ ٱلْخَٰلِدُونَ

34 We did not grant immortality to any human being before you. Should you die, are they then the immortal?

٣٥ كُلُّ نَفْسٍ ذَآئِقَةُ ٱلْمَوْتِ ۗ وَنَبْلُوكُم بِٱلشَّرِّ
وَٱلْخَيْرِ فِتْنَةً ۖ وَإِلَيْنَا تُرْجَعُونَ

35 Every soul will taste death. We burden you with adversity and prosperity—a test. And to Us you will be returned.

٣٦ وَإِذَا رَءَاكَ ٱلَّذِينَ كَفَرُوٓا۟ إِن يَتَّخِذُونَكَ إِلَّا
هُزُوًا أَهَـٰذَا ٱلَّذِى يَذْكُرُ ءَالِهَتَكُمْ وَهُم بِذِكْرِ
ٱلرَّحْمَـٰنِ هُمْ كَـٰفِرُونَ

36 When those who disbelieve see you, they treat you only with ridicule: “Is this the one who mentions your gods?” And they reject the mention of the Merciful.

٣٧ خُلِقَ ٱلْإِنسَـٰنُ مِنْ عَجَلٍ ۚ سَأُو۟رِيكُمْ ءَايَـٰتِى
فَلَا تَسْتَعْجِلُونِ

37 The human being was created of haste. I will show you My signs, so do not seek to rush Me.

٣٨ وَيَقُولُونَ مَتَىٰ هَـٰذَا ٱلْوَعْدُ إِن كُنتُمْ
صَـٰدِقِينَ

38 And they say, “When will this promise come true, if you are truthful?”

٣٩ لَوْ يَعْلَمُ ٱلَّذِينَ كَفَرُوا۟ حِينَ لَا يَكُفُّونَ عَن
وُجُوهِهِمُ ٱلنَّارَ وَلَا عَن ظُهُورِهِمْ وَلَا هُمْ
يُنصَرُونَ

39 If those who disbelieve only knew, when they cannot keep the fire off their faces and off their backs, and they will not be helped.

٤٠ بَلْ تَأْتِيهِم بَغْتَةً فَتَبْهَتُهُمْ فَلَا يَسْتَطِيعُونَ
رَدَّهَا وَلَا هُمْ يُنظَرُونَ

40 In fact, it will come upon them suddenly, and bewilder them. They will not be able to repel it, and they will not be reprieved.

٤١ وَلَقَدِ ٱسْتُهْزِئَ بِرُسُلٍ مِّن قَبْلِكَ فَحَاقَ
بِٱلَّذِينَ سَخِرُوا۟ مِنْهُم مَّا كَانُوا۟ بِهِۦ يَسْتَهْزِءُونَ

41 Messengers before you were also ridiculed, but those who jeered were surrounded by what they had ridiculed.

٤٢ قُلْ مَن يَكْلَؤُكُم بِٱلَّيْلِ وَٱلنَّهَارِ مِنَ ٱلرَّحْمَـٰنِ ۗ
بَلْ هُمْ عَن ذِكْرِ رَبِّهِم مُّعْرِضُونَ

42 Say, “Who guards you against the Merciful by night and by day?” But they turn away from the mention of their Lord.

٤٣ أَمْ لَهُمْ ءَالِهَةٌ تَمْنَعُهُم مِّن دُونِنَا ۚ لَا
يَسْتَطِيعُونَ نَصْرَ أَنفُسِهِمْ وَلَا هُم مِّنَّا
يُصْحَبُونَ

43 Or do they have gods who can defend them against Us? They cannot help themselves, nor will they be protected from Us.

٤٤ بَلْ مَتَّعْنَا هَـٰٓؤُلَآءِ وَءَابَآءَهُمْ حَتَّىٰ طَالَ
عَلَيْهِمُ ٱلْعُمُرُ ۗ أَفَلَا يَرَوْنَ أَنَّا نَأْتِى ٱلْأَرْضَ
نَنقُصُهَا مِنْ أَطْرَافِهَآ ۚ أَفَهُمُ ٱلْغَـٰلِبُونَ

44 We have given these enjoyments, and their ancestors, until time grew long upon them. Do they not see how We gradually reduce the land from its extremities? Are they then the victors?

٤٥ قُلْ إِنَّمَآ أُنذِرُكُم بِٱلْوَحْيِ ۚ وَلَا يَسْمَعُ ٱلصُّمُّ
ٱلدُّعَآءَ إِذَا مَا يُنذَرُونَ

45 Say, "I am warning you through inspiration." But the deaf cannot hear the call when they are being warned.

٤٦ وَلَئِن مَّسَّتْهُمْ نَفْحَةٌ مِّنْ عَذَابِ رَبِّكَ لَيَقُولُنَّ
يَٰوَيْلَنَآ إِنَّا كُنَّا ظَٰلِمِينَ

46 And when a breath of your Lord's punishment touches them, they say, "Woe to us, we were truly wicked."

٤٧ وَنَضَعُ ٱلْمَوَٰزِينَ ٱلْقِسْطَ لِيَوْمِ ٱلْقِيَٰمَةِ فَلَا
تُظْلَمُ نَفْسٌ شَيْـًٔا ۖ وَإِن كَانَ مِثْقَالَ حَبَّةٍ مِّنْ
خَرْدَلٍ أَتَيْنَا بِهَا ۗ وَكَفَىٰ بِنَا حَٰسِبِينَ

47 We will set up the scales of justice for the Day of Resurrection, so that no soul will suffer the least injustice. And even if it be the weight of a mustard-seed, We will bring it up. Sufficient are We as Reckoners.

٤٨ وَلَقَدْ ءَاتَيْنَا مُوسَىٰ وَهَٰرُونَ ٱلْفُرْقَانَ
وَضِيَآءً وَذِكْرًا لِّلْمُتَّقِينَ

48 We gave Moses and Aaron the Criterion, and illumination, and a reminder for the righteous.

٤٩ ٱلَّذِينَ يَخْشَوْنَ رَبَّهُم بِٱلْغَيْبِ وَهُم مِّنَ
ٱلسَّاعَةِ مُشْفِقُونَ

49 Those who fear their Lord in private, and are apprehensive of the Hour.

٥٠ وَهَٰذَا ذِكْرٌ مُّبَارَكٌ أَنزَلْنَٰهُ ۚ أَفَأَنتُمْ لَهُۥ مُنكِرُونَ

50 This too is a blessed message that We revealed. Are you going to deny it?

٥١ وَلَقَدْ ءَاتَيْنَآ إِبْرَٰهِيمَ رُشْدَهُۥ مِن قَبْلُ وَكُنَّا
بِهِۦ عَٰلِمِينَ

51 We gave Abraham his integrity formerly, and We knew him well.

٥٢ إِذْ قَالَ لِأَبِيهِ وَقَوْمِهِۦ مَا هَٰذِهِ ٱلتَّمَاثِيلُ ٱلَّتِىٓ
أَنتُمْ لَهَا عَٰكِفُونَ

52 When he said to his father and his people, "What are these statues to which you are devoted?"

٥٣ قَالُوا۟ وَجَدْنَآ ءَابَآءَنَا لَهَا عَٰبِدِينَ

53 They said, "We found our parents worshiping them."

٥٤ قَالَ لَقَدْ كُنتُمْ أَنتُمْ وَءَابَآؤُكُمْ فِى ضَلَٰلٍ
مُّبِينٍ

54 He said, "You and your parents are in evident error."

٥٥ قَالُوٓا۟ أَجِئْتَنَا بِٱلْحَقِّ أَمْ أَنتَ مِنَ ٱللَّٰعِبِينَ

55 They said, "Are you telling us the truth, or are you just playing?"

٥٦ قَالَ بَل رَّبُّكُمْ رَبُّ ٱلسَّمَٰوَٰتِ وَٱلْأَرْضِ ٱلَّذِى
فَطَرَهُنَّ وَأَنَا۠ عَلَىٰ ذَٰلِكُم مِّنَ ٱلشَّٰهِدِينَ

56 He said, "Your Lord is the Lord of the heavens and the earth, the One who created them, and I bear witness to that.

٥٧ وَتَٱللَّهِ لَأَكِيدَنَّ أَصۡنَٰمَكُم بَعۡدَ أَن تُوَلُّواْ
مُدۡبِرِينَ

57 “By Allah, I will have a plan for your statues after you have gone away.”

٥٨ فَجَعَلَهُمۡ جُذَٰذًا إِلَّا كَبِيرًا لَّهُمۡ لَعَلَّهُمۡ إِلَيۡهِ
يَرۡجِعُونَ

58 So he reduced them into pieces, except for their biggest, that they may return to it.

٥٩ قَالُواْ مَن فَعَلَ هَٰذَا بِـَٔالِهَتِنَآ إِنَّهُۥ لَمِنَ ٱلظَّٰلِمِينَ

59 They said, “Who did this to our gods? He is certainly one of the wrongdoers.”

٦٠ قَالُواْ سَمِعۡنَا فَتٗى يَذۡكُرُهُمۡ يُقَالُ لَهُۥٓ إِبۡرَٰهِيمُ

60 They said, “We heard a youth mentioning them. He is called Abraham.”

٦١ قَالُواْ فَأۡتُواْ بِهِۦ عَلَىٰٓ أَعۡيُنِ ٱلنَّاسِ لَعَلَّهُمۡ
يَشۡهَدُونَ

61 They said, “Bring him before the eyes of the people, so that they may witness.”

٦٢ قَالُوٓاْ ءَأَنتَ فَعَلۡتَ هَٰذَا بِـَٔالِهَتِنَا يَٰٓإِبۡرَٰهِيمُ

62 They said, “Are you the one who did this to our gods, O Abraham?”

٦٣ قَالَ بَلۡ فَعَلَهُۥ كَبِيرُهُمۡ هَٰذَا فَسۡـَٔلُوهُمۡ إِن
كَانُواْ يَنطِقُونَ

63 He said, “But it was this biggest of them that did it. Ask them, if they can speak.”

٦٤ فَرَجَعُوٓاْ إِلَىٰٓ أَنفُسِهِمۡ فَقَالُوٓاْ إِنَّكُمۡ أَنتُمُ
ٱلظَّٰلِمُونَ

64 Then they turned to one another, and said, “You yourselves are the wrongdoers.”

٦٥ ثُمَّ نُكِسُواْ عَلَىٰ رُءُوسِهِمۡ لَقَدۡ عَلِمۡتَ مَا
هَٰٓؤُلَآءِ يَنطِقُونَ

65 But they reverted to their old ideas: “You certainly know that these do not speak.”

٦٦ قَالَ أَفَتَعۡبُدُونَ مِن دُونِ ٱللَّهِ مَا لَا يَنفَعُكُمۡ
شَيۡـٔٗا وَلَا يَضُرُّكُمۡ

66 He said, “Do you worship, instead of Allah, what can neither benefit you in anything, nor harm you?

٦٧ أُفّٖ لَّكُمۡ وَلِمَا تَعۡبُدُونَ مِن دُونِ ٱللَّهِۖ أَفَلَا
تَعۡقِلُونَ

67 Fie on you, and on what you worship instead of Allah. Do you not understand?”

٦٨ قَالُواْ حَرِّقُوهُ وَٱنصُرُوٓاْ ءَالِهَتَكُمۡ إِن كُنتُمۡ
فَٰعِلِينَ

68 They said, “Burn him and support your gods, if you are going to act.”

٦٩ قُلۡنَا يَٰنَارُ كُونِي بَرۡدٗا وَسَلَٰمًا عَلَىٰٓ إِبۡرَٰهِيمَ

69 We said, “O fire, be coolness and safety upon Abraham.”

٧٠ وَأَرَادُواْ بِهِۦ كَيۡدٗا فَجَعَلۡنَٰهُمُ ٱلۡأَخۡسَرِينَ

70 They planned to harm him, but We made them the worst losers.

٧١ وَنَجَّيْنَٰهُ وَلُوطًا إِلَى ٱلْأَرْضِ ٱلَّتِى بَٰرَكْنَا فِيهَا
لِلْعَٰلَمِينَ

71 And We delivered him, and Lot, to the land that We blessed for all people.

٧٢ وَوَهَبْنَا لَهُۥٓ إِسْحَٰقَ وَيَعْقُوبَ نَافِلَةًۖ وَكُلًّا
جَعَلْنَا صَٰلِحِينَ

72 And We granted him Isaac and Jacob as a gift; and each We made righteous.

٧٣ وَجَعَلْنَٰهُمْ أَئِمَّةً يَهْدُونَ بِأَمْرِنَا وَأَوْحَيْنَآ
إِلَيْهِمْ فِعْلَ ٱلْخَيْرَٰتِ وَإِقَامَ ٱلصَّلَوٰةِ وَإِيتَآءَ
ٱلزَّكَوٰةِۖ وَكَانُوا۟ لَنَا عَٰبِدِينَ

73 And We made them leaders, guiding by Our command; and We inspired them to do good works, and to observe the prayer, and to give out charity. They were devoted servants to Us.

٧٤ وَلُوطًا ءَاتَيْنَٰهُ حُكْمًا وَعِلْمًا وَنَجَّيْنَٰهُ مِنَ
ٱلْقَرْيَةِ ٱلَّتِى كَانَت تَّعْمَلُ ٱلْخَبَٰٓئِثَۗ إِنَّهُمْ كَانُوا۟
قَوْمَ سَوْءٍ فَٰسِقِينَ

74 And Lot—We gave him judgment and knowledge, and We delivered him from the town that practiced the abominations. They were wicked and perverted people.

٧٥ وَأَدْخَلْنَٰهُ فِى رَحْمَتِنَآۖ إِنَّهُۥ مِنَ ٱلصَّٰلِحِينَ

75 And We admitted him into Our mercy; for He was one of the righteous.

٧٦ وَنُوحًا إِذْ نَادَىٰ مِن قَبْلُ فَٱسْتَجَبْنَا لَهُۥ
فَنَجَّيْنَٰهُ وَأَهْلَهُۥ مِنَ ٱلْكَرْبِ ٱلْعَظِيمِ

76 And Noah, when he called before. So We answered him, and delivered him and his family from the great disaster.

٧٧ وَنَصَرْنَٰهُ مِنَ ٱلْقَوْمِ ٱلَّذِينَ كَذَّبُوا۟ بِـَٔايَٰتِنَآۚ
إِنَّهُمْ كَانُوا۟ قَوْمَ سَوْءٍ فَأَغْرَقْنَٰهُمْ أَجْمَعِينَ

77 And We supported him against the people who rejected Our signs. They were an evil people, so We drowned them all.

٧٨ وَدَاوُۥدَ وَسُلَيْمَٰنَ إِذْ يَحْكُمَانِ فِى ٱلْحَرْثِ إِذْ
نَفَشَتْ فِيهِ غَنَمُ ٱلْقَوْمِ وَكُنَّا لِحُكْمِهِمْ شَٰهِدِينَ

78 And David and Solomon, when they gave judgment in the case of the field, when some people's sheep wandered therein by night; and We were witnesses to their judgment.

٧٩ فَفَهَّمْنَٰهَا سُلَيْمَٰنَۚ وَكُلًّا ءَاتَيْنَا حُكْمًا وَعِلْمًاۚ
وَسَخَّرْنَا مَعَ دَاوُۥدَ ٱلْجِبَالَ يُسَبِّحْنَ وَٱلطَّيْرَۚ
وَكُنَّا فَٰعِلِينَ

79 And so We made Solomon understand it, and to each We gave wisdom and knowledge. And We subjected the mountains along with David to sing Our praises, and the birds as well—surely We did.

80 And We taught him the making of shields for you, to protect you from your violence. Are you, then, appreciative?

٨٠ وَعَلَّمْنَٰهُ صَنْعَةَ لَبُوسٍ لَّكُمْ لِتُحْصِنَكُم مِّنۢ
بَأْسِكُمْ ۖ فَهَلْ أَنتُمْ شَٰكِرُونَ

81 And to Solomon the stormy wind, blowing at His command towards the land that We have blessed. We are aware of everything.

٨١ وَلِسُلَيْمَٰنَ ٱلرِّيحَ عَاصِفَةً تَجْرِى بِأَمْرِهِۦٓ إِلَى
ٱلْأَرْضِ ٱلَّتِى بَٰرَكْنَا فِيهَا ۚ وَكُنَّا بِكُلِّ شَىْءٍ
عَٰلِمِينَ

82 And of the devils were some that dived for him, and performed other, lesser tasks. But We kept them restrained.

٨٢ وَمِنَ ٱلشَّيَٰطِينِ مَن يَغُوصُونَ لَهُۥ وَيَعْمَلُونَ
عَمَلًا دُونَ ذَٰلِكَ ۖ وَكُنَّا لَهُمْ حَٰفِظِينَ

83 And Job, when he cried out to his Lord: "Great harm has afflicted me, and you are the Most Merciful of the merciful."

٨٣ وَأَيُّوبَ إِذْ نَادَىٰ رَبَّهُۥٓ أَنِّى مَسَّنِىَ ٱلضُّرُّ وَأَنتَ
أَرْحَمُ ٱلرَّٰحِمِينَ

84 So We answered him, lifted his suffering, and restored his family to him, and their like with them—a mercy from Us, and a reminder for the worshipers.

٨٤ فَٱسْتَجَبْنَا لَهُۥ فَكَشَفْنَا مَا بِهِۦ مِن ضُرٍّ ۖ
وَءَاتَيْنَٰهُ أَهْلَهُۥ وَمِثْلَهُم مَّعَهُمْ رَحْمَةً مِّنْ عِندِنَا
وَذِكْرَىٰ لِلْعَٰبِدِينَ

85 And Ishmael, and Enoch, and Ezekiel; each was one of the steadfast.

٨٥ وَإِسْمَٰعِيلَ وَإِدْرِيسَ وَذَا ٱلْكِفْلِ ۖ كُلٌّ مِّنَ
ٱلصَّٰبِرِينَ

86 And We admitted them into Our mercy. They were among the righteous.

٨٦ وَأَدْخَلْنَٰهُمْ فِى رَحْمَتِنَآ ۖ إِنَّهُم مِّنَ ٱلصَّٰلِحِينَ

87 And Jonah, when he stormed out in fury, thinking We had no power over him. But then He cried out in the darkness, "There is no god but You! Glory to You! I was one of the wrongdoers!"

٨٧ وَذَا ٱلنُّونِ إِذ ذَّهَبَ مُغَٰضِبًا فَظَنَّ أَن لَّن
نَّقْدِرَ عَلَيْهِ فَنَادَىٰ فِى ٱلظُّلُمَٰتِ أَن لَّآ إِلَٰهَ إِلَّآ
أَنتَ سُبْحَٰنَكَ إِنِّى كُنتُ مِنَ ٱلظَّٰلِمِينَ

88 So We answered him, and saved him from the affliction. Thus We save the faithful.

٨٨ فَٱسْتَجَبْنَا لَهُۥ وَنَجَّيْنَٰهُ مِنَ ٱلْغَمِّ ۚ وَكَذَٰلِكَ
نُۨجِى ٱلْمُؤْمِنِينَ

89 And Zechariah, when he called out to his Lord, "My Lord, do not leave me alone, even though you are the Best of heirs."

٨٩ وَزَكَرِيَّآ إِذْ نَادَىٰ رَبَّهُۥ رَبِّ لَا تَذَرْنِى فَرْدًا
وَأَنتَ خَيْرُ ٱلْوَٰرِثِينَ

٩٠ فَٱسْتَجَبْنَا لَهُۥ وَوَهَبْنَا لَهُۥ يَحْيَىٰ وَأَصْلَحْنَا لَهُۥ
زَوْجَهُۥٓ ۚ إِنَّهُمْ كَانُوا۟ يُسَٰرِعُونَ فِى ٱلْخَيْرَٰتِ
وَيَدْعُونَنَا رَغَبًا وَرَهَبًا ۖ وَكَانُوا۟ لَنَا خَٰشِعِينَ

90 So We answered him, and gave him John. And We cured his wife for him. They used to vie in doing righteous deeds, and used to call on Us in love and awe, and they used to humble themselves to Us.

٩١ وَٱلَّتِىٓ أَحْصَنَتْ فَرْجَهَا فَنَفَخْنَا فِيهَا مِن
رُّوحِنَا وَجَعَلْنَٰهَا وَٱبْنَهَآ ءَايَةً لِّلْعَٰلَمِينَ

91 And she who guarded her virginity. We breathed into her of Our spirit, and made her and her son a sign to the world.

٩٢ إِنَّ هَٰذِهِۦٓ أُمَّتُكُمْ أُمَّةً وَٰحِدَةً وَأَنَا۠ رَبُّكُمْ
فَٱعْبُدُونِ

92 This community of yours is one community, and I am your Lord, so worship Me.

٩٣ وَتَقَطَّعُوٓا۟ أَمْرَهُم بَيْنَهُمْ ۖ كُلٌّ إِلَيْنَا رَٰجِعُونَ

93 But they splintered themselves into factions. They will all return to Us.

٩٤ فَمَن يَعْمَلْ مِنَ ٱلصَّٰلِحَٰتِ وَهُوَ مُؤْمِنٌ فَلَا
كُفْرَانَ لِسَعْيِهِۦ وَإِنَّا لَهُۥ كَٰتِبُونَ

94 Whoever does righteous deeds, and is a believer, his effort will not be denied. We are writing it down for him.

٩٥ وَحَرَٰمٌ عَلَىٰ قَرْيَةٍ أَهْلَكْنَٰهَآ أَنَّهُمْ لَا يَرْجِعُونَ

95 There is a ban on the town that We had destroyed—that they will not return.

٩٦ حَتَّىٰٓ إِذَا فُتِحَتْ يَأْجُوجُ وَمَأْجُوجُ وَهُم
مِّن كُلِّ حَدَبٍ يَنسِلُونَ

96 Until, when Gog and Magog are let loose, and they swarm down from every mound.

٩٧ وَٱقْتَرَبَ ٱلْوَعْدُ ٱلْحَقُّ فَإِذَا هِىَ شَٰخِصَةٌ
أَبْصَٰرُ ٱلَّذِينَ كَفَرُوا۟ يَٰوَيْلَنَا قَدْ كُنَّا فِى غَفْلَةٍ مِّنْ
هَٰذَا بَلْ كُنَّا ظَٰلِمِينَ

97 The promise of truth has drawn near. The eyes of those who disbelieved will stare in horror: "Woe to us. We were oblivious to this. In fact, we were wrongdoers."

٩٨ إِنَّكُمْ وَمَا تَعْبُدُونَ مِن دُونِ ٱللَّهِ حَصَبُ
جَهَنَّمَ أَنتُمْ لَهَا وَٰرِدُونَ

98 You and what you worship besides Allah are fuel for Hell. You will descend into it.

٩٩ لَوْ كَانَ هَٰٓؤُلَآءِ ءَالِهَةً مَّا وَرَدُوهَا ۖ وَكُلٌّ فِيهَا
خَٰلِدُونَ

99 Had these been gods, they would not have descended into it. All will abide in it.

١٠٠ لَهُمْ فِيهَا زَفِيرٌ وَهُمْ فِيهَا لَا يَسْمَعُونَ

100 In it they will wail. In it they will not hear.

١٠١ إِنَّ ٱلَّذِينَ سَبَقَتْ لَهُم مِّنَّا ٱلْحُسْنَىٰٓ أُو۟لَـٰٓئِكَ
عَنْهَا مُبْعَدُونَ

101 As for those who deserved goodness from Us—these will be kept away from it.

١٠٢ لَا يَسْمَعُونَ حَسِيسَهَا ۖ وَهُمْ فِى مَا ٱشْتَهَتْ
أَنفُسُهُمْ خَـٰلِدُونَ

102 They will not hear its hissing, and they will forever abide in what their hearts desire.

١٠٣ لَا يَحْزُنُهُمُ ٱلْفَزَعُ ٱلْأَكْبَرُ وَتَتَلَقَّىٰهُمُ ٱلْمَلَـٰٓئِكَةُ
هَـٰذَا يَوْمُكُمُ ٱلَّذِى كُنتُمْ تُوعَدُونَ

103 The Supreme Fear will not worry them, and the angels will receive them: "This is your Day which you were promised."

١٠٤ يَوْمَ نَطْوِى ٱلسَّمَآءَ كَطَىِّ ٱلسِّجِلِّ لِلْكُتُبِ ۚ
كَمَا بَدَأْنَآ أَوَّلَ خَلْقٍ نُّعِيدُهُۥ ۚ وَعْدًا عَلَيْنَآ ۚ إِنَّا كُنَّا
فَـٰعِلِينَ

104 On the Day when We fold the heaven, like the folding of a book. Just as We began the first creation, We will repeat it—a promise binding on Us. We will act.

١٠٥ وَلَقَدْ كَتَبْنَا فِى ٱلزَّبُورِ مِنۢ بَعْدِ ٱلذِّكْرِ أَنَّ
ٱلْأَرْضَ يَرِثُهَا عِبَادِىَ ٱلصَّـٰلِحُونَ

105 We have written in the Psalms, after the Reminder, that the earth will be inherited by My righteous servants.

١٠٦ إِنَّ فِى هَـٰذَا لَبَلَـٰغًا لِّقَوْمٍ عَـٰبِدِينَ

106 Indeed, in this is a message for people who worship.

١٠٧ وَمَآ أَرْسَلْنَـٰكَ إِلَّا رَحْمَةً لِّلْعَـٰلَمِينَ

107 We did not send you except as mercy to mankind.

١٠٨ قُلْ إِنَّمَا يُوحَىٰٓ إِلَىَّ أَنَّمَآ إِلَـٰهُكُمْ إِلَـٰهٌ وَٰحِدٌ ۖ
فَهَلْ أَنتُم مُّسْلِمُونَ

108 Say, "It is revealed to me that your God is One God. Are you going to submit?"

١٠٩ فَإِن تَوَلَّوْا۟ فَقُلْ ءَاذَنتُكُمْ عَلَىٰ سَوَآءٍ ۖ وَإِنْ
أَدْرِىٓ أَقَرِيبٌ أَم بَعِيدٌ مَّا تُوعَدُونَ

109 But if they turn away, say, "I have informed you sufficiently. Although I do not know whether what you are promised is near or far."

١١٠ إِنَّهُۥ يَعْلَمُ ٱلْجَهْرَ مِنَ ٱلْقَوْلِ وَيَعْلَمُ مَا
تَكْتُمُونَ

110 He knows what is said openly, and He knows what you conceal.

١١١ وَإِنْ أَدْرِى لَعَلَّهُۥ فِتْنَةٌ لَّكُمْ وَمَتَـٰعٌ إِلَىٰ حِينٍ

111 "And I do not know whether it is perhaps a trial for you, and an enjoyment for a while."

١١٢ قَـٰلَ رَبِّ ٱحْكُم بِٱلْحَقِّ ۗ وَرَبُّنَا ٱلرَّحْمَـٰنُ
ٱلْمُسْتَعَانُ عَلَىٰ مَا تَصِفُونَ

112 He said, "My Lord, judge with justice." And, "Our Lord is the Gracious, Whose help is sought against what you allege."

22 The Pilgrimage الحج

بِسْمِ ٱللَّهِ ٱلرَّحْمَٰنِ ٱلرَّحِيمِ

In the name of Allah, the Gracious, the Merciful.

١ يَٰٓأَيُّهَا ٱلنَّاسُ ٱتَّقُوا۟ رَبَّكُمْ ۚ إِنَّ زَلْزَلَةَ ٱلسَّاعَةِ
شَىْءٌ عَظِيمٌ

1 O people, be conscious of your Lord. The quaking of the Hour is a tremendous thing.

٢ يَوْمَ تَرَوْنَهَا تَذْهَلُ كُلُّ مُرْضِعَةٍ عَمَّآ أَرْضَعَتْ
وَتَضَعُ كُلُّ ذَاتِ حَمْلٍ حَمْلَهَا وَتَرَى ٱلنَّاسَ
سُكَٰرَىٰ وَمَا هُم بِسُكَٰرَىٰ وَلَٰكِنَّ عَذَابَ ٱللَّهِ
شَدِيدٌ

2 On the Day when you will see it: every nursing mother will discard her infant, and every pregnant woman will abort her load, and you will see the people drunk, even though they are not drunk—but the punishment of Allah is severe.

٣ وَمِنَ ٱلنَّاسِ مَن يُجَٰدِلُ فِى ٱللَّهِ بِغَيْرِ عِلْمٍ
وَيَتَّبِعُ كُلَّ شَيْطَٰنٍ مَّرِيدٍ

3 Among the people is he who argues about Allah without knowledge, and follows every defiant devil.

٤ كُتِبَ عَلَيْهِ أَنَّهُۥ مَن تَوَلَّاهُ فَأَنَّهُۥ يُضِلُّهُۥ وَيَهْدِيهِ
إِلَىٰ عَذَابِ ٱلسَّعِيرِ

4 It was decreed for him, that whoever follows him—he will misguide him, and lead him to the torment of the Blaze.

٥ يَٰٓأَيُّهَا ٱلنَّاسُ إِن كُنتُمْ فِى رَيْبٍ مِّنَ ٱلْبَعْثِ
فَإِنَّا خَلَقْنَٰكُم مِّن تُرَابٍ ثُمَّ مِن نُّطْفَةٍ ثُمَّ مِنْ
عَلَقَةٍ ثُمَّ مِن مُّضْغَةٍ مُّخَلَّقَةٍ وَغَيْرِ مُخَلَّقَةٍ
لِّنُبَيِّنَ لَكُمْ ۚ وَنُقِرُّ فِى ٱلْأَرْحَامِ مَا نَشَآءُ إِلَىٰٓ
أَجَلٍ مُّسَمًّى ثُمَّ نُخْرِجُكُمْ طِفْلًا ثُمَّ لِتَبْلُغُوٓا۟
أَشُدَّكُمْ ۖ وَمِنكُم مَّن يُتَوَفَّىٰ وَمِنكُم مَّن يُرَدُّ
إِلَىٰٓ أَرْذَلِ ٱلْعُمُرِ لِكَيْلَا يَعْلَمَ مِنۢ بَعْدِ عِلْمٍ شَيْـًٔا ۚ
وَتَرَى ٱلْأَرْضَ هَامِدَةً فَإِذَآ أَنزَلْنَا عَلَيْهَا ٱلْمَآءَ
ٱهْتَزَّتْ وَرَبَتْ وَأَنۢبَتَتْ مِن كُلِّ زَوْجٍۭ بَهِيجٍ

5 O people! If you are in doubt about the Resurrection—We created you from dust, then from a small drop, then from a clinging clot, then from a lump of flesh, partly developed and partly undeveloped. In order to clarify things for you. And We settle in the wombs whatever We will for a designated term, and then We bring you out as infants, until you reach your full strength. And some of you will pass away, and some of you will be returned to the vilest age, so that he may not know, after having known. And you see the earth still; but when We send down water on it, it vibrates, and swells, and grows all kinds of lovely pairs.

٦ ذَٰلِكَ بِأَنَّ ٱللَّهَ هُوَ ٱلْحَقُّ وَأَنَّهُۥ يُحْىِ ٱلْمَوْتَىٰ
وَأَنَّهُۥ عَلَىٰ كُلِّ شَىْءٍ قَدِيرٌ

6 That is because Allah is the truth, and because He gives life to the dead, and because He is Capable of everything.

٧ وَأَنَّ ٱلسَّاعَةَ ءَاتِيَةٌ لَّا رَيْبَ فِيهَا وَأَنَّ ٱللَّهَ
يَبْعَثُ مَن فِى ٱلْقُبُورِ

7 And because the Hour is coming—there is no doubt about it—and because Allah will resurrect those in the graves.

٨ وَمِنَ ٱلنَّاسِ مَن يُجَٰدِلُ فِى ٱللَّهِ بِغَيْرِ عِلْمٍ
وَلَا هُدًى وَلَا كِتَٰبٍ مُّنِيرٍ

8 And among the people is he who argues about Allah without knowledge, or guidance, or an enlightening scripture.

٩ ثَانِىَ عِطْفِهِۦ لِيُضِلَّ عَن سَبِيلِ ٱللَّهِ ۖ لَهُۥ فِى
ٱلدُّنْيَا خِزْىٌ ۖ وَنُذِيقُهُۥ يَوْمَ ٱلْقِيَٰمَةِ عَذَابَ
ٱلْحَرِيقِ

9 Turning aside in contempt, to lead away from the path of Allah. He will have humiliation in this world, and on the Day of Resurrection We will make him taste the agony of burning.

١٠ ذَٰلِكَ بِمَا قَدَّمَتْ يَدَاكَ وَأَنَّ ٱللَّهَ لَيْسَ بِظَلَّٰمٍ
لِّلْعَبِيدِ

10 That is for what your hands have advanced, and because Allah is not unjust to the servants.

١١ وَمِنَ ٱلنَّاسِ مَن يَعْبُدُ ٱللَّهَ عَلَىٰ حَرْفٍ ۖ فَإِنْ
أَصَابَهُۥ خَيْرٌ ٱطْمَأَنَّ بِهِۦ ۖ وَإِنْ أَصَابَتْهُ فِتْنَةٌ
ٱنقَلَبَ عَلَىٰ وَجْهِهِۦ خَسِرَ ٱلدُّنْيَا وَٱلْءَاخِرَةَ ۚ
ذَٰلِكَ هُوَ ٱلْخُسْرَانُ ٱلْمُبِينُ

11 And among the people is he who worships Allah on edge. When something good comes his way, he is content with it. But when an ordeal strikes him, he makes a turnaround. He loses this world and the next. That is the obvious loss.

١٢ يَدْعُوا۟ مِن دُونِ ٱللَّهِ مَا لَا يَضُرُّهُۥ وَمَا لَا
يَنفَعُهُۥ ۚ ذَٰلِكَ هُوَ ٱلضَّلَٰلُ ٱلْبَعِيدُ

12 He invokes, instead of Allah, what can neither harm him nor benefit him. That is the far straying.

١٣ يَدْعُوا۟ لَمَن ضَرُّهُۥٓ أَقْرَبُ مِن نَّفْعِهِۦ ۚ لَبِئْسَ
ٱلْمَوْلَىٰ وَلَبِئْسَ ٱلْعَشِيرُ

13 He invokes one whose harm is closer than his benefit. What a miserable master. What a miserable companion.

١٤ إِنَّ ٱللَّهَ يُدْخِلُ ٱلَّذِينَ ءَامَنُوا۟ وَعَمِلُوا۟
ٱلصَّٰلِحَٰتِ جَنَّٰتٍ تَجْرِى مِن تَحْتِهَا ٱلْأَنْهَٰرُ ۚ إِنَّ
ٱللَّهَ يَفْعَلُ مَا يُرِيدُ

14 Allah will admit those who believe and do righteous deeds into Gardens beneath which rivers flow. Allah does whatever He wills.

١٥ مَن كَانَ يَظُنُّ أَن لَّن يَنصُرَهُ ٱللَّهُ فِى ٱلدُّنْيَا
وَٱلْـَٔاخِرَةِ فَلْيَمْدُدْ بِسَبَبٍ إِلَى ٱلسَّمَآءِ ثُمَّ
لْيَقْطَعْ فَلْيَنظُرْ هَلْ يُذْهِبَنَّ كَيْدُهُۥ مَا يَغِيظُ

15 Whoever thinks that Allah will not help him in this life and in the Hereafter—let him turn to heaven, then sever, and see if his cunning eliminates what enrages him.

١٦ وَكَذَٰلِكَ أَنزَلْنَٰهُ ءَايَٰتٍۭ بَيِّنَٰتٍ وَأَنَّ ٱللَّهَ يَهْدِى
مَن يُرِيدُ

16 Thus We revealed it as clarifying signs, and Allah guides whomever He wills.

١٧ إِنَّ ٱلَّذِينَ ءَامَنُوا۟ وَٱلَّذِينَ هَادُوا۟ وَٱلصَّٰبِـِٔينَ
وَٱلنَّصَٰرَىٰ وَٱلْمَجُوسَ وَٱلَّذِينَ أَشْرَكُوٓا۟ إِنَّ ٱللَّهَ
يَفْصِلُ بَيْنَهُمْ يَوْمَ ٱلْقِيَٰمَةِ ۚ إِنَّ ٱللَّهَ عَلَىٰ كُلِّ
شَىْءٍ شَهِيدٌ

17 Those who believe, and those who are Jewish, and the Sabeans, and the Christians, and the Zoroastrians, and the Polytheists—Allah will judge between them on the Day of Resurrection. Allah is witness to all things.

١٨ أَلَمْ تَرَ أَنَّ ٱللَّهَ يَسْجُدُ لَهُۥ مَن فِى ٱلسَّمَٰوَٰتِ
وَمَن فِى ٱلْأَرْضِ وَٱلشَّمْسُ وَٱلْقَمَرُ وَٱلنُّجُومُ
وَٱلْجِبَالُ وَٱلشَّجَرُ وَٱلدَّوَآبُّ وَكَثِيرٌ مِّنَ ٱلنَّاسِ ۖ
وَكَثِيرٌ حَقَّ عَلَيْهِ ٱلْعَذَابُ ۗ وَمَن يُهِنِ ٱللَّهُ فَمَا لَهُۥ
مِن مُّكْرِمٍ ۚ إِنَّ ٱللَّهَ يَفْعَلُ مَا يَشَآءُ ۩

18 Do you not realize that to Allah prostrates everyone in the heavens and everyone on earth, and the sun, and the moon, and the stars, and the mountains, and the trees, and the animals, and many of the people? But many are justly deserving of punishment. Whomever Allah shames, there is none to honor him. Allah does whatever He wills.

١٩ هَٰذَانِ خَصْمَانِ ٱخْتَصَمُوا۟ فِى رَبِّهِمْ ۖ فَٱلَّذِينَ
كَفَرُوا۟ قُطِّعَتْ لَهُمْ ثِيَابٌ مِّن نَّارٍ يُصَبُّ مِن
فَوْقِ رُءُوسِهِمُ ٱلْحَمِيمُ

19 Here are two adversaries feuding regarding their Lord. As for those who disbelieve, garments of fire will be tailored for them, and scalding water will be poured over their heads.

٢٠ يُصْهَرُ بِهِۦ مَا فِى بُطُونِهِمْ وَٱلْجُلُودُ

20 Melting their insides and their skins.

٢١ وَلَهُم مَّقَٰمِعُ مِنْ حَدِيدٍ

21 And they will have maces of iron.

٢٢ كُلَّمَآ أَرَادُوٓا۟ أَن يَخْرُجُوا۟ مِنْهَا مِنْ غَمٍّ
أُعِيدُوا۟ فِيهَا وَذُوقُوا۟ عَذَابَ ٱلْحَرِيقِ

22 Whenever they try to escape the gloom, they will be driven back to it: "Taste the suffering of burning."

٢٣ إِنَّ ٱللَّهَ يُدْخِلُ ٱلَّذِينَ ءَامَنُوا۟ وَعَمِلُوا۟
ٱلصَّٰلِحَٰتِ جَنَّٰتٍ تَجْرِى مِن تَحْتِهَا ٱلْأَنْهَٰرُ

23 But Allah will admit those who believe and do good deeds into Gardens beneath which rivers flow. They will be decorated therein with

يُحَلَّوْنَ فِيهَا مِنْ أَسَاوِرَ مِن ذَهَبٍ وَلُؤْلُؤًا ۖ
وَلِبَاسُهُمْ فِيهَا حَرِيرٌ

bracelets of gold and pearls, and their garments therein will be of silk.

٢٤ وَهُدُوٓا۟ إِلَى ٱلطَّيِّبِ مِنَ ٱلْقَوْلِ وَهُدُوٓا۟ إِلَىٰ
صِرَٰطِ ٱلْحَمِيدِ

24 They were guided to purity of speech. They were guided to the path of the Most Praised.

٢٥ إِنَّ ٱلَّذِينَ كَفَرُوا۟ وَيَصُدُّونَ عَن سَبِيلِ ٱللَّهِ
وَٱلْمَسْجِدِ ٱلْحَرَامِ ٱلَّذِى جَعَلْنَٰهُ لِلنَّاسِ سَوَآءً
ٱلْعَٰكِفُ فِيهِ وَٱلْبَادِ ۚ وَمَن يُرِدْ فِيهِ بِإِلْحَادٍۭ بِظُلْمٍ
نُّذِقْهُ مِنْ عَذَابٍ أَلِيمٍ

25 As for those who disbelieve and repel from Allah's path and from the Sacred Mosque—which We have designated for all mankind equally, whether residing therein or passing through—and seek to commit sacrilege therein—We will make him taste of a painful punishment.

٢٦ وَإِذْ بَوَّأْنَا لِإِبْرَٰهِيمَ مَكَانَ ٱلْبَيْتِ أَن لَّا تُشْرِكْ
بِى شَيْـًٔا وَطَهِّرْ بَيْتِىَ لِلطَّآئِفِينَ وَٱلْقَآئِمِينَ
وَٱلرُّكَّعِ ٱلسُّجُودِ

26 We showed Abraham the location of the House: "Do not associate anything with Me; and purify My House for those who circle around, and those who stand to pray, and those who kneel and prostrate."

٢٧ وَأَذِّن فِى ٱلنَّاسِ بِٱلْحَجِّ يَأْتُوكَ رِجَالًا وَعَلَىٰ
كُلِّ ضَامِرٍ يَأْتِينَ مِن كُلِّ فَجٍّ عَمِيقٍ

27 And announce the pilgrimage to humanity. They will come to you on foot, and on every transport. They will come from every distant point.

٢٨ لِّيَشْهَدُوا۟ مَنَٰفِعَ لَهُمْ وَيَذْكُرُوا۟ ٱسْمَ ٱللَّهِ فِىٓ
أَيَّامٍ مَّعْلُومَٰتٍ عَلَىٰ مَا رَزَقَهُم مِّنۢ بَهِيمَةِ
ٱلْأَنْعَٰمِ ۖ فَكُلُوا۟ مِنْهَا وَأَطْعِمُوا۟ ٱلْبَآئِسَ ٱلْفَقِيرَ

28 That they may witness the benefits for themselves, and celebrate the name of Allah during the appointed days, for providing them with the animal livestock. So eat from it, and feed the unfortunate poor.

٢٩ ثُمَّ لْيَقْضُوا۟ تَفَثَهُمْ وَلْيُوفُوا۟ نُذُورَهُمْ
وَلْيَطَّوَّفُوا۟ بِٱلْبَيْتِ ٱلْعَتِيقِ

29 Then let them perform their acts of cleansing, and fulfill their vows, and circle around the Ancient House.

٣٠ ذَٰلِكَ وَمَن يُعَظِّمْ حُرُمَٰتِ ٱللَّهِ فَهُوَ خَيْرٌ لَّهُۥ
عِندَ رَبِّهِۦ ۗ وَأُحِلَّتْ لَكُمُ ٱلْأَنْعَٰمُ إِلَّا مَا يُتْلَىٰ
عَلَيْكُمْ ۖ فَٱجْتَنِبُوا۟ ٱلرِّجْسَ مِنَ ٱلْأَوْثَٰنِ
وَٱجْتَنِبُوا۟ قَوْلَ ٱلزُّورِ

30 All that. Whoever venerates the sanctities of Allah—it is good for him with his Lord. All livestock are permitted to you, except what is recited to you. So stay away from the abomination of idols, and stay away from perjury.

٣١ حُنَفَآءَ لِلَّهِ غَيْرَ مُشْرِكِينَ بِهِۦۚ وَمَن يُشْرِكْ
بِٱللَّهِ فَكَأَنَّمَا خَرَّ مِنَ ٱلسَّمَآءِ فَتَخْطَفُهُ ٱلطَّيْرُ أَوْ
تَهْوِى بِهِ ٱلرِّيحُ فِى مَكَانٍ سَحِيقٍ

31 Being true to Allah, without associating anything with Him. Whoever associates anything with Allah—it is as though he has fallen from the sky, and is snatched by the birds, or is swept away by the wind to a distant abyss.

٣٢ ذَٰلِكَ وَمَن يُعَظِّمْ شَعَٰٓئِرَ ٱللَّهِ فَإِنَّهَا مِن تَقْوَى
ٱلْقُلُوبِ

32 So it is. Whoever venerates the sacraments of Allah—it is from the piety of the hearts.

٣٣ لَكُمْ فِيهَا مَنَٰفِعُ إِلَىٰٓ أَجَلٍ مُّسَمًّى ثُمَّ مَحِلُّهَآ
إِلَى ٱلْبَيْتِ ٱلْعَتِيقِ

33 In them are benefits for you until a certain time. Then their place is by the Ancient House.

٣٤ وَلِكُلِّ أُمَّةٍ جَعَلْنَا مَنسَكًا لِّيَذْكُرُوا۟ ٱسْمَ ٱللَّهِ
عَلَىٰ مَا رَزَقَهُم مِّنۢ بَهِيمَةِ ٱلْأَنْعَٰمِۗ فَإِلَٰهُكُمْ إِلَٰهٌ
وَٰحِدٌ فَلَهُۥٓ أَسْلِمُوا۟ۗ وَبَشِّرِ ٱلْمُخْبِتِينَ

34 We have appointed a rite for every nation, that they may commemorate Allah's name over the livestock He has provided for them. Your God is One God, so to Him submit, and announce good news to the humble.

٣٥ ٱلَّذِينَ إِذَا ذُكِرَ ٱللَّهُ وَجِلَتْ قُلُوبُهُمْ
وَٱلصَّٰبِرِينَ عَلَىٰ مَآ أَصَابَهُمْ وَٱلْمُقِيمِى ٱلصَّلَوٰةِ
وَمِمَّا رَزَقْنَٰهُمْ يُنفِقُونَ

35 Those whose hearts tremble when Allah is mentioned, and those who endure what has befallen them, and those who perform the prayer and spend from what We have provided for them.

٣٦ وَٱلْبُدْنَ جَعَلْنَٰهَا لَكُم مِّن شَعَٰٓئِرِ ٱللَّهِ لَكُمْ فِيهَا
خَيْرٌۖ فَٱذْكُرُوا۟ ٱسْمَ ٱللَّهِ عَلَيْهَا صَوَآفَّۖ فَإِذَا
وَجَبَتْ جُنُوبُهَا فَكُلُوا۟ مِنْهَا وَأَطْعِمُوا۟ ٱلْقَانِعَ
وَٱلْمُعْتَرَّۚ كَذَٰلِكَ سَخَّرْنَٰهَا لَكُمْ لَعَلَّكُمْ تَشْكُرُونَ

36 We have made the animal offerings emblems of Allah for you. In them is goodness for you. So pronounce Allah's name upon them as they line up. Then, when they have fallen on their sides, eat of them and feed the contented and the beggar. Thus We have subjected them to you, that you may be thankful.

٣٧ لَن يَنَالَ ٱللَّهَ لُحُومُهَا وَلَا دِمَآؤُهَا وَلَٰكِن
يَنَالُهُ ٱلتَّقْوَىٰ مِنكُمْۚ كَذَٰلِكَ سَخَّرَهَا لَكُمْ
لِتُكَبِّرُوا۟ ٱللَّهَ عَلَىٰ مَا هَدَىٰكُمْۗ وَبَشِّرِ ٱلْمُحْسِنِينَ

37 Neither their flesh, nor their blood, ever reaches Allah. What reaches Him is the righteousness from you. Thus He subdued them to you, that you may glorify Allah for guiding you.

And give good news to the charitable.

٣٨ إِنَّ ٱللَّهَ يُدَٰفِعُ عَنِ ٱلَّذِينَ ءَامَنُوٓاْۗ إِنَّ ٱللَّهَ لَا يُحِبُّ كُلَّ خَوَّانٍ كَفُورٍ

38 Allah defends those who believe. Allah does not love any ungrateful traitor.

٣٩ أُذِنَ لِلَّذِينَ يُقَٰتَلُونَ بِأَنَّهُمْ ظُلِمُواْۚ وَإِنَّ ٱللَّهَ عَلَىٰ نَصْرِهِمْ لَقَدِيرٌ

39 Permission is given to those who are fought against, and Allah is Able to give them victory.

٤٠ ٱلَّذِينَ أُخْرِجُواْ مِن دِيَٰرِهِم بِغَيْرِ حَقٍّ إِلَّآ أَن يَقُولُواْ رَبُّنَا ٱللَّهُۗ وَلَوْلَا دَفْعُ ٱللَّهِ ٱلنَّاسَ بَعْضَهُم بِبَعْضٍ لَّهُدِّمَتْ صَوَٰمِعُ وَبِيَعٌ وَصَلَوَٰتٌ وَمَسَٰجِدُ يُذْكَرُ فِيهَا ٱسْمُ ٱللَّهِ كَثِيرًاۗ وَلَيَنصُرَنَّ ٱللَّهُ مَن يَنصُرُهُۥٓۗ إِنَّ ٱللَّهَ لَقَوِىٌّ عَزِيزٌ

40 Those who were unjustly evicted from their homes, merely for saying, “Our Lord is Allah.” Were it not that Allah repels people by means of others: monasteries, churches, synagogues, and mosques—where the name of Allah is mentioned much—would have been demolished. Allah supports whoever supports Him. Allah is Strong and Mighty.

٤١ ٱلَّذِينَ إِن مَّكَّنَّٰهُمْ فِى ٱلْأَرْضِ أَقَامُواْ ٱلصَّلَوٰةَ وَءَاتَوُاْ ٱلزَّكَوٰةَ وَأَمَرُواْ بِٱلْمَعْرُوفِ وَنَهَوْاْ عَنِ ٱلْمُنكَرِۗ وَلِلَّهِ عَٰقِبَةُ ٱلْأُمُورِ

41 Those who, when We empower them in the land, observe the prayer, and give regular charity, and command what is right, and forbid what is wrong. To Allah belongs the outcome of events.

٤٢ وَإِن يُكَذِّبُوكَ فَقَدْ كَذَّبَتْ قَبْلَهُمْ قَوْمُ نُوحٍ وَعَادٌ وَثَمُودُ

42 If they deny you—before them the people of Noah, and Aad, and Thamood also denied.

٤٣ وَقَوْمُ إِبْرَٰهِيمَ وَقَوْمُ لُوطٍ

43 And the people of Abraham, and the people of Lot.

٤٤ وَأَصْحَٰبُ مَدْيَنَۖ وَكُذِّبَ مُوسَىٰ فَأَمْلَيْتُ لِلْكَٰفِرِينَ ثُمَّ أَخَذْتُهُمْۖ فَكَيْفَ كَانَ نَكِيرِ

44 And the inhabitants of Median. And Moses was denied. Then I reprieved those who disbelieved, but then I seized them. So how was My rejection?

٤٥ فَكَأَيِّن مِّن قَرْيَةٍ أَهْلَكْنَٰهَا وَهِىَ ظَالِمَةٌ فَهِىَ خَاوِيَةٌ عَلَىٰ عُرُوشِهَا وَبِئْرٍ مُّعَطَّلَةٍ وَقَصْرٍ مَّشِيدٍ

45 How many a town have We destroyed while it was doing wrong? They lie in ruins; with stilled wells, and lofty mansions.

٤٦ أَفَلَمْ يَسِيرُوا۟ فِى ٱلْأَرْضِ فَتَكُونَ لَهُمْ قُلُوبٌ
يَعْقِلُونَ بِهَآ أَوْ ءَاذَانٌ يَسْمَعُونَ بِهَا ۖ فَإِنَّهَا لَا
تَعْمَى ٱلْأَبْصَـٰرُ وَلَـٰكِن تَعْمَى ٱلْقُلُوبُ ٱلَّتِى فِى
ٱلصُّدُورِ

46 Have they not journeyed in the land, and had minds to reason with, or ears to listen with? It is not the eyes that go blind, but it is the hearts, within the chests, that go blind.

٤٧ وَيَسْتَعْجِلُونَكَ بِٱلْعَذَابِ وَلَن يُخْلِفَ ٱللَّهُ
وَعْدَهُۥ ۚ وَإِنَّ يَوْمًا عِندَ رَبِّكَ كَأَلْفِ سَنَةٍ مِّمَّا
تَعُدُّونَ

47 And they ask you to hasten the punishment. But Allah never breaks His promise. A day with your Lord is like a thousand years of your count.

٤٨ وَكَأَيِّن مِّن قَرْيَةٍ أَمْلَيْتُ لَهَا وَهِىَ ظَالِمَةٌ ثُمَّ
أَخَذْتُهَا وَإِلَىَّ ٱلْمَصِيرُ

48 How many a town have I reprieved, although it was unjust? Then I seized it. To Me is the destination.

٤٩ قُلْ يَـٰٓأَيُّهَا ٱلنَّاسُ إِنَّمَآ أَنَا۠ لَكُمْ نَذِيرٌ مُّبِينٌ

49 Say, “O people, I am only a plain warner to you.”

٥٠ فَٱلَّذِينَ ءَامَنُوا۟ وَعَمِلُوا۟ ٱلصَّـٰلِحَـٰتِ لَهُم
مَّغْفِرَةٌ وَرِزْقٌ كَرِيمٌ

50 Those who believe and work righteousness—for them is forgiveness and a generous provision.

٥١ وَٱلَّذِينَ سَعَوْا۟ فِىٓ ءَايَـٰتِنَا مُعَـٰجِزِينَ أُو۟لَـٰٓئِكَ
أَصْحَـٰبُ ٱلْجَحِيمِ

51 But those who strive against Our revelations—these are the inmates of Hell.

٥٢ وَمَآ أَرْسَلْنَا مِن قَبْلِكَ مِن رَّسُولٍ وَلَا نَبِىٍّ إِلَّآ
إِذَا تَمَنَّىٰٓ أَلْقَى ٱلشَّيْطَـٰنُ فِىٓ أُمْنِيَّتِهِۦ فَيَنسَخُ
ٱللَّهُ مَا يُلْقِى ٱلشَّيْطَـٰنُ ثُمَّ يُحْكِمُ ٱللَّهُ ءَايَـٰتِهِۦ ۗ
وَٱللَّهُ عَلِيمٌ حَكِيمٌ

52 We never sent a messenger before you, or a prophet, but when he had a desire Satan interfered in his wishes. But Allah nullifies what Satan interjects, and Allah affirms His revelations. Allah is Omniscient and Wise.

٥٣ لِّيَجْعَلَ مَا يُلْقِى ٱلشَّيْطَـٰنُ فِتْنَةً لِّلَّذِينَ فِى
قُلُوبِهِم مَّرَضٌ وَٱلْقَاسِيَةِ قُلُوبُهُمْ ۗ وَإِنَّ ٱلظَّـٰلِمِينَ
لَفِى شِقَاقٍۭ بَعِيدٍ

53 In order to make Satan’s suggestions a trial for those whose hearts are diseased, and those whose hearts are hardened. The wrongdoers are in profound discord.

٥٤ وَلِيَعْلَمَ ٱلَّذِينَ أُوتُوا۟ ٱلْعِلْمَ أَنَّهُ ٱلْحَقُّ مِن
رَّبِّكَ فَيُؤْمِنُوا۟ بِهِۦ فَتُخْبِتَ لَهُۥ قُلُوبُهُمْ ۗ وَإِنَّ ٱللَّهَ
لَهَادِ ٱلَّذِينَ ءَامَنُوٓا۟ إِلَىٰ صِرَٰطٍ مُّسْتَقِيمٍ

54 And so that those endowed with knowledge may know that it is the truth from your Lord, and so believe in it, and their hearts soften to it.

Allah guides those who believe to a straight path.

٥٥ وَلَا يَزَالُ ٱلَّذِينَ كَفَرُوا۟ فِى مِرْيَةٍ مِّنْهُ حَتَّىٰ
تَأْتِيَهُمُ ٱلسَّاعَةُ بَغْتَةً أَوْ يَأْتِيَهُمْ عَذَابُ يَوْمٍ
عَقِيمٍ

55 Those who disbelieve will continue to be hesitant about it, until the Hour comes upon them suddenly, or there comes to them the torment of a desolate Day.

٥٦ ٱلْمُلْكُ يَوْمَئِذٍ لِّلَّهِ يَحْكُمُ بَيْنَهُمْ ۚ فَٱلَّذِينَ
ءَامَنُوا۟ وَعَمِلُوا۟ ٱلصَّٰلِحَٰتِ فِى جَنَّٰتِ ٱلنَّعِيمِ

56 Sovereignty on that Day belongs to Allah; He will judge between them. Those who believe and do good deeds will be in the Gardens of Bliss.

٥٧ وَٱلَّذِينَ كَفَرُوا۟ وَكَذَّبُوا۟ بِـَٔايَٰتِنَا فَأُو۟لَٰٓئِكَ لَهُمْ
عَذَابٌ مُّهِينٌ

57 But those who disbelieve and reject Our revelations—these will have a humiliating punishment.

٥٨ وَٱلَّذِينَ هَاجَرُوا۟ فِى سَبِيلِ ٱللَّهِ ثُمَّ قُتِلُوٓا۟ أَوْ
مَاتُوا۟ لَيَرْزُقَنَّهُمُ ٱللَّهُ رِزْقًا حَسَنًا ۚ وَإِنَّ ٱللَّهَ لَهُوَ
خَيْرُ ٱلرَّٰزِقِينَ

58 Those who emigrate in Allah's cause, then get killed, or die, Allah will provide them with fine provisions. Allah is the Best of Providers.

٥٩ لَيُدْخِلَنَّهُم مُّدْخَلًا يَرْضَوْنَهُۥ ۗ وَإِنَّ ٱللَّهَ لَعَلِيمٌ
حَلِيمٌ

59 He will admit them an admittance that will please them. Allah is Knowing and Clement.

٦٠ ذَٰلِكَ وَمَنْ عَاقَبَ بِمِثْلِ مَا عُوقِبَ بِهِۦ ثُمَّ
بُغِىَ عَلَيْهِ لَيَنصُرَنَّهُ ٱللَّهُ ۗ إِنَّ ٱللَّهَ لَعَفُوٌّ غَفُورٌ

60 That is so! Whoever retaliates similarly to the affliction he was made to suffer, and then he is wronged again, Allah will definitely assist him. Allah is Pardoning and Forgiving.

٦١ ذَٰلِكَ بِأَنَّ ٱللَّهَ يُولِجُ ٱلَّيْلَ فِى ٱلنَّهَارِ وَيُولِجُ
ٱلنَّهَارَ فِى ٱلَّيْلِ وَأَنَّ ٱللَّهَ سَمِيعٌۢ بَصِيرٌ

61 That is because Allah merges the night into the day, and He merges the day into the night, and because Allah is Hearing and Seeing.

٦٢ ذَٰلِكَ بِأَنَّ ٱللَّهَ هُوَ ٱلْحَقُّ وَأَنَّ مَا يَدْعُونَ مِن
دُونِهِۦ هُوَ ٱلْبَٰطِلُ وَأَنَّ ٱللَّهَ هُوَ ٱلْعَلِىُّ ٱلْكَبِيرُ

62 That is because Allah is the Reality, and what they invoke besides Him is vanity, and because Allah is the Sublime, the Grand.

٦٣ أَلَمْ تَرَ أَنَّ ٱللَّهَ أَنزَلَ مِنَ ٱلسَّمَآءِ مَآءً
فَتُصْبِحُ ٱلْأَرْضُ مُخْضَرَّةً ۗ إِنَّ ٱللَّهَ لَطِيفٌ خَبِيرٌ

63 Do you not see that Allah sends down water from the sky, and the land becomes green? Allah is Kind and Aware.

٦٤ لَّهُۥ مَا فِى ٱلسَّمَٰوَٰتِ وَمَا فِى ٱلْأَرْضِ ۗ وَإِنَّ
ٱللَّهَ لَهُوَ ٱلْغَنِىُّ ٱلْحَمِيدُ

64 To Him belongs everything in the heavens and everything on earth. Allah is the Rich, the Praised.

٦٥ أَلَمْ تَرَ أَنَّ ٱللَّهَ سَخَّرَ لَكُم مَّا فِى ٱلْأَرْضِ
وَٱلْفُلْكَ تَجْرِى فِى ٱلْبَحْرِ بِأَمْرِهِۦ وَيُمْسِكُ
ٱلسَّمَآءَ أَن تَقَعَ عَلَى ٱلْأَرْضِ إِلَّا بِإِذْنِهِۦٓ ۗ إِنَّ ٱللَّهَ
بِٱلنَّاسِ لَرَءُوفٌ رَّحِيمٌ

65 Do you not see that Allah made everything on earth subservient to you? How the ships sail at sea by His command? That He holds up the sky lest it falls on earth—except by His permission? Allah is Gracious towards the people, Most Merciful.

٦٦ وَهُوَ ٱلَّذِىٓ أَحْيَاكُمْ ثُمَّ يُمِيتُكُمْ ثُمَّ يُحْيِيكُمْ ۗ
إِنَّ ٱلْإِنسَٰنَ لَكَفُورٌ

66 And it is He who gives you life, then makes you die, then revives you. The human being is unappreciative.

٦٧ لِّكُلِّ أُمَّةٍ جَعَلْنَا مَنسَكًا هُمْ نَاسِكُوهُ ۖ فَلَا
يُنَٰزِعُنَّكَ فِى ٱلْأَمْرِ ۚ وَٱدْعُ إِلَىٰ رَبِّكَ ۖ إِنَّكَ لَعَلَىٰ
هُدًى مُّسْتَقِيمٍ

67 For every congregation We have appointed acts of devotion, which they observe. So do not let them dispute with you in this matter. And invite to your Lord; you are upon a straight guidance.

٦٨ وَإِن جَٰدَلُوكَ فَقُلِ ٱللَّهُ أَعْلَمُ بِمَا تَعْمَلُونَ

68 But if they dispute with you, say, “Allah is fully aware of what you do.”

٦٩ ٱللَّهُ يَحْكُمُ بَيْنَكُمْ يَوْمَ ٱلْقِيَٰمَةِ فِيمَا كُنتُمْ
فِيهِ تَخْتَلِفُونَ

69 Allah will judge between you on the Day of Resurrection regarding what you disagree about.

٧٠ أَلَمْ تَعْلَمْ أَنَّ ٱللَّهَ يَعْلَمُ مَا فِى ٱلسَّمَآءِ
وَٱلْأَرْضِ ۗ إِنَّ ذَٰلِكَ فِى كِتَٰبٍ ۚ إِنَّ ذَٰلِكَ عَلَى ٱللَّهِ
يَسِيرٌ

70 Do you not know that Allah knows everything in the heavens and the earth? This is in a book. That is easy for Allah.

٧١ وَيَعْبُدُونَ مِن دُونِ ٱللَّهِ مَا لَمْ يُنَزِّلْ بِهِۦ
سُلْطَٰنًا وَمَا لَيْسَ لَهُم بِهِۦ عِلْمٌ ۗ وَمَا لِلظَّٰلِمِينَ
مِن نَّصِيرٍ

71 Yet they worship, besides Allah, things for which He sent down no warrant, and what they have no knowledge of. There is no savior for the transgressors.

٧٢ وَإِذَا تُتْلَىٰ عَلَيْهِمْ ءَايَٰتُنَا بَيِّنَٰتٍ تَعْرِفُ فِى
وُجُوهِ ٱلَّذِينَ كَفَرُوا۟ ٱلْمُنكَرَ ۖ يَكَادُونَ يَسْطُونَ
بِٱلَّذِينَ يَتْلُونَ عَلَيْهِمْ ءَايَٰتِنَا ۗ قُلْ أَفَأُنَبِّئُكُم بِشَرٍّ

72 And when Our Clear Verses are recited to them, you will recognize disgust on the faces of those who disbelieve. They nearly assault those who recite to them Our Verses. Say, “Shall I inform you of

مِّن ذَٰلِكُمُۗ ٱلنَّارُ وَعَدَهَا ٱللَّهُ ٱلَّذِينَ كَفَرُواْۖ
وَبِئۡسَ ٱلۡمَصِيرُ

something worse than that? The Fire! Allah has promised it to those who disbelieve. And what a wretched outcome!"

٧٣ يَٰٓأَيُّهَا ٱلنَّاسُ ضُرِبَ مَثَلٞ فَٱسۡتَمِعُواْ لَهُۥٓۚ إِنَّ
ٱلَّذِينَ تَدۡعُونَ مِن دُونِ ٱللَّهِ لَن يَخۡلُقُواْ ذُبَابٗا
وَلَوِ ٱجۡتَمَعُواْ لَهُۥۖ وَإِن يَسۡلُبۡهُمُ ٱلذُّبَابُ شَيۡـٔٗا لَّا
يَسۡتَنقِذُوهُ مِنۡهُۚ ضَعُفَ ٱلطَّالِبُ وَٱلۡمَطۡلُوبُ

73 O people! A parable is presented, so listen to it: Those you invoke besides Allah will never create a fly, even if they banded together for that purpose. And if the fly steals anything from them, they cannot recover it from it. Weak are the pursuer and the pursued.

٧٤ مَا قَدَرُواْ ٱللَّهَ حَقَّ قَدۡرِهِۦٓۚ إِنَّ ٱللَّهَ لَقَوِيٌّ
عَزِيزٌ

74 They do not value Allah as He should be valued. Allah is Strong and Powerful.

٧٥ ٱللَّهُ يَصۡطَفِي مِنَ ٱلۡمَلَٰٓئِكَةِ رُسُلٗا وَمِنَ
ٱلنَّاسِۚ إِنَّ ٱللَّهَ سَمِيعُۢ بَصِيرٞ

75 Allah chooses messengers from among the angels, and from among the people. Allah is Hearing and Seeing.

٧٦ يَعۡلَمُ مَا بَيۡنَ أَيۡدِيهِمۡ وَمَا خَلۡفَهُمۡۗ وَإِلَى ٱللَّهِ
تُرۡجَعُ ٱلۡأُمُورُ

76 He knows what is before them, and what is behind them. To Allah all matters are referred.

٧٧ يَٰٓأَيُّهَا ٱلَّذِينَ ءَامَنُواْ ٱرۡكَعُواْ وَٱسۡجُدُواْ
وَٱعۡبُدُواْ رَبَّكُمۡ وَٱفۡعَلُواْ ٱلۡخَيۡرَ لَعَلَّكُمۡ تُفۡلِحُونَ
۩

77 O you who believe! Kneel, and prostrate, and worship your Lord, and do good deeds, so that you may succeed.

٧٨ وَجَٰهِدُواْ فِي ٱللَّهِ حَقَّ جِهَادِهِۦۚ هُوَ ٱجۡتَبَىٰكُمۡ
وَمَا جَعَلَ عَلَيۡكُمۡ فِي ٱلدِّينِ مِنۡ حَرَجٖۚ مِّلَّةَ
أَبِيكُمۡ إِبۡرَٰهِيمَۚ هُوَ سَمَّىٰكُمُ ٱلۡمُسۡلِمِينَ مِن قَبۡلُ
وَفِي هَٰذَا لِيَكُونَ ٱلرَّسُولُ شَهِيدًا عَلَيۡكُمۡ
وَتَكُونُواْ شُهَدَآءَ عَلَى ٱلنَّاسِۚ فَأَقِيمُواْ ٱلصَّلَوٰةَ
وَءَاتُواْ ٱلزَّكَوٰةَ وَٱعۡتَصِمُواْ بِٱللَّهِ هُوَ مَوۡلَىٰكُمۡۖ
فَنِعۡمَ ٱلۡمَوۡلَىٰ وَنِعۡمَ ٱلنَّصِيرُ

78 And strive for Allah, with the striving due to Him. He has chosen you, and has not burdened you in religion—the faith of your father Abraham. It is he who named you Muslims before, and in this. So that the Messenger may be a witness over you, and you may be witnesses over the people. So pray regularly, and give regular charity, and cleave to Allah. He is your Protector. What an excellent Protector, and what an excellent Helper.

23 The Believers المؤمنون

بِسْمِ ٱللَّهِ ٱلرَّحْمَٰنِ ٱلرَّحِيمِ	In the name of Allah, the Gracious, the Merciful.
١ قَدْ أَفْلَحَ ٱلْمُؤْمِنُونَ	1 Successful are the believers.
٢ ٱلَّذِينَ هُمْ فِى صَلَاتِهِمْ خَٰشِعُونَ	2 Those who are humble in their prayers.
٣ وَٱلَّذِينَ هُمْ عَنِ ٱللَّغْوِ مُعْرِضُونَ	3 Those who avoid nonsense.
٤ وَٱلَّذِينَ هُمْ لِلزَّكَوٰةِ فَٰعِلُونَ	4 Those who work for charity.
٥ وَٱلَّذِينَ هُمْ لِفُرُوجِهِمْ حَٰفِظُونَ	5 Those who safeguard their chastity.
٦ إِلَّا عَلَىٰٓ أَزْوَٰجِهِمْ أَوْ مَا مَلَكَتْ أَيْمَٰنُهُمْ فَإِنَّهُمْ غَيْرُ مَلُومِينَ	6 Except from their spouses, or their dependents—for then they are free from blame.
٧ فَمَنِ ٱبْتَغَىٰ وَرَآءَ ذَٰلِكَ فَأُو۟لَٰٓئِكَ هُمُ ٱلْعَادُونَ	7 But whoever seeks anything beyond that—these are the transgressors.
٨ وَٱلَّذِينَ هُمْ لِأَمَٰنَٰتِهِمْ وَعَهْدِهِمْ رَٰعُونَ	8 Those who are faithful to their trusts and pledges.
٩ وَٱلَّذِينَ هُمْ عَلَىٰ صَلَوَٰتِهِمْ يُحَافِظُونَ	9 Those who safeguard their prayers.
١٠ أُو۟لَٰٓئِكَ هُمُ ٱلْوَٰرِثُونَ	10 These are the inheritors.
١١ ٱلَّذِينَ يَرِثُونَ ٱلْفِرْدَوْسَ هُمْ فِيهَا خَٰلِدُونَ	11 Who will inherit Paradise, wherein they will dwell forever.
١٢ وَلَقَدْ خَلَقْنَا ٱلْإِنسَٰنَ مِن سُلَٰلَةٍ مِّن طِينٍ	12 We created man from an extract of clay.
١٣ ثُمَّ جَعَلْنَٰهُ نُطْفَةً فِى قَرَارٍ مَّكِينٍ	13 Then We made him a seed, in a secure repository.
١٤ ثُمَّ خَلَقْنَا ٱلنُّطْفَةَ عَلَقَةً فَخَلَقْنَا ٱلْعَلَقَةَ مُضْغَةً فَخَلَقْنَا ٱلْمُضْغَةَ عِظَٰمًا فَكَسَوْنَا ٱلْعِظَٰمَ لَحْمًا ثُمَّ أَنشَأْنَٰهُ خَلْقًا ءَاخَرَ ۚ فَتَبَارَكَ ٱللَّهُ أَحْسَنُ ٱلْخَٰلِقِينَ	14 Then We developed the seed into a clot. Then We developed the clot into a lump. Then We developed the lump into bones. Then We clothed the bones with flesh. Then We produced it into another creature. Most Blessed is Allah, the Best of Creators.
١٥ ثُمَّ إِنَّكُم بَعْدَ ذَٰلِكَ لَمَيِّتُونَ	15 Then, after that, you will die.

١٦ ثُمَّ إِنَّكُمْ يَوْمَ ٱلْقِيَٰمَةِ تُبْعَثُونَ

16 Then, on the Day of Resurrection,
you will be resurrected.

١٧ وَلَقَدْ خَلَقْنَا فَوْقَكُمْ سَبْعَ طَرَآئِقَ وَمَا كُنَّا عَنِ
ٱلْخَلْقِ غَٰفِلِينَ

17 We created above you seven
pathways, and We are never
heedless of the creation.

١٨ وَأَنزَلْنَا مِنَ ٱلسَّمَآءِ مَآءًۢ بِقَدَرٍ فَأَسْكَنَّٰهُ فِى
ٱلْأَرْضِ ۖ وَإِنَّا عَلَىٰ ذَهَابٍۭ بِهِۦ لَقَٰدِرُونَ

18 And We sent down water from the
sky in proper quantity, and settled it
in the ground, and We are Able to
take it away.

١٩ فَأَنشَأْنَا لَكُم بِهِۦ جَنَّٰتٍ مِّن نَّخِيلٍ وَأَعْنَٰبٍ
لَّكُمْ فِيهَا فَوَٰكِهُ كَثِيرَةٌ وَمِنْهَا تَأْكُلُونَ

19 With it We produce for you
gardens of palms and vines, yielding
abundant fruit for you to eat.

٢٠ وَشَجَرَةً تَخْرُجُ مِن طُورِ سَيْنَآءَ تَنۢبُتُ
بِٱلدُّهْنِ وَصِبْغٍ لِّلْءَاكِلِينَ

20 And a tree springing out of Mount
Sinai, producing oil, and seasoning
for those who eat.

٢١ وَإِنَّ لَكُمْ فِى ٱلْأَنْعَٰمِ لَعِبْرَةً ۖ نُّسْقِيكُم مِّمَّا فِى
بُطُونِهَا وَلَكُمْ فِيهَا مَنَٰفِعُ كَثِيرَةٌ وَمِنْهَا تَأْكُلُونَ

21 And there is a lesson for you in
livestock: We give you to drink from
what is in their bellies, and you have
many benefits in them, and from
them you eat.

٢٢ وَعَلَيْهَا وَعَلَى ٱلْفُلْكِ تُحْمَلُونَ

22 And on them, and on the ships,
you are transported.

٢٣ وَلَقَدْ أَرْسَلْنَا نُوحًا إِلَىٰ قَوْمِهِۦ فَقَالَ يَٰقَوْمِ
ٱعْبُدُوا۟ ٱللَّهَ مَا لَكُم مِّنْ إِلَٰهٍ غَيْرُهُۥٓ ۖ أَفَلَا تَتَّقُونَ

23 We sent Noah to his people. He
said, "O my people, worship Allah,
you have no deity other than Him.
Will you not take heed?"

٢٤ فَقَالَ ٱلْمَلَؤُا۟ ٱلَّذِينَ كَفَرُوا۟ مِن قَوْمِهِۦ مَا هَٰذَآ
إِلَّا بَشَرٌ مِّثْلُكُمْ يُرِيدُ أَن يَتَفَضَّلَ عَلَيْكُمْ وَلَوْ
شَآءَ ٱللَّهُ لَأَنزَلَ مَلَٰٓئِكَةً مَّا سَمِعْنَا بِهَٰذَا فِىٓ
ءَابَآئِنَا ٱلْأَوَّلِينَ

24 But the notables of his people,
who disbelieved, said, "This is
nothing but a human like you, who
wants to gain superiority over you.
Had Allah willed, He would have
sent down angels. We never heard
of this from our forefathers of old.

٢٥ إِنْ هُوَ إِلَّا رَجُلٌۢ بِهِۦ جِنَّةٌ فَتَرَبَّصُوا۟ بِهِۦ حَتَّىٰ
حِينٍ

25 He is nothing but a man
possessed. Just ignore him for a
while."

٢٦ قَالَ رَبِّ ٱنصُرْنِى بِمَا كَذَّبُونِ

26 He said, "My Lord, help me, for
they have rejected me."

٢٧ فَأَوْحَيْنَآ إِلَيْهِ أَنِ ٱصْنَعِ ٱلْفُلْكَ بِأَعْيُنِنَا
وَوَحْيِنَا فَإِذَا جَآءَ أَمْرُنَا وَفَارَ ٱلتَّنُّورُ ۙ فَٱسْلُكْ
فِيهَا مِن كُلٍّ زَوْجَيْنِ ٱثْنَيْنِ وَأَهْلَكَ إِلَّا مَن
سَبَقَ عَلَيْهِ ٱلْقَوْلُ مِنْهُمْ ۖ وَلَا تُخَٰطِبْنِى فِى
ٱلَّذِينَ ظَلَمُوٓا۟ ۖ إِنَّهُم مُّغْرَقُونَ

27 So We inspired him: "Build the Ark under Our observation and by Our inspiration. And when Our decree comes to pass, and the oven boils over, load into it two pairs of every kind, together with your family, except those of them against whom the word has already been pronounced. And do not speak to me concerning those who did wrong; for they are to be drowned."

٢٨ فَإِذَا ٱسْتَوَيْتَ أَنتَ وَمَن مَّعَكَ عَلَى ٱلْفُلْكِ
فَقُلِ ٱلْحَمْدُ لِلَّهِ ٱلَّذِى نَجَّىٰنَا مِنَ ٱلْقَوْمِ ٱلظَّٰلِمِينَ

28 Then, when you and those with you are settled in the Ark, say, "Praise be to Allah, who has saved us from the wrongdoing people."

٢٩ وَقُل رَّبِّ أَنزِلْنِى مُنزَلًا مُّبَارَكًا وَأَنتَ خَيْرُ
ٱلْمُنزِلِينَ

29 And say, "My Lord, land me with a blessed landing, as you are the best of transporters."

٣٠ إِنَّ فِى ذَٰلِكَ لَءَايَٰتٍ وَإِن كُنَّا لَمُبْتَلِينَ

30 Surely in that are signs. We are always testing.

٣١ ثُمَّ أَنشَأْنَا مِنۢ بَعْدِهِمْ قَرْنًا ءَاخَرِينَ

31 Then, after them, We established another generation.

٣٢ فَأَرْسَلْنَا فِيهِمْ رَسُولًا مِّنْهُمْ أَنِ ٱعْبُدُوا۟ ٱللَّهَ
مَا لَكُم مِّنْ إِلَٰهٍ غَيْرُهُۥٓ ۖ أَفَلَا تَتَّقُونَ

32 And We sent among them a messenger from themselves: "Serve Allah. You have no god other than Him. Will you not be cautious?"

٣٣ وَقَالَ ٱلْمَلَأُ مِن قَوْمِهِ ٱلَّذِينَ كَفَرُوا۟ وَكَذَّبُوا۟
بِلِقَآءِ ٱلْءَاخِرَةِ وَأَتْرَفْنَٰهُمْ فِى ٱلْحَيَوٰةِ ٱلدُّنْيَا
مَا هَٰذَآ إِلَّا بَشَرٌ مِّثْلُكُمْ يَأْكُلُ مِمَّا تَأْكُلُونَ مِنْهُ
وَيَشْرَبُ مِمَّا تَشْرَبُونَ

33 But the dignitaries of his people, those who disbelieved and denied the meeting of the Hereafter, and We had indulged them in the present life, said, "This is nothing but a human like you; he eats what you eat, and he drinks what you drink.

٣٤ وَلَئِنْ أَطَعْتُم بَشَرًا مِّثْلَكُمْ إِنَّكُمْ إِذًا
لَّخَٰسِرُونَ

34 If you obey a human being like yourselves, then you will be losers.

٣٥ أَيَعِدُكُمْ أَنَّكُمْ إِذَا مِتُّمْ وَكُنتُمْ تُرَابًا وَعِظَٰمًا
أَنَّكُم مُّخْرَجُونَ

35 Does he promise you that when you have died and become dust and bones, you will be brought out?

٣٦ هَيْهَاتَ هَيْهَاتَ لِمَا تُوعَدُونَ

36 Farfetched, farfetched is what you are promised.

٣٧ إِنْ هِيَ إِلَّا حَيَاتُنَا ٱلدُّنْيَا نَمُوتُ وَنَحْيَا وَمَا
نَحْنُ بِمَبْعُوثِينَ

37 There is nothing but our life in this world. We die, and we live, and we are not resurrected.

٣٨ إِنْ هُوَ إِلَّا رَجُلٌ ٱفْتَرَىٰ عَلَى ٱللَّهِ كَذِبًا وَمَا
نَحْنُ لَهُۥ بِمُؤْمِنِينَ

38 He is nothing but a man, making up lies about Allah. We have no faith in him."

٣٩ قَالَ رَبِّ ٱنصُرْنِى بِمَا كَذَّبُونِ

39 He said, "My Lord, help me, for they have rejected me."

٤٠ قَالَ عَمَّا قَلِيلٍ لَّيُصْبِحُنَّ نَٰدِمِينَ

40 He said, "Soon they will be filled with regret."

٤١ فَأَخَذَتْهُمُ ٱلصَّيْحَةُ بِٱلْحَقِّ فَجَعَلْنَٰهُمْ غُثَآءً ۚ
فَبُعْدًا لِّلْقَوْمِ ٱلظَّٰلِمِينَ

41 Then the Blast struck them, justifiably, and We turned them into scum. So away with the wicked people.

٤٢ ثُمَّ أَنشَأْنَا مِنۢ بَعْدِهِمْ قُرُونًا ءَاخَرِينَ

42 Then, after them, We raised other generations.

٤٣ مَا تَسْبِقُ مِنْ أُمَّةٍ أَجَلَهَا وَمَا يَسْتَـْٔخِرُونَ

43 No nation can advance its time, nor can they postpone it.

٤٤ ثُمَّ أَرْسَلْنَا رُسُلَنَا تَتْرَا ۖ كُلَّ مَا جَآءَ أُمَّةً
رَّسُولُهَا كَذَّبُوهُ ۚ فَأَتْبَعْنَا بَعْضَهُم بَعْضًا
وَجَعَلْنَٰهُمْ أَحَادِيثَ ۚ فَبُعْدًا لِّقَوْمٍ لَّا يُؤْمِنُونَ

44 Then We sent Our messengers in succession. Every time a messenger came to his community, they called him a liar. So We made them follow one another, and made them history. So away with a people who do not believe.

٤٥ ثُمَّ أَرْسَلْنَا مُوسَىٰ وَأَخَاهُ هَٰرُونَ بِـَٔايَٰتِنَا
وَسُلْطَٰنٍ مُّبِينٍ

45 Then We sent Moses and his brother Aaron, with Our signs and a clear authority.

٤٦ إِلَىٰ فِرْعَوْنَ وَمَلَإِي۟هِۦ فَٱسْتَكْبَرُوا۟ وَكَانُوا۟
قَوْمًا عَالِينَ

46 To Pharaoh and his nobles, but they turned arrogant. They were oppressive people.

٤٧ فَقَالُوٓا۟ أَنُؤْمِنُ لِبَشَرَيْنِ مِثْلِنَا وَقَوْمُهُمَا لَنَا
عَٰبِدُونَ

47 They said, "Are we to believe in two mortals like us, and their people are our slaves?"

٤٨ فَكَذَّبُوهُمَا فَكَانُوا۟ مِنَ ٱلْمُهْلَكِينَ

48 So they called them liars, and thus were among those destroyed.

٤٩ وَلَقَدْ ءَاتَيْنَا مُوسَى ٱلْكِتَٰبَ لَعَلَّهُمْ يَهْتَدُونَ

49 And We gave Moses the Scripture, that they may be guided.

٥٠ وَجَعَلْنَا ٱبْنَ مَرْيَمَ وَأُمَّهُۥٓ ءَايَةً وَءَاوَيْنَٰهُمَآ
إِلَىٰ رَبْوَةٍ ذَاتِ قَرَارٍ وَمَعِينٍ

50 And We made Mary's son and his mother a sign, and We sheltered them on high ground with security and flowing springs.

٥١ يَٰٓأَيُّهَا ٱلرُّسُلُ كُلُوا۟ مِنَ ٱلطَّيِّبَٰتِ وَٱعْمَلُوا۟
صَٰلِحًا ۖ إِنِّى بِمَا تَعْمَلُونَ عَلِيمٌ

51 O messengers, eat of the good things, and act with integrity. I am aware of what you do.

٥٢ وَإِنَّ هَٰذِهِۦٓ أُمَّتُكُمْ أُمَّةً وَٰحِدَةً وَأَنَا۠ رَبُّكُمْ
فَٱتَّقُونِ

52 This nation of yours is one nation, and I am your Lord, so fear Me.

٥٣ فَتَقَطَّعُوٓا۟ أَمْرَهُم بَيْنَهُمْ زُبُرًا ۖ كُلُّ حِزْبٍۭ بِمَا
لَدَيْهِمْ فَرِحُونَ

53 But they tore themselves into sects; each party happy with what they have.

٥٤ فَذَرْهُمْ فِى غَمْرَتِهِمْ حَتَّىٰ حِينٍ

54 So leave them in their bewilderment until a time.

٥٥ أَيَحْسَبُونَ أَنَّمَا نُمِدُّهُم بِهِۦ مِن مَّالٍ وَبَنِينَ

55 Do they assume that, in furnishing them with wealth and children.

٥٦ نُسَارِعُ لَهُمْ فِى ٱلْخَيْرَٰتِ ۚ بَل لَّا يَشْعُرُونَ

56 We race to give them the good things? In fact, they have no idea.

٥٧ إِنَّ ٱلَّذِينَ هُم مِّنْ خَشْيَةِ رَبِّهِم مُّشْفِقُونَ

57 Those who, from awe of their Lord, are fearful.

٥٨ وَٱلَّذِينَ هُم بِـَٔايَٰتِ رَبِّهِمْ يُؤْمِنُونَ

58 And those who believe in their Lord's Verses.

٥٩ وَٱلَّذِينَ هُم بِرَبِّهِمْ لَا يُشْرِكُونَ

59 And those who associate no partners with their Lord.

٦٠ وَٱلَّذِينَ يُؤْتُونَ مَآ ءَاتَوا۟ وَّقُلُوبُهُمْ وَجِلَةٌ
أَنَّهُمْ إِلَىٰ رَبِّهِمْ رَٰجِعُونَ

60 And those who give what they give, while their hearts quake, knowing that to their Lord they will return.

٦١ أُو۟لَٰٓئِكَ يُسَٰرِعُونَ فِى ٱلْخَيْرَٰتِ وَهُمْ لَهَا
سَٰبِقُونَ

61 It is they who race towards goodness. It is they who will reach it first.

٦٢ وَلَا نُكَلِّفُ نَفْسًا إِلَّا وُسْعَهَا ۖ وَلَدَيْنَا كِتَٰبٌ
يَنطِقُ بِٱلْحَقِّ ۚ وَهُمْ لَا يُظْلَمُونَ

62 We never burden any soul beyond its capacity. And with Us is a record that tells the truth, and they will not be wronged.

٦٣ بَلْ قُلُوبُهُمْ فِى غَمْرَةٍ مِّنْ هَٰذَا وَلَهُمْ أَعْمَٰلٌ
مِّن دُونِ ذَٰلِكَ هُمْ لَهَا عَٰمِلُونَ

63 But their hearts are puzzled because of this; and they have deeds that do not conform to this, which they continue to perpetrate.

٦٤ حَتَّىٰٓ إِذَآ أَخَذْنَا مُتْرَفِيهِم بِٱلْعَذَابِ إِذَا هُمْ
يَجْـَٔرُونَ

64 Until, when We seize the decadent among them with torment, they begin to groan.

٦٥ لَا تَجْـَٔرُوا۟ ٱلْيَوْمَ ۖ إِنَّكُم مِّنَّا لَا تُنصَرُونَ

65 Do not groan today. You will receive no help from Us.

٦٦ قَدْ كَانَتْ ءَايَٰتِى تُتْلَىٰ عَلَيْكُمْ فَكُنتُمْ عَلَىٰٓ
أَعْقَٰبِكُمْ تَنكِصُونَ

66 My Verses were recited to you, but you turned back on your heels.

٦٧ مُسْتَكْبِرِينَ بِهِۦ سَٰمِرًا تَهْجُرُونَ

67 Arrogant towards it—talked nonsense about it—disregarded it.

٦٨ أَفَلَمْ يَدَّبَّرُوا۟ ٱلْقَوْلَ أَمْ جَآءَهُم مَّا لَمْ يَأْتِ
ءَابَآءَهُمُ ٱلْأَوَّلِينَ

68 Have they not pondered the Word? Or has there come to them what came not to their forefathers of old?

٦٩ أَمْ لَمْ يَعْرِفُوا۟ رَسُولَهُمْ فَهُمْ لَهُۥ مُنكِرُونَ

69 Or is it that they did not recognize their messenger, so they are denying him?

٧٠ أَمْ يَقُولُونَ بِهِۦ جِنَّةٌۢ ۚ بَلْ جَآءَهُم بِٱلْحَقِّ
وَأَكْثَرُهُمْ لِلْحَقِّ كَٰرِهُونَ

70 Or do they say, "He is possessed?" In fact, he brought them the truth, but most of them hate the truth.

٧١ وَلَوِ ٱتَّبَعَ ٱلْحَقُّ أَهْوَآءَهُمْ لَفَسَدَتِ ٱلسَّمَٰوَٰتُ
وَٱلْأَرْضُ وَمَن فِيهِنَّ ۚ بَلْ أَتَيْنَٰهُم بِذِكْرِهِمْ فَهُمْ
عَن ذِكْرِهِم مُّعْرِضُونَ

71 If the truth conformed to their desires, the heavens, the earth, and everyone in them would have gone to ruin. In fact, We have given them their message, but they keep avoiding their message.

٧٢ أَمْ تَسْـَٔلُهُمْ خَرْجًا فَخَرَاجُ رَبِّكَ خَيْرٌ ۖ وَهُوَ
خَيْرُ ٱلرَّٰزِقِينَ

72 Or are you asking them for a payment? The revenue from your Lord is better, and He is the Best of providers.

٧٣ وَإِنَّكَ لَتَدْعُوهُمْ إِلَىٰ صِرَٰطٍ مُّسْتَقِيمٍ

73 You are inviting them to a straight path.

٧٤ وَإِنَّ ٱلَّذِينَ لَا يُؤْمِنُونَ بِٱلْءَاخِرَةِ عَنِ
ٱلصِّرَٰطِ لَنَٰكِبُونَ

74 But those who do not believe in the Hereafter are swerving from the path.

٧٥ وَلَوْ رَحِمْنَٰهُمْ وَكَشَفْنَا مَا بِهِم مِّن ضُرٍّ لَّلَجُّوا۟
فِى طُغْيَٰنِهِمْ يَعْمَهُونَ

75 Even if We had mercy on them, and relieved their problems, they would still blindly persist in their defiance.

٧٦ وَلَقَدْ أَخَذْنَٰهُم بِٱلْعَذَابِ فَمَا ٱسْتَكَانُوا۟ لِرَبِّهِمْ
وَمَا يَتَضَرَّعُونَ

76 We have already gripped them with suffering, but they did not surrender to their Lord, nor did they humble themselves.

٧٧ حَتَّىٰٓ إِذَا فَتَحْنَا عَلَيْهِم بَابًا ذَا عَذَابٍ شَدِيدٍ
إِذَا هُمْ فِيهِ مُبْلِسُونَ

77 Until, when We have opened before them a gate of intense agony, at once they will despair.

٧٨ وَهُوَ ٱلَّذِىٓ أَنشَأَ لَكُمُ ٱلسَّمْعَ وَٱلْأَبْصَٰرَ
وَٱلْأَفْـِٔدَةَ ۚ قَلِيلًا مَّا تَشْكُرُونَ

78 It is He who produced for you the hearing, and the eyesight, and the feelings. But little gratitude you show.

٧٩ وَهُوَ ٱلَّذِى ذَرَأَكُمْ فِى ٱلْأَرْضِ وَإِلَيْهِ
تُحْشَرُونَ

79 And it is He who multiplied you on earth, and to Him you will be gathered.

٨٠ وَهُوَ ٱلَّذِى يُحْىِۦ وَيُمِيتُ وَلَهُ ٱخْتِلَٰفُ ٱلَّيْلِ
وَٱلنَّهَارِ ۚ أَفَلَا تَعْقِلُونَ

80 And it is He who gives life and brings death, and to Him is the alternation of night and day. Do you not understand?

٨١ بَلْ قَالُوا۟ مِثْلَ مَا قَالَ ٱلْأَوَّلُونَ

81 But they say the like of what the ancients said.

٨٢ قَالُوٓا۟ أَءِذَا مِتْنَا وَكُنَّا تُرَابًا وَعِظَٰمًا أَءِنَّا
لَمَبْعُوثُونَ

82 They say, “After we have died, and become dust and bones, will we be resurrected?

٨٣ لَقَدْ وُعِدْنَا نَحْنُ وَءَابَآؤُنَا هَٰذَا مِن قَبْلُ إِنْ
هَٰذَآ إِلَّآ أَسَٰطِيرُ ٱلْأَوَّلِينَ

83 We were promised this before—we and our ancestors—these are nothing but legends of the ancients.”

٨٤ قُل لِّمَنِ ٱلْأَرْضُ وَمَن فِيهَآ إِن كُنتُمْ تَعْلَمُونَ

84 Say, “To whom does the earth belong, and everyone in it, if you happen to know?”

٨٥ سَيَقُولُونَ لِلَّهِ ۚ قُلْ أَفَلَا تَذَكَّرُونَ

85 They will say, “To Allah.” Say, “Will you not reflect?”

٨٦ قُلْ مَن رَّبُّ ٱلسَّمَٰوَٰتِ ٱلسَّبْعِ وَرَبُّ ٱلْعَرْشِ
ٱلْعَظِيمِ

86 Say, “Who is the Lord of the seven heavens, and Lord of the Splendid Throne?”

٨٧ سَيَقُولُونَ لِلَّهِ ۚ قُلْ أَفَلَا تَتَّقُونَ

87 They will say, “To Allah.” Say, “Will you not become righteous?”

٨٨ قُلْ مَنۢ بِيَدِهِۦ مَلَكُوتُ كُلِّ شَىْءٍ وَهُوَ يُجِيرُ
وَلَا يُجَارُ عَلَيْهِ إِن كُنتُمْ تَعْلَمُونَ

88 Say, "In whose hand is the dominion of all things, and He protects and cannot be protected from, if you happen to know?"

٨٩ سَيَقُولُونَ لِلَّهِ ۚ قُلْ فَأَنَّىٰ تُسْحَرُونَ

89 They will say, "To Allah." Say, "Then are you bewitched?"

٩٠ بَلْ أَتَيْنَٰهُم بِٱلْحَقِّ وَإِنَّهُمْ لَكَٰذِبُونَ

90 In fact, We have given them the truth, and they are liars.

٩١ مَا ٱتَّخَذَ ٱللَّهُ مِن وَلَدٍ وَمَا كَانَ مَعَهُۥ مِنْ إِلَٰهٍ ۚ
إِذًا لَّذَهَبَ كُلُّ إِلَٰهٍۭ بِمَا خَلَقَ وَلَعَلَا بَعْضُهُمْ عَلَىٰ
بَعْضٍ ۚ سُبْحَٰنَ ٱللَّهِ عَمَّا يَصِفُونَ

91 Allah has never begotten a son, nor is there any god besides Him. Otherwise, each god would have taken away what it has created, and some of them would have gained supremacy over others. Glory be to Allah, far beyond what they describe.

٩٢ عَٰلِمِ ٱلْغَيْبِ وَٱلشَّهَٰدَةِ فَتَعَٰلَىٰ عَمَّا يُشْرِكُونَ

92 The Knower of the hidden and the manifest. He is exalted, far above what they associate.

٩٣ قُل رَّبِّ إِمَّا تُرِيَنِّى مَا يُوعَدُونَ

93 Say, "My Lord, if You would show me what they are promised.

٩٤ رَبِّ فَلَا تَجْعَلْنِى فِى ٱلْقَوْمِ ٱلظَّٰلِمِينَ

94 My Lord, do not place me among the wicked people."

٩٥ وَإِنَّا عَلَىٰٓ أَن نُّرِيَكَ مَا نَعِدُهُمْ لَقَٰدِرُونَ

95 We are surely Able to show you what We promise them.

٩٦ ٱدْفَعْ بِٱلَّتِى هِىَ أَحْسَنُ ٱلسَّيِّئَةَ ۚ نَحْنُ أَعْلَمُ
بِمَا يَصِفُونَ

96 Repel evil by what is better. We are aware of what they describe.

٩٧ وَقُل رَّبِّ أَعُوذُ بِكَ مِنْ هَمَزَٰتِ ٱلشَّيَٰطِينِ

97 And say, "My Lord, I seek refuge with You from the urgings of the devils.

٩٨ وَأَعُوذُ بِكَ رَبِّ أَن يَحْضُرُونِ

98 And I seek refuge with You, my Lord, lest they become present."

٩٩ حَتَّىٰٓ إِذَا جَآءَ أَحَدَهُمُ ٱلْمَوْتُ قَالَ رَبِّ
ٱرْجِعُونِ

99 Until, when death comes to one of them, he says, "My Lord, send me back.

١٠٠ لَعَلِّىٓ أَعْمَلُ صَٰلِحًا فِيمَا تَرَكْتُ ۚ كَلَّآ ۚ إِنَّهَا
كَلِمَةٌ هُوَ قَآئِلُهَا ۖ وَمِن وَرَآئِهِم بَرْزَخٌ إِلَىٰ يَوْمِ
يُبْعَثُونَ

100 That I may do right in what I have neglected." By no means! It is just a word that he utters. And behind them is a barrier, until the Day they are resurrected.

١٠١ فَإِذَا نُفِخَ فِى ٱلصُّورِ فَلَآ أَنسَابَ بَيْنَهُمْ
يَوْمَئِذٍ وَلَا يَتَسَآءَلُونَ

101 When the Horn is blown, no relations between them will exist on that Day, and they will not ask after one another.

١٠٢ فَمَن ثَقُلَتْ مَوَٰزِينُهُۥ فَأُو۟لَٰٓئِكَ هُمُ ٱلْمُفْلِحُونَ

102 Those whose scales are heavy—those are the successful.

١٠٣ وَمَنْ خَفَّتْ مَوَٰزِينُهُۥ فَأُو۟لَٰٓئِكَ ٱلَّذِينَ خَسِرُوٓا۟
أَنفُسَهُمْ فِى جَهَنَّمَ خَٰلِدُونَ

103 But those whose scales are light—those are they who have lost their souls; in Hell they will dwell forever.

١٠٤ تَلْفَحُ وُجُوهَهُمُ ٱلنَّارُ وَهُمْ فِيهَا كَٰلِحُونَ

104 The Fire lashes their faces, and therein they grimace.

١٠٥ أَلَمْ تَكُنْ ءَايَٰتِى تُتْلَىٰ عَلَيْكُمْ فَكُنتُم بِهَا
تُكَذِّبُونَ

105 "Were not My revelations recited to you, and you kept on rejecting them?"

١٠٦ قَالُوا۟ رَبَّنَا غَلَبَتْ عَلَيْنَا شِقْوَتُنَا وَكُنَّا قَوْمًا
ضَآلِّينَ

106 They will say, "Our Lord, our wretchedness prevailed over us, and we were a people astray.

١٠٧ رَبَّنَآ أَخْرِجْنَا مِنْهَا فَإِنْ عُدْنَا فَإِنَّا ظَٰلِمُونَ

107 Our Lord! Bring us out of this. If we ever returned, we would truly be evil."

١٠٨ قَالَ ٱخْسَـُٔوا۟ فِيهَا وَلَا تُكَلِّمُونِ

108 He will say, "Be despised therein, and do not speak to Me.

١٠٩ إِنَّهُۥ كَانَ فَرِيقٌ مِّنْ عِبَادِى يَقُولُونَ رَبَّنَآ
ءَامَنَّا فَٱغْفِرْ لَنَا وَٱرْحَمْنَا وَأَنتَ خَيْرُ ٱلرَّٰحِمِينَ

109 There was a group of My servants who would say, `Our Lord, we have believed, so forgive us, and have mercy on us; You are the Best of the merciful.'

١١٠ فَٱتَّخَذْتُمُوهُمْ سِخْرِيًّا حَتَّىٰٓ أَنسَوْكُمْ ذِكْرِى
وَكُنتُم مِّنْهُمْ تَضْحَكُونَ

110 But you made them a target of ridicule, until they made you forget My remembrance; and you used to laugh at them.

١١١ إِنِّى جَزَيْتُهُمُ ٱلْيَوْمَ بِمَا صَبَرُوٓا۟ أَنَّهُمْ هُمُ
ٱلْفَآئِزُونَ

111 Today, I have rewarded them for their endurance. They are the ones who are the triumphant."

١١٢ قَٰلَ كَمۡ لَبِثۡتُمۡ فِى ٱلۡأَرۡضِ عَدَدَ سِنِينَ

112 He will say, "How many years did you remain on earth?"

١١٣ قَالُواْ لَبِثۡنَا يَوۡمًا أَوۡ بَعۡضَ يَوۡمٍ فَسۡـَٔلِ
ٱلۡعَآدِّينَ

113 They will say, "We remained a day, or part of a day; but ask those who keep count."

١١٤ قَٰلَ إِن لَّبِثۡتُمۡ إِلَّا قَلِيلًاۖ لَّوۡ أَنَّكُمۡ كُنتُمۡ
تَعۡلَمُونَ

114 He will say, "You remained only for a little while, if you only knew.

١١٥ أَفَحَسِبۡتُمۡ أَنَّمَا خَلَقۡنَٰكُمۡ عَبَثًا وَأَنَّكُمۡ إِلَيۡنَا لَا
تُرۡجَعُونَ

115 Did you think that We created you in vain, and that to Us you will not be returned?"

١١٦ فَتَعَٰلَى ٱللَّهُ ٱلۡمَلِكُ ٱلۡحَقُّۖ لَآ إِلَٰهَ إِلَّا هُوَ رَبُّ
ٱلۡعَرۡشِ ٱلۡكَرِيمِ

116 So Exalted is Allah, the Ruler, the Real. There is no god except He, the Lord of the Noble Throne.

١١٧ وَمَن يَدۡعُ مَعَ ٱللَّهِ إِلَٰهًا ءَاخَرَ لَا بُرۡهَٰنَ لَهُۥ
بِهِۦ فَإِنَّمَا حِسَابُهُۥ عِندَ رَبِّهِۦٓۚ إِنَّهُۥ لَا يُفۡلِحُ
ٱلۡكَٰفِرُونَ

117 Whoever invokes another god besides Allah—he has no proof thereof—his reckoning rests with his Lord. The disbelievers will not succeed.

١١٨ وَقُل رَّبِّ ٱغۡفِرۡ وَٱرۡحَمۡ وَأَنتَ خَيۡرُ ٱلرَّٰحِمِينَ

118 And say, "My Lord, forgive and have mercy, for You are the Best of the merciful."

24 The Light النور

بِسۡمِ ٱللَّهِ ٱلرَّحۡمَٰنِ ٱلرَّحِيمِ

In the name of Allah, the Gracious, the Merciful.

١ سُورَةٌ أَنزَلۡنَٰهَا وَفَرَضۡنَٰهَا وَأَنزَلۡنَا فِيهَآ ءَايَٰتِۭ
بَيِّنَٰتٖ لَّعَلَّكُمۡ تَذَكَّرُونَ

1 A chapter that We have revealed, and made obligatory, and revealed in it clear Verses, that you may take heed.

٢ ٱلزَّانِيَةُ وَٱلزَّانِى فَٱجۡلِدُواْ كُلَّ وَٰحِدٖ مِّنۡهُمَا
مِاْئَةَ جَلۡدَةٖۖ وَلَا تَأۡخُذۡكُم بِهِمَا رَأۡفَةٞ فِى دِينِ
ٱللَّهِ إِن كُنتُمۡ تُؤۡمِنُونَ بِٱللَّهِ وَٱلۡيَوۡمِ ٱلۡءَاخِرِۖ
وَلۡيَشۡهَدۡ عَذَابَهُمَا طَآئِفَةٞ مِّنَ ٱلۡمُؤۡمِنِينَ

2 The adulteress and the adulterer—whip each one of them a hundred lashes, and let no pity towards them overcome you regarding Allah's Law, if you believe in Allah and the Last Day. And let a group of believers witness their punishment.

٣ ٱلزَّانِى لَا يَنكِحُ إِلَّا زَانِيَةً أَوْ مُشْرِكَةً وَٱلزَّانِيَةُ
لَا يَنكِحُهَآ إِلَّا زَانٍ أَوْ مُشْرِكٌ ۚ وَحُرِّمَ ذَٰلِكَ عَلَى
ٱلْمُؤْمِنِينَ

3 The adulterer shall marry none but an adulteress or an idolatress; and the adulteress shall marry none but an adulterer or an idolater. That has been prohibited for the believers.

٤ وَٱلَّذِينَ يَرْمُونَ ٱلْمُحْصَنَٰتِ ثُمَّ لَمْ يَأْتُوا۟
بِأَرْبَعَةِ شُهَدَآءَ فَٱجْلِدُوهُمْ ثَمَٰنِينَ جَلْدَةً وَلَا
تَقْبَلُوا۟ لَهُمْ شَهَٰدَةً أَبَدًا ۚ وَأُو۟لَٰٓئِكَ هُمُ ٱلْفَٰسِقُونَ

4 Those who accuse chaste women, then cannot bring four witnesses, whip them eighty lashes, and do not ever accept their testimony. For these are the immoral.

٥ إِلَّا ٱلَّذِينَ تَابُوا۟ مِنۢ بَعْدِ ذَٰلِكَ وَأَصْلَحُوا۟ فَإِنَّ
ٱللَّهَ غَفُورٌ رَّحِيمٌ

5 Except for those who repent afterwards, and reform; for Allah is Forgiving and Merciful.

٦ وَٱلَّذِينَ يَرْمُونَ أَزْوَٰجَهُمْ وَلَمْ يَكُن لَّهُمْ
شُهَدَآءُ إِلَّآ أَنفُسُهُمْ فَشَهَٰدَةُ أَحَدِهِمْ أَرْبَعُ
شَهَٰدَٰتٍۭ بِٱللَّهِ ۙ إِنَّهُۥ لَمِنَ ٱلصَّٰدِقِينَ

6 As for those who accuse their own spouses, but have no witnesses except themselves, the testimony of one of them is equivalent to four testimonies, if he swears by Allah that he is truthful.

٧ وَٱلْخَٰمِسَةُ أَنَّ لَعْنَتَ ٱللَّهِ عَلَيْهِ إِن كَانَ مِنَ
ٱلْكَٰذِبِينَ

7 And the fifth time, that Allah's curse be upon him, if he is a liar.

٨ وَيَدْرَؤُا۟ عَنْهَا ٱلْعَذَابَ أَن تَشْهَدَ أَرْبَعَ شَهَٰدَٰتٍۭ
بِٱللَّهِ ۙ إِنَّهُۥ لَمِنَ ٱلْكَٰذِبِينَ

8 But punishment shall be averted from her, if she swears four times by Allah, that he is a liar.

٩ وَٱلْخَٰمِسَةَ أَنَّ غَضَبَ ٱللَّهِ عَلَيْهَآ إِن كَانَ مِنَ
ٱلصَّٰدِقِينَ

9 And the fifth time, that Allah's wrath be upon her, if he is truthful.

١٠ وَلَوْلَا فَضْلُ ٱللَّهِ عَلَيْكُمْ وَرَحْمَتُهُۥ وَأَنَّ ٱللَّهَ
تَوَّابٌ حَكِيمٌ

10 Were it not for Allah's grace upon you, and His mercy, and that Allah is Conciliatory and Wise.

١١ إِنَّ ٱلَّذِينَ جَآءُو بِٱلْإِفْكِ عُصْبَةٌ مِّنكُمْ ۚ لَا
تَحْسَبُوهُ شَرًّا لَّكُم ۖ بَلْ هُوَ خَيْرٌ لَّكُمْ ۚ لِكُلِّ ٱمْرِئٍ
مِّنْهُم مَّا ٱكْتَسَبَ مِنَ ٱلْإِثْمِ ۚ وَٱلَّذِى تَوَلَّىٰ كِبْرَهُۥ
مِنْهُمْ لَهُۥ عَذَابٌ عَظِيمٌ

11 Those who perpetrated the slander are a band of you. Do not consider it bad for you, but it is good for you. Each person among them bears his share in the sin. As for him who played the major role—for him is a terrible punishment.

12 Why, when you heard about it, the believing men and women did not think well of one another, and say, “This is an obvious lie”?

١٢ لَّوْلَآ إِذْ سَمِعْتُمُوهُ ظَنَّ ٱلْمُؤْمِنُونَ وَٱلْمُؤْمِنَٰتُ بِأَنفُسِهِمْ خَيْرًا وَقَالُوا۟ هَٰذَآ إِفْكٌ مُّبِينٌ

13 Why did they not bring four witnesses to testify to it? If they fail to bring the witnesses, then in Allah’s sight, they are liars.

١٣ لَّوْلَا جَآءُو عَلَيْهِ بِأَرْبَعَةِ شُهَدَآءَ ۚ فَإِذْ لَمْ يَأْتُوا۟ بِٱلشُّهَدَآءِ فَأُو۟لَٰٓئِكَ عِندَ ٱللَّهِ هُمُ ٱلْكَٰذِبُونَ

14 Were it not for Allah’s favor upon you, and His mercy, in this world and the Hereafter, you would have suffered a great punishment for what you have ventured into.

١٤ وَلَوْلَا فَضْلُ ٱللَّهِ عَلَيْكُمْ وَرَحْمَتُهُۥ فِى ٱلدُّنْيَا وَٱلْءَاخِرَةِ لَمَسَّكُمْ فِى مَآ أَفَضْتُمْ فِيهِ عَذَابٌ عَظِيمٌ

15 When you rumored it with your tongues, and spoke with your mouths what you had no knowledge of, and you considered it trivial; but according to Allah, it is serious.

١٥ إِذْ تَلَقَّوْنَهُۥ بِأَلْسِنَتِكُمْ وَتَقُولُونَ بِأَفْوَاهِكُم مَّا لَيْسَ لَكُم بِهِۦ عِلْمٌ وَتَحْسَبُونَهُۥ هَيِّنًا وَهُوَ عِندَ ٱللَّهِ عَظِيمٌ

16 When you heard it, you should have said, “It is not for us to repeat this. By Your glory, this is a serious slander.”

١٦ وَلَوْلَآ إِذْ سَمِعْتُمُوهُ قُلْتُم مَّا يَكُونُ لَنَآ أَن نَّتَكَلَّمَ بِهَٰذَا سُبْحَٰنَكَ هَٰذَا بُهْتَٰنٌ عَظِيمٌ

17 Allah cautions you never to return to the like of it, if you are believers.

١٧ يَعِظُكُمُ ٱللَّهُ أَن تَعُودُوا۟ لِمِثْلِهِۦٓ أَبَدًا إِن كُنتُم مُّؤْمِنِينَ

18 Allah explains the Verses to you. Allah is Knowing and Wise.

١٨ وَيُبَيِّنُ ٱللَّهُ لَكُمُ ٱلْءَايَٰتِ ۚ وَٱللَّهُ عَلِيمٌ حَكِيمٌ

19 Those who love to see immorality spread among the believers—for them is a painful punishment, in this life and in the Hereafter. Allah knows, and you do not know.

١٩ إِنَّ ٱلَّذِينَ يُحِبُّونَ أَن تَشِيعَ ٱلْفَٰحِشَةُ فِى ٱلَّذِينَ ءَامَنُوا۟ لَهُمْ عَذَابٌ أَلِيمٌ فِى ٱلدُّنْيَا وَٱلْءَاخِرَةِ ۚ وَٱللَّهُ يَعْلَمُ وَأَنتُمْ لَا تَعْلَمُونَ

20 Were it not for Allah’s grace upon you, and His mercy, and that Allah is Clement and Merciful.

٢٠ وَلَوْلَا فَضْلُ ٱللَّهِ عَلَيْكُمْ وَرَحْمَتُهُۥ وَأَنَّ ٱللَّهَ رَءُوفٌ رَّحِيمٌ

21 O you who believe! Do not follow Satan’s footsteps. Whoever follows Satan’s footsteps—he advocates obscenity and immorality. Were it not for Allah’s grace towards you, and His mercy, not one of you would

٢١ يَٰٓأَيُّهَا ٱلَّذِينَ ءَامَنُوا۟ لَا تَتَّبِعُوا۟ خُطُوَٰتِ ٱلشَّيْطَٰنِ ۚ وَمَن يَتَّبِعْ خُطُوَٰتِ ٱلشَّيْطَٰنِ فَإِنَّهُۥ يَأْمُرُ بِٱلْفَحْشَآءِ وَٱلْمُنكَرِ ۚ وَلَوْلَا فَضْلُ ٱللَّهِ

عَلَيْكُمْ وَرَحْمَتُهُۥ مَا زَكَىٰ مِنكُم مِّنْ أَحَدٍ أَبَدًا
وَلَٰكِنَّ ٱللَّهَ يُزَكِّى مَن يَشَآءُ ۗ وَٱللَّهُ سَمِيعٌ عَلِيمٌ

have been pure, ever. But Allah purifies whomever He wills. Allah is All-Hearing, All-Knowing.

٢٢ وَلَا يَأْتَلِ أُو۟لُوا۟ ٱلْفَضْلِ مِنكُمْ وَٱلسَّعَةِ أَن
يُؤْتُوٓا۟ أُو۟لِى ٱلْقُرْبَىٰ وَٱلْمَسَٰكِينَ وَٱلْمُهَٰجِرِينَ فِى
سَبِيلِ ٱللَّهِ ۖ وَلْيَعْفُوا۟ وَلْيَصْفَحُوٓا۟ ۗ أَلَا تُحِبُّونَ أَن
يَغْفِرَ ٱللَّهُ لَكُمْ ۗ وَٱللَّهُ غَفُورٌ رَّحِيمٌ

22 Those of you who have affluence and means should not refuse to give to the relatives, and the needy, and the emigrants for the sake of Allah. And let them pardon, and let them overlook. Do you not love for Allah to pardon you? Allah is All-Forgiving, Most Merciful.

٢٣ إِنَّ ٱلَّذِينَ يَرْمُونَ ٱلْمُحْصَنَٰتِ ٱلْغَٰفِلَٰتِ
ٱلْمُؤْمِنَٰتِ لُعِنُوا۟ فِى ٱلدُّنْيَا وَٱلْءَاخِرَةِ وَلَهُمْ
عَذَابٌ عَظِيمٌ

23 Those who slander honorable, innocent, believing women are cursed in this life and in the Hereafter. They will have a terrible punishment.

٢٤ يَوْمَ تَشْهَدُ عَلَيْهِمْ أَلْسِنَتُهُمْ وَأَيْدِيهِمْ
وَأَرْجُلُهُم بِمَا كَانُوا۟ يَعْمَلُونَ

24 On the Day when their tongues, and their hands, and their feet will testify against them regarding what they used to do.

٢٥ يَوْمَئِذٍ يُوَفِّيهِمُ ٱللَّهُ دِينَهُمُ ٱلْحَقَّ وَيَعْلَمُونَ
أَنَّ ٱللَّهَ هُوَ ٱلْحَقُّ ٱلْمُبِينُ

25 On that Day, Allah will pay them their account in full, and they will know that Allah is the Evident Reality.

٢٦ ٱلْخَبِيثَٰتُ لِلْخَبِيثِينَ وَٱلْخَبِيثُونَ لِلْخَبِيثَٰتِ ۖ
وَٱلطَّيِّبَٰتُ لِلطَّيِّبِينَ وَٱلطَّيِّبُونَ لِلطَّيِّبَٰتِ ۚ أُو۟لَٰٓئِكَ
مُبَرَّءُونَ مِمَّا يَقُولُونَ ۖ لَهُم مَّغْفِرَةٌ وَرِزْقٌ كَرِيمٌ

26 Bad women are for bad men, and bad men are for bad women, and good women are for good men, and good men are for good women. Those are acquitted of what they say. There is forgiveness for them, and a generous provision.

٢٧ يَٰٓأَيُّهَا ٱلَّذِينَ ءَامَنُوا۟ لَا تَدْخُلُوا۟ بُيُوتًا غَيْرَ
بُيُوتِكُمْ حَتَّىٰ تَسْتَأْنِسُوا۟ وَتُسَلِّمُوا۟ عَلَىٰٓ أَهْلِهَا ۚ
ذَٰلِكُمْ خَيْرٌ لَّكُمْ لَعَلَّكُمْ تَذَكَّرُونَ

27 O you who believe! Do not enter homes other than your own, until you have asked permission and greeted their occupants. That is better for you, that you may be aware.

٢٨ فَإِن لَّمْ تَجِدُوا۟ فِيهَآ أَحَدًا فَلَا تَدْخُلُوهَا
حَتَّىٰ يُؤْذَنَ لَكُمْ ۖ وَإِن قِيلَ لَكُمُ ٱرْجِعُوا۟

28 And if you find no one in them, do not enter them until you are given permission. And if it is said to you, “Turn back,” then turn back. That is

فَٱرْجِعُوا۟ ۖ هُوَ أَزْكَىٰ لَكُمْ ۚ وَٱللَّهُ بِمَا تَعْمَلُونَ
عَلِيمٌ

more proper for you. Allah is aware of what you do.

٢٩ لَّيْسَ عَلَيْكُمْ جُنَاحٌ أَن تَدْخُلُوا۟ بُيُوتًا غَيْرَ
مَسْكُونَةٍ فِيهَا مَتَٰعٌ لَّكُمْ ۚ وَٱللَّهُ يَعْلَمُ مَا تُبْدُونَ
وَمَا تَكْتُمُونَ

29 There is no blame on you for entering uninhabited houses, in which are belongings of yours. Allah knows what you reveal and what you conceal.

٣٠ قُل لِّلْمُؤْمِنِينَ يَغُضُّوا۟ مِنْ أَبْصَٰرِهِمْ
وَيَحْفَظُوا۟ فُرُوجَهُمْ ۚ ذَٰلِكَ أَزْكَىٰ لَهُمْ ۗ إِنَّ ٱللَّهَ
خَبِيرٌۢ بِمَا يَصْنَعُونَ

30 Tell the believing men to restrain their looks, and to guard their privates. That is purer for them. Allah is cognizant of what they do.

٣١ وَقُل لِّلْمُؤْمِنَٰتِ يَغْضُضْنَ مِنْ أَبْصَٰرِهِنَّ
وَيَحْفَظْنَ فُرُوجَهُنَّ وَلَا يُبْدِينَ زِينَتَهُنَّ إِلَّا مَا
ظَهَرَ مِنْهَا ۖ وَلْيَضْرِبْنَ بِخُمُرِهِنَّ عَلَىٰ جُيُوبِهِنَّ ۖ
وَلَا يُبْدِينَ زِينَتَهُنَّ إِلَّا لِبُعُولَتِهِنَّ أَوْ ءَابَآئِهِنَّ أَوْ
ءَابَآءِ بُعُولَتِهِنَّ أَوْ أَبْنَآئِهِنَّ أَوْ أَبْنَآءِ بُعُولَتِهِنَّ أَوْ
إِخْوَٰنِهِنَّ أَوْ بَنِىٓ إِخْوَٰنِهِنَّ أَوْ بَنِىٓ أَخَوَٰتِهِنَّ أَوْ
نِسَآئِهِنَّ أَوْ مَا مَلَكَتْ أَيْمَٰنُهُنَّ أَوِ ٱلتَّٰبِعِينَ غَيْرِ
أُو۟لِى ٱلْإِرْبَةِ مِنَ ٱلرِّجَالِ أَوِ ٱلطِّفْلِ ٱلَّذِينَ لَمْ
يَظْهَرُوا۟ عَلَىٰ عَوْرَٰتِ ٱلنِّسَآءِ ۖ وَلَا يَضْرِبْنَ
بِأَرْجُلِهِنَّ لِيُعْلَمَ مَا يُخْفِينَ مِن زِينَتِهِنَّ ۚ وَتُوبُوٓا۟
إِلَى ٱللَّهِ جَمِيعًا أَيُّهَ ٱلْمُؤْمِنُونَ لَعَلَّكُمْ تُفْلِحُونَ

31 And tell the believing women to restrain their looks, and to guard their privates, and not display their beauty except what is apparent thereof, and to draw their coverings over their breasts, and not expose their beauty except to their husbands, their fathers, their husbands' fathers, their sons, their husbands' sons, their brothers, their brothers' sons, their sisters' sons, their women, what their right hands possess, their male attendants who have no sexual desires, or children who are not yet aware of the nakedness of women. And they should not strike their feet to draw attention to their hidden beauty. And repent to Allah, all of you believers, so that you may succeed.

٣٢ وَأَنكِحُوا۟ ٱلْأَيَٰمَىٰ مِنكُمْ وَٱلصَّٰلِحِينَ مِنْ
عِبَادِكُمْ وَإِمَآئِكُمْ ۚ إِن يَكُونُوا۟ فُقَرَآءَ يُغْنِهِمُ ٱللَّهُ
مِن فَضْلِهِۦ ۗ وَٱللَّهُ وَٰسِعٌ عَلِيمٌ

32 And wed the singles among you, and those who are fit among your servants and maids. If they are poor, Allah will enrich them from His bounty. Allah is All-Encompassing, All-Knowing.

٣٣ وَلْيَسْتَعْفِفِ ٱلَّذِينَ لَا يَجِدُونَ نِكَاحًا حَتَّىٰ
يُغْنِيَهُمُ ٱللَّهُ مِن فَضْلِهِۦ ۗ وَٱلَّذِينَ يَبْتَغُونَ

33 And let those who do not find the means to marry abstain, until Allah enriches them from His bounty. If

ٱلْكِتَٰبَ مِمَّا مَلَكَتْ أَيْمَٰنُكُمْ فَكَاتِبُوهُمْ إِنْ عَلِمْتُمْ
فِيهِمْ خَيْرًا ۖ وَءَاتُوهُم مِّن مَّالِ ٱللَّهِ ٱلَّذِىٓ
ءَاتَىٰكُمْ ۚ وَلَا تُكْرِهُوا۟ فَتَيَٰتِكُمْ عَلَى ٱلْبِغَآءِ إِنْ
أَرَدْنَ تَحَصُّنًا لِّتَبْتَغُوا۟ عَرَضَ ٱلْحَيَوٰةِ ٱلدُّنْيَا ۚ
وَمَن يُكْرِههُّنَّ فَإِنَّ ٱللَّهَ مِنۢ بَعْدِ إِكْرَٰهِهِنَّ غَفُورٌ
رَّحِيمٌ

any of your servants wish to be freed, grant them their wish, if you recognize some good in them. And give them of Allah's wealth which he has given you. And do not compel your girls to prostitution, seeking the materials of this life, if they desire to remain chaste. Should anyone compel them—after their compulsion, Allah is Forgiving and Merciful.

٣٤ وَلَقَدْ أَنزَلْنَآ إِلَيْكُمْ ءَايَٰتٍ مُّبَيِّنَٰتٍ وَمَثَلًا مِّنَ
ٱلَّذِينَ خَلَوْا۟ مِن قَبْلِكُمْ وَمَوْعِظَةً لِّلْمُتَّقِينَ

34 We have sent down to you clarifying revelations, and examples of those who passed on before you, and advice for the righteous.

٣٥ ٱللَّهُ نُورُ ٱلسَّمَٰوَٰتِ وَٱلْأَرْضِ ۚ مَثَلُ نُورِهِۦ
كَمِشْكَوٰةٍ فِيهَا مِصْبَاحٌ ۖ ٱلْمِصْبَاحُ فِى زُجَاجَةٍ ۖ
ٱلزُّجَاجَةُ كَأَنَّهَا كَوْكَبٌ دُرِّىٌّ يُوقَدُ مِن شَجَرَةٍ
مُّبَٰرَكَةٍ زَيْتُونَةٍ لَّا شَرْقِيَّةٍ وَلَا غَرْبِيَّةٍ يَكَادُ زَيْتُهَا
يُضِىٓءُ وَلَوْ لَمْ تَمْسَسْهُ نَارٌ ۚ نُّورٌ عَلَىٰ نُورٍ ۗ
يَهْدِى ٱللَّهُ لِنُورِهِۦ مَن يَشَآءُ ۚ وَيَضْرِبُ ٱللَّهُ
ٱلْأَمْثَٰلَ لِلنَّاسِ ۗ وَٱللَّهُ بِكُلِّ شَىْءٍ عَلِيمٌ

35 Allah is the Light of the heavens and the earth. The allegory of His light is that of a pillar on which is a lamp. The lamp is within a glass. The glass is like a brilliant planet, fueled by a blessed tree, an olive tree, neither eastern nor western. Its oil would almost illuminate, even if no fire has touched it. Light upon Light. Allah guides to His light whomever He wills. Allah thus cites the parables for the people. Allah is cognizant of everything.

٣٦ فِى بُيُوتٍ أَذِنَ ٱللَّهُ أَن تُرْفَعَ وَيُذْكَرَ فِيهَا
ٱسْمُهُۥ يُسَبِّحُ لَهُۥ فِيهَا بِٱلْغُدُوِّ وَٱلْءَاصَالِ

36 In houses which Allah has permitted to be raised, and His name is celebrated therein. He is glorified therein, morning and evening.

٣٧ رِجَالٌ لَّا تُلْهِيهِمْ تِجَٰرَةٌ وَلَا بَيْعٌ عَن ذِكْرِ ٱللَّهِ
وَإِقَامِ ٱلصَّلَوٰةِ وَإِيتَآءِ ٱلزَّكَوٰةِ ۙ يَخَافُونَ يَوْمًا
تَتَقَلَّبُ فِيهِ ٱلْقُلُوبُ وَٱلْأَبْصَٰرُ

37 By men who neither trading nor commerce distracts them from Allah's remembrance, and from performing the prayers, and from giving alms. They fear a Day when hearts and sights are overturned.

٣٨ لِيَجْزِيَهُمُ ٱللَّهُ أَحْسَنَ مَا عَمِلُوا۟ وَيَزِيدَهُم
مِّن فَضْلِهِۦ ۗ وَٱللَّهُ يَرْزُقُ مَن يَشَآءُ بِغَيْرِ حِسَابٍ

38 Allah will reward them according to the best of what they did, and He will increase them from His bounty.

Allah provides for whomever He wills without reckoning.

٣٩ وَٱلَّذِينَ كَفَرُوٓاْ أَعۡمَٰلُهُمۡ كَسَرَابِۭ بِقِيعَةٖ
يَحۡسَبُهُ ٱلظَّمۡـَٔانُ مَآءً حَتَّىٰٓ إِذَا جَآءَهُۥ لَمۡ يَجِدۡهُ
شَيۡـٔٗا وَوَجَدَ ٱللَّهَ عِندَهُۥ فَوَفَّىٰهُ حِسَابَهُۥۗ وَٱللَّهُ
سَرِيعُ ٱلۡحِسَابِ

39 As for those who disbelieve, their works are like a mirage in a desert. The thirsty assumes it is to be water. Until, when he has reached it, he finds it to be nothing, but there he finds Allah, Who settles his account in full. Allah is swift in reckoning.

٤٠ أَوۡ كَظُلُمَٰتٖ فِي بَحۡرٖ لُّجِّيّٖ يَغۡشَىٰهُ مَوۡجٞ مِّن
فَوۡقِهِۦ مَوۡجٞ مِّن فَوۡقِهِۦ سَحَابٞۚ ظُلُمَٰتُۢ بَعۡضُهَا
فَوۡقَ بَعۡضٍ إِذَآ أَخۡرَجَ يَدَهُۥ لَمۡ يَكَدۡ يَرَىٰهَاۗ وَمَن
لَّمۡ يَجۡعَلِ ٱللَّهُ لَهُۥ نُورٗا فَمَا لَهُۥ مِن نُّورٍ

40 Or like utter darkness in a vast ocean, covered by waves, above which are waves, above which is fog. Darkness upon darkness. If he brings out his hand, he will hardly see it. He to whom Allah has not granted a light has no light.

٤١ أَلَمۡ تَرَ أَنَّ ٱللَّهَ يُسَبِّحُ لَهُۥ مَن فِي ٱلسَّمَٰوَٰتِ
وَٱلۡأَرۡضِ وَٱلطَّيۡرُ صَٰٓفَّٰتٖۖ كُلّٞ قَدۡ عَلِمَ صَلَاتَهُۥ
وَتَسۡبِيحَهُۥۗ وَٱللَّهُ عَلِيمُۢ بِمَا يَفۡعَلُونَ

41 Do you not realize that Allah is glorified by whatever is in the heavens and the earth, and even by the birds in formation? Each knows its prayer and its manner of praise. Allah knows well what they do.

٤٢ وَلِلَّهِ مُلۡكُ ٱلسَّمَٰوَٰتِ وَٱلۡأَرۡضِۖ وَإِلَى ٱللَّهِ
ٱلۡمَصِيرُ

42 To Allah belongs the dominion of the heavens and the earth, and to Allah is the ultimate return.

٤٣ أَلَمۡ تَرَ أَنَّ ٱللَّهَ يُزۡجِي سَحَابٗا ثُمَّ يُؤَلِّفُ بَيۡنَهُۥ
ثُمَّ يَجۡعَلُهُۥ رُكَامٗا فَتَرَى ٱلۡوَدۡقَ يَخۡرُجُ مِنۡ
خِلَٰلِهِۦ وَيُنَزِّلُ مِنَ ٱلسَّمَآءِ مِن جِبَالٖ فِيهَا مِنۢ
بَرَدٖ فَيُصِيبُ بِهِۦ مَن يَشَآءُ وَيَصۡرِفُهُۥ عَن مَّن
يَشَآءُۖ يَكَادُ سَنَا بَرۡقِهِۦ يَذۡهَبُ بِٱلۡأَبۡصَٰرِ

43 Have you not seen how Allah propels the clouds, then brings them together, then piles them into a heap, and you see rain drops emerging from its midst? How He brings down loads of hail from the sky, striking with it whomever He wills, and diverting it from whomever He wills? The flash of its lightening almost snatches the sight away.

٤٤ يُقَلِّبُ ٱللَّهُ ٱلَّيۡلَ وَٱلنَّهَارَۚ إِنَّ فِي ذَٰلِكَ لَعِبۡرَةٗ
لِّأُوْلِي ٱلۡأَبۡصَٰرِ

44 Allah alternates the night and the day. In that is a lesson for those who have insight.

٤٥ وَٱللَّهُ خَلَقَ كُلَّ دَآبَّةٖ مِّن مَّآءٖۖ فَمِنۡهُم مَّن
يَمۡشِي عَلَىٰ بَطۡنِهِۦ وَمِنۡهُم مَّن يَمۡشِي عَلَىٰ

45 Allah created every living creature from water. Some of them crawl on their bellies, and some walk on two

رِجْلَيْنِ وَمِنْهُم مَّن يَمْشِى عَلَىٰٓ أَرْبَعٍ ۚ يَخْلُقُ
ٱللَّهُ مَا يَشَآءُ ۚ إِنَّ ٱللَّهَ عَلَىٰ كُلِّ شَىْءٍ قَدِيرٌ

feet, and others walk on four. Allah creates whatever He wills. Allah is Capable of everything.

٤٦ لَّقَدْ أَنزَلْنَآ ءَايَٰتٍ مُّبَيِّنَٰتٍ ۚ وَٱللَّهُ يَهْدِى مَن
يَشَآءُ إِلَىٰ صِرَٰطٍ مُّسْتَقِيمٍ

46 We sent down enlightening revelations, and Allah guides whomever He wills to a straight path.

٤٧ وَيَقُولُونَ ءَامَنَّا بِٱللَّهِ وَبِٱلرَّسُولِ وَأَطَعْنَا ثُمَّ
يَتَوَلَّىٰ فَرِيقٌ مِّنْهُم مِّنۢ بَعْدِ ذَٰلِكَ ۚ وَمَآ أُو۟لَٰٓئِكَ
بِٱلْمُؤْمِنِينَ

47 And they say, “We have believed in Allah and the Messenger, and we obey,” but some of them turn away afterwards. These are not believers.

٤٨ وَإِذَا دُعُوٓا۟ إِلَى ٱللَّهِ وَرَسُولِهِۦ لِيَحْكُمَ بَيْنَهُمْ
إِذَا فَرِيقٌ مِّنْهُم مُّعْرِضُونَ

48 And when they are called to Allah and His Messenger, in order to judge between them, some of them refuse.

٤٩ وَإِن يَكُن لَّهُمُ ٱلْحَقُّ يَأْتُوٓا۟ إِلَيْهِ مُذْعِنِينَ

49 But if justice is on their side, they accept it willingly.

٥٠ أَفِى قُلُوبِهِم مَّرَضٌ أَمِ ٱرْتَابُوٓا۟ أَمْ يَخَافُونَ
أَن يَحِيفَ ٱللَّهُ عَلَيْهِمْ وَرَسُولُهُۥ ۚ بَلْ أُو۟لَٰٓئِكَ هُمُ
ٱلظَّٰلِمُونَ

50 Is there sickness in their hearts? Or are they suspicious? Or do they fear that Allah may do them injustice? Or His Messenger? In fact, they themselves are the unjust.

٥١ إِنَّمَا كَانَ قَوْلَ ٱلْمُؤْمِنِينَ إِذَا دُعُوٓا۟ إِلَى ٱللَّهِ
وَرَسُولِهِۦ لِيَحْكُمَ بَيْنَهُمْ أَن يَقُولُوا۟ سَمِعْنَا
وَأَطَعْنَا ۚ وَأُو۟لَٰٓئِكَ هُمُ ٱلْمُفْلِحُونَ

51 The response of the believers, when they are called to Allah and His Messenger in order to judge between them, is to say, “We hear and we obey.” These are the successful.

٥٢ وَمَن يُطِعِ ٱللَّهَ وَرَسُولَهُۥ وَيَخْشَ ٱللَّهَ وَيَتَّقْهِ
فَأُو۟لَٰٓئِكَ هُمُ ٱلْفَآئِزُونَ

52 Whoever obeys Allah and His Messenger, and fears Allah, and is conscious of Him—these are the winners.

٥٣ وَأَقْسَمُوا۟ بِٱللَّهِ جَهْدَ أَيْمَٰنِهِمْ لَئِنْ أَمَرْتَهُمْ
لَيَخْرُجُنَّ ۖ قُل لَّا تُقْسِمُوا۟ ۖ طَاعَةٌ مَّعْرُوفَةٌ ۚ إِنَّ
ٱللَّهَ خَبِيرٌۢ بِمَا تَعْمَلُونَ

53 And they swear by Allah with their solemn oaths, that if you commanded them, they would mobilize. Say, “Do not swear. Obedience will be recognized. Allah is experienced with what you do.”

٥٤ قُلْ أَطِيعُوا۟ ٱللَّهَ وَأَطِيعُوا۟ ٱلرَّسُولَ ۖ فَإِن
تَوَلَّوْا۟ فَإِنَّمَا عَلَيْهِ مَا حُمِّلَ وَعَلَيْكُم مَّا حُمِّلْتُمْ ۖ

54 Say, “Obey Allah and obey the Messenger.” But if they turn away, then he is responsible for his

وَإِن تُطِيعُوهُ تَهْتَدُوا۟ ۚ وَمَا عَلَى ٱلرَّسُولِ إِلَّا
ٱلْبَلَٰغُ ٱلْمُبِينُ

obligations, and you are responsible for your obligations. And if you obey him, you will be guided. It is only incumbent on the Messenger to deliver the Clarifying Message.

٥٥ وَعَدَ ٱللَّهُ ٱلَّذِينَ ءَامَنُوا۟ مِنكُمْ وَعَمِلُوا۟
ٱلصَّٰلِحَٰتِ لَيَسْتَخْلِفَنَّهُمْ فِى ٱلْأَرْضِ كَمَا
ٱسْتَخْلَفَ ٱلَّذِينَ مِن قَبْلِهِمْ وَلَيُمَكِّنَنَّ لَهُمْ دِينَهُمُ
ٱلَّذِى ٱرْتَضَىٰ لَهُمْ وَلَيُبَدِّلَنَّهُم مِّنۢ بَعْدِ خَوْفِهِمْ
أَمْنًا ۚ يَعْبُدُونَنِى لَا يُشْرِكُونَ بِى شَيْـًٔا ۚ وَمَن كَفَرَ
بَعْدَ ذَٰلِكَ فَأُو۟لَٰٓئِكَ هُمُ ٱلْفَٰسِقُونَ

55 Allah has promised those of you who believe and do righteous deeds, that He will make them successors on earth, as He made those before them successors, and He will establish for them their religion—which He has approved for them—and He will substitute security in place of their fear. They worship Me, never associating anything with Me. But whoever disbelieves after that—these are the sinners.

٥٦ وَأَقِيمُوا۟ ٱلصَّلَوٰةَ وَءَاتُوا۟ ٱلزَّكَوٰةَ وَأَطِيعُوا۟
ٱلرَّسُولَ لَعَلَّكُمْ تُرْحَمُونَ

56 Pray regularly, and give regular charity, and obey the Messenger, so that you may receive mercy.

٥٧ لَا تَحْسَبَنَّ ٱلَّذِينَ كَفَرُوا۟ مُعْجِزِينَ فِى
ٱلْأَرْضِ ۚ وَمَأْوَىٰهُمُ ٱلنَّارُ ۖ وَلَبِئْسَ ٱلْمَصِيرُ

57 Never think that those who disbelieve can escape on earth. Their place is the Fire; a miserable destination.

٥٨ يَٰٓأَيُّهَا ٱلَّذِينَ ءَامَنُوا۟ لِيَسْتَـْٔذِنكُمُ ٱلَّذِينَ
مَلَكَتْ أَيْمَٰنُكُمْ وَٱلَّذِينَ لَمْ يَبْلُغُوا۟ ٱلْحُلُمَ مِنكُمْ
ثَلَٰثَ مَرَّٰتٍ ۚ مِّن قَبْلِ صَلَوٰةِ ٱلْفَجْرِ وَحِينَ
تَضَعُونَ ثِيَابَكُم مِّنَ ٱلظَّهِيرَةِ وَمِنۢ بَعْدِ صَلَوٰةِ
ٱلْعِشَآءِ ۚ ثَلَٰثُ عَوْرَٰتٍ لَّكُمْ ۚ لَيْسَ عَلَيْكُمْ وَلَا
عَلَيْهِمْ جُنَاحٌۢ بَعْدَهُنَّ ۚ طَوَّٰفُونَ عَلَيْكُم بَعْضُكُمْ
عَلَىٰ بَعْضٍ ۚ كَذَٰلِكَ يُبَيِّنُ ٱللَّهُ لَكُمُ ٱلْءَايَٰتِ ۗ
وَٱللَّهُ عَلِيمٌ حَكِيمٌ

58 O you who believe! Permission must be requested by your servants and those of you who have not reached puberty. On three occasions: before the Dawn Prayer, and at noon when you change your clothes, and after the Evening Prayer. These are three occasions of privacy for you. At other times, it is not wrong for you or them to intermingle with one another. Allah thus clarifies the revelations for you. Allah is Knowledgeable and Wise.

٥٩ وَإِذَا بَلَغَ ٱلْأَطْفَٰلُ مِنكُمُ ٱلْحُلُمَ فَلْيَسْتَـْٔذِنُوا۟
كَمَا ٱسْتَـْٔذَنَ ٱلَّذِينَ مِن قَبْلِهِمْ ۚ كَذَٰلِكَ يُبَيِّنُ ٱللَّهُ
لَكُمْ ءَايَٰتِهِۦ ۗ وَٱللَّهُ عَلِيمٌ حَكِيمٌ

59 When the children among you reach puberty, they must ask permission, as those before them asked permission. Allah thus

clarifies His revelations for you. Allah is Knowledgeable and Wise.

٦٠ وَٱلْقَوَٰعِدُ مِنَ ٱلنِّسَآءِ ٱلَّٰتِى لَا يَرْجُونَ نِكَاحًا
فَلَيْسَ عَلَيْهِنَّ جُنَاحٌ أَن يَضَعْنَ ثِيَابَهُنَّ غَيْرَ
مُتَبَرِّجَٰتٍۭ بِزِينَةٍ ۖ وَأَن يَسْتَعْفِفْنَ خَيْرٌ لَّهُنَّ ۗ
وَٱللَّهُ سَمِيعٌ عَلِيمٌ

60 Women past the age of childbearing, who have no desire for marriage, commit no wrong by taking off their outer clothing, provided they do not flaunt their finery. But to maintain modesty is better for them. Allah is Hearing and Knowing.

٦١ لَّيْسَ عَلَى ٱلْأَعْمَىٰ حَرَجٌ وَلَا عَلَى ٱلْأَعْرَجِ
حَرَجٌ وَلَا عَلَى ٱلْمَرِيضِ حَرَجٌ وَلَا عَلَىٰٓ أَنفُسِكُمْ
أَن تَأْكُلُوا۟ مِنۢ بُيُوتِكُمْ أَوْ بُيُوتِ ءَابَآئِكُمْ أَوْ
بُيُوتِ أُمَّهَٰتِكُمْ أَوْ بُيُوتِ إِخْوَٰنِكُمْ أَوْ بُيُوتِ
أَخَوَٰتِكُمْ أَوْ بُيُوتِ أَعْمَٰمِكُمْ أَوْ بُيُوتِ عَمَّٰتِكُمْ أَوْ
بُيُوتِ أَخْوَٰلِكُمْ أَوْ بُيُوتِ خَٰلَٰتِكُمْ أَوْ مَا مَلَكْتُم
مَّفَاتِحَهُۥٓ أَوْ صَدِيقِكُمْ ۚ لَيْسَ عَلَيْكُمْ جُنَاحٌ أَن
تَأْكُلُوا۟ جَمِيعًا أَوْ أَشْتَاتًا ۚ فَإِذَا دَخَلْتُم بُيُوتًا
فَسَلِّمُوا۟ عَلَىٰٓ أَنفُسِكُمْ تَحِيَّةً مِّنْ عِندِ ٱللَّهِ
مُبَٰرَكَةً طَيِّبَةً ۚ كَذَٰلِكَ يُبَيِّنُ ٱللَّهُ لَكُمُ ٱلْءَايَٰتِ
لَعَلَّكُمْ تَعْقِلُونَ

61 There is no blame on the blind, nor any blame on the lame, nor any blame on the sick, nor on yourselves for eating at your homes, or your fathers' homes, or your mothers' homes, or your brothers' homes, or your sisters' homes, or the homes of your paternal uncles, or the homes of your paternal aunts, or the homes of your maternal uncles, or the homes of your maternal aunts, or those whose keys you own, or the homes of your friends. You commit no wrong by eating together or separately. But when you enter any home, greet one another with a greeting from Allah, blessed and good. Allah thus explains the revelations for you, so that you may understand.

٦٢ إِنَّمَا ٱلْمُؤْمِنُونَ ٱلَّذِينَ ءَامَنُوا۟ بِٱللَّهِ وَرَسُولِهِۦ
وَإِذَا كَانُوا۟ مَعَهُۥ عَلَىٰٓ أَمْرٍ جَامِعٍ لَّمْ يَذْهَبُوا۟
حَتَّىٰ يَسْتَـْٔذِنُوهُ ۚ إِنَّ ٱلَّذِينَ يَسْتَـْٔذِنُونَكَ أُو۟لَٰٓئِكَ
ٱلَّذِينَ يُؤْمِنُونَ بِٱللَّهِ وَرَسُولِهِۦ ۚ فَإِذَا ٱسْتَـْٔذَنُوكَ
لِبَعْضِ شَأْنِهِمْ فَأْذَن لِّمَن شِئْتَ مِنْهُمْ وَٱسْتَغْفِرْ
لَهُمُ ٱللَّهَ ۚ إِنَّ ٱللَّهَ غَفُورٌ رَّحِيمٌ

62 The believers are those who believe in Allah and His Messenger, and when they are with him for a matter of common interest, they do not leave until they have asked him for permission. Those who ask your permission are those who believe in Allah and His Messenger. So when they ask your permission to attend to some affair of theirs, give permission to any of them you wish, and ask Allah's forgiveness for them. Allah is Forgiving and Merciful.

٦٣ لَّا تَجْعَلُوا۟ دُعَآءَ ٱلرَّسُولِ بَيْنَكُمْ كَدُعَآءِ
بَعْضِكُم بَعْضًا ۚ قَدْ يَعْلَمُ ٱللَّهُ ٱلَّذِينَ يَتَسَلَّلُونَ
مِنكُمْ لِوَاذًا ۚ فَلْيَحْذَرِ ٱلَّذِينَ يُخَالِفُونَ عَنْ
أَمْرِهِۦٓ أَن تُصِيبَهُمْ فِتْنَةٌ أَوْ يُصِيبَهُمْ عَذَابٌ
أَلِيمٌ

63 Do not address the Messenger in the same manner you address one another. Allah knows those of you who slip away using flimsy excuses. So let those who oppose his orders beware, lest an ordeal strikes them, or a painful punishment befalls them.

٦٤ أَلَآ إِنَّ لِلَّهِ مَا فِى ٱلسَّمَٰوَٰتِ وَٱلْأَرْضِ ۖ قَدْ
يَعْلَمُ مَآ أَنتُمْ عَلَيْهِ وَيَوْمَ يُرْجَعُونَ إِلَيْهِ
فَيُنَبِّئُهُم بِمَا عَمِلُوا۟ ۗ وَٱللَّهُ بِكُلِّ شَىْءٍ عَلِيمٌۢ

64 Surely, to Allah belongs everything in the heavens and the earth. He knows what you are about. And on the Day they are returned to Him, He will inform them of what they did. Allah has full knowledge of all things.

25 The Criterion الفرقان

بِسْمِ ٱللَّهِ ٱلرَّحْمَٰنِ ٱلرَّحِيمِ

In the name of Allah, the Gracious, the Merciful.

١ تَبَارَكَ ٱلَّذِى نَزَّلَ ٱلْفُرْقَانَ عَلَىٰ عَبْدِهِۦ لِيَكُونَ
لِلْعَٰلَمِينَ نَذِيرًا

1 Blessed is He who sent down the Criterion upon His servant, to be a warning to humanity.

٢ ٱلَّذِى لَهُۥ مُلْكُ ٱلسَّمَٰوَٰتِ وَٱلْأَرْضِ وَلَمْ يَتَّخِذْ
وَلَدًا وَلَمْ يَكُن لَّهُۥ شَرِيكٌ فِى ٱلْمُلْكِ وَخَلَقَ كُلَّ
شَىْءٍ فَقَدَّرَهُۥ تَقْدِيرًا

2 He to whom belongs the kingdom of the heavens and the earth, who took to Himself no son, who never had a partner in His kingship; who created everything and determined its measure.

٣ وَٱتَّخَذُوا۟ مِن دُونِهِۦٓ ءَالِهَةً لَّا يَخْلُقُونَ شَيْـًٔا
وَهُمْ يُخْلَقُونَ وَلَا يَمْلِكُونَ لِأَنفُسِهِمْ ضَرًّا وَلَا
نَفْعًا وَلَا يَمْلِكُونَ مَوْتًا وَلَا حَيَوٰةً وَلَا نُشُورًا

3 And yet, instead of Him, they produce for themselves gods that create nothing, but are themselves created; that have no power to harm or benefit themselves; and no power over life, death, or resurrection.

٤ وَقَالَ ٱلَّذِينَ كَفَرُوٓا۟ إِنْ هَٰذَآ إِلَّآ إِفْكٌ ٱفْتَرَىٰهُ
وَأَعَانَهُۥ عَلَيْهِ قَوْمٌ ءَاخَرُونَ ۖ فَقَدْ جَآءُو ظُلْمًا
وَزُورًا

4 Those who disbelieve say, “This is nothing but a lie that he made up, and others have helped him at it.” They have committed an injustice and a perjury.

٥ وَقَالُوٓاْ أَسَٰطِيرُ ٱلْأَوَّلِينَ ٱكْتَتَبَهَا فَهِىَ تُمْلَىٰ
عَلَيْهِ بُكْرَةً وَأَصِيلًا

5 And they say, "Tales of the ancients; he wrote them down; they are dictated to him morning and evening."

٦ قُلْ أَنزَلَهُ ٱلَّذِى يَعْلَمُ ٱلسِّرَّ فِى ٱلسَّمَٰوَٰتِ
وَٱلْأَرْضِ ۚ إِنَّهُۥ كَانَ غَفُورًا رَّحِيمًا

6 Say, "It was revealed by He who knows the Secret in the heavens and the earth. He is always Forgiving and Merciful."

٧ وَقَالُواْ مَالِ هَٰذَا ٱلرَّسُولِ يَأْكُلُ ٱلطَّعَامَ
وَيَمْشِى فِى ٱلْأَسْوَاقِ ۙ لَوْلَآ أُنزِلَ إِلَيْهِ مَلَكٌ
فَيَكُونَ مَعَهُۥ نَذِيرًا

7 And they say, "What sort of messenger is this, who eats food, and walks in the marketplaces? If only an angel was sent down with him, to be alongside him a warner."

٨ أَوْ يُلْقَىٰٓ إِلَيْهِ كَنزٌ أَوْ تَكُونُ لَهُۥ جَنَّةٌ يَأْكُلُ
مِنْهَا ۚ وَقَالَ ٱلظَّٰلِمُونَ إِن تَتَّبِعُونَ إِلَّا رَجُلًا
مَّسْحُورًا

8 Or, "If only a treasure was dropped on him." Or, "If only he had a garden from which he eats." The evildoers also say, "You are following but a man under spell."

٩ ٱنظُرْ كَيْفَ ضَرَبُواْ لَكَ ٱلْأَمْثَٰلَ فَضَلُّواْ فَلَا
يَسْتَطِيعُونَ سَبِيلًا

9 Look how they invent examples for you. They have gone astray, and cannot find a way.

١٠ تَبَارَكَ ٱلَّذِىٓ إِن شَآءَ جَعَلَ لَكَ خَيْرًا مِّن ذَٰلِكَ
جَنَّٰتٍ تَجْرِى مِن تَحْتِهَا ٱلْأَنْهَٰرُ وَيَجْعَل لَّكَ
قُصُورًۢا

10 Blessed is He who, if He wills, can provide you with better than that—gardens beneath which rivers flow—and He will give you palaces.

١١ بَلْ كَذَّبُواْ بِٱلسَّاعَةِ ۖ وَأَعْتَدْنَا لِمَن كَذَّبَ
بِٱلسَّاعَةِ سَعِيرًا

11 In fact, they have denied the Hour, and We have prepared for those who deny the Hour a Blaze.

١٢ إِذَا رَأَتْهُم مِّن مَّكَانٍۭ بَعِيدٍ سَمِعُواْ لَهَا تَغَيُّظًا
وَزَفِيرًا

12 When it sees them from a distant place, they will hear it raging and roaring.

١٣ وَإِذَآ أُلْقُواْ مِنْهَا مَكَانًا ضَيِّقًا مُّقَرَّنِينَ دَعَوْاْ
هُنَالِكَ ثُبُورًا

13 And when they are thrown into it, into a tight place, shackled, they will plead there for death.

١٤ لَّا تَدْعُواْ ٱلْيَوْمَ ثُبُورًا وَٰحِدًا وَٱدْعُواْ ثُبُورًا
كَثِيرًا

14 "Do not plead for one death today, but plead for a great many deaths."

١٥ قُلْ أَذَٰلِكَ خَيْرٌ أَمْ جَنَّةُ ٱلْخُلْدِ ٱلَّتِى وُعِدَ
ٱلْمُتَّقُونَ ۚ كَانَتْ لَهُمْ جَزَآءً وَمَصِيرًا

15 Say, "Is this better, or the Garden of Eternity promised to the

righteous? It is for them a reward and a destination.

١٦ لَّهُمْ فِيهَا مَا يَشَآءُونَ خَٰلِدِينَ ۚ كَانَ عَلَىٰ
رَبِّكَ وَعْدًا مَّسْـُٔولًا

16 They will have therein whatever they desire, forever. That is upon your Lord a binding promise.

١٧ وَيَوْمَ يَحْشُرُهُمْ وَمَا يَعْبُدُونَ مِن دُونِ ٱللَّهِ
فَيَقُولُ ءَأَنتُمْ أَضْلَلْتُمْ عِبَادِى هَٰٓؤُلَآءِ أَمْ هُمْ
ضَلُّوا۟ ٱلسَّبِيلَ

17 On the Day when He gathers them, and what they worshiped besides Allah, He will say, "Was it you who misled these servants of Mine, or was it they who lost the way?"

١٨ قَالُوا۟ سُبْحَٰنَكَ مَا كَانَ يَنۢبَغِى لَنَآ أَن نَّتَّخِذَ
مِن دُونِكَ مِنْ أَوْلِيَآءَ وَلَٰكِن مَّتَّعْتَهُمْ وَءَابَآءَهُمْ
حَتَّىٰ نَسُوا۟ ٱلذِّكْرَ وَكَانُوا۟ قَوْمًۢا بُورًا

18 They will say, "Glory be to You. It was not for us to take any lords besides You. But you gave them enjoyments, and their ancestors, until they forgot the Message, and became ruined people."

١٩ فَقَدْ كَذَّبُوكُم بِمَا تَقُولُونَ فَمَا تَسْتَطِيعُونَ
صَرْفًا وَلَا نَصْرًا ۚ وَمَن يَظْلِم مِّنكُمْ نُذِقْهُ عَذَابًا
كَبِيرًا

19 They have denied you because of what you say; so you can neither avert, nor help. Whoever among you commits injustice, We will make him taste a grievous punishment.

٢٠ وَمَآ أَرْسَلْنَا قَبْلَكَ مِنَ ٱلْمُرْسَلِينَ إِلَّآ إِنَّهُمْ
لَيَأْكُلُونَ ٱلطَّعَامَ وَيَمْشُونَ فِى ٱلْأَسْوَاقِ ۗ
وَجَعَلْنَا بَعْضَكُمْ لِبَعْضٍ فِتْنَةً أَتَصْبِرُونَ ۗ وَكَانَ
رَبُّكَ بَصِيرًا

20 We never sent any messengers before you, but they ate food and walked in the marketplaces. And We made some of you tempters for one another—will you be patient? Your Lord is always Observing.

٢١ وَقَالَ ٱلَّذِينَ لَا يَرْجُونَ لِقَآءَنَا لَوْلَآ أُنزِلَ
عَلَيْنَا ٱلْمَلَٰٓئِكَةُ أَوْ نَرَىٰ رَبَّنَا ۗ لَقَدِ ٱسْتَكْبَرُوا۟ فِىٓ
أَنفُسِهِمْ وَعَتَوْ عُتُوًّا كَبِيرًا

21 Those who do not expect to meet Us say, "If only the angels were sent down to us, or we could see our Lord." They have grown arrogant within themselves, and have become excessively defiant.

٢٢ يَوْمَ يَرَوْنَ ٱلْمَلَٰٓئِكَةَ لَا بُشْرَىٰ يَوْمَئِذٍ
لِّلْمُجْرِمِينَ وَيَقُولُونَ حِجْرًا مَّحْجُورًا

22 On the Day when they see the angels—there will be no good news for sinners on that Day; and they will say, "A protective refuge."

٢٣ وَقَدِمْنَآ إِلَىٰ مَا عَمِلُوا۟ مِنْ عَمَلٍ فَجَعَلْنَٰهُ
هَبَآءً مَّنثُورًا

23 We will proceed to the works they did, and will turn them into scattered dust.

٢٤ أَصْحَٰبُ ٱلْجَنَّةِ يَوْمَئِذٍ خَيْرٌ مُّسْتَقَرًّا
وَأَحْسَنُ مَقِيلًا

24 The companions of Paradise on that Day will be better lodged, and more fairly accommodated.

٢٥ وَيَوْمَ تَشَقَّقُ ٱلسَّمَآءُ بِٱلْغَمَٰمِ وَنُزِّلَ ٱلْمَلَٰٓئِكَةُ
تَنزِيلًا

25 The Day when the sky is cleft with clouds, and the angels are sent down in streams.

٢٦ ٱلْمُلْكُ يَوْمَئِذٍ ٱلْحَقُّ لِلرَّحْمَٰنِ ۚ وَكَانَ يَوْمًا
عَلَى ٱلْكَٰفِرِينَ عَسِيرًا

26 On that Day, true sovereignty will belong to the Merciful, and it will be a difficult Day for the disbelievers.

٢٧ وَيَوْمَ يَعَضُّ ٱلظَّالِمُ عَلَىٰ يَدَيْهِ يَقُولُ
يَٰلَيْتَنِى ٱتَّخَذْتُ مَعَ ٱلرَّسُولِ سَبِيلًا

27 On that Day, the wrongdoer will bite his hands, and say, "If only I had followed the way with the Messenger.

٢٨ يَٰوَيْلَتَىٰ لَيْتَنِى لَمْ أَتَّخِذْ فُلَانًا خَلِيلًا

28 Oh, woe to me; I wish I never took so-and-so for a friend.

٢٩ لَّقَدْ أَضَلَّنِى عَنِ ٱلذِّكْرِ بَعْدَ إِذْ جَآءَنِى ۗ وَكَانَ
ٱلشَّيْطَٰنُ لِلْإِنسَٰنِ خَذُولًا

29 He led me away from the Message after it had come to me; for Satan has always been a betrayer of man."

٣٠ وَقَالَ ٱلرَّسُولُ يَٰرَبِّ إِنَّ قَوْمِى ٱتَّخَذُوا۟ هَٰذَا
ٱلْقُرْءَانَ مَهْجُورًا

30 And the Messenger will say, "My Lord, my people have abandoned this Quran."

٣١ وَكَذَٰلِكَ جَعَلْنَا لِكُلِّ نَبِىٍّ عَدُوًّا مِّنَ
ٱلْمُجْرِمِينَ ۗ وَكَفَىٰ بِرَبِّكَ هَادِيًا وَنَصِيرًا

31 Likewise, to every prophet We assign enemies from among the wicked. But your Lord suffices as a Guide and Savior.

٣٢ وَقَالَ ٱلَّذِينَ كَفَرُوا۟ لَوْلَا نُزِّلَ عَلَيْهِ ٱلْقُرْءَانُ
جُمْلَةً وَٰحِدَةً ۚ كَذَٰلِكَ لِنُثَبِّتَ بِهِۦ فُؤَادَكَ ۖ وَرَتَّلْنَٰهُ
تَرْتِيلًا

32 Those who disbelieve say, "Why was the Quran not revealed to him at once?" Thus in order to strengthen your heart thereby, and We revealed it in stages.

٣٣ وَلَا يَأْتُونَكَ بِمَثَلٍ إِلَّا جِئْنَٰكَ بِٱلْحَقِّ وَأَحْسَنَ
تَفْسِيرًا

33 Whatever argument they come to you with, We provide you with the truth, and a better exposition.

٣٤ ٱلَّذِينَ يُحْشَرُونَ عَلَىٰ وُجُوهِهِمْ إِلَىٰ جَهَنَّمَ
أُو۟لَٰٓئِكَ شَرٌّ مَّكَانًا وَأَضَلُّ سَبِيلًا

34 Those who are herded into Hell on their faces—those are in a worse position, and further astray from the way.

٣٥ وَلَقَدْ ءَاتَيْنَا مُوسَى ٱلْكِتَٰبَ وَجَعَلْنَا مَعَهُۥٓ
أَخَاهُ هَٰرُونَ وَزِيرًا

35 We gave Moses the Scripture, and appointed his brother Aaron as his assistant.

٣٦ فَقُلْنَا ٱذْهَبَآ إِلَى ٱلْقَوْمِ ٱلَّذِينَ كَذَّبُوا۟ بِـَٔايَٰتِنَا
فَدَمَّرْنَٰهُمْ تَدْمِيرًا

36 We said, “Go to the people who rejected Our signs,” and We destroyed them completely.

٣٧ وَقَوْمَ نُوحٍ لَّمَّا كَذَّبُوا۟ ٱلرُّسُلَ أَغْرَقْنَٰهُمْ
وَجَعَلْنَٰهُمْ لِلنَّاسِ ءَايَةًۖ وَأَعْتَدْنَا لِلظَّٰلِمِينَ عَذَابًا
أَلِيمًا

37 And the people of Noah: when they rejected the messengers, We drowned them, and made them a lesson for mankind. We have prepared for the wrongdoers a painful retribution.

٣٨ وَعَادًا وَثَمُودَا۟ وَأَصْحَٰبَ ٱلرَّسِّ وَقُرُونًۢا بَيْنَ
ذَٰلِكَ كَثِيرًا

38 And Aad, and Thamood, and the inhabitants of Arras, and many generations in between.

٣٩ وَكُلًّا ضَرَبْنَا لَهُ ٱلْأَمْثَٰلَۖ وَكُلًّا تَبَّرْنَا تَتْبِيرًا

39 To each We presented the parables; and each We devastated utterly.

٤٠ وَلَقَدْ أَتَوْا۟ عَلَى ٱلْقَرْيَةِ ٱلَّتِىٓ أُمْطِرَتْ مَطَرَ
ٱلسَّوْءِۚ أَفَلَمْ يَكُونُوا۟ يَرَوْنَهَاۚ بَلْ كَانُوا۟ لَا
يَرْجُونَ نُشُورًا

40 And they came upon the city that was drenched by the terrible rain. Did they not see it? But they do not expect resurrection.

٤١ وَإِذَا رَأَوْكَ إِن يَتَّخِذُونَكَ إِلَّا هُزُوًا أَهَٰذَا
ٱلَّذِى بَعَثَ ٱللَّهُ رَسُولًا

41 And when they see you, they take you for nothing but mockery: “Is this the one Allah sent as a messenger?”

٤٢ إِن كَادَ لَيُضِلُّنَا عَنْ ءَالِهَتِنَا لَوْلَآ أَن صَبَرْنَا
عَلَيْهَاۚ وَسَوْفَ يَعْلَمُونَ حِينَ يَرَوْنَ ٱلْعَذَابَ
مَنْ أَضَلُّ سَبِيلًا

42 “He nearly led us away from our gods, had we not patiently adhered to them.” But they will know, when they witness the torment, who is further away from the way.

٤٣ أَرَءَيْتَ مَنِ ٱتَّخَذَ إِلَٰهَهُۥ هَوَىٰهُ أَفَأَنتَ تَكُونُ
عَلَيْهِ وَكِيلًا

43 Have you seen him who chose his desire as his god? Would you be an agent for him?

٤٤ أَمْ تَحْسَبُ أَنَّ أَكْثَرَهُمْ يَسْمَعُونَ أَوْ
يَعْقِلُونَۚ إِنْ هُمْ إِلَّا كَٱلْأَنْعَٰمِۖ بَلْ هُمْ أَضَلُّ
سَبِيلًا

44 Or do you assume that most of them hear or understand? They are just like cattle, but even more errant in their way.

٤٥ أَلَمْ تَرَ إِلَىٰ رَبِّكَ كَيْفَ مَدَّ ٱلظِّلَّ وَلَوْ شَآءَ
لَجَعَلَهُۥ سَاكِنًا ثُمَّ جَعَلْنَا ٱلشَّمْسَ عَلَيْهِ دَلِيلًا

45 Do you not see how your Lord extends the shadow? Had He willed, He could have made it still. And We made the sun a pointer to it.

٤٦ ثُمَّ قَبَضْنَٰهُ إِلَيْنَا قَبْضًا يَسِيرًا

46 Then We withdraw it towards Us gradually.

٤٧ وَهُوَ ٱلَّذِى جَعَلَ لَكُمُ ٱلَّيْلَ لِبَاسًا وَٱلنَّوْمَ
سُبَاتًا وَجَعَلَ ٱلنَّهَارَ نُشُورًا

47 And it is He who made the night a covering for you, and sleep for rest; and He made the day a revival.

٤٨ وَهُوَ ٱلَّذِىٓ أَرْسَلَ ٱلرِّيَٰحَ بُشْرًۢا بَيْنَ يَدَىْ
رَحْمَتِهِۦ ۚ وَأَنزَلْنَا مِنَ ٱلسَّمَآءِ مَآءً طَهُورًا

48 And it is He who sends the winds, bringing advance news of His mercy; and We send down from the sky pure water.

٤٩ لِّنُحْـِۧىَ بِهِۦ بَلْدَةً مَّيْتًا وَنُسْقِيَهُۥ مِمَّا خَلَقْنَآ
أَنْعَٰمًا وَأَنَاسِىَّ كَثِيرًا

49 To revive dead lands thereby, and to provide drink for the multitude of animals and humans We created.

٥٠ وَلَقَدْ صَرَّفْنَٰهُ بَيْنَهُمْ لِيَذَّكَّرُوا۟ فَأَبَىٰٓ أَكْثَرُ
ٱلنَّاسِ إِلَّا كُفُورًا

50 We have circulated it among them, that they may reflect, but most people persist in thanklessness.

٥١ وَلَوْ شِئْنَا لَبَعَثْنَا فِى كُلِّ قَرْيَةٍ نَّذِيرًا

51 Had We willed, We could have sent to every town a warner.

٥٢ فَلَا تُطِعِ ٱلْكَٰفِرِينَ وَجَٰهِدْهُم بِهِۦ جِهَادًا
كَبِيرًا

52 So do not obey the disbelievers, but strive against them with it, a mighty struggle.

٥٣ وَهُوَ ٱلَّذِى مَرَجَ ٱلْبَحْرَيْنِ هَٰذَا عَذْبٌ فُرَاتٌ
وَهَٰذَا مِلْحٌ أُجَاجٌ وَجَعَلَ بَيْنَهُمَا بَرْزَخًا وَحِجْرًا
مَّحْجُورًا

53 And it is He who merged the two seas; this one fresh and sweet, and that one salty and bitter; and He placed between them a barrier, and an impassable boundary.

٥٤ وَهُوَ ٱلَّذِى خَلَقَ مِنَ ٱلْمَآءِ بَشَرًا فَجَعَلَهُۥ نَسَبًا
وَصِهْرًا ۗ وَكَانَ رَبُّكَ قَدِيرًا

54 And it is He who, from fluid, created the human being. Then He made relationships through marriage and mating. Your Lord is Omnipotent.

٥٥ وَيَعْبُدُونَ مِن دُونِ ٱللَّهِ مَا لَا يَنفَعُهُمْ وَلَا
يَضُرُّهُمْ ۗ وَكَانَ ٱلْكَافِرُ عَلَىٰ رَبِّهِۦ ظَهِيرًا

55 And yet, instead of Allah, they serve what neither profits them nor harms them. The disbeliever has always turned his back on his Lord.

٥٦ وَمَآ أَرْسَلْنَٰكَ إِلَّا مُبَشِّرًا وَنَذِيرًا

56 We sent you only as a herald of good news and a warner.

٥٧ قُلْ مَآ أَسْـَٔلُكُمْ عَلَيْهِ مِنْ أَجْرٍ إِلَّا مَن شَآءَ أَن
يَتَّخِذَ إِلَىٰ رَبِّهِۦ سَبِيلًا

57 Say, "I ask of you no payment for this—only that whoever wills may take a path to his Lord."

٥٨ وَتَوَكَّلْ عَلَى ٱلْحَىِّ ٱلَّذِى لَا يَمُوتُ وَسَبِّحْ
بِحَمْدِهِۦ ۚ وَكَفَىٰ بِهِۦ بِذُنُوبِ عِبَادِهِۦ خَبِيرًا

58 And put your trust in the Living, the One who never dies; and celebrate His praise. He suffices as the All-Informed Knower of the faults of His creatures.

٥٩ ٱلَّذِى خَلَقَ ٱلسَّمَٰوَٰتِ وَٱلْأَرْضَ وَمَا بَيْنَهُمَا
فِى سِتَّةِ أَيَّامٍ ثُمَّ ٱسْتَوَىٰ عَلَى ٱلْعَرْشِ ۚ
ٱلرَّحْمَٰنُ فَسْـَٔلْ بِهِۦ خَبِيرًا

59 He who created the heavens and the earth and everything between them in six days, then settled on the Throne. The Most Merciful. Ask about Him a well-informed.

٦٠ وَإِذَا قِيلَ لَهُمُ ٱسْجُدُوا۟ لِلرَّحْمَٰنِ قَالُوا۟ وَمَا
ٱلرَّحْمَٰنُ أَنَسْجُدُ لِمَا تَأْمُرُنَا وَزَادَهُمْ نُفُورًا ۩

60 And when it is said to them, "Bow down to the Merciful," they say, "And what is the Merciful? Are we to bow down to whatever you command us?" And it increases their aversion.

٦١ تَبَارَكَ ٱلَّذِى جَعَلَ فِى ٱلسَّمَآءِ بُرُوجًا وَجَعَلَ
فِيهَا سِرَٰجًا وَقَمَرًا مُّنِيرًا

61 Blessed is He who placed constellations in the sky, and placed in it a lamp, and an illuminating moon.

٦٢ وَهُوَ ٱلَّذِى جَعَلَ ٱلَّيْلَ وَٱلنَّهَارَ خِلْفَةً لِّمَنْ
أَرَادَ أَن يَذَّكَّرَ أَوْ أَرَادَ شُكُورًا

62 And it is He who made the night and the day alternate—for whoever desires to reflect, or desires to show gratitude.

٦٣ وَعِبَادُ ٱلرَّحْمَٰنِ ٱلَّذِينَ يَمْشُونَ عَلَى ٱلْأَرْضِ
هَوْنًا وَإِذَا خَاطَبَهُمُ ٱلْجَٰهِلُونَ قَالُوا۟ سَلَٰمًا

63 The servants of the Merciful are those who walk the earth in humility, and when the ignorant address them, they say, "Peace."

٦٤ وَٱلَّذِينَ يَبِيتُونَ لِرَبِّهِمْ سُجَّدًا وَقِيَٰمًا

64 And those who pass the night prostrating themselves to their Lord and standing up.

٦٥ وَٱلَّذِينَ يَقُولُونَ رَبَّنَا ٱصْرِفْ عَنَّا عَذَابَ
جَهَنَّمَ ۖ إِنَّ عَذَابَهَا كَانَ غَرَامًا

65 And those who say, "Our Lord, avert from us the suffering of Hell, for its suffering is continuous.

٦٦ إِنَّهَا سَآءَتْ مُسْتَقَرًّا وَمُقَامًا

66 It is indeed a miserable residence and destination."

٦٧ وَٱلَّذِينَ إِذَآ أَنفَقُواْ لَمْ يُسْرِفُواْ وَلَمْ يَقْتُرُواْ
وَكَانَ بَيْنَ ذَٰلِكَ قَوَامًا

67 And those who, when they spend, are neither wasteful nor stingy, but choose a middle course between that.

٦٨ وَٱلَّذِينَ لَا يَدْعُونَ مَعَ ٱللَّهِ إِلَٰهًا ءَاخَرَ وَلَا
يَقْتُلُونَ ٱلنَّفْسَ ٱلَّتِى حَرَّمَ ٱللَّهُ إِلَّا بِٱلْحَقِّ وَلَا
يَزْنُونَ ۚ وَمَن يَفْعَلْ ذَٰلِكَ يَلْقَ أَثَامًا

68 And those who do not implore besides Allah any other god, and do not kill the soul which Allah has made sacred—except in the pursuit of justice—and do not commit adultery. Whoever does that will face penalties.

٦٩ يُضَٰعَفْ لَهُ ٱلْعَذَابُ يَوْمَ ٱلْقِيَٰمَةِ وَيَخْلُدْ فِيهِۦ
مُهَانًا

69 The punishment will be doubled for him on the Day of Resurrection, and he will dwell therein in humiliation forever.

٧٠ إِلَّا مَن تَابَ وَءَامَنَ وَعَمِلَ عَمَلًا صَٰلِحًا
فَأُوْلَٰٓئِكَ يُبَدِّلُ ٱللَّهُ سَيِّـَٔاتِهِمْ حَسَنَٰتٍ ۗ وَكَانَ ٱللَّهُ
غَفُورًا رَّحِيمًا

70 Except for those who repent, and believe, and do good deeds. These—Allah will replace their bad deeds with good deeds. Allah is ever Forgiving and Merciful.

٧١ وَمَن تَابَ وَعَمِلَ صَٰلِحًا فَإِنَّهُۥ يَتُوبُ إِلَى ٱللَّهِ
مَتَابًا

71 Whoever repents and acts righteously—has inclined towards Allah with repentance.

٧٢ وَٱلَّذِينَ لَا يَشْهَدُونَ ٱلزُّورَ وَإِذَا مَرُّواْ بِٱللَّغْوِ
مَرُّواْ كِرَامًا

72 And those who do not bear false witness; and when they come across indecencies, they pass by with dignity.

٧٣ وَٱلَّذِينَ إِذَا ذُكِّرُواْ بِـَٔايَٰتِ رَبِّهِمْ لَمْ يَخِرُّواْ
عَلَيْهَا صُمًّا وَعُمْيَانًا

73 And those who, when reminded of the revelations of their Lord, do not fall before them deaf and blind.

٧٤ وَٱلَّذِينَ يَقُولُونَ رَبَّنَا هَبْ لَنَا مِنْ أَزْوَٰجِنَا
وَذُرِّيَّٰتِنَا قُرَّةَ أَعْيُنٍ وَٱجْعَلْنَا لِلْمُتَّقِينَ إِمَامًا

74 And those who say, “Our Lord, grant us delight in our spouses and our children, and make us a good example for the righteous.”

٧٥ أُوْلَٰٓئِكَ يُجْزَوْنَ ٱلْغُرْفَةَ بِمَا صَبَرُواْ وَيُلَقَّوْنَ
فِيهَا تَحِيَّةً وَسَلَٰمًا

75 Those will be awarded the Chamber for their patience, and will be greeted therein with greetings and peace.

٧٦ خَٰلِدِينَ فِيهَا ۚ حَسُنَتْ مُسْتَقَرًّا وَمُقَامًا

76 Abiding therein forever—it is an excellent residence and destination.

٧٧ قُلْ مَا يَعْبَؤُا۟ بِكُمْ رَبِّى لَوْلَا دُعَآؤُكُمْ ۖ فَقَدْ كَذَّبْتُمْ فَسَوْفَ يَكُونُ لِزَامًۢا

77 Say, “What are you to my Lord without your prayers? You have denied the truth, and the inevitable will happen.”

26 The Poets الشعراء

بِسْمِ ٱللَّهِ ٱلرَّحْمَٰنِ ٱلرَّحِيمِ

In the name of Allah, the Gracious, the Merciful.

١ طسٓمٓ

1 Ta, Seen, Meem.

٢ تِلْكَ ءَايَٰتُ ٱلْكِتَٰبِ ٱلْمُبِينِ

2 These are the Verses of the Clarifying Book.

٣ لَعَلَّكَ بَٰخِعٌ نَّفْسَكَ أَلَّا يَكُونُوا۟ مُؤْمِنِينَ

3 Perhaps you will destroy yourself with grief, because they do not become believers.

٤ إِن نَّشَأْ نُنَزِّلْ عَلَيْهِم مِّنَ ٱلسَّمَآءِ ءَايَةً فَظَلَّتْ أَعْنَٰقُهُمْ لَهَا خَٰضِعِينَ

4 If We will, We can send down upon them a sign from heaven, at which their necks will stay bent in humility.

٥ وَمَا يَأْتِيهِم مِّن ذِكْرٍ مِّنَ ٱلرَّحْمَٰنِ مُحْدَثٍ إِلَّا كَانُوا۟ عَنْهُ مُعْرِضِينَ

5 No fresh reminder comes to them from the Most Merciful, but they turn their backs at it.

٦ فَقَدْ كَذَّبُوا۟ فَسَيَأْتِيهِمْ أَنۢبَٰٓؤُا۟ مَا كَانُوا۟ بِهِۦ يَسْتَهْزِءُونَ

6 They have denied the truth, but soon will come to them the news of what they ridiculed.

٧ أَوَلَمْ يَرَوْا۟ إِلَى ٱلْأَرْضِ كَمْ أَنۢبَتْنَا فِيهَا مِن كُلِّ زَوْجٍ كَرِيمٍ

7 Have they not seen the earth, and how many beautiful pairs We produced therein?

٨ إِنَّ فِى ذَٰلِكَ لَءَايَةً ۖ وَمَا كَانَ أَكْثَرُهُم مُّؤْمِنِينَ

8 Surely in this is a sign, but most of them are not believers.

٩ وَإِنَّ رَبَّكَ لَهُوَ ٱلْعَزِيزُ ٱلرَّحِيمُ

9 Most surely, your Lord is the Almighty, the Merciful.

١٠ وَإِذْ نَادَىٰ رَبُّكَ مُوسَىٰٓ أَنِ ٱئْتِ ٱلْقَوْمَ ٱلظَّٰلِمِينَ

10 Your Lord called to Moses, “Go to the tyrannical people.

١١ قَوْمَ فِرْعَوْنَ ۚ أَلَا يَتَّقُونَ

11 The people of Pharaoh. Will they not fear?”

١٢ قَالَ رَبِّ إِنِّىٓ أَخَافُ أَن يُكَذِّبُونِ	12 He said, “My Lord, I fear they will reject me.
١٣ وَيَضِيقُ صَدْرِى وَلَا يَنطَلِقُ لِسَانِى فَأَرْسِلْ إِلَىٰ هَٰرُونَ	13 And I become stressed, and my tongue is not fluent, so send Aaron too.
١٤ وَلَهُمْ عَلَىَّ ذَنۢبٌ فَأَخَافُ أَن يَقْتُلُونِ	14 And they have a charge against me, so I fear they will kill me.”
١٥ قَالَ كَلَّا ۖ فَٱذْهَبَا بِـَٔايَٰتِنَآ ۖ إِنَّا مَعَكُم مُّسْتَمِعُونَ	15 He said, “No. Go, both of you, with Our proofs. We will be with you, listening.
١٦ فَأْتِيَا فِرْعَوْنَ فَقُولَآ إِنَّا رَسُولُ رَبِّ ٱلْعَٰلَمِينَ	16 Go to Pharaoh, and say, ‘We are the Messengers of the Lord of the Worlds.
١٧ أَنْ أَرْسِلْ مَعَنَا بَنِىٓ إِسْرَٰٓءِيلَ	17 Let the Children of Israel go with us.’”
١٨ قَالَ أَلَمْ نُرَبِّكَ فِينَا وَلِيدًا وَلَبِثْتَ فِينَا مِنْ عُمُرِكَ سِنِينَ	18 He said, “Did we not raise you among us as a child, and you stayed among us for many of your years?
١٩ وَفَعَلْتَ فَعْلَتَكَ ٱلَّتِى فَعَلْتَ وَأَنتَ مِنَ ٱلْكَٰفِرِينَ	19 And you committed that deed you committed, and you were ungrateful.”
٢٠ قَالَ فَعَلْتُهَآ إِذًا وَأَنَا۠ مِنَ ٱلضَّآلِّينَ	20 He said, “I did it then, when I was of those astray.
٢١ فَفَرَرْتُ مِنكُمْ لَمَّا خِفْتُكُمْ فَوَهَبَ لِى رَبِّى حُكْمًا وَجَعَلَنِى مِنَ ٱلْمُرْسَلِينَ	21 And I fled from you when I feared you; but my Lord gave me wisdom, and made me one of the messengers.
٢٢ وَتِلْكَ نِعْمَةٌ تَمُنُّهَا عَلَىَّ أَنْ عَبَّدتَّ بَنِىٓ إِسْرَٰٓءِيلَ	22 Is that the favor you taunt me with, although you have enslaved the Children of Israel?”
٢٣ قَالَ فِرْعَوْنُ وَمَا رَبُّ ٱلْعَٰلَمِينَ	23 Pharaoh said, “And what is the Lord of the Worlds?”
٢٤ قَالَ رَبُّ ٱلسَّمَٰوَٰتِ وَٱلْأَرْضِ وَمَا بَيْنَهُمَآ ۖ إِن كُنتُم مُّوقِنِينَ	24 He said, “The Lord of the heavens and the earth, and everything between them, if you are aware.”
٢٥ قَالَ لِمَنْ حَوْلَهُۥٓ أَلَا تَسْتَمِعُونَ	25 He said to those around him, “Do you not hear?”
٢٦ قَالَ رَبُّكُمْ وَرَبُّ ءَابَآئِكُمُ ٱلْأَوَّلِينَ	26 He said, “Your Lord and the Lord of your ancestors of old.”

٢٧ قَالَ إِنَّ رَسُولَكُمُ ٱلَّذِىٓ أُرْسِلَ إِلَيْكُمْ لَمَجْنُونٌ	27 He said, "This messenger of yours, who is sent to you, is crazy."
٢٨ قَالَ رَبُّ ٱلْمَشْرِقِ وَٱلْمَغْرِبِ وَمَا بَيْنَهُمَآ ۖ إِن كُنتُمْ تَعْقِلُونَ	28 He said, "Lord of the East and the West, and everything between them, if you understand."
٢٩ قَالَ لَئِنِ ٱتَّخَذْتَ إِلَٰهًا غَيْرِى لَأَجْعَلَنَّكَ مِنَ ٱلْمَسْجُونِينَ	29 He said, "If you accept any god other than me, I will make you a prisoner."
٣٠ قَالَ أَوَلَوْ جِئْتُكَ بِشَىْءٍ مُّبِينٍ	30 He said, "What if I bring you something convincing?"
٣١ قَالَ فَأْتِ بِهِۦٓ إِن كُنتَ مِنَ ٱلصَّٰدِقِينَ	31 He said, "Bring it, if you are being truthful."
٣٢ فَأَلْقَىٰ عَصَاهُ فَإِذَا هِىَ ثُعْبَانٌ مُّبِينٌ	32 So he cast his staff; and it was a serpent, plain to see.
٣٣ وَنَزَعَ يَدَهُۥ فَإِذَا هِىَ بَيْضَآءُ لِلنَّٰظِرِينَ	33 And he pulled his hand; and it was white, for all to see.
٣٤ قَالَ لِلْمَلَإِ حَوْلَهُۥٓ إِنَّ هَٰذَا لَسَٰحِرٌ عَلِيمٌ	34 He said to the dignitaries around him, "This is a skilled magician.
٣٥ يُرِيدُ أَن يُخْرِجَكُم مِّنْ أَرْضِكُم بِسِحْرِهِۦ فَمَاذَا تَأْمُرُونَ	35 He intends to drive you out of your land with his magic, so what do you recommend?"
٣٦ قَالُوٓا۟ أَرْجِهْ وَأَخَاهُ وَٱبْعَثْ فِى ٱلْمَدَآئِنِ حَٰشِرِينَ	36 They said, "Delay him and his brother, and send recruiters to the cities.
٣٧ يَأْتُوكَ بِكُلِّ سَحَّارٍ عَلِيمٍ	37 To bring you every experienced magician."
٣٨ فَجُمِعَ ٱلسَّحَرَةُ لِمِيقَٰتِ يَوْمٍ مَّعْلُومٍ	38 So the magicians were gathered for the appointment on a specified day.
٣٩ وَقِيلَ لِلنَّاسِ هَلْ أَنتُم مُّجْتَمِعُونَ	39 And it was said to the people, "Are you all gathered?
٤٠ لَعَلَّنَا نَتَّبِعُ ٱلسَّحَرَةَ إِن كَانُوا۟ هُمُ ٱلْغَٰلِبِينَ	40 That we may follow the magicians, if they are the winners."
٤١ فَلَمَّا جَآءَ ٱلسَّحَرَةُ قَالُوا۟ لِفِرْعَوْنَ أَئِنَّ لَنَا لَأَجْرًا إِن كُنَّا نَحْنُ ٱلْغَٰلِبِينَ	41 When the magicians arrived, they said to Pharaoh, "Is there a reward for us, if we are the winners?"
٤٢ قَالَ نَعَمْ وَإِنَّكُمْ إِذًا لَّمِنَ ٱلْمُقَرَّبِينَ	42 He said, "Yes, and you will be among those favored."

٤٣ قَالَ لَهُم مُّوسَىٰٓ أَلْقُوا۟ مَآ أَنتُم مُّلْقُونَ

43 Moses said to them, “Present what you intend to present.”

٤٤ فَأَلْقَوْا۟ حِبَالَهُمْ وَعِصِيَّهُمْ وَقَالُوا۟ بِعِزَّةِ
فِرْعَوْنَ إِنَّا لَنَحْنُ ٱلْغَٰلِبُونَ

44 So they threw their ropes and their sticks, and said, “By the majesty of Pharaoh, we will be the winners.”

٤٥ فَأَلْقَىٰ مُوسَىٰ عَصَاهُ فَإِذَا هِىَ تَلْقَفُ مَا
يَأْفِكُونَ

45 Then Moses threw his staff, and behold, it began swallowing their trickery.

٤٦ فَأُلْقِىَ ٱلسَّحَرَةُ سَٰجِدِينَ

46 And the magicians fell down prostrating.

٤٧ قَالُوٓا۟ ءَامَنَّا بِرَبِّ ٱلْعَٰلَمِينَ

47 They said, “We have believed in the Lord of the Worlds.

٤٨ رَبِّ مُوسَىٰ وَهَٰرُونَ

48 The Lord of Moses and Aaron.”

٤٩ قَالَ ءَامَنتُمْ لَهُۥ قَبْلَ أَنْ ءَاذَنَ لَكُمْ ۖ إِنَّهُۥ
لَكَبِيرُكُمُ ٱلَّذِى عَلَّمَكُمُ ٱلسِّحْرَ فَلَسَوْفَ تَعْلَمُونَ ۚ
لَأُقَطِّعَنَّ أَيْدِيَكُمْ وَأَرْجُلَكُم مِّنْ خِلَٰفٍ
وَلَأُصَلِّبَنَّكُمْ أَجْمَعِينَ

49 He said, “Did you believe in Him before I have given you permission? He must be your chief, who taught you magic. You will soon know. I will cut off your hands and feet on opposite sides, and I will crucify you all.”

٥٠ قَالُوا۟ لَا ضَيْرَ ۖ إِنَّآ إِلَىٰ رَبِّنَا مُنقَلِبُونَ

50 They said, “No problem. To our Lord we will return.

٥١ إِنَّا نَطْمَعُ أَن يَغْفِرَ لَنَا رَبُّنَا خَطَٰيَٰنَآ أَن كُنَّآ
أَوَّلَ ٱلْمُؤْمِنِينَ

51 We are eager for our Lord to forgive us our sins, since we are the first of the believers.”

٥٢ وَأَوْحَيْنَآ إِلَىٰ مُوسَىٰٓ أَنْ أَسْرِ بِعِبَادِىٓ إِنَّكُم
مُّتَّبَعُونَ

52 And We inspired Moses: “Travel with My servants by night. You will be followed.”

٥٣ فَأَرْسَلَ فِرْعَوْنُ فِى ٱلْمَدَآئِنِ حَٰشِرِينَ

53 Pharaoh sent heralds to the cities.

٥٤ إِنَّ هَٰٓؤُلَآءِ لَشِرْذِمَةٌ قَلِيلُونَ

54 “These are a small gang.

٥٥ وَإِنَّهُمْ لَنَا لَغَآئِظُونَ

55 And they are enraging us.

٥٦ وَإِنَّا لَجَمِيعٌ حَٰذِرُونَ

56 But we are a vigilant multitude.”

٥٧ فَأَخْرَجْنَٰهُم مِّن جَنَّٰتٍ وَعُيُونٍ

57 So We drove them out of gardens and springs.

٥٨ وَكُنُوزٍ وَمَقَامٍ كَرِيمٍ

58 And treasures and noble dwellings.

٥٩ كَذَٰلِكَ وَأَوْرَثْنَٰهَا بَنِىٓ إِسْرَٰٓءِيلَ

59 So it was. And We made the Children of Israel inherit them.

٦٠ فَأَتْبَعُوهُم مُّشْرِقِينَ

60 And they pursued them at sunrise.

٦١ فَلَمَّا تَرَٰٓءَا ٱلْجَمْعَانِ قَالَ أَصْحَٰبُ مُوسَىٰٓ إِنَّا
لَمُدْرَكُونَ

61 When the two groups sighted each other, the followers of Moses said, “We are being overtaken.”

٦٢ قَالَ كَلَّآ ۖ إِنَّ مَعِىَ رَبِّى سَيَهْدِينِ

62 He said, “No; my Lord is with me, He will guide me.”

٦٣ فَأَوْحَيْنَآ إِلَىٰ مُوسَىٰٓ أَنِ ٱضْرِب بِّعَصَاكَ
ٱلْبَحْرَ ۖ فَٱنفَلَقَ فَكَانَ كُلُّ فِرْقٍ كَٱلطَّوْدِ ٱلْعَظِيمِ

63 We inspired Moses: “Strike the sea with your staff.” Whereupon it parted, and each part was like a huge hill.

٦٤ وَأَزْلَفْنَا ثَمَّ ٱلْءَاخَرِينَ

64 And there We brought the others near.

٦٥ وَأَنجَيْنَا مُوسَىٰ وَمَن مَّعَهُۥٓ أَجْمَعِينَ

65 And We saved Moses and those with him, all together.

٦٦ ثُمَّ أَغْرَقْنَا ٱلْءَاخَرِينَ

66 Then We drowned the others.

٦٧ إِنَّ فِى ذَٰلِكَ لَءَايَةً ۖ وَمَا كَانَ أَكْثَرُهُم
مُّؤْمِنِينَ

67 In that there is a sign, but most of them are not believers.

٦٨ وَإِنَّ رَبَّكَ لَهُوَ ٱلْعَزِيزُ ٱلرَّحِيمُ

68 Surely, your Lord is the Almighty, the Merciful.

٦٩ وَٱتْلُ عَلَيْهِمْ نَبَأَ إِبْرَٰهِيمَ

69 And relate to them the story of Abraham.

٧٠ إِذْ قَالَ لِأَبِيهِ وَقَوْمِهِۦ مَا تَعْبُدُونَ

70 When he said to his father and his people, “What do you worship?”

٧١ قَالُوا۟ نَعْبُدُ أَصْنَامًا فَنَظَلُّ لَهَا عَٰكِفِينَ

71 They said, “We worship idols, and we remain devoted to them.”

٧٢ قَالَ هَلْ يَسْمَعُونَكُمْ إِذْ تَدْعُونَ

72 He said, “Do they hear you when you pray?

٧٣ أَوْ يَنفَعُونَكُمْ أَوْ يَضُرُّونَ

73 Or do they benefit you, or harm you?”

٧٤ قَالُوا۟ بَلْ وَجَدْنَآ ءَابَآءَنَا كَذَٰلِكَ يَفْعَلُونَ

74 They said, “But we found our ancestors doing so.”

٧٥ قَالَ أَفَرَءَيْتُم مَّا كُنتُمْ تَعْبُدُونَ

75 He said, “Have you considered what you worship.

٧٦ أَنتُمْ وَءَابَآؤُكُمُ ٱلْأَقْدَمُونَ

76 You and your ancient ancestors?

٧٧ فَإِنَّهُمْ عَدُوٌّ لِّىٓ إِلَّا رَبَّ ٱلْعَٰلَمِينَ

77 They are enemies to me, but not so the Lord of the Worlds.

٧٨ ٱلَّذِى خَلَقَنِى فَهُوَ يَهْدِينِ

78 He who created me, and guides me.

٧٩ وَٱلَّذِى هُوَ يُطْعِمُنِى وَيَسْقِينِ

79 He who feeds me, and waters me.

٨٠ وَإِذَا مَرِضْتُ فَهُوَ يَشْفِينِ

80 And when I get sick, He heals me.

٨١ وَٱلَّذِى يُمِيتُنِى ثُمَّ يُحْيِينِ

81 He who makes me die, and then revives me.

٨٢ وَٱلَّذِىٓ أَطْمَعُ أَن يَغْفِرَ لِى خَطِيٓـَٔتِى يَوْمَ ٱلدِّينِ

82 He who, I hope, will forgive my sins on the Day of the Reckoning."

٨٣ رَبِّ هَبْ لِى حُكْمًا وَأَلْحِقْنِى بِٱلصَّٰلِحِينَ

83 "My Lord! Grant me wisdom, and include me with the righteous.

٨٤ وَٱجْعَل لِّى لِسَانَ صِدْقٍ فِى ٱلْءَاخِرِينَ

84 And give me a reputation of truth among the others.

٨٥ وَٱجْعَلْنِى مِن وَرَثَةِ جَنَّةِ ٱلنَّعِيمِ

85 And make me of the inheritors of the Garden of Bliss.

٨٦ وَٱغْفِرْ لِأَبِىٓ إِنَّهُۥ كَانَ مِنَ ٱلضَّآلِّينَ

86 And forgive my father—he was one of the misguided.

٨٧ وَلَا تُخْزِنِى يَوْمَ يُبْعَثُونَ

87 And do not disgrace me on the Day they are resurrected.

٨٨ يَوْمَ لَا يَنفَعُ مَالٌ وَلَا بَنُونَ

88 The Day when neither wealth nor children will help.

٨٩ إِلَّا مَنْ أَتَى ٱللَّهَ بِقَلْبٍ سَلِيمٍ

89 Except for him who comes to Allah with a sound heart."

٩٠ وَأُزْلِفَتِ ٱلْجَنَّةُ لِلْمُتَّقِينَ

90 And Paradise will be brought near for the righteous.

٩١ وَبُرِّزَتِ ٱلْجَحِيمُ لِلْغَاوِينَ

91 And the Blaze will be displayed to the deviators.

٩٢ وَقِيلَ لَهُمْ أَيْنَ مَا كُنتُمْ تَعْبُدُونَ

92 And it will be said to them, "Where are those you used to worship?"

٩٣ مِن دُونِ ٱللَّهِ هَلْ يَنصُرُونَكُمْ أَوْ يَنتَصِرُونَ

93 Besides Allah? Can they help you, or help themselves?"

٩٤ فَكُبْكِبُوا۟ فِيهَا هُمْ وَٱلْغَاوُۥنَ

94 Then they will be toppled into it, together with the seducers.

٩٥ وَجُنُودُ إِبْلِيسَ أَجْمَعُونَ

95 And the soldiers of Satan, all of them.

٩٦ قَالُواْ وَهُمْ فِيهَا يَخْتَصِمُونَ

96 They will say, as they feud in it.

٩٧ تَٱللَّهِ إِن كُنَّا لَفِى ضَلَٰلٍ مُّبِينٍ

97 “By Allah, We were in evident error.

٩٨ إِذْ نُسَوِّيكُم بِرَبِّ ٱلْعَٰلَمِينَ

98 For equating you with the Lord of the Worlds.

٩٩ وَمَآ أَضَلَّنَآ إِلَّا ٱلْمُجْرِمُونَ

99 No one misled us except the sinners.

١٠٠ فَمَا لَنَا مِن شَٰفِعِينَ

100 Now we have no intercessors.

١٠١ وَلَا صَدِيقٍ حَمِيمٍ

101 And no sincere friend.

١٠٢ فَلَوْ أَنَّ لَنَا كَرَّةً فَنَكُونَ مِنَ ٱلْمُؤْمِنِينَ

102 If only we could have another chance, we would be among the faithful.”

١٠٣ إِنَّ فِى ذَٰلِكَ لَءَايَةًۖ وَمَا كَانَ أَكْثَرُهُم
مُّؤْمِنِينَ

103 Surely in this is a sign, but most of them are not believers.

١٠٤ وَإِنَّ رَبَّكَ لَهُوَ ٱلْعَزِيزُ ٱلرَّحِيمُ

104 Your Lord is the Almighty, the Merciful.

١٠٥ كَذَّبَتْ قَوْمُ نُوحٍ ٱلْمُرْسَلِينَ

105 The people of Noah disbelieved the messengers.

١٠٦ إِذْ قَالَ لَهُمْ أَخُوهُمْ نُوحٌ أَلَا تَتَّقُونَ

106 Their brother Noah said to them, “Do you not fear?

١٠٧ إِنِّى لَكُمْ رَسُولٌ أَمِينٌ

107 I am to you a faithful messenger.

١٠٨ فَٱتَّقُواْ ٱللَّهَ وَأَطِيعُونِ

108 So fear Allah, and obey me.

١٠٩ وَمَآ أَسْـَٔلُكُمْ عَلَيْهِ مِنْ أَجْرٍۖ إِنْ أَجْرِىَ إِلَّا
عَلَىٰ رَبِّ ٱلْعَٰلَمِينَ

109 I ask of you no payment for this. My payment is only from the Lord of the Worlds.

١١٠ فَٱتَّقُواْ ٱللَّهَ وَأَطِيعُونِ

110 So fear Allah, and obey me.”

١١١ قَالُوٓاْ أَنُؤْمِنُ لَكَ وَٱتَّبَعَكَ ٱلْأَرْذَلُونَ

111 They said, “Shall we believe in you, when it is the lowliest who follow you?”

١١٢ قَالَ وَمَا عِلْمِى بِمَا كَانُواْ يَعْمَلُونَ

112 He said, “What do I know about what they do?

١١٣ إِنْ حِسَابُهُمْ إِلَّا عَلَىٰ رَبِّىۖ لَوْ تَشْعُرُونَ

113 Their account rests only with my Lord, if you have sense.

114 And I am not about to drive away the believers.

١١٤ وَمَآ أَنَا۠ بِطَارِدِ ٱلْمُؤْمِنِينَ

115 I am only a clear warner."

١١٥ إِنْ أَنَا۠ إِلَّا نَذِيرٌ مُّبِينٌ

116 They said, "If you do not refrain, O Noah, you will be stoned."

١١٦ قَالُوا۟ لَئِن لَّمْ تَنتَهِ يَٰنُوحُ لَتَكُونَنَّ مِنَ ٱلْمَرْجُومِينَ

117 He said, "My Lord, my people have denied me.

١١٧ قَالَ رَبِّ إِنَّ قَوْمِى كَذَّبُونِ

118 So judge between me and them decisively, and deliver me and the believers who are with me.

١١٨ فَٱفْتَحْ بَيْنِى وَبَيْنَهُمْ فَتْحًا وَنَجِّنِى وَمَن مَّعِىَ مِنَ ٱلْمُؤْمِنِينَ

119 So We delivered him and those with him in the laden Ark.

١١٩ فَأَنجَيْنَٰهُ وَمَن مَّعَهُۥ فِى ٱلْفُلْكِ ٱلْمَشْحُونِ

120 Then We drowned the rest.

١٢٠ ثُمَّ أَغْرَقْنَا بَعْدُ ٱلْبَاقِينَ

121 In that is a sign, but most of them are not believers.

١٢١ إِنَّ فِى ذَٰلِكَ لَءَايَةً ۖ وَمَا كَانَ أَكْثَرُهُم مُّؤْمِنِينَ

122 Your Lord is the Almighty, the Merciful.

١٢٢ وَإِنَّ رَبَّكَ لَهُوَ ٱلْعَزِيزُ ٱلرَّحِيمُ

123 Aad disbelieved the messengers.

١٢٣ كَذَّبَتْ عَادٌ ٱلْمُرْسَلِينَ

124 When their brother Hud said to them, "Do you not fear?

١٢٤ إِذْ قَالَ لَهُمْ أَخُوهُمْ هُودٌ أَلَا تَتَّقُونَ

125 I am to you a faithful messenger.

١٢٥ إِنِّى لَكُمْ رَسُولٌ أَمِينٌ

126 So fear Allah, and obey me.

١٢٦ فَٱتَّقُوا۟ ٱللَّهَ وَأَطِيعُونِ

127 I ask of you no payment for this. My payment is only from the Lord of the Worlds.

١٢٧ وَمَآ أَسْـَٔلُكُمْ عَلَيْهِ مِنْ أَجْرٍ ۖ إِنْ أَجْرِىَ إِلَّا عَلَىٰ رَبِّ ٱلْعَٰلَمِينَ

128 Do you build a monument on every height for vanity's sake?

١٢٨ أَتَبْنُونَ بِكُلِّ رِيعٍ ءَايَةً تَعْبَثُونَ

129 And you set up fortresses, hoping to live forever?

١٢٩ وَتَتَّخِذُونَ مَصَانِعَ لَعَلَّكُمْ تَخْلُدُونَ

130 And when you strike, you strike mercilessly?

١٣٠ وَإِذَا بَطَشْتُم بَطَشْتُمْ جَبَّارِينَ

131 So fear Allah, and obey me.

١٣١ فَٱتَّقُوا۟ ٱللَّهَ وَأَطِيعُونِ

١٣٢ وَٱتَّقُوا۟ ٱلَّذِىٓ أَمَدَّكُم بِمَا تَعْلَمُونَ	132 And reverence Him, who supplied you with everything you know.
١٣٣ أَمَدَّكُم بِأَنْعَٰمٍ وَبَنِينَ	133 He supplied you with livestock and children.
١٣٤ وَجَنَّٰتٍ وَعُيُونٍ	134 And gardens and springs.
١٣٥ إِنِّىٓ أَخَافُ عَلَيْكُمْ عَذَابَ يَوْمٍ عَظِيمٍ	135 I fear for you the punishment of an awesome Day."
١٣٦ قَالُوا۟ سَوَآءٌ عَلَيْنَآ أَوَعَظْتَ أَمْ لَمْ تَكُن مِّنَ ٱلْوَٰعِظِينَ	136 They said, "It is the same for us, whether you lecture us, or do not lecture.
١٣٧ إِنْ هَٰذَآ إِلَّا خُلُقُ ٱلْأَوَّلِينَ	137 This is nothing but morals of the ancients.
١٣٨ وَمَا نَحْنُ بِمُعَذَّبِينَ	138 And we will not be punished."
١٣٩ فَكَذَّبُوهُ فَأَهْلَكْنَٰهُمْ ۗ إِنَّ فِى ذَٰلِكَ لَءَايَةً ۖ وَمَا كَانَ أَكْثَرُهُم مُّؤْمِنِينَ	139 So they denied him, and We destroyed them. Surely in this is a sign, but most of them are not believers.
١٤٠ وَإِنَّ رَبَّكَ لَهُوَ ٱلْعَزِيزُ ٱلرَّحِيمُ	140 Your Lord is the Almighty, the Merciful.
١٤١ كَذَّبَتْ ثَمُودُ ٱلْمُرْسَلِينَ	141 Thamood disbelieved the messengers.
١٤٢ إِذْ قَالَ لَهُمْ أَخُوهُمْ صَٰلِحٌ أَلَا تَتَّقُونَ	142 When their brother Saleh said to them, "Do you not fear?
١٤٣ إِنِّى لَكُمْ رَسُولٌ أَمِينٌ	143 I am to you a faithful messenger.
١٤٤ فَٱتَّقُوا۟ ٱللَّهَ وَأَطِيعُونِ	144 So fear Allah, and obey me.
١٤٥ وَمَآ أَسْـَٔلُكُمْ عَلَيْهِ مِنْ أَجْرٍ ۖ إِنْ أَجْرِىَ إِلَّا عَلَىٰ رَبِّ ٱلْعَٰلَمِينَ	145 I ask of you no payment for it. My payment is only from the Lord of the Worlds.
١٤٦ أَتُتْرَكُونَ فِى مَا هَٰهُنَآ ءَامِنِينَ	146 Will you be left secure in what is here?
١٤٧ فِى جَنَّٰتٍ وَعُيُونٍ	147 In gardens and springs?
١٤٨ وَزُرُوعٍ وَنَخْلٍ طَلْعُهَا هَضِيمٌ	148 And fields, and palm-trees whose fruits are delicious?
١٤٩ وَتَنْحِتُونَ مِنَ ٱلْجِبَالِ بُيُوتًا فَٰرِهِينَ	149 And you skillfully carve houses in the mountains?

١٥٠ فَٱتَّقُوا۟ ٱللَّهَ وَأَطِيعُونِ	150 So fear Allah, and obey me.
١٥١ وَلَا تُطِيعُوٓا۟ أَمْرَ ٱلْمُسْرِفِينَ	151 And do not obey the command of the extravagant.
١٥٢ ٱلَّذِينَ يُفْسِدُونَ فِى ٱلْأَرْضِ وَلَا يُصْلِحُونَ	152 Who spread turmoil on earth, and do not reform."
١٥٣ قَالُوٓا۟ إِنَّمَآ أَنتَ مِنَ ٱلْمُسَحَّرِينَ	153 They said, "You are surely one of the bewitched.
١٥٤ مَآ أَنتَ إِلَّا بَشَرٌ مِّثْلُنَا فَأْتِ بِـَٔايَةٍ إِن كُنتَ مِنَ ٱلصَّـٰدِقِينَ	154 You are nothing but a man like us. So bring us a sign, if you are truthful.
١٥٥ قَالَ هَـٰذِهِۦ نَاقَةٌ لَّهَا شِرْبٌ وَلَكُمْ شِرْبُ يَوْمٍ مَّعْلُومٍ	155 He said, "This is a she-camel; she has her turn of drinking, and you have your turn of drinking—on a specified day.
١٥٦ وَلَا تَمَسُّوهَا بِسُوٓءٍ فَيَأْخُذَكُمْ عَذَابُ يَوْمٍ عَظِيمٍ	156 And do not touch her with harm, lest the punishment of a great day seizes you."
١٥٧ فَعَقَرُوهَا فَأَصْبَحُوا۟ نَـٰدِمِينَ	157 But they slaughtered her, and became full of remorse.
١٥٨ فَأَخَذَهُمُ ٱلْعَذَابُ ۗ إِنَّ فِى ذَٰلِكَ لَـَٔايَةً ۖ وَمَا كَانَ أَكْثَرُهُم مُّؤْمِنِينَ	158 So the punishment overtook them. Surely in this is a sign, but most of them are not believers.
١٥٩ وَإِنَّ رَبَّكَ لَهُوَ ٱلْعَزِيزُ ٱلرَّحِيمُ	159 Your Lord is the Almighty, the Merciful.
١٦٠ كَذَّبَتْ قَوْمُ لُوطٍ ٱلْمُرْسَلِينَ	160 The people of Lot disbelieved the messengers.
١٦١ إِذْ قَالَ لَهُمْ أَخُوهُمْ لُوطٌ أَلَا تَتَّقُونَ	161 When their brother Lot said to them, "Do you not fear?
١٦٢ إِنِّى لَكُمْ رَسُولٌ أَمِينٌ	162 I am to you a faithful messenger.
١٦٣ فَٱتَّقُوا۟ ٱللَّهَ وَأَطِيعُونِ	163 So fear Allah, and obey me.
١٦٤ وَمَآ أَسْـَٔلُكُمْ عَلَيْهِ مِنْ أَجْرٍ ۖ إِنْ أَجْرِىَ إِلَّا عَلَىٰ رَبِّ ٱلْعَـٰلَمِينَ	164 I ask of you no payment for it. My payment is only from the Lord of the Worlds.
١٦٥ أَتَأْتُونَ ٱلذُّكْرَانَ مِنَ ٱلْعَـٰلَمِينَ	165 Do you approach the males of the world?

166 And forsake the wives your Lord created for you? Indeed, you are intrusive people."

١٦٦ وَتَذَرُونَ مَا خَلَقَ لَكُمْ رَبُّكُم مِّنْ أَزْوَٰجِكُم ۚ
بَلْ أَنتُمْ قَوْمٌ عَادُونَ

167 They said, "Unless you refrain, O Lot, you will be expelled."

١٦٧ قَالُوا۟ لَئِن لَّمْ تَنتَهِ يَٰلُوطُ لَتَكُونَنَّ مِنَ
ٱلْمُخْرَجِينَ

168 He said, "I certainly deplore your conduct."

١٦٨ قَالَ إِنِّى لِعَمَلِكُم مِّنَ ٱلْقَالِينَ

169 "My Lord, save me and my family from what they do."

١٦٩ رَبِّ نَجِّنِى وَأَهْلِى مِمَّا يَعْمَلُونَ

170 So We saved him and his family, altogether.

١٧٠ فَنَجَّيْنَٰهُ وَأَهْلَهُۥٓ أَجْمَعِينَ

171 Except for an old woman among those who tarried.

١٧١ إِلَّا عَجُوزًا فِى ٱلْغَٰبِرِينَ

172 Then We destroyed the others.

١٧٢ ثُمَّ دَمَّرْنَا ٱلْءَاخَرِينَ

173 And We rained down on them a rain. Dreadful is the rain of those forewarned.

١٧٣ وَأَمْطَرْنَا عَلَيْهِم مَّطَرًا ۖ فَسَآءَ مَطَرُ
ٱلْمُنذَرِينَ

174 Surely in this is a sign, but most of them are not believers.

١٧٤ إِنَّ فِى ذَٰلِكَ لَءَايَةً ۖ وَمَا كَانَ أَكْثَرُهُم
مُّؤْمِنِينَ

175 Your Lord is the Almighty, the Merciful.

١٧٥ وَإِنَّ رَبَّكَ لَهُوَ ٱلْعَزِيزُ ٱلرَّحِيمُ

176 The People of the Woods disbelieved the messengers.

١٧٦ كَذَّبَ أَصْحَٰبُ لْـَٔيْكَةِ ٱلْمُرْسَلِينَ

177 When Shuaib said to them, "Do you not fear?

١٧٧ إِذْ قَالَ لَهُمْ شُعَيْبٌ أَلَا تَتَّقُونَ

178 I am to you a trustworthy messenger.

١٧٨ إِنِّى لَكُمْ رَسُولٌ أَمِينٌ

179 So fear Allah, and obey me.

١٧٩ فَٱتَّقُوا۟ ٱللَّهَ وَأَطِيعُونِ

180 I ask of you no payment for it. My payment is only from the Lord of the Worlds.

١٨٠ وَمَآ أَسْـَٔلُكُمْ عَلَيْهِ مِنْ أَجْرٍ ۖ إِنْ أَجْرِىَ إِلَّا
عَلَىٰ رَبِّ ٱلْعَٰلَمِينَ

181 Give full measure, and do not cheat.

١٨١ أَوْفُوا۟ ٱلْكَيْلَ وَلَا تَكُونُوا۟ مِنَ ٱلْمُخْسِرِينَ

182 And weigh with accurate scales.

١٨٢ وَزِنُوا۟ بِٱلْقِسْطَاسِ ٱلْمُسْتَقِيمِ

١٨٣ وَلَا تَبۡخَسُواْ ٱلنَّاسَ أَشۡيَآءَهُمۡ وَلَا تَعۡثَوۡاْ
فِي ٱلۡأَرۡضِ مُفۡسِدِينَ

183 And do not defraud people of their belongings, and do not work corruption in the land.

١٨٤ وَٱتَّقُواْ ٱلَّذِي خَلَقَكُمۡ وَٱلۡجِبِلَّةَ ٱلۡأَوَّلِينَ

184 And fear Him who created you and the masses of old."

١٨٥ قَالُوٓاْ إِنَّمَآ أَنتَ مِنَ ٱلۡمُسَحَّرِينَ

185 They said, "You are one of those bewitched.

١٨٦ وَمَآ أَنتَ إِلَّا بَشَرٞ مِّثۡلُنَا وَإِن نَّظُنُّكَ لَمِنَ
ٱلۡكَٰذِبِينَ

186 And you are nothing but a man like us; and we think that you are a liar.

١٨٧ فَأَسۡقِطۡ عَلَيۡنَا كِسَفٗا مِّنَ ٱلسَّمَآءِ إِن كُنتَ
مِنَ ٱلصَّٰدِقِينَ

187 So bring down on us pieces from the sky, if you are truthful."

١٨٨ قَالَ رَبِّيٓ أَعۡلَمُ بِمَا تَعۡمَلُونَ

188 He said, "My Lord is Well Aware of what you do."

١٨٩ فَكَذَّبُوهُ فَأَخَذَهُمۡ عَذَابُ يَوۡمِ ٱلظُّلَّةِۚ إِنَّهُۥ
كَانَ عَذَابَ يَوۡمٍ عَظِيمٍ

189 But they denied him. So the punishment of the day of gloom gripped them. It was the punishment of a great day.

١٩٠ إِنَّ فِي ذَٰلِكَ لَأٓيَةٗۖ وَمَا كَانَ أَكۡثَرُهُم
مُّؤۡمِنِينَ

190 Surely in this is a sign, but most of them are not believers.

١٩١ وَإِنَّ رَبَّكَ لَهُوَ ٱلۡعَزِيزُ ٱلرَّحِيمُ

191 Your Lord is the Almighty, the Merciful.

١٩٢ وَإِنَّهُۥ لَتَنزِيلُ رَبِّ ٱلۡعَٰلَمِينَ

192 It is a revelation from the Lord of the Worlds.

١٩٣ نَزَلَ بِهِ ٱلرُّوحُ ٱلۡأَمِينُ

193 The Honest Spirit came down with it.

١٩٤ عَلَىٰ قَلۡبِكَ لِتَكُونَ مِنَ ٱلۡمُنذِرِينَ

194 Upon your heart, that you may be one of the warners.

١٩٥ بِلِسَانٍ عَرَبِيّٖ مُّبِينٖ

195 In a clear Arabic tongue.

١٩٦ وَإِنَّهُۥ لَفِي زُبُرِ ٱلۡأَوَّلِينَ

196 And it is in the scriptures of the ancients.

١٩٧ أَوَلَمۡ يَكُن لَّهُمۡ ءَايَةً أَن يَعۡلَمَهُۥ عُلَمَٰٓؤُاْ بَنِيٓ
إِسۡرَٰٓءِيلَ

197 Is it not a sign for them that the scholars of the Children of Israel recognized it?

١٩٨ وَلَوۡ نَزَّلۡنَٰهُ عَلَىٰ بَعۡضِ ٱلۡأَعۡجَمِينَ

198 Had We revealed it to one of the foreigners.

١٩٩ فَقَرَأَهُۥ عَلَيْهِم مَّا كَانُوا۟ بِهِۦ مُؤْمِنِينَ	199 And he had recited it to them, they still would not have believed in it.
٢٠٠ كَذَٰلِكَ سَلَكْنَٰهُ فِى قُلُوبِ ٱلْمُجْرِمِينَ	200 Thus We make it pass through the hearts of the guilty.
٢٠١ لَا يُؤْمِنُونَ بِهِۦ حَتَّىٰ يَرَوُا۟ ٱلْعَذَابَ ٱلْأَلِيمَ	201 They will not believe in it until they witness the painful punishment.
٢٠٢ فَيَأْتِيَهُم بَغْتَةً وَهُمْ لَا يَشْعُرُونَ	202 It will come to them suddenly, while they are unaware.
٢٠٣ فَيَقُولُوا۟ هَلْ نَحْنُ مُنظَرُونَ	203 Then they will say, “Are we given any respite?”
٢٠٤ أَفَبِعَذَابِنَا يَسْتَعْجِلُونَ	204 Do they seek to hasten Our punishment?
٢٠٥ أَفَرَءَيْتَ إِن مَّتَّعْنَٰهُمْ سِنِينَ	205 Have you considered: if We let them enjoy themselves for some years.
٢٠٦ ثُمَّ جَآءَهُم مَّا كَانُوا۟ يُوعَدُونَ	206 Then there comes to them what they were promised.
٢٠٧ مَآ أَغْنَىٰ عَنْهُم مَّا كَانُوا۟ يُمَتَّعُونَ	207 Of what avail to them will be their past enjoyments?
٢٠٨ وَمَآ أَهْلَكْنَا مِن قَرْيَةٍ إِلَّا لَهَا مُنذِرُونَ	208 Never did We destroy a town, but it had warners.
٢٠٩ ذِكْرَىٰ وَمَا كُنَّا ظَٰلِمِينَ	209 As a reminder—We are never unjust.
٢١٠ وَمَا تَنَزَّلَتْ بِهِ ٱلشَّيَٰطِينُ	210 It was not the devils that revealed it.
٢١١ وَمَا يَنۢبَغِى لَهُمْ وَمَا يَسْتَطِيعُونَ	211 It is not in their interests, nor in their power.
٢١٢ إِنَّهُمْ عَنِ ٱلسَّمْعِ لَمَعْزُولُونَ	212 They are barred from hearing.
٢١٣ فَلَا تَدْعُ مَعَ ٱللَّهِ إِلَٰهًا ءَاخَرَ فَتَكُونَ مِنَ ٱلْمُعَذَّبِينَ	213 So do not pray to another god with Allah, else you will be of those tormented.
٢١٤ وَأَنذِرْ عَشِيرَتَكَ ٱلْأَقْرَبِينَ	214 And warn your close relatives.
٢١٥ وَٱخْفِضْ جَنَاحَكَ لِمَنِ ٱتَّبَعَكَ مِنَ ٱلْمُؤْمِنِينَ	215 And lower your wing to those of the believers who follow you.
٢١٦ فَإِنْ عَصَوْكَ فَقُلْ إِنِّى بَرِىٓءٌ مِّمَّا تَعْمَلُونَ	216 And if they disobey you, say, “I am innocent of what you do.”

٢١٧ وَتَوَكَّلْ عَلَى ٱلْعَزِيزِ ٱلرَّحِيمِ	217 And put your trust in the Almighty, the Merciful.
٢١٨ ٱلَّذِى يَرَىٰكَ حِينَ تَقُومُ	218 He Who sees you when you rise.
٢١٩ وَتَقَلُّبَكَ فِى ٱلسَّٰجِدِينَ	219 And your devotions amidst the worshipers.
٢٢٠ إِنَّهُۥ هُوَ ٱلسَّمِيعُ ٱلْعَلِيمُ	220 He is indeed the Hearer, the Aware.
٢٢١ هَلْ أُنَبِّئُكُمْ عَلَىٰ مَن تَنَزَّلُ ٱلشَّيَٰطِينُ	221 Shall I inform you upon whom the devils descend?
٢٢٢ تَنَزَّلُ عَلَىٰ كُلِّ أَفَّاكٍ أَثِيمٍ	222 They descend upon every sinful liar.
٢٢٣ يُلْقُونَ ٱلسَّمْعَ وَأَكْثَرُهُمْ كَٰذِبُونَ	223 They give ear, and most of them are liars.
٢٢٤ وَٱلشُّعَرَآءُ يَتَّبِعُهُمُ ٱلْغَاوُۥنَ	224 And as for the poets—the deviators follow them.
٢٢٥ أَلَمْ تَرَ أَنَّهُمْ فِى كُلِّ وَادٍ يَهِيمُونَ	225 Do you not see how they ramble in every style?
٢٢٦ وَأَنَّهُمْ يَقُولُونَ مَا لَا يَفْعَلُونَ	226 And how they say what they do not do?
٢٢٧ إِلَّا ٱلَّذِينَ ءَامَنُوا۟ وَعَمِلُوا۟ ٱلصَّٰلِحَٰتِ وَذَكَرُوا۟ ٱللَّهَ كَثِيرًا وَٱنتَصَرُوا۟ مِنۢ بَعْدِ مَا ظُلِمُوا۟ ۗ وَسَيَعْلَمُ ٱلَّذِينَ ظَلَمُوٓا۟ أَىَّ مُنقَلَبٍ يَنقَلِبُونَ	227 Except for those who believe, and do good deeds, and remember Allah frequently, and defend themselves after they are wronged. As for those who do wrong, they will know by what overturning they will be overturned.

27 The Ant النمل

بِسْمِ ٱللَّهِ ٱلرَّحْمَٰنِ ٱلرَّحِيمِ	In the name of Allah, the Gracious, the Merciful.
١ طسٓ ۚ تِلْكَ ءَايَٰتُ ٱلْقُرْءَانِ وَكِتَابٍ مُّبِينٍ	1 Ta, Seen. These are the Signs of the Quran—a book that makes things clear.
٢ هُدًى وَبُشْرَىٰ لِلْمُؤْمِنِينَ	2 Guidance and good news for the believers.

٣ ٱلَّذِينَ يُقِيمُونَ ٱلصَّلَوٰةَ وَيُؤْتُونَ ٱلزَّكَوٰةَ وَهُم
بِٱلْءَاخِرَةِ هُمْ يُوقِنُونَ

3 Those who observe the prayers, and give charity regularly, and are certain of the Hereafter.

٤ إِنَّ ٱلَّذِينَ لَا يُؤْمِنُونَ بِٱلْءَاخِرَةِ زَيَّنَّا لَهُمْ
أَعْمَٰلَهُمْ فَهُمْ يَعْمَهُونَ

4 As for those who do not believe in the Hereafter: We made their deeds appear good to them, so they wander aimlessly.

٥ أُو۟لَٰٓئِكَ ٱلَّذِينَ لَهُمْ سُوٓءُ ٱلْعَذَابِ وَهُمْ فِى
ٱلْءَاخِرَةِ هُمُ ٱلْأَخْسَرُونَ

5 It is they who will receive the grievous punishment—and in the Hereafter they will be the greatest losers.

٦ وَإِنَّكَ لَتُلَقَّى ٱلْقُرْءَانَ مِن لَّدُنْ حَكِيمٍ عَلِيمٍ

6 You are receiving the Quran from an All-Wise, All-Knowing.

٧ إِذْ قَالَ مُوسَىٰ لِأَهْلِهِۦٓ إِنِّىٓ ءَانَسْتُ نَارًا
سَـَٔاتِيكُم مِّنْهَا بِخَبَرٍ أَوْ ءَاتِيكُم بِشِهَابٍ قَبَسٍ
لَّعَلَّكُمْ تَصْطَلُونَ

7 When Moses said to his family, "I have glimpsed a fire. I will bring you some news from it; or bring you a firebrand, that you may warm yourselves."

٨ فَلَمَّا جَآءَهَا نُودِىَ أَنۢ بُورِكَ مَن فِى ٱلنَّارِ
وَمَنْ حَوْلَهَا وَسُبْحَٰنَ ٱللَّهِ رَبِّ ٱلْعَٰلَمِينَ

8 Then, when he reached it, he was called: "Blessed is He who is within the fire, and He who is around it, and glorified be Allah, Lord of the Worlds.

٩ يَٰمُوسَىٰٓ إِنَّهُۥٓ أَنَا ٱللَّهُ ٱلْعَزِيزُ ٱلْحَكِيمُ

9 O Moses, it is I, Allah, the Almighty, the Wise.

١٠ وَأَلْقِ عَصَاكَ ۚ فَلَمَّا رَءَاهَا تَهْتَزُّ كَأَنَّهَا جَآنٌّ
وَلَّىٰ مُدْبِرًا وَلَمْ يُعَقِّبْ ۚ يَٰمُوسَىٰ لَا تَخَفْ إِنِّى
لَا يَخَافُ لَدَىَّ ٱلْمُرْسَلُونَ

10 Throw down your staff." But when he saw it quivering, as though it were a demon, he turned around not looking back. "O Moses, do not fear; the messengers do not fear in My presence.

١١ إِلَّا مَن ظَلَمَ ثُمَّ بَدَّلَ حُسْنًۢا بَعْدَ سُوٓءٍ فَإِنِّى
غَفُورٌ رَّحِيمٌ

11 But whoever has done wrong, and then substituted goodness in place of evil. I am Forgiving and Merciful.

١٢ وَأَدْخِلْ يَدَكَ فِى جَيْبِكَ تَخْرُجْ بَيْضَآءَ مِنْ
غَيْرِ سُوٓءٍ ۖ فِى تِسْعِ ءَايَٰتٍ إِلَىٰ فِرْعَوْنَ
وَقَوْمِهِۦٓ ۚ إِنَّهُمْ كَانُوا۟ قَوْمًا فَٰسِقِينَ

12 Put your hand inside your pocket, and it will come out white, without blemish—among nine miracles to Pharaoh and his people, for they are immoral people."

١٣ فَلَمَّا جَآءَتْهُمْ ءَايَٰتُنَا مُبْصِرَةً قَالُوا۟ هَٰذَا
سِحْرٌ مُّبِينٌ

13 Yet when Our enlightening signs came to them, they said, “This is obvious witchcraft.”

١٤ وَجَحَدُوا۟ بِهَا وَٱسْتَيْقَنَتْهَآ أَنفُسُهُمْ ظُلْمًا
وَعُلُوًّا ۚ فَٱنظُرْ كَيْفَ كَانَ عَٰقِبَةُ ٱلْمُفْسِدِينَ

14 And they rejected them, although their souls were certain of them, out of wickedness and pride. So see how the outcome was for the mischief-makers.

١٥ وَلَقَدْ ءَاتَيْنَا دَاوُۥدَ وَسُلَيْمَٰنَ عِلْمًا ۖ وَقَالَا
ٱلْحَمْدُ لِلَّهِ ٱلَّذِى فَضَّلَنَا عَلَىٰ كَثِيرٍ مِّنْ عِبَادِهِ
ٱلْمُؤْمِنِينَ

15 And We gave David and Solomon knowledge. They said, “Praise Allah, who has favored us over many of His believing servants.”

١٦ وَوَرِثَ سُلَيْمَٰنُ دَاوُۥدَ ۖ وَقَالَ يَٰٓأَيُّهَا ٱلنَّاسُ
عُلِّمْنَا مَنطِقَ ٱلطَّيْرِ وَأُوتِينَا مِن كُلِّ شَىْءٍ ۖ إِنَّ
هَٰذَا لَهُوَ ٱلْفَضْلُ ٱلْمُبِينُ

16 And Solomon succeeded David. He said, “O people, we were taught the language of birds, and we were given from everything. This is indeed a real blessing.”

١٧ وَحُشِرَ لِسُلَيْمَٰنَ جُنُودُهُۥ مِنَ ٱلْجِنِّ وَٱلْإِنسِ
وَٱلطَّيْرِ فَهُمْ يُوزَعُونَ

17 To the service of Solomon were mobilized his troops of sprites, and men, and birds—all held in strict order.

١٨ حَتَّىٰٓ إِذَآ أَتَوْا۟ عَلَىٰ وَادِ ٱلنَّمْلِ قَالَتْ نَمْلَةٌ
يَٰٓأَيُّهَا ٱلنَّمْلُ ٱدْخُلُوا۟ مَسَٰكِنَكُمْ لَا يَحْطِمَنَّكُمْ
سُلَيْمَٰنُ وَجُنُودُهُۥ وَهُمْ لَا يَشْعُرُونَ

18 Until, when they came upon the Valley of Ants, an ant said, “O ants! Go into your nests, lest Solomon and his troops crush you without noticing.”

١٩ فَتَبَسَّمَ ضَاحِكًا مِّن قَوْلِهَا وَقَالَ رَبِّ
أَوْزِعْنِىٓ أَنْ أَشْكُرَ نِعْمَتَكَ ٱلَّتِىٓ أَنْعَمْتَ عَلَىَّ
وَعَلَىٰ وَٰلِدَىَّ وَأَنْ أَعْمَلَ صَٰلِحًا تَرْضَىٰهُ
وَأَدْخِلْنِى بِرَحْمَتِكَ فِى عِبَادِكَ ٱلصَّٰلِحِينَ

19 He smiled and laughed at her words, and said, “My Lord, direct me to be thankful for the blessings you have bestowed upon me and upon my parents, and to do good works that please You. And admit me, by Your grace, into the company of Your virtuous servants.”

٢٠ وَتَفَقَّدَ ٱلطَّيْرَ فَقَالَ مَا لِىَ لَآ أَرَى ٱلْهُدْهُدَ أَمْ
كَانَ مِنَ ٱلْغَآئِبِينَ

20 Then he inspected the birds, and said, “Why do I not see the hoopoe? Or is he among the absentees?

٢١ لَأُعَذِّبَنَّهُۥ عَذَابًا شَدِيدًا أَوْ لَأَا۟ذْبَحَنَّهُۥٓ أَوْ
لَيَأْتِيَنِّى بِسُلْطَٰنٍ مُّبِينٍ

21 I will punish him most severely, or slay him, unless he gives me a valid excuse.”

٢٢ فَمَكَثَ غَيْرَ بَعِيدٍ فَقَالَ أَحَطتُ بِمَا لَمْ تُحِطْ بِهِۦ وَجِئْتُكَ مِن سَبَإٍۭ بِنَبَإٍ يَقِينٍ

22 But he did not stay for long. He said, "I have learnt something you did not know. I have come to you from Sheba, with reliable information.

٢٣ إِنِّى وَجَدتُّ ٱمْرَأَةً تَمْلِكُهُمْ وَأُوتِيَتْ مِن كُلِّ شَىْءٍ وَلَهَا عَرْشٌ عَظِيمٌ

23 I found a woman ruling over them, and she was given of everything, and she has a magnificent throne.

٢٤ وَجَدتُّهَا وَقَوْمَهَا يَسْجُدُونَ لِلشَّمْسِ مِن دُونِ ٱللَّهِ وَزَيَّنَ لَهُمُ ٱلشَّيْطَٰنُ أَعْمَٰلَهُمْ فَصَدَّهُمْ عَنِ ٱلسَّبِيلِ فَهُمْ لَا يَهْتَدُونَ

24 I found her and her people worshiping the sun, instead of Allah. Satan made their conduct appear good to them, and diverted them from the path, so they are not guided.

٢٥ أَلَّا يَسْجُدُوا۟ لِلَّهِ ٱلَّذِى يُخْرِجُ ٱلْخَبْءَ فِى ٱلسَّمَٰوَٰتِ وَٱلْأَرْضِ وَيَعْلَمُ مَا تُخْفُونَ وَمَا تُعْلِنُونَ

25 If only they would worship Allah, who brings to light the mysteries of the heavens and the earth, and knows what you conceal and what you reveal.

٢٦ ٱللَّهُ لَآ إِلَٰهَ إِلَّا هُوَ رَبُّ ٱلْعَرْشِ ٱلْعَظِيمِ ۩

26 Allah—There is no god but He, the Lord of the Sublime Throne."

٢٧ قَالَ سَنَنظُرُ أَصَدَقْتَ أَمْ كُنتَ مِنَ ٱلْكَٰذِبِينَ

27 He said, "We will see, whether you have spoken the truth, or whether you are a liar.

٢٨ ٱذْهَب بِّكِتَٰبِى هَٰذَا فَأَلْقِهْ إِلَيْهِمْ ثُمَّ تَوَلَّ عَنْهُمْ فَٱنظُرْ مَاذَا يَرْجِعُونَ

28 Go with this letter of mine, and deliver it to them; then withdraw from them, and see how they respond."

٢٩ قَالَتْ يَٰٓأَيُّهَا ٱلْمَلَؤُا۟ إِنِّىٓ أُلْقِىَ إِلَىَّ كِتَٰبٌ كَرِيمٌ

29 She said, "O Counselors, a gracious letter was delivered to me.

٣٠ إِنَّهُۥ مِن سُلَيْمَٰنَ وَإِنَّهُۥ بِسْمِ ٱللَّهِ ٱلرَّحْمَٰنِ ٱلرَّحِيمِ

30 It is from Solomon, and it is, 'In the Name of Allah, the Gracious, the Merciful.

٣١ أَلَّا تَعْلُوا۟ عَلَىَّ وَأْتُونِى مُسْلِمِينَ

31 Do not defy me, and come to me submissively.'"

٣٢ قَالَتْ يَٰٓأَيُّهَا ٱلْمَلَؤُا۟ أَفْتُونِى فِىٓ أَمْرِى مَا كُنتُ قَاطِعَةً أَمْرًا حَتَّىٰ تَشْهَدُونِ

32 She said, "O counselors, advise me in this matter of mine. I never make a decision unless you are present."

٣٣ قَالُوا۟ نَحْنُ أُو۟لُوا۟ قُوَّةٍ وَأُو۟لُوا۟ بَأْسٍ شَدِيدٍ
وَٱلْأَمْرُ إِلَيْكِ فَٱنظُرِى مَاذَا تَأْمُرِينَ

33 They said, “We are a people of might and great courage, but the decision is yours, so consider what you wish to command.”

٣٤ قَالَتْ إِنَّ ٱلْمُلُوكَ إِذَا دَخَلُوا۟ قَرْيَةً أَفْسَدُوهَا
وَجَعَلُوٓا۟ أَعِزَّةَ أَهْلِهَآ أَذِلَّةً ۖ وَكَذَٰلِكَ يَفْعَلُونَ

34 She said, “When kings enter a city, they devastate it, and subjugate its dignified people. Thus they always do.

٣٥ وَإِنِّى مُرْسِلَةٌ إِلَيْهِم بِهَدِيَّةٍ فَنَاظِرَةٌۢ بِمَ
يَرْجِعُ ٱلْمُرْسَلُونَ

35 I am sending them a gift, and will see what the envoys bring back.”

٣٦ فَلَمَّا جَآءَ سُلَيْمَٰنَ قَالَ أَتُمِدُّونَنِ بِمَالٍ فَمَآ
ءَاتَىٰنِۦَ ٱللَّهُ خَيْرٌ مِّمَّآ ءَاتَىٰكُم بَلْ أَنتُم بِهَدِيَّتِكُمْ
تَفْرَحُونَ

36 When he came to Solomon, he said, “Are you supplying me with money? What Allah has given me is better than what He has given you. It is you who delight in your gift.

٣٧ ٱرْجِعْ إِلَيْهِمْ فَلَنَأْتِيَنَّهُم بِجُنُودٍ لَّا قِبَلَ لَهُم
بِهَا وَلَنُخْرِجَنَّهُم مِّنْهَآ أَذِلَّةً وَهُمْ صَٰغِرُونَ

37 Go back to them. We will come upon them with troops they cannot resist; and we will expel them from there, disgraced and humiliated.”

٣٨ قَالَ يَٰٓأَيُّهَا ٱلْمَلَؤُا۟ أَيُّكُمْ يَأْتِينِى بِعَرْشِهَا قَبْلَ
أَن يَأْتُونِى مُسْلِمِينَ

38 He said, “O notables, which one of you will bring me her throne before they come to me in submission?”

٣٩ قَالَ عِفْرِيتٌ مِّنَ ٱلْجِنِّ أَنَا۠ ءَاتِيكَ بِهِۦ قَبْلَ
أَن تَقُومَ مِن مَّقَامِكَ ۖ وَإِنِّى عَلَيْهِ لَقَوِىٌّ أَمِينٌ

39 An imp of the sprites said, “I will bring it to you before you rise from your seat. I am strong and reliable enough to do it.”

٤٠ قَالَ ٱلَّذِى عِندَهُۥ عِلْمٌ مِّنَ ٱلْكِتَٰبِ أَنَا۠ ءَاتِيكَ
بِهِۦ قَبْلَ أَن يَرْتَدَّ إِلَيْكَ طَرْفُكَ ۚ فَلَمَّا رَءَاهُ
مُسْتَقِرًّا عِندَهُۥ قَالَ هَٰذَا مِن فَضْلِ رَبِّى لِيَبْلُوَنِىٓ
ءَأَشْكُرُ أَمْ أَكْفُرُ ۖ وَمَن شَكَرَ فَإِنَّمَا يَشْكُرُ
لِنَفْسِهِۦ ۖ وَمَن كَفَرَ فَإِنَّ رَبِّى غَنِىٌّ كَرِيمٌ

40 He who had knowledge from the Book said, “I will bring it to you before your glance returns to you.” And when he saw it settled before him, he said, “This is from the grace of my Lord, to test me, whether I am grateful or ungrateful. He who is grateful, his gratitude is to his own credit; but he who is ungrateful—my Lord is Independent and Generous.”

٤١ قَالَ نَكِّرُوا۟ لَهَا عَرْشَهَا نَنظُرْ أَتَهْتَدِىٓ أَمْ
تَكُونُ مِنَ ٱلَّذِينَ لَا يَهْتَدُونَ

41 He said, “Disguise her throne for her, and we shall see whether she will be guided, or remains one of the misguided.”

٤٢ فَلَمَّا جَآءَتْ قِيلَ أَهَٰكَذَا عَرْشُكِ ۖ قَالَتْ كَأَنَّهُۥ
هُوَ ۚ وَأُوتِينَا ٱلْعِلْمَ مِن قَبْلِهَا وَكُنَّا مُسْلِمِينَ

42 When she arrived, it was said, “Is your throne like this?” She said, “As if this is it.” “We were given knowledge before her, and we were submissive.”

٤٣ وَصَدَّهَا مَا كَانَت تَّعْبُدُ مِن دُونِ ٱللَّهِ ۖ إِنَّهَا
كَانَتْ مِن قَوْمٍ كَٰفِرِينَ

43 But she was prevented by what she worshiped besides Allah; she belonged to a disbelieving people.

٤٤ قِيلَ لَهَا ٱدْخُلِى ٱلصَّرْحَ ۖ فَلَمَّا رَأَتْهُ حَسِبَتْهُ
لُجَّةً وَكَشَفَتْ عَن سَاقَيْهَا ۚ قَالَ إِنَّهُۥ صَرْحٌ
مُّمَرَّدٌ مِّن قَوَارِيرَ ۗ قَالَتْ رَبِّ إِنِّى ظَلَمْتُ نَفْسِى
وَأَسْلَمْتُ مَعَ سُلَيْمَٰنَ لِلَّهِ رَبِّ ٱلْعَٰلَمِينَ

44 It was said to her, “Go inside the palace.” And when she saw it, she thought it was a deep pond, and she bared her legs. He said, “It is a palace paved with glass.” She said, “My Lord, I have done wrong to myself, and I have submitted with Solomon, to Allah, Lord of the Worlds.”

٤٥ وَلَقَدْ أَرْسَلْنَآ إِلَىٰ ثَمُودَ أَخَاهُمْ صَٰلِحًا أَنِ
ٱعْبُدُوا۟ ٱللَّهَ فَإِذَا هُمْ فَرِيقَانِ يَخْتَصِمُونَ

45 And We sent to Thamood their brother Saleh: “Worship Allah.” But they became two disputing factions.

٤٦ قَالَ يَٰقَوْمِ لِمَ تَسْتَعْجِلُونَ بِٱلسَّيِّئَةِ قَبْلَ
ٱلْحَسَنَةِ ۖ لَوْلَا تَسْتَغْفِرُونَ ٱللَّهَ لَعَلَّكُمْ تُرْحَمُونَ

46 He said, “O my people, why are you quick to do evil rather than good? If only you would seek Allah’s forgiveness, so that you may be shown mercy.”

٤٧ قَالُوا۟ ٱطَّيَّرْنَا بِكَ وَبِمَن مَّعَكَ ۚ قَالَ طَٰٓئِرُكُمْ
عِندَ ٱللَّهِ ۖ بَلْ أَنتُمْ قَوْمٌ تُفْتَنُونَ

47 They said, “We consider you an ill omen, and those with you.” He said, “Your omen is with Allah. In fact, you are a people being tested.”

٤٨ وَكَانَ فِى ٱلْمَدِينَةِ تِسْعَةُ رَهْطٍ يُفْسِدُونَ
فِى ٱلْأَرْضِ وَلَا يُصْلِحُونَ

48 In the city was a gang of nine who made mischief in the land and did no good.

٤٩ قَالُوا۟ تَقَاسَمُوا۟ بِٱللَّهِ لَنُبَيِّتَنَّهُۥ وَأَهْلَهُۥ ثُمَّ
لَنَقُولَنَّ لِوَلِيِّهِۦ مَا شَهِدْنَا مَهْلِكَ أَهْلِهِۦ وَإِنَّا
لَصَٰدِقُونَ

49 They said, “Swear by Allah to one another that we will attack him and his family by night, and then tell his guardian, 'We did not witness the murder of his family, and we are being truthful.'“

٥٠ وَمَكَرُوا۟ مَكْرًا وَمَكَرْنَا مَكْرًا وَهُمْ لَا يَشْعُرُونَ

50 They planned a plan, and We planned a plan, but they did not notice.

٥١ فَٱنظُرْ كَيْفَ كَانَ عَٰقِبَةُ مَكْرِهِمْ أَنَّا دَمَّرْنَٰهُمْ
وَقَوْمَهُمْ أَجْمَعِينَ

51 So note the outcome of their planning; We destroyed them and their people, altogether.

٥٢ فَتِلْكَ بُيُوتُهُمْ خَاوِيَةًۢ بِمَا ظَلَمُوٓا۟ ۗ إِنَّ فِى
ذَٰلِكَ لَءَايَةً لِّقَوْمٍ يَعْلَمُونَ

52 Here are their homes, in ruins, on account of their iniquities. Surely in this is a sign for people who know.

٥٣ وَأَنجَيْنَا ٱلَّذِينَ ءَامَنُوا۟ وَكَانُوا۟ يَتَّقُونَ

53 And We saved those who believed and were pious.

٥٤ وَلُوطًا إِذْ قَالَ لِقَوْمِهِۦٓ أَتَأْتُونَ ٱلْفَٰحِشَةَ
وَأَنتُمْ تُبْصِرُونَ

54 And Lot, when he said to his people, “Do you commit lewdness with open eyes?

٥٥ أَئِنَّكُمْ لَتَأْتُونَ ٱلرِّجَالَ شَهْوَةً مِّن دُونِ
ٱلنِّسَآءِ ۚ بَلْ أَنتُمْ قَوْمٌ تَجْهَلُونَ

55 Do you lust after men instead of women? You are truly ignorant people.”

٥٦ فَمَا كَانَ جَوَابَ قَوْمِهِۦٓ إِلَّآ أَن قَالُوٓا۟ أَخْرِجُوٓا۟
ءَالَ لُوطٍ مِّن قَرْيَتِكُمْ ۖ إِنَّهُمْ أُنَاسٌ يَتَطَهَّرُونَ

56 But the only response of his people was to say, “Expel the family of Lot from your town. They are purist people.”

٥٧ فَأَنجَيْنَٰهُ وَأَهْلَهُۥٓ إِلَّا ٱمْرَأَتَهُۥ قَدَّرْنَٰهَا مِنَ
ٱلْغَٰبِرِينَ

57 So We saved him and his family, except for his wife, whom We destined to be among the laggards.

٥٨ وَأَمْطَرْنَا عَلَيْهِم مَّطَرًا ۖ فَسَآءَ مَطَرُ
ٱلْمُنذَرِينَ

58 And We rained upon them a rain. Miserable was the rain of those forewarned.

٥٩ قُلِ ٱلْحَمْدُ لِلَّهِ وَسَلَٰمٌ عَلَىٰ عِبَادِهِ ٱلَّذِينَ
ٱصْطَفَىٰٓ ۗ ءَآللَّهُ خَيْرٌ أَمَّا يُشْرِكُونَ

59 Say, “Praise Allah, and peace be upon His servants whom He has selected. Is Allah better, or what they associate?”

٦٠ أَمَّنْ خَلَقَ ٱلسَّمَٰوَٰتِ وَٱلْأَرْضَ وَأَنزَلَ لَكُم مِّنَ
ٱلسَّمَآءِ مَآءً فَأَنۢبَتْنَا بِهِۦ حَدَآئِقَ ذَاتَ بَهْجَةٍ مَّا
كَانَ لَكُمْ أَن تُنۢبِتُوا۟ شَجَرَهَآ ۗ أَءِلَٰهٌ مَّعَ ٱللَّهِ ۚ بَلْ
هُمْ قَوْمٌ يَعْدِلُونَ

60 Or, who created the heavens and the earth, and rains down water from the sky for you? With it We produce gardens full of beauty, whose trees you could not have produced. Is there another god with Allah? But they are a people who equate.

٦١ أَمَّن جَعَلَ ٱلْأَرْضَ قَرَارًا وَجَعَلَ خِلَٰلَهَآ أَنْهَٰرًا
وَجَعَلَ لَهَا رَوَٰسِىَ وَجَعَلَ بَيْنَ ٱلْبَحْرَيْنِ حَاجِزًا ۗ
أَءِلَٰهٌ مَّعَ ٱللَّهِ ۚ بَلْ أَكْثَرُهُمْ لَا يَعْلَمُونَ

61 Or, who made the earth habitable, and made rivers flow through it, and set mountains on it, and placed a partition between the two seas? Is

there another god with Allah? But most of them do not know.

٦٢ أَمَّن يُجِيبُ ٱلْمُضْطَرَّ إِذَا دَعَاهُ وَيَكْشِفُ
ٱلسُّوٓءَ وَيَجْعَلُكُمْ خُلَفَآءَ ٱلْأَرْضِ ۗ أَءِلَٰهٌ مَّعَ ٱللَّهِ ۚ
قَلِيلًا مَّا تَذَكَّرُونَ

62 Or, who answers the one in need when he prays to Him, and relieves adversity, and makes you successors on earth? Is there another god with Allah? How hardly you pay attention.

٦٣ أَمَّن يَهْدِيكُمْ فِى ظُلُمَٰتِ ٱلْبَرِّ وَٱلْبَحْرِ وَمَن
يُرْسِلُ ٱلرِّيَٰحَ بُشْرًۢا بَيْنَ يَدَىْ رَحْمَتِهِۦٓ ۗ أَءِلَٰهٌ مَّعَ
ٱللَّهِ ۚ تَعَٰلَى ٱللَّهُ عَمَّا يُشْرِكُونَ

63 Or, who guides you through the darkness of land and sea, and who sends the winds as heralds of His mercy? Is there another god with Allah? Most exalted is Allah, above what they associate.

٦٤ أَمَّن يَبْدَؤُا۟ ٱلْخَلْقَ ثُمَّ يُعِيدُهُۥ وَمَن يَرْزُقُكُم
مِّنَ ٱلسَّمَآءِ وَٱلْأَرْضِ ۗ أَءِلَٰهٌ مَّعَ ٱللَّهِ ۚ قُلْ هَاتُوا۟
بُرْهَٰنَكُمْ إِن كُنتُمْ صَٰدِقِينَ

64 Or, who originates the creation and then repeats it, and who gives you livelihood from the sky and the earth? Is there another god with Allah? Say, "Produce your evidence, if you are truthful."

٦٥ قُل لَّا يَعْلَمُ مَن فِى ٱلسَّمَٰوَٰتِ وَٱلْأَرْضِ
ٱلْغَيْبَ إِلَّا ٱللَّهُ ۚ وَمَا يَشْعُرُونَ أَيَّانَ يُبْعَثُونَ

65 Say, "No one in the heavens or on earth knows the future except Allah; and they do not perceive when they will be resurrected."

٦٦ بَلِ ٱدَّٰرَكَ عِلْمُهُمْ فِى ٱلْءَاخِرَةِ ۚ بَلْ هُمْ فِى
شَكٍّ مِّنْهَا ۖ بَلْ هُم مِّنْهَا عَمُونَ

66 In fact, their knowledge of the Hereafter is confused. In fact, they are in doubt about it. In fact, they are blind to it.

٦٧ وَقَالَ ٱلَّذِينَ كَفَرُوٓا۟ أَءِذَا كُنَّا تُرَٰبًا وَءَابَآؤُنَآ
أَئِنَّا لَمُخْرَجُونَ

67 Those who disbelieve say, "When we have become dust, and our ancestors, shall we be brought out?

٦٨ لَقَدْ وُعِدْنَا هَٰذَا نَحْنُ وَءَابَآؤُنَا مِن قَبْلُ إِنْ
هَٰذَآ إِلَّآ أَسَٰطِيرُ ٱلْأَوَّلِينَ

68 We were promised that before, we and our ancestors—these are nothing but legends of the ancients."

٦٩ قُلْ سِيرُوا۟ فِى ٱلْأَرْضِ فَٱنظُرُوا۟ كَيْفَ كَانَ
عَٰقِبَةُ ٱلْمُجْرِمِينَ

69 Say, travel through the earth, and observe the fate of the guilty."

٧٠ وَلَا تَحْزَنْ عَلَيْهِمْ وَلَا تَكُن فِى ضَيْقٍ مِّمَّا
يَمْكُرُونَ

70 But do not grieve over them, and do not be troubled by what they plot.

٧١ وَيَقُولُونَ مَتَىٰ هَٰذَا ٱلْوَعْدُ إِن كُنتُمْ صَٰدِقِينَ

71 And they say, “When is this promise, if you are truthful?”

٧٢ قُلْ عَسَىٰٓ أَن يَكُونَ رَدِفَ لَكُم بَعْضُ ٱلَّذِى
تَسْتَعْجِلُونَ

72 Say, “Perhaps some of what you are impatient for has drawn near.”

٧٣ وَإِنَّ رَبَّكَ لَذُو فَضْلٍ عَلَى ٱلنَّاسِ وَلَٰكِنَّ
أَكْثَرَهُمْ لَا يَشْكُرُونَ

73 Your Lord is gracious towards humanity, but most of them are not thankful.

٧٤ وَإِنَّ رَبَّكَ لَيَعْلَمُ مَا تُكِنُّ صُدُورُهُمْ وَمَا
يُعْلِنُونَ

74 And your Lord knows what their hearts conceal, and what they reveal.

٧٥ وَمَا مِنْ غَآئِبَةٍ فِى ٱلسَّمَآءِ وَٱلْأَرْضِ إِلَّا فِى
كِتَٰبٍ مُّبِينٍ

75 There is no mystery in the heaven and the earth, but it is in a Clear Book.

٧٦ إِنَّ هَٰذَا ٱلْقُرْءَانَ يَقُصُّ عَلَىٰ بَنِىٓ إِسْرَٰٓءِيلَ
أَكْثَرَ ٱلَّذِى هُمْ فِيهِ يَخْتَلِفُونَ

76 This Quran relates to the Children of Israel most of what they differ about.

٧٧ وَإِنَّهُۥ لَهُدًى وَرَحْمَةٌ لِّلْمُؤْمِنِينَ

77 And it is guidance and mercy for the believers.

٧٨ إِنَّ رَبَّكَ يَقْضِى بَيْنَهُم بِحُكْمِهِۦ ۚ وَهُوَ ٱلْعَزِيزُ
ٱلْعَلِيمُ

78 Your Lord will judge between them by His wisdom. He is the Almighty, the All-Knowing.

٧٩ فَتَوَكَّلْ عَلَى ٱللَّهِ ۖ إِنَّكَ عَلَى ٱلْحَقِّ ٱلْمُبِينِ

79 So rely on Allah. You are upon the clear truth.

٨٠ إِنَّكَ لَا تُسْمِعُ ٱلْمَوْتَىٰ وَلَا تُسْمِعُ ٱلصُّمَّ
ٱلدُّعَآءَ إِذَا وَلَّوْا۟ مُدْبِرِينَ

80 You cannot make the dead hear, nor can you make the deaf hear the call if they turn their backs and flee.

٨١ وَمَآ أَنتَ بِهَٰدِى ٱلْعُمْىِ عَن ضَلَٰلَتِهِمْ ۖ إِن
تُسْمِعُ إِلَّا مَن يُؤْمِنُ بِـَٔايَٰتِنَا فَهُم مُّسْلِمُونَ

81 Nor can you guide the blind out of their straying. You can make no one listen, except those who believe in Our verses; for they are Muslims.

٨٢ وَإِذَا وَقَعَ ٱلْقَوْلُ عَلَيْهِمْ أَخْرَجْنَا لَهُمْ دَآبَّةً
مِّنَ ٱلْأَرْضِ تُكَلِّمُهُمْ أَنَّ ٱلنَّاسَ كَانُوا۟ بِـَٔايَٰتِنَا لَا
يُوقِنُونَ

82 And when the Word has fallen on them, We will bring out for them from the earth a creature which will say to them that the people are uncertain of Our revelations.

٨٣ وَيَوْمَ نَحْشُرُ مِن كُلِّ أُمَّةٍ فَوْجًا مِّمَّن يُكَذِّبُ
بِـَٔايَٰتِنَا فَهُمْ يُوزَعُونَ

83 On the Day when We gather from every community a group of those

who rejected Our revelations; and they will be restrained.

٨٤ حَتَّىٰٓ إِذَا جَآءُو قَالَ أَكَذَّبْتُم بِـَٔايَٰتِى وَلَمْ
تُحِيطُوا۟ بِهَا عِلْمًا أَمَّاذَا كُنتُمْ تَعْمَلُونَ

84 Until, when they arrive, He will say, “Did you reject My revelations without comprehending them? Or what is it you were doing?”

٨٥ وَوَقَعَ ٱلْقَوْلُ عَلَيْهِم بِمَا ظَلَمُوا۟ فَهُمْ لَا
يَنطِقُونَ

85 The Word will come down upon them for their wrongdoing, and they will not speak.

٨٦ أَلَمْ يَرَوْا۟ أَنَّا جَعَلْنَا ٱلَّيْلَ لِيَسْكُنُوا۟ فِيهِ
وَٱلنَّهَارَ مُبْصِرًا ۚ إِنَّ فِى ذَٰلِكَ لَءَايَٰتٍ لِّقَوْمٍ
يُؤْمِنُونَ

86 Do they not see that We made the night for them to rest therein, and the day for visibility? Surely in that are signs for people who believe.

٨٧ وَيَوْمَ يُنفَخُ فِى ٱلصُّورِ فَفَزِعَ مَن فِى
ٱلسَّمَٰوَٰتِ وَمَن فِى ٱلْأَرْضِ إِلَّا مَن شَآءَ ٱللَّهُ ۚ
وَكُلٌّ أَتَوْهُ دَٰخِرِينَ

87 On the Day when the Trumpet is blown, everyone in the heavens and the earth will be horrified, except whomever Allah wills; and everyone will come before Him in humility.

٨٨ وَتَرَى ٱلْجِبَالَ تَحْسَبُهَا جَامِدَةً وَهِىَ تَمُرُّ مَرَّ
ٱلسَّحَابِ ۚ صُنْعَ ٱللَّهِ ٱلَّذِىٓ أَتْقَنَ كُلَّ شَىْءٍ ۚ إِنَّهُۥ
خَبِيرٌۢ بِمَا تَفْعَلُونَ

88 And you see the mountains, and imagine them fixed, yet they pass, as the passing of the clouds—the making of Allah, who has perfected everything. He is fully Informed of what you do.

٨٩ مَن جَآءَ بِٱلْحَسَنَةِ فَلَهُۥ خَيْرٌ مِّنْهَا وَهُم مِّن
فَزَعٍ يَوْمَئِذٍ ءَامِنُونَ

89 Whoever brings a virtue will receive better than it—and they will be safe from the horrors of that Day.

٩٠ وَمَن جَآءَ بِٱلسَّيِّئَةِ فَكُبَّتْ وُجُوهُهُمْ فِى
ٱلنَّارِ هَلْ تُجْزَوْنَ إِلَّا مَا كُنتُمْ تَعْمَلُونَ

90 But whoever brings evil—their faces will be tumbled into the Fire. Will you be rewarded except for what you used to do?

٩١ إِنَّمَآ أُمِرْتُ أَنْ أَعْبُدَ رَبَّ هَٰذِهِ ٱلْبَلْدَةِ ٱلَّذِى
حَرَّمَهَا وَلَهُۥ كُلُّ شَىْءٍ ۖ وَأُمِرْتُ أَنْ أَكُونَ مِنَ
ٱلْمُسْلِمِينَ

91 “I was commanded to worship the Lord of this town, who has sanctified it, and to Whom everything belongs; and I was commanded to be of those who submit.

٩٢ وَأَنْ أَتْلُوَا۟ ٱلْقُرْءَانَ ۖ فَمَنِ ٱهْتَدَىٰ فَإِنَّمَا
يَهْتَدِى لِنَفْسِهِۦ ۖ وَمَن ضَلَّ فَقُلْ إِنَّمَآ أَنَا۠ مِنَ
ٱلْمُنذِرِينَ

92 And to recite the Quran." Whoever is guided—is guided to his own advantage. And whoever goes astray, then say, "I am one of the warners."

٩٣ وَقُلِ ٱلْحَمْدُ لِلَّهِ سَيُرِيكُمْ ءَايَٰتِهِۦ
فَتَعْرِفُونَهَا ۚ وَمَا رَبُّكَ بِغَٰفِلٍ عَمَّا تَعْمَلُونَ

93 And say, "Praise belongs to Allah; He will show you His signs, and you will recognize them. Your Lord is not heedless of what you do."

28 History القصص

بِسْمِ ٱللَّهِ ٱلرَّحْمَٰنِ ٱلرَّحِيمِ

In the name of Allah, the Gracious, the Merciful.

١ طسٓمٓ

1 Ta, Seen, Meem.

٢ تِلْكَ ءَايَٰتُ ٱلْكِتَٰبِ ٱلْمُبِينِ

2 These are the Verses of the Clear Book.

٣ نَتْلُوا۟ عَلَيْكَ مِن نَّبَإِ مُوسَىٰ وَفِرْعَوْنَ بِٱلْحَقِّ
لِقَوْمٍ يُؤْمِنُونَ

3 We narrate to you from the history of Moses and Pharaoh—in truth—for people who believe.

٤ إِنَّ فِرْعَوْنَ عَلَا فِى ٱلْأَرْضِ وَجَعَلَ أَهْلَهَا
شِيَعًا يَسْتَضْعِفُ طَآئِفَةً مِّنْهُمْ يُذَبِّحُ أَبْنَآءَهُمْ
وَيَسْتَحْىِۦ نِسَآءَهُمْ ۚ إِنَّهُۥ كَانَ مِنَ ٱلْمُفْسِدِينَ

4 Pharaoh exalted himself in the land, and divided its people into factions. He persecuted a group of them, slaughtering their sons, while sparing their daughters. He was truly a corrupter.

٥ وَنُرِيدُ أَن نَّمُنَّ عَلَى ٱلَّذِينَ ٱسْتُضْعِفُوا۟ فِى
ٱلْأَرْضِ وَنَجْعَلَهُمْ أَئِمَّةً وَنَجْعَلَهُمُ ٱلْوَٰرِثِينَ

5 But We desired to favor those who were oppressed in the land, and to make them leaders, and to make them the inheritors.

٦ وَنُمَكِّنَ لَهُمْ فِى ٱلْأَرْضِ وَنُرِىَ فِرْعَوْنَ وَهَٰمَٰنَ
وَجُنُودَهُمَا مِنْهُم مَّا كَانُوا۟ يَحْذَرُونَ

6 And to establish them in the land; and to show Pharaoh, Hamaan, and their troops, the very thing they feared.

٧ وَأَوْحَيْنَآ إِلَىٰٓ أُمِّ مُوسَىٰٓ أَنْ أَرْضِعِيهِ ۖ فَإِذَا
خِفْتِ عَلَيْهِ فَأَلْقِيهِ فِى ٱلْيَمِّ وَلَا تَخَافِى وَلَا

7 We inspired the mother of Moses: "Nurse him; then, when you fear for him, cast him into the river, and do not fear, nor grieve; We will return

تَحْزَنِىٓ ۖ إِنَّا رَآدُّوهُ إِلَيْكِ وَجَاعِلُوهُ مِنَ ٱلْمُرْسَلِينَ

him to you, and make him one of the messengers."

٨ فَٱلْتَقَطَهُۥٓ ءَالُ فِرْعَوْنَ لِيَكُونَ لَهُمْ عَدُوًّا وَحَزَنًا ۗ إِنَّ فِرْعَوْنَ وَهَٰمَٰنَ وَجُنُودَهُمَا كَانُوا۟ خَٰطِـِٔينَ

8 Pharaoh's household picked him up, to be an opponent and a sorrow for them. Pharaoh, Hamaan, and their troops were sinners.

٩ وَقَالَتِ ٱمْرَأَتُ فِرْعَوْنَ قُرَّتُ عَيْنٍ لِّى وَلَكَ ۖ لَا تَقْتُلُوهُ عَسَىٰٓ أَن يَنفَعَنَآ أَوْ نَتَّخِذَهُۥ وَلَدًا وَهُمْ لَا يَشْعُرُونَ

9 Pharaoh's wife said, "An eye's delight for me and for you. Do not kill him; perhaps he will be useful to us, or we may adopt him as a son." But they did not foresee.

١٠ وَأَصْبَحَ فُؤَادُ أُمِّ مُوسَىٰ فَٰرِغًا ۖ إِن كَادَتْ لَتُبْدِى بِهِۦ لَوْلَآ أَن رَّبَطْنَا عَلَىٰ قَلْبِهَا لِتَكُونَ مِنَ ٱلْمُؤْمِنِينَ

10 The heart of Moses' mother became vacant. She was about to disclose him, had We not steadied her heart, that she may remain a believer.

١١ وَقَالَتْ لِأُخْتِهِۦ قُصِّيهِ ۖ فَبَصُرَتْ بِهِۦ عَن جُنُبٍ وَهُمْ لَا يَشْعُرُونَ

11 She said to his sister, "Trail him." So she watched him from afar, and they were unaware.

١٢ وَحَرَّمْنَا عَلَيْهِ ٱلْمَرَاضِعَ مِن قَبْلُ فَقَالَتْ هَلْ أَدُلُّكُمْ عَلَىٰٓ أَهْلِ بَيْتٍ يَكْفُلُونَهُۥ لَكُمْ وَهُمْ لَهُۥ نَٰصِحُونَ

12 We forbade him breastfeeding at first. So she said, "Shall I tell you about a family that can raise him for you, and will look after him?"

١٣ فَرَدَدْنَٰهُ إِلَىٰٓ أُمِّهِۦ كَىْ تَقَرَّ عَيْنُهَا وَلَا تَحْزَنَ وَلِتَعْلَمَ أَنَّ وَعْدَ ٱللَّهِ حَقٌّ وَلَٰكِنَّ أَكْثَرَهُمْ لَا يَعْلَمُونَ

13 Thus We returned him to his mother, that she may be comforted, and not grieve, and know that Allah's promise is true. But most of them do not know.

١٤ وَلَمَّا بَلَغَ أَشُدَّهُۥ وَٱسْتَوَىٰٓ ءَاتَيْنَٰهُ حُكْمًا وَعِلْمًا ۚ وَكَذَٰلِكَ نَجْزِى ٱلْمُحْسِنِينَ

14 And when he reached his maturity, and became established, We gave him wisdom and knowledge. Thus do We reward the virtuous.

١٥ وَدَخَلَ ٱلْمَدِينَةَ عَلَىٰ حِينِ غَفْلَةٍ مِّنْ أَهْلِهَا فَوَجَدَ فِيهَا رَجُلَيْنِ يَقْتَتِلَانِ هَٰذَا مِن شِيعَتِهِۦ وَهَٰذَا مِنْ عَدُوِّهِۦ ۖ فَٱسْتَغَٰثَهُ ٱلَّذِى مِن شِيعَتِهِۦ عَلَى ٱلَّذِى مِنْ عَدُوِّهِۦ فَوَكَزَهُۥ مُوسَىٰ فَقَضَىٰ

15 Once he entered the city, unnoticed by its people. He found in it two men fighting—one of his own sect, and one from his enemies. The one of his sect solicited his assistance against the one from his enemies; so Moses punched him,

عَلَيْهِۖ قَالَ هَٰذَا مِنْ عَمَلِ ٱلشَّيْطَٰنِۖ إِنَّهُۥ عَدُوٌّ
مُّضِلٌّ مُّبِينٌ

and put an end to him. He said, "This is of Satan's doing; he is an enemy that openly misleads."

١٦ قَالَ رَبِّ إِنِّى ظَلَمْتُ نَفْسِى فَٱغْفِرْ لِى فَغَفَرَ
لَهُۥٓۚ إِنَّهُۥ هُوَ ٱلْغَفُورُ ٱلرَّحِيمُ

16 He said, "My Lord, I have wronged myself, so forgive me." So He forgave him. He is the Forgiver, the Merciful.

١٧ قَالَ رَبِّ بِمَآ أَنْعَمْتَ عَلَىَّ فَلَنْ أَكُونَ ظَهِيرًا
لِّلْمُجْرِمِينَ

17 He said, "My Lord, in as much as you have favored me, I will never be a supporter of the criminals."

١٨ فَأَصْبَحَ فِى ٱلْمَدِينَةِ خَآئِفًا يَتَرَقَّبُ فَإِذَا
ٱلَّذِى ٱسْتَنصَرَهُۥ بِٱلْأَمْسِ يَسْتَصْرِخُهُۥۚ قَالَ لَهُۥ
مُوسَىٰٓ إِنَّكَ لَغَوِىٌّ مُّبِينٌ

18 The next morning, he went about in the city, fearful and vigilant, when the man who had sought his assistance the day before was shouting out to him. Moses said to him, "You are clearly a troublemaker."

١٩ فَلَمَّآ أَنْ أَرَادَ أَن يَبْطِشَ بِٱلَّذِى هُوَ عَدُوٌّ لَّهُمَا
قَالَ يَٰمُوسَىٰٓ أَتُرِيدُ أَن تَقْتُلَنِى كَمَا قَتَلْتَ نَفْسًۢا
بِٱلْأَمْسِۖ إِن تُرِيدُ إِلَّآ أَن تَكُونَ جَبَّارًا فِى
ٱلْأَرْضِ وَمَا تُرِيدُ أَن تَكُونَ مِنَ ٱلْمُصْلِحِينَ

19 As he was about to strike the one who was their enemy, he said, "O Moses, do you intend to kill me, as you killed someone yesterday? You only want to be a bully in the land, and do not want to be a peacemaker."

٢٠ وَجَآءَ رَجُلٌ مِّنْ أَقْصَا ٱلْمَدِينَةِ يَسْعَىٰ قَالَ
يَٰمُوسَىٰٓ إِنَّ ٱلْمَلَأَ يَأْتَمِرُونَ بِكَ لِيَقْتُلُوكَ فَٱخْرُجْ
إِنِّى لَكَ مِنَ ٱلنَّٰصِحِينَ

20 And a man came from the farthest part of the city running. He said, "O Moses, the authorities are considering killing you, so leave; I am giving you good advice."

٢١ فَخَرَجَ مِنْهَا خَآئِفًا يَتَرَقَّبُۖ قَالَ رَبِّ نَجِّنِى
مِنَ ٱلْقَوْمِ ٱلظَّٰلِمِينَ

21 So he left, fearful and vigilant. He said, "My Lord, deliver me from the wrongdoing people."

٢٢ وَلَمَّا تَوَجَّهَ تِلْقَآءَ مَدْيَنَ قَالَ عَسَىٰ رَبِّىٓ أَن
يَهْدِيَنِى سَوَآءَ ٱلسَّبِيلِ

22 As he headed towards Median, he said, "Perhaps my Lord will guide me to the right way."

٢٣ وَلَمَّا وَرَدَ مَآءَ مَدْيَنَ وَجَدَ عَلَيْهِ أُمَّةً مِّنَ
ٱلنَّاسِ يَسْقُونَ وَوَجَدَ مِن دُونِهِمُ ٱمْرَأَتَيْنِ
تَذُودَانِۖ قَالَ مَا خَطْبُكُمَاۖ قَالَتَا لَا نَسْقِى حَتَّىٰ
يُصْدِرَ ٱلرِّعَآءُۖ وَأَبُونَا شَيْخٌ كَبِيرٌ

23 And when he arrived at the waters of Median, he found there a crowd of people drawing water, and he noticed two women waiting on the side. He said, "What is the matter with you?" They said, "We cannot

draw water until the shepherds depart, and our father is a very old man."

٢٤ فَسَقَىٰ لَهُمَا ثُمَّ تَوَلَّىٰٓ إِلَى ٱلظِّلِّ فَقَالَ رَبِّ
إِنِّى لِمَآ أَنزَلْتَ إِلَىَّ مِنْ خَيْرٍ فَقِيرٌ

24 So he drew water for them, and then withdrew to the shade, and said, "My Lord, I am in dire need of whatever good you might send down to me."

٢٥ فَجَآءَتْهُ إِحْدَىٰهُمَا تَمْشِى عَلَى ٱسْتِحْيَآءٍ
قَالَتْ إِنَّ أَبِى يَدْعُوكَ لِيَجْزِيَكَ أَجْرَ مَا سَقَيْتَ
لَنَا ۚ فَلَمَّا جَآءَهُۥ وَقَصَّ عَلَيْهِ ٱلْقَصَصَ قَالَ لَا
تَخَفْ ۖ نَجَوْتَ مِنَ ٱلْقَوْمِ ٱلظَّٰلِمِينَ

25 Then, one of the two women approached him, walking bashfully. She said, "My father is calling you, to reward you for drawing water for us." And when he came to him, and told him the story, he said, "Do not fear, you have escaped from the wrongdoing people."

٢٦ قَالَتْ إِحْدَىٰهُمَا يَٰٓأَبَتِ ٱسْتَـْٔجِرْهُ ۖ إِنَّ خَيْرَ مَنِ
ٱسْتَـْٔجَرْتَ ٱلْقَوِىُّ ٱلْأَمِينُ

26 One of the two women said, "Father, hire him; the best employee for you is the strong and trustworthy."

٢٧ قَالَ إِنِّىٓ أُرِيدُ أَنْ أُنكِحَكَ إِحْدَى ٱبْنَتَىَّ
هَٰتَيْنِ عَلَىٰٓ أَن تَأْجُرَنِى ثَمَٰنِىَ حِجَجٍ ۖ فَإِنْ
أَتْمَمْتَ عَشْرًا فَمِنْ عِندِكَ ۖ وَمَآ أُرِيدُ أَنْ أَشُقَّ
عَلَيْكَ ۚ سَتَجِدُنِىٓ إِن شَآءَ ٱللَّهُ مِنَ ٱلصَّٰلِحِينَ

27 He said, "I want to marry you to one of these two daughters of mine, provided you work for me for eight years. But if you complete ten, that is up to you. I do not intend to impose any hardship on you. You will find me, Allah willing, one of the righteous."

٢٨ قَالَ ذَٰلِكَ بَيْنِى وَبَيْنَكَ ۖ أَيَّمَا ٱلْأَجَلَيْنِ
قَضَيْتُ فَلَا عُدْوَٰنَ عَلَىَّ ۖ وَٱللَّهُ عَلَىٰ مَا نَقُولُ
وَكِيلٌ

28 He said, "Let this be an agreement between you and me. Whichever of the two terms I fulfill, there shall be no reprisal against me; and Allah is witness over what we say."

٢٩ فَلَمَّا قَضَىٰ مُوسَى ٱلْأَجَلَ وَسَارَ بِأَهْلِهِۦٓ
ءَانَسَ مِن جَانِبِ ٱلطُّورِ نَارًا قَالَ لِأَهْلِهِ ٱمْكُثُوٓا۟
إِنِّىٓ ءَانَسْتُ نَارًا لَّعَلِّىٓ ءَاتِيكُم مِّنْهَا بِخَبَرٍ أَوْ
جَذْوَةٍ مِّنَ ٱلنَّارِ لَعَلَّكُمْ تَصْطَلُونَ

29 When Moses had completed the term, and departed with his family, he noticed a fire by the side of the Mount. He said to his family, "Stay here, I have glimpsed a fire. Perhaps I can bring you some information from there, or an ember from the fire, that you may warm yourselves."

٣٠ فَلَمَّآ أَتَىٰهَا نُودِىَ مِن شَٰطِئِ ٱلْوَادِ ٱلْأَيْمَنِ فِى
ٱلْبُقْعَةِ ٱلْمُبَٰرَكَةِ مِنَ ٱلشَّجَرَةِ أَن يَٰمُوسَىٰٓ إِنِّىٓ
أَنَا ٱللَّهُ رَبُّ ٱلْعَٰلَمِينَ

30 When he reached it, he was called from the right side of the valley, at the Blessed Spot, from the bush: "O Moses, it is I, Allah, the Lord of the Worlds.

٣١ وَأَنْ أَلْقِ عَصَاكَ ۖ فَلَمَّا رَءَاهَا تَهْتَزُّ كَأَنَّهَا جَآنٌّ
وَلَّىٰ مُدْبِرًا وَلَمْ يُعَقِّبْ ۚ يَٰمُوسَىٰٓ أَقْبِلْ وَلَا
تَخَفْ ۖ إِنَّكَ مِنَ ٱلْءَامِنِينَ

31 Throw down your staff." And when he saw it wiggling, as if it were possessed, he turned his back to flee, and did not look back. "O Moses, come forward, and do not fear, you are perfectly safe.

٣٢ ٱسْلُكْ يَدَكَ فِى جَيْبِكَ تَخْرُجْ بَيْضَآءَ مِنْ
غَيْرِ سُوٓءٍ وَٱضْمُمْ إِلَيْكَ جَنَاحَكَ مِنَ ٱلرَّهْبِ ۖ
فَذَٰنِكَ بُرْهَٰنَانِ مِن رَّبِّكَ إِلَىٰ فِرْعَوْنَ وَمَلَإِي۟هِۦٓ ۚ
إِنَّهُمْ كَانُوا۟ قَوْمًا فَٰسِقِينَ

32 Put your hand inside your pocket, and it will come out white, without blemish. And press your arm to your side, against fear. These are two proofs from your Lord, to Pharaoh and his dignitaries. They are truly sinful people."

٣٣ قَالَ رَبِّ إِنِّى قَتَلْتُ مِنْهُمْ نَفْسًا فَأَخَافُ أَن
يَقْتُلُونِ

33 He said, "My Lord, I have killed one of them, and I fear they will kill me.

٣٤ وَأَخِى هَٰرُونُ هُوَ أَفْصَحُ مِنِّى لِسَانًا فَأَرْسِلْهُ
مَعِىَ رِدْءًا يُصَدِّقُنِىٓ ۖ إِنِّىٓ أَخَافُ أَن يُكَذِّبُونِ

34 And my brother Aaron, he is more eloquent than me, so send him with me, to help me, and to confirm my words, for I fear they will reject me."

٣٥ قَالَ سَنَشُدُّ عَضُدَكَ بِأَخِيكَ وَنَجْعَلُ لَكُمَا
سُلْطَٰنًا فَلَا يَصِلُونَ إِلَيْكُمَا ۚ بِـَٔايَٰتِنَآ أَنتُمَا وَمَنِ
ٱتَّبَعَكُمَا ٱلْغَٰلِبُونَ

35 He said, "We will strengthen your arm with your brother, and We will give you authority, so they will not touch you. By virtue of Our signs, you and those who follow you will be the triumphant."

٣٦ فَلَمَّا جَآءَهُم مُّوسَىٰ بِـَٔايَٰتِنَا بَيِّنَٰتٍ قَالُوا۟ مَا
هَٰذَآ إِلَّا سِحْرٌ مُّفْتَرًى وَمَا سَمِعْنَا بِهَٰذَا فِىٓ
ءَابَآئِنَا ٱلْأَوَّلِينَ

36 But when Moses came to them with Our signs, clear and manifest, they said, "This is nothing but fabricated magic, and We never heard of this from our ancestors of old."

٣٧ وَقَالَ مُوسَىٰ رَبِّىٓ أَعْلَمُ بِمَن جَآءَ بِٱلْهُدَىٰ
مِنْ عِندِهِۦ وَمَن تَكُونُ لَهُۥ عَٰقِبَةُ ٱلدَّارِ ۖ إِنَّهُۥ لَا
يُفْلِحُ ٱلظَّٰلِمُونَ

37 Moses said, "My Lord is well aware of him who brings guidance from Him, and him who will have the

sequel of the abode. The wrongdoers will not succeed."

٣٨ وَقَالَ فِرْعَوْنُ يَٰٓأَيُّهَا ٱلْمَلَأُ مَا عَلِمْتُ لَكُم مِّنْ
إِلَٰهٍ غَيْرِى فَأَوْقِدْ لِى يَٰهَٰمَٰنُ عَلَى ٱلطِّينِ فَٱجْعَل
لِّى صَرْحًا لَّعَلِّىٓ أَطَّلِعُ إِلَىٰٓ إِلَٰهِ مُوسَىٰ وَإِنِّى
لَأَظُنُّهُۥ مِنَ ٱلْكَٰذِبِينَ

38 Pharaoh said, "O nobles, I know of no god for you other than me. So fire-up the bricks for me O Hamaan, and build me a tower, that I may ascend to the God of Moses, though I think he is a liar."

٣٩ وَٱسْتَكْبَرَ هُوَ وَجُنُودُهُۥ فِى ٱلْأَرْضِ بِغَيْرِ
ٱلْحَقِّ وَظَنُّوٓا۟ أَنَّهُمْ إِلَيْنَا لَا يُرْجَعُونَ

39 He and his troops acted arrogantly in the land, with no justification. They thought they would not be returned to Us.

٤٠ فَأَخَذْنَٰهُ وَجُنُودَهُۥ فَنَبَذْنَٰهُمْ فِى ٱلْيَمِّ ۖ فَٱنظُرْ
كَيْفَ كَانَ عَٰقِبَةُ ٱلظَّٰلِمِينَ

40 So We seized him, and his troops, and We threw them into the sea. Observe, therefore, what was the end of the oppressors.

٤١ وَجَعَلْنَٰهُمْ أَئِمَّةً يَدْعُونَ إِلَى ٱلنَّارِ ۖ وَيَوْمَ
ٱلْقِيَٰمَةِ لَا يُنصَرُونَ

41 And We made them leaders calling to the Fire. And on Resurrection Day, they will not be saved.

٤٢ وَأَتْبَعْنَٰهُمْ فِى هَٰذِهِ ٱلدُّنْيَا لَعْنَةً ۖ وَيَوْمَ
ٱلْقِيَٰمَةِ هُم مِّنَ ٱلْمَقْبُوحِينَ

42 And We pursued them in this world with a curse. And on Resurrection Day, they will be among the despised.

٤٣ وَلَقَدْ ءَاتَيْنَا مُوسَى ٱلْكِتَٰبَ مِنۢ بَعْدِ مَآ
أَهْلَكْنَا ٱلْقُرُونَ ٱلْأُولَىٰ بَصَآئِرَ لِلنَّاسِ وَهُدًى
وَرَحْمَةً لَّعَلَّهُمْ يَتَذَكَّرُونَ

43 We gave Moses the Scripture after We had annihilated the previous generations; as an illumination for mankind, and guidance, and mercy, so that they may remember.

٤٤ وَمَا كُنتَ بِجَانِبِ ٱلْغَرْبِىِّ إِذْ قَضَيْنَآ إِلَىٰ
مُوسَى ٱلْأَمْرَ وَمَا كُنتَ مِنَ ٱلشَّٰهِدِينَ

44 You were not on the Western Side when We decreed the command to Moses, nor were you among the witnesses.

٤٥ وَلَٰكِنَّآ أَنشَأْنَا قُرُونًا فَتَطَاوَلَ عَلَيْهِمُ ٱلْعُمُرُ ۚ
وَمَا كُنتَ ثَاوِيًا فِىٓ أَهْلِ مَدْيَنَ تَتْلُوا۟ عَلَيْهِمْ
ءَايَٰتِنَا وَلَٰكِنَّا كُنَّا مُرْسِلِينَ

45 But We established many generations, and time took its toll on them. Nor were you among the people of Median, reciting Our revelations to them. But We kept sending messengers.

٤٦ وَمَا كُنتَ بِجَانِبِ ٱلطُّورِ إِذْ نَادَيْنَا وَلَٰكِن
رَّحْمَةً مِّن رَّبِّكَ لِتُنذِرَ قَوْمًا مَّآ أَتَىٰهُم مِّن نَّذِيرٍ
مِّن قَبْلِكَ لَعَلَّهُمْ يَتَذَكَّرُونَ

46 Nor were you by the side of the Mount when We proclaimed. Rather, it was a mercy from your Lord, that you may warn people who received no warner before you, so that they may take heed.

٤٧ وَلَوْلَآ أَن تُصِيبَهُم مُّصِيبَةٌۢ بِمَا قَدَّمَتْ
أَيْدِيهِمْ فَيَقُولُوا۟ رَبَّنَا لَوْلَآ أَرْسَلْتَ إِلَيْنَا رَسُولًا
فَنَتَّبِعَ ءَايَٰتِكَ وَنَكُونَ مِنَ ٱلْمُؤْمِنِينَ

47 Otherwise, if a calamity befell them as a result of what their hands have perpetrated, they would say, “Our Lord, if only You had sent us a messenger, we would have followed Your revelations, and been among the believers.”

٤٨ فَلَمَّا جَآءَهُمُ ٱلْحَقُّ مِنْ عِندِنَا قَالُوا۟ لَوْلَآ
أُوتِىَ مِثْلَ مَآ أُوتِىَ مُوسَىٰٓ ۚ أَوَلَمْ يَكْفُرُوا۟ بِمَآ
أُوتِىَ مُوسَىٰ مِن قَبْلُ ۖ قَالُوا۟ سِحْرَانِ تَظَٰهَرَا
وَقَالُوٓا۟ إِنَّا بِكُلٍّ كَٰفِرُونَ

48 But when the truth came to them from Us, they said, “If only he was given the like of what was given to Moses.” Did they not disbelieve in what was given to Moses in the past? They said, “Two works of magic backing one another.” And they said, “We are disbelieving in both.”

٤٩ قُلْ فَأْتُوا۟ بِكِتَٰبٍ مِّنْ عِندِ ٱللَّهِ هُوَ أَهْدَىٰ
مِنْهُمَآ أَتَّبِعْهُ إِن كُنتُمْ صَٰدِقِينَ

49 Say, “Then bring a scripture from Allah, more conductive to guidance than both, and I will follow it, if you are truthful.”

٥٠ فَإِن لَّمْ يَسْتَجِيبُوا۟ لَكَ فَٱعْلَمْ أَنَّمَا يَتَّبِعُونَ
أَهْوَآءَهُمْ ۚ وَمَنْ أَضَلُّ مِمَّنِ ٱتَّبَعَ هَوَىٰهُ بِغَيْرِ
هُدًى مِّنَ ٱللَّهِ ۚ إِنَّ ٱللَّهَ لَا يَهْدِى ٱلْقَوْمَ ٱلظَّٰلِمِينَ

50 But if they fail to respond to you, know that they follow their fancies. And who is more lost than him who follows his fancy without guidance from Allah? Allah does not guide the unjust people.

٥١ وَلَقَدْ وَصَّلْنَا لَهُمُ ٱلْقَوْلَ لَعَلَّهُمْ يَتَذَكَّرُونَ

51 We have delivered the Word to them, that they may remember.

٥٢ ٱلَّذِينَ ءَاتَيْنَٰهُمُ ٱلْكِتَٰبَ مِن قَبْلِهِۦ هُم بِهِۦ
يُؤْمِنُونَ

52 Those to whom We gave the Scripture before it believe in it.

٥٣ وَإِذَا يُتْلَىٰ عَلَيْهِمْ قَالُوٓا۟ ءَامَنَّا بِهِۦٓ إِنَّهُ ٱلْحَقُّ
مِن رَّبِّنَآ إِنَّا كُنَّا مِن قَبْلِهِۦ مُسْلِمِينَ

53 When it is recited to them, they say, “We have believed in it; it is the truth from our Lord; we were Muslims prior to it.”

٥٤ أُوْلَٰٓئِكَ يُؤْتَوْنَ أَجْرَهُم مَّرَّتَيْنِ بِمَا صَبَرُواْ
وَيَدْرَءُونَ بِٱلْحَسَنَةِ ٱلسَّيِّئَةَ وَمِمَّا رَزَقْنَٰهُمْ
يُنفِقُونَ

54 These will be given their reward twice, because they persevered; and they counter evil with good; and from Our provisions to them, they give.

٥٥ وَإِذَا سَمِعُواْ ٱللَّغْوَ أَعْرَضُواْ عَنْهُ وَقَالُواْ لَنَآ
أَعْمَٰلُنَا وَلَكُمْ أَعْمَٰلُكُمْ سَلَٰمٌ عَلَيْكُمْ لَا نَبْتَغِى
ٱلْجَٰهِلِينَ

55 And when they hear vain talk, they avoid it, and say, “We have our deeds, and you have your deeds; peace be upon you; we do not desire the ignorant.”

٥٦ إِنَّكَ لَا تَهْدِى مَنْ أَحْبَبْتَ وَلَٰكِنَّ ٱللَّهَ يَهْدِى
مَن يَشَآءُ ۚ وَهُوَ أَعْلَمُ بِٱلْمُهْتَدِينَ

56 You cannot guide whom you love, but Allah guides whom He wills, and He knows best those who are guided.

٥٧ وَقَالُوٓاْ إِن نَّتَّبِعِ ٱلْهُدَىٰ مَعَكَ نُتَخَطَّفْ مِنْ
أَرْضِنَآ ۚ أَوَلَمْ نُمَكِّن لَّهُمْ حَرَمًا ءَامِنًا يُجْبَىٰٓ إِلَيْهِ
ثَمَرَٰتُ كُلِّ شَىْءٍ رِّزْقًا مِّن لَّدُنَّا وَلَٰكِنَّ أَكْثَرَهُمْ لَا
يَعْلَمُونَ

57 And they say, “If we follow the guidance with you, we will be snatched from our land.” Did We not establish for them a Safe Sanctuary, to which are brought all kinds of fruits, as provision from Ourselves? But most of them do not know.

٥٨ وَكَمْ أَهْلَكْنَا مِن قَرْيَةٍۭ بَطِرَتْ مَعِيشَتَهَا ۖ
فَتِلْكَ مَسَٰكِنُهُمْ لَمْ تُسْكَن مِّنۢ بَعْدِهِمْ إِلَّا قَلِيلًا ۖ
وَكُنَّا نَحْنُ ٱلْوَٰرِثِينَ

58 And how many a city did We destroy for turning unappreciative of its livelihood? Here are their homes, uninhabited after them, except for a few. And We became the Inheritors.

٥٩ وَمَا كَانَ رَبُّكَ مُهْلِكَ ٱلْقُرَىٰ حَتَّىٰ يَبْعَثَ فِىٓ
أُمِّهَا رَسُولًا يَتْلُواْ عَلَيْهِمْ ءَايَٰتِنَا ۚ وَمَا كُنَّا
مُهْلِكِى ٱلْقُرَىٰٓ إِلَّا وَأَهْلُهَا ظَٰلِمُونَ

59 Your Lord never destroys cities without first sending a messenger in their midst, reciting to them Our revelations. And We never destroy the cities, unless their people are wrongdoers.

٦٠ وَمَآ أُوتِيتُم مِّن شَىْءٍ فَمَتَٰعُ ٱلْحَيَوٰةِ ٱلدُّنْيَا
وَزِينَتُهَا ۚ وَمَا عِندَ ٱللَّهِ خَيْرٌ وَأَبْقَىٰٓ ۚ أَفَلَا
تَعْقِلُونَ

60 Whatever thing you are given is but the material of this world, and its glitter. But what is with Allah is better, and longer lasting. Do you not comprehend?

٦١ أَفَمَن وَعَدْنَٰهُ وَعْدًا حَسَنًا فَهُوَ لَٰقِيهِ كَمَن
مَّتَّعْنَٰهُ مَتَٰعَ ٱلْحَيَوٰةِ ٱلدُّنْيَا ثُمَّ هُوَ يَوْمَ ٱلْقِيَٰمَةِ
مِنَ ٱلْمُحْضَرِينَ

61 Can someone to whom We have made a fine promise—which he will attain—be equal to someone to whom We have given enjoyments in this world, but who will be, on

Resurrection Day, among the arraigned?

٦٢ وَيَوْمَ يُنَادِيهِمْ فَيَقُولُ أَيْنَ شُرَكَآءِىَ ٱلَّذِينَ
كُنتُمْ تَزْعُمُونَ

62 On the Day when He will call to them, and say, "Where are My associates whom you used to claim?"

٦٣ قَالَ ٱلَّذِينَ حَقَّ عَلَيْهِمُ ٱلْقَوْلُ رَبَّنَا هَٰٓؤُلَآءِ
ٱلَّذِينَ أَغْوَيْنَآ أَغْوَيْنَٰهُمْ كَمَا غَوَيْنَا ۖ تَبَرَّأْنَآ إِلَيْكَ ۖ
مَا كَانُوٓا۟ إِيَّانَا يَعْبُدُونَ

63 Those against whom the sentence is justified will say, "Our Lord, these are they whom we misled. We misled them, as we were misled. We beg Your forgiveness; it was not us they used to worship."

٦٤ وَقِيلَ ٱدْعُوا۟ شُرَكَآءَكُمْ فَدَعَوْهُمْ فَلَمْ
يَسْتَجِيبُوا۟ لَهُمْ وَرَأَوُا۟ ٱلْعَذَابَ ۚ لَوْ أَنَّهُمْ كَانُوا۟
يَهْتَدُونَ

64 And it will be said, "Call on your partners." And they will call on them, but they will not respond to them. And they will see the suffering. If only they were guided.

٦٥ وَيَوْمَ يُنَادِيهِمْ فَيَقُولُ مَاذَآ أَجَبْتُمُ
ٱلْمُرْسَلِينَ

65 On the Day when He will call to them, and say, "What did you answer the Messengers?"

٦٦ فَعَمِيَتْ عَلَيْهِمُ ٱلْأَنۢبَآءُ يَوْمَئِذٍ فَهُمْ لَا
يَتَسَآءَلُونَ

66 They will be blinded by the facts on that Day, and they will not question each other.

٦٧ فَأَمَّا مَن تَابَ وَءَامَنَ وَعَمِلَ صَٰلِحًا فَعَسَىٰٓ
أَن يَكُونَ مِنَ ٱلْمُفْلِحِينَ

67 But he who repents, and believes, and does righteous deeds, may well be among the winners.

٦٨ وَرَبُّكَ يَخْلُقُ مَا يَشَآءُ وَيَخْتَارُ ۗ مَا كَانَ لَهُمُ
ٱلْخِيَرَةُ ۚ سُبْحَٰنَ ٱللَّهِ وَتَعَٰلَىٰ عَمَّا يُشْرِكُونَ

68 Your Lord creates whatever He wills, and He chooses. The choice is not theirs. Glory be to Allah, and exalted be He above the associations they make.

٦٩ وَرَبُّكَ يَعْلَمُ مَا تُكِنُّ صُدُورُهُمْ وَمَا يُعْلِنُونَ

69 And your Lord knows what their hearts conceal, and what they reveal.

٧٠ وَهُوَ ٱللَّهُ لَآ إِلَٰهَ إِلَّا هُوَ ۖ لَهُ ٱلْحَمْدُ فِى ٱلْأُولَىٰ
وَٱلْءَاخِرَةِ ۖ وَلَهُ ٱلْحُكْمُ وَإِلَيْهِ تُرْجَعُونَ

70 And He is Allah. There is no god but He. To Him belongs all praise in this life, and in the next. And His is the decision, and to Him you will be returned.

٧١ قُلْ أَرَءَيْتُمْ إِن جَعَلَ ٱللَّهُ عَلَيْكُمُ ٱلَّيْلَ
سَرْمَدًا إِلَىٰ يَوْمِ ٱلْقِيَٰمَةِ مَنْ إِلَٰهٌ غَيْرُ ٱللَّهِ
يَأْتِيكُم بِضِيَآءٍ ۖ أَفَلَا تَسْمَعُونَ

71 Say, "Have you considered? Had Allah made the night perpetual over you until the Day of Resurrection, which god other than Allah will bring you illumination? Do you not hear?"

٧٢ قُلْ أَرَءَيْتُمْ إِن جَعَلَ ٱللَّهُ عَلَيْكُمُ ٱلنَّهَارَ
سَرْمَدًا إِلَىٰ يَوْمِ ٱلْقِيَٰمَةِ مَنْ إِلَٰهٌ غَيْرُ ٱللَّهِ
يَأْتِيكُم بِلَيْلٍ تَسْكُنُونَ فِيهِ ۖ أَفَلَا تُبْصِرُونَ

72 Say, "Have you considered? Had Allah made the day perpetual over you until the Day of Resurrection, which god other than Allah will bring you night to rest in? Do you not see?"

٧٣ وَمِن رَّحْمَتِهِۦ جَعَلَ لَكُمُ ٱلَّيْلَ وَٱلنَّهَارَ
لِتَسْكُنُوا۟ فِيهِ وَلِتَبْتَغُوا۟ مِن فَضْلِهِۦ وَلَعَلَّكُمْ
تَشْكُرُونَ

73 It is out of His mercy that He made for you the night and the day, that you may rest in it, and seek some of His bounty; and that you may give thanks.

٧٤ وَيَوْمَ يُنَادِيهِمْ فَيَقُولُ أَيْنَ شُرَكَآءِىَ ٱلَّذِينَ
كُنتُمْ تَزْعُمُونَ

74 On the Day when He will call to them, and say, "Where are My associates whom you used to claim?"

٧٥ وَنَزَعْنَا مِن كُلِّ أُمَّةٍ شَهِيدًا فَقُلْنَا هَاتُوا۟
بُرْهَٰنَكُمْ فَعَلِمُوٓا۟ أَنَّ ٱلْحَقَّ لِلَّهِ وَضَلَّ عَنْهُم مَّا
كَانُوا۟ يَفْتَرُونَ

75 And We will draw out from every community a witness, and say, "Produce your evidence." Then they will realize that the truth is Allah's, and those they used to invent have forsaken them.

٧٦ إِنَّ قَٰرُونَ كَانَ مِن قَوْمِ مُوسَىٰ فَبَغَىٰ
عَلَيْهِمْ ۖ وَءَاتَيْنَٰهُ مِنَ ٱلْكُنُوزِ مَآ إِنَّ مَفَاتِحَهُۥ
لَتَنُوٓأُ بِٱلْعُصْبَةِ أُو۟لِى ٱلْقُوَّةِ إِذْ قَالَ لَهُۥ قَوْمُهُۥ لَا
تَفْرَحْ ۖ إِنَّ ٱللَّهَ لَا يُحِبُّ ٱلْفَرِحِينَ

76 Quaroon belonged to the clan of Moses, but he oppressed them. We had given him treasures, the keys of which would weigh down a group of strong men. His people said to him, "Do not exult; Allah does not love the exultant.

٧٧ وَٱبْتَغِ فِيمَآ ءَاتَىٰكَ ٱللَّهُ ٱلدَّارَ ٱلْءَاخِرَةَ ۖ وَلَا
تَنسَ نَصِيبَكَ مِنَ ٱلدُّنْيَا ۖ وَأَحْسِن كَمَآ أَحْسَنَ
ٱللَّهُ إِلَيْكَ ۖ وَلَا تَبْغِ ٱلْفَسَادَ فِى ٱلْأَرْضِ ۖ إِنَّ ٱللَّهَ
لَا يُحِبُّ ٱلْمُفْسِدِينَ

77 But seek, with what Allah has given you, the Home of the Hereafter, and do not neglect your share of this world. And be charitable, as Allah has been charitable to you. And do not seek corruption in the land. Allah does not like the seekers of corruption."

٧٨ قَالَ إِنَّمَآ أُوتِيتُهُۥ عَلَىٰ عِلْمٍ عِندِىٓ ۚ أَوَلَمْ
يَعْلَمْ أَنَّ ٱللَّهَ قَدْ أَهْلَكَ مِن قَبْلِهِۦ مِنَ ٱلْقُرُونِ
مَنْ هُوَ أَشَدُّ مِنْهُ قُوَّةً وَأَكْثَرُ جَمْعًا ۚ وَلَا يُسْـَٔلُ
عَن ذُنُوبِهِمُ ٱلْمُجْرِمُونَ

78 He said, "I was given all this on account of knowledge I possess." Did he not know that Allah destroyed many generations before him, who were stronger than he, and possessed greater riches? But the guilty will not be asked about their sins.

٧٩ فَخَرَجَ عَلَىٰ قَوْمِهِۦ فِى زِينَتِهِۦ ۖ قَالَ ٱلَّذِينَ
يُرِيدُونَ ٱلْحَيَوٰةَ ٱلدُّنْيَا يَـٰلَيْتَ لَنَا مِثْلَ مَآ أُوتِىَ
قَـٰرُونُ إِنَّهُۥ لَذُو حَظٍّ عَظِيمٍ

79 And he went out before his people in his splendor. Those who desired the worldly life said, "If only we possessed the likes of what Quaroon was given. He is indeed very fortunate."

٨٠ وَقَالَ ٱلَّذِينَ أُوتُوا۟ ٱلْعِلْمَ وَيْلَكُمْ ثَوَابُ ٱللَّهِ
خَيْرٌ لِّمَنْ ءَامَنَ وَعَمِلَ صَـٰلِحًا وَلَا يُلَقَّىٰهَآ إِلَّا
ٱلصَّـٰبِرُونَ

80 But those who were given knowledge said, "Woe to you! The reward of Allah is better for those who believe and do righteous deeds." Yet none attains it except the steadfast.

٨١ فَخَسَفْنَا بِهِۦ وَبِدَارِهِ ٱلْأَرْضَ فَمَا كَانَ لَهُۥ مِن
فِئَةٍ يَنصُرُونَهُۥ مِن دُونِ ٱللَّهِ وَمَا كَانَ مِنَ
ٱلْمُنتَصِرِينَ

81 So We caused the earth to cave in on him and his mansion. He had no company to save him from Allah, and he could not defend himself.

٨٢ وَأَصْبَحَ ٱلَّذِينَ تَمَنَّوْا۟ مَكَانَهُۥ بِٱلْأَمْسِ
يَقُولُونَ وَيْكَأَنَّ ٱللَّهَ يَبْسُطُ ٱلرِّزْقَ لِمَن يَشَآءُ
مِنْ عِبَادِهِۦ وَيَقْدِرُ ۖ لَوْلَآ أَن مَّنَّ ٱللَّهُ عَلَيْنَا
لَخَسَفَ بِنَا ۖ وَيْكَأَنَّهُۥ لَا يُفْلِحُ ٱلْكَـٰفِرُونَ

82 Those who had wished they were in his position the day before were saying, "Indeed, it is Allah who spreads the bounty to whomever He wills of His servants, and restricts it. Had Allah not been gracious to us, He would have caved in on us. No wonder the ungrateful never prosper."

٨٣ تِلْكَ ٱلدَّارُ ٱلْـَٔاخِرَةُ نَجْعَلُهَا لِلَّذِينَ لَا
يُرِيدُونَ عُلُوًّا فِى ٱلْأَرْضِ وَلَا فَسَادًا ۚ وَٱلْعَـٰقِبَةُ
لِلْمُتَّقِينَ

83 That Home of the Hereafter—We assign it for those who seek no superiority on earth, nor corruption. And the outcome is for the cautious.

٨٤ مَن جَآءَ بِٱلْحَسَنَةِ فَلَهُۥ خَيْرٌ مِّنْهَا ۖ وَمَن جَآءَ
بِٱلسَّيِّئَةِ فَلَا يُجْزَى ٱلَّذِينَ عَمِلُوا۟ ٱلسَّيِّـَٔاتِ إِلَّا مَا
كَانُوا۟ يَعْمَلُونَ

84 Whoever brings a virtue will receive better than it. But whoever brings evil—the evildoers will be rewarded only according to what they used to do.

٨٥ إِنَّ ٱلَّذِى فَرَضَ عَلَيْكَ ٱلْقُرْءَانَ لَرَآدُّكَ إِلَىٰ
مَعَادٍ ۚ قُل رَّبِّىٓ أَعْلَمُ مَن جَآءَ بِٱلْهُدَىٰ وَمَنْ هُوَ
فِى ضَلَٰلٍ مُّبِينٍ

85 He Who ordained the Quran for you will return you Home. Say, "My Lord knows best who comes with guidance, and who is in manifest error."

٨٦ وَمَا كُنتَ تَرْجُوٓا۟ أَن يُلْقَىٰٓ إِلَيْكَ ٱلْكِتَٰبُ إِلَّا
رَحْمَةً مِّن رَّبِّكَ ۖ فَلَا تَكُونَنَّ ظَهِيرًا لِّلْكَٰفِرِينَ

86 You did not expect the Scripture to be transmitted to you, except as mercy from your Lord. Therefore, do not be a supporter of the disbelievers.

٨٧ وَلَا يَصُدُّنَّكَ عَنْ ءَايَٰتِ ٱللَّهِ بَعْدَ إِذْ أُنزِلَتْ
إِلَيْكَ ۖ وَٱدْعُ إِلَىٰ رَبِّكَ ۖ وَلَا تَكُونَنَّ مِنَ
ٱلْمُشْرِكِينَ

87 And do not let them divert you from Allah's revelations after they have been revealed to you. And pray to your Lord, and never be of the polytheists.

٨٨ وَلَا تَدْعُ مَعَ ٱللَّهِ إِلَٰهًا ءَاخَرَ ۘ لَآ إِلَٰهَ إِلَّا هُوَ ۚ
كُلُّ شَىْءٍ هَالِكٌ إِلَّا وَجْهَهُۥ ۚ لَهُ ٱلْحُكْمُ وَإِلَيْهِ
تُرْجَعُونَ

88 And do not invoke with Allah any other god. There is no god but He. All things perish, except His presence. His is the judgment, and to Him you will be returned.

29 The Spider العنكبوت

بِسْمِ ٱللَّهِ ٱلرَّحْمَٰنِ ٱلرَّحِيمِ

In the name of Allah, the Gracious, the Merciful.

١ الٓمٓ

1 Alif, Lam, Meem.

٢ أَحَسِبَ ٱلنَّاسُ أَن يُتْرَكُوٓا۟ أَن يَقُولُوٓا۟ ءَامَنَّا
وَهُمْ لَا يُفْتَنُونَ

2 Have the people supposed that they will be left alone to say, "We believe," without being put to the test?

٣ وَلَقَدْ فَتَنَّا ٱلَّذِينَ مِن قَبْلِهِمْ ۖ فَلَيَعْلَمَنَّ ٱللَّهُ
ٱلَّذِينَ صَدَقُوا۟ وَلَيَعْلَمَنَّ ٱلْكَٰذِبِينَ

3 We have tested those before them. Allah will surely know the truthful, and He will surely know the liars.

٤ أَمْ حَسِبَ ٱلَّذِينَ يَعْمَلُونَ ٱلسَّيِّـَٔاتِ أَن
يَسْبِقُونَا ۚ سَآءَ مَا يَحْكُمُونَ

4 Or do those who commit sins think they can fool Us? Terrible is their opinion!

٥ مَن كَانَ يَرْجُوا۟ لِقَآءَ ٱللَّهِ فَإِنَّ أَجَلَ ٱللَّهِ
لَءَاتٍ ۚ وَهُوَ ٱلسَّمِيعُ ٱلْعَلِيمُ

5 Whoever looks forward to the meeting with Allah—the appointed time of Allah is coming. He is the All-Hearing, the All-Knowing.

٦ وَمَن جَٰهَدَ فَإِنَّمَا يُجَٰهِدُ لِنَفْسِهِۦٓ ۚ إِنَّ ٱللَّهَ لَغَنِىٌّ
عَنِ ٱلْعَٰلَمِينَ

6 Whoever strives, strives only for himself. Allah is Independent of the beings.

٧ وَٱلَّذِينَ ءَامَنُوا۟ وَعَمِلُوا۟ ٱلصَّٰلِحَٰتِ لَنُكَفِّرَنَّ
عَنْهُمْ سَيِّـَٔاتِهِمْ وَلَنَجْزِيَنَّهُمْ أَحْسَنَ ٱلَّذِى كَانُوا۟
يَعْمَلُونَ

7 Those who believe and do righteous deeds—We will remit their sins, and We will reward them according to the best of what they used to do.

٨ وَوَصَّيْنَا ٱلْإِنسَٰنَ بِوَٰلِدَيْهِ حُسْنًا ۖ وَإِن جَٰهَدَاكَ
لِتُشْرِكَ بِى مَا لَيْسَ لَكَ بِهِۦ عِلْمٌ فَلَا تُطِعْهُمَآ ۚ
إِلَىَّ مَرْجِعُكُمْ فَأُنَبِّئُكُم بِمَا كُنتُمْ تَعْمَلُونَ

8 We have advised the human being to be good to his parents. But if they urge you to associate with Me something you have no knowledge of, do not obey them. To Me is your return; and I will inform you of what you used to do.

٩ وَٱلَّذِينَ ءَامَنُوا۟ وَعَمِلُوا۟ ٱلصَّٰلِحَٰتِ لَنُدْخِلَنَّهُمْ
فِى ٱلصَّٰلِحِينَ

9 Those who believe and do good works—We will admit them into the company of the righteous.

١٠ وَمِنَ ٱلنَّاسِ مَن يَقُولُ ءَامَنَّا بِٱللَّهِ فَإِذَآ
أُوذِىَ فِى ٱللَّهِ جَعَلَ فِتْنَةَ ٱلنَّاسِ كَعَذَابِ ٱللَّهِ
وَلَئِن جَآءَ نَصْرٌ مِّن رَّبِّكَ لَيَقُولُنَّ إِنَّا كُنَّا مَعَكُمْ ۚ
أَوَلَيْسَ ٱللَّهُ بِأَعْلَمَ بِمَا فِى صُدُورِ ٱلْعَٰلَمِينَ

10 Among the people is he who says, "We have believed in Allah." Yet when he is harmed on Allah's account, he equates the people's persecution with Allah's retribution. And if help comes from your Lord, he says, "We were actually with you." Is not Allah aware of what is inside the hearts of the people?

١١ وَلَيَعْلَمَنَّ ٱللَّهُ ٱلَّذِينَ ءَامَنُوا۟ وَلَيَعْلَمَنَّ
ٱلْمُنَٰفِقِينَ

11 Allah certainly knows those who believe, and He certainly knows the hypocrites.

١٢ وَقَالَ ٱلَّذِينَ كَفَرُوا۟ لِلَّذِينَ ءَامَنُوا۟ ٱتَّبِعُوا۟ سَبِيلَنَا وَلْنَحْمِلْ خَطَٰيَٰكُمْ وَمَا هُم بِحَٰمِلِينَ مِنْ خَطَٰيَٰهُم مِّن شَىْءٍ ۖ إِنَّهُمْ لَكَٰذِبُونَ	12 Those who disbelieve say to those who believe, "Follow our way, and we will carry your sins." In no way can they carry any of their sins. They are liars.
١٣ وَلَيَحْمِلُنَّ أَثْقَالَهُمْ وَأَثْقَالًا مَّعَ أَثْقَالِهِمْ ۖ وَلَيُسْـَٔلُنَّ يَوْمَ ٱلْقِيَٰمَةِ عَمَّا كَانُوا۟ يَفْتَرُونَ	13 They will carry their own loads, and other loads with their own. And they will be questioned on the Day of Resurrection concerning what they used to fabricate.
١٤ وَلَقَدْ أَرْسَلْنَا نُوحًا إِلَىٰ قَوْمِهِۦ فَلَبِثَ فِيهِمْ أَلْفَ سَنَةٍ إِلَّا خَمْسِينَ عَامًا فَأَخَذَهُمُ ٱلطُّوفَانُ وَهُمْ ظَٰلِمُونَ	14 We sent Noah to his people, and He stayed among them for a thousand years minus fifty years. Then the Deluge swept them; for they were wrongdoers.
١٥ فَأَنجَيْنَٰهُ وَأَصْحَٰبَ ٱلسَّفِينَةِ وَجَعَلْنَٰهَآ ءَايَةً لِّلْعَٰلَمِينَ	15 But We saved him, together with the company of the Ark, and We made it a sign for all peoples.
١٦ وَإِبْرَٰهِيمَ إِذْ قَالَ لِقَوْمِهِ ٱعْبُدُوا۟ ٱللَّهَ وَٱتَّقُوهُ ۖ ذَٰلِكُمْ خَيْرٌ لَّكُمْ إِن كُنتُمْ تَعْلَمُونَ	16 And Abraham, when he said to his people, "Worship Allah, and fear Him. That is better for you, if you only knew.
١٧ إِنَّمَا تَعْبُدُونَ مِن دُونِ ٱللَّهِ أَوْثَٰنًا وَتَخْلُقُونَ إِفْكًا ۚ إِنَّ ٱلَّذِينَ تَعْبُدُونَ مِن دُونِ ٱللَّهِ لَا يَمْلِكُونَ لَكُمْ رِزْقًا فَٱبْتَغُوا۟ عِندَ ٱللَّهِ ٱلرِّزْقَ وَٱعْبُدُوهُ وَٱشْكُرُوا۟ لَهُۥٓ ۖ إِلَيْهِ تُرْجَعُونَ	17 You worship idols besides Allah, and you fabricate falsehoods. Those you worship, instead of Allah, cannot provide you with livelihood. So seek your livelihood from Allah, and worship Him, and thank Him. To Him you will be returned."
١٨ وَإِن تُكَذِّبُوا۟ فَقَدْ كَذَّبَ أُمَمٌ مِّن قَبْلِكُمْ ۖ وَمَا عَلَى ٱلرَّسُولِ إِلَّا ٱلْبَلَٰغُ ٱلْمُبِينُ	18 If you disbelieve, communities before you have also disbelieved. The Messenger is only responsible for clear transmission.
١٩ أَوَلَمْ يَرَوْا۟ كَيْفَ يُبْدِئُ ٱللَّهُ ٱلْخَلْقَ ثُمَّ يُعِيدُهُۥٓ ۚ إِنَّ ذَٰلِكَ عَلَى ٱللَّهِ يَسِيرٌ	19 Have they not seen how Allah originates the creation, and then reproduces it? This is easy for Allah.
٢٠ قُلْ سِيرُوا۟ فِى ٱلْأَرْضِ فَٱنظُرُوا۟ كَيْفَ بَدَأَ ٱلْخَلْقَ ۚ ثُمَّ ٱللَّهُ يُنشِئُ ٱلنَّشْأَةَ ٱلْـَٔاخِرَةَ ۚ إِنَّ ٱللَّهَ عَلَىٰ كُلِّ شَىْءٍ قَدِيرٌ	20 Say, "Roam the earth, and observe how He originated the creation." Then Allah will bring about the next existence. Allah has power over all things."

٢١ يُعَذِّبُ مَن يَشَآءُ وَيَرۡحَمُ مَن يَشَآءُۖ وَإِلَيۡهِ
تُقۡلَبُونَ

21 He punishes whom He wills, and He grants mercy to whom He wills, and to Him you will be restored.

٢٢ وَمَآ أَنتُم بِمُعۡجِزِينَ فِي ٱلۡأَرۡضِ وَلَا فِي
ٱلسَّمَآءِۖ وَمَا لَكُم مِّن دُونِ ٱللَّهِ مِن وَلِيّٖ وَلَا
نَصِيرٖ

22 You cannot escape, on earth or in the heaven; and you have no protector and no savior besides Allah.

٢٣ وَٱلَّذِينَ كَفَرُواْ بِـَٔايَٰتِ ٱللَّهِ وَلِقَآئِهِۦٓ أُوْلَٰٓئِكَ
يَئِسُواْ مِن رَّحۡمَتِي وَأُوْلَٰٓئِكَ لَهُمۡ عَذَابٌ أَلِيمٞ

23 Those who disbelieved in Allah's signs and His encounter—these have despaired of My mercy. For them is a painful torment.

٢٤ فَمَا كَانَ جَوَابَ قَوۡمِهِۦٓ إِلَّآ أَن قَالُواْ ٱقۡتُلُوهُ
أَوۡ حَرِّقُوهُ فَأَنجَىٰهُ ٱللَّهُ مِنَ ٱلنَّارِۚ إِنَّ فِي ذَٰلِكَ
لَأٓيَٰتٖ لِّقَوۡمٖ يُؤۡمِنُونَ

24 But the only response from his people was their saying, "Kill him, or burn him." But Allah saved him from the fire. Surely in that are signs for people who believe.

٢٥ وَقَالَ إِنَّمَا ٱتَّخَذۡتُم مِّن دُونِ ٱللَّهِ أَوۡثَٰنٗا
مَّوَدَّةَ بَيۡنِكُمۡ فِي ٱلۡحَيَوٰةِ ٱلدُّنۡيَاۖ ثُمَّ يَوۡمَ
ٱلۡقِيَٰمَةِ يَكۡفُرُ بَعۡضُكُم بِبَعۡضٖ وَيَلۡعَنُ بَعۡضُكُم
بَعۡضٗا وَمَأۡوَىٰكُمُ ٱلنَّارُ وَمَا لَكُم مِّن نَّٰصِرِينَ

25 And he said, "You have chosen idols instead of Allah, out of affection for one another in the worldly life. But then, on the Day of Resurrection, you will disown one another, and curse one another. Your destiny is Hell, and you will have no saviors."

٢٦ فَـَٔامَنَ لَهُۥ لُوطٞۘ وَقَالَ إِنِّي مُهَاجِرٌ إِلَىٰ رَبِّيٓۖ
إِنَّهُۥ هُوَ ٱلۡعَزِيزُ ٱلۡحَكِيمُ

26 Then Lot believed in him, and said, "I am emigrating to my Lord. He is the Noble, the Wise."

٢٧ وَوَهَبۡنَا لَهُۥٓ إِسۡحَٰقَ وَيَعۡقُوبَ وَجَعَلۡنَا فِي
ذُرِّيَّتِهِ ٱلنُّبُوَّةَ وَٱلۡكِتَٰبَ وَءَاتَيۡنَٰهُ أَجۡرَهُۥ فِي
ٱلدُّنۡيَاۖ وَإِنَّهُۥ فِي ٱلۡأٓخِرَةِ لَمِنَ ٱلصَّٰلِحِينَ

27 And We granted him Isaac and Jacob, and conferred on his descendants the Prophethood and the Book, and gave him his reward in this life; and in the Hereafter he will be among the upright.

٢٨ وَلُوطًا إِذۡ قَالَ لِقَوۡمِهِۦٓ إِنَّكُمۡ لَتَأۡتُونَ ٱلۡفَٰحِشَةَ
مَا سَبَقَكُم بِهَا مِنۡ أَحَدٖ مِّنَ ٱلۡعَٰلَمِينَ

28 And Lot, when he said to his people, "You are committing an obscenity not perpetrated before you by anyone in the whole world.

٢٩ أَئِنَّكُمۡ لَتَأۡتُونَ ٱلرِّجَالَ وَتَقۡطَعُونَ ٱلسَّبِيلَ
وَتَأۡتُونَ فِي نَادِيكُمُ ٱلۡمُنكَرَۖ فَمَا كَانَ جَوَابَ

29 You approach men, and cut off the way, and commit lewdness in your gatherings." But the only response

قَوْمِهِۦٓ إِلَّآ أَن قَالُوا۟ ٱئْتِنَا بِعَذَابِ ٱللَّهِ إِن كُنتَ
مِنَ ٱلصَّٰدِقِينَ

from his people was to say, "Bring upon us Allah's punishment, if you are truthful."

٣٠ قَالَ رَبِّ ٱنصُرْنِى عَلَى ٱلْقَوْمِ ٱلْمُفْسِدِينَ

30 He said, "My Lord, help me against the people of corruption."

٣١ وَلَمَّا جَآءَتْ رُسُلُنَآ إِبْرَٰهِيمَ بِٱلْبُشْرَىٰ قَالُوٓا۟
إِنَّا مُهْلِكُوٓا۟ أَهْلِ هَٰذِهِ ٱلْقَرْيَةِ ۖ إِنَّ أَهْلَهَا كَانُوا۟
ظَٰلِمِينَ

31 And when Our envoys brought Abraham the good news, they said, "We are going to destroy the people of this town; its people are wrongdoers."

٣٢ قَالَ إِنَّ فِيهَا لُوطًا ۚ قَالُوا۟ نَحْنُ أَعْلَمُ بِمَن
فِيهَا ۖ لَنُنَجِّيَنَّهُۥ وَأَهْلَهُۥٓ إِلَّا ٱمْرَأَتَهُۥ كَانَتْ مِنَ
ٱلْغَٰبِرِينَ

32 He said, "Yet Lot is in it." They said, "We are well aware of who is in it. We will save him, and his family, except for his wife, who will remain behind."

٣٣ وَلَمَّآ أَن جَآءَتْ رُسُلُنَا لُوطًا سِىٓءَ بِهِمْ
وَضَاقَ بِهِمْ ذَرْعًا وَقَالُوا۟ لَا تَخَفْ وَلَا تَحْزَنْ ۖ
إِنَّا مُنَجُّوكَ وَأَهْلَكَ إِلَّا ٱمْرَأَتَكَ كَانَتْ مِنَ
ٱلْغَٰبِرِينَ

33 Then, when Our envoys came to Lot, they were mistreated, and he was troubled and distressed on their account. They said, "Do not fear, nor grieve. We will save you and your family, except for your wife, who will remain behind."

٣٤ إِنَّا مُنزِلُونَ عَلَىٰٓ أَهْلِ هَٰذِهِ ٱلْقَرْيَةِ رِجْزًا مِّنَ
ٱلسَّمَآءِ بِمَا كَانُوا۟ يَفْسُقُونَ

34 "We will bring down upon the people of this town a scourge from heaven, because of their wickedness."

٣٥ وَلَقَد تَّرَكْنَا مِنْهَآ ءَايَةًۢ بَيِّنَةً لِّقَوْمٍ يَعْقِلُونَ

35 And We left behind a clear trace of it, for people who understand.

٣٦ وَإِلَىٰ مَدْيَنَ أَخَاهُمْ شُعَيْبًا فَقَالَ يَٰقَوْمِ
ٱعْبُدُوا۟ ٱللَّهَ وَٱرْجُوا۟ ٱلْيَوْمَ ٱلْءَاخِرَ وَلَا تَعْثَوْا۟
فِى ٱلْأَرْضِ مُفْسِدِينَ

36 And to Median, their brother Shuaib. He said, "O my people, worship Allah and anticipate the Last Day, and do not spread corruption in the land."

٣٧ فَكَذَّبُوهُ فَأَخَذَتْهُمُ ٱلرَّجْفَةُ فَأَصْبَحُوا۟ فِى
دَارِهِمْ جَٰثِمِينَ

37 But they rejected him, so the tremor overtook them, and they were left motionless in their homes.

٣٨ وَعَادًا وَثَمُودَا۟ وَقَد تَّبَيَّنَ لَكُم مِّن مَّسَٰكِنِهِمْ ۖ
وَزَيَّنَ لَهُمُ ٱلشَّيْطَٰنُ أَعْمَٰلَهُمْ فَصَدَّهُمْ عَنِ
ٱلسَّبِيلِ وَكَانُوا۟ مُسْتَبْصِرِينَ

38 And Aad and Thamood. It has become clear to you from their dwellings. Satan embellished for them their deeds, barring them from

the path, even though they could see.

٣٩ وَقَٰرُونَ وَفِرۡعَوۡنَ وَهَٰمَٰنَۖ وَلَقَدۡ جَآءَهُم
مُّوسَىٰ بِٱلۡبَيِّنَٰتِ فَٱسۡتَكۡبَرُواْ فِى ٱلۡأَرۡضِ وَمَا
كَانُواْ سَٰبِقِينَ

39 And Quaroon, and Pharaoh, and Hamaan—Moses went to them with clear arguments, but they acted arrogantly in the land. And they could not get ahead.

٤٠ فَكُلًّا أَخَذۡنَا بِذَنۢبِهِۦۖ فَمِنۡهُم مَّنۡ أَرۡسَلۡنَا عَلَيۡهِ
حَاصِبٗا وَمِنۡهُم مَّنۡ أَخَذَتۡهُ ٱلصَّيۡحَةُ وَمِنۡهُم مَّنۡ
خَسَفۡنَا بِهِ ٱلۡأَرۡضَ وَمِنۡهُم مَّنۡ أَغۡرَقۡنَاۚ وَمَا كَانَ
ٱللَّهُ لِيَظۡلِمَهُمۡ وَلَٰكِن كَانُوٓاْ أَنفُسَهُمۡ يَظۡلِمُونَ

40 Each We seized by his sin. Against some We sent a sandstorm. Some were struck by the Blast. Some We caused the ground to cave in beneath them. And some We drowned. It was not Allah who wronged them, but it was they who wronged their own selves.

٤١ مَثَلُ ٱلَّذِينَ ٱتَّخَذُواْ مِن دُونِ ٱللَّهِ أَوۡلِيَآءَ
كَمَثَلِ ٱلۡعَنكَبُوتِ ٱتَّخَذَتۡ بَيۡتٗاۖ وَإِنَّ أَوۡهَنَ
ٱلۡبُيُوتِ لَبَيۡتُ ٱلۡعَنكَبُوتِۖ لَوۡ كَانُواْ يَعۡلَمُونَ

41 The likeness of those who take to themselves protectors other than Allah is that of the spider. It builds a house. But the most fragile of houses is the spider's house. If they only knew.

٤٢ إِنَّ ٱللَّهَ يَعۡلَمُ مَا يَدۡعُونَ مِن دُونِهِۦ مِن
شَىۡءٖۚ وَهُوَ ٱلۡعَزِيزُ ٱلۡحَكِيمُ

42 Allah knows what they invoke besides Him. He is the Almighty, the Wise.

٤٣ وَتِلۡكَ ٱلۡأَمۡثَٰلُ نَضۡرِبُهَا لِلنَّاسِۖ وَمَا يَعۡقِلُهَآ إِلَّا
ٱلۡعَٰلِمُونَ

43 These examples—We put them forward to the people; but none grasps them except the learned.

٤٤ خَلَقَ ٱللَّهُ ٱلسَّمَٰوَٰتِ وَٱلۡأَرۡضَ بِٱلۡحَقِّۚ إِنَّ فِى
ذَٰلِكَ لَأٓيَةٗ لِّلۡمُؤۡمِنِينَ

44 Allah created the heavens and the earth with truth. Surely in that is a sign for the believers.

٤٥ ٱتۡلُ مَآ أُوحِىَ إِلَيۡكَ مِنَ ٱلۡكِتَٰبِ وَأَقِمِ
ٱلصَّلَوٰةَۖ إِنَّ ٱلصَّلَوٰةَ تَنۡهَىٰ عَنِ ٱلۡفَحۡشَآءِ
وَٱلۡمُنكَرِۗ وَلَذِكۡرُ ٱللَّهِ أَكۡبَرُۗ وَٱللَّهُ يَعۡلَمُ مَا
تَصۡنَعُونَ

45 Recite what is revealed to you of the Scripture, and perform the prayer. The prayer prevents indecencies and evils. And the remembrance of Allah is greater. And Allah knows what you do.

٤٦ وَلَا تُجَٰدِلُوٓاْ أَهۡلَ ٱلۡكِتَٰبِ إِلَّا بِٱلَّتِى هِىَ
أَحۡسَنُ إِلَّا ٱلَّذِينَ ظَلَمُواْ مِنۡهُمۡۖ وَقُولُوٓاْ ءَامَنَّا

46 And do not argue with the People of the Scripture except in the best manner possible, except those who do wrong among them. And say, "We believe in what was revealed to

بِٱلَّذِىٓ أُنزِلَ إِلَيْنَا وَأُنزِلَ إِلَيْكُمْ وَإِلَٰهُنَا وَإِلَٰهُكُمْ
وَٰحِدٌ وَنَحْنُ لَهُۥ مُسْلِمُونَ

us, and in what was revealed to you; and our God and your God is One; and to Him we are submissive."

٤٧ وَكَذَٰلِكَ أَنزَلْنَآ إِلَيْكَ ٱلْكِتَٰبَ ۚ فَٱلَّذِينَ ءَاتَيْنَٰهُمُ
ٱلْكِتَٰبَ يُؤْمِنُونَ بِهِۦ ۖ وَمِنْ هَٰٓؤُلَآءِ مَن يُؤْمِنُ
بِهِۦ ۚ وَمَا يَجْحَدُ بِـَٔايَٰتِنَآ إِلَّا ٱلْكَٰفِرُونَ

47 Likewise, We revealed to you the Scripture. Those to whom We gave the Scripture believe in it, and some of these believe in it. None renounce Our communications except the disbelievers.

٤٨ وَمَا كُنتَ تَتْلُوا۟ مِن قَبْلِهِۦ مِن كِتَٰبٍ وَلَا
تَخُطُّهُۥ بِيَمِينِكَ ۖ إِذًا لَّٱرْتَابَ ٱلْمُبْطِلُونَ

48 You did not read any scripture before this, nor did you write it down with your right hand; otherwise the falsifiers would have doubted.

٤٩ بَلْ هُوَ ءَايَٰتٌۢ بَيِّنَٰتٌ فِى صُدُورِ ٱلَّذِينَ أُوتُوا۟
ٱلْعِلْمَ ۚ وَمَا يَجْحَدُ بِـَٔايَٰتِنَآ إِلَّا ٱلظَّٰلِمُونَ

49 In fact, it is clear signs in the hearts of those given knowledge. No one renounce Our signs except the unjust.

٥٠ وَقَالُوا۟ لَوْلَآ أُنزِلَ عَلَيْهِ ءَايَٰتٌ مِّن رَّبِّهِۦ ۖ قُلْ
إِنَّمَا ٱلْءَايَٰتُ عِندَ ٱللَّهِ وَإِنَّمَآ أَنَا۠ نَذِيرٌ مُّبِينٌ

50 And they said, "If only a miracle from his Lord was sent down to him." Say, "Miracles are only with Allah, and I am only a clear warner."

٥١ أَوَلَمْ يَكْفِهِمْ أَنَّآ أَنزَلْنَا عَلَيْكَ ٱلْكِتَٰبَ يُتْلَىٰ
عَلَيْهِمْ ۚ إِنَّ فِى ذَٰلِكَ لَرَحْمَةً وَذِكْرَىٰ لِقَوْمٍ
يُؤْمِنُونَ

51 Does it not suffice them that We revealed to you the Scripture, which is recited to them? In that is mercy and a reminder for people who believe.

٥٢ قُلْ كَفَىٰ بِٱللَّهِ بَيْنِى وَبَيْنَكُمْ شَهِيدًا ۖ يَعْلَمُ
مَا فِى ٱلسَّمَٰوَٰتِ وَٱلْأَرْضِ ۗ وَٱلَّذِينَ ءَامَنُوا۟
بِٱلْبَٰطِلِ وَكَفَرُوا۟ بِٱللَّهِ أُو۟لَٰٓئِكَ هُمُ ٱلْخَٰسِرُونَ

52 Say, "Allah suffices as witness between you and me. He knows everything in the heavens and the Earth. Those who believe in vanity and reject Allah—it is they who are the losers."

٥٣ وَيَسْتَعْجِلُونَكَ بِٱلْعَذَابِ ۚ وَلَوْلَآ أَجَلٌ مُّسَمًّى
لَّجَآءَهُمُ ٱلْعَذَابُ وَلَيَأْتِيَنَّهُم بَغْتَةً وَهُمْ لَا
يَشْعُرُونَ

53 And they urge you to hasten the punishment. Were it not for a specified time, the punishment would have come to them. But it will come upon them suddenly, while they are unaware.

٥٤ يَسْتَعْجِلُونَكَ بِٱلْعَذَابِ وَإِنَّ جَهَنَّمَ لَمُحِيطَةٌۢ
بِٱلْكَٰفِرِينَ

54 They urge you to hasten the punishment. But Hell will engulf the disbelievers.

٥٥ يَوْمَ يَغْشَىٰهُمُ ٱلْعَذَابُ مِن فَوْقِهِمْ وَمِن
تَحْتِ أَرْجُلِهِمْ وَيَقُولُ ذُوقُوا۟ مَا كُنتُمْ تَعْمَلُونَ

55 On the Day when the punishment will envelop them, from above them, and from beneath their feet, He will say, “Taste what you used to do!”

٥٦ يَـٰعِبَادِىَ ٱلَّذِينَ ءَامَنُوٓا۟ إِنَّ أَرْضِى وَٰسِعَةٌ
فَإِيَّـٰىَ فَٱعْبُدُونِ

56 O My servants who have believed: My earth is vast, so worship Me alone.

٥٧ كُلُّ نَفْسٍ ذَآئِقَةُ ٱلْمَوْتِ ۖ ثُمَّ إِلَيْنَا تُرْجَعُونَ

57 Every soul will taste death. Then to Us you will be returned.

٥٨ وَٱلَّذِينَ ءَامَنُوا۟ وَعَمِلُوا۟ ٱلصَّـٰلِحَـٰتِ لَنُبَوِّئَنَّهُم
مِّنَ ٱلْجَنَّةِ غُرَفًا تَجْرِى مِن تَحْتِهَا ٱلْأَنْهَـٰرُ
خَـٰلِدِينَ فِيهَا ۚ نِعْمَ أَجْرُ ٱلْعَـٰمِلِينَ

58 Those who believe and work righteousness—We will settle them in Paradise, in mansions under which rivers flow, dwelling therein forever. Excellent is the compensation for the workers.

٥٩ ٱلَّذِينَ صَبَرُوا۟ وَعَلَىٰ رَبِّهِمْ يَتَوَكَّلُونَ

59 Those who endure patiently, and in their Lord they trust.

٦٠ وَكَأَيِّن مِّن دَآبَّةٍ لَّا تَحْمِلُ رِزْقَهَا ٱللَّهُ يَرْزُقُهَا
وَإِيَّاكُمْ ۚ وَهُوَ ٱلسَّمِيعُ ٱلْعَلِيمُ

60 How many a creature there is that does not carry its provision? Allah provides for them, and for you. He is the Hearer, the Knowledgeable.

٦١ وَلَئِن سَأَلْتَهُم مَّنْ خَلَقَ ٱلسَّمَـٰوَٰتِ وَٱلْأَرْضَ
وَسَخَّرَ ٱلشَّمْسَ وَٱلْقَمَرَ لَيَقُولُنَّ ٱللَّهُ ۖ فَأَنَّىٰ
يُؤْفَكُونَ

61 And if you asked them, “Who created the heavens and the earth and regulated the sun and the moon?” They would say, “Allah.” Why then do they deviate?

٦٢ ٱللَّهُ يَبْسُطُ ٱلرِّزْقَ لِمَن يَشَآءُ مِنْ عِبَادِهِۦ
وَيَقْدِرُ لَهُۥٓ ۚ إِنَّ ٱللَّهَ بِكُلِّ شَىْءٍ عَلِيمٌ

62 Allah expands the provision for whomever He wills of His servants, and restricts it. Allah is Cognizant of all things.

٦٣ وَلَئِن سَأَلْتَهُم مَّن نَّزَّلَ مِنَ ٱلسَّمَآءِ مَآءً
فَأَحْيَا بِهِ ٱلْأَرْضَ مِنۢ بَعْدِ مَوْتِهَا لَيَقُولُنَّ ٱللَّهُ ۚ
قُلِ ٱلْحَمْدُ لِلَّهِ ۚ بَلْ أَكْثَرُهُمْ لَا يَعْقِلُونَ

63 And if you asked them, “Who sends water down from the sky, with which He revives the earth after it had died?” They would say, “Allah.” Say, “Praise be to Allah.” But most of them do not understand.

٦٤ وَمَا هَـٰذِهِ ٱلْحَيَوٰةُ ٱلدُّنْيَآ إِلَّا لَهْوٌ وَلَعِبٌ ۚ وَإِنَّ
ٱلدَّارَ ٱلْـَٔاخِرَةَ لَهِىَ ٱلْحَيَوَانُ ۚ لَوْ كَانُوا۟
يَعْلَمُونَ

64 The life of this world is nothing but diversion and play, and the Home of the Hereafter is the Life, if they only knew.

٦٥ فَإِذَا رَكِبُوا۟ فِى ٱلْفُلْكِ دَعَوُا۟ ٱللَّهَ مُخْلِصِينَ
لَهُ ٱلدِّينَ فَلَمَّا نَجَّىٰهُمْ إِلَى ٱلْبَرِّ إِذَا هُمْ يُشْرِكُونَ

65 When they embark on a vessel, they pray to Allah, devoting their faith to Him; but once He has delivered them safely to land, they attribute partners to Him.

٦٦ لِيَكْفُرُوا۟ بِمَآ ءَاتَيْنَٰهُمْ وَلِيَتَمَتَّعُوا۟ ۖ فَسَوْفَ
يَعْلَمُونَ

66 To be ungrateful for what We have given them, and to enjoy themselves. They will surely come to know.

٦٧ أَوَلَمْ يَرَوْا۟ أَنَّا جَعَلْنَا حَرَمًا ءَامِنًا وَيُتَخَطَّفُ
ٱلنَّاسُ مِنْ حَوْلِهِمْ ۚ أَفَبِٱلْبَٰطِلِ يُؤْمِنُونَ وَبِنِعْمَةِ
ٱللَّهِ يَكْفُرُونَ

67 Do they not see that We established a Secure Sanctuary, while all around them the people are being carried away? Do they believe in falsehood, and reject the blessings of Allah?

٦٨ وَمَنْ أَظْلَمُ مِمَّنِ ٱفْتَرَىٰ عَلَى ٱللَّهِ كَذِبًا أَوْ
كَذَّبَ بِٱلْحَقِّ لَمَّا جَآءَهُۥٓ ۚ أَلَيْسَ فِى جَهَنَّمَ مَثْوًى
لِّلْكَٰفِرِينَ

68 And who does greater wrong than he who fabricates lies and attributes them to Allah, or calls the truth a lie when it has come to him? Is there not in Hell a dwelling for the blasphemers?

٦٩ وَٱلَّذِينَ جَٰهَدُوا۟ فِينَا لَنَهْدِيَنَّهُمْ سُبُلَنَا ۚ وَإِنَّ
ٱللَّهَ لَمَعَ ٱلْمُحْسِنِينَ

69 As for those who strive for Us—We will guide them in Our ways. Allah is with the doers of good.

30 The Romans الروم

بِسْمِ ٱللَّهِ ٱلرَّحْمَٰنِ ٱلرَّحِيمِ

In the name of Allah, the Gracious, the Merciful.

١ الٓمٓ

1 Alif, Lam, Meem.

٢ غُلِبَتِ ٱلرُّومُ

2 The Romans have been defeated.

٣ فِىٓ أَدْنَى ٱلْأَرْضِ وَهُم مِّنۢ بَعْدِ غَلَبِهِمْ
سَيَغْلِبُونَ

3 In a nearby territory. But following their defeat, they will be victorious.

٤ فِى بِضْعِ سِنِينَ ۗ لِلَّهِ ٱلْأَمْرُ مِن قَبْلُ وَمِنۢ بَعْدُ ۚ
وَيَوْمَئِذٍ يَفْرَحُ ٱلْمُؤْمِنُونَ

4 In a few years. The matter is up to Allah, in the past, and in the future. On that day, the believers will rejoice.

٥ بِنَصْرِ ٱللَّهِ ۚ يَنصُرُ مَن يَشَآءُ ۖ وَهُوَ ٱلْعَزِيزُ
ٱلرَّحِيمُ

5 In Allah's support. He supports whomever He wills. He is the Almighty, the Merciful.

٦ وَعْدَ ٱللَّهِ ۖ لَا يُخْلِفُ ٱللَّهُ وَعْدَهُۥ وَلَٰكِنَّ أَكْثَرَ
ٱلنَّاسِ لَا يَعْلَمُونَ

6 The promise of Allah—Allah never breaks His promise, but most people do not know.

٧ يَعْلَمُونَ ظَٰهِرًا مِّنَ ٱلْحَيَوٰةِ ٱلدُّنْيَا وَهُمْ عَنِ
ٱلْءَاخِرَةِ هُمْ غَٰفِلُونَ

7 They know an outer aspect of the worldly life, but they are heedless of the Hereafter.

٨ أَوَلَمْ يَتَفَكَّرُوا۟ فِىٓ أَنفُسِهِم ۗ مَّا خَلَقَ ٱللَّهُ
ٱلسَّمَٰوَٰتِ وَٱلْأَرْضَ وَمَا بَيْنَهُمَآ إِلَّا بِٱلْحَقِّ وَأَجَلٍ
مُّسَمًّى ۗ وَإِنَّ كَثِيرًا مِّنَ ٱلنَّاسِ بِلِقَآئِ رَبِّهِمْ
لَكَٰفِرُونَ

8 Do they not reflect within themselves? Allah did not create the heavens and the earth, and what is between them, except with reason, and for a specific duration. But most people, regarding meeting their Lord, are disbelievers.

٩ أَوَلَمْ يَسِيرُوا۟ فِى ٱلْأَرْضِ فَيَنظُرُوا۟ كَيْفَ كَانَ
عَٰقِبَةُ ٱلَّذِينَ مِن قَبْلِهِمْ ۚ كَانُوٓا۟ أَشَدَّ مِنْهُمْ قُوَّةً
وَأَثَارُوا۟ ٱلْأَرْضَ وَعَمَرُوهَآ أَكْثَرَ مِمَّا عَمَرُوهَا
وَجَآءَتْهُمْ رُسُلُهُم بِٱلْبَيِّنَٰتِ ۖ فَمَا كَانَ ٱللَّهُ
لِيَظْلِمَهُمْ وَلَٰكِن كَانُوٓا۟ أَنفُسَهُمْ يَظْلِمُونَ

9 Have they not travelled the earth and seen how those before them ended up? They were more powerful than them, and they cultivated the land and developed it more than they developed it, and their messengers came to them with clear signs. Allah would never wrong them, but they used to wrong themselves.

١٠ ثُمَّ كَانَ عَٰقِبَةَ ٱلَّذِينَ أَسَٰٓـُٔوا۟ ٱلسُّوٓأَىٰٓ أَن كَذَّبُوا۟
بِـَٔايَٰتِ ٱللَّهِ وَكَانُوا۟ بِهَا يَسْتَهْزِءُونَ

10 Then, evil was the end of those who committed evil. That is because they rejected Allah's revelations, and used to ridicule them.

١١ ٱللَّهُ يَبْدَؤُا۟ ٱلْخَلْقَ ثُمَّ يُعِيدُهُۥ ثُمَّ إِلَيْهِ
تُرْجَعُونَ

11 Allah originates creation, and then repeats it. Then to Him you will be returned.

١٢ وَيَوْمَ تَقُومُ ٱلسَّاعَةُ يُبْلِسُ ٱلْمُجْرِمُونَ

12 On the Day when the Hour takes place, the guilty will despair.

١٣ وَلَمْ يَكُن لَّهُم مِّن شُرَكَآئِهِمْ شُفَعَٰٓؤُا۟ وَكَانُوا۟
بِشُرَكَآئِهِمْ كَٰفِرِينَ

13 They will have no intercessors from among their idols, and they will disown their partners.

١٤ وَيَوْمَ تَقُومُ ٱلسَّاعَةُ يَوْمَئِذٍ يَتَفَرَّقُونَ

14 On the Day when the Hour takes place—on that Day they will separate.

١٥ فَأَمَّا ٱلَّذِينَ ءَامَنُوا۟ وَعَمِلُوا۟ ٱلصَّٰلِحَٰتِ فَهُمْ
فِى رَوْضَةٍ يُحْبَرُونَ

15 As for those who believed and did good deeds—they will be delighted in meadows.

١٦ وَأَمَّا ٱلَّذِينَ كَفَرُوا۟ وَكَذَّبُوا۟ بِـَٔايَٰتِنَا وَلِقَآئِ
ٱلْءَاخِرَةِ فَأُو۟لَٰٓئِكَ فِى ٱلْعَذَابِ مُحْضَرُونَ

16 But as for those who disbelieved, and rejected Our signs and the encounter of the Hereafter—those will be hauled into the torment.

١٧ فَسُبْحَٰنَ ٱللَّهِ حِينَ تُمْسُونَ وَحِينَ
تُصْبِحُونَ

17 So glorify Allah when you retire at night, and when you rise in the morning.

١٨ وَلَهُ ٱلْحَمْدُ فِى ٱلسَّمَٰوَٰتِ وَٱلْأَرْضِ وَعَشِيًّا
وَحِينَ تُظْهِرُونَ

18 His is the praise in the heavens and on earth, and in the evening, and when you reach midday.

١٩ يُخْرِجُ ٱلْحَىَّ مِنَ ٱلْمَيِّتِ وَيُخْرِجُ ٱلْمَيِّتَ مِنَ
ٱلْحَىِّ وَيُحْىِ ٱلْأَرْضَ بَعْدَ مَوْتِهَا ۚ وَكَذَٰلِكَ
تُخْرَجُونَ

19 He brings the living out of the dead, and He brings the dead out of the living, and He revives the land after it had died. Likewise you will be resurrected.

٢٠ وَمِنْ ءَايَٰتِهِۦٓ أَنْ خَلَقَكُم مِّن تُرَابٍ ثُمَّ إِذَآ
أَنتُم بَشَرٌ تَنتَشِرُونَ

20 And of His signs is that He created you from dust; and behold, you become humans spreading out.

٢١ وَمِنْ ءَايَٰتِهِۦٓ أَنْ خَلَقَ لَكُم مِّنْ أَنفُسِكُمْ
أَزْوَٰجًا لِّتَسْكُنُوٓا۟ إِلَيْهَا وَجَعَلَ بَيْنَكُم مَّوَدَّةً
وَرَحْمَةً ۚ إِنَّ فِى ذَٰلِكَ لَءَايَٰتٍ لِّقَوْمٍ يَتَفَكَّرُونَ

21 And of His signs is that He created for you mates from among yourselves, so that you may find tranquility in them; and He planted love and compassion between you. In this are signs for people who reflect.

٢٢ وَمِنْ ءَايَٰتِهِۦ خَلْقُ ٱلسَّمَٰوَٰتِ وَٱلْأَرْضِ
وَٱخْتِلَٰفُ أَلْسِنَتِكُمْ وَأَلْوَٰنِكُمْ ۚ إِنَّ فِى ذَٰلِكَ
لَءَايَٰتٍ لِّلْعَٰلِمِينَ

22 And of His signs is the creation of the heavens and the earth, and the diversity of your languages and colors. In this are signs for those who know.

٢٣ وَمِنْ ءَايَٰتِهِۦ مَنَامُكُم بِٱلَّيْلِ وَٱلنَّهَارِ
وَٱبْتِغَآؤُكُم مِّن فَضْلِهِۦٓ ۚ إِنَّ فِى ذَٰلِكَ لَءَايَٰتٍ
لِّقَوْمٍ يَسْمَعُونَ

23 And of His signs are your sleep by night and day, and your pursuit of His bounty. In this are signs for people who listen.

٢٤ وَمِنْ ءَايَٰتِهِۦ يُرِيكُمُ ٱلْبَرْقَ خَوْفًا وَطَمَعًا
وَيُنَزِّلُ مِنَ ٱلسَّمَآءِ مَآءً فَيُحْىِۦ بِهِ ٱلْأَرْضَ بَعْدَ
مَوْتِهَآ ۚ إِنَّ فِى ذَٰلِكَ لَءَايَٰتٍ لِّقَوْمٍ يَعْقِلُونَ

24 And of His signs is that He shows you the lightning, causing fear and hope. And He brings down water from the sky, and with it He revives the earth after it was dead. In this are signs for people who understand.

٢٥ وَمِنْ ءَايَٰتِهِۦٓ أَن تَقُومَ ٱلسَّمَآءُ وَٱلْأَرْضُ
بِأَمْرِهِۦ ۚ ثُمَّ إِذَا دَعَاكُمْ دَعْوَةً مِّنَ ٱلْأَرْضِ إِذَآ
أَنتُمْ تَخْرُجُونَ

25 And of His signs is that the heaven and the earth stand at His disposal. And then, when He calls you out of the earth, you will emerge at once.

٢٦ وَلَهُۥ مَن فِى ٱلسَّمَٰوَٰتِ وَٱلْأَرْضِ ۖ كُلٌّ لَّهُۥ
قَٰنِتُونَ

26 To Him belongs everyone in the heavens and the earth. All are submissive to Him.

٢٧ وَهُوَ ٱلَّذِى يَبْدَؤُا۟ ٱلْخَلْقَ ثُمَّ يُعِيدُهُۥ وَهُوَ
أَهْوَنُ عَلَيْهِ ۚ وَلَهُ ٱلْمَثَلُ ٱلْأَعْلَىٰ فِى ٱلسَّمَٰوَٰتِ
وَٱلْأَرْضِ ۚ وَهُوَ ٱلْعَزِيزُ ٱلْحَكِيمُ

27 It is He who initiates creation, and then repeats it, something easy for Him. His is the highest attribute, in the heavens and the earth. He is the Almighty, the Wise.

٢٨ ضَرَبَ لَكُم مَّثَلًا مِّنْ أَنفُسِكُمْ ۖ هَل لَّكُم مِّن
مَّا مَلَكَتْ أَيْمَٰنُكُم مِّن شُرَكَآءَ فِى مَا رَزَقْنَٰكُمْ
فَأَنتُمْ فِيهِ سَوَآءٌ تَخَافُونَهُمْ كَخِيفَتِكُمْ
أَنفُسَكُمْ ۚ كَذَٰلِكَ نُفَصِّلُ ٱلْءَايَٰتِ لِقَوْمٍ يَعْقِلُونَ

28 He illustrates an example for you, from your own selves: do you make your servants full partners in the wealth We have given you? Do you revere them as you revere one another? We thus explain the revelations for a people who understand.

٢٩ بَلِ ٱتَّبَعَ ٱلَّذِينَ ظَلَمُوٓا۟ أَهْوَآءَهُم بِغَيْرِ عِلْمٍ ۖ
فَمَن يَهْدِى مَنْ أَضَلَّ ٱللَّهُ ۖ وَمَا لَهُم مِّن نَّٰصِرِينَ

29 Yet the wrongdoers follow their desires without knowledge. But who can guide whom Allah leaves astray? They will have no helpers.

٣٠ فَأَقِمْ وَجْهَكَ لِلدِّينِ حَنِيفًا ۚ فِطْرَتَ ٱللَّهِ
ٱلَّتِى فَطَرَ ٱلنَّاسَ عَلَيْهَا ۚ لَا تَبْدِيلَ لِخَلْقِ ٱللَّهِ ۚ
ذَٰلِكَ ٱلدِّينُ ٱلْقَيِّمُ وَلَٰكِنَّ أَكْثَرَ ٱلنَّاسِ لَا يَعْلَمُونَ

30 So devote yourself to the religion of monotheism—the natural instinct Allah has instilled in mankind. There is no altering Allah's creation. This is the true religion, but most people do not know.

٣١ مُنِيبِينَ إِلَيْهِ وَٱتَّقُوهُ وَأَقِيمُوا۟ ٱلصَّلَوٰةَ وَلَا
تَكُونُوا۟ مِنَ ٱلْمُشْرِكِينَ

31 Turning towards Him—and be conscious of Him, and perform the prayer, and do not be of the idolaters.

٣٢ مِنَ ٱلَّذِينَ فَرَّقُوا۟ دِينَهُمْ وَكَانُوا۟ شِيَعًا ۖ كُلُّ
حِزْبٍۭ بِمَا لَدَيْهِمْ فَرِحُونَ

32 Of those who divided their religion, and became sects; each faction pleased with what they have.

٣٣ وَإِذَا مَسَّ ٱلنَّاسَ ضُرٌّ دَعَوْا۟ رَبَّهُم مُّنِيبِينَ
إِلَيْهِ ثُمَّ إِذَآ أَذَاقَهُم مِّنْهُ رَحْمَةً إِذَا فَرِيقٌ مِّنْهُم
بِرَبِّهِمْ يُشْرِكُونَ

33 When affliction touches the people, they call on their Lord, turning to Him in repentance. But then, when He gives them a taste of His mercy, some of them attribute partners to their Lord.

٣٤ لِيَكْفُرُوا۟ بِمَآ ءَاتَيْنَٰهُمْ ۚ فَتَمَتَّعُوا۟ فَسَوْفَ
تَعْلَمُونَ

34 To show ingratitude for what We have given them. Indulge yourselves—you will surely know.

٣٥ أَمْ أَنزَلْنَا عَلَيْهِمْ سُلْطَٰنًا فَهُوَ يَتَكَلَّمُ بِمَا كَانُوا۟
بِهِۦ يُشْرِكُونَ

35 Have We sent down to them any authority, which speaks in support of their idols?

٣٦ وَإِذَآ أَذَقْنَا ٱلنَّاسَ رَحْمَةً فَرِحُوا۟ بِهَا ۖ وَإِن
تُصِبْهُمْ سَيِّئَةٌۢ بِمَا قَدَّمَتْ أَيْدِيهِمْ إِذَا هُمْ
يَقْنَطُونَ

36 When We give people a taste of mercy, they rejoice in it. But when adversity befalls them, because of what their hands have perpetrated, they begin to despair.

٣٧ أَوَلَمْ يَرَوْا۟ أَنَّ ٱللَّهَ يَبْسُطُ ٱلرِّزْقَ لِمَن يَشَآءُ
وَيَقْدِرُ ۚ إِنَّ فِى ذَٰلِكَ لَءَايَٰتٍ لِّقَوْمٍ يُؤْمِنُونَ

37 Do they not see that Allah expands the provision for whomever He wills, or restricts it? Surely in this are signs for people who believe.

٣٨ فَـَٔاتِ ذَا ٱلْقُرْبَىٰ حَقَّهُۥ وَٱلْمِسْكِينَ وَٱبْنَ
ٱلسَّبِيلِ ۚ ذَٰلِكَ خَيْرٌ لِّلَّذِينَ يُرِيدُونَ وَجْهَ ٱللَّهِ ۖ
وَأُو۟لَٰٓئِكَ هُمُ ٱلْمُفْلِحُونَ

38 So give the relative his rights, and the destitute, and the wayfarer. That is best for those who seek Allah's presence. Those are the prosperous.

٣٩ وَمَآ ءَاتَيْتُم مِّن رِّبًا لِّيَرْبُوَا۟ فِىٓ أَمْوَٰلِ ٱلنَّاسِ
فَلَا يَرْبُوا۟ عِندَ ٱللَّهِ ۖ وَمَآ ءَاتَيْتُم مِّن زَكَوٰةٍ
تُرِيدُونَ وَجْهَ ٱللَّهِ فَأُو۟لَٰٓئِكَ هُمُ ٱلْمُضْعِفُونَ

39 The usury you practice, seeking thereby to multiply people's wealth, will not multiply with Allah. But what you give in charity, desiring Allah's approval—these are the multipliers.

٤٠ ٱللَّهُ ٱلَّذِى خَلَقَكُمْ ثُمَّ رَزَقَكُمْ ثُمَّ يُمِيتُكُمْ ثُمَّ
يُحْيِيكُمْ ۖ هَلْ مِن شُرَكَآئِكُم مَّن يَفْعَلُ مِن
ذَٰلِكُم مِّن شَىْءٍ ۚ سُبْحَٰنَهُۥ وَتَعَٰلَىٰ عَمَّا يُشْرِكُونَ

40 Allah is He who created you, then provides for you, then makes you die, then brings you back to life. Can any of your idols do any of that? Glorified is He, and Exalted above what they associate.

٤١ ظَهَرَ ٱلْفَسَادُ فِى ٱلْبَرِّ وَٱلْبَحْرِ بِمَا كَسَبَتْ
أَيْدِى ٱلنَّاسِ لِيُذِيقَهُم بَعْضَ ٱلَّذِى عَمِلُوا۟ لَعَلَّهُمْ
يَرْجِعُونَ

41 Corruption has appeared on land and sea, because of what people's hands have earned, in order to make them taste some of what they have done, so that they might return.

٤٢ قُلْ سِيرُوا۟ فِى ٱلْأَرْضِ فَٱنظُرُوا۟ كَيْفَ كَانَ
عَٰقِبَةُ ٱلَّذِينَ مِن قَبْلُ ۚ كَانَ أَكْثَرُهُم مُّشْرِكِينَ

42 Say, "Roam the earth, and observe the fate of those who came before. Most of them were idolaters."

٤٣ فَأَقِمْ وَجْهَكَ لِلدِّينِ ٱلْقَيِّمِ مِن قَبْلِ أَن يَأْتِىَ
يَوْمٌ لَّا مَرَدَّ لَهُۥ مِنَ ٱللَّهِ ۖ يَوْمَئِذٍ يَصَّدَّعُونَ

43 So devote yourself to the upright religion, before there comes from Allah a Day that cannot be averted. On that Day, they will be shocked.

٤٤ مَن كَفَرَ فَعَلَيْهِ كُفْرُهُۥ ۖ وَمَنْ عَمِلَ صَٰلِحًا
فَلِأَنفُسِهِمْ يَمْهَدُونَ

44 Whoever disbelieves, upon him falls his disbelief. And whoever acts righteously—they are preparing for themselves.

٤٥ لِيَجْزِىَ ٱلَّذِينَ ءَامَنُوا۟ وَعَمِلُوا۟ ٱلصَّٰلِحَٰتِ مِن
فَضْلِهِۦٓ ۚ إِنَّهُۥ لَا يُحِبُّ ٱلْكَٰفِرِينَ

45 So that He may reward those who have believed and done the righteous deeds out of His bounty. Indeed, He does not love the ungrateful.

٤٦ وَمِنْ ءَايَٰتِهِۦٓ أَن يُرْسِلَ ٱلرِّيَاحَ مُبَشِّرَٰتٍ
وَلِيُذِيقَكُم مِّن رَّحْمَتِهِۦ وَلِتَجْرِىَ ٱلْفُلْكُ بِأَمْرِهِۦ
وَلِتَبْتَغُوا۟ مِن فَضْلِهِۦ وَلَعَلَّكُمْ تَشْكُرُونَ

46 And of His signs is that He sends the winds bearing good news, to give you a taste of His mercy, and so that the ships may sail by His command, and so that you may seek of His bounty, and so that you may give thanks.

٤٧ وَلَقَدْ أَرْسَلْنَا مِن قَبْلِكَ رُسُلًا إِلَىٰ قَوْمِهِمْ
فَجَآءُوهُم بِٱلْبَيِّنَٰتِ فَٱنتَقَمْنَا مِنَ ٱلَّذِينَ
أَجْرَمُوا۟ ۖ وَكَانَ حَقًّا عَلَيْنَا نَصْرُ ٱلْمُؤْمِنِينَ

47 Before you, We sent messengers to their people. They came to them with clear proofs. Then We took revenge on those who sinned. It is incumbent on Us to help the believers.

٤٨ ٱللَّهُ ٱلَّذِى يُرْسِلُ ٱلرِّيَٰحَ فَتُثِيرُ سَحَابًا
فَيَبْسُطُهُۥ فِى ٱلسَّمَآءِ كَيْفَ يَشَآءُ وَيَجْعَلُهُۥ
كِسَفًا فَتَرَى ٱلْوَدْقَ يَخْرُجُ مِنْ خِلَٰلِهِۦ ۖ فَإِذَآ

48 Allah is He who sends the winds. They stir up clouds. Then He spreads them in the sky as He wills. And He breaks them apart. Then you see rain drops issuing from their midst. Then, when He makes it fall

أَصَابَ بِهِۦ مَن يَشَآءُ مِنْ عِبَادِهِۦٓ إِذَا هُمْ
يَسْتَبْشِرُونَ

upon whom He wills of His servants, behold, they rejoice.

٤٩ وَإِن كَانُوا۟ مِن قَبْلِ أَن يُنَزَّلَ عَلَيْهِم مِّن
قَبْلِهِۦ لَمُبْلِسِينَ

49 Although they were before this—before it was sent down upon them—in despair.

٥٠ فَٱنظُرْ إِلَىٰٓ ءَاثَٰرِ رَحْمَتِ ٱللَّهِ كَيْفَ يُحْىِ
ٱلْأَرْضَ بَعْدَ مَوْتِهَآ ۚ إِنَّ ذَٰلِكَ لَمُحْىِ ٱلْمَوْتَىٰ ۖ
وَهُوَ عَلَىٰ كُلِّ شَىْءٍ قَدِيرٌ

50 So observe the effects of Allah's mercy—how He revives the earth after it was dead. Indeed, He is the Reviver of the dead. He is Capable of everything.

٥١ وَلَئِنْ أَرْسَلْنَا رِيحًا فَرَأَوْهُ مُصْفَرًّا لَّظَلُّوا۟ مِنۢ
بَعْدِهِۦ يَكْفُرُونَ

51 But if We send a wind, and they see it turning things yellow, they would continue thereafter to disbelieve.

٥٢ فَإِنَّكَ لَا تُسْمِعُ ٱلْمَوْتَىٰ وَلَا تُسْمِعُ ٱلصُّمَّ
ٱلدُّعَآءَ إِذَا وَلَّوْا۟ مُدْبِرِينَ

52 You cannot make the dead hear, nor can you make the deaf hear the call when they turn away.

٥٣ وَمَآ أَنتَ بِهَٰدِ ٱلْعُمْىِ عَن ضَلَٰلَتِهِمْ ۖ إِن تُسْمِعُ
إِلَّا مَن يُؤْمِنُ بِـَٔايَٰتِنَا فَهُم مُّسْلِمُونَ

53 Nor can you guide the blind out of their error. You can make hear only those who believe in Our signs, and so have submitted.

٥٤ ٱللَّهُ ٱلَّذِى خَلَقَكُم مِّن ضَعْفٍ ثُمَّ جَعَلَ مِنۢ
بَعْدِ ضَعْفٍ قُوَّةً ثُمَّ جَعَلَ مِنۢ بَعْدِ قُوَّةٍ ضَعْفًا
وَشَيْبَةً ۚ يَخْلُقُ مَا يَشَآءُ ۖ وَهُوَ ٱلْعَلِيمُ ٱلْقَدِيرُ

54 Allah is He Who created you weak, then after weakness gave you strength, then after strength gave you weakness and gray hair. He creates whatever He wills. He is the Omniscient, the Omnipotent.

٥٥ وَيَوْمَ تَقُومُ ٱلسَّاعَةُ يُقْسِمُ ٱلْمُجْرِمُونَ مَا
لَبِثُوا۟ غَيْرَ سَاعَةٍ ۚ كَذَٰلِكَ كَانُوا۟ يُؤْفَكُونَ

55 On the Day when the Hour takes place, the sinners will swear they had stayed but an hour. Thus they were deluded.

٥٦ وَقَالَ ٱلَّذِينَ أُوتُوا۟ ٱلْعِلْمَ وَٱلْإِيمَٰنَ لَقَدْ لَبِثْتُمْ
فِى كِتَٰبِ ٱللَّهِ إِلَىٰ يَوْمِ ٱلْبَعْثِ ۖ فَهَٰذَا يَوْمُ
ٱلْبَعْثِ وَلَٰكِنَّكُمْ كُنتُمْ لَا تَعْلَمُونَ

56 But those endowed with knowledge and faith will say, "You remained in Allah's Book until the Day of Resurrection. This is the Day of Resurrection, but you did not know."

٥٧ فَيَوْمَئِذٍ لَّا يَنفَعُ ٱلَّذِينَ ظَلَمُوا۟ مَعْذِرَتُهُمْ وَلَا
هُمْ يُسْتَعْتَبُونَ

57 On that Day, the sinners' excuses will not benefit them, nor will they be excused.

٥٨ وَلَقَدْ ضَرَبْنَا لِلنَّاسِ فِى هَٰذَا ٱلْقُرْءَانِ مِن كُلِّ مَثَلٍ ۚ وَلَئِن جِئْتَهُم بِـَٔايَةٍ لَّيَقُولَنَّ ٱلَّذِينَ كَفَرُوٓا۟ إِنْ أَنتُمْ إِلَّا مُبْطِلُونَ	58 We have cited in this Quran for the people every sort of parable. But even if you bring them a miracle, those who disbelieve will say, "You are nothing but fakers."
٥٩ كَذَٰلِكَ يَطْبَعُ ٱللَّهُ عَلَىٰ قُلُوبِ ٱلَّذِينَ لَا يَعْلَمُونَ	59 Allah thus seals the hearts of those who do not know.
٦٠ فَٱصْبِرْ إِنَّ وَعْدَ ٱللَّهِ حَقٌّ ۖ وَلَا يَسْتَخِفَّنَّكَ ٱلَّذِينَ لَا يُوقِنُونَ	60 So be patient. The promise of Allah is true. And do not let those who lack certainty belittle you.

31 Luqman لقمان

بِسْمِ ٱللَّهِ ٱلرَّحْمَٰنِ ٱلرَّحِيمِ	In the name of Allah, the Gracious, the Merciful.
١ الٓمٓ	1 Alif, Lam, Meem.
٢ تِلْكَ ءَايَٰتُ ٱلْكِتَٰبِ ٱلْحَكِيمِ	2 These are the Verses of the Wise Book.
٣ هُدًى وَرَحْمَةً لِّلْمُحْسِنِينَ	3 A guide and a mercy for the righteous.
٤ ٱلَّذِينَ يُقِيمُونَ ٱلصَّلَوٰةَ وَيُؤْتُونَ ٱلزَّكَوٰةَ وَهُم بِٱلْءَاخِرَةِ هُمْ يُوقِنُونَ	4 Those who observe the prayer, and pay the obligatory charity, and are certain of the Hereafter.
٥ أُو۟لَٰٓئِكَ عَلَىٰ هُدًى مِّن رَّبِّهِمْ ۖ وَأُو۟لَٰٓئِكَ هُمُ ٱلْمُفْلِحُونَ	5 These are upon guidance from their Lord. These are the successful.
٦ وَمِنَ ٱلنَّاسِ مَن يَشْتَرِى لَهْوَ ٱلْحَدِيثِ لِيُضِلَّ عَن سَبِيلِ ٱللَّهِ بِغَيْرِ عِلْمٍ وَيَتَّخِذَهَا هُزُوًا ۚ أُو۟لَٰٓئِكَ لَهُمْ عَذَابٌ مُّهِينٌ	6 Among the people is he who trades in distracting tales; intending, without knowledge, to lead away from Allah's way, and to make a mockery of it. These will have a humiliating punishment.
٧ وَإِذَا تُتْلَىٰ عَلَيْهِ ءَايَٰتُنَا وَلَّىٰ مُسْتَكْبِرًا كَأَن لَّمْ يَسْمَعْهَا كَأَنَّ فِىٓ أُذُنَيْهِ وَقْرًا ۖ فَبَشِّرْهُ بِعَذَابٍ أَلِيمٍ	7 And when Our Verses are recited to him, he turns away in pride, as though he did not hear them, as though there is deafness in his ears. So inform him of a painful punishment.

٨ إِنَّ ٱلَّذِينَ ءَامَنُوا۟ وَعَمِلُوا۟ ٱلصَّـٰلِحَـٰتِ لَهُمْ
جَنَّـٰتُ ٱلنَّعِيمِ

8 As for those who believe and do good deeds—for them are the Gardens of Bliss.

٩ خَـٰلِدِينَ فِيهَا ۖ وَعْدَ ٱللَّهِ حَقًّا ۚ وَهُوَ ٱلْعَزِيزُ
ٱلْحَكِيمُ

9 Dwelling therein forever. The promise of Allah is true. He is the Mighty, the Wise.

١٠ خَلَقَ ٱلسَّمَـٰوَٰتِ بِغَيْرِ عَمَدٍ تَرَوْنَهَا ۖ وَأَلْقَىٰ فِى
ٱلْأَرْضِ رَوَٰسِىَ أَن تَمِيدَ بِكُمْ وَبَثَّ فِيهَا مِن كُلِّ
دَآبَّةٍ ۚ وَأَنزَلْنَا مِنَ ٱلسَّمَآءِ مَآءً فَأَنۢبَتْنَا فِيهَا مِن
كُلِّ زَوْجٍ كَرِيمٍ

10 He created the heavens without pillars that you can see, and placed stabilizers on earth lest it shifts with you, and scattered throughout it all kinds of creatures. And from the sky We sent down water, and caused to grow therein of every noble pair.

١١ هَـٰذَا خَلْقُ ٱللَّهِ فَأَرُونِى مَاذَا خَلَقَ ٱلَّذِينَ مِن
دُونِهِۦ ۚ بَلِ ٱلظَّـٰلِمُونَ فِى ضَلَـٰلٍ مُّبِينٍ

11 Such is Allah's creation. Now show me what those besides Him have created. In fact, the wicked are in obvious error.

١٢ وَلَقَدْ ءَاتَيْنَا لُقْمَـٰنَ ٱلْحِكْمَةَ أَنِ ٱشْكُرْ لِلَّهِ ۚ
وَمَن يَشْكُرْ فَإِنَّمَا يَشْكُرُ لِنَفْسِهِۦ ۖ وَمَن كَفَرَ فَإِنَّ
ٱللَّهَ غَنِىٌّ حَمِيدٌ

12 We endowed Luqman with wisdom: "Give thanks to Allah." Whoever is appreciative—is appreciative for the benefit of his own soul. And whoever is unappreciative—Allah is Sufficient and Praiseworthy.

١٣ وَإِذْ قَالَ لُقْمَـٰنُ لِٱبْنِهِۦ وَهُوَ يَعِظُهُۥ يَـٰبُنَىَّ لَا
تُشْرِكْ بِٱللَّهِ ۖ إِنَّ ٱلشِّرْكَ لَظُلْمٌ عَظِيمٌ

13 When Luqman said to his son, as he advised him, "O my son, do not associate anything with Allah, for idolatry is a terrible wrong."

١٤ وَوَصَّيْنَا ٱلْإِنسَـٰنَ بِوَٰلِدَيْهِ حَمَلَتْهُ أُمُّهُۥ وَهْنًا
عَلَىٰ وَهْنٍ وَفِصَـٰلُهُۥ فِى عَامَيْنِ أَنِ ٱشْكُرْ لِى
وَلِوَٰلِدَيْكَ إِلَىَّ ٱلْمَصِيرُ

14 We have entrusted the human being with the care of his parents. His mother carried him through hardship upon hardship, weaning him in two years. So give thanks to Me, and to your parents. To Me is the destination.

١٥ وَإِن جَـٰهَدَاكَ عَلَىٰٓ أَن تُشْرِكَ بِى مَا لَيْسَ لَكَ
بِهِۦ عِلْمٌ فَلَا تُطِعْهُمَا ۖ وَصَاحِبْهُمَا فِى ٱلدُّنْيَا
مَعْرُوفًا ۖ وَٱتَّبِعْ سَبِيلَ مَنْ أَنَابَ إِلَىَّ ۚ ثُمَّ إِلَىَّ
مَرْجِعُكُمْ فَأُنَبِّئُكُم بِمَا كُنتُمْ تَعْمَلُونَ

15 But if they strive to have you associate with Me something of which you have no knowledge, do not obey them. But keep them company in this life, in kindness, and follow the path of him who turns to

Me. Then to Me is your return; and I will inform you of what you used to do.

١٦ يَٰبُنَيَّ إِنَّهَآ إِن تَكُ مِثْقَالَ حَبَّةٍ مِّنْ خَرْدَلٍ
فَتَكُن فِى صَخْرَةٍ أَوْ فِى ٱلسَّمَٰوَٰتِ أَوْ فِى
ٱلْأَرْضِ يَأْتِ بِهَا ٱللَّهُ ۚ إِنَّ ٱللَّهَ لَطِيفٌ خَبِيرٌ

16 “O my son, even if it were the weight of a mustard-seed, in a rock, or in the heavens, or on earth, Allah will bring it to light. Allah is Kind and Expert.

١٧ يَٰبُنَيَّ أَقِمِ ٱلصَّلَوٰةَ وَأْمُرْ بِٱلْمَعْرُوفِ وَٱنْهَ عَنِ
ٱلْمُنكَرِ وَٱصْبِرْ عَلَىٰ مَآ أَصَابَكَ ۖ إِنَّ ذَٰلِكَ مِنْ
عَزْمِ ٱلْأُمُورِ

17 O my son, observe the prayer, advocate righteousness, forbid evil, and be patient over what has befallen you. These are of the most honorable traits.

١٨ وَلَا تُصَعِّرْ خَدَّكَ لِلنَّاسِ وَلَا تَمْشِ فِى
ٱلْأَرْضِ مَرَحًا ۖ إِنَّ ٱللَّهَ لَا يُحِبُّ كُلَّ مُخْتَالٍ
فَخُورٍ

18 And do not treat people with arrogance, nor walk proudly on earth. Allah does not love the arrogant showoffs.

١٩ وَٱقْصِدْ فِى مَشْيِكَ وَٱغْضُضْ مِن صَوْتِكَ ۚ
إِنَّ أَنكَرَ ٱلْأَصْوَٰتِ لَصَوْتُ ٱلْحَمِيرِ

19 And moderate your stride, and lower your voice. The most repulsive of voices is the donkey’s voice.”

٢٠ أَلَمْ تَرَوْا۟ أَنَّ ٱللَّهَ سَخَّرَ لَكُم مَّا فِى ٱلسَّمَٰوَٰتِ
وَمَا فِى ٱلْأَرْضِ وَأَسْبَغَ عَلَيْكُمْ نِعَمَهُۥ ظَٰهِرَةً
وَبَاطِنَةً ۗ وَمِنَ ٱلنَّاسِ مَن يُجَٰدِلُ فِى ٱللَّهِ بِغَيْرِ
عِلْمٍ وَلَا هُدًى وَلَا كِتَٰبٍ مُّنِيرٍ

20 Do you not see how Allah placed at your service everything in the heavens and the earth? How He showered you with His blessings, both outward and inward? Yet among the people is he who argues about Allah without knowledge, without guidance, and without an enlightening Scripture.

٢١ وَإِذَا قِيلَ لَهُمُ ٱتَّبِعُوا۟ مَآ أَنزَلَ ٱللَّهُ قَالُوا۟ بَلْ
نَتَّبِعُ مَا وَجَدْنَا عَلَيْهِ ءَابَآءَنَآ ۚ أَوَلَوْ كَانَ
ٱلشَّيْطَٰنُ يَدْعُوهُمْ إِلَىٰ عَذَابِ ٱلسَّعِيرِ

21 And when it is said to them, “Follow what Allah has revealed,” they say, “Rather, we follow what we found our parents devoted to.” Even if Satan is calling them to the suffering of the Blaze?

٢٢ وَمَن يُسْلِمْ وَجْهَهُۥٓ إِلَى ٱللَّهِ وَهُوَ مُحْسِنٌ
فَقَدِ ٱسْتَمْسَكَ بِٱلْعُرْوَةِ ٱلْوُثْقَىٰ ۗ وَإِلَى ٱللَّهِ
عَٰقِبَةُ ٱلْأُمُورِ

22 Whoever submits himself wholly to Allah, and is a doer of good, has grasped the most trustworthy handle. With Allah rests the outcome of all events.

٢٣ وَمَن كَفَرَ فَلَا يَحْزُنكَ كُفْرُهُۥٓ ۚ إِلَيْنَا مَرْجِعُهُمْ فَنُنَبِّئُهُم بِمَا عَمِلُوٓا۟ ۚ إِنَّ ٱللَّهَ عَلِيمٌۢ بِذَاتِ ٱلصُّدُورِ

23 Whoever disbelieves—let not his disbelief sadden you. To Us is their return. Then We will inform them of what they did. Allah knows what lies within the hearts.

٢٤ نُمَتِّعُهُمْ قَلِيلًا ثُمَّ نَضْطَرُّهُمْ إِلَىٰ عَذَابٍ غَلِيظٍ

24 We give them a little comfort; then We compel them to a harsh torment.

٢٥ وَلَئِن سَأَلْتَهُم مَّنْ خَلَقَ ٱلسَّمَٰوَٰتِ وَٱلْأَرْضَ لَيَقُولُنَّ ٱللَّهُ ۚ قُلِ ٱلْحَمْدُ لِلَّهِ ۚ بَلْ أَكْثَرُهُمْ لَا يَعْلَمُونَ

25 And if you ask them, “Who created the heavens and the earth?” They will say, “Allah.” Say, “Praise be to Allah.” But most of them do not know.

٢٦ لِلَّهِ مَا فِى ٱلسَّمَٰوَٰتِ وَٱلْأَرْضِ ۚ إِنَّ ٱللَّهَ هُوَ ٱلْغَنِىُّ ٱلْحَمِيدُ

26 To Allah belongs everything in the heavens and the earth. Allah is the Rich, the Praised.

٢٧ وَلَوْ أَنَّمَا فِى ٱلْأَرْضِ مِن شَجَرَةٍ أَقْلَٰمٌ وَٱلْبَحْرُ يَمُدُّهُۥ مِنۢ بَعْدِهِۦ سَبْعَةُ أَبْحُرٍ مَّا نَفِدَتْ كَلِمَٰتُ ٱللَّهِ ۗ إِنَّ ٱللَّهَ عَزِيزٌ حَكِيمٌ

27 If all the trees on earth were pens, filled by the ocean, with seven more oceans besides, the Words of Allah would not run out. Allah is Majestic and Wise.

٢٨ مَّا خَلْقُكُمْ وَلَا بَعْثُكُمْ إِلَّا كَنَفْسٍ وَٰحِدَةٍ ۗ إِنَّ ٱللَّهَ سَمِيعٌۢ بَصِيرٌ

28 Your creation and your resurrection are only as a single soul. Allah is Hearing and Seeing.

٢٩ أَلَمْ تَرَ أَنَّ ٱللَّهَ يُولِجُ ٱلَّيْلَ فِى ٱلنَّهَارِ وَيُولِجُ ٱلنَّهَارَ فِى ٱلَّيْلِ وَسَخَّرَ ٱلشَّمْسَ وَٱلْقَمَرَ كُلٌّ يَجْرِىٓ إِلَىٰٓ أَجَلٍ مُّسَمًّى وَأَنَّ ٱللَّهَ بِمَا تَعْمَلُونَ خَبِيرٌ

29 Have you not seen how Allah merges the night into the day, and merges the day into the night? That He subjected the sun and the moon, each running for a stated term? And that Allah is Cognizant of everything you do?

٣٠ ذَٰلِكَ بِأَنَّ ٱللَّهَ هُوَ ٱلْحَقُّ وَأَنَّ مَا يَدْعُونَ مِن دُونِهِ ٱلْبَٰطِلُ وَأَنَّ ٱللَّهَ هُوَ ٱلْعَلِىُّ ٱلْكَبِيرُ

30 That is because Allah is the Reality, and what they worship besides Him is falsehood, and because Allah is the Exalted, the Supreme.

٣١ أَلَمْ تَرَ أَنَّ ٱلْفُلْكَ تَجْرِى فِى ٱلْبَحْرِ بِنِعْمَتِ ٱللَّهِ لِيُرِيَكُم مِّنْ ءَايَٰتِهِۦٓ ۚ إِنَّ فِى ذَٰلِكَ لَءَايَٰتٍ لِّكُلِّ صَبَّارٍ شَكُورٍ

31 Have you not seen how the ships sail through the sea, by the grace of Allah, to show you of His wonders? In that are signs for every persevering, thankful person.

٣٢ وَإِذَا غَشِيَهُم مَّوْجٌ كَٱلظُّلَلِ دَعَوُاْ ٱللَّهَ
مُخْلِصِينَ لَهُ ٱلدِّينَ فَلَمَّا نَجَّىٰهُمْ إِلَى ٱلْبَرِّ فَمِنْهُم
مُّقْتَصِدٌ ۚ وَمَا يَجْحَدُ بِـَٔايَٰتِنَآ إِلَّا كُلُّ خَتَّارٍ كَفُورٍ

32 When waves, like canopies, cover them, they call upon Allah, devoting their religion to Him. But when He has delivered them to dry land, some of them waver. No one renounces Our revelations except the treacherous blasphemer.

٣٣ يَٰٓأَيُّهَا ٱلنَّاسُ ٱتَّقُواْ رَبَّكُمْ وَٱخْشَوْاْ يَوْمًا لَّا
يَجْزِى وَالِدٌ عَن وَلَدِهِۦ وَلَا مَوْلُودٌ هُوَ جَازٍ عَن
وَالِدِهِۦ شَيْـًٔا ۚ إِنَّ وَعْدَ ٱللَّهِ حَقٌّ ۖ فَلَا تَغُرَّنَّكُمُ
ٱلْحَيَوٰةُ ٱلدُّنْيَا وَلَا يَغُرَّنَّكُم بِٱللَّهِ ٱلْغَرُورُ

33 O people! Be conscious of your Lord, and dread a Day when no parent can avail his child, nor can a child avail his parent, in anything. The promise of Allah is true. Therefore, do not let this life deceive you, nor let illusions deceive you regarding Allah.

٣٤ إِنَّ ٱللَّهَ عِندَهُۥ عِلْمُ ٱلسَّاعَةِ وَيُنَزِّلُ ٱلْغَيْثَ
وَيَعْلَمُ مَا فِى ٱلْأَرْحَامِ ۖ وَمَا تَدْرِى نَفْسٌ مَّاذَا
تَكْسِبُ غَدًا ۖ وَمَا تَدْرِى نَفْسٌۢ بِأَىِّ أَرْضٍ تَمُوتُ ۚ
إِنَّ ٱللَّهَ عَلِيمٌ خَبِيرٌۢ

34 With Allah rests the knowledge of the Hour. He sends down the rain, and He knows what the wombs contain. No soul knows what it will reap tomorrow, and no soul knows in what land it will die. Allah is All-Knowing, Well-Informed.

32 Prostration السجدة

بِسْمِ ٱللَّهِ ٱلرَّحْمَٰنِ ٱلرَّحِيمِ

In the name of Allah, the Gracious, the Merciful.

١ الٓمٓ

1 Alif, Lam, Meem.

٢ تَنزِيلُ ٱلْكِتَٰبِ لَا رَيْبَ فِيهِ مِن رَّبِّ ٱلْعَٰلَمِينَ

2 The revelation of the Book, without a doubt, is from the Lord of the Universe.

٣ أَمْ يَقُولُونَ ٱفْتَرَىٰهُ ۚ بَلْ هُوَ ٱلْحَقُّ مِن رَّبِّكَ
لِتُنذِرَ قَوْمًا مَّآ أَتَىٰهُم مِّن نَّذِيرٍ مِّن قَبْلِكَ لَعَلَّهُمْ
يَهْتَدُونَ

3 Yet they say, "He made it up." In fact, it is the Truth from your Lord, to warn a people who received no warner before you, that they may be guided.

٤ ٱللَّهُ ٱلَّذِى خَلَقَ ٱلسَّمَٰوَٰتِ وَٱلْأَرْضَ وَمَا بَيْنَهُمَا
فِى سِتَّةِ أَيَّامٍ ثُمَّ ٱسْتَوَىٰ عَلَى ٱلْعَرْشِ ۖ مَا لَكُم
مِّن دُونِهِۦ مِن وَلِىٍّ وَلَا شَفِيعٍ ۚ أَفَلَا تَتَذَكَّرُونَ

4 Allah is He who created the heavens and the earth and everything between them in six days, and then established Himself

on the Throne. Apart from Him, you have no master and no intercessor. Will you not reflect?

٥ يُدَبِّرُ ٱلْأَمْرَ مِنَ ٱلسَّمَآءِ إِلَى ٱلْأَرْضِ ثُمَّ يَعْرُجُ
إِلَيْهِ فِى يَوْمٍ كَانَ مِقْدَارُهُۥٓ أَلْفَ سَنَةٍ مِّمَّا
تَعُدُّونَ

5 He regulates all affairs, from the heavens, to the earth. Then it ascends to Him on a Day the length of which is a thousand years by your count.

٦ ذَٰلِكَ عَٰلِمُ ٱلْغَيْبِ وَٱلشَّهَٰدَةِ ٱلْعَزِيزُ ٱلرَّحِيمُ

6 That is the Knower of the Invisible and the Visible, the Powerful, the Merciful.

٧ ٱلَّذِىٓ أَحْسَنَ كُلَّ شَىْءٍ خَلَقَهُۥ ۖ وَبَدَأَ خَلْقَ
ٱلْإِنسَٰنِ مِن طِينٍ

7 He who perfected everything He created, and originated the creation of man from clay.

٨ ثُمَّ جَعَلَ نَسْلَهُۥ مِن سُلَٰلَةٍ مِّن مَّآءٍ مَّهِينٍ

8 Then made his reproduction from an extract of an insignificant fluid.

٩ ثُمَّ سَوَّىٰهُ وَنَفَخَ فِيهِ مِن رُّوحِهِۦ ۖ وَجَعَلَ لَكُمُ
ٱلسَّمْعَ وَٱلْأَبْصَٰرَ وَٱلْأَفْـِٔدَةَ ۚ قَلِيلًا مَّا تَشْكُرُونَ

9 Then He proportioned him, and breathed into him of His Spirit. Then He gave you the hearing, and the eyesight, and the brains—but rarely do you give thanks.

١٠ وَقَالُوٓا۟ أَءِذَا ضَلَلْنَا فِى ٱلْأَرْضِ أَءِنَّا لَفِى
خَلْقٍ جَدِيدٍۭ ۚ بَلْ هُم بِلِقَآءِ رَبِّهِمْ كَٰفِرُونَ

10 And they say, “When we are lost into the earth, shall we be in a new creation?” In fact, they deny the meeting with their Lord.

١١ قُلْ يَتَوَفَّىٰكُم مَّلَكُ ٱلْمَوْتِ ٱلَّذِى وُكِّلَ بِكُمْ ثُمَّ
إِلَىٰ رَبِّكُمْ تُرْجَعُونَ

11 Say, “The angel of death put in charge of you will reclaim you. Then to your Lord you will be returned.”

١٢ وَلَوْ تَرَىٰٓ إِذِ ٱلْمُجْرِمُونَ نَاكِسُوا۟ رُءُوسِهِمْ
عِندَ رَبِّهِمْ رَبَّنَآ أَبْصَرْنَا وَسَمِعْنَا فَٱرْجِعْنَا نَعْمَلْ
صَٰلِحًا إِنَّا مُوقِنُونَ

12 If only you could see the guilty, bowing their heads before their Lord: “Our Lord, we have seen and we have heard, so send us back, and we will act righteously; we are now convinced.”

١٣ وَلَوْ شِئْنَا لَءَاتَيْنَا كُلَّ نَفْسٍ هُدَىٰهَا وَلَٰكِنْ
حَقَّ ٱلْقَوْلُ مِنِّى لَأَمْلَأَنَّ جَهَنَّمَ مِنَ ٱلْجِنَّةِ
وَٱلنَّاسِ أَجْمَعِينَ

13 Had We willed, We could have given every soul its guidance, but the declaration from Me will come true: “I will fill Hell with jinn and humans, altogether.”

١٤ فَذُوقُوا۟ بِمَا نَسِيتُمْ لِقَآءَ يَوْمِكُمْ هَٰذَآ إِنَّا
نَسِينَٰكُمْ ۖ وَذُوقُوا۟ عَذَابَ ٱلْخُلْدِ بِمَا كُنتُمْ
تَعْمَلُونَ

14 So taste, because you forgot the meeting of this Day of yours; We have forgotten you; so taste the eternal torment for what you used to do.

١٥ إِنَّمَا يُؤْمِنُ بِـَٔايَٰتِنَا ٱلَّذِينَ إِذَا ذُكِّرُوا۟ بِهَا خَرُّوا۟
سُجَّدًا وَسَبَّحُوا۟ بِحَمْدِ رَبِّهِمْ وَهُمْ لَا
يَسْتَكْبِرُونَ ۩

15 They believe in Our communications, those who, when reminded of them, fall down prostrate, and glorify their Lord with praise, and are not proud.

١٦ تَتَجَافَىٰ جُنُوبُهُمْ عَنِ ٱلْمَضَاجِعِ يَدْعُونَ
رَبَّهُمْ خَوْفًا وَطَمَعًا وَمِمَّا رَزَقْنَٰهُمْ يُنفِقُونَ

16 Their sides shun their beds, as they pray to their Lord, out of reverence and hope; and from Our provisions to them, they give.

١٧ فَلَا تَعْلَمُ نَفْسٌ مَّآ أُخْفِىَ لَهُم مِّن قُرَّةِ أَعْيُنٍ
جَزَآءًۢ بِمَا كَانُوا۟ يَعْمَلُونَ

17 No soul knows what eye's delight awaits them—a reward for what they used to do.

١٨ أَفَمَن كَانَ مُؤْمِنًا كَمَن كَانَ فَاسِقًا ۚ لَّا
يَسْتَوُۥنَ

18 Is someone who is faithful like someone who is a sinner? They are not equal.

١٩ أَمَّا ٱلَّذِينَ ءَامَنُوا۟ وَعَمِلُوا۟ ٱلصَّٰلِحَٰتِ فَلَهُمْ
جَنَّٰتُ ٱلْمَأْوَىٰ نُزُلًۢا بِمَا كَانُوا۟ يَعْمَلُونَ

19 As for those who believe and do righteous deeds, for them are the Gardens of Shelter—hospitality for what they used to do.

٢٠ وَأَمَّا ٱلَّذِينَ فَسَقُوا۟ فَمَأْوَىٰهُمُ ٱلنَّارُ ۖ كُلَّمَآ
أَرَادُوٓا۟ أَن يَخْرُجُوا۟ مِنْهَآ أُعِيدُوا۟ فِيهَا وَقِيلَ
لَهُمْ ذُوقُوا۟ عَذَابَ ٱلنَّارِ ٱلَّذِى كُنتُم بِهِۦ تُكَذِّبُونَ

20 But as for those who transgressed, their shelter is the Fire. Every time they try to get out of it, they will be brought back into it, and it will be said to them, "Taste the suffering of the Fire which you used to deny."

٢١ وَلَنُذِيقَنَّهُم مِّنَ ٱلْعَذَابِ ٱلْأَدْنَىٰ دُونَ ٱلْعَذَابِ
ٱلْأَكْبَرِ لَعَلَّهُمْ يَرْجِعُونَ

21 We will make them taste the lesser torment, prior to the greater torment, so that they may return.

٢٢ وَمَنْ أَظْلَمُ مِمَّن ذُكِّرَ بِـَٔايَٰتِ رَبِّهِۦ ثُمَّ أَعْرَضَ
عَنْهَآ ۚ إِنَّا مِنَ ٱلْمُجْرِمِينَ مُنتَقِمُونَ

22 Who is more wrong than he, who, when reminded of his Lord's revelations, turns away from them? We will certainly wreak vengeance upon the criminals.

٢٣ وَلَقَدْ ءَاتَيْنَا مُوسَى ٱلْكِتَٰبَ فَلَا تَكُن فِى مِرْيَةٍ مِّن لِّقَآئِهِۦ ۖ وَجَعَلْنَٰهُ هُدًى لِّبَنِىٓ إِسْرَٰٓءِيلَ

23 We gave Moses the Book; so do not be in doubt regarding His encounter; and We made it a guidance for the Children of Israel.

٢٤ وَجَعَلْنَا مِنْهُمْ أَئِمَّةً يَهْدُونَ بِأَمْرِنَا لَمَّا صَبَرُوا۟ ۖ وَكَانُوا۟ بِـَٔايَٰتِنَا يُوقِنُونَ

24 And We appointed leaders from among them, guiding by Our command, as long as they persevered and were certain of Our communications.

٢٥ إِنَّ رَبَّكَ هُوَ يَفْصِلُ بَيْنَهُمْ يَوْمَ ٱلْقِيَٰمَةِ فِيمَا كَانُوا۟ فِيهِ يَخْتَلِفُونَ

25 Your Lord will judge between them on the Day of Resurrection regarding everything they had disputed.

٢٦ أَوَلَمْ يَهْدِ لَهُمْ كَمْ أَهْلَكْنَا مِن قَبْلِهِم مِّنَ ٱلْقُرُونِ يَمْشُونَ فِى مَسَٰكِنِهِمْ ۚ إِنَّ فِى ذَٰلِكَ لَءَايَٰتٍ ۖ أَفَلَا يَسْمَعُونَ

26 Is it not a lesson for them, how many generations We have destroyed before them, in whose habitations they walk? Surely in that are signs. Do they not hear?

٢٧ أَوَلَمْ يَرَوْا۟ أَنَّا نَسُوقُ ٱلْمَآءَ إِلَى ٱلْأَرْضِ ٱلْجُرُزِ فَنُخْرِجُ بِهِۦ زَرْعًا تَأْكُلُ مِنْهُ أَنْعَٰمُهُمْ وَأَنفُسُهُمْ ۖ أَفَلَا يُبْصِرُونَ

27 Do they not see how We conduct the water to a dry land, and with it We produce vegetation, from which their livestock eat, and themselves? Do they not see?

٢٨ وَيَقُولُونَ مَتَىٰ هَٰذَا ٱلْفَتْحُ إِن كُنتُمْ صَٰدِقِينَ

28 And they say, “When is this victory, if you are truthful?”

٢٩ قُلْ يَوْمَ ٱلْفَتْحِ لَا يَنفَعُ ٱلَّذِينَ كَفَرُوٓا۟ إِيمَٰنُهُمْ وَلَا هُمْ يُنظَرُونَ

29 Say, “On the day of victory, the faith of those who disbelieved will be of no avail to them, and they will not be granted respite.”

٣٠ فَأَعْرِضْ عَنْهُمْ وَٱنتَظِرْ إِنَّهُم مُّنتَظِرُونَ

30 So turn away from them, and wait. They too are waiting.

33 The Confederates الأحزاب

بِسْمِ ٱللَّهِ ٱلرَّحْمَٰنِ ٱلرَّحِيمِ

In the name of Allah, the Gracious, the Merciful.

١ يَٰٓأَيُّهَا ٱلنَّبِىُّ ٱتَّقِ ٱللَّهَ وَلَا تُطِعِ ٱلْكَٰفِرِينَ وَٱلْمُنَٰفِقِينَ ۗ إِنَّ ٱللَّهَ كَانَ عَلِيمًا حَكِيمًا

1 O Prophet! Fear Allah, and do not obey the unbelievers and the hypocrites. Allah is Knowledgeable and Wise.

٢ وَٱتَّبِعْ مَا يُوحَىٰٓ إِلَيْكَ مِن رَّبِّكَ ۚ إِنَّ ٱللَّهَ كَانَ
بِمَا تَعْمَلُونَ خَبِيرًا

2 And follow what is revealed to you from your Lord. Allah is fully aware of what you do.

٣ وَتَوَكَّلْ عَلَى ٱللَّهِ ۚ وَكَفَىٰ بِٱللَّهِ وَكِيلًا

3 And put your trust in Allah. Allah is enough as a trustee.

٤ مَّا جَعَلَ ٱللَّهُ لِرَجُلٍ مِّن قَلْبَيْنِ فِى جَوْفِهِۦ ۚ
وَمَا جَعَلَ أَزْوَٰجَكُمُ ٱلَّٰٓـِٔى تُظَٰهِرُونَ مِنْهُنَّ
أُمَّهَٰتِكُمْ ۚ وَمَا جَعَلَ أَدْعِيَآءَكُمْ أَبْنَآءَكُمْ ۚ ذَٰلِكُمْ
قَوْلُكُم بِأَفْوَٰهِكُمْ ۖ وَٱللَّهُ يَقُولُ ٱلْحَقَّ وَهُوَ
يَهْدِى ٱلسَّبِيلَ

4 Allah did not place two hearts inside any man's body. Nor did He make your wives whom you equate with your mothers, your actual mothers. Nor did He make your adopted sons, your actual sons. These are your words coming out of your mouths. Allah speaks the truth, and guides to the path.

٥ ٱدْعُوهُمْ لِءَابَآئِهِمْ هُوَ أَقْسَطُ عِندَ ٱللَّهِ ۚ فَإِن
لَّمْ تَعْلَمُوٓا۟ ءَابَآءَهُمْ فَإِخْوَٰنُكُمْ فِى ٱلدِّينِ
وَمَوَٰلِيكُمْ ۚ وَلَيْسَ عَلَيْكُمْ جُنَاحٌ فِيمَآ أَخْطَأْتُم
بِهِۦ وَلَٰكِن مَّا تَعَمَّدَتْ قُلُوبُكُمْ ۚ وَكَانَ ٱللَّهُ غَفُورًا
رَّحِيمًا

5 Call them after their fathers; that is more equitable with Allah. But if you do not know their fathers, then your brethren in faith and your friends. There is no blame on you if you err therein, barring what your hearts premeditates. Allah is Forgiving and Merciful.

٦ ٱلنَّبِىُّ أَوْلَىٰ بِٱلْمُؤْمِنِينَ مِنْ أَنفُسِهِمْ ۖ وَأَزْوَٰجُهُۥٓ
أُمَّهَٰتُهُمْ ۗ وَأُو۟لُوا۟ ٱلْأَرْحَامِ بَعْضُهُمْ أَوْلَىٰ بِبَعْضٍ
فِى كِتَٰبِ ٱللَّهِ مِنَ ٱلْمُؤْمِنِينَ وَٱلْمُهَٰجِرِينَ إِلَّآ أَن
تَفْعَلُوٓا۟ إِلَىٰٓ أَوْلِيَآئِكُم مَّعْرُوفًا ۚ كَانَ ذَٰلِكَ فِى
ٱلْكِتَٰبِ مَسْطُورًا

6 The Prophet is more caring of the believers than they are of themselves, and his wives are mothers to them. And blood-relatives are closer to one another in Allah's Book than the believers or the emigrants, though you should do good to your friends. That is inscribed in the Book.

٧ وَإِذْ أَخَذْنَا مِنَ ٱلنَّبِيِّـۧنَ مِيثَٰقَهُمْ وَمِنكَ وَمِن
نُّوحٍ وَإِبْرَٰهِيمَ وَمُوسَىٰ وَعِيسَى ٱبْنِ مَرْيَمَ ۖ
وَأَخَذْنَا مِنْهُم مِّيثَٰقًا غَلِيظًا

7 Recall that We received a pledge from the prophets, and from you, and from Noah, and Abraham, and Moses, and Jesus son of Mary. We received from them a solemn pledge.

٨ لِّيَسْـَٔلَ ٱلصَّٰدِقِينَ عَن صِدْقِهِمْ ۚ وَأَعَدَّ
لِلْكَٰفِرِينَ عَذَابًا أَلِيمًا

8 That He may ask the sincere about their sincerity. He has prepared for the disbelievers a painful punishment.

٩ يَٰٓأَيُّهَا ٱلَّذِينَ ءَامَنُواْ ٱذْكُرُواْ نِعْمَةَ ٱللَّهِ عَلَيْكُمْ
إِذْ جَآءَتْكُمْ جُنُودٌ فَأَرْسَلْنَا عَلَيْهِمْ رِيحًا
وَجُنُودًا لَّمْ تَرَوْهَا ۚ وَكَانَ ٱللَّهُ بِمَا تَعْمَلُونَ
بَصِيرًا

9 O you who believe! Remember Allah's blessings upon you, when forces came against you, and We sent against them a wind, and forces you did not see. Allah is Observant of what you do.

١٠ إِذْ جَآءُوكُم مِّن فَوْقِكُمْ وَمِنْ أَسْفَلَ مِنكُمْ
وَإِذْ زَاغَتِ ٱلْأَبْصَٰرُ وَبَلَغَتِ ٱلْقُلُوبُ ٱلْحَنَاجِرَ
وَتَظُنُّونَ بِٱللَّهِ ٱلظُّنُونَا۠

10 When they came upon you, from above you, and from beneath you; and the eyes became dazed, and the hearts reached the throats, and you harbored doubts about Allah.

١١ هُنَالِكَ ٱبْتُلِىَ ٱلْمُؤْمِنُونَ وَزُلْزِلُواْ زِلْزَالًا
شَدِيدًا

11 There and then the believers were tested, and were shaken most severely.

١٢ وَإِذْ يَقُولُ ٱلْمُنَٰفِقُونَ وَٱلَّذِينَ فِى قُلُوبِهِم
مَّرَضٌ مَّا وَعَدَنَا ٱللَّهُ وَرَسُولُهُۥٓ إِلَّا غُرُورًا

12 When the hypocrites and those in whose hearts is sickness said, "Allah and His Messenger promised us nothing but illusion."

١٣ وَإِذْ قَالَت طَّآئِفَةٌ مِّنْهُمْ يَٰٓأَهْلَ يَثْرِبَ لَا مُقَامَ
لَكُمْ فَٱرْجِعُواْ ۚ وَيَسْتَـْٔذِنُ فَرِيقٌ مِّنْهُمُ ٱلنَّبِىَّ
يَقُولُونَ إِنَّ بُيُوتَنَا عَوْرَةٌ وَمَا هِىَ بِعَوْرَةٍ ۖ إِن
يُرِيدُونَ إِلَّا فِرَارًا

13 And when a group of them said, "O people of Yathrib, you cannot make a stand, so retreat." And a faction of them asked the Prophet to excuse them, saying, "Our homes are exposed," although they were not exposed. They only wanted to flee.

١٤ وَلَوْ دُخِلَتْ عَلَيْهِم مِّنْ أَقْطَارِهَا ثُمَّ سُئِلُواْ
ٱلْفِتْنَةَ لَءَاتَوْهَا وَمَا تَلَبَّثُواْ بِهَآ إِلَّا يَسِيرًا

14 Had it been invaded from its sides, and they were asked to dissent, they would have done so with little hesitation.

١٥ وَلَقَدْ كَانُواْ عَٰهَدُواْ ٱللَّهَ مِن قَبْلُ لَا يُوَلُّونَ
ٱلْأَدْبَٰرَ ۚ وَكَانَ عَهْدُ ٱللَّهِ مَسْـُٔولًا

15 Although they had made a pledged to Allah, in the past, that they will not turn their backs. A pledge to Allah is a responsibility.

١٦ قُل لَّن يَنفَعَكُمُ ٱلْفِرَارُ إِن فَرَرْتُم مِّنَ ٱلْمَوْتِ
أَوِ ٱلْقَتْلِ وَإِذًا لَّا تُمَتَّعُونَ إِلَّا قَلِيلًا

16 Say, "Flight will not benefit you, if you flee from death or killing, even then you will be given only brief enjoyment."

١٧ قُلْ مَن ذَا ٱلَّذِى يَعْصِمُكُم مِّنَ ٱللَّهِ إِنْ أَرَادَ
بِكُمْ سُوٓءًا أَوْ أَرَادَ بِكُمْ رَحْمَةً ۚ وَلَا يَجِدُونَ لَهُم
مِّن دُونِ ٱللَّهِ وَلِيًّا وَلَا نَصِيرًا

17 Say, "Who is it who will shield you from Allah, if He intends adversity for you, or intends mercy for you?" Besides Allah, they will find for themselves neither friend nor helper.

١٨ قَدْ يَعْلَمُ ٱللَّهُ ٱلْمُعَوِّقِينَ مِنكُمْ وَٱلْقَآئِلِينَ
لِإِخْوَٰنِهِمْ هَلُمَّ إِلَيْنَا ۖ وَلَا يَأْتُونَ ٱلْبَأْسَ إِلَّا قَلِيلًا

18 Allah already knows the hinderers among you, and those who say to their brethren, "Come and join us." Rarely do they mobilize for battle.

١٩ أَشِحَّةً عَلَيْكُمْ ۖ فَإِذَا جَآءَ ٱلْخَوْفُ رَأَيْتَهُمْ
يَنظُرُونَ إِلَيْكَ تَدُورُ أَعْيُنُهُمْ كَٱلَّذِى يُغْشَىٰ
عَلَيْهِ مِنَ ٱلْمَوْتِ ۖ فَإِذَا ذَهَبَ ٱلْخَوْفُ سَلَقُوكُم
بِأَلْسِنَةٍ حِدَادٍ أَشِحَّةً عَلَى ٱلْخَيْرِ ۚ أُو۟لَٰٓئِكَ لَمْ
يُؤْمِنُوا۟ فَأَحْبَطَ ٱللَّهُ أَعْمَٰلَهُمْ ۚ وَكَانَ ذَٰلِكَ عَلَى
ٱللَّهِ يَسِيرًا

19 Being stingy towards you. And when fear approaches, you see them staring at you—their eyes rolling—like someone fainting at death. Then, when panic is over, they whip you with sharp tongues. They resent you any good. These have never believed, so Allah has nullified their works; a matter easy for Allah.

٢٠ يَحْسَبُونَ ٱلْأَحْزَابَ لَمْ يَذْهَبُوا۟ ۖ وَإِن يَأْتِ
ٱلْأَحْزَابُ يَوَدُّوا۟ لَوْ أَنَّهُم بَادُونَ فِى ٱلْأَعْرَابِ
يَسْـَٔلُونَ عَنْ أَنۢبَآئِكُمْ ۖ وَلَوْ كَانُوا۟ فِيكُم مَّا قَٰتَلُوٓا۟
إِلَّا قَلِيلًا

20 They assumed that the confederates had not withdrawn. But were the confederates to advance, they would wish they were in the desert with the Bedouins, inquiring about your news. And if they were among you, they would have done little fighting.

٢١ لَّقَدْ كَانَ لَكُمْ فِى رَسُولِ ٱللَّهِ أُسْوَةٌ حَسَنَةٌ
لِّمَن كَانَ يَرْجُوا۟ ٱللَّهَ وَٱلْيَوْمَ ٱلْءَاخِرَ وَذَكَرَ ٱللَّهَ
كَثِيرًا

21 You have an excellent example in the Messenger of Allah; for anyone who seeks Allah and the Last Day, and remembers Allah frequently.

٢٢ وَلَمَّا رَءَا ٱلْمُؤْمِنُونَ ٱلْأَحْزَابَ قَالُوا۟ هَٰذَا مَا
وَعَدَنَا ٱللَّهُ وَرَسُولُهُۥ وَصَدَقَ ٱللَّهُ وَرَسُولُهُۥ ۚ وَمَا
زَادَهُمْ إِلَّآ إِيمَٰنًا وَتَسْلِيمًا

22 And when the believers saw the confederates, they said, "This is what Allah and His messenger have promised us; and Allah and His messenger have told the truth." And it only increased them in faith and submission.

٢٣ مِّنَ ٱلْمُؤْمِنِينَ رِجَالٌ صَدَقُوا۟ مَا عَـٰهَدُوا۟ ٱللَّهَ
عَلَيْهِ ۖ فَمِنْهُم مَّن قَضَىٰ نَحْبَهُۥ وَمِنْهُم مَّن
يَنتَظِرُ ۖ وَمَا بَدَّلُوا۟ تَبْدِيلًا

23 Of the believers are men who are true to what they pledged to Allah. Some of them have fulfilled their vows; and some are still waiting, and never wavering.

٢٤ لِّيَجْزِىَ ٱللَّهُ ٱلصَّـٰدِقِينَ بِصِدْقِهِمْ وَيُعَذِّبَ
ٱلْمُنَـٰفِقِينَ إِن شَآءَ أَوْ يَتُوبَ عَلَيْهِمْ ۚ إِنَّ ٱللَّهَ
كَانَ غَفُورًا رَّحِيمًا

24 That Allah may reward the truthful for their truthfulness; and punish the hypocrites, if He wills, or pardon them. Allah is Forgiving and Merciful.

٢٥ وَرَدَّ ٱللَّهُ ٱلَّذِينَ كَفَرُوا۟ بِغَيْظِهِمْ لَمْ يَنَالُوا۟
خَيْرًا ۚ وَكَفَى ٱللَّهُ ٱلْمُؤْمِنِينَ ٱلْقِتَالَ ۚ وَكَانَ ٱللَّهُ
قَوِيًّا عَزِيزًا

25 Allah repelled the disbelievers in their rage; they gained no advantage. Allah thus spared the believers combat. Allah is Strong and Mighty.

٢٦ وَأَنزَلَ ٱلَّذِينَ ظَـٰهَرُوهُم مِّنْ أَهْلِ ٱلْكِتَـٰبِ مِن
صَيَاصِيهِمْ وَقَذَفَ فِى قُلُوبِهِمُ ٱلرُّعْبَ فَرِيقًا
تَقْتُلُونَ وَتَأْسِرُونَ فَرِيقًا

26 And He brought down from their strongholds those of the People of the Book who backed them, and He threw terror into their hearts. Some of them you killed, and others you took captive.

٢٧ وَأَوْرَثَكُمْ أَرْضَهُمْ وَدِيَـٰرَهُمْ وَأَمْوَٰلَهُمْ وَأَرْضًا
لَّمْ تَطَـُٔوهَا ۚ وَكَانَ ٱللَّهُ عَلَىٰ كُلِّ شَىْءٍ قَدِيرًا

27 And He made you inherit their land, and their homes, and their possessions, and a region you have never stepped on. Allah has power over all things.

٢٨ يَـٰٓأَيُّهَا ٱلنَّبِىُّ قُل لِّأَزْوَٰجِكَ إِن كُنتُنَّ تُرِدْنَ
ٱلْحَيَوٰةَ ٱلدُّنْيَا وَزِينَتَهَا فَتَعَالَيْنَ أُمَتِّعْكُنَّ
وَأُسَرِّحْكُنَّ سَرَاحًا جَمِيلًا

28 O Prophet! Say to your wives, “If you desire the life of this world and its finery, then let me compensate you, and release you kindly.

٢٩ وَإِن كُنتُنَّ تُرِدْنَ ٱللَّهَ وَرَسُولَهُۥ وَٱلدَّارَ
ٱلْـَٔاخِرَةَ فَإِنَّ ٱللَّهَ أَعَدَّ لِلْمُحْسِنَـٰتِ مِنكُنَّ أَجْرًا
عَظِيمًا

29 But if you desire Allah, His Messenger, and the Home of the Hereafter, then Allah has prepared for the righteous among you a magnificent compensation.”

٣٠ يَـٰنِسَآءَ ٱلنَّبِىِّ مَن يَأْتِ مِنكُنَّ بِفَـٰحِشَةٍ مُّبَيِّنَةٍ
يُضَـٰعَفْ لَهَا ٱلْعَذَابُ ضِعْفَيْنِ ۚ وَكَانَ ذَٰلِكَ عَلَى
ٱللَّهِ يَسِيرًا

30 O wives of the Prophet! Whoever of you commits a proven indecency, the punishment for her will be doubled. And that would be easy for Allah.

٣١ وَمَن يَقْنُتْ مِنكُنَّ لِلَّهِ وَرَسُولِهِۦ وَتَعْمَلْ
صَٰلِحًا نُّؤْتِهَآ أَجْرَهَا مَرَّتَيْنِ وَأَعْتَدْنَا لَهَا رِزْقًا
كَرِيمًا

31 But whoever of you remains obedient to Allah and His Messenger, and acts righteously, We will give her a double reward; and We have prepared for her a generous provision.

٣٢ يَٰنِسَآءَ ٱلنَّبِيِّ لَسْتُنَّ كَأَحَدٍ مِّنَ ٱلنِّسَآءِ ۚ إِنِ
ٱتَّقَيْتُنَّ فَلَا تَخْضَعْنَ بِٱلْقَوْلِ فَيَطْمَعَ ٱلَّذِى فِى
قَلْبِهِۦ مَرَضٌ وَقُلْنَ قَوْلًا مَّعْرُوفًا

32 O wives of the Prophet! You are not like any other women, if you observe piety. So do not speak too softly, lest the sick at heart lusts after you, but speak in an appropriate manner.

٣٣ وَقَرْنَ فِى بُيُوتِكُنَّ وَلَا تَبَرَّجْنَ تَبَرُّجَ
ٱلْجَٰهِلِيَّةِ ٱلْأُولَىٰ ۖ وَأَقِمْنَ ٱلصَّلَوٰةَ وَءَاتِينَ
ٱلزَّكَوٰةَ وَأَطِعْنَ ٱللَّهَ وَرَسُولَهُۥٓ ۚ إِنَّمَا يُرِيدُ ٱللَّهُ
لِيُذْهِبَ عَنكُمُ ٱلرِّجْسَ أَهْلَ ٱلْبَيْتِ وَيُطَهِّرَكُمْ
تَطْهِيرًا

33 And settle in your homes; and do not display yourselves, as in the former days of ignorance. And perform the prayer, and give regular charity, and obey Allah and His Messenger. Allah desires to remove all impurity from you, O People of the Household, and to purify you thoroughly.

٣٤ وَٱذْكُرْنَ مَا يُتْلَىٰ فِى بُيُوتِكُنَّ مِنْ ءَايَٰتِ
ٱللَّهِ وَٱلْحِكْمَةِ ۚ إِنَّ ٱللَّهَ كَانَ لَطِيفًا خَبِيرًا

34 And remember what is recited in your homes of Allah's revelations and wisdom. Allah is Kind and Informed.

٣٥ إِنَّ ٱلْمُسْلِمِينَ وَٱلْمُسْلِمَٰتِ وَٱلْمُؤْمِنِينَ
وَٱلْمُؤْمِنَٰتِ وَٱلْقَٰنِتِينَ وَٱلْقَٰنِتَٰتِ وَٱلصَّٰدِقِينَ
وَٱلصَّٰدِقَٰتِ وَٱلصَّٰبِرِينَ وَٱلصَّٰبِرَٰتِ وَٱلْخَٰشِعِينَ
وَٱلْخَٰشِعَٰتِ وَٱلْمُتَصَدِّقِينَ وَٱلْمُتَصَدِّقَٰتِ
وَٱلصَّٰٓئِمِينَ وَٱلصَّٰٓئِمَٰتِ وَٱلْحَٰفِظِينَ فُرُوجَهُمْ
وَٱلْحَٰفِظَٰتِ وَٱلذَّٰكِرِينَ ٱللَّهَ كَثِيرًا وَٱلذَّٰكِرَٰتِ أَعَدَّ
ٱللَّهُ لَهُم مَّغْفِرَةً وَأَجْرًا عَظِيمًا

35 Muslim men and Muslim women, believing men and believing women, obedient men and obedient women, truthful men and truthful women, patient men and patient women, humble men and humble women, charitable men and charitable women, fasting men and fasting women, men who guard their chastity and women who guard, men who remember Allah frequently and women who remember—Allah has prepared for them a pardon, and an immense reward.

٣٦ وَمَا كَانَ لِمُؤْمِنٍ وَلَا مُؤْمِنَةٍ إِذَا قَضَى ٱللَّهُ
وَرَسُولُهُۥٓ أَمْرًا أَن يَكُونَ لَهُمُ ٱلْخِيَرَةُ مِنْ

36 It is not for any believer, man or woman, when Allah and His Messenger have decided a matter,

أَمْرِهِمْ ۗ وَمَن يَعْصِ ٱللَّهَ وَرَسُولَهُۥ فَقَدْ ضَلَّ
ضَلَٰلًا مُّبِينًا

to have liberty of choice in their decision. Whoever disobeys Allah and His Messenger has gone far astray.

٣٧ وَإِذْ تَقُولُ لِلَّذِىٓ أَنْعَمَ ٱللَّهُ عَلَيْهِ وَأَنْعَمْتَ
عَلَيْهِ أَمْسِكْ عَلَيْكَ زَوْجَكَ وَٱتَّقِ ٱللَّهَ وَتُخْفِى
فِى نَفْسِكَ مَا ٱللَّهُ مُبْدِيهِ وَتَخْشَى ٱلنَّاسَ
وَٱللَّهُ أَحَقُّ أَن تَخْشَىٰهُ ۖ فَلَمَّا قَضَىٰ زَيْدٌ مِّنْهَا
وَطَرًا زَوَّجْنَٰكَهَا لِكَىْ لَا يَكُونَ عَلَى ٱلْمُؤْمِنِينَ
حَرَجٌ فِىٓ أَزْوَٰجِ أَدْعِيَآئِهِمْ إِذَا قَضَوْا۟ مِنْهُنَّ
وَطَرًا ۚ وَكَانَ أَمْرُ ٱللَّهِ مَفْعُولًا

37 When you said to him whom Allah had blessed, and you had favored, "Keep your wife to yourself, and fear Allah." But you hid within yourself what Allah was to reveal. And you feared the people, but it was Allah you were supposed to fear. Then, when Zaid ended his relationship with her, We gave her to you in marriage, that there may be no restriction for believers regarding the wives of their adopted sons, when their relationship has ended. The command of Allah was fulfilled.

٣٨ مَّا كَانَ عَلَى ٱلنَّبِىِّ مِنْ حَرَجٍ فِيمَا فَرَضَ
ٱللَّهُ لَهُۥ ۖ سُنَّةَ ٱللَّهِ فِى ٱلَّذِينَ خَلَوْا۟ مِن قَبْلُ ۚ
وَكَانَ أَمْرُ ٱللَّهِ قَدَرًا مَّقْدُورًا

38 There is no blame on the Prophet regarding what Allah has ordained for him. Such is the pattern of Allah among those who passed before. The command of Allah is an absolute decree.

٣٩ ٱلَّذِينَ يُبَلِّغُونَ رِسَٰلَٰتِ ٱللَّهِ وَيَخْشَوْنَهُۥ وَلَا
يَخْشَوْنَ أَحَدًا إِلَّا ٱللَّهَ ۗ وَكَفَىٰ بِٱللَّهِ حَسِيبًا

39 Those who deliver the messages of Allah, and fear Him, and never fear anyone except Allah. Allah is sufficient as a reckoner.

٤٠ مَّا كَانَ مُحَمَّدٌ أَبَآ أَحَدٍ مِّن رِّجَالِكُمْ وَلَٰكِن
رَّسُولَ ٱللَّهِ وَخَاتَمَ ٱلنَّبِيِّۦنَ ۗ وَكَانَ ٱللَّهُ بِكُلِّ
شَىْءٍ عَلِيمًا

40 Muhammad is not the father of any of your men; but he is the Messenger of Allah, and the seal of the prophets. Allah is Cognizant of everything.

٤١ يَٰٓأَيُّهَا ٱلَّذِينَ ءَامَنُوا۟ ٱذْكُرُوا۟ ٱللَّهَ ذِكْرًا كَثِيرًا

41 O you who believe, remember Allah with frequent remembrance.

٤٢ وَسَبِّحُوهُ بُكْرَةً وَأَصِيلًا

42 And glorify Him morning and evening.

٤٣ هُوَ ٱلَّذِى يُصَلِّى عَلَيْكُمْ وَمَلَٰٓئِكَتُهُۥ لِيُخْرِجَكُم
مِّنَ ٱلظُّلُمَٰتِ إِلَى ٱلنُّورِ ۚ وَكَانَ بِٱلْمُؤْمِنِينَ رَحِيمًا

43 It is He who reaches out to you, and His angels, to bring you out of darkness into the light. And He is Ever-Merciful towards the believers.

٤٤ تَحِيَّتُهُمْ يَوْمَ يَلْقَوْنَهُۥ سَلَٰمٌ ۚ وَأَعَدَّ لَهُمْ أَجْرًا
كَرِيمًا

44 Their greeting on the Day they meet Him is, “Peace,” and He has prepared for them a generous reward.

٤٥ يَٰٓأَيُّهَا ٱلنَّبِىُّ إِنَّآ أَرْسَلْنَٰكَ شَٰهِدًا وَمُبَشِّرًا
وَنَذِيرًا

45 O prophet! We have sent you as a witness, and a bearer of good news, and a warner.

٤٦ وَدَاعِيًا إِلَى ٱللَّهِ بِإِذْنِهِۦ وَسِرَاجًا مُّنِيرًا

46 And a caller towards Allah by His leave, and an illuminating beacon.

٤٧ وَبَشِّرِ ٱلْمُؤْمِنِينَ بِأَنَّ لَهُم مِّنَ ٱللَّهِ فَضْلًا
كَبِيرًا

47 And give the believers the good news that for them is a great reward.

٤٨ وَلَا تُطِعِ ٱلْكَٰفِرِينَ وَٱلْمُنَٰفِقِينَ وَدَعْ أَذَىٰهُمْ
وَتَوَكَّلْ عَلَى ٱللَّهِ ۚ وَكَفَىٰ بِٱللَّهِ وَكِيلًا

48 And do not obey the blasphemers and the hypocrites, and ignore their insults, and rely on Allah. Allah is a sufficient protector.

٤٩ يَٰٓأَيُّهَا ٱلَّذِينَ ءَامَنُوٓا۟ إِذَا نَكَحْتُمُ ٱلْمُؤْمِنَٰتِ ثُمَّ
طَلَّقْتُمُوهُنَّ مِن قَبْلِ أَن تَمَسُّوهُنَّ فَمَا لَكُمْ
عَلَيْهِنَّ مِنْ عِدَّةٍ تَعْتَدُّونَهَا ۖ فَمَتِّعُوهُنَّ
وَسَرِّحُوهُنَّ سَرَاحًا جَمِيلًا

49 O you who believe! When you marry believing women, but then divorce them before you have touched them, there is no waiting period for you to observe in respect to them; but compensate them, and release them in a graceful manner.

٥٠ يَٰٓأَيُّهَا ٱلنَّبِىُّ إِنَّآ أَحْلَلْنَا لَكَ أَزْوَٰجَكَ ٱلَّٰتِىٓ
ءَاتَيْتَ أُجُورَهُنَّ وَمَا مَلَكَتْ يَمِينُكَ مِمَّآ أَفَآءَ
ٱللَّهُ عَلَيْكَ وَبَنَاتِ عَمِّكَ وَبَنَاتِ عَمَّٰتِكَ وَبَنَاتِ
خَالِكَ وَبَنَاتِ خَٰلَٰتِكَ ٱلَّٰتِى هَاجَرْنَ مَعَكَ وَٱمْرَأَةً
مُّؤْمِنَةً إِن وَهَبَتْ نَفْسَهَا لِلنَّبِىِّ إِنْ أَرَادَ ٱلنَّبِىُّ
أَن يَسْتَنكِحَهَا خَالِصَةً لَّكَ مِن دُونِ ٱلْمُؤْمِنِينَ ۗ
قَدْ عَلِمْنَا مَا فَرَضْنَا عَلَيْهِمْ فِىٓ أَزْوَٰجِهِمْ وَمَا
مَلَكَتْ أَيْمَٰنُهُمْ لِكَيْلَا يَكُونَ عَلَيْكَ حَرَجٌ ۗ وَكَانَ
ٱللَّهُ غَفُورًا رَّحِيمًا

50 O Prophet! We have permitted to you your wives to whom you have given their dowries, and those you already have, as granted to you by Allah, and the daughters of your paternal uncle, and the daughters of your paternal aunts, and the daughters of your maternal uncle, and the daughters of your maternal aunts who emigrated with you, and a believing woman who has offered herself to the Prophet, if the Prophet desires to marry her, exclusively for you, and not for the believers. We know what We have ordained for them regarding their wives and those their right-hands possess. This

is to spare you any difficulty. Allah is Forgiving and Merciful.

٥١ تُرْجِى مَن تَشَآءُ مِنْهُنَّ وَتُـْٔوِىٓ إِلَيْكَ مَن
تَشَآءُ ۖ وَمَنِ ٱبْتَغَيْتَ مِمَّنْ عَزَلْتَ فَلَا جُنَاحَ
عَلَيْكَ ۚ ذَٰلِكَ أَدْنَىٰٓ أَن تَقَرَّ أَعْيُنُهُنَّ وَلَا يَحْزَنَّ
وَيَرْضَيْنَ بِمَآ ءَاتَيْتَهُنَّ كُلُّهُنَّ ۚ وَٱللَّهُ يَعْلَمُ مَا
فِى قُلُوبِكُمْ ۚ وَكَانَ ٱللَّهُ عَلِيمًا حَلِيمًا

51 You may defer any of them you wish, and receive any of them you wish. Should you desire any of those you had deferred, there is no blame on you. This is more proper, so that they will be comforted, and not be grieved, and be content with what you have given each one of them. Allah knows what is within your hearts. Allah is Omniscient and Clement.

٥٢ لَّا يَحِلُّ لَكَ ٱلنِّسَآءُ مِنۢ بَعْدُ وَلَآ أَن تَبَدَّلَ
بِهِنَّ مِنْ أَزْوَٰجٍ وَلَوْ أَعْجَبَكَ حُسْنُهُنَّ إِلَّا مَا
مَلَكَتْ يَمِينُكَ ۗ وَكَانَ ٱللَّهُ عَلَىٰ كُلِّ شَىْءٍ رَّقِيبًا

52 Beyond that, no other women are permissible for you, nor can you exchange them for other wives, even if you admire their beauty, except those you already have. Allah is Watchful over all things.

٥٣ يَٰٓأَيُّهَا ٱلَّذِينَ ءَامَنُوا۟ لَا تَدْخُلُوا۟ بُيُوتَ ٱلنَّبِىِّ
إِلَّآ أَن يُؤْذَنَ لَكُمْ إِلَىٰ طَعَامٍ غَيْرَ نَٰظِرِينَ إِنَىٰهُ
وَلَٰكِنْ إِذَا دُعِيتُمْ فَٱدْخُلُوا۟ فَإِذَا طَعِمْتُمْ
فَٱنتَشِرُوا۟ وَلَا مُسْتَـْٔنِسِينَ لِحَدِيثٍ ۚ إِنَّ ذَٰلِكُمْ
كَانَ يُؤْذِى ٱلنَّبِىَّ فَيَسْتَحْىِۦ مِنكُمْ ۖ وَٱللَّهُ لَا
يَسْتَحْىِۦ مِنَ ٱلْحَقِّ ۚ وَإِذَا سَأَلْتُمُوهُنَّ مَتَٰعًا
فَسْـَٔلُوهُنَّ مِن وَرَآءِ حِجَابٍ ۚ ذَٰلِكُمْ أَطْهَرُ
لِقُلُوبِكُمْ وَقُلُوبِهِنَّ ۚ وَمَا كَانَ لَكُمْ أَن تُؤْذُوا۟
رَسُولَ ٱللَّهِ وَلَآ أَن تَنكِحُوٓا۟ أَزْوَٰجَهُۥ مِنۢ بَعْدِهِۦٓ
أَبَدًا ۚ إِنَّ ذَٰلِكُمْ كَانَ عِندَ ٱللَّهِ عَظِيمًا

53 O you who believe! Do not enter the homes of the Prophet, unless you are given permission to come for a meal; and do not wait for its preparation. And when you are invited, go in. And when you have eaten, disperse, without lingering for conversation. This irritates the Prophet, and he shies away from you, but Allah does not shy away from the truth. And when you ask his wives for something, ask them from behind a screen; that is purer for your hearts and their hearts. You must never offend the Messenger of Allah, nor must you ever marry his wives after him, for that would be an enormity with Allah.

٥٤ إِن تُبْدُوا۟ شَيْـًٔا أَوْ تُخْفُوهُ فَإِنَّ ٱللَّهَ كَانَ بِكُلِّ
شَىْءٍ عَلِيمًا

54 Whether you declare a thing, or hide it, Allah is Aware of all things.

٥٥ لَّا جُنَاحَ عَلَيْهِنَّ فِىٓ ءَابَآئِهِنَّ وَلَآ أَبْنَآئِهِنَّ وَلَآ
إِخْوَٰنِهِنَّ وَلَآ أَبْنَآءِ إِخْوَٰنِهِنَّ وَلَآ أَبْنَآءِ أَخَوَٰتِهِنَّ
وَلَا نِسَآئِهِنَّ وَلَا مَا مَلَكَتْ أَيْمَٰنُهُنَّ ۗ وَٱتَّقِينَ ٱللَّهَ ۚ
إِنَّ ٱللَّهَ كَانَ عَلَىٰ كُلِّ شَىْءٍ شَهِيدًا

55 There is no blame on them concerning their fathers, or their sons, or their brothers, or their brothers' sons, or their sisters' sons, or their women, or their female servants. But they should remain conscious of Allah. Allah is Witness over all things.

٥٦ إِنَّ ٱللَّهَ وَمَلَٰٓئِكَتَهُۥ يُصَلُّونَ عَلَى ٱلنَّبِىِّ ۚ يَٰٓأَيُّهَا
ٱلَّذِينَ ءَامَنُوا۟ صَلُّوا۟ عَلَيْهِ وَسَلِّمُوا۟ تَسْلِيمًا

56 Allah and His angels give blessings to the Prophet. O you who believe, call for blessings on him, and greet him with a prayer of peace.

٥٧ إِنَّ ٱلَّذِينَ يُؤْذُونَ ٱللَّهَ وَرَسُولَهُۥ لَعَنَهُمُ ٱللَّهُ
فِى ٱلدُّنْيَا وَٱلْءَاخِرَةِ وَأَعَدَّ لَهُمْ عَذَابًا مُّهِينًا

57 Those who insult Allah and His Messenger, Allah has cursed them in this life and in the Hereafter, and has prepared for them a demeaning punishment.

٥٨ وَٱلَّذِينَ يُؤْذُونَ ٱلْمُؤْمِنِينَ وَٱلْمُؤْمِنَٰتِ بِغَيْرِ
مَا ٱكْتَسَبُوا۟ فَقَدِ ٱحْتَمَلُوا۟ بُهْتَٰنًا وَإِثْمًا مُّبِينًا

58 Those who harm believing men and believing women, for acts they did not commit, bear the burden of perjury and a flagrant sin.

٥٩ يَٰٓأَيُّهَا ٱلنَّبِىُّ قُل لِّأَزْوَٰجِكَ وَبَنَاتِكَ وَنِسَآءِ
ٱلْمُؤْمِنِينَ يُدْنِينَ عَلَيْهِنَّ مِن جَلَٰبِيبِهِنَّ ۚ ذَٰلِكَ
أَدْنَىٰٓ أَن يُعْرَفْنَ فَلَا يُؤْذَيْنَ ۗ وَكَانَ ٱللَّهُ غَفُورًا
رَّحِيمًا

59 O Prophet! Tell your wives, and your daughters, and the women of the believers, to lengthen their garments. That is more proper, so they will be recognized and not harassed. Allah is Forgiving and Merciful.

٦٠ لَّئِن لَّمْ يَنتَهِ ٱلْمُنَٰفِقُونَ وَٱلَّذِينَ فِى قُلُوبِهِم
مَّرَضٌ وَٱلْمُرْجِفُونَ فِى ٱلْمَدِينَةِ لَنُغْرِيَنَّكَ بِهِمْ
ثُمَّ لَا يُجَاوِرُونَكَ فِيهَآ إِلَّا قَلِيلًا

60 If the hypocrites, and those with sickness in their hearts, and the rumormongers in the City, do not desist, We will incite you against them; then they will not be your neighbors there except for a short while.

٦١ مَّلْعُونِينَ ۖ أَيْنَمَا ثُقِفُوٓا۟ أُخِذُوا۟ وَقُتِّلُوا۟ تَقْتِيلًا

61 They are cursed; wherever they are found, they should be captured and killed outright.

٦٢ سُنَّةَ ٱللَّهِ فِى ٱلَّذِينَ خَلَوْا۟ مِن قَبْلُ ۖ وَلَن
تَجِدَ لِسُنَّةِ ٱللَّهِ تَبْدِيلًا

62 Such has been Allah's precedent with those who passed away before. You will find no change in Allah's system.

٦٣ يَسْـَٔلُكَ ٱلنَّاسُ عَنِ ٱلسَّاعَةِ ۖ قُلْ إِنَّمَا عِلْمُهَا
عِندَ ٱللَّهِ ۚ وَمَا يُدْرِيكَ لَعَلَّ ٱلسَّاعَةَ تَكُونُ قَرِيبًا

63 The people ask you about the Hour. Say, "The knowledge thereof rests with Allah. But what do you know? Perhaps the hour is near."

٦٤ إِنَّ ٱللَّهَ لَعَنَ ٱلْكَٰفِرِينَ وَأَعَدَّ لَهُمْ سَعِيرًا

64 Allah has cursed the disbelievers, and has prepared for them a Blaze.

٦٥ خَٰلِدِينَ فِيهَآ أَبَدًا ۖ لَّا يَجِدُونَ وَلِيًّا وَلَا
نَصِيرًا

65 Dwelling therein forever, not finding a protector or a savior.

٦٦ يَوْمَ تُقَلَّبُ وُجُوهُهُمْ فِى ٱلنَّارِ يَقُولُونَ
يَٰلَيْتَنَآ أَطَعْنَا ٱللَّهَ وَأَطَعْنَا ٱلرَّسُولَا۠

66 The Day when their faces are flipped into the Fire, they will say, "If only we had obeyed Allah and obeyed the Messenger."

٦٧ وَقَالُوا۟ رَبَّنَآ إِنَّآ أَطَعْنَا سَادَتَنَا وَكُبَرَآءَنَا
فَأَضَلُّونَا ٱلسَّبِيلَا۠

67 And they will say, "Lord, we have obeyed our superiors and our dignitaries, but they led us away from the way.

٦٨ رَبَّنَآ ءَاتِهِمْ ضِعْفَيْنِ مِنَ ٱلْعَذَابِ وَٱلْعَنْهُمْ
لَعْنًا كَبِيرًا

68 Lord, give them double the punishment, and curse them with a great curse."

٦٩ يَٰٓأَيُّهَا ٱلَّذِينَ ءَامَنُوا۟ لَا تَكُونُوا۟ كَٱلَّذِينَ ءَاذَوْا۟
مُوسَىٰ فَبَرَّأَهُ ٱللَّهُ مِمَّا قَالُوا۟ ۚ وَكَانَ عِندَ ٱللَّهِ
وَجِيهًا

69 O you who believe! Do not be like those who abused Moses; but Allah cleared him of what they said. He was distinguished with Allah.

٧٠ يَٰٓأَيُّهَا ٱلَّذِينَ ءَامَنُوا۟ ٱتَّقُوا۟ ٱللَّهَ وَقُولُوا۟ قَوْلًا
سَدِيدًا

70 O you who believe! Be conscious of Allah, and speak in a straightforward manner.

٧١ يُصْلِحْ لَكُمْ أَعْمَٰلَكُمْ وَيَغْفِرْ لَكُمْ ذُنُوبَكُمْ ۗ
وَمَن يُطِعِ ٱللَّهَ وَرَسُولَهُۥ فَقَدْ فَازَ فَوْزًا عَظِيمًا

71 He will rectify your conduct for you, and will forgive you your sins. Whoever obeys Allah and His Messenger has won a great victory.

٧٢ إِنَّا عَرَضْنَا ٱلْأَمَانَةَ عَلَى ٱلسَّمَٰوَٰتِ وَٱلْأَرْضِ
وَٱلْجِبَالِ فَأَبَيْنَ أَن يَحْمِلْنَهَا وَأَشْفَقْنَ مِنْهَا
وَحَمَلَهَا ٱلْإِنسَٰنُ ۖ إِنَّهُۥ كَانَ ظَلُومًا جَهُولًا

72 We offered the Trust to the heavens, and the earth, and the mountains; but they refused to bear it, and were apprehensive of it; but

the human being accepted it. He was unfair and ignorant.

٧٣ لِّيُعَذِّبَ ٱللَّهُ ٱلْمُنَٰفِقِينَ وَٱلْمُنَٰفِقَٰتِ
وَٱلْمُشْرِكِينَ وَٱلْمُشْرِكَٰتِ وَيَتُوبَ ٱللَّهُ عَلَى
ٱلْمُؤْمِنِينَ وَٱلْمُؤْمِنَٰتِ ۗ وَكَانَ ٱللَّهُ غَفُورًا رَّحِيمًا

73 Allah will punish the hypocrites, men and women, and the idolaters, men and women. And Allah will redeem the believers, men and women. Allah is Ever-Forgiving, Most Merciful.

34 Sheba سبإ

بِسْمِ ٱللَّهِ ٱلرَّحْمَٰنِ ٱلرَّحِيمِ

In the name of Allah, the Gracious, the Merciful.

١ ٱلْحَمْدُ لِلَّهِ ٱلَّذِى لَهُۥ مَا فِى ٱلسَّمَٰوَٰتِ وَمَا فِى
ٱلْأَرْضِ وَلَهُ ٱلْحَمْدُ فِى ٱلْءَاخِرَةِ ۚ وَهُوَ ٱلْحَكِيمُ
ٱلْخَبِيرُ

1 Praise be to Allah, to Whom belongs everything in the heavens and the earth; and praise be to Him in the Hereafter. He is the Wise, the Expert.

٢ يَعْلَمُ مَا يَلِجُ فِى ٱلْأَرْضِ وَمَا يَخْرُجُ مِنْهَا
وَمَا يَنزِلُ مِنَ ٱلسَّمَآءِ وَمَا يَعْرُجُ فِيهَا ۚ وَهُوَ
ٱلرَّحِيمُ ٱلْغَفُورُ

2 He knows what penetrates into the earth, and what comes out of it, and what descends from the sky, and what ascends to it. He is the Merciful, the Forgiving.

٣ وَقَالَ ٱلَّذِينَ كَفَرُوا۟ لَا تَأْتِينَا ٱلسَّاعَةُ ۖ قُلْ بَلَىٰ
وَرَبِّى لَتَأْتِيَنَّكُمْ عَٰلِمِ ٱلْغَيْبِ ۖ لَا يَعْزُبُ عَنْهُ
مِثْقَالُ ذَرَّةٍ فِى ٱلسَّمَٰوَٰتِ وَلَا فِى ٱلْأَرْضِ وَلَآ
أَصْغَرُ مِن ذَٰلِكَ وَلَآ أَكْبَرُ إِلَّا فِى كِتَٰبٍ مُّبِينٍ

3 Those who disbelieve say, "The Hour will not come upon us." Say, "Yes indeed, by my Lord, it will come upon you. He is the Knower of the unseen." Not an atom's weight in the heavens and the earth, or anything smaller or larger, escapes His knowledge. All are in a Clear Record.

٤ لِّيَجْزِىَ ٱلَّذِينَ ءَامَنُوا۟ وَعَمِلُوا۟ ٱلصَّٰلِحَٰتِ ۚ
أُو۟لَٰٓئِكَ لَهُم مَّغْفِرَةٌ وَرِزْقٌ كَرِيمٌ

4 That He may recompense those who believe and do good works. Those will have forgiveness, and a generous provision.

٥ وَٱلَّذِينَ سَعَوْ فِىٓ ءَايَٰتِنَا مُعَٰجِزِينَ أُو۟لَٰٓئِكَ لَهُمْ
عَذَابٌ مِّن رِّجْزٍ أَلِيمٌ

5 As for those who strive against Our revelations, seeking to undermine them—for them is a punishment of a painful plague.

٦ وَيَرَى ٱلَّذِينَ أُوتُوا۟ ٱلْعِلْمَ ٱلَّذِىٓ أُنزِلَ إِلَيْكَ مِن
رَّبِّكَ هُوَ ٱلْحَقَّ وَيَهْدِىٓ إِلَىٰ صِرَٰطِ ٱلْعَزِيزِ
ٱلْحَمِيدِ

6 Those who received knowledge know that what is revealed to you from your Lord is the truth; and it guides to the path of the Majestic, the Praiseworthy.

٧ وَقَالَ ٱلَّذِينَ كَفَرُوا۟ هَلْ نَدُلُّكُمْ عَلَىٰ رَجُلٍ
يُنَبِّئُكُمْ إِذَا مُزِّقْتُمْ كُلَّ مُمَزَّقٍ إِنَّكُمْ لَفِى خَلْقٍ
جَدِيدٍ

7 Those who disbelieved said, “Shall we point out to you a man, who will tell you that, once torn into shreds, you will be in a new creation?

٨ أَفْتَرَىٰ عَلَى ٱللَّهِ كَذِبًا أَم بِهِۦ جِنَّةٌۢ ۗ بَلِ ٱلَّذِينَ
لَا يُؤْمِنُونَ بِٱلْءَاخِرَةِ فِى ٱلْعَذَابِ وَٱلضَّلَٰلِ
ٱلْبَعِيدِ

8 Did he invent a lie about Allah, or is there madness in him?” Indeed, those who do not believe in the Hereafter are in torment, and far astray.

٩ أَفَلَمْ يَرَوْا۟ إِلَىٰ مَا بَيْنَ أَيْدِيهِمْ وَمَا خَلْفَهُم
مِّنَ ٱلسَّمَآءِ وَٱلْأَرْضِ ۚ إِن نَّشَأْ نَخْسِفْ بِهِمُ
ٱلْأَرْضَ أَوْ نُسْقِطْ عَلَيْهِمْ كِسَفًا مِّنَ ٱلسَّمَآءِ ۚ إِنَّ
فِى ذَٰلِكَ لَءَايَةً لِّكُلِّ عَبْدٍ مُّنِيبٍ

9 Do they not reflect upon what lies before them and behind them, of the heaven and the earth? If We will, We can make the earth cave in beneath them, or make pieces of the sky fall down on them. In that is a sign for every devout servant.

١٠ وَلَقَدْ ءَاتَيْنَا دَاوُۥدَ مِنَّا فَضْلًا ۖ يَٰجِبَالُ أَوِّبِى
مَعَهُۥ وَٱلطَّيْرَ ۖ وَأَلَنَّا لَهُ ٱلْحَدِيدَ

10 We bestowed upon David favor from Us: “O mountains, and birds: echo with him.” And We softened iron for him.

١١ أَنِ ٱعْمَلْ سَٰبِغَٰتٍ وَقَدِّرْ فِى ٱلسَّرْدِ ۖ وَٱعْمَلُوا۟
صَٰلِحًا ۖ إِنِّى بِمَا تَعْمَلُونَ بَصِيرٌ

11 “Make coats of armor, and measure the links well; and work righteousness. I am Observant of everything you do.”

١٢ وَلِسُلَيْمَٰنَ ٱلرِّيحَ غُدُوُّهَا شَهْرٌ وَرَوَاحُهَا شَهْرٌ ۖ
وَأَسَلْنَا لَهُۥ عَيْنَ ٱلْقِطْرِ ۖ وَمِنَ ٱلْجِنِّ مَن يَعْمَلُ
بَيْنَ يَدَيْهِ بِإِذْنِ رَبِّهِۦ ۖ وَمَن يَزِغْ مِنْهُمْ عَنْ أَمْرِنَا
نُذِقْهُ مِنْ عَذَابِ ٱلسَّعِيرِ

12 And for Solomon the wind—its outward journey was one month, and its return journey was one month. And We made a spring of tar flow for him. And there were sprites that worked under him, by the leave of his Lord. But whoever of them swerved from Our command, We make him taste of the punishment of the Inferno.

١٣ يَعْمَلُونَ لَهُۥ مَا يَشَآءُ مِن مَّحَٰرِيبَ وَتَمَٰثِيلَ
وَجِفَانٍ كَٱلْجَوَابِ وَقُدُورٍ رَّاسِيَٰتٍ ۚ ٱعْمَلُوٓا۟ ءَالَ
دَاوُۥدَ شُكْرًا ۚ وَقَلِيلٌ مِّنْ عِبَادِىَ ٱلشَّكُورُ

13 They made for him whatever he wished: sanctuaries, statues, bowls like pools, and heavy cauldrons. "O House of David, work with appreciation," but a few of My servants are appreciative.

١٤ فَلَمَّا قَضَيْنَا عَلَيْهِ ٱلْمَوْتَ مَا دَلَّهُمْ عَلَىٰ
مَوْتِهِۦٓ إِلَّا دَآبَّةُ ٱلْأَرْضِ تَأْكُلُ مِنسَأَتَهُۥ ۖ فَلَمَّا خَرَّ
تَبَيَّنَتِ ٱلْجِنُّ أَن لَّوْ كَانُوا۟ يَعْلَمُونَ ٱلْغَيْبَ مَا
لَبِثُوا۟ فِى ٱلْعَذَابِ ٱلْمُهِينِ

14 Then, when We decreed death for him, nothing indicated his death to them except an earthworm eating at his staff. Then, when he fell down, it became clear to the sprites that, had they known the unseen, they would not have remained in the demeaning torment.

١٥ لَقَدْ كَانَ لِسَبَإٍ فِى مَسْكَنِهِمْ ءَايَةٌ ۖ جَنَّتَانِ
عَن يَمِينٍ وَشِمَالٍ ۖ كُلُوا۟ مِن رِّزْقِ رَبِّكُمْ
وَٱشْكُرُوا۟ لَهُۥ ۚ بَلْدَةٌ طَيِّبَةٌ وَرَبٌّ غَفُورٌ

15 In Sheba's homeland there used to be a wonder: two gardens, on the right, and on the left. "Eat of your Lord's provision, and give thanks to Him." A good land, and a forgiving Lord.

١٦ فَأَعْرَضُوا۟ فَأَرْسَلْنَا عَلَيْهِمْ سَيْلَ ٱلْعَرِمِ
وَبَدَّلْنَٰهُم بِجَنَّتَيْهِمْ جَنَّتَيْنِ ذَوَاتَىْ أُكُلٍ خَمْطٍ
وَأَثْلٍ وَشَىْءٍ مِّن سِدْرٍ قَلِيلٍ

16 But they turned away, so We unleashed against them the flood of the dam; and We substituted their two gardens with two gardens of bitter fruits, thorny shrubs, and meager harvest.

١٧ ذَٰلِكَ جَزَيْنَٰهُم بِمَا كَفَرُوا۟ ۖ وَهَلْ نُجَٰزِىٓ إِلَّا
ٱلْكَفُورَ

17 We thus penalized them for their ingratitude. Would We penalize any but the ungrateful?

١٨ وَجَعَلْنَا بَيْنَهُمْ وَبَيْنَ ٱلْقُرَى ٱلَّتِى بَٰرَكْنَا فِيهَا
قُرًى ظَٰهِرَةً وَقَدَّرْنَا فِيهَا ٱلسَّيْرَ ۖ سِيرُوا۟ فِيهَا
لَيَالِىَ وَأَيَّامًا ءَامِنِينَ

18 Between them and the towns We had blessed, We placed prominent towns, and We made the travel between them easy. "Travel between them by night and day, in safety."

١٩ فَقَالُوا۟ رَبَّنَا بَٰعِدْ بَيْنَ أَسْفَارِنَا وَظَلَمُوٓا۟
أَنفُسَهُمْ فَجَعَلْنَٰهُمْ أَحَادِيثَ وَمَزَّقْنَٰهُمْ كُلَّ
مُمَزَّقٍ ۚ إِنَّ فِى ذَٰلِكَ لَءَايَٰتٍ لِّكُلِّ صَبَّارٍ شَكُورٍ

19 But they said, "Our Lord, lengthen the distances of our journeys." They wronged themselves; so We made them history, and We scattered them in every direction. In this are lessons

for every steadfast and appreciative person.

٢٠ وَلَقَدْ صَدَّقَ عَلَيْهِمْ إِبْلِيسُ ظَنَّهُۥ فَٱتَّبَعُوهُ إِلَّا
فَرِيقًا مِّنَ ٱلْمُؤْمِنِينَ

20 Satan was correct in his assessment of them. They followed him, except for a group of believers.

٢١ وَمَا كَانَ لَهُۥ عَلَيْهِم مِّن سُلْطَٰنٍ إِلَّا لِنَعْلَمَ مَن
يُؤْمِنُ بِٱلْءَاخِرَةِ مِمَّنْ هُوَ مِنْهَا فِى شَكٍّ ۗ
وَرَبُّكَ عَلَىٰ كُلِّ شَىْءٍ حَفِيظٌ

21 He had no authority over them; except that We willed to distinguish him who believes in the Hereafter, from him who is doubtful about it. Your Lord is Guardian over all things.

٢٢ قُلِ ٱدْعُوا۟ ٱلَّذِينَ زَعَمْتُم مِّن دُونِ ٱللَّهِ ۖ لَا
يَمْلِكُونَ مِثْقَالَ ذَرَّةٍ فِى ٱلسَّمَٰوَٰتِ وَلَا فِى
ٱلْأَرْضِ وَمَا لَهُمْ فِيهِمَا مِن شِرْكٍ وَمَا لَهُۥ مِنْهُم
مِّن ظَهِيرٍ

22 Say, "Call upon those whom you claim besides Allah. They possess not an atom's weight in the heavens or the earth, and they possess no share of either, and He has no backers from among them."

٢٣ وَلَا تَنفَعُ ٱلشَّفَٰعَةُ عِندَهُۥٓ إِلَّا لِمَنْ أَذِنَ لَهُۥ ۚ
حَتَّىٰٓ إِذَا فُزِّعَ عَن قُلُوبِهِمْ قَالُوا۟ مَاذَا قَالَ
رَبُّكُمْ ۖ قَالُوا۟ ٱلْحَقَّ ۖ وَهُوَ ٱلْعَلِىُّ ٱلْكَبِيرُ

23 Intercession with Him is of no value, except for someone He has permitted. Until, when fear has subsided from their hearts, they will say, "What did your Lord say?" They will say, "The truth, and He is the High, the Great."

٢٤ قُلْ مَن يَرْزُقُكُم مِّنَ ٱلسَّمَٰوَٰتِ وَٱلْأَرْضِ ۖ قُلِ
ٱللَّهُ ۖ وَإِنَّآ أَوْ إِيَّاكُمْ لَعَلَىٰ هُدًى أَوْ فِى ضَلَٰلٍ
مُّبِينٍ

24 Say, "Who provides for you from the heavens and the earth?" Say, "Allah. And Either you, or we, are rightly guided, or in evident error."

٢٥ قُل لَّا تُسْـَٔلُونَ عَمَّآ أَجْرَمْنَا وَلَا نُسْـَٔلُ عَمَّا
تَعْمَلُونَ

25 Say, "You will not be asked about our misdeeds, nor will we be asked about what you do."

٢٦ قُلْ يَجْمَعُ بَيْنَنَا رَبُّنَا ثُمَّ يَفْتَحُ بَيْنَنَا بِٱلْحَقِّ
وَهُوَ ٱلْفَتَّاحُ ٱلْعَلِيمُ

26 Say, "Our Lord will bring us together; then He will judge between us equitably. He is the All-Knowing Judge."

٢٧ قُلْ أَرُونِىَ ٱلَّذِينَ أَلْحَقْتُم بِهِۦ شُرَكَآءَ ۖ كَلَّا ۚ
بَلْ هُوَ ٱللَّهُ ٱلْعَزِيزُ ٱلْحَكِيمُ

27 Say, "Show me those you have attached to Him as associates. No indeed! But He is Allah, the Powerful, the Wise."

٢٨ وَمَآ أَرْسَلْنَٰكَ إِلَّا كَآفَّةً لِّلنَّاسِ بَشِيرًا وَنَذِيرًا
وَلَٰكِنَّ أَكْثَرَ ٱلنَّاسِ لَا يَعْلَمُونَ

28 We sent you only universally to all people, a herald and warner, but most people do not know.

٢٩ وَيَقُولُونَ مَتَىٰ هَٰذَا ٱلْوَعْدُ إِن كُنتُمْ صَٰدِقِينَ

29 And they say, "When is this promise due, if you are truthful?"

٣٠ قُل لَّكُم مِّيعَادُ يَوْمٍ لَّا تَسْتَـْٔخِرُونَ عَنْهُ
سَاعَةً وَلَا تَسْتَقْدِمُونَ

30 Say, "You are promised a Day, which you cannot postpone by one hour, nor bring forward."

٣١ وَقَالَ ٱلَّذِينَ كَفَرُوا۟ لَن نُّؤْمِنَ بِهَٰذَا ٱلْقُرْءَانِ
وَلَا بِٱلَّذِى بَيْنَ يَدَيْهِ ۗ وَلَوْ تَرَىٰٓ إِذِ ٱلظَّٰلِمُونَ
مَوْقُوفُونَ عِندَ رَبِّهِمْ يَرْجِعُ بَعْضُهُمْ إِلَىٰ بَعْضٍ
ٱلْقَوْلَ يَقُولُ ٱلَّذِينَ ٱسْتُضْعِفُوا۟ لِلَّذِينَ
ٱسْتَكْبَرُوا۟ لَوْلَآ أَنتُمْ لَكُنَّا مُؤْمِنِينَ

31 Those who disbelieve say, "We will never believe in this Quran, nor in what came before it." If you could only see the wrongdoers, captive before their Lord, throwing back allegations at one another. Those who were oppressed will say to those who were arrogant, "Were it not for you, we would have been believers."

٣٢ قَالَ ٱلَّذِينَ ٱسْتَكْبَرُوا۟ لِلَّذِينَ ٱسْتُضْعِفُوٓا۟
أَنَحْنُ صَدَدْنَٰكُمْ عَنِ ٱلْهُدَىٰ بَعْدَ إِذْ جَآءَكُم ۖ بَلْ
كُنتُم مُّجْرِمِينَ

32 Those who were arrogant will say to those who were oppressed, "Was it us who turned you away from guidance when it came to you? No indeed, you yourselves were sinful."

٣٣ وَقَالَ ٱلَّذِينَ ٱسْتُضْعِفُوا۟ لِلَّذِينَ ٱسْتَكْبَرُوا۟
بَلْ مَكْرُ ٱلَّيْلِ وَٱلنَّهَارِ إِذْ تَأْمُرُونَنَآ أَن نَّكْفُرَ بِٱللَّهِ
وَنَجْعَلَ لَهُۥٓ أَندَادًا ۚ وَأَسَرُّوا۟ ٱلنَّدَامَةَ لَمَّا رَأَوُا۟
ٱلْعَذَابَ وَجَعَلْنَا ٱلْأَغْلَٰلَ فِىٓ أَعْنَاقِ ٱلَّذِينَ
كَفَرُوا۟ ۚ هَلْ يُجْزَوْنَ إِلَّا مَا كَانُوا۟ يَعْمَلُونَ

33 And those who were oppressed will say to those who were arrogant, "It was your scheming by night and day; as you instructed us to reject Allah, and to set up rivals to Him." They will hide their remorse when they see the retribution. We will put yokes around the necks of those who disbelieved. Will they be repaid for anything other than what they used to do?

٣٤ وَمَآ أَرْسَلْنَا فِى قَرْيَةٍ مِّن نَّذِيرٍ إِلَّا قَالَ
مُتْرَفُوهَآ إِنَّا بِمَآ أُرْسِلْتُم بِهِۦ كَٰفِرُونَ

34 We sent no warner to any town, without its affluent saying, "We reject what you are sent with."

٣٥ وَقَالُوا۟ نَحْنُ أَكْثَرُ أَمْوَٰلًا وَأَوْلَٰدًا وَمَا نَحْنُ
بِمُعَذَّبِينَ

35 And they say, "We have more wealth and more children, and we will not be punished."

٣٦ قُلْ إِنَّ رَبِّى يَبْسُطُ ٱلرِّزْقَ لِمَن يَشَآءُ وَيَقْدِرُ
وَلَٰكِنَّ أَكْثَرَ ٱلنَّاسِ لَا يَعْلَمُونَ

36 Say, "My Lord spreads out His bounty to whomever He wills, or restricts it; but most people do not know."

٣٧ وَمَآ أَمْوَٰلُكُمْ وَلَآ أَوْلَٰدُكُم بِٱلَّتِى تُقَرِّبُكُمْ
عِندَنَا زُلْفَىٰٓ إِلَّا مَنْ ءَامَنَ وَعَمِلَ صَٰلِحًا فَأُو۟لَٰٓئِكَ
لَهُمْ جَزَآءُ ٱلضِّعْفِ بِمَا عَمِلُوا۟ وَهُمْ فِى ٱلْغُرُفَٰتِ
ءَامِنُونَ

37 It is neither your wealth nor your children that bring you closer to Us, but it is he who believes and does good deeds. These will have a double reward for what they did; and they will reside in the Chambers, in peace and security.

٣٨ وَٱلَّذِينَ يَسْعَوْنَ فِىٓ ءَايَٰتِنَا مُعَٰجِزِينَ أُو۟لَٰٓئِكَ
فِى ٱلْعَذَابِ مُحْضَرُونَ

38 But those who work against Our revelations, seeking to undermine them—those will be summoned to the punishment.

٣٩ قُلْ إِنَّ رَبِّى يَبْسُطُ ٱلرِّزْقَ لِمَن يَشَآءُ مِنْ
عِبَادِهِۦ وَيَقْدِرُ لَهُۥ ۚ وَمَآ أَنفَقْتُم مِّن شَىْءٍ فَهُوَ
يُخْلِفُهُۥ ۖ وَهُوَ خَيْرُ ٱلرَّٰزِقِينَ

39 Say, "My Lord extends the provision to whomever He wills of His servants, or withholds it. Anything you spend, He will replace it. He is the Best of providers."

٤٠ وَيَوْمَ يَحْشُرُهُمْ جَمِيعًا ثُمَّ يَقُولُ لِلْمَلَٰٓئِكَةِ
أَهَٰٓؤُلَآءِ إِيَّاكُمْ كَانُوا۟ يَعْبُدُونَ

40 On the Day when He gathers them all together, then say to the angels, "Was it you these used to worship?"

٤١ قَالُوا۟ سُبْحَٰنَكَ أَنتَ وَلِيُّنَا مِن دُونِهِم ۖ بَلْ
كَانُوا۟ يَعْبُدُونَ ٱلْجِنَّ ۖ أَكْثَرُهُم بِهِم مُّؤْمِنُونَ

41 They will say, "Be You glorified; You are our Master, not them. In fact, they used to worship the jinn, and most of them had faith in them."

٤٢ فَٱلْيَوْمَ لَا يَمْلِكُ بَعْضُكُمْ لِبَعْضٍ نَّفْعًا وَلَا
ضَرًّا وَنَقُولُ لِلَّذِينَ ظَلَمُوا۟ ذُوقُوا۟ عَذَابَ ٱلنَّارِ
ٱلَّتِى كُنتُم بِهَا تُكَذِّبُونَ

42 "Today, none of you has the power to profit or harm the other." And We will say to those who did wrong, "Taste the agony of the Fire which you used to deny."

٤٣ وَإِذَا تُتْلَىٰ عَلَيْهِمْ ءَايَٰتُنَا بَيِّنَٰتٍ قَالُوا۟ مَا هَٰذَآ
إِلَّا رَجُلٌ يُرِيدُ أَن يَصُدَّكُمْ عَمَّا كَانَ يَعْبُدُ
ءَابَآؤُكُمْ وَقَالُوا۟ مَا هَٰذَآ إِلَّآ إِفْكٌ مُّفْتَرًى ۚ وَقَالَ
ٱلَّذِينَ كَفَرُوا۟ لِلْحَقِّ لَمَّا جَآءَهُمْ إِنْ هَٰذَآ إِلَّا
سِحْرٌ مُّبِينٌ

43 And when Our enlightening Verses are recited to them, they say, "This is nothing but a man who wants to divert you from what your ancestors used to worship." And they say, "This is nothing but a fabricated lie." And when the Truth comes to them, the blasphemers say

of the Truth, “This is nothing but plain magic.”

٤٤ وَمَآ ءَاتَيْنَٰهُم مِّن كُتُبٍ يَدْرُسُونَهَا ۖ وَمَآ
أَرْسَلْنَآ إِلَيْهِمْ قَبْلَكَ مِن نَّذِيرٍ

44 But We gave them no book to study, and We did not send them any warner before you.

٤٥ وَكَذَّبَ ٱلَّذِينَ مِن قَبْلِهِمْ وَمَا بَلَغُوا۟ مِعْشَارَ
مَآ ءَاتَيْنَٰهُمْ فَكَذَّبُوا۟ رُسُلِى ۖ فَكَيْفَ كَانَ نَكِيرِ

45 Those before them also denied the Truth, yet they have not attained one-tenth of what We had given them. They rejected My messengers, so how was My disapproval?

٤٦ قُلْ إِنَّمَآ أَعِظُكُم بِوَٰحِدَةٍ ۖ أَن تَقُومُوا۟ لِلَّهِ
مَثْنَىٰ وَفُرَٰدَىٰ ثُمَّ تَتَفَكَّرُوا۟ ۚ مَا بِصَاحِبِكُم مِّن
جِنَّةٍ ۚ إِنْ هُوَ إِلَّا نَذِيرٌ لَّكُم بَيْنَ يَدَىْ عَذَابٍ
شَدِيدٍ

46 Say, “I offer you a single advice: devote yourselves to Allah, in pairs, or individually; and reflect. There is no madness in your friend. He is just a warner to you, before the advent of a severe punishment.”

٤٧ قُلْ مَا سَأَلْتُكُم مِّنْ أَجْرٍ فَهُوَ لَكُمْ ۖ إِنْ أَجْرِىَ
إِلَّا عَلَى ٱللَّهِ ۖ وَهُوَ عَلَىٰ كُلِّ شَىْءٍ شَهِيدٌ

47 Say, “Whatever compensation I have asked of you, is yours. My compensation comes only from Allah, and He is Witness over all things.”

٤٨ قُلْ إِنَّ رَبِّى يَقْذِفُ بِٱلْحَقِّ عَلَّٰمُ ٱلْغُيُوبِ

48 Say, “My Lord projects the truth. He is the Knower of the Unseen.”

٤٩ قُلْ جَآءَ ٱلْحَقُّ وَمَا يُبْدِئُ ٱلْبَٰطِلُ وَمَا يُعِيدُ

49 Say, “The Truth has come; while falsehood can neither originate, nor regenerate.”

٥٠ قُلْ إِن ضَلَلْتُ فَإِنَّمَآ أَضِلُّ عَلَىٰ نَفْسِى ۖ وَإِنِ
ٱهْتَدَيْتُ فَبِمَا يُوحِىٓ إِلَىَّ رَبِّىٓ ۚ إِنَّهُۥ سَمِيعٌ
قَرِيبٌ

50 Say, “If I err, I err only to my own loss; but if I am guided, it is by what my Lord inspires me. He is Hearing and Near.”

٥١ وَلَوْ تَرَىٰٓ إِذْ فَزِعُوا۟ فَلَا فَوْتَ وَأُخِذُوا۟ مِن
مَّكَانٍ قَرِيبٍ

51 If you could only see when they are terrified, and there is no escape, and they are seized from a nearby place.

٥٢ وَقَالُوٓا۟ ءَامَنَّا بِهِۦ وَأَنَّىٰ لَهُمُ ٱلتَّنَاوُشُ مِن
مَّكَانٍۭ بَعِيدٍ

52 And they say, “We have believed in it.” But how can they attain it from a distant place?

٥٣ وَقَدْ كَفَرُوا۟ بِهِۦ مِن قَبْلُ ۖ وَيَقْذِفُونَ بِٱلْغَيْبِ
مِن مَّكَانٍۭ بَعِيدٍ

53 They have rejected it in the past, and made allegations from a far-off place.

٥٤ وَحِيلَ بَيْنَهُمْ وَبَيْنَ مَا يَشْتَهُونَ كَمَا فُعِلَ
بِأَشْيَاعِهِم مِّن قَبْلُ ۚ إِنَّهُمْ كَانُوا۟ فِى شَكٍّ مُّرِيبٍۭ

54 A barrier will be placed between them and what they desire, as was done formerly with their counterparts. They were in disturbing doubt.

35 Originator فاطر

بِسْمِ ٱللَّهِ ٱلرَّحْمَٰنِ ٱلرَّحِيمِ

In the name of Allah, the Gracious, the Merciful.

١ ٱلْحَمْدُ لِلَّهِ فَاطِرِ ٱلسَّمَٰوَٰتِ وَٱلْأَرْضِ جَاعِلِ
ٱلْمَلَٰٓئِكَةِ رُسُلًا أُو۟لِىٓ أَجْنِحَةٍ مَّثْنَىٰ وَثُلَٰثَ وَرُبَٰعَ ۚ
يَزِيدُ فِى ٱلْخَلْقِ مَا يَشَآءُ ۚ إِنَّ ٱللَّهَ عَلَىٰ كُلِّ
شَىْءٍ قَدِيرٌ

1 Praise be to Allah, Originator of the heavens and the earth, Maker of the angels messengers with wings—double, triple, and quadruple. He adds to creation as He wills. Allah is Able to do all things.

٢ مَّا يَفْتَحِ ٱللَّهُ لِلنَّاسِ مِن رَّحْمَةٍ فَلَا مُمْسِكَ
لَهَا ۖ وَمَا يُمْسِكْ فَلَا مُرْسِلَ لَهُۥ مِنۢ بَعْدِهِۦ ۚ وَهُوَ
ٱلْعَزِيزُ ٱلْحَكِيمُ

2 Whatever mercy Allah unfolds for the people, none can withhold it. And if He withholds it, none can release it thereafter. He is the Exalted in Power, Full of Wisdom.

٣ يَٰٓأَيُّهَا ٱلنَّاسُ ٱذْكُرُوا۟ نِعْمَتَ ٱللَّهِ عَلَيْكُمْ ۚ هَلْ
مِنْ خَٰلِقٍ غَيْرُ ٱللَّهِ يَرْزُقُكُم مِّنَ ٱلسَّمَآءِ
وَٱلْأَرْضِ ۚ لَآ إِلَٰهَ إِلَّا هُوَ ۖ فَأَنَّىٰ تُؤْفَكُونَ

3 O people! Remember Allah's blessings upon you. Is there a creator other than Allah who provides for you from the heaven and the earth? There is no god but He. So how are you misled?

٤ وَإِن يُكَذِّبُوكَ فَقَدْ كُذِّبَتْ رُسُلٌ مِّن قَبْلِكَ ۚ
وَإِلَى ٱللَّهِ تُرْجَعُ ٱلْأُمُورُ

4 If they reject you, messengers before you were also rejected. To Allah all matters are returned.

٥ يَٰٓأَيُّهَا ٱلنَّاسُ إِنَّ وَعْدَ ٱللَّهِ حَقٌّ ۖ فَلَا تَغُرَّنَّكُمُ
ٱلْحَيَوٰةُ ٱلدُّنْيَا ۖ وَلَا يَغُرَّنَّكُم بِٱللَّهِ ٱلْغَرُورُ

5 O people! The promise of Allah is true; so let not the lowly life seduce you, and let not the Tempter tempt you away from Allah.

٦ إِنَّ ٱلشَّيْطَٰنَ لَكُمْ عَدُوٌّ فَٱتَّخِذُوهُ عَدُوًّا ۚ إِنَّمَا
يَدْعُوا۟ حِزْبَهُۥ لِيَكُونُوا۟ مِنْ أَصْحَٰبِ ٱلسَّعِيرِ

6 Satan is an enemy to you, so treat him as an enemy. He only invites his

gang to be among the inmates of the Inferno.

٧ ٱلَّذِينَ كَفَرُوا۟ لَهُمْ عَذَابٌ شَدِيدٌ ۖ وَٱلَّذِينَ
ءَامَنُوا۟ وَعَمِلُوا۟ ٱلصَّـٰلِحَـٰتِ لَهُم مَّغْفِرَةٌ وَأَجْرٌ
كَبِيرٌ

7 Those who disbelieve will suffer a harsh punishment, but those who believe and do righteous deeds will have forgiveness and a great reward.

٨ أَفَمَن زُيِّنَ لَهُۥ سُوٓءُ عَمَلِهِۦ فَرَءَاهُ حَسَنًا ۖ فَإِنَّ
ٱللَّهَ يُضِلُّ مَن يَشَآءُ وَيَهْدِى مَن يَشَآءُ ۖ فَلَا
تَذْهَبْ نَفْسُكَ عَلَيْهِمْ حَسَرَٰتٍ ۚ إِنَّ ٱللَّهَ عَلِيمٌۢ
بِمَا يَصْنَعُونَ

8 What of him whose evil deed was made attractive to him, and so he regards it as good? Allah leads astray whomever He wills, and He guides whomever He wills. Therefore, do not waste yourself sorrowing over them. Allah knows exactly what they do.

٩ وَٱللَّهُ ٱلَّذِىٓ أَرْسَلَ ٱلرِّيَـٰحَ فَتُثِيرُ سَحَابًا
فَسُقْنَـٰهُ إِلَىٰ بَلَدٍ مَّيِّتٍ فَأَحْيَيْنَا بِهِ ٱلْأَرْضَ بَعْدَ
مَوْتِهَا ۚ كَذَٰلِكَ ٱلنُّشُورُ

9 Allah is He who sends the winds, which agitate clouds, which We drive to a dead land, and thereby revive the ground after it had died. Likewise is the Resurrection.

١٠ مَن كَانَ يُرِيدُ ٱلْعِزَّةَ فَلِلَّهِ ٱلْعِزَّةُ جَمِيعًا ۚ إِلَيْهِ
يَصْعَدُ ٱلْكَلِمُ ٱلطَّيِّبُ وَٱلْعَمَلُ ٱلصَّـٰلِحُ يَرْفَعُهُۥ ۚ
وَٱلَّذِينَ يَمْكُرُونَ ٱلسَّيِّـَٔاتِ لَهُمْ عَذَابٌ شَدِيدٌ ۖ
وَمَكْرُ أُو۟لَـٰٓئِكَ هُوَ يَبُورُ

10 Whoever desires honor—all honor belongs to Allah. To Him ascends speech that is pure, and He elevates righteous conduct. As for those who plot evil, a terrible punishment awaits them, and the planning of these will fail.

١١ وَٱللَّهُ خَلَقَكُم مِّن تُرَابٍ ثُمَّ مِن نُّطْفَةٍ ثُمَّ
جَعَلَكُمْ أَزْوَٰجًا ۚ وَمَا تَحْمِلُ مِنْ أُنثَىٰ وَلَا تَضَعُ
إِلَّا بِعِلْمِهِۦ ۚ وَمَا يُعَمَّرُ مِن مُّعَمَّرٍ وَلَا يُنقَصُ مِنْ
عُمُرِهِۦٓ إِلَّا فِى كِتَـٰبٍ ۚ إِنَّ ذَٰلِكَ عَلَى ٱللَّهِ يَسِيرٌ

11 Allah created you from dust, then from a small drop; then He made you pairs. No female conceives, or delivers, except with His knowledge. No living thing advances in years, or its life is shortened, except it be in a Record. That is surely easy for Allah.

١٢ وَمَا يَسْتَوِى ٱلْبَحْرَانِ هَـٰذَا عَذْبٌ فُرَاتٌ سَآئِغٌ
شَرَابُهُۥ وَهَـٰذَا مِلْحٌ أُجَاجٌ ۖ وَمِن كُلٍّ تَأْكُلُونَ
لَحْمًا طَرِيًّا وَتَسْتَخْرِجُونَ حِلْيَةً تَلْبَسُونَهَا ۖ
وَتَرَى ٱلْفُلْكَ فِيهِ مَوَاخِرَ لِتَبْتَغُوا۟ مِن فَضْلِهِۦ
وَلَعَلَّكُمْ تَشْكُرُونَ

12 The two seas are not the same. One is fresh, sweet, good to drink, while the other is salty and bitter. Yet from each you eat tender meat, and extract jewelry which you wear. And you see the ships plowing through them, so that you may seek of His bounty, so that you may give thanks.

١٣ يُولِجُ ٱلَّيْلَ فِى ٱلنَّهَارِ وَيُولِجُ ٱلنَّهَارَ فِى ٱلَّيْلِ
وَسَخَّرَ ٱلشَّمْسَ وَٱلْقَمَرَ كُلٌّ يَجْرِى لِأَجَلٍ
مُّسَمًّى ۚ ذَٰلِكُمُ ٱللَّهُ رَبُّكُمْ لَهُ ٱلْمُلْكُ ۚ وَٱلَّذِينَ
تَدْعُونَ مِن دُونِهِۦ مَا يَمْلِكُونَ مِن قِطْمِيرٍ

13 He merges the night into the day, and He merges the day into the night; and He regulates the sun and the moon, each running for a stated term. Such is Allah, your Lord; His is the sovereignty. As for those you call upon besides Him, they do not possess a speck.

١٤ إِن تَدْعُوهُمْ لَا يَسْمَعُوا۟ دُعَآءَكُمْ وَلَوْ سَمِعُوا۟
مَا ٱسْتَجَابُوا۟ لَكُمْ ۖ وَيَوْمَ ٱلْقِيَٰمَةِ يَكْفُرُونَ
بِشِرْكِكُمْ ۚ وَلَا يُنَبِّئُكَ مِثْلُ خَبِيرٍ

14 If you pray to them, they cannot hear your prayer. And even if they heard, they would not answer you. And on the Day of Resurrection, they will reject your partnership. None informs you like an Expert.

١٥ يَٰٓأَيُّهَا ٱلنَّاسُ أَنتُمُ ٱلْفُقَرَآءُ إِلَى ٱللَّهِ ۖ وَٱللَّهُ هُوَ
ٱلْغَنِىُّ ٱلْحَمِيدُ

15 O people! It is you who are the poor, in need of Allah; while Allah is the Rich, the Praiseworthy.

١٦ إِن يَشَأْ يُذْهِبْكُمْ وَيَأْتِ بِخَلْقٍ جَدِيدٍ

16 If He wills, He can do away with you, and produce a new creation.

١٧ وَمَا ذَٰلِكَ عَلَى ٱللَّهِ بِعَزِيزٍ

17 And that would not be difficult for Allah.

١٨ وَلَا تَزِرُ وَازِرَةٌ وِزْرَ أُخْرَىٰ ۚ وَإِن تَدْعُ مُثْقَلَةٌ
إِلَىٰ حِمْلِهَا لَا يُحْمَلْ مِنْهُ شَىْءٌ وَلَوْ كَانَ ذَا
قُرْبَىٰٓ ۗ إِنَّمَا تُنذِرُ ٱلَّذِينَ يَخْشَوْنَ رَبَّهُم بِٱلْغَيْبِ
وَأَقَامُوا۟ ٱلصَّلَوٰةَ ۚ وَمَن تَزَكَّىٰ فَإِنَّمَا يَتَزَكَّىٰ
لِنَفْسِهِۦ ۚ وَإِلَى ٱللَّهِ ٱلْمَصِيرُ

18 No burdened soul can carry the burden of another. Even if one weighted down calls for help with its burden, nothing can be lifted from it, even if they were related. You are to warn those who fear their Lord inwardly, and perform the prayer. He who purifies himself purifies himself for his own good. To Allah is the ultimate return.

١٩ وَمَا يَسْتَوِى ٱلْأَعْمَىٰ وَٱلْبَصِيرُ

19 Not equal are the blind and the seeing.

٢٠ وَلَا ٱلظُّلُمَٰتُ وَلَا ٱلنُّورُ

20 Nor are the darkness and the light.

٢١ وَلَا ٱلظِّلُّ وَلَا ٱلْحَرُورُ

21 Nor are the shade and the torrid heat.

٢٢ وَمَا يَسْتَوِى ٱلْأَحْيَآءُ وَلَا ٱلْأَمْوَٰتُ ۚ إِنَّ ٱللَّهَ
يُسْمِعُ مَن يَشَآءُ ۖ وَمَآ أَنتَ بِمُسْمِعٍ مَّن فِى
ٱلْقُبُورِ

22 Nor are equal the living and the dead. Allah causes whomever He wills to hear, but you cannot make those in the graves hear.

٢٣ إِنْ أَنتَ إِلَّا نَذِيرٌ

23 You are only a warner.

٢٤ إِنَّآ أَرْسَلْنَٰكَ بِٱلْحَقِّ بَشِيرًا وَنَذِيرًا ۚ وَإِن مِّنْ
أُمَّةٍ إِلَّا خَلَا فِيهَا نَذِيرٌ

24 We sent you with the truth; a bearer of good news, and a warner. There is no community but a warner has passed through it.

٢٥ وَإِن يُكَذِّبُوكَ فَقَدْ كَذَّبَ ٱلَّذِينَ مِن قَبْلِهِمْ
جَآءَتْهُمْ رُسُلُهُم بِٱلْبَيِّنَٰتِ وَبِٱلزُّبُرِ وَبِٱلْكِتَٰبِ
ٱلْمُنِيرِ

25 If they disbelieve you, those before them also disbelieved. Their messengers came to them with the clear proofs, with the Psalms, and with the Enlightening Scripture.

٢٦ ثُمَّ أَخَذْتُ ٱلَّذِينَ كَفَرُوا۟ ۖ فَكَيْفَ كَانَ نَكِيرِ

26 Then I seized those who disbelieved—so how was My rejection?

٢٧ أَلَمْ تَرَ أَنَّ ٱللَّهَ أَنزَلَ مِنَ ٱلسَّمَآءِ مَآءً
فَأَخْرَجْنَا بِهِۦ ثَمَرَٰتٍ مُّخْتَلِفًا أَلْوَٰنُهَا ۚ وَمِنَ
ٱلْجِبَالِ جُدَدٌۢ بِيضٌ وَحُمْرٌ مُّخْتَلِفٌ أَلْوَٰنُهَا
وَغَرَابِيبُ سُودٌ

27 Have you not seen that Allah sends down water from the sky? With it We produce fruits of various colors. And in the mountains are streaks of white and red—varying in their hue—and pitch-black.

٢٨ وَمِنَ ٱلنَّاسِ وَٱلدَّوَآبِّ وَٱلْأَنْعَٰمِ مُخْتَلِفٌ
أَلْوَٰنُهُۥ كَذَٰلِكَ ۗ إِنَّمَا يَخْشَى ٱللَّهَ مِنْ عِبَادِهِ
ٱلْعُلَمَٰٓؤُا۟ ۗ إِنَّ ٱللَّهَ عَزِيزٌ غَفُورٌ

28 Likewise, human beings, animals, and livestock come in various colors. From among His servants, the learned fear Allah. Allah is Almighty, Oft-Forgiving.

٢٩ إِنَّ ٱلَّذِينَ يَتْلُونَ كِتَٰبَ ٱللَّهِ وَأَقَامُوا۟ ٱلصَّلَوٰةَ
وَأَنفَقُوا۟ مِمَّا رَزَقْنَٰهُمْ سِرًّا وَعَلَانِيَةً يَرْجُونَ
تِجَٰرَةً لَّن تَبُورَ

29 Those who recite the Book of Allah, and perform the prayer, and spend of what We have provided for them, secretly and publicly, expect a trade that will not fail.

٣٠ لِيُوَفِّيَهُمْ أُجُورَهُمْ وَيَزِيدَهُم مِّن فَضْلِهِۦٓ ۚ
إِنَّهُۥ غَفُورٌ شَكُورٌ

30 He will pay them their dues in full, and will increase them from His bounty. He is Forgiving and Appreciative.

٣١ وَٱلَّذِىٓ أَوْحَيْنَآ إِلَيْكَ مِنَ ٱلْكِتَٰبِ هُوَ ٱلْحَقُّ
مُصَدِّقًا لِّمَا بَيْنَ يَدَيْهِ ۗ إِنَّ ٱللَّهَ بِعِبَادِهِۦ لَخَبِيرٌۢ
بَصِيرٌ

31 What We inspired in you, of the Book, is the truth, confirming what preceded it. Allah is Well-Informed of His servants, All-Seeing.

٣٢ ثُمَّ أَوْرَثْنَا ٱلْكِتَٰبَ ٱلَّذِينَ ٱصْطَفَيْنَا مِنْ
عِبَادِنَا ۖ فَمِنْهُمْ ظَالِمٌ لِّنَفْسِهِۦ وَمِنْهُم مُّقْتَصِدٌ
وَمِنْهُمْ سَابِقٌۢ بِٱلْخَيْرَٰتِ بِإِذْنِ ٱللَّهِ ۚ ذَٰلِكَ هُوَ
ٱلْفَضْلُ ٱلْكَبِيرُ

32 Then We passed the Book to those of Our servants whom We chose. Some of them wrong their souls, and some follow a middle course, and some are in the foremost in good deeds by Allah's leave; that is the greatest blessing.

٣٣ جَنَّٰتُ عَدْنٍ يَدْخُلُونَهَا يُحَلَّوْنَ فِيهَا مِنْ
أَسَاوِرَ مِن ذَهَبٍ وَلُؤْلُؤًا ۖ وَلِبَاسُهُمْ فِيهَا حَرِيرٌ

33 The Gardens of Eden, which they will enter. They will be adorned therein with gold bracelets and pearls, and their garments therein will be of silk.

٣٤ وَقَالُوا۟ ٱلْحَمْدُ لِلَّهِ ٱلَّذِىٓ أَذْهَبَ عَنَّا ٱلْحَزَنَ ۖ
إِنَّ رَبَّنَا لَغَفُورٌ شَكُورٌ

34 And they will say, "Praise Allah, who has lifted all sorrow from us. Our Lord is Most Forgiving, Most Appreciative.

٣٥ ٱلَّذِىٓ أَحَلَّنَا دَارَ ٱلْمُقَامَةِ مِن فَضْلِهِۦ لَا يَمَسُّنَا
فِيهَا نَصَبٌ وَلَا يَمَسُّنَا فِيهَا لُغُوبٌ

35 He Who settled us in the Home of Permanence, by His grace, where boredom will not touch us, and fatigue will not afflict us."

٣٦ وَٱلَّذِينَ كَفَرُوا۟ لَهُمْ نَارُ جَهَنَّمَ لَا يُقْضَىٰ
عَلَيْهِمْ فَيَمُوتُوا۟ وَلَا يُخَفَّفُ عَنْهُم مِّنْ عَذَابِهَا ۚ
كَذَٰلِكَ نَجْزِى كُلَّ كَفُورٍ

36 As for those who disbelieve, for them is the Fire of Hell, wherein they will never be finished off and die, nor will its punishment be lightened for them. Thus We will repay every ingrate.

٣٧ وَهُمْ يَصْطَرِخُونَ فِيهَا رَبَّنَآ أَخْرِجْنَا نَعْمَلْ
صَٰلِحًا غَيْرَ ٱلَّذِى كُنَّا نَعْمَلُ ۚ أَوَلَمْ نُعَمِّرْكُم مَّا
يَتَذَكَّرُ فِيهِ مَن تَذَكَّرَ وَجَآءَكُمُ ٱلنَّذِيرُ ۖ فَذُوقُوا۟
فَمَا لِلظَّٰلِمِينَ مِن نَّصِيرٍ

37 And they will scream therein, "Our Lord, let us out, and we will act righteously, differently from the way we used to act." Did We not give you a life long enough, in which anyone who wanted to understand would have understood? And the warner did come to you. So taste. The evildoers will have no helper.

٣٨ إِنَّ ٱللَّهَ عَٰلِمُ غَيْبِ ٱلسَّمَٰوَٰتِ وَٱلْأَرْضِ ۚ إِنَّهُۥ
عَلِيمٌۢ بِذَاتِ ٱلصُّدُورِ

38 Allah is the Knower of the future of the heavens and the earth. He knows what the hearts contain.

٣٩ هُوَ ٱلَّذِى جَعَلَكُمْ خَلَٰٓئِفَ فِى ٱلْأَرْضِ ۚ فَمَن
كَفَرَ فَعَلَيْهِ كُفْرُهُۥ ۖ وَلَا يَزِيدُ ٱلْكَٰفِرِينَ كُفْرُهُمْ
عِندَ رَبِّهِمْ إِلَّا مَقْتًا ۖ وَلَا يَزِيدُ ٱلْكَٰفِرِينَ كُفْرُهُمْ
إِلَّا خَسَارًا

39 It is He who made you successors on earth. Whoever disbelieves, his disbelief will recoil upon him. The disbelief of the disbelievers adds only to their Lord's disfavor of them. The disbelief of the disbelievers adds only to their perdition.

٤٠ قُلْ أَرَءَيْتُمْ شُرَكَآءَكُمُ ٱلَّذِينَ تَدْعُونَ مِن
دُونِ ٱللَّهِ أَرُونِى مَاذَا خَلَقُوا۟ مِنَ ٱلْأَرْضِ أَمْ لَهُمْ
شِرْكٌ فِى ٱلسَّمَٰوَٰتِ أَمْ ءَاتَيْنَٰهُمْ كِتَٰبًا فَهُمْ عَلَىٰ
بَيِّنَتٍ مِّنْهُ ۚ بَلْ إِن يَعِدُ ٱلظَّٰلِمُونَ بَعْضُهُم بَعْضًا
إِلَّا غُرُورًا

40 Say, “Have you considered those partners of yours that you worship instead of Allah? Show me what they have created on earth. Or do they have any share in the heavens?” Or have We given them a book whose clear teachings they follow? In fact, the wrongdoers promise one another nothing but delusions.

٤١ إِنَّ ٱللَّهَ يُمْسِكُ ٱلسَّمَٰوَٰتِ وَٱلْأَرْضَ أَن تَزُولَا ۚ
وَلَئِن زَالَتَآ إِنْ أَمْسَكَهُمَا مِنْ أَحَدٍ مِّنۢ بَعْدِهِۦٓ ۚ
إِنَّهُۥ كَانَ حَلِيمًا غَفُورًا

41 Allah holds the heavens and the earth, lest they fall apart. And were they to fall apart, there is none to hold them together except He. He is Most Clement, Most Forgiving.

٤٢ وَأَقْسَمُوا۟ بِٱللَّهِ جَهْدَ أَيْمَٰنِهِمْ لَئِن جَآءَهُمْ
نَذِيرٌ لَّيَكُونُنَّ أَهْدَىٰ مِنْ إِحْدَى ٱلْأُمَمِ ۖ فَلَمَّا
جَآءَهُمْ نَذِيرٌ مَّا زَادَهُمْ إِلَّا نُفُورًا

42 And they swore by Allah with their solemn oaths, that if a warner came to them, they would be more guided than any other people. Yet when a warner came to them, it only increased them in aversion.

٤٣ ٱسْتِكْبَارًا فِى ٱلْأَرْضِ وَمَكْرَ ٱلسَّيِّئِ ۚ وَلَا
يَحِيقُ ٱلْمَكْرُ ٱلسَّيِّئُ إِلَّا بِأَهْلِهِۦ ۚ فَهَلْ يَنظُرُونَ
إِلَّا سُنَّتَ ٱلْأَوَّلِينَ ۚ فَلَن تَجِدَ لِسُنَّتِ ٱللَّهِ تَبْدِيلًا ۖ
وَلَن تَجِدَ لِسُنَّتِ ٱللَّهِ تَحْوِيلًا

43 Priding themselves on earth, and scheming evil. But evil scheming overwhelms none but its authors. Do they expect anything but the precedent of the ancients? You will not find any change in Allah’s practice, and you will not find any substitute to Allah’s practice.

٤٤ أَوَلَمْ يَسِيرُوا۟ فِى ٱلْأَرْضِ فَيَنظُرُوا۟ كَيْفَ
كَانَ عَٰقِبَةُ ٱلَّذِينَ مِن قَبْلِهِمْ وَكَانُوٓا۟ أَشَدَّ مِنْهُمْ

44 Have they not journeyed in the land and observed the fate of those who preceded them? They were

قُوَّةً ۚ وَمَا كَانَ ٱللَّهُ لِيُعْجِزَهُۥ مِن شَىْءٍ فِى
ٱلسَّمَٰوَٰتِ وَلَا فِى ٱلْأَرْضِ ۚ إِنَّهُۥ كَانَ عَلِيمًا قَدِيرًا

superior to them in strength. But nothing can defeat Allah in the heavens or on Earth. He is indeed Omniscient and Omnipotent.

٤٥ وَلَوْ يُؤَاخِذُ ٱللَّهُ ٱلنَّاسَ بِمَا كَسَبُوا۟ مَا تَرَكَ
عَلَىٰ ظَهْرِهَا مِن دَآبَّةٍ وَلَٰكِن يُؤَخِّرُهُمْ إِلَىٰٓ أَجَلٍ
مُّسَمًّى ۖ فَإِذَا جَآءَ أَجَلُهُمْ فَإِنَّ ٱللَّهَ كَانَ بِعِبَادِهِۦ
بَصِيرًۢا

45 If Allah were to punish the people for what they have earned, He would not leave a single living creature on its surface. But He defers them until a stated time. Then, when their time has arrived—Allah is Observant of His creatures.

36 Ya-Seen يس

بِسْمِ ٱللَّهِ ٱلرَّحْمَٰنِ ٱلرَّحِيمِ

In the name of Allah, the Gracious, the Merciful.

١ يسٓ

1 Ya, Seen.

٢ وَٱلْقُرْءَانِ ٱلْحَكِيمِ

2 By the Wise Quran.

٣ إِنَّكَ لَمِنَ ٱلْمُرْسَلِينَ

3 You are one of the messengers.

٤ عَلَىٰ صِرَٰطٍ مُّسْتَقِيمٍ

4 On a straight path.

٥ تَنزِيلَ ٱلْعَزِيزِ ٱلرَّحِيمِ

5 The revelation of the Almighty, the Merciful.

٦ لِتُنذِرَ قَوْمًا مَّآ أُنذِرَ ءَابَآؤُهُمْ فَهُمْ غَٰفِلُونَ

6 To warn a people whose ancestors were not warned, and so they are unaware.

٧ لَقَدْ حَقَّ ٱلْقَوْلُ عَلَىٰٓ أَكْثَرِهِمْ فَهُمْ لَا يُؤْمِنُونَ

7 The Word was realized against most of them, for they do not believe.

٨ إِنَّا جَعَلْنَا فِىٓ أَعْنَٰقِهِمْ أَغْلَٰلًا فَهِىَ إِلَى
ٱلْأَذْقَانِ فَهُم مُّقْمَحُونَ

8 We placed shackles around their necks, up to their chins, so they are stiff-necked.

٩ وَجَعَلْنَا مِنۢ بَيْنِ أَيْدِيهِمْ سَدًّا وَمِنْ خَلْفِهِمْ
سَدًّا فَأَغْشَيْنَٰهُمْ فَهُمْ لَا يُبْصِرُونَ

9 And We placed a barrier in front of them, and a barrier behind them, and We have enshrouded them, so they cannot see.

١٠ وَسَوَآءٌ عَلَيۡهِمۡ ءَأَنذَرۡتَهُمۡ أَمۡ لَمۡ تُنذِرۡهُمۡ لَا
يُؤۡمِنُونَ

10 It is the same for them, whether you warn them, or do not warn them—they will not believe.

١١ إِنَّمَا تُنذِرُ مَنِ ٱتَّبَعَ ٱلذِّكۡرَ وَخَشِيَ ٱلرَّحۡمَٰنَ
بِٱلۡغَيۡبِۖ فَبَشِّرۡهُ بِمَغۡفِرَةٖ وَأَجۡرٖ كَرِيمٍ

11 You warn only him who follows the Message, and fears the Most Gracious inwardly. So give him good news of forgiveness, and a generous reward.

١٢ إِنَّا نَحۡنُ نُحۡيِ ٱلۡمَوۡتَىٰ وَنَكۡتُبُ مَا قَدَّمُواْ
وَءَاثَٰرَهُمۡۚ وَكُلَّ شَيۡءٍ أَحۡصَيۡنَٰهُ فِيٓ إِمَامٖ مُّبِينٖ

12 It is We who revive the dead; and We write down what they have forwarded, and their traces. We have tallied all things in a Clear Record.

١٣ وَٱضۡرِبۡ لَهُم مَّثَلًا أَصۡحَٰبَ ٱلۡقَرۡيَةِ إِذۡ جَآءَهَا
ٱلۡمُرۡسَلُونَ

13 And cite for them the parable of the landlords of the town—when the messengers came to it.

١٤ إِذۡ أَرۡسَلۡنَآ إِلَيۡهِمُ ٱثۡنَيۡنِ فَكَذَّبُوهُمَا فَعَزَّزۡنَا
بِثَالِثٖ فَقَالُوٓاْ إِنَّآ إِلَيۡكُم مُّرۡسَلُونَ

14 We sent them two messengers, but they denied them both, so We reinforced them with a third. They said, "We are messengers to you."

١٥ قَالُواْ مَآ أَنتُمۡ إِلَّا بَشَرٞ مِّثۡلُنَا وَمَآ أَنزَلَ
ٱلرَّحۡمَٰنُ مِن شَيۡءٍ إِنۡ أَنتُمۡ إِلَّا تَكۡذِبُونَ

15 They said, "You are nothing but humans like us, and the Gracious did not send down anything; you are only lying."

١٦ قَالُواْ رَبُّنَا يَعۡلَمُ إِنَّآ إِلَيۡكُمۡ لَمُرۡسَلُونَ

16 They said, "Our Lord knows that we are messengers to you.

١٧ وَمَا عَلَيۡنَآ إِلَّا ٱلۡبَلَٰغُ ٱلۡمُبِينُ

17 And our only duty is clear communication."

١٨ قَالُوٓاْ إِنَّا تَطَيَّرۡنَا بِكُمۡۖ لَئِن لَّمۡ تَنتَهُواْ
لَنَرۡجُمَنَّكُمۡ وَلَيَمَسَّنَّكُم مِّنَّا عَذَابٌ أَلِيمٞ

18 They said, "We see an evil omen in you; if you do not give up, we will stone you, and a painful punishment from us will befall you."

١٩ قَالُواْ طَٰٓئِرُكُم مَّعَكُمۡۚ أَئِن ذُكِّرۡتُمۚ بَلۡ أَنتُمۡ
قَوۡمٞ مُّسۡرِفُونَ

19 They said, "Your evil omen is upon you. Is it because you were reminded? But you are an extravagant people."

٢٠ وَجَآءَ مِنۡ أَقۡصَا ٱلۡمَدِينَةِ رَجُلٞ يَسۡعَىٰ قَالَ
يَٰقَوۡمِ ٱتَّبِعُواْ ٱلۡمُرۡسَلِينَ

20 Then a man came running from the remotest part of the city. He said, "O my people, follow the messengers.

٢١ ٱتَّبِعُوا۟ مَن لَّا يَسْـَٔلُكُمْ أَجْرًا وَهُم مُّهْتَدُونَ

21 Follow those who ask you of no wage, and are themselves guided.

٢٢ وَمَا لِىَ لَآ أَعْبُدُ ٱلَّذِى فَطَرَنِى وَإِلَيْهِ
تُرْجَعُونَ

22 "And why should I not worship Him Who created me, and to Whom you will be returned?

٢٣ ءَأَتَّخِذُ مِن دُونِهِۦٓ ءَالِهَةً إِن يُرِدْنِ ٱلرَّحْمَٰنُ
بِضُرٍّ لَّا تُغْنِ عَنِّى شَفَٰعَتُهُمْ شَيْـًٔا وَلَا يُنقِذُونِ

23 Shall I take other gods instead of Him? If the Merciful desires harm for me, their intercession will not avail me at all, nor will they save me.

٢٤ إِنِّىٓ إِذًا لَّفِى ضَلَٰلٍ مُّبِينٍ

24 In that case, I would be completely lost.

٢٥ إِنِّىٓ ءَامَنتُ بِرَبِّكُمْ فَٱسْمَعُونِ

25 I have believed in your Lord, so listen to me."

٢٦ قِيلَ ٱدْخُلِ ٱلْجَنَّةَ ۖ قَالَ يَٰلَيْتَ قَوْمِى
يَعْلَمُونَ

26 It was said, "Enter Paradise." He said, "If only my people knew.

٢٧ بِمَا غَفَرَ لِى رَبِّى وَجَعَلَنِى مِنَ ٱلْمُكْرَمِينَ

27 How my Lord has forgiven me, and made me one of the honored."

٢٨ وَمَآ أَنزَلْنَا عَلَىٰ قَوْمِهِۦ مِنۢ بَعْدِهِۦ مِن جُندٍ
مِّنَ ٱلسَّمَآءِ وَمَا كُنَّا مُنزِلِينَ

28 After him, We sent down no hosts from heaven to his people; nor would We ever send any down.

٢٩ إِن كَانَتْ إِلَّا صَيْحَةً وَٰحِدَةً فَإِذَا هُمْ
خَٰمِدُونَ

29 It was just one Cry, and they were stilled.

٣٠ يَٰحَسْرَةً عَلَى ٱلْعِبَادِ ۚ مَا يَأْتِيهِم مِّن رَّسُولٍ
إِلَّا كَانُوا۟ بِهِۦ يَسْتَهْزِءُونَ

30 Alas for the servants. No messenger ever came to them, but they ridiculed him.

٣١ أَلَمْ يَرَوْا۟ كَمْ أَهْلَكْنَا قَبْلَهُم مِّنَ ٱلْقُرُونِ أَنَّهُمْ
إِلَيْهِمْ لَا يَرْجِعُونَ

31 Have they not considered how many generations We destroyed before them; and that unto them they will not return?

٣٢ وَإِن كُلٌّ لَّمَّا جَمِيعٌ لَّدَيْنَا مُحْضَرُونَ

32 All of them, every single one of them, will be arraigned before Us.

٣٣ وَءَايَةٌ لَّهُمُ ٱلْأَرْضُ ٱلْمَيْتَةُ أَحْيَيْنَٰهَا
وَأَخْرَجْنَا مِنْهَا حَبًّا فَمِنْهُ يَأْكُلُونَ

33 And there is a sign for them in the dead land: We give it life, and produce from it grains from which they eat.

٣٤ وَجَعَلْنَا فِيهَا جَنَّٰتٍ مِّن نَّخِيلٍ وَأَعْنَٰبٍ
وَفَجَّرْنَا فِيهَا مِنَ ٱلْعُيُونِ

34 And We place in it gardens of palm-trees and vines, and cause springs to gush out of it.

٣٥ لِيَأْكُلُوا۟ مِن ثَمَرِهِۦ وَمَا عَمِلَتْهُ أَيْدِيهِمْ ۖ أَفَلَا
يَشْكُرُونَ

35 That they may eat from its fruits, although their hands did not make it. Will they not be appreciative?

٣٦ سُبْحَٰنَ ٱلَّذِى خَلَقَ ٱلْأَزْوَٰجَ كُلَّهَا مِمَّا تُنۢبِتُ
ٱلْأَرْضُ وَمِنْ أَنفُسِهِمْ وَمِمَّا لَا يَعْلَمُونَ

36 Glory be to Him who created all the pairs; of what the earth produces, and of their own selves, and of what they do not know.

٣٧ وَءَايَةٌ لَّهُمُ ٱلَّيْلُ نَسْلَخُ مِنْهُ ٱلنَّهَارَ فَإِذَا هُم
مُّظْلِمُونَ

37 Another sign for them is the night: We strip the day out of it—and they are in darkness.

٣٨ وَٱلشَّمْسُ تَجْرِى لِمُسْتَقَرٍّ لَّهَا ۚ ذَٰلِكَ تَقْدِيرُ
ٱلْعَزِيزِ ٱلْعَلِيمِ

38 And the sun runs towards its destination. Such is the design of the Almighty, the All-Knowing.

٣٩ وَٱلْقَمَرَ قَدَّرْنَٰهُ مَنَازِلَ حَتَّىٰ عَادَ كَٱلْعُرْجُونِ
ٱلْقَدِيمِ

39 And the moon: We have disposed it in phases, until it returns like the old twig.

٤٠ لَا ٱلشَّمْسُ يَنۢبَغِى لَهَآ أَن تُدْرِكَ ٱلْقَمَرَ وَلَا
ٱلَّيْلُ سَابِقُ ٱلنَّهَارِ ۚ وَكُلٌّ فِى فَلَكٍ يَسْبَحُونَ

40 The sun is not to overtake the moon, nor is the night to outpace the day. Each floats in an orbit.

٤١ وَءَايَةٌ لَّهُمْ أَنَّا حَمَلْنَا ذُرِّيَّتَهُمْ فِى ٱلْفُلْكِ
ٱلْمَشْحُونِ

41 Another sign for them is that We carried their offspring in the laden Ark.

٤٢ وَخَلَقْنَا لَهُم مِّن مِّثْلِهِۦ مَا يَرْكَبُونَ

42 And We created for them the like of it, in which they ride.

٤٣ وَإِن نَّشَأْ نُغْرِقْهُمْ فَلَا صَرِيخَ لَهُمْ وَلَا هُمْ
يُنقَذُونَ

43 If We will, We can drown them—with no screaming to be heard from them, nor will they be saved.

٤٤ إِلَّا رَحْمَةً مِّنَّا وَمَتَٰعًا إِلَىٰ حِينٍ

44 Except by a mercy from Us, and enjoyment for a while.

٤٥ وَإِذَا قِيلَ لَهُمُ ٱتَّقُوا۟ مَا بَيْنَ أَيْدِيكُمْ وَمَا
خَلْفَكُمْ لَعَلَّكُمْ تُرْحَمُونَ

45 Yet when it is said to them, “Beware of what lies before you, and what lies behind you, that you may receive mercy.”

٤٦ وَمَا تَأْتِيهِم مِّنْ ءَايَةٍ مِّنْ ءَايَٰتِ رَبِّهِمْ إِلَّا
كَانُوا۟ عَنْهَا مُعْرِضِينَ

46 Yet never came to them a sign of their Lord’s signs, but they turned away from it.

٤٧ وَإِذَا قِيلَ لَهُمْ أَنفِقُوا۟ مِمَّا رَزَقَكُمُ ٱللَّهُ قَالَ
ٱلَّذِينَ كَفَرُوا۟ لِلَّذِينَ ءَامَنُوٓا۟ أَنُطْعِمُ مَن لَّوْ يَشَآءُ
ٱللَّهُ أَطْعَمَهُۥٓ إِنْ أَنتُمْ إِلَّا فِى ضَلَٰلٍ مُّبِينٍ

47 And when it is said to them, "Spend of what Allah has provided for you," those who disbelieve say to those who believe, "Shall we feed someone whom Allah could feed, if He so willed? You must be deeply misguided."

٤٨ وَيَقُولُونَ مَتَىٰ هَٰذَا ٱلْوَعْدُ إِن كُنتُمْ صَٰدِقِينَ

48 And they say, "When will this promise be, if you are truthful?"

٤٩ مَا يَنظُرُونَ إِلَّا صَيْحَةً وَٰحِدَةً تَأْخُذُهُمْ
وَهُمْ يَخِصِّمُونَ

49 All they can expect is a single blast, which will seize them while they feud.

٥٠ فَلَا يَسْتَطِيعُونَ تَوْصِيَةً وَلَآ إِلَىٰٓ أَهْلِهِمْ
يَرْجِعُونَ

50 They will not be able to make a will, nor will they return to their families.

٥١ وَنُفِخَ فِى ٱلصُّورِ فَإِذَا هُم مِّنَ ٱلْأَجْدَاثِ إِلَىٰ
رَبِّهِمْ يَنسِلُونَ

51 The Trumpet will be blown, then behold, they will rush from the tombs to their Lord.

٥٢ قَالُوا۟ يَٰوَيْلَنَا مَنۢ بَعَثَنَا مِن مَّرْقَدِنَا ۜ هَٰذَا مَا
وَعَدَ ٱلرَّحْمَٰنُ وَصَدَقَ ٱلْمُرْسَلُونَ

52 They will say, "Woe to us! Who resurrected us from our resting-place?" This is what the Most Gracious had promised, and the messengers have spoken the truth."

٥٣ إِن كَانَتْ إِلَّا صَيْحَةً وَٰحِدَةً فَإِذَا هُمْ جَمِيعٌ
لَّدَيْنَا مُحْضَرُونَ

53 It will be but a single scream; and behold, they will all be brought before Us.

٥٤ فَٱلْيَوْمَ لَا تُظْلَمُ نَفْسٌ شَيْـًٔا وَلَا تُجْزَوْنَ إِلَّا
مَا كُنتُمْ تَعْمَلُونَ

54 On that Day, no soul will be wronged in the least, and you will be recompensed only for what you used to do.

٥٥ إِنَّ أَصْحَٰبَ ٱلْجَنَّةِ ٱلْيَوْمَ فِى شُغُلٍ فَٰكِهُونَ

55 The inhabitants of Paradise, on that Day, will be happily busy.

٥٦ هُمْ وَأَزْوَٰجُهُمْ فِى ظِلَٰلٍ عَلَى ٱلْأَرَآئِكِ
مُتَّكِـُٔونَ

56 They and their spouses, in shades, reclining on couches.

٥٧ لَهُمْ فِيهَا فَٰكِهَةٌ وَلَهُم مَّا يَدَّعُونَ

57 They will have therein fruits. They will have whatever they call for.

٥٨ سَلَٰمٌ قَوْلًا مِّن رَّبٍّ رَّحِيمٍ

58 Peace—a saying from a Most Merciful Lord.

٥٩ وَٱمْتَٰزُوا۟ ٱلْيَوْمَ أَيُّهَا ٱلْمُجْرِمُونَ

59 But step aside today, you criminals.

٦٠ أَلَمْ أَعْهَدْ إِلَيْكُمْ يَٰبَنِىٓ ءَادَمَ أَن لَّا تَعْبُدُوا۟
ٱلشَّيْطَٰنَ ۖ إِنَّهُۥ لَكُمْ عَدُوٌّ مُّبِينٌ

60 Did I not covenant with you, O Children of Adam, that you shall not serve the devil? That he is your sworn enemy?

٦١ وَأَنِ ٱعْبُدُونِى ۚ هَٰذَا صِرَٰطٌ مُّسْتَقِيمٌ

61 And that you shall serve Me? This is a straight path.

٦٢ وَلَقَدْ أَضَلَّ مِنكُمْ جِبِلًّا كَثِيرًا ۖ أَفَلَمْ تَكُونُوا۟
تَعْقِلُونَ

62 He has misled a great multitude of you. Did you not understand?

٦٣ هَٰذِهِۦ جَهَنَّمُ ٱلَّتِى كُنتُمْ تُوعَدُونَ

63 This is Hellfire, which you were promised.

٦٤ ٱصْلَوْهَا ٱلْيَوْمَ بِمَا كُنتُمْ تَكْفُرُونَ

64 Roast in it today, because you persistently disbelieved.

٦٥ ٱلْيَوْمَ نَخْتِمُ عَلَىٰٓ أَفْوَٰهِهِمْ وَتُكَلِّمُنَآ أَيْدِيهِمْ
وَتَشْهَدُ أَرْجُلُهُم بِمَا كَانُوا۟ يَكْسِبُونَ

65 On this Day, We will seal their mouths, and their hands will speak to Us, and their feet will testify to everything they had done.

٦٦ وَلَوْ نَشَآءُ لَطَمَسْنَا عَلَىٰٓ أَعْيُنِهِمْ فَٱسْتَبَقُوا۟
ٱلصِّرَٰطَ فَأَنَّىٰ يُبْصِرُونَ

66 If We will, We can blind their eyes as they rush towards the path—but how will they see?

٦٧ وَلَوْ نَشَآءُ لَمَسَخْنَٰهُمْ عَلَىٰ مَكَانَتِهِمْ فَمَا
ٱسْتَطَٰعُوا۟ مُضِيًّا وَلَا يَرْجِعُونَ

67 And if We will, We can cripple them in their place; so they can neither move forward, nor go back.

٦٨ وَمَن نُّعَمِّرْهُ نُنَكِّسْهُ فِى ٱلْخَلْقِ ۖ أَفَلَا يَعْقِلُونَ

68 Whomever We grant old age, We reverse his development. Do they not understand?

٦٩ وَمَا عَلَّمْنَٰهُ ٱلشِّعْرَ وَمَا يَنۢبَغِى لَهُۥٓ ۚ إِنْ هُوَ إِلَّا
ذِكْرٌ وَقُرْءَانٌ مُّبِينٌ

69 We did not teach him poetry, nor is it proper for him. It is only a reminder, and a Clear Quran.

٧٠ لِّيُنذِرَ مَن كَانَ حَيًّا وَيَحِقَّ ٱلْقَوْلُ عَلَى
ٱلْكَٰفِرِينَ

70 That he may warn whoever is alive, and prove the Word against the faithless.

٧١ أَوَلَمْ يَرَوْا۟ أَنَّا خَلَقْنَا لَهُم مِّمَّا عَمِلَتْ أَيْدِينَآ
أَنْعَٰمًا فَهُمْ لَهَا مَٰلِكُونَ

71 Have they not seen that We created for them, of Our Handiwork, livestock that they own?

٧٢ وَذَلَّلْنَٰهَا لَهُمْ فَمِنْهَا رَكُوبُهُمْ وَمِنْهَا يَأْكُلُونَ

72 And We subdued them for them. Some they ride, and some they eat.

٧٣ وَلَهُمْ فِيهَا مَنَٰفِعُ وَمَشَارِبُ ۖ أَفَلَا يَشْكُرُونَ	73 And they have in them other benefits, and drinks. Will they not give thanks?
٧٤ وَٱتَّخَذُواْ مِن دُونِ ٱللَّهِ ءَالِهَةً لَّعَلَّهُمْ يُنصَرُونَ	74 Yet they have taken to themselves gods other than Allah, that perhaps they may be helped.
٧٥ لَا يَسْتَطِيعُونَ نَصْرَهُمْ وَهُمْ لَهُمْ جُندٌ مُّحْضَرُونَ	75 They cannot help them, although they are arrayed as troops for them.
٧٦ فَلَا يَحْزُنكَ قَوْلُهُمْ ۘ إِنَّا نَعْلَمُ مَا يُسِرُّونَ وَمَا يُعْلِنُونَ	76 So let their words not sadden you. We know what they conceal, and what they reveal.
٧٧ أَوَلَمْ يَرَ ٱلْإِنسَٰنُ أَنَّا خَلَقْنَٰهُ مِن نُّطْفَةٍ فَإِذَا هُوَ خَصِيمٌ مُّبِينٌ	77 Does the human being not consider that We created him from a seed? Yet he becomes a fierce adversary.
٧٨ وَضَرَبَ لَنَا مَثَلًا وَنَسِىَ خَلْقَهُۥ ۖ قَالَ مَن يُحْىِ ٱلْعِظَٰمَ وَهِىَ رَمِيمٌ	78 And he produces arguments against Us, and he forgets his own creation. He says, "Who will revive the bones when they have decayed?"
٧٩ قُلْ يُحْيِيهَا ٱلَّذِىٓ أَنشَأَهَآ أَوَّلَ مَرَّةٍ ۖ وَهُوَ بِكُلِّ خَلْقٍ عَلِيمٌ	79 Say, "He who initiated them in the first instance will revive them. He has knowledge of every creation."
٨٠ ٱلَّذِى جَعَلَ لَكُم مِّنَ ٱلشَّجَرِ ٱلْأَخْضَرِ نَارًا فَإِذَآ أَنتُم مِّنْهُ تُوقِدُونَ	80 He who produced fuel for you from the green trees, with which you kindle a fire.
٨١ أَوَلَيْسَ ٱلَّذِى خَلَقَ ٱلسَّمَٰوَٰتِ وَٱلْأَرْضَ بِقَٰدِرٍ عَلَىٰٓ أَن يَخْلُقَ مِثْلَهُم ۚ بَلَىٰ وَهُوَ ٱلْخَلَّٰقُ ٱلْعَلِيمُ	81 Is not He who created the heavens and the earth able to create the like of them? Certainly. He is the Supreme All-Knowing Creator.
٨٢ إِنَّمَآ أَمْرُهُۥٓ إِذَآ أَرَادَ شَيْـًٔا أَن يَقُولَ لَهُۥ كُن فَيَكُونُ	82 His command, when He wills a thing, is to say to it, "Be," and it comes to be.
٨٣ فَسُبْحَٰنَ ٱلَّذِى بِيَدِهِۦ مَلَكُوتُ كُلِّ شَىْءٍ وَإِلَيْهِ تُرْجَعُونَ	83 So glory be to Him in whose hand is the dominion of everything, and to Him you will be returned.

37 The Aligners الصافات

بِسْمِ ٱللَّهِ ٱلرَّحْمَٰنِ ٱلرَّحِيمِ

In the name of Allah, the Gracious, the Merciful.

١ وَٱلصَّٰٓفَّٰتِ صَفًّا

1 By the aligners aligning.

٢ فَٱلزَّٰجِرَٰتِ زَجْرًا

2 And the drivers driving.

٣ فَٱلتَّٰلِيَٰتِ ذِكْرًا

3 And the reciters of the Reminder.

٤ إِنَّ إِلَٰهَكُمْ لَوَٰحِدٌ

4 Your God is indeed One.

٥ رَّبُّ ٱلسَّمَٰوَٰتِ وَٱلْأَرْضِ وَمَا بَيْنَهُمَا وَرَبُّ ٱلْمَشَٰرِقِ

5 Lord of the heavens and the earth, and everything between them; and Lord of the Easts.

٦ إِنَّا زَيَّنَّا ٱلسَّمَآءَ ٱلدُّنْيَا بِزِينَةٍ ٱلْكَوَاكِبِ

6 We have adorned the lower heaven with the beauty of the planets.

٧ وَحِفْظًا مِّن كُلِّ شَيْطَٰنٍ مَّارِدٍ

7 And guarded it against every defiant devil.

٨ لَّا يَسَّمَّعُونَ إِلَى ٱلْمَلَإِ ٱلْأَعْلَىٰ وَيُقْذَفُونَ مِن كُلِّ جَانِبٍ

8 They cannot eavesdrop on the Supernal Elite, for they get bombarded from every side.

٩ دُحُورًا ۖ وَلَهُمْ عَذَابٌ وَاصِبٌ

9 Repelled—they will have a lingering torment.

١٠ إِلَّا مَنْ خَطِفَ ٱلْخَطْفَةَ فَأَتْبَعَهُۥ شِهَابٌ ثَاقِبٌ

10 Except for him who snatches a fragment—he gets pursued by a piercing projectile.

١١ فَٱسْتَفْتِهِمْ أَهُمْ أَشَدُّ خَلْقًا أَم مَّنْ خَلَقْنَآ ۚ إِنَّا خَلَقْنَٰهُم مِّن طِينٍ لَّازِبٍ

11 Inquire of them, "Are they more difficult to create, or the others We created?" We created them from sticky clay.

١٢ بَلْ عَجِبْتَ وَيَسْخَرُونَ

12 But you wonder, and they ridicule.

١٣ وَإِذَا ذُكِّرُوا۟ لَا يَذْكُرُونَ

13 And when reminded, they pay no attention.

١٤ وَإِذَا رَأَوْا۟ ءَايَةً يَسْتَسْخِرُونَ

14 And when they see a sign, they ridicule.

١٥ وَقَالُوٓا۟ إِنْ هَٰذَآ إِلَّا سِحْرٌ مُّبِينٌ

15 And they say, "This is nothing but plain magic.

١٦ أَءِذَا مِتْنَا وَكُنَّا تُرَابًا وَعِظَٰمًا أَءِنَّا لَمَبْعُوثُونَ	16 When we have died and become dust and bones, shall we be resurrected?
١٧ أَوَءَابَآؤُنَا ٱلْأَوَّلُونَ	17 And our ancestors of old?"
١٨ قُلْ نَعَمْ وَأَنتُمْ دَٰخِرُونَ	18 Say, "Yes indeed, and you will be totally subdued."
١٩ فَإِنَّمَا هِىَ زَجْرَةٌ وَٰحِدَةٌ فَإِذَا هُمْ يَنظُرُونَ	19 It will be a single nudge, and they will be staring.
٢٠ وَقَالُوا۟ يَٰوَيْلَنَا هَٰذَا يَوْمُ ٱلدِّينِ	20 They will say, "Woe to us. This is the Day of Judgment."
٢١ هَٰذَا يَوْمُ ٱلْفَصْلِ ٱلَّذِى كُنتُم بِهِۦ تُكَذِّبُونَ	21 "This is the Day of Separation which you used to deny.
٢٢ ٱحْشُرُوا۟ ٱلَّذِينَ ظَلَمُوا۟ وَأَزْوَٰجَهُمْ وَمَا كَانُوا۟ يَعْبُدُونَ	22 Gather those who did wrong, and their mates, and what they used to worship.
٢٣ مِن دُونِ ٱللَّهِ فَٱهْدُوهُمْ إِلَىٰ صِرَٰطِ ٱلْجَحِيمِ	23 Besides Allah, and lead them to the way to Hell.
٢٤ وَقِفُوهُمْ ۖ إِنَّهُم مَّسْـُٔولُونَ	24 And stop them. They are to be questioned."
٢٥ مَا لَكُمْ لَا تَنَاصَرُونَ	25 What is the matter with you? Why do you not help one another?
٢٦ بَلْ هُمُ ٱلْيَوْمَ مُسْتَسْلِمُونَ	26 In fact, on that Day, they will be submissive.
٢٧ وَأَقْبَلَ بَعْضُهُمْ عَلَىٰ بَعْضٍ يَتَسَآءَلُونَ	27 They will come to one another, questioning one another.
٢٨ قَالُوٓا۟ إِنَّكُمْ كُنتُمْ تَأْتُونَنَا عَنِ ٱلْيَمِينِ	28 They will say, "You used to come at us from the right."
٢٩ قَالُوا۟ بَل لَّمْ تَكُونُوا۟ مُؤْمِنِينَ	29 They will say, "You yourselves were not believers.
٣٠ وَمَا كَانَ لَنَا عَلَيْكُم مِّن سُلْطَٰنٍۭ ۖ بَلْ كُنتُمْ قَوْمًا طَٰغِينَ	30 We had no authority over you. You yourselves were rebellious people.
٣١ فَحَقَّ عَلَيْنَا قَوْلُ رَبِّنَآ ۖ إِنَّا لَذَآئِقُونَ	31 The Word of our Lord has been realized against us. We are tasting it.
٣٢ فَأَغْوَيْنَٰكُمْ إِنَّا كُنَّا غَٰوِينَ	32 We seduced you. We were seducers."

٣٣ فَإِنَّهُمْ يَوْمَئِذٍ فِى ٱلْعَذَابِ مُشْتَرِكُونَ	33 On that Day, they will share in the punishment.
٣٤ إِنَّا كَذَٰلِكَ نَفْعَلُ بِٱلْمُجْرِمِينَ	34 Thus We deal with the sinners.
٣٥ إِنَّهُمْ كَانُوٓا۟ إِذَا قِيلَ لَهُمْ لَآ إِلَٰهَ إِلَّا ٱللَّهُ يَسْتَكْبِرُونَ	35 When it was said to them, "There is no god except Allah," they grew arrogant.
٣٦ وَيَقُولُونَ أَئِنَّا لَتَارِكُوٓا۟ ءَالِهَتِنَا لِشَاعِرٍ مَّجْنُونٍۭ	36 And said, "Are we to abandon our gods for a mad poet?"
٣٧ بَلْ جَآءَ بِٱلْحَقِّ وَصَدَّقَ ٱلْمُرْسَلِينَ	37 In fact, he came with the truth, and he confirmed the messengers.
٣٨ إِنَّكُمْ لَذَآئِقُوا۟ ٱلْعَذَابِ ٱلْأَلِيمِ	38 Most assuredly, you will taste the painful punishment.
٣٩ وَمَا تُجْزَوْنَ إِلَّا مَا كُنتُمْ تَعْمَلُونَ	39 And you will be repaid only for what you used to do.
٤٠ إِلَّا عِبَادَ ٱللَّهِ ٱلْمُخْلَصِينَ	40 Except for Allah's sincere servants.
٤١ أُو۟لَٰٓئِكَ لَهُمْ رِزْقٌ مَّعْلُومٌ	41 For them is a known provision.
٤٢ فَوَٰكِهُ ۖ وَهُم مُّكْرَمُونَ	42 Fruits; and they will be honored.
٤٣ فِى جَنَّٰتِ ٱلنَّعِيمِ	43 In the Gardens of Bliss.
٤٤ عَلَىٰ سُرُرٍ مُّتَقَٰبِلِينَ	44 On furnishings, facing one another.
٤٥ يُطَافُ عَلَيْهِم بِكَأْسٍ مِّن مَّعِينٍۭ	45 They will be offered a cup of pure drink.
٤٦ بَيْضَآءَ لَذَّةٍ لِّلشَّٰرِبِينَ	46 White; a delight to those who drink.
٤٧ لَا فِيهَا غَوْلٌ وَلَا هُمْ عَنْهَا يُنزَفُونَ	47 Never polluted, and never intoxicating.
٤٨ وَعِندَهُمْ قَٰصِرَٰتُ ٱلطَّرْفِ عِينٌ	48 With them will be bashful women with lovely eyes.
٤٩ كَأَنَّهُنَّ بَيْضٌ مَّكْنُونٌ	49 As if they were closely guarded pearls.
٥٠ فَأَقْبَلَ بَعْضُهُمْ عَلَىٰ بَعْضٍ يَتَسَآءَلُونَ	50 Then they will approach one another, questioning.
٥١ قَالَ قَآئِلٌ مِّنْهُمْ إِنِّى كَانَ لِى قَرِينٌ	51 One of them will say, "I used to have a friend.

٥٢ يَقُولُ أَءِنَّكَ لَمِنَ ٱلْمُصَدِّقِينَ	52 Who used to say, "Are you of those who believe?
٥٣ أَءِذَا مِتْنَا وَكُنَّا تُرَابًا وَعِظَٰمًا أَءِنَّا لَمَدِينُونَ	53 That after we die and become dust and bones, we will be called to account?"
٥٤ قَالَ هَلْ أَنتُم مُّطَّلِعُونَ	54 He will say, "Will you have a look?"
٥٥ فَٱطَّلَعَ فَرَءَاهُ فِى سَوَآءِ ٱلْجَحِيمِ	55 He will look, and will see him in the pit of Hell.
٥٦ قَالَ تَٱللَّهِ إِن كِدتَّ لَتُرْدِينِ	56 He will say, "By Allah, you almost ruined me.
٥٧ وَلَوْلَا نِعْمَةُ رَبِّى لَكُنتُ مِنَ ٱلْمُحْضَرِينَ	57 Were it not for the grace of my Lord, I would have been among the arraigned."
٥٨ أَفَمَا نَحْنُ بِمَيِّتِينَ	58 "We will not die.
٥٩ إِلَّا مَوْتَتَنَا ٱلْأُولَىٰ وَمَا نَحْنُ بِمُعَذَّبِينَ	59 Except for our first death, and we will not be punished."
٦٠ إِنَّ هَٰذَا لَهُوَ ٱلْفَوْزُ ٱلْعَظِيمُ	60 This is the supreme triumph.
٦١ لِمِثْلِ هَٰذَا فَلْيَعْمَلِ ٱلْعَٰمِلُونَ	61 For the like of this let the workers work.
٦٢ أَذَٰلِكَ خَيْرٌ نُّزُلًا أَمْ شَجَرَةُ ٱلزَّقُّومِ	62 Is this a better hospitality, or the Tree of Bitterness?
٦٣ إِنَّا جَعَلْنَٰهَا فِتْنَةً لِّلظَّٰلِمِينَ	63 We made it an ordeal for the unjust.
٦٤ إِنَّهَا شَجَرَةٌ تَخْرُجُ فِىٓ أَصْلِ ٱلْجَحِيمِ	64 It is a tree that grows from the bottom of Hell.
٦٥ طَلْعُهَا كَأَنَّهُۥ رُءُوسُ ٱلشَّيَٰطِينِ	65 Its fruits are like the devils' heads.
٦٦ فَإِنَّهُمْ لَءَاكِلُونَ مِنْهَا فَمَالِـُٔونَ مِنْهَا ٱلْبُطُونَ	66 They will eat from it, and fill their bellies with it.
٦٧ ثُمَّ إِنَّ لَهُمْ عَلَيْهَا لَشَوْبًا مِّنْ حَمِيمٍ	67 Then, on top of it, they will have a brew of boiling liquid.
٦٨ ثُمَّ إِنَّ مَرْجِعَهُمْ لَإِلَى ٱلْجَحِيمِ	68 Then their return will be to the Blaze.
٦٩ إِنَّهُمْ أَلْفَوْا۟ ءَابَآءَهُمْ ضَآلِّينَ	69 They had found their parents astray.
٧٠ فَهُمْ عَلَىٰٓ ءَاثَٰرِهِمْ يُهْرَعُونَ	70 And rushed along in their footsteps.

71 And most of the ancients before
them went astray.

٧١ وَلَقَدْ ضَلَّ قَبْلَهُمْ أَكْثَرُ ٱلْأَوَّلِينَ

72 Even though We sent messengers
to warn them.

٧٢ وَلَقَدْ أَرْسَلْنَا فِيهِم مُّنذِرِينَ

73 So observe the end of those who
were warned.

٧٣ فَٱنظُرْ كَيْفَ كَانَ عَٰقِبَةُ ٱلْمُنذَرِينَ

74 Except for the sincere servants of
Allah.

٧٤ إِلَّا عِبَادَ ٱللَّهِ ٱلْمُخْلَصِينَ

75 And Noah called out to Us, and
We are the Best of responders.

٧٥ وَلَقَدْ نَادَىٰنَا نُوحٌ فَلَنِعْمَ ٱلْمُجِيبُونَ

76 And We saved him and his family
from the great calamity.

٧٦ وَنَجَّيْنَٰهُ وَأَهْلَهُۥ مِنَ ٱلْكَرْبِ ٱلْعَظِيمِ

77 And We made his descendants
the survivors.

٧٧ وَجَعَلْنَا ذُرِّيَّتَهُۥ هُمُ ٱلْبَاقِينَ

78 And We left mention of him among
those who succeeded.

٧٨ وَتَرَكْنَا عَلَيْهِ فِى ٱلْءَاخِرِينَ

79 Peace be upon Noah among all
people.

٧٩ سَلَٰمٌ عَلَىٰ نُوحٍ فِى ٱلْعَٰلَمِينَ

80 We thus reward the righteous.

٨٠ إِنَّا كَذَٰلِكَ نَجْزِى ٱلْمُحْسِنِينَ

81 He was one of Our believing
servants.

٨١ إِنَّهُۥ مِنْ عِبَادِنَا ٱلْمُؤْمِنِينَ

82 Then We drowned the others.

٨٢ ثُمَّ أَغْرَقْنَا ٱلْءَاخَرِينَ

83 Of his kind was Abraham.

٨٣ وَإِنَّ مِن شِيعَتِهِۦ لَإِبْرَٰهِيمَ

84 When he came to his Lord with a
sound heart.

٨٤ إِذْ جَآءَ رَبَّهُۥ بِقَلْبٍ سَلِيمٍ

85 He said to his father and his
people, “What are you worshiping?

٨٥ إِذْ قَالَ لِأَبِيهِ وَقَوْمِهِۦ مَاذَا تَعْبُدُونَ

86 Is it falsified gods, instead of Allah,
that you want?

٨٦ أَئِفْكًا ءَالِهَةً دُونَ ٱللَّهِ تُرِيدُونَ

87 So what is your opinion about the
Lord of the Worlds?”

٨٧ فَمَا ظَنُّكُم بِرَبِّ ٱلْعَٰلَمِينَ

88 Then he took a glance at the stars.

٨٨ فَنَظَرَ نَظْرَةً فِى ٱلنُّجُومِ

89 And said, “I am sick.”

٨٩ فَقَالَ إِنِّى سَقِيمٌ

90 But they turned their backs on
him, and went away.

٩٠ فَتَوَلَّوْا۟ عَنْهُ مُدْبِرِينَ

٩١ فَرَاغَ إِلَىٰٓ ءَالِهَتِهِمۡ فَقَالَ أَلَا تَأۡكُلُونَ

91 Then he turned to their gods, and said, “will you not eat?

٩٢ مَا لَكُمۡ لَا تَنطِقُونَ

92 What is it with you, that you do not speak?”

٩٣ فَرَاغَ عَلَيۡهِمۡ ضَرۡبَۢا بِٱلۡيَمِينِ

93 Then he turned on them, striking with his right hand.

٩٤ فَأَقۡبَلُوٓاْ إِلَيۡهِ يَزِفُّونَ

94 And they came running towards him.

٩٥ قَالَ أَتَعۡبُدُونَ مَا تَنۡحِتُونَ

95 He said, “Do you worship what you carve?

٩٦ وَٱللَّهُ خَلَقَكُمۡ وَمَا تَعۡمَلُونَ

96 When Allah created you, and what you manufacture?”

٩٧ قَالُواْ ٱبۡنُواْ لَهُۥ بُنۡيَٰنٗا فَأَلۡقُوهُ فِي ٱلۡجَحِيمِ

97 They said, “Build a pyre for him, and throw him into the furnace.”

٩٨ فَأَرَادُواْ بِهِۦ كَيۡدٗا فَجَعَلۡنَٰهُمُ ٱلۡأَسۡفَلِينَ

98 They wished him ill, but We made them the losers.

٩٩ وَقَالَ إِنِّي ذَاهِبٌ إِلَىٰ رَبِّي سَيَهۡدِينِ

99 He said, “I am going towards my Lord, and He will guide me.”

١٠٠ رَبِّ هَبۡ لِي مِنَ ٱلصَّٰلِحِينَ

100 “My Lord, give me one of the righteous.”

١٠١ فَبَشَّرۡنَٰهُ بِغُلَٰمٍ حَلِيمٖ

101 So We gave him good news of a clement boy.

١٠٢ فَلَمَّا بَلَغَ مَعَهُ ٱلسَّعۡيَ قَالَ يَٰبُنَيَّ إِنِّيٓ أَرَىٰ
فِي ٱلۡمَنَامِ أَنِّيٓ أَذۡبَحُكَ فَٱنظُرۡ مَاذَا تَرَىٰۚ قَالَ
يَٰٓأَبَتِ ٱفۡعَلۡ مَا تُؤۡمَرُۖ سَتَجِدُنِيٓ إِن شَآءَ ٱللَّهُ
مِنَ ٱلصَّٰبِرِينَ

102 Then, when he was old enough to accompany him, he said, “O My son, I see in a dream that I am sacrificing you; see what you think.” He said, “O my Father, do as you are commanded; you will find me, Allah willing, one of the steadfast.”

١٠٣ فَلَمَّآ أَسۡلَمَا وَتَلَّهُۥ لِلۡجَبِينِ

103 Then, when they had submitted, and he put his forehead down.

١٠٤ وَنَٰدَيۡنَٰهُ أَن يَٰٓإِبۡرَٰهِيمُ

104 We called out to him, “O Abraham!

١٠٥ قَدۡ صَدَّقۡتَ ٱلرُّءۡيَآۚ إِنَّا كَذَٰلِكَ نَجۡزِي
ٱلۡمُحۡسِنِينَ

105 You have fulfilled the vision.” Thus We reward the doers of good.

١٠٦ إِنَّ هَٰذَا لَهُوَ ٱلۡبَلَٰٓؤُاْ ٱلۡمُبِينُ

106 This was certainly an evident test.

١٠٧ وَفَدَيْنَٰهُ بِذِبْحٍ عَظِيمٍ	107 And We redeemed him with a great sacrifice.
١٠٨ وَتَرَكْنَا عَلَيْهِ فِى ٱلْءَاخِرِينَ	108 And We left with him for later generations.
١٠٩ سَلَٰمٌ عَلَىٰٓ إِبْرَٰهِيمَ	109 Peace be upon Abraham.
١١٠ كَذَٰلِكَ نَجْزِى ٱلْمُحْسِنِينَ	110 Thus We reward the doers of good.
١١١ إِنَّهُۥ مِنْ عِبَادِنَا ٱلْمُؤْمِنِينَ	111 He was one of Our believing servants.
١١٢ وَبَشَّرْنَٰهُ بِإِسْحَٰقَ نَبِيًّا مِّنَ ٱلصَّٰلِحِينَ	112 And We gave him good news of Isaac, a prophet, one of the righteous.
١١٣ وَبَٰرَكْنَا عَلَيْهِ وَعَلَىٰٓ إِسْحَٰقَ ۚ وَمِن ذُرِّيَّتِهِمَا مُحْسِنٌ وَظَالِمٌ لِّنَفْسِهِۦ مُبِينٌ	113 And We blessed him, and Isaac. But among their descendants are some who are righteous, and some who are clearly unjust to themselves.
١١٤ وَلَقَدْ مَنَنَّا عَلَىٰ مُوسَىٰ وَهَٰرُونَ	114 And We blessed Moses and Aaron.
١١٥ وَنَجَّيْنَٰهُمَا وَقَوْمَهُمَا مِنَ ٱلْكَرْبِ ٱلْعَظِيمِ	115 And We delivered them and their people from the terrible disaster.
١١٦ وَنَصَرْنَٰهُمْ فَكَانُوا۟ هُمُ ٱلْغَٰلِبِينَ	116 And We supported them, and so they were the victors.
١١٧ وَءَاتَيْنَٰهُمَا ٱلْكِتَٰبَ ٱلْمُسْتَبِينَ	117 And We gave them the Clarifying Scripture.
١١٨ وَهَدَيْنَٰهُمَا ٱلصِّرَٰطَ ٱلْمُسْتَقِيمَ	118 And We guided them upon the straight path.
١١٩ وَتَرَكْنَا عَلَيْهِمَا فِى ٱلْءَاخِرِينَ	119 And We left with them for later generations.
١٢٠ سَلَٰمٌ عَلَىٰ مُوسَىٰ وَهَٰرُونَ	120 Peace be upon Moses and Aaron.
١٢١ إِنَّا كَذَٰلِكَ نَجْزِى ٱلْمُحْسِنِينَ	121 Thus We reward the righteous.
١٢٢ إِنَّهُمَا مِنْ عِبَادِنَا ٱلْمُؤْمِنِينَ	122 They were of Our believing servants.
١٢٣ وَإِنَّ إِلْيَاسَ لَمِنَ ٱلْمُرْسَلِينَ	123 Also Elijah was one of the messengers.

١٢٤ إِذْ قَالَ لِقَوْمِهِۦٓ أَلَا تَتَّقُونَ
124 He said to his people, “Do you not fear?

١٢٥ أَتَدْعُونَ بَعْلًا وَتَذَرُونَ أَحْسَنَ ٱلْخَٰلِقِينَ
125 Do you call on Baal, and forsake the Best of creators?

١٢٦ ٱللَّهَ رَبَّكُمْ وَرَبَّ ءَابَآئِكُمُ ٱلْأَوَّلِينَ
126 Allah is your Lord, and the Lord of your ancestors.”

١٢٧ فَكَذَّبُوهُ فَإِنَّهُمْ لَمُحْضَرُونَ
127 But they called him a liar, and thus they will be brought forward.

١٢٨ إِلَّا عِبَادَ ٱللَّهِ ٱلْمُخْلَصِينَ
128 Except for Allah’s sincere servants.

١٢٩ وَتَرَكْنَا عَلَيْهِ فِى ٱلْءَاخِرِينَ
129 And We left with him for later generations.

١٣٠ سَلَٰمٌ عَلَىٰٓ إِلْ يَاسِينَ
130 Peace be upon the House of Elijah.

١٣١ إِنَّا كَذَٰلِكَ نَجْزِى ٱلْمُحْسِنِينَ
131 Thus We reward the virtuous.

١٣٢ إِنَّهُۥ مِنْ عِبَادِنَا ٱلْمُؤْمِنِينَ
132 He was one of Our believing servants.

١٣٣ وَإِنَّ لُوطًا لَّمِنَ ٱلْمُرْسَلِينَ
133 And Lot was one of the messengers.

١٣٤ إِذْ نَجَّيْنَٰهُ وَأَهْلَهُۥٓ أَجْمَعِينَ
134 We saved him and his family, all of them.

١٣٥ إِلَّا عَجُوزًا فِى ٱلْغَٰبِرِينَ
135 Except for an old woman who lagged behind.

١٣٦ ثُمَّ دَمَّرْنَا ٱلْءَاخَرِينَ
136 Then We annihilated the others.

١٣٧ وَإِنَّكُمْ لَتَمُرُّونَ عَلَيْهِم مُّصْبِحِينَ
137 You pass by them in the morning.

١٣٨ وَبِٱلَّيْلِ ۚ أَفَلَا تَعْقِلُونَ
138 And at night. Do you not understand?

١٣٩ وَإِنَّ يُونُسَ لَمِنَ ٱلْمُرْسَلِينَ
139 And Jonah was one of the messengers.

١٤٠ إِذْ أَبَقَ إِلَى ٱلْفُلْكِ ٱلْمَشْحُونِ
140 When he fled to the laden boat.

١٤١ فَسَاهَمَ فَكَانَ مِنَ ٱلْمُدْحَضِينَ
141 He gambled and lost.

١٤٢ فَٱلْتَقَمَهُ ٱلْحُوتُ وَهُوَ مُلِيمٌ
142 Then the fish swallowed him, and he was to blame.

١٤٣ فَلَوْلَآ أَنَّهُۥ كَانَ مِنَ ٱلْمُسَبِّحِينَ
143 Had he not been one of those who praised.

١٤٤ لَلَبِثَ فِى بَطْنِهِۦٓ إِلَىٰ يَوْمِ يُبْعَثُونَ	144 He would have stayed in its belly until the Day they are raised.
١٤٥ فَنَبَذْنَٰهُ بِٱلْعَرَآءِ وَهُوَ سَقِيمٌ	145 Then We threw him into the wilderness, and he was sick.
١٤٦ وَأَنۢبَتْنَا عَلَيْهِ شَجَرَةً مِّن يَقْطِينٍ	146 And We made a gourd tree grow over him.
١٤٧ وَأَرْسَلْنَٰهُ إِلَىٰ مِاْئَةِ أَلْفٍ أَوْ يَزِيدُونَ	147 Then We sent him to a hundred thousand, or more.
١٤٨ فَـَٔامَنُوا۟ فَمَتَّعْنَٰهُمْ إِلَىٰ حِينٍ	148 And they believed, so We gave them enjoyment for a while.
١٤٩ فَٱسْتَفْتِهِمْ أَلِرَبِّكَ ٱلْبَنَاتُ وَلَهُمُ ٱلْبَنُونَ	149 Ask them, “Are the daughters for your Lord, while for them the sons?”
١٥٠ أَمْ خَلَقْنَا ٱلْمَلَٰٓئِكَةَ إِنَٰثًا وَهُمْ شَٰهِدُونَ	150 Or did We create the angels females, as they witnessed?”
١٥١ أَلَآ إِنَّهُم مِّنْ إِفْكِهِمْ لَيَقُولُونَ	151 No indeed! It is one of their lies when they say.
١٥٢ وَلَدَ ٱللَّهُ وَإِنَّهُمْ لَكَٰذِبُونَ	152 “Allah has begotten.” They are indeed lying.
١٥٣ أَصْطَفَى ٱلْبَنَاتِ عَلَى ٱلْبَنِينَ	153 So He preferred girls over boys?
١٥٤ مَا لَكُمْ كَيْفَ تَحْكُمُونَ	154 What is the matter with you? How do you judge?
١٥٥ أَفَلَا تَذَكَّرُونَ	155 Will you not reflect?
١٥٦ أَمْ لَكُمْ سُلْطَٰنٌ مُّبِينٌ	156 Or do you have some clear proof?
١٥٧ فَأْتُوا۟ بِكِتَٰبِكُمْ إِن كُنتُمْ صَٰدِقِينَ	157 Then bring your book, if you are telling the truth.
١٥٨ وَجَعَلُوا۟ بَيْنَهُۥ وَبَيْنَ ٱلْجِنَّةِ نَسَبًا ۚ وَلَقَدْ عَلِمَتِ ٱلْجِنَّةُ إِنَّهُمْ لَمُحْضَرُونَ	158 And they invented a relationship between Him and the jinn. But the jinn know that they will be arraigned.
١٥٩ سُبْحَٰنَ ٱللَّهِ عَمَّا يَصِفُونَ	159 Allah be glorified, far above what they allege.
١٦٠ إِلَّا عِبَادَ ٱللَّهِ ٱلْمُخْلَصِينَ	160 Except for Allah’s sincere servants.
١٦١ فَإِنَّكُمْ وَمَا تَعْبُدُونَ	161 Surely, you and what you serve.
١٦٢ مَآ أَنتُمْ عَلَيْهِ بِفَٰتِنِينَ	162 Cannot seduce away from Him.

١٦٣ إِلَّا مَنْ هُوَ صَالِ ٱلْجَحِيمِ	163 Except for he who will be roasting in Hell.
١٦٤ وَمَا مِنَّآ إِلَّا لَهُۥ مَقَامٌ مَّعْلُومٌ	164 “There is not one of us but has an assigned position.
١٦٥ وَإِنَّا لَنَحْنُ ٱلصَّآفُّونَ	165 And we are the arrangers.
١٦٦ وَإِنَّا لَنَحْنُ ٱلْمُسَبِّحُونَ	166 And we are the glorifiers.”
١٦٧ وَإِن كَانُوا۟ لَيَقُولُونَ	167 Even though they used to say.
١٦٨ لَوْ أَنَّ عِندَنَا ذِكْرًا مِّنَ ٱلْأَوَّلِينَ	168 “Had we received advice from the ancients.
١٦٩ لَكُنَّا عِبَادَ ٱللَّهِ ٱلْمُخْلَصِينَ	169 We would have been Allah's faithful servants.”
١٧٠ فَكَفَرُوا۟ بِهِۦ ۖ فَسَوْفَ يَعْلَمُونَ	170 But they rejected it, so they will find out.
١٧١ وَلَقَدْ سَبَقَتْ كَلِمَتُنَا لِعِبَادِنَا ٱلْمُرْسَلِينَ	171 Our Word has already gone out to our servant messengers.
١٧٢ إِنَّهُمْ لَهُمُ ٱلْمَنصُورُونَ	172 It is they who will be supported.
١٧٣ وَإِنَّ جُندَنَا لَهُمُ ٱلْغَٰلِبُونَ	173 And Our troops will be the victors.
١٧٤ فَتَوَلَّ عَنْهُمْ حَتَّىٰ حِينٍ	174 So disregard them for a while.
١٧٥ وَأَبْصِرْهُمْ فَسَوْفَ يُبْصِرُونَ	175 And watch them—they will soon see.
١٧٦ أَفَبِعَذَابِنَا يَسْتَعْجِلُونَ	176 Are they seeking to hasten Our punishment?
١٧٧ فَإِذَا نَزَلَ بِسَاحَتِهِمْ فَسَآءَ صَبَاحُ ٱلْمُنذَرِينَ	177 When it descends into their yard, miserable will be the morning of those forewarned.
١٧٨ وَتَوَلَّ عَنْهُمْ حَتَّىٰ حِينٍ	178 So avoid them for a while.
١٧٩ وَأَبْصِرْ فَسَوْفَ يُبْصِرُونَ	179 And watch—they will soon see.
١٨٠ سُبْحَٰنَ رَبِّكَ رَبِّ ٱلْعِزَّةِ عَمَّا يَصِفُونَ	180 Exalted be your Lord, the Lord of Glory, beyond their allegations.
١٨١ وَسَلَٰمٌ عَلَى ٱلْمُرْسَلِينَ	181 And peace be upon the messengers.
١٨٢ وَٱلْحَمْدُ لِلَّهِ رَبِّ ٱلْعَٰلَمِينَ	182 And praise be to Allah, the Lord of the Worlds.

38 Saad ص

بِسْمِ ٱللَّهِ ٱلرَّحْمَٰنِ ٱلرَّحِيمِ

In the name of Allah, the Gracious, the Merciful.

١ صٓ ۚ وَٱلْقُرْءَانِ ذِى ٱلذِّكْرِ

1 Saad. By the renowned Quran.

٢ بَلِ ٱلَّذِينَ كَفَرُوا۟ فِى عِزَّةٍ وَشِقَاقٍ

2 Those who disbelieve are steeped in arrogance and defiance.

٣ كَمْ أَهْلَكْنَا مِن قَبْلِهِم مِّن قَرْنٍ فَنَادَوا۟ وَّلَاتَ
حِينَ مَنَاصٍ

3 How many generations have We destroyed before them? They cried out when it was too late to escape.

٤ وَعَجِبُوٓا۟ أَن جَآءَهُم مُّنذِرٌ مِّنْهُمْ ۖ وَقَالَ
ٱلْكَٰفِرُونَ هَٰذَا سَٰحِرٌ كَذَّابٌ

4 And they marveled that a warner has come to them from among them. The disbelievers said, “This is a lying magician.”

٥ أَجَعَلَ ٱلْءَالِهَةَ إِلَٰهًا وَٰحِدًا ۖ إِنَّ هَٰذَا لَشَىْءٌ
عُجَابٌ

5 “Did he turn all the gods into one God? This is something strange.”

٦ وَٱنطَلَقَ ٱلْمَلَأُ مِنْهُمْ أَنِ ٱمْشُوا۟ وَٱصْبِرُوا۟ عَلَىٰٓ
ءَالِهَتِكُمْ ۖ إِنَّ هَٰذَا لَشَىْءٌ يُرَادُ

6 The notables among them announced: “Go on, and hold fast to your gods. This is something planned.

٧ مَا سَمِعْنَا بِهَٰذَا فِى ٱلْمِلَّةِ ٱلْءَاخِرَةِ إِنْ هَٰذَآ
إِلَّا ٱخْتِلَٰقٌ

7 We never heard of this in the former faith. This is nothing but a fabrication.

٨ أَءُنزِلَ عَلَيْهِ ٱلذِّكْرُ مِنۢ بَيْنِنَا ۚ بَلْ هُمْ فِى شَكٍّ
مِّن ذِكْرِى ۖ بَل لَّمَّا يَذُوقُوا۟ عَذَابِ

8 Was the message sent down to him, out of all of us?” In fact, they are doubtful of My warning. In fact, they have not yet tasted My punishment.

٩ أَمْ عِندَهُمْ خَزَآئِنُ رَحْمَةِ رَبِّكَ ٱلْعَزِيزِ ٱلْوَهَّابِ

9 Or do they possess the treasuries of the mercy of your Lord—the Majestic, the Giver?

١٠ أَمْ لَهُم مُّلْكُ ٱلسَّمَٰوَٰتِ وَٱلْأَرْضِ وَمَا بَيْنَهُمَا ۖ
فَلْيَرْتَقُوا۟ فِى ٱلْأَسْبَٰبِ

10 Or do they possess the sovereignty of the heavens and the earth and what is between them? Then let them ascend the ropes.

١١ جُندٌ مَّا هُنَالِكَ مَهْزُومٌ مِّنَ ٱلْأَحْزَابِ

11 An army of confederates will be defeated there.

١٢ كَذَّبَتْ قَبْلَهُمْ قَوْمُ نُوحٍ وَعَادٌ وَفِرْعَوْنُ ذُو ٱلْأَوْتَادِ

12 Before them the people of Noah denied the truth; as did Aad, and Pharaoh of the Stakes.

١٣ وَثَمُودُ وَقَوْمُ لُوطٍ وَأَصْحَٰبُ لْـَٔيْكَةِ ۚ أُو۟لَٰٓئِكَ ٱلْأَحْزَابُ

13 And Thamood, and the people of Lot, and the dwellers of the Woods—these were the confederates.

١٤ إِن كُلٌّ إِلَّا كَذَّبَ ٱلرُّسُلَ فَحَقَّ عِقَابِ

14 None of them but denied the messengers, so My retribution was deserved.

١٥ وَمَا يَنظُرُ هَٰٓؤُلَآءِ إِلَّا صَيْحَةً وَٰحِدَةً مَّا لَهَا مِن فَوَاقٍ

15 These can expect only a single scream, from which there is no recovery.

١٦ وَقَالُوا۟ رَبَّنَا عَجِّل لَّنَا قِطَّنَا قَبْلَ يَوْمِ ٱلْحِسَابِ

16 And they say, “Our Lord, hasten Your writ upon us, before the Day of Account.”

١٧ ٱصْبِرْ عَلَىٰ مَا يَقُولُونَ وَٱذْكُرْ عَبْدَنَا دَاوُۥدَ ذَا ٱلْأَيْدِ ۖ إِنَّهُۥٓ أَوَّابٌ

17 Be patient in the face of what they say, and mention Our servant David, the resourceful. He was obedient.

١٨ إِنَّا سَخَّرْنَا ٱلْجِبَالَ مَعَهُۥ يُسَبِّحْنَ بِٱلْعَشِىِّ وَٱلْإِشْرَاقِ

18 We committed the mountains to glorify with him, in the evening and at daybreak.

١٩ وَٱلطَّيْرَ مَحْشُورَةً ۖ كُلٌّ لَّهُۥٓ أَوَّابٌ

19 And the birds, gathered together. All obedient to him.

٢٠ وَشَدَدْنَا مُلْكَهُۥ وَءَاتَيْنَٰهُ ٱلْحِكْمَةَ وَفَصْلَ ٱلْخِطَابِ

20 And We strengthened his kingdom, and gave him wisdom and decisive speech.

٢١ وَهَلْ أَتَىٰكَ نَبَؤُا۟ ٱلْخَصْمِ إِذْ تَسَوَّرُوا۟ ٱلْمِحْرَابَ

21 Has the story of the two disputants reached you? When they scaled the sanctuary?

٢٢ إِذْ دَخَلُوا۟ عَلَىٰ دَاوُۥدَ فَفَزِعَ مِنْهُمْ ۖ قَالُوا۟ لَا تَخَفْ ۖ خَصْمَانِ بَغَىٰ بَعْضُنَا عَلَىٰ بَعْضٍ فَٱحْكُم بَيْنَنَا بِٱلْحَقِّ وَلَا تُشْطِطْ وَٱهْدِنَآ إِلَىٰ سَوَآءِ ٱلصِّرَٰطِ

22 When they entered upon David, and he was startled by them. They said, “Do not fear. Two disputants; one of us has wronged the other; so judge between us fairly, and do not be biased, and guide us to the straight way.”

٢٣ إِنَّ هَٰذَآ أَخِى لَهُۥ تِسۡعٌ وَتِسۡعُونَ نَعۡجَةً وَلِىَ
نَعۡجَةٌ وَٰحِدَةٌ فَقَالَ أَكۡفِلۡنِيهَا وَعَزَّنِى فِى
ٱلۡخِطَابِ

23 “This brother of mine has ninety nine ewes, and I have one ewe, and he said, ‘Entrust it to me,’ and he pressured me with words.”

٢٤ قَالَ لَقَدۡ ظَلَمَكَ بِسُؤَالِ نَعۡجَتِكَ إِلَىٰ
نِعَاجِهِۦۖ وَإِنَّ كَثِيرًا مِّنَ ٱلۡخُلَطَآءِ لَيَبۡغِى
بَعۡضُهُمۡ عَلَىٰ بَعۡضٍ إِلَّا ٱلَّذِينَ ءَامَنُواْ وَعَمِلُواْ
ٱلصَّٰلِحَٰتِ وَقَلِيلٌ مَّا هُمۡۗ وَظَنَّ دَاوُۥدُ أَنَّمَا فَتَنَّٰهُ
فَٱسۡتَغۡفَرَ رَبَّهُۥ وَخَرَّ رَاكِعًا وَأَنَابَ ۩

24 He said, “He has done you wrong by asking your ewe in addition to his ewes. Many partners take advantage of one another, except those who believe and do good deeds, but these are so few.” David realized that We were testing him, so he sought forgiveness from his Lord, and fell down to his knees, and repented.

٢٥ فَغَفَرۡنَا لَهُۥ ذَٰلِكَۖ وَإِنَّ لَهُۥ عِندَنَا لَزُلۡفَىٰ وَحُسۡنَ
مَـَٔابٍ

25 So We forgave him that. And for him is nearness to Us, and a good place of return.

٢٦ يَٰدَاوُۥدُ إِنَّا جَعَلۡنَٰكَ خَلِيفَةً فِى ٱلۡأَرۡضِ
فَٱحۡكُم بَيۡنَ ٱلنَّاسِ بِٱلۡحَقِّ وَلَا تَتَّبِعِ ٱلۡهَوَىٰ
فَيُضِلَّكَ عَن سَبِيلِ ٱللَّهِۚ إِنَّ ٱلَّذِينَ يَضِلُّونَ عَن
سَبِيلِ ٱللَّهِ لَهُمۡ عَذَابٌ شَدِيدُۢ بِمَا نَسُواْ يَوۡمَ
ٱلۡحِسَابِ

26 “O David, We made you a ruler in the land, so judge between the people with justice, and do not follow desire, lest it diverts you from Allah’s path. Those who stray from Allah’s path will have a painful punishment, for having ignored the Day of Account.”

٢٧ وَمَا خَلَقۡنَا ٱلسَّمَآءَ وَٱلۡأَرۡضَ وَمَا بَيۡنَهُمَا
بَٰطِلًاۚ ذَٰلِكَ ظَنُّ ٱلَّذِينَ كَفَرُواْۚ فَوَيۡلٌ لِّلَّذِينَ
كَفَرُواْ مِنَ ٱلنَّارِ

27 We did not create the heaven and the earth and everything between them in vain. That is the assumption of those who disbelieve—so woe to those who disbelieve because of the Fire.

٢٨ أَمۡ نَجۡعَلُ ٱلَّذِينَ ءَامَنُواْ وَعَمِلُواْ ٱلصَّٰلِحَٰتِ
كَٱلۡمُفۡسِدِينَ فِى ٱلۡأَرۡضِ أَمۡ نَجۡعَلُ ٱلۡمُتَّقِينَ
كَٱلۡفُجَّارِ

28 Or are We to treat those who believe and do righteous deeds like those who make trouble on earth? Or are We to treat the pious like the shameless?

٢٩ كِتَٰبٌ أَنزَلۡنَٰهُ إِلَيۡكَ مُبَٰرَكٌ لِّيَدَّبَّرُوٓاْ ءَايَٰتِهِۦ
وَلِيَتَذَكَّرَ أُوْلُواْ ٱلۡأَلۡبَٰبِ

29 A blessed Book that We sent down to you, that they may ponder its Verses, and for those with intelligence to take heed.

٣٠ وَوَهَبْنَا لِدَاوُۥدَ سُلَيْمَٰنَ ۚ نِعْمَ ٱلْعَبْدُ ۖ إِنَّهُۥٓ أَوَّابٌ

30 And We granted David, Solomon, an excellent servant. He was penitent.

٣١ إِذْ عُرِضَ عَلَيْهِ بِٱلْعَشِىِّ ٱلصَّٰفِنَٰتُ ٱلْجِيَادُ

31 When the beautiful horses were paraded before him in the evening.

٣٢ فَقَالَ إِنِّىٓ أَحْبَبْتُ حُبَّ ٱلْخَيْرِ عَن ذِكْرِ رَبِّى
حَتَّىٰ تَوَارَتْ بِٱلْحِجَابِ

32 He said, “I have preferred the love of niceties to the remembrance of my Lord—until it disappeared behind the veil.

٣٣ رُدُّوهَا عَلَىَّ ۖ فَطَفِقَ مَسْحًۢا بِٱلسُّوقِ
وَٱلْأَعْنَاقِ

33 Bring them back to me.” And he began caressing their legs and necks.

٣٤ وَلَقَدْ فَتَنَّا سُلَيْمَٰنَ وَأَلْقَيْنَا عَلَىٰ كُرْسِيِّهِۦ
جَسَدًا ثُمَّ أَنَابَ

34 We tested Solomon, and placed a body on his throne; then he repented.

٣٥ قَالَ رَبِّ ٱغْفِرْ لِى وَهَبْ لِى مُلْكًا لَّا يَنۢبَغِى
لِأَحَدٍ مِّنۢ بَعْدِىٓ ۖ إِنَّكَ أَنتَ ٱلْوَهَّابُ

35 He said, “My Lord, forgive me, and grant me a kingdom never to be attained by anyone after me. You are the Giver.”

٣٦ فَسَخَّرْنَا لَهُ ٱلرِّيحَ تَجْرِى بِأَمْرِهِۦ رُخَآءً
حَيْثُ أَصَابَ

36 So We placed the wind at his service, blowing gently by his command, wherever he directed.

٣٧ وَٱلشَّيَٰطِينَ كُلَّ بَنَّآءٍ وَغَوَّاصٍ

37 And the demons—every builder and diver.

٣٨ وَءَاخَرِينَ مُقَرَّنِينَ فِى ٱلْأَصْفَادِ

38 And others fettered in chains.

٣٩ هَٰذَا عَطَآؤُنَا فَٱمْنُنْ أَوْ أَمْسِكْ بِغَيْرِ حِسَابٍ

39 “This is Our gift; so give generously, or withhold; without account.”

٤٠ وَإِنَّ لَهُۥ عِندَنَا لَزُلْفَىٰ وَحُسْنَ مَـَٔابٍ

40 For him is nearness to Us, and a beautiful resort.

٤١ وَٱذْكُرْ عَبْدَنَآ أَيُّوبَ إِذْ نَادَىٰ رَبَّهُۥٓ أَنِّى مَسَّنِىَ
ٱلشَّيْطَٰنُ بِنُصْبٍ وَعَذَابٍ

41 And mention Our servant Job, when he called out to his Lord, “Satan has afflicted me with hardship and pain.”

٤٢ ٱرْكُضْ بِرِجْلِكَ ۖ هَٰذَا مُغْتَسَلٌۢ بَارِدٌ وَشَرَابٌ

42 “Stamp with your foot—here is cool water to wash with, and to drink.”

٤٣ وَوَهَبْنَا لَهُۥٓ أَهْلَهُۥ وَمِثْلَهُم مَّعَهُمْ رَحْمَةً مِّنَّا وَذِكْرَىٰ لِأُولِى ٱلْأَلْبَٰبِ	43 And We restored his family for him, and their like with them; as a mercy from Us, and a lesson for those who possess insight.
٤٤ وَخُذْ بِيَدِكَ ضِغْثًا فَٱضْرِب بِّهِۦ وَلَا تَحْنَثْ إِنَّا وَجَدْنَٰهُ صَابِرًا ۚ نِّعْمَ ٱلْعَبْدُ ۖ إِنَّهُۥٓ أَوَّابٌ	44 "Take with your hand a bundle, and strike with it, and do not break your oath." We found him patient. What an excellent servant! He was obedient.
٤٥ وَٱذْكُرْ عِبَٰدَنَآ إِبْرَٰهِيمَ وَإِسْحَٰقَ وَيَعْقُوبَ أُولِى ٱلْأَيْدِى وَٱلْأَبْصَٰرِ	45 And mention Our servants Abraham, Isaac, and Jacob—endowed with ability and vision.
٤٦ إِنَّآ أَخْلَصْنَٰهُم بِخَالِصَةٍ ذِكْرَى ٱلدَّارِ	46 We distinguished them with a distinct quality: the remembrance of the Home.
٤٧ وَإِنَّهُمْ عِندَنَا لَمِنَ ٱلْمُصْطَفَيْنَ ٱلْأَخْيَارِ	47 To Us they are among the chosen, the outstanding.
٤٨ وَٱذْكُرْ إِسْمَٰعِيلَ وَٱلْيَسَعَ وَذَا ٱلْكِفْلِ ۖ وَكُلٌّ مِّنَ ٱلْأَخْيَارِ	48 And mention Ishmael, Elisha, and Ezekiel; all are among the outstanding.
٤٩ هَٰذَا ذِكْرٌ ۚ وَإِنَّ لِلْمُتَّقِينَ لَحُسْنَ مَـَٔابٍ	49 This is a reminder. The devout will have a good place of return.
٥٠ جَنَّٰتِ عَدْنٍ مُّفَتَّحَةً لَّهُمُ ٱلْأَبْوَٰبُ	50 The Gardens of Eden, with their doors wide-open for them.
٥١ مُتَّكِـِٔينَ فِيهَا يَدْعُونَ فِيهَا بِفَٰكِهَةٍ كَثِيرَةٍ وَشَرَابٍ	51 Relaxing therein, and calling for abundant fruit and beverage.
٥٢ وَعِندَهُمْ قَٰصِرَٰتُ ٱلطَّرْفِ أَتْرَابٌ	52 With them will be attendants with modest gaze, of same age.
٥٣ هَٰذَا مَا تُوعَدُونَ لِيَوْمِ ٱلْحِسَابِ	53 This is what you are promised for the Day of Account.
٥٤ إِنَّ هَٰذَا لَرِزْقُنَا مَا لَهُۥ مِن نَّفَادٍ	54 Such is Our bounty, inexhaustible.
٥٥ هَٰذَا ۚ وَإِنَّ لِلطَّٰغِينَ لَشَرَّ مَـَٔابٍ	55 All This. But the transgressors will have a miserable return.
٥٦ جَهَنَّمَ يَصْلَوْنَهَا فَبِئْسَ ٱلْمِهَادُ	56 Hell; in which they will roast; what a miserable abode!
٥٧ هَٰذَا فَلْيَذُوقُوهُ حَمِيمٌ وَغَسَّاقٌ	57 All this. Let them taste it—boiling and bitter cold.

٥٨ وَءَاخَرُ مِن شَكْلِهِۦٓ أَزْوَٰجٌ

58 And similar torments of diverse kinds.

٥٩ هَٰذَا فَوْجٌ مُّقْتَحِمٌ مَّعَكُمْ ۖ لَا مَرْحَبًۢا بِهِمْ ۚ
إِنَّهُمْ صَالُوا۟ ٱلنَّارِ

59 "This is a crowd rushing headlong with you." There is no welcome for them. They will be scorched by the Fire.

٦٠ قَالُوا۟ بَلْ أَنتُمْ لَا مَرْحَبًۢا بِكُمْ ۖ أَنتُمْ قَدَّمْتُمُوهُ
لَنَا ۖ فَبِئْسَ ٱلْقَرَارُ

60 They will say, "But it is you! There is no welcome for you! It is you who brought it upon us! What a miserable end!"

٦١ قَالُوا۟ رَبَّنَا مَن قَدَّمَ لَنَا هَٰذَا فَزِدْهُ عَذَابًا
ضِعْفًا فِى ٱلنَّارِ

61 They will say, "Our Lord, whoever brought this upon us, give him double torment in the Fire."

٦٢ وَقَالُوا۟ مَا لَنَا لَا نَرَىٰ رِجَالًا كُنَّا نَعُدُّهُم مِّنَ
ٱلْأَشْرَارِ

62 And they will say, "What is it with us that we do not see men we used to count among the wicked?

٦٣ أَتَّخَذْنَٰهُمْ سِخْرِيًّا أَمْ زَاغَتْ عَنْهُمُ ٱلْأَبْصَٰرُ

63 Did we take them for mockery, or have our eyes swerved from them?

٦٤ إِنَّ ذَٰلِكَ لَحَقٌّ تَخَاصُمُ أَهْلِ ٱلنَّارِ

64 This is certainly true—the feuding of the people of the Fire.

٦٥ قُلْ إِنَّمَآ أَنَا۠ مُنذِرٌ ۖ وَمَا مِنْ إِلَٰهٍ إِلَّا ٱللَّهُ ٱلْوَٰحِدُ
ٱلْقَهَّارُ

65 Say, "I am only a warner, and there is no god except Allah—the One, the Conqueror.

٦٦ رَبُّ ٱلسَّمَٰوَٰتِ وَٱلْأَرْضِ وَمَا بَيْنَهُمَا ٱلْعَزِيزُ
ٱلْغَفَّٰرُ

66 The Lord of the heavens and the earth, and everything between them; the Mighty, the Forgiver."

٦٧ قُلْ هُوَ نَبَؤٌا۟ عَظِيمٌ

67 Say, "It is a message of great importance.

٦٨ أَنتُمْ عَنْهُ مُعْرِضُونَ

68 From which you are turning away.

٦٩ مَا كَانَ لِىَ مِنْ عِلْمٍۭ بِٱلْمَلَإِ ٱلْأَعْلَىٰٓ إِذْ
يَخْتَصِمُونَ

69 I have no knowledge of the Highest Assembly as they dispute.

٧٠ إِن يُوحَىٰٓ إِلَىَّ إِلَّآ أَنَّمَآ أَنَا۠ نَذِيرٌ مُّبِينٌ

70 It is only revealed to me that I am a clear warner."

٧١ إِذْ قَالَ رَبُّكَ لِلْمَلَٰٓئِكَةِ إِنِّى خَٰلِقٌۢ بَشَرًا مِّن
طِينٍ

71 Your Lord said to the angels, "I am creating a human being from clay.

٧٢ فَإِذَا سَوَّيْتُهُۥ وَنَفَخْتُ فِيهِ مِن رُّوحِى فَقَعُوا۟
لَهُۥ سَٰجِدِينَ

72 When I have formed him, and breathed into him of My spirit, fall prostrate before him.

٧٣ فَسَجَدَ ٱلْمَلَٰٓئِكَةُ كُلُّهُمْ أَجْمَعُونَ

73 So the angels fell prostrate, all of them.

٧٤ إِلَّآ إِبْلِيسَ ٱسْتَكْبَرَ وَكَانَ مِنَ ٱلْكَٰفِرِينَ

74 Except for Satan. He was too proud, and one of the faithless.

٧٥ قَالَ يَٰٓإِبْلِيسُ مَا مَنَعَكَ أَن تَسْجُدَ لِمَا خَلَقْتُ
بِيَدَىَّ ۖ أَسْتَكْبَرْتَ أَمْ كُنتَ مِنَ ٱلْعَالِينَ

75 He said, “O Satan, what prevented you from prostrating before what I created with My Own hands? Are you too proud, or were you one of the exalted?”

٧٦ قَالَ أَنَا۠ خَيْرٌ مِّنْهُ ۖ خَلَقْتَنِى مِن نَّارٍ وَخَلَقْتَهُۥ
مِن طِينٍ

76 He said, “I am better than he; You created me from fire, and You created him from clay.”

٧٧ قَالَ فَٱخْرُجْ مِنْهَا فَإِنَّكَ رَجِيمٌ

77 He said, “Then get out of here! You are an outcast!

٧٨ وَإِنَّ عَلَيْكَ لَعْنَتِىٓ إِلَىٰ يَوْمِ ٱلدِّينِ

78 And My curse will be upon you until the Day of Judgment.”

٧٩ قَالَ رَبِّ فَأَنظِرْنِىٓ إِلَىٰ يَوْمِ يُبْعَثُونَ

79 He said, “Lord, defer me until the Day they are resurrected.”

٨٠ قَالَ فَإِنَّكَ مِنَ ٱلْمُنظَرِينَ

80 He said, “You are one of those deferred.

٨١ إِلَىٰ يَوْمِ ٱلْوَقْتِ ٱلْمَعْلُومِ

81 Until the Day of the Time Appointed.”

٨٢ قَالَ فَبِعِزَّتِكَ لَأُغْوِيَنَّهُمْ أَجْمَعِينَ

82 He said, “By Your majesty, I will seduce them all.

٨٣ إِلَّا عِبَادَكَ مِنْهُمُ ٱلْمُخْلَصِينَ

83 Except for your loyal servants among them.”

٨٤ قَالَ فَٱلْحَقُّ وَٱلْحَقَّ أَقُولُ

84 He said, “The truth is, and I say the truth.

٨٥ لَأَمْلَأَنَّ جَهَنَّمَ مِنكَ وَمِمَّن تَبِعَكَ مِنْهُمْ
أَجْمَعِينَ

85 I will fill Hell with you, and with every one of them who follows you.”

٨٦ قُلْ مَآ أَسْـَٔلُكُمْ عَلَيْهِ مِنْ أَجْرٍ وَمَآ أَنَا۠ مِنَ
ٱلْمُتَكَلِّفِينَ

86 Say, “I ask of you no wage for this, and I am not a pretender.

٨٧ إِنْ هُوَ إِلَّا ذِكْرٌ لِّلْعَٰلَمِينَ

87 It is but a reminder to mankind.

٨٨ وَلَتَعۡلَمُنَّ نَبَأَهُۥ بَعۡدَ حِينِۭ

88 And you will know its message
after a while."

39 Throngs الزمر

بِسۡمِ ٱللَّهِ ٱلرَّحۡمَٰنِ ٱلرَّحِيمِ

In the name of Allah, the Gracious, the Merciful.

١ تَنزِيلُ ٱلۡكِتَٰبِ مِنَ ٱللَّهِ ٱلۡعَزِيزِ ٱلۡحَكِيمِ

1 The revelation of the Book is from Allah, the Mighty and Wise.

٢ إِنَّآ أَنزَلۡنَآ إِلَيۡكَ ٱلۡكِتَٰبَ بِٱلۡحَقِّ فَٱعۡبُدِ ٱللَّهَ
مُخۡلِصٗا لَّهُ ٱلدِّينَ

2 We sent down to you the Book with the truth, so serve Allah, devoting your religion to Him.

٣ أَلَا لِلَّهِ ٱلدِّينُ ٱلۡخَالِصُۚ وَٱلَّذِينَ ٱتَّخَذُواْ مِن
دُونِهِۦٓ أَوۡلِيَآءَ مَا نَعۡبُدُهُمۡ إِلَّا لِيُقَرِّبُونَآ إِلَى ٱللَّهِ
زُلۡفَىٰٓ إِنَّ ٱللَّهَ يَحۡكُمُ بَيۡنَهُمۡ فِي مَا هُمۡ فِيهِ
يَخۡتَلِفُونَۗ إِنَّ ٱللَّهَ لَا يَهۡدِي مَنۡ هُوَ كَٰذِبٞ كَفَّارٞ

3 Is not to Allah that sincere faith is due? As for those who take guardians besides Him, "We only worship them that they may bring us nearer to Allah." Allah will judge between them regarding their differences. Allah does not guide the lying blasphemer.

٤ لَّوۡ أَرَادَ ٱللَّهُ أَن يَتَّخِذَ وَلَدٗا لَّٱصۡطَفَىٰ مِمَّا
يَخۡلُقُ مَا يَشَآءُۚ سُبۡحَٰنَهُۥۖ هُوَ ٱللَّهُ ٱلۡوَٰحِدُ ٱلۡقَهَّارُ

4 If Allah wanted to have a son, He could have selected from His creation at will. Glory be to Him. He is Allah, the One, the Prevailing.

٥ خَلَقَ ٱلسَّمَٰوَٰتِ وَٱلۡأَرۡضَ بِٱلۡحَقِّۖ يُكَوِّرُ ٱلَّيۡلَ
عَلَى ٱلنَّهَارِ وَيُكَوِّرُ ٱلنَّهَارَ عَلَى ٱلَّيۡلِۖ وَسَخَّرَ
ٱلشَّمۡسَ وَٱلۡقَمَرَۖ كُلّٞ يَجۡرِي لِأَجَلٖ مُّسَمًّىۗ أَلَا
هُوَ ٱلۡعَزِيزُ ٱلۡغَفَّٰرُ

5 He created the heavens and the earth with reason. He wraps the night around the day, and He wraps the day around the night. And He regulates the sun and the moon, each running along a specific course. He is indeed the Almighty, the Forgiver.

٦ خَلَقَكُم مِّن نَّفۡسٖ وَٰحِدَةٖ ثُمَّ جَعَلَ مِنۡهَا
زَوۡجَهَا وَأَنزَلَ لَكُم مِّنَ ٱلۡأَنۡعَٰمِ ثَمَٰنِيَةَ أَزۡوَٰجٖۚ
يَخۡلُقُكُمۡ فِي بُطُونِ أُمَّهَٰتِكُمۡ خَلۡقٗا مِّنۢ بَعۡدِ خَلۡقٖ
فِي ظُلُمَٰتٖ ثَلَٰثٖۚ ذَٰلِكُمُ ٱللَّهُ رَبُّكُمۡ لَهُ ٱلۡمُلۡكُۖ لَآ
إِلَٰهَ إِلَّا هُوَۖ فَأَنَّىٰ تُصۡرَفُونَ

6 He created you from one person, then made from it its mate, and brought down livestock for you—eight kinds in pairs. He creates you in the wombs of your mothers, in successive formations, in a triple darkness. Such is Allah, your Lord. His is the kingdom. There is no god but He. So what made you deviate?

٧ إِن تَكْفُرُوا۟ فَإِنَّ ٱللَّهَ غَنِىٌّ عَنكُمْ ۖ وَلَا يَرْضَىٰ
لِعِبَادِهِ ٱلْكُفْرَ ۖ وَإِن تَشْكُرُوا۟ يَرْضَهُ لَكُمْ ۗ وَلَا تَزِرُ
وَازِرَةٌ وِزْرَ أُخْرَىٰ ۗ ثُمَّ إِلَىٰ رَبِّكُم مَّرْجِعُكُمْ
فَيُنَبِّئُكُم بِمَا كُنتُمْ تَعْمَلُونَ ۚ إِنَّهُۥ عَلِيمٌۢ بِذَاتِ
ٱلصُّدُورِ

7 If you disbelieve, Allah is Independent of you, yet He does not approve ingratitude on the part of His servants. And if you are thankful, He will approve that in you. No bearer of burden can bear the burden of another. Then to your Lord is your return; and He will inform you of what you used to do. He is aware of what the hearts contain.

٨ وَإِذَا مَسَّ ٱلْإِنسَٰنَ ضُرٌّ دَعَا رَبَّهُۥ مُنِيبًا إِلَيْهِ ثُمَّ
إِذَا خَوَّلَهُۥ نِعْمَةً مِّنْهُ نَسِىَ مَا كَانَ يَدْعُوٓا۟ إِلَيْهِ
مِن قَبْلُ وَجَعَلَ لِلَّهِ أَندَادًا لِّيُضِلَّ عَن سَبِيلِهِۦ ۚ
قُلْ تَمَتَّعْ بِكُفْرِكَ قَلِيلًا ۖ إِنَّكَ مِنْ أَصْحَٰبِ ٱلنَّارِ

8 When some adversity touches the human being, he prays to his Lord, repenting to Him. But then, when He confers on him a grace of His, he forgets what he was praying for before, and he attributes rivals to Allah, in order to lead astray from His way. Say, "Enjoy your disbelief for a little while; you will be among the inmates of the Fire."

٩ أَمَّنْ هُوَ قَٰنِتٌ ءَانَآءَ ٱلَّيْلِ سَاجِدًا وَقَآئِمًا
يَحْذَرُ ٱلْءَاخِرَةَ وَيَرْجُوا۟ رَحْمَةَ رَبِّهِۦ ۗ قُلْ هَلْ
يَسْتَوِى ٱلَّذِينَ يَعْلَمُونَ وَٱلَّذِينَ لَا يَعْلَمُونَ ۗ إِنَّمَا
يَتَذَكَّرُ أُو۟لُوا۟ ٱلْأَلْبَٰبِ

9 Is he who worships devoutly during the watches of the night, prostrating himself and standing up, mindful of the Hereafter, and placing his hope in the mercy of his Lord? Say, "Are those who know and those who do not know equal?" Only those possessed of reason will remember.

١٠ قُلْ يَٰعِبَادِ ٱلَّذِينَ ءَامَنُوا۟ ٱتَّقُوا۟ رَبَّكُمْ ۚ لِلَّذِينَ
أَحْسَنُوا۟ فِى هَٰذِهِ ٱلدُّنْيَا حَسَنَةٌ ۗ وَأَرْضُ ٱللَّهِ
وَٰسِعَةٌ ۗ إِنَّمَا يُوَفَّى ٱلصَّٰبِرُونَ أَجْرَهُم بِغَيْرِ
حِسَابٍ

10 Say, "O My devotees who have believed, keep your duty to your Lord. For those who do good in this world, is goodness. And Allah's earth is vast. The steadfast will be paid their wages in full, without reckoning."

١١ قُلْ إِنِّىٓ أُمِرْتُ أَنْ أَعْبُدَ ٱللَّهَ مُخْلِصًا لَّهُ
ٱلدِّينَ

11 Say, "I was commanded to serve Allah, devoting my religion exclusively to Him.

١٢ وَأُمِرْتُ لِأَنْ أَكُونَ أَوَّلَ ٱلْمُسْلِمِينَ

12 And I was commanded to be the first of those who submit."

١٣ قُلْ إِنِّيٓ أَخَافُ إِنْ عَصَيْتُ رَبِّي عَذَابَ يَوْمٍ
عَظِيمٍ

13 Say, "I fear, if I disobeyed my Lord, the punishment of a horrendous Day."

١٤ قُلِ ٱللَّهَ أَعْبُدُ مُخْلِصًا لَّهُۥ دِينِي

14 Say, "It is Allah I worship, sincere in my faith in Him."

١٥ فَٱعْبُدُوا۟ مَا شِئْتُم مِّن دُونِهِۦ ۗ قُلْ إِنَّ
ٱلْخَٰسِرِينَ ٱلَّذِينَ خَسِرُوٓا۟ أَنفُسَهُمْ وَأَهْلِيهِمْ
يَوْمَ ٱلْقِيَٰمَةِ ۗ أَلَا ذَٰلِكَ هُوَ ٱلْخُسْرَانُ ٱلْمُبِينُ

15 "But you can worship whatever you wish besides Him." Say, "The losers are those who lose their souls and their people on the Day of Resurrection." That is indeed the obvious loss.

١٦ لَهُم مِّن فَوْقِهِمْ ظُلَلٌ مِّنَ ٱلنَّارِ وَمِن تَحْتِهِمْ
ظُلَلٌ ۚ ذَٰلِكَ يُخَوِّفُ ٱللَّهُ بِهِۦ عِبَادَهُۥ ۚ يَٰعِبَادِ
فَٱتَّقُونِ

16 They will have layers of Fire above them, and layers beneath them. That is how Allah strikes fear into His servants—"O My servants! Beware of Me!"

١٧ وَٱلَّذِينَ ٱجْتَنَبُوا۟ ٱلطَّٰغُوتَ أَن يَعْبُدُوهَا
وَأَنَابُوٓا۟ إِلَى ٱللَّهِ لَهُمُ ٱلْبُشْرَىٰ ۚ فَبَشِّرْ عِبَادِ

17 As for those who avoid the worship of idols, and devote themselves to Allah—theirs is the good news. So give good news to My servants.

١٨ ٱلَّذِينَ يَسْتَمِعُونَ ٱلْقَوْلَ فَيَتَّبِعُونَ أَحْسَنَهُۥٓ ۚ
أُو۟لَٰٓئِكَ ٱلَّذِينَ هَدَىٰهُمُ ٱللَّهُ ۖ وَأُو۟لَٰٓئِكَ هُمْ أُو۟لُوا۟
ٱلْأَلْبَٰبِ

18 Those who listen to the Word, and follow the best of it. These are they whom Allah has guided. These are they who possess intellect.

١٩ أَفَمَنْ حَقَّ عَلَيْهِ كَلِمَةُ ٱلْعَذَابِ أَفَأَنتَ تُنقِذُ
مَن فِي ٱلنَّارِ

19 What about someone who has deserved the sentence of punishment? Is it you who can save those in the Fire?

٢٠ لَٰكِنِ ٱلَّذِينَ ٱتَّقَوْا۟ رَبَّهُمْ لَهُمْ غُرَفٌ مِّن فَوْقِهَا
غُرَفٌ مَّبْنِيَّةٌ تَجْرِي مِن تَحْتِهَا ٱلْأَنْهَٰرُ ۖ وَعْدَ
ٱللَّهِ ۖ لَا يُخْلِفُ ٱللَّهُ ٱلْمِيعَادَ

20 But those who fear their Lord will have mansions upon mansions, built high, with streams flowing beneath them. The promise of Allah; and Allah never breaks a promise.

٢١ أَلَمْ تَرَ أَنَّ ٱللَّهَ أَنزَلَ مِنَ ٱلسَّمَآءِ مَآءً فَسَلَكَهُۥ
يَنَٰبِيعَ فِي ٱلْأَرْضِ ثُمَّ يُخْرِجُ بِهِۦ زَرْعًا مُّخْتَلِفًا
أَلْوَٰنُهُۥ ثُمَّ يَهِيجُ فَتَرَىٰهُ مُصْفَرًّا ثُمَّ يَجْعَلُهُۥ
حُطَٰمًا ۚ إِنَّ فِي ذَٰلِكَ لَذِكْرَىٰ لِأُو۟لِي ٱلْأَلْبَٰبِ

21 Have you not considered how Allah sends down water from the sky, then He makes it flow into underground wells, then He produces with it plants of various colors, then they wither and you see

them yellowing, then He turns them into debris? Surely in this is a reminder for those with understanding.

٢٢ أَفَمَن شَرَحَ ٱللَّهُ صَدْرَهُۥ لِلْإِسْلَٰمِ فَهُوَ عَلَىٰ
نُورٍ مِّن رَّبِّهِۦ ۚ فَوَيْلٌ لِّلْقَٰسِيَةِ قُلُوبُهُم مِّن ذِكْرِ
ٱللَّهِ ۚ أُو۟لَٰٓئِكَ فِى ضَلَٰلٍ مُّبِينٍ

22 What about someone whose heart Allah has opened to Islam, so that he follows a light from His Lord? Woe to those whose hearts are hardened against the mention of Allah. Those are in manifest error.

٢٣ ٱللَّهُ نَزَّلَ أَحْسَنَ ٱلْحَدِيثِ كِتَٰبًا مُّتَشَٰبِهًا
مَّثَانِىَ تَقْشَعِرُّ مِنْهُ جُلُودُ ٱلَّذِينَ يَخْشَوْنَ رَبَّهُمْ
ثُمَّ تَلِينُ جُلُودُهُمْ وَقُلُوبُهُمْ إِلَىٰ ذِكْرِ ٱللَّهِ ۚ ذَٰلِكَ
هُدَى ٱللَّهِ يَهْدِى بِهِۦ مَن يَشَآءُ ۚ وَمَن يُضْلِلِ
ٱللَّهُ فَمَا لَهُۥ مِنْ هَادٍ

23 Allah has sent down the best of narrations: a Scripture consistent and paired. The skins of those who reverence their Lord shiver from it, then their skins and their hearts soften up to the remembrance of Allah. Such is Allah's guidance; He guides with it whomever He wills. But whomever Allah leaves astray, for him there is no guide.

٢٤ أَفَمَن يَتَّقِى بِوَجْهِهِۦ سُوٓءَ ٱلْعَذَابِ يَوْمَ
ٱلْقِيَٰمَةِ ۚ وَقِيلَ لِلظَّٰلِمِينَ ذُوقُوا۟ مَا كُنتُمْ
تَكْسِبُونَ

24 What about someone who covers his face against the terrible misery of the Day of Resurrection? To the evildoers it will be said, "Taste what you used to earn."

٢٥ كَذَّبَ ٱلَّذِينَ مِن قَبْلِهِمْ فَأَتَىٰهُمُ ٱلْعَذَابُ مِنْ
حَيْثُ لَا يَشْعُرُونَ

25 Those before them also denied the truth, so the penalty came upon them from where they did not perceive.

٢٦ فَأَذَاقَهُمُ ٱللَّهُ ٱلْخِزْىَ فِى ٱلْحَيَوٰةِ ٱلدُّنْيَا ۖ
وَلَعَذَابُ ٱلْءَاخِرَةِ أَكْبَرُ ۚ لَوْ كَانُوا۟ يَعْلَمُونَ

26 Allah made them taste disgrace in the present life, but the punishment of the Hereafter is worse, if they only knew.

٢٧ وَلَقَدْ ضَرَبْنَا لِلنَّاسِ فِى هَٰذَا ٱلْقُرْءَانِ مِن
كُلِّ مَثَلٍ لَّعَلَّهُمْ يَتَذَكَّرُونَ

27 We have cited in this Quran for mankind every ideal, that they may take heed.

٢٨ قُرْءَانًا عَرَبِيًّا غَيْرَ ذِى عِوَجٍ لَّعَلَّهُمْ يَتَّقُونَ

28 An Arabic Quran, without any defect, so they may become righteous.

٢٩ ضَرَبَ ٱللَّهُ مَثَلًا رَّجُلًا فِيهِ شُرَكَآءُ
مُتَشَٰكِسُونَ وَرَجُلًا سَلَمًا لِّرَجُلٍ هَلْ يَسْتَوِيَانِ
مَثَلًا ۚ ٱلْحَمْدُ لِلَّهِ ۚ بَلْ أَكْثَرُهُمْ لَا يَعْلَمُونَ

29 Allah cites the example of a man shared by partners at odds, and a man belonging exclusively to one man. Are they equal in status? Praise be to Allah, but most of them do not know.

٣٠ إِنَّكَ مَيِّتٌ وَإِنَّهُم مَّيِّتُونَ

30 You will die, and they will die.

٣١ ثُمَّ إِنَّكُمْ يَوْمَ ٱلْقِيَٰمَةِ عِندَ رَبِّكُمْ تَخْتَصِمُونَ

31 Then, on the Day of Resurrection, you will be quarrelling before your Lord.

٣٢ فَمَنْ أَظْلَمُ مِمَّن كَذَبَ عَلَى ٱللَّهِ وَكَذَّبَ
بِٱلصِّدْقِ إِذْ جَآءَهُۥٓ ۚ أَلَيْسَ فِى جَهَنَّمَ مَثْوًى
لِّلْكَٰفِرِينَ

32 Who is more evil than he who lies about Allah, and denies the truth when it has come to him? Is there not in Hell room for the ungrateful?

٣٣ وَٱلَّذِى جَآءَ بِٱلصِّدْقِ وَصَدَّقَ بِهِۦٓ ۙ أُو۟لَٰٓئِكَ
هُمُ ٱلْمُتَّقُونَ

33 But he who promotes the truth, and testifies to it—these are the righteous.

٣٤ لَهُم مَّا يَشَآءُونَ عِندَ رَبِّهِمْ ۚ ذَٰلِكَ جَزَآءُ
ٱلْمُحْسِنِينَ

34 They will have whatever they please with their Lord. Such is the reward for the virtuous.

٣٥ لِيُكَفِّرَ ٱللَّهُ عَنْهُمْ أَسْوَأَ ٱلَّذِى عَمِلُوا۟
وَيَجْزِيَهُمْ أَجْرَهُم بِأَحْسَنِ ٱلَّذِى كَانُوا۟ يَعْمَلُونَ

35 Allah will acquit them of the worst of their deeds, and will reward them according to the best of what they used to do.

٣٦ أَلَيْسَ ٱللَّهُ بِكَافٍ عَبْدَهُۥ ۖ وَيُخَوِّفُونَكَ بِٱلَّذِينَ
مِن دُونِهِۦ ۚ وَمَن يُضْلِلِ ٱللَّهُ فَمَا لَهُۥ مِنْ هَادٍ

36 Is Allah not enough for His servant? And they frighten you with those besides Him. Whomever Allah sends astray, for him there is no guide.

٣٧ وَمَن يَهْدِ ٱللَّهُ فَمَا لَهُۥ مِن مُّضِلٍّ ۗ أَلَيْسَ ٱللَّهُ
بِعَزِيزٍ ذِى ٱنتِقَامٍ

37 And whomever Allah guides, for him there is no misleader. Is Allah not Powerful and Vengeful?

٣٨ وَلَئِن سَأَلْتَهُم مَّنْ خَلَقَ ٱلسَّمَٰوَٰتِ وَٱلْأَرْضَ
لَيَقُولُنَّ ٱللَّهُ ۚ قُلْ أَفَرَءَيْتُم مَّا تَدْعُونَ مِن دُونِ
ٱللَّهِ إِنْ أَرَادَنِىَ ٱللَّهُ بِضُرٍّ هَلْ هُنَّ كَٰشِفَٰتُ ضُرِّهِۦٓ
أَوْ أَرَادَنِى بِرَحْمَةٍ هَلْ هُنَّ مُمْسِكَٰتُ رَحْمَتِهِۦ ۚ
قُلْ حَسْبِىَ ٱللَّهُ ۖ عَلَيْهِ يَتَوَكَّلُ ٱلْمُتَوَكِّلُونَ

38 And if you asked them, “Who created the heavens and the earth?” they would say, “Allah.” Say, “Have you seen those you pray to instead of Allah? If Allah willed any harm for me, can they lift His harm? And if He willed a blessing for me, can they hold back His mercy?” Say, “Allah

suffices for me. On Him the reliant
rely."

٣٩ قُلْ يَٰقَوْمِ ٱعْمَلُوا۟ عَلَىٰ مَكَانَتِكُمْ إِنِّى عَٰمِلٌۖ
فَسَوْفَ تَعْلَمُونَ

39 Say: "O my people, work according to your ability; and so will I. Then you will know.

٤٠ مَن يَأْتِيهِ عَذَابٌ يُخْزِيهِ وَيَحِلُّ عَلَيْهِ عَذَابٌ
مُّقِيمٌ

40 Who will receive a humiliating punishment, and on whom will fall a lasting torment."

٤١ إِنَّآ أَنزَلْنَا عَلَيْكَ ٱلْكِتَٰبَ لِلنَّاسِ بِٱلْحَقِّۖ فَمَنِ
ٱهْتَدَىٰ فَلِنَفْسِهِۦۖ وَمَن ضَلَّ فَإِنَّمَا يَضِلُّ عَلَيْهَاۖ
وَمَآ أَنتَ عَلَيْهِم بِوَكِيلٍ

41 We sent down upon you the Book for mankind in truth. He who follows guidance does so for the good of his soul. And he who strays in error does so to its detriment. You are not their overseer.

٤٢ ٱللَّهُ يَتَوَفَّى ٱلْأَنفُسَ حِينَ مَوْتِهَا وَٱلَّتِى لَمْ
تَمُتْ فِى مَنَامِهَاۖ فَيُمْسِكُ ٱلَّتِى قَضَىٰ عَلَيْهَا
ٱلْمَوْتَ وَيُرْسِلُ ٱلْأُخْرَىٰٓ إِلَىٰٓ أَجَلٍ مُّسَمًّىۚ إِنَّ
فِى ذَٰلِكَ لَءَايَٰتٍ لِّقَوْمٍ يَتَفَكَّرُونَ

42 Allah takes the souls at the time of their death, and those that have not died during their sleep. He retains those for which He has decreed death, and He releases the others until a predetermined time. In that are signs for people who reflect.

٤٣ أَمِ ٱتَّخَذُوا۟ مِن دُونِ ٱللَّهِ شُفَعَآءَۚ قُلْ أَوَلَوْ
كَانُوا۟ لَا يَمْلِكُونَ شَيْـًٔا وَلَا يَعْقِلُونَ

43 Or have they chosen intercessors other than Allah? Say, "Even though they have no power over anything, and are devoid of reason?"

٤٤ قُل لِّلَّهِ ٱلشَّفَٰعَةُ جَمِيعًاۖ لَّهُۥ مُلْكُ ٱلسَّمَٰوَٰتِ
وَٱلْأَرْضِۖ ثُمَّ إِلَيْهِ تُرْجَعُونَ

44 Say, "All intercession is up to Allah. To Him belongs the kingdom of the heavens and the earth. Then to Him you will be returned."

٤٥ وَإِذَا ذُكِرَ ٱللَّهُ وَحْدَهُ ٱشْمَأَزَّتْ قُلُوبُ ٱلَّذِينَ
لَا يُؤْمِنُونَ بِٱلْءَاخِرَةِۖ وَإِذَا ذُكِرَ ٱلَّذِينَ مِن
دُونِهِۦٓ إِذَا هُمْ يَسْتَبْشِرُونَ

45 When Allah alone is mentioned, the hearts of those who do not believe in the Hereafter shrink with resentment. But when those other than Him are mentioned, they become filled with joy.

٤٦ قُلِ ٱللَّهُمَّ فَاطِرَ ٱلسَّمَٰوَٰتِ وَٱلْأَرْضِ عَٰلِمَ
ٱلْغَيْبِ وَٱلشَّهَٰدَةِ أَنتَ تَحْكُمُ بَيْنَ عِبَادِكَ فِى مَا
كَانُوا۟ فِيهِ يَخْتَلِفُونَ

46 Say, "Our God, Initiator of the heavens and the earth, Knower of all secrets and declarations. You will judge between your servants regarding what they had differed about."

٤٧ وَلَوْ أَنَّ لِلَّذِينَ ظَلَمُوا۟ مَا فِى ٱلْأَرْضِ جَمِيعًا وَمِثْلَهُۥ مَعَهُۥ لَٱفْتَدَوْا۟ بِهِۦ مِن سُوٓءِ ٱلْعَذَابِ يَوْمَ ٱلْقِيَٰمَةِ ۚ وَبَدَا لَهُم مِّنَ ٱللَّهِ مَا لَمْ يَكُونُوا۟ يَحْتَسِبُونَ	47 If those who did wrong owned everything on earth, and the like of it with it, they would redeem themselves with it from the terrible suffering on the Day of Resurrection. But there will appear to them from Allah what they never anticipated.
٤٨ وَبَدَا لَهُمْ سَيِّـَٔاتُ مَا كَسَبُوا۟ وَحَاقَ بِهِم مَّا كَانُوا۟ بِهِۦ يَسْتَهْزِءُونَ	48 There will appear to them the evils of their deeds, and they will be surrounded by what they used to ridicule.
٤٩ فَإِذَا مَسَّ ٱلْإِنسَٰنَ ضُرٌّ دَعَانَا ثُمَّ إِذَا خَوَّلْنَٰهُ نِعْمَةً مِّنَّا قَالَ إِنَّمَآ أُوتِيتُهُۥ عَلَىٰ عِلْمٍۭ ۚ بَلْ هِىَ فِتْنَةٌ وَلَٰكِنَّ أَكْثَرَهُمْ لَا يَعْلَمُونَ	49 When adversity touches the human being, he calls on Us. But then, when We favor him with a blessing from Us, he says, “I have attained this by virtue of my knowledge.” However, it is a test, but most of them do not know.
٥٠ قَدْ قَالَهَا ٱلَّذِينَ مِن قَبْلِهِمْ فَمَآ أَغْنَىٰ عَنْهُم مَّا كَانُوا۟ يَكْسِبُونَ	50 Those before them said it, but what they had earned did not avail them.
٥١ فَأَصَابَهُمْ سَيِّـَٔاتُ مَا كَسَبُوا۟ ۚ وَٱلَّذِينَ ظَلَمُوا۟ مِنْ هَٰٓؤُلَآءِ سَيُصِيبُهُمْ سَيِّـَٔاتُ مَا كَسَبُوا۟ وَمَا هُم بِمُعْجِزِينَ	51 The evils of their deeds caught up with them. And the wrongdoers among these will also be afflicted by the evils of what they earned, and they cannot prevent it.
٥٢ أَوَلَمْ يَعْلَمُوٓا۟ أَنَّ ٱللَّهَ يَبْسُطُ ٱلرِّزْقَ لِمَن يَشَآءُ وَيَقْدِرُ ۚ إِنَّ فِى ذَٰلِكَ لَءَايَٰتٍ لِّقَوْمٍ يُؤْمِنُونَ	52 Do they not know that Allah extends the provision to whomever He wills, and constricts it? In that are signs for people who believe.
٥٣ قُلْ يَٰعِبَادِىَ ٱلَّذِينَ أَسْرَفُوا۟ عَلَىٰٓ أَنفُسِهِمْ لَا تَقْنَطُوا۟ مِن رَّحْمَةِ ٱللَّهِ ۚ إِنَّ ٱللَّهَ يَغْفِرُ ٱلذُّنُوبَ جَمِيعًا ۚ إِنَّهُۥ هُوَ ٱلْغَفُورُ ٱلرَّحِيمُ	53 Say, “O My servants who have transgressed against themselves: do not despair of Allah’s mercy, for Allah forgives all sins. He is indeed the Forgiver, the Clement.”
٥٤ وَأَنِيبُوٓا۟ إِلَىٰ رَبِّكُمْ وَأَسْلِمُوا۟ لَهُۥ مِن قَبْلِ أَن يَأْتِيَكُمُ ٱلْعَذَابُ ثُمَّ لَا تُنصَرُونَ	54 And turn to your Lord, and submit to Him, before the retribution comes upon you. Then you will not be helped.

٥٥ وَٱتَّبِعُوٓا۟ أَحْسَنَ مَآ أُنزِلَ إِلَيْكُم مِّن رَّبِّكُم مِّن
قَبْلِ أَن يَأْتِيَكُمُ ٱلْعَذَابُ بَغْتَةً وَأَنتُمْ لَا
تَشْعُرُونَ

55 And follow the best of what was revealed to you from your Lord, before the punishment comes upon you suddenly, while you are unaware.

٥٦ أَن تَقُولَ نَفْسٌ يَٰحَسْرَتَىٰ عَلَىٰ مَا فَرَّطتُ
فِى جَنۢبِ ٱللَّهِ وَإِن كُنتُ لَمِنَ ٱلسَّٰخِرِينَ

56 So that a soul may not say, “How sorry I am, for having neglected my duty to Allah, and for having been of the scoffers.”

٥٧ أَوْ تَقُولَ لَوْ أَنَّ ٱللَّهَ هَدَىٰنِى لَكُنتُ مِنَ
ٱلْمُتَّقِينَ

57 Or say, “Had Allah guided me; I would have been of the pious.”

٥٨ أَوْ تَقُولَ حِينَ تَرَى ٱلْعَذَابَ لَوْ أَنَّ لِى كَرَّةً
فَأَكُونَ مِنَ ٱلْمُحْسِنِينَ

58 Or say, when it sees the penalty, “If only I had another chance, I would be of the virtuous.”

٥٩ بَلَىٰ قَدْ جَآءَتْكَ ءَايَٰتِى فَكَذَّبْتَ بِهَا
وَٱسْتَكْبَرْتَ وَكُنتَ مِنَ ٱلْكَٰفِرِينَ

59 Yes indeed! My Verses did come to you, but you called them lies, turned arrogant, and were of the faithless.

٦٠ وَيَوْمَ ٱلْقِيَٰمَةِ تَرَى ٱلَّذِينَ كَذَبُوا۟ عَلَى ٱللَّهِ
وُجُوهُهُم مُّسْوَدَّةٌ ۚ أَلَيْسَ فِى جَهَنَّمَ مَثْوًى
لِّلْمُتَكَبِّرِينَ

60 On the Day of Resurrection, you will see those who told lies about Allah with their faces blackened. Is there not a place in Hell for the arrogant?

٦١ وَيُنَجِّى ٱللَّهُ ٱلَّذِينَ ٱتَّقَوْا۟ بِمَفَازَتِهِمْ لَا
يَمَسُّهُمُ ٱلسُّوٓءُ وَلَا هُمْ يَحْزَنُونَ

61 And Allah will save those who maintained righteousness to their place of salvation. No harm will touch them, nor will they grieve.

٦٢ ٱللَّهُ خَٰلِقُ كُلِّ شَىْءٍ ۖ وَهُوَ عَلَىٰ كُلِّ شَىْءٍ
وَكِيلٌ

62 Allah is the Creator of all things, and He is in Charge of all things.

٦٣ لَّهُۥ مَقَالِيدُ ٱلسَّمَٰوَٰتِ وَٱلْأَرْضِ ۗ وَٱلَّذِينَ كَفَرُوا۟
بِـَٔايَٰتِ ٱللَّهِ أُو۟لَٰٓئِكَ هُمُ ٱلْخَٰسِرُونَ

63 To Him belong the reins of the heavens and the earth. But those who blaspheme against the revelations of Allah—it is they who are the losers.

٦٤ قُلْ أَفَغَيْرَ ٱللَّهِ تَأْمُرُوٓنِّىٓ أَعْبُدُ أَيُّهَا ٱلْجَٰهِلُونَ

64 Say, “Is it other than Allah you instruct me to worship, you ignorant ones?”

٦٥ وَلَقَدْ أُوحِىَ إِلَيْكَ وَإِلَى ٱلَّذِينَ مِن قَبْلِكَ لَئِنْ أَشْرَكْتَ لَيَحْبَطَنَّ عَمَلُكَ وَلَتَكُونَنَّ مِنَ ٱلْخَٰسِرِينَ	65 It was revealed to you, and to those before you, that if you idolize, your works will be in vain, and you will be of the losers.
٦٦ بَلِ ٱللَّهَ فَٱعْبُدْ وَكُن مِّنَ ٱلشَّٰكِرِينَ	66 Rather, worship Allah, and be of the appreciative.
٦٧ وَمَا قَدَرُوا۟ ٱللَّهَ حَقَّ قَدْرِهِۦ وَٱلْأَرْضُ جَمِيعًا قَبْضَتُهُۥ يَوْمَ ٱلْقِيَٰمَةِ وَٱلسَّمَٰوَٰتُ مَطْوِيَّٰتٌۢ بِيَمِينِهِۦ ۚ سُبْحَٰنَهُۥ وَتَعَٰلَىٰ عَمَّا يُشْرِكُونَ	67 They have not esteemed Allah as He ought to be esteemed. The entire earth will be in His grip on the Day of Resurrection, and the heavens will be folded in His right. Immaculate is He, and Transcendent He is beyond the associations they make.
٦٨ وَنُفِخَ فِى ٱلصُّورِ فَصَعِقَ مَن فِى ٱلسَّمَٰوَٰتِ وَمَن فِى ٱلْأَرْضِ إِلَّا مَن شَآءَ ٱللَّهُ ۖ ثُمَّ نُفِخَ فِيهِ أُخْرَىٰ فَإِذَا هُمْ قِيَامٌ يَنظُرُونَ	68 And the Trumpet will be sounded, whereupon everyone in the heavens and the earth will be stunned, except whomever Allah wills. Then it will be sounded another time, whereupon they will rise up, looking on.
٦٩ وَأَشْرَقَتِ ٱلْأَرْضُ بِنُورِ رَبِّهَا وَوُضِعَ ٱلْكِتَٰبُ وَجِا۟ىٓءَ بِٱلنَّبِيِّۦنَ وَٱلشُّهَدَآءِ وَقُضِىَ بَيْنَهُم بِٱلْحَقِّ وَهُمْ لَا يُظْلَمُونَ	69 And the earth will shine with the Light of its Lord; and the Book will be put in place; and the prophets and the witnesses will be brought in; and Judgment will be passed among them equitably, and they will not be wronged.
٧٠ وَوُفِّيَتْ كُلُّ نَفْسٍ مَّا عَمِلَتْ وَهُوَ أَعْلَمُ بِمَا يَفْعَلُونَ	70 And every soul will be fully compensated for what it had done. He is well aware of what they do.
٧١ وَسِيقَ ٱلَّذِينَ كَفَرُوٓا۟ إِلَىٰ جَهَنَّمَ زُمَرًا ۖ حَتَّىٰٓ إِذَا جَآءُوهَا فُتِحَتْ أَبْوَٰبُهَا وَقَالَ لَهُمْ خَزَنَتُهَآ أَلَمْ يَأْتِكُمْ رُسُلٌ مِّنكُمْ يَتْلُونَ عَلَيْكُمْ ءَايَٰتِ رَبِّكُمْ وَيُنذِرُونَكُمْ لِقَآءَ يَوْمِكُمْ هَٰذَا ۚ قَالُوا۟ بَلَىٰ وَلَٰكِنْ حَقَّتْ كَلِمَةُ ٱلْعَذَابِ عَلَى ٱلْكَٰفِرِينَ	71 Those who disbelieved will be driven to Hell in throngs. Until, when they have reached it, and its gates are opened, its keepers will say to them, “Did not messengers from among you come to you, reciting to you the revelations of your Lord, and warning you of the meeting of this Day of yours?” They will say, “Yes, but the verdict of punishment is justified against the disbelievers.”

٧٢ قِيلَ ٱدْخُلُوٓا۟ أَبْوَٰبَ جَهَنَّمَ خَٰلِدِينَ فِيهَا ۖ
فَبِئْسَ مَثْوَى ٱلْمُتَكَبِّرِينَ

72 It will be said, "Enter the gates of Hell, to abide therein eternally." How wretched is the destination of the arrogant.

٧٣ وَسِيقَ ٱلَّذِينَ ٱتَّقَوْا۟ رَبَّهُمْ إِلَى ٱلْجَنَّةِ زُمَرًا ۖ
حَتَّىٰٓ إِذَا جَآءُوهَا وَفُتِحَتْ أَبْوَٰبُهَا وَقَالَ لَهُمْ
خَزَنَتُهَا سَلَٰمٌ عَلَيْكُمْ طِبْتُمْ فَٱدْخُلُوهَا خَٰلِدِينَ

73 And those who feared their Lord will be led to Paradise in throngs. Until, when they have reached it, and its gates are opened, its keepers will say to them, "Peace be upon you, you have been good, so enter it, to abide therein eternally."

٧٤ وَقَالُوا۟ ٱلْحَمْدُ لِلَّهِ ٱلَّذِى صَدَقَنَا وَعْدَهُۥ
وَأَوْرَثَنَا ٱلْأَرْضَ نَتَبَوَّأُ مِنَ ٱلْجَنَّةِ حَيْثُ نَشَآءُ ۖ
فَنِعْمَ أَجْرُ ٱلْعَٰمِلِينَ

74 And they will say, "Praise be to Allah, who has fulfilled His promise to us, and made us inherit the land, enjoying Paradise as we please." How excellent is the reward of the workers.

٧٥ وَتَرَى ٱلْمَلَٰٓئِكَةَ حَآفِّينَ مِنْ حَوْلِ ٱلْعَرْشِ
يُسَبِّحُونَ بِحَمْدِ رَبِّهِمْ ۖ وَقُضِىَ بَيْنَهُم بِٱلْحَقِّ
وَقِيلَ ٱلْحَمْدُ لِلَّهِ رَبِّ ٱلْعَٰلَمِينَ

75 And you will see the angels hovering around the Throne, glorifying their Lord with praise. And it will be judged between them equitably, and it will be said, "Praise be to Allah, Lord of the Worlds."

40 Forgiver غافر

بِسْمِ ٱللَّهِ ٱلرَّحْمَٰنِ ٱلرَّحِيمِ

In the name of Allah, the Gracious, the Merciful.

١ حمٓ

1 Ha, Meem.

٢ تَنزِيلُ ٱلْكِتَٰبِ مِنَ ٱللَّهِ ٱلْعَزِيزِ ٱلْعَلِيمِ

2 The sending down of the Scripture is from Allah the Almighty, the Omniscient.

٣ غَافِرِ ٱلذَّنۢبِ وَقَابِلِ ٱلتَّوْبِ شَدِيدِ ٱلْعِقَابِ ذِى
ٱلطَّوْلِ ۖ لَآ إِلَٰهَ إِلَّا هُوَ ۖ إِلَيْهِ ٱلْمَصِيرُ

3 Forgiver of sins, Accepter of repentance, Severe in punishment, Bountiful in bounty. There is no god but He. To Him is the ultimate return.

٤ مَا يُجَٰدِلُ فِىٓ ءَايَٰتِ ٱللَّهِ إِلَّا ٱلَّذِينَ كَفَرُوا۟ فَلَا
يَغْرُرْكَ تَقَلُّبُهُمْ فِى ٱلْبِلَٰدِ

4 None argues against Allah's revelations except those who disbelieve. So do not be impressed by their activities in the land.

٥ كَذَّبَتْ قَبْلَهُمْ قَوْمُ نُوحٍ وَٱلْأَحْزَابُ مِنۢ
بَعْدِهِمْۖ وَهَمَّتْ كُلُّ أُمَّةٍۭ بِرَسُولِهِمْ لِيَأْخُذُوهُۖ
وَجَٰدَلُوا۟ بِٱلْبَٰطِلِ لِيُدْحِضُوا۟ بِهِ ٱلْحَقَّ فَأَخَذْتُهُمْۖ
فَكَيْفَ كَانَ عِقَابِ

5 Before them the people of Noah rejected the truth, as did the confederates after them. Every community plotted against their messenger, to capture him. And they argued with falsehood, to defeat with it the truth. But I seized them. What a punishment it was!

٦ وَكَذَٰلِكَ حَقَّتْ كَلِمَتُ رَبِّكَ عَلَى ٱلَّذِينَ كَفَرُوٓا۟
أَنَّهُمْ أَصْحَٰبُ ٱلنَّارِ

6 Thus the sentence of your Lord became realized against those who disbelieve, that they are to be inmates of the Fire.

٧ ٱلَّذِينَ يَحْمِلُونَ ٱلْعَرْشَ وَمَنْ حَوْلَهُۥ يُسَبِّحُونَ
بِحَمْدِ رَبِّهِمْ وَيُؤْمِنُونَ بِهِۦ وَيَسْتَغْفِرُونَ لِلَّذِينَ
ءَامَنُوا۟ رَبَّنَا وَسِعْتَ كُلَّ شَىْءٍ رَّحْمَةً وَعِلْمًا
فَٱغْفِرْ لِلَّذِينَ تَابُوا۟ وَٱتَّبَعُوا۟ سَبِيلَكَ وَقِهِمْ
عَذَابَ ٱلْجَحِيمِ

7 Those who carry the Throne, and those around it, glorify their Lord with praise, and believe in Him, and ask for forgiveness for those who believe: "Our Lord, You have encompassed everything in mercy and knowledge; so forgive those who repent and follow Your path, and protect them from the agony of the Blaze.

٨ رَبَّنَا وَأَدْخِلْهُمْ جَنَّٰتِ عَدْنٍ ٱلَّتِى وَعَدتَّهُمْ
وَمَن صَلَحَ مِنْ ءَابَآئِهِمْ وَأَزْوَٰجِهِمْ وَذُرِّيَّٰتِهِمْۚ
إِنَّكَ أَنتَ ٱلْعَزِيزُ ٱلْحَكِيمُ

8 And admit them, Our Lord, into the Gardens of Eternity, which You have promised them, and the righteous among their parents, and their spouses, and their offspring. You are indeed the Almighty, the Most Wise.

٩ وَقِهِمُ ٱلسَّيِّـَٔاتِۚ وَمَن تَقِ ٱلسَّيِّـَٔاتِ يَوْمَئِذٍ
فَقَدْ رَحِمْتَهُۥۚ وَذَٰلِكَ هُوَ ٱلْفَوْزُ ٱلْعَظِيمُ

9 And shield them from the evil deeds. Whomever You shield from the evil deeds, on that Day, You have had mercy on him. That is the supreme achievement."

١٠ إِنَّ ٱلَّذِينَ كَفَرُوا۟ يُنَادَوْنَ لَمَقْتُ ٱللَّهِ أَكْبَرُ مِن
مَّقْتِكُمْ أَنفُسَكُمْ إِذْ تُدْعَوْنَ إِلَى ٱلْإِيمَٰنِ
فَتَكْفُرُونَ

10 Those who disbelieved will be addressed, "The loathing of Allah is greater than your loathing of yourselves—for you were invited to the faith, but you refused."

١١ قَالُوا۟ رَبَّنَآ أَمَتَّنَا ٱثْنَتَيْنِ وَأَحْيَيْتَنَا ٱثْنَتَيْنِ
فَٱعْتَرَفْنَا بِذُنُوبِنَا فَهَلْ إِلَىٰ خُرُوجٍ مِّن سَبِيلٍ

11 They will say, "Our Lord, you made us die twice, and twice you

gave us life. Now we acknowledge our sins. Is there any way out?"

١٢ ذَٰلِكُم بِأَنَّهُۥٓ إِذَا دُعِىَ ٱللَّهُ وَحْدَهُۥ كَفَرْتُمْ ۖ وَإِن
يُشْرَكْ بِهِۦ تُؤْمِنُوا۟ ۚ فَٱلْحُكْمُ لِلَّهِ ٱلْعَلِىِّ ٱلْكَبِيرِ

12 That is because when Allah alone was called upon, you disbelieved; but when others were associated with Him, you believed. Judgment rests with Allah the Sublime, the Majestic.

١٣ هُوَ ٱلَّذِى يُرِيكُمْ ءَايَٰتِهِۦ وَيُنَزِّلُ لَكُم مِّنَ
ٱلسَّمَآءِ رِزْقًا ۚ وَمَا يَتَذَكَّرُ إِلَّا مَن يُنِيبُ

13 It is He who shows you His wonders, and sends down sustenance from the sky for you. But none pays heed except the repentant.

١٤ فَٱدْعُوا۟ ٱللَّهَ مُخْلِصِينَ لَهُ ٱلدِّينَ وَلَوْ كَرِهَ
ٱلْكَٰفِرُونَ

14 So call upon Allah, with sincere devotion to Him, even though the disbelievers resent it.

١٥ رَفِيعُ ٱلدَّرَجَٰتِ ذُو ٱلْعَرْشِ يُلْقِى ٱلرُّوحَ مِنْ
أَمْرِهِۦ عَلَىٰ مَن يَشَآءُ مِنْ عِبَادِهِۦ لِيُنذِرَ يَوْمَ
ٱلتَّلَاقِ

15 Exalted in rank, Owner of the Throne. He conveys the Spirit, by His command, upon whomever He wills of His servants, to warn of the Day of Encounter.

١٦ يَوْمَ هُم بَٰرِزُونَ ۖ لَا يَخْفَىٰ عَلَى ٱللَّهِ مِنْهُمْ
شَىْءٌ ۚ لِّمَنِ ٱلْمُلْكُ ٱلْيَوْمَ ۖ لِلَّهِ ٱلْوَٰحِدِ ٱلْقَهَّارِ

16 The Day when they will emerge, nothing about them will be concealed from Allah. "To whom does the sovereignty belong today?" "To Allah, the One, the Irresistible."

١٧ ٱلْيَوْمَ تُجْزَىٰ كُلُّ نَفْسٍۭ بِمَا كَسَبَتْ ۚ لَا ظُلْمَ
ٱلْيَوْمَ ۚ إِنَّ ٱللَّهَ سَرِيعُ ٱلْحِسَابِ

17 On that Day, every soul will be recompensed for what it had earned. There will be no injustice on that Day. Allah is quick to settle accounts.

١٨ وَأَنذِرْهُمْ يَوْمَ ٱلْـَٔازِفَةِ إِذِ ٱلْقُلُوبُ لَدَى
ٱلْحَنَاجِرِ كَٰظِمِينَ ۚ مَا لِلظَّٰلِمِينَ مِنْ حَمِيمٍ وَلَا
شَفِيعٍ يُطَاعُ

18 And warn them of the Day of Imminence, when the hearts are at the throats, choking them. The evildoers will have no intimate friend, and no intercessor to be obeyed.

١٩ يَعْلَمُ خَآئِنَةَ ٱلْأَعْيُنِ وَمَا تُخْفِى ٱلصُّدُورُ

19 He knows the deceptions of the eyes, and what the hearts conceal.

٢٠ وَٱللَّهُ يَقۡضِى بِٱلۡحَقِّۖ وَٱلَّذِينَ يَدۡعُونَ مِن
دُونِهِۦ لَا يَقۡضُونَ بِشَىۡءٍۗ إِنَّ ٱللَّهَ هُوَ ٱلسَّمِيعُ
ٱلۡبَصِيرُ

20 Allah judges with justice, while those whom they invoke besides Him cannot judge with anything. It is Allah who is the Hearing, the Seeing.

٢١ أَوَلَمۡ يَسِيرُواْ فِى ٱلۡأَرۡضِ فَيَنظُرُواْ كَيۡفَ
كَانَ عَٰقِبَةُ ٱلَّذِينَ كَانُواْ مِن قَبۡلِهِمۡۚ كَانُواْ هُمۡ
أَشَدَّ مِنۡهُمۡ قُوَّةً وَءَاثَارًا فِى ٱلۡأَرۡضِ فَأَخَذَهُمُ
ٱللَّهُ بِذُنُوبِهِمۡ وَمَا كَانَ لَهُم مِّنَ ٱللَّهِ مِن وَاقٍ

21 Have they not travelled through the earth, and seen the consequences for those before them? They were stronger than them, and they left more impact on earth. But Allah seized them for their sins, and they had no defender against Allah.

٢٢ ذَٰلِكَ بِأَنَّهُمۡ كَانَت تَّأۡتِيهِمۡ رُسُلُهُم بِٱلۡبَيِّنَٰتِ
فَكَفَرُواْ فَأَخَذَهُمُ ٱللَّهُۚ إِنَّهُۥ قَوِىٌّ شَدِيدُ ٱلۡعِقَابِ

22 That is because their messengers used to come to them with clear proofs, but they disbelieved, so Allah seized them. He is Strong, Severe in retribution.

٢٣ وَلَقَدۡ أَرۡسَلۡنَا مُوسَىٰ بِـَٔايَٰتِنَا وَسُلۡطَٰنٍ مُّبِينٍ

23 We sent Moses with Our signs, and a clear authority.

٢٤ إِلَىٰ فِرۡعَوۡنَ وَهَٰمَٰنَ وَقَٰرُونَ فَقَالُواْ سَٰحِرٌ
كَذَّابٌ

24 To Pharaoh, Hamaan, and Quaroon. But they said, “A lying sorcerer.”

٢٥ فَلَمَّا جَآءَهُم بِٱلۡحَقِّ مِنۡ عِندِنَا قَالُواْ ٱقۡتُلُوٓاْ
أَبۡنَآءَ ٱلَّذِينَ ءَامَنُواْ مَعَهُۥ وَٱسۡتَحۡيُواْ نِسَآءَهُمۡۚ
وَمَا كَيۡدُ ٱلۡكَٰفِرِينَ إِلَّا فِى ضَلَٰلٍ

25 Then, when he came to them with the truth from Us, they said, “Kill the sons of those who have believed with him, and spare their daughters.” But the scheming of the unbelievers can only go astray.

٢٦ وَقَالَ فِرۡعَوۡنُ ذَرُونِىٓ أَقۡتُلۡ مُوسَىٰ وَلۡيَدۡعُ
رَبَّهُۥٓۖ إِنِّىٓ أَخَافُ أَن يُبَدِّلَ دِينَكُمۡ أَوۡ أَن يُظۡهِرَ
فِى ٱلۡأَرۡضِ ٱلۡفَسَادَ

26 Pharaoh said, “Leave me to kill Moses, and let him appeal to his Lord. I fear he may change your religion, or spread disorder in the land.”

٢٧ وَقَالَ مُوسَىٰٓ إِنِّى عُذۡتُ بِرَبِّى وَرَبِّكُم مِّن
كُلِّ مُتَكَبِّرٍ لَّا يُؤۡمِنُ بِيَوۡمِ ٱلۡحِسَابِ

27 Moses said, “I have sought the protection of my Lord and your Lord, from every tyrant who does not believe in the Day of Account.”

٢٨ وَقَالَ رَجُلٌ مُّؤۡمِنٌ مِّنۡ ءَالِ فِرۡعَوۡنَ يَكۡتُمُ
إِيمَٰنَهُۥٓ أَتَقۡتُلُونَ رَجُلًا أَن يَقُولَ رَبِّىَ ٱللَّهُ وَقَدۡ

28 A believing man from Pharaoh's family, who had concealed his faith, said, “Are you going to kill a man for

جَآءَكُم بِٱلْبَيِّنَٰتِ مِن رَّبِّكُمْ ۖ وَإِن يَكُ كَٰذِبًا فَعَلَيْهِ كَذِبُهُۥ ۖ وَإِن يَكُ صَادِقًا يُصِبْكُم بَعْضُ ٱلَّذِى يَعِدُكُمْ ۖ إِنَّ ٱللَّهَ لَا يَهْدِى مَنْ هُوَ مُسْرِفٌ كَذَّابٌ	saying, `My Lord is Allah,' and he has brought you clear proofs from your Lord? If he is a liar, his lying will rebound upon him; but if he is truthful, then some of what he promises you will befall you. Allah does not guide the extravagant imposter.
٢٩ يَٰقَوْمِ لَكُمُ ٱلْمُلْكُ ٱلْيَوْمَ ظَٰهِرِينَ فِى ٱلْأَرْضِ فَمَن يَنصُرُنَا مِنۢ بَأْسِ ٱللَّهِ إِن جَآءَنَا ۚ قَالَ فِرْعَوْنُ مَآ أُرِيكُمْ إِلَّا مَآ أَرَىٰ وَمَآ أَهْدِيكُمْ إِلَّا سَبِيلَ ٱلرَّشَادِ	29 O my people! Yours is the dominion today, supreme in the land; but who will help us against Allah's might, should it fall upon us?" Pharaoh said, "I do not show you except what I see, and I do not guide you except to the path of prudence."
٣٠ وَقَالَ ٱلَّذِىٓ ءَامَنَ يَٰقَوْمِ إِنِّىٓ أَخَافُ عَلَيْكُم مِّثْلَ يَوْمِ ٱلْأَحْزَابِ	30 The one who had believed said, "O my people, I fear for you the like of the day of the confederates.
٣١ مِثْلَ دَأْبِ قَوْمِ نُوحٍ وَعَادٍ وَثَمُودَ وَٱلَّذِينَ مِنۢ بَعْدِهِمْ ۚ وَمَا ٱللَّهُ يُرِيدُ ظُلْمًا لِّلْعِبَادِ	31 Like the fate of the people of Noah, and Aad, and Thamood, and those after them. Allah wants no injustice for the servants.
٣٢ وَيَٰقَوْمِ إِنِّىٓ أَخَافُ عَلَيْكُمْ يَوْمَ ٱلتَّنَادِ	32 O my people, I fear for you the Day of Calling Out.
٣٣ يَوْمَ تُوَلُّونَ مُدْبِرِينَ مَا لَكُم مِّنَ ٱللَّهِ مِنْ عَاصِمٍ ۗ وَمَن يُضْلِلِ ٱللَّهُ فَمَا لَهُۥ مِنْ هَادٍ	33 The Day when you will turn and flee, having no defender against Allah. Whomever Allah misguides has no guide."
٣٤ وَلَقَدْ جَآءَكُمْ يُوسُفُ مِن قَبْلُ بِٱلْبَيِّنَٰتِ فَمَا زِلْتُمْ فِى شَكٍّ مِّمَّا جَآءَكُم بِهِۦ ۖ حَتَّىٰٓ إِذَا هَلَكَ قُلْتُمْ لَن يَبْعَثَ ٱللَّهُ مِنۢ بَعْدِهِۦ رَسُولًا ۚ كَذَٰلِكَ يُضِلُّ ٱللَّهُ مَنْ هُوَ مُسْرِفٌ مُّرْتَابٌ	34 Joseph had come to you with clear revelations, but you continued to doubt what he came to you with. Until, when he perished, you said, "Allah will never send a messenger after him." Thus Allah leads astray the outrageous skeptic.
٣٥ ٱلَّذِينَ يُجَٰدِلُونَ فِىٓ ءَايَٰتِ ٱللَّهِ بِغَيْرِ سُلْطَٰنٍ أَتَىٰهُمْ ۖ كَبُرَ مَقْتًا عِندَ ٱللَّهِ وَعِندَ ٱلَّذِينَ ءَامَنُوا۟ ۚ كَذَٰلِكَ يَطْبَعُ ٱللَّهُ عَلَىٰ كُلِّ قَلْبِ مُتَكَبِّرٍ جَبَّارٍ	35 Those who argue against Allah's revelations, without any proof having come to them—a heinous sin in the sight of Allah, and of those who believe. Thus Allah seals the heart of every proud bully.

٣٦ وَقَالَ فِرْعَوْنُ يَٰهَٰمَٰنُ ٱبْنِ لِى صَرْحًا لَّعَلِّىٓ
أَبْلُغُ ٱلْأَسْبَٰبَ

36 And Pharaoh said, “O Hamaan, build me a tower, that I may reach the pathways.

٣٧ أَسْبَٰبَ ٱلسَّمَٰوَٰتِ فَأَطَّلِعَ إِلَىٰٓ إِلَٰهِ مُوسَىٰ
وَإِنِّى لَأَظُنُّهُۥ كَٰذِبًا ۚ وَكَذَٰلِكَ زُيِّنَ لِفِرْعَوْنَ سُوٓءُ
عَمَلِهِۦ وَصُدَّ عَنِ ٱلسَّبِيلِ ۚ وَمَا كَيْدُ فِرْعَوْنَ إِلَّا
فِى تَبَابٍ

37 The pathways of the heavens, so that I may glance at the God of Moses; though I think he is lying.” Thus Pharaoh’s evil deeds were made to appear good to him, and he was averted from the path. Pharaoh's guile was only in defeat.

٣٨ وَقَالَ ٱلَّذِىٓ ءَامَنَ يَٰقَوْمِ ٱتَّبِعُونِ أَهْدِكُمْ
سَبِيلَ ٱلرَّشَادِ

38 The one who had believed said, “O my people, follow me, and I will guide you to the path of rectitude.”

٣٩ يَٰقَوْمِ إِنَّمَا هَٰذِهِ ٱلْحَيَوٰةُ ٱلدُّنْيَا مَتَٰعٌ وَإِنَّ
ٱلْءَاخِرَةَ هِىَ دَارُ ٱلْقَرَارِ

39 “O my people, the life of this world is nothing but fleeting enjoyment, but the Hereafter is the Home of Permanence.

٤٠ مَنْ عَمِلَ سَيِّئَةً فَلَا يُجْزَىٰٓ إِلَّا مِثْلَهَا ۖ وَمَنْ
عَمِلَ صَٰلِحًا مِّن ذَكَرٍ أَوْ أُنثَىٰ وَهُوَ مُؤْمِنٌ
فَأُو۟لَٰٓئِكَ يَدْخُلُونَ ٱلْجَنَّةَ يُرْزَقُونَ فِيهَا بِغَيْرِ
حِسَابٍ

40 Whoever commits a sin will be repaid only with its like. But whoever works righteousness, whether male or female, and is a believer—these will enter Paradise, where they will be provided for without account.

٤١ وَيَٰقَوْمِ مَا لِىٓ أَدْعُوكُمْ إِلَى ٱلنَّجَوٰةِ
وَتَدْعُونَنِىٓ إِلَى ٱلنَّارِ

41 O my people, how is it that I call you to salvation, and you call me to the Fire?

٤٢ تَدْعُونَنِى لِأَكْفُرَ بِٱللَّهِ وَأُشْرِكَ بِهِۦ مَا لَيْسَ
لِى بِهِۦ عِلْمٌ وَأَنَا۠ أَدْعُوكُمْ إِلَى ٱلْعَزِيزِ ٱلْغَفَّٰرِ

42 You call me to reject Allah, and to associate with Him what I have no knowledge of, while I call you to the Mighty Forgiver.

٤٣ لَا جَرَمَ أَنَّمَا تَدْعُونَنِىٓ إِلَيْهِ لَيْسَ لَهُۥ دَعْوَةٌ
فِى ٱلدُّنْيَا وَلَا فِى ٱلْءَاخِرَةِ وَأَنَّ مَرَدَّنَآ إِلَى
ٱللَّهِ وَأَنَّ ٱلْمُسْرِفِينَ هُمْ أَصْحَٰبُ ٱلنَّارِ

43 Without a doubt, what you call me to has no say in this world, or in the Hereafter; and our turning back is to Allah; and the transgressors are the inmates of the Fire.

٤٤ فَسَتَذْكُرُونَ مَآ أَقُولُ لَكُمْ ۚ وَأُفَوِّضُ أَمْرِىٓ
إِلَى ٱللَّهِ ۚ إِنَّ ٱللَّهَ بَصِيرٌۢ بِٱلْعِبَادِ

44 You will remember what I am telling you, so I commit my case to Allah. Allah is Observant of the servants.”

٤٥ فَوَقَىٰهُ ٱللَّهُ سَيِّـَٔاتِ مَا مَكَرُواْۖ وَحَاقَ بِـَٔالِ
فِرْعَوْنَ سُوٓءُ ٱلْعَذَابِ

45 So Allah protected him from the evils of their scheming, while a terrible torment besieged Pharaoh's clan.

٤٦ ٱلنَّارُ يُعْرَضُونَ عَلَيْهَا غُدُوًّا وَعَشِيًّاۖ وَيَوْمَ
تَقُومُ ٱلسَّاعَةُ أَدْخِلُوٓاْ ءَالَ فِرْعَوْنَ أَشَدَّ
ٱلْعَذَابِ

46 The Fire. They will be exposed to it morning and evening. And on the Day the Hour takes place: "Admit the clan of Pharaoh to the most intense agony."

٤٧ وَإِذْ يَتَحَآجُّونَ فِى ٱلنَّارِ فَيَقُولُ ٱلضُّعَفَٰٓؤُاْ
لِلَّذِينَ ٱسْتَكْبَرُوٓاْ إِنَّا كُنَّا لَكُمْ تَبَعًا فَهَلْ أَنتُم
مُّغْنُونَ عَنَّا نَصِيبًا مِّنَ ٱلنَّارِ

47 As they quarrel in the Fire, the weak will say to those who were arrogant, "We were followers of yours; will you then spare us a portion of the Fire?"

٤٨ قَالَ ٱلَّذِينَ ٱسْتَكْبَرُوٓاْ إِنَّا كُلٌّ فِيهَآ إِنَّ ٱللَّهَ
قَدْ حَكَمَ بَيْنَ ٱلْعِبَادِ

48 Those who were arrogant will say, "We are all in it; Allah has judged between the servants."

٤٩ وَقَالَ ٱلَّذِينَ فِى ٱلنَّارِ لِخَزَنَةِ جَهَنَّمَ ٱدْعُواْ
رَبَّكُمْ يُخَفِّفْ عَنَّا يَوْمًا مِّنَ ٱلْعَذَابِ

49 And those in the Fire will say to the keepers of Hell, "Call to your Lord to lessen our suffering for one day."

٥٠ قَالُوٓاْ أَوَلَمْ تَكُ تَأْتِيكُمْ رُسُلُكُم بِٱلْبَيِّنَٰتِۖ
قَالُواْ بَلَىٰۚ قَالُواْ فَٱدْعُواْۗ وَمَا دُعَٰٓؤُاْ ٱلْكَٰفِرِينَ إِلَّا
فِى ضَلَٰلٍ

50 They will say, "Did not your messengers come to you with clear signs?" They will say, "Yes." They will say, "Then pray, but the prayers of the disbelievers will always be in vain."

٥١ إِنَّا لَنَنصُرُ رُسُلَنَا وَٱلَّذِينَ ءَامَنُواْ فِى ٱلْحَيَوٰةِ
ٱلدُّنْيَا وَيَوْمَ يَقُومُ ٱلْأَشْهَٰدُ

51 Most surely We will support Our messengers and those who believe, in this life, and on the Day the witnesses arise.

٥٢ يَوْمَ لَا يَنفَعُ ٱلظَّٰلِمِينَ مَعْذِرَتُهُمْۖ وَلَهُمُ ٱللَّعْنَةُ
وَلَهُمْ سُوٓءُ ٱلدَّارِ

52 The Day when their excuses will not profit the wrongdoers, and the curse will be upon them, and they will have the Home of Misery.

٥٣ وَلَقَدْ ءَاتَيْنَا مُوسَى ٱلْهُدَىٰ وَأَوْرَثْنَا بَنِىٓ
إِسْرَٰٓءِيلَ ٱلْكِتَٰبَ

53 We gave Moses guidance, and made the Children of Israel inherit the Scripture.

٥٤ هُدًى وَذِكْرَىٰ لِأُوْلِى ٱلْأَلْبَٰبِ

54 A guide and a reminder for those endowed with reason.

٥٥ فَٱصْبِرْ إِنَّ وَعْدَ ٱللَّهِ حَقٌّ وَٱسْتَغْفِرْ لِذَنۢبِكَ
وَسَبِّحْ بِحَمْدِ رَبِّكَ بِٱلْعَشِىِّ وَٱلْإِبْكَٰرِ

55 So be patient. The promise of Allah is true. And ask forgiveness for your sin, and proclaim the praise of your Lord evening and morning.

٥٦ إِنَّ ٱلَّذِينَ يُجَٰدِلُونَ فِىٓ ءَايَٰتِ ٱللَّهِ بِغَيْرِ
سُلْطَٰنٍ أَتَىٰهُمْ ۙ إِن فِى صُدُورِهِمْ إِلَّا كِبْرٌ مَّا هُم
بِبَٰلِغِيهِ ۚ فَٱسْتَعِذْ بِٱللَّهِ ۖ إِنَّهُۥ هُوَ ٱلسَّمِيعُ ٱلْبَصِيرُ

56 Those who dispute regarding Allah's revelations without any authority having come to them—there is nothing in their hearts but the feeling of greatness, which they will never attain. So seek refuge in Allah; for He is the All-Hearing, the All-Seeing.

٥٧ لَخَلْقُ ٱلسَّمَٰوَٰتِ وَٱلْأَرْضِ أَكْبَرُ مِنْ خَلْقِ
ٱلنَّاسِ وَلَٰكِنَّ أَكْثَرَ ٱلنَّاسِ لَا يَعْلَمُونَ

57 Certainly the creation of the heavens and the earth is greater than the creation of humanity, but most people do not know.

٥٨ وَمَا يَسْتَوِى ٱلْأَعْمَىٰ وَٱلْبَصِيرُ وَٱلَّذِينَ
ءَامَنُوا۟ وَعَمِلُوا۟ ٱلصَّٰلِحَٰتِ وَلَا ٱلْمُسِىٓءُ ۚ قَلِيلًا
مَّا تَتَذَكَّرُونَ

58 Not equal are the blind and the seeing. Nor are those who believe and work righteousness equal to the sinners. How little you reflect.

٥٩ إِنَّ ٱلسَّاعَةَ لَءَاتِيَةٌ لَّا رَيْبَ فِيهَا وَلَٰكِنَّ أَكْثَرَ
ٱلنَّاسِ لَا يُؤْمِنُونَ

59 Indeed, the Hour is coming; there is no doubt about it; but most people do not believe.

٦٠ وَقَالَ رَبُّكُمُ ٱدْعُونِىٓ أَسْتَجِبْ لَكُمْ ۚ إِنَّ
ٱلَّذِينَ يَسْتَكْبِرُونَ عَنْ عِبَادَتِى سَيَدْخُلُونَ
جَهَنَّمَ دَاخِرِينَ

60 Your Lord has said, "Pray to Me, and I will respond to you. But those who are too proud to worship Me will enter Hell forcibly."

٦١ ٱللَّهُ ٱلَّذِى جَعَلَ لَكُمُ ٱلَّيْلَ لِتَسْكُنُوا۟ فِيهِ
وَٱلنَّهَارَ مُبْصِرًا ۚ إِنَّ ٱللَّهَ لَذُو فَضْلٍ عَلَى ٱلنَّاسِ
وَلَٰكِنَّ أَكْثَرَ ٱلنَّاسِ لَا يَشْكُرُونَ

61 It is Allah Who made the night for you, that you may rest therein; and the day allowing sight. Allah is gracious towards the people, but most people do not give thanks.

٦٢ ذَٰلِكُمُ ٱللَّهُ رَبُّكُمْ خَٰلِقُ كُلِّ شَىْءٍ لَّآ إِلَٰهَ إِلَّا
هُوَ ۖ فَأَنَّىٰ تُؤْفَكُونَ

62 Such is Allah, your Lord, Creator of all things. There is no god except Him; so how could you turn away?

٦٣ كَذَٰلِكَ يُؤْفَكُ ٱلَّذِينَ كَانُوا۟ بِـَٔايَٰتِ ٱللَّهِ
يَجْحَدُونَ

63 Thus are turned away those who dispute the signs of Allah.

٦٤ ٱللَّهُ ٱلَّذِى جَعَلَ لَكُمُ ٱلْأَرْضَ قَرَارًا وَٱلسَّمَآءَ
بِنَآءً وَصَوَّرَكُمْ فَأَحْسَنَ صُوَرَكُمْ وَرَزَقَكُم مِّنَ
ٱلطَّيِّبَٰتِ ۚ ذَٰلِكُمُ ٱللَّهُ رَبُّكُمْ ۖ فَتَبَارَكَ ٱللَّهُ رَبُّ
ٱلْعَٰلَمِينَ

64 It is Allah who made the earth a habitat for you, and the sky a structure. And He designed you, and designed you well; and He provided you with the good things. Such is Allah, your Lord; so Blessed is Allah, Lord of the Worlds.

٦٥ هُوَ ٱلْحَىُّ لَآ إِلَٰهَ إِلَّا هُوَ فَٱدْعُوهُ مُخْلِصِينَ لَهُ
ٱلدِّينَ ۗ ٱلْحَمْدُ لِلَّهِ رَبِّ ٱلْعَٰلَمِينَ

65 He is the Living One. There is no god except He. So pray to Him, devoting your religion to Him. Praise be to Allah, the Lord of the Worlds.

٦٦ قُلْ إِنِّى نُهِيتُ أَنْ أَعْبُدَ ٱلَّذِينَ تَدْعُونَ مِن
دُونِ ٱللَّهِ لَمَّا جَآءَنِىَ ٱلْبَيِّنَٰتُ مِن رَّبِّى وَأُمِرْتُ
أَنْ أُسْلِمَ لِرَبِّ ٱلْعَٰلَمِينَ

66 Say, “I was prohibited from worshiping those you invoke besides Allah, now that clear revelations have come to me from my Lord; and I was commanded to submit to the Lord of the Worlds.”

٦٧ هُوَ ٱلَّذِى خَلَقَكُم مِّن تُرَابٍ ثُمَّ مِن نُّطْفَةٍ ثُمَّ
مِنْ عَلَقَةٍ ثُمَّ يُخْرِجُكُمْ طِفْلًا ثُمَّ لِتَبْلُغُوٓا۟
أَشُدَّكُمْ ثُمَّ لِتَكُونُوا۟ شُيُوخًا ۚ وَمِنكُم مَّن
يُتَوَفَّىٰ مِن قَبْلُ ۖ وَلِتَبْلُغُوٓا۟ أَجَلًا مُّسَمًّى وَلَعَلَّكُمْ
تَعْقِلُونَ

67 It is He who created you from dust, then from a seed, then from an embryo, then He brings you out as an infant, then He lets you reach your maturity, then you become elderly—although some of you die sooner—so that you may reach a predetermined age, so that you may understand.

٦٨ هُوَ ٱلَّذِى يُحْىِۦ وَيُمِيتُ ۖ فَإِذَا قَضَىٰٓ أَمْرًا
فَإِنَّمَا يَقُولُ لَهُۥ كُن فَيَكُونُ

68 It is He who gives life and death; and when He decides on a thing, He just says to it, “Be,” and it comes to be.

٦٩ أَلَمْ تَرَ إِلَى ٱلَّذِينَ يُجَٰدِلُونَ فِىٓ ءَايَٰتِ ٱللَّهِ
أَنَّىٰ يُصْرَفُونَ

69 Have you not observed those who dispute regarding Allah's revelations, how they have deviated?

٧٠ ٱلَّذِينَ كَذَّبُوا۟ بِٱلْكِتَٰبِ وَبِمَآ أَرْسَلْنَا بِهِۦ رُسُلَنَا ۖ
فَسَوْفَ يَعْلَمُونَ

70 Those who call the Book a lie, and what We sent Our messengers with—they will surely know.

٧١ إِذِ ٱلْأَغْلَٰلُ فِىٓ أَعْنَٰقِهِمْ وَٱلسَّلَٰسِلُ يُسْحَبُونَ

71 When the yokes are around their necks, and they will be dragged by the chains.

٧٢ فِى ٱلْحَمِيمِ ثُمَّ فِى ٱلنَّارِ يُسْجَرُونَ

72 Into the boiling water, then in the Fire they will be consumed.

٧٣ ثُمَّ قِيلَ لَهُمْ أَيْنَ مَا كُنتُمْ تُشْرِكُونَ

73 Then it will be said to them, “Where are those you used to deify?

٧٤ مِن دُونِ ٱللَّهِ قَالُوا۟ ضَلُّوا۟ عَنَّا بَل لَّمْ نَكُن
نَّدْعُوا۟ مِن قَبْلُ شَيْـًٔا كَذَٰلِكَ يُضِلُّ ٱللَّهُ ٱلْكَٰفِرِينَ

74 Instead of Allah?” They will say, “They have abandoned us. In fact, we were praying to nothing before.” Thus Allah sends the disbelievers astray.

٧٥ ذَٰلِكُم بِمَا كُنتُمْ تَفْرَحُونَ فِى ٱلْأَرْضِ بِغَيْرِ
ٱلْحَقِّ وَبِمَا كُنتُمْ تَمْرَحُونَ

75 That is because you used to rejoice on earth in other than the truth, and because you used to behave with vanity.

٧٦ ٱدْخُلُوٓا۟ أَبْوَٰبَ جَهَنَّمَ خَٰلِدِينَ فِيهَا فَبِئْسَ
مَثْوَى ٱلْمُتَكَبِّرِينَ

76 Enter the gates of Hell, to remain therein forever. What a terrible dwelling for the arrogant.

٧٧ فَٱصْبِرْ إِنَّ وَعْدَ ٱللَّهِ حَقٌّ فَإِمَّا نُرِيَنَّكَ بَعْضَ
ٱلَّذِى نَعِدُهُمْ أَوْ نَتَوَفَّيَنَّكَ فَإِلَيْنَا يُرْجَعُونَ

77 So be patient. The promise of Allah is true. Whether We show you some of what We have promised them, or take you to Us, to Us they will be returned.

٧٨ وَلَقَدْ أَرْسَلْنَا رُسُلًا مِّن قَبْلِكَ مِنْهُم مَّن
قَصَصْنَا عَلَيْكَ وَمِنْهُم مَّن لَّمْ نَقْصُصْ عَلَيْكَ
وَمَا كَانَ لِرَسُولٍ أَن يَأْتِىَ بِـَٔايَةٍ إِلَّا بِإِذْنِ ٱللَّهِ
فَإِذَا جَآءَ أَمْرُ ٱللَّهِ قُضِىَ بِٱلْحَقِّ وَخَسِرَ هُنَالِكَ
ٱلْمُبْطِلُونَ

78 We sent messengers before you. Some of them We told you about, and some We did not tell you about. No messenger can bring a miracle except by leave of Allah. Then, when the command of Allah is issued, fair judgment will be passed, and there and then the seekers of vanity will lose.

٧٩ ٱللَّهُ ٱلَّذِى جَعَلَ لَكُمُ ٱلْأَنْعَٰمَ لِتَرْكَبُوا۟ مِنْهَا
وَمِنْهَا تَأْكُلُونَ

79 Allah is He who created the domestic animals for you—some for you to ride, and some you eat.

٨٠ وَلَكُمْ فِيهَا مَنَٰفِعُ وَلِتَبْلُغُوا۟ عَلَيْهَا حَاجَةً فِى
صُدُورِكُمْ وَعَلَيْهَا وَعَلَى ٱلْفُلْكِ تُحْمَلُونَ

80 And in them you have other benefits as well, and through them you satisfy your needs. And on them, and on the ships, you are transported.

٨١ وَيُرِيكُمْ ءَايَٰتِهِۦ فَأَىَّ ءَايَٰتِ ٱللَّهِ تُنكِرُونَ

81 And He shows you His signs. So which of Allah’s signs will you deny?

٨٢ أَفَلَمْ يَسِيرُوا۟ فِى ٱلْأَرْضِ فَيَنظُرُوا۟ كَيْفَ
كَانَ عَٰقِبَةُ ٱلَّذِينَ مِن قَبْلِهِمْ كَانُوٓا۟ أَكْثَرَ مِنْهُمْ

82 Have they not journeyed through the land, and seen the outcome for those before them? They were more

وَأَشَدَّ قُوَّةً وَءَاثَارًا فِى ٱلْأَرْضِ فَمَآ أَغْنَىٰ
عَنْهُم مَّا كَانُوا۟ يَكْسِبُونَ

numerous than they, and had greater power and influence in the land. But what they had achieved availed them nothing.

٨٣ فَلَمَّا جَآءَتْهُمْ رُسُلُهُم بِٱلْبَيِّنَٰتِ فَرِحُوا۟ بِمَا
عِندَهُم مِّنَ ٱلْعِلْمِ وَحَاقَ بِهِم مَّا كَانُوا۟ بِهِۦ
يَسْتَهْزِءُونَ

83 When their messengers came to them with clear proofs, they rejoiced in the knowledge they had, and the very things they used to ridicule besieged them.

٨٤ فَلَمَّا رَأَوْا۟ بَأْسَنَا قَالُوٓا۟ ءَامَنَّا بِٱللَّهِ وَحْدَهُۥ
وَكَفَرْنَا بِمَا كُنَّا بِهِۦ مُشْرِكِينَ

84 Then, when they witnessed Our might, they said, “We believe in Allah alone, and we reject what we used to associate with Him.”

٨٥ فَلَمْ يَكُ يَنفَعُهُمْ إِيمَٰنُهُمْ لَمَّا رَأَوْا۟ بَأْسَنَا ۖ
سُنَّتَ ٱللَّهِ ٱلَّتِى قَدْ خَلَتْ فِى عِبَادِهِۦ ۖ وَخَسِرَ
هُنَالِكَ ٱلْكَٰفِرُونَ

85 But their faith could not help them once they witnessed Our might. This has been Allah’s way of dealing with His servants. And there and then the disbelievers lost.

41 Detailed فصلت

بِسْمِ ٱللَّهِ ٱلرَّحْمَٰنِ ٱلرَّحِيمِ

In the name of Allah, the Gracious, the Merciful.

١ حمٓ

1 Ha, Meem.

٢ تَنزِيلٌ مِّنَ ٱلرَّحْمَٰنِ ٱلرَّحِيمِ

2 A revelation from the Most Gracious, the Most Merciful.

٣ كِتَٰبٌ فُصِّلَتْ ءَايَٰتُهُۥ قُرْءَانًا عَرَبِيًّا لِّقَوْمٍ
يَعْلَمُونَ

3 A Scripture whose Verses are detailed, a Quran in Arabic for people who know.

٤ بَشِيرًا وَنَذِيرًا فَأَعْرَضَ أَكْثَرُهُمْ فَهُمْ لَا
يَسْمَعُونَ

4 Bringing good news, and giving warnings. But most of them turn away, so they do not listen.

٥ وَقَالُوا۟ قُلُوبُنَا فِىٓ أَكِنَّةٍ مِّمَّا تَدْعُونَآ إِلَيْهِ
وَفِىٓ ءَاذَانِنَا وَقْرٌ وَمِنۢ بَيْنِنَا وَبَيْنِكَ حِجَابٌ
فَٱعْمَلْ إِنَّنَا عَٰمِلُونَ

5 And they say, “Our hearts are screened from what you call us to, and in our ears is deafness, and between us and you is a barrier. So do what you want, and so will we.”

٦ قُلْ إِنَّمَآ أَنَا۠ بَشَرٌ مِّثْلُكُمْ يُوحَىٰٓ إِلَىَّ أَنَّمَآ
إِلَٰهُكُمْ إِلَٰهٌ وَٰحِدٌ فَٱسْتَقِيمُوٓا۟ إِلَيْهِ وَٱسْتَغْفِرُوهُ ۗ
وَوَيْلٌ لِّلْمُشْرِكِينَ

6 Say, "I am only a human like you; it is inspired in me that your God is One God. So be upright towards Him, and seek forgiveness from Him." And woe to the idolaters.

٧ ٱلَّذِينَ لَا يُؤْتُونَ ٱلزَّكَوٰةَ وَهُم بِٱلْءَاخِرَةِ هُمْ
كَٰفِرُونَ

7 Those who do not pay the alms; and regarding the Hereafter, they are disbelievers.

٨ إِنَّ ٱلَّذِينَ ءَامَنُوا۟ وَعَمِلُوا۟ ٱلصَّٰلِحَٰتِ لَهُمْ أَجْرٌ
غَيْرُ مَمْنُونٍ

8 As for those who believe and do righteous deeds—for them is a reward uninterrupted.

٩ قُلْ أَئِنَّكُمْ لَتَكْفُرُونَ بِٱلَّذِى خَلَقَ ٱلْأَرْضَ فِى
يَوْمَيْنِ وَتَجْعَلُونَ لَهُۥٓ أَندَادًا ۚ ذَٰلِكَ رَبُّ ٱلْعَٰلَمِينَ

9 Say, "Do you reject the One who created the earth in two days? And you attribute equals to Him? That is the Lord of the Universe."

١٠ وَجَعَلَ فِيهَا رَوَٰسِىَ مِن فَوْقِهَا وَبَٰرَكَ فِيهَا
وَقَدَّرَ فِيهَآ أَقْوَٰتَهَا فِىٓ أَرْبَعَةِ أَيَّامٍ سَوَآءً
لِّلسَّآئِلِينَ

10 He placed stabilizers over it; and blessed it; and planned its provisions in four days, equally to the seekers.

١١ ثُمَّ ٱسْتَوَىٰٓ إِلَى ٱلسَّمَآءِ وَهِىَ دُخَانٌ فَقَالَ
لَهَا وَلِلْأَرْضِ ٱئْتِيَا طَوْعًا أَوْ كَرْهًا قَالَتَآ أَتَيْنَا
طَآئِعِينَ

11 Then He turned to the sky, and it was smoke, and said to it and to the earth, "Come, willingly or unwillingly." They said, "We come willingly."

١٢ فَقَضَىٰهُنَّ سَبْعَ سَمَٰوَاتٍ فِى يَوْمَيْنِ وَأَوْحَىٰ
فِى كُلِّ سَمَآءٍ أَمْرَهَا ۚ وَزَيَّنَّا ٱلسَّمَآءَ ٱلدُّنْيَا
بِمَصَٰبِيحَ وَحِفْظًا ۚ ذَٰلِكَ تَقْدِيرُ ٱلْعَزِيزِ ٱلْعَلِيمِ

12 So He completed them as seven universes in two days, and He assigned to each universe its laws. And We decorated the lower universe with lamps, and for protection. That is the design of the Almighty, the All-Knowing.

١٣ فَإِنْ أَعْرَضُوا۟ فَقُلْ أَنذَرْتُكُمْ صَٰعِقَةً مِّثْلَ
صَٰعِقَةِ عَادٍ وَثَمُودَ

13 But if they turn away, say, "I have warned you of a thunderbolt, like the thunderbolt of Aad and Thamood."

١٤ إِذْ جَآءَتْهُمُ ٱلرُّسُلُ مِنۢ بَيْنِ أَيْدِيهِمْ وَمِنْ
خَلْفِهِمْ أَلَّا تَعْبُدُوٓا۟ إِلَّا ٱللَّهَ ۖ قَالُوا۟ لَوْ شَآءَ رَبُّنَا
لَأَنزَلَ مَلَٰٓئِكَةً فَإِنَّا بِمَآ أُرْسِلْتُم بِهِۦ كَٰفِرُونَ

14 Their messengers came to them, from before them and from behind them, saying, "Do not worship anyone but Allah." They said, "Had our Lord willed, He would have sent

down angels; Therefore, we reject what you are sent with.”

١٥ فَأَمَّا عَادٌ فَٱسْتَكْبَرُوا۟ فِى ٱلْأَرْضِ بِغَيْرِ ٱلْحَقِّ وَقَالُوا۟ مَنْ أَشَدُّ مِنَّا قُوَّةً ۖ أَوَلَمْ يَرَوْا۟ أَنَّ ٱللَّهَ ٱلَّذِى خَلَقَهُمْ هُوَ أَشَدُّ مِنْهُمْ قُوَّةً ۖ وَكَانُوا۟ بِـَٔايَٰتِنَا يَجْحَدُونَ

15 As for Aad, they turned arrogant on earth, and opposed justice, and said, “Who is more powerful than us?” Have they not considered that Allah, who created them, is more powerful than they? And they went on denying Our revelations.

١٦ فَأَرْسَلْنَا عَلَيْهِمْ رِيحًا صَرْصَرًا فِىٓ أَيَّامٍ نَّحِسَاتٍ لِّنُذِيقَهُمْ عَذَابَ ٱلْخِزْىِ فِى ٱلْحَيَوٰةِ ٱلدُّنْيَا ۖ وَلَعَذَابُ ٱلْءَاخِرَةِ أَخْزَىٰ ۖ وَهُمْ لَا يُنصَرُونَ

16 So We unleashed upon them a screaming wind, for a few miserable days, to make them taste the punishment of shame in this life; but the punishment of the Hereafter is more shameful; and they will not be saved.

١٧ وَأَمَّا ثَمُودُ فَهَدَيْنَٰهُمْ فَٱسْتَحَبُّوا۟ ٱلْعَمَىٰ عَلَى ٱلْهُدَىٰ فَأَخَذَتْهُمْ صَٰعِقَةُ ٱلْعَذَابِ ٱلْهُونِ بِمَا كَانُوا۟ يَكْسِبُونَ

17 And as for Thamood, We guided them, but they preferred blindness over guidance. So the thunderbolt of the humiliating punishment seized them, because of what they used to earn.

١٨ وَنَجَّيْنَا ٱلَّذِينَ ءَامَنُوا۟ وَكَانُوا۟ يَتَّقُونَ

18 And We saved those who believed and were righteous.

١٩ وَيَوْمَ يُحْشَرُ أَعْدَآءُ ٱللَّهِ إِلَى ٱلنَّارِ فَهُمْ يُوزَعُونَ

19 The Day when Allah’s enemies are herded into the Fire, forcibly.

٢٠ حَتَّىٰٓ إِذَا مَا جَآءُوهَا شَهِدَ عَلَيْهِمْ سَمْعُهُمْ وَأَبْصَٰرُهُمْ وَجُلُودُهُم بِمَا كَانُوا۟ يَعْمَلُونَ

20 Until, when they have reached it, their hearing, and their sight, and their skins will testify against them regarding what they used to do.

٢١ وَقَالُوا۟ لِجُلُودِهِمْ لِمَ شَهِدتُّمْ عَلَيْنَا ۖ قَالُوٓا۟ أَنطَقَنَا ٱللَّهُ ٱلَّذِىٓ أَنطَقَ كُلَّ شَىْءٍ وَهُوَ خَلَقَكُمْ أَوَّلَ مَرَّةٍ وَإِلَيْهِ تُرْجَعُونَ

21 And they will say to their skins, “Why did you testify against us?” They will say, “Allah, Who made all things speak, made us speak. It is He who created you the first time, and to Him you are returned.”

٢٢ وَمَا كُنتُمْ تَسْتَتِرُونَ أَن يَشْهَدَ عَلَيْكُمْ
سَمْعُكُمْ وَلَآ أَبْصَٰرُكُمْ وَلَا جُلُودُكُمْ وَلَٰكِن ظَنَنتُمْ
أَنَّ ٱللَّهَ لَا يَعْلَمُ كَثِيرًا مِّمَّا تَعْمَلُونَ

22 You were unable to hide yourselves from your hearing, and your sight, and your skins, to prevent them from testifying against you, and you imagined that Allah was unaware of much of what you do.

٢٣ وَذَٰلِكُمْ ظَنُّكُمُ ٱلَّذِى ظَنَنتُم بِرَبِّكُمْ أَرْدَىٰكُمْ
فَأَصْبَحْتُم مِّنَ ٱلْخَٰسِرِينَ

23 It is that thought of yours about your Lord that led you to ruin—so you became of the losers.

٢٤ فَإِن يَصْبِرُوا۟ فَٱلنَّارُ مَثْوًى لَّهُمْ ۖ وَإِن
يَسْتَعْتِبُوا۟ فَمَا هُم مِّنَ ٱلْمُعْتَبِينَ

24 If they endure patiently, the Fire will be their residence; and if they make up excuses, they will not be pardoned.

٢٥ وَقَيَّضْنَا لَهُمْ قُرَنَآءَ فَزَيَّنُوا۟ لَهُم مَّا بَيْنَ
أَيْدِيهِمْ وَمَا خَلْفَهُمْ وَحَقَّ عَلَيْهِمُ ٱلْقَوْلُ فِىٓ
أُمَمٍ قَدْ خَلَتْ مِن قَبْلِهِم مِّنَ ٱلْجِنِّ وَٱلْإِنسِ ۖ
إِنَّهُمْ كَانُوا۟ خَٰسِرِينَ

25 We had assigned companions for them, who glamorized to them what was in front of them, and what was behind them. And the Word proved true against them in communities of jinn and humans that have passed away before them. They were losers.

٢٦ وَقَالَ ٱلَّذِينَ كَفَرُوا۟ لَا تَسْمَعُوا۟ لِهَٰذَا ٱلْقُرْءَانِ
وَٱلْغَوْا۟ فِيهِ لَعَلَّكُمْ تَغْلِبُونَ

26 Those who disbelieve say, “Do not listen to this Quran, and talk over it, so that you may prevail.”

٢٧ فَلَنُذِيقَنَّ ٱلَّذِينَ كَفَرُوا۟ عَذَابًا شَدِيدًا
وَلَنَجْزِيَنَّهُمْ أَسْوَأَ ٱلَّذِى كَانُوا۟ يَعْمَلُونَ

27 We will make those who disbelieve taste an intense agony, and We will recompense them according to the worst of what they used to do.

٢٨ ذَٰلِكَ جَزَآءُ أَعْدَآءِ ٱللَّهِ ٱلنَّارُ ۖ لَهُمْ فِيهَا دَارُ
ٱلْخُلْدِ ۖ جَزَآءًۢ بِمَا كَانُوا۟ بِـَٔايَٰتِنَا يَجْحَدُونَ

28 Such is the recompense of Allah’s enemies—the Fire—where they will have their permanent home, in recompense for having disregarded Our revelations.

٢٩ وَقَالَ ٱلَّذِينَ كَفَرُوا۟ رَبَّنَآ أَرِنَا ٱلَّذَيْنِ أَضَلَّانَا
مِنَ ٱلْجِنِّ وَٱلْإِنسِ نَجْعَلْهُمَا تَحْتَ أَقْدَامِنَا
لِيَكُونَا مِنَ ٱلْأَسْفَلِينَ

29 Those who disbelieved will say, “Our Lord, show us those who led us astray—among jinn and humans—and we will trample them under our feet, so they become of the lowest.”

٣٠ إِنَّ ٱلَّذِينَ قَالُواْ رَبُّنَا ٱللَّهُ ثُمَّ ٱسْتَقَٰمُواْ تَتَنَزَّلُ
عَلَيْهِمُ ٱلْمَلَٰٓئِكَةُ أَلَّا تَخَافُواْ وَلَا تَحْزَنُواْ وَأَبْشِرُواْ
بِٱلْجَنَّةِ ٱلَّتِى كُنتُمْ تُوعَدُونَ

30 Surely, those who say: "Our Lord is Allah," and then go straight, the angels will descend upon them: "Do not fear, and do not grieve, but rejoice in the news of the Garden which you were promised.

٣١ نَحْنُ أَوْلِيَآؤُكُمْ فِى ٱلْحَيَوٰةِ ٱلدُّنْيَا وَفِى
ٱلْءَاخِرَةِ ۖ وَلَكُمْ فِيهَا مَا تَشْتَهِىٓ أَنفُسُكُمْ
وَلَكُمْ فِيهَا مَا تَدَّعُونَ

31 We are your allies in this life and in the Hereafter, wherein you will have whatever your souls desire, and you will have therein whatever you call for.

٣٢ نُزُلًا مِّنْ غَفُورٍ رَّحِيمٍ

32 As Hospitality from an All-Forgiving, Merciful One."

٣٣ وَمَنْ أَحْسَنُ قَوْلًا مِّمَّن دَعَآ إِلَى ٱللَّهِ وَعَمِلَ
صَٰلِحًا وَقَالَ إِنَّنِى مِنَ ٱلْمُسْلِمِينَ

33 And who is better in speech than someone who calls to Allah, and acts with integrity, and says, "I am of those who submit"?

٣٤ وَلَا تَسْتَوِى ٱلْحَسَنَةُ وَلَا ٱلسَّيِّئَةُ ۚ ٱدْفَعْ
بِٱلَّتِى هِىَ أَحْسَنُ فَإِذَا ٱلَّذِى بَيْنَكَ وَبَيْنَهُۥ عَدَٰوَةٌ
كَأَنَّهُۥ وَلِىٌّ حَمِيمٌ

34 Good and evil are not equal. Repel evil with good, and the person who was your enemy becomes like an intimate friend.

٣٥ وَمَا يُلَقَّىٰهَآ إِلَّا ٱلَّذِينَ صَبَرُواْ وَمَا يُلَقَّىٰهَآ إِلَّا
ذُو حَظٍّ عَظِيمٍ

35 But none will attain it except those who persevere, and none will attain it except the very fortunate.

٣٦ وَإِمَّا يَنزَغَنَّكَ مِنَ ٱلشَّيْطَٰنِ نَزْغٌ فَٱسْتَعِذْ
بِٱللَّهِ ۖ إِنَّهُۥ هُوَ ٱلسَّمِيعُ ٱلْعَلِيمُ

36 When a temptation from the Devil provokes you, seek refuge in Allah; He is the Hearer, the Knower.

٣٧ وَمِنْ ءَايَٰتِهِ ٱلَّيْلُ وَٱلنَّهَارُ وَٱلشَّمْسُ وَٱلْقَمَرُ ۚ
لَا تَسْجُدُواْ لِلشَّمْسِ وَلَا لِلْقَمَرِ وَٱسْجُدُواْ لِلَّهِ
ٱلَّذِى خَلَقَهُنَّ إِن كُنتُمْ إِيَّاهُ تَعْبُدُونَ

37 And of His signs are the night and the day, and the sun and the moon. Do not bow down to the sun, nor to the moon, but bow down to Allah, Who created them both, if it is Him that you serve.

٣٨ فَإِنِ ٱسْتَكْبَرُواْ فَٱلَّذِينَ عِندَ رَبِّكَ يُسَبِّحُونَ
لَهُۥ بِٱلَّيْلِ وَٱلنَّهَارِ وَهُمْ لَا يَسْـَٔمُونَ ۩

38 But if they are too proud—those in the presence of your Lord praise Him night and day, and without ever tiring.

٣٩ وَمِنْ ءَايَٰتِهِۦٓ أَنَّكَ تَرَى ٱلْأَرْضَ خَٰشِعَةً فَإِذَآ
أَنزَلْنَا عَلَيْهَا ٱلْمَآءَ ٱهْتَزَّتْ وَرَبَتْ ۚ إِنَّ ٱلَّذِىٓ

39 And of His signs is that you see the land still. But when We send down water upon it, it stirs and

أَحْيَاهَا لَمُحْيِ ٱلْمَوْتَىٰٓ ۚ إِنَّهُۥ عَلَىٰ كُلِّ شَىْءٍ
قَدِيرٌ

grows. Surely, He Who revived it will revive the dead. He is Able to do all things.

٤٠ إِنَّ ٱلَّذِينَ يُلْحِدُونَ فِىٓ ءَايَٰتِنَا لَا يَخْفَوْنَ
عَلَيْنَآ ۗ أَفَمَن يُلْقَىٰ فِى ٱلنَّارِ خَيْرٌ أَم مَّن يَأْتِىٓ
ءَامِنًا يَوْمَ ٱلْقِيَٰمَةِ ۚ ٱعْمَلُوا۟ مَا شِئْتُمْ ۖ إِنَّهُۥ بِمَا
تَعْمَلُونَ بَصِيرٌ

40 Those who despise Our revelations are not hidden from Us. Is he who is hurled into the Fire better? Or he who arrives safely on the Day of Resurrection? Do as you please; He is Seeing of everything you do.

٤١ إِنَّ ٱلَّذِينَ كَفَرُوا۟ بِٱلذِّكْرِ لَمَّا جَآءَهُمْ ۖ وَإِنَّهُۥ
لَكِتَٰبٌ عَزِيزٌ

41 Those who reject the Reminder when it has come to them—it is an invincible Book.

٤٢ لَّا يَأْتِيهِ ٱلْبَٰطِلُ مِنۢ بَيْنِ يَدَيْهِ وَلَا مِنْ
خَلْفِهِۦ ۖ تَنزِيلٌ مِّنْ حَكِيمٍ حَمِيدٍ

42 Falsehood cannot approach it, from before it or behind it. It is a revelation from One Wise and Praiseworthy.

٤٣ مَّا يُقَالُ لَكَ إِلَّا مَا قَدْ قِيلَ لِلرُّسُلِ مِن
قَبْلِكَ ۚ إِنَّ رَبَّكَ لَذُو مَغْفِرَةٍ وَذُو عِقَابٍ أَلِيمٍ

43 Nothing is said to you but was said to the Messengers before you: your Lord is Possessor of Forgiveness, and Possessor of Painful Repayment.

٤٤ وَلَوْ جَعَلْنَٰهُ قُرْءَانًا أَعْجَمِيًّا لَّقَالُوا۟ لَوْلَا
فُصِّلَتْ ءَايَٰتُهُۥٓ ۖ ءَا۬عْجَمِىٌّ وَعَرَبِىٌّ ۗ قُلْ هُوَ
لِلَّذِينَ ءَامَنُوا۟ هُدًى وَشِفَآءٌ ۖ وَٱلَّذِينَ لَا يُؤْمِنُونَ
فِىٓ ءَاذَانِهِمْ وَقْرٌ وَهُوَ عَلَيْهِمْ عَمًى ۚ أُو۟لَٰٓئِكَ
يُنَادَوْنَ مِن مَّكَانٍۭ بَعِيدٍ

44 Had We made it a Quran in a foreign language, they would have said, “If only its verses were made clear.” Non-Arabic and an Arab? Say, “For those who believe, it is guidance and healing. But as for those who do not believe: there is heaviness in their ears, and it is blindness for them. These are being called from a distant place.”

٤٥ وَلَقَدْ ءَاتَيْنَا مُوسَى ٱلْكِتَٰبَ فَٱخْتُلِفَ فِيهِ ۗ
وَلَوْلَا كَلِمَةٌ سَبَقَتْ مِن رَّبِّكَ لَقُضِىَ بَيْنَهُمْ ۚ
وَإِنَّهُمْ لَفِى شَكٍّ مِّنْهُ مُرِيبٍ

45 We gave Moses the Book, but disputes arose concerning it. Were it not for a prior decree from your Lord, judgment would have been pronounced between them. But they are in perplexing doubt concerning it.

٤٦ مَّنْ عَمِلَ صَٰلِحًا فَلِنَفْسِهِۦ ۖ وَمَنْ أَسَآءَ
فَعَلَيْهَا ۗ وَمَا رَبُّكَ بِظَلَّٰمٍ لِّلْعَبِيدِ

46 Whoever acts righteously does so for himself; and whoever works evil does so against himself. Your Lord is not unjust to the servants.

٤٧ إِلَيْهِ يُرَدُّ عِلْمُ ٱلسَّاعَةِ ۚ وَمَا تَخْرُجُ مِن ثَمَرَٰتٍ
مِّنْ أَكْمَامِهَا وَمَا تَحْمِلُ مِنْ أُنثَىٰ وَلَا تَضَعُ إِلَّا
بِعِلْمِهِۦ ۚ وَيَوْمَ يُنَادِيهِمْ أَيْنَ شُرَكَآءِى قَالُوٓا۟
ءَاذَنَّٰكَ مَا مِنَّا مِن شَهِيدٍ

47 To Him is referred the knowledge of the Hour. No fruit emerges from its sheath, and no female conceives or delivers, except with His knowledge. And on the Day when He calls out to them, "Where are My associates?" They will say, "We admit to you, none of us is a witness."

٤٨ وَضَلَّ عَنْهُم مَّا كَانُوا۟ يَدْعُونَ مِن قَبْلُ ۖ
وَظَنُّوا۟ مَا لَهُم مِّن مَّحِيصٍ

48 What they used to pray to before will forsake them, and they will realize that they have no escape.

٤٩ لَّا يَسْـَٔمُ ٱلْإِنسَٰنُ مِن دُعَآءِ ٱلْخَيْرِ وَإِن مَّسَّهُ
ٱلشَّرُّ فَيَـُٔوسٌ قَنُوطٌ

49 The human being never tires of praying for good things; but when adversity afflicts him, he despairs and loses hope.

٥٠ وَلَئِنْ أَذَقْنَٰهُ رَحْمَةً مِّنَّا مِنۢ بَعْدِ ضَرَّآءَ مَسَّتْهُ
لَيَقُولَنَّ هَٰذَا لِى وَمَآ أَظُنُّ ٱلسَّاعَةَ قَآئِمَةً وَلَئِن
رُّجِعْتُ إِلَىٰ رَبِّىٓ إِنَّ لِى عِندَهُۥ لَلْحُسْنَىٰ ۚ
فَلَنُنَبِّئَنَّ ٱلَّذِينَ كَفَرُوا۟ بِمَا عَمِلُوا۟ وَلَنُذِيقَنَّهُم مِّنْ
عَذَابٍ غَلِيظٍ

50 And when We let him taste a mercy from Us, after the adversity that had afflicted him, he will say, "This is mine, and I do not think that the Hour is coming; and even if I am returned to my Lord, I will have the very best with Him." We will inform those who disbelieve of what they did, and We will make them taste an awful punishment.

٥١ وَإِذَآ أَنْعَمْنَا عَلَى ٱلْإِنسَٰنِ أَعْرَضَ وَنَـَٔا
بِجَانِبِهِۦ وَإِذَا مَسَّهُ ٱلشَّرُّ فَذُو دُعَآءٍ عَرِيضٍ

51 When We provide comfort for the human being, he withdraws and distances himself; but when adversity befalls him, he starts lengthy prayers.

٥٢ قُلْ أَرَءَيْتُمْ إِن كَانَ مِنْ عِندِ ٱللَّهِ ثُمَّ كَفَرْتُم
بِهِۦ مَنْ أَضَلُّ مِمَّنْ هُوَ فِى شِقَاقٍۭ بَعِيدٍ

52 Say, "Have you considered? If it is from Allah and you reject it—who is further astray than he who is cutoff and alienated?"

٥٣ سَنُرِيهِمْ ءَايَٰتِنَا فِى ٱلْءَافَاقِ وَفِىٓ أَنفُسِهِمْ
حَتَّىٰ يَتَبَيَّنَ لَهُمْ أَنَّهُ ٱلْحَقُّ ۗ أَوَلَمْ يَكْفِ بِرَبِّكَ
أَنَّهُۥ عَلَىٰ كُلِّ شَىْءٍ شَهِيدٌ

53 We will show them Our proofs on the horizons, and in their very souls, until it becomes clear to them that it is the truth. Is it not sufficient that your Lord is witness over everything?

٥٤ أَلَآ إِنَّهُمْ فِى مِرْيَةٍ مِّن لِّقَآءِ رَبِّهِمْ ۗ أَلَآ إِنَّهُۥ
بِكُلِّ شَىْءٍ مُّحِيطٌۢ

54 Surely they are in doubt about the encounter with their Lord. Surely He comprehends everything.

42 Consultation الشورى

بِسْمِ ٱللَّهِ ٱلرَّحْمَٰنِ ٱلرَّحِيمِ

In the name of Allah, the Gracious, the Merciful.

١ حمٓ

1 Ha, Meem.

٢ عٓسٓقٓ

2 Ayn, Seen, Qaf.

٣ كَذَٰلِكَ يُوحِىٓ إِلَيْكَ وَإِلَى ٱلَّذِينَ مِن قَبْلِكَ
ٱللَّهُ ٱلْعَزِيزُ ٱلْحَكِيمُ

3 Thus He inspires you, and those before you—Allah the Almighty, the Wise.

٤ لَهُۥ مَا فِى ٱلسَّمَٰوَٰتِ وَمَا فِى ٱلْأَرْضِ ۖ وَهُوَ
ٱلْعَلِىُّ ٱلْعَظِيمُ

4 To him belongs everything in the heavens and everything on earth. He is the Sublime, the Magnificent.

٥ تَكَادُ ٱلسَّمَٰوَٰتُ يَتَفَطَّرْنَ مِن فَوْقِهِنَّ ۚ
وَٱلْمَلَٰٓئِكَةُ يُسَبِّحُونَ بِحَمْدِ رَبِّهِمْ وَيَسْتَغْفِرُونَ
لِمَن فِى ٱلْأَرْضِ ۗ أَلَآ إِنَّ ٱللَّهَ هُوَ ٱلْغَفُورُ ٱلرَّحِيمُ

5 The heavens above them almost burst apart, while the angels glorify the praises of their Lord, and ask forgiveness for those on earth. Allah is indeed the Forgiver, the Merciful.

٦ وَٱلَّذِينَ ٱتَّخَذُوا۟ مِن دُونِهِۦٓ أَوْلِيَآءَ ٱللَّهُ
حَفِيظٌ عَلَيْهِمْ وَمَآ أَنتَ عَلَيْهِم بِوَكِيلٍ

6 As for those who take masters other than Him: Allah is in charge of them, and you are not responsible for them.

٧ وَكَذَٰلِكَ أَوْحَيْنَآ إِلَيْكَ قُرْءَانًا عَرَبِيًّا لِّتُنذِرَ أُمَّ
ٱلْقُرَىٰ وَمَنْ حَوْلَهَا وَتُنذِرَ يَوْمَ ٱلْجَمْعِ لَا رَيْبَ
فِيهِ ۚ فَرِيقٌ فِى ٱلْجَنَّةِ وَفَرِيقٌ فِى ٱلسَّعِيرِ

7 Thus We inspired you with an Arabic Quran, that you may warn the Central City and whoever is around it, and to warn of the Day of Assembly, of which there is no doubt; a group in the Garden, and a group in the Furnace.

٨ وَلَوْ شَآءَ ٱللَّهُ لَجَعَلَهُمْ أُمَّةً وَٰحِدَةً وَلَٰكِن
يُدْخِلُ مَن يَشَآءُ فِى رَحْمَتِهِۦ ۚ وَٱلظَّٰلِمُونَ مَا
لَهُم مِّن وَلِىٍّ وَلَا نَصِيرٍ

8 Had Allah willed, He could have made them one community, but He admits into His mercy whomever He wills. As for the wrongdoers, they will have no protector and no savior.

٩ أَمِ ٱتَّخَذُوا۟ مِن دُونِهِۦٓ أَوْلِيَآءَ ۖ فَٱللَّهُ هُوَ ٱلْوَلِىُّ
وَهُوَ يُحْىِ ٱلْمَوْتَىٰ وَهُوَ عَلَىٰ كُلِّ شَىْءٍ قَدِيرٌ

9 Or have they adopted protectors besides him? But Allah is the Protector, and He gives life to the dead, and He has power over all things.

١٠ وَمَا ٱخْتَلَفْتُمْ فِيهِ مِن شَىْءٍ فَحُكْمُهُۥٓ إِلَى
ٱللَّهِ ۚ ذَٰلِكُمُ ٱللَّهُ رَبِّى عَلَيْهِ تَوَكَّلْتُ وَإِلَيْهِ أُنِيبُ

10 Whatever matter you differ about, its judgment rests with Allah. “Such is Allah, my Lord, in Whom I trust, and unto Him I repent.”

١١ فَاطِرُ ٱلسَّمَٰوَٰتِ وَٱلْأَرْضِ ۚ جَعَلَ لَكُم مِّنْ
أَنفُسِكُمْ أَزْوَٰجًا وَمِنَ ٱلْأَنْعَٰمِ أَزْوَٰجًا ۖ يَذْرَؤُكُمْ
فِيهِ ۚ لَيْسَ كَمِثْلِهِۦ شَىْءٌ ۖ وَهُوَ ٱلسَّمِيعُ ٱلْبَصِيرُ

11 Originator of the heavens and the earth. He made for you mates from among yourselves, and pairs of animals, by means of which He multiplies you. There is nothing like Him. He is the Hearing, the Seeing.

١٢ لَهُۥ مَقَالِيدُ ٱلسَّمَٰوَٰتِ وَٱلْأَرْضِ ۖ يَبْسُطُ ٱلرِّزْقَ
لِمَن يَشَآءُ وَيَقْدِرُ ۚ إِنَّهُۥ بِكُلِّ شَىْءٍ عَلِيمٌ

12 To Him belongs absolute control of the heavens and the earth. He spreads the bounties to whomever He wills, or reduces it. He is aware of all things.

١٣ شَرَعَ لَكُم مِّنَ ٱلدِّينِ مَا وَصَّىٰ بِهِۦ نُوحًا
وَٱلَّذِىٓ أَوْحَيْنَآ إِلَيْكَ وَمَا وَصَّيْنَا بِهِۦٓ إِبْرَٰهِيمَ
وَمُوسَىٰ وَعِيسَىٰٓ ۖ أَنْ أَقِيمُوا۟ ٱلدِّينَ وَلَا
تَتَفَرَّقُوا۟ فِيهِ ۚ كَبُرَ عَلَى ٱلْمُشْرِكِينَ مَا تَدْعُوهُمْ
إِلَيْهِ ۚ ٱللَّهُ يَجْتَبِىٓ إِلَيْهِ مَن يَشَآءُ وَيَهْدِىٓ إِلَيْهِ
مَن يُنِيبُ

13 He prescribed for you the same religion He enjoined upon Noah, and what We inspired to you, and what We enjoined upon Abraham, and Moses, and Jesus: “You shall uphold the religion, and be not divided therein.” As for the idolaters, what you call them to is outrageous to them. Allah chooses to Himself whom He wills, and He guides to Himself whoever repents.

١٤ وَمَا تَفَرَّقُوٓا۟ إِلَّا مِنۢ بَعْدِ مَا جَآءَهُمُ ٱلْعِلْمُ
بَغْيًۢا بَيْنَهُمْ ۚ وَلَوْلَا كَلِمَةٌ سَبَقَتْ مِن رَّبِّكَ إِلَىٰٓ

14 They became divided only after knowledge came to them, out of resentment among themselves. Were it not for a predetermined decision from your Lord, judgment would have been pronounced

أَجَلٍ مُّسَمًّى لَّقُضِىَ بَيْنَهُمْ ۚ وَإِنَّ ٱلَّذِينَ أُورِثُوا۟
ٱلْكِتَـٰبَ مِنۢ بَعْدِهِمْ لَفِى شَكٍّ مِّنْهُ مُرِيبٍ

between them. Indeed, those who were made to inherit the Book after them are in grave doubt about it.

١٥ فَلِذَٰلِكَ فَٱدْعُ ۖ وَٱسْتَقِمْ كَمَآ أُمِرْتَ ۖ وَلَا تَتَّبِعْ
أَهْوَآءَهُمْ ۖ وَقُلْ ءَامَنتُ بِمَآ أَنزَلَ ٱللَّهُ مِن
كِتَـٰبٍ ۖ وَأُمِرْتُ لِأَعْدِلَ بَيْنَكُمُ ۖ ٱللَّهُ رَبُّنَا وَرَبُّكُمْ ۖ
لَنَآ أَعْمَـٰلُنَا وَلَكُمْ أَعْمَـٰلُكُمْ ۖ لَا حُجَّةَ بَيْنَنَا وَبَيْنَكُمُ ۖ
ٱللَّهُ يَجْمَعُ بَيْنَنَا ۖ وَإِلَيْهِ ٱلْمَصِيرُ

15 To this go on inviting, and be upright as you were commanded, and do not follow their inclinations, and say, "I believe in whatever Book Allah has sent down, and I was commanded to judge between you equitably. Allah is our Lord and your Lord. We have our deeds, and you have your deeds. Let there be no quarrel between us and you. Allah will bring us together, and to Him is the ultimate return."

١٦ وَٱلَّذِينَ يُحَآجُّونَ فِى ٱللَّهِ مِنۢ بَعْدِ مَا
ٱسْتُجِيبَ لَهُۥ حُجَّتُهُمْ دَاحِضَةٌ عِندَ رَبِّهِمْ
وَعَلَيْهِمْ غَضَبٌ وَلَهُمْ عَذَابٌ شَدِيدٌ

16 As for those who dispute about Allah after having answered His call, their argument is invalid with their Lord; and upon them falls wrath; and a grievous torment awaits them.

١٧ ٱللَّهُ ٱلَّذِىٓ أَنزَلَ ٱلْكِتَـٰبَ بِٱلْحَقِّ وَٱلْمِيزَانَ ۗ وَمَا
يُدْرِيكَ لَعَلَّ ٱلسَّاعَةَ قَرِيبٌ

17 It is Allah who revealed the Book with the truth, and the Balance. And what will make you realize that perhaps the Hour is near?

١٨ يَسْتَعْجِلُ بِهَا ٱلَّذِينَ لَا يُؤْمِنُونَ بِهَا ۖ وَٱلَّذِينَ
ءَامَنُوا۟ مُشْفِقُونَ مِنْهَا وَيَعْلَمُونَ أَنَّهَا ٱلْحَقُّ ۗ أَلَآ
إِنَّ ٱلَّذِينَ يُمَارُونَ فِى ٱلسَّاعَةِ لَفِى ضَلَـٰلٍۭ بَعِيدٍ

18 Those who do not believe in it seek to hasten it; but those who believe are apprehensive of it, and they know it to be the truth. Absolutely, those who question the Hour are in distant error.

١٩ ٱللَّهُ لَطِيفٌۢ بِعِبَادِهِۦ يَرْزُقُ مَن يَشَآءُ ۖ وَهُوَ
ٱلْقَوِىُّ ٱلْعَزِيزُ

19 Allah is kind towards His worshipers. He provides for whomever He wills. He is the Powerful, the Honorable.

٢٠ مَن كَانَ يُرِيدُ حَرْثَ ٱلْـَٔاخِرَةِ نَزِدْ لَهُۥ فِى
حَرْثِهِۦ ۖ وَمَن كَانَ يُرِيدُ حَرْثَ ٱلدُّنْيَا نُؤْتِهِۦ
مِنْهَا وَمَا لَهُۥ فِى ٱلْـَٔاخِرَةِ مِن نَّصِيبٍ

20 Whoever desires the harvest of the Hereafter, We increase for him his harvest; and whoever desires the harvest of this world, We give him thereof, and he has no share of the Hereafter.

٢١ أَمْ لَهُمْ شُرَكَٰٓؤُاْ شَرَعُواْ لَهُم مِّنَ ٱلدِّينِ مَا لَمْ
يَأْذَنۢ بِهِ ٱللَّهُۚ وَلَوْلَا كَلِمَةُ ٱلْفَصْلِ لَقُضِىَ بَيْنَهُمْۗ
وَإِنَّ ٱلظَّٰلِمِينَ لَهُمْ عَذَابٌ أَلِيمٌ

21 Or is it that they have partners who litigate for them religious laws never authorized by Allah? Were it not for the conclusive decision, it would have been settled between them. The wicked will have a painful punishment.

٢٢ تَرَى ٱلظَّٰلِمِينَ مُشْفِقِينَ مِمَّا كَسَبُواْ وَهُوَ
وَاقِعٌۢ بِهِمْۗ وَٱلَّذِينَ ءَامَنُواْ وَعَمِلُواْ ٱلصَّٰلِحَٰتِ
فِى رَوْضَاتِ ٱلْجَنَّاتِۖ لَهُم مَّا يَشَآءُونَ عِندَ
رَبِّهِمْۚ ذَٰلِكَ هُوَ ٱلْفَضْلُ ٱلْكَبِيرُ

22 You will see the unjust terrified of what they have earned, and it will befall them. As for those who believe and do good deeds, they will be in the Meadows of the Gardens; they will have whatever they please in the presence of their Lord; that is the supreme blessing.

٢٣ ذَٰلِكَ ٱلَّذِى يُبَشِّرُ ٱللَّهُ عِبَادَهُ ٱلَّذِينَ ءَامَنُواْ
وَعَمِلُواْ ٱلصَّٰلِحَٰتِۗ قُل لَّآ أَسْـَٔلُكُمْ عَلَيْهِ أَجْرًا إِلَّا
ٱلْمَوَدَّةَ فِى ٱلْقُرْبَىٰۗ وَمَن يَقْتَرِفْ حَسَنَةً نَّزِدْ لَهُۥ
فِيهَا حُسْنًاۚ إِنَّ ٱللَّهَ غَفُورٌ شَكُورٌ

23 That is the good news Allah gives to His servants who believe and do good deeds. Say, "I ask of you no wage for it, except affection among the near of kin." Whoever does a good deed, We will increase its goodness for him. Allah is Forgiving and Appreciative.

٢٤ أَمْ يَقُولُونَ ٱفْتَرَىٰ عَلَى ٱللَّهِ كَذِبًاۖ فَإِن يَشَإِ
ٱللَّهُ يَخْتِمْ عَلَىٰ قَلْبِكَۗ وَيَمْحُ ٱللَّهُ ٱلْبَٰطِلَ
وَيُحِقُّ ٱلْحَقَّ بِكَلِمَٰتِهِۦٓۚ إِنَّهُۥ عَلِيمٌۢ بِذَاتِ ٱلصُّدُورِ

24 Or do they say, "He forged a lie about Allah." If Allah so willed, He could have sealed your heart. But Allah obliterates the false, and confirm the true by His Words. He knows what is in the hearts.

٢٥ وَهُوَ ٱلَّذِى يَقْبَلُ ٱلتَّوْبَةَ عَنْ عِبَادِهِۦ وَيَعْفُواْ
عَنِ ٱلسَّيِّـَٔاتِ وَيَعْلَمُ مَا تَفْعَلُونَ

25 It is He who accepts the repentance of His worshipers, and remits the sins, and knows what you do.

٢٦ وَيَسْتَجِيبُ ٱلَّذِينَ ءَامَنُواْ وَعَمِلُواْ ٱلصَّٰلِحَٰتِ
وَيَزِيدُهُم مِّن فَضْلِهِۦۚ وَٱلْكَٰفِرُونَ لَهُمْ عَذَابٌ
شَدِيدٌ

26 And He answers those who believe and do good deeds, and He increases them of His grace. But the disbelievers will suffer a terrible punishment.

٢٧ وَلَوْ بَسَطَ ٱللَّهُ ٱلرِّزْقَ لِعِبَادِهِۦ لَبَغَوْا۟ فِى
ٱلْأَرْضِ وَلَٰكِن يُنَزِّلُ بِقَدَرٍ مَّا يَشَآءُ ۚ إِنَّهُۥ بِعِبَادِهِۦ
خَبِيرٌۢ بَصِيرٌ

27 If Allah were to increase the provision to His servants, they would transgress on earth; but He sends down in precise measure whatever He wills. Surely, regarding His servants, He is Expert and Observant.

٢٨ وَهُوَ ٱلَّذِى يُنَزِّلُ ٱلْغَيْثَ مِنۢ بَعْدِ مَا قَنَطُوا۟
وَيَنشُرُ رَحْمَتَهُۥ ۚ وَهُوَ ٱلْوَلِىُّ ٱلْحَمِيدُ

28 It is He who brings down the rain after they have despaired, and unfolds His mercy. He is the Guardian, the Praised.

٢٩ وَمِنْ ءَايَٰتِهِۦ خَلْقُ ٱلسَّمَٰوَٰتِ وَٱلْأَرْضِ وَمَا
بَثَّ فِيهِمَا مِن دَآبَّةٍ ۚ وَهُوَ عَلَىٰ جَمْعِهِمْ إِذَا
يَشَآءُ قَدِيرٌ

29 And of His signs are the creation of the heavens and the earth, and the creatures He has spread throughout them; and He is Able to gather them at will.

٣٠ وَمَآ أَصَٰبَكُم مِّن مُّصِيبَةٍ فَبِمَا كَسَبَتْ
أَيْدِيكُمْ وَيَعْفُوا۟ عَن كَثِيرٍ

30 Whatever misfortune befalls you, it is because of what your hands have earned; and yet He pardons much.

٣١ وَمَآ أَنتُم بِمُعْجِزِينَ فِى ٱلْأَرْضِ ۖ وَمَا لَكُم
مِّن دُونِ ٱللَّهِ مِن وَلِىٍّ وَلَا نَصِيرٍ

31 You are not the ones to interfere on earth; and besides Allah, you have no ally, and no helper.

٣٢ وَمِنْ ءَايَٰتِهِ ٱلْجَوَارِ فِى ٱلْبَحْرِ كَٱلْأَعْلَٰمِ

32 And of His signs are the ships sailing the sea like flags.

٣٣ إِن يَشَأْ يُسْكِنِ ٱلرِّيحَ فَيَظْلَلْنَ رَوَاكِدَ عَلَىٰ
ظَهْرِهِۦٓ ۚ إِنَّ فِى ذَٰلِكَ لَءَايَٰتٍ لِّكُلِّ صَبَّارٍ شَكُورٍ

33 If He willed, He could have stilled the winds, leaving them motionless on its surface. Surely in that are signs for every disciplined, grateful person.

٣٤ أَوْ يُوبِقْهُنَّ بِمَا كَسَبُوا۟ وَيَعْفُ عَن كَثِيرٍ

34 Or He could wreck them, because of what they have earned. And yet He pardons much.

٣٥ وَيَعْلَمَ ٱلَّذِينَ يُجَٰدِلُونَ فِىٓ ءَايَٰتِنَا مَا لَهُم
مِّن مَّحِيصٍ

35 Those who dispute Our signs know that there is no asylum for them.

٣٦ فَمَآ أُوتِيتُم مِّن شَىْءٍ فَمَتَٰعُ ٱلْحَيَوٰةِ ٱلدُّنْيَا ۖ
وَمَا عِندَ ٱللَّهِ خَيْرٌ وَأَبْقَىٰ لِلَّذِينَ ءَامَنُوا۟ وَعَلَىٰ
رَبِّهِمْ يَتَوَكَّلُونَ

36 Whatever thing you are given is only the provision of this life. But what Allah possesses is better and more lasting for those who believe and rely on their Lord.

٣٧ وَٱلَّذِينَ يَجْتَنِبُونَ كَبَٰٓئِرَ ٱلْإِثْمِ وَٱلْفَوَٰحِشَ
وَإِذَا مَا غَضِبُواْ هُمْ يَغْفِرُونَ

37 And those who avoid major sins and indecencies; and if they become angry, they forgive.

٣٨ وَٱلَّذِينَ ٱسْتَجَابُواْ لِرَبِّهِمْ وَأَقَامُواْ ٱلصَّلَوٰةَ
وَأَمْرُهُمْ شُورَىٰ بَيْنَهُمْ وَمِمَّا رَزَقْنَٰهُمْ يُنفِقُونَ

38 And those who respond to their Lord, and pray regularly, and conduct their affairs by mutual consultation, and give of what We have provided them.

٣٩ وَٱلَّذِينَ إِذَآ أَصَابَهُمُ ٱلْبَغْىُ هُمْ يَنتَصِرُونَ

39 And those who, when wronged, defend themselves.

٤٠ وَجَزَٰٓؤُاْ سَيِّئَةٍ سَيِّئَةٌ مِّثْلُهَا ۖ فَمَنْ عَفَا وَأَصْلَحَ
فَأَجْرُهُۥ عَلَى ٱللَّهِ ۚ إِنَّهُۥ لَا يُحِبُّ ٱلظَّٰلِمِينَ

40 The repayment of a bad action is one equivalent to it. But whoever pardons and makes reconciliation, his reward lies with Allah. He does not love the unjust.

٤١ وَلَمَنِ ٱنتَصَرَ بَعْدَ ظُلْمِهِۦ فَأُوْلَٰٓئِكَ مَا عَلَيْهِم
مِّن سَبِيلٍ

41 As for those who retaliate after being wronged, there is no blame on them.

٤٢ إِنَّمَا ٱلسَّبِيلُ عَلَى ٱلَّذِينَ يَظْلِمُونَ ٱلنَّاسَ
وَيَبْغُونَ فِى ٱلْأَرْضِ بِغَيْرِ ٱلْحَقِّ ۚ أُوْلَٰٓئِكَ لَهُمْ
عَذَابٌ أَلِيمٌ

42 Blame lies on those who wrong people, and commit aggression in the land without right. These will have a painful punishment.

٤٣ وَلَمَن صَبَرَ وَغَفَرَ إِنَّ ذَٰلِكَ لَمِنْ عَزْمِ ٱلْأُمُورِ

43 But whoever endures patiently and forgives—that is a sign of real resolve.

٤٤ وَمَن يُضْلِلِ ٱللَّهُ فَمَا لَهُۥ مِن وَلِىٍّ مِّنۢ بَعْدِهِۦ ۗ
وَتَرَى ٱلظَّٰلِمِينَ لَمَّا رَأَوُاْ ٱلْعَذَابَ يَقُولُونَ هَلْ
إِلَىٰ مَرَدٍّ مِّن سَبِيلٍ

44 Whoever Allah leaves astray has no protector apart from Him. And you will see the transgressors, when they see the torment, saying, "Is there a way of going back?"

٤٥ وَتَرَىٰهُمْ يُعْرَضُونَ عَلَيْهَا خَٰشِعِينَ مِنَ ٱلذُّلِّ
يَنظُرُونَ مِن طَرْفٍ خَفِىٍّ ۗ وَقَالَ ٱلَّذِينَ ءَامَنُوٓاْ
إِنَّ ٱلْخَٰسِرِينَ ٱلَّذِينَ خَسِرُوٓاْ أَنفُسَهُمْ وَأَهْلِيهِمْ
يَوْمَ ٱلْقِيَٰمَةِ ۗ أَلَآ إِنَّ ٱلظَّٰلِمِينَ فِى عَذَابٍ مُّقِيمٍ

45 And you will see them exposed to it, cowering from disgrace, looking with concealed eyes. Those who believed will say, "The losers are those who lost themselves and their families on the Day of Resurrection." Indeed, the evildoers are in a lasting torment.

٤٦ وَمَا كَانَ لَهُم مِّنْ أَوْلِيَآءَ يَنصُرُونَهُم مِّن
دُونِ ٱللَّهِ ۗ وَمَن يُضْلِلِ ٱللَّهُ فَمَا لَهُۥ مِن سَبِيلٍ

46 They will have no allies to support them against Allah. Whomever Allah leaves astray has no way out.

٤٧ ٱسْتَجِيبُوا۟ لِرَبِّكُم مِّن قَبْلِ أَن يَأْتِىَ يَوْمٌ لَّا
مَرَدَّ لَهُۥ مِنَ ٱللَّهِ ۚ مَا لَكُم مِّن مَّلْجَإٍ يَوْمَئِذٍ وَمَا
لَكُم مِّن نَّكِيرٍ

47 Respond to your Lord before there comes from Allah a Day that cannot be turned back. You will have no refuge on that Day, and no possibility of denial.

٤٨ فَإِنْ أَعْرَضُوا۟ فَمَآ أَرْسَلْنَٰكَ عَلَيْهِمْ حَفِيظًا ۖ
إِنْ عَلَيْكَ إِلَّا ٱلْبَلَٰغُ ۗ وَإِنَّآ إِذَآ أَذَقْنَا ٱلْإِنسَٰنَ مِنَّا
رَحْمَةً فَرِحَ بِهَا ۖ وَإِن تُصِبْهُمْ سَيِّئَةٌۢ بِمَا قَدَّمَتْ
أَيْدِيهِمْ فَإِنَّ ٱلْإِنسَٰنَ كَفُورٌ

48 But if they turn away—We did not send you as a guardian over them. Your only duty is communication. Whenever We let man taste mercy from Us, he rejoices in it; but when misfortune befalls them, as a consequence of what their hands have perpetrated, man turns blasphemous.

٤٩ لِّلَّهِ مُلْكُ ٱلسَّمَٰوَٰتِ وَٱلْأَرْضِ ۚ يَخْلُقُ مَا يَشَآءُ ۚ
يَهَبُ لِمَن يَشَآءُ إِنَٰثًا وَيَهَبُ لِمَن يَشَآءُ ٱلذُّكُورَ

49 To Allah belongs the dominion of the heavens and the earth. He creates whatever He wills. He grants daughters to whomever He wills, and He grants sons to whomever He wills.

٥٠ أَوْ يُزَوِّجُهُمْ ذُكْرَانًا وَإِنَٰثًا ۖ وَيَجْعَلُ مَن يَشَآءُ
عَقِيمًا ۚ إِنَّهُۥ عَلِيمٌ قَدِيرٌ

50 Or He combines them together, males and females; and He renders whomever He wills sterile. He is Knowledgeable and Capable.

٥١ وَمَا كَانَ لِبَشَرٍ أَن يُكَلِّمَهُ ٱللَّهُ إِلَّا وَحْيًا أَوْ مِن
وَرَآئِ حِجَابٍ أَوْ يُرْسِلَ رَسُولًا فَيُوحِىَ بِإِذْنِهِۦ
مَا يَشَآءُ ۚ إِنَّهُۥ عَلِىٌّ حَكِيمٌ

51 It is not for any human that Allah should speak to him, except by inspiration, or from behind a veil, or by sending a messenger to reveal by His permission whatever He wills. He is All-High, All-Wise.

٥٢ وَكَذَٰلِكَ أَوْحَيْنَآ إِلَيْكَ رُوحًا مِّنْ أَمْرِنَا ۚ مَا
كُنتَ تَدْرِى مَا ٱلْكِتَٰبُ وَلَا ٱلْإِيمَٰنُ وَلَٰكِن جَعَلْنَٰهُ
نُورًا نَّهْدِى بِهِۦ مَن نَّشَآءُ مِنْ عِبَادِنَا ۚ وَإِنَّكَ
لَتَهْدِىٓ إِلَىٰ صِرَٰطٍ مُّسْتَقِيمٍ

52 We thus inspired you spiritually, by Our command. You did not know what the Scripture is, nor what faith is, but We made it a light, with which We guide whomever We will of Our servants. You surely guide to a straight path.

٥٣ صِرَٰطِ ٱللَّهِ ٱلَّذِى لَهُۥ مَا فِى ٱلسَّمَٰوَٰتِ وَمَا فِى ٱلْأَرْضِ ۗ أَلَآ إِلَى ٱللَّهِ تَصِيرُ ٱلْأُمُورُ	53 The path of Allah, to whom belongs everything in the heavens and everything on earth. Indeed, to Allah all matters revert.

43 Decorations الزخرف

بِسْمِ ٱللَّهِ ٱلرَّحْمَٰنِ ٱلرَّحِيمِ	In the name of Allah, the Gracious, the Merciful.
١ حمٓ	1 Ha, Meem.
٢ وَٱلْكِتَٰبِ ٱلْمُبِينِ	2 By the Book that makes things clear.
٣ إِنَّا جَعَلْنَٰهُ قُرْءَٰنًا عَرَبِيًّا لَّعَلَّكُمْ تَعْقِلُونَ	3 We made it an Arabic Quran, so that you may understand.
٤ وَإِنَّهُۥ فِىٓ أُمِّ ٱلْكِتَٰبِ لَدَيْنَا لَعَلِىٌّ حَكِيمٌ	4 And it is with Us, in the Source Book, sublime and wise.
٥ أَفَنَضْرِبُ عَنكُمُ ٱلذِّكْرَ صَفْحًا أَن كُنتُمْ قَوْمًا مُّسْرِفِينَ	5 Shall We hold back the Reminder from you, since you are a transgressing people?
٦ وَكَمْ أَرْسَلْنَا مِن نَّبِىٍّ فِى ٱلْأَوَّلِينَ	6 How many a prophet did We send to the ancients?
٧ وَمَا يَأْتِيهِم مِّن نَّبِىٍّ إِلَّا كَانُوا۟ بِهِۦ يَسْتَهْزِءُونَ	7 No messenger came to them, but they ridiculed him.
٨ فَأَهْلَكْنَآ أَشَدَّ مِنْهُم بَطْشًا وَمَضَىٰ مَثَلُ ٱلْأَوَّلِينَ	8 We destroyed people more powerful than they, and so the example of the ancients has passed away.
٩ وَلَئِن سَأَلْتَهُم مَّنْ خَلَقَ ٱلسَّمَٰوَٰتِ وَٱلْأَرْضَ لَيَقُولُنَّ خَلَقَهُنَّ ٱلْعَزِيزُ ٱلْعَلِيمُ	9 And if you asked them, “Who created the heavens and the earth?” They would say, “The Mighty, the Knower created them.”
١٠ ٱلَّذِى جَعَلَ لَكُمُ ٱلْأَرْضَ مَهْدًا وَجَعَلَ لَكُمْ فِيهَا سُبُلًا لَّعَلَّكُمْ تَهْتَدُونَ	10 He who made the earth a habitat for you, and traced pathways for you on it, that you may be guided.
١١ وَٱلَّذِى نَزَّلَ مِنَ ٱلسَّمَآءِ مَآءًۢ بِقَدَرٍ فَأَنشَرْنَا بِهِۦ بَلْدَةً مَّيْتًا ۚ كَذَٰلِكَ تُخْرَجُونَ	11 He who sends down water from the sky in due proportion; and so We revive thereby a dead land. Thus you will be brought out.

١٢ وَٱلَّذِى خَلَقَ ٱلْأَزْوَٰجَ كُلَّهَا وَجَعَلَ لَكُم مِّنَ
ٱلْفُلْكِ وَٱلْأَنْعَٰمِ مَا تَرْكَبُونَ

12 He Who created all the pairs; and provided you with ships, and animals on which you ride.

١٣ لِتَسْتَوُۥا۟ عَلَىٰ ظُهُورِهِۦ ثُمَّ تَذْكُرُوا۟ نِعْمَةَ
رَبِّكُمْ إِذَا ٱسْتَوَيْتُمْ عَلَيْهِ وَتَقُولُوا۟ سُبْحَٰنَ ٱلَّذِى
سَخَّرَ لَنَا هَٰذَا وَمَا كُنَّا لَهُۥ مُقْرِنِينَ

13 That you may mount their backs, and remember the favor of your Lord as you sit firmly upon them, and say, “Glory be to Him Who placed these at our service; surely we could not have done it by ourselves.

١٤ وَإِنَّآ إِلَىٰ رَبِّنَا لَمُنقَلِبُونَ

14 And surely, to our Lord we will return.”

١٥ وَجَعَلُوا۟ لَهُۥ مِنْ عِبَادِهِۦ جُزْءًا ۚ إِنَّ ٱلْإِنسَٰنَ
لَكَفُورٌ مُّبِينٌ

15 Yet they turn one of His servants into a part of Him. Man is clearly ungrateful.

١٦ أَمِ ٱتَّخَذَ مِمَّا يَخْلُقُ بَنَاتٍ وَأَصْفَىٰكُم بِٱلْبَنِينَ

16 Or has He chosen for Himself daughters from what He creates, and favored you with sons?

١٧ وَإِذَا بُشِّرَ أَحَدُهُم بِمَا ضَرَبَ لِلرَّحْمَٰنِ مَثَلًا
ظَلَّ وَجْهُهُۥ مُسْوَدًّا وَهُوَ كَظِيمٌ

17 Yet when one of them is given news of what he attributes to the Most Gracious, his face darkens, and he suppresses grief.

١٨ أَوَمَن يُنَشَّؤُا۟ فِى ٱلْحِلْيَةِ وَهُوَ فِى ٱلْخِصَامِ
غَيْرُ مُبِينٍ

18 “Someone brought up to be beautiful, and unable to help in a fight?”

١٩ وَجَعَلُوا۟ ٱلْمَلَٰٓئِكَةَ ٱلَّذِينَ هُمْ عِبَٰدُ ٱلرَّحْمَٰنِ
إِنَٰثًا ۚ أَشَهِدُوا۟ خَلْقَهُمْ ۚ سَتُكْتَبُ شَهَٰدَتُهُمْ
وَيُسْـَٔلُونَ

19 And they appoint the angels, who are servants to the Most Gracious, as females. Have they witnessed their creation? Their claim will be recorded, and they will be questioned.

٢٠ وَقَالُوا۟ لَوْ شَآءَ ٱلرَّحْمَٰنُ مَا عَبَدْنَٰهُم ۗ مَّا لَهُم
بِذَٰلِكَ مِنْ عِلْمٍ ۖ إِنْ هُمْ إِلَّا يَخْرُصُونَ

20 And they say, “Had the Most Gracious willed, we would not have worshiped them.” But they have no knowledge of that; they are merely guessing.

٢١ أَمْ ءَاتَيْنَٰهُمْ كِتَٰبًا مِّن قَبْلِهِۦ فَهُم بِهِۦ
مُسْتَمْسِكُونَ

21 Or have We given them a book prior to this one, to which they adhere?

٢٢ بَلْ قَالُوٓا۟ إِنَّا وَجَدْنَآ ءَابَآءَنَا عَلَىٰٓ أُمَّةٍ وَإِنَّا
عَلَىٰٓ ءَاثَـٰرِهِم مُّهْتَدُونَ

22 But they say, “We found our parents on a course, and we are guided in their footsteps.”

٢٣ وَكَذَٰلِكَ مَآ أَرْسَلْنَا مِن قَبْلِكَ فِى قَرْيَةٍ مِّن
نَّذِيرٍ إِلَّا قَالَ مُتْرَفُوهَآ إِنَّا وَجَدْنَآ ءَابَآءَنَا عَلَىٰٓ
أُمَّةٍ وَإِنَّا عَلَىٰٓ ءَاثَـٰرِهِم مُّقْتَدُونَ

23 Likewise, We sent no warner before you to any town, but the wealthy among them said, “We found our parents on a course, and we are following in their footsteps.”

٢٤ قَـٰلَ أَوَلَوْ جِئْتُكُم بِأَهْدَىٰ مِمَّا وَجَدتُّمْ عَلَيْهِ
ءَابَآءَكُمْ ۖ قَالُوٓا۟ إِنَّا بِمَآ أُرْسِلْتُم بِهِۦ كَـٰفِرُونَ

24 He would say, “Even if I bring you better guidance than what you found your parents following?” They would say, “We reject what you are sent with.”

٢٥ فَٱنتَقَمْنَا مِنْهُمْ ۖ فَٱنظُرْ كَيْفَ كَانَ عَـٰقِبَةُ
ٱلْمُكَذِّبِينَ

25 So We wreaked vengeance upon them. Behold, then, what was the fate of those who deny.

٢٦ وَإِذْ قَالَ إِبْرَٰهِيمُ لِأَبِيهِ وَقَوْمِهِۦٓ إِنَّنِى بَرَآءٌ
مِّمَّا تَعْبُدُونَ

26 When Abraham said to his father and his people, “I am innocent of what you worship.

٢٧ إِلَّا ٱلَّذِى فَطَرَنِى فَإِنَّهُۥ سَيَهْدِينِ

27 Except for He who created me, for He will guide me.”

٢٨ وَجَعَلَهَا كَلِمَةًۢ بَاقِيَةً فِى عَقِبِهِۦ لَعَلَّهُمْ
يَرْجِعُونَ

28 And he made it an enduring word in his progeny, so that they may return.

٢٩ بَلْ مَتَّعْتُ هَـٰٓؤُلَآءِ وَءَابَآءَهُمْ حَتَّىٰ جَآءَهُمُ
ٱلْحَقُّ وَرَسُولٌ مُّبِينٌ

29 I gave these and their forefathers some enjoyment, until the truth and a manifest messenger came to them.

٣٠ وَلَمَّا جَآءَهُمُ ٱلْحَقُّ قَالُوا۟ هَـٰذَا سِحْرٌ وَإِنَّا بِهِۦ
كَـٰفِرُونَ

30 But when the truth came to them, they said, “This is sorcery, and we refuse to believe in it.”

٣١ وَقَالُوا۟ لَوْلَا نُزِّلَ هَـٰذَا ٱلْقُرْءَانُ عَلَىٰ رَجُلٍ مِّنَ
ٱلْقَرْيَتَيْنِ عَظِيمٍ

31 They also said, “If only this Quran was sent down to a man of importance from the two cities.”

٣٢ أَهُمْ يَقْسِمُونَ رَحْمَتَ رَبِّكَ ۚ نَحْنُ قَسَمْنَا
بَيْنَهُم مَّعِيشَتَهُمْ فِى ٱلْحَيَوٰةِ ٱلدُّنْيَا ۚ وَرَفَعْنَا
بَعْضَهُمْ فَوْقَ بَعْضٍ دَرَجَـٰتٍ لِّيَتَّخِذَ بَعْضُهُم

32 Is it they who allocate the mercy of your Lord? It is We who have allocated their livelihood in this life, and We elevated some of them in rank above others, that some of them would take others in service.

بَعْضًا سُخْرِيًّا ۗ وَرَحْمَتُ رَبِّكَ خَيْرٌ مِّمَّا يَجْمَعُونَ	But your Lord's mercy is better than what they amass.
٣٣ وَلَوْلَآ أَن يَكُونَ ٱلنَّاسُ أُمَّةً وَٰحِدَةً لَّجَعَلْنَا لِمَن يَكْفُرُ بِٱلرَّحْمَٰنِ لِبُيُوتِهِمْ سُقُفًا مِّن فِضَّةٍ وَمَعَارِجَ عَلَيْهَا يَظْهَرُونَ	33 Were it not that humanity would become a single community, We would have provided those who disbelieve in the Most Gracious with roofs of silver to their houses, and stairways by which they ascend.
٣٤ وَلِبُيُوتِهِمْ أَبْوَٰبًا وَسُرُرًا عَلَيْهَا يَتَّكِـُٔونَ	34 And doors to their houses, and furnishings on which they recline.
٣٥ وَزُخْرُفًا ۚ وَإِن كُلُّ ذَٰلِكَ لَمَّا مَتَٰعُ ٱلْحَيَوٰةِ ٱلدُّنْيَا ۚ وَٱلْءَاخِرَةُ عِندَ رَبِّكَ لِلْمُتَّقِينَ	35 And decorations. Yet all that is nothing but the stuff of this life. Yet the Hereafter, with your Lord, is for the righteous.
٣٦ وَمَن يَعْشُ عَن ذِكْرِ ٱلرَّحْمَٰنِ نُقَيِّضْ لَهُۥ شَيْطَٰنًا فَهُوَ لَهُۥ قَرِينٌ	36 Whoever shuns the remembrance of the Most Gracious, We assign for him a devil, to be his companion.
٣٧ وَإِنَّهُمْ لَيَصُدُّونَهُمْ عَنِ ٱلسَّبِيلِ وَيَحْسَبُونَ أَنَّهُم مُّهْتَدُونَ	37 They hinder them from the path, though they think they are guided.
٣٨ حَتَّىٰٓ إِذَا جَآءَنَا قَالَ يَٰلَيْتَ بَيْنِى وَبَيْنَكَ بُعْدَ ٱلْمَشْرِقَيْنِ فَبِئْسَ ٱلْقَرِينُ	38 Until, when He comes to Us, he will say, "If only there were between me and you the distance of the two Easts." What an evil companion!
٣٩ وَلَن يَنفَعَكُمُ ٱلْيَوْمَ إِذ ظَّلَمْتُمْ أَنَّكُمْ فِى ٱلْعَذَابِ مُشْتَرِكُونَ	39 It will not benefit you on that Day, since you did wrong. You are partners in the suffering.
٤٠ أَفَأَنتَ تُسْمِعُ ٱلصُّمَّ أَوْ تَهْدِى ٱلْعُمْىَ وَمَن كَانَ فِى ضَلَٰلٍ مُّبِينٍ	40 Can you make the deaf hear, or guide the blind, and him who is in evident error?
٤١ فَإِمَّا نَذْهَبَنَّ بِكَ فَإِنَّا مِنْهُم مُّنتَقِمُونَ	41 Even if We take you away, We will wreak vengeance upon them.
٤٢ أَوْ نُرِيَنَّكَ ٱلَّذِى وَعَدْنَٰهُمْ فَإِنَّا عَلَيْهِم مُّقْتَدِرُونَ	42 Or show you what We have promised them; for We have absolute power over them.
٤٣ فَٱسْتَمْسِكْ بِٱلَّذِىٓ أُوحِىَ إِلَيْكَ ۖ إِنَّكَ عَلَىٰ صِرَٰطٍ مُّسْتَقِيمٍ	43 So adhere to what is revealed to you. You are upon a straight path.

٤٤ وَإِنَّهُۥ لَذِكْرٌ لَّكَ وَلِقَوْمِكَ ۖ وَسَوْفَ تُسْـَٔلُونَ

44 It is a message for you, and for your people; and you will be questioned.

٤٥ وَسْـَٔلْ مَنْ أَرْسَلْنَا مِن قَبْلِكَ مِن رُّسُلِنَآ
أَجَعَلْنَا مِن دُونِ ٱلرَّحْمَٰنِ ءَالِهَةً يُعْبَدُونَ

45 Ask those of Our messengers We sent before you: “Did We appoint gods besides the Most Gracious to be worshiped?”

٤٦ وَلَقَدْ أَرْسَلْنَا مُوسَىٰ بِـَٔايَٰتِنَآ إِلَىٰ فِرْعَوْنَ
وَمَلَإِي۟هِۦ فَقَالَ إِنِّى رَسُولُ رَبِّ ٱلْعَٰلَمِينَ

46 We sent Moses with Our revelations to Pharaoh and his dignitaries. He said, “I am the Messenger of the Lord of the Worlds.”

٤٧ فَلَمَّا جَآءَهُم بِـَٔايَٰتِنَآ إِذَا هُم مِّنْهَا يَضْحَكُونَ

47 But when he showed them Our signs, they started laughing at them.

٤٨ وَمَا نُرِيهِم مِّنْ ءَايَةٍ إِلَّا هِىَ أَكْبَرُ مِنْ أُخْتِهَا ۖ
وَأَخَذْنَٰهُم بِٱلْعَذَابِ لَعَلَّهُمْ يَرْجِعُونَ

48 Each sign We showed them was more marvelous than its counterpart. And We afflicted them with the plagues, so that they may repent.

٤٩ وَقَالُوا۟ يَٰٓأَيُّهَ ٱلسَّاحِرُ ٱدْعُ لَنَا رَبَّكَ بِمَا عَهِدَ
عِندَكَ إِنَّنَا لَمُهْتَدُونَ

49 They said, “O sorcerer, pray to your Lord for us, according to His pledge to you, and then we will be guided.”

٥٠ فَلَمَّا كَشَفْنَا عَنْهُمُ ٱلْعَذَابَ إِذَا هُمْ يَنكُثُونَ

50 But when We lifted the torment from them, they immediately broke their promise.

٥١ وَنَادَىٰ فِرْعَوْنُ فِى قَوْمِهِۦ قَالَ يَٰقَوْمِ أَلَيْسَ
لِى مُلْكُ مِصْرَ وَهَٰذِهِ ٱلْأَنْهَٰرُ تَجْرِى مِن تَحْتِىٓ ۖ
أَفَلَا تُبْصِرُونَ

51 Pharaoh proclaimed among his people, saying, “O my people, do I not own the Kingdom of Egypt, and these rivers flow beneath me? Do you not see?

٥٢ أَمْ أَنَا۠ خَيْرٌ مِّنْ هَٰذَا ٱلَّذِى هُوَ مَهِينٌ وَلَا يَكَادُ
يُبِينُ

52 Am I not better than this miserable wretch, who can barely express himself?

٥٣ فَلَوْلَآ أُلْقِىَ عَلَيْهِ أَسْوِرَةٌ مِّن ذَهَبٍ أَوْ جَآءَ
مَعَهُ ٱلْمَلَٰٓئِكَةُ مُقْتَرِنِينَ

53 Why are bracelets of gold not dropped on him, or they angels came with him in procession?”

٥٤ فَٱسْتَخَفَّ قَوْمَهُۥ فَأَطَاعُوهُ ۚ إِنَّهُمْ كَانُوا۟ قَوْمًا
فَٰسِقِينَ

54 Thus he fooled his people, and they obeyed him. They were wicked people.

٥٥ فَلَمَّآ ءَاسَفُونَا ٱنتَقَمْنَا مِنْهُمْ فَأَغْرَقْنَٰهُمْ
أَجْمَعِينَ

55 And when they provoked Our wrath, We took retribution from them, and We drowned them all.

٥٦ فَجَعَلْنَٰهُمْ سَلَفًا وَمَثَلًا لِّلْءَاخِرِينَ

56 Thus We made them a precedent and an example for the others.

٥٧ وَلَمَّا ضُرِبَ ٱبْنُ مَرْيَمَ مَثَلًا إِذَا قَوْمُكَ مِنْهُ
يَصِدُّونَ

57 And when the son of Mary was cited as an example, your people opposed.

٥٨ وَقَالُوٓا۟ ءَأَٰلِهَتُنَا خَيْرٌ أَمْ هُوَ ۚ مَا ضَرَبُوهُ لَكَ
إِلَّا جَدَلًۢا ۚ بَلْ هُمْ قَوْمٌ خَصِمُونَ

58 They said, “Are our gods better, or he?” They cited him only for argument. In fact, they are a quarrelsome people.

٥٩ إِنْ هُوَ إِلَّا عَبْدٌ أَنْعَمْنَا عَلَيْهِ وَجَعَلْنَٰهُ مَثَلًا
لِّبَنِىٓ إِسْرَٰٓءِيلَ

59 He was just a servant whom We blessed, and We made him an example for the Children of Israel.

٦٠ وَلَوْ نَشَآءُ لَجَعَلْنَا مِنكُم مَّلَٰٓئِكَةً فِى ٱلْأَرْضِ
يَخْلُفُونَ

60 Had We willed, We would have made of you angels to be successors on earth.

٦١ وَإِنَّهُۥ لَعِلْمٌ لِّلسَّاعَةِ فَلَا تَمْتَرُنَّ بِهَا وَٱتَّبِعُونِ ۚ
هَٰذَا صِرَٰطٌ مُّسْتَقِيمٌ

61 He is a portent of the Hour, so have no doubt about it, and follow Me. This is a straight way.

٦٢ وَلَا يَصُدَّنَّكُمُ ٱلشَّيْطَٰنُ ۖ إِنَّهُۥ لَكُمْ عَدُوٌّ مُّبِينٌ

62 And let not Satan divert you. He is an open enemy to you.

٦٣ وَلَمَّا جَآءَ عِيسَىٰ بِٱلْبَيِّنَٰتِ قَالَ قَدْ جِئْتُكُم
بِٱلْحِكْمَةِ وَلِأُبَيِّنَ لَكُم بَعْضَ ٱلَّذِى تَخْتَلِفُونَ
فِيهِ ۖ فَٱتَّقُوا۟ ٱللَّهَ وَأَطِيعُونِ

63 When Jesus came with the clarifications, he said, “I have come to you with wisdom, and to clarify for you some of what you differ about. So fear Allah, and obey me.

٦٤ إِنَّ ٱللَّهَ هُوَ رَبِّى وَرَبُّكُمْ فَٱعْبُدُوهُ ۚ هَٰذَا
صِرَٰطٌ مُّسْتَقِيمٌ

64 Allah is my Lord and your Lord, so worship Him—this is a straight path.”

٦٥ فَٱخْتَلَفَ ٱلْأَحْزَابُ مِنۢ بَيْنِهِمْ ۖ فَوَيْلٌ لِّلَّذِينَ
ظَلَمُوا۟ مِنْ عَذَابِ يَوْمٍ أَلِيمٍ

65 But the factions differed among themselves. So woe to the wrongdoers from the suffering of a painful Day.

٦٦ هَلْ يَنظُرُونَ إِلَّا ٱلسَّاعَةَ أَن تَأْتِيَهُم بَغْتَةً
وَهُمْ لَا يَشْعُرُونَ

66 Are they only waiting for the Hour to come upon them suddenly, while they are unaware?

٦٧ ٱلْأَخِلَّآءُ يَوْمَئِذٍۭ بَعْضُهُمْ لِبَعْضٍ عَدُوٌّ إِلَّا ٱلْمُتَّقِينَ	67 On that Day, friends will be enemies of one another, except for the righteous.
٦٨ يَٰعِبَادِ لَا خَوْفٌ عَلَيْكُمُ ٱلْيَوْمَ وَلَآ أَنتُمْ تَحْزَنُونَ	68 O My servants, you have nothing to fear on that Day, nor will you grieve.
٦٩ ٱلَّذِينَ ءَامَنُوا۟ بِـَٔايَٰتِنَا وَكَانُوا۟ مُسْلِمِينَ	69 Those who believed in Our revelations, and were submissive.
٧٠ ٱدْخُلُوا۟ ٱلْجَنَّةَ أَنتُمْ وَأَزْوَٰجُكُمْ تُحْبَرُونَ	70 Enter the Garden, you and your spouses, Joyfully.
٧١ يُطَافُ عَلَيْهِم بِصِحَافٍ مِّن ذَهَبٍ وَأَكْوَابٍ ۖ وَفِيهَا مَا تَشْتَهِيهِ ٱلْأَنفُسُ وَتَلَذُّ ٱلْأَعْيُنُ ۖ وَأَنتُمْ فِيهَا خَٰلِدُونَ	71 They will be served around with trays of gold, and cups. Therein is whatever the souls desire and delights the eyes. Therein you will stay forever.
٧٢ وَتِلْكَ ٱلْجَنَّةُ ٱلَّتِىٓ أُورِثْتُمُوهَا بِمَا كُنتُمْ تَعْمَلُونَ	72 Such is the Garden you are made to inherit, because of what you used to do.
٧٣ لَكُمْ فِيهَا فَٰكِهَةٌ كَثِيرَةٌ مِّنْهَا تَأْكُلُونَ	73 Therein you will have abundant fruit, from which you eat.
٧٤ إِنَّ ٱلْمُجْرِمِينَ فِى عَذَابِ جَهَنَّمَ خَٰلِدُونَ	74 As for the sinners, they will be in the torment of Hell forever.
٧٥ لَا يُفَتَّرُ عَنْهُمْ وَهُمْ فِيهِ مُبْلِسُونَ	75 It will never be eased for them. In it, they will be devastated.
٧٦ وَمَا ظَلَمْنَٰهُمْ وَلَٰكِن كَانُوا۟ هُمُ ٱلظَّٰلِمِينَ	76 We did them no injustice, but it was they who were the unjust.
٧٧ وَنَادَوْا۟ يَٰمَٰلِكُ لِيَقْضِ عَلَيْنَا رَبُّكَ ۖ قَالَ إِنَّكُم مَّٰكِثُونَ	77 And they will cry, “O Malek, let your Lord finish us off.” He will say, “You are staying.”
٧٨ لَقَدْ جِئْنَٰكُم بِٱلْحَقِّ وَلَٰكِنَّ أَكْثَرَكُمْ لِلْحَقِّ كَٰرِهُونَ	78 We have given you the truth, but most of you hate the truth.
٧٩ أَمْ أَبْرَمُوٓا۟ أَمْرًا فَإِنَّا مُبْرِمُونَ	79 Have they contrived some scheme? We too are contriving.
٨٠ أَمْ يَحْسَبُونَ أَنَّا لَا نَسْمَعُ سِرَّهُمْ وَنَجْوَىٰهُم ۚ بَلَىٰ وَرُسُلُنَا لَدَيْهِمْ يَكْتُبُونَ	80 Or do they think that We cannot hear their secrets and their conspiracies? Yes indeed, Our messengers are by them, writing down.

٨١ قُلْ إِن كَانَ لِلرَّحْمَٰنِ وَلَدٌ فَأَنَا أَوَّلُ ٱلْعَٰبِدِينَ	81 Say, "If the Most Gracious had a son, I would be the first to worship."
٨٢ سُبْحَٰنَ رَبِّ ٱلسَّمَٰوَٰتِ وَٱلْأَرْضِ رَبِّ ٱلْعَرْشِ عَمَّا يَصِفُونَ	82 Glorified be the Lord of the heavens and the earth, the Lord of the Throne, beyond what they describe.
٨٣ فَذَرْهُمْ يَخُوضُوا۟ وَيَلْعَبُوا۟ حَتَّىٰ يُلَٰقُوا۟ يَوْمَهُمُ ٱلَّذِى يُوعَدُونَ	83 So leave them to blunder and play, until they encounter their Day which they are promised.
٨٤ وَهُوَ ٱلَّذِى فِى ٱلسَّمَآءِ إِلَٰهٌ وَفِى ٱلْأَرْضِ إِلَٰهٌ ۚ وَهُوَ ٱلْحَكِيمُ ٱلْعَلِيمُ	84 It is He who is Allah in heaven, and Allah on earth. He is the Wise, the Knower.
٨٥ وَتَبَارَكَ ٱلَّذِى لَهُۥ مُلْكُ ٱلسَّمَٰوَٰتِ وَٱلْأَرْضِ وَمَا بَيْنَهُمَا وَعِندَهُۥ عِلْمُ ٱلسَّاعَةِ وَإِلَيْهِ تُرْجَعُونَ	85 And blessed is He Who has sovereignty over the heavens and the earth and what is between them. He alone has knowledge of the Hour, and to Him you will be returned.
٨٦ وَلَا يَمْلِكُ ٱلَّذِينَ يَدْعُونَ مِن دُونِهِ ٱلشَّفَٰعَةَ إِلَّا مَن شَهِدَ بِٱلْحَقِّ وَهُمْ يَعْلَمُونَ	86 Those they invoke besides Him are incapable of intercession; only those who testify to the truth and have knowledge.
٨٧ وَلَئِن سَأَلْتَهُم مَّنْ خَلَقَهُمْ لَيَقُولُنَّ ٱللَّهُ ۖ فَأَنَّىٰ يُؤْفَكُونَ	87 And if you asked them, "Who created them?", they would say, "Allah." Why then do they deviate?
٨٨ وَقِيلِهِۦ يَٰرَبِّ إِنَّ هَٰٓؤُلَآءِ قَوْمٌ لَّا يُؤْمِنُونَ	88 As for his statement: "My Lord, these are a people who do not believe."
٨٩ فَٱصْفَحْ عَنْهُمْ وَقُلْ سَلَٰمٌ ۚ فَسَوْفَ يَعْلَمُونَ	89 Pardon them, and say, "Peace." They will come to know.

44 Smoke الدخان

بِسْمِ ٱللَّهِ ٱلرَّحْمَٰنِ ٱلرَّحِيمِ	In the name of Allah, the Gracious, the Merciful.
١ حمٓ	1 Ha, Meem.
٢ وَٱلْكِتَٰبِ ٱلْمُبِينِ	2 By the Enlightening Scripture.

٣ إِنَّآ أَنزَلْنَٰهُ فِى لَيْلَةٍ مُّبَٰرَكَةٍ ۚ إِنَّا كُنَّا مُنذِرِينَ	3 We have revealed it on a Blessed Night—We have warned.
٤ فِيهَا يُفْرَقُ كُلُّ أَمْرٍ حَكِيمٍ	4 In it is distinguished every wise command.
٥ أَمْرًا مِّنْ عِندِنَآ ۚ إِنَّا كُنَّا مُرْسِلِينَ	5 A decree from Us. We have been sending messages.
٦ رَحْمَةً مِّن رَّبِّكَ ۚ إِنَّهُۥ هُوَ ٱلسَّمِيعُ ٱلْعَلِيمُ	6 As mercy from your Lord. He is the Hearer, the Knower.
٧ رَبِّ ٱلسَّمَٰوَٰتِ وَٱلْأَرْضِ وَمَا بَيْنَهُمَآ ۖ إِن كُنتُم مُّوقِنِينَ	7 Lord of the heavens and the earth and what is between them, if you know for sure.
٨ لَآ إِلَٰهَ إِلَّا هُوَ يُحْىِۦ وَيُمِيتُ ۖ رَبُّكُمْ وَرَبُّ ءَابَآئِكُمُ ٱلْأَوَّلِينَ	8 There is no god but He. He gives life and causes death—your Lord and Lord of your ancestors of old.
٩ بَلْ هُمْ فِى شَكٍّ يَلْعَبُونَ	9 Yet they play around in doubt.
١٠ فَٱرْتَقِبْ يَوْمَ تَأْتِى ٱلسَّمَآءُ بِدُخَانٍ مُّبِينٍ	10 So watch out for the Day when the sky produces a visible smoke.
١١ يَغْشَى ٱلنَّاسَ ۖ هَٰذَا عَذَابٌ أَلِيمٌ	11 Enveloping mankind; this is a painful punishment.
١٢ رَّبَّنَا ٱكْشِفْ عَنَّا ٱلْعَذَابَ إِنَّا مُؤْمِنُونَ	12 "Our Lord, lift the torment from us, we are believers."
١٣ أَنَّىٰ لَهُمُ ٱلذِّكْرَىٰ وَقَدْ جَآءَهُمْ رَسُولٌ مُّبِينٌ	13 But how can they be reminded? An enlightening messenger has already come to them.
١٤ ثُمَّ تَوَلَّوْا۟ عَنْهُ وَقَالُوا۟ مُعَلَّمٌ مَّجْنُونٌ	14 But they turned away from him, and said, "Educated, but crazy!"
١٥ إِنَّا كَاشِفُوا۟ ٱلْعَذَابِ قَلِيلًا ۚ إِنَّكُمْ عَآئِدُونَ	15 We will ease the punishment a little, but you will revert.
١٦ يَوْمَ نَبْطِشُ ٱلْبَطْشَةَ ٱلْكُبْرَىٰٓ إِنَّا مُنتَقِمُونَ	16 The Day when We launch the Great Assault—We will avenge.
١٧ وَلَقَدْ فَتَنَّا قَبْلَهُمْ قَوْمَ فِرْعَوْنَ وَجَآءَهُمْ رَسُولٌ كَرِيمٌ	17 Before them We tested the people of Pharaoh; a noble messenger came to them.
١٨ أَنْ أَدُّوٓا۟ إِلَىَّ عِبَادَ ٱللَّهِ ۖ إِنِّى لَكُمْ رَسُولٌ أَمِينٌ	18 Saying, "Hand over Allah's servants to me. I am an honest messenger to you."

١٩ وَأَن لَّا تَعْلُوا۟ عَلَى ٱللَّهِ ۖ إِنِّىٓ ءَاتِيكُم بِسُلْطَٰنٍ
مُّبِينٍ

19 And, "Do not exalt yourselves
above Allah. I come to you with clear
authority.

٢٠ وَإِنِّى عُذْتُ بِرَبِّى وَرَبِّكُمْ أَن تَرْجُمُونِ

20 I have taken refuge in my Lord
and your Lord, lest you stone me.

٢١ وَإِن لَّمْ تُؤْمِنُوا۟ لِى فَٱعْتَزِلُونِ

21 But if you do not believe in me,
keep away from me."

٢٢ فَدَعَا رَبَّهُۥٓ أَنَّ هَٰٓؤُلَآءِ قَوْمٌ مُّجْرِمُونَ

22 He appealed to his Lord: "These
are a sinful people."

٢٣ فَأَسْرِ بِعِبَادِى لَيْلًا إِنَّكُم مُّتَّبَعُونَ

23 "Set out with My servants by
night—you will be followed.

٢٤ وَٱتْرُكِ ٱلْبَحْرَ رَهْوًا ۖ إِنَّهُمْ جُندٌ مُّغْرَقُونَ

24 And cross the sea quickly; they
are an army to be drowned."

٢٥ كَمْ تَرَكُوا۟ مِن جَنَّٰتٍ وَعُيُونٍ

25 How many gardens and fountains
did they leave behind?

٢٦ وَزُرُوعٍ وَمَقَامٍ كَرِيمٍ

26 And plantations, and splendid
buildings.

٢٧ وَنَعْمَةٍ كَانُوا۟ فِيهَا فَٰكِهِينَ

27 And comforts they used to enjoy.

٢٨ كَذَٰلِكَ ۖ وَأَوْرَثْنَٰهَا قَوْمًا ءَاخَرِينَ

28 So it was; and We passed it on to
another people.

٢٩ فَمَا بَكَتْ عَلَيْهِمُ ٱلسَّمَآءُ وَٱلْأَرْضُ وَمَا كَانُوا۟
مُنظَرِينَ

29 Neither heaven nor earth wept
over them, nor were they reprieved.

٣٠ وَلَقَدْ نَجَّيْنَا بَنِىٓ إِسْرَٰٓءِيلَ مِنَ ٱلْعَذَابِ
ٱلْمُهِينِ

30 And We delivered the Children of
Israel from the humiliating
persecution.

٣١ مِن فِرْعَوْنَ ۚ إِنَّهُۥ كَانَ عَالِيًا مِّنَ ٱلْمُسْرِفِينَ

31 From Pharaoh. He was a
transgressing tyrant.

٣٢ وَلَقَدِ ٱخْتَرْنَٰهُمْ عَلَىٰ عِلْمٍ عَلَى ٱلْعَٰلَمِينَ

32 And We chose them knowingly
over all other people.

٣٣ وَءَاتَيْنَٰهُم مِّنَ ٱلْءَايَٰتِ مَا فِيهِ بَلَٰٓؤٌا۟ مُّبِينٌ

33 And We gave them many signs, in
which was an obvious test.

٣٤ إِنَّ هَٰٓؤُلَآءِ لَيَقُولُونَ

34 These people say.

٣٥ إِنْ هِىَ إِلَّا مَوْتَتُنَا ٱلْأُولَىٰ وَمَا نَحْنُ
بِمُنشَرِينَ

35 "There is nothing but our first
death, and we will not be
resurrected.

٣٦ فَأْتُوا۟ بِـَٔابَآئِنَآ إِن كُنتُمْ صَـٰدِقِينَ

36 Bring back our ancestors, if you are truthful."

٣٧ أَهُمْ خَيْرٌ أَمْ قَوْمُ تُبَّعٍ وَٱلَّذِينَ مِن قَبْلِهِمْ ۚ
أَهْلَكْنَـٰهُمْ ۖ إِنَّهُمْ كَانُوا۟ مُجْرِمِينَ

37 Are they better, or the people of Tubba and those before them? We annihilated them. They were evildoers.

٣٨ وَمَا خَلَقْنَا ٱلسَّمَـٰوَٰتِ وَٱلْأَرْضَ وَمَا بَيْنَهُمَا
لَـٰعِبِينَ

38 We did not create the heavens and the earth and what is between them to play.

٣٩ مَا خَلَقْنَـٰهُمَآ إِلَّا بِٱلْحَقِّ وَلَـٰكِنَّ أَكْثَرَهُمْ لَا
يَعْلَمُونَ

39 We created them only for a specific purpose, but most of them do not know.

٤٠ إِنَّ يَوْمَ ٱلْفَصْلِ مِيقَـٰتُهُمْ أَجْمَعِينَ

40 The Day of Sorting Out is the appointed time for them all.

٤١ يَوْمَ لَا يُغْنِى مَوْلًى عَن مَّوْلًى شَيْـًٔا وَلَا هُمْ
يُنصَرُونَ

41 The Day when no friend will avail a friend in any way, and they will not be helped.

٤٢ إِلَّا مَن رَّحِمَ ٱللَّهُ ۚ إِنَّهُۥ هُوَ ٱلْعَزِيزُ ٱلرَّحِيمُ

42 Except for him upon whom Allah has mercy. He is the Mighty, the Merciful.

٤٣ إِنَّ شَجَرَتَ ٱلزَّقُّومِ

43 The Tree of Bitterness.

٤٤ طَعَامُ ٱلْأَثِيمِ

44 The food of the sinner.

٤٥ كَٱلْمُهْلِ يَغْلِى فِى ٱلْبُطُونِ

45 Like molten lead; boiling inside the bellies.

٤٦ كَغَلْىِ ٱلْحَمِيمِ

46 Like the boiling of seething water.

٤٧ خُذُوهُ فَٱعْتِلُوهُ إِلَىٰ سَوَآءِ ٱلْجَحِيمِ

47 Seize him and drag him into the midst of Hell!

٤٨ ثُمَّ صُبُّوا۟ فَوْقَ رَأْسِهِۦ مِنْ عَذَابِ ٱلْحَمِيمِ

48 Then pour over his head the suffering of the Inferno!

٤٩ ذُقْ إِنَّكَ أَنتَ ٱلْعَزِيزُ ٱلْكَرِيمُ

49 Taste! You who were powerful and noble.

٥٠ إِنَّ هَـٰذَا مَا كُنتُم بِهِۦ تَمْتَرُونَ

50 This is what you used to doubt.

٥١ إِنَّ ٱلْمُتَّقِينَ فِى مَقَامٍ أَمِينٍ

51 As for the righteous, they will be in a secure place.

٥٢ فِى جَنَّـٰتٍ وَعُيُونٍ

52 Amidst gardens and springs.

٥٣ يَلْبَسُونَ مِن سُندُسٍ وَإِسْتَبْرَقٍ مُّتَقَٰبِلِينَ

53 Dressed in silk and brocade, facing one another.

٥٤ كَذَٰلِكَ وَزَوَّجْنَٰهُم بِحُورٍ عِينٍ

54 So it is, and We will wed them to lovely companions.

٥٥ يَدْعُونَ فِيهَا بِكُلِّ فَٰكِهَةٍ ءَامِنِينَ

55 They will call therein for every kind of fruit, in peace and security.

٥٦ لَا يَذُوقُونَ فِيهَا ٱلْمَوْتَ إِلَّا ٱلْمَوْتَةَ ٱلْأُولَىٰ ۖ
وَوَقَىٰهُمْ عَذَابَ ٱلْجَحِيمِ

56 Therein they will not taste death, beyond the first death; and He will protect them from the torment of Hell.

٥٧ فَضْلًا مِّن رَّبِّكَ ۚ ذَٰلِكَ هُوَ ٱلْفَوْزُ ٱلْعَظِيمُ

57 A favor from your Lord. That is the supreme salvation.

٥٨ فَإِنَّمَا يَسَّرْنَٰهُ بِلِسَانِكَ لَعَلَّهُمْ يَتَذَكَّرُونَ

58 We made it easy in your language, so that they may remember.

٥٩ فَٱرْتَقِبْ إِنَّهُم مُّرْتَقِبُونَ

59 So wait and watch. They too are waiting and watching.

45 Kneeling الجاثية

بِسْمِ ٱللَّهِ ٱلرَّحْمَٰنِ ٱلرَّحِيمِ

In the name of Allah, the Gracious, the Merciful.

١ حمٓ

1 Ha, Meem.

٢ تَنزِيلُ ٱلْكِتَٰبِ مِنَ ٱللَّهِ ٱلْعَزِيزِ ٱلْحَكِيمِ

2 The revelation of the Book is from Allah, the Exalted in Might, the Wise.

٣ إِنَّ فِى ٱلسَّمَٰوَٰتِ وَٱلْأَرْضِ لَءَايَٰتٍ لِّلْمُؤْمِنِينَ

3 In the heavens and the earth are proofs for the believers.

٤ وَفِى خَلْقِكُمْ وَمَا يَبُثُّ مِن دَآبَّةٍ ءَايَٰتٌ لِّقَوْمٍ
يُوقِنُونَ

4 And in your own creation, and in the creatures He scattered, are signs for people of firm faith.

٥ وَٱخْتِلَٰفِ ٱلَّيْلِ وَٱلنَّهَارِ وَمَآ أَنزَلَ ٱللَّهُ مِنَ
ٱلسَّمَآءِ مِن رِّزْقٍ فَأَحْيَا بِهِ ٱلْأَرْضَ بَعْدَ مَوْتِهَا
وَتَصْرِيفِ ٱلرِّيَٰحِ ءَايَٰتٌ لِّقَوْمٍ يَعْقِلُونَ

5 And in the alternation of night and day, and in the sustenance Allah sends down from the sky, with which He revives the earth after its death, and in the circulation of the winds, are marvels for people who reason.

٦ تِلْكَ ءَايَٰتُ ٱللَّهِ نَتْلُوهَا عَلَيْكَ بِٱلْحَقِّ ۖ فَبِأَىِّ
حَدِيثٍۭ بَعْدَ ٱللَّهِ وَءَايَٰتِهِۦ يُؤْمِنُونَ

6 These are Allah's Verses which We recite to you in truth. In which

message, after Allah and His revelations, will they believe?

٧ وَيْلٌ لِّكُلِّ أَفَّاكٍ أَثِيمٍ

7 Woe to every sinful liar.

٨ يَسْمَعُ ءَايَٰتِ ٱللَّهِ تُتْلَىٰ عَلَيْهِ ثُمَّ يُصِرُّ
مُسْتَكْبِرًا كَأَن لَّمْ يَسْمَعْهَا ۖ فَبَشِّرْهُ بِعَذَابٍ أَلِيمٍ

8 Who hears Allah's revelations being recited to him, yet he persists arrogantly, as though he did not hear them. Announce to him a painful punishment.

٩ وَإِذَا عَلِمَ مِنْ ءَايَٰتِنَا شَيْـًٔا ٱتَّخَذَهَا هُزُوًا ۚ
أُو۟لَٰٓئِكَ لَهُمْ عَذَابٌ مُّهِينٌ

9 And when he learns something of Our revelations, he takes them in mockery. For such there is a shameful punishment.

١٠ مِّن وَرَآئِهِمْ جَهَنَّمُ ۖ وَلَا يُغْنِى عَنْهُم مَّا
كَسَبُوا۟ شَيْـًٔا وَلَا مَا ٱتَّخَذُوا۟ مِن دُونِ ٱللَّهِ
أَوْلِيَآءَ ۖ وَلَهُمْ عَذَابٌ عَظِيمٌ

10 Beyond them lies Hell. What they have earned will not benefit them at all, nor will those they adopted as lords instead of Allah. They will have a terrible punishment.

١١ هَٰذَا هُدًى ۖ وَٱلَّذِينَ كَفَرُوا۟ بِـَٔايَٰتِ رَبِّهِمْ لَهُمْ
عَذَابٌ مِّن رِّجْزٍ أَلِيمٌ

11 This is guidance. Those who blaspheme their Lord's revelations will have a punishment of agonizing pain.

١٢ ٱللَّهُ ٱلَّذِى سَخَّرَ لَكُمُ ٱلْبَحْرَ لِتَجْرِىَ ٱلْفُلْكُ
فِيهِ بِأَمْرِهِۦ وَلِتَبْتَغُوا۟ مِن فَضْلِهِۦ وَلَعَلَّكُمْ
تَشْكُرُونَ

12 It is Allah who placed the sea at your service, so that ships may run through it by His command, and that you may seek of His bounty, and that you may give thanks.

١٣ وَسَخَّرَ لَكُم مَّا فِى ٱلسَّمَٰوَٰتِ وَمَا فِى ٱلْأَرْضِ
جَمِيعًا مِّنْهُ ۚ إِنَّ فِى ذَٰلِكَ لَءَايَٰتٍ لِّقَوْمٍ
يَتَفَكَّرُونَ

13 And He placed at your service whatever is in the heavens and whatever is on earth—all is from Him. In that are signs for a people who think.

١٤ قُل لِّلَّذِينَ ءَامَنُوا۟ يَغْفِرُوا۟ لِلَّذِينَ لَا يَرْجُونَ
أَيَّامَ ٱللَّهِ لِيَجْزِىَ قَوْمًۢا بِمَا كَانُوا۟ يَكْسِبُونَ

14 Tell those who believe to forgive those who do not hope for the Days of Allah. He will fully recompense people for whatever they have earned.

١٥ مَنْ عَمِلَ صَٰلِحًا فَلِنَفْسِهِۦ ۖ وَمَنْ أَسَآءَ
فَعَلَيْهَا ۖ ثُمَّ إِلَىٰ رَبِّكُمْ تُرْجَعُونَ

15 Whoever does a good deed, it is for his soul; and whoever commits evil, it is against it; then to your Lord you will be returned.

١٦ وَلَقَدْ ءَاتَيْنَا بَنِىٓ إِسْرَٰٓءِيلَ ٱلْكِتَـٰبَ وَٱلْحُكْمَ
وَٱلنُّبُوَّةَ وَرَزَقْنَـٰهُم مِّنَ ٱلطَّيِّبَـٰتِ وَفَضَّلْنَـٰهُمْ عَلَى
ٱلْعَـٰلَمِينَ

16 We gave the Children of Israel the Book, and wisdom, and prophecy; and We provided them with the good things; and We gave them advantage over all other people.

١٧ وَءَاتَيْنَـٰهُم بَيِّنَـٰتٍ مِّنَ ٱلْأَمْرِ ۖ فَمَا ٱخْتَلَفُوٓا۟ إِلَّا
مِنۢ بَعْدِ مَا جَآءَهُمُ ٱلْعِلْمُ بَغْيًۢا بَيْنَهُمْ ۚ إِنَّ رَبَّكَ
يَقْضِى بَيْنَهُمْ يَوْمَ ٱلْقِيَـٰمَةِ فِيمَا كَانُوا۟ فِيهِ
يَخْتَلِفُونَ

17 And We gave them precise rulings. They fell into dispute only after knowledge came to them, out of mutual rivalry. Your Lord will judge between them on the Day of Resurrection regarding the things they differed about.

١٨ ثُمَّ جَعَلْنَـٰكَ عَلَىٰ شَرِيعَةٍ مِّنَ ٱلْأَمْرِ فَٱتَّبِعْهَا
وَلَا تَتَّبِعْ أَهْوَآءَ ٱلَّذِينَ لَا يَعْلَمُونَ

18 Then We set you upon a pathway of faith, so follow it, and do not follow the inclinations of those who do not know.

١٩ إِنَّهُمْ لَن يُغْنُوا۟ عَنكَ مِنَ ٱللَّهِ شَيْـًٔا ۚ وَإِنَّ
ٱلظَّـٰلِمِينَ بَعْضُهُمْ أَوْلِيَآءُ بَعْضٍ ۖ وَٱللَّهُ وَلِىُّ
ٱلْمُتَّقِينَ

19 They will not help you against Allah in any way. The wrongdoers are allies of one another, while Allah is the Protector of the righteous.

٢٠ هَـٰذَا بَصَـٰٓئِرُ لِلنَّاسِ وَهُدًى وَرَحْمَةٌ لِّقَوْمٍ
يُوقِنُونَ

20 This is an illumination for mankind, and guidance, and mercy for people who believe with certainty.

٢١ أَمْ حَسِبَ ٱلَّذِينَ ٱجْتَرَحُوا۟ ٱلسَّيِّـَٔاتِ أَن
نَّجْعَلَهُمْ كَٱلَّذِينَ ءَامَنُوا۟ وَعَمِلُوا۟ ٱلصَّـٰلِحَـٰتِ
سَوَآءً مَّحْيَاهُمْ وَمَمَاتُهُمْ ۚ سَآءَ مَا يَحْكُمُونَ

21 Do those who perpetrate the evil deeds assume that We will regard them as equal to those who believe and do righteous deeds, whether in their life or their death? Evil is their judgment!

٢٢ وَخَلَقَ ٱللَّهُ ٱلسَّمَـٰوَٰتِ وَٱلْأَرْضَ بِٱلْحَقِّ
وَلِتُجْزَىٰ كُلُّ نَفْسٍۭ بِمَا كَسَبَتْ وَهُمْ لَا يُظْلَمُونَ

22 Allah created the heavens and the earth with justice, so that every soul will be repaid for what it has earned. And they will not be wronged.

٢٣ أَفَرَءَيْتَ مَنِ ٱتَّخَذَ إِلَـٰهَهُۥ هَوَىٰهُ وَأَضَلَّهُ ٱللَّهُ
عَلَىٰ عِلْمٍ وَخَتَمَ عَلَىٰ سَمْعِهِۦ وَقَلْبِهِۦ وَجَعَلَ
عَلَىٰ بَصَرِهِۦ غِشَـٰوَةً فَمَن يَهْدِيهِ مِنۢ بَعْدِ ٱللَّهِ ۚ
أَفَلَا تَذَكَّرُونَ

23 Have you considered him who has taken his desire for his god? Allah has knowingly led him astray, and has sealed his hearing and his heart, and has placed a veil over his vision. Who will guide him after Allah? Will you not reflect?

٢٤ وَقَالُواْ مَا هِىَ إِلَّا حَيَاتُنَا ٱلدُّنْيَا نَمُوتُ
وَنَحْيَا وَمَا يُهْلِكُنَآ إِلَّا ٱلدَّهْرُۚ وَمَا لَهُم بِذَٰلِكَ مِنْ
عِلْمٍۖ إِنْ هُمْ إِلَّا يَظُنُّونَ

24 And they say, "There is nothing but this our present life; we die and we live, and nothing destroys us except time." But they have no knowledge of that; they are only guessing.

٢٥ وَإِذَا تُتْلَىٰ عَلَيْهِمْ ءَايَٰتُنَا بَيِّنَٰتٍ مَّا كَانَ
حُجَّتَهُمْ إِلَّآ أَن قَالُواْ ٱئْتُواْ بِـَٔابَآئِنَآ إِن كُنتُمْ
صَٰدِقِينَ

25 When Our clarifying Verses are recited to them, their only argument is to say, "Bring back our ancestors, if you are truthful."

٢٦ قُلِ ٱللَّهُ يُحْيِيكُمْ ثُمَّ يُمِيتُكُمْ ثُمَّ يَجْمَعُكُمْ
إِلَىٰ يَوْمِ ٱلْقِيَٰمَةِ لَا رَيْبَ فِيهِ وَلَٰكِنَّ أَكْثَرَ ٱلنَّاسِ
لَا يَعْلَمُونَ

26 Say, "Allah gives you life, then He makes you die; then He gathers you for the Day of Resurrection, about which there is no doubt. But most people do not know."

٢٧ وَلِلَّهِ مُلْكُ ٱلسَّمَٰوَٰتِ وَٱلْأَرْضِۚ وَيَوْمَ تَقُومُ
ٱلسَّاعَةُ يَوْمَئِذٍ يَخْسَرُ ٱلْمُبْطِلُونَ

27 To Allah belongs the kingship of the heavens and the earth. On the Day when the Hour takes place, on that Day the falsifiers will lose.

٢٨ وَتَرَىٰ كُلَّ أُمَّةٍ جَاثِيَةًۚ كُلُّ أُمَّةٍ تُدْعَىٰٓ إِلَىٰ
كِتَٰبِهَا ٱلْيَوْمَ تُجْزَوْنَ مَا كُنتُمْ تَعْمَلُونَ

28 You will see every community on its knees; every community will be called to its Book: "Today you are being repaid for what you used to do.

٢٩ هَٰذَا كِتَٰبُنَا يَنطِقُ عَلَيْكُم بِٱلْحَقِّۚ إِنَّا كُنَّا
نَسْتَنسِخُ مَا كُنتُمْ تَعْمَلُونَ

29 This Book of Ours speaks about you in truth. We have been transcribing what you have been doing."

٣٠ فَأَمَّا ٱلَّذِينَ ءَامَنُواْ وَعَمِلُواْ ٱلصَّٰلِحَٰتِ
فَيُدْخِلُهُمْ رَبُّهُمْ فِى رَحْمَتِهِۦۚ ذَٰلِكَ هُوَ ٱلْفَوْزُ
ٱلْمُبِينُ

30 As for those who believed and did righteous deeds, their Lord will admit them into His mercy. That is the clear triumph.

٣١ وَأَمَّا ٱلَّذِينَ كَفَرُوٓاْ أَفَلَمْ تَكُنْ ءَايَٰتِى تُتْلَىٰ
عَلَيْكُمْ فَٱسْتَكْبَرْتُمْ وَكُنتُمْ قَوْمًا مُّجْرِمِينَ

31 But as for those who disbelieved: "Were My revelations not recited to you? But you turned arrogant, and were guilty people."

٣٢ وَإِذَا قِيلَ إِنَّ وَعْدَ ٱللَّهِ حَقٌّ وَٱلسَّاعَةُ لَا
رَيْبَ فِيهَا قُلْتُم مَّا نَدْرِى مَا ٱلسَّاعَةُ إِن نَّظُنُّ
إِلَّا ظَنًّا وَمَا نَحْنُ بِمُسْتَيْقِنِينَ

32 And when it was said, "The promise of Allah is true, and of the Hour there is no doubt," you said, "We do not know what the Hour is; we think it is only speculation; we are not convinced."

٣٣ وَبَدَا لَهُمْ سَيِّـَٔاتُ مَا عَمِلُوا۟ وَحَاقَ بِهِم مَّا
كَانُوا۟ بِهِۦ يَسْتَهْزِءُونَ

33 The evils of what they did will become evident to them, and the very thing they ridiculed will haunt them.

٣٤ وَقِيلَ ٱلْيَوْمَ نَنسَىٰكُمْ كَمَا نَسِيتُمْ لِقَآءَ
يَوْمِكُمْ هَٰذَا وَمَأْوَىٰكُمُ ٱلنَّارُ وَمَا لَكُم مِّن
نَّٰصِرِينَ

34 And it will be said, "Today We forget you, as you forgot the encounter of this Day of yours. Your abode is the Fire, and there are no saviors for you.

٣٥ ذَٰلِكُم بِأَنَّكُمُ ٱتَّخَذْتُمْ ءَايَٰتِ ٱللَّهِ هُزُوًا
وَغَرَّتْكُمُ ٱلْحَيَوٰةُ ٱلدُّنْيَا ۚ فَٱلْيَوْمَ لَا يُخْرَجُونَ
مِنْهَا وَلَا هُمْ يُسْتَعْتَبُونَ

35 That is because you took Allah's revelations for a joke, and the worldly life lured you." So today they will not be brought out of it, and they will not be allowed to repent.

٣٦ فَلِلَّهِ ٱلْحَمْدُ رَبِّ ٱلسَّمَٰوَٰتِ وَرَبِّ ٱلْأَرْضِ رَبِّ
ٱلْعَٰلَمِينَ

36 Praise belongs to Allah; Lord of the heavens, Lord of the earth, Lord of humanity.

٣٧ وَلَهُ ٱلْكِبْرِيَآءُ فِى ٱلسَّمَٰوَٰتِ وَٱلْأَرْضِ ۖ وَهُوَ
ٱلْعَزِيزُ ٱلْحَكِيمُ

37 To Him belongs all supremacy in the heavens and the earth. He is the Majestic, the Wise.

46 The Dunes الأحقاف

بِسْمِ ٱللَّهِ ٱلرَّحْمَٰنِ ٱلرَّحِيمِ

In the name of Allah, the Gracious, the Merciful.

١ حمٓ

1 Ha, Meem.

٢ تَنزِيلُ ٱلْكِتَٰبِ مِنَ ٱللَّهِ ٱلْعَزِيزِ ٱلْحَكِيمِ

2 The sending down of the Scripture is from Allah, the Honorable, the Wise.

٣ مَا خَلَقْنَا ٱلسَّمَٰوَٰتِ وَٱلْأَرْضَ وَمَا بَيْنَهُمَآ إِلَّا
بِٱلْحَقِّ وَأَجَلٍ مُّسَمًّى ۚ وَٱلَّذِينَ كَفَرُوا۟ عَمَّآ
أُنذِرُوا۟ مُعْرِضُونَ

3 We did not create the heavens and the earth and what lies between them except with reason, and for a finite period. But the blasphemers

continue to ignore the warnings they receive.

٤ قُلْ أَرَءَيْتُم مَّا تَدْعُونَ مِن دُونِ ٱللَّهِ أَرُونِى
مَاذَا خَلَقُوا۟ مِنَ ٱلْأَرْضِ أَمْ لَهُمْ شِرْكٌ فِى
ٱلسَّمَـٰوَٰتِ ۖ ٱئْتُونِى بِكِتَـٰبٍ مِّن قَبْلِ هَـٰذَآ أَوْ أَثَـٰرَةٍ
مِّنْ عِلْمٍ إِن كُنتُمْ صَـٰدِقِينَ

4 Say, “Have you considered those you worship instead of Allah? Show me which portion of the earth they have created. Or do they own a share of the heavens? Bring me a scripture prior to this one, or some trace of knowledge, if you are truthful.”

٥ وَمَنْ أَضَلُّ مِمَّن يَدْعُوا۟ مِن دُونِ ٱللَّهِ مَن لَّا
يَسْتَجِيبُ لَهُۥٓ إِلَىٰ يَوْمِ ٱلْقِيَـٰمَةِ وَهُمْ عَن دُعَآئِهِمْ
غَـٰفِلُونَ

5 Who is more wrong than him who invokes, besides Allah, those who will not answer him until the Day of Resurrection, and are heedless of their prayers?

٦ وَإِذَا حُشِرَ ٱلنَّاسُ كَانُوا۟ لَهُمْ أَعْدَآءً وَكَانُوا۟
بِعِبَادَتِهِمْ كَـٰفِرِينَ

6 And when humanity is gathered, they will be enemies to them, and will renounce their worship of them.

٧ وَإِذَا تُتْلَىٰ عَلَيْهِمْ ءَايَـٰتُنَا بَيِّنَـٰتٍ قَالَ ٱلَّذِينَ
كَفَرُوا۟ لِلْحَقِّ لَمَّا جَآءَهُمْ هَـٰذَا سِحْرٌ مُّبِينٌ

7 When Our revelations are recited to them, plain and clear, those who disbelieve say of the truth when it has come to them, “This is obviously magic.”

٨ أَمْ يَقُولُونَ ٱفْتَرَىٰهُ ۖ قُلْ إِنِ ٱفْتَرَيْتُهُۥ فَلَا
تَمْلِكُونَ لِى مِنَ ٱللَّهِ شَيْـًٔا ۖ هُوَ أَعْلَمُ بِمَا
تُفِيضُونَ فِيهِ ۖ كَفَىٰ بِهِۦ شَهِيدًۢا بَيْنِى وَبَيْنَكُمْ ۖ
وَهُوَ ٱلْغَفُورُ ٱلرَّحِيمُ

8 Or do they say, “He invented it himself”? Say, “If I invented it myself, there is nothing you can do to protect me from Allah. He knows well what you are engaged in. He is sufficient witness between me and you. He is the Forgiver, the Merciful.”

٩ قُلْ مَا كُنتُ بِدْعًا مِّنَ ٱلرُّسُلِ وَمَآ أَدْرِى مَا
يُفْعَلُ بِى وَلَا بِكُمْ ۖ إِنْ أَتَّبِعُ إِلَّا مَا يُوحَىٰٓ إِلَىَّ
وَمَآ أَنَا۠ إِلَّا نَذِيرٌ مُّبِينٌ

9 Say, “I am not different from the other messengers; and I do not know what will be done with me, or with you. I only follow what is inspired in me, and I am only a clear warner.”

١٠ قُلْ أَرَءَيْتُمْ إِن كَانَ مِنْ عِندِ ٱللَّهِ وَكَفَرْتُم
بِهِۦ وَشَهِدَ شَاهِدٌ مِّنۢ بَنِىٓ إِسْرَٰٓءِيلَ عَلَىٰ مِثْلِهِۦ

10 Say, “Have you considered? What if it is from Allah and you disbelieve in it? A witness from the Children of Israel testified to its like, and has

فَـَٔامَنَ وَٱسْتَكْبَرْتُمْ ۖ إِنَّ ٱللَّهَ لَا يَهْدِى ٱلْقَوْمَ
ٱلظَّٰلِمِينَ

believed, while you turned arrogant. Allah does not guide the unjust people."

١١ وَقَالَ ٱلَّذِينَ كَفَرُوا۟ لِلَّذِينَ ءَامَنُوا۟ لَوْ كَانَ
خَيْرًا مَّا سَبَقُونَآ إِلَيْهِ ۚ وَإِذْ لَمْ يَهْتَدُوا۟ بِهِۦ
فَسَيَقُولُونَ هَٰذَآ إِفْكٌ قَدِيمٌ

11 Those who disbelieve say to those who believe, "If it were anything good, they would not have preceded us to it." And since they were not guided by it, they will say, "This is an ancient lie."

١٢ وَمِن قَبْلِهِۦ كِتَٰبُ مُوسَىٰٓ إِمَامًا وَرَحْمَةً ۚ
وَهَٰذَا كِتَٰبٌ مُّصَدِّقٌ لِّسَانًا عَرَبِيًّا لِّيُنذِرَ ٱلَّذِينَ
ظَلَمُوا۟ وَبُشْرَىٰ لِلْمُحْسِنِينَ

12 And before it was the Book of Moses, a model and a mercy. And this is a confirming Book, in the Arabic language, to warn those who do wrong—and good news for the doers of good.

١٣ إِنَّ ٱلَّذِينَ قَالُوا۟ رَبُّنَا ٱللَّهُ ثُمَّ ٱسْتَقَٰمُوا۟ فَلَا
خَوْفٌ عَلَيْهِمْ وَلَا هُمْ يَحْزَنُونَ

13 Those who say, "Our Lord is Allah," then lead a righteous life—they have nothing to fear, nor shall they grieve.

١٤ أُو۟لَٰٓئِكَ أَصْحَٰبُ ٱلْجَنَّةِ خَٰلِدِينَ فِيهَا جَزَآءًۢ
بِمَا كَانُوا۟ يَعْمَلُونَ

14 These are the inhabitants of Paradise, where they will dwell forever—a reward for what they used to do.

١٥ وَوَصَّيْنَا ٱلْإِنسَٰنَ بِوَٰلِدَيْهِ إِحْسَٰنًا ۖ حَمَلَتْهُ أُمُّهُۥ
كُرْهًا وَوَضَعَتْهُ كُرْهًا ۖ وَحَمْلُهُۥ وَفِصَٰلُهُۥ ثَلَٰثُونَ
شَهْرًا ۚ حَتَّىٰٓ إِذَا بَلَغَ أَشُدَّهُۥ وَبَلَغَ أَرْبَعِينَ سَنَةً
قَالَ رَبِّ أَوْزِعْنِىٓ أَنْ أَشْكُرَ نِعْمَتَكَ ٱلَّتِىٓ أَنْعَمْتَ
عَلَىَّ وَعَلَىٰ وَٰلِدَىَّ وَأَنْ أَعْمَلَ صَٰلِحًا تَرْضَىٰهُ
وَأَصْلِحْ لِى فِى ذُرِّيَّتِىٓ ۖ إِنِّى تُبْتُ إِلَيْكَ وَإِنِّى
مِنَ ٱلْمُسْلِمِينَ

15 We have enjoined upon man kindness to his parents. His mother carried him with difficulty, and delivered him with difficulty. His bearing and weaning takes thirty months. Until, when he has attained his maturity, and has reached forty years, he says, "Lord, enable me to appreciate the blessings You have bestowed upon me and upon my parents, and to act with righteousness, pleasing You. And improve my children for me. I have sincerely repented to You, and I am of those who have surrendered."

١٦ أُوْلَٰٓئِكَ ٱلَّذِينَ نَتَقَبَّلُ عَنۡهُمۡ أَحۡسَنَ مَا عَمِلُواْ
وَنَتَجَاوَزُ عَن سَيِّـَٔاتِهِمۡ فِىٓ أَصۡحَٰبِ ٱلۡجَنَّةِۖ
وَعۡدَ ٱلصِّدۡقِ ٱلَّذِى كَانُواْ يُوعَدُونَ

16 Those are they from whom We accept the best of their deeds, and We overlook their misdeeds, among the dwellers of Paradise—the promise of truth which they are promised.

١٧ وَٱلَّذِى قَالَ لِوَٰلِدَيۡهِ أُفّٖ لَّكُمَآ أَتَعِدَانِنِىٓ أَنۡ
أُخۡرَجَ وَقَدۡ خَلَتِ ٱلۡقُرُونُ مِن قَبۡلِى وَهُمَا
يَسۡتَغِيثَانِ ٱللَّهَ وَيۡلَكَ ءَامِنۡ إِنَّ وَعۡدَ ٱللَّهِ حَقّٞ
فَيَقُولُ مَا هَٰذَآ إِلَّآ أَسَٰطِيرُ ٱلۡأَوَّلِينَ

17 As for him who says to his parents, "Enough of you! Are you promising me that I will be raised up, when generations have passed away before me?" While they cry for Allah's help, "Woe to you! Believe! The promise of Allah is true!" But he says, "These are nothing but tales of the ancients."

١٨ أُوْلَٰٓئِكَ ٱلَّذِينَ حَقَّ عَلَيۡهِمُ ٱلۡقَوۡلُ فِىٓ أُمَمٖ قَدۡ
خَلَتۡ مِن قَبۡلِهِم مِّنَ ٱلۡجِنِّ وَٱلۡإِنسِۖ إِنَّهُمۡ كَانُواْ
خَٰسِرِينَ

18 Those are they upon whom the sentence is justified, among the communities that have passed away before them, of jinn and humans. They are truly losers.

١٩ وَلِكُلّٖ دَرَجَٰتٞ مِّمَّا عَمِلُواْۖ وَلِيُوَفِّيَهُمۡ أَعۡمَٰلَهُمۡ
وَهُمۡ لَا يُظۡلَمُونَ

19 There are degrees for everyone, according to what they have done, and He will repay them for their works in full, and they will not be wronged.

٢٠ وَيَوۡمَ يُعۡرَضُ ٱلَّذِينَ كَفَرُواْ عَلَى ٱلنَّارِ
أَذۡهَبۡتُمۡ طَيِّبَٰتِكُمۡ فِى حَيَاتِكُمُ ٱلدُّنۡيَا
وَٱسۡتَمۡتَعۡتُم بِهَا فَٱلۡيَوۡمَ تُجۡزَوۡنَ عَذَابَ ٱلۡهُونِ
بِمَا كُنتُمۡ تَسۡتَكۡبِرُونَ فِى ٱلۡأَرۡضِ بِغَيۡرِ ٱلۡحَقِّ
وَبِمَا كُنتُمۡ تَفۡسُقُونَ

20 On the Day when the faithless will be paraded before the Fire: "You have squandered your good in your worldly life, and you took pleasure in them. So today you are being repaid with the torment of shame, because of your unjust arrogance on earth, and because you used to sin."

٢١ وَٱذۡكُرۡ أَخَا عَادٍ إِذۡ أَنذَرَ قَوۡمَهُۥ بِٱلۡأَحۡقَافِ
وَقَدۡ خَلَتِ ٱلنُّذُرُ مِنۢ بَيۡنِ يَدَيۡهِ وَمِنۡ خَلۡفِهِۦٓ أَلَّا
تَعۡبُدُوٓاْ إِلَّا ٱللَّهَ إِنِّىٓ أَخَافُ عَلَيۡكُمۡ عَذَابَ يَوۡمٍ
عَظِيمٍ

21 And mention the brother of Aad, as he warned his people at the dunes. Warnings have passed away before him, and after him: "Worship none but Allah; I fear for you the punishment of a tremendous Day."

٢٢ قَالُوٓا۟ أَجِئْتَنَا لِتَأْفِكَنَا عَنْ ءَالِهَتِنَا فَأْتِنَا بِمَا
تَعِدُنَآ إِن كُنتَ مِنَ ٱلصَّـٰدِقِينَ

22 They said, "Did you come to us to divert us from our gods? Then bring us what you threaten us with, if you are being truthful."

٢٣ قَالَ إِنَّمَا ٱلْعِلْمُ عِندَ ٱللَّهِ وَأُبَلِّغُكُم مَّآ أُرْسِلْتُ
بِهِۦ وَلَـٰكِنِّىٓ أَرَىٰكُمْ قَوْمًا تَجْهَلُونَ

23 He said, "The knowledge is only with Allah, and I inform you of what I was sent with; but I see you are an ignorant people."

٢٤ فَلَمَّا رَأَوْهُ عَارِضًا مُّسْتَقْبِلَ أَوْدِيَتِهِمْ قَالُوا۟
هَـٰذَا عَارِضٌ مُّمْطِرُنَا ۚ بَلْ هُوَ مَا ٱسْتَعْجَلْتُم بِهِۦ ۖ
رِيحٌ فِيهَا عَذَابٌ أَلِيمٌ

24 Then, when they saw a cloud approaching their valley, they said, "This is a cloud that will bring us rain." "In fact, it is what you were impatient for: a wind in which is grievous suffering."

٢٥ تُدَمِّرُ كُلَّ شَىْءٍۭ بِأَمْرِ رَبِّهَا فَأَصْبَحُوا۟ لَا يُرَىٰٓ
إِلَّا مَسَـٰكِنُهُمْ ۚ كَذَٰلِكَ نَجْزِى ٱلْقَوْمَ ٱلْمُجْرِمِينَ

25 It will destroy everything by the command of its Lord. And when the morning came upon them, there was nothing to be seen except their dwellings. Thus We requite the guilty people.

٢٦ وَلَقَدْ مَكَّنَّـٰهُمْ فِيمَآ إِن مَّكَّنَّـٰكُمْ فِيهِ وَجَعَلْنَا
لَهُمْ سَمْعًا وَأَبْصَـٰرًا وَأَفْـِٔدَةً فَمَآ أَغْنَىٰ عَنْهُمْ
سَمْعُهُمْ وَلَآ أَبْصَـٰرُهُمْ وَلَآ أَفْـِٔدَتُهُم مِّن شَىْءٍ إِذْ
كَانُوا۟ يَجْحَدُونَ بِـَٔايَـٰتِ ٱللَّهِ وَحَاقَ بِهِم مَّا كَانُوا۟
بِهِۦ يَسْتَهْزِءُونَ

26 We had empowered them in the same way as We empowered you; and We gave them the hearing, and the sight, and the minds. But neither their hearing, nor their sight, nor their minds availed them in any way. That is because they disregarded the revelations of Allah; and so they became surrounded by what they used to ridicule.

٢٧ وَلَقَدْ أَهْلَكْنَا مَا حَوْلَكُم مِّنَ ٱلْقُرَىٰ وَصَرَّفْنَا
ٱلْـَٔايَـٰتِ لَعَلَّهُمْ يَرْجِعُونَ

27 We have destroyed many townships around you, and diversified the signs, so that they may return.

٢٨ فَلَوْلَا نَصَرَهُمُ ٱلَّذِينَ ٱتَّخَذُوا۟ مِن دُونِ ٱللَّهِ
قُرْبَانًا ءَالِهَةًۢ ۖ بَلْ ضَلُّوا۟ عَنْهُمْ ۚ وَذَٰلِكَ إِفْكُهُمْ
وَمَا كَانُوا۟ يَفْتَرُونَ

28 Why then did the idols, whom they worshiped as means of nearness to Allah, not help them? In fact, they abandoned them. It was their lie, a fabrication of their own making.

٢٩ وَإِذْ صَرَفْنَآ إِلَيْكَ نَفَرًا مِّنَ ٱلْجِنِّ يَسْتَمِعُونَ
ٱلْقُرْءَانَ فَلَمَّا حَضَرُوهُ قَالُوٓا۟ أَنصِتُوا۟ ۖ فَلَمَّا
قُضِىَ وَلَّوْا۟ إِلَىٰ قَوْمِهِم مُّنذِرِينَ

29 Recall when We dispatched towards you a number of jinn, to listen to the Quran. When they came in its presence, they said, “Pay attention!” Then, when it was concluded, they rushed to their people, warning them.

٣٠ قَالُوا۟ يَٰقَوْمَنَآ إِنَّا سَمِعْنَا كِتَٰبًا أُنزِلَ مِنۢ بَعْدِ
مُوسَىٰ مُصَدِّقًا لِّمَا بَيْنَ يَدَيْهِ يَهْدِىٓ إِلَى ٱلْحَقِّ
وَإِلَىٰ طَرِيقٍ مُّسْتَقِيمٍ

30 They said, “O our people, we have heard a Scripture, sent down after Moses, confirming what came before it. It guides to the truth, and to a straight path.

٣١ يَٰقَوْمَنَآ أَجِيبُوا۟ دَاعِىَ ٱللَّهِ وَءَامِنُوا۟ بِهِۦ يَغْفِرْ
لَكُم مِّن ذُنُوبِكُمْ وَيُجِرْكُم مِّنْ عَذَابٍ أَلِيمٍ

31 O our people! Answer the caller to Allah, and believe in Him; and He will forgive you your sins, and will save you from a painful punishment.”

٣٢ وَمَن لَّا يُجِبْ دَاعِىَ ٱللَّهِ فَلَيْسَ بِمُعْجِزٍ فِى
ٱلْأَرْضِ وَلَيْسَ لَهُۥ مِن دُونِهِۦٓ أَوْلِيَآءُ ۚ أُو۟لَٰٓئِكَ فِى
ضَلَٰلٍ مُّبِينٍ

32 He who does not answer the caller to Allah will not escape on earth, and has no protectors besides Him. Those are in obvious error.

٣٣ أَوَلَمْ يَرَوْا۟ أَنَّ ٱللَّهَ ٱلَّذِى خَلَقَ ٱلسَّمَٰوَٰتِ
وَٱلْأَرْضَ وَلَمْ يَعْىَ بِخَلْقِهِنَّ بِقَٰدِرٍ عَلَىٰٓ أَن
يُحْۦِىَ ٱلْمَوْتَىٰ ۚ بَلَىٰٓ إِنَّهُۥ عَلَىٰ كُلِّ شَىْءٍ قَدِيرٌ

33 Do they not realize that Allah, who created the heavens and the earth, and was never tired by creating them, is Able to revive the dead? Yes indeed; He is Capable of everything.

٣٤ وَيَوْمَ يُعْرَضُ ٱلَّذِينَ كَفَرُوا۟ عَلَى ٱلنَّارِ أَلَيْسَ
هَٰذَا بِٱلْحَقِّ ۖ قَالُوا۟ بَلَىٰ وَرَبِّنَا ۚ قَالَ فَذُوقُوا۟
ٱلْعَذَابَ بِمَا كُنتُمْ تَكْفُرُونَ

34 On the Day when those who disbelieved are presented to the Fire: “Is this not real?” They will say, “Yes, indeed, by our Lord.” He will say, “Then taste the suffering for having disbelieved.”

٣٥ فَٱصْبِرْ كَمَا صَبَرَ أُو۟لُوا۟ ٱلْعَزْمِ مِنَ ٱلرُّسُلِ وَلَا
تَسْتَعْجِل لَّهُمْ ۚ كَأَنَّهُمْ يَوْمَ يَرَوْنَ مَا يُوعَدُونَ
لَمْ يَلْبَثُوٓا۟ إِلَّا سَاعَةً مِّن نَّهَارٍۭ ۚ بَلَٰغٌ ۚ فَهَلْ يُهْلَكُ إِلَّا
ٱلْقَوْمُ ٱلْفَٰسِقُونَ

35 So be patient, as the messengers with resolve were patient, and do not be hasty regarding them. On the Day when they witness what they are promised, it will seem as if they had lasted only for an hour of a day. A proclamation: Will any be destroyed except the sinful people?

47 Muhammad محمد

بِسْمِ ٱللَّهِ ٱلرَّحْمَٰنِ ٱلرَّحِيمِ

In the name of Allah, the Gracious, the Merciful.

١ ٱلَّذِينَ كَفَرُوا۟ وَصَدُّوا۟ عَن سَبِيلِ ٱللَّهِ أَضَلَّ
أَعْمَٰلَهُمْ

1 Those who disbelieve and repel from the path of Allah—He nullifies their works.

٢ وَٱلَّذِينَ ءَامَنُوا۟ وَعَمِلُوا۟ ٱلصَّٰلِحَٰتِ وَءَامَنُوا۟
بِمَا نُزِّلَ عَلَىٰ مُحَمَّدٍ وَهُوَ ٱلْحَقُّ مِن رَّبِّهِمْ ۙ كَفَّرَ
عَنْهُمْ سَيِّـَٔاتِهِمْ وَأَصْلَحَ بَالَهُمْ

2 While those who believe, and work righteousness, and believe in what was sent down to Muhammad—and it is the truth from their Lord—He remits their sins, and relieves their concerns.

٣ ذَٰلِكَ بِأَنَّ ٱلَّذِينَ كَفَرُوا۟ ٱتَّبَعُوا۟ ٱلْبَٰطِلَ وَأَنَّ
ٱلَّذِينَ ءَامَنُوا۟ ٱتَّبَعُوا۟ ٱلْحَقَّ مِن رَّبِّهِمْ ۚ كَذَٰلِكَ
يَضْرِبُ ٱللَّهُ لِلنَّاسِ أَمْثَٰلَهُمْ

3 That is because those who disbelieve follow falsehoods, while those who believe follow the truth from their Lord. Allah thus cites for the people their examples.

٤ فَإِذَا لَقِيتُمُ ٱلَّذِينَ كَفَرُوا۟ فَضَرْبَ ٱلرِّقَابِ
حَتَّىٰٓ إِذَآ أَثْخَنتُمُوهُمْ فَشُدُّوا۟ ٱلْوَثَاقَ فَإِمَّا مَنًّۢا
بَعْدُ وَإِمَّا فِدَآءً حَتَّىٰ تَضَعَ ٱلْحَرْبُ أَوْزَارَهَا ۚ
ذَٰلِكَ وَلَوْ يَشَآءُ ٱللَّهُ لَٱنتَصَرَ مِنْهُمْ وَلَٰكِن لِّيَبْلُوَا۟
بَعْضَكُم بِبَعْضٍ ۗ وَٱلَّذِينَ قُتِلُوا۟ فِى سَبِيلِ ٱللَّهِ
فَلَن يُضِلَّ أَعْمَٰلَهُمْ

4 When you encounter those who disbelieve, strike at their necks. Then, when you have routed them, bind them firmly. Then, either release them by grace, or by ransom, until war lays down its burdens. Had Allah willed, He could have defeated them Himself, but He thus tests some of you by means of others. As for those who are killed in the way of Allah, He will not let their deeds go to waste.

٥ سَيَهْدِيهِمْ وَيُصْلِحُ بَالَهُمْ

5 He will guide them, and will improve their state of mind.

٦ وَيُدْخِلُهُمُ ٱلْجَنَّةَ عَرَّفَهَا لَهُمْ

6 And will admit them into Paradise, which He has identified for them.

٧ يَٰٓأَيُّهَا ٱلَّذِينَ ءَامَنُوٓا۟ إِن تَنصُرُوا۟ ٱللَّهَ يَنصُرْكُمْ
وَيُثَبِّتْ أَقْدَامَكُمْ

7 O you who believe! If you support Allah, He will support you, and will strengthen your foothold.

٨ وَٱلَّذِينَ كَفَرُوا۟ فَتَعْسًا لَّهُمْ وَأَضَلَّ أَعْمَـٰلَهُمْ

8 But as for those who disbelieve, for them is perdition, and He will waste their deeds.

٩ ذَٰلِكَ بِأَنَّهُمْ كَرِهُوا۟ مَآ أَنزَلَ ٱللَّهُ فَأَحْبَطَ
أَعْمَـٰلَهُمْ

9 That is because they hated what Allah revealed, so He nullified their deeds.

١٠ أَفَلَمْ يَسِيرُوا۟ فِى ٱلْأَرْضِ فَيَنظُرُوا۟ كَيْفَ
كَانَ عَـٰقِبَةُ ٱلَّذِينَ مِن قَبْلِهِمْ ۖ دَمَّرَ ٱللَّهُ عَلَيْهِمْ ۖ
وَلِلْكَـٰفِرِينَ أَمْثَـٰلُهَا

10 Have they not journeyed through the earth and seen the consequences for those before them? Allah poured destruction upon them, and for the unbelievers is something comparable.

١١ ذَٰلِكَ بِأَنَّ ٱللَّهَ مَوْلَى ٱلَّذِينَ ءَامَنُوا۟ وَأَنَّ
ٱلْكَـٰفِرِينَ لَا مَوْلَىٰ لَهُمْ

11 That is because Allah is the Master of those who believe, while the disbelievers have no master.

١٢ إِنَّ ٱللَّهَ يُدْخِلُ ٱلَّذِينَ ءَامَنُوا۟ وَعَمِلُوا۟
ٱلصَّـٰلِحَـٰتِ جَنَّـٰتٍ تَجْرِى مِن تَحْتِهَا ٱلْأَنْهَـٰرُ ۖ
وَٱلَّذِينَ كَفَرُوا۟ يَتَمَتَّعُونَ وَيَأْكُلُونَ كَمَا تَأْكُلُ
ٱلْأَنْعَـٰمُ وَٱلنَّارُ مَثْوًى لَّهُمْ

12 Allah will admit those who believe and do good deeds into gardens beneath which rivers flow. As for those who disbelieve, they enjoy themselves, and eat as cattle eat, and the Fire will be their dwelling.

١٣ وَكَأَيِّن مِّن قَرْيَةٍ هِىَ أَشَدُّ قُوَّةً مِّن قَرْيَتِكَ
ٱلَّتِىٓ أَخْرَجَتْكَ أَهْلَكْنَـٰهُمْ فَلَا نَاصِرَ لَهُمْ

13 How many a town was more powerful than your town which evicted you? We destroyed them, and there was no helper for them.

١٤ أَفَمَن كَانَ عَلَىٰ بَيِّنَةٍ مِّن رَّبِّهِۦ كَمَن زُيِّنَ لَهُۥ
سُوٓءُ عَمَلِهِۦ وَٱتَّبَعُوٓا۟ أَهْوَآءَهُم

14 Is he who stands upon evidence from his Lord, like someone whose evil deed is made to appear good to him? And they follow their own desires?

١٥ مَّثَلُ ٱلْجَنَّةِ ٱلَّتِى وُعِدَ ٱلْمُتَّقُونَ ۖ فِيهَآ أَنْهَـٰرٌ
مِّن مَّآءٍ غَيْرِ ءَاسِنٍ وَأَنْهَـٰرٌ مِّن لَّبَنٍ لَّمْ يَتَغَيَّرْ
طَعْمُهُۥ وَأَنْهَـٰرٌ مِّنْ خَمْرٍ لَّذَّةٍ لِّلشَّـٰرِبِينَ وَأَنْهَـٰرٌ مِّنْ
عَسَلٍ مُّصَفًّى ۖ وَلَهُمْ فِيهَا مِن كُلِّ ٱلثَّمَرَٰتِ
وَمَغْفِرَةٌ مِّن رَّبِّهِمْ ۖ كَمَنْ هُوَ خَـٰلِدٌ فِى ٱلنَّارِ
وَسُقُوا۟ مَآءً حَمِيمًا فَقَطَّعَ أَمْعَآءَهُمْ

15 The likeness of the Garden promised to the righteous: in it are rivers of pure water, and rivers of milk forever fresh, and rivers of wine delightful to the drinkers, and rivers of strained honey. And therein they will have of every fruit, and forgiveness from their Lord. Like one abiding in the Fire forever, and are given to drink boiling water, that cuts-up their bowels?

١٦ وَمِنْهُم مَّن يَسْتَمِعُ إِلَيْكَ حَتَّىٰٓ إِذَا خَرَجُوا۟
مِنْ عِندِكَ قَالُوا۟ لِلَّذِينَ أُوتُوا۟ ٱلْعِلْمَ مَاذَا قَالَ
ءَانِفًا ۚ أُو۟لَـٰٓئِكَ ٱلَّذِينَ طَبَعَ ٱللَّهُ عَلَىٰ قُلُوبِهِمْ
وَٱتَّبَعُوٓا۟ أَهْوَآءَهُمْ

16 Among them are those who listen to you, but when they leave your presence, they say to those given knowledge, “What did he say just now?” Those are they whose hearts Allah has sealed, and they follow their own desires.

١٧ وَٱلَّذِينَ ٱهْتَدَوْا۟ زَادَهُمْ هُدًى وَءَاتَىٰهُمْ
تَقْوَىٰهُمْ

17 As for those who are guided, He increases them in guidance, and He has granted them their righteousness.

١٨ فَهَلْ يَنظُرُونَ إِلَّا ٱلسَّاعَةَ أَن تَأْتِيَهُم بَغْتَةً ۖ
فَقَدْ جَآءَ أَشْرَاطُهَا ۚ فَأَنَّىٰ لَهُمْ إِذَا جَآءَتْهُمْ
ذِكْرَىٰهُمْ

18 Are they just waiting until the Hour comes to them suddenly? Its tokens have already come. But how will they be reminded when it has come to them?

١٩ فَٱعْلَمْ أَنَّهُۥ لَآ إِلَـٰهَ إِلَّا ٱللَّهُ وَٱسْتَغْفِرْ لِذَنۢبِكَ
وَلِلْمُؤْمِنِينَ وَٱلْمُؤْمِنَـٰتِ ۗ وَٱللَّهُ يَعْلَمُ مُتَقَلَّبَكُمْ
وَمَثْوَىٰكُمْ

19 Know that there is no god but Allah, and ask forgiveness for your sin, and for the believing men and believing women. Allah knows your movements, and your resting-place.

٢٠ وَيَقُولُ ٱلَّذِينَ ءَامَنُوا۟ لَوْلَا نُزِّلَتْ سُورَةٌ ۖ فَإِذَآ
أُنزِلَتْ سُورَةٌ مُّحْكَمَةٌ وَذُكِرَ فِيهَا ٱلْقِتَالُ ۙ رَأَيْتَ
ٱلَّذِينَ فِى قُلُوبِهِم مَّرَضٌ يَنظُرُونَ إِلَيْكَ نَظَرَ
ٱلْمَغْشِىِّ عَلَيْهِ مِنَ ٱلْمَوْتِ ۖ فَأَوْلَىٰ لَهُمْ

20 Those who believe say, “If only a chapter is sent down.” Yet when a decisive chapter is sent down, and fighting is mentioned in it, you see those in whose hearts is sickness looking at you with the look of someone fainting at death. So woe to them!

٢١ طَاعَةٌ وَقَوْلٌ مَّعْرُوفٌ ۚ فَإِذَا عَزَمَ ٱلْأَمْرُ فَلَوْ
صَدَقُوا۟ ٱللَّهَ لَكَانَ خَيْرًا لَّهُمْ

21 Obedience and upright speech. Then, when the matter is settled, being true to Allah would have been better for them.

٢٢ فَهَلْ عَسَيْتُمْ إِن تَوَلَّيْتُمْ أَن تُفْسِدُوا۟ فِى
ٱلْأَرْضِ وَتُقَطِّعُوٓا۟ أَرْحَامَكُمْ

22 If you turn away, you are likely to make mischief on earth, and sever your family ties.

٢٣ أُو۟لَـٰٓئِكَ ٱلَّذِينَ لَعَنَهُمُ ٱللَّهُ فَأَصَمَّهُمْ وَأَعْمَىٰٓ
أَبْصَـٰرَهُمْ

23 Those are they whom Allah has cursed. He made them deaf, and blinded their sight.

٢٤ أَفَلَا يَتَدَبَّرُونَ ٱلْقُرْءَانَ أَمْ عَلَىٰ قُلُوبٍ أَقْفَالُهَآ	24 Will they not ponder the Quran? Or are there locks upon their hearts?
٢٥ إِنَّ ٱلَّذِينَ ٱرْتَدُّوا۟ عَلَىٰٓ أَدْبَٰرِهِم مِّنۢ بَعْدِ مَا تَبَيَّنَ لَهُمُ ٱلْهُدَى ۙ ٱلشَّيْطَٰنُ سَوَّلَ لَهُمْ وَأَمْلَىٰ لَهُمْ	25 Those who reverted after the guidance became clear to them—Satan has enticed them, and has given them latitude.
٢٦ ذَٰلِكَ بِأَنَّهُمْ قَالُوا۟ لِلَّذِينَ كَرِهُوا۟ مَا نَزَّلَ ٱللَّهُ سَنُطِيعُكُمْ فِى بَعْضِ ٱلْأَمْرِ ۖ وَٱللَّهُ يَعْلَمُ إِسْرَارَهُمْ	26 That is because they said to those who hated what Allah has revealed, “We will obey you in certain matters.” But Allah knows their secret thoughts.
٢٧ فَكَيْفَ إِذَا تَوَفَّتْهُمُ ٱلْمَلَٰٓئِكَةُ يَضْرِبُونَ وُجُوهَهُمْ وَأَدْبَٰرَهُمْ	27 How about when the angels take them at death, beating their faces and their backs?
٢٨ ذَٰلِكَ بِأَنَّهُمُ ٱتَّبَعُوا۟ مَآ أَسْخَطَ ٱللَّهَ وَكَرِهُوا۟ رِضْوَٰنَهُۥ فَأَحْبَطَ أَعْمَٰلَهُمْ	28 That is because they pursued what displeases Allah, and they disliked His approval, so He nullified their works.
٢٩ أَمْ حَسِبَ ٱلَّذِينَ فِى قُلُوبِهِم مَّرَضٌ أَن لَّن يُخْرِجَ ٱللَّهُ أَضْغَٰنَهُمْ	29 Do those in whose hearts is sickness think that Allah will not expose their malice?
٣٠ وَلَوْ نَشَآءُ لَأَرَيْنَٰكَهُمْ فَلَعَرَفْتَهُم بِسِيمَٰهُمْ ۚ وَلَتَعْرِفَنَّهُمْ فِى لَحْنِ ٱلْقَوْلِ ۚ وَٱللَّهُ يَعْلَمُ أَعْمَٰلَكُمْ	30 Had We willed, We could have shown them to you, and you would have recognized them by their marks. Yet you will recognize them by their tone of speech. And Allah knows your actions.
٣١ وَلَنَبْلُوَنَّكُمْ حَتَّىٰ نَعْلَمَ ٱلْمُجَٰهِدِينَ مِنكُمْ وَٱلصَّٰبِرِينَ وَنَبْلُوَا۟ أَخْبَارَكُمْ	31 We will certainly test you, until We know those among you who strive, and those who are steadfast, and We will test your reactions.
٣٢ إِنَّ ٱلَّذِينَ كَفَرُوا۟ وَصَدُّوا۟ عَن سَبِيلِ ٱللَّهِ وَشَآقُّوا۟ ٱلرَّسُولَ مِنۢ بَعْدِ مَا تَبَيَّنَ لَهُمُ ٱلْهُدَىٰ لَن يَضُرُّوا۟ ٱللَّهَ شَيْـًٔا وَسَيُحْبِطُ أَعْمَٰلَهُمْ	32 Those who disbelieve, and hinder from the path of Allah, and oppose the Messenger after guidance has become clear to them—they will not hurt Allah in the least, but He will nullify their deeds.

٣٣ يَٰٓأَيُّهَا ٱلَّذِينَ ءَامَنُوٓاْ أَطِيعُواْ ٱللَّهَ وَأَطِيعُواْ
ٱلرَّسُولَ وَلَا تُبْطِلُوٓاْ أَعْمَٰلَكُمْ

33 O you who believe! Obey Allah, and obey the Messenger, and do not let your deeds go to waste.

٣٤ إِنَّ ٱلَّذِينَ كَفَرُواْ وَصَدُّواْ عَن سَبِيلِ ٱللَّهِ ثُمَّ
مَاتُواْ وَهُمْ كُفَّارٌ فَلَن يَغْفِرَ ٱللَّهُ لَهُمْ

34 Those who disbelieve, and hinder from Allah's path, and then die as disbelievers—Allah will not forgive them.

٣٥ فَلَا تَهِنُواْ وَتَدْعُوٓاْ إِلَى ٱلسَّلْمِ وَأَنتُمُ
ٱلْأَعْلَوْنَ وَٱللَّهُ مَعَكُمْ وَلَن يَتِرَكُمْ أَعْمَٰلَكُمْ

35 So do not waver and call for peace while you have the upper hand. Allah is with you, and He will not waste your efforts.

٣٦ إِنَّمَا ٱلْحَيَوٰةُ ٱلدُّنْيَا لَعِبٌ وَلَهْوٌ ۚ وَإِن تُؤْمِنُواْ
وَتَتَّقُواْ يُؤْتِكُمْ أُجُورَكُمْ وَلَا يَسْـَٔلْكُمْ أَمْوَٰلَكُمْ

36 The life of this world is nothing but play and pastime. But if you have faith and lead a righteous life, He will grant you your rewards, and He will not ask you for your possessions.

٣٧ إِن يَسْـَٔلْكُمُوهَا فَيُحْفِكُمْ تَبْخَلُواْ وَيُخْرِجْ
أَضْغَٰنَكُمْ

37 Were He to ask you for it, and press you, you would become tightfisted, and He would expose your unwillingness.

٣٨ هَٰٓأَنتُمْ هَٰٓؤُلَآءِ تُدْعَوْنَ لِتُنفِقُواْ فِى سَبِيلِ
ٱللَّهِ فَمِنكُم مَّن يَبْخَلُ ۖ وَمَن يَبْخَلْ فَإِنَّمَا يَبْخَلُ
عَن نَّفْسِهِۦ ۚ وَٱللَّهُ ٱلْغَنِىُّ وَأَنتُمُ ٱلْفُقَرَآءُ ۚ وَإِن
تَتَوَلَّوْاْ يَسْتَبْدِلْ قَوْمًا غَيْرَكُمْ ثُمَّ لَا يَكُونُوٓاْ
أَمْثَٰلَكُم

38 Here you are, being called to spend in the cause of Allah. Among you are those who withhold; but whoever withholds is withholding against his own soul. Allah is the Rich, while you are the needy. And if you turn away, He will replace you with another people, and they will not be like you.

48 Victory الفتح

بِسْمِ ٱللَّهِ ٱلرَّحْمَٰنِ ٱلرَّحِيمِ

In the name of Allah, the Gracious, the Merciful.

١ إِنَّا فَتَحْنَا لَكَ فَتْحًا مُّبِينًا

1 We have granted you a conspicuous victory.

٢ لِّيَغْفِرَ لَكَ ٱللَّهُ مَا تَقَدَّمَ مِن ذَنۢبِكَ وَمَا تَأَخَّرَ
وَيُتِمَّ نِعْمَتَهُۥ عَلَيْكَ وَيَهْدِيَكَ صِرَٰطًا مُّسْتَقِيمًا

2 That Allah may forgive you your sin, past and to come, and complete His favors upon you, and guide you in a straight path.

٣ وَيَنصُرَكَ ٱللَّهُ نَصْرًا عَزِيزًا

3 And help you with an unwavering support.

٤ هُوَ ٱلَّذِىٓ أَنزَلَ ٱلسَّكِينَةَ فِى قُلُوبِ ٱلْمُؤْمِنِينَ
لِيَزْدَادُوٓا۟ إِيمَٰنًا مَّعَ إِيمَٰنِهِمْ ۗ وَلِلَّهِ جُنُودُ ٱلسَّمَٰوَٰتِ
وَٱلْأَرْضِ ۚ وَكَانَ ٱللَّهُ عَلِيمًا حَكِيمًا

4 It is He who sent down tranquility into the hearts of the believers, to add faith to their faith. To Allah belong the forces of the heavens and the earth. Allah is Knowing and Wise.

٥ لِّيُدْخِلَ ٱلْمُؤْمِنِينَ وَٱلْمُؤْمِنَٰتِ جَنَّٰتٍ تَجْرِى
مِن تَحْتِهَا ٱلْأَنْهَٰرُ خَٰلِدِينَ فِيهَا وَيُكَفِّرَ عَنْهُمْ
سَيِّـَٔاتِهِمْ ۚ وَكَانَ ذَٰلِكَ عِندَ ٱللَّهِ فَوْزًا عَظِيمًا

5 He will admit the believers, male and female, into Gardens beneath which rivers flow, to abide therein forever, and He will remit their sins. That, with Allah, is a great triumph.

٦ وَيُعَذِّبَ ٱلْمُنَٰفِقِينَ وَٱلْمُنَٰفِقَٰتِ وَٱلْمُشْرِكِينَ
وَٱلْمُشْرِكَٰتِ ٱلظَّآنِّينَ بِٱللَّهِ ظَنَّ ٱلسَّوْءِ ۚ عَلَيْهِمْ
دَآئِرَةُ ٱلسَّوْءِ ۖ وَغَضِبَ ٱللَّهُ عَلَيْهِمْ وَلَعَنَهُمْ
وَأَعَدَّ لَهُمْ جَهَنَّمَ ۖ وَسَآءَتْ مَصِيرًا

6 And He will punish the hypocrites, male and female, and the idolaters, male and female, those who harbor evil thoughts about Allah. They are surrounded by evil; and Allah is angry with them, and has cursed them, and has prepared for them Hell—a miserable destination.

٧ وَلِلَّهِ جُنُودُ ٱلسَّمَٰوَٰتِ وَٱلْأَرْضِ ۚ وَكَانَ ٱللَّهُ
عَزِيزًا حَكِيمًا

7 To Allah belong the troops of the heavens and the earth. Allah is Mighty and Wise.

٨ إِنَّآ أَرْسَلْنَٰكَ شَٰهِدًا وَمُبَشِّرًا وَنَذِيرًا

8 We sent you as a witness, and a bearer of good news, and a warner.

٩ لِّتُؤْمِنُوا۟ بِٱللَّهِ وَرَسُولِهِۦ وَتُعَزِّرُوهُ وَتُوَقِّرُوهُ
وَتُسَبِّحُوهُ بُكْرَةً وَأَصِيلًا

9 That you may believe in Allah and His Messenger, and support Him, and honor Him, and praise Him morning and evening.

١٠ إِنَّ ٱلَّذِينَ يُبَايِعُونَكَ إِنَّمَا يُبَايِعُونَ ٱللَّهَ يَدُ
ٱللَّهِ فَوْقَ أَيْدِيهِمْ ۚ فَمَن نَّكَثَ فَإِنَّمَا يَنكُثُ عَلَىٰ
نَفْسِهِۦ ۖ وَمَنْ أَوْفَىٰ بِمَا عَٰهَدَ عَلَيْهُ ٱللَّهَ
فَسَيُؤْتِيهِ أَجْرًا عَظِيمًا

10 Those who pledge allegiance to you are pledging allegiance to Allah. The hand of Allah is over their hands. Whoever breaks his pledge breaks it to his own loss. And whoever fulfills his covenant with Allah, He will grant him a great reward.

١١ سَيَقُولُ لَكَ ٱلْمُخَلَّفُونَ مِنَ ٱلْأَعْرَابِ شَغَلَتْنَآ
أَمْوَٰلُنَا وَأَهْلُونَا فَٱسْتَغْفِرْ لَنَا ۚ يَقُولُونَ بِأَلْسِنَتِهِم

11 The Desert-Arabs who remained behind will say to you, "Our belongings and our families have

preoccupied us, so ask forgiveness for us." They say with their tongues what is not in their hearts. Say, "Who can avail you anything against Allah, if He desires loss for you, or desires gain for you?" In fact, Allah is Informed of what you do.

مَّا لَيْسَ فِى قُلُوبِهِمْ ۚ قُلْ فَمَن يَمْلِكُ لَكُم مِّنَ
ٱللَّهِ شَيْـًٔا إِنْ أَرَادَ بِكُمْ ضَرًّا أَوْ أَرَادَ بِكُمْ نَفْعًۢا ۚ
بَلْ كَانَ ٱللَّهُ بِمَا تَعْمَلُونَ خَبِيرًۢا

12 But you thought that the Messenger and the believers will never return to their families, and this seemed fine to your hearts; and you harbored evil thoughts, and were uncivilized people.

١٢ بَلْ ظَنَنتُمْ أَن لَّن يَنقَلِبَ ٱلرَّسُولُ
وَٱلْمُؤْمِنُونَ إِلَىٰٓ أَهْلِيهِمْ أَبَدًا وَزُيِّنَ ذَٰلِكَ فِى
قُلُوبِكُمْ وَظَنَنتُمْ ظَنَّ ٱلسَّوْءِ وَكُنتُمْ قَوْمًۢا بُورًا

13 He who does not believe in Allah and His Messenger—We have prepared for the disbelievers a Blazing Fire.

١٣ وَمَن لَّمْ يُؤْمِنۢ بِٱللَّهِ وَرَسُولِهِۦ فَإِنَّآ أَعْتَدْنَا
لِلْكَٰفِرِينَ سَعِيرًا

14 To Allah belongs the kingdom of the heavens and the earth. He forgives whomever He wills, and He punishes whomever He wills. Allah is Forgiving and Merciful.

١٤ وَلِلَّهِ مُلْكُ ٱلسَّمَٰوَٰتِ وَٱلْأَرْضِ ۚ يَغْفِرُ لِمَن
يَشَآءُ وَيُعَذِّبُ مَن يَشَآءُ ۚ وَكَانَ ٱللَّهُ غَفُورًا
رَّحِيمًا

15 Those who lagged behind will say when you depart to collect the gains, "Let us follow you." They want to change the Word of Allah. Say, "You will not follow us; Allah has said so before." Then they will say, "But you are jealous of us." In fact, they understand only a little.

١٥ سَيَقُولُ ٱلْمُخَلَّفُونَ إِذَا ٱنطَلَقْتُمْ إِلَىٰ مَغَانِمَ
لِتَأْخُذُوهَا ذَرُونَا نَتَّبِعْكُمْ ۖ يُرِيدُونَ أَن يُبَدِّلُوا۟
كَلَٰمَ ٱللَّهِ ۚ قُل لَّن تَتَّبِعُونَا كَذَٰلِكُمْ قَالَ ٱللَّهُ مِن
قَبْلُ ۖ فَسَيَقُولُونَ بَلْ تَحْسُدُونَنَا ۚ بَلْ كَانُوا۟ لَا
يَفْقَهُونَ إِلَّا قَلِيلًا

16 Say to the Desert-Arabs who lagged behind, "You will be called against a people of great might; you will fight them, unless they submit. If you obey, Allah will give you a fine reward. But if you turn away, as you turned away before, He will punish you with a painful punishment."

١٦ قُل لِّلْمُخَلَّفِينَ مِنَ ٱلْأَعْرَابِ سَتُدْعَوْنَ إِلَىٰ
قَوْمٍ أُو۟لِى بَأْسٍ شَدِيدٍ تُقَٰتِلُونَهُمْ أَوْ يُسْلِمُونَ ۖ
فَإِن تُطِيعُوا۟ يُؤْتِكُمُ ٱللَّهُ أَجْرًا حَسَنًا ۖ وَإِن
تَتَوَلَّوْا۟ كَمَا تَوَلَّيْتُم مِّن قَبْلُ يُعَذِّبْكُمْ عَذَابًا
أَلِيمًا

17 There is no blame on the blind, nor any blame on the lame, nor any blame on the sick. Whoever obeys Allah and His Messenger—He will

١٧ لَّيْسَ عَلَى ٱلْأَعْمَىٰ حَرَجٌ وَلَا عَلَى ٱلْأَعْرَجِ
حَرَجٌ وَلَا عَلَى ٱلْمَرِيضِ حَرَجٌ ۗ وَمَن يُطِعِ ٱللَّهَ

وَرَسُولَهُۥ يُدْخِلْهُ جَنَّٰتٍ تَجْرِى مِن تَحْتِهَا ٱلْأَنْهَٰرُ ۖ
وَمَن يَتَوَلَّ يُعَذِّبْهُ عَذَابًا أَلِيمًا

admit him into gardens beneath which rivers flow; but whoever turns away—He will punish him with a painful punishment.

١٨ لَّقَدْ رَضِىَ ٱللَّهُ عَنِ ٱلْمُؤْمِنِينَ إِذْ يُبَايِعُونَكَ
تَحْتَ ٱلشَّجَرَةِ فَعَلِمَ مَا فِى قُلُوبِهِمْ فَأَنزَلَ
ٱلسَّكِينَةَ عَلَيْهِمْ وَأَثَٰبَهُمْ فَتْحًا قَرِيبًا

18 Allah was pleased with the believers, when they pledged allegiance to you under the tree. He knew what was in their hearts, and sent down serenity upon them, and rewarded them with an imminent conquest.

١٩ وَمَغَانِمَ كَثِيرَةً يَأْخُذُونَهَا ۗ وَكَانَ ٱللَّهُ عَزِيزًا
حَكِيمًا

19 And abundant gains for them to capture. Allah is Mighty and Wise.

٢٠ وَعَدَكُمُ ٱللَّهُ مَغَانِمَ كَثِيرَةً تَأْخُذُونَهَا فَعَجَّلَ
لَكُمْ هَٰذِهِۦ وَكَفَّ أَيْدِىَ ٱلنَّاسِ عَنكُمْ وَلِتَكُونَ
ءَايَةً لِّلْمُؤْمِنِينَ وَيَهْدِيَكُمْ صِرَٰطًا مُّسْتَقِيمًا

20 Allah has promised you abundant gains, which you will capture. He has expedited this for you, and has restrained people's hands from you; that it may be a sign to the believers, and that He may guide you on a straight path.

٢١ وَأُخْرَىٰ لَمْ تَقْدِرُوا۟ عَلَيْهَا قَدْ أَحَاطَ ٱللَّهُ بِهَا ۚ
وَكَانَ ٱللَّهُ عَلَىٰ كُلِّ شَىْءٍ قَدِيرًا

21 And other things, of which you were incapable, but Allah has encompassed them. Allah is Capable of everything.

٢٢ وَلَوْ قَٰتَلَكُمُ ٱلَّذِينَ كَفَرُوا۟ لَوَلَّوُا۟ ٱلْأَدْبَٰرَ ثُمَّ لَا
يَجِدُونَ وَلِيًّا وَلَا نَصِيرًا

22 If those who disbelieve had fought you, they would have turned back and fled, then found neither protector nor helper.

٢٣ سُنَّةَ ٱللَّهِ ٱلَّتِى قَدْ خَلَتْ مِن قَبْلُ ۖ وَلَن تَجِدَ
لِسُنَّةِ ٱللَّهِ تَبْدِيلًا

23 It is Allah's pattern, ongoing since the past. You will never find any change in Allah's pattern.

٢٤ وَهُوَ ٱلَّذِى كَفَّ أَيْدِيَهُمْ عَنكُمْ وَأَيْدِيَكُمْ
عَنْهُم بِبَطْنِ مَكَّةَ مِنۢ بَعْدِ أَنْ أَظْفَرَكُمْ عَلَيْهِمْ ۚ
وَكَانَ ٱللَّهُ بِمَا تَعْمَلُونَ بَصِيرًا

24 It is He who withheld their hands from you, and your hands from them, in the valley of Mecca, after giving you advantage over them. Allah is Observer of what you do.

٢٥ هُمُ ٱلَّذِينَ كَفَرُوا۟ وَصَدُّوكُمْ عَنِ ٱلْمَسْجِدِ
ٱلْحَرَامِ وَٱلْهَدْىَ مَعْكُوفًا أَن يَبْلُغَ مَحِلَّهُۥ ۚ وَلَوْلَا

25 It is they who disbelieved, and barred you from the Sacred Mosque, and prevented the offering from reaching its destination. Were it not

رِجَالٌ مُّؤْمِنُونَ وَنِسَآءٌ مُّؤْمِنَٰتٌ لَّمْ تَعْلَمُوهُمْ
أَن تَطَـُٔوهُمْ فَتُصِيبَكُم مِّنْهُم مَّعَرَّةٌۢ بِغَيْرِ عِلْمٍۖ
لِّيُدْخِلَ ٱللَّهُ فِى رَحْمَتِهِۦ مَن يَشَآءُۚ لَوْ تَزَيَّلُوا۟
لَعَذَّبْنَا ٱلَّذِينَ كَفَرُوا۟ مِنْهُمْ عَذَابًا أَلِيمًا

for faithful men and faithful women, whom you did not know, you were about to hurt them, and became guilty of an unintentional crime. Thus Allah admits into His mercy whomever He wills. Had they dispersed, We would have punished those who disbelieved among them with a painful penalty.

٢٦ إِذْ جَعَلَ ٱلَّذِينَ كَفَرُوا۟ فِى قُلُوبِهِمُ ٱلْحَمِيَّةَ
حَمِيَّةَ ٱلْجَٰهِلِيَّةِ فَأَنزَلَ ٱللَّهُ سَكِينَتَهُۥ عَلَىٰ
رَسُولِهِۦ وَعَلَى ٱلْمُؤْمِنِينَ وَأَلْزَمَهُمْ كَلِمَةَ
ٱلتَّقْوَىٰ وَكَانُوٓا۟ أَحَقَّ بِهَا وَأَهْلَهَاۚ وَكَانَ ٱللَّهُ بِكُلِّ
شَىْءٍ عَلِيمًا

26 Those who disbelieved filled their hearts with rage—the rage of the days of ignorance. But Allah sent His serenity down upon His Messenger, and upon the believers, and imposed on them the words of righteousness—of which they were most worthy and deserving. Allah is aware of everything.

٢٧ لَّقَدْ صَدَقَ ٱللَّهُ رَسُولَهُ ٱلرُّءْيَا بِٱلْحَقِّۖ
لَتَدْخُلُنَّ ٱلْمَسْجِدَ ٱلْحَرَامَ إِن شَآءَ ٱللَّهُ ءَامِنِينَ
مُحَلِّقِينَ رُءُوسَكُمْ وَمُقَصِّرِينَ لَا تَخَافُونَۖ
فَعَلِمَ مَا لَمْ تَعْلَمُوا۟ فَجَعَلَ مِن دُونِ ذَٰلِكَ فَتْحًا
قَرِيبًا

27 Allah has fulfilled His Messenger's vision in truth: "You will enter the Sacred Mosque, Allah willing, in security, heads shaven, or hair cut short, not fearing. He knew what you did not know, and has granted besides that an imminent victory."

٢٨ هُوَ ٱلَّذِىٓ أَرْسَلَ رَسُولَهُۥ بِٱلْهُدَىٰ وَدِينِ ٱلْحَقِّ
لِيُظْهِرَهُۥ عَلَى ٱلدِّينِ كُلِّهِۦۚ وَكَفَىٰ بِٱللَّهِ شَهِيدًا

28 It is He who sent His Messenger with the guidance and the religion of truth, to make it prevail over all religions. Allah suffices as Witness.

٢٩ مُّحَمَّدٌ رَّسُولُ ٱللَّهِۚ وَٱلَّذِينَ مَعَهُۥٓ أَشِدَّآءُ
عَلَى ٱلْكُفَّارِ رُحَمَآءُ بَيْنَهُمْۖ تَرَىٰهُمْ رُكَّعًا سُجَّدًا
يَبْتَغُونَ فَضْلًا مِّنَ ٱللَّهِ وَرِضْوَٰنًاۖ سِيمَاهُمْ فِى
وُجُوهِهِم مِّنْ أَثَرِ ٱلسُّجُودِۚ ذَٰلِكَ مَثَلُهُمْ فِى
ٱلتَّوْرَىٰةِۚ وَمَثَلُهُمْ فِى ٱلْإِنجِيلِ كَزَرْعٍ أَخْرَجَ
شَطْـَٔهُۥ فَـَٔازَرَهُۥ فَٱسْتَغْلَظَ فَٱسْتَوَىٰ عَلَىٰ سُوقِهِۦ
يُعْجِبُ ٱلزُّرَّاعَ لِيَغِيظَ بِهِمُ ٱلْكُفَّارَۗ وَعَدَ ٱللَّهُ

29 Muhammad is the Messenger of Allah. Those with him are stern against the disbelievers, yet compassionate amongst themselves. You see them kneeling, prostrating, seeking blessings from Allah and approval. Their marks are on their faces from the effects of prostration. Such is their description in the Torah, and their description in the Gospel: like a plant that sprouts, becomes strong, grows thick, and rests on its stem, impressing the

ٱلَّذِينَ ءَامَنُوا۟ وَعَمِلُوا۟ ٱلصَّٰلِحَٰتِ مِنْهُم مَّغْفِرَةً وَأَجْرًا عَظِيمًۢا	farmers. Through them He enrages the disbelievers. Allah has promised those among them who believe and do good deeds forgiveness and a great reward.

49 The Chambers الحجرات

بِسْمِ ٱللَّهِ ٱلرَّحْمَٰنِ ٱلرَّحِيمِ	In the name of Allah, the Gracious, the Merciful.
١ يَٰٓأَيُّهَا ٱلَّذِينَ ءَامَنُوا۟ لَا تُقَدِّمُوا۟ بَيْنَ يَدَىِ ٱللَّهِ وَرَسُولِهِۦ ۖ وَٱتَّقُوا۟ ٱللَّهَ ۚ إِنَّ ٱللَّهَ سَمِيعٌ عَلِيمٌ	1 O you who believe! Do not place your opinions above that of Allah and His Messenger, and fear Allah. Allah is Hearing and Knowing.
٢ يَٰٓأَيُّهَا ٱلَّذِينَ ءَامَنُوا۟ لَا تَرْفَعُوٓا۟ أَصْوَٰتَكُمْ فَوْقَ صَوْتِ ٱلنَّبِىِّ وَلَا تَجْهَرُوا۟ لَهُۥ بِٱلْقَوْلِ كَجَهْرِ بَعْضِكُمْ لِبَعْضٍ أَن تَحْبَطَ أَعْمَٰلُكُمْ وَأَنتُمْ لَا تَشْعُرُونَ	2 O you who believe! Do not raise your voices above the voice of the Prophet, and do not speak loudly to him, as you speak loudly to one another, lest your works be in vain without you realizing.
٣ إِنَّ ٱلَّذِينَ يَغُضُّونَ أَصْوَٰتَهُمْ عِندَ رَسُولِ ٱللَّهِ أُو۟لَٰٓئِكَ ٱلَّذِينَ ٱمْتَحَنَ ٱللَّهُ قُلُوبَهُمْ لِلتَّقْوَىٰ ۚ لَهُم مَّغْفِرَةٌ وَأَجْرٌ عَظِيمٌ	3 Those who lower their voices before Allah's Messenger—those are they whose hearts Allah has tested for piety. They will have forgiveness and a great reward.
٤ إِنَّ ٱلَّذِينَ يُنَادُونَكَ مِن وَرَآءِ ٱلْحُجُرَٰتِ أَكْثَرُهُمْ لَا يَعْقِلُونَ	4 Those who call you from behind the chambers—most of them do not understand.
٥ وَلَوْ أَنَّهُمْ صَبَرُوا۟ حَتَّىٰ تَخْرُجَ إِلَيْهِمْ لَكَانَ خَيْرًا لَّهُمْ ۚ وَٱللَّهُ غَفُورٌ رَّحِيمٌ	5 Had they remained patient until you came out to them, it would have been better for them. But Allah is Forgiving and Merciful.
٦ يَٰٓأَيُّهَا ٱلَّذِينَ ءَامَنُوٓا۟ إِن جَآءَكُمْ فَاسِقٌۢ بِنَبَإٍ فَتَبَيَّنُوٓا۟ أَن تُصِيبُوا۟ قَوْمًۢا بِجَهَٰلَةٍ فَتُصْبِحُوا۟ عَلَىٰ مَا فَعَلْتُمْ نَٰدِمِينَ	6 O you who believe! If a troublemaker brings you any news, investigate, lest you harm people out of ignorance, and you become regretful for what you have done.
٧ وَٱعْلَمُوٓا۟ أَنَّ فِيكُمْ رَسُولَ ٱللَّهِ ۚ لَوْ يُطِيعُكُمْ فِى كَثِيرٍ مِّنَ ٱلْأَمْرِ لَعَنِتُّمْ وَلَٰكِنَّ ٱللَّهَ حَبَّبَ	7 And know that among you is the Messenger of Allah. Had he obeyed you in many things, you would have

إِلَيْكُمُ ٱلْإِيمَٰنَ وَزَيَّنَهُۥ فِى قُلُوبِكُمْ وَكَرَّهَ إِلَيْكُمُ
ٱلْكُفْرَ وَٱلْفُسُوقَ وَٱلْعِصْيَانَ ۚ أُو۟لَٰٓئِكَ هُمُ
ٱلرَّٰشِدُونَ

suffered hardship. But Allah has given you the love of faith, and adorned it in your hearts, and made disbelief, mischief, and rebellion hateful to you. These are the rightly guided.

٨ فَضْلًا مِّنَ ٱللَّهِ وَنِعْمَةً ۚ وَٱللَّهُ عَلِيمٌ حَكِيمٌ

8 A Grace and Favor from Allah. Allah is Knowing and Wise.

٩ وَإِن طَآئِفَتَانِ مِنَ ٱلْمُؤْمِنِينَ ٱقْتَتَلُوا۟
فَأَصْلِحُوا۟ بَيْنَهُمَا ۖ فَإِنۢ بَغَتْ إِحْدَىٰهُمَا عَلَى
ٱلْأُخْرَىٰ فَقَٰتِلُوا۟ ٱلَّتِى تَبْغِى حَتَّىٰ تَفِىٓءَ إِلَىٰٓ
أَمْرِ ٱللَّهِ ۚ فَإِن فَآءَتْ فَأَصْلِحُوا۟ بَيْنَهُمَا بِٱلْعَدْلِ
وَأَقْسِطُوٓا۟ ۖ إِنَّ ٱللَّهَ يُحِبُّ ٱلْمُقْسِطِينَ

9 If two groups of believers fight each other, reconcile between them. But if one group aggresses against the other, fight the aggressing group until it complies with Allah's command. Once it has complied, reconcile between them with justice, and be equitable. Allah loves the equitable.

١٠ إِنَّمَا ٱلْمُؤْمِنُونَ إِخْوَةٌ فَأَصْلِحُوا۟ بَيْنَ
أَخَوَيْكُمْ ۚ وَٱتَّقُوا۟ ٱللَّهَ لَعَلَّكُمْ تُرْحَمُونَ

10 The believers are brothers, so reconcile between your brothers, and remain conscious of Allah, so that you may receive mercy.

١١ يَٰٓأَيُّهَا ٱلَّذِينَ ءَامَنُوا۟ لَا يَسْخَرْ قَوْمٌ مِّن قَوْمٍ
عَسَىٰٓ أَن يَكُونُوا۟ خَيْرًا مِّنْهُمْ وَلَا نِسَآءٌ مِّن
نِّسَآءٍ عَسَىٰٓ أَن يَكُنَّ خَيْرًا مِّنْهُنَّ ۖ وَلَا تَلْمِزُوٓا۟
أَنفُسَكُمْ وَلَا تَنَابَزُوا۟ بِٱلْأَلْقَٰبِ ۖ بِئْسَ ٱلِٱسْمُ
ٱلْفُسُوقُ بَعْدَ ٱلْإِيمَٰنِ ۚ وَمَن لَّمْ يَتُبْ فَأُو۟لَٰٓئِكَ هُمُ
ٱلظَّٰلِمُونَ

11 O you who believe! No people shall ridicule other people, for they may be better than they. Nor shall any women ridicule other women, for they may be better than they. Nor shall you slander one another, nor shall you insult one another with names. Evil is the return to wickedness after having attained faith. Whoever does not repent—these are the wrongdoers.

١٢ يَٰٓأَيُّهَا ٱلَّذِينَ ءَامَنُوا۟ ٱجْتَنِبُوا۟ كَثِيرًا مِّنَ ٱلظَّنِّ
إِنَّ بَعْضَ ٱلظَّنِّ إِثْمٌ ۖ وَلَا تَجَسَّسُوا۟ وَلَا يَغْتَب
بَّعْضُكُم بَعْضًا ۚ أَيُحِبُّ أَحَدُكُمْ أَن يَأْكُلَ لَحْمَ
أَخِيهِ مَيْتًا فَكَرِهْتُمُوهُ ۚ وَٱتَّقُوا۟ ٱللَّهَ ۚ إِنَّ ٱللَّهَ
تَوَّابٌ رَّحِيمٌ

12 O you who believe! Avoid most suspicion—some suspicion is sinful. And do not spy on one another, nor backbite one another. Would any of you like to eat the flesh of his dead brother? You would detest it. So remain mindful of Allah. Allah is Most Relenting, Most Merciful.

١٣ يَٰٓأَيُّهَا ٱلنَّاسُ إِنَّا خَلَقْنَٰكُم مِّن ذَكَرٍ وَأُنثَىٰ وَجَعَلْنَٰكُمْ شُعُوبًا وَقَبَآئِلَ لِتَعَارَفُوٓا۟ ۚ إِنَّ أَكْرَمَكُمْ عِندَ ٱللَّهِ أَتْقَىٰكُمْ ۚ إِنَّ ٱللَّهَ عَلِيمٌ خَبِيرٌ

13 O people! We created you from a male and a female, and made you races and tribes, that you may know one another. The best among you in the sight of Allah is the most righteous. Allah is All-Knowing, Well-Experienced.

١٤ قَالَتِ ٱلْأَعْرَابُ ءَامَنَّا ۖ قُل لَّمْ تُؤْمِنُوا۟ وَلَٰكِن قُولُوٓا۟ أَسْلَمْنَا وَلَمَّا يَدْخُلِ ٱلْإِيمَٰنُ فِى قُلُوبِكُمْ ۖ وَإِن تُطِيعُوا۟ ٱللَّهَ وَرَسُولَهُۥ لَا يَلِتْكُم مِّنْ أَعْمَٰلِكُمْ شَيْـًٔا ۚ إِنَّ ٱللَّهَ غَفُورٌ رَّحِيمٌ

14 The Desert-Arabs say, “We have believed.” Say, “You have not believed; but say, ‘We have submitted,’ for faith has not yet entered into your hearts. But if you obey Allah and His Messenger, He will not diminish any of your deeds. Allah is Forgiving and Merciful.”

١٥ إِنَّمَا ٱلْمُؤْمِنُونَ ٱلَّذِينَ ءَامَنُوا۟ بِٱللَّهِ وَرَسُولِهِۦ ثُمَّ لَمْ يَرْتَابُوا۟ وَجَٰهَدُوا۟ بِأَمْوَٰلِهِمْ وَأَنفُسِهِمْ فِى سَبِيلِ ٱللَّهِ ۚ أُو۟لَٰٓئِكَ هُمُ ٱلصَّٰدِقُونَ

15 The believers are those who believe in Allah and His Messenger, and then have not doubted, and strive for Allah’s cause with their wealth and their persons. These are the sincere.

١٦ قُلْ أَتُعَلِّمُونَ ٱللَّهَ بِدِينِكُمْ وَٱللَّهُ يَعْلَمُ مَا فِى ٱلسَّمَٰوَٰتِ وَمَا فِى ٱلْأَرْضِ ۚ وَٱللَّهُ بِكُلِّ شَىْءٍ عَلِيمٌ

16 Say, “Are you going to teach Allah about your religion, when Allah knows everything in the heavens and the earth, and Allah is aware of all things?”

١٧ يَمُنُّونَ عَلَيْكَ أَنْ أَسْلَمُوا۟ ۖ قُل لَّا تَمُنُّوا۟ عَلَىَّ إِسْلَٰمَكُم ۖ بَلِ ٱللَّهُ يَمُنُّ عَلَيْكُمْ أَنْ هَدَىٰكُمْ لِلْإِيمَٰنِ إِن كُنتُمْ صَٰدِقِينَ

17 They regarded it a favor to you that they have submitted. Say, “Do not consider your submission a favor to me; it is Allah who has done you a favor by guiding you to the faith, if you are sincere.”

١٨ إِنَّ ٱللَّهَ يَعْلَمُ غَيْبَ ٱلسَّمَٰوَٰتِ وَٱلْأَرْضِ ۚ وَٱللَّهُ بَصِيرٌۢ بِمَا تَعْمَلُونَ

18 Allah knows the secrets of the heavens and the earth, and Allah is seeing of everything you do.

50 Qaf ق

بِسْمِ ٱللَّهِ ٱلرَّحْمَٰنِ ٱلرَّحِيمِ

In the name of Allah, the Gracious, the Merciful.

١ قٓ ۚ وَٱلْقُرْءَانِ ٱلْمَجِيدِ

1 Qaf. By the Glorious Quran.

٢ بَلْ عَجِبُوٓا۟ أَن جَآءَهُم مُّنذِرٌ مِّنْهُمْ فَقَالَ
ٱلْكَٰفِرُونَ هَٰذَا شَىْءٌ عَجِيبٌ

2 They marveled that a warner has come to them from among them. The disbelievers say, “This is something strange.

٣ أَءِذَا مِتْنَا وَكُنَّا تُرَابًا ۖ ذَٰلِكَ رَجْعٌۢ بَعِيدٌ

3 When we have died and become dust? This is a farfetched return.”

٤ قَدْ عَلِمْنَا مَا تَنقُصُ ٱلْأَرْضُ مِنْهُمْ ۖ وَعِندَنَا
كِتَٰبٌ حَفِيظٌۢ

4 We know what the earth consumes of them, and with Us is a comprehensive book.

٥ بَلْ كَذَّبُوا۟ بِٱلْحَقِّ لَمَّا جَآءَهُمْ فَهُمْ فِىٓ أَمْرٍ
مَّرِيجٍ

5 But they denied the truth when it has come to them, so they are in a confused state.

٦ أَفَلَمْ يَنظُرُوٓا۟ إِلَى ٱلسَّمَآءِ فَوْقَهُمْ كَيْفَ بَنَيْنَٰهَا
وَزَيَّنَّٰهَا وَمَا لَهَا مِن فُرُوجٍ

6 Have they not observed the sky above them, how We constructed it, and decorated it, and it has no cracks?

٧ وَٱلْأَرْضَ مَدَدْنَٰهَا وَأَلْقَيْنَا فِيهَا رَوَٰسِىَ وَأَنۢبَتْنَا
فِيهَا مِن كُلِّ زَوْجٍۭ بَهِيجٍ

7 And the earth, how We spread it out, and set on it mountains, and grew in it all kinds of delightful pairs?

٨ تَبْصِرَةً وَذِكْرَىٰ لِكُلِّ عَبْدٍ مُّنِيبٍ

8 A lesson and a reminder for every penitent worshiper.

٩ وَنَزَّلْنَا مِنَ ٱلسَّمَآءِ مَآءً مُّبَٰرَكًا فَأَنۢبَتْنَا بِهِۦ
جَنَّٰتٍ وَحَبَّ ٱلْحَصِيدِ

9 And We brought down from the sky blessed water, and produced with it gardens and grain to harvest.

١٠ وَٱلنَّخْلَ بَاسِقَٰتٍ لَّهَا طَلْعٌ نَّضِيدٌ

10 And the soaring palm trees, with clustered dates.

١١ رِّزْقًا لِّلْعِبَادِ ۖ وَأَحْيَيْنَا بِهِۦ بَلْدَةً مَّيْتًا ۚ كَذَٰلِكَ
ٱلْخُرُوجُ

11 As sustenance for the servants. And We revive thereby a dead town. Likewise is the resurrection.

١٢ كَذَّبَتْ قَبْلَهُمْ قَوْمُ نُوحٍ وَأَصْحَٰبُ ٱلرَّسِّ
وَثَمُودُ

12 Before them the people of Noah denied the truth, and so did the dwellers of Russ, and Thamood.

١٣ وَعَادٌ وَفِرْعَوْنُ وَإِخْوَٰنُ لُوطٍ

13 And Aad, and Pharaoh, and the brethren of Lot.

١٤ وَأَصْحَٰبُ ٱلْأَيْكَةِ وَقَوْمُ تُبَّعٍ ۚ كُلٌّ كَذَّبَ
ٱلرُّسُلَ فَحَقَّ وَعِيدِ

14 And the Dwellers of the Woods, and the people of Tubba. They all rejected the messengers, so My threat came true.

١٥ أَفَعَيِينَا بِٱلْخَلْقِ ٱلْأَوَّلِ ۚ بَلْ هُمْ فِى لَبْسٍ مِّنْ خَلْقٍ جَدِيدٍ

15 Were We fatigued by the first creation? But they are in doubt of a new creation.

١٦ وَلَقَدْ خَلَقْنَا ٱلْإِنسَٰنَ وَنَعْلَمُ مَا تُوَسْوِسُ بِهِۦ نَفْسُهُۥ ۖ وَنَحْنُ أَقْرَبُ إِلَيْهِ مِنْ حَبْلِ ٱلْوَرِيدِ

16 We created the human being, and We know what his soul whispers to him. We are nearer to him than his jugular vein.

١٧ إِذْ يَتَلَقَّى ٱلْمُتَلَقِّيَانِ عَنِ ٱلْيَمِينِ وَعَنِ ٱلشِّمَالِ قَعِيدٌ

17 As the two receivers receive, seated to the right and to the left.

١٨ مَّا يَلْفِظُ مِن قَوْلٍ إِلَّا لَدَيْهِ رَقِيبٌ عَتِيدٌ

18 Not a word does he utter, but there is a watcher by him, ready.

١٩ وَجَآءَتْ سَكْرَةُ ٱلْمَوْتِ بِٱلْحَقِّ ۖ ذَٰلِكَ مَا كُنتَ مِنْهُ تَحِيدُ

19 The daze of death has come in truth: "This is what you tried to evade."

٢٠ وَنُفِخَ فِى ٱلصُّورِ ۚ ذَٰلِكَ يَوْمُ ٱلْوَعِيدِ

20 And the Trumpet is blown: "This is the Promised Day."

٢١ وَجَآءَتْ كُلُّ نَفْسٍ مَّعَهَا سَآئِقٌ وَشَهِيدٌ

21 And every soul will come forward, accompanied by a driver and a witness.

٢٢ لَّقَدْ كُنتَ فِى غَفْلَةٍ مِّنْ هَٰذَا فَكَشَفْنَا عَنكَ غِطَآءَكَ فَبَصَرُكَ ٱلْيَوْمَ حَدِيدٌ

22 "You were in neglect of this, so We lifted your screen from you, and your vision today is keen."

٢٣ وَقَالَ قَرِينُهُۥ هَٰذَا مَا لَدَىَّ عَتِيدٌ

23 And His escort will say, "This is what I have ready with me."

٢٤ أَلْقِيَا فِى جَهَنَّمَ كُلَّ كَفَّارٍ عَنِيدٍ

24 "Throw into Hell every stubborn disbeliever.

٢٥ مَّنَّاعٍ لِّلْخَيْرِ مُعْتَدٍ مُّرِيبٍ

25 Preventer of good, aggressor, doubter.

٢٦ ٱلَّذِى جَعَلَ مَعَ ٱللَّهِ إِلَٰهًا ءَاخَرَ فَأَلْقِيَاهُ فِى ٱلْعَذَابِ ٱلشَّدِيدِ

26 Who fabricated another god with Allah; toss him into the intense agony."

٢٧ قَالَ قَرِينُهُۥ رَبَّنَا مَآ أَطْغَيْتُهُۥ وَلَٰكِن كَانَ فِى ضَلَٰلٍ بَعِيدٍ

27 His escort will say, "Our Lord, I did not make him rebel, but he was far astray."

٢٨ قَالَ لَا تَخْتَصِمُوا۟ لَدَىَّ وَقَدْ قَدَّمْتُ إِلَيْكُم بِٱلْوَعِيدِ

28 He will say, "Do not feud in My presence—I had warned you in advance.

٢٩ مَا يُبَدَّلُ ٱلْقَوْلُ لَدَىَّ وَمَآ أَنَا۠ بِظَلَّٰمٍ لِّلْعَبِيدِ

29 The decree from Me will not be changed, and I am not unjust to the servants."

٣٠ يَوْمَ نَقُولُ لِجَهَنَّمَ هَلِ ٱمْتَلَأْتِ وَتَقُولُ هَلْ
مِن مَّزِيدٍ

30 On the Day when We will say to Hell, "Are you full?" And it will say, "Are there any more?"

٣١ وَأُزْلِفَتِ ٱلْجَنَّةُ لِلْمُتَّقِينَ غَيْرَ بَعِيدٍ

31 And Paradise will be brought closer to the pious, not far away.

٣٢ هَٰذَا مَا تُوعَدُونَ لِكُلِّ أَوَّابٍ حَفِيظٍ

32 "This is what you were promised—for every careful penitent.

٣٣ مَّنْ خَشِىَ ٱلرَّحْمَٰنَ بِٱلْغَيْبِ وَجَآءَ بِقَلْبٍ
مُّنِيبٍ

33 Who inwardly feared the Most Gracious, and came with a repentant heart.

٣٤ ٱدْخُلُوهَا بِسَلَٰمٍ ۖ ذَٰلِكَ يَوْمُ ٱلْخُلُودِ

34 Enter it in peace. This is the Day of Eternity."

٣٥ لَهُم مَّا يَشَآءُونَ فِيهَا وَلَدَيْنَا مَزِيدٌ

35 Therein they will have whatever they desire—and We have even more.

٣٦ وَكَمْ أَهْلَكْنَا قَبْلَهُم مِّن قَرْنٍ هُمْ أَشَدُّ مِنْهُم
بَطْشًا فَنَقَّبُوا۟ فِى ٱلْبِلَٰدِ هَلْ مِن مَّحِيصٍ

36 How many generations before them, who were more powerful than they, did We destroy? They explored the lands—was there any escape?

٣٧ إِنَّ فِى ذَٰلِكَ لَذِكْرَىٰ لِمَن كَانَ لَهُۥ قَلْبٌ أَوْ
أَلْقَى ٱلسَّمْعَ وَهُوَ شَهِيدٌ

37 In that is a reminder for whoever possesses a heart, or cares to listen and witness.

٣٨ وَلَقَدْ خَلَقْنَا ٱلسَّمَٰوَٰتِ وَٱلْأَرْضَ وَمَا بَيْنَهُمَا
فِى سِتَّةِ أَيَّامٍ وَمَا مَسَّنَا مِن لُّغُوبٍ

38 We created the heavens and the earth and what is between them in six days, and no fatigue touched Us.

٣٩ فَٱصْبِرْ عَلَىٰ مَا يَقُولُونَ وَسَبِّحْ بِحَمْدِ رَبِّكَ
قَبْلَ طُلُوعِ ٱلشَّمْسِ وَقَبْلَ ٱلْغُرُوبِ

39 So endure what they say, and proclaim the praises of your Lord before the rising of the sun, and before sunset.

٤٠ وَمِنَ ٱلَّيْلِ فَسَبِّحْهُ وَأَدْبَٰرَ ٱلسُّجُودِ

40 And glorify Him during the night, and at the end of devotions.

٤١ وَٱسْتَمِعْ يَوْمَ يُنَادِ ٱلْمُنَادِ مِن مَّكَانٍ قَرِيبٍ

41 And listen for the Day when the caller calls from a nearby place.

٤٢ يَوْمَ يَسْمَعُونَ ٱلصَّيْحَةَ بِٱلْحَقِّ ۚ ذَٰلِكَ يَوْمُ
ٱلْخُرُوجِ

42 The Day when they will hear the Shout in all truth. That is the Day of Emergence.

٤٣ إِنَّا نَحْنُ نُحْيِۦ وَنُمِيتُ وَإِلَيْنَا ٱلْمَصِيرُ

43 It is We who control life and death, and to Us is the destination.

٤٤ يَوْمَ تَشَقَّقُ ٱلْأَرْضُ عَنْهُمْ سِرَاعًاۚ ذَٰلِكَ حَشْرٌ
عَلَيْنَا يَسِيرٌ

44 The Day when the earth will crack for them at once. That is an easy gathering for Us.

٤٥ نَّحْنُ أَعْلَمُ بِمَا يَقُولُونَۖ وَمَآ أَنتَ عَلَيْهِم
بِجَبَّارٍۖ فَذَكِّرْ بِٱلْقُرْءَانِ مَن يَخَافُ وَعِيدِ

45 We are fully aware of what they say, and you are not a dictator over them. So remind by the Quran whoever fears My warning.

51 The Spreaders الذاريات

بِسْمِ ٱللَّهِ ٱلرَّحْمَٰنِ ٱلرَّحِيمِ

In the name of Allah, the Gracious, the Merciful.

١ وَٱلذَّٰرِيَٰتِ ذَرْوًا

1 By the spreaders spreading.

٢ فَٱلْحَٰمِلَٰتِ وِقْرًا

2 And those carrying loads.

٣ فَٱلْجَٰرِيَٰتِ يُسْرًا

3 And those moving gently.

٤ فَٱلْمُقَسِّمَٰتِ أَمْرًا

4 And those distributing as commanded.

٥ إِنَّمَا تُوعَدُونَ لَصَادِقٌ

5 What you are promised is true.

٦ وَإِنَّ ٱلدِّينَ لَوَٰقِعٌ

6 Judgment will take place.

٧ وَٱلسَّمَآءِ ذَاتِ ٱلْحُبُكِ

7 By the sky that is woven.

٨ إِنَّكُمْ لَفِى قَوْلٍ مُّخْتَلِفٍ

8 You differ in what you say.

٩ يُؤْفَكُ عَنْهُ مَنْ أُفِكَ

9 Averted from it is he who is averted.

١٠ قُتِلَ ٱلْخَرَّٰصُونَ

10 Perish the imposters.

١١ ٱلَّذِينَ هُمْ فِى غَمْرَةٍ سَاهُونَ

11 Those who are dazed in ignorance.

١٢ يَسْـَٔلُونَ أَيَّانَ يَوْمُ ٱلدِّينِ

12 They ask, “When is the Day of Judgment?”

١٣ يَوْمَ هُمْ عَلَى ٱلنَّارِ يُفْتَنُونَ

13 The Day they are presented to the Fire.

١٤ ذُوقُوا۟ فِتْنَتَكُمْ هَٰذَا ٱلَّذِى كُنتُم بِهِۦ
تَسْتَعْجِلُونَ

14 "Taste your ordeal. This is what
you used to challenge."

١٥ إِنَّ ٱلْمُتَّقِينَ فِى جَنَّٰتٍ وَعُيُونٍ

15 But the pious are amidst gardens
and springs.

١٦ ءَاخِذِينَ مَآ ءَاتَىٰهُمْ رَبُّهُمْ ۚ إِنَّهُمْ كَانُوا۟ قَبْلَ
ذَٰلِكَ مُحْسِنِينَ

16 Receiving what their Lord has
given them. They were virtuous
before that.

١٧ كَانُوا۟ قَلِيلًا مِّنَ ٱلَّيْلِ مَا يَهْجَعُونَ

17 They used to sleep a little at night.

١٨ وَبِٱلْأَسْحَارِ هُمْ يَسْتَغْفِرُونَ

18 And at dawn, they would pray for
pardon.

١٩ وَفِىٓ أَمْوَٰلِهِمْ حَقٌّ لِّلسَّآئِلِ وَٱلْمَحْرُومِ

19 And in their wealth, there was a
share for the beggar and the
deprived.

٢٠ وَفِى ٱلْأَرْضِ ءَايَٰتٌ لِّلْمُوقِنِينَ

20 And on earth are signs for the
convinced.

٢١ وَفِىٓ أَنفُسِكُمْ ۚ أَفَلَا تُبْصِرُونَ

21 And within yourselves. Do you not
see?

٢٢ وَفِى ٱلسَّمَآءِ رِزْقُكُمْ وَمَا تُوعَدُونَ

22 And in the heaven is your
livelihood, and what you are
promised.

٢٣ فَوَرَبِّ ٱلسَّمَآءِ وَٱلْأَرْضِ إِنَّهُۥ لَحَقٌّ مِّثْلَ مَآ
أَنَّكُمْ تَنطِقُونَ

23 By the Lord of the heaven and the
earth, it is as true as the fact that
you speak.

٢٤ هَلْ أَتَىٰكَ حَدِيثُ ضَيْفِ إِبْرَٰهِيمَ ٱلْمُكْرَمِينَ

24 Has the story of Abraham's
honorable guests reached you?

٢٥ إِذْ دَخَلُوا۟ عَلَيْهِ فَقَالُوا۟ سَلَٰمًا ۖ قَالَ سَلَٰمٌ قَوْمٌ
مُّنكَرُونَ

25 When they entered upon him, they
said, "Peace." He said, "Peace,
strangers."

٢٦ فَرَاغَ إِلَىٰٓ أَهْلِهِۦ فَجَآءَ بِعِجْلٍ سَمِينٍ

26 Then he slipped away to his
family, and brought a fatted calf.

٢٧ فَقَرَّبَهُۥٓ إِلَيْهِمْ قَالَ أَلَا تَأْكُلُونَ

27 He set it before them. He said,
"Will you not eat?"

٢٨ فَأَوْجَسَ مِنْهُمْ خِيفَةً ۖ قَالُوا۟ لَا تَخَفْ ۖ
وَبَشَّرُوهُ بِغُلَٰمٍ عَلِيمٍ

28 And he harbored fear of them.
They said, "Do not fear," and they
announced to him the good news of
a knowledgeable boy.

٢٩ فَأَقْبَلَتِ ٱمْرَأَتُهُۥ فِى صَرَّةٍ فَصَكَّتْ وَجْهَهَا وَقَالَتْ عَجُوزٌ عَقِيمٌ

29 His wife came forward crying. She clasped her face, and said, “A barren old woman?”

٣٠ قَالُوا۟ كَذَٰلِكِ قَالَ رَبُّكِ ۖ إِنَّهُۥ هُوَ ٱلْحَكِيمُ ٱلْعَلِيمُ

30 They said, “Thus spoke your Lord. He is the Wise, the Knowing.”

٣١ قَالَ فَمَا خَطْبُكُمْ أَيُّهَا ٱلْمُرْسَلُونَ

31 He said, “What is your business, O envoys?”

٣٢ قَالُوٓا۟ إِنَّآ أُرْسِلْنَآ إِلَىٰ قَوْمٍ مُّجْرِمِينَ

32 They said, “We are sent to a people guilty of sin.”

٣٣ لِنُرْسِلَ عَلَيْهِمْ حِجَارَةً مِّن طِينٍ

33 “To unleash upon them rocks of clay.”

٣٤ مُّسَوَّمَةً عِندَ رَبِّكَ لِلْمُسْرِفِينَ

34 “Marked by your Lord for the excessive.”

٣٥ فَأَخْرَجْنَا مَن كَانَ فِيهَا مِنَ ٱلْمُؤْمِنِينَ

35 We evacuated all the believers who were in it.

٣٦ فَمَا وَجَدْنَا فِيهَا غَيْرَ بَيْتٍ مِّنَ ٱلْمُسْلِمِينَ

36 But found in it only one household of Muslims.

٣٧ وَتَرَكْنَا فِيهَآ ءَايَةً لِّلَّذِينَ يَخَافُونَ ٱلْعَذَابَ ٱلْأَلِيمَ

37 And We left in it a sign for those who fear the painful punishment.

٣٨ وَفِى مُوسَىٰٓ إِذْ أَرْسَلْنَٰهُ إِلَىٰ فِرْعَوْنَ بِسُلْطَٰنٍ مُّبِينٍ

38 And in Moses. We sent him to Pharaoh with a clear authority.

٣٩ فَتَوَلَّىٰ بِرُكْنِهِۦ وَقَالَ سَٰحِرٌ أَوْ مَجْنُونٌ

39 But he turned away with his warlords, and said, “A sorcerer or a madman.”

٤٠ فَأَخَذْنَٰهُ وَجُنُودَهُۥ فَنَبَذْنَٰهُمْ فِى ٱلْيَمِّ وَهُوَ مُلِيمٌ

40 So We seized him and his troops, and threw them into the sea, and He was to blame.

٤١ وَفِى عَادٍ إِذْ أَرْسَلْنَا عَلَيْهِمُ ٱلرِّيحَ ٱلْعَقِيمَ

41 And in Aad. We unleashed against them the devastating wind.

٤٢ مَا تَذَرُ مِن شَىْءٍ أَتَتْ عَلَيْهِ إِلَّا جَعَلَتْهُ كَٱلرَّمِيمِ

42 It spared nothing it came upon, but rendered it like decayed ruins.

٤٣ وَفِى ثَمُودَ إِذْ قِيلَ لَهُمْ تَمَتَّعُوا۟ حَتَّىٰ حِينٍ

43 And in Thamood. They were told, “Enjoy yourselves for a while.”

٤٤ فَعَتَوْا۟ عَنْ أَمْرِ رَبِّهِمْ فَأَخَذَتْهُمُ ٱلصَّٰعِقَةُ
وَهُمْ يَنظُرُونَ

44 But they defied the command of their Lord, so the lightning struck them as they looked on.

٤٥ فَمَا ٱسْتَطَٰعُوا۟ مِن قِيَامٍ وَمَا كَانُوا۟ مُنتَصِرِينَ

45 They could not rise up, nor could they find help.

٤٦ وَقَوْمَ نُوحٍ مِّن قَبْلُ ۖ إِنَّهُمْ كَانُوا۟ قَوْمًا
فَٰسِقِينَ

46 And before that, the people of Noah. They were immoral people.

٤٧ وَٱلسَّمَآءَ بَنَيْنَٰهَا بِأَيْي۟دٍ وَإِنَّا لَمُوسِعُونَ

47 We constructed the universe with power, and We are expanding it.

٤٨ وَٱلْأَرْضَ فَرَشْنَٰهَا فَنِعْمَ ٱلْمَٰهِدُونَ

48 And the earth—We spread it out—How well We prepared it!

٤٩ وَمِن كُلِّ شَىْءٍ خَلَقْنَا زَوْجَيْنِ لَعَلَّكُمْ
تَذَكَّرُونَ

49 We created all things in pairs, so that you may reflect and ponder.

٥٠ فَفِرُّوٓا۟ إِلَى ٱللَّهِ ۖ إِنِّى لَكُم مِّنْهُ نَذِيرٌ مُّبِينٌ

50 "So flee towards Allah. I am to you from Him a clear warner."

٥١ وَلَا تَجْعَلُوا۟ مَعَ ٱللَّهِ إِلَٰهًا ءَاخَرَ ۖ إِنِّى لَكُم مِّنْهُ
نَذِيرٌ مُّبِينٌ

51 "And do not set up any other god with Allah. I am to you from Him a clear warner."

٥٢ كَذَٰلِكَ مَآ أَتَى ٱلَّذِينَ مِن قَبْلِهِم مِّن رَّسُولٍ
إِلَّا قَالُوا۟ سَاحِرٌ أَوْ مَجْنُونٌ

52 Likewise, no messenger came to those before them, but they said, "A sorcerer or a madman."

٥٣ أَتَوَاصَوْا۟ بِهِۦ ۚ بَلْ هُمْ قَوْمٌ طَاغُونَ

53 Did they recommend it to one another? In fact, they are rebellious people.

٥٤ فَتَوَلَّ عَنْهُمْ فَمَآ أَنتَ بِمَلُومٍ

54 So turn away from them; you are not to blame.

٥٥ وَذَكِّرْ فَإِنَّ ٱلذِّكْرَىٰ تَنفَعُ ٱلْمُؤْمِنِينَ

55 And remind, for the reminder benefits the believers.

٥٦ وَمَا خَلَقْتُ ٱلْجِنَّ وَٱلْإِنسَ إِلَّا لِيَعْبُدُونِ

56 I did not create the jinn and the humans except to worship Me.

٥٧ مَآ أُرِيدُ مِنْهُم مِّن رِّزْقٍ وَمَآ أُرِيدُ أَن
يُطْعِمُونِ

57 I need no livelihood from them, nor do I need them to feed Me.

٥٨ إِنَّ ٱللَّهَ هُوَ ٱلرَّزَّاقُ ذُو ٱلْقُوَّةِ ٱلْمَتِينُ

58 Allah is the Provider, the One with Power, the Strong.

٥٩ فَإِنَّ لِلَّذِينَ ظَلَمُوا۟ ذَنُوبًا مِّثْلَ ذَنُوبِ أَصْحَـٰبِهِمْ فَلَا يَسْتَعْجِلُونِ	59 Those who do wrong will have their turn, like the turn of their counterparts, so let them not rush Me.
٦٠ فَوَيْلٌ لِّلَّذِينَ كَفَرُوا۟ مِن يَوْمِهِمُ ٱلَّذِى يُوعَدُونَ	60 So woe to those who disbelieve because of that Day of theirs which they are promised.

52 The Mount الطور

بِسْمِ ٱللَّهِ ٱلرَّحْمَـٰنِ ٱلرَّحِيمِ	In the name of Allah, the Gracious, the Merciful.
١ وَٱلطُّورِ	1 By the Mount.
٢ وَكِتَـٰبٍ مَّسْطُورٍ	2 And a Book inscribed.
٣ فِى رَقٍّ مَّنشُورٍ	3 In a published scroll.
٤ وَٱلْبَيْتِ ٱلْمَعْمُورِ	4 And the frequented House.
٥ وَٱلسَّقْفِ ٱلْمَرْفُوعِ	5 And the elevated roof.
٦ وَٱلْبَحْرِ ٱلْمَسْجُورِ	6 And the seething sea.
٧ إِنَّ عَذَابَ رَبِّكَ لَوَٰقِعٌ	7 The punishment of your Lord is coming.
٨ مَّا لَهُۥ مِن دَافِعٍ	8 There is nothing to avert it.
٩ يَوْمَ تَمُورُ ٱلسَّمَآءُ مَوْرًا	9 On the Day when the heaven sways in agitation.
١٠ وَتَسِيرُ ٱلْجِبَالُ سَيْرًا	10 And the mountains go into motion.
١١ فَوَيْلٌ يَوْمَئِذٍ لِّلْمُكَذِّبِينَ	11 Woe on that Day to the deniers.
١٢ ٱلَّذِينَ هُمْ فِى خَوْضٍ يَلْعَبُونَ	12 Those who play with speculation.
١٣ يَوْمَ يُدَعُّونَ إِلَىٰ نَارِ جَهَنَّمَ دَعًّا	13 The Day when they are shoved into the Fire of Hell forcefully.
١٤ هَـٰذِهِ ٱلنَّارُ ٱلَّتِى كُنتُم بِهَا تُكَذِّبُونَ	14 “This is the Fire which you used to deny.
١٥ أَفَسِحْرٌ هَـٰذَآ أَمْ أَنتُمْ لَا تُبْصِرُونَ	15 Is this magic, or do you not see?

١٦ ٱصْلَوْهَا فَٱصْبِرُوٓا۟ أَوْ لَا تَصْبِرُوا۟ سَوَآءٌ عَلَيْكُمْ ۖ إِنَّمَا تُجْزَوْنَ مَا كُنتُمْ تَعْمَلُونَ	16 Burn in it. Whether you are patient, or impatient, it is the same for you. You are only being repaid for what you used to do."
١٧ إِنَّ ٱلْمُتَّقِينَ فِى جَنَّٰتٍ وَنَعِيمٍ	17 But the righteous will be amid gardens and bliss.
١٨ فَٰكِهِينَ بِمَآ ءَاتَىٰهُمْ رَبُّهُمْ وَوَقَىٰهُمْ رَبُّهُمْ عَذَابَ ٱلْجَحِيمِ	18 Enjoying what their Lord has given them, and their Lord has spared them the suffering of Hell.
١٩ كُلُوا۟ وَٱشْرَبُوا۟ هَنِيٓـًٔۢا بِمَا كُنتُمْ تَعْمَلُونَ	19 Eat and drink happily, for what you used to do.
٢٠ مُتَّكِـِٔينَ عَلَىٰ سُرُرٍ مَّصْفُوفَةٍ ۖ وَزَوَّجْنَٰهُم بِحُورٍ عِينٍ	20 Relaxing on luxurious furnishings; and We will couple them with gorgeous spouses.
٢١ وَٱلَّذِينَ ءَامَنُوا۟ وَٱتَّبَعَتْهُمْ ذُرِّيَّتُهُم بِإِيمَٰنٍ أَلْحَقْنَا بِهِمْ ذُرِّيَّتَهُمْ وَمَآ أَلَتْنَٰهُم مِّنْ عَمَلِهِم مِّن شَىْءٍ ۚ كُلُّ ٱمْرِئٍۭ بِمَا كَسَبَ رَهِينٌ	21 Those who believed, and their offspring followed them in faith—We will unite them with their offspring, and We will not deprive them of any of their works. Every person is hostage to what he has earned.
٢٢ وَأَمْدَدْنَٰهُم بِفَٰكِهَةٍ وَلَحْمٍ مِّمَّا يَشْتَهُونَ	22 And We will supply them with fruit, and meat; such as they desire.
٢٣ يَتَنَٰزَعُونَ فِيهَا كَأْسًا لَّا لَغْوٌ فِيهَا وَلَا تَأْثِيمٌ	23 They will exchange therein a cup; wherein is neither harm, nor sin.
٢٤ وَيَطُوفُ عَلَيْهِمْ غِلْمَانٌ لَّهُمْ كَأَنَّهُمْ لُؤْلُؤٌ مَّكْنُونٌ	24 Serving them will be youths like hidden pearls.
٢٥ وَأَقْبَلَ بَعْضُهُمْ عَلَىٰ بَعْضٍ يَتَسَآءَلُونَ	25 And they will approach one another, inquiring.
٢٦ قَالُوٓا۟ إِنَّا كُنَّا قَبْلُ فِىٓ أَهْلِنَا مُشْفِقِينَ	26 They will say, "Before this, we were fearful for our families.
٢٧ فَمَنَّ ٱللَّهُ عَلَيْنَا وَوَقَىٰنَا عَذَابَ ٱلسَّمُومِ	27 But Allah blessed us, and spared us the agony of the Fiery Winds.
٢٨ إِنَّا كُنَّا مِن قَبْلُ نَدْعُوهُ ۖ إِنَّهُۥ هُوَ ٱلْبَرُّ ٱلرَّحِيمُ	28 Before this, we used to pray to Him. He is the Good, the Compassionate."
٢٩ فَذَكِّرْ فَمَآ أَنتَ بِنِعْمَتِ رَبِّكَ بِكَاهِنٍ وَلَا مَجْنُونٍ	29 So remind. By the grace of your Lord, you are neither a soothsayer, nor a madman.

٣٠ أَمْ يَقُولُونَ شَاعِرٌ نَّتَرَبَّصُ بِهِۦ رَيْبَ ٱلْمَنُونِ

30 Or do they say, “A poet—we await for him a calamity of time”?

٣١ قُلْ تَرَبَّصُوا۟ فَإِنِّى مَعَكُم مِّنَ ٱلْمُتَرَبِّصِينَ

31 Say, “Go on waiting; I will be waiting with you.”

٣٢ أَمْ تَأْمُرُهُمْ أَحْلَٰمُهُم بِهَٰذَآ ۚ أَمْ هُمْ قَوْمٌ
طَاغُونَ

32 Or is it that their dreams compel them to this? Or are they aggressive people?

٣٣ أَمْ يَقُولُونَ تَقَوَّلَهُۥ ۚ بَل لَّا يُؤْمِنُونَ

33 Or do they say, “He made it up”? Rather, they do not believe.

٣٤ فَلْيَأْتُوا۟ بِحَدِيثٍ مِّثْلِهِۦٓ إِن كَانُوا۟ صَٰدِقِينَ

34 So let them produce a discourse like it, if they are truthful.

٣٥ أَمْ خُلِقُوا۟ مِنْ غَيْرِ شَىْءٍ أَمْ هُمُ ٱلْخَٰلِقُونَ

35 Or were they created out of nothing? Or are they the creators?

٣٦ أَمْ خَلَقُوا۟ ٱلسَّمَٰوَٰتِ وَٱلْأَرْضَ ۚ بَل لَّا يُوقِنُونَ

36 Or did they create the heavens and the earth? In fact, they are not certain.

٣٧ أَمْ عِندَهُمْ خَزَآئِنُ رَبِّكَ أَمْ هُمُ ٱلْمُصَۣيْطِرُونَ

37 Or do they possess the treasuries of your Lord? Or are they the controllers?

٣٨ أَمْ لَهُمْ سُلَّمٌ يَسْتَمِعُونَ فِيهِ ۖ فَلْيَأْتِ
مُسْتَمِعُهُم بِسُلْطَٰنٍ مُّبِينٍ

38 Or do they have a stairway by means of which they listen? Then let their listener produce a clear proof.

٣٩ أَمْ لَهُ ٱلْبَنَٰتُ وَلَكُمُ ٱلْبَنُونَ

39 Or for Him the daughters, and for you the sons?

٤٠ أَمْ تَسْـَٔلُهُمْ أَجْرًا فَهُم مِّن مَّغْرَمٍ مُّثْقَلُونَ

40 Or do you demand a payment from them, and they are burdened by debt?

٤١ أَمْ عِندَهُمُ ٱلْغَيْبُ فَهُمْ يَكْتُبُونَ

41 Or do they know the future, and they are writing it down?

٤٢ أَمْ يُرِيدُونَ كَيْدًا ۖ فَٱلَّذِينَ كَفَرُوا۟ هُمُ
ٱلْمَكِيدُونَ

42 Or are they planning a conspiracy? The conspiracy will befall the disbelievers.

٤٣ أَمْ لَهُمْ إِلَٰهٌ غَيْرُ ٱللَّهِ ۚ سُبْحَٰنَ ٱللَّهِ عَمَّا
يُشْرِكُونَ

43 Or do they have a god besides Allah? Allah transcends what they associate.

٤٤ وَإِن يَرَوْا۟ كِسْفًا مِّنَ ٱلسَّمَآءِ سَاقِطًا يَقُولُوا۟
سَحَابٌ مَّرْكُومٌ

44 Even if they were to see lumps of the sky falling down, they would say, “A mass of clouds.”

٤٥ فَذَرْهُمْ حَتَّىٰ يُلَٰقُوا۟ يَوْمَهُمُ ٱلَّذِى فِيهِ يُصْعَقُونَ	45 So leave them until they meet their Day in which they will be stunned.
٤٦ يَوْمَ لَا يُغْنِى عَنْهُمْ كَيْدُهُمْ شَيْـًٔا وَلَا هُمْ يُنصَرُونَ	46 The Day when their ploys will avail them nothing; and they will not be helped.
٤٧ وَإِنَّ لِلَّذِينَ ظَلَمُوا۟ عَذَابًا دُونَ ذَٰلِكَ وَلَٰكِنَّ أَكْثَرَهُمْ لَا يَعْلَمُونَ	47 For those who do wrong, there is a punishment besides that; but most of them do not know.
٤٨ وَٱصْبِرْ لِحُكْمِ رَبِّكَ فَإِنَّكَ بِأَعْيُنِنَا ۖ وَسَبِّحْ بِحَمْدِ رَبِّكَ حِينَ تَقُومُ	48 So patiently await the decision of your Lord, for you are before Our Eyes; and proclaim the praises of your Lord when you arise.
٤٩ وَمِنَ ٱلَّيْلِ فَسَبِّحْهُ وَإِدْبَٰرَ ٱلنُّجُومِ	49 And glorify Him during the night, and at the receding of the stars.

53 The Star النجم

بِسْمِ ٱللَّهِ ٱلرَّحْمَٰنِ ٱلرَّحِيمِ	In the name of Allah, the Gracious, the Merciful.
١ وَٱلنَّجْمِ إِذَا هَوَىٰ	1 By the star as it goes down.
٢ مَا ضَلَّ صَاحِبُكُمْ وَمَا غَوَىٰ	2 Your friend has not gone astray, nor has he erred.
٣ وَمَا يَنطِقُ عَنِ ٱلْهَوَىٰٓ	3 Nor does he speak out of desire.
٤ إِنْ هُوَ إِلَّا وَحْىٌ يُوحَىٰ	4 It is but a revelation revealed.
٥ عَلَّمَهُۥ شَدِيدُ ٱلْقُوَىٰ	5 Taught to him by the Extremely Powerful.
٦ ذُو مِرَّةٍ فَٱسْتَوَىٰ	6 The one of vigor. He settled.
٧ وَهُوَ بِٱلْأُفُقِ ٱلْأَعْلَىٰ	7 While he was at the highest horizon.
٨ ثُمَّ دَنَا فَتَدَلَّىٰ	8 Then he came near, and hovered around.
٩ فَكَانَ قَابَ قَوْسَيْنِ أَوْ أَدْنَىٰ	9 He was within two bows' length, or closer.
١٠ فَأَوْحَىٰٓ إِلَىٰ عَبْدِهِۦ مَآ أَوْحَىٰ	10 Then He revealed to His servant what He revealed.

١١ مَا كَذَبَ ٱلْفُؤَادُ مَا رَأَىٰٓ

11 The heart did not lie about what it saw.

١٢ أَفَتُمَٰرُونَهُۥ عَلَىٰ مَا يَرَىٰ

12 Will you dispute with him concerning what he saw?

١٣ وَلَقَدْ رَءَاهُ نَزْلَةً أُخْرَىٰ

13 He saw him on another descent.

١٤ عِندَ سِدْرَةِ ٱلْمُنتَهَىٰ

14 At the Lotus Tree of the Extremity.

١٥ عِندَهَا جَنَّةُ ٱلْمَأْوَىٰٓ

15 Near which is the Garden of Repose.

١٦ إِذْ يَغْشَى ٱلسِّدْرَةَ مَا يَغْشَىٰ

16 As there covered the Lotus Tree what covered it.

١٧ مَا زَاغَ ٱلْبَصَرُ وَمَا طَغَىٰ

17 The sight did not waver, nor did it exceed.

١٨ لَقَدْ رَأَىٰ مِنْ ءَايَٰتِ رَبِّهِ ٱلْكُبْرَىٰٓ

18 He saw some of the Great Signs of his Lord.

١٩ أَفَرَءَيْتُمُ ٱللَّٰتَ وَٱلْعُزَّىٰ

19 Have you considered al-Lat and al-Uzza?

٢٠ وَمَنَوٰةَ ٱلثَّالِثَةَ ٱلْأُخْرَىٰٓ

20 And Manat, the third one, the other?

٢١ أَلَكُمُ ٱلذَّكَرُ وَلَهُ ٱلْأُنثَىٰ

21 Are you to have the males, and He the females?

٢٢ تِلْكَ إِذًا قِسْمَةٌ ضِيزَىٰٓ

22 What a bizarre distribution.

٢٣ إِنْ هِىَ إِلَّآ أَسْمَآءٌ سَمَّيْتُمُوهَآ أَنتُمْ
وَءَابَآؤُكُم مَّآ أَنزَلَ ٱللَّهُ بِهَا مِن سُلْطَٰنٍ ۚ إِن
يَتَّبِعُونَ إِلَّا ٱلظَّنَّ وَمَا تَهْوَى ٱلْأَنفُسُ ۖ وَلَقَدْ
جَآءَهُم مِّن رَّبِّهِمُ ٱلْهُدَىٰٓ

23 These are nothing but names, which you have devised, you and your ancestors, for which Allah sent down no authority. They follow nothing but assumptions, and what the ego desires, even though guidance has come to them from their Lord.

٢٤ أَمْ لِلْإِنسَٰنِ مَا تَمَنَّىٰ

24 Or is the human being to have whatever he desires?

٢٥ فَلِلَّهِ ٱلْءَاخِرَةُ وَٱلْأُولَىٰ

25 To Allah belong the Last and the First.

٢٦ وَكَم مِّن مَّلَكٍ فِى ٱلسَّمَٰوَٰتِ لَا تُغْنِى
شَفَٰعَتُهُمْ شَيْـًٔا إِلَّا مِنۢ بَعْدِ أَن يَأْذَنَ ٱللَّهُ لِمَن
يَشَآءُ وَيَرْضَىٰٓ

26 How many an angel is there in the heavens whose intercession avails nothing, except after Allah gives

permission to whomever He wills,
and approves?

٢٧ إِنَّ ٱلَّذِينَ لَا يُؤْمِنُونَ بِٱلْـَٔاخِرَةِ لَيُسَمُّونَ
ٱلْمَلَـٰٓئِكَةَ تَسْمِيَةَ ٱلْأُنثَىٰ

27 Those who do not believe in the Hereafter give the angels the names of females.

٢٨ وَمَا لَهُم بِهِۦ مِنْ عِلْمٍ ۖ إِن يَتَّبِعُونَ إِلَّا ٱلظَّنَّ ۖ
وَإِنَّ ٱلظَّنَّ لَا يُغْنِى مِنَ ٱلْحَقِّ شَيْـًٔا

28 They have no knowledge of that. They only follow assumptions, and assumptions are no substitute for the truth.

٢٩ فَأَعْرِضْ عَن مَّن تَوَلَّىٰ عَن ذِكْرِنَا وَلَمْ يُرِدْ
إِلَّا ٱلْحَيَوٰةَ ٱلدُّنْيَا

29 So avoid him who has turned away from Our remembrance, and desires nothing but the present life.

٣٠ ذَٰلِكَ مَبْلَغُهُم مِّنَ ٱلْعِلْمِ ۚ إِنَّ رَبَّكَ هُوَ أَعْلَمُ
بِمَن ضَلَّ عَن سَبِيلِهِۦ وَهُوَ أَعْلَمُ بِمَنِ ٱهْتَدَىٰ

30 That is the extent of their knowledge. Your Lord knows best who has strayed from His path, and He knows best who has accepted guidance.

٣١ وَلِلَّهِ مَا فِى ٱلسَّمَـٰوَٰتِ وَمَا فِى ٱلْأَرْضِ
لِيَجْزِىَ ٱلَّذِينَ أَسَـٰٓـُٔوا۟ بِمَا عَمِلُوا۟ وَيَجْزِىَ ٱلَّذِينَ
أَحْسَنُوا۟ بِٱلْحُسْنَى

31 To Allah belongs whatever is in the heavens and whatever is on earth. He will repay those who do evil according to their deeds, and recompense those who do good with the best.

٣٢ ٱلَّذِينَ يَجْتَنِبُونَ كَبَـٰٓئِرَ ٱلْإِثْمِ وَٱلْفَوَٰحِشَ إِلَّا
ٱللَّمَمَ ۚ إِنَّ رَبَّكَ وَٰسِعُ ٱلْمَغْفِرَةِ ۚ هُوَ أَعْلَمُ بِكُمْ إِذْ
أَنشَأَكُم مِّنَ ٱلْأَرْضِ وَإِذْ أَنتُمْ أَجِنَّةٌ فِى بُطُونِ
أُمَّهَـٰتِكُمْ ۖ فَلَا تُزَكُّوٓا۟ أَنفُسَكُمْ ۖ هُوَ أَعْلَمُ بِمَنِ
ٱتَّقَىٰٓ

32 Those who avoid gross sins and indecencies—except for minor lapses—your Lord is of Vast Forgiveness. He knows you well, ever since He created you from the earth, and ever since you were embryos in your mothers' wombs. So do not acclaim your own virtue; He is fully aware of the righteous.

٣٣ أَفَرَءَيْتَ ٱلَّذِى تَوَلَّىٰ

33 Have you considered him who turned away?

٣٤ وَأَعْطَىٰ قَلِيلًا وَأَكْدَىٰٓ

34 And gave a little, and held back?

٣٥ أَعِندَهُۥ عِلْمُ ٱلْغَيْبِ فَهُوَ يَرَىٰٓ

35 Does he possess knowledge of the unseen, and can therefore foresee?

٣٦ أَمْ لَمْ يُنَبَّأْ بِمَا فِى صُحُفِ مُوسَىٰ

36 Or was he not informed of what is in the Scrolls of Moses?

٣٧ وَإِبْرَٰهِيمَ ٱلَّذِى وَفَّىٰٓ

37 And of Abraham, who fulfilled?

٣٨ أَلَّا تَزِرُ وَازِرَةٌ وِزْرَ أُخْرَىٰ

38 That no soul bears the burdens of another soul.

٣٩ وَأَن لَّيْسَ لِلْإِنسَٰنِ إِلَّا مَا سَعَىٰ

39 And that the human being attains only what he strives for.

٤٠ وَأَنَّ سَعْيَهُۥ سَوْفَ يُرَىٰ

40 And that his efforts will be witnessed.

٤١ ثُمَّ يُجْزَىٰهُ ٱلْجَزَآءَ ٱلْأَوْفَىٰ

41 Then he will be rewarded for it the fullest reward.

٤٢ وَأَنَّ إِلَىٰ رَبِّكَ ٱلْمُنتَهَىٰ

42 And that to your Lord is the finality.

٤٣ وَأَنَّهُۥ هُوَ أَضْحَكَ وَأَبْكَىٰ

43 And that it is He who causes laughter and weeping.

٤٤ وَأَنَّهُۥ هُوَ أَمَاتَ وَأَحْيَا

44 And that it is He who gives death and life.

٤٥ وَأَنَّهُۥ خَلَقَ ٱلزَّوْجَيْنِ ٱلذَّكَرَ وَٱلْأُنثَىٰ

45 And that it is He who created the two kinds—the male and the female.

٤٦ مِن نُّطْفَةٍ إِذَا تُمْنَىٰ

46 From a sperm drop, when emitted.

٤٧ وَأَنَّ عَلَيْهِ ٱلنَّشْأَةَ ٱلْأُخْرَىٰ

47 And that upon Him is the next existence.

٤٨ وَأَنَّهُۥ هُوَ أَغْنَىٰ وَأَقْنَىٰ

48 And that it is He who enriches and impoverishes.

٤٩ وَأَنَّهُۥ هُوَ رَبُّ ٱلشِّعْرَىٰ

49 And that it is He who is the Lord of Sirius.

٥٠ وَأَنَّهُۥٓ أَهْلَكَ عَادًا ٱلْأُولَىٰ

50 And that it is He who destroyed the first Aad.

٥١ وَثَمُودَاْ فَمَآ أَبْقَىٰ

51 And Thamood, sparing no one.

٥٢ وَقَوْمَ نُوحٍ مِّن قَبْلُ ۖ إِنَّهُمْ كَانُواْ هُمْ أَظْلَمَ
وَأَطْغَىٰ

52 And the people of Noah before that; for they were most unjust and most oppressive.

٥٣ وَٱلْمُؤْتَفِكَةَ أَهْوَىٰ

53 And He toppled the ruined cities.

٥٤ فَغَشَّىٰهَا مَا غَشَّىٰ

54 And covered them with whatever covered them.

٥٥ فَبِأَىِّ ءَالَآءِ رَبِّكَ تَتَمَارَىٰ

55 So which of your Lord's marvels can you deny?

٥٦ هَٰذَا نَذِيرٌ مِّنَ ٱلنُّذُرِ ٱلْأُولَىٰٓ

56 This is a warning, just like the first warnings.

٥٧ أَزِفَتِ ٱلْءَازِفَةُ

57 The inevitable is imminent.

٥٨ لَيْسَ لَهَا مِن دُونِ ٱللَّهِ كَاشِفَةٌ

58 None besides Allah can unveil it.

٥٩ أَفَمِنْ هَٰذَا ٱلْحَدِيثِ تَعْجَبُونَ

59 Do you marvel at this discourse?

٦٠ وَتَضْحَكُونَ وَلَا تَبْكُونَ

60 And laugh, and do not weep?

٦١ وَأَنتُمْ سَٰمِدُونَ

61 Lost in your frivolity?

٦٢ فَٱسْجُدُوا۟ لِلَّهِ وَٱعْبُدُوا۟ ۩

62 So bow down to Allah, and worship!

54 The Moon القمر

بِسْمِ ٱللَّهِ ٱلرَّحْمَٰنِ ٱلرَّحِيمِ

In the name of Allah, the Gracious, the Merciful.

١ ٱقْتَرَبَتِ ٱلسَّاعَةُ وَٱنشَقَّ ٱلْقَمَرُ

1 The Hour has drawn near, and the moon has split.

٢ وَإِن يَرَوْا۟ ءَايَةً يُعْرِضُوا۟ وَيَقُولُوا۟ سِحْرٌ مُّسْتَمِرٌّ

2 Yet whenever they see a miracle, they turn away, and say, “Continuous magic.”

٣ وَكَذَّبُوا۟ وَٱتَّبَعُوٓا۟ أَهْوَآءَهُمْ ۚ وَكُلُّ أَمْرٍ مُّسْتَقِرٌّ

3 They lied, and followed their opinions, but everything has its time.

٤ وَلَقَدْ جَآءَهُم مِّنَ ٱلْأَنۢبَآءِ مَا فِيهِ مُزْدَجَرٌ

4 And there came to them news containing a deterrent.

٥ حِكْمَةٌۢ بَٰلِغَةٌ ۖ فَمَا تُغْنِ ٱلنُّذُرُ

5 Profound wisdom—but warnings are of no avail.

٦ فَتَوَلَّ عَنْهُمْ ۘ يَوْمَ يَدْعُ ٱلدَّاعِ إِلَىٰ شَىْءٍ نُّكُرٍ

6 So turn away from them. On the Day when the Caller calls to something terrible.

٧ خُشَّعًا أَبْصَٰرُهُمْ يَخْرُجُونَ مِنَ ٱلْأَجْدَاثِ كَأَنَّهُمْ جَرَادٌ مُّنتَشِرٌ

7 Their eyes humiliated, they will emerge from the graves, as if they were swarming locusts.

٨ مُّهْطِعِينَ إِلَى ٱلدَّاعِ ۖ يَقُولُ ٱلْكَٰفِرُونَ هَٰذَا يَوْمٌ عَسِرٌ

8 Scrambling towards the Caller, the disbelievers will say, “This is a difficult Day.”

٩ كَذَّبَتْ قَبْلَهُمْ قَوْمُ نُوحٍ فَكَذَّبُوا۟ عَبْدَنَا وَقَالُوا۟ مَجْنُونٌ وَٱزْدُجِرَ	9 Before them the people of Noah disbelieved. They rejected Our servant, and said, "Crazy," and he was rebuked.
١٠ فَدَعَا رَبَّهُۥٓ أَنِّى مَغْلُوبٌ فَٱنتَصِرْ	10 So he appealed to his Lord, "I am overwhelmed, so help me."
١١ فَفَتَحْنَآ أَبْوَٰبَ ٱلسَّمَآءِ بِمَآءٍ مُّنْهَمِرٍ	11 So We opened the floodgates of heaven with water pouring down.
١٢ وَفَجَّرْنَا ٱلْأَرْضَ عُيُونًا فَٱلْتَقَى ٱلْمَآءُ عَلَىٰٓ أَمْرٍ قَدْ قُدِرَ	12 And We made the earth burst with springs, and the waters met for a purpose already destined.
١٣ وَحَمَلْنَٰهُ عَلَىٰ ذَاتِ أَلْوَٰحٍ وَدُسُرٍ	13 And We carried him on a craft of planks and nails.
١٤ تَجْرِى بِأَعْيُنِنَا جَزَآءً لِّمَن كَانَ كُفِرَ	14 Sailing before Our eyes; a reward for him who was rejected.
١٥ وَلَقَد تَّرَكْنَٰهَآ ءَايَةً فَهَلْ مِن مُّدَّكِرٍ	15 And We left it as a sign. Is there anyone who would take heed?
١٦ فَكَيْفَ كَانَ عَذَابِى وَنُذُرِ	16 So how were My punishment and My warnings?
١٧ وَلَقَدْ يَسَّرْنَا ٱلْقُرْءَانَ لِلذِّكْرِ فَهَلْ مِن مُّدَّكِرٍ	17 We made the Quran easy to learn. Is there anyone who would learn?
١٨ كَذَّبَتْ عَادٌ فَكَيْفَ كَانَ عَذَابِى وَنُذُرِ	18 Aad denied the truth. So how were My punishment and My warnings?
١٩ إِنَّآ أَرْسَلْنَا عَلَيْهِمْ رِيحًا صَرْصَرًا فِى يَوْمِ نَحْسٍ مُّسْتَمِرٍّ	19 We unleashed upon them a screaming wind, on a day of unrelenting misery.
٢٠ تَنزِعُ ٱلنَّاسَ كَأَنَّهُمْ أَعْجَازُ نَخْلٍ مُّنقَعِرٍ	20 Plucking the people away, as though they were trunks of uprooted palm-trees.
٢١ فَكَيْفَ كَانَ عَذَابِى وَنُذُرِ	21 So how were My punishment and My warnings?
٢٢ وَلَقَدْ يَسَّرْنَا ٱلْقُرْءَانَ لِلذِّكْرِ فَهَلْ مِن مُّدَّكِرٍ	22 We made the Quran easy to remember. Is there anyone who would remember?
٢٣ كَذَّبَتْ ثَمُودُ بِٱلنُّذُرِ	23 Thamood rejected the warnings.
٢٤ فَقَالُوٓا۟ أَبَشَرًا مِّنَّا وَٰحِدًا نَّتَّبِعُهُۥٓ إِنَّآ إِذًا لَّفِى ضَلَٰلٍ وَسُعُرٍ	24 They said, "Are we to follow one of us, a human being? We would then go astray, and end up in Hell.

٢٥ أَءُلْقِىَ ٱلذِّكْرُ عَلَيْهِ مِنۢ بَيْنِنَا بَلْ هُوَ كَذَّابٌ أَشِرٌ

25 Was the message given to him, out of all of us? In fact, he is a wicked liar."

٢٦ سَيَعْلَمُونَ غَدًا مَّنِ ٱلْكَذَّابُ ٱلْأَشِرُ

26 They will know tomorrow who the wicked liar is.

٢٧ إِنَّا مُرْسِلُوا۟ ٱلنَّاقَةِ فِتْنَةً لَّهُمْ فَٱرْتَقِبْهُمْ وَٱصْطَبِرْ

27 We are sending the she-camel as a test for them; so watch them and be patient.

٢٨ وَنَبِّئْهُمْ أَنَّ ٱلْمَآءَ قِسْمَةٌۢ بَيْنَهُمْ ۖ كُلُّ شِرْبٍ مُّحْتَضَرٌ

28 And inform them that the water is to be shared between them; each share of drink made available.

٢٩ فَنَادَوْا۟ صَاحِبَهُمْ فَتَعَاطَىٰ فَعَقَرَ

29 But they called their friend, and he dared, and he slaughtered.

٣٠ فَكَيْفَ كَانَ عَذَابِى وَنُذُرِ

30 So how were My punishment and My warnings?

٣١ إِنَّآ أَرْسَلْنَا عَلَيْهِمْ صَيْحَةً وَٰحِدَةً فَكَانُوا۟ كَهَشِيمِ ٱلْمُحْتَظِرِ

31 We sent against them a single Scream, and they became like crushed hay.

٣٢ وَلَقَدْ يَسَّرْنَا ٱلْقُرْءَانَ لِلذِّكْرِ فَهَلْ مِن مُّدَّكِرٍ

32 We made the Quran easy to understand. Is there anyone who would understand?

٣٣ كَذَّبَتْ قَوْمُ لُوطٍۭ بِٱلنُّذُرِ

33 The people of Lot rejected the warnings.

٣٤ إِنَّآ أَرْسَلْنَا عَلَيْهِمْ حَاصِبًا إِلَّآ ءَالَ لُوطٍ ۖ نَّجَّيْنَٰهُم بِسَحَرٍ

34 We unleashed upon them a shower of stones, except for the family of Lot; We rescued them at dawn.

٣٥ نِّعْمَةً مِّنْ عِندِنَا ۚ كَذَٰلِكَ نَجْزِى مَن شَكَرَ

35 A blessing from Us. Thus We reward the thankful.

٣٦ وَلَقَدْ أَنذَرَهُم بَطْشَتَنَا فَتَمَارَوْا۟ بِٱلنُّذُرِ

36 He had warned them of Our onslaught, but they dismissed the warnings.

٣٧ وَلَقَدْ رَٰوَدُوهُ عَن ضَيْفِهِۦ فَطَمَسْنَآ أَعْيُنَهُمْ فَذُوقُوا۟ عَذَابِى وَنُذُرِ

37 They even lusted for his guest, so We obliterated their eyes. "So taste My punishment and My warnings."

٣٨ وَلَقَدْ صَبَّحَهُم بُكْرَةً عَذَابٌ مُّسْتَقِرٌّ

38 Early morning brought upon them enduring punishment.

٣٩ فَذُوقُوا۟ عَذَابِى وَنُذُرِ

39 So taste My punishment and My warnings.

٤٠ وَلَقَدْ يَسَّرْنَا ٱلْقُرْءَانَ لِلذِّكْرِ فَهَلْ مِن مُّدَّكِرٍ

40 We made the Quran easy to memorize. Is there anyone who would memorize?

٤١ وَلَقَدْ جَآءَ ءَالَ فِرْعَوْنَ ٱلنُّذُرُ

41 The warnings also came to the people of Pharaoh.

٤٢ كَذَّبُوا۟ بِـَٔايَـٰتِنَا كُلِّهَا فَأَخَذْنَـٰهُمْ أَخْذَ عَزِيزٍ
مُّقْتَدِرٍ

42 They rejected Our signs, all of them, so We seized them—the seizure of an Almighty Omnipotent.

٤٣ أَكُفَّارُكُمْ خَيْرٌ مِّنْ أُو۟لَـٰٓئِكُمْ أَمْ لَكُم بَرَآءَةٌ فِى
ٱلزُّبُرِ

43 Are your unbelievers better than all those? Or do you have immunity in the scriptures?

٤٤ أَمْ يَقُولُونَ نَحْنُ جَمِيعٌ مُّنتَصِرٌ

44 Or do they say, “We are united, and we will be victorious”?

٤٥ سَيُهْزَمُ ٱلْجَمْعُ وَيُوَلُّونَ ٱلدُّبُرَ

45 The multitude will be defeated, and they will turn their backs.

٤٦ بَلِ ٱلسَّاعَةُ مَوْعِدُهُمْ وَٱلسَّاعَةُ أَدْهَىٰ وَأَمَرُّ

46 The Hour is their appointed time—the Hour is more disastrous, and most bitter.

٤٧ إِنَّ ٱلْمُجْرِمِينَ فِى ضَلَـٰلٍ وَسُعُرٍ

47 The wicked are in confusion and madness.

٤٨ يَوْمَ يُسْحَبُونَ فِى ٱلنَّارِ عَلَىٰ وُجُوهِهِمْ
ذُوقُوا۟ مَسَّ سَقَرَ

48 The Day when they are dragged upon their faces into the Fire: “Taste the touch of Saqar.”

٤٩ إِنَّا كُلَّ شَىْءٍ خَلَقْنَـٰهُ بِقَدَرٍ

49 Everything We created is precisely measured.

٥٠ وَمَآ أَمْرُنَآ إِلَّا وَٰحِدَةٌ كَلَمْحٍۭ بِٱلْبَصَرِ

50 And Our command is but once, like the twinkling of an eye.

٥١ وَلَقَدْ أَهْلَكْنَآ أَشْيَاعَكُمْ فَهَلْ مِن مُّدَّكِرٍ

51 We have destroyed your likes. Is there anyone who would ponder?

٥٢ وَكُلُّ شَىْءٍ فَعَلُوهُ فِى ٱلزُّبُرِ

52 Everything they have done is in the Books.

٥٣ وَكُلُّ صَغِيرٍ وَكَبِيرٍ مُّسْتَطَرٌ

53 Everything, small or large, is written down.

٥٤ إِنَّ ٱلْمُتَّقِينَ فِى جَنَّـٰتٍ وَنَهَرٍ

54 The righteous will be amidst gardens and rivers.

٥٥ فِى مَقْعَدِ صِدْقٍ عِندَ مَلِيكٍ مُّقْتَدِرٍۭ

55 In an assembly of virtue, in the presence of an Omnipotent King.

55 The Compassionate الرحمن

بِسْمِ ٱللَّهِ ٱلرَّحْمَٰنِ ٱلرَّحِيمِ
In the name of Allah, the Gracious, the Merciful.

١ ٱلرَّحْمَٰنُ
1 The Compassionate.

٢ عَلَّمَ ٱلْقُرْءَانَ
2 Has taught the Quran.

٣ خَلَقَ ٱلْإِنسَٰنَ
3 He created man.

٤ عَلَّمَهُ ٱلْبَيَانَ
4 And taught him clear expression.

٥ ٱلشَّمْسُ وَٱلْقَمَرُ بِحُسْبَانٍ
5 The sun and the moon move according to plan.

٦ وَٱلنَّجْمُ وَٱلشَّجَرُ يَسْجُدَانِ
6 And the stars and the trees prostrate themselves.

٧ وَٱلسَّمَآءَ رَفَعَهَا وَوَضَعَ ٱلْمِيزَانَ
7 And the sky, He raised; and He set up the balance.

٨ أَلَّا تَطْغَوْا۟ فِى ٱلْمِيزَانِ
8 So do not transgress in the balance.

٩ وَأَقِيمُوا۟ ٱلْوَزْنَ بِٱلْقِسْطِ وَلَا تُخْسِرُوا۟ ٱلْمِيزَانَ
9 But maintain the weights with justice, and do not violate the balance.

١٠ وَٱلْأَرْضَ وَضَعَهَا لِلْأَنَامِ
10 And the earth; He set up for the creatures.

١١ فِيهَا فَٰكِهَةٌ وَٱلنَّخْلُ ذَاتُ ٱلْأَكْمَامِ
11 In it are fruits, and palms in clusters.

١٢ وَٱلْحَبُّ ذُو ٱلْعَصْفِ وَٱلرَّيْحَانُ
12 And grains in the blades, and fragrant plants.

١٣ فَبِأَىِّ ءَالَآءِ رَبِّكُمَا تُكَذِّبَانِ
13 So which of your Lord's marvels will you deny?

١٤ خَلَقَ ٱلْإِنسَٰنَ مِن صَلْصَٰلٍ كَٱلْفَخَّارِ
14 He created man from hard clay, like bricks.

١٥ وَخَلَقَ ٱلْجَآنَّ مِن مَّارِجٍ مِّن نَّارٍ
15 And created the jinn from a fusion of fire.

١٦ فَبِأَىِّ ءَالَآءِ رَبِّكُمَا تُكَذِّبَانِ
16 So which of your Lord's marvels will you deny?

١٧ رَبُّ ٱلْمَشْرِقَيْنِ وَرَبُّ ٱلْمَغْرِبَيْنِ
17 Lord of the two Easts and Lord of the two Wests.

١٨ فَبِأَيِّ ءَالَآءِ رَبِّكُمَا تُكَذِّبَانِ

18 So which of your Lord's marvels will you deny?

١٩ مَرَجَ ٱلْبَحْرَيْنِ يَلْتَقِيَانِ

19 He merged the two seas, converging together.

٢٠ بَيْنَهُمَا بَرْزَخٌ لَّا يَبْغِيَانِ

20 Between them is a barrier, which they do not overrun.

٢١ فَبِأَيِّ ءَالَآءِ رَبِّكُمَا تُكَذِّبَانِ

21 So which of your Lord's marvels will you deny?

٢٢ يَخْرُجُ مِنْهُمَا ٱللُّؤْلُؤُ وَٱلْمَرْجَانُ

22 From them emerge pearls and coral.

٢٣ فَبِأَيِّ ءَالَآءِ رَبِّكُمَا تُكَذِّبَانِ

23 So which of your Lord's marvels will you deny?

٢٤ وَلَهُ ٱلْجَوَارِ ٱلْمُنشَـَٔاتُ فِى ٱلْبَحْرِ كَٱلْأَعْلَٰمِ

24 His are the ships, raised above the sea like landmarks.

٢٥ فَبِأَيِّ ءَالَآءِ رَبِّكُمَا تُكَذِّبَانِ

25 So which of your Lord's marvels will you deny?

٢٦ كُلُّ مَنْ عَلَيْهَا فَانٍ

26 Everyone upon it is perishing.

٢٧ وَيَبْقَىٰ وَجْهُ رَبِّكَ ذُو ٱلْجَلَٰلِ وَٱلْإِكْرَامِ

27 But will remain the Presence of your Lord, Full of Majesty and Splendor.

٢٨ فَبِأَيِّ ءَالَآءِ رَبِّكُمَا تُكَذِّبَانِ

28 So which of your Lord's marvels will you deny?

٢٩ يَسْـَٔلُهُۥ مَن فِى ٱلسَّمَٰوَٰتِ وَٱلْأَرْضِ ۚ كُلَّ يَوْمٍ
هُوَ فِى شَأْنٍ

29 Everyone in the heavens and the earth asks Him. Every day He is managing.

٣٠ فَبِأَيِّ ءَالَآءِ رَبِّكُمَا تُكَذِّبَانِ

30 So which of your Lord's marvels will you deny?

٣١ سَنَفْرُغُ لَكُمْ أَيُّهَ ٱلثَّقَلَانِ

31 We will attend to you, O prominent two.

٣٢ فَبِأَيِّ ءَالَآءِ رَبِّكُمَا تُكَذِّبَانِ

32 So which of your Lord's marvels will you deny?

٣٣ يَٰمَعْشَرَ ٱلْجِنِّ وَٱلْإِنسِ إِنِ ٱسْتَطَعْتُمْ أَن
تَنفُذُوا۟ مِنْ أَقْطَارِ ٱلسَّمَٰوَٰتِ وَٱلْأَرْضِ فَٱنفُذُوا۟ ۚ
لَا تَنفُذُونَ إِلَّا بِسُلْطَٰنٍ

33 O society of jinn and humans! If you can pass through the bounds of the heavens and the earth, go ahead and pass. But you will not pass except with authorization.

٣٤ فَبِأَيِّ ءَالَآءِ رَبِّكُمَا تُكَذِّبَانِ

34 So which of your Lord's marvels will you deny?

٣٥ يُرْسَلُ عَلَيْكُمَا شُوَاظٌ مِّن نَّارٍ وَنُحَاسٌ فَلَا تَنتَصِرَانِ	35 You will be bombarded with flares of fire and brass, and you will not succeed.
٣٦ فَبِأَيِّ ءَالَآءِ رَبِّكُمَا تُكَذِّبَانِ	36 So which of your Lord's marvels will you deny?
٣٧ فَإِذَا ٱنشَقَّتِ ٱلسَّمَآءُ فَكَانَتْ وَرْدَةً كَٱلدِّهَانِ	37 When the sky splits apart, and becomes rose, like paint.
٣٨ فَبِأَيِّ ءَالَآءِ رَبِّكُمَا تُكَذِّبَانِ	38 So which of your Lord's marvels will you deny?
٣٩ فَيَوْمَئِذٍ لَّا يُسْـَٔلُ عَن ذَنبِهِۦٓ إِنسٌ وَلَا جَآنٌّ	39 On that Day, no human and no jinn will be asked about his sins.
٤٠ فَبِأَيِّ ءَالَآءِ رَبِّكُمَا تُكَذِّبَانِ	40 So which of your Lord's marvels will you deny?
٤١ يُعْرَفُ ٱلْمُجْرِمُونَ بِسِيمَٰهُمْ فَيُؤْخَذُ بِٱلنَّوَٰصِى وَٱلْأَقْدَامِ	41 The guilty will be recognized by their marks; they will be taken by the forelocks and the feet.
٤٢ فَبِأَيِّ ءَالَآءِ رَبِّكُمَا تُكَذِّبَانِ	42 So which of your Lord's marvels will you deny?
٤٣ هَٰذِهِۦ جَهَنَّمُ ٱلَّتِى يُكَذِّبُ بِهَا ٱلْمُجْرِمُونَ	43 This is Hell that the guilty denied.
٤٤ يَطُوفُونَ بَيْنَهَا وَبَيْنَ حَمِيمٍ ءَانٍ	44 They circulate between it and between a seething bath.
٤٥ فَبِأَيِّ ءَالَآءِ رَبِّكُمَا تُكَذِّبَانِ	45 So which of your Lord's marvels will you deny?
٤٦ وَلِمَنْ خَافَ مَقَامَ رَبِّهِۦ جَنَّتَانِ	46 But for him who feared the standing of his Lord are two gardens.
٤٧ فَبِأَيِّ ءَالَآءِ رَبِّكُمَا تُكَذِّبَانِ	47 So which of your Lord's marvels will you deny?
٤٨ ذَوَاتَآ أَفْنَانٍ	48 Full of varieties.
٤٩ فَبِأَيِّ ءَالَآءِ رَبِّكُمَا تُكَذِّبَانِ	49 So which of your Lord's marvels will you deny?
٥٠ فِيهِمَا عَيْنَانِ تَجْرِيَانِ	50 In them are two flowing springs.
٥١ فَبِأَيِّ ءَالَآءِ رَبِّكُمَا تُكَذِّبَانِ	51 So which of your Lord's marvels will you deny?
٥٢ فِيهِمَا مِن كُلِّ فَٰكِهَةٍ زَوْجَانِ	52 In them are fruits of every kind, in pairs.

٥٣ فَبِأَيِّ ءَالَآءِ رَبِّكُمَا تُكَذِّبَانِ

53 So which of your Lord's marvels will you deny?

٥٤ مُتَّكِـِٔينَ عَلَىٰ فُرُشٍۭ بَطَآئِنُهَا مِنْ إِسْتَبْرَقٍ ۚ
وَجَنَى ٱلْجَنَّتَيْنِ دَانٍ

54 Reclining on furnishings lined with brocade, and the fruits of the two gardens are near at hand.

٥٥ فَبِأَيِّ ءَالَآءِ رَبِّكُمَا تُكَذِّبَانِ

55 So which of your Lord's marvels will you deny?

٥٦ فِيهِنَّ قَٰصِرَٰتُ ٱلطَّرْفِ لَمْ يَطْمِثْهُنَّ إِنسٌ
قَبْلَهُمْ وَلَا جَآنٌّ

56 In them are maidens restraining their glances, untouched before by any man or jinn.

٥٧ فَبِأَيِّ ءَالَآءِ رَبِّكُمَا تُكَذِّبَانِ

57 So which of your Lord's marvels will you deny?

٥٨ كَأَنَّهُنَّ ٱلْيَاقُوتُ وَٱلْمَرْجَانُ

58 As though they were rubies and corals.

٥٩ فَبِأَيِّ ءَالَآءِ رَبِّكُمَا تُكَذِّبَانِ

59 So which of your Lord's marvels will you deny?

٦٠ هَلْ جَزَآءُ ٱلْإِحْسَٰنِ إِلَّا ٱلْإِحْسَٰنُ

60 Is the reward of goodness anything but goodness?

٦١ فَبِأَيِّ ءَالَآءِ رَبِّكُمَا تُكَذِّبَانِ

61 So which of your Lord's marvels will you deny?

٦٢ وَمِن دُونِهِمَا جَنَّتَانِ

62 And beneath them are two gardens.

٦٣ فَبِأَيِّ ءَالَآءِ رَبِّكُمَا تُكَذِّبَانِ

63 So which of your Lord's marvels will you deny?

٦٤ مُدْهَآمَّتَانِ

64 Deep green.

٦٥ فَبِأَيِّ ءَالَآءِ رَبِّكُمَا تُكَذِّبَانِ

65 So which of your Lord's marvels will you deny?

٦٦ فِيهِمَا عَيْنَانِ نَضَّاخَتَانِ

66 In them are two gushing springs.

٦٧ فَبِأَيِّ ءَالَآءِ رَبِّكُمَا تُكَذِّبَانِ

67 So which of your Lord's marvels will you deny?

٦٨ فِيهِمَا فَٰكِهَةٌ وَنَخْلٌ وَرُمَّانٌ

68 In them are fruits, and date-palms, and pomegranates.

٦٩ فَبِأَيِّ ءَالَآءِ رَبِّكُمَا تُكَذِّبَانِ

69 So which of your Lord's marvels will you deny?

٧٠ فِيهِنَّ خَيْرَٰتٌ حِسَانٌ

70 In them are good and beautiful ones.

٧١ فَبِأَيِّ ءَالَآءِ رَبِّكُمَا تُكَذِّبَانِ

71 So which of your Lord's marvels will you deny?

٧٢ حُورٌ مَّقْصُورَٰتٌ فِى ٱلْخِيَامِ

72 Companions, secluded in the tents.

٧٣ فَبِأَيِّ ءَالَآءِ رَبِّكُمَا تُكَذِّبَانِ

73 So which of your Lord's marvels will you deny?

٧٤ لَمْ يَطْمِثْهُنَّ إِنسٌ قَبْلَهُمْ وَلَا جَآنٌّ

74 Whom no human has touched before, nor jinn.

٧٥ فَبِأَيِّ ءَالَآءِ رَبِّكُمَا تُكَذِّبَانِ

75 So which of your Lord's marvels will you deny?

٧٦ مُتَّكِـِٔينَ عَلَىٰ رَفْرَفٍ خُضْرٍ وَعَبْقَرِىٍّ حِسَانٍ

76 Reclining on green cushions, and exquisite carpets.

٧٧ فَبِأَيِّ ءَالَآءِ رَبِّكُمَا تُكَذِّبَانِ

77 So which of your Lord's marvels will you deny?

٧٨ تَبَٰرَكَ ٱسْمُ رَبِّكَ ذِى ٱلْجَلَٰلِ وَٱلْإِكْرَامِ

78 Blessed be the name of your Lord, Full of Majesty and Splendor.

56 The Inevitable الواقعة

بِسْمِ ٱللَّهِ ٱلرَّحْمَٰنِ ٱلرَّحِيمِ

In the name of Allah, the Gracious, the Merciful.

١ إِذَا وَقَعَتِ ٱلْوَاقِعَةُ

1 When the inevitable occurs.

٢ لَيْسَ لِوَقْعَتِهَا كَاذِبَةٌ

2 Of its occurrence, there is no denial.

٣ خَافِضَةٌ رَّافِعَةٌ

3 Bringing low, raising high.

٤ إِذَا رُجَّتِ ٱلْأَرْضُ رَجًّا

4 When the earth is shaken with a shock.

٥ وَبُسَّتِ ٱلْجِبَالُ بَسًّا

5 And the mountains are crushed and crumbled.

٦ فَكَانَتْ هَبَآءً مُّنۢبَثًّا

6 And they become scattered dust.

٧ وَكُنتُمْ أَزْوَٰجًا ثَلَٰثَةً

7 And you become three classes.

٨ فَأَصْحَٰبُ ٱلْمَيْمَنَةِ مَآ أَصْحَٰبُ ٱلْمَيْمَنَةِ

8 Those on the Right—what of those on the Right?

٩ وَأَصْحَٰبُ ٱلْمَشْـَٔمَةِ مَآ أَصْحَٰبُ ٱلْمَشْـَٔمَةِ

9 And those on the Left—what of those on the Left?

١٠ وَٱلسَّٰبِقُونَ ٱلسَّٰبِقُونَ

10 And the forerunners, the forerunners.

١١ أُوْلَٰٓئِكَ ٱلْمُقَرَّبُونَ

11 Those are the nearest.

١٢ فِى جَنَّٰتِ ٱلنَّعِيمِ

12 In the Gardens of Bliss.

١٣ ثُلَّةٌ مِّنَ ٱلْأَوَّلِينَ

13 A throng from the ancients.

١٤ وَقَلِيلٌ مِّنَ ٱلْءَاخِرِينَ

14 And a small band from the latecomers.

١٥ عَلَىٰ سُرُرٍ مَّوْضُونَةٍ

15 On luxurious furnishings.

١٦ مُّتَّكِـِٔينَ عَلَيْهَا مُتَقَٰبِلِينَ

16 Reclining on them, facing one another.

١٧ يَطُوفُ عَلَيْهِمْ وِلْدَٰنٌ مُّخَلَّدُونَ

17 Serving them will be immortalized youth.

١٨ بِأَكْوَابٍ وَأَبَارِيقَ وَكَأْسٍ مِّن مَّعِينٍ

18 With cups, pitchers, and sparkling drinks.

١٩ لَّا يُصَدَّعُونَ عَنْهَا وَلَا يُنزِفُونَ

19 Causing them neither headache, nor intoxication.

٢٠ وَفَٰكِهَةٍ مِّمَّا يَتَخَيَّرُونَ

20 And fruits of their choice.

٢١ وَلَحْمِ طَيْرٍ مِّمَّا يَشْتَهُونَ

21 And meat of birds that they may desire.

٢٢ وَحُورٌ عِينٌ

22 And lovely companions.

٢٣ كَأَمْثَٰلِ ٱللُّؤْلُؤِ ٱلْمَكْنُونِ

23 The likenesses of treasured pearls.

٢٤ جَزَآءًۢ بِمَا كَانُوا۟ يَعْمَلُونَ

24 As a reward for what they used to do.

٢٥ لَا يَسْمَعُونَ فِيهَا لَغْوًا وَلَا تَأْثِيمًا

25 Therein they will hear no nonsense, and no accusations.

٢٦ إِلَّا قِيلًا سَلَٰمًا سَلَٰمًا

26 But only the greeting: “Peace, peace.”

٢٧ وَأَصْحَٰبُ ٱلْيَمِينِ مَآ أَصْحَٰبُ ٱلْيَمِينِ

27 And those on the Right—what of those on the Right?

٢٨ فِى سِدْرٍ مَّخْضُودٍ

28 In lush orchards.

٢٩ وَطَلْحٍ مَّنضُودٍ

29 And sweet-smelling plants.

٣٠ وَظِلٍّ مَّمْدُودٍ

30 And extended shade.

٣١ وَمَآءٍ مَّسْكُوبٍ	31 And outpouring water.
٣٢ وَفَٰكِهَةٍ كَثِيرَةٍ	32 And abundant fruit.
٣٣ لَّا مَقْطُوعَةٍ وَلَا مَمْنُوعَةٍ	33 Neither withheld, nor forbidden.
٣٤ وَفُرُشٍ مَّرْفُوعَةٍ	34 And uplifted mattresses.
٣٥ إِنَّآ أَنشَأْنَٰهُنَّ إِنشَآءً	35 We have created them of special creation.
٣٦ فَجَعَلْنَٰهُنَّ أَبْكَارًا	36 And made them virgins.
٣٧ عُرُبًا أَتْرَابًا	37 Tender and un-aging.
٣٨ لِّأَصْحَٰبِ ٱلْيَمِينِ	38 For those on the Right.
٣٩ ثُلَّةٌ مِّنَ ٱلْأَوَّلِينَ	39 A throng from the ancients.
٤٠ وَثُلَّةٌ مِّنَ ٱلْءَاخِرِينَ	40 And a throng from the latecomers.
٤١ وَأَصْحَٰبُ ٱلشِّمَالِ مَآ أَصْحَٰبُ ٱلشِّمَالِ	41 And those on the Left—what of those on the Left?
٤٢ فِى سَمُومٍ وَحَمِيمٍ	42 Amid searing wind and boiling water.
٤٣ وَظِلٍّ مِّن يَحْمُومٍ	43 And a shadow of thick smoke.
٤٤ لَّا بَارِدٍ وَلَا كَرِيمٍ	44 Neither cool, nor refreshing.
٤٥ إِنَّهُمْ كَانُوا۟ قَبْلَ ذَٰلِكَ مُتْرَفِينَ	45 They had lived before that in luxury.
٤٦ وَكَانُوا۟ يُصِرُّونَ عَلَى ٱلْحِنثِ ٱلْعَظِيمِ	46 And they used to persist in immense wrongdoing.
٤٧ وَكَانُوا۟ يَقُولُونَ أَئِذَا مِتْنَا وَكُنَّا تُرَابًا وَعِظَٰمًا أَءِنَّا لَمَبْعُوثُونَ	47 And they used to say, “When we are dead and turned into dust and bones, are we to be resurrected?
٤٨ أَوَءَابَآؤُنَا ٱلْأَوَّلُونَ	48 And our ancient ancestors too?”
٤٩ قُلْ إِنَّ ٱلْأَوَّلِينَ وَٱلْءَاخِرِينَ	49 Say, “The first and the last.
٥٠ لَمَجْمُوعُونَ إِلَىٰ مِيقَٰتِ يَوْمٍ مَّعْلُومٍ	50 Will be gathered for the appointment of a familiar Day.”
٥١ ثُمَّ إِنَّكُمْ أَيُّهَا ٱلضَّآلُّونَ ٱلْمُكَذِّبُونَ	51 Then you, you misguided, who deny the truth.

٥٢ لَـَٔاكِلُونَ مِن شَجَرٍ مِّن زَقُّومٍ	52 Will be eating from the Tree of Bitterness.
٥٣ فَمَالِـُٔونَ مِنْهَا ٱلْبُطُونَ	53 Will be filling your bellies with it.
٥٤ فَشَٰرِبُونَ عَلَيْهِ مِنَ ٱلْحَمِيمِ	54 Will be drinking on top of it boiling water.
٥٥ فَشَٰرِبُونَ شُرْبَ ٱلْهِيمِ	55 Drinking like thirsty camels drink.
٥٦ هَٰذَا نُزُلُهُمْ يَوْمَ ٱلدِّينِ	56 That is their hospitality on the Day of Retribution.
٥٧ نَحْنُ خَلَقْنَٰكُمْ فَلَوْلَا تُصَدِّقُونَ	57 We created you—if only you would believe!
٥٨ أَفَرَءَيْتُم مَّا تُمْنُونَ	58 Have you seen what you ejaculate?
٥٩ ءَأَنتُمْ تَخْلُقُونَهُۥٓ أَمْ نَحْنُ ٱلْخَٰلِقُونَ	59 Is it you who create it, or are We the Creator?
٦٠ نَحْنُ قَدَّرْنَا بَيْنَكُمُ ٱلْمَوْتَ وَمَا نَحْنُ بِمَسْبُوقِينَ	60 We have decreed death among you, and We will not be outstripped.
٦١ عَلَىٰٓ أَن نُّبَدِّلَ أَمْثَٰلَكُمْ وَنُنشِئَكُمْ فِى مَا لَا تَعْلَمُونَ	61 In replacing you with your likes, and transforming you into what you do not know.
٦٢ وَلَقَدْ عَلِمْتُمُ ٱلنَّشْأَةَ ٱلْأُولَىٰ فَلَوْلَا تَذَكَّرُونَ	62 You have known the first formation; if only you would remember.
٦٣ أَفَرَءَيْتُم مَّا تَحْرُثُونَ	63 Have you seen what you cultivate?
٦٤ ءَأَنتُمْ تَزْرَعُونَهُۥٓ أَمْ نَحْنُ ٱلزَّٰرِعُونَ	64 Is it you who make it grow, or are We the Grower?
٦٥ لَوْ نَشَآءُ لَجَعَلْنَٰهُ حُطَٰمًا فَظَلْتُمْ تَفَكَّهُونَ	65 If We will, We can turn it into rubble; then you will lament.
٦٦ إِنَّا لَمُغْرَمُونَ	66 “We are penalized.
٦٧ بَلْ نَحْنُ مَحْرُومُونَ	67 No, we are being deprived.”
٦٨ أَفَرَءَيْتُمُ ٱلْمَآءَ ٱلَّذِى تَشْرَبُونَ	68 Have you seen the water you drink?
٦٩ ءَأَنتُمْ أَنزَلْتُمُوهُ مِنَ ٱلْمُزْنِ أَمْ نَحْنُ ٱلْمُنزِلُونَ	69 Is it you who sent it down from the clouds, or are We the Sender?

٧٠ لَوْ نَشَآءُ جَعَلْنَٰهُ أُجَاجًا فَلَوْلَا تَشْكُرُونَ

70 If We will, We can make it salty. Will you not be thankful?

٧١ أَفَرَءَيْتُمُ ٱلنَّارَ ٱلَّتِى تُورُونَ

71 Have you seen the fire you kindle?

٧٢ ءَأَنتُمْ أَنشَأْتُمْ شَجَرَتَهَآ أَمْ نَحْنُ ٱلْمُنشِـُٔونَ

72 Is it you who produce its tree, or are We the Producer?

٧٣ نَحْنُ جَعَلْنَٰهَا تَذْكِرَةً وَمَتَٰعًا لِّلْمُقْوِينَ

73 We have made it a reminder, and a comfort for the users.

٧٤ فَسَبِّحْ بِٱسْمِ رَبِّكَ ٱلْعَظِيمِ

74 So glorify the Name of your Great Lord.

٧٥ فَلَآ أُقْسِمُ بِمَوَٰقِعِ ٱلنُّجُومِ

75 I swear by the locations of the stars.

٧٦ وَإِنَّهُۥ لَقَسَمٌ لَّوْ تَعْلَمُونَ عَظِيمٌ

76 It is an oath, if you only knew, that is tremendous.

٧٧ إِنَّهُۥ لَقُرْءَانٌ كَرِيمٌ

77 It is a noble Quran.

٧٨ فِى كِتَٰبٍ مَّكْنُونٍ

78 In a well-protected Book.

٧٩ لَّا يَمَسُّهُۥٓ إِلَّا ٱلْمُطَهَّرُونَ

79 None can grasp it except the purified.

٨٠ تَنزِيلٌ مِّن رَّبِّ ٱلْعَٰلَمِينَ

80 A revelation from the Lord of the Worlds.

٨١ أَفَبِهَٰذَا ٱلْحَدِيثِ أَنتُم مُّدْهِنُونَ

81 Is it this discourse that you take so lightly?

٨٢ وَتَجْعَلُونَ رِزْقَكُمْ أَنَّكُمْ تُكَذِّبُونَ

82 And you make it your livelihood to deny it?

٨٣ فَلَوْلَآ إِذَا بَلَغَتِ ٱلْحُلْقُومَ

83 So when it has reached the throat.

٨٤ وَأَنتُمْ حِينَئِذٍ تَنظُرُونَ

84 As you are looking on.

٨٥ وَنَحْنُ أَقْرَبُ إِلَيْهِ مِنكُمْ وَلَٰكِن لَّا تُبْصِرُونَ

85 We are nearer to it than you are, but you do not see.

٨٦ فَلَوْلَآ إِن كُنتُمْ غَيْرَ مَدِينِينَ

86 If you are not held to account.

٨٧ تَرْجِعُونَهَآ إِن كُنتُمْ صَٰدِقِينَ

87 Then bring it back, if you are truthful.

٨٨ فَأَمَّآ إِن كَانَ مِنَ ٱلْمُقَرَّبِينَ

88 But if he is one of those brought near.

٨٩ فَرَوْحٌ وَرَيْحَانٌ وَجَنَّتُ نَعِيمٍ

89 Then happiness, and flowers, and Garden of Delights.

٩٠ وَأَمَّآ إِن كَانَ مِنْ أَصْحَٰبِ ٱلْيَمِينِ	90 And if he is one of those on the Right.
٩١ فَسَلَٰمٌ لَّكَ مِنْ أَصْحَٰبِ ٱلْيَمِينِ	91 Then, “Peace upon you,” from those on the Right.
٩٢ وَأَمَّآ إِن كَانَ مِنَ ٱلْمُكَذِّبِينَ ٱلضَّآلِّينَ	92 But if he is one of the deniers, the mistaken.
٩٣ فَنُزُلٌ مِّنْ حَمِيمٍ	93 Then a welcome of Inferno.
٩٤ وَتَصْلِيَةُ جَحِيمٍ	94 And burning in Hell.
٩٥ إِنَّ هَٰذَا لَهُوَ حَقُّ ٱلْيَقِينِ	95 This is the certain truth.
٩٦ فَسَبِّحْ بِٱسْمِ رَبِّكَ ٱلْعَظِيمِ	96 So glorify the Name of your Lord, the Magnificent

57 Iron الحديد

بِسْمِ ٱللَّهِ ٱلرَّحْمَٰنِ ٱلرَّحِيمِ	In the name of Allah, the Gracious, the Merciful.
١ سَبَّحَ لِلَّهِ مَا فِى ٱلسَّمَٰوَٰتِ وَٱلْأَرْضِ ۖ وَهُوَ ٱلْعَزِيزُ ٱلْحَكِيمُ	1 Glorifying Allah is everything in the heavens and the earth. He is the Almighty, the Wise.
٢ لَهُۥ مُلْكُ ٱلسَّمَٰوَٰتِ وَٱلْأَرْضِ ۖ يُحْىِۦ وَيُمِيتُ ۖ وَهُوَ عَلَىٰ كُلِّ شَىْءٍ قَدِيرٌ	2 To Him belongs the kingdom of the heavens and the earth. He gives life and causes death, and He has power over all things.
٣ هُوَ ٱلْأَوَّلُ وَٱلْءَاخِرُ وَٱلظَّٰهِرُ وَٱلْبَاطِنُ ۖ وَهُوَ بِكُلِّ شَىْءٍ عَلِيمٌ	3 He is the First and the Last, and the Outer and the Inner, and He has knowledge of all things.
٤ هُوَ ٱلَّذِى خَلَقَ ٱلسَّمَٰوَٰتِ وَٱلْأَرْضَ فِى سِتَّةِ أَيَّامٍ ثُمَّ ٱسْتَوَىٰ عَلَى ٱلْعَرْشِ ۚ يَعْلَمُ مَا يَلِجُ فِى ٱلْأَرْضِ وَمَا يَخْرُجُ مِنْهَا وَمَا يَنزِلُ مِنَ ٱلسَّمَآءِ وَمَا يَعْرُجُ فِيهَا ۖ وَهُوَ مَعَكُمْ أَيْنَ مَا كُنتُمْ ۚ وَٱللَّهُ بِمَا تَعْمَلُونَ بَصِيرٌ	4 It is He who created the heavens and the earth in six days, then settled over the Throne. He knows what penetrates into the earth, and what comes out of it, and what descends from the sky, and what ascends to it. And He is with you wherever you may be. Allah is Seeing of everything you do.
٥ لَّهُۥ مُلْكُ ٱلسَّمَٰوَٰتِ وَٱلْأَرْضِ ۚ وَإِلَى ٱللَّهِ تُرْجَعُ ٱلْأُمُورُ	5 To Him belongs the kingship of the heavens and the earth, and to Allah all matters are referred.

٦ يُولِجُ ٱلَّيْلَ فِى ٱلنَّهَارِ وَيُولِجُ ٱلنَّهَارَ فِى ٱلَّيْلِ ۚ
وَهُوَ عَلِيمٌۢ بِذَاتِ ٱلصُّدُورِ

6 He merges the night into the day, and He merges the day into the night; and He knows what the hearts contains.

٧ ءَامِنُوا۟ بِٱللَّهِ وَرَسُولِهِۦ وَأَنفِقُوا۟ مِمَّا جَعَلَكُم
مُّسْتَخْلَفِينَ فِيهِ ۖ فَٱلَّذِينَ ءَامَنُوا۟ مِنكُمْ
وَأَنفَقُوا۟ لَهُمْ أَجْرٌ كَبِيرٌ

7 Believe in Allah and His Messenger, and spend from what He made you inherit. Those among you who believe and give will have a great reward.

٨ وَمَا لَكُمْ لَا تُؤْمِنُونَ بِٱللَّهِ ۙ وَٱلرَّسُولُ يَدْعُوكُمْ
لِتُؤْمِنُوا۟ بِرَبِّكُمْ وَقَدْ أَخَذَ مِيثَٰقَكُمْ إِن كُنتُم
مُّؤْمِنِينَ

8 What is the matter with you that you do not believe in Allah, when the Messenger calls you to believe in your Lord, and He has received a pledge from you, if you are believers?

٩ هُوَ ٱلَّذِى يُنَزِّلُ عَلَىٰ عَبْدِهِۦٓ ءَايَٰتٍۭ بَيِّنَٰتٍ
لِّيُخْرِجَكُم مِّنَ ٱلظُّلُمَٰتِ إِلَى ٱلنُّورِ ۚ وَإِنَّ ٱللَّهَ
بِكُمْ لَرَءُوفٌ رَّحِيمٌ

9 It is He who sends down upon His servant clear revelations, to bring you out of darkness into the light. Allah is Gentle towards you, Most Compassionate.

١٠ وَمَا لَكُمْ أَلَّا تُنفِقُوا۟ فِى سَبِيلِ ٱللَّهِ وَلِلَّهِ
مِيرَٰثُ ٱلسَّمَٰوَٰتِ وَٱلْأَرْضِ ۚ لَا يَسْتَوِى مِنكُم مَّنْ
أَنفَقَ مِن قَبْلِ ٱلْفَتْحِ وَقَٰتَلَ ۚ أُو۟لَٰٓئِكَ أَعْظَمُ
دَرَجَةً مِّنَ ٱلَّذِينَ أَنفَقُوا۟ مِنۢ بَعْدُ وَقَٰتَلُوا۟ ۚ وَكُلًّا
وَعَدَ ٱللَّهُ ٱلْحُسْنَىٰ ۚ وَٱللَّهُ بِمَا تَعْمَلُونَ خَبِيرٌ

10 And why is it that you do not spend in the cause of Allah, when to Allah belongs the inheritance of the heavens and the earth? Not equal among you are those who contributed before the conquest, and fought. Those are higher in rank than those who contributed afterwards, and fought. But Allah promises both a good reward. Allah is Well Experienced in what you do.

١١ مَّن ذَا ٱلَّذِى يُقْرِضُ ٱللَّهَ قَرْضًا حَسَنًا
فَيُضَٰعِفَهُۥ لَهُۥ وَلَهُۥٓ أَجْرٌ كَرِيمٌ

11 Who is he who will lend Allah a loan of goodness, that He may double it for him, and will have a generous reward?

١٢ يَوْمَ تَرَى ٱلْمُؤْمِنِينَ وَٱلْمُؤْمِنَٰتِ يَسْعَىٰ
نُورُهُم بَيْنَ أَيْدِيهِمْ وَبِأَيْمَٰنِهِم بُشْرَىٰكُمُ ٱلْيَوْمَ
جَنَّٰتٌ تَجْرِى مِن تَحْتِهَا ٱلْأَنْهَٰرُ خَٰلِدِينَ فِيهَا ۚ
ذَٰلِكَ هُوَ ٱلْفَوْزُ ٱلْعَظِيمُ

12 On the Day when you see the believing men and believing women—their light radiating ahead of them, and to their right: "Good news for you today: gardens beneath which rivers flow, dwelling

therein forever. That is the great triumph."

١٣ يَوْمَ يَقُولُ ٱلْمُنَٰفِقُونَ وَٱلْمُنَٰفِقَٰتُ لِلَّذِينَ
ءَامَنُوا۟ ٱنظُرُونَا نَقْتَبِسْ مِن نُّورِكُمْ قِيلَ
ٱرْجِعُوا۟ وَرَآءَكُمْ فَٱلْتَمِسُوا۟ نُورًا فَضُرِبَ بَيْنَهُم
بِسُورٍ لَّهُۥ بَابٌۢ بَاطِنُهُۥ فِيهِ ٱلرَّحْمَةُ وَظَٰهِرُهُۥ مِن
قِبَلِهِ ٱلْعَذَابُ

13 On the Day when the hypocritical men and hypocritical women will say to those who believed, "Wait for us; let us absorb some of your light." It will be said, "Go back behind you, and seek light." A wall will be raised between them, in which is a door; within it is mercy, and outside it is agony.

١٤ يُنَادُونَهُمْ أَلَمْ نَكُن مَّعَكُمْ ۖ قَالُوا۟ بَلَىٰ وَلَٰكِنَّكُمْ
فَتَنتُمْ أَنفُسَكُمْ وَتَرَبَّصْتُمْ وَٱرْتَبْتُمْ وَغَرَّتْكُمُ
ٱلْأَمَانِىُّ حَتَّىٰ جَآءَ أَمْرُ ٱللَّهِ وَغَرَّكُم بِٱللَّهِ
ٱلْغَرُورُ

14 They will call to them, "Were we not with you?" They will say, "Yes, but you cheated your souls, and waited, and doubted, and became deluded by wishful thinking, until the command of Allah arrived; and arrogance deceived you regarding Allah."

١٥ فَٱلْيَوْمَ لَا يُؤْخَذُ مِنكُمْ فِدْيَةٌ وَلَا مِنَ ٱلَّذِينَ
كَفَرُوا۟ ۚ مَأْوَىٰكُمُ ٱلنَّارُ ۖ هِىَ مَوْلَىٰكُمْ ۖ وَبِئْسَ
ٱلْمَصِيرُ

15 "Therefore, today no ransom will be accepted from you, nor from those who disbelieved. The Fire is your refuge. It is your companion—what an evil fate!"

١٦ أَلَمْ يَأْنِ لِلَّذِينَ ءَامَنُوٓا۟ أَن تَخْشَعَ قُلُوبُهُمْ
لِذِكْرِ ٱللَّهِ وَمَا نَزَلَ مِنَ ٱلْحَقِّ وَلَا يَكُونُوا۟
كَٱلَّذِينَ أُوتُوا۟ ٱلْكِتَٰبَ مِن قَبْلُ فَطَالَ عَلَيْهِمُ
ٱلْأَمَدُ فَقَسَتْ قُلُوبُهُمْ ۖ وَكَثِيرٌ مِّنْهُمْ فَٰسِقُونَ

16 Is it not time for those who believe to surrender their hearts to the remembrance of Allah, and to the truth that has come down, and not be like those who were given the Book previously, but time became prolonged for them, so their hearts hardened, and many of them are sinners?

١٧ ٱعْلَمُوٓا۟ أَنَّ ٱللَّهَ يُحْىِ ٱلْأَرْضَ بَعْدَ مَوْتِهَا ۚ قَدْ
بَيَّنَّا لَكُمُ ٱلْءَايَٰتِ لَعَلَّكُمْ تَعْقِلُونَ

17 Know that Allah revives the earth after its death. We thus explain the revelations for you, so that you may understand.

١٨ إِنَّ ٱلْمُصَّدِّقِينَ وَٱلْمُصَّدِّقَٰتِ وَأَقْرَضُوا۟ ٱللَّهَ
قَرْضًا حَسَنًا يُضَٰعَفُ لَهُمْ وَلَهُمْ أَجْرٌ كَرِيمٌ

18 The charitable men and charitable women, who have loaned Allah a loan of righteousness—it will be multiplied for them, and for them is a generous reward.

١٩ وَٱلَّذِينَ ءَامَنُواْ بِٱللَّهِ وَرُسُلِهِۦٓ أُوْلَٰٓئِكَ هُمُ
ٱلصِّدِّيقُونَۖ وَٱلشُّهَدَآءُ عِندَ رَبِّهِمۡ لَهُمۡ أَجۡرُهُمۡ
وَنُورُهُمۡۖ وَٱلَّذِينَ كَفَرُواْ وَكَذَّبُواْ بِـَٔايَٰتِنَآ أُوْلَٰٓئِكَ
أَصۡحَٰبُ ٱلۡجَحِيمِ

19 Those who believe in Allah and His messengers—these are the sincere and the witnesses with their Lord; they will have their reward and their light. But as for those who disbelieve and deny Our revelations—these are the inmates of the Blaze.

٢٠ ٱعۡلَمُوٓاْ أَنَّمَا ٱلۡحَيَوٰةُ ٱلدُّنۡيَا لَعِبٞ وَلَهۡوٞ وَزِينَةٞ
وَتَفَاخُرُۢ بَيۡنَكُمۡ وَتَكَاثُرٞ فِي ٱلۡأَمۡوَٰلِ وَٱلۡأَوۡلَٰدِۖ
كَمَثَلِ غَيۡثٍ أَعۡجَبَ ٱلۡكُفَّارَ نَبَاتُهُۥ ثُمَّ يَهِيجُ
فَتَرَىٰهُ مُصۡفَرّٗا ثُمَّ يَكُونُ حُطَٰمٗاۖ وَفِي ٱلۡأٓخِرَةِ
عَذَابٞ شَدِيدٞ وَمَغۡفِرَةٞ مِّنَ ٱللَّهِ وَرِضۡوَٰنٞۚ وَمَا
ٱلۡحَيَوٰةُ ٱلدُّنۡيَآ إِلَّا مَتَٰعُ ٱلۡغُرُورِ

20 Know that the worldly life is only play, and distraction, and glitter, and boasting among you, and rivalry in wealth and children. It is like a rainfall that produces plants, and delights the disbelievers. But then it withers, and you see it yellowing, and then it becomes debris. While in the Hereafter there is severe agony, and forgiveness from Allah, and acceptance. The life of this world is nothing but enjoyment of vanity.

٢١ سَابِقُوٓاْ إِلَىٰ مَغۡفِرَةٖ مِّن رَّبِّكُمۡ وَجَنَّةٍ عَرۡضُهَا
كَعَرۡضِ ٱلسَّمَآءِ وَٱلۡأَرۡضِ أُعِدَّتۡ لِلَّذِينَ ءَامَنُواْ
بِٱللَّهِ وَرُسُلِهِۦۚ ذَٰلِكَ فَضۡلُ ٱللَّهِ يُؤۡتِيهِ مَن
يَشَآءُۚ وَٱللَّهُ ذُو ٱلۡفَضۡلِ ٱلۡعَظِيمِ

21 Race towards forgiveness from your Lord; and a Garden as vast as the heavens and the earth, prepared for those who believe in Allah and His messengers. That is the grace of Allah; He bestows it on whomever He wills. Allah is the Possessor of Immense Grace.

٢٢ مَآ أَصَابَ مِن مُّصِيبَةٖ فِي ٱلۡأَرۡضِ وَلَا فِيٓ
أَنفُسِكُمۡ إِلَّا فِي كِتَٰبٖ مِّن قَبۡلِ أَن نَّبۡرَأَهَآۚ إِنَّ
ذَٰلِكَ عَلَى ٱللَّهِ يَسِيرٞ

22 No calamity occurs on earth, or in your souls, but it is in a Book, even before We make it happen. That is easy for Allah.

٢٣ لِّكَيۡلَا تَأۡسَوۡاْ عَلَىٰ مَا فَاتَكُمۡ وَلَا تَفۡرَحُواْ بِمَآ
ءَاتَىٰكُمۡۗ وَٱللَّهُ لَا يُحِبُّ كُلَّ مُخۡتَالٖ فَخُورٍ

23 That you may not sorrow over what eludes you, nor exult over what He has given you. Allah does not love the proud snob.

٢٤ ٱلَّذِينَ يَبۡخَلُونَ وَيَأۡمُرُونَ ٱلنَّاسَ بِٱلۡبُخۡلِۗ
وَمَن يَتَوَلَّ فَإِنَّ ٱللَّهَ هُوَ ٱلۡغَنِيُّ ٱلۡحَمِيدُ

24 Those who are stingy, and induce people to be stingy. Whoever turns away—Allah is the Independent, the Praiseworthy.

٢٥ لَقَدْ أَرْسَلْنَا رُسُلَنَا بِٱلْبَيِّنَٰتِ وَأَنزَلْنَا مَعَهُمُ
ٱلْكِتَٰبَ وَٱلْمِيزَانَ لِيَقُومَ ٱلنَّاسُ بِٱلْقِسْطِ ۖ وَأَنزَلْنَا
ٱلْحَدِيدَ فِيهِ بَأْسٌ شَدِيدٌ وَمَنَٰفِعُ لِلنَّاسِ وَلِيَعْلَمَ
ٱللَّهُ مَن يَنصُرُهُۥ وَرُسُلَهُۥ بِٱلْغَيْبِ ۚ إِنَّ ٱللَّهَ قَوِىٌّ
عَزِيزٌ

25 We sent Our messengers with the clear proofs, and We sent down with them the Book and the Balance, that humanity may uphold justice. And We sent down iron, in which is violent force, and benefits for humanity. That Allah may know who supports Him and His messengers invisibly. Allah is Strong and Powerful.

٢٦ وَلَقَدْ أَرْسَلْنَا نُوحًا وَإِبْرَٰهِيمَ وَجَعَلْنَا فِى
ذُرِّيَّتِهِمَا ٱلنُّبُوَّةَ وَٱلْكِتَٰبَ ۖ فَمِنْهُم مُّهْتَدٍ ۖ وَكَثِيرٌ
مِّنْهُمْ فَٰسِقُونَ

26 We sent Noah and Abraham, and established in their line Prophethood and the Scripture. Some of them are guided, but many of them are sinners.

٢٧ ثُمَّ قَفَّيْنَا عَلَىٰٓ ءَاثَٰرِهِم بِرُسُلِنَا وَقَفَّيْنَا
بِعِيسَى ٱبْنِ مَرْيَمَ وَءَاتَيْنَٰهُ ٱلْإِنجِيلَ وَجَعَلْنَا
فِى قُلُوبِ ٱلَّذِينَ ٱتَّبَعُوهُ رَأْفَةً وَرَحْمَةً
وَرَهْبَانِيَّةً ٱبْتَدَعُوهَا مَا كَتَبْنَٰهَا عَلَيْهِمْ إِلَّا
ٱبْتِغَآءَ رِضْوَٰنِ ٱللَّهِ فَمَا رَعَوْهَا حَقَّ رِعَايَتِهَا ۖ
فَـَٔاتَيْنَا ٱلَّذِينَ ءَامَنُوا۟ مِنْهُمْ أَجْرَهُمْ ۖ وَكَثِيرٌ
مِّنْهُمْ فَٰسِقُونَ

27 Then We sent in their wake Our messengers, and followed up with Jesus son of Mary, and We gave him the Gospel, and instilled in the hearts of those who followed him compassion and mercy. But as for the monasticism which they invented—We did not ordain it for them—only to seek Allah's approval. But they did not observe it with its due observance. So We gave those of them who believed their reward, but many of them are sinful.

٢٨ يَٰٓأَيُّهَا ٱلَّذِينَ ءَامَنُوا۟ ٱتَّقُوا۟ ٱللَّهَ وَءَامِنُوا۟
بِرَسُولِهِۦ يُؤْتِكُمْ كِفْلَيْنِ مِن رَّحْمَتِهِۦ وَيَجْعَل
لَّكُمْ نُورًا تَمْشُونَ بِهِۦ وَيَغْفِرْ لَكُمْ ۚ وَٱللَّهُ غَفُورٌ
رَّحِيمٌ

28 O you who believe! Fear Allah, and believe in His Messenger: He will give you a double portion of His mercy, and will give you a light by which you walk, and will forgive you. Allah is Forgiving and Merciful.

٢٩ لِّئَلَّا يَعْلَمَ أَهْلُ ٱلْكِتَٰبِ أَلَّا يَقْدِرُونَ عَلَىٰ
شَىْءٍ مِّن فَضْلِ ٱللَّهِ ۙ وَأَنَّ ٱلْفَضْلَ بِيَدِ ٱللَّهِ
يُؤْتِيهِ مَن يَشَآءُ ۚ وَٱللَّهُ ذُو ٱلْفَضْلِ ٱلْعَظِيمِ

29 That the People of the Book may know that they have no power whatsoever over Allah's grace, and that all grace is in Allah's hand; He gives it to whomever He wills. Allah is Possessor of Great Grace.

58 The Argument المجادلة

بِسْمِ ٱللَّهِ ٱلرَّحْمَٰنِ ٱلرَّحِيمِ

In the name of Allah, the Gracious, the Merciful.

١ قَدْ سَمِعَ ٱللَّهُ قَوْلَ ٱلَّتِى تُجَٰدِلُكَ فِى زَوْجِهَا
وَتَشْتَكِىٓ إِلَى ٱللَّهِ وَٱللَّهُ يَسْمَعُ تَحَاوُرَكُمَآ ۚ إِنَّ
ٱللَّهَ سَمِيعٌۢ بَصِيرٌ

1 Allah has heard the statement of she who argued with you concerning her husband, as she complained to Allah. Allah heard your conversation. Allah is Hearing and Seeing.

٢ ٱلَّذِينَ يُظَٰهِرُونَ مِنكُم مِّن نِّسَآئِهِم مَّا هُنَّ
أُمَّهَٰتِهِمْ ۖ إِنْ أُمَّهَٰتُهُمْ إِلَّا ٱلَّٰٓـِٔى وَلَدْنَهُمْ ۚ وَإِنَّهُمْ
لَيَقُولُونَ مُنكَرًا مِّنَ ٱلْقَوْلِ وَزُورًا ۚ وَإِنَّ ٱللَّهَ
لَعَفُوٌّ غَفُورٌ

2 Those of you who estrange their wives by equating them with their mothers—they are not their mothers. Their mothers are none else but those who gave birth to them. What they say is evil, and a blatant lie. But Allah is Pardoning and Forgiving.

٣ وَٱلَّذِينَ يُظَٰهِرُونَ مِن نِّسَآئِهِمْ ثُمَّ يَعُودُونَ
لِمَا قَالُوا۟ فَتَحْرِيرُ رَقَبَةٍ مِّن قَبْلِ أَن يَتَمَآسَّا ۚ
ذَٰلِكُمْ تُوعَظُونَ بِهِۦ ۚ وَٱللَّهُ بِمَا تَعْمَلُونَ خَبِيرٌ

3 Those who estrange their wives by equating them with their mothers, then go back on what they said, must set free a slave before they may touch one another. To this you are exhorted, and Allah is well aware of what you do.

٤ فَمَن لَّمْ يَجِدْ فَصِيَامُ شَهْرَيْنِ مُتَتَابِعَيْنِ مِن
قَبْلِ أَن يَتَمَآسَّا ۖ فَمَن لَّمْ يَسْتَطِعْ فَإِطْعَامُ
سِتِّينَ مِسْكِينًا ۚ ذَٰلِكَ لِتُؤْمِنُوا۟ بِٱللَّهِ وَرَسُولِهِۦ ۚ
وَتِلْكَ حُدُودُ ٱللَّهِ ۗ وَلِلْكَٰفِرِينَ عَذَابٌ أَلِيمٌ

4 But whoever cannot find the means must fast for two consecutive months before they may touch one another. And if he is unable, then the feeding of sixty needy people. This, in order that you affirm your faith in Allah and His Messenger. These are the ordinances of Allah. The unbelievers will have a painful punishment.

٥ إِنَّ ٱلَّذِينَ يُحَآدُّونَ ٱللَّهَ وَرَسُولَهُۥ كُبِتُوا۟ كَمَا
كُبِتَ ٱلَّذِينَ مِن قَبْلِهِمْ ۚ وَقَدْ أَنزَلْنَآ ءَايَٰتٍۭ
بَيِّنَٰتٍ ۚ وَلِلْكَٰفِرِينَ عَذَابٌ مُّهِينٌ

5 Those who oppose Allah and His Messenger will be subdued, as those before them were subdued. We have revealed clear messages. The unbelievers will have a demeaning punishment.

٦ يَوْمَ يَبْعَثُهُمُ ٱللَّهُ جَمِيعًا فَيُنَبِّئُهُم بِمَا عَمِلُوٓا۟ ۚ
أَحْصَىٰهُ ٱللَّهُ وَنَسُوهُ ۚ وَٱللَّهُ عَلَىٰ كُلِّ شَىْءٍ
شَهِيدٌ

6 On the Day when Allah resurrects them all, and informs them of what they did. Allah has kept count of it, but they have forgotten it. Allah is Witness over everything.

٧ أَلَمْ تَرَ أَنَّ ٱللَّهَ يَعْلَمُ مَا فِى ٱلسَّمَٰوَٰتِ وَمَا فِى
ٱلْأَرْضِ ۖ مَا يَكُونُ مِن نَّجْوَىٰ ثَلَٰثَةٍ إِلَّا هُوَ
رَابِعُهُمْ وَلَا خَمْسَةٍ إِلَّا هُوَ سَادِسُهُمْ وَلَآ أَدْنَىٰ
مِن ذَٰلِكَ وَلَآ أَكْثَرَ إِلَّا هُوَ مَعَهُمْ أَيْنَ مَا كَانُوا۟ ۖ
ثُمَّ يُنَبِّئُهُم بِمَا عَمِلُوا۟ يَوْمَ ٱلْقِيَٰمَةِ ۚ إِنَّ ٱللَّهَ بِكُلِّ
شَىْءٍ عَلِيمٌ

7 Do you not realize that Allah knows everything in the heavens and everything on earth? There is no secret counsel between three, but He is their fourth; nor between five, but He is their sixth; nor less than that, nor more, but He is with them wherever they may be. Then, on the Day of Resurrection, He will inform them of what they did. Allah has knowledge of everything.

٨ أَلَمْ تَرَ إِلَى ٱلَّذِينَ نُهُوا۟ عَنِ ٱلنَّجْوَىٰ ثُمَّ
يَعُودُونَ لِمَا نُهُوا۟ عَنْهُ وَيَتَنَٰجَوْنَ بِٱلْإِثْمِ
وَٱلْعُدْوَٰنِ وَمَعْصِيَتِ ٱلرَّسُولِ وَإِذَا جَآءُوكَ
حَيَّوْكَ بِمَا لَمْ يُحَيِّكَ بِهِ ٱللَّهُ وَيَقُولُونَ فِىٓ
أَنفُسِهِمْ لَوْلَا يُعَذِّبُنَا ٱللَّهُ بِمَا نَقُولُ ۚ حَسْبُهُمْ
جَهَنَّمُ يَصْلَوْنَهَا ۖ فَبِئْسَ ٱلْمَصِيرُ

8 Have you noted those who were prohibited from conspiring secretly, but then reverted to what they were prohibited from? They conspire to commit sin, and aggression, and defiance of the Messenger. And when they come to you, they greet you with a greeting that Allah never greeted you with. And they say within themselves, "Why does Allah not punish us for what we say?" Hell is enough for them. They will roast in it. What a miserable destiny!

٩ يَٰٓأَيُّهَا ٱلَّذِينَ ءَامَنُوٓا۟ إِذَا تَنَٰجَيْتُمْ فَلَا تَتَنَٰجَوْا۟
بِٱلْإِثْمِ وَٱلْعُدْوَٰنِ وَمَعْصِيَتِ ٱلرَّسُولِ وَتَنَٰجَوْا۟
بِٱلْبِرِّ وَٱلتَّقْوَىٰ ۖ وَٱتَّقُوا۟ ٱللَّهَ ٱلَّذِىٓ إِلَيْهِ تُحْشَرُونَ

9 O you who believe! When you converse secretly, do not converse in sin, and aggression, and disobedience of the Messenger; but converse in virtue and piety; And fear Allah, to Whom you will be gathered.

١٠ إِنَّمَا ٱلنَّجْوَىٰ مِنَ ٱلشَّيْطَٰنِ لِيَحْزُنَ ٱلَّذِينَ
ءَامَنُوا۟ وَلَيْسَ بِضَآرِّهِمْ شَيْـًٔا إِلَّا بِإِذْنِ ٱللَّهِ ۚ
وَعَلَى ٱللَّهِ فَلْيَتَوَكَّلِ ٱلْمُؤْمِنُونَ

10 Conspiracies are from Satan, that he may dishearten those who believe; but he will not harm them in the least, except by leave of Allah. So let the believers put their trust in Allah.

١١ يَٰٓأَيُّهَا ٱلَّذِينَ ءَامَنُوٓاْ إِذَا قِيلَ لَكُمْ تَفَسَّحُواْ
فِى ٱلْمَجَٰلِسِ فَٱفْسَحُواْ يَفْسَحِ ٱللَّهُ لَكُمْۖ وَإِذَا
قِيلَ ٱنشُزُواْ فَٱنشُزُواْ يَرْفَعِ ٱللَّهُ ٱلَّذِينَ ءَامَنُواْ
مِنكُمْ وَٱلَّذِينَ أُوتُواْ ٱلْعِلْمَ دَرَجَٰتٍۚ وَٱللَّهُ بِمَا
تَعْمَلُونَ خَبِيرٌ

11 O you who believe! When you are told to make room in your gatherings, make room; Allah will make room for you. And when you are told to disperse, disperse. Allah elevates those among you who believe, and those given knowledge, many steps. Allah is Aware of what you do.

١٢ يَٰٓأَيُّهَا ٱلَّذِينَ ءَامَنُوٓاْ إِذَا نَٰجَيْتُمُ ٱلرَّسُولَ
فَقَدِّمُواْ بَيْنَ يَدَىْ نَجْوَىٰكُمْ صَدَقَةًۚ ذَٰلِكَ خَيْرٌ
لَّكُمْ وَأَطْهَرُۚ فَإِن لَّمْ تَجِدُواْ فَإِنَّ ٱللَّهَ غَفُورٌ
رَّحِيمٌ

12 O you who believe! When you converse privately with the Messenger, offer something in charity before your conversation. That is better for you, and purer. But if you do not find the means—Allah is Forgiving and Merciful.

١٣ ءَأَشْفَقْتُمْ أَن تُقَدِّمُواْ بَيْنَ يَدَىْ نَجْوَىٰكُمْ
صَدَقَٰتٍۚ فَإِذْ لَمْ تَفْعَلُواْ وَتَابَ ٱللَّهُ عَلَيْكُمْ
فَأَقِيمُواْ ٱلصَّلَوٰةَ وَءَاتُواْ ٱلزَّكَوٰةَ وَأَطِيعُواْ ٱللَّهَ
وَرَسُولَهُۥۚ وَٱللَّهُ خَبِيرٌۢ بِمَا تَعْمَلُونَ

13 Are you reluctant to offer charity before your conversation? If you do not do so, and Allah pardons you, then perform the prayer, and give alms, and obey Allah and His Messenger. Allah is Aware of what you do.

١٤ أَلَمْ تَرَ إِلَى ٱلَّذِينَ تَوَلَّوْاْ قَوْمًا غَضِبَ ٱللَّهُ
عَلَيْهِم مَّا هُم مِّنكُمْ وَلَا مِنْهُمْ وَيَحْلِفُونَ عَلَى
ٱلْكَذِبِ وَهُمْ يَعْلَمُونَ

14 Have you considered those who befriended a people with whom Allah has become angry? They are not of you, nor of them. And they swear to a lie while they know.

١٥ أَعَدَّ ٱللَّهُ لَهُمْ عَذَابًا شَدِيدًاۖ إِنَّهُمْ سَآءَ مَا
كَانُواْ يَعْمَلُونَ

15 Allah has prepared for them a terrible punishment. Evil is what they used to do.

١٦ ٱتَّخَذُوٓاْ أَيْمَٰنَهُمْ جُنَّةً فَصَدُّواْ عَن سَبِيلِ ٱللَّهِ
فَلَهُمْ عَذَابٌ مُّهِينٌ

16 They took their oaths as a screen, and prevented others from Allah's path. They will have a shameful punishment.

١٧ لَّن تُغْنِىَ عَنْهُمْ أَمْوَٰلُهُمْ وَلَآ أَوْلَٰدُهُم مِّنَ ٱللَّهِ
شَيْـًٔاۚ أُوْلَٰٓئِكَ أَصْحَٰبُ ٱلنَّارِۖ هُمْ فِيهَا خَٰلِدُونَ

17 Neither their possessions nor their children will avail them anything against Allah. These are the inhabitants of the Fire, dwelling therein forever.

١٨ يَوْمَ يَبْعَثُهُمُ ٱللَّهُ جَمِيعًا فَيَحْلِفُونَ لَهُۥ كَمَا
يَحْلِفُونَ لَكُمْ ۖ وَيَحْسَبُونَ أَنَّهُمْ عَلَىٰ شَىْءٍ ۚ أَلَآ
إِنَّهُمْ هُمُ ٱلْكَـٰذِبُونَ

18 On the Day when Allah will resurrect them altogether—they will swear to Him, as they swear to you, thinking that they are upon something. Indeed, they themselves are the liars.

١٩ ٱسْتَحْوَذَ عَلَيْهِمُ ٱلشَّيْطَـٰنُ فَأَنسَىٰهُمْ ذِكْرَ ٱللَّهِ ۚ
أُو۟لَـٰٓئِكَ حِزْبُ ٱلشَّيْطَـٰنِ ۚ أَلَآ إِنَّ حِزْبَ ٱلشَّيْطَـٰنِ
هُمُ ٱلْخَـٰسِرُونَ

19 Satan has taken hold of them, and so has caused them to forget the remembrance of Allah. These are the partisans of Satan. Indeed, it is Satan's partisans who are the losers.

٢٠ إِنَّ ٱلَّذِينَ يُحَآدُّونَ ٱللَّهَ وَرَسُولَهُۥٓ أُو۟لَـٰٓئِكَ فِى
ٱلْأَذَلِّينَ

20 Those who oppose Allah and His Messenger are among the lowliest.

٢١ كَتَبَ ٱللَّهُ لَأَغْلِبَنَّ أَنَا۠ وَرُسُلِىٓ ۚ إِنَّ ٱللَّهَ قَوِىٌّ
عَزِيزٌ

21 Allah has written: "I will certainly prevail, I and My messengers." Allah is Strong and Mighty.

٢٢ لَّا تَجِدُ قَوْمًا يُؤْمِنُونَ بِٱللَّهِ وَٱلْيَوْمِ ٱلْـَٔاخِرِ
يُوَآدُّونَ مَنْ حَآدَّ ٱللَّهَ وَرَسُولَهُۥ وَلَوْ كَانُوٓا۟
ءَابَآءَهُمْ أَوْ أَبْنَآءَهُمْ أَوْ إِخْوَٰنَهُمْ أَوْ عَشِيرَتَهُمْ ۚ
أُو۟لَـٰٓئِكَ كَتَبَ فِى قُلُوبِهِمُ ٱلْإِيمَـٰنَ وَأَيَّدَهُم بِرُوحٍ
مِّنْهُ ۖ وَيُدْخِلُهُمْ جَنَّـٰتٍ تَجْرِى مِن تَحْتِهَا ٱلْأَنْهَـٰرُ
خَـٰلِدِينَ فِيهَا ۚ رَضِىَ ٱللَّهُ عَنْهُمْ وَرَضُوا۟ عَنْهُ ۚ
أُو۟لَـٰٓئِكَ حِزْبُ ٱللَّهِ ۚ أَلَآ إِنَّ حِزْبَ ٱللَّهِ هُمُ
ٱلْمُفْلِحُونَ

22 You will not find a people who believe in Allah and the Last Day, loving those who oppose Allah and His Messenger, even if they were their parents, or their children, or their siblings, or their close relatives. These—He has inscribed faith in their hearts, and has supported them with a spirit from Him. And He will admit them into Gardens beneath which rivers flow, wherein they will dwell forever. Allah is pleased with them, and they are pleased with Him. These are the partisans of Allah. Indeed, it is Allah's partisans who are the successful.

59 The Mobilization الحشر

بِسْمِ ٱللَّهِ ٱلرَّحْمَـٰنِ ٱلرَّحِيمِ

In the name of Allah, the Gracious, the Merciful.

١ سَبَّحَ لِلَّهِ مَا فِى ٱلسَّمَٰوَٰتِ وَمَا فِى ٱلْأَرْضِ ۖ
وَهُوَ ٱلْعَزِيزُ ٱلْحَكِيمُ

1 Glorifying Allah is all that exists in the heavens and the earth. He is the Almighty, the Most Wise.

٢ هُوَ ٱلَّذِىٓ أَخْرَجَ ٱلَّذِينَ كَفَرُوا۟ مِنْ أَهْلِ ٱلْكِتَٰبِ
مِن دِيَٰرِهِمْ لِأَوَّلِ ٱلْحَشْرِ ۚ مَا ظَنَنتُمْ أَن
يَخْرُجُوا۟ ۖ وَظَنُّوٓا۟ أَنَّهُم مَّانِعَتُهُمْ حُصُونُهُم مِّنَ
ٱللَّهِ فَأَتَىٰهُمُ ٱللَّهُ مِنْ حَيْثُ لَمْ يَحْتَسِبُوا۟ ۖ
وَقَذَفَ فِى قُلُوبِهِمُ ٱلرُّعْبَ ۚ يُخْرِبُونَ بُيُوتَهُم
بِأَيْدِيهِمْ وَأَيْدِى ٱلْمُؤْمِنِينَ فَٱعْتَبِرُوا۟ يَٰٓأُو۟لِى
ٱلْأَبْصَٰرِ

2 It is He who evicted those who disbelieved among the People of the Book from their homes at the first mobilization. You did not think they would leave, and they thought their fortresses would protect them from Allah. But Allah came at them from where they never expected, and threw terror into their hearts. They wrecked their homes with their own hands, and by the hands of the believers. Therefore, take a lesson, O you who have insight.

٣ وَلَوْلَآ أَن كَتَبَ ٱللَّهُ عَلَيْهِمُ ٱلْجَلَآءَ لَعَذَّبَهُمْ
فِى ٱلدُّنْيَا ۖ وَلَهُمْ فِى ٱلْءَاخِرَةِ عَذَابُ ٱلنَّارِ

3 Had Allah not decreed exile for them, He would have punished them in this life. But in the Hereafter they will have the punishment of the Fire.

٤ ذَٰلِكَ بِأَنَّهُمْ شَآقُّوا۟ ٱللَّهَ وَرَسُولَهُۥ ۖ وَمَن يُشَآقِّ
ٱللَّهَ فَإِنَّ ٱللَّهَ شَدِيدُ ٱلْعِقَابِ

4 That is because they opposed Allah and His Messenger. Whoever opposes Allah—Allah is stern in retribution.

٥ مَا قَطَعْتُم مِّن لِّينَةٍ أَوْ تَرَكْتُمُوهَا قَآئِمَةً عَلَىٰٓ
أُصُولِهَا فَبِإِذْنِ ٱللَّهِ وَلِيُخْزِىَ ٱلْفَٰسِقِينَ

5 Whether you cut down a tree, or leave it standing on its trunk, it is by Allah's will. He will surely disgrace the sinners.

٦ وَمَآ أَفَآءَ ٱللَّهُ عَلَىٰ رَسُولِهِۦ مِنْهُمْ فَمَآ
أَوْجَفْتُمْ عَلَيْهِ مِنْ خَيْلٍ وَلَا رِكَابٍ وَلَٰكِنَّ ٱللَّهَ
يُسَلِّطُ رُسُلَهُۥ عَلَىٰ مَن يَشَآءُ ۚ وَٱللَّهُ عَلَىٰ كُلِّ
شَىْءٍ قَدِيرٌ

6 Whatever Allah has bestowed upon His Messenger from them; you spurred neither horse nor camel for them, but Allah gives authority to His messengers over whomever He will. Allah is Able to do all things.

٧ مَّآ أَفَآءَ ٱللَّهُ عَلَىٰ رَسُولِهِۦ مِنْ أَهْلِ ٱلْقُرَىٰ
فَلِلَّهِ وَلِلرَّسُولِ وَلِذِى ٱلْقُرْبَىٰ وَٱلْيَتَٰمَىٰ
وَٱلْمَسَٰكِينِ وَٱبْنِ ٱلسَّبِيلِ كَىْ لَا يَكُونَ دُولَةًۢ
بَيْنَ ٱلْأَغْنِيَآءِ مِنكُمْ ۚ وَمَآ ءَاتَىٰكُمُ ٱلرَّسُولُ

7 Whatever Allah restored to His Messenger from the inhabitants of the villages belongs to Allah, and to the Messenger, and to the relatives, and to the orphans, and to the poor, and to the wayfarer; so that it may not circulate solely between the

فَخُذُوهُ وَمَا نَهَىٰكُمْ عَنْهُ فَٱنتَهُوا۟ ۚ وَٱتَّقُوا۟ ٱللَّهَ ۖ
إِنَّ ٱللَّهَ شَدِيدُ ٱلْعِقَابِ

wealthy among you. Whatever the Messenger gives you, accept it; and whatever he forbids you, abstain from it. And fear Allah. Allah is severe in punishment.

٨ لِلْفُقَرَآءِ ٱلْمُهَـٰجِرِينَ ٱلَّذِينَ أُخْرِجُوا۟ مِن
دِيَـٰرِهِمْ وَأَمْوَٰلِهِمْ يَبْتَغُونَ فَضْلًا مِّنَ ٱللَّهِ
وَرِضْوَٰنًا وَيَنصُرُونَ ٱللَّهَ وَرَسُولَهُۥٓ ۚ أُو۟لَـٰٓئِكَ هُمُ
ٱلصَّـٰدِقُونَ

8 To the poor refugees who were driven out of their homes and their possessions, as they sought the favor of Allah and His approval, and came to the aid of Allah and His Messenger. These are the sincere.

٩ وَٱلَّذِينَ تَبَوَّءُو ٱلدَّارَ وَٱلْإِيمَـٰنَ مِن قَبْلِهِمْ
يُحِبُّونَ مَنْ هَاجَرَ إِلَيْهِمْ وَلَا يَجِدُونَ فِى
صُدُورِهِمْ حَاجَةً مِّمَّآ أُوتُوا۟ وَيُؤْثِرُونَ عَلَىٰٓ
أَنفُسِهِمْ وَلَوْ كَانَ بِهِمْ خَصَاصَةٌ ۚ وَمَن يُوقَ
شُحَّ نَفْسِهِۦ فَأُو۟لَـٰٓئِكَ هُمُ ٱلْمُفْلِحُونَ

9 And those who, before them, had settled in the homeland, and had accepted faith. They love those who emigrated to them, and find no hesitation in their hearts in helping them. They give them priority over themselves, even if they themselves are needy. Whoever is protected from his natural greed—it is they who are the successful.

١٠ وَٱلَّذِينَ جَآءُو مِنۢ بَعْدِهِمْ يَقُولُونَ رَبَّنَا ٱغْفِرْ
لَنَا وَلِإِخْوَٰنِنَا ٱلَّذِينَ سَبَقُونَا بِٱلْإِيمَـٰنِ وَلَا تَجْعَلْ
فِى قُلُوبِنَا غِلًّا لِّلَّذِينَ ءَامَنُوا۟ رَبَّنَآ إِنَّكَ رَءُوفٌ
رَّحِيمٌ

10 And those who came after them, saying, “Our Lord, forgive us, and our brethren who preceded us in faith, and leave no malice in our hearts towards those who believe. Our Lord, You are Clement and Merciful.”

١١ أَلَمْ تَرَ إِلَى ٱلَّذِينَ نَافَقُوا۟ يَقُولُونَ لِإِخْوَٰنِهِمُ
ٱلَّذِينَ كَفَرُوا۟ مِنْ أَهْلِ ٱلْكِتَـٰبِ لَئِنْ أُخْرِجْتُمْ
لَنَخْرُجَنَّ مَعَكُمْ وَلَا نُطِيعُ فِيكُمْ أَحَدًا أَبَدًا وَإِن
قُوتِلْتُمْ لَنَنصُرَنَّكُمْ وَٱللَّهُ يَشْهَدُ إِنَّهُمْ لَكَـٰذِبُونَ

11 Have you not considered those who act hypocritically? They say to their brethren who disbelieved among the People of the Book, “If you are evicted, we will leave with you, and will not obey anyone against you; and should anyone fight you, we will certainly support you.” But Allah bears witness that they are liars.

١٢ لَئِنْ أُخْرِجُوا۟ لَا يَخْرُجُونَ مَعَهُمْ وَلَئِن
قُوتِلُوا۟ لَا يَنصُرُونَهُمْ وَلَئِن نَّصَرُوهُمْ لَيُوَلُّنَّ
ٱلْأَدْبَٰرَ ثُمَّ لَا يُنصَرُونَ

12 If they are evicted, they will not leave with them; and if anyone fights them, they will not support them; and if they go to their aid, they will turn their backs and flee; then they will receive no support.

١٣ لَأَنتُمْ أَشَدُّ رَهْبَةً فِى صُدُورِهِم مِّنَ ٱللَّهِ ۚ
ذَٰلِكَ بِأَنَّهُمْ قَوْمٌ لَّا يَفْقَهُونَ

13 Fear of you is more intense in their hearts than fear of Allah. That is because they are a people who do not understand.

١٤ لَا يُقَٰتِلُونَكُمْ جَمِيعًا إِلَّا فِى قُرًى مُّحَصَّنَةٍ أَوْ
مِن وَرَآءِ جُدُرٍۭ ۚ بَأْسُهُم بَيْنَهُمْ شَدِيدٌ ۚ تَحْسَبُهُمْ
جَمِيعًا وَقُلُوبُهُمْ شَتَّىٰ ۚ ذَٰلِكَ بِأَنَّهُمْ قَوْمٌ لَّا
يَعْقِلُونَ

14 They will not fight you all together except from fortified strongholds, or from behind walls. Their hostility towards each other is severe. You would think they are united, but their hearts are diverse. That is because they are a people who do not understand.

١٥ كَمَثَلِ ٱلَّذِينَ مِن قَبْلِهِمْ قَرِيبًا ۖ ذَاقُوا۟ وَبَالَ
أَمْرِهِمْ وَلَهُمْ عَذَابٌ أَلِيمٌ

15 Like those shortly before them. They experienced the consequences of their decisions. For them is a painful punishment.

١٦ كَمَثَلِ ٱلشَّيْطَٰنِ إِذْ قَالَ لِلْإِنسَٰنِ ٱكْفُرْ فَلَمَّا
كَفَرَ قَالَ إِنِّى بَرِىٓءٌ مِّنكَ إِنِّىٓ أَخَافُ ٱللَّهَ رَبَّ
ٱلْعَٰلَمِينَ

16 Like the devil, when he says to the human being, “Disbelieve.” But when he has disbelieved, he says, “I am innocent of you; I fear Allah, the Lord of the Worlds.”

١٧ فَكَانَ عَٰقِبَتَهُمَآ أَنَّهُمَا فِى ٱلنَّارِ خَٰلِدَيْنِ فِيهَا ۚ
وَذَٰلِكَ جَزَٰٓؤُا۟ ٱلظَّٰلِمِينَ

17 The ultimate end for both of them is the Fire, where they will dwell forever. Such is the requital for the wrongdoers.

١٨ يَٰٓأَيُّهَا ٱلَّذِينَ ءَامَنُوا۟ ٱتَّقُوا۟ ٱللَّهَ وَلْتَنظُرْ نَفْسٌ
مَّا قَدَّمَتْ لِغَدٍ ۖ وَٱتَّقُوا۟ ٱللَّهَ ۚ إِنَّ ٱللَّهَ خَبِيرٌۢ بِمَا
تَعْمَلُونَ

18 O you who believe! Fear Allah, and let every soul consider what it has forwarded for the morrow, and fear Allah. Allah is Aware of what you do.

١٩ وَلَا تَكُونُوا۟ كَٱلَّذِينَ نَسُوا۟ ٱللَّهَ فَأَنسَىٰهُمْ
أَنفُسَهُمْ ۚ أُو۟لَٰٓئِكَ هُمُ ٱلْفَٰسِقُونَ

19 And do not be like those who forgot Allah, so He made them forget themselves. These are the sinners.

٢٠ لَا يَسْتَوِىٓ أَصْحَـٰبُ ٱلنَّارِ وَأَصْحَـٰبُ ٱلْجَنَّةِ ۚ
أَصْحَـٰبُ ٱلْجَنَّةِ هُمُ ٱلْفَآئِزُونَ

20 Not equal are the inhabitants of the Fire and the inhabitants of Paradise. It is the inhabitants of Paradise who are the winners.

٢١ لَوْ أَنزَلْنَا هَـٰذَا ٱلْقُرْءَانَ عَلَىٰ جَبَلٍ لَّرَأَيْتَهُۥ
خَـٰشِعًا مُّتَصَدِّعًا مِّنْ خَشْيَةِ ٱللَّهِ ۚ وَتِلْكَ ٱلْأَمْثَـٰلُ
نَضْرِبُهَا لِلنَّاسِ لَعَلَّهُمْ يَتَفَكَّرُونَ

21 Had We sent this Quran down on a mountain, you would have seen it trembling, crumbling in awe of Allah. These parables We cite for the people, so that they may reflect.

٢٢ هُوَ ٱللَّهُ ٱلَّذِى لَآ إِلَـٰهَ إِلَّا هُوَ ۖ عَـٰلِمُ ٱلْغَيْبِ
وَٱلشَّهَـٰدَةِ ۖ هُوَ ٱلرَّحْمَـٰنُ ٱلرَّحِيمُ

22 He is Allah. There is no god but He, the Knower of secrets and declarations. He is the Compassionate, the Merciful.

٢٣ هُوَ ٱللَّهُ ٱلَّذِى لَآ إِلَـٰهَ إِلَّا هُوَ ٱلْمَلِكُ ٱلْقُدُّوسُ
ٱلسَّلَـٰمُ ٱلْمُؤْمِنُ ٱلْمُهَيْمِنُ ٱلْعَزِيزُ ٱلْجَبَّارُ ٱلْمُتَكَبِّرُ ۚ
سُبْحَـٰنَ ٱللَّهِ عَمَّا يُشْرِكُونَ

23 He is Allah; besides Whom there is no god; the Sovereign, the Holy, the Peace-Giver, the Faith-Giver, the Overseer, the Almighty, the Omnipotent, the Overwhelming. Glory be to Allah, beyond what they associate.

٢٤ هُوَ ٱللَّهُ ٱلْخَـٰلِقُ ٱلْبَارِئُ ٱلْمُصَوِّرُ ۖ لَهُ ٱلْأَسْمَآءُ
ٱلْحُسْنَىٰ ۚ يُسَبِّحُ لَهُۥ مَا فِى ٱلسَّمَـٰوَٰتِ وَٱلْأَرْضِ ۖ
وَهُوَ ٱلْعَزِيزُ ٱلْحَكِيمُ

24 He is Allah; the Creator, the Maker, the Designer. His are the Most Beautiful Names. Whatever is in the heavens and the earth glorifies Him. He is the Majestic, the Wise.

60 The Woman Tested الممتحنة

بِسْمِ ٱللَّهِ ٱلرَّحْمَـٰنِ ٱلرَّحِيمِ

In the name of Allah, the Gracious, the Merciful.

١ يَـٰٓأَيُّهَا ٱلَّذِينَ ءَامَنُوا۟ لَا تَتَّخِذُوا۟ عَدُوِّى
وَعَدُوَّكُمْ أَوْلِيَآءَ تُلْقُونَ إِلَيْهِم بِٱلْمَوَدَّةِ وَقَدْ
كَفَرُوا۟ بِمَا جَآءَكُم مِّنَ ٱلْحَقِّ يُخْرِجُونَ
ٱلرَّسُولَ وَإِيَّاكُمْ ۙ أَن تُؤْمِنُوا۟ بِٱللَّهِ رَبِّكُمْ إِن
كُنتُمْ خَرَجْتُمْ جِهَـٰدًا فِى سَبِيلِى وَٱبْتِغَآءَ
مَرْضَاتِى ۚ تُسِرُّونَ إِلَيْهِم بِٱلْمَوَدَّةِ وَأَنَا۠ أَعْلَمُ بِمَآ

1 O you who believe! Do not take My enemies and your enemies for supporters, offering them affection, when they have disbelieved in what has come to you of the Truth. They have expelled the Messenger, and you, because you believed in Allah, your Lord. If you have mobilized to strive for My cause, seeking My

أَخْفَيْتُمْ وَمَآ أَعْلَنتُمْ ۚ وَمَن يَفْعَلْهُ مِنكُمْ فَقَدْ
ضَلَّ سَوَآءَ ٱلسَّبِيلِ

approval, how can you secretly love them? I know what you conceal and what you reveal. Whoever among you does that has strayed from the right way.

٢ إِن يَثْقَفُوكُمْ يَكُونُوا۟ لَكُمْ أَعْدَآءً وَيَبْسُطُوٓا۟
إِلَيْكُمْ أَيْدِيَهُمْ وَأَلْسِنَتَهُم بِٱلسُّوٓءِ وَوَدُّوا۟ لَوْ
تَكْفُرُونَ

2 Whenever they encounter you, they treat you as enemies, and they stretch their hands and tongues against you with malice. They wish that you would disbelieve.

٣ لَن تَنفَعَكُمْ أَرْحَامُكُمْ وَلَآ أَوْلَٰدُكُمْ ۚ يَوْمَ
ٱلْقِيَٰمَةِ يَفْصِلُ بَيْنَكُمْ ۚ وَٱللَّهُ بِمَا تَعْمَلُونَ بَصِيرٌ

3 Neither your relatives nor your children will benefit you on the Day of Resurrection. He will separate between you. Allah is Observant of what you do.

٤ قَدْ كَانَتْ لَكُمْ أُسْوَةٌ حَسَنَةٌ فِىٓ إِبْرَٰهِيمَ
وَٱلَّذِينَ مَعَهُۥٓ إِذْ قَالُوا۟ لِقَوْمِهِمْ إِنَّا بُرَءَٰٓؤُا۟ مِنكُمْ
وَمِمَّا تَعْبُدُونَ مِن دُونِ ٱللَّهِ كَفَرْنَا بِكُمْ وَبَدَا
بَيْنَنَا وَبَيْنَكُمُ ٱلْعَدَٰوَةُ وَٱلْبَغْضَآءُ أَبَدًا حَتَّىٰ
تُؤْمِنُوا۟ بِٱللَّهِ وَحْدَهُۥٓ إِلَّا قَوْلَ إِبْرَٰهِيمَ لِأَبِيهِ
لَأَسْتَغْفِرَنَّ لَكَ وَمَآ أَمْلِكُ لَكَ مِنَ ٱللَّهِ مِن
شَىْءٍ ۖ رَّبَّنَا عَلَيْكَ تَوَكَّلْنَا وَإِلَيْكَ أَنَبْنَا وَإِلَيْكَ
ٱلْمَصِيرُ

4 You have had an excellent example in Abraham and those with him; when they said to their people, “We are quit of you, and what you worship apart from Allah. We denounce you. Enmity and hatred has surfaced between us and you, forever, until you believe in Allah alone.” Except for the words of Abraham to his father, “I will ask forgiveness for you, though I have no power from Allah to do anything for you.” “Our Lord, in You we trust, and to You we repent, and to You is the ultimate resort.

٥ رَبَّنَا لَا تَجْعَلْنَا فِتْنَةً لِّلَّذِينَ كَفَرُوا۟ وَٱغْفِرْ لَنَا
رَبَّنَآ ۖ إِنَّكَ أَنتَ ٱلْعَزِيزُ ٱلْحَكِيمُ

5 Our Lord, do not make us a target for those who disbelieve, and forgive us, our Lord. You are indeed the Mighty and Wise.”

٦ لَقَدْ كَانَ لَكُمْ فِيهِمْ أُسْوَةٌ حَسَنَةٌ لِّمَن كَانَ
يَرْجُوا۟ ٱللَّهَ وَٱلْيَوْمَ ٱلْءَاخِرَ ۚ وَمَن يَتَوَلَّ فَإِنَّ
ٱللَّهَ هُوَ ٱلْغَنِىُّ ٱلْحَمِيدُ

6 There is an excellent example in them for you—for anyone who seeks Allah and the Last Day. But whoever turns away—Allah is the Self-Sufficient, the Most Praised.

٧ عَسَى ٱللَّهُ أَن يَجْعَلَ بَيْنَكُمْ وَبَيْنَ ٱلَّذِينَ
عَادَيْتُم مِّنْهُم مَّوَدَّةً ۚ وَٱللَّهُ قَدِيرٌ ۚ وَٱللَّهُ غَفُورٌ
رَّحِيمٌ

7 Perhaps Allah will plant affection between you and those of them you consider enemies. Allah is Capable. Allah is Forgiving and Merciful.

٨ لَّا يَنْهَىٰكُمُ ٱللَّهُ عَنِ ٱلَّذِينَ لَمْ يُقَـٰتِلُوكُمْ فِى
ٱلدِّينِ وَلَمْ يُخْرِجُوكُم مِّن دِيَـٰرِكُمْ أَن تَبَرُّوهُمْ
وَتُقْسِطُوٓا۟ إِلَيْهِمْ ۚ إِنَّ ٱللَّهَ يُحِبُّ ٱلْمُقْسِطِينَ

8 As for those who have not fought against you for your religion, nor expelled you from your homes, Allah does not prohibit you from dealing with them kindly and equitably. Allah loves the equitable.

٩ إِنَّمَا يَنْهَىٰكُمُ ٱللَّهُ عَنِ ٱلَّذِينَ قَـٰتَلُوكُمْ فِى
ٱلدِّينِ وَأَخْرَجُوكُم مِّن دِيَـٰرِكُمْ وَظَـٰهَرُوا۟ عَلَىٰٓ
إِخْرَاجِكُمْ أَن تَوَلَّوْهُمْ ۚ وَمَن يَتَوَلَّهُمْ فَأُو۟لَـٰٓئِكَ
هُمُ ٱلظَّـٰلِمُونَ

9 But Allah prohibits you from befriending those who fought against you over your religion, and expelled you from your homes, and aided in your expulsion. Whoever takes them for friends—these are the wrongdoers.

١٠ يَـٰٓأَيُّهَا ٱلَّذِينَ ءَامَنُوٓا۟ إِذَا جَآءَكُمُ ٱلْمُؤْمِنَـٰتُ
مُهَـٰجِرَٰتٍ فَٱمْتَحِنُوهُنَّ ۖ ٱللَّهُ أَعْلَمُ بِإِيمَـٰنِهِنَّ ۖ فَإِنْ
عَلِمْتُمُوهُنَّ مُؤْمِنَـٰتٍ فَلَا تَرْجِعُوهُنَّ إِلَى ٱلْكُفَّارِ ۖ
لَا هُنَّ حِلٌّ لَّهُمْ وَلَا هُمْ يَحِلُّونَ لَهُنَّ ۖ وَءَاتُوهُم
مَّآ أَنفَقُوا۟ ۚ وَلَا جُنَاحَ عَلَيْكُمْ أَن تَنكِحُوهُنَّ إِذَآ
ءَاتَيْتُمُوهُنَّ أُجُورَهُنَّ ۚ وَلَا تُمْسِكُوا۟ بِعِصَمِ
ٱلْكَوَافِرِ وَسْـَٔلُوا۟ مَآ أَنفَقْتُمْ وَلْيَسْـَٔلُوا۟ مَآ أَنفَقُوا۟ ۚ
ذَٰلِكُمْ حُكْمُ ٱللَّهِ ۖ يَحْكُمُ بَيْنَكُمْ ۚ وَٱللَّهُ عَلِيمٌ
حَكِيمٌ

10 O you who believe! When believing women come to you emigrating, test them. Allah is Aware of their faith. And if you find them to be faithful, do not send them back to the unbelievers. They are not lawful for them, nor are they lawful for them. But give them what they have spent. You are not at fault if you marry them, provided you give them their compensation. And do not hold on to ties with unbelieving women, but demand what you have spent, and let them demand what they have spent. This is the rule of Allah; He rules among you. Allah is Knowing and Wise.

١١ وَإِن فَاتَكُمْ شَىْءٌ مِّنْ أَزْوَٰجِكُمْ إِلَى ٱلْكُفَّارِ
فَعَاقَبْتُمْ فَـَٔاتُوا۟ ٱلَّذِينَ ذَهَبَتْ أَزْوَٰجُهُم مِّثْلَ مَآ
أَنفَقُوا۟ ۚ وَٱتَّقُوا۟ ٱللَّهَ ٱلَّذِىٓ أَنتُم بِهِۦ مُؤْمِنُونَ

11 If any of your wives desert you to the unbelievers, and you decide to penalize them, give those whose wives have gone away the equivalent of what they had spent. And fear Allah, in whom you are believers.

١٢ يَٰٓأَيُّهَا ٱلنَّبِيُّ إِذَا جَآءَكَ ٱلْمُؤْمِنَٰتُ يُبَايِعْنَكَ
عَلَىٰٓ أَن لَّا يُشْرِكْنَ بِٱللَّهِ شَيْـًٔا وَلَا يَسْرِقْنَ وَلَا
يَزْنِينَ وَلَا يَقْتُلْنَ أَوْلَٰدَهُنَّ وَلَا يَأْتِينَ بِبُهْتَٰنٍ
يَفْتَرِينَهُۥ بَيْنَ أَيْدِيهِنَّ وَأَرْجُلِهِنَّ وَلَا يَعْصِينَكَ
فِى مَعْرُوفٍ ۙ فَبَايِعْهُنَّ وَٱسْتَغْفِرْ لَهُنَّ ٱللَّهَ ۖ إِنَّ
ٱللَّهَ غَفُورٌ رَّحِيمٌ

12 O prophet! If believing women come to you, pledging allegiance to you, on condition that they will not associate anything with Allah, nor steal, nor commit adultery, nor kill their children, nor commit perjury as to parenthood, nor disobey you in anything righteous, accept their allegiance and ask Allah's forgiveness for them. Allah is Forgiving and Merciful.

١٣ يَٰٓأَيُّهَا ٱلَّذِينَ ءَامَنُوا۟ لَا تَتَوَلَّوْا۟ قَوْمًا غَضِبَ
ٱللَّهُ عَلَيْهِمْ قَدْ يَئِسُوا۟ مِنَ ٱلْءَاخِرَةِ كَمَا يَئِسَ
ٱلْكُفَّارُ مِنْ أَصْحَٰبِ ٱلْقُبُورِ

13 O you who believe! Do not befriend people with whom Allah has become angry, and have despaired of the Hereafter, as the faithless have despaired of the occupants of the graves.

61 Column الصف

بِسْمِ ٱللَّهِ ٱلرَّحْمَٰنِ ٱلرَّحِيمِ

In the name of Allah, the Gracious, the Merciful.

١ سَبَّحَ لِلَّهِ مَا فِى ٱلسَّمَٰوَٰتِ وَمَا فِى ٱلْأَرْضِ ۖ
وَهُوَ ٱلْعَزِيزُ ٱلْحَكِيمُ

1 Everything in the heavens and the earth praises Allah. He is the Almighty, the Wise.

٢ يَٰٓأَيُّهَا ٱلَّذِينَ ءَامَنُوا۟ لِمَ تَقُولُونَ مَا لَا تَفْعَلُونَ

2 O you who believe! Why do you say what you do not do?

٣ كَبُرَ مَقْتًا عِندَ ٱللَّهِ أَن تَقُولُوا۟ مَا لَا تَفْعَلُونَ

3 It is most hateful to Allah that you say what you do not do.

٤ إِنَّ ٱللَّهَ يُحِبُّ ٱلَّذِينَ يُقَٰتِلُونَ فِى سَبِيلِهِۦ
صَفًّا كَأَنَّهُم بُنْيَٰنٌ مَّرْصُوصٌ

4 Allah loves those who fight in His cause, in ranks, as though they were a compact structure.

٥ وَإِذْ قَالَ مُوسَىٰ لِقَوْمِهِۦ يَٰقَوْمِ لِمَ تُؤْذُونَنِى
وَقَد تَّعْلَمُونَ أَنِّى رَسُولُ ٱللَّهِ إِلَيْكُمْ ۖ فَلَمَّا
زَاغُوٓا۟ أَزَاغَ ٱللَّهُ قُلُوبَهُمْ ۚ وَٱللَّهُ لَا يَهْدِى ٱلْقَوْمَ
ٱلْفَٰسِقِينَ

5 When Moses said to his people, "O my people, why do you hurt me, although you know that I am Allah's Messenger to you?" And when they swerved, Allah swerved their hearts. Allah does not guide the sinful people.

٦ وَإِذْ قَالَ عِيسَى ٱبْنُ مَرْيَمَ يَٰبَنِىٓ إِسْرَٰٓءِيلَ
إِنِّى رَسُولُ ٱللَّهِ إِلَيْكُم مُّصَدِّقًا لِّمَا بَيْنَ يَدَىَّ
مِنَ ٱلتَّوْرَىٰةِ وَمُبَشِّرًۢا بِرَسُولٍ يَأْتِى مِنۢ بَعْدِى
ٱسْمُهُۥٓ أَحْمَدُ ۖ فَلَمَّا جَآءَهُم بِٱلْبَيِّنَٰتِ قَالُوا۟ هَٰذَا
سِحْرٌ مُّبِينٌ

6 And when Jesus son of Mary said, “O Children of Israel, I am Allah’s Messenger to you, confirming what preceded me of the Torah, and announcing good news of a messenger who will come after me, whose name is Ahmad.” But when he showed them the miracles, they said, “This is obvious sorcery.”

٧ وَمَنْ أَظْلَمُ مِمَّنِ ٱفْتَرَىٰ عَلَى ٱللَّهِ ٱلْكَذِبَ
وَهُوَ يُدْعَىٰٓ إِلَى ٱلْإِسْلَٰمِ ۚ وَٱللَّهُ لَا يَهْدِى ٱلْقَوْمَ
ٱلظَّٰلِمِينَ

7 And who is a greater wrongdoer than he who attributes falsehoods to Allah, when he is being invited to Islam? Allah does not guide the wrongdoing people.

٨ يُرِيدُونَ لِيُطْفِـُٔوا۟ نُورَ ٱللَّهِ بِأَفْوَٰهِهِمْ وَٱللَّهُ
مُتِمُّ نُورِهِۦ وَلَوْ كَرِهَ ٱلْكَٰفِرُونَ

8 They want to extinguish Allah’s Light with their mouths; but Allah will complete His Light, even though the disbelievers dislike it.

٩ هُوَ ٱلَّذِىٓ أَرْسَلَ رَسُولَهُۥ بِٱلْهُدَىٰ وَدِينِ ٱلْحَقِّ
لِيُظْهِرَهُۥ عَلَى ٱلدِّينِ كُلِّهِۦ وَلَوْ كَرِهَ ٱلْمُشْرِكُونَ

9 It is He who sent His Messenger with the guidance and the true religion, to make it prevail over all religions, even though the idolaters dislike it.

١٠ يَٰٓأَيُّهَا ٱلَّذِينَ ءَامَنُوا۟ هَلْ أَدُلُّكُمْ عَلَىٰ تِجَٰرَةٍ
تُنجِيكُم مِّنْ عَذَابٍ أَلِيمٍ

10 O you who believe! Shall I inform you of a trade that will save you from a painful torment?

١١ تُؤْمِنُونَ بِٱللَّهِ وَرَسُولِهِۦ وَتُجَٰهِدُونَ فِى
سَبِيلِ ٱللَّهِ بِأَمْوَٰلِكُمْ وَأَنفُسِكُمْ ۚ ذَٰلِكُمْ خَيْرٌ لَّكُمْ
إِن كُنتُمْ تَعْلَمُونَ

11 That you believe in Allah and His Messenger, and strive in the cause of Allah with your possessions and yourselves. That is best for you, if you only knew.

١٢ يَغْفِرْ لَكُمْ ذُنُوبَكُمْ وَيُدْخِلْكُمْ جَنَّٰتٍ تَجْرِى
مِن تَحْتِهَا ٱلْأَنْهَٰرُ وَمَسَٰكِنَ طَيِّبَةً فِى جَنَّٰتِ
عَدْنٍ ۚ ذَٰلِكَ ٱلْفَوْزُ ٱلْعَظِيمُ

12 He will forgive you your sins; and will admit you into gardens beneath which rivers flow, and into beautiful mansions in the Gardens of Eden. That is the supreme success.

١٣ وَأُخْرَىٰ تُحِبُّونَهَا ۖ نَصْرٌ مِّنَ ٱللَّهِ وَفَتْحٌ
قَرِيبٌ ۗ وَبَشِّرِ ٱلْمُؤْمِنِينَ

13 And something else you love: support from Allah, and imminent victory. So give good news to the believers.

١٤ يَٰٓأَيُّهَا ٱلَّذِينَ ءَامَنُوا۟ كُونُوٓا۟ أَنصَارَ ٱللَّهِ كَمَا
قَالَ عِيسَى ٱبْنُ مَرْيَمَ لِلْحَوَارِيِّـۧنَ مَنْ أَنصَارِىٓ
إِلَى ٱللَّهِ ۖ قَالَ ٱلْحَوَارِيُّونَ نَحْنُ أَنصَارُ ٱللَّهِ ۖ
فَـَٔامَنَت طَّآئِفَةٌ مِّنۢ بَنِىٓ إِسْرَٰٓءِيلَ وَكَفَرَت
طَّآئِفَةٌ ۖ فَأَيَّدْنَا ٱلَّذِينَ ءَامَنُوا۟ عَلَىٰ عَدُوِّهِمْ
فَأَصْبَحُوا۟ ظَٰهِرِينَ

14 O you who believe! Be supporters of Allah, as Jesus son of Mary said to the disciples, “Who are my supporters towards Allah?” The disciples said, “We are Allah's supporters.” So a group of the Children of Israel believed, while another group disbelieved. We supported those who believed against their foe, so they became dominant.

62 Friday الجمعة

بِسْمِ ٱللَّهِ ٱلرَّحْمَٰنِ ٱلرَّحِيمِ

In the name of Allah, the Gracious, the Merciful.

١ يُسَبِّحُ لِلَّهِ مَا فِى ٱلسَّمَٰوَٰتِ وَمَا فِى ٱلْأَرْضِ
ٱلْمَلِكِ ٱلْقُدُّوسِ ٱلْعَزِيزِ ٱلْحَكِيمِ

1 Everything in the heavens and the earth glorifies Allah the Sovereign, the Holy, the Almighty, the Wise.

٢ هُوَ ٱلَّذِى بَعَثَ فِى ٱلْأُمِّيِّـۧنَ رَسُولًا مِّنْهُمْ
يَتْلُوا۟ عَلَيْهِمْ ءَايَٰتِهِۦ وَيُزَكِّيهِمْ وَيُعَلِّمُهُمُ ٱلْكِتَٰبَ
وَٱلْحِكْمَةَ وَإِن كَانُوا۟ مِن قَبْلُ لَفِى ضَلَٰلٍ مُّبِينٍ

2 It is He who sent among the unlettered a messenger from themselves; reciting His revelations to them, and purifying them, and teaching them the Scripture and wisdom; although they were in obvious error before that.

٣ وَءَاخَرِينَ مِنْهُمْ لَمَّا يَلْحَقُوا۟ بِهِمْ ۚ وَهُوَ ٱلْعَزِيزُ
ٱلْحَكِيمُ

3 And others from them, who have not yet joined them. He is the Glorious, the Wise.

٤ ذَٰلِكَ فَضْلُ ٱللَّهِ يُؤْتِيهِ مَن يَشَآءُ ۚ وَٱللَّهُ ذُو
ٱلْفَضْلِ ٱلْعَظِيمِ

4 That is Allah’s grace, which He grants to whomever He wills. Allah is Possessor of limitless grace.

٥ مَثَلُ ٱلَّذِينَ حُمِّلُوا۟ ٱلتَّوْرَىٰةَ ثُمَّ لَمْ يَحْمِلُوهَا
كَمَثَلِ ٱلْحِمَارِ يَحْمِلُ أَسْفَارًۢا ۚ بِئْسَ مَثَلُ ٱلْقَوْمِ
ٱلَّذِينَ كَذَّبُوا۟ بِـَٔايَٰتِ ٱللَّهِ ۚ وَٱللَّهُ لَا يَهْدِى ٱلْقَوْمَ
ٱلظَّٰلِمِينَ

5 The example of those who were entrusted with the Torah, but then failed to uphold it, is like the donkey carrying works of literature. Miserable is the example of the people who denounce Allah’s revelations. Allah does not guide the wrongdoing people.

٦ قُلْ يَٰٓأَيُّهَا ٱلَّذِينَ هَادُوٓا۟ إِن زَعَمْتُمْ أَنَّكُمْ
أَوْلِيَآءُ لِلَّهِ مِن دُونِ ٱلنَّاسِ فَتَمَنَّوُا۟ ٱلْمَوْتَ إِن
كُنتُمْ صَٰدِقِينَ

6 Say, "O you who follow Judaism; if you claim to be the chosen of Allah, to the exclusion of the rest of mankind, then wish for death if you are sincere."

٧ وَلَا يَتَمَنَّوْنَهُۥٓ أَبَدًۢا بِمَا قَدَّمَتْ أَيْدِيهِمْ ۚ وَٱللَّهُ
عَلِيمٌۢ بِٱلظَّٰلِمِينَ

7 But they will not wish for it, ever, due to what their hands have advanced. Allah knows well the wrongdoers.

٨ قُلْ إِنَّ ٱلْمَوْتَ ٱلَّذِى تَفِرُّونَ مِنْهُ فَإِنَّهُۥ
مُلَٰقِيكُمْ ۖ ثُمَّ تُرَدُّونَ إِلَىٰ عَٰلِمِ ٱلْغَيْبِ وَٱلشَّهَٰدَةِ
فَيُنَبِّئُكُم بِمَا كُنتُمْ تَعْمَلُونَ

8 Say, "The death from which you flee will catch up with you; then you will be returned to the Knower of the Invisible and the Visible, and He will inform you of what you used to do."

٩ يَٰٓأَيُّهَا ٱلَّذِينَ ءَامَنُوٓا۟ إِذَا نُودِىَ لِلصَّلَوٰةِ مِن
يَوْمِ ٱلْجُمُعَةِ فَٱسْعَوْا۟ إِلَىٰ ذِكْرِ ٱللَّهِ وَذَرُوا۟
ٱلْبَيْعَ ۚ ذَٰلِكُمْ خَيْرٌ لَّكُمْ إِن كُنتُمْ تَعْلَمُونَ

9 O you who believe! When the call is made for prayer on Congregation Day, hasten to the remembrance of Allah, and drop all business. That is better for you, if you only knew.

١٠ فَإِذَا قُضِيَتِ ٱلصَّلَوٰةُ فَٱنتَشِرُوا۟ فِى ٱلْأَرْضِ
وَٱبْتَغُوا۟ مِن فَضْلِ ٱللَّهِ وَٱذْكُرُوا۟ ٱللَّهَ كَثِيرًا
لَّعَلَّكُمْ تُفْلِحُونَ

10 Then, when the prayer is concluded, disperse through the land, and seek Allah's bounty, and remember Allah much, so that you may prosper.

١١ وَإِذَا رَأَوْا۟ تِجَٰرَةً أَوْ لَهْوًا ٱنفَضُّوٓا۟ إِلَيْهَا
وَتَرَكُوكَ قَآئِمًا ۚ قُلْ مَا عِندَ ٱللَّهِ خَيْرٌ مِّنَ ٱللَّهْوِ
وَمِنَ ٱلتِّجَٰرَةِ ۚ وَٱللَّهُ خَيْرُ ٱلرَّٰزِقِينَ

11 Yet whenever they come across some business, or some entertainment, they scramble towards it, and leave you standing. Say, "What is with Allah is better than entertainment and business; and Allah is the Best of providers."

63 The Hypocrites المنافقون

بِسْمِ ٱللَّهِ ٱلرَّحْمَٰنِ ٱلرَّحِيمِ

In the name of Allah, the Gracious, the Merciful.

١ إِذَا جَآءَكَ ٱلْمُنَٰفِقُونَ قَالُوا۟ نَشْهَدُ إِنَّكَ لَرَسُولُ
ٱللَّهِ ۗ وَٱللَّهُ يَعْلَمُ إِنَّكَ لَرَسُولُهُۥ وَٱللَّهُ يَشْهَدُ إِنَّ
ٱلْمُنَٰفِقِينَ لَكَٰذِبُونَ

1 When the hypocrites come to you, they say, "We bear witness that you are Allah's Messenger." Allah knows that you are His Messenger, and

Allah bears witness that the hypocrites are liars.

٢ ٱتَّخَذُوٓاْ أَيۡمَٰنَهُمۡ جُنَّةٗ فَصَدُّواْ عَن سَبِيلِ ٱللَّهِۚ
إِنَّهُمۡ سَآءَ مَا كَانُواْ يَعۡمَلُونَ

2 They treat their oaths as a cover, and so they repel others from Allah's path. Evil is what they do.

٣ ذَٰلِكَ بِأَنَّهُمۡ ءَامَنُواْ ثُمَّ كَفَرُواْ فَطُبِعَ عَلَىٰ
قُلُوبِهِمۡ فَهُمۡ لَا يَفۡقَهُونَ

3 That is because they believed, and then disbelieved; so their hearts were sealed, and they cannot understand.

٤ وَإِذَا رَأَيۡتَهُمۡ تُعۡجِبُكَ أَجۡسَامُهُمۡۖ وَإِن يَقُولُواْ
تَسۡمَعۡ لِقَوۡلِهِمۡۖ كَأَنَّهُمۡ خُشُبٞ مُّسَنَّدَةٞۖ يَحۡسَبُونَ
كُلَّ صَيۡحَةٍ عَلَيۡهِمۡۚ هُمُ ٱلۡعَدُوُّ فَٱحۡذَرۡهُمۡۚ
قَٰتَلَهُمُ ٱللَّهُۖ أَنَّىٰ يُؤۡفَكُونَ

4 When you see them, their appearance impresses you. And when they speak, you listen to what they say. They are like propped-up timber. They think every shout is aimed at them. They are the enemy, so beware of them. Allah condemns them; how deluded they are!

٥ وَإِذَا قِيلَ لَهُمۡ تَعَالَوۡاْ يَسۡتَغۡفِرۡ لَكُمۡ رَسُولُ ٱللَّهِ
لَوَّوۡاْ رُءُوسَهُمۡ وَرَأَيۡتَهُمۡ يَصُدُّونَ وَهُم
مُّسۡتَكۡبِرُونَ

5 And when it is said to them, "Come, the Messenger of Allah will ask forgiveness for you," they bend their heads, and you see them turning away arrogantly.

٦ سَوَآءٌ عَلَيۡهِمۡ أَسۡتَغۡفَرۡتَ لَهُمۡ أَمۡ لَمۡ تَسۡتَغۡفِرۡ
لَهُمۡ لَن يَغۡفِرَ ٱللَّهُ لَهُمۡۚ إِنَّ ٱللَّهَ لَا يَهۡدِي ٱلۡقَوۡمَ
ٱلۡفَٰسِقِينَ

6 It is the same for them, whether you ask forgiveness for them, or do not ask forgiveness for them; Allah will not forgive them. Allah does not guide the sinful people.

٧ هُمُ ٱلَّذِينَ يَقُولُونَ لَا تُنفِقُواْ عَلَىٰ مَنۡ عِندَ
رَسُولِ ٱللَّهِ حَتَّىٰ يَنفَضُّواْۗ وَلِلَّهِ خَزَآئِنُ
ٱلسَّمَٰوَٰتِ وَٱلۡأَرۡضِ وَلَٰكِنَّ ٱلۡمُنَٰفِقِينَ لَا يَفۡقَهُونَ

7 It is they who say: "Do not spend anything on those who side with Allah's Messenger, unless they have dispersed." To Allah belong the treasures of the heavens and the earth, but the hypocrites do not understand.

٨ يَقُولُونَ لَئِن رَّجَعۡنَآ إِلَى ٱلۡمَدِينَةِ لَيُخۡرِجَنَّ
ٱلۡأَعَزُّ مِنۡهَا ٱلۡأَذَلَّۚ وَلِلَّهِ ٱلۡعِزَّةُ وَلِرَسُولِهِۦ
وَلِلۡمُؤۡمِنِينَ وَلَٰكِنَّ ٱلۡمُنَٰفِقِينَ لَا يَعۡلَمُونَ

8 They say, "If we return to the City, the more powerful therein will evict the weak." But power belongs to Allah, and His Messenger, and the believers; but the hypocrites do not know.

٩ يَٰٓأَيُّهَا ٱلَّذِينَ ءَامَنُوا۟ لَا تُلْهِكُمْ أَمْوَٰلُكُمْ وَلَآ
أَوْلَٰدُكُمْ عَن ذِكْرِ ٱللَّهِ ۚ وَمَن يَفْعَلْ ذَٰلِكَ فَأُو۟لَٰٓئِكَ
هُمُ ٱلْخَٰسِرُونَ

9 O you who believe! Let neither your possessions nor your children distract you from the remembrance of Allah. Whoever does that—these are the losers.

١٠ وَأَنفِقُوا۟ مِن مَّا رَزَقْنَٰكُم مِّن قَبْلِ أَن يَأْتِىَ
أَحَدَكُمُ ٱلْمَوْتُ فَيَقُولَ رَبِّ لَوْلَآ أَخَّرْتَنِىٓ إِلَىٰٓ
أَجَلٍ قَرِيبٍ فَأَصَّدَّقَ وَأَكُن مِّنَ ٱلصَّٰلِحِينَ

10 And give from what We have provided for you, before death approaches one of you, and he says, “My Lord, if only You would delay me for a short while, so that I may be charitable, and be one of the righteous.”

١١ وَلَن يُؤَخِّرَ ٱللَّهُ نَفْسًا إِذَا جَآءَ أَجَلُهَا ۚ وَٱللَّهُ
خَبِيرٌۢ بِمَا تَعْمَلُونَ

11 But Allah will not delay a soul when its time has come. Allah is Informed of what you do.

64 Gathering التغابن

بِسْمِ ٱللَّهِ ٱلرَّحْمَٰنِ ٱلرَّحِيمِ

In the name of Allah, the Gracious, the Merciful.

١ يُسَبِّحُ لِلَّهِ مَا فِى ٱلسَّمَٰوَٰتِ وَمَا فِى ٱلْأَرْضِ ۖ
لَهُ ٱلْمُلْكُ وَلَهُ ٱلْحَمْدُ ۖ وَهُوَ عَلَىٰ كُلِّ شَىْءٍ
قَدِيرٌ

1 Everything in the heavens and the earth praises Allah. To Him belongs the Kingdom, and to Him all praise is due, and He is Able to do all things.

٢ هُوَ ٱلَّذِى خَلَقَكُمْ فَمِنكُمْ كَافِرٌ وَمِنكُم مُّؤْمِنٌ ۚ
وَٱللَّهُ بِمَا تَعْمَلُونَ بَصِيرٌ

2 It is He who created you. Some of you are unbelievers, and some of you are believers. And Allah perceives what you do.

٣ خَلَقَ ٱلسَّمَٰوَٰتِ وَٱلْأَرْضَ بِٱلْحَقِّ وَصَوَّرَكُمْ
فَأَحْسَنَ صُوَرَكُمْ ۖ وَإِلَيْهِ ٱلْمَصِيرُ

3 He created the heavens and the earth with truth, and He designed you, and designed you well, and to Him is the final return.

٤ يَعْلَمُ مَا فِى ٱلسَّمَٰوَٰتِ وَٱلْأَرْضِ وَيَعْلَمُ مَا
تُسِرُّونَ وَمَا تُعْلِنُونَ ۚ وَٱللَّهُ عَلِيمٌۢ بِذَاتِ
ٱلصُّدُورِ

4 He knows everything in the heavens and the earth, and He knows what you conceal and what you reveal. And Allah knows what is within the hearts.

٥ أَلَمْ يَأْتِكُمْ نَبَؤُا۟ ٱلَّذِينَ كَفَرُوا۟ مِن قَبْلُ فَذَاقُوا۟
وَبَالَ أَمْرِهِمْ وَلَهُمْ عَذَابٌ أَلِيمٌ

5 Has the news not reached you, of those who disbelieved before? They tasted the ill consequences of their

conduct, and a painful torment awaits them.

٦ ذَٰلِكَ بِأَنَّهُۥ كَانَت تَّأۡتِيهِمۡ رُسُلُهُم بِٱلۡبَيِّنَٰتِ
فَقَالُوٓاْ أَبَشَرٞ يَهۡدُونَنَا فَكَفَرُواْ وَتَوَلَّواْۚ
وَّٱسۡتَغۡنَى ٱللَّهُۚ وَٱللَّهُ غَنِيٌّ حَمِيدٞ

6 That is because their messengers came to them with clear explanations, but they said, “Are human beings going to guide us?” So they disbelieved and turned away. But Allah is in no need. Allah is Independent and Praiseworthy.

٧ زَعَمَ ٱلَّذِينَ كَفَرُوٓاْ أَن لَّن يُبۡعَثُواْۚ قُلۡ بَلَىٰ
وَرَبِّي لَتُبۡعَثُنَّ ثُمَّ لَتُنَبَّؤُنَّ بِمَا عَمِلۡتُمۡۚ وَذَٰلِكَ
عَلَى ٱللَّهِ يَسِيرٞ

7 Those who disbelieve claim that they will not be resurrected. Say, “Yes indeed, by my Lord, you will be resurrected; then you will be informed of everything you did; and that is easy for Allah.”

٨ فَـَٔامِنُواْ بِٱللَّهِ وَرَسُولِهِۦ وَٱلنُّورِ ٱلَّذِيٓ أَنزَلۡنَاۚ
وَٱللَّهُ بِمَا تَعۡمَلُونَ خَبِيرٞ

8 So believe in Allah and His Messenger, and the Light which We sent down. Allah is Aware of everything you do.

٩ يَوۡمَ يَجۡمَعُكُمۡ لِيَوۡمِ ٱلۡجَمۡعِۖ ذَٰلِكَ يَوۡمُ
ٱلتَّغَابُنِۗ وَمَن يُؤۡمِنۢ بِٱللَّهِ وَيَعۡمَلۡ صَٰلِحٗا يُكَفِّرۡ
عَنۡهُ سَيِّـَٔاتِهِۦ وَيُدۡخِلۡهُ جَنَّٰتٖ تَجۡرِي مِن تَحۡتِهَا
ٱلۡأَنۡهَٰرُ خَٰلِدِينَ فِيهَآ أَبَدٗاۚ ذَٰلِكَ ٱلۡفَوۡزُ ٱلۡعَظِيمُ

9 The Day when He gathers you for the Day of Gathering—that is the Day of Mutual Exchange. Whoever believes in Allah and acts with integrity, He will remit his misdeeds, and will admit him into gardens beneath which rivers flow, to dwell therein forever. That is the supreme achievement.

١٠ وَٱلَّذِينَ كَفَرُواْ وَكَذَّبُواْ بِـَٔايَٰتِنَآ أُوْلَٰٓئِكَ أَصۡحَٰبُ
ٱلنَّارِ خَٰلِدِينَ فِيهَاۖ وَبِئۡسَ ٱلۡمَصِيرُ

10 But as for those who disbelieve and denounce Our revelations—these are the inmates of the Fire, dwelling therein forever; and what a miserable fate!

١١ مَآ أَصَابَ مِن مُّصِيبَةٍ إِلَّا بِإِذۡنِ ٱللَّهِۗ وَمَن
يُؤۡمِنۢ بِٱللَّهِ يَهۡدِ قَلۡبَهُۥۚ وَٱللَّهُ بِكُلِّ شَيۡءٍ عَلِيمٞ

11 No disaster occurs except by Allah’s leave. Whoever believes in Allah, He guides his heart. Allah is Aware of everything.

١٢ وَأَطِيعُواْ ٱللَّهَ وَأَطِيعُواْ ٱلرَّسُولَۚ فَإِن
تَوَلَّيۡتُمۡ فَإِنَّمَا عَلَىٰ رَسُولِنَا ٱلۡبَلَٰغُ ٱلۡمُبِينُ

12 So obey Allah, and obey the Messenger. But if you turn away—it is only incumbent on Our Messenger to deliver the clear message.

١٣ ٱللَّهُ لَآ إِلَٰهَ إِلَّا هُوَۚ وَعَلَى ٱللَّهِ فَلۡيَتَوَكَّلِ
ٱلۡمُؤۡمِنُونَ

13 Allah, there is no god but He; and in Allah let the believers put their trust.

١٤ يَٰٓأَيُّهَا ٱلَّذِينَ ءَامَنُوٓاْ إِنَّ مِنۡ أَزۡوَٰجِكُمۡ
وَأَوۡلَٰدِكُمۡ عَدُوّٗا لَّكُمۡ فَٱحۡذَرُوهُمۡۚ وَإِن تَعۡفُواْ
وَتَصۡفَحُواْ وَتَغۡفِرُواْ فَإِنَّ ٱللَّهَ غَفُورٞ رَّحِيمٌ

14 O you who believe! Among your wives and your children are enemies to you, so beware of them. But if you pardon, and overlook, and forgive—Allah is Forgiver and Merciful.

١٥ إِنَّمَآ أَمۡوَٰلُكُمۡ وَأَوۡلَٰدُكُمۡ فِتۡنَةٞۚ وَٱللَّهُ عِندَهُۥٓ أَجۡرٌ
عَظِيمٞ

15 Your possessions and your children are a test, but with Allah is a splendid reward.

١٦ فَٱتَّقُواْ ٱللَّهَ مَا ٱسۡتَطَعۡتُمۡ وَٱسۡمَعُواْ وَأَطِيعُواْ
وَأَنفِقُواْ خَيۡرٗا لِّأَنفُسِكُمۡۗ وَمَن يُوقَ شُحَّ نَفۡسِهِۦ
فَأُوْلَٰٓئِكَ هُمُ ٱلۡمُفۡلِحُونَ

16 So be conscious of Allah as much as you can, and listen, and obey, and give for your own good. He who is protected from his stinginess—these are the prosperous.

١٧ إِن تُقۡرِضُواْ ٱللَّهَ قَرۡضًا حَسَنٗا يُضَٰعِفۡهُ لَكُمۡ
وَيَغۡفِرۡ لَكُمۡۚ وَٱللَّهُ شَكُورٌ حَلِيمٌ

17 If you lend Allah a good loan, He will multiply it for you, and will forgive you. Allah is Appreciative and Forbearing.

١٨ عَٰلِمُ ٱلۡغَيۡبِ وَٱلشَّهَٰدَةِ ٱلۡعَزِيزُ ٱلۡحَكِيمُ

18 The Knower of the Unseen and the Seen, the Almighty, the Wise.

65 Divorce الطلاق

بِسۡمِ ٱللَّهِ ٱلرَّحۡمَٰنِ ٱلرَّحِيمِ

In the name of Allah, the Gracious, the Merciful.

١ يَٰٓأَيُّهَا ٱلنَّبِيُّ إِذَا طَلَّقۡتُمُ ٱلنِّسَآءَ فَطَلِّقُوهُنَّ
لِعِدَّتِهِنَّ وَأَحۡصُواْ ٱلۡعِدَّةَۖ وَٱتَّقُواْ ٱللَّهَ رَبَّكُمۡۖ لَا
تُخۡرِجُوهُنَّ مِنۢ بُيُوتِهِنَّ وَلَا يَخۡرُجۡنَ إِلَّآ أَن
يَأۡتِينَ بِفَٰحِشَةٖ مُّبَيِّنَةٖۚ وَتِلۡكَ حُدُودُ ٱللَّهِۚ وَمَن
يَتَعَدَّ حُدُودَ ٱللَّهِ فَقَدۡ ظَلَمَ نَفۡسَهُۥۚ لَا تَدۡرِي لَعَلَّ
ٱللَّهَ يُحۡدِثُ بَعۡدَ ذَٰلِكَ أَمۡرٗا

1 O Prophet! If any of you divorce women, divorce them during their period of purity, and calculate their term. And be pious before Allah, your Lord. And do not evict them from their homes, nor shall they leave, unless they have committed a proven adultery. These are the limits of Allah—whoever oversteps Allah's limits has wronged his own soul. You never know; Allah may afterwards bring about a new situation.

٢ فَإِذَا بَلَغْنَ أَجَلَهُنَّ فَأَمْسِكُوهُنَّ بِمَعْرُوفٍ أَوْ
فَارِقُوهُنَّ بِمَعْرُوفٍ وَأَشْهِدُوا۟ ذَوَىْ عَدْلٍ مِّنكُمْ
وَأَقِيمُوا۟ ٱلشَّهَـٰدَةَ لِلَّهِ ۚ ذَٰلِكُمْ يُوعَظُ بِهِۦ مَن كَانَ
يُؤْمِنُ بِٱللَّهِ وَٱلْيَوْمِ ٱلْـَٔاخِرِ ۚ وَمَن يَتَّقِ ٱللَّهَ
يَجْعَل لَّهُۥ مَخْرَجًا

2 Once they have reached their term, either retain them honorably, or separate from them honorably. And call to witness two just people from among you, and give upright testimony for Allah. By that is exhorted whoever believes in Allah and the Last Day. And whoever fears Allah—He will make a way out for him.

٣ وَيَرْزُقْهُ مِنْ حَيْثُ لَا يَحْتَسِبُ ۚ وَمَن يَتَوَكَّلْ
عَلَى ٱللَّهِ فَهُوَ حَسْبُهُۥٓ ۚ إِنَّ ٱللَّهَ بَـٰلِغُ أَمْرِهِۦ ۚ قَدْ
جَعَلَ ٱللَّهُ لِكُلِّ شَىْءٍ قَدْرًا

3 And will provide for him from where he never expected. Whoever relies on Allah—He will suffice him. Allah will accomplish His purpose. Allah has set a measure to all things.

٤ وَٱلَّـٰٓـِٔى يَئِسْنَ مِنَ ٱلْمَحِيضِ مِن نِّسَآئِكُمْ إِنِ
ٱرْتَبْتُمْ فَعِدَّتُهُنَّ ثَلَـٰثَةُ أَشْهُرٍ وَٱلَّـٰٓـِٔى لَمْ يَحِضْنَ ۚ
وَأُو۟لَـٰتُ ٱلْأَحْمَالِ أَجَلُهُنَّ أَن يَضَعْنَ حَمْلَهُنَّ ۚ
وَمَن يَتَّقِ ٱللَّهَ يَجْعَل لَّهُۥ مِنْ أَمْرِهِۦ يُسْرًا

4 As for those of your women who have reached menopause, if you have any doubts, their term shall be three months—and also for those who have not menstruated. As for those who are pregnant, their term shall be until they have delivered. Whoever fears Allah—He will make things easy for him.

٥ ذَٰلِكَ أَمْرُ ٱللَّهِ أَنزَلَهُۥٓ إِلَيْكُمْ ۚ وَمَن يَتَّقِ ٱللَّهَ
يُكَفِّرْ عَنْهُ سَيِّـَٔاتِهِۦ وَيُعْظِمْ لَهُۥٓ أَجْرًا

5 This is the ordinance of Allah, which He sent down to you. Whoever fears Allah—He will remit his sins, and will amplify his reward.

٦ أَسْكِنُوهُنَّ مِنْ حَيْثُ سَكَنتُم مِّن وُجْدِكُمْ وَلَا
تُضَآرُّوهُنَّ لِتُضَيِّقُوا۟ عَلَيْهِنَّ ۚ وَإِن كُنَّ أُو۟لَـٰتِ
حَمْلٍ فَأَنفِقُوا۟ عَلَيْهِنَّ حَتَّىٰ يَضَعْنَ حَمْلَهُنَّ ۚ
فَإِنْ أَرْضَعْنَ لَكُمْ فَـَٔاتُوهُنَّ أُجُورَهُنَّ ۖ وَأْتَمِرُوا۟
بَيْنَكُم بِمَعْرُوفٍ ۖ وَإِن تَعَاسَرْتُمْ فَسَتُرْضِعُ لَهُۥٓ
أُخْرَىٰ

6 Allow them to reside where you reside, according to your means, and do not harass them in order to make things difficult for them. If they are pregnant, spend on them until they give birth. And if they nurse your infant, give them their payment. And conduct your relation in amity. But if you disagree, then let another woman nurse him.

٧ لِيُنفِقْ ذُو سَعَةٍ مِّن سَعَتِهِۦ ۖ وَمَن قُدِرَ عَلَيْهِ
رِزْقُهُۥ فَلْيُنفِقْ مِمَّآ ءَاتَىٰهُ ٱللَّهُ ۚ لَا يُكَلِّفُ ٱللَّهُ

7 The wealthy shall spend according to his means; and he whose resources are restricted shall spend according to what Allah has given

نَفْسًا إِلَّا مَآ ءَاتَىٰهَا ۚ سَيَجْعَلُ ٱللَّهُ بَعْدَ عُسْرٍ
يُسْرًا

him. Allah never burdens a soul beyond what He has given it. Allah will bring ease after hardship.

٨ وَكَأَيِّن مِّن قَرْيَةٍ عَتَتْ عَنْ أَمْرِ رَبِّهَا وَرُسُلِهِۦ
فَحَاسَبْنَٰهَا حِسَابًا شَدِيدًا وَعَذَّبْنَٰهَا عَذَابًا نُّكْرًا

8 How many a town defied the command of its Lord and His messengers? So We held it strictly accountable, and We punished it with a dreadful punishment.

٩ فَذَاقَتْ وَبَالَ أَمْرِهَا وَكَانَ عَٰقِبَةُ أَمْرِهَا خُسْرًا

9 It tasted the result of its decisions, and the outcome of its decisions was perdition.

١٠ أَعَدَّ ٱللَّهُ لَهُمْ عَذَابًا شَدِيدًا ۖ فَٱتَّقُوا۟ ٱللَّهَ
يَٰٓأُو۟لِى ٱلْأَلْبَٰبِ ٱلَّذِينَ ءَامَنُوا۟ ۚ قَدْ أَنزَلَ ٱللَّهُ
إِلَيْكُمْ ذِكْرًا

10 Allah has prepared for them a severe retribution. So beware of Allah, O you who possess intellect and have faith. Allah has sent down to you a Reminder.

١١ رَّسُولًا يَتْلُوا۟ عَلَيْكُمْ ءَايَٰتِ ٱللَّهِ مُبَيِّنَٰتٍ
لِّيُخْرِجَ ٱلَّذِينَ ءَامَنُوا۟ وَعَمِلُوا۟ ٱلصَّٰلِحَٰتِ مِنَ
ٱلظُّلُمَٰتِ إِلَى ٱلنُّورِ ۚ وَمَن يُؤْمِنۢ بِٱللَّهِ وَيَعْمَلْ
صَٰلِحًا يُدْخِلْهُ جَنَّٰتٍ تَجْرِى مِن تَحْتِهَا ٱلْأَنْهَٰرُ
خَٰلِدِينَ فِيهَآ أَبَدًا ۖ قَدْ أَحْسَنَ ٱللَّهُ لَهُۥ رِزْقًا

11 A messenger who recites to you Allah's Verses, clear and distinct, that he may bring those who believe and work righteousness from darkness into light. Whoever believes in Allah and acts with integrity, He will admit him into gardens beneath which rivers flow, therein to abide forever. Allah has given him an excellent provision.

١٢ ٱللَّهُ ٱلَّذِى خَلَقَ سَبْعَ سَمَٰوَٰتٍ وَمِنَ ٱلْأَرْضِ
مِثْلَهُنَّ يَتَنَزَّلُ ٱلْأَمْرُ بَيْنَهُنَّ لِتَعْلَمُوٓا۟ أَنَّ ٱللَّهَ عَلَىٰ
كُلِّ شَىْءٍ قَدِيرٌ وَأَنَّ ٱللَّهَ قَدْ أَحَاطَ بِكُلِّ شَىْءٍ
عِلْمًۢا

12 Allah is He Who created seven heavens, and their like of earth. The command descends through them, so that you may know that Allah is Capable of everything, and that Allah Encompasses everything in knowledge.

66 Prohibition التحريم

بِسْمِ ٱللَّهِ ٱلرَّحْمَٰنِ ٱلرَّحِيمِ

In the name of Allah, the Gracious, the Merciful.

١ يَٰٓأَيُّهَا ٱلنَّبِىُّ لِمَ تُحَرِّمُ مَآ أَحَلَّ ٱللَّهُ لَكَ ۖ تَبْتَغِى
مَرْضَاتَ أَزْوَٰجِكَ ۚ وَٱللَّهُ غَفُورٌ رَّحِيمٌ

1 O prophet! Why do you prohibit what Allah has permitted for you,

seeking to please your wives? Allah is Forgiving and Merciful.

٢ قَدْ فَرَضَ ٱللَّهُ لَكُمْ تَحِلَّةَ أَيْمَٰنِكُمْ ۚ وَٱللَّهُ
مَوْلَىٰكُمْ ۖ وَهُوَ ٱلْعَلِيمُ ٱلْحَكِيمُ

2 Allah has decreed for you the dissolution of your oaths. Allah is your Master. He is the All-Knowing, the Most Wise.

٣ وَإِذْ أَسَرَّ ٱلنَّبِىُّ إِلَىٰ بَعْضِ أَزْوَٰجِهِۦ حَدِيثًا
فَلَمَّا نَبَّأَتْ بِهِۦ وَأَظْهَرَهُ ٱللَّهُ عَلَيْهِ عَرَّفَ بَعْضَهُۥ
وَأَعْرَضَ عَنۢ بَعْضٍ ۖ فَلَمَّا نَبَّأَهَا بِهِۦ قَالَتْ مَنْ
أَنۢبَأَكَ هَٰذَا ۖ قَالَ نَبَّأَنِىَ ٱلْعَلِيمُ ٱلْخَبِيرُ

3 The Prophet told something in confidence to one of his wives. But when she disclosed it, and Allah made it known to him; he communicated part of it, and he avoided another part. Then, when he informed her of it, she said, "Who informed you of this?" He said, "The All-Knowing, the All-Informed, informed me."

٤ إِن تَتُوبَآ إِلَى ٱللَّهِ فَقَدْ صَغَتْ قُلُوبُكُمَا ۖ وَإِن
تَظَٰهَرَا عَلَيْهِ فَإِنَّ ٱللَّهَ هُوَ مَوْلَىٰهُ وَجِبْرِيلُ
وَصَٰلِحُ ٱلْمُؤْمِنِينَ ۖ وَٱلْمَلَٰٓئِكَةُ بَعْدَ ذَٰلِكَ ظَهِيرٌ

4 If you repent to Allah, then your hearts have listened. But if you band together against him, then Allah is his Ally, as is Gabriel, and the righteous believers. In addition, the angels will assist him.

٥ عَسَىٰ رَبُّهُۥٓ إِن طَلَّقَكُنَّ أَن يُبْدِلَهُۥٓ أَزْوَٰجًا خَيْرًا
مِّنكُنَّ مُسْلِمَٰتٍ مُّؤْمِنَٰتٍ قَٰنِتَٰتٍ تَٰٓئِبَٰتٍ عَٰبِدَٰتٍ
سَٰٓئِحَٰتٍ ثَيِّبَٰتٍ وَأَبْكَارًا

5 Perhaps, if he divorces you, his Lord will give him in exchange wives better than you: submissive, believing, obedient, penitent, devout, fasting—previously married, or virgins.

٦ يَٰٓأَيُّهَا ٱلَّذِينَ ءَامَنُوا۟ قُوٓا۟ أَنفُسَكُمْ وَأَهْلِيكُمْ
نَارًا وَقُودُهَا ٱلنَّاسُ وَٱلْحِجَارَةُ عَلَيْهَا مَلَٰٓئِكَةٌ
غِلَاظٌ شِدَادٌ لَّا يَعْصُونَ ٱللَّهَ مَآ أَمَرَهُمْ
وَيَفْعَلُونَ مَا يُؤْمَرُونَ

6 O you who believe! Protect yourselves and your families from a Fire, whose fuel is people and stones. Over it are angels, fierce and powerful. They never disobey Allah in anything He commands them, and they carry out whatever they are commanded.

٧ يَٰٓأَيُّهَا ٱلَّذِينَ كَفَرُوا۟ لَا تَعْتَذِرُوا۟ ٱلْيَوْمَ ۖ إِنَّمَا
تُجْزَوْنَ مَا كُنتُمْ تَعْمَلُونَ

7 O you who disbelieved! Make no excuses today. You are being repaid for what you used to do.

٨ يَٰٓأَيُّهَا ٱلَّذِينَ ءَامَنُوا۟ تُوبُوٓا۟ إِلَى ٱللَّهِ تَوْبَةً
نَّصُوحًا عَسَىٰ رَبُّكُمْ أَن يُكَفِّرَ عَنكُمْ سَيِّـَٔاتِكُمْ
وَيُدْخِلَكُمْ جَنَّٰتٍ تَجْرِى مِن تَحْتِهَا ٱلْأَنْهَٰرُ يَوْمَ
لَا يُخْزِى ٱللَّهُ ٱلنَّبِىَّ وَٱلَّذِينَ ءَامَنُوا۟ مَعَهُۥ ۖ
نُورُهُمْ يَسْعَىٰ بَيْنَ أَيْدِيهِمْ وَبِأَيْمَٰنِهِمْ يَقُولُونَ
رَبَّنَآ أَتْمِمْ لَنَا نُورَنَا وَٱغْفِرْ لَنَآ ۖ إِنَّكَ عَلَىٰ كُلِّ
شَىْءٍ قَدِيرٌ

8 O you who believe! Repent to Allah with sincere repentance. Perhaps your Lord will remit your sins, and admit you into gardens beneath which rivers flow, on the Day when Allah will not disappoint the Prophet and those who believed with him. Their light streaming before them, and to their right, they will say, "Our Lord, complete our light for us, and forgive us; You are capable of all things."

٩ يَٰٓأَيُّهَا ٱلنَّبِىُّ جَٰهِدِ ٱلْكُفَّارَ وَٱلْمُنَٰفِقِينَ وَٱغْلُظْ
عَلَيْهِمْ ۚ وَمَأْوَىٰهُمْ جَهَنَّمُ ۖ وَبِئْسَ ٱلْمَصِيرُ

9 O prophet! Strive hard against the disbelievers and the hypocrites, and be stern with them. Their abode is Hell. What a miserable destination!

١٠ ضَرَبَ ٱللَّهُ مَثَلًا لِّلَّذِينَ كَفَرُوا۟ ٱمْرَأَتَ نُوحٍ
وَٱمْرَأَتَ لُوطٍ ۖ كَانَتَا تَحْتَ عَبْدَيْنِ مِنْ عِبَادِنَا
صَٰلِحَيْنِ فَخَانَتَاهُمَا فَلَمْ يُغْنِيَا عَنْهُمَا مِنَ ٱللَّهِ
شَيْـًٔا وَقِيلَ ٱدْخُلَا ٱلنَّارَ مَعَ ٱلدَّٰخِلِينَ

10 Allah illustrates an example of those who disbelieve: the wife of Noah and the wife of Lot. They were under two of Our righteous servants, but they betrayed them. They availed them nothing against Allah, and it was said, "Enter the Fire with those who are entering."

١١ وَضَرَبَ ٱللَّهُ مَثَلًا لِّلَّذِينَ ءَامَنُوا۟ ٱمْرَأَتَ
فِرْعَوْنَ إِذْ قَالَتْ رَبِّ ٱبْنِ لِى عِندَكَ بَيْتًا فِى
ٱلْجَنَّةِ وَنَجِّنِى مِن فِرْعَوْنَ وَعَمَلِهِۦ وَنَجِّنِى مِنَ
ٱلْقَوْمِ ٱلظَّٰلِمِينَ

11 And Allah illustrates an example of those who believe: the wife of Pharaoh, when she said, "My Lord, build for me, with you, a house in Paradise, and save me from Pharaoh and his works, and save me from the wrongdoing people."

١٢ وَمَرْيَمَ ٱبْنَتَ عِمْرَٰنَ ٱلَّتِىٓ أَحْصَنَتْ فَرْجَهَا
فَنَفَخْنَا فِيهِ مِن رُّوحِنَا وَصَدَّقَتْ بِكَلِمَٰتِ رَبِّهَا
وَكُتُبِهِۦ وَكَانَتْ مِنَ ٱلْقَٰنِتِينَ

12 And Mary, the daughter of Imran, who guarded her womb, and so We breathed into her of Our Spirit; and she believed in the truth of her Lord's Words and His Books, and was one of the devout.

67 Sovereignty الملك

بِسْمِ ٱللَّهِ ٱلرَّحْمَٰنِ ٱلرَّحِيمِ

In the name of Allah, the Gracious, the Merciful.

١ تَبَٰرَكَ ٱلَّذِى بِيَدِهِ ٱلْمُلْكُ وَهُوَ عَلَىٰ كُلِّ شَىْءٍ
قَدِيرٌ

1 Blessed is He in whose hand is the sovereignty, and Who has power over everything.

٢ ٱلَّذِى خَلَقَ ٱلْمَوْتَ وَٱلْحَيَوٰةَ لِيَبْلُوَكُمْ أَيُّكُمْ
أَحْسَنُ عَمَلًا ۚ وَهُوَ ٱلْعَزِيزُ ٱلْغَفُورُ

2 He who created death and life—to test you—as to which of you is better in conduct. He is the Almighty, the Forgiving.

٣ ٱلَّذِى خَلَقَ سَبْعَ سَمَٰوَٰتٍ طِبَاقًا ۖ مَّا تَرَىٰ فِى
خَلْقِ ٱلرَّحْمَٰنِ مِن تَفَٰوُتٍ ۖ فَٱرْجِعِ ٱلْبَصَرَ هَلْ
تَرَىٰ مِن فُطُورٍ

3 He who created seven heavens in layers. You see no discrepancy in the creation of the Compassionate. Look again. Can you see any cracks?

٤ ثُمَّ ٱرْجِعِ ٱلْبَصَرَ كَرَّتَيْنِ يَنقَلِبْ إِلَيْكَ ٱلْبَصَرُ
خَاسِئًا وَهُوَ حَسِيرٌ

4 Then look again, and again, and your sight will return to you dazzled and exhausted.

٥ وَلَقَدْ زَيَّنَّا ٱلسَّمَآءَ ٱلدُّنْيَا بِمَصَٰبِيحَ وَجَعَلْنَٰهَا
رُجُومًا لِّلشَّيَٰطِينِ ۖ وَأَعْتَدْنَا لَهُمْ عَذَابَ ٱلسَّعِيرِ

5 We have adorned the lower heaven with lanterns, and made them missiles against the devils; and We have prepared for them the punishment of the Blaze.

٦ وَلِلَّذِينَ كَفَرُوا۟ بِرَبِّهِمْ عَذَابُ جَهَنَّمَ ۖ وَبِئْسَ
ٱلْمَصِيرُ

6 For those who reject their Lord, there is the torment of Hell. What an evil destination!

٧ إِذَآ أُلْقُوا۟ فِيهَا سَمِعُوا۟ لَهَا شَهِيقًا وَهِىَ تَفُورُ

7 When they are thrown into it, they will hear it roaring, as it seethes.

٨ تَكَادُ تَمَيَّزُ مِنَ ٱلْغَيْظِ ۖ كُلَّمَآ أُلْقِىَ فِيهَا فَوْجٌ
سَأَلَهُمْ خَزَنَتُهَآ أَلَمْ يَأْتِكُمْ نَذِيرٌ

8 It almost bursts with fury. Every time a batch is thrown into it, its keepers will ask them, “Has no warner come to you?”

٩ قَالُوا۟ بَلَىٰ قَدْ جَآءَنَا نَذِيرٌ فَكَذَّبْنَا وَقُلْنَا مَا
نَزَّلَ ٱللَّهُ مِن شَىْءٍ إِنْ أَنتُمْ إِلَّا فِى ضَلَٰلٍ كَبِيرٍ

9 They will say, “Yes, a warner did come to us, but we disbelieved, and said, ‘Allah did not send down anything; you are very much mistaken.’”

١٠ وَقَالُوا۟ لَوْ كُنَّا نَسْمَعُ أَوْ نَعْقِلُ مَا كُنَّا فِىٓ
أَصْحَٰبِ ٱلسَّعِيرِ

10 And they will say, “Had we listened or reasoned, we would not have been among the inmates of the Blaze.”

١١ فَٱعْتَرَفُوا۟ بِذَنۢبِهِمْ فَسُحْقًا لِّأَصْحَٰبِ ٱلسَّعِيرِ

11 So they will acknowledge their sins. So away with the inmates of the Blaze.

١٢ إِنَّ ٱلَّذِينَ يَخْشَوْنَ رَبَّهُم بِٱلْغَيْبِ لَهُم مَّغْفِرَةٌ
وَأَجْرٌ كَبِيرٌ

12 As for those who fear their Lord in secret—for them is forgiveness and a great reward.

١٣ وَأَسِرُّوا۟ قَوْلَكُمْ أَوِ ٱجْهَرُوا۟ بِهِۦٓ ۖ إِنَّهُۥ عَلِيمٌۢ
بِذَاتِ ٱلصُّدُورِ

13 Whether you keep your words secret, or declare them—He is Aware of the inner thoughts.

١٤ أَلَا يَعْلَمُ مَنْ خَلَقَ وَهُوَ ٱللَّطِيفُ ٱلْخَبِيرُ

14 Would He not know, He Who created? He is the Refined, the Expert.

١٥ هُوَ ٱلَّذِى جَعَلَ لَكُمُ ٱلْأَرْضَ ذَلُولًا فَٱمْشُوا۟
فِى مَنَاكِبِهَا وَكُلُوا۟ مِن رِّزْقِهِۦ ۖ وَإِلَيْهِ ٱلنُّشُورُ

15 It is He who made the earth manageable for you, so travel its regions, and eat of His provisions. To Him is the Resurgence.

١٦ ءَأَمِنتُم مَّن فِى ٱلسَّمَآءِ أَن يَخْسِفَ بِكُمُ
ٱلْأَرْضَ فَإِذَا هِىَ تَمُورُ

16 Are you confident that the One in heaven will not cause the earth to collapse beneath you as it spins?

١٧ أَمْ أَمِنتُم مَّن فِى ٱلسَّمَآءِ أَن يُرْسِلَ عَلَيْكُمْ
حَاصِبًا ۖ فَسَتَعْلَمُونَ كَيْفَ نَذِيرِ

17 Or are you confident that the One in Heaven will not unleash against you a violent storm? Then you will know what My warning is like.

١٨ وَلَقَدْ كَذَّبَ ٱلَّذِينَ مِن قَبْلِهِمْ فَكَيْفَ كَانَ
نَكِيرِ

18 Those before them also denied the truth; and how was My disapproval?

١٩ أَوَلَمْ يَرَوْا۟ إِلَى ٱلطَّيْرِ فَوْقَهُمْ صَٰٓفَّٰتٍ
وَيَقْبِضْنَ ۚ مَا يُمْسِكُهُنَّ إِلَّا ٱلرَّحْمَٰنُ ۚ إِنَّهُۥ بِكُلِّ
شَىْءٍۭ بَصِيرٌ

19 Have they not seen the birds above them, spreading their wings, and folding them? None holds them except the Compassionate. He is Perceiver of everything.

٢٠ أَمَّنْ هَٰذَا ٱلَّذِى هُوَ جُندٌ لَّكُمْ يَنصُرُكُم مِّن
دُونِ ٱلرَّحْمَٰنِ ۚ إِنِ ٱلْكَٰفِرُونَ إِلَّا فِى غُرُورٍ

20 Or who is this who is a force for you to protect you against the Compassionate? The disbelievers are in nothing but delusion.

٢١ أَمَّنْ هَٰذَا ٱلَّذِى يَرْزُقُكُمْ إِنْ أَمْسَكَ رِزْقَهُۥ ۚ بَل
لَّجُّوا۟ فِى عُتُوٍّ وَنُفُورٍ

21 Or who is this that will provide for you, if He withholds His provision? Yet they persist in defiance and aversion.

٢٢ أَفَمَن يَمْشِى مُكِبًّا عَلَىٰ وَجْهِهِۦٓ أَهْدَىٰٓ أَمَّن
يَمْشِى سَوِيًّا عَلَىٰ صِرَٰطٍ مُّسْتَقِيمٍ

22 Is he who walks bent on his own design better guided, or he who walks upright on a straight path?

٢٣ قُلْ هُوَ ٱلَّذِىٓ أَنشَأَكُمْ وَجَعَلَ لَكُمُ ٱلسَّمْعَ
وَٱلْأَبْصَٰرَ وَٱلْأَفْـِٔدَةَ ۖ قَلِيلًا مَّا تَشْكُرُونَ

23 Say, "It is He who produced you; and made for you the hearing, and the vision, and the organs. But rarely do you give thanks."

٢٤ قُلْ هُوَ ٱلَّذِى ذَرَأَكُمْ فِى ٱلْأَرْضِ وَإِلَيْهِ
تُحْشَرُونَ

24 Say, "It is He who scattered you on earth, and to Him you will be rounded up."

٢٥ وَيَقُولُونَ مَتَىٰ هَٰذَا ٱلْوَعْدُ إِن كُنتُمْ صَٰدِقِينَ

25 And they say, "When will this promise be fulfilled, if you are truthful?"

٢٦ قُلْ إِنَّمَا ٱلْعِلْمُ عِندَ ٱللَّهِ وَإِنَّمَآ أَنَا۠ نَذِيرٌ مُّبِينٌ

26 Say, "Knowledge is with Allah, and I am only a clear warner."

٢٧ فَلَمَّا رَأَوْهُ زُلْفَةً سِيٓـَٔتْ وُجُوهُ ٱلَّذِينَ كَفَرُوا۟
وَقِيلَ هَٰذَا ٱلَّذِى كُنتُم بِهِۦ تَدَّعُونَ

27 But when they see it approaching, the faces of those who disbelieved will turn gloomy, and it will be said, "This is what you used to call for."

٢٨ قُلْ أَرَءَيْتُمْ إِنْ أَهْلَكَنِىَ ٱللَّهُ وَمَن مَّعِىَ أَوْ
رَحِمَنَا فَمَن يُجِيرُ ٱلْكَٰفِرِينَ مِنْ عَذَابٍ أَلِيمٍ

28 Say, "Have you considered? Should Allah make me perish, and those with me; or else He bestows His mercy on us; who will protect the disbelievers from an agonizing torment?"

٢٩ قُلْ هُوَ ٱلرَّحْمَٰنُ ءَامَنَّا بِهِۦ وَعَلَيْهِ تَوَكَّلْنَا ۖ
فَسَتَعْلَمُونَ مَنْ هُوَ فِى ضَلَٰلٍ مُّبِينٍ

29 Say, "He is the Compassionate. We have faith in Him, and in Him we trust. Soon you will know who is in evident error."

٣٠ قُلْ أَرَءَيْتُمْ إِنْ أَصْبَحَ مَآؤُكُمْ غَوْرًا فَمَن
يَأْتِيكُم بِمَآءٍ مَّعِينٍ

30 Say, "Have you considered? If your water drains away, who will bring you pure running water?"

68 The Pen القلم

بِسْمِ ٱللَّهِ ٱلرَّحْمَٰنِ ٱلرَّحِيمِ

In the name of Allah, the Gracious, the Merciful.

١ نٓ ۚ وَٱلْقَلَمِ وَمَا يَسْطُرُونَ

1 Noon. By the pen, and by what they inscribe.

٢ مَآ أَنتَ بِنِعْمَةِ رَبِّكَ بِمَجْنُونٍ

2 By the grace of your Lord, you are not insane.

٣ وَإِنَّ لَكَ لَأَجْرًا غَيْرَ مَمْنُونٍ

3 In fact, you will have a reward that will never end.

٤ وَإِنَّكَ لَعَلَىٰ خُلُقٍ عَظِيمٍ

4 And you are of a great moral character.

٥ فَسَتُبْصِرُ وَيُبْصِرُونَ

5 You will see, and they will see.

٦ بِأَييِّكُمُ ٱلْمَفْتُونُ

6 Which of you is the afflicted.

٧ إِنَّ رَبَّكَ هُوَ أَعْلَمُ بِمَن ضَلَّ عَن سَبِيلِهِۦ وَهُوَ
أَعْلَمُ بِٱلْمُهْتَدِينَ

7 Your Lord knows best who has strayed from His path, and He knows best the well-guided.

٨ فَلَا تُطِعِ ٱلْمُكَذِّبِينَ

8 So do not obey the deniers.

٩ وَدُّوا۟ لَوْ تُدْهِنُ فَيُدْهِنُونَ

9 They would like you to compromise, so they would compromise.

١٠ وَلَا تُطِعْ كُلَّ حَلَّافٍ مَّهِينٍ

10 And do not obey any vile swearer.

١١ هَمَّازٍ مَّشَّآءٍۭ بِنَمِيمٍ

11 Backbiter, spreader of slander.

١٢ مَّنَّاعٍ لِّلْخَيْرِ مُعْتَدٍ أَثِيمٍ

12 Preventer of good, transgressor, sinner.

١٣ عُتُلٍّۭ بَعْدَ ذَٰلِكَ زَنِيمٍ

13 Rude and fake besides.

١٤ أَن كَانَ ذَا مَالٍ وَبَنِينَ

14 Just because he has money and children.

١٥ إِذَا تُتْلَىٰ عَلَيْهِ ءَايَٰتُنَا قَالَ أَسَٰطِيرُ ٱلْأَوَّلِينَ

15 When Our Verses are recited to him, he says, “Myths of the ancients!”

١٦ سَنَسِمُهُۥ عَلَى ٱلْخُرْطُومِ

16 We will brand him on the muzzle.

١٧ إِنَّا بَلَوْنَٰهُمْ كَمَا بَلَوْنَآ أَصْحَٰبَ ٱلْجَنَّةِ إِذْ
أَقْسَمُوا۟ لَيَصْرِمُنَّهَا مُصْبِحِينَ

17 We tested them, as We tested the owners of the garden, when they vowed to harvest it in the morning.

١٨ وَلَا يَسْتَثْنُونَ

18 Without any reservation.

١٩ فَطَافَ عَلَيْهَا طَآئِفٌ مِّن رَّبِّكَ وَهُمْ نَآئِمُونَ

19 But a calamity from your Lord went around it while they slept.

٢٠ فَأَصْبَحَتْ كَٱلصَّرِيمِ

20 And in the morning it was as if picked.

٢١ فَتَنَادَوْاْ مُصْبِحِينَ

21 In the morning, they called to one another.

٢٢ أَنِ ٱغْدُواْ عَلَىٰ حَرْثِكُمْ إِن كُنتُمْ صَٰرِمِينَ

22 “Go early to your plantation, if you are going to harvest.”

٢٣ فَٱنطَلَقُواْ وَهُمْ يَتَخَٰفَتُونَ

23 So off they went, murmuring to one another.

٢٤ أَن لَّا يَدْخُلَنَّهَا ٱلْيَوْمَ عَلَيْكُم مِّسْكِينٌ

24 “No poor person is to enter it upon you today.”

٢٥ وَغَدَوْاْ عَلَىٰ حَرْدٍ قَٰدِرِينَ

25 And early they went, resolved in intent.

٢٦ فَلَمَّا رَأَوْهَا قَالُوٓاْ إِنَّا لَضَآلُّونَ

26 But when they saw it, they said, “We were wrong.

٢٧ بَلْ نَحْنُ مَحْرُومُونَ

27 We are now deprived.”

٢٨ قَالَ أَوْسَطُهُمْ أَلَمْ أَقُل لَّكُمْ لَوْلَا تُسَبِّحُونَ

28 The most reasonable of them said, “Did I not say to you, ‘if only you would glorify?’”

٢٩ قَالُواْ سُبْحَٰنَ رَبِّنَآ إِنَّا كُنَّا ظَٰلِمِينَ

29 They said, “Glory to our Lord—We were indeed in the wrong.”

٣٠ فَأَقْبَلَ بَعْضُهُمْ عَلَىٰ بَعْضٍ يَتَلَٰوَمُونَ

30 Then they turned to one another, blaming one another.

٣١ قَالُواْ يَٰوَيْلَنَآ إِنَّا كُنَّا طَٰغِينَ

31 They said, “Woe to us—we were indeed domineering.

٣٢ عَسَىٰ رَبُّنَآ أَن يُبْدِلَنَا خَيْرًا مِّنْهَآ إِنَّآ إِلَىٰ رَبِّنَا رَٰغِبُونَ

32 Perhaps our Lord will give us a better substitute for it. We are turning to our Lord.”

٣٣ كَذَٰلِكَ ٱلْعَذَابُ ۖ وَلَعَذَابُ ٱلْءَاخِرَةِ أَكْبَرُ ۚ لَوْ كَانُواْ يَعْلَمُونَ

33 Such is the punishment; but the punishment of the Hereafter is greater, if they only knew.

٣٤ إِنَّ لِلْمُتَّقِينَ عِندَ رَبِّهِمْ جَنَّٰتِ ٱلنَّعِيمِ

34 For the righteous are Gardens of Delight with their Lord.

٣٥ أَفَنَجْعَلُ ٱلْمُسْلِمِينَ كَٱلْمُجْرِمِينَ

35 Shall We treat the Muslims like the villains?

٣٦ مَا لَكُمْ كَيْفَ تَحْكُمُونَ

36 What is the matter with you? How do you judge?

٣٧ أَمْ لَكُمْ كِتَٰبٌ فِيهِ تَدْرُسُونَ

37 Or do you have a scripture in which you study.

٣٨ إِنَّ لَكُمْ فِيهِ لَمَا تَخَيَّرُونَ

38 Wherein there is whatever you choose?

٣٩ أَمْ لَكُمْ أَيْمَٰنٌ عَلَيْنَا بَٰلِغَةٌ إِلَىٰ يَوْمِ ٱلْقِيَٰمَةِ ۙ إِنَّ
لَكُمْ لَمَا تَحْكُمُونَ

39 Or do you have oaths from Us, binding until the Day of Resurrection, that you will have whatever you demand?

٤٠ سَلْهُمْ أَيُّهُم بِذَٰلِكَ زَعِيمٌ

40 Ask them, which of them will guarantee that.

٤١ أَمْ لَهُمْ شُرَكَآءُ فَلْيَأْتُوا۟ بِشُرَكَآئِهِمْ إِن كَانُوا۟
صَٰدِقِينَ

41 Or do they have partners? Then let them produce their partners, if they are truthful.

٤٢ يَوْمَ يُكْشَفُ عَن سَاقٍ وَيُدْعَوْنَ إِلَى
ٱلسُّجُودِ فَلَا يَسْتَطِيعُونَ

42 On the Day when the Shin will be exposed, and they will be called to bow down, but they will be unable.

٤٣ خَٰشِعَةً أَبْصَٰرُهُمْ تَرْهَقُهُمْ ذِلَّةٌ ۖ وَقَدْ كَانُوا۟
يُدْعَوْنَ إِلَى ٱلسُّجُودِ وَهُمْ سَٰلِمُونَ

43 Their eyes subdued, shame will cover them. They were invited to bow down when they were sound.

٤٤ فَذَرْنِى وَمَن يُكَذِّبُ بِهَٰذَا ٱلْحَدِيثِ ۖ
سَنَسْتَدْرِجُهُم مِّنْ حَيْثُ لَا يَعْلَمُونَ

44 So leave Me to those who reject this discourse; We will proceed against them gradually, from where they do not know.

٤٥ وَأُمْلِى لَهُمْ ۚ إِنَّ كَيْدِى مَتِينٌ

45 And I will give them respite. My plan is firm.

٤٦ أَمْ تَسْـَٔلُهُمْ أَجْرًا فَهُم مِّن مَّغْرَمٍ مُّثْقَلُونَ

46 Or do you ask them for a fee, so they are burdened with debt?

٤٧ أَمْ عِندَهُمُ ٱلْغَيْبُ فَهُمْ يَكْتُبُونَ

47 Or do they know the future, and so they write it down?

٤٨ فَٱصْبِرْ لِحُكْمِ رَبِّكَ وَلَا تَكُن كَصَاحِبِ
ٱلْحُوتِ إِذْ نَادَىٰ وَهُوَ مَكْظُومٌ

48 So wait patiently for the Decision of your Lord, and do not be like the Fellow of the Fish who cried out in despair.

٤٩ لَّوْلَآ أَن تَدَٰرَكَهُۥ نِعْمَةٌ مِّن رَّبِّهِۦ لَنُبِذَ بِٱلْعَرَآءِ
وَهُوَ مَذْمُومٌ

49 Were it not for his Lord's favor that reached him, he would have been thrown into the wilderness, fully despised.

٥٠ فَٱجْتَبَٰهُ رَبُّهُۥ فَجَعَلَهُۥ مِنَ ٱلصَّٰلِحِينَ

50 But his Lord chose him, and made him one of the righteous.

٥١ وَإِن يَكَادُ ٱلَّذِينَ كَفَرُوا۟ لَيُزْلِقُونَكَ بِأَبْصَٰرِهِمْ
لَمَّا سَمِعُوا۟ ٱلذِّكْرَ وَيَقُولُونَ إِنَّهُۥ لَمَجْنُونٌ

51 Those who disbelieve almost stab you with their glances when they hear the message, and say, "He is crazy!"

٥٢ وَمَا هُوَ إِلَّا ذِكْرٌ لِّلْعَٰلَمِينَ

52 But it is no less than a reminder to all the Worlds.

69 The Reality الحاقة

بِسْمِ ٱللَّهِ ٱلرَّحْمَٰنِ ٱلرَّحِيمِ

In the name of Allah, the Gracious, the Merciful.

١ ٱلْحَآقَّةُ

1 The Reality.

٢ مَا ٱلْحَآقَّةُ

2 What is the Reality?

٣ وَمَآ أَدْرَىٰكَ مَا ٱلْحَآقَّةُ

3 What will make you understand what the Reality is?

٤ كَذَّبَتْ ثَمُودُ وَعَادٌۢ بِٱلْقَارِعَةِ

4 Thamood and Aad denied the Catastrophe.

٥ فَأَمَّا ثَمُودُ فَأُهْلِكُوا۟ بِٱلطَّاغِيَةِ

5 As for Thamood, they were annihilated by the Overwhelming.

٦ وَأَمَّا عَادٌ فَأُهْلِكُوا۟ بِرِيحٍ صَرْصَرٍ عَاتِيَةٍ

6 And as for Aad; they were annihilated by a furious, roaring wind.

٧ سَخَّرَهَا عَلَيْهِمْ سَبْعَ لَيَالٍ وَثَمَٰنِيَةَ أَيَّامٍ
حُسُومًا فَتَرَى ٱلْقَوْمَ فِيهَا صَرْعَىٰ كَأَنَّهُمْ
أَعْجَازُ نَخْلٍ خَاوِيَةٍ

7 He unleashed it upon them for seven nights and eight days, in succession. You could see the people tossed around, as though they were stumps of hollow palm-trees.

٨ فَهَلْ تَرَىٰ لَهُم مِّنۢ بَاقِيَةٍ

8 Can you see any remnant of them?

٩ وَجَآءَ فِرْعَوْنُ وَمَن قَبْلَهُۥ وَٱلْمُؤْتَفِكَٰتُ
بِٱلْخَاطِئَةِ

9 Then Pharaoh came, and those before him, and the Overturned Cities steeped in sin.

١٠ فَعَصَوْا۟ رَسُولَ رَبِّهِمْ فَأَخَذَهُمْ أَخْذَةً رَّابِيَةً

10 But they disobeyed the messenger of their Lord, so He seized them with an overpowering grip.

١١ إِنَّا لَمَّا طَغَا ٱلْمَآءُ حَمَلْنَٰكُمْ فِى ٱلْجَارِيَةِ	11 When the waters overflowed, We carried you in the cruising ship.
١٢ لِنَجْعَلَهَا لَكُمْ تَذْكِرَةً وَتَعِيَهَآ أُذُنٌ وَٰعِيَةٌ	12 To make it a lesson for you—so that retaining ears may retain it.
١٣ فَإِذَا نُفِخَ فِى ٱلصُّورِ نَفْخَةٌ وَٰحِدَةٌ	13 Then, when the Trumpet is sounded a single time.
١٤ وَحُمِلَتِ ٱلْأَرْضُ وَٱلْجِبَالُ فَدُكَّتَا دَكَّةً وَٰحِدَةً	14 And the earth and the mountains are lifted up, and crushed, with a single crush.
١٥ فَيَوْمَئِذٍ وَقَعَتِ ٱلْوَاقِعَةُ	15 On that Day, the Event will come to pass.
١٦ وَٱنشَقَّتِ ٱلسَّمَآءُ فَهِىَ يَوْمَئِذٍ وَاهِيَةٌ	16 And the heaven will crack; so on that Day it will be frail.
١٧ وَٱلْمَلَكُ عَلَىٰٓ أَرْجَآئِهَا ۚ وَيَحْمِلُ عَرْشَ رَبِّكَ فَوْقَهُمْ يَوْمَئِذٍ ثَمَٰنِيَةٌ	17 And the angels will be ranged around its borders, while eight will be carrying the Throne of your Lord above them that Day.
١٨ يَوْمَئِذٍ تُعْرَضُونَ لَا تَخْفَىٰ مِنكُمْ خَافِيَةٌ	18 On that Day you will be exposed, and no secret of yours will remain hidden.
١٩ فَأَمَّا مَنْ أُوتِىَ كِتَٰبَهُۥ بِيَمِينِهِۦ فَيَقُولُ هَآؤُمُ ٱقْرَءُوا۟ كِتَٰبِيَهْ	19 As for him who is given his book in his right hand, he will say, “Here, take my book and read it.
٢٠ إِنِّى ظَنَنتُ أَنِّى مُلَٰقٍ حِسَابِيَهْ	20 I knew I would be held accountable.”
٢١ فَهُوَ فِى عِيشَةٍ رَّاضِيَةٍ	21 So he will be in pleasant living.
٢٢ فِى جَنَّةٍ عَالِيَةٍ	22 In a lofty Garden.
٢٣ قُطُوفُهَا دَانِيَةٌ	23 Its pickings are within reach.
٢٤ كُلُوا۟ وَٱشْرَبُوا۟ هَنِيٓـًٔا بِمَآ أَسْلَفْتُمْ فِى ٱلْأَيَّامِ ٱلْخَالِيَةِ	24 “Eat and drink merrily for what you did in the days gone by.”
٢٥ وَأَمَّا مَنْ أُوتِىَ كِتَٰبَهُۥ بِشِمَالِهِۦ فَيَقُولُ يَٰلَيْتَنِى لَمْ أُوتَ كِتَٰبِيَهْ	25 But as for him who is given his book in his left hand, he will say, “I wish I was never given my book.
٢٦ وَلَمْ أَدْرِ مَا حِسَابِيَهْ	26 And never knew what my account was.
٢٧ يَٰلَيْتَهَا كَانَتِ ٱلْقَاضِيَةَ	27 If only it was the end.

٢٨ مَآ أَغْنَىٰ عَنِّى مَالِيَهْ ۜ

28 My money cannot avail me.

٢٩ هَلَكَ عَنِّى سُلْطَٰنِيَهْ

29 My power has vanished from me."

٣٠ خُذُوهُ فَغُلُّوهُ

30 "Take him and shackle him.

٣١ ثُمَّ ٱلْجَحِيمَ صَلُّوهُ

31 Then scorch him in the Blaze.

٣٢ ثُمَّ فِى سِلْسِلَةٍ ذَرْعُهَا سَبْعُونَ ذِرَاعًا فَٱسْلُكُوهُ

32 Then in a chain which length is seventy cubits tie him up.

٣٣ إِنَّهُۥ كَانَ لَا يُؤْمِنُ بِٱللَّهِ ٱلْعَظِيمِ

33 For he would not believe in Allah the Great.

٣٤ وَلَا يَحُضُّ عَلَىٰ طَعَامِ ٱلْمِسْكِينِ

34 Nor would he advocate the feeding of the destitute.

٣٥ فَلَيْسَ لَهُ ٱلْيَوْمَ هَٰهُنَا حَمِيمٌ

35 So he has no friend here today.

٣٦ وَلَا طَعَامٌ إِلَّا مِنْ غِسْلِينٍ

36 And no food except scum.

٣٧ لَّا يَأْكُلُهُۥٓ إِلَّا ٱلْخَٰطِـُٔونَ

37 Which only the sinners eat."

٣٨ فَلَآ أُقْسِمُ بِمَا تُبْصِرُونَ

38 Indeed, I swear by what you see.

٣٩ وَمَا لَا تُبْصِرُونَ

39 And by what you do not see.

٤٠ إِنَّهُۥ لَقَوْلُ رَسُولٍ كَرِيمٍ

40 It is the speech of a noble messenger.

٤١ وَمَا هُوَ بِقَوْلِ شَاعِرٍ ۚ قَلِيلًا مَّا تُؤْمِنُونَ

41 And it is not the speech of a poet—little do you believe.

٤٢ وَلَا بِقَوْلِ كَاهِنٍ ۚ قَلِيلًا مَّا تَذَكَّرُونَ

42 Nor is it the speech of a soothsayer—little do you take heed.

٤٣ تَنزِيلٌ مِّن رَّبِّ ٱلْعَٰلَمِينَ

43 It is a revelation from the Lord of the Worlds.

٤٤ وَلَوْ تَقَوَّلَ عَلَيْنَا بَعْضَ ٱلْأَقَاوِيلِ

44 Had he falsely attributed some statements to Us.

٤٥ لَأَخَذْنَا مِنْهُ بِٱلْيَمِينِ

45 We would have seized him by the right arm.

٤٦ ثُمَّ لَقَطَعْنَا مِنْهُ ٱلْوَتِينَ

46 Then slashed his lifeline.

٤٧ فَمَا مِنكُم مِّنْ أَحَدٍ عَنْهُ حَٰجِزِينَ

47 And none of you could have restrained Us from him.

٤٨ وَإِنَّهُۥ لَتَذْكِرَةٌ لِّلْمُتَّقِينَ

48 Surely, it is a message for the righteous.

٤٩ وَإِنَّا لَنَعْلَمُ أَنَّ مِنكُم مُّكَذِّبِينَ	49 And We know that some of you will reject it.
٥٠ وَإِنَّهُۥ لَحَسْرَةٌ عَلَى ٱلْكَٰفِرِينَ	50 And it is surely a source of grief for the unbelievers.
٥١ وَإِنَّهُۥ لَحَقُّ ٱلْيَقِينِ	51 Yet it is the absolute truth.
٥٢ فَسَبِّحْ بِٱسْمِ رَبِّكَ ٱلْعَظِيمِ	52 So glorify the name of your Lord, the Magnificent.

70 Ways of Ascent المعارج

بِسْمِ ٱللَّهِ ٱلرَّحْمَٰنِ ٱلرَّحِيمِ	In the name of Allah, the Gracious, the Merciful.
١ سَأَلَ سَآئِلٌۢ بِعَذَابٍ وَاقِعٍ	1 A questioner questioned the imminent torment.
٢ لِّلْكَٰفِرِينَ لَيْسَ لَهُۥ دَافِعٌ	2 For the disbelievers; none can repel it.
٣ مِّنَ ٱللَّهِ ذِى ٱلْمَعَارِجِ	3 From Allah, Lord of the Ways of Ascent.
٤ تَعْرُجُ ٱلْمَلَٰٓئِكَةُ وَٱلرُّوحُ إِلَيْهِ فِى يَوْمٍ كَانَ مِقْدَارُهُۥ خَمْسِينَ أَلْفَ سَنَةٍ	4 Unto Him the angels and the Spirit ascend on a Day the duration of which is fifty thousand years.
٥ فَٱصْبِرْ صَبْرًا جَمِيلًا	5 So be patient, with sweet patience.
٦ إِنَّهُمْ يَرَوْنَهُۥ بَعِيدًا	6 They see it distant.
٧ وَنَرَىٰهُ قَرِيبًا	7 But We see it near.
٨ يَوْمَ تَكُونُ ٱلسَّمَآءُ كَٱلْمُهْلِ	8 On the Day when the sky will be like molten brass.
٩ وَتَكُونُ ٱلْجِبَالُ كَٱلْعِهْنِ	9 And the mountains will be like tufted wool.
١٠ وَلَا يَسْـَٔلُ حَمِيمٌ حَمِيمًا	10 No friend will care about his friend.
١١ يُبَصَّرُونَهُمْ ۚ يَوَدُّ ٱلْمُجْرِمُ لَوْ يَفْتَدِى مِنْ عَذَابِ يَوْمِئِذٍۭ بِبَنِيهِ	11 They will be shown each other. The criminal wishes he would be redeemed from the punishment of that Day by his children.
١٢ وَصَٰحِبَتِهِۦ وَأَخِيهِ	12 And his spouse, and his brother.

13 And his family that sheltered him.	١٣ وَفَصِيلَتِهِ ٱلَّتِى تُـْٔوِيهِ
14 And everyone on earth, in order to save him.	١٤ وَمَن فِى ٱلْأَرْضِ جَمِيعًا ثُمَّ يُنجِيهِ
15 By no means! It is a Raging Fire.	١٥ كَلَّآ ۖ إِنَّهَا لَظَىٰ
16 It strips away the scalps.	١٦ نَزَّاعَةً لِّلشَّوَىٰ
17 It invites him who once turned his back and fled.	١٧ تَدْعُوا۟ مَنْ أَدْبَرَ وَتَوَلَّىٰ
18 And accumulated and hoarded.	١٨ وَجَمَعَ فَأَوْعَىٰٓ
19 Man was created restless.	١٩ إِنَّ ٱلْإِنسَٰنَ خُلِقَ هَلُوعًا
20 Touched by adversity, he is fretful.	٢٠ إِذَا مَسَّهُ ٱلشَّرُّ جَزُوعًا
21 Touched by good, he is ungenerous.	٢١ وَإِذَا مَسَّهُ ٱلْخَيْرُ مَنُوعًا
22 Except the prayerful.	٢٢ إِلَّا ٱلْمُصَلِّينَ
23 Those who are constant at their prayers.	٢٣ ٱلَّذِينَ هُمْ عَلَىٰ صَلَاتِهِمْ دَآئِمُونَ
24 And those in whose wealth is a rightful share.	٢٤ وَٱلَّذِينَ فِىٓ أَمْوَٰلِهِمْ حَقٌّ مَّعْلُومٌ
25 For the beggar and the deprived.	٢٥ لِّلسَّآئِلِ وَٱلْمَحْرُومِ
26 And those who affirm the Day of Judgment.	٢٦ وَٱلَّذِينَ يُصَدِّقُونَ بِيَوْمِ ٱلدِّينِ
27 And those who fear the punishment of their Lord.	٢٧ وَٱلَّذِينَ هُم مِّنْ عَذَابِ رَبِّهِم مُّشْفِقُونَ
28 Their Lord's punishment is not to be taken for granted.	٢٨ إِنَّ عَذَابَ رَبِّهِمْ غَيْرُ مَأْمُونٍ
29 And those who guard their chastity.	٢٩ وَٱلَّذِينَ هُمْ لِفُرُوجِهِمْ حَٰفِظُونَ
30 Except from their spouses or those living under their control, for then they are free of blame.	٣٠ إِلَّا عَلَىٰٓ أَزْوَٰجِهِمْ أَوْ مَا مَلَكَتْ أَيْمَٰنُهُمْ فَإِنَّهُمْ غَيْرُ مَلُومِينَ
31 But whoever seeks to go beyond that—these are the transgressors.	٣١ فَمَنِ ٱبْتَغَىٰ وَرَآءَ ذَٰلِكَ فَأُو۟لَٰٓئِكَ هُمُ ٱلْعَادُونَ
32 And those who honor their trusts and their pledges.	٣٢ وَٱلَّذِينَ هُمْ لِأَمَٰنَٰتِهِمْ وَعَهْدِهِمْ رَٰعُونَ

٣٣ وَٱلَّذِينَ هُم بِشَهَٰدَٰتِهِمْ قَآئِمُونَ	33 And those who stand by their testimonies.
٣٤ وَٱلَّذِينَ هُمْ عَلَىٰ صَلَاتِهِمْ يُحَافِظُونَ	34 And those who are dedicated to their prayers.
٣٥ أُوْلَٰٓئِكَ فِى جَنَّٰتٍ مُّكْرَمُونَ	35 These will be honored in Gardens.
٣٦ فَمَالِ ٱلَّذِينَ كَفَرُوا۟ قِبَلَكَ مُهْطِعِينَ	36 What is with those who disbelieve, stretching their necks towards you.
٣٧ عَنِ ٱلْيَمِينِ وَعَنِ ٱلشِّمَالِ عِزِينَ	37 From the right, and from the left, banding together?
٣٨ أَيَطْمَعُ كُلُّ ٱمْرِئٍ مِّنْهُمْ أَن يُدْخَلَ جَنَّةَ نَعِيمٍ	38 Is every one of them aspiring to be admitted into a Garden of Bliss?
٣٩ كَلَّآ ۖ إِنَّا خَلَقْنَٰهُم مِّمَّا يَعْلَمُونَ	39 No indeed! We created them from what they know.
٤٠ فَلَآ أُقْسِمُ بِرَبِّ ٱلْمَشَٰرِقِ وَٱلْمَغَٰرِبِ إِنَّا لَقَٰدِرُونَ	40 I swear by the Lord of the Easts and the Wests, that We are Able.
٤١ عَلَىٰٓ أَن نُّبَدِّلَ خَيْرًا مِّنْهُمْ وَمَا نَحْنُ بِمَسْبُوقِينَ	41 To replace them with better than they, and We are not to be outdone.
٤٢ فَذَرْهُمْ يَخُوضُوا۟ وَيَلْعَبُوا۟ حَتَّىٰ يُلَٰقُوا۟ يَوْمَهُمُ ٱلَّذِى يُوعَدُونَ	42 So leave them to blunder and play, until they meet their Day which they are promised.
٤٣ يَوْمَ يَخْرُجُونَ مِنَ ٱلْأَجْدَاثِ سِرَاعًا كَأَنَّهُمْ إِلَىٰ نُصُبٍ يُوفِضُونَ	43 The Day when they will emerge from the tombs in a rush, as though they were hurrying towards a target.
٤٤ خَٰشِعَةً أَبْصَٰرُهُمْ تَرْهَقُهُمْ ذِلَّةٌ ۚ ذَٰلِكَ ٱلْيَوْمُ ٱلَّذِى كَانُوا۟ يُوعَدُونَ	44 Their eyes cast down; overwhelmed by humiliation. This is the Day which they were promised.

71 Noah نوح

بِسْمِ ٱللَّهِ ٱلرَّحْمَٰنِ ٱلرَّحِيمِ	In the name of Allah, the Gracious, the Merciful.
١ إِنَّآ أَرْسَلْنَا نُوحًا إِلَىٰ قَوْمِهِۦٓ أَنْ أَنذِرْ قَوْمَكَ مِن قَبْلِ أَن يَأْتِيَهُمْ عَذَابٌ أَلِيمٌ	1 We sent Noah to his people: “Warn your people before there comes upon them a painful punishment.”
٢ قَالَ يَٰقَوْمِ إِنِّى لَكُمْ نَذِيرٌ مُّبِينٌ	2 He said, “O my people, I am to you a clear warner.

٣ أَنِ ٱعْبُدُوا۟ ٱللَّهَ وَٱتَّقُوهُ وَأَطِيعُونِ

3 Worship Allah and reverence Him, and obey me.

٤ يَغْفِرْ لَكُم مِّن ذُنُوبِكُمْ وَيُؤَخِّرْكُمْ إِلَىٰٓ أَجَلٍ مُّسَمًّى ۚ إِنَّ أَجَلَ ٱللَّهِ إِذَا جَآءَ لَا يُؤَخَّرُ ۖ لَوْ كُنتُمْ تَعْلَمُونَ

4 And He will forgive you of your sins, and reprieve you until a stated term. Allah's term cannot be deferred once it has arrived, if you only knew."

٥ قَالَ رَبِّ إِنِّى دَعَوْتُ قَوْمِى لَيْلًا وَنَهَارًا

5 He said, "My Lord, I have called my people night and day.

٦ فَلَمْ يَزِدْهُمْ دُعَآءِىٓ إِلَّا فِرَارًا

6 But my call added only to their flight.

٧ وَإِنِّى كُلَّمَا دَعَوْتُهُمْ لِتَغْفِرَ لَهُمْ جَعَلُوٓا۟ أَصَٰبِعَهُمْ فِىٓ ءَاذَانِهِمْ وَٱسْتَغْشَوْا۟ ثِيَابَهُمْ وَأَصَرُّوا۟ وَٱسْتَكْبَرُوا۟ ٱسْتِكْبَارًا

7 Whenever I called them to Your forgiveness, they thrust their fingers into their ears, and wrapped themselves in their garments, and insisted, and became more and more arrogant.

٨ ثُمَّ إِنِّى دَعَوْتُهُمْ جِهَارًا

8 Then I called them openly.

٩ ثُمَّ إِنِّىٓ أَعْلَنتُ لَهُمْ وَأَسْرَرْتُ لَهُمْ إِسْرَارًا

9 Then I appealed to them publicly, and I spoke to them privately.

١٠ فَقُلْتُ ٱسْتَغْفِرُوا۟ رَبَّكُمْ إِنَّهُۥ كَانَ غَفَّارًا

10 I said, 'Ask your Lord for forgiveness; He is Forgiving.

١١ يُرْسِلِ ٱلسَّمَآءَ عَلَيْكُم مِّدْرَارًا

11 He will let loose the sky upon you in torrents.

١٢ وَيُمْدِدْكُم بِأَمْوَٰلٍ وَبَنِينَ وَيَجْعَل لَّكُمْ جَنَّٰتٍ وَيَجْعَل لَّكُمْ أَنْهَٰرًا

12 And provide you with wealth and children, and allot for you gardens, and allot for you rivers.

١٣ مَّا لَكُمْ لَا تَرْجُونَ لِلَّهِ وَقَارًا

13 What is the matter with you, that you do not appreciate Allah's Greatness?

١٤ وَقَدْ خَلَقَكُمْ أَطْوَارًا

14 Although He created you in stages.

١٥ أَلَمْ تَرَوْا۟ كَيْفَ خَلَقَ ٱللَّهُ سَبْعَ سَمَٰوَٰتٍ طِبَاقًا

15 Do you not realize that Allah created seven heavens in layers?

١٦ وَجَعَلَ ٱلْقَمَرَ فِيهِنَّ نُورًا وَجَعَلَ ٱلشَّمْسَ سِرَاجًا

16 And He set the moon in their midst for light, and He made the sun a lamp.

١٧ وَٱللَّهُ أَنۢبَتَكُم مِّنَ ٱلْأَرْضِ نَبَاتًا

17 And Allah germinated you from the earth like plants.

١٨ ثُمَّ يُعِيدُكُمْ فِيهَا وَيُخْرِجُكُمْ إِخْرَاجًا	18 Then He will return you into it, and will bring you out again.
١٩ وَٱللَّهُ جَعَلَ لَكُمُ ٱلْأَرْضَ بِسَاطًا	19 And Allah made the earth a spread for you.
٢٠ لِّتَسْلُكُوا۟ مِنْهَا سُبُلًا فِجَاجًا	20 That you may travel its diverse roads.'"
٢١ قَالَ نُوحٌ رَّبِّ إِنَّهُمْ عَصَوْنِى وَٱتَّبَعُوا۟ مَن لَّمْ يَزِدْهُ مَالُهُۥ وَوَلَدُهُۥٓ إِلَّا خَسَارًا	21 Noah said, "My Lord, they have defied me, and followed him whose wealth and children increase him only in perdition."
٢٢ وَمَكَرُوا۟ مَكْرًا كُبَّارًا	22 And they schemed outrageous schemes.
٢٣ وَقَالُوا۟ لَا تَذَرُنَّ ءَالِهَتَكُمْ وَلَا تَذَرُنَّ وَدًّا وَلَا سُوَاعًا وَلَا يَغُوثَ وَيَعُوقَ وَنَسْرًا	23 And they said, "Do not give up your gods; do not give up Wadd, nor Souwa, nor Yaghoos, and Yaooq, and Nassr.
٢٤ وَقَدْ أَضَلُّوا۟ كَثِيرًا ۖ وَلَا تَزِدِ ٱلظَّٰلِمِينَ إِلَّا ضَلَٰلًا	24 They have misled many, so do not increase the wrongdoers except in confusion."
٢٥ مِّمَّا خَطِيٓـَٔـٰتِهِمْ أُغْرِقُوا۟ فَأُدْخِلُوا۟ نَارًا فَلَمْ يَجِدُوا۟ لَهُم مِّن دُونِ ٱللَّهِ أَنصَارًا	25 Because of their wrongs, they were drowned, and were hurled into a Fire. They did not find apart from Allah any helpers.
٢٦ وَقَالَ نُوحٌ رَّبِّ لَا تَذَرْ عَلَى ٱلْأَرْضِ مِنَ ٱلْكَٰفِرِينَ دَيَّارًا	26 Noah said, "My Lord, do not leave of the unbelievers a single dweller on earth.
٢٧ إِنَّكَ إِن تَذَرْهُمْ يُضِلُّوا۟ عِبَادَكَ وَلَا يَلِدُوٓا۟ إِلَّا فَاجِرًا كَفَّارًا	27 If You leave them, they will mislead your servants, and will breed only wicked unbelievers.
٢٨ رَّبِّ ٱغْفِرْ لِى وَلِوَٰلِدَىَّ وَلِمَن دَخَلَ بَيْتِىَ مُؤْمِنًا وَلِلْمُؤْمِنِينَ وَٱلْمُؤْمِنَٰتِ وَلَا تَزِدِ ٱلظَّٰلِمِينَ إِلَّا تَبَارًا	28 My Lord! Forgive me and my parents, and anyone who enters my home in faith, and all the believing men and believing women; and do not increase the wrongdoers except in perdition."

72 The Jinn الجن

بِسْمِ ٱللَّهِ ٱلرَّحْمَٰنِ ٱلرَّحِيمِ	In the name of Allah, the Gracious, the Merciful.
١ قُلْ أُوحِىَ إِلَىَّ أَنَّهُ ٱسْتَمَعَ نَفَرٌ مِّنَ ٱلْجِنِّ فَقَالُوٓا۟ إِنَّا سَمِعْنَا قُرْءَانًا عَجَبًا	1 Say, "It was revealed to me that a band of jinn listened in, and said, 'We have heard a wondrous Quran.
٢ يَهْدِىٓ إِلَى ٱلرُّشْدِ فَـَٔامَنَّا بِهِۦ ۖ وَلَن نُّشْرِكَ بِرَبِّنَآ أَحَدًا	2 It guides to rectitude, so we have believed in it; and we will never associate anyone with our Lord.
٣ وَأَنَّهُۥ تَعَٰلَىٰ جَدُّ رَبِّنَا مَا ٱتَّخَذَ صَٰحِبَةً وَلَا وَلَدًا	3 And Exalted is the Grandeur of our Lord—He never had a mate, nor a child.
٤ وَأَنَّهُۥ كَانَ يَقُولُ سَفِيهُنَا عَلَى ٱللَّهِ شَطَطًا	4 But the fools among us used to say nonsense about Allah.
٥ وَأَنَّا ظَنَنَّآ أَن لَّن تَقُولَ ٱلْإِنسُ وَٱلْجِنُّ عَلَى ٱللَّهِ كَذِبًا	5 And we thought that humans and jinn would never utter lies about Allah.
٦ وَأَنَّهُۥ كَانَ رِجَالٌ مِّنَ ٱلْإِنسِ يَعُوذُونَ بِرِجَالٍ مِّنَ ٱلْجِنِّ فَزَادُوهُمْ رَهَقًا	6 Some individual humans used to seek power through some individual jinn, but they only increased them in confusion.
٧ وَأَنَّهُمْ ظَنُّوا۟ كَمَا ظَنَنتُمْ أَن لَّن يَبْعَثَ ٱللَّهُ أَحَدًا	7 They thought, as you thought, that Allah would never resurrect anyone.
٨ وَأَنَّا لَمَسْنَا ٱلسَّمَآءَ فَوَجَدْنَٰهَا مُلِئَتْ حَرَسًا شَدِيدًا وَشُهُبًا	8 We probed the heaven, and found it filled with stern guards and projectiles.
٩ وَأَنَّا كُنَّا نَقْعُدُ مِنْهَا مَقَٰعِدَ لِلسَّمْعِ ۖ فَمَن يَسْتَمِعِ ٱلْـَٔانَ يَجِدْ لَهُۥ شِهَابًا رَّصَدًا	9 We used to take up positions to listen in; but whoever listens now finds a projectile in wait for him.
١٠ وَأَنَّا لَا نَدْرِىٓ أَشَرٌّ أُرِيدَ بِمَن فِى ٱلْأَرْضِ أَمْ أَرَادَ بِهِمْ رَبُّهُمْ رَشَدًا	10 We do not know whether ill is intended for those on earth, or if their Lord intends goodness for them.
١١ وَأَنَّا مِنَّا ٱلصَّٰلِحُونَ وَمِنَّا دُونَ ذَٰلِكَ ۖ كُنَّا طَرَآئِقَ قِدَدًا	11 Some of us are righteous, but some of us are less than that; we follow divergent paths.

١٢ وَأَنَّا ظَنَنَّآ أَن لَّن نُّعْجِزَ ٱللَّهَ فِى ٱلْأَرْضِ وَلَن
نُّعْجِزَهُۥ هَرَبًا

12 We realized that we cannot defeat Allah on earth, and that we cannot escape Him by fleeing.

١٣ وَأَنَّا لَمَّا سَمِعْنَا ٱلْهُدَىٰٓ ءَامَنَّا بِهِۦ ۖ فَمَن يُؤْمِنۢ
بِرَبِّهِۦ فَلَا يَخَافُ بَخْسًا وَلَا رَهَقًا

13 And when we heard the guidance, we believed in it. Whoever believes in his Lord fears neither loss, nor burden.

١٤ وَأَنَّا مِنَّا ٱلْمُسْلِمُونَ وَمِنَّا ٱلْقَٰسِطُونَ ۖ فَمَنْ
أَسْلَمَ فَأُو۟لَٰٓئِكَ تَحَرَّوْا۟ رَشَدًا

14 Among us are those who are submitting, and among us are the compromisers. As for those who have submitted—it is they who pursue rectitude.

١٥ وَأَمَّا ٱلْقَٰسِطُونَ فَكَانُوا۟ لِجَهَنَّمَ حَطَبًا

15 But as for the compromisers—they will be firewood for Hell.'"

١٦ وَأَلَّوِ ٱسْتَقَٰمُوا۟ عَلَى ٱلطَّرِيقَةِ لَأَسْقَيْنَٰهُم مَّآءً
غَدَقًا

16 Had they kept true to the Path, We would have given them plenty water to drink.

١٧ لِّنَفْتِنَهُمْ فِيهِ ۚ وَمَن يُعْرِضْ عَن ذِكْرِ رَبِّهِۦ
يَسْلُكْهُ عَذَابًا صَعَدًا

17 To test them with it. Whoever turns away from the remembrance of his Lord, He will direct him to torment ever mounting.

١٨ وَأَنَّ ٱلْمَسَٰجِدَ لِلَّهِ فَلَا تَدْعُوا۟ مَعَ ٱللَّهِ أَحَدًا

18 The places of worship are for Allah. So do not call, besides Allah, upon anyone else.

١٩ وَأَنَّهُۥ لَمَّا قَامَ عَبْدُ ٱللَّهِ يَدْعُوهُ كَادُوا۟ يَكُونُونَ
عَلَيْهِ لِبَدًا

19 And when the servant of Allah got up calling on Him, they almost fell on him in a mass.

٢٠ قُلْ إِنَّمَآ أَدْعُوا۟ رَبِّى وَلَآ أُشْرِكُ بِهِۦٓ أَحَدًا

20 Say, "I pray only to my Lord, and I never associate anyone with Him."

٢١ قُلْ إِنِّى لَآ أَمْلِكُ لَكُمْ ضَرًّا وَلَا رَشَدًا

21 Say, "It is not in my power to harm you, nor to bring you to right conduct."

٢٢ قُلْ إِنِّى لَن يُجِيرَنِى مِنَ ٱللَّهِ أَحَدٌ وَلَنْ أَجِدَ
مِن دُونِهِۦ مُلْتَحَدًا

22 Say, "No one can protect me from Allah, and I will not find any refuge except with Him.

٢٣ إِلَّا بَلَٰغًا مِّنَ ٱللَّهِ وَرِسَٰلَٰتِهِۦ ۚ وَمَن يَعْصِ ٱللَّهَ
وَرَسُولَهُۥ فَإِنَّ لَهُۥ نَارَ جَهَنَّمَ خَٰلِدِينَ فِيهَآ أَبَدًا

23 Except for a proclamation from Allah and His messages. He who defies Allah and His Messenger—for him is the Fire of Hell, in which they will dwell forever."

٢٤ حَتَّىٰٓ إِذَا رَأَوْا۟ مَا يُوعَدُونَ فَسَيَعْلَمُونَ مَنْ أَضْعَفُ نَاصِرًا وَأَقَلُّ عَدَدًا

24 Until, when they see what they were promised, they will know who is weaker in helpers, and fewer in numbers.

٢٥ قُلْ إِنْ أَدْرِىٓ أَقَرِيبٌ مَّا تُوعَدُونَ أَمْ يَجْعَلُ لَهُۥ رَبِّىٓ أَمَدًا

25 Say, “I do not know whether what you are promised is near, or whether my Lord will extend it for a period.”

٢٦ عَٰلِمُ ٱلْغَيْبِ فَلَا يُظْهِرُ عَلَىٰ غَيْبِهِۦٓ أَحَدًا

26 The Knower of the Invisible; He does not disclose His Invisible to anyone.

٢٧ إِلَّا مَنِ ٱرْتَضَىٰ مِن رَّسُولٍ فَإِنَّهُۥ يَسْلُكُ مِنۢ بَيْنِ يَدَيْهِ وَمِنْ خَلْفِهِۦ رَصَدًا

27 Except to a Messenger of His choosing. He then dispatches guards before him and behind him.

٢٨ لِّيَعْلَمَ أَن قَدْ أَبْلَغُوا۟ رِسَٰلَٰتِ رَبِّهِمْ وَأَحَاطَ بِمَا لَدَيْهِمْ وَأَحْصَىٰ كُلَّ شَىْءٍ عَدَدًۢا

28 That He may know that they have conveyed the messages of their Lord. He encompasses what they have, and has tallied everything by number.

73 The Enwrapped المزمل

بِسْمِ ٱللَّهِ ٱلرَّحْمَٰنِ ٱلرَّحِيمِ

In the name of Allah, the Gracious, the Merciful.

١ يَٰٓأَيُّهَا ٱلْمُزَّمِّلُ

1 O you Enwrapped one.

٢ قُمِ ٱلَّيْلَ إِلَّا قَلِيلًا

2 Stay up during the night, except a little.

٣ نِّصْفَهُۥٓ أَوِ ٱنقُصْ مِنْهُ قَلِيلًا

3 For half of it, or reduce it a little.

٤ أَوْ زِدْ عَلَيْهِ وَرَتِّلِ ٱلْقُرْءَانَ تَرْتِيلًا

4 Or add to it; and chant the Quran rhythmically.

٥ إِنَّا سَنُلْقِى عَلَيْكَ قَوْلًا ثَقِيلًا

5 We are about to give you a heavy message.

٦ إِنَّ نَاشِئَةَ ٱلَّيْلِ هِىَ أَشَدُّ وَطْـًٔا وَأَقْوَمُ قِيلًا

6 The vigil of night is more effective, and better suited for recitation.

٧ إِنَّ لَكَ فِى ٱلنَّهَارِ سَبْحًا طَوِيلًا

7 In the daytime, you have lengthy work to do.

٨ وَٱذْكُرِ ٱسْمَ رَبِّكَ وَتَبَتَّلْ إِلَيْهِ تَبْتِيلًا

8 So remember the Name of your Lord, and devote yourself to Him wholeheartedly.

٩ رَّبُّ ٱلْمَشْرِقِ وَٱلْمَغْرِبِ لَآ إِلَٰهَ إِلَّا هُوَ فَٱتَّخِذْهُ
وَكِيلًا

9 Lord of the East and the West. There is no god but He, so take Him as a Trustee.

١٠ وَٱصْبِرْ عَلَىٰ مَا يَقُولُونَ وَٱهْجُرْهُمْ هَجْرًا
جَمِيلًا

10 And endure patiently what they say, and withdraw from them politely.

١١ وَذَرْنِى وَٱلْمُكَذِّبِينَ أُو۟لِى ٱلنَّعْمَةِ وَمَهِّلْهُمْ
قَلِيلًا

11 And leave Me to those who deny the truth, those of luxury, and give them a brief respite.

١٢ إِنَّ لَدَيْنَآ أَنكَالًا وَجَحِيمًا

12 With Us are shackles, and a Fierce Fire.

١٣ وَطَعَامًا ذَا غُصَّةٍ وَعَذَابًا أَلِيمًا

13 And food that chokes, and a painful punishment.

١٤ يَوْمَ تَرْجُفُ ٱلْأَرْضُ وَٱلْجِبَالُ وَكَانَتِ ٱلْجِبَالُ
كَثِيبًا مَّهِيلًا

14 On the Day when the earth and the mountains tremble, and the mountains become heaps of sand.

١٥ إِنَّآ أَرْسَلْنَآ إِلَيْكُمْ رَسُولًا شَٰهِدًا عَلَيْكُمْ كَمَآ
أَرْسَلْنَآ إِلَىٰ فِرْعَوْنَ رَسُولًا

15 We have sent to you a messenger, a witness over you, as We sent to Pharaoh a messenger.

١٦ فَعَصَىٰ فِرْعَوْنُ ٱلرَّسُولَ فَأَخَذْنَٰهُ أَخْذًا
وَبِيلًا

16 But Pharaoh defied the Messenger, so We seized him with a terrible seizing.

١٧ فَكَيْفَ تَتَّقُونَ إِن كَفَرْتُمْ يَوْمًا يَجْعَلُ
ٱلْوِلْدَٰنَ شِيبًا

17 So how will you, if you persist in unbelief, save yourself from a Day which will turn the children gray-haired?

١٨ ٱلسَّمَآءُ مُنفَطِرٌۢ بِهِۦ ۚ كَانَ وَعْدُهُۥ مَفْعُولًا

18 The heaven will shatter thereby. His promise is always fulfilled.

١٩ إِنَّ هَٰذِهِۦ تَذْكِرَةٌ ۖ فَمَن شَآءَ ٱتَّخَذَ إِلَىٰ رَبِّهِۦ
سَبِيلًا

19 This is a reminder. So whoever wills, let him take a path to his Lord.

٢٠ إِنَّ رَبَّكَ يَعْلَمُ أَنَّكَ تَقُومُ أَدْنَىٰ مِن ثُلُثَىِ
ٱلَّيْلِ وَنِصْفَهُۥ وَثُلُثَهُۥ وَطَآئِفَةٌ مِّنَ ٱلَّذِينَ مَعَكَ ۚ
وَٱللَّهُ يُقَدِّرُ ٱلَّيْلَ وَٱلنَّهَارَ ۚ عَلِمَ أَن لَّن تُحْصُوهُ
فَتَابَ عَلَيْكُمْ ۖ فَٱقْرَءُوا۟ مَا تَيَسَّرَ مِنَ ٱلْقُرْءَانِ ۚ
عَلِمَ أَن سَيَكُونُ مِنكُم مَّرْضَىٰ ۙ وَءَاخَرُونَ

20 Your Lord knows that you stay up nearly two-thirds of the night, or half of it, or one-third of it, along with a group of those with you. Allah designed the night and the day. He knows that you are unable to sustain it, so He has pardoned you. So read of the Quran what is possible for you. He knows that some of you

يَضْرِبُونَ فِى ٱلْأَرْضِ يَبْتَغُونَ مِن فَضْلِ ٱللَّهِ ۙ
وَءَاخَرُونَ يُقَـٰتِلُونَ فِى سَبِيلِ ٱللَّهِ ۖ فَٱقْرَءُوا۟ مَا
تَيَسَّرَ مِنْهُ ۚ وَأَقِيمُوا۟ ٱلصَّلَوٰةَ وَءَاتُوا۟ ٱلزَّكَوٰةَ
وَأَقْرِضُوا۟ ٱللَّهَ قَرْضًا حَسَنًا ۚ وَمَا تُقَدِّمُوا۟
لِأَنفُسِكُم مِّنْ خَيْرٍ تَجِدُوهُ عِندَ ٱللَّهِ هُوَ خَيْرًا
وَأَعْظَمَ أَجْرًا ۚ وَٱسْتَغْفِرُوا۟ ٱللَّهَ ۖ إِنَّ ٱللَّهَ غَفُورٌ
رَّحِيمٌۢ

may be ill; and others travelling through the land, seeking Allah's bounty; and others fighting in Allah's cause. So read of it what is possible for you, and observe the prayers, and give regular charity, and lend Allah a generous loan. Whatever good you advance for yourselves, you will find it with Allah, better and generously rewarded. And seek Allah's forgiveness, for Allah is Forgiving and Merciful.

74 The Enrobed المدثر

بِسْمِ ٱللَّهِ ٱلرَّحْمَـٰنِ ٱلرَّحِيمِ

In the name of Allah, the Gracious, the Merciful.

يَـٰٓأَيُّهَا ٱلْمُدَّثِّرُ ١
1 O you Enrobed one.

قُمْ فَأَنذِرْ ٢
2 Arise and warn.

وَرَبَّكَ فَكَبِّرْ ٣
3 And magnify your Lord.

وَثِيَابَكَ فَطَهِّرْ ٤
4 And purify your clothes.

وَٱلرُّجْزَ فَٱهْجُرْ ٥
5 And abandon abominations.

وَلَا تَمْنُن تَسْتَكْثِرُ ٦
6 And show no favor seeking gain.

وَلِرَبِّكَ فَٱصْبِرْ ٧
7 And be constant for your Lord.

فَإِذَا نُقِرَ فِى ٱلنَّاقُورِ ٨
8 When the Trumpet is blown.

فَذَٰلِكَ يَوْمَئِذٍ يَوْمٌ عَسِيرٌ ٩
9 That Day will be a difficult day.

عَلَى ٱلْكَـٰفِرِينَ غَيْرُ يَسِيرٍ ١٠
10 For the disbelievers—not easy.

ذَرْنِى وَمَنْ خَلَقْتُ وَحِيدًا ١١
11 Leave Me to him whom I created alone.

وَجَعَلْتُ لَهُۥ مَالًا مَّمْدُودًا ١٢
12 And gave him vast wealth.

وَبَنِينَ شُهُودًا ١٣
13 And children as witnesses.

وَمَهَّدتُّ لَهُۥ تَمْهِيدًا ١٤
14 And smoothed things for him.

١٥ ثُمَّ يَطْمَعُ أَنْ أَزِيدَ

15 Then he wants Me to add yet more!

١٦ كَلَّآ ۖ إِنَّهُۥ كَانَ لِءَايَٰتِنَا عَنِيدًا

16 By no means! He was stubborn towards Our revelations.

١٧ سَأُرْهِقُهُۥ صَعُودًا

17 I will exhaust him increasingly.

١٨ إِنَّهُۥ فَكَّرَ وَقَدَّرَ

18 He thought and analyzed.

١٩ فَقُتِلَ كَيْفَ قَدَّرَ

19 May he perish, how he analyzed.

٢٠ ثُمَّ قُتِلَ كَيْفَ قَدَّرَ

20 Again: may he perish, how he analyzed.

٢١ ثُمَّ نَظَرَ

21 Then he looked.

٢٢ ثُمَّ عَبَسَ وَبَسَرَ

22 Then he frowned and whined.

٢٣ ثُمَّ أَدْبَرَ وَٱسْتَكْبَرَ

23 Then he turned back and was proud.

٢٤ فَقَالَ إِنْ هَٰذَآ إِلَّا سِحْرٌ يُؤْثَرُ

24 And said, "This is nothing but magic from the past.

٢٥ إِنْ هَٰذَآ إِلَّا قَوْلُ ٱلْبَشَرِ

25 This is nothing but the word of a mortal."

٢٦ سَأُصْلِيهِ سَقَرَ

26 I will roast him in Saqar.

٢٧ وَمَآ أَدْرَىٰكَ مَا سَقَرُ

27 But what will explain to you what Saqar is?

٢٨ لَا تُبْقِى وَلَا تَذَرُ

28 It neither leaves, nor spares.

٢٩ لَوَّاحَةٌ لِّلْبَشَرِ

29 It scorches the flesh.

٣٠ عَلَيْهَا تِسْعَةَ عَشَرَ

30 Over it are Nineteen.

٣١ وَمَا جَعَلْنَآ أَصْحَٰبَ ٱلنَّارِ إِلَّا مَلَٰٓئِكَةً ۙ وَمَا
جَعَلْنَا عِدَّتَهُمْ إِلَّا فِتْنَةً لِّلَّذِينَ كَفَرُوا۟ لِيَسْتَيْقِنَ
ٱلَّذِينَ أُوتُوا۟ ٱلْكِتَٰبَ وَيَزْدَادَ ٱلَّذِينَ ءَامَنُوٓا۟
إِيمَٰنًا ۙ وَلَا يَرْتَابَ ٱلَّذِينَ أُوتُوا۟ ٱلْكِتَٰبَ
وَٱلْمُؤْمِنُونَ ۙ وَلِيَقُولَ ٱلَّذِينَ فِى قُلُوبِهِم مَّرَضٌ
وَٱلْكَٰفِرُونَ مَاذَآ أَرَادَ ٱللَّهُ بِهَٰذَا مَثَلًا ۚ كَذَٰلِكَ
يُضِلُّ ٱللَّهُ مَن يَشَآءُ وَيَهْدِى مَن يَشَآءُ ۚ وَمَا

31 We have appointed only angels to be wardens of the Fire, and caused their number to be a stumbling block for those who disbelieve; so that those given the Scripture may attain certainty; and those who believe may increase in faith; and those given the Scripture and the believers may not doubt; and those in whose hearts is sickness and the unbelievers may say, "What did Allah intend by this parable?" Thus

يَعْلَمُ جُنُودَ رَبِّكَ إِلَّا هُوَ ۚ وَمَا هِىَ إِلَّا ذِكْرَىٰ لِلْبَشَرِ	Allah leads astray whom He wills, and guides whom He wills. None knows the soldiers of your Lord except He. This is nothing but a reminder for the mortals.
٣٢ كَلَّا وَٱلْقَمَرِ	32 Nay! By the moon.
٣٣ وَٱلَّيْلِ إِذْ أَدْبَرَ	33 And the night as it retreats.
٣٤ وَٱلصُّبْحِ إِذَآ أَسْفَرَ	34 And the morning as it lights up.
٣٥ إِنَّهَا لَإِحْدَى ٱلْكُبَرِ	35 It is one of the greatest.
٣٦ نَذِيرًا لِّلْبَشَرِ	36 A warning to the mortals.
٣٧ لِمَن شَآءَ مِنكُمْ أَن يَتَقَدَّمَ أَوْ يَتَأَخَّرَ	37 To whomever among you wishes to advance, or regress.
٣٨ كُلُّ نَفْسٍۭ بِمَا كَسَبَتْ رَهِينَةٌ	38 Every soul is hostage to what it has earned.
٣٩ إِلَّآ أَصْحَٰبَ ٱلْيَمِينِ	39 Except for those on the Right.
٤٠ فِى جَنَّٰتٍ يَتَسَآءَلُونَ	40 In Gardens, inquiring.
٤١ عَنِ ٱلْمُجْرِمِينَ	41 About the guilty.
٤٢ مَا سَلَكَكُمْ فِى سَقَرَ	42 “What drove you into Saqar?”
٤٣ قَالُوا۟ لَمْ نَكُ مِنَ ٱلْمُصَلِّينَ	43 They will say, “We were not of those who prayed.
٤٤ وَلَمْ نَكُ نُطْعِمُ ٱلْمِسْكِينَ	44 Nor did we feed the destitute.
٤٥ وَكُنَّا نَخُوضُ مَعَ ٱلْخَآئِضِينَ	45 And we used to indulge with those who indulge.
٤٦ وَكُنَّا نُكَذِّبُ بِيَوْمِ ٱلدِّينِ	46 And we used to deny the Day of Judgment.
٤٧ حَتَّىٰٓ أَتَىٰنَا ٱلْيَقِينُ	47 Until the Inevitable came upon us.”
٤٨ فَمَا تَنفَعُهُمْ شَفَٰعَةُ ٱلشَّٰفِعِينَ	48 But the intercession of intercessors will not help them.
٤٩ فَمَا لَهُمْ عَنِ ٱلتَّذْكِرَةِ مُعْرِضِينَ	49 Why are they turning away from the Reminder?
٥٠ كَأَنَّهُمْ حُمُرٌ مُّسْتَنفِرَةٌ	50 As though they were panicked donkeys.

٥١ فَرَّتْ مِن قَسْوَرَةٍۭ	51 Fleeing from a lion?
٥٢ بَلْ يُرِيدُ كُلُّ ٱمْرِئٍ مِّنْهُمْ أَن يُؤْتَىٰ صُحُفًا مُّنَشَّرَةً	52 Yet every one of them desires to be given scrolls unrolled.
٥٣ كَلَّا ۖ بَل لَّا يَخَافُونَ ٱلْـَٔاخِرَةَ	53 No indeed! But they do not fear the Hereafter.
٥٤ كَلَّآ إِنَّهُۥ تَذْكِرَةٌ	54 Nevertheless, it is a reminder.
٥٥ فَمَن شَآءَ ذَكَرَهُۥ	55 So whoever wills, shall remember it.
٥٦ وَمَا يَذْكُرُونَ إِلَّآ أَن يَشَآءَ ٱللَّهُ ۚ هُوَ أَهْلُ ٱلتَّقْوَىٰ وَأَهْلُ ٱلْمَغْفِرَةِ	56 But they will not remember, unless Allah wills. He is the Source of Righteousness, and the Source of Forgiveness.

75 Resurrection القيامة

بِسْمِ ٱللَّهِ ٱلرَّحْمَٰنِ ٱلرَّحِيمِ	In the name of Allah, the Gracious, the Merciful.
١ لَآ أُقْسِمُ بِيَوْمِ ٱلْقِيَٰمَةِ	1 I swear by the Day of Resurrection.
٢ وَلَآ أُقْسِمُ بِٱلنَّفْسِ ٱللَّوَّامَةِ	2 And I swear by the blaming soul.
٣ أَيَحْسَبُ ٱلْإِنسَٰنُ أَلَّن نَّجْمَعَ عِظَامَهُۥ	3 Does man think that We will not reassemble his bones?
٤ بَلَىٰ قَٰدِرِينَ عَلَىٰٓ أَن نُّسَوِّىَ بَنَانَهُۥ	4 Yes indeed; We are Able to reconstruct his fingertips.
٥ بَلْ يُرِيدُ ٱلْإِنسَٰنُ لِيَفْجُرَ أَمَامَهُۥ	5 But man wants to deny what is ahead of him.
٦ يَسْـَٔلُ أَيَّانَ يَوْمُ ٱلْقِيَٰمَةِ	6 He asks, “When is the Day of Resurrection?”
٧ فَإِذَا بَرِقَ ٱلْبَصَرُ	7 When vision is dazzled.
٨ وَخَسَفَ ٱلْقَمَرُ	8 And the moon is eclipsed.
٩ وَجُمِعَ ٱلشَّمْسُ وَٱلْقَمَرُ	9 And the sun and the moon are joined together.
١٠ يَقُولُ ٱلْإِنسَٰنُ يَوْمَئِذٍ أَيْنَ ٱلْمَفَرُّ	10 On that Day, man will say, “Where is the escape?”

١١ كَلَّا لَا وَزَرَ

11 No indeed! There is no refuge.

١٢ إِلَىٰ رَبِّكَ يَوْمَئِذٍ ٱلْمُسْتَقَرُّ

12 To your Lord on that Day is the settlement.

١٣ يُنَبَّؤُا۟ ٱلْإِنسَٰنُ يَوْمَئِذٍۭ بِمَا قَدَّمَ وَأَخَّرَ

13 On that Day man will be informed of everything he put forward, and everything he left behind.

١٤ بَلِ ٱلْإِنسَٰنُ عَلَىٰ نَفْسِهِۦ بَصِيرَةٌ

14 And man will be evidence against himself.

١٥ وَلَوْ أَلْقَىٰ مَعَاذِيرَهُۥ

15 Even as he presents his excuses.

١٦ لَا تُحَرِّكْ بِهِۦ لِسَانَكَ لِتَعْجَلَ بِهِۦٓ

16 Do not wag your tongue with it, to hurry on with it.

١٧ إِنَّ عَلَيْنَا جَمْعَهُۥ وَقُرْءَانَهُۥ

17 Upon Us is its collection and its recitation.

١٨ فَإِذَا قَرَأْنَٰهُ فَٱتَّبِعْ قُرْءَانَهُۥ

18 Then, when We have recited it, follow its recitation.

١٩ ثُمَّ إِنَّ عَلَيْنَا بَيَانَهُۥ

19 Then upon Us is its explanation.

٢٠ كَلَّا بَلْ تُحِبُّونَ ٱلْعَاجِلَةَ

20 Alas, you love the fleeting life.

٢١ وَتَذَرُونَ ٱلْءَاخِرَةَ

21 And you disregard the Hereafter.

٢٢ وُجُوهٌ يَوْمَئِذٍ نَّاضِرَةٌ

22 Faces on that Day will be radiant.

٢٣ إِلَىٰ رَبِّهَا نَاظِرَةٌ

23 Looking towards their Lord.

٢٤ وَوُجُوهٌ يَوْمَئِذٍۭ بَاسِرَةٌ

24 And faces on that Day will be gloomy.

٢٥ تَظُنُّ أَن يُفْعَلَ بِهَا فَاقِرَةٌ

25 Realizing that a back-breaker has befallen them.

٢٦ كَلَّآ إِذَا بَلَغَتِ ٱلتَّرَاقِىَ

26 Indeed, when it has reached the breast-bones.

٢٧ وَقِيلَ مَنْ ۜ رَاقٍ

27 And it is said, “Who is the healer?”

٢٨ وَظَنَّ أَنَّهُ ٱلْفِرَاقُ

28 And He realizes that it is the parting.

٢٩ وَٱلْتَفَّتِ ٱلسَّاقُ بِٱلسَّاقِ

29 And leg is entwined with leg.

٣٠ إِلَىٰ رَبِّكَ يَوْمَئِذٍ ٱلْمَسَاقُ

30 To your Lord on that Day is the drive.

٣١ فَلَا صَدَّقَ وَلَا صَلَّىٰ

31 He neither believed nor prayed.

٣٢ وَلَٰكِن كَذَّبَ وَتَوَلَّىٰ	32 But he denied and turned away.
٣٣ ثُمَّ ذَهَبَ إِلَىٰٓ أَهْلِهِۦ يَتَمَطَّىٰٓ	33 Then he went to his family, full of pride.
٣٤ أَوْلَىٰ لَكَ فَأَوْلَىٰ	34 Woe to you; and woe.
٣٥ ثُمَّ أَوْلَىٰ لَكَ فَأَوْلَىٰٓ	35 Then again: Woe to you; and woe.
٣٦ أَيَحْسَبُ ٱلْإِنسَٰنُ أَن يُتْرَكَ سُدًى	36 Does man think that he will be left without purpose?
٣٧ أَلَمْ يَكُ نُطْفَةً مِّن مَّنِيٍّ يُمْنَىٰ	37 Was he not a drop of ejaculated semen?
٣٨ ثُمَّ كَانَ عَلَقَةً فَخَلَقَ فَسَوَّىٰ	38 Then he became a clot. And He created and proportioned?
٣٩ فَجَعَلَ مِنْهُ ٱلزَّوْجَيْنِ ٱلذَّكَرَ وَٱلْأُنثَىٰٓ	39 And made of him the two sexes, the male and the female?
٤٠ أَلَيْسَ ذَٰلِكَ بِقَٰدِرٍ عَلَىٰٓ أَن يُحْـِۧىَ ٱلْمَوْتَىٰ	40 Is He not Able to revive the dead?

76 Man الإنسان

بِسْمِ ٱللَّهِ ٱلرَّحْمَٰنِ ٱلرَّحِيمِ	In the name of Allah, the Gracious, the Merciful.
١ هَلْ أَتَىٰ عَلَى ٱلْإِنسَٰنِ حِينٌ مِّنَ ٱلدَّهْرِ لَمْ يَكُن شَيْـًٔا مَّذْكُورًا	1 Has there come upon man a period of time when he was nothing to be mentioned?
٢ إِنَّا خَلَقْنَا ٱلْإِنسَٰنَ مِن نُّطْفَةٍ أَمْشَاجٍ نَّبْتَلِيهِ فَجَعَلْنَٰهُ سَمِيعًۢا بَصِيرًا	2 We created man from a liquid mixture, to test him; and We made him hearing and seeing.
٣ إِنَّا هَدَيْنَٰهُ ٱلسَّبِيلَ إِمَّا شَاكِرًا وَإِمَّا كَفُورًا	3 We guided him to the way, be he appreciative or unappreciative.
٤ إِنَّآ أَعْتَدْنَا لِلْكَٰفِرِينَ سَلَٰسِلَا۟ وَأَغْلَٰلًا وَسَعِيرًا	4 We have prepared for the faithless chains, and yokes, and a Searing Fire.
٥ إِنَّ ٱلْأَبْرَارَ يَشْرَبُونَ مِن كَأْسٍ كَانَ مِزَاجُهَا كَافُورًا	5 But the righteous will drink from a cup whose mixture is aroma.
٦ عَيْنًا يَشْرَبُ بِهَا عِبَادُ ٱللَّهِ يُفَجِّرُونَهَا تَفْجِيرًا	6 A spring from which the servants of Allah will drink, making it gush abundantly.

7 They fulfill their vows, and dread a Day whose ill is widespread.	٧ يُوفُونَ بِٱلنَّذْرِ وَيَخَافُونَ يَوْمًا كَانَ شَرُّهُۥ مُسْتَطِيرًا
8 And they feed, for the love of Him, the poor, and the orphan, and the captive.	٨ وَيُطْعِمُونَ ٱلطَّعَامَ عَلَىٰ حُبِّهِۦ مِسْكِينًا وَيَتِيمًا وَأَسِيرًا
9 "We only feed you for the sake of Allah. We want from you neither compensation, nor gratitude.	٩ إِنَّمَا نُطْعِمُكُمْ لِوَجْهِ ٱللَّهِ لَا نُرِيدُ مِنكُمْ جَزَآءً وَلَا شُكُورًا
10 We dread from our Lord a frowning grim Day."	١٠ إِنَّا نَخَافُ مِن رَّبِّنَا يَوْمًا عَبُوسًا قَمْطَرِيرًا
11 So Allah will protect them from the ills of that Day, and will grant them radiance and joy.	١١ فَوَقَىٰهُمُ ٱللَّهُ شَرَّ ذَٰلِكَ ٱلْيَوْمِ وَلَقَّىٰهُمْ نَضْرَةً وَسُرُورًا
12 And will reward them for their patience with a Garden and silk.	١٢ وَجَزَىٰهُم بِمَا صَبَرُوا۟ جَنَّةً وَحَرِيرًا
13 Reclining therein on the thrones; experiencing therein neither sun, nor frost.	١٣ مُّتَّكِـِٔينَ فِيهَا عَلَى ٱلْأَرَآئِكِ ۖ لَا يَرَوْنَ فِيهَا شَمْسًا وَلَا زَمْهَرِيرًا
14 Its shade hovering over them, and its fruit brought low within reach.	١٤ وَدَانِيَةً عَلَيْهِمْ ظِلَٰلُهَا وَذُلِّلَتْ قُطُوفُهَا تَذْلِيلًا
15 Passing around them are vessels of silver, and cups of crystal.	١٥ وَيُطَافُ عَلَيْهِم بِـَٔانِيَةٍ مِّن فِضَّةٍ وَأَكْوَابٍ كَانَتْ قَوَارِيرَا۠
16 Crystal of silver—they measured them exactly.	١٦ قَوَارِيرَا۟ مِن فِضَّةٍ قَدَّرُوهَا تَقْدِيرًا
17 They will be served therein with a cup whose flavor is Zanjabeel.	١٧ وَيُسْقَوْنَ فِيهَا كَأْسًا كَانَ مِزَاجُهَا زَنجَبِيلًا
18 A spring therein named Salsabeel.	١٨ عَيْنًا فِيهَا تُسَمَّىٰ سَلْسَبِيلًا
19 Passing among them are eternalized youths. If you see them, you would think them sprinkled pearls.	١٩ وَيَطُوفُ عَلَيْهِمْ وِلْدَٰنٌ مُّخَلَّدُونَ إِذَا رَأَيْتَهُمْ حَسِبْتَهُمْ لُؤْلُؤًا مَّنثُورًا
20 Wherever you look, you see bliss, and a vast kingdom.	٢٠ وَإِذَا رَأَيْتَ ثَمَّ رَأَيْتَ نَعِيمًا وَمُلْكًا كَبِيرًا

٢١ عَٰلِيَهُمْ ثِيَابُ سُندُسٍ خُضْرٌ وَإِسْتَبْرَقٌ ۖ
وَحُلُّوٓا۟ أَسَاوِرَ مِن فِضَّةٍ وَسَقَىٰهُمْ رَبُّهُمْ شَرَابًا
طَهُورًا

21 Upon them are garments of green silk, and satin. And they will be adorned with bracelets of silver. And their Lord will offer them a pure drink.

٢٢ إِنَّ هَٰذَا كَانَ لَكُمْ جَزَآءً وَكَانَ سَعْيُكُم
مَّشْكُورًا

22 “This is a reward for you. Your efforts are well appreciated.”

٢٣ إِنَّا نَحْنُ نَزَّلْنَا عَلَيْكَ ٱلْقُرْءَانَ تَنزِيلًا

23 It is We who sent down the Quran upon you—a gradual revelation.

٢٤ فَٱصْبِرْ لِحُكْمِ رَبِّكَ وَلَا تُطِعْ مِنْهُمْ ءَاثِمًا أَوْ
كَفُورًا

24 So be patient for the decision of your Lord, and do not obey the sinner or the blasphemer among them.

٢٥ وَٱذْكُرِ ٱسْمَ رَبِّكَ بُكْرَةً وَأَصِيلًا

25 And mention the Name of your Lord, morning and evening.

٢٦ وَمِنَ ٱلَّيْلِ فَٱسْجُدْ لَهُۥ وَسَبِّحْهُ لَيْلًا طَوِيلًا

26 And for part of the night, prostrate yourself to Him, and glorify Him long into the night.

٢٧ إِنَّ هَٰٓؤُلَآءِ يُحِبُّونَ ٱلْعَاجِلَةَ وَيَذَرُونَ
وَرَآءَهُمْ يَوْمًا ثَقِيلًا

27 As for these: they love the fleeting life, and leave behind a Heavy Day.

٢٨ نَّحْنُ خَلَقْنَٰهُمْ وَشَدَدْنَآ أَسْرَهُمْ ۖ وَإِذَا شِئْنَا
بَدَّلْنَآ أَمْثَٰلَهُمْ تَبْدِيلًا

28 We created them, and strengthened their frame; and whenever We will, We can replace them with others like them.

٢٩ إِنَّ هَٰذِهِۦ تَذْكِرَةٌ ۖ فَمَن شَآءَ ٱتَّخَذَ إِلَىٰ رَبِّهِۦ
سَبِيلًا

29 This is a reminder; so whoever wills, let him take a path to his Lord.

٣٠ وَمَا تَشَآءُونَ إِلَّآ أَن يَشَآءَ ٱللَّهُ ۚ إِنَّ ٱللَّهَ كَانَ
عَلِيمًا حَكِيمًا

30 Yet you cannot will, unless Allah wills. Allah is Knowing and Wise.

٣١ يُدْخِلُ مَن يَشَآءُ فِى رَحْمَتِهِۦ ۚ وَٱلظَّٰلِمِينَ
أَعَدَّ لَهُمْ عَذَابًا أَلِيمًا

31 He admits into His mercy whomever He wills. But as for the wrongdoers, He has prepared for them a painful punishment.

77 The Unleashed المرسلات

بِسْمِ ٱللَّهِ ٱلرَّحْمَٰنِ ٱلرَّحِيمِ	In the name of Allah, the Gracious, the Merciful.
١ وَٱلْمُرْسَلَٰتِ عُرْفًا	1 By those unleashed in succession.
٢ فَٱلْعَٰصِفَٰتِ عَصْفًا	2 Storming turbulently.
٣ وَٱلنَّٰشِرَٰتِ نَشْرًا	3 Scattering far and wide.
٤ فَٱلْفَٰرِقَٰتِ فَرْقًا	4 Separating decisively.
٥ فَٱلْمُلْقِيَٰتِ ذِكْرًا	5 Delivering a message.
٦ عُذْرًا أَوْ نُذْرًا	6 Excusing or warning.
٧ إِنَّمَا تُوعَدُونَ لَوَٰقِعٌ	7 Surely what you are promised will happen.
٨ فَإِذَا ٱلنُّجُومُ طُمِسَتْ	8 When the stars are obliterated.
٩ وَإِذَا ٱلسَّمَآءُ فُرِجَتْ	9 And the sky is fractured.
١٠ وَإِذَا ٱلْجِبَالُ نُسِفَتْ	10 And the mountains are blown away.
١١ وَإِذَا ٱلرُّسُلُ أُقِّتَتْ	11 And the messengers are alerted.
١٢ لِأَىِّ يَوْمٍ أُجِّلَتْ	12 Until which day is it deferred?
١٣ لِيَوْمِ ٱلْفَصْلِ	13 Until the Day of Decision.
١٤ وَمَآ أَدْرَىٰكَ مَا يَوْمُ ٱلْفَصْلِ	14 And what will teach you what the Day of Decision is?
١٥ وَيْلٌ يَوْمَئِذٍ لِّلْمُكَذِّبِينَ	15 Woe on that Day to the liars.
١٦ أَلَمْ نُهْلِكِ ٱلْأَوَّلِينَ	16 Did We not destroy the ancients?
١٧ ثُمَّ نُتْبِعُهُمُ ٱلْءَاخِرِينَ	17 Then succeeded them with the others?
١٨ كَذَٰلِكَ نَفْعَلُ بِٱلْمُجْرِمِينَ	18 This is how We deal with the guilty.
١٩ وَيْلٌ يَوْمَئِذٍ لِّلْمُكَذِّبِينَ	19 Woe on that Day to the rejecters.
٢٠ أَلَمْ نَخْلُقكُّم مِّن مَّآءٍ مَّهِينٍ	20 Did We not create you from an insignificant fluid?

٢١ فَجَعَلْنَٰهُ فِى قَرَارٍ مَّكِينٍ	21 Then lodged it in a secure place?
٢٢ إِلَىٰ قَدَرٍ مَّعْلُومٍ	22 For a known term?
٢٣ فَقَدَرْنَا فَنِعْمَ ٱلْقَٰدِرُونَ	23 We measured precisely. We are the best to measure.
٢٤ وَيْلٌ يَوْمَئِذٍ لِّلْمُكَذِّبِينَ	24 Woe on that Day to the falsifiers.
٢٥ أَلَمْ نَجْعَلِ ٱلْأَرْضَ كِفَاتًا	25 Did We not make the earth a homestead?
٢٦ أَحْيَآءً وَأَمْوَٰتًا	26 For the living and the dead?
٢٧ وَجَعَلْنَا فِيهَا رَوَٰسِىَ شَٰمِخَٰتٍ وَأَسْقَيْنَٰكُم مَّآءً فُرَاتًا	27 And set on it lofty mountains, and given you pure water to drink?
٢٨ وَيْلٌ يَوْمَئِذٍ لِّلْمُكَذِّبِينَ	28 Woe on that Day to the deniers.
٢٩ ٱنطَلِقُوٓا۟ إِلَىٰ مَا كُنتُم بِهِۦ تُكَذِّبُونَ	29 "Proceed to what you used to deny."
٣٠ ٱنطَلِقُوٓا۟ إِلَىٰ ظِلٍّ ذِى ثَلَٰثِ شُعَبٍ	30 "Proceed to a shadow of three different masses."
٣١ لَّا ظَلِيلٍ وَلَا يُغْنِى مِنَ ٱللَّهَبِ	31 Offering no shade, and unavailing against the flames.
٣٢ إِنَّهَا تَرْمِى بِشَرَرٍ كَٱلْقَصْرِ	32 It shoots sparks as castles.
٣٣ كَأَنَّهُۥ جِمَٰلَتٌ صُفْرٌ	33 As if they were yellow camels.
٣٤ وَيْلٌ يَوْمَئِذٍ لِّلْمُكَذِّبِينَ	34 Woe on that Day to the liars.
٣٥ هَٰذَا يَوْمُ لَا يَنطِقُونَ	35 This is a Day when they will not speak.
٣٦ وَلَا يُؤْذَنُ لَهُمْ فَيَعْتَذِرُونَ	36 And they will not be allowed to apologize.
٣٧ وَيْلٌ يَوْمَئِذٍ لِّلْمُكَذِّبِينَ	37 Woe on that Day to the rejecters.
٣٨ هَٰذَا يَوْمُ ٱلْفَصْلِ ۖ جَمَعْنَٰكُمْ وَٱلْأَوَّلِينَ	38 This is the Day of Separation; We have gathered you, together with the ancients.
٣٩ فَإِن كَانَ لَكُمْ كَيْدٌ فَكِيدُونِ	39 So if you have a strategy, use it against Me.
٤٠ وَيْلٌ يَوْمَئِذٍ لِّلْمُكَذِّبِينَ	40 Woe on that Day to the falsifiers.

٤١ إِنَّ ٱلْمُتَّقِينَ فِى ظِلَٰلٍ وَعُيُونٍ	41 The righteous will be amidst shades and fountains.
٤٢ وَفَوَٰكِهَ مِمَّا يَشْتَهُونَ	42 And fruits as they desire.
٤٣ كُلُوا۟ وَٱشْرَبُوا۟ هَنِيٓـًٔۢا بِمَا كُنتُمْ تَعْمَلُونَ	43 "Eat and drink pleasantly, for what you used to do."
٤٤ إِنَّا كَذَٰلِكَ نَجْزِى ٱلْمُحْسِنِينَ	44 This is how We reward the doers of good.
٤٥ وَيْلٌ يَوْمَئِذٍ لِّلْمُكَذِّبِينَ	45 Woe on that Day to the deniers.
٤٦ كُلُوا۟ وَتَمَتَّعُوا۟ قَلِيلًا إِنَّكُم مُّجْرِمُونَ	46 "Eat and enjoy yourselves a little; you are indeed criminals."
٤٧ وَيْلٌ يَوْمَئِذٍ لِّلْمُكَذِّبِينَ	47 Woe on that Day to the liars.
٤٨ وَإِذَا قِيلَ لَهُمُ ٱرْكَعُوا۟ لَا يَرْكَعُونَ	48 And when it is said to them, "Kneel", they do not kneel.
٤٩ وَيْلٌ يَوْمَئِذٍ لِّلْمُكَذِّبِينَ	49 Woe on that Day to the rejecters.
٥٠ فَبِأَىِّ حَدِيثٍۭ بَعْدَهُۥ يُؤْمِنُونَ	50 In what message, beyond this, will they believe?

78 The Event النبا

بِسْمِ ٱللَّهِ ٱلرَّحْمَٰنِ ٱلرَّحِيمِ	In the name of Allah, the Gracious, the Merciful.
١ عَمَّ يَتَسَآءَلُونَ	1 What are they asking one another about?
٢ عَنِ ٱلنَّبَإِ ٱلْعَظِيمِ	2 About the Great Event.
٣ ٱلَّذِى هُمْ فِيهِ مُخْتَلِفُونَ	3 About which they disagree.
٤ كَلَّا سَيَعْلَمُونَ	4 Surely, they will find out.
٥ ثُمَّ كَلَّا سَيَعْلَمُونَ	5 Most certainly, they will find out.
٦ أَلَمْ نَجْعَلِ ٱلْأَرْضَ مِهَٰدًا	6 Did We not make the earth a cradle?
٧ وَٱلْجِبَالَ أَوْتَادًا	7 And the mountains pegs?
٨ وَخَلَقْنَٰكُمْ أَزْوَٰجًا	8 And created you in pairs?
٩ وَجَعَلْنَا نَوْمَكُمْ سُبَاتًا	9 And made your sleep for rest?

١٠ وَجَعَلْنَا ٱلَّيْلَ لِبَاسًا	10 And made the night a cover?
١١ وَجَعَلْنَا ٱلنَّهَارَ مَعَاشًا	11 And made the day for livelihood?
١٢ وَبَنَيْنَا فَوْقَكُمْ سَبْعًا شِدَادًا	12 And built above you seven strong ones?
١٣ وَجَعَلْنَا سِرَاجًا وَهَّاجًا	13 And placed a blazing lamp?
١٤ وَأَنزَلْنَا مِنَ ٱلْمُعْصِرَٰتِ مَآءً ثَجَّاجًا	14 And brought down from the clouds pouring water?
١٥ لِّنُخْرِجَ بِهِۦ حَبًّا وَنَبَاتًا	15 To produce with it grains and vegetation?
١٦ وَجَنَّٰتٍ أَلْفَافًا	16 And luxuriant gardens?
١٧ إِنَّ يَوْمَ ٱلْفَصْلِ كَانَ مِيقَٰتًا	17 The Day of Sorting has been appointed.
١٨ يَوْمَ يُنفَخُ فِى ٱلصُّورِ فَتَأْتُونَ أَفْوَاجًا	18 The Day when the Trumpet is blown, and you will come in droves.
١٩ وَفُتِحَتِ ٱلسَّمَآءُ فَكَانَتْ أَبْوَٰبًا	19 And the sky is opened up, and becomes gateways.
٢٠ وَسُيِّرَتِ ٱلْجِبَالُ فَكَانَتْ سَرَابًا	20 And the mountains are set in motion, and become a mirage.
٢١ إِنَّ جَهَنَّمَ كَانَتْ مِرْصَادًا	21 Hell is lying in ambush.
٢٢ لِّلطَّٰغِينَ مَـَٔابًا	22 For the oppressors, a destination.
٢٣ لَّٰبِثِينَ فِيهَآ أَحْقَابًا	23 Where they will remain for eons.
٢٤ لَّا يَذُوقُونَ فِيهَا بَرْدًا وَلَا شَرَابًا	24 They will taste therein neither coolness, nor drink.
٢٥ إِلَّا حَمِيمًا وَغَسَّاقًا	25 Except boiling water, and freezing hail.
٢٦ جَزَآءً وِفَاقًا	26 A fitting requital.
٢٧ إِنَّهُمْ كَانُوا۟ لَا يَرْجُونَ حِسَابًا	27 For they were not anticipating any reckoning.
٢٨ وَكَذَّبُوا۟ بِـَٔايَٰتِنَا كِذَّابًا	28 And they denied Our signs utterly.
٢٩ وَكُلَّ شَىْءٍ أَحْصَيْنَٰهُ كِتَٰبًا	29 But We have enumerated everything in writing.
٣٠ فَذُوقُوا۟ فَلَن نَّزِيدَكُمْ إِلَّا عَذَابًا	30 So taste! We will increase you only in suffering.

٣١ إِنَّ لِلْمُتَّقِينَ مَفَازًا

31 But for the righteous there is triumph.

٣٢ حَدَآئِقَ وَأَعْنَٰبًا

32 Gardens and vineyards.

٣٣ وَكَوَاعِبَ أَتْرَابًا

33 And splendid spouses, well matched.

٣٤ وَكَأْسًا دِهَاقًا

34 And delicious drinks.

٣٥ لَّا يَسْمَعُونَ فِيهَا لَغْوًا وَلَا كِذَّٰبًا

35 They will hear therein neither gossip, nor lies.

٣٦ جَزَآءً مِّن رَّبِّكَ عَطَآءً حِسَابًا

36 A reward from your Lord, a fitting gift.

٣٧ رَّبِّ ٱلسَّمَٰوَٰتِ وَٱلْأَرْضِ وَمَا بَيْنَهُمَا ٱلرَّحْمَٰنِ ۖ
لَا يَمْلِكُونَ مِنْهُ خِطَابًا

37 Lord of the heavens and the earth, and everything between them—The Most Merciful—none can argue with Him.

٣٨ يَوْمَ يَقُومُ ٱلرُّوحُ وَٱلْمَلَٰٓئِكَةُ صَفًّا ۖ لَّا
يَتَكَلَّمُونَ إِلَّا مَنْ أَذِنَ لَهُ ٱلرَّحْمَٰنُ وَقَالَ صَوَابًا

38 On the Day when the Spirit and the angels stand in row. They will not speak, unless it be one permitted by the Most Merciful, and he will say what is right.

٣٩ ذَٰلِكَ ٱلْيَوْمُ ٱلْحَقُّ ۖ فَمَن شَآءَ ٱتَّخَذَ إِلَىٰ رَبِّهِۦ
مَـَٔابًا

39 That is the Day of Reality. So whoever wills, let him take a way back to his Lord.

٤٠ إِنَّآ أَنذَرْنَٰكُمْ عَذَابًا قَرِيبًا يَوْمَ يَنظُرُ ٱلْمَرْءُ مَا
قَدَّمَتْ يَدَاهُ وَيَقُولُ ٱلْكَافِرُ يَٰلَيْتَنِى كُنتُ تُرَٰبًۢا

40 We have warned you of a near punishment—the Day when a person will observe what his hands have produced, and the faithless will say, "O, I wish I were dust."

79 The Snatchers النازعات

بِسْمِ ٱللَّهِ ٱلرَّحْمَٰنِ ٱلرَّحِيمِ

In the name of Allah, the Gracious, the Merciful.

١ وَٱلنَّٰزِعَٰتِ غَرْقًا

1 By those who snatch violently.

٢ وَٱلنَّٰشِطَٰتِ نَشْطًا

2 And those who remove gently.

٣ وَٱلسَّٰبِحَٰتِ سَبْحًا

3 And those who glide smoothly.

٤ فَٱلسَّٰبِقَٰتِ سَبْقًا

4 And those who race swiftly.

٥ فَٱلْمُدَبِّرَٰتِ أَمْرًا	5 And those who regulate events.
٦ يَوْمَ تَرْجُفُ ٱلرَّاجِفَةُ	6 On the Day when the Quake quakes.
٧ تَتْبَعُهَا ٱلرَّادِفَةُ	7 And is followed by the Successor.
٨ قُلُوبٌ يَوْمَئِذٍ وَاجِفَةٌ	8 Hearts on that Day will be pounding.
٩ أَبْصَٰرُهَا خَٰشِعَةٌ	9 Their sights downcast.
١٠ يَقُولُونَ أَءِنَّا لَمَرْدُودُونَ فِى ٱلْحَافِرَةِ	10 They say, “Are we to be restored to the original condition?
١١ أَءِذَا كُنَّا عِظَٰمًا نَّخِرَةً	11 When we have become hollow bones?”
١٢ قَالُوا۟ تِلْكَ إِذًا كَرَّةٌ خَاسِرَةٌ	12 They say, “This is a losing proposition.”
١٣ فَإِنَّمَا هِىَ زَجْرَةٌ وَٰحِدَةٌ	13 But it will be only a single nudge.
١٤ فَإِذَا هُم بِٱلسَّاهِرَةِ	14 And they will be awake.
١٥ هَلْ أَتَىٰكَ حَدِيثُ مُوسَىٰٓ	15 Has the story of Moses reached you?
١٦ إِذْ نَادَىٰهُ رَبُّهُۥ بِٱلْوَادِ ٱلْمُقَدَّسِ طُوًى	16 When His Lord called out to him in the sacred valley of Tuwa.
١٧ ٱذْهَبْ إِلَىٰ فِرْعَوْنَ إِنَّهُۥ طَغَىٰ	17 “Go to Pharaoh—he has transgressed.”
١٨ فَقُلْ هَل لَّكَ إِلَىٰٓ أَن تَزَكَّىٰ	18 And say, “Do you care to be cleansed?
١٩ وَأَهْدِيَكَ إِلَىٰ رَبِّكَ فَتَخْشَىٰ	19 And I will guide you to your Lord, and you will turn reverent.”
٢٠ فَأَرَىٰهُ ٱلْءَايَةَ ٱلْكُبْرَىٰ	20 He showed him the Greatest Miracle.
٢١ فَكَذَّبَ وَعَصَىٰ	21 But he denied and defied.
٢٢ ثُمَّ أَدْبَرَ يَسْعَىٰ	22 Then turned his back, and tried.
٢٣ فَحَشَرَ فَنَادَىٰ	23 And gathered and proclaimed.
٢٤ فَقَالَ أَنَا۠ رَبُّكُمُ ٱلْأَعْلَىٰ	24 He said, “I am your Lord, the most high.”

٢٥ فَأَخَذَهُ ٱللَّهُ نَكَالَ ٱلْـَٔاخِرَةِ وَٱلْأُولَىٰٓ	25 So Allah seized him with an exemplary punishment, in the last and in the first.
٢٦ إِنَّ فِى ذَٰلِكَ لَعِبْرَةً لِّمَن يَخْشَىٰٓ	26 In this is a lesson for whoever fears.
٢٧ ءَأَنتُمْ أَشَدُّ خَلْقًا أَمِ ٱلسَّمَآءُ ۚ بَنَىٰهَا	27 Are you more difficult to create, or the heaven? He constructed it.
٢٨ رَفَعَ سَمْكَهَا فَسَوَّىٰهَا	28 He raised its masses, and proportioned it.
٢٩ وَأَغْطَشَ لَيْلَهَا وَأَخْرَجَ ضُحَىٰهَا	29 And He dimmed its night, and brought out its daylight.
٣٠ وَٱلْأَرْضَ بَعْدَ ذَٰلِكَ دَحَىٰهَآ	30 And the earth after that He spread.
٣١ أَخْرَجَ مِنْهَا مَآءَهَا وَمَرْعَىٰهَا	31 And from it, He produced its water and its pasture.
٣٢ وَٱلْجِبَالَ أَرْسَىٰهَا	32 And the mountains, He anchored.
٣٣ مَتَٰعًا لَّكُمْ وَلِأَنْعَٰمِكُمْ	33 A source of enjoyment for you and for your animals.
٣٤ فَإِذَا جَآءَتِ ٱلطَّآمَّةُ ٱلْكُبْرَىٰ	34 But when the Great Cataclysm arrives.
٣٥ يَوْمَ يَتَذَكَّرُ ٱلْإِنسَٰنُ مَا سَعَىٰ	35 A Day when man will remember what he has endeavored.
٣٦ وَبُرِّزَتِ ٱلْجَحِيمُ لِمَن يَرَىٰ	36 And Hell will be displayed to whoever sees.
٣٧ فَأَمَّا مَن طَغَىٰ	37 As for him who was defiant.
٣٨ وَءَاثَرَ ٱلْحَيَوٰةَ ٱلدُّنْيَا	38 And preferred the life of this world.
٣٩ فَإِنَّ ٱلْجَحِيمَ هِىَ ٱلْمَأْوَىٰ	39 Then Hell is the shelter.
٤٠ وَأَمَّا مَنْ خَافَ مَقَامَ رَبِّهِۦ وَنَهَى ٱلنَّفْسَ عَنِ ٱلْهَوَىٰ	40 But as for him who feared the Standing of his Lord, and restrained the self from desires.
٤١ فَإِنَّ ٱلْجَنَّةَ هِىَ ٱلْمَأْوَىٰ	41 Then Paradise is the shelter.
٤٢ يَسْـَٔلُونَكَ عَنِ ٱلسَّاعَةِ أَيَّانَ مُرْسَىٰهَا	42 They ask you about the Hour, "When will it take place?"
٤٣ فِيمَ أَنتَ مِن ذِكْرَىٰهَآ	43 You have no knowledge of it.
٤٤ إِلَىٰ رَبِّكَ مُنتَهَىٰهَآ	44 To your Lord is its finality.

٤٥ إِنَّمَآ أَنتَ مُنذِرُ مَن يَخْشَىٰهَا	45 You are just a warner for whoever dreads it.
٤٦ كَأَنَّهُمْ يَوْمَ يَرَوْنَهَا لَمْ يَلْبَثُوٓاْ إِلَّا عَشِيَّةً أَوْ ضُحَىٰهَا	46 On the Day when they witness it—as though they only stayed an evening, or its morning.

80 He Frowned عبس

بِسْمِ ٱللَّهِ ٱلرَّحْمَٰنِ ٱلرَّحِيمِ	In the name of Allah, the Gracious, the Merciful.
١ عَبَسَ وَتَوَلَّىٰٓ	1 He frowned and turned away.
٢ أَن جَآءَهُ ٱلْأَعْمَىٰ	2 When the blind man approached him.
٣ وَمَا يُدْرِيكَ لَعَلَّهُۥ يَزَّكَّىٰٓ	3 But how do you know? Perhaps he was seeking to purify himself.
٤ أَوْ يَذَّكَّرُ فَتَنفَعَهُ ٱلذِّكْرَىٰٓ	4 Or be reminded, and the message would benefit him.
٥ أَمَّا مَنِ ٱسْتَغْنَىٰ	5 But as for him who was indifferent.
٦ فَأَنتَ لَهُۥ تَصَدَّىٰ	6 You gave him your attention.
٧ وَمَا عَلَيْكَ أَلَّا يَزَّكَّىٰ	7 Though you are not liable if he does not purify himself.
٨ وَأَمَّا مَن جَآءَكَ يَسْعَىٰ	8 But as for him who came to you seeking.
٩ وَهُوَ يَخْشَىٰ	9 In awe.
١٠ فَأَنتَ عَنْهُ تَلَهَّىٰ	10 To him you were inattentive.
١١ كَلَّآ إِنَّهَا تَذْكِرَةٌ	11 Do not. This is a Lesson.
١٢ فَمَن شَآءَ ذَكَرَهُۥ	12 Whoever wills, shall remember it.
١٣ فِى صُحُفٍ مُّكَرَّمَةٍ	13 On honorable pages.
١٤ مَّرْفُوعَةٍ مُّطَهَّرَةٍۭ	14 Exalted and purified.
١٥ بِأَيْدِى سَفَرَةٍ	15 By the hands of scribes.
١٦ كِرَامٍۭ بَرَرَةٍ	16 Noble and devoted.
١٧ قُتِلَ ٱلْإِنسَٰنُ مَآ أَكْفَرَهُۥ	17 Perish man! How thankless he is!

١٨ مِنْ أَيِّ شَيْءٍ خَلَقَهُۥ	18 From what did He create him?
١٩ مِن نُّطْفَةٍ خَلَقَهُۥ فَقَدَّرَهُۥ	19 From a sperm drop He created him, and enabled him.
٢٠ ثُمَّ ٱلسَّبِيلَ يَسَّرَهُۥ	20 Then He eased the way for him.
٢١ ثُمَّ أَمَاتَهُۥ فَأَقْبَرَهُۥ	21 Then He puts him to death, and buries him.
٢٢ ثُمَّ إِذَا شَآءَ أَنشَرَهُۥ	22 Then, when He wills, He will resurrect him.
٢٣ كَلَّا لَمَّا يَقْضِ مَآ أَمَرَهُۥ	23 But no, he did not fulfill what He has commanded him.
٢٤ فَلْيَنظُرِ ٱلْإِنسَٰنُ إِلَىٰ طَعَامِهِۦٓ	24 Let man consider his food.
٢٥ أَنَّا صَبَبْنَا ٱلْمَآءَ صَبًّا	25 We pour down water in abundance.
٢٦ ثُمَّ شَقَقْنَا ٱلْأَرْضَ شَقًّا	26 Then crack the soil open.
٢٧ فَأَنۢبَتْنَا فِيهَا حَبًّا	27 And grow in it grains.
٢٨ وَعِنَبًا وَقَضْبًا	28 And grapes and herbs.
٢٩ وَزَيْتُونًا وَنَخْلًا	29 And olives and dates.
٣٠ وَحَدَآئِقَ غُلْبًا	30 And luscious gardens.
٣١ وَفَٰكِهَةً وَأَبًّا	31 And fruits and vegetables.
٣٢ مَّتَٰعًا لَّكُمْ وَلِأَنْعَٰمِكُمْ	32 Enjoyment for you, and for your livestock.
٣٣ فَإِذَا جَآءَتِ ٱلصَّآخَّةُ	33 But when the Deafening Noise comes to pass.
٣٤ يَوْمَ يَفِرُّ ٱلْمَرْءُ مِنْ أَخِيهِ	34 The Day when a person will flee from his brother.
٣٥ وَأُمِّهِۦ وَأَبِيهِ	35 And his mother and his father.
٣٦ وَصَٰحِبَتِهِۦ وَبَنِيهِ	36 And his consort and his children.
٣٧ لِكُلِّ ٱمْرِئٍ مِّنْهُمْ يَوْمَئِذٍ شَأْنٌ يُغْنِيهِ	37 Every one of them, on that Day, will have enough to preoccupy him.
٣٨ وُجُوهٌ يَوْمَئِذٍ مُّسْفِرَةٌ	38 Faces on that Day will be radiant.
٣٩ ضَاحِكَةٌ مُّسْتَبْشِرَةٌ	39 Laughing and rejoicing.

٤٠ وَوُجُوهٌ يَوْمَئِذٍ عَلَيْهَا غَبَرَةٌ	40 And Faces on that Day will be covered with misery.
٤١ تَرْهَقُهَا قَتَرَةٌ	41 Overwhelmed by remorse.
٤٢ أُوْلَٰٓئِكَ هُمُ ٱلْكَفَرَةُ ٱلْفَجَرَةُ	42 These are the faithless, the vicious.

81 The Rolling التكوير

بِسْمِ ٱللَّهِ ٱلرَّحْمَٰنِ ٱلرَّحِيمِ	In the name of Allah, the Gracious, the Merciful.
١ إِذَا ٱلشَّمْسُ كُوِّرَتْ	1 When the sun is rolled up.
٢ وَإِذَا ٱلنُّجُومُ ٱنكَدَرَتْ	2 When the stars are dimmed.
٣ وَإِذَا ٱلْجِبَالُ سُيِّرَتْ	3 When the mountains are set in motion.
٤ وَإِذَا ٱلْعِشَارُ عُطِّلَتْ	4 When the relationships are suspended.
٥ وَإِذَا ٱلْوُحُوشُ حُشِرَتْ	5 When the beasts are gathered.
٦ وَإِذَا ٱلْبِحَارُ سُجِّرَتْ	6 When the oceans are set aflame.
٧ وَإِذَا ٱلنُّفُوسُ زُوِّجَتْ	7 When the souls are paired.
٨ وَإِذَا ٱلْمَوْءُۥدَةُ سُئِلَتْ	8 When the girl, buried alive, is asked:
٩ بِأَىِّ ذَنۢبٍ قُتِلَتْ	9 For what crime was she killed?
١٠ وَإِذَا ٱلصُّحُفُ نُشِرَتْ	10 When the records are made public.
١١ وَإِذَا ٱلسَّمَآءُ كُشِطَتْ	11 When the sky is peeled away.
١٢ وَإِذَا ٱلْجَحِيمُ سُعِّرَتْ	12 When the Fire is set ablaze.
١٣ وَإِذَا ٱلْجَنَّةُ أُزْلِفَتْ	13 When Paradise is brought near.
١٤ عَلِمَتْ نَفْسٌ مَّآ أَحْضَرَتْ	14 Each soul will know what it has readied.
١٥ فَلَآ أُقْسِمُ بِٱلْخُنَّسِ	15 I swear by the galaxies.
١٦ ٱلْجَوَارِ ٱلْكُنَّسِ	16 Precisely running their courses.

١٧ وَٱلَّيْلِ إِذَا عَسْعَسَ	17 And by the night as it recedes.
١٨ وَٱلصُّبْحِ إِذَا تَنَفَّسَ	18 And by the morn as it breathes.
١٩ إِنَّهُۥ لَقَوْلُ رَسُولٍ كَرِيمٍ	19 This is the speech of a noble messenger.
٢٠ ذِى قُوَّةٍ عِندَ ذِى ٱلْعَرْشِ مَكِينٍ	20 Endowed with power, eminent with the Lord of the Throne.
٢١ مُّطَاعٍ ثَمَّ أَمِينٍ	21 Obeyed and honest.
٢٢ وَمَا صَاحِبُكُم بِمَجْنُونٍ	22 Your friend is not possessed.
٢٣ وَلَقَدْ رَءَاهُ بِٱلْأُفُقِ ٱلْمُبِينِ	23 He saw him on the luminous horizon.
٢٤ وَمَا هُوَ عَلَى ٱلْغَيْبِ بِضَنِينٍ	24 And He does not withhold knowledge of the Unseen.
٢٥ وَمَا هُوَ بِقَوْلِ شَيْطَٰنٍ رَّجِيمٍ	25 And it is not the word of an accursed devil.
٢٦ فَأَيْنَ تَذْهَبُونَ	26 So where are you heading?
٢٧ إِنْ هُوَ إِلَّا ذِكْرٌ لِّلْعَٰلَمِينَ	27 It is only a Reminder to all mankind.
٢٨ لِمَن شَآءَ مِنكُمْ أَن يَسْتَقِيمَ	28 To whoever of you wills to go straight.
٢٩ وَمَا تَشَآءُونَ إِلَّآ أَن يَشَآءَ ٱللَّهُ رَبُّ ٱلْعَٰلَمِينَ	29 But you cannot will, unless Allah wills—The Lord of the Worlds.

82 The Shattering الانفطار

بِسْمِ ٱللَّهِ ٱلرَّحْمَٰنِ ٱلرَّحِيمِ	In the name of Allah, the Gracious, the Merciful.
١ إِذَا ٱلسَّمَآءُ ٱنفَطَرَتْ	1 When the sky breaks apart.
٢ وَإِذَا ٱلْكَوَاكِبُ ٱنتَثَرَتْ	2 When the planets are scattered.
٣ وَإِذَا ٱلْبِحَارُ فُجِّرَتْ	3 When the oceans are exploded.
٤ وَإِذَا ٱلْقُبُورُ بُعْثِرَتْ	4 When the tombs are strewn around.
٥ عَلِمَتْ نَفْسٌ مَّا قَدَّمَتْ وَأَخَّرَتْ	5 Each soul will know what it has advanced, and what it has deferred.

٦ يَٰٓأَيُّهَا ٱلۡإِنسَٰنُ مَا غَرَّكَ بِرَبِّكَ ٱلۡكَرِيمِ	6 O man! What deluded you concerning your Lord, the Most Generous?
٧ ٱلَّذِي خَلَقَكَ فَسَوَّىٰكَ فَعَدَلَكَ	7 He Who created you, and formed you, and proportioned you?
٨ فِيٓ أَيِّ صُورَةٖ مَّا شَآءَ رَكَّبَكَ	8 In whatever shape He willed, He assembled you.
٩ كَلَّا بَلۡ تُكَذِّبُونَ بِٱلدِّينِ	9 But you reject the religion.
١٠ وَإِنَّ عَلَيۡكُمۡ لَحَٰفِظِينَ	10 Though over you are watchers.
١١ كِرَامٗا كَٰتِبِينَ	11 Honest recorders.
١٢ يَعۡلَمُونَ مَا تَفۡعَلُونَ	12 They know everything you do.
١٣ إِنَّ ٱلۡأَبۡرَارَ لَفِي نَعِيمٖ	13 The virtuous will be in bliss.
١٤ وَإِنَّ ٱلۡفُجَّارَ لَفِي جَحِيمٖ	14 While the wicked will be in Hell.
١٥ يَصۡلَوۡنَهَا يَوۡمَ ٱلدِّينِ	15 They will enter it on the Day of Justice.
١٦ وَمَا هُمۡ عَنۡهَا بِغَآئِبِينَ	16 And they will not be absent from it.
١٧ وَمَآ أَدۡرَىٰكَ مَا يَوۡمُ ٱلدِّينِ	17 But what will convey to you what the Day of Justice is?
١٨ ثُمَّ مَآ أَدۡرَىٰكَ مَا يَوۡمُ ٱلدِّينِ	18 Then again, what will convey to you what the Day of Justice is?
١٩ يَوۡمَ لَا تَمۡلِكُ نَفۡسٞ لِّنَفۡسٖ شَيۡـٔٗاۖ وَٱلۡأَمۡرُ يَوۡمَئِذٖ لِّلَّهِ	19 The Day when no soul will avail another soul anything; and the decision on that Day is Allah's.

83 The Defrauders المطففين

بِسۡمِ ٱللَّهِ ٱلرَّحۡمَٰنِ ٱلرَّحِيمِ	In the name of Allah, the Gracious, the Merciful.
١ وَيۡلٞ لِّلۡمُطَفِّفِينَ	1 Woe to the defrauders.
٢ ٱلَّذِينَ إِذَا ٱكۡتَالُواْ عَلَى ٱلنَّاسِ يَسۡتَوۡفُونَ	2 Those who, when they take a measure from people, they take in full.
٣ وَإِذَا كَالُوهُمۡ أَو وَّزَنُوهُمۡ يُخۡسِرُونَ	3 But when they measure or weigh to others, they cheat.

٤ أَلَا يَظُنُّ أُولَٰٓئِكَ أَنَّهُم مَّبْعُوثُونَ	4 Do these not know that they will be resurrected?
٥ لِيَوْمٍ عَظِيمٍ	5 For a Great Day?
٦ يَوْمَ يَقُومُ ٱلنَّاسُ لِرَبِّ ٱلْعَٰلَمِينَ	6 The Day when mankind will stand before the Lord of the Worlds?
٧ كَلَّآ إِنَّ كِتَٰبَ ٱلْفُجَّارِ لَفِى سِجِّينٍ	7 Not at all. The record of the wicked is in Sijjeen.
٨ وَمَآ أَدْرَىٰكَ مَا سِجِّينٌ	8 But how can you know what Sijjeen is?
٩ كِتَٰبٌ مَّرْقُومٌ	9 A numerical book.
١٠ وَيْلٌ يَوْمَئِذٍ لِّلْمُكَذِّبِينَ	10 Woe on that Day to the deniers.
١١ ٱلَّذِينَ يُكَذِّبُونَ بِيَوْمِ ٱلدِّينِ	11 Those who deny the Day of Reckoning.
١٢ وَمَا يُكَذِّبُ بِهِۦٓ إِلَّا كُلُّ مُعْتَدٍ أَثِيمٍ	12 But none denies it except the sinful aggressor.
١٣ إِذَا تُتْلَىٰ عَلَيْهِ ءَايَٰتُنَا قَالَ أَسَٰطِيرُ ٱلْأَوَّلِينَ	13 When Our revelations are recited to him, he says, "Legends of the ancients."
١٤ كَلَّا ۖ بَلْ ۜ رَانَ عَلَىٰ قُلُوبِهِم مَّا كَانُوا۟ يَكْسِبُونَ	14 Not at all. Their hearts have become corroded by what they used to earn.
١٥ كَلَّآ إِنَّهُمْ عَن رَّبِّهِمْ يَوْمَئِذٍ لَّمَحْجُوبُونَ	15 Not at all. On that Day, they will be screened from their Lord.
١٦ ثُمَّ إِنَّهُمْ لَصَالُوا۟ ٱلْجَحِيمِ	16 Then they will roast in Hell.
١٧ ثُمَّ يُقَالُ هَٰذَا ٱلَّذِى كُنتُم بِهِۦ تُكَذِّبُونَ	17 Then it will be said, "This is what you used to deny."
١٨ كَلَّآ إِنَّ كِتَٰبَ ٱلْأَبْرَارِ لَفِى عِلِّيِّينَ	18 No indeed; the record of the righteous is in Elliyyeen.
١٩ وَمَآ أَدْرَىٰكَ مَا عِلِّيُّونَ	19 But how can you know what Elliyyoon is?
٢٠ كِتَٰبٌ مَّرْقُومٌ	20 A numerical book.
٢١ يَشْهَدُهُ ٱلْمُقَرَّبُونَ	21 Witnessed by those brought near.
٢٢ إِنَّ ٱلْأَبْرَارَ لَفِى نَعِيمٍ	22 Indeed, the righteous will be amid bliss.

٢٣ عَلَى ٱلْأَرَآئِكِ يَنظُرُونَ	23 On thrones, looking on.
٢٤ تَعْرِفُ فِى وُجُوهِهِمْ نَضْرَةَ ٱلنَّعِيمِ	24 You will recognize on their faces the radiance of bliss.
٢٥ يُسْقَوْنَ مِن رَّحِيقٍ مَّخْتُومٍ	25 They will be given to drink a sealed wine.
٢٦ خِتَٰمُهُۥ مِسْكٌ ۚ وَفِى ذَٰلِكَ فَلْيَتَنَافَسِ ٱلْمُتَنَٰفِسُونَ	26 Whose seal is musk—this is what competitors should compete for.
٢٧ وَمِزَاجُهُۥ مِن تَسْنِيمٍ	27 Its mixture is of Tasneem.
٢٨ عَيْنًا يَشْرَبُ بِهَا ٱلْمُقَرَّبُونَ	28 A spring from which those brought near drink.
٢٩ إِنَّ ٱلَّذِينَ أَجْرَمُوا۟ كَانُوا۟ مِنَ ٱلَّذِينَ ءَامَنُوا۟ يَضْحَكُونَ	29 Those who committed crimes used to laugh at those who believed.
٣٠ وَإِذَا مَرُّوا۟ بِهِمْ يَتَغَامَزُونَ	30 And when they passed by them, they would wink at one another.
٣١ وَإِذَا ٱنقَلَبُوٓا۟ إِلَىٰٓ أَهْلِهِمُ ٱنقَلَبُوا۟ فَكِهِينَ	31 And when they went back to their families, they would go back exulting.
٣٢ وَإِذَا رَأَوْهُمْ قَالُوٓا۟ إِنَّ هَٰٓؤُلَآءِ لَضَآلُّونَ	32 And if they saw them, they would say, "These people are lost."
٣٣ وَمَآ أُرْسِلُوا۟ عَلَيْهِمْ حَٰفِظِينَ	33 Yet they were not sent as guardians over them.
٣٤ فَٱلْيَوْمَ ٱلَّذِينَ ءَامَنُوا۟ مِنَ ٱلْكُفَّارِ يَضْحَكُونَ	34 But on that Day, those who believed will laugh at the unbelievers.
٣٥ عَلَى ٱلْأَرَآئِكِ يَنظُرُونَ	35 On luxurious furnishings, looking on.
٣٦ هَلْ ثُوِّبَ ٱلْكُفَّارُ مَا كَانُوا۟ يَفْعَلُونَ	36 Have the unbelievers been repaid for what they used to do?

84 The Rupture الانشقاق

بِسْمِ ٱللَّهِ ٱلرَّحْمَٰنِ ٱلرَّحِيمِ	In the name of Allah, the Gracious, the Merciful.
١ إِذَا ٱلسَّمَآءُ ٱنشَقَّتْ	1 When the sky is ruptured.

٢ وَأَذِنَتْ لِرَبِّهَا وَحُقَّتْ	2 And hearkens to its Lord, as it must.
٣ وَإِذَا ٱلْأَرْضُ مُدَّتْ	3 And when the earth is leveled out.
٤ وَأَلْقَتْ مَا فِيهَا وَتَخَلَّتْ	4 And casts out what is in it, and becomes empty.
٥ وَأَذِنَتْ لِرَبِّهَا وَحُقَّتْ	5 And hearkens to its Lord, as it must.
٦ يَٰٓأَيُّهَا ٱلْإِنسَٰنُ إِنَّكَ كَادِحٌ إِلَىٰ رَبِّكَ كَدْحًا فَمُلَٰقِيهِ	6 O man! You are laboring towards your Lord, and you will meet Him.
٧ فَأَمَّا مَنْ أُوتِىَ كِتَٰبَهُۥ بِيَمِينِهِۦ	7 As for him who is given his book in his right hand.
٨ فَسَوْفَ يُحَاسَبُ حِسَابًا يَسِيرًا	8 He will have an easy settlement.
٩ وَيَنقَلِبُ إِلَىٰٓ أَهْلِهِۦ مَسْرُورًا	9 And will return to his family delighted.
١٠ وَأَمَّا مَنْ أُوتِىَ كِتَٰبَهُۥ وَرَآءَ ظَهْرِهِۦ	10 But as for him who is given his book behind his back.
١١ فَسَوْفَ يَدْعُوا۟ ثُبُورًا	11 He will call for death.
١٢ وَيَصْلَىٰ سَعِيرًا	12 And will enter the Blaze.
١٣ إِنَّهُۥ كَانَ فِىٓ أَهْلِهِۦ مَسْرُورًا	13 He used to be happy among his family.
١٤ إِنَّهُۥ ظَنَّ أَن لَّن يَحُورَ	14 He thought he would never return.
١٥ بَلَىٰٓ إِنَّ رَبَّهُۥ كَانَ بِهِۦ بَصِيرًا	15 In fact, his Lord was watching him.
١٦ فَلَآ أُقْسِمُ بِٱلشَّفَقِ	16 I swear by the twilight.
١٧ وَٱلَّيْلِ وَمَا وَسَقَ	17 And by the night, and what it covers.
١٨ وَٱلْقَمَرِ إِذَا ٱتَّسَقَ	18 And by the moon, as it grows full.
١٩ لَتَرْكَبُنَّ طَبَقًا عَن طَبَقٍ	19 You will mount stage by stage.
٢٠ فَمَا لَهُمْ لَا يُؤْمِنُونَ	20 What is the matter with them that they do not believe?
٢١ وَإِذَا قُرِئَ عَلَيْهِمُ ٱلْقُرْءَانُ لَا يَسْجُدُونَ ۩	21 And when the Quran is read to them, they do not bow down?

٢٢ بَلِ ٱلَّذِينَ كَفَرُوا۟ يُكَذِّبُونَ	22 In fact, those who disbelieve are in denial.
٢٣ وَٱللَّهُ أَعْلَمُ بِمَا يُوعُونَ	23 But Allah knows what they hide inside.
٢٤ فَبَشِّرْهُم بِعَذَابٍ أَلِيمٍ	24 So inform them of a painful punishment.
٢٥ إِلَّا ٱلَّذِينَ ءَامَنُوا۟ وَعَمِلُوا۟ ٱلصَّٰلِحَٰتِ لَهُمْ أَجْرٌ غَيْرُ مَمْنُونٍ	25 Except those who believe and do good deeds; they will have an undiminished reward.

85 The Constellations البروج

بِسْمِ ٱللَّهِ ٱلرَّحْمَٰنِ ٱلرَّحِيمِ	In the name of Allah, the Gracious, the Merciful.
١ وَٱلسَّمَآءِ ذَاتِ ٱلْبُرُوجِ	1 By the sky with the constellations.
٢ وَٱلْيَوْمِ ٱلْمَوْعُودِ	2 And by the Promised Day.
٣ وَشَاهِدٍ وَمَشْهُودٍ	3 And by the witness and the witnessed.
٤ قُتِلَ أَصْحَٰبُ ٱلْأُخْدُودِ	4 Destroyed were the People of the Trench.
٥ ٱلنَّارِ ذَاتِ ٱلْوَقُودِ	5 The fire supplied with fuel.
٦ إِذْ هُمْ عَلَيْهَا قُعُودٌ	6 While they sat around it.
٧ وَهُمْ عَلَىٰ مَا يَفْعَلُونَ بِٱلْمُؤْمِنِينَ شُهُودٌ	7 And were witnessing what they did to the believers.
٨ وَمَا نَقَمُوا۟ مِنْهُمْ إِلَّآ أَن يُؤْمِنُوا۟ بِٱللَّهِ ٱلْعَزِيزِ ٱلْحَمِيدِ	8 They begrudged them only because they believed in Allah the Almighty, the Praiseworthy.
٩ ٱلَّذِى لَهُۥ مُلْكُ ٱلسَّمَٰوَٰتِ وَٱلْأَرْضِ ۚ وَٱللَّهُ عَلَىٰ كُلِّ شَىْءٍ شَهِيدٌ	9 To Whom belongs the sovereignty of the heavens and the earth. Allah is witness over everything.
١٠ إِنَّ ٱلَّذِينَ فَتَنُوا۟ ٱلْمُؤْمِنِينَ وَٱلْمُؤْمِنَٰتِ ثُمَّ لَمْ يَتُوبُوا۟ فَلَهُمْ عَذَابُ جَهَنَّمَ وَلَهُمْ عَذَابُ ٱلْحَرِيقِ	10 Those who tempt the believers, men and women, then do not repent; for them is the punishment of Hell; for them is the punishment of Burning.

١١ إِنَّ ٱلَّذِينَ ءَامَنُوا۟ وَعَمِلُوا۟ ٱلصَّٰلِحَٰتِ لَهُمْ جَنَّٰتٌ تَجْرِى مِن تَحْتِهَا ٱلْأَنْهَٰرُ ۚ ذَٰلِكَ ٱلْفَوْزُ ٱلْكَبِيرُ	11 Those who believe and do righteous deeds will have Gardens beneath which rivers flow. That is the great triumph.
١٢ إِنَّ بَطْشَ رَبِّكَ لَشَدِيدٌ	12 The onslaught of your Lord is severe.
١٣ إِنَّهُۥ هُوَ يُبْدِئُ وَيُعِيدُ	13 It is He who begins and repeats.
١٤ وَهُوَ ٱلْغَفُورُ ٱلْوَدُودُ	14 And He is the Forgiving, the Loving.
١٥ ذُو ٱلْعَرْشِ ٱلْمَجِيدُ	15 Possessor of the Glorious Throne.
١٦ فَعَّالٌ لِّمَا يُرِيدُ	16 Doer of whatever He wills.
١٧ هَلْ أَتَىٰكَ حَدِيثُ ٱلْجُنُودِ	17 Has there come to you the story of the legions?
١٨ فِرْعَوْنَ وَثَمُودَ	18 Of Pharaoh and Thamood?
١٩ بَلِ ٱلَّذِينَ كَفَرُوا۟ فِى تَكْذِيبٍ	19 In fact, those who disbelieve are in denial.
٢٠ وَٱللَّهُ مِن وَرَآئِهِم مُّحِيطٌۢ	20 And Allah encloses them from beyond.
٢١ بَلْ هُوَ قُرْءَانٌ مَّجِيدٌ	21 In fact, it is a Glorious Quran.
٢٢ فِى لَوْحٍ مَّحْفُوظٍۭ	22 In a Preserved Tablet.

86 The Nightly Visitor الطارق

بِسْمِ ٱللَّهِ ٱلرَّحْمَٰنِ ٱلرَّحِيمِ	In the name of Allah, the Gracious, the Merciful.
١ وَٱلسَّمَآءِ وَٱلطَّارِقِ	1 By the sky and at-Tariq.
٢ وَمَآ أَدْرَىٰكَ مَا ٱلطَّارِقُ	2 But what will let you know what at-Tariq is?
٣ ٱلنَّجْمُ ٱلثَّاقِبُ	3 The Piercing Star.
٤ إِن كُلُّ نَفْسٍ لَّمَّا عَلَيْهَا حَافِظٌ	4 There is no soul without a Protector over it.
٥ فَلْيَنظُرِ ٱلْإِنسَٰنُ مِمَّ خُلِقَ	5 Let man consider what he was created from.

٦ خُلِقَ مِن مَّآءٍ دَافِقٍ	6 He was created from gushing liquid.
٧ يَخْرُجُ مِنۢ بَيْنِ ٱلصُّلْبِ وَٱلتَّرَآئِبِ	7 Issuing from between the backbone and the breastbones.
٨ إِنَّهُۥ عَلَىٰ رَجْعِهِۦ لَقَادِرٌ	8 He is certainly able to return him.
٩ يَوْمَ تُبْلَى ٱلسَّرَآئِرُ	9 On the Day when the secrets are disclosed.
١٠ فَمَا لَهُۥ مِن قُوَّةٍ وَلَا نَاصِرٍ	10 He will have no strength, and no supporter.
١١ وَٱلسَّمَآءِ ذَاتِ ٱلرَّجْعِ	11 By the sky that returns.
١٢ وَٱلْأَرْضِ ذَاتِ ٱلصَّدْعِ	12 And the earth that cracks open.
١٣ إِنَّهُۥ لَقَوْلٌ فَصْلٌ	13 It is a Decisive Word.
١٤ وَمَا هُوَ بِٱلْهَزْلِ	14 It is no joke.
١٥ إِنَّهُمْ يَكِيدُونَ كَيْدًا	15 They plot and scheme.
١٦ وَأَكِيدُ كَيْدًا	16 But I plot and scheme.
١٧ فَمَهِّلِ ٱلْكَٰفِرِينَ أَمْهِلْهُمْ رُوَيْدًۢا	17 Therefore, give the blasphemers respite, a brief respite.

87 The Most High الأعلى

بِسْمِ ٱللَّهِ ٱلرَّحْمَٰنِ ٱلرَّحِيمِ	In the name of Allah, the Gracious, the Merciful.
١ سَبِّحِ ٱسْمَ رَبِّكَ ٱلْأَعْلَى	1 Praise the Name of your Lord, the Most High.
٢ ٱلَّذِى خَلَقَ فَسَوَّىٰ	2 He who creates and regulates.
٣ وَٱلَّذِى قَدَّرَ فَهَدَىٰ	3 He who measures and guides.
٤ وَٱلَّذِىٓ أَخْرَجَ ٱلْمَرْعَىٰ	4 He who produces the pasture.
٥ فَجَعَلَهُۥ غُثَآءً أَحْوَىٰ	5 And then turns it into light debris.
٦ سَنُقْرِئُكَ فَلَا تَنسَىٰٓ	6 We will make you read, so do not forget.

7 Except what Allah wills. He knows what is declared, and what is hidden.	٧ إِلَّا مَا شَآءَ ٱللَّهُ ۚ إِنَّهُۥ يَعْلَمُ ٱلْجَهْرَ وَمَا يَخْفَىٰ
8 We will ease you into the Easy Way.	٨ وَنُيَسِّرُكَ لِلْيُسْرَىٰ
9 So remind, if reminding helps.	٩ فَذَكِّرْ إِن نَّفَعَتِ ٱلذِّكْرَىٰ
10 The reverent will remember.	١٠ سَيَذَّكَّرُ مَن يَخْشَىٰ
11 But the wretched will avoid it.	١١ وَيَتَجَنَّبُهَا ٱلْأَشْقَى
12 He who will enter the Gigantic Fire.	١٢ ٱلَّذِى يَصْلَى ٱلنَّارَ ٱلْكُبْرَىٰ
13 Where he will neither die, nor live.	١٣ ثُمَّ لَا يَمُوتُ فِيهَا وَلَا يَحْيَىٰ
14 Successful is he who purifies himself.	١٤ قَدْ أَفْلَحَ مَن تَزَكَّىٰ
15 And mentions the name of his Lord, and prays.	١٥ وَذَكَرَ ٱسْمَ رَبِّهِۦ فَصَلَّىٰ
16 But you prefer the present life.	١٦ بَلْ تُؤْثِرُونَ ٱلْحَيَوٰةَ ٱلدُّنْيَا
17 Though the Hereafter is better, and more lasting.	١٧ وَٱلْءَاخِرَةُ خَيْرٌ وَأَبْقَىٰٓ
18 This is in the former scriptures.	١٨ إِنَّ هَٰذَا لَفِى ٱلصُّحُفِ ٱلْأُولَىٰ
19 The Scriptures of Abraham and Moses.	١٩ صُحُفِ إِبْرَٰهِيمَ وَمُوسَىٰ

88 The Overwhelming الغاشية

In the name of Allah, the Gracious, the Merciful.	بِسْمِ ٱللَّهِ ٱلرَّحْمَٰنِ ٱلرَّحِيمِ
1 Has there come to you the news of the overwhelming?	١ هَلْ أَتَىٰكَ حَدِيثُ ٱلْغَٰشِيَةِ
2 Faces on that Day will be shamed.	٢ وُجُوهٌ يَوْمَئِذٍ خَٰشِعَةٌ
3 Laboring and exhausted.	٣ عَامِلَةٌ نَّاصِبَةٌ
4 Roasting in a scorching Fire.	٤ تَصْلَىٰ نَارًا حَامِيَةً
5 Given to drink from a flaming spring.	٥ تُسْقَىٰ مِنْ عَيْنٍ ءَانِيَةٍ

٦ لَّيْسَ لَهُمْ طَعَامٌ إِلَّا مِن ضَرِيعٍ	6 They will have no food except thorns.
٧ لَّا يُسْمِنُ وَلَا يُغْنِى مِن جُوعٍ	7 That neither nourishes, nor satisfies hunger.
٨ وُجُوهٌ يَوْمَئِذٍ نَّاعِمَةٌ	8 Faces on that Day will be joyful.
٩ لِّسَعْيِهَا رَاضِيَةٌ	9 Satisfied with their endeavor.
١٠ فِى جَنَّةٍ عَالِيَةٍ	10 In a lofty Garden.
١١ لَّا تَسْمَعُ فِيهَا لَٰغِيَةً	11 In it you will hear no nonsense.
١٢ فِيهَا عَيْنٌ جَارِيَةٌ	12 In it is a flowing spring.
١٣ فِيهَا سُرُرٌ مَّرْفُوعَةٌ	13 In it are raised beds.
١٤ وَأَكْوَابٌ مَّوْضُوعَةٌ	14 And cups set in place.
١٥ وَنَمَارِقُ مَصْفُوفَةٌ	15 And cushions set in rows.
١٦ وَزَرَابِىُّ مَبْثُوثَةٌ	16 And carpets spread around.
١٧ أَفَلَا يَنظُرُونَ إِلَى ٱلْإِبِلِ كَيْفَ خُلِقَتْ	17 Do they not look at the camels—how they are created?
١٨ وَإِلَى ٱلسَّمَآءِ كَيْفَ رُفِعَتْ	18 And at the sky—how it is raised?
١٩ وَإِلَى ٱلْجِبَالِ كَيْفَ نُصِبَتْ	19 And at the mountains—how they are installed?
٢٠ وَإِلَى ٱلْأَرْضِ كَيْفَ سُطِحَتْ	20 And at the earth—how it is spread out?
٢١ فَذَكِّرْ إِنَّمَآ أَنتَ مُذَكِّرٌ	21 So remind. You are only a reminder.
٢٢ لَّسْتَ عَلَيْهِم بِمُصَيْطِرٍ	22 You have no control over them.
٢٣ إِلَّا مَن تَوَلَّىٰ وَكَفَرَ	23 But whoever turns away and disbelieves.
٢٤ فَيُعَذِّبُهُ ٱللَّهُ ٱلْعَذَابَ ٱلْأَكْبَرَ	24 Allah will punish him with the greatest punishment.
٢٥ إِنَّ إِلَيْنَآ إِيَابَهُمْ	25 To Us is their return.
٢٦ ثُمَّ إِنَّ عَلَيْنَا حِسَابَهُم	26 Then upon Us rests their reckoning.

89 The Dawn الفجر

بِسْمِ ٱللَّهِ ٱلرَّحْمَٰنِ ٱلرَّحِيمِ	In the name of Allah, the Gracious, the Merciful.
١ وَٱلْفَجْرِ	1 By the daybreak.
٢ وَلَيَالٍ عَشْرٍ	2 And ten nights.
٣ وَٱلشَّفْعِ وَٱلْوَتْرِ	3 And the even and the odd.
٤ وَٱلَّيْلِ إِذَا يَسْرِ	4 And the night as it recedes.
٥ هَلْ فِى ذَٰلِكَ قَسَمٌ لِّذِى حِجْرٍ	5 Is there in this an oath for a rational person?
٦ أَلَمْ تَرَ كَيْفَ فَعَلَ رَبُّكَ بِعَادٍ	6 Have you not seen how your Lord dealt with Aad?
٧ إِرَمَ ذَاتِ ٱلْعِمَادِ	7 Erum of the pillars.
٨ ٱلَّتِى لَمْ يُخْلَقْ مِثْلُهَا فِى ٱلْبِلَٰدِ	8 The like of which was never created in the land.
٩ وَثَمُودَ ٱلَّذِينَ جَابُوا۟ ٱلصَّخْرَ بِٱلْوَادِ	9 And Thamood—those who carved the rocks in the valley.
١٠ وَفِرْعَوْنَ ذِى ٱلْأَوْتَادِ	10 And Pharaoh of the Stakes.
١١ ٱلَّذِينَ طَغَوْا۟ فِى ٱلْبِلَٰدِ	11 Those who committed excesses in the lands.
١٢ فَأَكْثَرُوا۟ فِيهَا ٱلْفَسَادَ	12 And spread much corruption therein.
١٣ فَصَبَّ عَلَيْهِمْ رَبُّكَ سَوْطَ عَذَابٍ	13 So your Lord poured down upon them a scourge of punishment.
١٤ إِنَّ رَبَّكَ لَبِٱلْمِرْصَادِ	14 Your Lord is on the lookout.
١٥ فَأَمَّا ٱلْإِنسَٰنُ إِذَا مَا ٱبْتَلَىٰهُ رَبُّهُۥ فَأَكْرَمَهُۥ وَنَعَّمَهُۥ فَيَقُولُ رَبِّىٓ أَكْرَمَنِ	15 As for man, whenever his Lord tests him, and honors him, and prospers him, he says, "My Lord has honored me."
١٦ وَأَمَّآ إِذَا مَا ٱبْتَلَىٰهُ فَقَدَرَ عَلَيْهِ رِزْقَهُۥ فَيَقُولُ رَبِّىٓ أَهَٰنَنِ	16 But whenever He tests him, and restricts his livelihood for him, he says, "My Lord has insulted me."
١٧ كَلَّا ۖ بَل لَّا تُكْرِمُونَ ٱلْيَتِيمَ	17 Not at all. But you do not honor the orphan.

١٨ وَلَا تَحَٰٓضُّونَ عَلَىٰ طَعَامِ ٱلْمِسْكِينِ	18 And you do not urge the feeding of the poor.
١٩ وَتَأْكُلُونَ ٱلتُّرَاثَ أَكْلًا لَّمًّا	19 And you devour inheritance with all greed.
٢٠ وَتُحِبُّونَ ٱلْمَالَ حُبًّا جَمًّا	20 And you love wealth with immense love.
٢١ كَلَّآ إِذَا دُكَّتِ ٱلْأَرْضُ دَكًّا دَكًّا	21 No—when the earth is leveled, pounded, and crushed.
٢٢ وَجَآءَ رَبُّكَ وَٱلْمَلَكُ صَفًّا صَفًّا	22 And your Lord comes, with the angels, row after row.
٢٣ وَجِاْىٓءَ يَوْمَئِذٍۭ بِجَهَنَّمَ ۚ يَوْمَئِذٍ يَتَذَكَّرُ ٱلْإِنسَٰنُ وَأَنَّىٰ لَهُ ٱلذِّكْرَىٰ	23 And on that Day, Hell is brought forward. On that Day, man will remember, but how will remembrance avail him?
٢٤ يَقُولُ يَٰلَيْتَنِى قَدَّمْتُ لِحَيَاتِى	24 He will say, "If only I had forwarded for my life."
٢٥ فَيَوْمَئِذٍ لَّا يُعَذِّبُ عَذَابَهُۥٓ أَحَدٌ	25 On that Day, none will punish as He punishes.
٢٦ وَلَا يُوثِقُ وَثَاقَهُۥٓ أَحَدٌ	26 And none will shackle as He shackles.
٢٧ يَٰٓأَيَّتُهَا ٱلنَّفْسُ ٱلْمُطْمَئِنَّةُ	27 But as for you, O tranquil soul.
٢٨ ٱرْجِعِىٓ إِلَىٰ رَبِّكِ رَاضِيَةً مَّرْضِيَّةً	28 Return to your Lord, pleased and accepted.
٢٩ فَٱدْخُلِى فِى عِبَٰدِى	29 Enter among My servants.
٣٠ وَٱدْخُلِى جَنَّتِى	30 Enter My Paradise.

90 The Land البلد

بِسْمِ ٱللَّهِ ٱلرَّحْمَٰنِ ٱلرَّحِيمِ	In the name of Allah, the Gracious, the Merciful.
١ لَآ أُقْسِمُ بِهَٰذَا ٱلْبَلَدِ	1 I swear by this land.
٢ وَأَنتَ حِلٌّۢ بِهَٰذَا ٱلْبَلَدِ	2 And you are a resident of this land.
٣ وَوَالِدٍ وَمَا وَلَدَ	3 And by a father and what he fathered.
٤ لَقَدْ خَلَقْنَا ٱلْإِنسَٰنَ فِى كَبَدٍ	4 We created man in distress.

٥ أَيَحْسَبُ أَن لَّن يَقْدِرَ عَلَيْهِ أَحَدٌ

5 Does he think that no one has power over him?

٦ يَقُولُ أَهْلَكْتُ مَالًا لُّبَدًا

6 He says, “I have used up so much money.”

٧ أَيَحْسَبُ أَن لَّمْ يَرَهُۥٓ أَحَدٌ

7 Does he think that no one sees him?

٨ أَلَمْ نَجْعَل لَّهُۥ عَيْنَيْنِ

8 Did We not give him two eyes?

٩ وَلِسَانًا وَشَفَتَيْنِ

9 And a tongue, and two lips?

١٠ وَهَدَيْنَٰهُ ٱلنَّجْدَيْنِ

10 And We showed him the two ways?

١١ فَلَا ٱقْتَحَمَ ٱلْعَقَبَةَ

11 But he did not brave the ascent.

١٢ وَمَآ أَدْرَىٰكَ مَا ٱلْعَقَبَةُ

12 And what will explain to you what the ascent is?

١٣ فَكُّ رَقَبَةٍ

13 The freeing of a slave.

١٤ أَوْ إِطْعَٰمٌ فِى يَوْمٍ ذِى مَسْغَبَةٍ

14 Or the feeding on a day of hunger.

١٥ يَتِيمًا ذَا مَقْرَبَةٍ

15 An orphan near of kin.

١٦ أَوْ مِسْكِينًا ذَا مَتْرَبَةٍ

16 Or a destitute in the dust.

١٧ ثُمَّ كَانَ مِنَ ٱلَّذِينَ ءَامَنُوا۟ وَتَوَاصَوْا۟ بِٱلصَّبْرِ
وَتَوَاصَوْا۟ بِٱلْمَرْحَمَةِ

17 Then he becomes of those who believe, and advise one another to patience, and advise one another to kindness.

١٨ أُو۟لَٰٓئِكَ أَصْحَٰبُ ٱلْمَيْمَنَةِ

18 These are the people of happiness.

١٩ وَٱلَّذِينَ كَفَرُوا۟ بِـَٔايَٰتِنَا هُمْ أَصْحَٰبُ ٱلْمَشْـَٔمَةِ

19 But as for those who defy Our revelations—these are the people of misery.

٢٠ عَلَيْهِمْ نَارٌ مُّؤْصَدَةٌۢ

20 Upon them is a padlocked Fire.

91 The Sun الشمس

بِسْمِ ٱللَّهِ ٱلرَّحْمَٰنِ ٱلرَّحِيمِ

In the name of Allah, the Gracious, the Merciful.

١ وَٱلشَّمْسِ وَضُحَىٰهَا

1 By the sun and its radiance.

2 And the moon as it follows it.	٢ وَٱلْقَمَرِ إِذَا تَلَىٰهَا
3 And the day as it reveals it.	٣ وَٱلنَّهَارِ إِذَا جَلَّىٰهَا
4 And the night as it conceals it.	٤ وَٱلَّيْلِ إِذَا يَغْشَىٰهَا
5 And the sky and He who built it.	٥ وَٱلسَّمَآءِ وَمَا بَنَىٰهَا
6 And the earth and He who spread it.	٦ وَٱلْأَرْضِ وَمَا طَحَىٰهَا
7 And the soul and He who proportioned it.	٧ وَنَفْسٍ وَمَا سَوَّىٰهَا
8 And inspired it with its wickedness and its righteousness.	٨ فَأَلْهَمَهَا فُجُورَهَا وَتَقْوَىٰهَا
9 Successful is he who purifies it.	٩ قَدْ أَفْلَحَ مَن زَكَّىٰهَا
10 Failing is he who corrupts it.	١٠ وَقَدْ خَابَ مَن دَسَّىٰهَا
11 Thamood denied in its pride.	١١ كَذَّبَتْ ثَمُودُ بِطَغْوَىٰهَآ
12 When it followed its most wicked.	١٢ إِذِ ٱنۢبَعَثَ أَشْقَىٰهَا
13 The messenger of Allah said to them, “This is the she-camel of Allah, so let her drink.”	١٣ فَقَالَ لَهُمْ رَسُولُ ٱللَّهِ نَاقَةَ ٱللَّهِ وَسُقْيَٰهَا
14 But they called him a liar, and hamstrung her. So their Lord crushed them for their sin, and leveled it.	١٤ فَكَذَّبُوهُ فَعَقَرُوهَا فَدَمْدَمَ عَلَيْهِمْ رَبُّهُم بِذَنۢبِهِمْ فَسَوَّىٰهَا
15 And He does not fear its sequel.	١٥ وَلَا يَخَافُ عُقْبَٰهَا

92 The Night الليل

In the name of Allah, the Gracious, the Merciful.	بِسْمِ ٱللَّهِ ٱلرَّحْمَٰنِ ٱلرَّحِيمِ
1 By the night as it covers.	١ وَٱلَّيْلِ إِذَا يَغْشَىٰ
2 And the day as it reveals.	٢ وَٱلنَّهَارِ إِذَا تَجَلَّىٰ
3 And He who created the male and the female.	٣ وَمَا خَلَقَ ٱلذَّكَرَ وَٱلْأُنثَىٰٓ

٤ إِنَّ سَعْيَكُمْ لَشَتَّىٰ	4 Your endeavors are indeed diverse.
٥ فَأَمَّا مَنْ أَعْطَىٰ وَٱتَّقَىٰ	5 As for him who gives and is righteous.
٦ وَصَدَّقَ بِٱلْحُسْنَىٰ	6 And confirms goodness.
٧ فَسَنُيَسِّرُهُۥ لِلْيُسْرَىٰ	7 We will ease his way towards ease.
٨ وَأَمَّا مَنۢ بَخِلَ وَٱسْتَغْنَىٰ	8 But as for him who is stingy and complacent.
٩ وَكَذَّبَ بِٱلْحُسْنَىٰ	9 And denies goodness.
١٠ فَسَنُيَسِّرُهُۥ لِلْعُسْرَىٰ	10 We will ease his way towards difficulty.
١١ وَمَا يُغْنِى عَنْهُ مَالُهُۥٓ إِذَا تَرَدَّىٰٓ	11 And his money will not avail him when he plummets.
١٢ إِنَّ عَلَيْنَا لَلْهُدَىٰ	12 It is upon Us to guide.
١٣ وَإِنَّ لَنَا لَلْـَٔاخِرَةَ وَٱلْأُولَىٰ	13 And to Us belong the Last and the First.
١٤ فَأَنذَرْتُكُمْ نَارًا تَلَظَّىٰ	14 I have warned you of a Fierce Blaze.
١٥ لَا يَصْلَىٰهَآ إِلَّا ٱلْأَشْقَى	15 None will burn in it except the very wicked.
١٦ ٱلَّذِى كَذَّبَ وَتَوَلَّىٰ	16 He who denies and turns away.
١٧ وَسَيُجَنَّبُهَا ٱلْأَتْقَى	17 But the devout will avoid it.
١٨ ٱلَّذِى يُؤْتِى مَالَهُۥ يَتَزَكَّىٰ	18 He who gives his money to become pure.
١٩ وَمَا لِأَحَدٍ عِندَهُۥ مِن نِّعْمَةٍ تُجْزَىٰٓ	19 Seeking no favor in return.
٢٠ إِلَّا ٱبْتِغَآءَ وَجْهِ رَبِّهِ ٱلْأَعْلَىٰ	20 Only seeking the acceptance of his Lord, the Most High.
٢١ وَلَسَوْفَ يَرْضَىٰ	21 And he will be satisfied.

93 Morning Light الضحى

بِسْمِ ٱللَّهِ ٱلرَّحْمَٰنِ ٱلرَّحِيمِ	In the name of Allah, the Gracious, the Merciful.

١ وَٱلضُّحَىٰ	1 By the morning light.
٢ وَٱلَّيْلِ إِذَا سَجَىٰ	2 And the night as it settles.
٣ مَا وَدَّعَكَ رَبُّكَ وَمَا قَلَىٰ	3 Your Lord did not abandon you, nor did He forget.
٤ وَلَلْءَاخِرَةُ خَيْرٌ لَّكَ مِنَ ٱلْأُولَىٰ	4 The Hereafter is better for you than the First.
٥ وَلَسَوْفَ يُعْطِيكَ رَبُّكَ فَتَرْضَىٰٓ	5 And your Lord will give you, and you will be satisfied.
٦ أَلَمْ يَجِدْكَ يَتِيمًا فَـَٔاوَىٰ	6 Did He not find you orphaned, and sheltered you?
٧ وَوَجَدَكَ ضَآلًّا فَهَدَىٰ	7 And found you wandering, and guided you?
٨ وَوَجَدَكَ عَآئِلًا فَأَغْنَىٰ	8 And found you in need, and enriched you?
٩ فَأَمَّا ٱلْيَتِيمَ فَلَا تَقْهَرْ	9 Therefore, do not mistreat the orphan.
١٠ وَأَمَّا ٱلسَّآئِلَ فَلَا تَنْهَرْ	10 Nor rebuff the seeker.
١١ وَأَمَّا بِنِعْمَةِ رَبِّكَ فَحَدِّثْ	11 But proclaim the blessings of your Lord.

94 The Soothing الشرح

بِسْمِ ٱللَّهِ ٱلرَّحْمَٰنِ ٱلرَّحِيمِ	In the name of Allah, the Gracious, the Merciful.
١ أَلَمْ نَشْرَحْ لَكَ صَدْرَكَ	1 Did We not soothe your heart?
٢ وَوَضَعْنَا عَنكَ وِزْرَكَ	2 And lift from you your burden.
٣ ٱلَّذِىٓ أَنقَضَ ظَهْرَكَ	3 Which weighed down your back?
٤ وَرَفَعْنَا لَكَ ذِكْرَكَ	4 And raised for you your reputation?
٥ فَإِنَّ مَعَ ٱلْعُسْرِ يُسْرًا	5 With hardship comes ease.
٦ إِنَّ مَعَ ٱلْعُسْرِ يُسْرًا	6 With hardship comes ease.
٧ فَإِذَا فَرَغْتَ فَٱنصَبْ	7 When your work is done, turn to devotion.

وَإِلَىٰ رَبِّكَ فَٱرْغَب ٨	8 And to your Lord turn for everything.

95 The Fig التين

بِسْمِ ٱللَّهِ ٱلرَّحْمَٰنِ ٱلرَّحِيمِ	In the name of Allah, the Gracious, the Merciful.
وَٱلتِّينِ وَٱلزَّيْتُونِ ١	1 By the fig and the olive.
وَطُورِ سِينِينَ ٢	2 And Mount Sinai.
وَهَٰذَا ٱلْبَلَدِ ٱلْأَمِينِ ٣	3 And this safe land.
لَقَدْ خَلَقْنَا ٱلْإِنسَٰنَ فِىٓ أَحْسَنِ تَقْوِيمٍ ٤	4 We created man in the best design.
ثُمَّ رَدَدْنَٰهُ أَسْفَلَ سَٰفِلِينَ ٥	5 Then reduced him to the lowest of the low.
إِلَّا ٱلَّذِينَ ءَامَنُوا۟ وَعَمِلُوا۟ ٱلصَّٰلِحَٰتِ فَلَهُمْ أَجْرٌ غَيْرُ مَمْنُونٍ ٦	6 Except those who believe and do righteous deeds; for them is a reward without end.
فَمَا يُكَذِّبُكَ بَعْدُ بِٱلدِّينِ ٧	7 So why do you still reject the religion?
أَلَيْسَ ٱللَّهُ بِأَحْكَمِ ٱلْحَٰكِمِينَ ٨	8 Is Allah not the Wisest of the wise?

96 Clot العلق

بِسْمِ ٱللَّهِ ٱلرَّحْمَٰنِ ٱلرَّحِيمِ	In the name of Allah, the Gracious, the Merciful.
ٱقْرَأْ بِٱسْمِ رَبِّكَ ٱلَّذِى خَلَقَ ١	1 Read: In the Name of your Lord who created.
خَلَقَ ٱلْإِنسَٰنَ مِنْ عَلَقٍ ٢	2 Created man from a clot.
ٱقْرَأْ وَرَبُّكَ ٱلْأَكْرَمُ ٣	3 Read: And your Lord is the Most Generous.
ٱلَّذِى عَلَّمَ بِٱلْقَلَمِ ٤	4 He who taught by the pen.
عَلَّمَ ٱلْإِنسَٰنَ مَا لَمْ يَعْلَمْ ٥	5 Taught man what he never knew.
كَلَّآ إِنَّ ٱلْإِنسَٰنَ لَيَطْغَىٰٓ ٦	6 In fact, man oversteps all bounds.

٧ أَن رَّءَاهُ ٱسْتَغْنَىٰٓ	7 When he considers himself exempt.
٨ إِنَّ إِلَىٰ رَبِّكَ ٱلرُّجْعَىٰٓ	8 But to your Lord is the return.
٩ أَرَءَيْتَ ٱلَّذِى يَنْهَىٰ	9 Have you seen him who prevents?
١٠ عَبْدًا إِذَا صَلَّىٰٓ	10 A servant when he prays?
١١ أَرَءَيْتَ إِن كَانَ عَلَى ٱلْهُدَىٰٓ	11 Do you think he is upon guidance?
١٢ أَوْ أَمَرَ بِٱلتَّقْوَىٰٓ	12 Or advocates righteousness?
١٣ أَرَءَيْتَ إِن كَذَّبَ وَتَوَلَّىٰٓ	13 Do you see how he disbelieved and turned away?
١٤ أَلَمْ يَعْلَم بِأَنَّ ٱللَّهَ يَرَىٰ	14 Does he not know that Allah sees?
١٥ كَلَّا لَئِن لَّمْ يَنتَهِ لَنَسْفَعًۢا بِٱلنَّاصِيَةِ	15 No. If he does not desist, We will drag him by the forelock.
١٦ نَاصِيَةٍ كَٰذِبَةٍ خَاطِئَةٍ	16 A deceitful, sinful forelock.
١٧ فَلْيَدْعُ نَادِيَهُۥ	17 Let him call on his gang.
١٨ سَنَدْعُ ٱلزَّبَانِيَةَ	18 We will call the Guards.
١٩ كَلَّا لَا تُطِعْهُ وَٱسْجُدْ وَٱقْتَرِب ۩	19 No, do not obey him; but kneel down, and come near.

97 Decree القدر

بِسْمِ ٱللَّهِ ٱلرَّحْمَٰنِ ٱلرَّحِيمِ	In the name of Allah, the Gracious, the Merciful.
١ إِنَّآ أَنزَلْنَٰهُ فِى لَيْلَةِ ٱلْقَدْرِ	1 We sent it down on the Night of Decree.
٢ وَمَآ أَدْرَىٰكَ مَا لَيْلَةُ ٱلْقَدْرِ	2 But what will convey to you what the Night of Decree is?
٣ لَيْلَةُ ٱلْقَدْرِ خَيْرٌ مِّنْ أَلْفِ شَهْرٍ	3 The Night of Decree is better than a thousand months.
٤ تَنَزَّلُ ٱلْمَلَٰٓئِكَةُ وَٱلرُّوحُ فِيهَا بِإِذْنِ رَبِّهِم مِّن كُلِّ أَمْرٍ	4 In it descend the angels and the Spirit, by the leave of their Lord, with every command.
٥ سَلَٰمٌ هِىَ حَتَّىٰ مَطْلَعِ ٱلْفَجْرِ	5 Peace it is; until the rise of dawn.

98 Clear Evidence البينة

بِسْمِ ٱللَّهِ ٱلرَّحْمَٰنِ ٱلرَّحِيمِ

In the name of Allah, the Gracious, the Merciful.

١ لَمْ يَكُنِ ٱلَّذِينَ كَفَرُوا۟ مِنْ أَهْلِ ٱلْكِتَٰبِ
وَٱلْمُشْرِكِينَ مُنفَكِّينَ حَتَّىٰ تَأْتِيَهُمُ ٱلْبَيِّنَةُ

1 Those who disbelieved among the People of the Scripture, and the Polytheists, were not apart, until the Clear Evidence came to them.

٢ رَسُولٌ مِّنَ ٱللَّهِ يَتْلُوا۟ صُحُفًا مُّطَهَّرَةً

2 A messenger from Allah reciting purified scripts.

٣ فِيهَا كُتُبٌ قَيِّمَةٌ

3 In them are valuable writings.

٤ وَمَا تَفَرَّقَ ٱلَّذِينَ أُوتُوا۟ ٱلْكِتَٰبَ إِلَّا مِنۢ بَعْدِ مَا
جَآءَتْهُمُ ٱلْبَيِّنَةُ

4 Those who were given the Scripture did not splinter, except after the Clear Evidence came to them.

٥ وَمَآ أُمِرُوٓا۟ إِلَّا لِيَعْبُدُوا۟ ٱللَّهَ مُخْلِصِينَ لَهُ
ٱلدِّينَ حُنَفَآءَ وَيُقِيمُوا۟ ٱلصَّلَوٰةَ وَيُؤْتُوا۟ ٱلزَّكَوٰةَ ۚ
وَذَٰلِكَ دِينُ ٱلْقَيِّمَةِ

5 They were commanded only to worship Allah, devoting their faith to Him alone, and to practice regular prayer, and to give alms. That is the upright religion.

٦ إِنَّ ٱلَّذِينَ كَفَرُوا۟ مِنْ أَهْلِ ٱلْكِتَٰبِ وَٱلْمُشْرِكِينَ
فِى نَارِ جَهَنَّمَ خَٰلِدِينَ فِيهَآ ۚ أُو۟لَٰٓئِكَ هُمْ شَرُّ
ٱلْبَرِيَّةِ

6 Those who disbelieve among the People of the Scripture, and the Polytheists, will be in the Fire of Hell, where they will abide forever. These are the worst of creatures.

٧ إِنَّ ٱلَّذِينَ ءَامَنُوا۟ وَعَمِلُوا۟ ٱلصَّٰلِحَٰتِ أُو۟لَٰٓئِكَ
هُمْ خَيْرُ ٱلْبَرِيَّةِ

7 As for those who believe and lead a righteous life—these are the best of creatures.

٨ جَزَآؤُهُمْ عِندَ رَبِّهِمْ جَنَّٰتُ عَدْنٍ تَجْرِى مِن
تَحْتِهَا ٱلْأَنْهَٰرُ خَٰلِدِينَ فِيهَآ أَبَدًا ۖ رَّضِىَ ٱللَّهُ
عَنْهُمْ وَرَضُوا۟ عَنْهُ ۚ ذَٰلِكَ لِمَنْ خَشِىَ رَبَّهُۥ

8 Their reward is with their Lord: Gardens of Eternity beneath which rivers flow, where they will abide forever. Allah is pleased with them, and they are pleased with Him. That is for whoever fears His Lord.

99 The Quake الزلزلة

بِسْمِ ٱللَّهِ ٱلرَّحْمَٰنِ ٱلرَّحِيمِ

In the name of Allah, the Gracious, the Merciful.

١ إِذَا زُلْزِلَتِ ٱلْأَرْضُ زِلْزَالَهَا	1 When the earth is shaken with its quake.
٢ وَأَخْرَجَتِ ٱلْأَرْضُ أَثْقَالَهَا	2 And the earth brings out its loads.
٣ وَقَالَ ٱلْإِنسَٰنُ مَا لَهَا	3 And man says, “What is the matter with it?”
٤ يَوْمَئِذٍ تُحَدِّثُ أَخْبَارَهَا	4 On that Day, it will tell its tales.
٥ بِأَنَّ رَبَّكَ أَوْحَىٰ لَهَا	5 For your Lord will have inspired it.
٦ يَوْمَئِذٍ يَصْدُرُ ٱلنَّاسُ أَشْتَاتًا لِّيُرَوْا۟ أَعْمَٰلَهُمْ	6 On that Day, the people will emerge in droves, to be shown their works.
٧ فَمَن يَعْمَلْ مِثْقَالَ ذَرَّةٍ خَيْرًا يَرَهُۥ	7 Whoever has done an atom's weight of good will see it.
٨ وَمَن يَعْمَلْ مِثْقَالَ ذَرَّةٍ شَرًّا يَرَهُۥ	8 And whoever has done an atom's weight of evil will see it.

100 The Racers العاديات

بِسْمِ ٱللَّهِ ٱلرَّحْمَٰنِ ٱلرَّحِيمِ	In the name of Allah, the Gracious, the Merciful.
١ وَٱلْعَٰدِيَٰتِ ضَبْحًا	1 By the racers panting.
٢ فَٱلْمُورِيَٰتِ قَدْحًا	2 Igniting sparks.
٣ فَٱلْمُغِيرَٰتِ صُبْحًا	3 Raiding at dawn.
٤ فَأَثَرْنَ بِهِۦ نَقْعًا	4 Raising clouds of dust.
٥ فَوَسَطْنَ بِهِۦ جَمْعًا	5 Storming into the midst.
٦ إِنَّ ٱلْإِنسَٰنَ لِرَبِّهِۦ لَكَنُودٌ	6 Indeed, the human being is ungrateful to his Lord.
٧ وَإِنَّهُۥ عَلَىٰ ذَٰلِكَ لَشَهِيدٌ	7 And he bears witness to that.
٨ وَإِنَّهُۥ لِحُبِّ ٱلْخَيْرِ لَشَدِيدٌ	8 And he is fierce in his love of wealth.
٩ أَفَلَا يَعْلَمُ إِذَا بُعْثِرَ مَا فِى ٱلْقُبُورِ	9 Does he not know? When the contents of the graves are scattered around.

١٠ وَحُصِّلَ مَا فِى ٱلصُّدُورِ	10 And the contents of the hearts are obtained.
١١ إِنَّ رَبَّهُم بِهِمْ يَوْمَئِذٍ لَّخَبِيرٌۢ	11 Their Lord, on that Day, is fully informed of them.

101 The Shocker القارعة

بِسْمِ ٱللَّهِ ٱلرَّحْمَٰنِ ٱلرَّحِيمِ	In the name of Allah, the Gracious, the Merciful.
١ ٱلْقَارِعَةُ	1 The Shocker.
٢ مَا ٱلْقَارِعَةُ	2 What is the Shocker?
٣ وَمَآ أَدْرَىٰكَ مَا ٱلْقَارِعَةُ	3 What will explain to you what the Shocker is?
٤ يَوْمَ يَكُونُ ٱلنَّاسُ كَٱلْفَرَاشِ ٱلْمَبْثُوثِ	4 The Day when the people will be like scattered moths.
٥ وَتَكُونُ ٱلْجِبَالُ كَٱلْعِهْنِ ٱلْمَنفُوشِ	5 And the mountains will be like tufted wool.
٦ فَأَمَّا مَن ثَقُلَتْ مَوَٰزِينُهُۥ	6 As for he whose scales are heavy.
٧ فَهُوَ فِى عِيشَةٍ رَّاضِيَةٍ	7 He will be in a pleasant life.
٨ وَأَمَّا مَنْ خَفَّتْ مَوَٰزِينُهُۥ	8 But as for he whose scales are light.
٩ فَأُمُّهُۥ هَاوِيَةٌ	9 His home is the Abyss.
١٠ وَمَآ أَدْرَىٰكَ مَا هِيَهْ	10 Do you know what it is?
١١ نَارٌ حَامِيَةٌۢ	11 A Raging Fire.

102 Abundance التكاثر

بِسْمِ ٱللَّهِ ٱلرَّحْمَٰنِ ٱلرَّحِيمِ	In the name of Allah, the Gracious, the Merciful.
١ أَلْهَىٰكُمُ ٱلتَّكَاثُرُ	1 Abundance distracts you.
٢ حَتَّىٰ زُرْتُمُ ٱلْمَقَابِرَ	2 Until you visit the graveyards.
٣ كَلَّا سَوْفَ تَعْلَمُونَ	3 Indeed, you will know.

٤ ثُمَّ كَلَّا سَوْفَ تَعْلَمُونَ	4 Certainly, you will know.
٥ كَلَّا لَوْ تَعْلَمُونَ عِلْمَ ٱلْيَقِينِ	5 If you knew with knowledge of certainty.
٦ لَتَرَوُنَّ ٱلْجَحِيمَ	6 You would see the Inferno.
٧ ثُمَّ لَتَرَوُنَّهَا عَيْنَ ٱلْيَقِينِ	7 Then you will see it with the eye of certainty.
٨ ثُمَّ لَتُسْـَٔلُنَّ يَوْمَئِذٍ عَنِ ٱلنَّعِيمِ	8 Then, on that Day, you will be questioned about the Bliss.

103 Time العصر

بِسْمِ ٱللَّهِ ٱلرَّحْمَٰنِ ٱلرَّحِيمِ	In the name of Allah, the Gracious, the Merciful.
١ وَٱلْعَصْرِ	1 By Time.
٢ إِنَّ ٱلْإِنسَٰنَ لَفِى خُسْرٍ	2 The human being is in loss.
٣ إِلَّا ٱلَّذِينَ ءَامَنُوا۟ وَعَمِلُوا۟ ٱلصَّٰلِحَٰتِ وَتَوَاصَوْا۟ بِٱلْحَقِّ وَتَوَاصَوْا۟ بِٱلصَّبْرِ	3 Except those who believe, and do good works, and encourage truth, and recommend patience.

104 The Backbiter الهمزة

بِسْمِ ٱللَّهِ ٱلرَّحْمَٰنِ ٱلرَّحِيمِ	In the name of Allah, the Gracious, the Merciful.
١ وَيْلٌ لِّكُلِّ هُمَزَةٍ لُّمَزَةٍ	1 Woe to every slanderer backbiter.
٢ ٱلَّذِى جَمَعَ مَالًا وَعَدَّدَهُۥ	2 Who gathers wealth and counts it over.
٣ يَحْسَبُ أَنَّ مَالَهُۥٓ أَخْلَدَهُۥ	3 Thinking that his wealth has made him immortal.
٤ كَلَّا ۖ لَيُنۢبَذَنَّ فِى ٱلْحُطَمَةِ	4 By no means. He will be thrown into the Crusher.
٥ وَمَآ أَدْرَىٰكَ مَا ٱلْحُطَمَةُ	5 And what will make you realize what the Crusher is?
٦ نَارُ ٱللَّهِ ٱلْمُوقَدَةُ	6 Allah's kindled Fire.
٧ ٱلَّتِى تَطَّلِعُ عَلَى ٱلْأَفْـِٔدَةِ	7 That laps to the hearts.

٨ إِنَّهَا عَلَيْهِم مُّؤْصَدَةٌ	8 It closes in on them.
٩ فِى عَمَدٍ مُّمَدَّدَةٍۭ	9 In extended columns.

105 The Elephant الفيل

بِسْمِ ٱللَّهِ ٱلرَّحْمَٰنِ ٱلرَّحِيمِ	In the name of Allah, the Gracious, the Merciful.
١ أَلَمْ تَرَ كَيْفَ فَعَلَ رَبُّكَ بِأَصْحَٰبِ ٱلْفِيلِ	1 Have you not considered how your Lord dealt with the People of the Elephant?
٢ أَلَمْ يَجْعَلْ كَيْدَهُمْ فِى تَضْلِيلٍ	2 Did He not make their plan go wrong?
٣ وَأَرْسَلَ عَلَيْهِمْ طَيْرًا أَبَابِيلَ	3 He sent against them swarms of birds.
٤ تَرْمِيهِم بِحِجَارَةٍ مِّن سِجِّيلٍ	4 Throwing at them rocks of baked clay.
٥ فَجَعَلَهُمْ كَعَصْفٍ مَّأْكُولٍۭ	5 Leaving them like chewed-up leaves.

106 Quraish قريش

بِسْمِ ٱللَّهِ ٱلرَّحْمَٰنِ ٱلرَّحِيمِ	In the name of Allah, the Gracious, the Merciful.
١ لِإِيلَٰفِ قُرَيْشٍ	1 For the security of Quraish.
٢ إِۦلَٰفِهِمْ رِحْلَةَ ٱلشِّتَآءِ وَٱلصَّيْفِ	2 Their security during winter and summer journeys.
٣ فَلْيَعْبُدُوا۟ رَبَّ هَٰذَا ٱلْبَيْتِ	3 Let them worship the Lord of this House.
٤ ٱلَّذِىٓ أَطْعَمَهُم مِّن جُوعٍ وَءَامَنَهُم مِّنْ خَوْفٍۭ	4 Who has fed them against hunger, and has secured them against fear.

107 Assistance الماعون

بِسْمِ ٱللَّهِ ٱلرَّحْمَٰنِ ٱلرَّحِيمِ	In the name of Allah, the Gracious, the Merciful.

١ أَرَءَيْتَ ٱلَّذِى يُكَذِّبُ بِٱلدِّينِ	1 Have you considered him who denies the religion?
٢ فَذَٰلِكَ ٱلَّذِى يَدُعُّ ٱلْيَتِيمَ	2 It is he who mistreats the orphan.
٣ وَلَا يَحُضُّ عَلَىٰ طَعَامِ ٱلْمِسْكِينِ	3 And does not encourage the feeding of the poor.
٤ فَوَيْلٌ لِّلْمُصَلِّينَ	4 So woe to those who pray.
٥ ٱلَّذِينَ هُمْ عَن صَلَاتِهِمْ سَاهُونَ	5 Those who are heedless of their prayers.
٦ ٱلَّذِينَ هُمْ يُرَآءُونَ	6 Those who put on the appearance.
٧ وَيَمْنَعُونَ ٱلْمَاعُونَ	7 And withhold the assistance.

108 Plenty الكوثر

بِسْمِ ٱللَّهِ ٱلرَّحْمَٰنِ ٱلرَّحِيمِ	In the name of Allah, the Gracious, the Merciful.
١ إِنَّآ أَعْطَيْنَٰكَ ٱلْكَوْثَرَ	1 We have given you plenty.
٢ فَصَلِّ لِرَبِّكَ وَٱنْحَرْ	2 So pray to your Lord and sacrifice.
٣ إِنَّ شَانِئَكَ هُوَ ٱلْأَبْتَرُ	3 He who hates you is the loser.

109 The Disbelievers الكافرون

بِسْمِ ٱللَّهِ ٱلرَّحْمَٰنِ ٱلرَّحِيمِ	In the name of Allah, the Gracious, the Merciful.
١ قُلْ يَٰٓأَيُّهَا ٱلْكَٰفِرُونَ	1 Say, “O disbelievers.
٢ لَآ أَعْبُدُ مَا تَعْبُدُونَ	2 I do not worship what you worship.
٣ وَلَآ أَنتُمْ عَٰبِدُونَ مَآ أَعْبُدُ	3 Nor do you worship what I worship.
٤ وَلَآ أَنَا۠ عَابِدٌ مَّا عَبَدتُّمْ	4 Nor do I serve what you serve.
٥ وَلَآ أَنتُمْ عَٰبِدُونَ مَآ أَعْبُدُ	5 Nor do you serve what I serve.
٦ لَكُمْ دِينُكُمْ وَلِىَ دِينِ	6 You have your way, and I have my way.”

110 Victory النصر

بِسْمِ ٱللَّهِ ٱلرَّحْمَٰنِ ٱلرَّحِيمِ	In the name of Allah, the Gracious, the Merciful.
١ إِذَا جَآءَ نَصْرُ ٱللَّهِ وَٱلْفَتْحُ	1 When there comes Allah's victory, and conquest.
٢ وَرَأَيْتَ ٱلنَّاسَ يَدْخُلُونَ فِى دِينِ ٱللَّهِ أَفْوَاجًا	2 And you see the people entering Allah's religion in multitudes.
٣ فَسَبِّحْ بِحَمْدِ رَبِّكَ وَٱسْتَغْفِرْهُ ۚ إِنَّهُۥ كَانَ تَوَّابًۢا	3 Then celebrate the praise of your Lord, and seek His forgiveness. He is the Accepter of Repentance.

111 Thorns المسد

بِسْمِ ٱللَّهِ ٱلرَّحْمَٰنِ ٱلرَّحِيمِ	In the name of Allah, the Gracious, the Merciful.
١ تَبَّتْ يَدَآ أَبِى لَهَبٍ وَتَبَّ	1 Condemned are the hands of Abee Lahab, and he is condemned.
٢ مَآ أَغْنَىٰ عَنْهُ مَالُهُۥ وَمَا كَسَبَ	2 His wealth did not avail him, nor did what he acquired.
٣ سَيَصْلَىٰ نَارًا ذَاتَ لَهَبٍ	3 He will burn in a Flaming Fire.
٤ وَٱمْرَأَتُهُۥ حَمَّالَةَ ٱلْحَطَبِ	4 And his wife—the firewood carrier.
٥ فِى جِيدِهَا حَبْلٌ مِّن مَّسَدٍۭ	5 Around her neck is a rope of thorns.

112 Monotheism الإخلاص

بِسْمِ ٱللَّهِ ٱلرَّحْمَٰنِ ٱلرَّحِيمِ	In the name of Allah, the Gracious, the Merciful.
١ قُلْ هُوَ ٱللَّهُ أَحَدٌ	1 Say, "He is Allah, the One.
٢ ٱللَّهُ ٱلصَّمَدُ	2 Allah, the Absolute.
٣ لَمْ يَلِدْ وَلَمْ يُولَدْ	3 He begets not, nor was He begotten.
٤ وَلَمْ يَكُن لَّهُۥ كُفُوًا أَحَدٌۢ	4 And there is nothing comparable to Him."

113 Daybreak الفلق

بِسْمِ ٱللَّهِ ٱلرَّحْمَٰنِ ٱلرَّحِيمِ	In the name of Allah, the Gracious, the Merciful.
١ قُلْ أَعُوذُ بِرَبِّ ٱلْفَلَقِ	1 Say, "I take refuge with the Lord of Daybreak.
٢ مِن شَرِّ مَا خَلَقَ	2 From the evil of what He created.
٣ وَمِن شَرِّ غَاسِقٍ إِذَا وَقَبَ	3 And from the evil of the darkness as it gathers.
٤ وَمِن شَرِّ ٱلنَّفَّٰثَٰتِ فِى ٱلْعُقَدِ	4 And from the evil of those who practice sorcery.
٥ وَمِن شَرِّ حَاسِدٍ إِذَا حَسَدَ	5 And from the evil of an envious when he envies."

114 Mankind الناس

بِسْمِ ٱللَّهِ ٱلرَّحْمَٰنِ ٱلرَّحِيمِ	In the name of Allah, the Gracious, the Merciful.
١ قُلْ أَعُوذُ بِرَبِّ ٱلنَّاسِ	1 Say, "I seek refuge in the Lord of mankind.
٢ مَلِكِ ٱلنَّاسِ	2 The King of mankind.
٣ إِلَٰهِ ٱلنَّاسِ	3 The God of mankind.
٤ مِن شَرِّ ٱلْوَسْوَاسِ ٱلْخَنَّاسِ	4 From the evil of the sneaky whisperer.
٥ ٱلَّذِى يُوَسْوِسُ فِى صُدُورِ ٱلنَّاسِ	5 Who whispers into the hearts of people.
٦ مِنَ ٱلْجِنَّةِ وَٱلنَّاسِ	6 From among jinn and among people."

Made in the USA
Columbia, SC
02 April 2022

58431255R00365